A History of the
People's Action Party
1985–2021

A History of the
People's Action Party
1985–2021

SHASHI JAYAKUMAR

NUS PRESS
SINGAPORE

Published by:

NUS Press
National University of Singapore
AS3-01-02, 3 Arts Link
Singapore 117569

Fax: (65) 6774-0652
E-mail: nusbooks@nus.edu.sg
Website: http://nuspress.nus.edu.sg

ISBN 978-981-325-128-1 (casebound)

National Library Board, Singapore Cataloguing in Publication Data
Name(s): Jayakumar, Shashi.
Title: A history of the People's Action Party, 1985-2021 / Shashi Jayakumar.
Description: Singapore : NUS Press, [2022] | Includes bibliographical
    references and index.
Identifier(s): OCN 1164363746 | ISBN 978-981-32-5128-1 (hardcover)
Subject(s): LCSH: People's Action Party (Singapore)--History. | Political
    parties--Singapore--History. | Singapore--Politics and government.
Classification: DDC 324.25957--dc23

The text in the background of the cover is taken from the Constitution
of the People's Action Party.

Designed by: Nur Nelani Jinadasa
Printed by: Mainland Press Pte Ltd

To

Mum and Dad with all my love

Contents

Acknowledgements

This book has taken a considerable amount of time to write. My only defence is that writing about the past is difficult, especially, I have now come to realise, for historians.

Numerous debts have been incurred in the course of this journey.

Firstly, I am grateful to serving and former MPs, Party leaders, and other individuals who played a part in these events for speaking to me on record. The interviews that I conducted have been listed in the bibliography. Beyond this, however, the path has been illuminated by dozens of Party officials, MPs, activists and cadres who spoke on background, and who assisted in clarifying various points of detail and historical incidents. This book would have been poorer without their clarifications and frank insights. I have respected their wishes not to be named.

It would not have been possible to understand the inner workings of the PAP, its machinery, and its evolutions, if not for many conversations over the years with former Organising Secretaries of the Party: Tang See Chim, Dr Ow Chin Hock and Lau Ping Sum. I am in their debt. Lau Ping Sum in particular has patiently answered hundreds of queries, in addition giving advice on my translations from Chinese to English (which I take primary responsibility for).

The unsung and dedicated staff at the National Archives of Singapore rarely receive recognition they deserve. I would like to thank them for facilitating my requests for access to papers and files. Equally helpful—and extremely patient—has been indefatigable Florence Tan-Ler.

The anonymous reviewers of this book made me think much harder about what I was trying to say—their comments helped considerably. Peter Schoppert and Lena Qua from NUS Press shepherded this project—no more than an idea in 2011—through to publication ten years later. Sunandini Lal and Anne Sanow have saved me from many, many errors (those which remain are my own). I am also grateful to the research assistants I have worked with over this time: these include Christine Chan, Beatrice Lee, Clement Liew, Benjamin Low, Daryl Ong, Angela Poh and Ong Wei Zhong.

Various individuals have shared their expertise and deep knowledge. Conversations with the late S.R. Nathan made me ponder the nature of leadership and the wielding of power. Prof. Chan Heng Chee's asides to me provided perspectives I would not otherwise have come by. The same should be said (particularly when it came to whom to ask and where to look) for Sonny Yap and Leong Weng Kam, who shared their views in the earlier phase of research. I am also grateful to Assoc. Prof. Terence Ho, Assoc. Prof. Eugene Tan and Assoc. Prof. Shandre Thangavelu when it came to untangling and interpreting various issues of policy. Bobby Yap has patiently shared his knowledge of aspects of grassroots organisations and their work. Assoc. Prof. Rahul Sagar has been a keenly supportive presence throughout.

My thinking when it comes to the earlier, pre-1980, history of Singapore and of the Party (which inevitably informs writing on the more recent period) has evolved over time, in part due to many productive conversations with Assoc. Prof. Albert Lau.

I would like to thank Prof. Kishore Mahbubani for giving me a home at the Lee Kuan Yew School of Public Policy, where I was a research fellow from 2011–14. Subsequently, Ambassadors Barry Desker and Ong Keng Yong provided an equally congenial environment at the S. Rajaratnam School of International Studies (RSIS) and supported my work.

This volume would not have been written without the love and support of my family and especially my understanding (*very* understanding) wife Miranda.

Readers might find a very small number of paragraphs familiar. While this project has been under way for some time, certain elements first found their way into publication via a shorter primer on the PAP co-authored with Assoc. Prof. Albert Lau (*Singapore Chronicles: PAP*), which was published in 2019 by the Straits Times Press, under the auspices of the Institute of Policy Studies, National University of Singapore. The work here has of course been extensively reworked, updated and expanded since then.

List of Abbreviations

4G leadership   Fourth-Generation Leadership

AMP   Association of Muslim Professionals
ASG   Assistant Secretary-General

BG   Brigadier General
BG (Res)   Brigadier General (Reservist)

CC   Community Centre [later Community Club]
CCC   Citizens' Consultative Committee
CCMC   Community Centre Management Committee
CDC   Community Development Council
CEC   Central Executive Committee
Col.   Colonel
ComCare   Community Care Endowment Fund
CPF   Central Provident Fund
CRC   Cost Review Committee

DPM   Deputy Prime Minister
1DPM   First Deputy Prime Minister
2DPM   Second Deputy Prime Minister

ERC   Economic Review Committee
ESC   Economic Strategies Committee
ESM   Emeritus Senior Minister

GE   General Election
GPC   Government Parliamentary Committee
GRC   Group Representation Constituency

GRO	Grassroots Organisations
GST	Goods and Services Tax
HDB	Housing and Development Board
HQ Exco	HQ Executive Committee
IPS	Institute of Policy Studies
ISA	Internal Security Act
ISD	Internal Security Department
MAB	Malay Affairs Bureau
MCD	Ministry of Community Development
Mendaki	Council for Education of Muslim Children
MITA	Ministry of Information and the Arts
MM	Minister Mentor
MOE	Ministry of Education
MOS	Minister of State
MP	Member of Parliament
MRT	Mass Rapid Transit
NCMP	Non-Constituency Member of Parliament
NMP	Nominated Member of Parliament
NS	National Service
NSP	National Solidarity Party
NTU	Nanyang Technological University
NTUC	National Trades Union Congress
NUS	National University of Singapore
OB markers	Out-of-bounds markers
OS	Organising Secretary
1OS	First Organising Secretary
2OS	Second Organising Secretary
OSC	Our Singapore Conversation
PA	People's Association PCF - PAP Community Foundation
PEA	Parliamentary Elections Act
PGP	Pioneer Generation Package

PM   Prime Minister
PR   Permanent Resident
PSP   Progress Singapore Party

RADM   Rear Admiral
RC   Residents' Committee
RSC   Remaking Singapore Committee

S21   Singapore 21
SDA   Singapore Democratic Alliance
SDP   Singapore Democratic Party
SG   Secretary-General
SMC   Single Member Constituency
SM   Senior Minister
SMS   Senior Minister of State
SPP   Singapore People's Party

WP   The Workers' Party

YP   Young PAP
YP21   Young PAP 21 initiative

Introduction

The People's Action Party (PAP) has been the subject of scholarly interest for almost the entire length of its existence. Early studies include *The People's Action Party of Singapore* (Thomas Bellows, 1970),[1] *Singapore's People's Action Party: Its History, Organization and Leadership* (Pang Cheng Lian, 1971) and *The Dynamics of One Party Dominance: The PAP at the Grass-Roots* (Chan Heng Chee, 1976). More recent treatments are *Singapore Politics under the People's Action Party* (Robert Milne and Diane Mauzy, 2002) and *Men in White: The Untold Story of Singapore's Ruling Political Party* (Sonny Yap, Leong Weng Kam and Richard Lim, 2009). There have also been accounts of the Party as well as memoirs and reminiscences by former PAP MPs. Examples are *The PAP Story: The Pioneering Years* (Fong Sip Chee, 1979) and *We Also Served: Reflections of Singapore's Former PAP MPs* (eds Chiang Hai Ding and Rohan Kamis, 2014).

The present book aims to contribute to the body of work above by providing a narrative and analytical history of the PAP from 1985 to 2021, beginning with the aftermath of the 1984 general election. This election saw the PAP suffer a 12.9 per cent vote swing against it. The week or so between the election result and the announcement of the new Cabinet (with Goh Chok Tong chosen as first deputy prime minister, in effect the political successor to Prime Minister Lee Kuan Yew) was to shape the nation's history. Given the period's significance, I have chosen to begin the narrative from this point.[2]

Although the book uses a broadly chronological treatment, certain thematic areas are covered—and analysed—within the chronological umbrella. These include, for example, Party recruitment selection; the PAP's unending—indeed existential—search for talent; Party organs and reorganisations that occurred from time to time; and the individuals who were part of this apparatus. Also covered are the various PAP organs (including the PAP Central Executive Committee, Party branches, Young PAP and the Women's Wing) and the PAP's relationship to parapolitical bodies such as grass-roots organisations.

There are, of course, various themes and topics that are recurrent and evolving, and which necessarily feature across chapters. These include, for example, the PAP's view and treatment of the Opposition, as well as the painstaking internal preparations for elections (and the rigorous post-mortems that invariably follow).

Given that the PAP has governed Singapore without interruption from 1959, it has been necessary to give also a sense of not just the Party in government, but the PAP as government. At various points, the text examines critical issues of policy (economic development, housing, transport, cost of living) as well as matters relating to the sociopolitical backdrop (including the government's evolving relationship with the people and civil society, and challenges to governance posed by social media).

The PAP's seeing itself as much more than an "ordinary" political party—as a national institution, or perhaps even as the only institution with the credentials to take the country forward—is an issue inextricably linked with the very longevity of the Party itself. I have avoided attempting to provide one single set of definitive answers as to why the Party has consistently won the people's mandate at each election from 1959. However, several themes suggest themselves. Some of these build on observations from PAP leaders. Not generally prone to excesses of nostalgic reflections, key individuals within the Party could on important occasions—such as significant anniversaries—look back on the past and comment with some perspicacity on why the PAP remained in power.

In 1979, on the occasion of the 25th anniversary of the Party, PM Lee Kuan Yew, secretary-general of the Party, reflected on this issue and on what lessons the PAP had learnt from some 20 years in government.[3] The principles he laid out automatically suggest themselves to a reader with even a passing appreciation of the PAP's history. One theme Lee highlighted included staying clean. The PAP's ruthless insistence on an untainted and corruption-free government—indeed a clean Singapore—is well known, and some examples of this are given in the chapters that follow. Lee also touched on the PAP's consistent policymaking; in securing the long-term interests of the people, the PAP rejected soft options and did not court popularity.[4]

The second generation of leaders saw the PAP's durability in largely similar terms. In 2004, on the occasion of the 50th anniversary of the Party, PAP chairman Dr Tony Tan put forward three fundamental principles for the PAP s dominance and longevity. These were honesty, incorruptibility and competence in government; an orderly system of renewal, and trust and identification of the Party with the needs, hopes and aspirations of the people.[5]

These themes have repeatedly surfaced in my research and interviews. One, highlighted by Dr Tony Tan above, and which I would suggest is in the core DNA of the Party, is renewal. As relevant chapters attempt to show, the Party has consistently attempted to co-opt the very best and brightest individuals, making concerted attempts (well before an election) to scour the landscape for those willing to serve. It has continued to co-opt from the top ranks of the civil service and the armed forces (even as it has continued to find it something of a challenge to bring in high-calibre individuals from the private sector). The Party in the contemporary period might not quite be able to claim the monopoly on talent that it once had, but there is a general acceptance on the part of the public that it has sieved and sifted out extremely qualified individuals in a thoroughly meritocratic process, with the top ranks of the leadership peopled by individuals judged to have the right qualities and skills to lead and take the country forward.

There have been fitful attempts to reinvigorate Party organs and institutions—indeed, references to these efforts can be found in Party publications and files going back to the late 1950s—but it is people, not structures, that are central to the Party's rejuvenation. There is a certain ruthlessness to this. Members of Parliament who are backbenchers without being elevated to political office have, since the 1980s, tended to serve no more than three terms on average (sometimes less). Until the 1980s, this provoked a degree of unhappiness on the part of some affected MPs, and incomprehension on the part of the people, some of whom assumed that the MPs had somehow failed or done something "wrong". Now, however, there is a wider acceptance amongst all concerned that this is inevitable and necessary and is in fact how the Party continually maintains its vigour. The clinical aspect of renewal can occasionally be glimpsed, too, in the top ranks. Witness, for example, the striking retirement of several ministers immediately after the 2011 general election. Not all the retirements had been anticipated, and it seemed that some of the ministers (those who had helmed the hot-button ministries in charge of issues that had seen serious public dissatisfaction) had been dropped.

The year 2011 also saw the bowing out from the PAP Central Executive Committee of Minister Mentor Lee Kuan Yew and Senior Minister Goh Chok Tong. As the penultimate chapter of the book shows, this was something agreed on by PM Lee Hsien Loong, Lee Kuan Yew and Goh Chok Tong: their instinct in the face of an electoral reverse was not to hold back change but to accelerate it and give the newer generation of Party leaders a freer hand to push on with renewal. Very similar thinking was at play in the last weeks of 1984 following a similar electoral reverse.

A second theme I would put forward (often cited by observers, and equally often discussed within the Party) is realism in communication. The Party has made consistent attempts to explain policy in a manner that carries the ground, even when it comes to unpalatable policy moves. The PAP government does not attempt to sugar-coat, or make promises that it cannot keep. Over time, and certainly since the turn of the millennium, a more consultative style has been adopted, with the Party more consistent in its attempts to explain policy in a manner that carries the ground, even when it comes to unpalatable policy moves. Despite the perception that the PAP government is top-down in its policymaking, one of its calling cards when it comes to thinking through critical evolutions (calibrations in the opening up of society, for example) is the inclusive nature of gathering views and feedback from different levels. When it comes to the directions of society, initiatives such as Singapore 21 (S21; 1999), Remaking Singapore (2002–03) and Our Singapore Conversation (2012–13) come to mind.

Notwithstanding a certain degree of opening up, the PAP does not like to lose control of public discourse. Historically, it has made strenuous attempts to set the tone and the agenda for the discussion of issues relating to policy and the public interest, both in and out of elections. Perhaps partly on account of its innate desire for control, the PAP government has been keenly aware of the challenges posed by disruptive developments such as the Internet and, more recently, social media. While some regulatory control has been exercised, this has on the whole been applied with a reasonably light touch. The Party has itself evolved its approach and become appreciably better over time in using the Internet and social media to communicate, with many MPs and ministers using these as one means to keep in touch with the people.

A third and somewhat overlooked theme that suggests itself is innovation. The leadership has never been averse to tinkering with aspects of the democratic model. Beginning from the 1980s the PAP government introduced changes that allowed for more diverse voices in Parliament. These changes included the introduction of the Non-Constituency Member of Parliament (NCMP) and Nominated Member of Parliament (NMP) schemes. A different, standout innovation would be Group Representation Constituencies (GRCs), introduced before the 1988 election. There was pushback from the Opposition, predictably. But there was also resistance from prominent figures of minority races within the PAP establishment, who felt that they could carry the ground in an election on their own. However, from the point of view of Lee Kuan Yew, GRCs were the only way to guarantee continued minority representation in Parliament. Now, three decades on, it might appear that Lee and the PAP leadership (whom Lee brought round to his point of view) were prescient in many respects.

It is, of course, tempting to suggest that the main reason for the PAP's success and longevity is its consistent ability to deliver growth and to distribute the rewards that come with growth to the people. This is both correct and an oversimplification. The Party has indeed been able to deliver an improved standard of living for the vast majority of the people. There have, however, been bumps in the road. The 1985–86 recession saw the PAP government convene a high-level committee that expeditiously decided on course corrections, including wage restraint and cuts in employers' Central Provident Fund contributions. Some of the bumps have not been particular to Singapore (the 1985–86 recession had at its heart a mix of external and indigenous factors) but linked to developments in the region and the wider world. The PAP government has never attempted to insulate itself from global or regional headwinds (the 1997–98 Asian Financial Crisis being one example) and has instead used various crises as an opportunity to remake, rethink and reinvent—the 2001–03 Economic Review Committee (ERC), the 2009–10 Economic Strategies Committee (ESC) and the 2016–17 Committee for the Future Economy (CFE) being cases in point.[6]

It is interesting that some of the areas that the Party has put in some of the hardest yards, and which are very germane to the Party's success—delivering growth and prosperity, communication and Party renewal, for example—are also areas that have proven to be points of some stress in recent years. From the 1990s, expectations have risen on the part of an ever more affluent and educated populace. The Party has on various occasions made attempts to explain to the people that expectations have to be moderated, even as moves were initiated (particularly in housing) to cater to material aspirations for "the good life".

As both government and Party, the PAP has upped its game in terms of understanding and relating to the aspirations of the electorate (the major part of which comprises citizens born in the post-independence period), but something of a loop has been created. The PAP government must not just be seen to be listening; it has to cater to a generation that wants some sense that its feedback has genuinely fed into the policymaking process. As this generation demands a greater stake in shaping the nation, resisting policy moves they find unpalatable (the 2013 uproar over the Population White Paper being a case in point), a key issue when it comes to the PAP government's durability may well be how well it can facilitate this participatory sense, remaining attuned to aspirations while simultaneously managing expectations. And all this while, it will have to retain the ability and indeed the authority to deliver policy doses that might not be universally welcomed even if for the long-term good of the body politic.

There have been stresses on renewal, too. Even though the Party has continued to draw on the pool of army generals and high-level civil servants, it cannot (as noted earlier) be said to have successfully cracked the problem of bringing in successful individuals from the private sector. Separately, netizens are all too ready to scrutinise the credentials and attributes of candidates presenting themselves for election and pointing out weaknesses (some illusory, some real).

The PAP began its existence as a party imbued by Fabian Socialist ideals, but it has never approached ideology as dogma. Faced with the exigencies of dealing with growth and employment issues, it learned from a very early stage to temper any notions of an ideal socialist utopia with a healthy appreciation of market forces and the idea that there should be no crutch mentality at any level of society. This strain of pragmatism persisted. It is the continuation of this strain—simply put, a lack of dogmatism—that enabled a rapid reinvention and reappraisal after the 2011 general election. Observers discussed at the time whether the initiatives introduced after 2011 (MediShield Life and the Pioneer Generation Package, for example) cumulatively added up to a shift to the left. It is perhaps possible to glimpse thinking reflective of a government knowing that realities had changed, with a concomitant realisation that there should be a preparedness to make important policy moves without some of the earlier microscopic scrutiny and gatekeeping (such as means-testing for social assistance programmes) that in earlier years might have been applied. It may be possible to sense, too, some of the Party's own 2011 election post-mortem thinking percolating down into these policy moves. It was a major conclusion of the post-mortem (as discussed in the penultimate chapter) that the Party had to find ways to enhance the well-being of all Singaporeans—not just those in the lower-income group it has traditionally been most concerned with, but also those in the middle. And as the Party leadership internally acknowledged at the time, besides requiring significant resources, this would have to be effected without turning populist.

Beneath the veneer of 62 years of dominance, longevity should be seen therefore as fragile—something that is constantly tended to (witness the meticulous manner with which the Party delves into election post-mortems, and within this, the seriousness with which the challenge of the rising Opposition is treated in the recent era). As the penultimate chapter shows, the degree of ground-level engagement that the Party went to in order to win back lost ground from 2011 to 2015 represented in some ways an unprecedented effort.

The 2015 election saw an exceptional result for the PAP, returned to power with a vote share of 69.9 per cent. Policy moves in the years leading up to 2015 and work put in at the ground level by individual PAP MPs were key factors. But there was also a confluence of circumstances—some unique and never to be repeated—that played into the 2015 result. The death of Lee Kuan Yew on 23 March 2015 was one. SG50 (Singapore's celebrations for its 50th year of independence, which buoyed the national mood), was another.

Party leaders acknowledged, both before and after the 2015 election victory, that a reservoir of trust is integral to the straight talking that the PAP has always deployed in its communications with the people. The PAP attempts to improve people's lives and at the same time takes hard policy decisions—increasingly, the two will have to reconcile within this reservoir.[7]

The question is whether the Party's vote share—and by implication its support levels—will at some point return to the mean. And if so, what will this mean? Will support levels for the only governing party that Singapore has ever known eventually rest at an equilibrium? Or will Singapore see (notwithstanding an increased tempo and intensity of work done on the ground by the Party) an inexorable slide in favour of the Opposition? The final chapter (which sees key leaders interviewed) asks these and other critical questions relating to Singapore's future.

The text of this book was largely complete by the time of the 2020 general election, held on 10 July. The election saw substantial gains—or the recovery of lost ground—by opposition parties (which together took 38.76 per cent of the vote against the PAP's 61.24 per cent). The remarkable aspect was not, it could be argued, the fact that the election was held even while Singapore grappled with the COVID-19 pandemic, nor even the slide in support for the PAP (which had acknowledged that replicating the 2015 result was impossible). Most noteworthy was a certain *kind* of sentiment evident on the ground and in the online space during the campaign, as well as the reaction of the PAP that acknowledged the changing mood of the times. Whether this sentiment signifies a profound generational shift in attitudes, or a reaction to the PAP's style (or both), is certain to be analysed in the course of the soul-searching promised both by the PAP and the Workers' Party (the key force in the reinvigorated opposition).

It would have been remiss to ignore the most salient of these developments. The final part of this work forms a coda examining the 2020 general election, with some thoughts offered on the PAP's—and by implication Singapore's—future. The next chapter of the PAP story promises a new premier leading a team of younger generation leaders; this much is known. What is largely unknowable at present is the degree to which this new team will in the years ahead be attuned to the aspirations of the younger generation, and how this team responds to a more effective challenge from the Opposition. If it hopes to maintain dominance and extend its longevity, it will have to achieve all this, all the while navigating Singapore through a world that, at the time of writing, looks to be irrevocably changed.

Note on Sources

Key Party leaders consented to interviews. These included PM Lee Hsien Loong and former Prime Ministers Lee Kuan Yew and Goh Chok Tong, several ministers past and present, as well as current and former MPs. I am also grateful to PAP officials responsible for the Party archive for making files available, as I am to relevant government agencies for making accessible files dealing with aspects of certain policies.[8] In addition, standard sources (including newspaper articles and the official Singapore Parliamentary Reports) that inform histories of the period have been used throughout.

Notes

1   Bellows began working on his doctoral dissertation on the PAP (which became the basis for his subsequent book) in the mid-1960s. Thomas J. Bellows, "The Singapore Party System: The First Two Decades" (PhD dissertation, Yale University, 1968).

2   It is hoped that the earlier history of the Party, itself a rich topic with many under-explored areas (notwithstanding the work done by historians, researchers and political scientists mentioned above in the text), will itself soon receive the comprehensive treatment it deserves.

3   Lee Kuan Yew, "What of the Past is Relevant to the Future?", in *People's Action Party 1954–1979. Petir 25th Anniversary Issue* (Singapore: Central Executive Committee, People's Action Party, 1979), pp. 30–43.

4   Lee also stressed the importance of clear signalling to the Party's supporters and intra-Party unity: "We have been a coherent united group not given to cliques and factionalism. . . . We learned never to confuse our supporters by needless infighting and open dissension. We argued and thrashed out our differences in private. In public we never contradicted each other." "What of the Past is Relevant to the Future?", p. 38.

5   Dr Tony Tan, "Three Fundamental Principles", in *PAP 50: Five Decades of the People's Action Party* (Singapore: People's Action Party, 2004), p. 8.

6   The text also addresses at select points "rethinking" in a different guise. This concerns various infrequent episodes where aspects of the very model underpinning the approach to growth and the economy are reconsidered. These episodes are important moments: some of the issues concern the role that market forces should play within the economy both generally and in particular sectors (housing, for example).

7   "We are fortunate to have inherited a legacy of strong trust between the people and the PAP. The Party built this trust painstakingly over more than 60 years, through the efforts of Party leaders, MPs, activists, Party members. We did so by working with Singaporeans and delivering results, but also working through difficult policies." Secretary-General Lee Hsien Loong, speech at PAP Awards and Convention, 19 Nov. 2017. https://www.pap. org.sg/conference-convention/pap-awards-and-convention-2017-transcript-of-speech-by-secretary-general-lee-hsien-loong/ (accessed 29 Jan. 2021).

8   Where files and documents from the PAP archive have been made available to me, I have cited these in the notes and given their origins ("PAP archive"). Other sources have included government memoranda, exchanges of letters, file notes, or documents pertaining to aspects of policy. Those that have been made available to me for the purpose of this book are distinguished from source citations from materials in the National Archives that are publicly accessible by the addition of "made available to the author", and I have also wherever practicable provided file references. More details on the sources used are provided in the bibliography.

Chapter 1

1985–88: Transition, Renewal, Renovation

Prosperity is a precious thing. Delivered consistently over a period of time by a competent government, it does not just raise living standards—it seeds belief on the part of the people that there is a future for themselves and their children. All the more so in a nation still young and with pangs of painful separation in recent memory.

The PAP government had from independence delivered prosperity. GDP growth averaged 9.76 per cent from 1965 to 1984.[1] GDP per capita, which was approximately US$500 in 1965, stood at just over US$7,200 in 1984.[2] The uplift went beyond simple numbers. Singapore's first prime minister, Lee Kuan Yew, was to look back and observe that the Party "had transformed lives of the people . . . the PAP stayed in power because they trusted us and had confidence in us. They trusted in the ability of the PAP to deliver what it promised."[3]

The ability to deliver makes the majority appreciative of government; it can also attenuate the chafing and frictions that arise when one party has the monopoly on power, making the task for the political opposition all the more difficult. The PAP's vote shares in the general elections of 1972, 1976, and 1980 were 70.4, 74.1, and 77.7 per cent respectively, with opposition parties in Singapore not being able to mount challenges credible enough to see even one of their number elected to Parliament across this period. By-elections in 1979 to speed up the pace of renewal within the PAP also saw a wipe-out, with the PAP winning all seven seats at stake and 72.69 per cent of the vote.[4] Rising affluence seemed set to continue into the 1980s: the years 1980 to 1984 saw real wages increasing at an average of almost 8 per cent annually.[5] Although there were some signs that there might be an increased desire on the part of the people for an opposition (seen in the election in 1981 of Joshua Benjamin Jeyaretnam, secretary-general of the Workers' Party to the parliamentary seat of Anson in a by-election), the PAP's grip on power seemed set to continue.

December 1984: The Aftermath

The 1984 general election (held on 22 December 1984), which saw a 12.9 per cent vote swing against the Party compared to the 1980 election, was therefore a surprise and a serious setback.[6] As Goh Chok Tong, minister for defence and second minister for health (and also first assistant secretary-general in the PAP Central Executive Committee, as well as chairman of the PAP General Elections Committee for the

1984 general election) was to note a few days after the result, "this general election has proven a little scary in the sense that many of us misjudged the mood of the population. There was nearly a swing that resulted in something which all of us did not want. It nearly happened in this election."[7]

Goh had "misjudged the degree of the swing".[8] Besides the desire on the part of the people for some check on the PAP in Parliament, there was also the issue of proposed policies that had not gone down well: the unpopular Graduate Mothers' Scheme and, separately, proposals embedded within what became known as the Howe Yoon Chong report. The former had put graduate mothers with three or more children at the top of the waiting list for primary school entry, followed by those with two children; while the latter (not implemented at the time of its first airing in March 1984 on account of the public outcry) suggested a number of avenues to prepare for Singapore's ageing population, including a suggestion that the minimum withdrawal age for Singaporeans' Central Provident Fund (CPF) savings might have to be raised from 55 to 60.[9]

The PAP would now have to deal with two Opposition members in Parliament. J.B. Jeyaretnam had retained his Anson seat with an increased majority, while Chiam See Tong, secretary-general of the Singapore Democratic Party (SDP), defeated the highly credentialled Mah Bow Tan to become an elected MP at the fourth time of asking.[10] The Party leadership now had to put together its internal post-mortem analysis, examine what went wrong and think through its future course. But on the critical issue of leadership succession, there was considerably less time. Before the election, Lee Kuan Yew had wanted the issue of his successor settled. The result convinced him not to delay.

A mere nine days separated Polling Day from the official announcement of the new Cabinet on 31 December. Looking back much later on these critical few days, Goh Chok Tong was to note that there were some (including even senior figures within the Party) who felt that the vote swing against the PAP necessitated a rethink, and that the handover to the new leaders should be pushed back. But according to Goh, Lee's thinking was that this was "all the more reason we should push ahead with self-renewal . . . the ground is changing. Better move faster with self-renewal. So you chaps go and choose a leader. Whoever you choose, I would appoint him".[11]

Lee had seen how the younger leaders had performed as ministers and in other capacities over the course of the previous years. He had seen how Goh Chok Tong performed as first organising secretary and second assistant secretary-general. This included Goh's work on earlier initiatives within the Party concerning internal renovation of Party structures. Goh had been a key figure in an internal PAP task force from 1977 to 1979 led by MP Hwang Soo Jin that ostensibly examined various matters related to Party organisation, but which in reality functioned also to break in new, promising figures who were slated for higher things.[12]

From the late 1970s, regular lunches with younger-generation leaders also helped Lee in forming his impressions. The lunch sessions included Goh Chok Tong and Lim Chee Onn (who were brought together by their work as Party organising secretaries), Dr Tony Tan (who was less involved in Party work and who lunched separately with Lee), and occasionally S. Dhanabalan.[13] Lee was also interested in the younger ministers' views of each other. Goh Chok Tong recalls occasions in the lead-up to the succession process being settled, when Lee would ask the younger ministers for submissions on paper: "Leaving yourself out, who do you rank?"[14]

The story of Lee's own preference of Dr Tony Tan for his successor has been told elsewhere.[15] This preference was well known within the private circle of Lee, Goh Chok Tong and Dr Tony Tan himself. Goh Chok Tong confirms that Lee had, in fact, told him privately that he preferred Dr Tony Tan.[16] But Lee also felt strongly that he should not pick his own successor. As he was to note in 1990, "the chances of success are much better if you select a group of people, any one of whom could be your successor. Let them contend amongst themselves and decide who will be the leader".[17] Lee never wavered from this, writing in his memoirs:

> I asked the younger Ministers to decide among themselves whom they would support as Prime Minister. I had helped to select them as MPs and appointed them as ministers. I wanted my successor to have the support of his peers. I had seen how Deng Xiaoping had failed with his appointees, Hu Yaobang and Zhao Ziyang. I also remembered how Anthony Eden, chosen by Winston Churchill, failed.[18]

Lee thus chose to take a hands-off approach in the last week of 1984 while the younger ministers attempted to grapple with the issue of choosing a *primus inter pares*. Dr Tony Tan recalled:

> We knew we had a setback. I can tell you my own feelings at the time were in view of this thing. My own feeling was that if we had hesitated, people would have lost confidence in us. So despite the election setback, we had to press ahead with self-renewal and proceed with what we had intended to do before the elections which was that Dr Goh and Raja would step down as deputy prime minister and two of the younger ministers will take their place. I felt that very strongly.
>
> I told them that we have to go ahead. Because this is a point if you hesitate you are lost. But of course it wasn't easy at the time because we were new, this was the first time that this had happened to us. There were a lot of uncertainties. And, you know, when you have a setback like this, you have a lot of criticism, people telling you you did this, you lost this because you were too arrogant, because you did this and you were wrong, and so on and so forth. Any number of people will tell you any number of reasons why you were wrong. And we went round, we talked about it at Party HQ, no decision, we talked about it. I remember one office, probably Goh Chok Tong's office because he was organising secretary at that time, we went to his place, talked about it, no decision. PM Lee I think talked a little bit about it in Cabinet or something, but still, I mean it sort of went on for a week, ten days.[19]

Dr Tony Tan (who at the time held the finance and trade and industry portfolios) played a critical role in forcing matters to resolution. He convened a post-dinner meeting of the younger leaders at his home on 30 December 1984.[20] The deliberations that night were to settle the issue of the deputy premiership and effectively choose Lee's successor. Early on in the meeting, Dr Tan ruled himself out of the reckoning. Those present decided on Goh Chok Tong, who, arriving late from another meeting, agreed to do the job.[21]

The following day, Goh Chok Tong communicated to PM Lee what had transpired: first, that the seven key ministers who formed the core of the next-generation leadership together with a select group of other MPs and officeholders had met, and that they were all unanimous in their decision that Goh move up to become first deputy prime minister (1DPM). Goh added that the group was divided on whether Ong Teng Cheong (minister without portfolio and secretary-general of the National Trades Union Congress) should move up to be second deputy prime minister (2DPM). Goh made known to PM Lee that he had decided Ong should be 2DPM to help him reach out to the Chinese-educated ground.[22]

Other documents show Goh Chok Tong submitting the final Cabinet list to PM Lee on 29 December 1984, the day *before* the 30 December meeting at Dr Tony Tan's house.[23] It is significant that this list already had Goh Chok Tong as 1DPM. This casts a somewhat different light on the 30 December 1984 gathering. This meeting may simply have set the final seal on a series of informal consultations that had been ongoing—deliberations that had already come close to settling on Goh as 1DPM. It also suggests that being chosen on that evening at Dr Tony Tan's house could not have come as a surprise to Goh himself.

There remains the question as to why Goh needed to reiterate to Lee, in his note of 31 December, the unanimity of the younger ministers in choosing him (Goh) as 1DPM, especially when the Cabinet list of 29 December sent to PM Lee gives the appearance of having settled the issue. In the absence of further information, one can only surmise that those concerned agreed that a meeting between the younger ministers was necessary in order to decide the succession issue once and for all, to confirm that Goh was indeed the unanimous choice (as well as settling the issue of the second deputy PM). If this interpretation is accepted, it would appear that it was not simply Dr Tony Tan who brought the ministers together that night of 30 December 1984; the generally felt need for absolute finality was the other force at work.[24]

New Directions

Goh clearly set out the terms of the understanding between PM Lee and the new team in his first press conference as 1DPM-designate on 31 December 1984. The younger ministers would run the show and would not be overruled by PM Lee unless the issues were so critical as to touch on the very survival of the country.[25] Effectively, the country (and, as we shall see, the Party) was now led by 1DPM Goh and the younger team. In the course of his brief speech at the swearing in of the Cabinet on 2 January 1985,

PM Lee confirmed what Goh had said: the younger leaders had now settled on a new striker, leaving Lee, who had played striker and in other positions from 1959 until 1984, to play goalkeeper.[26] New directions and new relationships with the electorate were to flow from their thinking. These will be examined in the following pages.

Style, Substance, Feedback

> For the PAP to suffer such a setback, there must be something amiss in the feedback the party leaders are getting. If there are kinks in the feedback machinery, they should be ironed out, and quickly.

> —*Straits Times* Editorial, "The Need to Listen", 31 December 1984

The election post-mortem task force, convened by 1DPM Goh and chaired by 2DPM Ong Teng Cheong, comprised younger MPs who had been brought in at the 1980 and 1984 elections.[27] The final report was written up by BG Lee Hsien Loong. It was the result not only of internal soul-searching but also field visits to branches, which had to submit returns to detailed questionnaires given to them. Trenchant throughout in its assessments, the report stated that the PAP government had "tempted fate" through its policies (or policy suggestions): "The CPF proposal suggested that people could not be trusted to look after their own money even in old age. The graduate mothers policy . . . implied that not every citizen's child would be equally talented or valued, and worse, that parents too were not equal." The report went even further, stating, "Had it not been for the tremendous depth of support which PAP enjoyed, we would have been voted out of office."[28]

Disposing of the deeply unpopular Graduate Mothers' Scheme was a relatively straightforward issue. In February 1985 Dr Tony Tan, who had held the education portfolio for not much more than a month, announced that he was reviewing the policy.[29] Parliament then heard from Dr Tan in May that he was recommending to Cabinet that the scheme be scrapped.[30] The issue of raising the withdrawal age for CPF funds from 55 to 60 (the key thrust of the Howe Yoon Chong report) was not raised again—for the time being.[31]

This backing down was limited in scope. Party leaders had, in fact, arrived very quickly at the conclusion that there was no need for a rethink of major policies. As the post-mortem report was to note: "The substance of PAP policy should not change. [We] may have to delay implementing particularly unpopular policies, but should never implement an unsound policy for the sake of popularity. Better to stand firm."[32]

This is echoed in 1DPM Goh's first public expressions of his thinking in the early weeks of his new office, which were to set the tone for the way the government engaged the people in the post-1984 period. Goh was clear that while there had been a sizeable protest vote, he did not think that people differed fundamentally on policy.[33] Goh noted that he would like "to encourage greater participation of Singaporeans in shaping the destiny of Singapore. . . . Singaporeans want to participate in determining the course of Singapore and we should encourage their participation."

While being prepared to concede that the PAP had misjudged the size of the swing, Goh chose to tie this to the point that grassroots organisations should be strengthened. The idea of poor networks and sensing mechanisms was also to come up in the PAP post-mortem report:

> The PAP had no reliable means of gauging public support, even during the campaign itself. We depended upon feedback from the branches, which was minimal and unreliable. None of the branches, not even those in what turned out to be marginal constituencies, felt any sense of alarm. They depended on impressions from house to house visits, and mistook courtesy for support. Short of having an intelligence network, or conducting public opinion polls, it will probably be difficult to improve the situation substantially.[34]

One or two of the more acute observers saw, early, which remedies were likely. On 30 December 1984, even before Goh's official appointment as 1DPM, Chan Heng Chee, a political science lecturer at National University of Singapore (NUS), noted that "the election results have turned up a classic case of the protest vote. It is not a vote to turn the PAP government out".[35] Chan (who later was to play her own part in the feedback structures to be created) observed, "There will probably be a restructuring of the PAP's party organisation and its network of feedback institutions in the following months, and a move to develop channels for citizen participation in policy-making."

The Feedback Unit

By early January 1985, ideas on how to rectify the lack of accurate feedback mechanisms were crystallising in 1DPM Goh's mind. On 16 January 1985 he lunched with PM Lee. At this meeting Goh raised the idea of reviving in some form the Central Complaints Bureau, which had been disbanded in 1980.[36]

Subsequent to this lunch, on 22 January 1985, DPM Goh wrote to Minister for Community Development S. Dhanabalan and Minister for Communications and Information Dr Yeo Ning Hong, suggesting the revival of the Central Complaints Bureau but adding that its name should be changed to "Public Consultation Unit" and it should be given "new form and objectives":

> To receive and document suggestions from the public on how to make Singapore a better place to live in, in particular, feedback on government policies and how they can be improved for common good. . . . Prime Minister thinks the proposal is worth a try, even though it may outlive its usefulness after a few years.[37]

In a sign of the urgency 1DPM Goh felt, S. Dhanabalan was asked to work out the details and put up a proposal to the Cabinet within two weeks. In their discussions at this time, the leadership recognised that people wanted a more participative style of government and wanted to have a say before major government policies were adopted. In addition, there was some recognition of the need for a more effective machinery through which people could seek redress for genuine grievances, especially in cases where ministries implemented policies overly rigidly.[38]

It is useful to consider how in the time from the leadership initially discussing the concept (February 1985) to the actual unveiling of the unit (April 1985), there had been subtle but important changes in thinking. The idea of a clearinghouse for complaints against the public bureaucracy was still present, but more muted.[39] There was a shift to the idea of explaining policy to a new generation, whose expectations were vastly different from those of older Singaporeans. This was reflected in Minister S. Dhanabalan's comments during the press conference on 15 April 1985 where the unit was officially unveiled:

> *The electorate itself is younger. It is better educated. The experience of the younger electorate, their life experience, is quite different. They can only remember a period of continuous growth and stability. It's not their fault. They just happen to be born, or they happen to grow up in a more fortunate time in our history. Their expectations are higher, as it should be. And because of these things, it is necessary to use existing channels of communication more effectively and in new and more imaginative ways in order to communicate with the people. This will be the main task of the Feedback Unit.*[40]

Dhanabalan cautioned (following the thinking of the still-gestating 1984 general election PAP post-mortem report) that "the establishment of the Feedback Unit does not mean that the Government intends to govern by conducting referenda or opinion polls on every issue".[41] While the leadership was stating its commitment to consultation, it was taking pains to delimit clearly its parameters.[42]

As Dhanabalan explained, educating people on national problems was the key aim of the meetings, forums and other activities organised by the Feedback Unit. It is no coincidence that this aspect—education—also features in the 1984 general election PAP post-mortem report:

> *The other side of consultation is education. . . . It is critical for the population to understand the limits of what is feasible. Otherwise, the government will always be under pressure to do the impossible. Whether the voters take an active part in the policy process, or whether they merely endorse a government every five years, it will help tremendously if they can distinguish a mirage from a vision. The evidence so far is that they cannot. Education of the voters is therefore a critical task of government, and especially of the Feedback Unit which has just been formed.*[43]

It also appears that some care was taken to make sure that feedback was not seen as being driven from the top. The Feedback Unit's Supervisory Panel was populated with individuals who would bolster the credentials of the unit by being a genuine listening ear for ground concerns. Outspoken Ayer Rajah MP Tan Cheng Bock was appointed chairman of the panel. Three other backbenchers were on the panel—Othman Haron

Eusofe, Dr Dixie Tan and Goh Choon Kang. Another two panel members were the community leaders Chang Meng Teng and Kenneth Chen.[44]

The leadership had acted quickly to shore up one vulnerability. The general response from the public and the press was that this was a large step in the right direction. Only one nagging doubt seems to have surfaced at that time, one that did not appear particularly significant but (as we will see) was to assume greater importance. The issue was this: if the intention was to invite feedback on matters of genuine importance, it seemed like only those who were well educated or could express themselves well could actually avail themselves of these new mechanisms. Others might have views, but be unable to express themselves. Tellingly, this theme was first enunciated by the Chinese-language press. *Shin Min Daily News* commented: "On the other hand, to the broad masses, the Feedback Unit looks like a central body beyond their reach and, in the eyes of the general public, it is another government department, giving them a feeling of austere aloofness."[45]

Just how useful were the mechanisms created, and whom did they reach out to? What about the less well educated, who were not comfortable with the newfound— and what some saw as new-fangled—mechanisms? This was an issue which was to recur in various forms throughout the 1980s and beyond.

PAP Renewal and Reorganisation, 1985–88

Goh Chok Tong's elevation to the deputy premiership entailed not just more political responsibility. As he made clear, he had at the same time been given full control of the PAP "as its *de facto* leader".[46] Goh began a programme of Party internal self-examination, reorganisation and expansion that was unprecedented in scale. This will now be examined, together with his discussions on the subject with PM Lee, which provides insights into the interplay between the two men.

On 24 January 1985 Goh wrote to PM Lee, suggesting the formation of a new committee within the Party HQ to be named the HQ Executive Committee (HQ Exco). The HQ Exco would assist the organising secretaries and HQ staff "to think out and implement ways and means of ensuring that the Party continues to enjoy popular support and occupy political high ground".[47] Goh suggested that the HQ Exco and working committees could have the same two-year lifespan as the Central Executive Committee (CEC). They would be appointed by the CEC and answer to it.

As Goh observed to Lee, the proposal to revitalise the workings of PAP HQ was not completely new. The HQ Exco proposal formalised the work of an earlier ad hoc task force (also chaired by Goh) established in February 1983. The key people involved in conceptualising this earlier task force were Goh, Lee and Ch'ng Jit Koon. Ch'ng (parliamentary secretary in the Prime Minister's Office) had come up with the early draft for the task force concept and sent his plan to PM Lee.[48] Ch'ng, who was closely connected to the Chinese-speaking ground, had in mind improving communication between the government and people through constituency walkabouts and dialogue sessions by younger MPs and ministers.[49] These began from October 1982, even before the task force officially began its work. Goh's ideas, which were to fuse with Ch'ng's, concerned a task force (with subcommittees concerned with constituency relations, branch liaison and information) to revitalise PAP branches.[50]

Writing to PM Lee in January 1985 on the proposed HQ Exco, Goh recalled this earlier initiative and noted that he had found it helpful and effective.

PM Lee replied a day later to say he approved the formation of the HQ Exco and its various working committees. But in response to Goh's suggestions for organising secretaries and key positions within the HQ Exco and subcommittees, Lee had this to say:

> *I have reservations on the over-burdening of the few key digits you have on these committees. If the same people are used over and over again, they cannot push all their jobs as expeditiously. Whether it is in HQ Executive Committee or in the working Committees, do not include a person just for form's sake. He must be there to make a contribution.*[51]

Lee was also prepared to offer further views on those people—in particular the younger generation coming through—who could be used, adding, "In a year and a half, you will know the quality of the 1984 batch and can use them."

The final makeup of the HQ Exco and its subcommittees is given in Table 1.1, together with a description of their functions.[52]

The formation of the HQ Exco, which was to meet bimonthly, was the core plank of Goh's plan to reorganise the Party. But Goh attached little fanfare to it at the time. He wrote to CEC members on 8 February 1985, stating simply that "the Party must be revitalized and our members imbued with a new mission and a new zeal", and that Secretary-General Lee had agreed with his suggestion to form the HQ Exco and its working committees, to assist the organising secretaries and the HQ staff.[53]

The committees under the HQ Exco wasted no time in getting to work. By April 1985 the Publicity and Publications Committee was reviewing the quality and cost effectiveness of publishing *Petir*.[54] Separately, by April 1985 the Branch Liaison Committee had come up with its own action plan to engage Party branches.[55]

Space precludes a full study of the working methods of the HQ Exco, its committees and the organising secretaries in this volume. It is apparent however that a key theme in Goh's thinking—attempting to reconnect with the ground (as we have already seen with the Feedback Unit, which stood outside of the Party) quickly manifested within the Party too. On 28 September 1985, First Organising Secretary (1OS) Ow Chin Hock wrote to various MPs and ministers:

> *The Objectives of our Party for the immediate future will be:*
> *(a) To focus the attention of our people, particularly the younger*
> *generation, on the basics of what makes Singapore tick.*
> *(b) To build up the image of the New Cabinet as a firm, fair, strong and*
> *understanding government, and the only choice for Singapore.*
> *(c) To forge a new accord and bond between our leaders and our people.*

Table 1.1 HQ Exco and Subcommittees, 1985

Name	Chairman	Purpose
HQ Exco Committee Chairman: Goh Chok Tong Members: Ahmad Mattar, Ch'ng Jit Koon, Chua Sian Chin, S. Jayakumar Secretary: Lau Ping Sum		
Branch Liaison Committee	Dr Ow Chin Hock	To strengthen rapport with branches and members through greater political participation by members and informal visits to branches by Party leaders
Constituency Relations Committee	Wong Kan Seng	To strengthen relations between the government and the people through constituency tours, seminars, forums, and dialogue sessions
Publicity and Publications Committee	Lim Boon Heng	To publish Petir and present and explain policies, ideologies, and activities of the Party and the government
Information Committee	Yeo Cheow Tong	To monitor ground political activities
Political Education Committee	Dr Wan Soon Bee	To organise political talks for Party members and train Party activists
Education Committee	Ho Kah Leong	To coordinate and plan BEST (Basic Education for Skills Training)* classes at NTUC (National Trades Union Congress) and PAP centres and administer kindergarten classes
Social and Recreational Committee	Dr Lee Boon Yang	To organise social and recreational activities and promote greater interaction and cohesiveness amongst members and supporters
Malay Affairs Bureau	Ahmad Mattar	To discuss matters of interest pertaining to the Malay-Muslim community in Singapore and make recommendations for the improvement of the community's welfare
District Committees		Seven district committees were formed to further the interests of the Party through district-based activities, to promote cooperation and fraternity among branches, and to monitor ground political activities.[†]

* BEST (Basic Education for Skills Training) was a programme run by the National Trades Union Congress (NTUC), with further support provided by the Vocational and Industrial Training Board (VITB) and the Institute of Technical Education (ITE), from 1982 until 2009 that provided English and arithmetic classes for workers who did not complete a Primary Six education. Completion of BEST would usually allow the participant to enrol in further skills training courses.

[†] The district committees at that time were Suburban West, Suburban East, Central, and Suburban North. These were later changed to align with the boundaries of the present-day Community Development Councils.

> *To achieve the above objectives, we must not only strengthen our relationship*
> *with existing organisations (e.g., constituency organisations, trade unions, etc.), but*
> *also establish a new frontier in building up rapport with various groups of opinion*
> *makers and opinion multipliers.*

Ow went on in the letter to identify the target groups—17 in all—and to note which MP had been assigned to lead which action team.[56] Ow requested that events such as dialogue sessions and tea parties be planned, "and as many members as possible of these target groups should be won over . . . also, leaders who are pro-government should be identified and they can be co-opted into organising activities for the group, or recruited into the resource pool of the Party HQ".[57]

Unfortunately, there is no real sense of the ongoing work of this initiative, precise details of the progress made, or when it ceased to function. But the mere fact of its existence is significant. These early moves in 1985 prefigured (or may even have segued into) the later ministerial engagement sessions and walkabouts, and the 1987 dialogue sessions associated with the Agenda for Action. The move to reach out to "target groups" should also not be regarded as a brand-new initiative. In the PAP archive there are extant letters from MPs and ministers to 1OS Ow, noting their appointment, detailing the progress they made, and in some cases observing that the appointments to head the action teams dovetailed with work that was already ongoing separately. 2DPM Ong Teng Cheng wrote on 15 November 1985 in reply to OS Ow Chin Hock, noting that he had been appointed team leader for three groups: trade unions, clan associations and taxi drivers. He noted that for unions, he already had a team of nine union MPs working closely with him, and affiliated unions had recently agreed to appoint 21 of the 24 new MPs as their union advisers.[58]

The public consultation and engagement (even as it built on earlier outreach work) from early 1985 clearly had something of an impact.[59] One commentator noted that 1DPM Goh and BG Lee took on the role of chief communicators for the Party, engaging in dialogue sessions with university students, professional groups, business leaders and the press,

> *[With Goh and Lee] striving to bridge the gap between government and the*
> *people. Both men invested time and energy in public forums before strategic*
> *elites such as university students, graduate alumni, professional groups, the press*
> *corps, and Chinese business leaders to elaborate on their vision of society and*
> *their perceptions and solutions to national problems. The adoption of a more*
> *consultative and consensus-seeking political style.[60]*

The Centre and the Branches

1DPM Goh spearheaded the Party reorganisation with a sense of urgency. His method of working was to float ideas (which in many cases had been first discussed with MPs or grassroots or Party activists) with PM Lee personally, and then to move quickly to table recommendations before the full Party CEC once Lee had signalled general agreement. Goh's ideas extended beyond modifying the Party structure at HQ level. He also thought more deeply in terms of how the Party had to change, in what direction, and how far.

In a 13 May 1986 memo to PM Lee, Goh laid out what he saw as the issues:

> *One major problem we will face is sagging spirit and vitality in the Party. This is due mainly to increasing frustration of Party members at their lack of role and prestige in the process of Government.*
>
> *I shall spend the next few months tackling this problem, finalising the programmes to attract new members and inject vitality into the Party, before the Party Conference in November.*
>
> *The process has already started, with several groups being asked to give a critical, detached view of the Party, and to make recommendations. Before we put the various proposals into a coherent manifesto for rallying Singaporeans in general, and Party members, in particular, I thought you might wish to glance through the following papers to see the main ideas being discussed.*

Goh ended the note by saying to PM Lee: "My plan is to discuss the above documents with MPs and Branch Committee members, and use the process of discussion, to mobilise them, Party members and others, behind an action programme for the Party. This action programme will be the manifesto of the Party for the next decade."[61]

The three papers Goh appended to this note were: (i) a paper titled "PAP's Public Image and How It Can Be Improved", authored by a resource panel of six high-ranking branch members (but all non-MPs);[62] (ii) an outline of the PAP Youth Wing, written by Lee Hsien Loong; and (iii) a paper on parliamentary committees by Dr Hong Hai.

The Youth Wing and Parliamentary Committees concept will be discussed later. What we are concerned with here is the paper "PAP's Public Image and How It Can Be Improved". It is possible to glimpse within this hard-hitting paper some of the 1984 election post-mortem that was ongoing at the PAP branch level.

The paper noted that after 25 years of PAP government, the lines between the Party and government had been blurred and that "the party is perceived, not as a party of the people, but a party of the government".

> *The image of the party, therefore, is formed by people's impression of the government. There is a perception that government policies are implemented without regard for the impact it has on people and that the government or party leaders are not willing to listen or consider alternatives. There is also the feeling that the opinions of the masses are not important, a result of the overly publicised policy of meritocracy and more recently the publicity over the selection of party candidates. They are insulted by the implied affront to their intelligence and are developing a "we'll show you" attitude.*[63]

The paper was particularly scathing on the neglect by PAP leadership of the branches:

> *The role of the branches and HQ is unclear. Unless an election is coming, most branches have been relegated to opening once a week for MPS [meet-the-people sessions]. The attitude of the branches towards HQ is also poor. Sometimes nothing important is ever discussed. Meetings at HQ degenerate to listening to announcements or directives . . . the few times discussions have taken place, no follow-up action is seen to be taken by ministers or senior party leaders, not even a note to say why the idea needs to be rejected. As a result HQ meetings are tolerated rather than viewed as a valuable means for discussions and information.*

The 1984 election post-mortem report had similarly noted that branches were moribund:

> *The party branches, on the other hand, are presently rather dormant outfits. Between elections, they run kindergarten classes and meet the people sessions, but often do little else. This is not a reflection on the dedication or commitment of the branch members, but a result of the branches being given no functional role to play.*[64]

This malaise at the branch level is something that had, at its roots, the historical treatment accorded to the branches since the 1960s. Former PAP MPs interviewed by the author stressed the importance of the historical legacy of the July 1961 split with PAP left-wing assemblymen, who, led by Lim Chin Siong and Lee Siew Choh, would go on to form the Barisan Sosialis. Many branches transferred overnight their allegiance, assets and members to what became the Barisan.[65] The memory of this split was to linger in the organisational thinking within the PAP leadership, with branches never being given too much influence or power.[66] The core of the Party lay in the CEC—the leadership, the direction, the politics.

Naturally, the threat of the branches being captured had receded by the 1980s. The thrust of large parts of the paper on the PAP's public image was to suggest, essentially, that politics should be reintroduced into the branches. The role of the branches had to be redefined: a branch "must be involved in politics and should be the focal point for political expression". The activists also noted that branches should be the focal point for disseminating Party and not just government policies and "should serve as a platform for political expression".[67]

The 1984 reverse made the Party leadership—and Goh in particular—more amenable to listening to the pleas from branch and grassroots leaders. The well-being and morale of the branches was debated at the CEC in August 1985, with Goh emphasising that in order to revitalise the Party, branch committees in particular had to be given a sense of contribution and influence.[68] The measures taken included the following:

- Branches were from 1985 allowed (through the district committees) to put up resolutions for consideration at Party conferences.[69]
- Links with HQ were improved through the Branch Liaison Committee.

- Goh personally briefed new MPs on how to organise their constituency activities with the Party branch as the focal point.[70]
- CEC agreed that the Party base had to be broadened. Recruitment targets were given to branches to broaden the Party base: a target of 50 members, including Youth Wing members, per branch by the end of 1986, and another 150 members in 1987 and 1988.[71]

Other incremental moves were made that did go some way to addressing the concern of depoliticisation of the branches. 1OS Ow Chin Hock and OS (Special Duties) Lau Ping Sum started holding meetings at neutral venues where branch members would come together and discuss issues of policy.[72] In 1985 Ow also began on his own initiative to tabulate and analyse data on the types of problems residents brought with them when meeting their MP at the weekly meet-the-people sessions in the PAP-run constituencies. This enabled the Party HQ to get a better fix on the nature of the problems that people faced on the ground, and also a better idea of the profile of people facing particular types of problems.[73] This eventually became a formalised arrangement, with branches tasked to submit individual returns of these analyses to the bimonthly branch secretary meetings at HQ. Finally, the HQ Exco's Information Committee, whose role was to monitor Opposition ground political activities and to work out political lines to counter such activities, appears to have taken steps to get branches to be more organised in operating their own committees to systematically monitor and gather feedback on the activities of opposition political parties within their constituencies.[74]

The picture that emerges from changes in 1985–86 is that some aspects of the long-standing neglect of the branches were lifted, with Goh Chok Tong as the primary architect. The branches, however, may have wanted more substantive change. The writers of the paper on the public image of the PAP were convinced that the various non-PAP grassroots organisations competed with the branches for media attention: "With the lack of visibility and status associated with being a party branch member, the grassroots organisations and leaders tend to attract more attention." The paper also noted that it was important to start integrating the various grassroots organisations within the Party, as some "have become too independent".[75] The writers of the report also suggested upgrading the Party profile and making the lines between the Party and government more distinct. The same concerns had been raised in the post-mortem report for the 1984 general election:

> *Campaigning will be easier if we have the support of the grassroots leadership, if we have a strong constituency apparatus of party branches. The grassroots organisations such as the RCs [Residents' Committees], CCMCs [Community Centre Management Committees] and CCCs [Citizens' Consultative Committees] must be firm supporters of the government, able to mobilise votes on its behalf. This is not the case, especially with the RCs, which have developed into rather apolitical organisations. Many RC members are reluctant to be identified with the PAP. This weakens our base substantially.[76]*

Lee's own views on the directions the Party had to take can be summed up in an intervention at the CEC's 24 July 1986 meeting, when changes to Party organisation were being discussed:

> *Secretary-General stated that it was up to the younger leaders to decide on the changes and innovations to be made to the Party organisation. However, he cautioned against a violent shift because striking too strident a note would arouse resentment and retaliation from the opposition supporters. The mystique of an elite group providing mutual help, as in the case of Freemasonry, was more effective.*[77]

1DPM Goh had no violent shifts in mind, and here it is useful to consider the things which Goh did *not* do in his reorganisation of the Party at this time, and what suggestions the leadership, collectively, were uncomfortable with. The CEC took the view that grassroots leaders should be encouraged to openly identify with the PAP, and that individual grassroots leaders should be encouraged to join the Party. In addition, there was some emphasis placed from 1986 onwards on getting grassroots organisations to organise activities jointly with the Party, through the PAP Community Foundation (PCF).[78] But the Party leadership felt that bringing the grassroots organisations too closely within the ambit of the Party would create more problems than it would solve. Civil servants, for example, would find it difficult to join RCs if they were brought within the PAP party structure.[79]

In his thinking of how the Party should evolve, 1DPM Goh chose not to make moves that would in effect have changed the relationship between the Party and the organisations it depended on. The Party continued to rely on non-Party organisations. The CCCs, RCs and the People's Association were left largely untouched. The setting up of the Feedback Unit in April 1985 was itself evidence of continued reliance on parapolitical organisations. These organisations combined had a greater outreach and were capable of reaching far beyond what the branches could do. And if in the minds of the people these were seen as part of the PAP, it was wholly not a bad thing. PM Lee had on 14 May written to Goh, commenting on the internal paper "The Public Image of the PAP". He noted (with reference to a suggestion that the Party and government should be made more distinct):

> *The question is what are the premises of your generation? Do you believe the younger generation? Do you believe the younger generation should be given their heads? Or are you sceptical? If you are sceptical, then the people's identification of government and party does little harm. It makes it more unlikely for people to vote another party in to form the government. It may happen, but only over a longer period of time. . . . However, you may want to make partial concessions to their proposals to win more such activists into the party and then slowly educate them into the facts of life.*[80]

To sum up: the Party leadership, while sympathetic to the branches, was not completely in agreement with all of what branches wanted. Some concerns could be seen to, but there were others that could not be addressed as the Party leadership was determined that reform would proceed in a circumspect manner, without radical tinkering. And even in areas where solutions had been attempted, there were no quick fixes. Calls to revitalise the branches were a recurring theme through the middle and late 1980s, as we shall see. And certain key issues—perceived neglect by HQ,[81] branches' role in shaping government policy, and differences in view on the role of the grassroots organisations—were to remain through the remainder of the 1980s and into the 1990s.[82]

Party Centralisation and Party Organs

1DPM Goh's primary instincts in Party reorganisation were above all centralising ones, as can be seen from the creation of the HQ Exco. Other Party bodies were formed during the second half of the 1980s, which deserve attention because they were to change for good the face of the PAP.

The PAP Community Foundation (PCF)

Party records reveal that the CEC had in February 1983 approved the formation of a Foundation which would take over the kindergarten and other education activities of the PAP branches. The branches were not legal entities, but several had built up sizeable reserves through the running of kindergartens. The decision was taken that these funds should be used for education, but that a separate organisation, related to the Party but non-political, would front these educational and other social activities. The actual incorporation of the PAP Community Foundation (the name settled on) was not formally tabled before the CEC until March 1986. It appears that the delay was on account of the need to first regularise the position of the branches.

S. Dhanabalan was elected Party treasurer in 1984. Like Goh Chok Tong, he had useful private sector experience. He quickly got to grips with modernising internal Party accounting practices, then turning his attention to the branches.[83] Dhanabalan recalled:

> [The branches] were all controlled by the MP, by the local committee, and to take it out and put it into a central organization where they would lose control was not an easy thing. So it was quite a delicate exercise, and we had to go and talk to the MPs, we got them together, we went to particular branches to assure them that this money was still available for them to run education programmes and so on, but they had to all be transferred into a central fund. And after quite a bit of persuasion, and I would say probably with a lot of misgivings, they agreed. And all the funds were then transferred to PCF.[84]

All branches transferred their accumulated financial assets to the PCF in 1987.[85] From this date, all education and social activities of the Party were conducted through the PCF.[86] Although these were to be its primary roles, the PCF served other useful functions too. As the paper on the incorporation of the PCF tabled at the March 1986 CEC meeting notes:

> In most constituencies there are no separate branch offices. The education centre (kindergarten) serves as the branch office and is identified as the centre of branch activities. If the educational centres come under the Foundation and the Foundation is not clearly identified with the Party in name and logo, the Party will have almost no physical presence in the constituency. It is therefore recommended that the Foundation be openly identified with the Party.[87]

The PCF was therefore *of* the Party, but intentionally distanced from politics. Internal Party discussion at this time had acknowledged the need to mitigate the austere image of the Party and for the Party to show its "human side". This was best done through the PCF and its social programmes.[88] In an April 1986 *Petir* article representing the first open airing of the PCF concept, Acting Minister for Community Development and Minister of State for Communications and Information Wong Kan Seng mused that in order to make the Party more "human" and "approachable", the PAP could not just remain as it was but had to remake its image into that of "a large compassionate social institution", and suggested that the proposed foundation was the logical way forward.[89]

People who might not necessarily have wanted to be involved with politics or any political party were thus brought indirectly into contact with the Party through social activities (such as Family Days, or walk-a-jogs to raise funds for charity and the PCF) and also through the charitable thrust of the PCF (bursary awards, for example). These activities helped to soften the image of the Party from the mid-1980s onwards.

We now turn to other aspects of institution-building that had the aim of refreshing the Party, broadening its base and renewing its appeal.

The Youth Wing

1DPM Goh, like PM Lee, did not feel that many MPs would emerge from the branches. Goh had been discussing with then-Acting Minister for Trade and Industry BG Lee Hsien Loong a concept that would, if it worked, renew PAP ranks, refresh the branches, and surface professionals and potential MPs. The idea—forming a PAP Youth Wing— would also change the nature and makeup of many of the branches for good.

BG Lee had set out the case for a Youth Wing to DPM Goh in the early months of 1986. Goh urged him to proceed but made one key observation: "Few existing youthful members have leadership potential, I think. They may be envious of newcomers. It is therefore better to invite potential youth leaders to be Party members first, before you entrench old ones in the Youth Committee."[90]

The CEC approved the formation of the Youth Wing at its 24 July 1986 meeting, with BG Lee as its first chairman.[91] PM Lee Hsien Loong recalled that bringing in new and young members into the existing system was by no means easy to accomplish. While they could always join as Party members, there was a certain social dynamic at work in the branches that could make it difficult for newcomers—however enthusiastic—to fit in. Branches sometimes held established groups of people who had been together for a long time.[92] The atmosphere could be cliquish. It was not easy for young people to break into a branch, find themselves welcome, or make themselves useful. "We were worried that the Party was getting old and out of date," observed PM Lee, looking back on the period.[93] A more direct way was needed to bring young people into the Party.

Success often depended at the branch level on whether there were one or two more active individuals who could get a group to coalesce around them. At some branches, the changes wrought by the arrival of the Youth Wing did not go down well and led to resentment. This was confirmed by George Yeo, who took over as chairman of the Youth Wing in 1991 and who was generally credited within the Party with taking Young PAP further and building on the foundations set by Lee Hsien Loong. Yeo touched on the issue of resistance at the branch level:

> At the branch level we had partial success, a lot depending on the particular branch. . . . Especially in branches where there are long-serving branch secretaries or those in any position of responsibility. They would want the young people to serve their time. Of course, young people with so many conflicting pressures on their time would be very repulsed by such an attitude. So I would say one-third to half of the branches had difficulty getting the MP and the branch secretaries to accept the Young PAP. Then over time, when the younger MPs coming in, the problem gradually corrected itself. In my case, I decided to force the change by telling my branch members that henceforth, the Young PAP person should be responsible for everything, from cleaning the toilet, opening the door. . . . Week in, week out, there's always a group who are there, typing letters, making sure that things are properly done. Then the older members can relax a bit, [don't] come when you didn't feel like it. And a few weeks, problems here and there, but eventually it worked very well and older members were very happy about it. They were relieved of the responsibility.[94]

There were other points of resentment. When the Youth Wing was formed, the monthly branch secretaries' meeting was (coincidentally) cut to once every three months. The frequency had to be raised to bimonthly in order to correct the impression held by some branch secretaries that the Youth Wing had become more important than senior activists.[95] Despite these issues, the Youth Wing (renamed Young PAP in 1993) grew. By late 1988, it had 2,000 members.[96] Key in its initial impetus was a calibrated mix of political and social activity. Many younger individuals were initially not very politically conscious and more comfortable taking part in social activities such as those organised (for example) by the People's Association Youth Movement. The politics had to be introduced gradually.

The Youth Wing did, however, succeed to an extent in repoliticising Party discourse. It organised the first Party convention in 1987, the first of its kind. This convention coincided with the debate on the National Agenda work group report. The Youth Wing held sessions within the convention to discuss the report; these sessions were held to have been quite successful in getting Party members to understand issues from a national perspective.

The Youth Wing had a certain attraction, as it could be a path to becoming an MP. Some individuals who became the earliest—and core—members of the Youth Wing were already active in the branches. In the 1988 general election, five candidates were put forward as coming from the Youth Wing. Two of them, John Chen and Choo Wee Khiang, had been with the Youth Wing since the beginning. Chen was the branch secretary in Hong Kah. The others—Davinder Singh, K. Shanmugam and Abdul Nasser Kamaruddin—were young candidates who went through the interview process and became members of the Youth Wing Central Committee. They were presented as Youth Wing members.

The Women's Wing

The last female MP, Chan Choy Siong, had stepped down in 1970 as the PAP member of parliament for Delta Constituency. Women had from that point not figured prominently on the political scene for many years. Branches in the 1970s and 1980s were male-dominated. Even at the time of the inauguration of the Women's Wing in April 1989, it was telling that all 81 PAP branch secretaries were men.

There seems to have been no impetus to change this state of affairs for a considerable length of time. Indeed, there may even have been some uncertainty within the Party leadership over whether women could, or should, be MPs. This changed around the time when Goh Chok Tong began serious efforts to bring in women—1984, the year when three female MPs were elected.[97] In 1986 Goh broached the idea of a Women's Wing with Dr Aline Wong and Dr Dixie Tan.[98] The idea was not taken up at that point for two reasons: Wong and Tan were busy with their MP duties and their careers; and in addition, there was a concern that the Women's Wing might be pushed into a supporting or backroom role.[99] But Wong subsequently took up the idea again when the recruitment drive of the Youth Wing showed that it was possible to surface women with a genuine interest in politics.[100] She drafted the initial proposal paper (which Goh personally approved) on the Women's Wing, which was put before the CEC on 4 December 1988.[101]

It is not difficult to understand Goh's personal interest in the subject. Just as with the formation of the Youth Wing, he felt that the base of people that the Party could tap on needed to be broadened. People could be brought into serious discussions of issues; some might become useful resource persons, and a few might make the jump to MP. But at least the Party would have access to a much wider pool of people than formerly, and the Party could decide how each would be used. Goh's sense was that the lack of a good network within the circles of qualified women was responsible for the PAP not being able to field more women candidates at the 1988 elections.[102]

Dr Aline Wong, looking back on these events, shed light on Goh's thinking:

> *So he told me actually that at that point of time . . . it was important to find more women MPs and also to build up a group of women supporters who need not necessarily join the Party as a member straight away but who would form some kind of a resource pool so that whenever we needed, we could tap ideas and expertise … we could have a list of these people to turn to. That's all the terms of reference he gave me.*[103]

It is clear that the Party leadership did not see the Women's Wing as discussing concerns of particular interest to women only; if it was to be formed, the wing had to fall in line with the objectives of other arms of the Party, particularly the Youth Wing. It had to get women to discuss national issues, help to transmit values to the young, and help the poor.[104]

As with the case of the Youth Wing, it was necessary to work hard to overcome issues at the branch level:

> *So the next step was to go around the branches and the districts to persuade both MPs and the grassroots to form the women's committee. So among the four women MPs, I would go around as much as possible, especially when a Women's Wing branch committee was inaugurated. So I took the opportunity to explain to them the mission, the objectives and so on of the Women's Wing and to get to know the male MPs, the local MPs. So for the first two years or so we were going around the branches . . . even up to the end of the third year or even up to the fifth year, not every branch, there were still a few branches without a Women's Wing committee and I was still disappointed. I remember feeling quite upset with my male colleagues. After two, three years after we had organised so many things. Branches had been invited to witness what we do, but several still could not form a committee.*[105]

The Women's Wing faced an additional level of resistance in the form of scepticism from some within the Party rank and file. This was partly on account of the long absence of women from national politics, and also on account of the concern some felt that the Party's energies were better spent on consolidating the Youth Wing.[106] Finally, some appear to have felt that the Women's Wing would find it difficult to be influential as Aline Wong was not on the CEC, whilst Youth Wing Chairman BG Lee was.[107] Wong and the other female MPs and activists persevered. It was to take many years before scepticism was broken down completely and branches fully accepted the presence of women's committees.

Recruitment: Other Aspects

We have already seen how the attempts in 1985–86 to revitalise the Party included enhanced recruitment efforts by the Party at the branch level. Even before this, DPM Goh decided that the system of screening and recruiting cadres should also be looked at afresh.

Cadres, Professionals and Ordinary People

Cadres made up a small number (not exceeding 1,000) of the Party membership.[108] They represented the Party elite, carefully screened and selected, with the ultimate power of electing the Party CEC. DPM Goh's concern appears to have been that many cadre members were essentially dormant, playing no constructive role at the branch level—nor, for that matter, anywhere else within the Party. Goh flagged the problem to Lee in June 1984 when he suggested dropping from the Party register cadres who had not attended the last two Party conferences without good reason, and who were in addition not known to be active in the Party branch or community organisations closely associated with the Party.[109]

The first task —the cleaning up of cadre lists—was relatively uncomplicated. PM Lee signalled his assent, suggesting only that in recommendations for cadre membership, priority be given to the recommendations of some of the newer MPs elected in 1980 or since the last cadre admission exercise. Implicit in this was the idea that newer MPs should be allowed to have their own supporters within the cadre membership.[110]

The second task was the actual renewal of the cadre ranks. This was considerably more involved. A selection exercise for cadre membership was held in August 1985, the first since early 1982. Three selection committees chaired by Dr Tony Tan, S. Dhanabalan and Prof. S. Jayakumar (with Tan as overall chairman) considered a total of 139 candidates put forward by the branches. The criterion for consideration was that candidates should have at least three years of membership in their branch (exceptional candidates with less than three years could be considered). Of the 139 candidates, 96, or 69.1 per cent, received "A" to "C" grades ("C" being deemed "acceptable") and were recommended for cadre membership.

Not all branch members and activists could make the jump to cadres. The less obvious but perhaps more significant point gleaned from this exercise is that even fewer cadres could be considered MP material. In the 1985 exercise, of the 139 individuals put forward by the branches, just 36 were tertiary educated. Only one candidate received an "A", which meant that the candidate was of potential MP calibre.[111] This points to the real issue within the Party: the renewal of MPs, and the question of where the next generation of MPs and ministers would come from. This had already caused a considerable degree of angst within the Party and was to remain a thorny issue.

The Party leadership had by the mid-1980s come to firmly hold the idea that the professional classes—the likely core of future MPs—would not come through the branches. Indeed, in the post-1984 period, PM Lee also took the view that many professionals and high-fliers did not want to be openly identified with the Party. This likely reflected the consensus within the CEC.[112]

What of the view from the branches? By 1985–86, thinking at the ground level appears to have come round to accepting that professionals would generally not be attracted to the branches. But the reason advanced by the branches was different: the system discouraged professionals from joining the Party in the branches because of the belief that if one was good enough, one would be asked to join anyway by Party leaders. This bypassed the need to "do time" in the branch.[113] The writers of the paper "The Public Image of the PAP" submitted to the PAP leadership in April 1986 implicitly accepted that this would not be changed but still insisted on the need to review the process of developing Party leadership. The report proposed not discarding the selection system, but that

> a parallel system could be put into place so that branches can nominate candidates for election to be considered by the CEC. It may be that such a system already exists. However, no one perceives or believes it does.

> The Party must compromise and allow a few candidates to be pushed up this way. Many believe that, unlike the past, there are now sufficient safeguards to ensure that the branches cannot dominate the CEC. It is now time, therefore, to reverse some of the depoliticisation of the branches.

> A second modification to the Party's system of selecting candidates is that where candidates are selected by the party's leaders, this should be done many years before the next election, and all must pass through the branch from day one, not when their nominations are imminent. During this period of time, party leaders should observe their progress as they work with other branch leaders. If the latter do not accept the candidate, the party leaders should seriously reconsider the individual's candidacy.[114]

Despite PM Lee's scepticism, he appears by this point to have been willing to allow certain concessions. He wrote to Goh in response to the paper: "You can agree that to make the Branches a path to MP-ship, that one-quarter to one-third of the next batch of candidates will be nominated or will come from the Branches."[115] This should not be read as a change of heart but as Lee for his part reacting to the 1984 election reverse, and to the Party post-mortem report, which had made the following point:

> The constant emphasis on quality of PAP candidates was turned against PAP. . . . We were accused of forgetting that our roots should lie in the ordinary people, the common man. Our candidates were written off as having no feel for the problems of the ordinary man in the street, unlike the less well qualified opposition MPs, who might be incoherent but were at least sincere. . . . The PAP must find some visible way to demonstrate that it has ordinary people in its inner circles, and for the people to identify themselves with the candidates even though the candidates are not poor or ill educated. This is a serious problem.

The Mechanics of Renewal

The 1984 reverse clearly gave a fresh impetus to the renewal process and lent added urgency to finding suitable candidates to be fielded at the next election. As early as December 1986, 1DPM Goh—who had since the early 1980s been in charge of selection—wrote to all PAP MPs confirming that the Party was building up a register of potential candidates for future elections, and that details of suitable persons should be sent to him.[116]

Considerable light has been shed on how MPs were spotted, recruited and interviewed through media features over the past decades and in the published recollections of present and former ministers and MPs. Coverage of the actual selection process included a series of detailed features by the *Straits Times* in June 1984. The newspaper highlighted several stages in the process and identified the key persons involved in selection:

- The initial (and exploratory) "tea sessions" would see several ministers present. Issues would be introduced for discussion. The key ministers involved at this stage would usually be Goh Chok Tong, Dr Yeo Ning Hong and Prof. S. Jayakumar.[117]
- Promising candidates from the first round would be invited for a session with a second group—this time with Dr Tony Tan (minister for trade and industry), Ong Teng Cheong (minister without portfolio) and S. Dhanabalan (minister for foreign affairs and culture). Dr Yeo or Prof. S. Jayakumar would sit in as linkman.[118] This was a more in-depth session.
- After a certain number of tea sessions (sometimes as many as three), there would be a shortlisting exercise. Those making the cut would have a one-to-one meeting with Goh Chok Tong. Candidates would be asked to consider standing.[119]
- The actual selection process would then begin. The selection panel at this stage was for much of the 1970s and 1980s headed by Lim Kim San.[120] In this committee were Ong Pang Boon, Chua Sian Chin and Ong Teng Cheong. Goh's team from the exploratory tea sessions also sat in.[121] This committee would rank the candidates in order of merit.
- The next stage was with the PM and other Cabinet ministers.[122] The panel would be thoroughly familiar with the candidates by this stage.
- The final stage was meeting the full membership of the PAP CEC. After this, the selection procedure formally ended.[123]
- Several months before the election, candidates approved by the CEC would be deployed to shadow sitting MPs.[124]

What has been provided above is a snapshot of procedures and processes in the mid-1980s. The following pages, based on interviews with former MPs and ministers, attempt to trace the evolution of these processes through the 1980s, to shed some light on the thinking of Party leadership in operating the selection mechanisms, and to give a sense of the process as the candidates themselves went through it.

The process was less structured in the late 1970s and early 1980s. Up to around 1979–80, many candidates were not even aware that they had been spotted; a few were not even aware until well into the proceedings what they were being interviewed for. Chandra Das, who was elected MP for Chong Boon in 1980, recalls being summoned to the Istana in 1979 with no explanation given. He thought that he was being asked to brief PM Lee on a forthcoming trip to Bangladesh:

> I got a call [in early 1979] come to Istana, four o'clock, "see PM." . . . So when I went there, I saw Eugene Yap sitting in the room.[125] Then Goh Chok Tong peeked out of his room and said "Come in." I said "No, I am going to see the PM Lee." He said "No, come in." So I walked into the room. The whole bunch was there—then I realized something was happening.[126]

This "something" was an interview by the full CEC—a considerable surprise to Das and others put in that situation, who not been through any interviews prior to this.

Das declined to run in the 1979 by-elections, explaining that he had become managing director of Intraco (the government-linked state trading enterprise) and needed time to settle down in the job:

> Then Goh Chok Tong came out. He said, "Why the hell you didn't say yes?" I told him the truth. I never considered . . . so that's where it ended. Anyway, Chok Tong says, we'll call you. So the subject was closed. Never broached again until August 1980. I went with Goh Chok Tong to Burma. We were playing golf with the deputy prime minister of Burma. After the game I was in the changing room. Goh Chok Tong came up to me, he said, "When you go back, you go and report to Ahmad Mattar." I said "Why?" He said, "We're fielding you. You go and report." That's how I got into politics.[127]

Where the selectors were convinced that an individual might make a good MP, it seems to have been a recurring theme that the individual would be asked, and then asked again if the initial response was negative. Wong Kan Seng had worked at the Ministry of Defence until 1981, when he left for the private sector. He attended tea sessions in 1982 but indicated that he could not stand on account of his young family:

> So I was asked to recommend some people who can. It was said if everybody gives me that answer that they have no alternative, then where do we find people? So I gave one name. So that person was called up for a tea session and eventually asked to consider. Said he can't. Of course he didn't know that I gave the name. He said he can't do that because he's just taken on a new assignment in the company and so on and his children were very young, younger than mine. So he was asked "Who do you suggest?" So he suggested

*my name. So ran in a circle. Then [Goh Chok Tong] called me up and said,
"Hey, you know you recommended so-and-so and I asked him. He said he
can't. And I asked him who, he said you." So if everybody gives that answer
then if I go further down the line and then who do I get? Surely, we don't want
somebody further down below to do the job. So I went back and discussed it
quite seriously with my wife.*[128]

Civil service experience, or work in government-linked organisations, helped
individuals like Wong Kan Seng get noticed.[129] Some with such experience had worked
closely with PAP leaders.[130] They could be fast-tracked through the process. When S.
Dhanabalan (who had worked under Hon Sui Sen in EDB and DBS) went through
the selection process, he went straight to see Dr Toh Chin Chye and after that to the
Party CEC.[131] There were many others deemed to have promise who could bypass
tea sessions and be asked straight away to consider standing as a candidate. Dr Dixie
Tan, a GP in private practice, was asked by her good friend Dr Tay Eng Soon (then
minister of state for education) to stand for the 1984 elections while the two families
were having dinner.[132]

Records of returned scholars were sifted through in order to spot candidates. Some
might have been completely unknown to PAP leaders until that point. One such
individual was Dr Yeo Ning Hong, then a returned scholar and an R&D manager at
a pharmaceutical firm. He was asked as a first step to have lunch with S. Dhanabalan,
then minister for foreign affairs, in early 1980.[133]

All PAP MPs were asked to bring in their own friends and contacts. Goh Chok
Tong duly did so upon coming into the Party, recommending Othman Haron Eusofe,
Dr Tan Cheng Bock and Dr Wan Soon Bee, all of whom made it through the interview
process. When leading the recruitment process in the 1980s, Goh similarly asked
others to recommend people: "This is what you call casting the net. So every MP
is a fisherman."[134] Even as the process became more structured through the 1980s,
this casting of the net continued and indeed was amplified. And those who fell out
of the process at the various stages were not simply discarded. Goh felt strongly that
they could be useful as a feedback network.[135] In the mid-1980s, 2,000 people were
identified as potentials after a search that lasted six years. Of these, between 300 and
400 were seen by DPM Goh.[136] Goh personally found 31 of the 60 candidates fielded
in the three elections of 1980, 1984 and 1988.[137]

Information from the interviews and biodata of potentials was cross-checked with
other sources. PM Lee and 1DPM Goh would occasionally write to people who knew
the candidates, telling them that the individual in question was under consideration
and asking for views. Questions posed included whether the individual had integrity
and was willing to serve the community. Sometimes incidents or anecdotes were asked
for that might support some of the views given. Those asked to provide information
usually took the task seriously and wrote detailed responses.[138] By the time the candidate
in question had to come before the CEC, the feedback and responses had been received
and scrutinised. The responses themselves influenced the way the CEC proceeded to
interview the candidate.[139]

Approximately seven of every ten persons approached agreed to be considered. But the process of sieving out was such that by the time candidates had reached the Lim Kim San panel, just under half were in the running. At the end of the process, which culminated in the CEC interviews, one in five who began would "clear" the process.[140] The interview with the CEC was no mere formality.[141] The CEC took into account many factors, including whether the candidate (promising as he or she might be) would be better off serving the country where he or she was at that point. Individuals may have been doing critical jobs where they worked—particularly in the civil service. On several occasions the CEC would decide not to field such individuals, especially if it had formed the view that the individual was not a sure bet for higher office. Others might be asked to consider serving in alternative capacities within the Party.[142]

Fresh avenues to tap into for the candidate search opened up as the 1980s progressed. These included the Youth Wing, as noted earlier. In addition, Goh Chok Tong's consultative approach and desire to widen the base the PAP could tap into led, as the 1980s progressed, to the formation of institutions where members of the public could contribute their views directly. This in turn enabled PAP leaders to spot people and assess their calibre. Within the Government Parliamentary Committees (GPCs), set up in 1987, members of the public were invited to sit on resource panels. From the 1988 slate, three individuals (Dr Hong Hai, Lew Syn Pau and Seet Ai Mee) were members of GPC resource panels.[143] Their performance as panel members was not necessarily what first brought them to the attention of the PAP leadership, but their role did give the Party the chance to confirm their potential.[144]

Goh was prepared to consider people who were not in the normal mould of PAP candidates, including a sprinkling of "angry young men". One individual whom Goh seems to have been particularly keen on—repeatedly inviting him for meetings and interviews—ran a magazine that had been criticised by the Ministry of Culture. He was asked to stand as an MP in the 1984 elections, but in the end he could not do so because of his fundamental disagreements with policy and his fear of having to toe the Party line.[145]

The pathways Malay/Muslim MPs in particular had to navigate could be particularly fraught. They carried the aspirations of the Malay community into Parliament and were expected by the community to articulate deeply felt issues and grievances. But there was also the expectation by the PAP leadership that Malay MPs would lead Singaporean Malays/Muslims to a better future in overcoming problems within the community.

Some of the problems were socio-educational in nature. Drug abuse within the Malay community had been an issue from the 1970s, and there were also growing concerns from that time about Malay involvement in gangs.[146]

The broader issue, however, was underachievement in education. This matter was increasingly discussed in public settings following the findings of the 1980 census, which painted a stark picture of academic underperformance. Besides the minuscule number of Malay graduates, Malays were disproportionately high-represented amongst those who had not attained qualifications beyond having completed primary school.[147] PM Lee gave a public airing to the issue in 1981, before this, bringing Malay community leaders into confidence, sharing with them historical data on academic underperformance in the Malay community.[148] Subsequently, in 1981, a group of Malay MPs led by Ahmad Mattar, acting minister for social affairs (and also minister in charge of Muslim affairs) formed Mendaki (the Council for Education of Muslim Children), with Mattar as its founding president.[149]

These moves in the educational sphere, and the beginnings of open discussion of the core issues, were positive. But on another issue, which cut much deeper, things were considerably more complex. This was loyalty.

From 1967 and up to the early 1980s, Malays (unlike other races) were not subject to universal conscription into National Service that applied to other races. The majority of Malays who were called up were posted to Vigilante Corps, the Singapore Civil Defence Force (after its formation in 1982), or to the police (rather than to the armed forces). Those who did serve in the armed forces were not posted to sensitive units.[150] Malays who did not serve National Service sometimes encountered difficulties on attempting to join the workforce, finding that many employers preferred those who had served National Service.[151] The perception was that the government did not want to place Singapore Malays in a conflicted position in the event that war broke out with Malaysia over (to give the most likely driver of any conflict) water, which Singapore depended on its neighbour for.[152] The issue of exclusion continued to simmer in the 1980s (and indeed beyond), not in the form of sustained outcry, but through consistent murmurings from the Malay community. Unlike the education issue, there was little data on hand, and precisely how far-reaching the exclusion was, and how exactly the policy was implemented, were unknown.

They were unknown but certainly felt by the MPs themselves. Many in their earlier lives had been teachers or journalists—professions that made them attuned to issues or ground sentiment in the Malay community.[153] Several were already well known by the grassroots on account of their volunteer work in Malay/Muslim organisations. They knew that, until the early 1980s, segments of the Malay ground were suspicious of the PAP.[154] Several themselves were critical of aspects of government policy that had an impact on the Malay/Muslim community and had in fact declined the PAP's overtures when initially approached.[155] A few had had personal run-ins with the authorities.[156] Some had been directly affected by the government policies described above. Abdullah Tarmugi had been the best recruit in his National Service platoon, but was baffled when recruits he had outperformed were sent to the prestigious Officer Cadet School, and he was not (and informed that he was released from fulltime National Service duties to boot). The sense of resentment—that he was not trusted—lingered, with Tarmugi raising the incident to PM Lee Kuan Yew when interviewed before the PAP selection committee.[157]

Tarmugi's was just one example of prospective candidates raising issues felt personally, and by the community, at the selection process. Yatiman Yusof, who was to serve as an MP from 1984 to 2006 and would rise to senior parliamentary secretary, recalls his experience:

I had been a teacher and then became a Berita Harian *journalist. I had already been approached many times by the PAP, as far back as the late 1970s. Each time I said no. In 1984 I went to Cambridge for a short journalism fellowship. S. Dhanabalan called me and told me to come back to Singapore. I returned and straightaway went to the Istana—into a room with three ministers and Lee Kuan Yew. PM Lee said, "I'm looking for people who are honest and for people who are willing to stand up who are willing to criticize the government where we are wrong." I responded with issues that were on my mind. Government support for Mendaki was one. I felt that the government should allow a portion of contributions by Malays to their CPF [Central Provident Fund] accounts to go to Mendaki, but government had been slow to act. I also said that Ahmad Mattar had been acting minister since 1977, for seven years. If he couldn't do the job, he should not have been made acting minister for so long. Finally I asked why weren't Malays called up to serve national service, and why were our loyalties being questioned. PM Lee was very upset when I raised the issue of Malays in the army. He said if Malaysia cut off Singapore's water supply and Singapore had to deploy, "you will be asked to pull the trigger against your cousins and brothers". I responded that loyalty and whether they pulled the trigger depended on how the government treated them. Singaporean Malays had to be treated justly and given opportunities. "You have to make the first move. Show them you trust them."*[158]

Personal reservations meant that the Party leadership was rebuffed—sometimes repeatedly—by prospective Malay/Muslim individuals identified as possible candidates. As with other candidates, the Party could be very persistent. Yatiman Yusof was first approached in 1978 and was asked again and again over the following years to reconsider, until the point he was summoned back from Cambridge in 1984.[159] Zainul Abidin Rasheed was first approached in 1976 but only agreed to be fielded almost 20 years later, for the 1997 general election. He did not have a grievance as such, but felt that he could do work to better the Malay/Muslim community outside of the Party.[160]

The general approach taken by PM Lee, (and later adopted by 1DPM Goh) when it came to selection was to approach individuals from all races who had the capacity to serve and who were men and women of integrity. Being critical of the policies of the PAP government was of little consequence if the Party leadership saw evidence of the individual in question being prepared to be constructive. This thrust was carried on by BG Lee Hsien Loong and Prof. S. Jayakumar, who by the 1988 election had been entrusted by Goh with the job of overseeing recruitment and selection.[161]

Throughout the 1980s there was also some emphasis placed on making sure that at least a handful of candidates came through the old way of "doing time" in the branches.[162] Still, the candidates surfaced with this type of experience never did reach the level of one-third to one-quarter that had been discussed between Goh and Lee in their May 1986 exchange. Few of the candidates surfaced in the slates for 1984, 1988 and 1991 were Party stalwarts, and branch complaints were to continue right through the 1990s and into the 2000s. Of the 19 who stood in 1988, ten had joined the PAP within the previous two years: five each in 1987 and 1988.[163] The bald fact was that the PAP continued to find the majority of its candidates from outside the branches, and this was what rankled within certain quarters of the Party.

We now turn to the types of people brought in over three elections—1984, 1988 and 1991 (see Appendix One, Tables 1.2, 1.3 and 1.4).

The 1984 batch was a watershed. As the *Straits Times* commented, "for the first time in its self-renewal exercise, the People's Action Party is presenting an all-graduate cast of 24 new candidates, with more likely to come". The candidates were superbly qualified on paper. Several held multiple degrees or doctorates, and seven could boast first class degrees.[164] The 1988 batch was equally impressive. Five held doctorates, and seven held first class honours degrees.[165]

While each slate across this period had a handful of scholars or technocrats, many of the candidates put up across these three elections had experience in PAP branches, the grassroots or voluntary organisations.

- From the 1984 batch, six could be said to have been active in PAP branches.[166] Another seven had grassroots experience outside the PAP, or experience in voluntary or cultural organisations that could be considered significant.[167]
- Four candidates in 1988 were closely identified with PAP branches.[168] Another four had significant experience in grassroots, cultural, or voluntary work outside the PAP.[169]
- In the 1991 batch, six individuals were closely associated with the branches or PAP organisations.[170] All of the 12 candidates fielded had significant experience in grassroots or voluntary organisations, save Lim Hng Kiang (who was a civil servant before being fielded).
- There were three new Chinese-educated candidates fielded in the 1984 election, four in the 1988 election, and one in 1991.[171] All eight Malay candidates fielded in 1984, 1988 and 1991 had extensive experience in Malay–Muslim voluntary religious or cultural organisations.

Nuances not immediately apparent from a simple reading of the data in Tables 1.2, 1.3 and 1.4 are present throughout. The Chinese-educated candidates, for example, were by no means a homogeneous group. Some, but not all, were effectively bilingual. While this was a quality the PAP prized highly amongst potential candidates, the leadership realised that these individuals might not necessarily be the ones to carry the Chinese ground. Other Chinese-educated MPs, such as the "coffeeshop MPs", who will be dealt with in chapter 3, could be more effective mobilisers and more effective in winning back seats that had been lost.

Goh's consultative style and the perceived approachability of the newer-generation PAP leaders led to more people being willing to come forward and serve as MPs. But also emerging within the entire leadership as the 1980s wore on was the recognition that change was needed too when it came to approaching individuals who were of ministerial calibre. The sense of this change comes not through a scrutiny of candidates' biodata, but from the recollections and viewpoints of those who went through the process.[172]

George Yeo, who was fielded in 1988 and who would go on to hold several ministerial positions, had been a near-contemporary of BG Lee Hsien Loong at Cambridge. Yeo characterised himself as well as many others of his generation as being "sceptical":

> I was two years Hsien Loong's junior in university. Lee Kuan Yew would have heard of me from Hsien Loong and knew about my student activities. Political activities in Cambridge. Mr Lee knew that Hsien Loong had to take on some position of national leadership and wanted those in his generation to join him. So I think naturally I came within their radar screen. I remember I wrote an article for the armed forces journal, Pointer. Somehow PM Lee got to see it, and I was asked through his office to send a copy to Goh Chok Tong, who was then defence minister and DPM. I was pleasantly surprised and flattered that PM Lee read what I wrote.[173]

In the end, it was a direct suggestion put to Yeo by Goh Chok Tong, who was at the time defence minister:

> I did see myself possibly going into politics at some point in time. But I was then too young, still not established and had no children. But Goh Chok Tong was very determined to pull me in and asked me a number of times. I knew he had gone back to PM Lee because in one of his conversations with me, he said, "PM said, he's getting old, and if you were to join earlier, there would be a chance to learn from him." I knew that argument came from PM. It wouldn't have come from Goh Chok Tong.

Yeo's political sensibilities were different from those of the old guard. In the energetic attempts of the Party leadership to get him to serve, it may be possible to glimpse beginnings of the thinking that was to bring in people later in the 1990s and 2000s who had views quite different from the Party, or who had been extremely critical of it.[174]

The Central Executive Committee, 1980–92

The CEC, the nerve centre of the Party and its ultimate decision-making authority, screened election candidates at the final stage, and also made the decisions, just prior to elections, on which MPs would be retired. Critical decisions, including the setting up of new Party bodies during this period (the HQ Exco, PCF, Women's Wing and Youth Wing), were taken by the CEC. By the early 1980s Lee Kuan Yew as secretary-general was increasingly sharing his thinking with Goh Chok Tong, and later (by the mid- to late 1980s) allowing Goh to decide on many Party matters while making his views known.

Perhaps the most important part of the CEC's decision-making concerned its own renewal: who would stand down, who would be co-opted and who (and how many) would be renominated from the CEC. As the 1980s progressed, the CEC gradually reduced the number of names it put forward for renomination. At the November 1982 conference the CEC renominated ten of its 14 existing members for the new CEC, leaving MPs to nominate eight from amongst themselves. But four years later, the outgoing CEC renominated only the six CEC office-holders for election into the next CEC. (MPs came together themselves prior to the Party conference to nominate the others for the slate.) It was Goh Chok Tong (supported by PM Lee) who was responsible for this change and for allowing MPs to select more CEC members. The thinking behind this was that CEC candidates had to have their acceptability tested among MPs and cadres.[175] MPs generally responded by voting in the existing CEC and other Cabinet office-holders, although from time to time voting did reveal occasional surprises. When Tan Cheng Bock was voted into the 19th CEC on 23 November 1986, he was the only backbencher. He remained in the CEC for ten years—in an indication, perhaps, that the other MPs felt that he could give the Party leadership a view from the ground in his forthright style, not just as a backbencher but also as the chairman of the Feedback Unit Supervisory Panel (1985–89).[176]

The actual voting into the CEC was done by cadres at the Party conference, which was a biennial affair from 1982. Cadres directly elected 12 CEC members, as provided for by the Party constitution. Under the Party constitution, six members could be co-opted into the CEC. The usual practice was for the secretary-general to co-opt, sometimes immediately after the vote, the two individuals not directly elected but with the next-highest votes. The prerogative to co-opt additional members (usually at the first CEC meeting following the Party conference) was occasionally exercised through the 1980s. There were occasions when individuals who had not been on the nomination list at the Party conference were later co-opted by the CEC. This appears to have been used especially to bring in younger MPs and ministers who might not have their own support base within the rank and file of Party cadres, but who the CEC felt should be brought in on account of their being seen as part of the core leadership, or because they represented the younger MPs.[177]

In 1957, voting cards for the Party conference were sent to the addresses of the unions controlled by the Communists—a mistake that cost the PAP moderates dear when they lost control of the CEC. Subsequent changes to the system designed to prevent a recurrence left an imprint that endured. The voting cards now came in three parts: (1) the admission slip, (2) the voting slip, and (3) one's own part of the slip. The organising secretary would prepare two lists showing those who had been elected: one with the number of votes and one without. Only the secretary-general and assistant secretary-general (besides the organising secretary) saw the former. Other aspects of the conference show an exceedingly well-controlled set of proceedings. While theoretically nominations from the floor were solicited, there were in practice none from the 1970s onwards.

Differences within the CEC on the pace of renewal were known by the early 1980s and acknowledged by Lee, who was to refer to these disagreements on various occasions.[178] The individual who would have felt this most keenly was Dr Toh Chin Chye, the chairman of the PAP from the time of its founding in 1954. Lee decided that Toh would step down from the chairmanship at the Party conference on 7 December 1980, although he remained a CEC member.[179] Lee, writing in his memoirs, said that Toh had to be dropped to prevent a split in the leadership, as Toh and others in the old guard (including Ong Pang Boon) disagreed with the manner and the pace of renewal.[180]

At this point we should consider the entry into politics of Col. Lee Hsien Loong, PM Lee's son, who had been spotted and approached by Goh Chok Tong.[181]

Lee went through two preliminary interviews in May and July 1984.[182] In the write-up where he was asked to describe himself and his character (a standard requirement and submitted by Lee in advance of the second interview), Col. Lee had observed:

> *The political process in Singapore requires two major responsibilities from MPs: maintaining rapport with and the confidence of the population, especially through grassroots organisations and trade unions, and helping to formulate and gain support for national policies. The first is a precondition to the second, which is more an analytical problem, but one needing sensitivity and emotional commitment to solve. There is little need for charismatic rabble rousing, to mobilize the population against deep social injustices. However, though the style may be more subdued, the depth of mutual understanding between the rulers and the ruled cannot be less. The challenge is therefore to renew and strengthen the bond.*[183]

The assessment of Lee at the preliminary interview stage was that he knew his mind—he was an asset who had thought through his choice and who knew what he was in for.[184]

> *Asked about his philosophy and attitude towards life, he said that he was deeply influenced by Prime Minister. They both share the same set of values and priorities and have the same temperaments. His approach is pragmatic but not dogmatic. He is inclined towards being flexible. He believes that it is more important to establish the correct general directions rather than to operate on fixed rules.*[185]

By then a brigadier-general, Lee Hsien Loong was interviewed by the CEC (the final interview stage) on 13 August 1984. Ong Pang Boon during this meeting raised a reservation on BG Lee's candidature. In noting that this was the first time a high-ranking Singapore Armed Forces (SAF) officer was resigning and then standing immediately for election, Ong suggested it might be better to field BG Lee only after he had spent some time in a civilian career. Goh Chok Tong suggested to Ong Teng Cheong, who chaired the meeting, that Lee's candidature should be approved without reservation, since there had been no actual objection to Lee's candidature on its merits, but the attention of Secretary-General Lee Kuan Yew (who had absented himself from the 13 August selection meeting and all earlier meetings where his son was interviewed) should be drawn to the point Ong had raised.[186]

Ong Pang Boon's reservation should be considered in its context. On 12 August 1984, at a time when there was already public speculation that Lee Hsien Loong might be fielded, Ong gave a speech in his constituency at Hong Lim Green Community Centre. In this speech Ong touched on several issues, including political succession and also political dynasties:

> *Without the people's support, and without men of dedication, integrity, ability and stamina coming forward to lead, no system can survive or last long . . . hereditary appointment of political leaders is no solution to the problem of political succession. Such appointed leaders do not enjoy the support and respect of the people, for the simple reason that they come not from the grassroots. As a result, they do not gain the support of the people.*[187]

Ong Pang Boon recalled that he had around this time been receiving a great deal of comment from the ground—especially the Chinese-educated grassroots—concerning BG Lee's prospective candidature. Many felt that while BG Lee was certainly highly qualified, it seemed that PM Lee was simply selecting his son for office. Ong realised that it was difficult to convey this sense—which would be viewed as criticism—to PM Lee. He thus chose to do it indirectly, through his speech, and also through his suggestion at the CEC that qualified as BG Lee was, it might be useful for him to spend time first in the public or private sector, in order for those on the ground to appreciate his abilities. Ong was clear, looking back, that he was not trying to oppose BG Lee's entry into politics.[188]

The leadership saw Ong's comments as a veiled criticism directed at both BG Lee's prospective candidature and the second-generation PAP leadership as a whole. A reply was required. This came primarily from Goh Chok Tong, who observed a few days later (when queried on the PAP's leadership selection methods, and specifically on comments made by Ong Pang Boon and also Dr Toh Chin Chye widely taken as being critical of the move to bring in technocrats to be next-generation leaders): "Technocrats are not test-tube babies manufactured in the clinically-clean laboratories of universities. They are the sons and daughters of Singapore, leading a very Singaporean life."[189]

Goh Chok Tong and PM Lee were exchanging notes on this issue even as it bubbled to the surface of public view. Goh told Lee that he and the younger generation of leaders had decided to "obliquely reply" to criticisms but to avoid open confrontation.[190] On BG Lee's candidature, Goh wrote to PM Lee observing that it was the younger generation of leaders who had wanted BG Lee to stand, even before PM Lee had raised the subject. For his part, Lee was cheered by Goh's decision to publicly reply to Ong Pang Boon. Writing to Goh (with younger ministers Ong Teng

Cheong, S. Dhanabalan and Dr Tony Tan copied), Lee observed: "You have to stand up and speak back to those old guards who obliquely criticize and downgrade you . . . you will be taken seriously as leaders on your own right. They cannot be allowed to get away with it. Chok Tong's reply enhances his stature." Lee added that he was puzzled why Ong Pang Boon had chosen to make BG Lee's candidature an issue. Lee observed to Goh that Ong might think he "could muster public support. I cannot believe he can be right."[191]

PM Lee chose in his 19 August 1984 National Day Rally speech to address this issue:

> *There have been differences of views within the PAP leadership on the pace and the method of self-renewal. Some believe the pace of self-renewal is too fast, that it could generate anxiety and uncertainty amongst some old guard MPs. Some prefer more recruitment of talent through the PAP branches, promoting activists and loyalists. Unfortunately, we tried this for years with such meagre results. . . . Well, I am prepared to try all approaches and will tap PAP and other grassroots activists to add to the pool of talent. But Dr Goh Keng Swee, S. Rajaratnam and I believe there can be no slowing down of self-renewal.*[192]

PM Lee intimated to Goh and the second-generation leaders that this was intended as a rebuttal to Ong Pang Boon and Toh Chin Chye. His intention, as he privately made known to Goh Chok Tong and the younger generation of leaders, was to make clear to Ong Pang Boon and Toh Chin Chye that he was prepared for conflict—a more serious conflict than simply the intra-party airing of differences of opinion—with them over the issue.[193]

It was Law Minister E.W. Barker, who was on friendly terms with Ong Pang Boon, who smoothed matters. Barker spoke to Ong (with the knowledge of PM Lee and Goh Chok Tong), later reporting back to Lee and Goh that Ong Pang Boon had had to make an issue of BG Lee's candidature, raising it only because he felt it was for the good of the Party and the SAF. PM Lee was not entirely convinced but was brought round to accepting that Ong had decided to avoid an open rupture after Ong made a second speech on 25 August 1984, at a dinner marking the 25th anniversary of the PAP Telok Ayer Branch. Ong noted on this occasion how those in the grassroots Citizens' Consultative Committees "like him, desire to pass on the baton to the younger generation".[194]

The message sent to the media by PM Lee throughout the period of these CEC and Cabinet changes (particularly in the early to mid-1980s) was consistent: the old guard stepping aside from leadership positions, or stepping down altogether, in order to allow the younger-generation leaders to assume higher profiles and take on leadership roles.[195] The new generation was the best that could be found, the old guard had discharged its responsibilities, and it was time to move on.[196] On 30 September 1984, the second generation of leaders were elected at the Party conference into the CEC. Lee Kuan Yew, who remained secretary-general, was now the only old guard leader in the CEC.

Lee made a distinction between old guard members with reservations on the pace of reform, and others who actively helped the younger leaders. Party Treasurer Chua Sian Chin, for example, was not renominated going into the 30 September Party conference, which marked the point where all the old guard CEC office-holders, save for Lee himself, were retired. But subsequently Lee and Goh decided to co-opt him, as he had voluntarily stepped aside and as he could be useful, particularly in setting up PCF.[197] There were other old guard members who accepted the pace of renewal, including Ho Kah Leong and Ch'ng Jit Koon. They remained in the CEC until 1986 and 2000 respectively.

Even if Dr Toh Chin Chye and Ong Pang Boon eventually had to accept change, their personal relationships with Lee had passed the point beyond which they could be restored. Lee evidently found it preferable to rely on Goh Chok Tong to communicate with them. On 11 August 1988, when the Party was preparing for the coming general election, Lee wrote to Goh:

> *After the CEC meeting, I shall write to Toh Chin Chye, Ong Pang Boon and Jek Yeun Thong to tell them that the CEC will not be putting them up for re-election, and thank them for their contribution. It would be better if when you meet them you could also speak to them. I think they will not enjoy a face to face meeting with me.*[198]

Exit Management

Renewal meant that individuals with vast accumulated experience, and who had given much of their working lives to the Party, were asked to step down. By the 1980s, the secretive and seemingly sudden nature of the exits had given rise to increasing public comment and was becoming a cause of concern within the Party rank and file. Many MPs who felt that they had served the Party faithfully through difficult times (particularly those who had been through the 1950s and 1960s) felt cast aside without due acknowledgement of their contributions.[199] Many had difficulty settling outside of politics, or even finding gainful employment.

It was at the time of the announcement of the new MPs for the 1988 elections, and the retirements of those who were stepping down, that the issue was first seriously aired and addressed by the Party leadership.[200] During the PAP rally to introduce new candidates and bid farewell to the 14 MPs retiring, 1DPM Goh asked: "Why should an MP retiring from a life of public service have to feel unwanted or misunderstood by the public? It should not be, but it is often the case in Singapore."[201] Goh further noted that many MPs felt let down: "They have served the party loyally for many years, and their retirement was often sudden, unexpected, and unceremonious."[202]

The tributes that Lee and Goh paid to the old guard on this occasion, and the remedies suggested by Goh (including a dinner in honour of retiring MPs and inviting retired MPs to important Party functions), went some way towards reducing the grievances that MPs may have felt. The issue did not simply pertain to recognising the contributions of past MPs. As was observed at the time, perceived shabby treatment of former MPs might deter people from joining and hinder self-renewal. This perhaps explains why 1DPM Goh did not let the issue drop, broaching it again at the CEC soon after the 1988 election:

> *Retired MPs who have a full-time job will face less economic difficulty. However, ex-office holders who have given many years to public service may find re-entry into private sector difficult if they need to work to fulfil their family and financial commitments. It is demeaning to them to go job hunting after having been held in high esteem by the public for many years.*
>
> *This gives rise to the public perception that the Party does not care much about or look after its retired MPs and office holders once they stepped down. This may dissuade others from joining the Party and serving as MPs/office holders. There is therefore a need for the Party to manage the exit/retirement of these MPs/office holders well, so that their retirement is seen as a gracious one.*[203]

Goh suggested that Party leaders should help such retired office-holders find jobs in government-owned or other companies if assistance was needed. But these arrangements never became institutionalised. Rather, it was a series of informal networks that occasionally operated to look after the well-being and employment of MPs and office-holders who had left the scene.

There exist within the ranks of former PAP MPs differing views on how well the issue of retired MPs was treated. The issue comes up often in discussions within the various groups of retired MPs who still meet informally to reminisce and renew their bonds. Some measure of dissatisfaction (or sadness) exists, particularly on the part of those who were asked to retire without much notice given.[204] The fact is that exit management could never be handled to the satisfaction of all concerned simply because decisions on MPs to be retired, and the numbers of MPs to be retired, were taken late. The CEC continued to interview and consider candidates until close to the election. It might make late decisions to increase the number of MPs to be retired if it found numbers of high-quality candidates who it felt should be fielded rather than being told to wait until the next election. This also meant that some incumbent MPs did not know whether they would be fielded, or asked to stand down, until very close to nomination day.[205] This was a problem that could not be fixed.

1DPM Goh was more successful in his suggestion that the Party formally institute various levels of Party awards to reward its staunchest supporters.[206] By 1988, the Party had formally instituted such a system.[207] The awards included the following:

- PAP Distinguished Service Medal (DSM; for exceptional service)
- PAP Commendation Medal
- PAP Long Service Awards (15 and 25 years)[208]

At the January 1988 Party convention (the occasion of the first Party awards ceremony), 239 older Party members received long service medals, with Lee himself noting "their unwavering loyalty and support through the ups and downs in the Party's fortunes. Without them the Singapore you know today would not have emerged."[209]

The second awards ceremony was held on 24 February 1990. For the first time, other than awarding the Commendation, Long Service and Youth Awards, the Party also awarded the Distinguished Service Medal (DSM), the highest award it could give. The DSM recipients in 1990 were S. Rajaratnam and Lim Kim San. Lee presented these in his capacity as secretary-general of the Party, and he personally wrote the citations for them.[210]

PM Lee as secretary-general allowed Goh to take the lead in the late 1980s move for better recognition of service to the Party. Lee did lead, however, in certain aspects of renewal even at this stage. Key amongst them was guiding new MPs on how they should conduct themselves in their station, particularly at this important juncture when so many of their forbears were leaving the scene. PM Lee wrote on 29 September 1988 to all PAP MPs:

> One valuable product of a hard-fought election battle is the feeling of solidarity between the candidates who fought together in that battle. After the carnage, the survivors recognise and count the lucky ones, and do not forget those plucky colleagues who were downed. A deep sense of comradeship is forged between party stalwarts, winners and losers. This was missed in the 1980 elections. Two casualties in 1984 were sobering experiences. So were the many keenly fought constituencies in 1988. But it was not a life and death struggle.
>
> Your relationships with the older MPs, including what you say of your predecessors in your constituencies, will help to make or mar the spirit of camaraderie between MPs. Some of you are better qualified than your predecessors in your constituencies and the older back-benchers, Parliamentary Secretaries, and Ministers of State. That you have better minds and more rigorous training should not delude you into believing that you have the better temperament or a finer touch for people and politics. The older MPs have gone through many battles. They survived because they were politically the fittest. They have that keen sense for people, as individuals and in groups.
>
> . . . It will help you and the Party if a certain humility and modesty enables easier relationships between you and the older MPs from whom you can pick up useful tips. Never be heard to complain about the poor branch committee, or CCC, or MC, or community centre facilities. The older MP did his best.
>
> . . . Life is transient. You come in as MP. You may or may not make a Parl Sec or a Minister. However it turns out, inevitably, you in turn, with the

passing of the years, will make way for a new crop of MPs. Your achievement
is in making things better whilst you are in charge as MP. So discharge your
duty to your constituents, your fellow Singaporeans. Be a credit to government
and party.[211]

1985–88: Summing Up

The period 1985–88 was a time when the Party attempted to recover from a serious
electoral reverse. It was also a time when many experienced hands were exiting from
the scene, leaving power increasingly in the hands of the younger leaders. PM Lee and
1DPM Goh spent much of this period looking within the Party and addressing issues
of its organisation, vitality and spirit.

What can be made of Party organisation at this time and its results? Given the speed
with which some moves were made, it is clear that 1DPM Goh had had in advance a
clear idea of what he wanted to do, and had thought deeply about these issues before
becoming 1DPM in 1985. Goh had since the late 1970s been part of efforts to reform
and reorganise the Party. He knew what had been done then—and also what had
been left undone. Earlier efforts had not gone to the extent of constituting new Party
institutions. Goh and his younger team did so, with the formation of the HQ Exco and
the Youth and Women's Wing, making for better control from the centre (in the case
of the HQ Exco) and broadening the Party base by the end of the decade. A further
observation is that there were issues which were important to Goh and the younger
leaders, and which they took a personal interest in, but which PM Lee and the older
generation simply had neither the time nor the resources to look into. Recognising
service to the Party was one such aspect, but only one in a slew of moves which fell
generally within the wider "softening" of the Party image that was attempted in the late
1980s. Other facets included recognition for service to the Party, and the formation of
the PCF and social activities that were introduced.

Earlier internal PAP task forces usually had a clear terminus. The one led by Hwang
Soo Jin, for example, began work in 1977, submitted its final report in December 1978
and then disbanded in April 1979. Goh's effort to revitalise the Party, on the other
hand, never formally ended. It reached across to the 1990s as well, and as we shall see,
issues regarding the image of the Party, recruitment and the status of the branches
continued to be debated. It should be added, too, that many of Goh's ideas in 1985–88
took a great deal of time to come to fruition, and that some issues had to be tackled
again and again.[212]

All in all, the Party was greatly strengthened by the rejuvenation of 1985–88. Some
of the newer leaders with experience in the corporate world were important players
in regularising various Party functions and methods. Men like Goh Chok Tong, S.
Dhanabalan and Dr Tony Tan—to name just some—used their experience and sense
of urgency to make for changes that were needed at this time of the Party's evolution.

In his speech at the Party convention on 23 January 1988, PM Lee observed that the
period from 1984 had been "a time for stock-taking and auditing. This is also the time
for new directions and new courses of action."[213] What he left unsaid, but which was

understood at the time, was that the Party was now better placed to face the challenges of the remainder of the 1980s through to the 1990s, and to face the Opposition—be it in Parliament or in electoral battlegrounds. These issues will now be examined.

Notes

1   Author's calculations, based on World Bank data ("GDP Growth [Annual %]—Singapore"). Available at https://data.worldbank.org/indicator/NY.GDP.MKTP. KD.ZG?end=2018&locations=SG (accessed 23 Jan. 2021).

2   World Bank, "GDP Per Capita [Current US$]—Singapore". Available at https://data. worldbank.org/indicator/NY.GDP.PCAP.CD?end=1984&locations=SG&start=1965 (accessed 6 July 2020). See also "An Economic History of Singapore, 1965–2065", keynote address by Ravi Menon, Managing Director of the Monetary Authority of Singapore, at the Singapore Economic Review Conference 2015, Singapore, 5 Aug. 2015. Available at https://www.bis.org/review/r150807b.htm (accessed 5 Dec. 2020).

3   Lee Kuan Yew, interview with the author, 28 Dec. 2011.

4   Author's calculations based on data from the website of the Elections Department of Singapore, available at https://www.eld.gov.sg/elections_past_parliamentary.html and https://www.eld.gov.sg/elections_past_by.html (accessed 12 July 2020). For information on elections, also useful is the unofficial resource http://www.singapore- elections.com.

5   Lim Chong Yah, *Singapore's National Wages Council: An Insider's View* (Singapore: World Scientific, 2014); see p. 197 for 1980–84 real wage data (inclusive of employee's CPF contributions).

6   The 12.9% swing against the PAP refers to the decrease in valid votes (excluding spoilt votes) from 77.7% (1980) to 64.8% (1984).

7   "My Two Goals—By the Striker", *Straits Times*, 1 Jan. 1985.

8   Ibid. Lee Kuan Yew conceded in his memoirs that the vote swing had been "more than I had anticipated". Lee Kuan Yew, *From Third World to First: The Singapore Story 1965–2000* (Singapore: Times Editions, 2000), p. 158.

9   *Report of the Committee on the Problems of the Aged* (Singapore: Ministry of Health, 1984). Available at https://www.nas.gov.sg/archivesonline/government_records/record-details/ c09bde19-86b3-11e7-83df-0050568939ad (accessed 23 Jan. 2021). This committee was headed by Howe Yoon Chong, the minister for health.

10 Chiam had earlier been unsuccessful in his attempts at the 1976 and 1980 elections (which had seen him stand in Cairnhill [1976] and Potong Pasir [1980]) as well as in the 1979 by-elections (Potong Pasir).

11 Goh Chok Tong, interview with the author, 22 June 2012. There were other considerations too. The departure of Deputy Prime Minister (DPM) Goh Keng Swee (who did not stand in the 1984 elections and retired from politics) played a key role in influencing Lee's thinking. Noting that Goh Keng Swee was a convinced proponent of self-renewal, he (Goh Chok Tong) suggested that Goh Keng Swee "forced" the issue: "If Goh Keng Swee had not left, I don't think PM Lee would have asked us to choose a leader in 1984 . . . he would probably have waited till 1987, 1988." Goh Chok Tong suggested that this was the key factor which led Lee to decide to appoint a younger minister as

DPM, as appointing an experienced minister would have entrenched the old guard even further.

12   The task force cleaned up several aspects of Party practice (including branches acting too independently, especially when it came to management of finances). It also revamped *Petir*, the Party publication, and had a role in introducing political education within the Party. Sizing up newer MPs to assess their future potential was also an important aspect, on which Hwang Soo Jin regularly communicated directly with PM Lee. Hwang was regularly asked by PM Lee to do detailed rankings of individuals, including Goh Chok Tong and other potential office-holders. It is worth noting that PM Lee (rather than relying on the PAP organising secretary at that time, Tang See Chim) chose for this task someone who lay outside the apex of the Party's power apparatus. Hwang, while effectively bilingual, was also not generally perceived as being tied to any existing established base (English- or Chinese-educated) within the Party. For details on this task force, its aims and its composition, see Sonny Yap, Richard Lim and Leong Weng Kam, *Men in White: The Untold Story of Singapore's Ruling Party* (Singapore: Singapore Press Holdings, 2009), pp. 393–6. I am grateful to Hwang Soo Jin for shedding light on the workings of the task force. Hwang Soo Jin, interview with the author, 24 Feb. 2014.

13   Goh Chok Tong, interview with the author, 22 June 2012. Lim Chee Onn had been the secretary-general of the National Trades Union Congress (NTUC) from 1979 and minister without portfolio (from 1980) until his resignation from these positions in April and July 1983 (respectively). Lim also resigned as PAP vice-chairman and second organising secretary in October that year. His stepping aside from the first echelon of new PAP leaders (although he remained an MP until 1992) was on account of his style of management within NTUC and in particular his attempts to modernise the unions and renew the ranks of union leaders. This brought him into conflict with older-generation unionists, with the president of Singapore and former NTUC Secretary-General Devan Nair himself intervening against Lim. Lim's replacement as NTUC secretary-general was Ong Teng Cheong. See Edwin Lee, *Singapore: The Unexpected Nation* (Singapore: Institute of Southeast Asian Studies, 2008), pp. 462–3.

14   Goh Chok Tong, interview with the author, 22 June 2012. Goh further observed: "And you can be sure, SM had also been asking older MPs, older Ministers to rank us. . . . We had peer rankings."

15   Yap et al., *Men in White*, pp. 420–3.

16   Goh Chok Tong, interview with the author, 22 June 2012.

17   "Preserving Singapore's Unique Political Culture", *Straits Times*, 26 Nov. 1990. Quoted in D.K. Mauzy and R.S. Milne, *Singapore Politics under the People's Action Party* (London: Routledge, 2002), p. 114.

18   Lee Kuan Yew, *From Third World to First*, p. 744. Lee locates this meeting of the younger ministers to choose the next prime minister as having taken place after the 1988 elections (p. 744). However, this should be read as after the 1984 election.

19   Dr Tony Tan, interview with the author, 11 July 2013. See also Yap et al., *Men in White*, pp. 420–1.

20   Yap et al., *Men in White*, pp. 420–3.

21 The outline of what happened at the meeting at Dr Tony Tan's home was given in a talk by then Minister for Home Affairs Prof. S. Jayakumar to MPs of the City North District on 17 January 1987. Subsequently, on 9 February 1987, Prof. Jayakumar wrote to PM Lee, attaching an edited version of the talk. Jayakumar noted that the objective of the talk was "to give our cadres some idea of how we, though not composed of persons who were comrades-in-arms at the outset, are developing into a team and are working as a team". He further noted that the edited version had been "tested" with the pre-Cabinet group of ministers. All of them save Yeo Ning Hong and Wong Kan Seng (who both thought the information should be kept a "mystery") agreed with publication, as did most of the MPs present at the talk. Jayakumar asked whether PM Lee objected to publication in *Petir*, or to the story being picked up by the media. Lee replied the following day: "The old guard never believed in openness of their deliberative processes as a plus. Indeed, it was to our advantage to keep our inner workings secret: so our disagreements, our methods of settling them and who supports whom and belongs to which faction—were screened off from view. It suited the mood of those times. Furthermore, it made no sense to disclose to our adversaries, the Communists or the British, how we operated. The new guard must establish that although they were not 'present at the creation' and that no Big Bang brought all of you together, as it did the old guard, nevertheless, you are becoming a closely knit team, through careful building up of working relationships, through the testing of each person's capacity and temperament against each other in real life situations." Lee concluded by stating that there was, on balance, "little lost by publishing, and perhaps some gain in credibility". Correspondence between PM Lee and Prof. S. Jayakumar, 9–10 Feb. 1987 (PAP archive). See "The New Guard Leadership" (interview with Prof. S. Jayakumar), *Petir*, Mar. 1987, pp. 5–9, esp. 7–8; also "New Guard Have Forged Own Working Style" and "New Guard a Cohesive Team", *Straits Times*, 16 Mar. 1987.

22 Goh Chok Tong to PM Lee Kuan Yew, 31 Dec. 1984 (National Archives of Singapore), made available to the author. The "seven younger Ministers" were Goh Chok Tong, Dr Tony Tan, Ong Teng Cheong, S. Dhanabalan, Prof. S. Jayakumar, Ahmad Mattar and Dr Yeo Ning Hong. The others present (Lee Yock Suan, Dr Tay Eng Soon, Dr Wan Soon Bee, Ch'ng Jit Koon and BG Lee Hsien Loong) were all, with the exception of Lee Hsien Loong, ministers of state. "Unanimous Choice of Chok Tong as 1DPM 'a Watershed'", *Straits Times*, 16 Mar. 1987; "New Guard Have Forged Own Working Style".

23 Goh Chok Tong to Lee Kuan Yew, 29 Dec. 1984 (National Archives of Singapore), made available to the author.

24 There were several discussions on the Cabinet line-up in late December, with the thinking on the line-up continuing to be refined until the last minute. Lee provided input and had given the younger team his assessment of the strengths of each candidate and who could take senior positions; the younger team took these views into account. Dr Tony Tan, interview with the author, 11 July 2013.

25 "My Two Goals—By the Striker".

26 "Political Transition: From Striker to Goalkeeper", speech by PM Lee Kuan Yew at the swearing-in of Cabinet on 2 January 1985 at the Istana. *The Papers of Lee Kuan Yew:*

Speeches, Interviews and Dialogues, Vol. 9: 1981–1987 (Singapore: Cengage Learning Asia, 2012), p. 380.

27   Besides 2DPM Ong, the Post-mortem Task Force members were Dr Yeo Ning Hong, Lee Yock Suan, Yeo Cheow Tong, Wong Kan Seng, BG Lee Hsien Loong, Dr Lee Boon Yang, Lim Boon Heng, Yatiman Yusof and Tan Guan Seng.

28   *1984 General Election PAP Post-mortem Report* (PAP archive).

29   Tan's admission was (for the era, at least) striking: "I don't believe that we never make mistakes, that government is infallible. From time to time we make errors in policy and administration . . . and where it won't be morally right to continue, we should examine policies; and if changes are necessary, I think we should be honest about it." "Graduate Mums: A Delicate Matter to Be Handled Carefully", *Straits Times*, 4 Feb. 1985.

30   "Graduate Mums Scheme to Go: Tony Tan", *Straits Times*, 26 Mar. 1985.

31   The basic problem of retirement adequacy remained, however. The government was to go some way to addressing this in 1987 when it introduced the CPF Minimum Sum Scheme, which prevented individuals from withdrawing all their CPF funds at one fell swoop at the age of 55 (a minimum sum had to be retained in one's CPF Retirement Account, with monthly payments coming from this sum after the age of 60).

32   *1984 General Election PAP Post-mortem Report*.

33   "My Two Goals—By the Striker".

34   *1984 General Election PAP Post-mortem Report*.

35   Chan Heng Chee, "Unlikely PAP Will Regain 100% Control", *Straits Times*, 30 Dec. 1984. The January 1985 poll conducted by the Straits Times Press Research and Information Department found that 80% of those polled agreed that people voted for the Opposition to show their protest against certain PAP policies. But only 6% did not want a PAP government ("Two Main Reasons for Loss of Support", *Straits Times*, 10 Apr. 1985). Chan also correctly saw that the election result persuaded Party leaders that "a new political style was necessary to deal with the repoliticized, more articulate, and better-educated population who had enjoyed a continuous period of stability and affluence". Chan Heng Chee, "Postscript: Politics in Singapore, 1984–1986", in *Government and Politics of Singapore*, ed. Jon S.T. Quah, Chan Heng Chee and Seah Chee Meow (Singapore: Oxford University Press, 1987), p. 312.

36   Housed within the Ministry for Social Affairs, the bureau, originally set up to handle complaints by individuals against the public sector, had seen the number of complaints dwindle as the public began to make complaints directly to relevant government agencies or to the press. "Complaints Bureau Being Run Down", *Straits Times*, 24 May 1980.

37   1DPM Goh Chok Tong to Minister (Community Development) S. Dhanabalan and Minister for Communications and Information Dr Yeo Ning Hong, 22 Jan. 1985 (National Archives of Singapore), made available to the author.

38   The name for the unit that Goh had first considered, and which the leadership initially approved, was "Confer". But at some point soon after February 1984, this name was dropped. Goh Chok Tong later recalled, "We were deliberating how to call this unit. Rajaratnam said, what is it, what is the purpose of this? I said, 'Well it is to get feedback.' [Rajaratnam] said, 'Well call it Feedback Unit'. Raja contributed to the

name of the unit. So we called it Feedback Unit. So that was the start." Goh Chok Tong, interview with the author, 22 June 2012.

39   Dhanabalan noted during the 15 April 1985 press conference that unveiled the Feedback Unit that the unit would work with civil servants to grow "a political feel on the part of civil servants so that when they formulate . . . or implement policies, they will be aware of the political repercussions and impact of policies". "Transcript of Press Conference on the Feedback Unit, MCD, Chaired by Mr S. Dhanabalan" (National Archives of Singapore), made available to the author.

40   Ibid. See also "Open Line for Better Decisions", *Straits Times*, 17 Apr. 1985; "Cheng Bock to Guide Panel", *Straits Times*, 17 Apr. 1985; and "A Vital Bridge Can Now Be Built", *Straits Times*, 17 Apr. 1985.

41   "Open Line for Better Decisions".

42   Just as the newly chosen 1DPM Goh had himself done at his 31 December 1984 press conference: "I hope you do not expect that new style means consultation on every policy, every small measure." "My Two Goals—By the Striker".

43   *1984 General Election PAP Post-mortem Report.*

44   "Cheng Bock to Guide Panel", *Straits Times*, 17 Apr. 1985. Chang Meng Teng was the chairman of Tanah Merah Citizens' Consultative Committee (CCC), while Kenneth Chen was the vice-chairman of Potong Pasir CCC.

45   "Feedback Unit Should Go Down to the Masses", *Shin Min Daily News*, 22 Apr. 1985, translated in *Straits Times*, 3 May 1985.

46   "Our Deal with the PM", *Straits Times*, 6 Jan. 1985.

47   Memo from First Organising Secretary (1OS) Goh Chok Tong to Secretary-General (SG) Lee Kuan Yew, 24 Jan. 1985 (PAP archive).

48   Ch'ng Jit Koon to Lee Kuan Yew, "Draft Proposal to Streamline the Communication Network between the Government and the People", 30 Dec. 1982 (PAP archive).

49   For Ch'ng's account of the origins of these walkabouts, see *Up Close with Lee Kuan Yew: Insights from Colleagues and Friends* (Singapore: Marshall Cavendish, 2016), pp. 75–6.

50   This task force comprised Goh Chok Tong (chairman), Dr Tony Tan, Lim Chee Onn, Ahmad Matter, Prof. S. Jayakumar, Ch'ng Jit Koon and Yeo Ning Hong (secretary). It was smaller than the 1985 HQ Exco, with just three subcommittees: an Information Committee chaired by Prof. S. Jayakumar, a Constituency Relations Committee chaired by Ch'ng Jit Koon, and a Branch Liaison Committee chaired by Yeo Ning Hong. "Establishment of Task Force" (paper drafted by 1OS Goh Chok Tong and approved at 11 Feb. 1983 CEC meeting) (PAP archive). Some details of this earlier task force were made public. "PAP Task Force", *Straits Times*, 19 Mar. 1983.

51   SG Lee Kuan Yew to 1OS Goh Chok Tong, 25 Jan. 1985 (PAP archive).

52   Some, but not all, of the details of the formation of the HQ Exco were made public on 4 March 1985. "Chok Tong to Head 'Leadership' Committee of PAP", *Straits Times*, 5 Mar. 1985. The information in Table 1.1 detailing the composition of the HQ Exco, and the makeup and purpose of the subcommittees, derives from contemporary documents in the PAP archive.

53   Goh Chok Tong to CEC members, 8 Feb. 1985 (PAP archive).

54   The subcommittee concluded that *Petir* should be made more vivid and timely and should be published bimonthly from 1985. 1OS Ow Chin Hock to Chairman, HQ Exco, Goh Chok Tong, 19 Apr. 1985 (PAP archive).

55   1OS Ow Chin Hock to Chairman, HQ Executive Committee Goh Chok Tong, 19 Apr. 1985 (PAP archive). This plan is no longer extant in the archives, but some sense of what was planned can be gathered from other sources and is discussed later in this chapter.

56   The target groups included, inter alia, professional associations, community organisations, trade unions, staff members and students of tertiary institutions, journalists and editors, civil servants, taxi drivers, youth groups, cultural organisations and clan associations. 1OS Dr Ow Chin Hock to various MPs and ministers, memo "Target Groups of Opinion Makers", 28 Sept. 1985 (PAP archive).

57   1OS Ow was acting on the direction of Assistant Secretary-General Goh Chok Tong. Ow wrote to Goh on 28 December 1985, confirming the MPs who had been appointed to lead the "action teams" that would engage the target groups. 1OS Dr Ow Chin Hock to Assistant Secretary-General (ASG) Goh Chok Tong, 28 Dec. 1985 (PAP archive).

58   Separately, Ong noted that he had been in close contact with clan associations through Ch'ng Jit Koon since late 1984. Ong further noted that six new MPs had been briefed and advised to accept invitations as advisers to some of these clan associations (BG Lee, Dr Lee Boon Yang, Goh Choon Kang, Chng Hee Kok, Tan Guan Seng and Yu-Foo Yee Shoon). 2DPM Ong Teng Cheong to 1OS Dr Ow Chin Hock, 15 Nov. 1985 (PAP archive).

59   An example is the dialogue session that 1DPM Goh and Minister for Community Development S. Dhanabalan had with 1,000 community leaders on 8 February 1985, where the idea of the Feedback Unit was publicly broached. The *Straits Times* noted that dialogue sessions themselves were intended as a series "to be held over the next two years as part of efforts to listen to, and act on, suggestions from the ground". "Feedback Plus Action", *Straits Times*, 10 Feb. 1985.

60   Chan Heng Chee, "Singapore in 1985: Managing Political Transition and Economic Recession", *Asian Survey* 26, 2, *A Survey of Asia in 1985: Part 2* (Feb. 1986): 158–67, esp. 161.

61   ASG Goh Chok Tong to SG Lee Kuan Yew, 13 May 1986 (PAP archive).

62   These were a mix of CCC and CCMC chairmen, members and secretaries. Two were cadre members. They were guided in their work by Wong Kan Seng and Ow Chin Hock. References following the paper are from the original version; a (less hard-hitting) summary was later published in *Petir* ("Improving the Party's Image", Dec. 1986, pp. 11–2) and summarised in the press. "Six Offer Ideas to Enhance PAP's Image", *Straits Times*, 12 Dec. 1986.

63   "The PAP's Public Image and How It Can Be Improved", 24 Apr. 1986 (PAP archive).

64   *1984 General Election PAP Post-mortem Report*.

65   Interviews with multiple former PAP MPs and retired former staff of PAP HQ. For a sense of how autonomously the branches had operated prior to the 1961 "Big Split", see Lee Khoon Choy, Transcript of Oral History Interview, Accession Number 000022, Reel 48, pp. 420–3 (National Archives of Singapore). Available at https://www.nas.gov.sg/archivesonline/oral_history_interviews/interview/000022 (accessed 23 Jan. 2021).

66   Observations on central control, relative neglect of the branches, and the historical reasons
      for this have been made in previous studies of the PAP and its leaders. As Thomas Bellows
      observed in 1967, when the schism with the pro-communist faction within the PAP and
      the split from the Barisan (which involved the defection of some of the Party branches)
      were still recent memories: "In recent years, as the only party in Singapore to have
      utilized mass party organizational techniques, the PAP has come to believe that the
      development of such an organization has fatal dangers implicit in it if the titular heads
      of the party cannot be assured of its absolute loyalty. Therefore, it has decided that the
      institutions to mould and integrate society, to encourage participation and expressions of
      support by the citizenry, should be governmental bodies rather the political party and its
      adjunct organisations. Party organisation is now being de-emphasized." Thomas J. Bellows,
      "The Singapore Party System", *Journal of Southeast Asian History* 8, 1 (Mar. 1967):
      122–38, at p. 130.
67   "The PAP's Public Image and How It Can Be Improved".
68   Minutes of PAP Central Executive Committee Meeting, 13 Aug. 1985 (PAP archive).
69   The Youth Wing was given a similar right. PAP Central Executive Committee, "Some
      Changes to Party Organisation", tabled at 24 July 1986 CEC meeting (PAP archive). At
      the PAP Party conference in January 1988, more than 120 resolutions were submitted
      from branches. It does not appear as if this measure was particularly long-lived: MPs
      from the era interviewed by the author point to a lack of meaningful resolutions from the
      branches. These eventually dried up altogether.
70   Minutes of PAP Central Executive Committee Meeting, 13 Aug. 1985.
71   "Some Changes to Party Organisation".
72   Dr Ow Chin Hock, interview with the author, 2 Nov. 2012.
73   Ibid. For details of the analysis exercise, see also "Fewer People Seeking Help at MP
      Sessions", *Straits Times*, 27 June 1992.
74   Yeo Cheow Tong (Chairman, Information Committee) to all PAP MPs, 15 Mar. 1985
      (PAP archive). Yeo noted that the Information Committee under the HQ Exco committee
      would regularly liaise directly with each branch feedback committee, rather than setting up
      another bureaucracy involving written reports. Yeo also noted that each Branch Feedback
      Committee "would also monitor the 'political mood' within the constituency".
75   "The PAP's Public Image and How It Can Be Improved".
76   *1984 General Election PAP Post-mortem Report.*
77   Minutes of PAP Central Executive Committee Meeting, 24 July 1986 (PAP archive).
78   Ibid.
79   Minutes of PAP Central Executive Committee Meeting, 13 Aug. 1985 (PAP archive).
80   SG Lee Kuan Yew to ASG Goh Chok Tong, 14 May 1986 (PAP archive).
81   A particular, and recurring, complaint was that CEC members and office-holders seldom
      visited the branches. Visits to the branches were conducted by district chairmen, who were
      seen as being "only" backbenchers. The HQ Exco regrouped PAP branches to coincide
      with the seven CCC districts. The idea was that district chairmen would now be part
      of the control and information network. But these district chairmen were from 1985
      appointed by the HQ Exco instead of the branches in each district. 1OS Goh Chok Tong
      to Secretary-General Lee Kuan Yew, 24 Jan. 1985 (PAP archive).

82   Peh Chin Hua, a Chinese-educated candidate and long-serving branch member in
      Kim Seng who stood in Jalan Besar Group Representation Constituency (GRC) in the
      September 1988 elections, had complained at the 24 January 1988 Party conference
      that the PAP had built up the grassroots organisations, only to be overshadowed by
      them: "Therefore, we should bring the PAP into the limelight so that its role in making
      national policies can be apparent." "Time to Come Out from the Shade", *Straits Times*,
      25 Jan. 1988.

83   Before S. Dhanabalan regularised Party finances in late 1985, the Party's holdings in shares
      and bonds were registered in the names of various nominee companies and individuals
      who were or had been members of the CEC. The share scrips and transfer forms were
      kept personally by the treasurer. S. Dhanabalan to CEC members, memo, "Opening of
      Custodian Account for the Party's Investments in Securities", 17 Oct. 1985 (PAP archive).

84   S. Dhanabalan, interview with the author, 14 May 2013.

85   S. Dhanabalan (treasurer) to CEC members, 11 June 1987 (PAP archive). PAP HQ
      contributed just $1,000 back to each branch, to enable each branch to start a new bank
      account for political activities. Before this, in the lead-up to the actual incorporation of the
      PCF, Dhanabalan required branches to start submitting accounts to Party HQ in order to
      establish their financial positions and to prepare them for auditing—the first time these
      checks had been carried out.

86   It took some time for all the kindergarten classes run by branches to actually come under
      PCF control. "$1m Start for PAP Foundation", *Straits Times*, 15 May 1986. Subsequently,
      Dr Tay Eng Soon (chairman of PCF, 1990–93) and Arthur Beng (first chairman of the
      kindergarten committee) were to play key roles in bringing PAP kindergartens onto the
      modern stage, gradually improving training, teacher education and pedagogy.

87   "The PAP Foundation", paper tabled at 3 Mar. 1986 CEC meeting (PAP archive).

88   Minutes of PAP Central Executive Committee Meeting, 24 July 1986 (PAP archive).

89   Wong Kan Seng, "A Soft Touch to Hard-Headedness", *Petir*, Apr. 1986, p. 6.

90   "Youth Committee" (memo from Goh Chok Tong to BG Lee Hsien Loong), 11 Apr.
      1986; memo and paper "PAP Youth Wing" (BG Lee Hsien Loong to 1DPM Goh Chok
      Tong), 6 May 1986 (PAP archive). BG Lee noted to Goh that he had first discussed the
      concept with other young ministers and Organising Secretary (Special Duties) Lau Ping
      Sum. Lau was the secretary of the working group set up by BG Lee that brought the idea
      of the Youth Wing into being (Lau Ping Sum, personal communication, 27 Oct. 2020).

91   Minutes of PAP Central Executive Committee Meeting, 24 July 1986. The idea was not
      completely new: Goh Choon Kang, who stood for the seat of Braddell Heights in the
      1984 elections, had called for the PAP to renew its ranks through the formation of a
      Youth Wing when speaking at the PAP Party conference on 30 September 1984. "Care for
      Retirees and Set up New Youth Wing", *Straits Times*, 8 Nov. 1984.

92   A small number of branches had in the 1970s and early 1980s youth groups or branch
      youth wings. These included Whampoa (under Dr Augustine Tan in the 1970s) and Chay
      Wai Chuen in Queenstown (1980s). Chay had been in the Whampoa youth wing and
      took the idea with him to Queenstown (Lau Ping Sum, personal communication, 27
      Oct. 2020). See Chay Wai Chuen, Transcript of Oral History Interview (Special Project,

Queenstown), Accession Number 003144/01, Disc 1, pp. 7–8 (National Archives of Singapore, accessed 25 Jan. 2021).

93 PM Lee Hsien Loong, interview with the author, 1 Dec. 2015.

94 George Yeo, interview with the author, 11 Oct. 2012.

95 Memo, "Appointment of Organising Secretaries", 22 Nov. 1991 (PAP archive). PAP sources also note that the frequent accompanying of Youth Wing Exco members on overseas trips with BG Yeo caused resentment among long-serving branch members, who may not have had similar opportunities.

96 "PAP Youth Challenged to Double Membership", *Straits Times*, 29 Oct. 1988.

97 No women were interviewed in 1980. The situation in 1984 was different: the three who were in the end asked to stand were part of a larger pool of women potentials who surfaced. "Two More Women May Stand on PAP Ticket", *Straits Times*, 14 June 1984.

98 "Chok Tong Sets 3 Challenges for the Party's Women's Wing", *Straits Times*, 3 July 1989.

99 1DPM Goh did not drop the idea: he publicly said in Oct.1987 that a Women's Wing would come into being after the Youth Wing had got off the ground. "PAP's Women's Wing to Define Role in Singapore Politics", *Straits Times*, 26 Apr. 1989.

100 "Backup for the Party for Most of Its 34 Years", *Straits Times*, 26 Apr. 1989.

101 "Concept Paper on PAP Women's Wing", tabled on 4 Dec. 1988, PAP Central Executive Committee meeting (PAP archive).

102 Goh Chok Tong, interview with the author, 30 Jan. 2013. Goh had hoped to field three more women candidates (in addition to Dr Dixie Tan, Dr Aline Wong and Yu-Foo Yee Shoon, who were fielded in 1984 and again in 1988) but was able to find only one: Dr Seet Ai Mee, who stood successfully in Bukit Gombak. "Chok Tong Sets 3 Challenges for the Party's Women's Wing".

103 Dr Aline Wong, interview with the author, 27 Dec. 2012.

104 These were the objectives 1DPM Goh publicly set for it when he launched the Women's Wing on 2 July 1989. "Chok Tong Sets 3 Challenges for the Party's Women's Wing". The leadership of the Women's Wing was not necessarily in complete agreement with the three objectives—particularly the second and third—as these could be seen as showing the Party's somewhat traditional perception of the role of women. Dr Aline Wong, personal communication, 3 Dec. 2020.

105 Dr Aline Wong, interview with the author, 27 Dec. 2012.

106 There appears to have been some belief within the Party rank and file that women were uninterested in politics. This may partly have had to do with the activities of the Women's Committees (WEC) of the People's Association. Individuals joining the WECs were women mainly interested in social and recreational activities, rather than in political participation. Dr Aline Wong, personal communication, 3 Dec. 2020.

107 "PAP's Women's Wing to Define Role in Singapore Politics", *Straits Times*, 26 Apr. 1989. Aline Wong would be co-opted into the CEC in 1990.

108 This decision was taken by the CEC at its 11 March 1982 meeting.

109 In a small number of cases, there seem to have been unnamed individuals ("malcontents") whose continued membership would be regarded as an embarrassment

to the Party. Exchange of letters between 1OS Goh Chok Tong and SG Lee Kuan Yew, 12 and 13 June 1984 (PAP archive). By the time the CEC in 1986 came round to removing dormant cadres, the threshold of absence from Party conferences (that would lead to removal) had risen from two to three.

110 The cadres had to be known quantities, too. Goh's submission on cadres in June 1984 to Lee, subsequently approved by the CEC, suggested that nominees should have been known to their MPs for at least three years and should preferably have been Party members also for at least three years.

111 *Report on Cadre Promotion Exercise 1985*, tabled at the 13 Mar. 1986 CEC meeting (PAP archive). In addition, of the 96 appointed cadres, more than half had not gone beyond secondary education. "96 from All Walks of Life Appointed PAP Cadres", *Straits Times*, 17 May 1986.

112 PM Lee made this observation at the 24 July 1986 CEC meeting when changes in Party organisation were being debated. Minutes of PAP Central Executive Committee Meeting, 24 July 1986 (PAP archive).

113 "The PAP's Public Image and How It Can Be Improved".

114 Ibid.

115 SG Lee Kuan Yew to ASG Goh Chok Tong, 14 May 1986 (PAP archive).

116 "Candidates" (memo from ASG Goh Chok Tong to all PAP MPs), 15 Dec. 1986 (PAP archive).

117 "Afternoon Tea that Can Change Lives", *Straits Times*, 3 June 1984.

118 Ibid.

119 "Lest I Become an Embarrassment", *Straits Times*, 10 June 1984.

120 Lim Kim San, a retired PAP minister (as well as former chairman of the Housing and Development Board, and widely credited with the success of Singapore's public housing programme) was known for his acumen as well as his shrewd assessments of people. See Lam Peng Er, "The Organisational Utility Men", in *Lee's Lieutenants: Singapore's Old Guard*, Rev. ed., ed. Lam Peng Er and Kevin Tan (Singapore: Straits Times Press, 2018), pp. 71–2, 76–7. See also "MPs, Yes, but Non Yes-Men", *Straits Times*, 10 June 1984.

121 "Day of Nerves and Frank Talk", *Straits Times*, 17 June 1984.

122 Ibid.

123 Some also went through psychological tests. In 1980 most of the 18 new candidates also went through psychological testing lasting one and a half days each. In 1984 some were put through the same examinations. The psychological assessment was for those whom the Party leaders did not know well but who had the potential to be office-bearers. It was also used with the small number of candidates for whom Party leaders might have had lingering doubts. "Under the Microscope", *Straits Times*, 24 June 1984.

124 The "shadowing" process involved sitting in on meet-the-people sessions and attending community functions. Not all potential candidates stayed in one constituency during the shadowing process, and not all were necessarily fielded in the end. "New Faces Make the Rounds with PAP MPs", *Straits Times*, 28 July 1988.

125 Eugene Yap was at the time the chief chemist of Fraser and Neave, a soft drink manufacturer. Yap was fielded in the February 1979 by-election, serving as MP until 2001.

126 S. Chandra Das, interview with the author, 16 Nov. 2012.

127 Ibid.

128 Wong Kan Seng, interview with the author, 16 Apr. 2013.

129 Wong had been head of the Navy Personnel Department in Mindef under Dr Goh Keng Swee and had been tasked with dealing with the issue of Vietnamese refugee boats entering Singapore waters in 1975. Goh, impressed with Wong's determination in executing instructions to speedily provision the boats and ensure that they moved on from Singapore, suggested to PM Lee Kuan Yew and Goh Chok Tong that Wong should be considered as a PAP candidate (Goh Chok Tong, personal communication, 12 June 2017). See also Lee, *Singapore: The Unexpected Nation*, p. 460.

130 Lim Hng Kiang, a Singapore Armed Forces and President's scholar, was drafted into the Ministry of National Development in early 1988 to assume the newly created post of deputy secretary (on the Administrative Service track). "National Development Ministry Reorganises", *Straits Times*, 8 Jan. 1988. Lim worked closely with S. Dhanabalan (who had taken over the National Development portfolio in 1987 following the suicide of Teh Cheang Wan) on two key policy issues that were to be introduced in 1989: Town Councils and the Ethnic Integration Policy. He was fielded in the 1991 election (Lim Hng Kiang, interview with the author, 30 Mar. 2021).

131 S. Dhanabalan, interview with the author, 14 May 2013.

132 "How Dixie Puts House in Order First", *Straits Times*, 1 July 1984.

133 "Beneficiary Repays His Debt", *Straits Times*, 10 June 1984, p. 18.

134 Goh Chok Tong, interview with the author, 22 June 2012. 1DPM Goh seems to have made it a particular point to ask those who said no to at least suggest names—their friends and contacts—who could be considered, outlining frankly the dangers of not having anyone to take Singapore through to the 1990s and beyond. "Afternoon Tea that Can Change Lives".

135 Goh Chok Tong, interview with the author, 22 June 2012.

136 "Afternoon Tea that Can Change Lives".

137 This was a fact revealed by then PM Lee in 1988. "Prime Minister's Assessment of Goh Chok Tong", *Straits Times*, 24 Aug. 1988. See also Lee, *Unexpected Nation*, pp. 457–60, for a discussion of the men brought in at this time who became senior politicians.

138 Some candidates were also required to submit essays about themselves. Prior to joining the Party in August 1988, George Yeo had to write a short piece describing his core values. Asad-ul Iqbal Latif and Lee Huay Leng (eds), *George Yeo on Bonsai, Banyan and the Tao* (Singapore: World Scientific, 2015), p. 3.

139 Interviews with multiple former ministers involved in candidate selection at the final stages.

140 "Few Stumble on the Home Stretch", *Straits Times*, 1 July 1984.

141 In many instances at the CEC round, Lee Kuan Yew took the role of lead interviewer. This could make for interesting exchanges. K. Shanmugam recalled many years later in 2020 the experience of being grilled by Lee at his 1987 CEC interview. Shanmugam, then a young 28-year-old lawyer, said something at the interview that sent Lee "into the stratosphere". Lee proceeded to grill Shanmugam on the (undisclosed) issue for 45 intense minutes. "I was saved by the fact that I was young, young enough not to be

intimidated by him [Lee], because I didn't know enough. Five years later, knowing what I knew about him, I would have been far more circumspect." "How K. Shanmugam, the Man Who Upholds Some of S'pore's Hardest Laws, Deals with a Crisis", Mothership.sg, 17 June 2020. https://mothership.sg/2020/06/k-shanmugam-interview-covid/ (accessed 6 Mar. 2021). Shanmugam was fielded in Sembawang GRC in the 1988 general election and would go on to hold ministerial positions for law, foreign affairs and home affairs.

142 Interviews with multiple former ministers involved in candidate selection at the final stages.

143 "New Faces Make the Rounds with PAP MPs", *Straits Times*, 28 July 1988. Each GPC had between 10 and 15 resource panel members who were members of the public. All told, there were 100 resource panel members across all GPCs. "Chok Tong: Time to Get Back to Consensus-Building Task", *Straits Times*, 31 July 1988.

144 Dr Hong Hai was, in fact, responsible for drafting the initial concept paper for GPCs which he submitted to Goh Chok Tong in 1986. GPCs and their genesis will be discussed in chapter 2.

145 "Why PAP Invited the 'Angry Young Man'", *Straits Times*, 10 June 1984. There is a useful discussion of the people brought in by Goh Chok Tong in Lee, *Singapore: Unexpected Nation*, pp. 457–61.

146 For the drug problem within the Malay community from the 1970s, see Francis Heng Hua Mong, "Ethnicity and Drug Abuse: The Case of the Singapore Malays" (PhD dissertation, University of Hull, 1994), pp. 15, 31–5, 339–40 (and pp. 302–4 for drug abusers' membership of secret societies and gangs). More generally, for Malay involvement in gangs (an issue that received more publicity from the late 1980s onwards, but which had been present earlier), see Sukmawati bte Haji Sirat, "Trends in Malay Political Leadership: The People's Action Party's Malay Political Leaders and the Integration of the Singapore Malays" (PhD dissertation, University of South Carolina, 1995), pp. 43–4, 229, 245. See also Mohamad Maidin Bin Packer, Oral History Interview (in Malay), Accession Number 003180 (National Archives of Singapore). Available at https://www.nas.gov.sg/archivesonline/oral_history_interviews/record-details/52112bc5-1161-11e3-83d5-0050568939ad (accessed 23 Jan. 2021). In Reels 2–4 and 8 a useful analysis is given of problems with the Malay community in the 1980s. Maidin Packer was a PAP MP from 1991 to 2006, rising to become senior parliamentary secretary.

147 According to the census, there were only 679 Malay university graduates (1.5% of the total number of graduates) in 1980. Khoo Chian Kim, *Census of Population 1980, Singapore: Release No. 3. Literacy and Education* (Singapore: Department of Statistics, 1981), p. 15. 48% of Malays above the age of 14 had only primary level education (see *Census of Population 1980*, pp. 20–1; author's calculations). All this meant, of course, that Malays were underrepresented in the ranks of white collar professionals.

148 Lee Kuan Yew, *From Third World to First*, pp. 238–9; National Day Rally Speech by Prime Minister Lee Kuan Yew (in Malay), 16 Aug. 1981.

149 On the formation of Mendaki, see Wan Hussin Zoohri, "Education from 1959 to 2014: The Seeds of the Formation of Mendaki", in *Majulah!, 50 Years of Malay/Muslim Community in Singapore*, ed. Zainul Abidin Rasheed and Norshahril Saat (Singapore: World Scientific, 2016), pp. 159–77, esp. 165–8.

150 For the rationale, see Norman Vasu and Nur Diyanah Binte Anwar, "The Maligned Malays and National Service", in *National Service in Singapore,* ed. Ho Shu Huang and Graham Ong-Webb (Singapore: World Scientific, 2019), pp. 203–25. See also Pang Eng Fong, "The Economic Status of Malay Muslims in Singapore", *Journal of the Institute of Muslim Minority Affairs* 3, 2 (1981): 148–61.

151 Abdullah Tarmugi, Transcript of Oral History Interview (in Malay), Reel 2, Accession Number 3179/06, pp. 25–6 (National Archives of Singapore). Available at https://www.nas.gov.sg/archivesonline/oral_history_interviews/record-details/29ff0f59-1161-11e3-83d5-0050568939ad (accessed 23 Jan. 2021). Tarmugi was a PAP MP from 1984 to 2011. He rose to become minister for community development and sports and minister in charge of Muslim affairs, also serving as Speaker of Parliament (2002–11).

152 The matter received a public airing in February/March 1987 when Second Minister for Defence BG Lee Hsien Loong observed that "if there is a conflict, if the SAF [Singapore Armed Forces] is called upon to defend our homeland, we don't want to put any of our soldiers in a difficult position where his emotions for the nation may come in conflict with his emotions for his religion, because these are two very strong fundamentals, and if they are not compatible, then they will be two very strong destructive forces in opposite directions." Singapore Parliamentary Debates, 17 Mar. 1987, col. 375. BG Lee was repeating (and using the opportunity to clarify) comments he had made at a grassroots forum at Yuhua constituency on 22 February 1987. "Candid Views Exchanged on Racial Harmony", *Straits Times*, 23 Feb. 1987.

153 Malay MPs who had been in the teaching profession (or trained as teachers) included Sidek Saniff, Wan Hussin Zoohri, Shaari Tadin, Abbas Abu Amin, Saidi Shariff, Harun Ghani, Ibrahim Othman and Zainal Sapari. Both Hawazi Daipi and Yatiman Yusof were teachers before becoming journalists. Other journalists included Mohamad Maidin Bin Packer, Zainul Abidin Rasheed and Abdullah Tarmugi. Another PAP MP, Nasser Kamaruddin, was a senior newscaster with the Singapore Broadcasting Corporation. From an earlier era, Othman Wok (a member of the PAP's first generation of leaders and minister for social affairs from 1963 to 1977) had also been a journalist (with *Utusan Melayu*).

154 Author interviews with multiple former PAP Malay/Muslim MPs. Another issue that caused resentment (which could linger for decades, and which affected all races) was the demolition of villages (kampungs) to make way for high-rise Housing and Development Board (HDB) housing, which in some cases meant the dispersal of communities that had lived in an area for generations. Wan Hussin Zoohri (a PAP MP from 1980 to 1991), for example, had to deal with unhappiness by Malays angered by the changes in a predominantly Malay area, Kampong Ubi, as it transformed into a housing estate; the other issue Zoohri had to deal with, the demolition of a cherished mosque, was another issue occurring elsewhere that had to be dealt with sensitively. See *The Story of Kampong Ubi*, ed. Shirley Tan-Oehler (Singapore: People's Action Party Kampong Ubi Branch and PAP Community Foundation, Kampong Ubi Branch, 1993).

155 See, for example, Sidek Saniff, *Life Reflections at Eighty* (Singapore: Opus Editorial, 2018), pp. 168–70. Sidek Saniff was a PAP MP from 1976 to 2011, rising to become senior minister of state.

156 In 1974 Yatiman Yusof was briefly detained by the Internal Security Department for alleged anti-state activity, which effectively ended his teaching career. Yatiman Yusof, interview with the author, 21 Oct. 2020.

157 Abdullah Tarmugi, Transcript of Oral History Interview (in Malay), Accession Number 3179/06, Reel 2, pp. 27–8 (National Archives of Singapore). Several from the Malay/Muslim community who became PAP MPs, looking back, were adamant that the issue of Malay loyalty should not arise. See, for example, Wan Hussin Bin Haji Zoohri, Transcript of Oral History Interview (in Malay), Accession Number 002862/12, Reel 9, pp. 84–5 (National Archives of Singapore); and Mohamad Maidin Bin Packer Mohd, Oral History Interview (in Malay), Reel 3, 05:32–07:20 and 37:28–38:19, Accession Number 003180 (National Archives of Singapore). Available at https://www.nas.gov.sg/archivesonline/oral_history_interviews/record-details/9b4ec773-1160-11e3-83d5-0050568939ad and https://www.nas.gov.sg/archivesonline/oral_history_interviews/record-details/4fc0ea0c-1161-11e3-83d5-0050568939ad (accessed 23 Jan. 2021).

158 Yatiman Yusof, interview with the author, 21 Oct. 2020. The change that Yatiman mooted—allowing a portion of individual CPF contributions by Malays/Muslims to go to Mendaki—did in fact take place in 1984. The other point raised—Dr Ahmad Mattar's long stint as acting minister—was a sore point within the Malay community and was raised by other prospective candidates when interviewed by the party leadership. See Zulkifli Mohammed, Transcript of Oral History Interview, Accession Number 003256/3, Reel 2, p. 44 (National Archives of Singapore). Available at https://www.nas.gov.sg/archivesonline/oral_history_interviews/record-details/59cb7d2b-1160-11e3-83d5-0050568939ad (accessed 23 Jan. 2021). Zulkifli Mohammed was a PAP MP from 1984 to 1996. He was also the nephew of Othman Wok.

159 Yatiman Yusof, interview with the author, 21 Oct. 2020. Zulkifli Mohammed (to give another example of several) was first approached in 1976 and then again asked to stand in the 1980 general election (he declined to be considered after reaching the final interview stage) but agreed to be fielded in 1984. What swung his thinking was a personal approach by Goh Chok Tong. Zulkifli Mohammed was convinced of Goh's sincerity and agreed to be fielded. Zulkifli Mohammed, Transcript of Oral History Interview, Reel 2, Accession Number 003256/3, pp. 41–3.

160 Zainul Abidin Rasheed, personal communication, 20 Nov. 2020. Besides being editor of *Berita Harian* (1976–96), he was also to be CEO of Mendaki (1990–93) and president of MUIS (Majlis Ugama Islam Singapura; the Islamic Religious Council of Singapore; 1991–96). The idea of working to advance the Malay community from the "outside" at least for a time, rather than through the PAP, was in the minds of several others who were subsequently persuaded to become PAP MPs. See, for example, Abdullah Tarmugi, Transcript of Oral History Interview (in Malay), Accession Number 3179/06, Reel 2, p. 34.

161 "BG Lee Tells What PAP Looks for in New Candidates", *Straits Times*, 18 Aug. 1988.

162 It does not necessarily follow that all of the candidates with PAP branch affiliations were pushed up solely on account of their work at the branches. Ho Tat Kin and Wang Kai Yuen were PhD holders, while Koh Lam Son and Arthur Beng were medical doctors.

These men had qualifications that in any case might have brought them to the attention of the PAP selectors.

163 "PAP Fielding 17 New Candidates", *Straits Times*, 21 Aug. 1988.

164 The class of 1980 included three non-graduates. "The Class of '84", *Straits Times*, 18 Oct. 1984.

165 Unlike the 1984 batch, two in the 1988 batch had not attended university: Peh Chin Hua and Charles Chong, "PAP Fielding 17 New Candidates", *Straits Times*, 21 Aug. 1988.

166 Yu-Foo Yee Shoon, Ho Tat Kin, Wang Kai Yuen, Arthur Beng, Philip Tan and Koh Lam Son.

167 Dr Dixie Tan, S. Vasoo, Zulkifli Mohammed, Heng Chiang Meng, Yatiman Yusof, Abdullah Tarmugi and Ibrahim Othman.

168 Peh Chin Hua, Chay Wai Chuen, Low Seow Chay and Peter Sung.

169 Ong Chit Chung, Loh Meng See, Choo Wee Khiang and Kenneth Chen.

170 Michael Lim, Harun Bin A. Ghani, R. Sinnakaruppan and Matthias Yao had experience or positions of leadership in PAP branches. Mohamad Maidin Bin Packer was the chairman of the Malay Affairs Advisory Committee for Aljunied GRC. Koo Tsai Kee was a committee member of the PAP Community Foundation.

171 Yu-Foo Yee Shoon, Goh Choon Kang and Tang Guan Seng in 1984; Low Seow Chay, John Chen, Peh Chin Hua and Choo Wee Khiang in 1988. From the 1991 batch of new candidates, only Dr Ker Sin Tze was Chinese educated.

172 When interviewed just before the elections, Yeo noted that he had "a duty to represent those in my generation, their hopes and fears", while noting the cynicism that many young people felt towards the government. "My Task Ahead by BG Yeo", *Straits Times*, 20 Aug. 1988.

173 George Yeo, interview with the author, 11 Oct. 2012. The short article that played a role in getting him noticed was "The Military and the Nation State", *Pointer* 6, 3 (Jan. 1981). See also "How I Got BG Yeo to Join the Team—and What a Catch!", *Straits Times*, 21 Jan. 1989. For Yeo's student involvement in protest activities against the Singapore government (having to do particularly with the issue of detentions in Singapore of activists under the Internal Security Act), see "Articles in CUMSA Newsletter", in *George Yeo on Bonsai, Banyan and the Tao*, ed. Latif and Lee, pp. 623–7.

174 Yeo openly admitted to having misgivings about joining the PAP but ultimately concluded that he had "a duty to represent those in my generation, their hopes and fears". "My Task Ahead by BG Yeo".

175 Minutes of PAP Central Executive Committee Meeting, 29 Oct. 1986 (PAP archive).

176 Not that the CEC appears at this stage to have been against backbenchers being voted in. The 1984 General Election Post-mortem Committee, chaired by 2DPM Ong Teng Cheong, had noted in its report, "The PAP must find some visible way to demonstrate that it has ordinary people in its inner circles." *1984 General Election PAP Post-mortem Report*.

177 Dr Yeo Ning Hong and Dr Wan Soon Bee were, for example, co-opted in March 1983. "Two Joining PAP Central Executive Committee", *Straits Times*, 4 Mar. 1983. Dr Ow

Chin Hock, 1OS from 1985 and a key figure in the conference proceedings, commented that he told Goh Chok Tong that the co-opting of additional individuals who had not even been nominated should not be allowed. Dr Ow Chin Hock, interview with the author, 2 Nov. 2012.

178 For example, at the 7 December 1980 Party conference. "Watershed for PAP", *Straits Times*, 25 Mar. 1981.

179 Toh was also dropped from the new Cabinet in early January 1981.

180 Lee Kuan Yew, *From Third World to First*, p. 742.

181 Peh Shing Huei, *Tall Order: The Goh Chok Tong Story*, Vol. 1 (Singapore: World Scientific, 2018), p. 159.

182 The panel for the first interview (18 May 1984) consisted of Lim Kim San, 1OS Goh Chok Tong, Dr Yeo Ning Hong (notetaker), Ong Pang Boon, Chua Sian Chin and Ong Teng Cheong, with Prof. S. Jayakumar in attendance. The panel for the second interview (18 July 1984) consisted of 1OS Goh Chok Tong, 2DPM S. Rajaratnam, Teh Cheang Wan, Dr Tony Tan and Dr Yeo Ning Hong (notetaker).

183 Lee Hsien Loong, Personal Statement to PAP Central Executive Committee, 2 June 1984 (PAP archive).

184 Interview notes, Lee Hsien Loong, candidate interview panels, 18 May 1984 and 18 July 1984 (PAP archive).

185 Ibid.

186 Minutes of PAP Central Executive Committee Meeting, 13 Aug. 1984 (PAP archive). For Lee Kuan Yew's thoughts on his son entering politics and making his way through the PAP selection process, see Peh Shing Huei, *Tall Order*, pp. 159–64.

187 Excerpts from speech by Ong Pang Boon, Minister for the Environment, at Hong Lim Green Community Centre, 12 Aug. 1984. "王邦文部长演词全文", *Lianhe Zaobao*, 13 Aug. 1984. For an English summary, see "A Warning on the Appointment of Political Leaders", *Singapore Monitor*, 14 Aug. 1984.

188 Ong Pang Boon, interview with the author, 9 Jan. 2020.

189 "Chok Tong Gives His Replies to Queries on the Future", *Straits Times*, 19 Aug. 1984.

190 Another reply from a younger-generation leader came in the form of a talk at this time to Party activists by Minister without Portfolio and NTUC Secretary-General Ong Teng Cheong, who was also Party chairman. Ong (in a nod to how many old guard MPs being retired before the 1984 election had made their grievances known in public settings, or who had been reluctant to orientate their successors on the ground), observed that "public lectures will only damage their own image and betray their real attitudes towards self-renewal. Worse, they could be accused of committing a treacherous parting act to undermine their own successors, to disrupt [the] self-renewal process and weaken the Party." "Teng Cheong: Retire Gracefully, With Dignity", *Petir*, Sept. 1984, p. 1.

191 Correspondence between PM Lee Kuan Yew and Goh Chok Tong (cc Ong Teng Cheong, S. Dhanabalan, Dr Tony Tan), 20–21 Aug. 1984 (National Archives of Singapore).

192 "Introducing Safeguards to Protect Singaporeans", PM Lee Kuan Yew, National Day Rally Speech, 19 Aug. 1984, *National Day Rally Speeches: 50 Years of Nationhood in Singapore 1966–2015* (National Archives of Singapore and Cengage Learning Asia,

2017), pp. 111–9, esp. 114. As Lee noted to Goh and the younger ministers, it was *Lianhe Zaobao* (the main Chinese-language daily newspaper) that realised the significance of the critical passage in Lee's National Day Rally speech, carrying this as its back page headline. "总理与两位副总理皆认为 党和政府自我更新步伐不可以放慢" [Prime Minister and the two deputy prime ministers think that the pace of Party and government self-renewal cannot slow down], *Lianhe Zaobao*, 20 Aug. 1984.

193 Correspondence between PM Lee Kuan Yew and Goh Chok Tong (cc Ong Teng Cheong, S. Dhanabalan, Dr Tony Tan), 20–21 Aug. 1984 (National Archives of Singapore). Lee was concerned enough to tell Goh he should consider bringing in new cadre members in case differences on the issue of succession and renewal came into the open and the issue came to a vote at the coming Party conference in September: "You and I have to make certain that the majority of the present MPs who are not being retired, are solidly with us in any showdown. The counting of heads of cadre members may also become crucial. If I am not around, the old guards may challenge your right to the leadership." Goh, in reply, wrote: "I don't think we should rush in cadre members nominated by MPs before Sep 84. It will be seen as 'packing' and a sign of weakness." Correspondence between PM Lee Kuan Yew and 1DPM Goh Chok Tong (cc Ong Teng Cheong, S. Dhanabalan, Dr Tony Tan), 20–21 Aug. 1984 (National Archives of Singapore), made available to the author.

194 Exchange of letters between PM Lee Kuan Yew and Goh Chok Tong (cc Ong Teng Cheong, S. Dhanabalan, Dr Tony Tan), 28–30 Aug. 1984 (National Archives of Singapore), made available to the author. For Ong Pang Boon's Telok Ayer speech, see "王邦文促请想成为新一代党领袖者 关注年轻选民期望" [Ong Pang Boon urges those who aspire to be the new generation of party leaders to pay attention to the expectations of young voters], *Lianhe Zaobao*, 26 Aug. 1984. The issue of the pace of renewal, and the feelings of the PAP old guard who retired (or who were asked to step aside) was something Ong Pang Boon felt deeply. On the occasion of his 90th birthday dinner on 23 March 2019, Ong (by then Singapore's last surviving old guard leader) alluded to the pain of renewal using a well-known Chinese idiom, 长江后浪催前浪 ("the rear waves of the Yangtze drive on those before"; literally, the later generation will replace the earlier). Ong continued, "I believe that leadership renewal is crucial to the success of all organizations, including political parties. But I also believe that, like the orderly waves of the Yangtze River, the renewal process must be well paced and sensitively executed so as to avoid unnecessary unhappiness among the older members." Speech delivered by Comrade Ong Pang Boon, 23 Mar. 2019. Available at https://www.facebook.com/watch/?v=426187534823690 (accessed 23 Jan. 2021). See also "Old Guard Leader Ong Pang Boon Honoured for His Contributions to Singapore on His 90th Birthday", *Straits Times*, 24 Mar. 2019.

195 "Turning Point for the PAP", *Straits Times*, 11 Jan. 1981.

196 "By handing over power whilst we are still alert and fully in charge, we are able to ensure that our successors have the basic attributes to be entrusted with power. It is reckless to hang on and to have power wrested from us when we have become feeble. Then we shall have no say in who our successors are." "Principles of Leadership for a

Stable Government and Dynamic Society", *PM Lee Kuan Yew, speech at the Dinner for the Establishment, 25 Sept. 1984, The Papers of Lee Kuan Yew: Speeches, Interviews and Dialogues, Vol. 9: 1981–1987*, p. 335.

197 Letter from Lee Kuan Yew to Goh Chok Tong, 11 Oct. 1984 (PAP archive). Chua was co-opted back into the CEC in February 1985. In describing his meeting with Chua, Lee wrote somewhat cryptically, "I explained how the momentum of events had forced the new guards to assert their group interests."

198 SG Lee Kuan Yew to ASG Goh Chok Tong, 11 Aug. 1988 (PAP archive). Neither Dr Toh, Ong Pang Boon nor Jek Yeun Thong was fielded in the September 1988 general election, with all retiring from politics. Their single seat constituencies (Rochor, Telok Ayer and Queenstown) were all absorbed into GRCs. In retirement, Toh would occasionally come out with biting criticisms of the Party. See Lam Peng Er, "The Organisational Utility Men", in *Lee's Lieutenants: Singapore's Old Guard*, ed. Lam Peng Er and Kevin Tan (Sydney: Allen & Unwin), pp. 42–79, esp. 64–7.

199 The angst occasionally could be glimpsed publicly. Chor Yeok Eng, who had been a PAP assemblyman for Jurong from 1959 to 1963, and then MP for Bukit Timah from 1966 to 1984, lashed out at the PAP's renewal policies in his speech (with the press present) at the Bukit Timah National Day Dinner on 31 August 1984. His successor, Dr Wang Kai Yuen, had in hand a statement drafted by PM Lee Kuan Yew paying tribute to Chor's contributions. Wang had planned to include this tribute as part of his own speech, but decided not to use the statement following Chor's outburst. Wang Kai Yuen, "The Country Boy", in *We Also Served: Reflections of Singapore's Former PAP MPs*, ed. Chiang Hai Ding and Rohan Kamis (Singapore: Straits Times Press Pte Ltd, 2014), p. 340.

200 A sense of the magnitude of the ongoing renewal process can be seen by examining the list of MPs retired by the CEC in 1988. Amongst the 14 MPs who stepped down (with the dates when they first became MPs in parentheses) were: Dr Yeoh Ghim Seng (1966), S. Rajaratnam (1959), E.W. Barker (1963), Phua Bah Lee (1968), Ong Pang Boon (1959), Dr Toh Chin Chye (1959), Jek Yeun Thong (1963), Fong Sip Chee (1963) and Tang See Chim (1966).

201 "Chok Tong's Handsome Tribute to 14 Veterans", *Straits Times*, 22 Aug. 1988. See also "Chok Tong's Approach to Retiring MPs Praised", *Straits Times*, 22 Aug. 1988.

202 "Chok Tong's Approach to Retiring MPs Praised". Clearly, Goh recognised that something had to be done—and said—to assuage the feelings of the old guard, many of whom felt unceremoniously discarded even though they had been with the PAP since the beginning and had seen it through its darkest days. For a public airing of this sense of grievance by a high-profile PAP figure who had been with the Party from the start, see "Treat the Old Guard with Dignity: Pang Boon", *Straits Times*, 5 Oct. 1980.

203 *Exit Management of Retired PAP MPs* (prepared by Wong Kan Seng and approved by Goh Chok Tong), tabled at 19 Oct. 1988 PAP Central Executive Committee meeting (PAP archive).

204 Wan Hussin Zoohri remembers: "Just two weeks before the 1991 GE, I received a call from Chok Tong, who was now the prime minister. We spoke for 10 minutes during which he surprised me by asking me to step aside for new blood. I could not understand

it. There had been no news about me being replaced, no murmurs about stepping down. It came quite suddenly. I had thought I could stay longer and contribute". "Wan Hussin Zoohri, The Teacher", in *We Also Served*, ed. Chiang Hai Ding and Rohan Kamis, p. 303. Wan Hussin Zoohri's account is unusually frank, but typical of the short, painful experience many MPs being retired had to go through.

205 Individuals (both incumbent MPs and new candidates) who were on the "final" list of candidates to be fielded were given the PAP's "election box" by Party HQ (which included the required forms, the Candidates' Handbook which contained important information for the candidates to understand, and briefs on policy matters that had been prepared). But even those given the election box close to Nomination Day could receive a (inevitably wrenching) last-minute notice that their candidature had been withdrawn, with an instruction to return the box to HQ. This might occur, for example, when a new candidate the PAP had tried to persuade for some time to stand had finally agreed to be fielded. When this happened, the candidate withdrawn would sometimes be personally called up (especially from the 1990s) by the PM, who might explain what had happened. On other occasions, however, the disappointed individual could not be afforded a direct explanation by the Party top brass (which sometimes had the effect of helping to soothe matters somewhat) owing to the other pressures on the Party leadership leading up to Nomination Day. Author interview with former PAP MPs and Party HQ officials, 4 Apr. 2021.

206 Memo from Goh Chok Tong to Secretary-General Lee, enclosing paper (drafted by Ch'ng Jit Koon, chairman of the PAP Awards Committee) on Party Awards to be considered by the CEC, 9 Dec. 1987 (PAP archive).

207 The moves to recognise service to the Party formalised existing mechanisms which had previously operated in an informal manner. Various categories of Long Service Awards had been given out in the past but on an ad hoc basis—for example, during the PAP's 25th anniversary in 1979.

208 The CEC agreed that DSM Awards would be kept to a minimum. The Commendation Medal was for Party members who had served not less than five years as office-bearers in the Party organisation, or for Party members who had served more than ten years in grassroots organisations, or for non-Party members or organisations which had served the Party and/or nation (at the discretion of the CEC).

209 Speech by PM Lee at the Party convention, 23 Jan. 1988 (PAP archive).

210 Personal communications from Party sources with knowledge of Party awards in 1990. Dr Toh Chin Chye was not awarded a DSM, although he was awarded the Order of Nila Utama (First Class) in the National Day Honours list that year together with other members of the PAP old guard such as Ong Pang Boon and E.W. Barker. S. Rajaratnam was singled out for special recognition with the Order of Temasek (First Class). "National Day Honours List 1990", *Straits Times*, 9 Aug. 1990. Ong Pang Boon was recognised with the PAP DSM 31 years after his retirement from politics, in 2019. "Top Party Honours for Ong Pang Boon", *Straits Times*, 11 Nov. 2019.

211 "Grassroots Experience" (letter from Secretary-General Lee Kuan Yew to all new PAP MPs), 29 Sept. 1988 (PAP archive).

212 There were, for example, proposals put forward by Goh to recruit outstanding professionals into the Party, as cadres attached to HQ, without having to "do time" in the branches. Other suggestions at this time including getting able branch members to serve in the various HQ Exco subcommittees. Other proposals, such as getting more full-time staff to do public relations and Party strategy and political research, came into being only much later.

213 PM Lee's speech at the PAP convention, 23 Jan. 1988 (PAP archive).

Chapter 2

1987–91: The Polity in Transition

Ways have to be found to enable the people to make more decisions for themselves. More responsibility must be placed on the electorate to understand problems, weigh alternatives, decide, and live with the consequences of the decisions. . . . If this succeeds, the popular mood will be channelled to constructive purposes. If it does not, the mood may turn restive, and disenchantment may lead to opposition for its own sake.

—PAP Central Executive Committee Report October 1984–October 1986[1]

Setting the Agenda

The right to rule, the 1984 PAP election post-mortem report noted, had not been transferred automatically from the PAP old guard to the new. In observing that over 200,000 voters cast their votes for the first time in 1984, the report commented that this group of mainly younger voters, not bonded to the PAP leadership as the older generation had been, saw the struggles of the independence period as only a lesson in history:

> *The most important priority of the new leadership must be to establish a close rapport with the people, to win the right to rule. We must present policies and goals which people will endorse, and gain legitimacy by being identified with these goals. . . . Gradually, mutual confidence must be built up between the rulers and the ruled.*[2]

How this should be done was discussed by the Party leadership as early as July 1986, in the course of deliberations on a Party manifesto. The CEC agreed that the manifesto would spell out long-term objectives, reflect the hopes and aspirations of people, and serve as a rallying point for them.[3] Subsequently, discussions on the outline of the Party manifesto were widened to include the district chairmen and the MPs themselves in late 1986 and early 1987. BG Lee then announced the manifesto, the National Agenda (which became known as the Agenda for Action), on 18 February 1987.[4] The effort was presented as an attempt to build consensus on national issues in order to achieve a realisation of Vision 1999, which had originally been introduced during the

1984 election campaign.[5] Also detailed was a series of engagement and consultation measures that was unprecedented in scope. Besides a new series of walkabouts and dialogue sessions by ministers, there were to be Feedback Unit sessions to get views from professionals on specialised areas (these included health care, culture and the arts). The Ministry of Community Development would also conduct national education seminars for thousands of grassroots leaders. As BG Lee pointed out, Party manifestos were usually dry and vague documents, but "the National Agenda is the opposite of all this, and unlike other election manifestos, would not be quickly forgotten." It was, he said, a document prepared "not for the party but for the whole nation".[6]

The thought, preparation and effort put into the Agenda for Action initiative of 1987–88 show that the Party was determined not to repeat earlier mistakes. The original Agenda for Action had been introduced late in the 1984 general election campaign.[7] There had initially been doubt in some quarters of the Party leadership over whether a manifesto was necessary. PM Lee had early in 1984 written to Goh, informing him that he (Lee) did not place great weight on a manifesto. It was only in December 1984, during the campaign itself, that Lee suggested to Goh that the future Singapore, which Singaporeans could build for themselves, should be spelled out. He added that the younger leaders should project their vision of Singapore for the 1980s and 1990s.[8] The actual reception to this earlier Agenda—known also as Vision 1999—was mixed. There were criticisms that the people were bogged down by more mundane concerns and were unable to relate to somewhat grandiose visions of a Singapore that would not materialise for some time to come.[9] Indeed, the PAP post-mortem report for the 1984 general election noted that the Agenda for Action and accompanying Vision 1999 (an ambitious economic and cultural blueprint that would take Singapore to the millennium and beyond) was introduced too late and too hastily: "A practical programme, linked to tangible, down to earth objectives, might have rallied the people better."[10]

There was from the beginning an attempt to make the 1987–88 Agenda more grounded in contemporary concerns, even as the overall vision for Singapore remained. The initial part of the National Agenda effort saw a series of direct questions posed to the people through various forums: questions on Singapore's vulnerability, nation-building, political stability and the role of the Party, challenges of population trends, the limits of growth, and economic, social, and cultural objectives.[11] Unsurprisingly, the National Agenda effort was described by Party leaders as a general exercise in public education; one designed to get Singaporeans looking at national problems facing the nation in order to understand them better.[12] Indeed, 2DPM Ong Teng Cheong had no qualms in calling it a "public education exercise for all Singaporeans".[13] BG Lee Hsien Loong (chairman of the Manifesto Committee) commented in a note to all PAP MPs on 31 January 1987: "If properly done, we will also educate Singaporeans in some basic facts of life, and win legitimacy and authority for the Party's goals."[14] BG Lee also wrote: "At the end of the process, if all goes well, we will have been seen to have made a considerable effort at consultation, the public will have a better understanding of the major issues, and the Party will have a Manifesto which had legitimacy and acceptance."[15]

The decision was taken early on to use the apparatus of government to support the effort (a prefiguration of later attempts by the Party to galvanise the people in national consultation exercises). The Feedback Unit, for example, was brought in to organise dialogue sessions. The Party reasoning was that the subjects in the manifesto were genuine national concerns, except the part on the Party's role. BG Lee was clear that the use of the state machinery and civil service was entirely justified, pointing out that this was not just a Party agenda but a national one, and that the whole nation had to be mobilised to achieve the goals therein.[16] As 1DPM Goh was to remark in February 1988 at the beginning of the parliamentary debate on the Agenda for Action report: "It represents not just the programme of the governing Party, but the priorities of the entire nation."[17] This approach perhaps marked a recognition, too, that a manifesto that was purely a Party document would have limited appeal. After the 1984 electoral result, the PAP needed something to make sure fissures did not widen. As one commentator noted, the decision of the PAP to discuss the National Agenda with the people was the "culmination of this approach" of forging a new consensus, and "for a political party to invite public participation in the formulation of its party manifesto was totally unprecedented".[18]

On the ground, the National Agenda feedback and consultation efforts were a continuation of ongoing, systematic efforts aimed at reconnecting before the next general election. Younger PAP MPs and leaders began from early 1986 to hold meetings with Party activists to explain policy and get feedback, with some of the key individuals involved (BG Lee, Wong Kan Seng and Yeo Cheow Tong) later becoming members of the Manifesto Committee. These individuals led National Agenda discussions in various branches.[19] All the districts had submitted their input by the end of July 1987. The first draft of the manifesto was discussed at the PAP Youth Wing convention on 19–20 September 1987, with the final draft endorsed by the Party convention on 23 January 1988. Lee in his speech at the convention noted that the National Agenda had been thoroughly discussed before being refined into the Agenda for Action. This ensured, as PM Lee noted at the convention, that the Agenda for Action "had been heard by a wide cross-section of Singaporeans and have won acceptance. The National Agenda is a consensus document."[20]

The effort to get the Agenda recognised as a national document, one seen and supported by the people, did not end there, however. The Green Paper on the Agenda for Action was presented to Parliament on 15 February 1988 and adopted on 25 February.[21] 1DPM Goh announced in Parliament that the goals of the Agenda for Action would be implemented through six specific advisory councils, each headed by a minister, that would prepare reports for the government on key issues.[22] These advisory councils were again (like the Agenda effort itself) an important prefiguration of how the government was to involve the people in its decision-making through the Goh premiership and beyond. The reports of these advisory councils were themselves in some cases to have important implications and will be dealt with presently.[23]

A quarter of a century before (beginning in late 1962), Lee Kuan Yew and the PAP had sought to mobilise the people through walkabouts and constituency tours that were (for that time) unprecedented in scope. The succeeding generation of leaders chose to do things differently, and it is possible within the framework of the National Agenda discussions to glimpse something of the technocratic inclination of the younger generation of leaders. Here were politicians still finding their feet, keen to engage, but also keen to do this through an orderly process and in a systematised manner. But there was the political savvy to realise that face-to-face contact could not be abandoned. Besides the various dialogue sessions organised by the Feedback Unit and Young PAP, the Party decided to organise a series of ministerial walkabouts. The new series of walkabouts began in early 1987 and drew to a close in November 1988.[24] The young office-holders involved in these walkabouts—Wong Kan Seng, Yeo Cheow Tong, Lee Hsien Loong and Lee Boon Yang—were leading members of the second-generation leadership and also members of the PAP Manifesto Committee. By the time the 1987–88 series had concluded, 77 of the 79 constituencies had been covered, with many walkabouts concluding with a dialogue session focusing on a main theme of the Agenda (examples included multiracialism or population issues). BG Lee publicly noted, "the aim was to let Cabinet ministers familiarize themselves with the constituencies and their problems as well as to discuss the National Agenda with the public".[25] As the *Straits Times* reported, comparing the walkabouts with an earlier series (which had spanned 1982–84), "there will be fewer frills this time, like lion and dragon dancing—and more serious talk".[26]

Conveying the sense of urgency which accompanied the Agenda for Action programme and discussions in 1987–88 is not a simple matter; with the passage of time, much of the import of these discussions and feedback sessions was diminished. Suffice it to say, however, that the key aim of the Party after its internal restructuring in 1985–87 was to reclaim the high ground and to convince the people that it was the only choice for successfully seeing the country through the challenges to come. (As we shall see, a similar attempt to regain the high ground was to be made after the 1991 general election.) In addition, it could be observed that within Party thinking there was the concern that existing efforts to communicate might not have had the desired effect. When Dr Tan Cheng Bock, first chairman of the Feedback Supervisory Panel, was quizzed on the subject in April 1987, he noted that there were still problems in the feedback process. Dr Tan, already well known for being in touch with the ground and for being exceptionally sympathetic to the concerns of the ordinary people, also commented that his main concern was whether the government could cope with the rising expectations of Singaporeans—an issue that if not handled carefully could spell trouble in the next election.[27]

Strands of Thinking and Change

Goh Chok Tong was, as we have seen, the principal architect of Party reorganisation in the 1980s. It was PM Lee, however, who had the key role in originating a number of major changes of a constitutional and parliamentary nature in the 1980s that were to change the political landscape for good. These include the Group Representation Constituency (GRC) system, the Non-Constituency Members of Parliament (NCMP) and Nominated Member of Parliament (NMP) schemes, and the elected presidency.

The public story of their implementation is well known. What follows is an attempt to trace the origins of these ideas. Rather than seeing these ideas in isolation, it is useful to examine the chronology of Lee's thinking on major changes during this critical period of the early 1980s.

One strand of Lee's thinking was the NCMP scheme, implemented in 1984 through amendments to the Constitution and the Parliamentary Elections Act before the general election that year. The idea was to allow up to three "best-loser" Opposition MPs (who had come closest at the polls to securing parliamentary seats) to take places in Parliament. This would guarantee an Opposition presence in Parliament.

If Lee thought that the scheme might satisfy the desire of the people for an Opposition, or decrease the chances of PAP MPs being knocked out at the ballot box now that there was the certainty of Opposition representation, he was mistaken. The outcome of the 1984 general election provided confirmation to PM Lee and his colleagues that an elected Opposition presence would likely be a fixture. The result was also critical in reviving discussions between PM Lee and the younger ministers on far-reaching parliamentary and constitutional changes.

PM Lee's remarks at the customary post-election press conference, in the early hours of 23 December 1984, were significant. Aiming his comments at the younger voters, Lee observed that the result showed a "highly sophisticated" electorate with "an unexpectedly subtle understanding of how to use one vote to maximum effect", voting for the Opposition and thereby pressuring the PAP government. As Lee went on to observe: "It is necessary to try and put some safeguards into the way in which people use their votes to bargain, to coerce, to push, to jostle and get what they want, without running the risk of losing the services of government because one day, by mistake, they will lose the services of the government."[28]

PM Goh took a more moderate posture, making it known at the Cabinet swearing-in on 31 December 1984 that he and his younger Cabinet colleagues felt that the existing system had worked well, and that they remained to be convinced of the need for changes to the voting system.[29]

Lee was fully aware and sensitive to these differences in thinking. His method of refining proposals detailed in the following pages was to discuss his ideas through notes exchanged with the younger ministers, and also through group discussions. Lee was clear that it was the younger ministers who, as the next leaders, would have to live with the changes and thus had to be comfortable with them.[30]

The Elected Presidency

Some of Lee's key considerations—a "freak" election resulting in "bad" government, and recognition that there existed a growing desire for a check on the PAP—appear to have stemmed from the 1981 Anson by-election result. Interviews for this book with former Cabinet ministers show that by late 1981, the idea of what would happen to Singapore in the event of "bad government" had begun to preoccupy PM Lee.[31] At this time, Lee broached the idea of an elected president with the law minister, E.W. Barker. Other members of Cabinet, particularly the younger ministers, were brought into the discussions by 1982.[32] In his 19 August 1984 National Day Rally speech, Lee noted that a mechanism was being worked out where the president could block a profligate government drawing on the reserves.[33] What the internal record and recollections of ministers show is that there were strong and occasionally heated disagreements on these subjects, particularly on the scope of powers to be given to the elected president. PM Lee's initial idea was for an extremely powerful elected president, but he eventually allowed the thinking of the younger ministers (who would have to live with any system implemented) to prevail. These ideas, which provided for an elected president with blocking powers (a "second key") over the use of financial reserves and key assets, and the appointment of key public service officers, were the foundations of the 1988 White Paper on the elected president scheme.[34] The proposals in fact represented a considerable dilution of the wide-ranging powers initially envisaged by PM Lee. But even so, objections were raised to the White Paper by individuals such as Ong Pang Boon. Ong had been privy to the internal discussions on the matter while still a Cabinet minister. In 1988, as a backbencher, Ong argued that the present system had worked well (without a president with wide-ranging powers), and that there had been no indication that younger, second-generation leaders had any "profligate tendency" that might necessitate the creation of a blocking mechanism.[35]

Beneath this thrust of his objections, it is possible to see another concern: the possibility that Lee Kuan Yew might become president. In what should be seen as Ong's final shot in his political parting of ways with Lee Kuan Yew, he remarked: "In the nature of power politics, another centre of power will emerge around the President, especially if the elected President has been a towering political leader for a long time. Ipso facto, the power and status of future Prime Ministers would correspondingly be reduced."[36]

It appears that Ong did not want this to happen: "Under a dominant PAP President, can a second or third generation Prime Minister ever come of age as to be able to govern independently without having to lean on the President's crutches?"[37]

PM Lee found it necessary during his National Day Rally speech of 14 August 1988 (two days after Ong had spoken in Parliament) to tackle Ong's suggestion that Lee might overshadow a future PM if he became the president:

> It has been suggested that this way I will have control. In other words, I will still control the Prime Minister. It's two centres of power. You know the Constitution of the PAP and the way the Central Executive is constituted, the mechanics of the system and the Constitution of Singapore. If you read that carefully, and Mr Ong Pang Boon does know how the party was run because he was the organizing secretary for many years, he will know both the mechanics, which are in the Constitution, and the dynamics, which is in the inter-personal relations between the office holders. Given me and my links with so many people, all I got to do is to stay Secretary-General of the PAP. I don't have to be President. I stay Secretary-General of the PAP and I can decide, I will have a very strong last word on policy. I don't have to be President and I am not looking for a job. Please believe me.[38]

The elected presidency concept was to continue to evolve, beyond the 1988 White Paper. In August 1990 a second White Paper was presented in Parliament. Additional roles were introduced for the elected president. These included strengthening the elected president's ability to check abuses of power on the part of the Executive when it came to detentions under the Internal Security Act. Powers were also given to the elected president to allow him to check possible abuses by the Executive as regards the making of prohibition orders under the Maintenance of Religious Harmony Act.[39]

A select committee was appointed to look into issues and make recommendations, and to receive written representations and receive oral evidence.[40] There were some significant changes made to the final bill based on the Report of the Select Committee, including those pertaining to attributes and qualifications required for prospective candidates for the elected presidency.[41]

The bill on the elected presidency was passed in Parliament in January 1991, with incumbent President Wee Kim Wee exercising, from the end of November that year, the powers of the elected president (including the newfound roles relating to safeguarding the reserves and integrity of the public services commenced) until his stepping down on 1 September 1993.

An important institution had thus been formed, but formed perhaps in a way that lent itself to a degree of interpretation. The actual arrangements when it came to safeguarding Singapore's reserves, particularly the precise role of the elected president in this regard, took a considerable length of time to be ironed out. Ong Teng Cheong, who succeeded Wee Kim Wee, recognised this, observing in his inauguration speech that the provisions behind the elected presidency had yet to be "fully tested out" and that both president and the government would have to "feel their way forward".[42] Also telling (perhaps more so than many realised at the time) was Ong's stated determination to do the job he had been entrusted to do, accounting first and foremost to the higher interests of all Singaporeans.[43]

Ong's vision of his role was not something that ruffled the leadership, it seemed, in 1993. And certainly not SM Lee Kuan Yew.[44] Lee observed that Ong should as president remain true to his character, also noting that Ong "would have to take a stand against the Government which may be very unpopular with many of the government supporters. And he must be prepared to do that. So his job is not to be popular. His job is to be strong."[45]

Group Representation Constituencies: The Race Issue

GRCs were first publicly mooted by Lim Boon Heng, MP for Kebun Baru, on 24 January 1987.[46] The idea, first presented as a concept of "Team MPs", essentially meant the establishment of constituencies larger than single-member constituencies, represented by not one but three MPs. Voters would be casting their votes for the entire team.

In the initial few weeks of the idea's presentation, GRCs were linked, curiously, to town councils (dealt with further below). The reasoning that was put out was that voters had to live with the choice of Opposition MPs they might choose to vote in.

The slate voted in would have a shared responsibility for administering the town council. As one commentator noted, "the initial lukewarm, if not negative, public response to the Team MPs scheme compelled the PAP government to reveal the real, though unstated, goal of the scheme and to modify somewhat the original intention of linking the scheme with the Town Councils".[47] The actual rationale then emerged, with government leaders suggesting that stipulating one member of the slate be of a minority race would be a way to ensure that there would always be minorities represented in Parliament.[48] This argument was most forcefully put forward by PM Lee in his National Day Rally speech on 16 August 1987.[49] His key point was that minority, and particularly Malay, candidates would be edged out by candidates who had a command of Mandarin or dialects.[50]

Some Opposition figures saw the proposal as a direct reaction to the 1984 general election reverse: a plot designed to hobble the Opposition and make sure the PAP remained in power while sweeping all seats.[51] Given these charges, the PAP released Cabinet papers on the origins of the Team MPs proposal on 21 January 1988.[52] The intention here was to show that the idea had been gestating for some time, even before 1984.[53] The Cabinet papers showed that PM Lee had thought of "twinning" (which would have required a slate of two MPs from one party, with one being a Malay) in 1982, and tried to persuade his Cabinet colleagues to move on the issue. The exchanges showed that Malay MPs and younger ministers (in particular Dr Ahmad Mattar, then the acting minister for social affairs) had objected.[54] A key concern was that the proposed changes implied that Malay MPs might not be electable on their own merits; this might in turn lead to a loss of confidence on the part of ethnic minority MPs.[55] Lee allowed the younger team to have their way but noted that he was prepared "to let the lesson be learnt the painful way".[56]

Of all the changes wrought in the late 1980s, the Team MPs/GRC concept was the hardest to push through. The results of the 1984 election brought the issue to the fore again in the thinking of the leadership. Issues of race had played out in ways that could not be disregarded and which, in the view of PM Lee, vindicated his observations on Singapore society and the possibilities of latent communalism resurfacing. In Chong Boon, the PAP candidate, Chandra Das, won 56 per cent of the vote against the Singapore Democratic Party (SDP) candidate, Ling How Doong. Chandra Das recalled:

> *1984 was very close. I was the incumbent. For four years I actually worked the ground very hard. We had a very good network, with good ground sensing. If we had not had that, I would have lost the election. . . . The campaign was a tough campaign—a dirty campaign. He [Ling] never spoke one word of English in his campaign. He just kept on saying "this guy can't speak Chinese" . . . that was his line of campaigning.*
>
> *. . . the campaign was going entirely in Chinese, and I had decided . . . those days they gave us a lot of independence. We ran the campaign ourselves. Apart from printing posters, the campaign was left entire to MPs. And so I decided*

I would have no rallies. But I would only go through house to house, personal campaigning. But the way it was going round . . . the Chinese part I couldn't handle. So Goh Chok Tong wanted to come down. So I said no. So I had a rally on a Thursday. Election was Saturday. So that it appears on Friday newspapers. So I was the only one at the rally speaking in English and Malay and some Tamil. But the rest of my speakers. . . . I think I had the best bunch of Chinese speakers you can ever find. Ong Teng Cheong. Lee Hsien Loong. Ch'ng Jit Koon. Ch'ng Jit Koon never speaks at rallies. Koh Lip Lin. And in dialects and Mandarin. And also my hawkers, my chairmen. And Ho Kah Leong as well. The whole bunch of Chinese-educated leaders in the Party. I am still certain until today that swung it. If I did not have that . . . I mean I won quite narrowly. It was between winning or losing. So that gave the PM Lee a big fright.[57]

What had happened at Chong Boon left an imprint not just on Chandra Das, but on the Party leadership.[58] The PAP view was that Ling had campaigned along communal lines, allegedly asking residents in Mandarin and dialect on his house-to-house visits whether "that Indian man" had paid a visit.[59] Though denied by Ling, the comment was used by the PAP later, in 1988, to support the case for GRCs, and to suggest that the Opposition might have no compunctions about campaigning along racial lines. The PAP found it convenient to resurface this issue as it could then cast doubt on the multiracial credentials of Ling's party, the SDP. A series of letters to the *Straits Times* were written by PAP MPs in January and February 1988 that decried Ling's alleged communalism and the SDP's apparent lack of multiracialism. The letters also attempted to undermine Ling further by questioning his comments that democracy was the rule by majority, that the Chinese were the majority in Singapore, and that there was nothing wrong if people voted along racial lines.[60] At the core of this was a blunt exchange of letters between the PAP MP and Senior Parliamentary Secretary Phua Bah Lee and the SDP's Chiam See Tong on the issue of the SDP's stance on race and racial campaigning.[61] Party records show that PM Lee was the prime mover behind Phua Bah Lee's letters to the *Straits Times* questioning the SDP's multiracial credentials. It was Lee who directed that Phua should ask in his letter that Chiam repudiate Ling's statement, and that Phua's letter should repeat in full what Ling had said about Chinese majority rule, so that people would be reminded of it.[62] It is clear that the danger of losing capable ethnic minority MPs for reasons that had nothing to do with their quality or calibre as individuals was felt most by PM Lee himself.

PM Lee succeeded in bringing most of the younger ministers in the post-1984 period round to his thinking on the team MPs/GRC issue.[63] But there was still the issue of how to convince the ground. This aroused emotions especially among the minorities. The Party approach was to reach out to the key organisations representing minorities, outlining the dangers of what would happen over the longer term if trends were left unchecked. For the Indian community, a key role was played by Chandra Das. He had seen first-hand what could happen when voting followed communal lines and had already raised the need to tackle the problem through the Team MPs proposal, before problems mounted or before ethnic minority MPs were entirely absent from Parliament.[64] His approach was to tirelessly seek support from the organisations representing the Indian community. This needed deft handling:

> So I asked for a meeting. Of all the presidents, secretaries and treasurers of about thirty-odd Indian organisations. So I asked Kandasamy to arrange.[65] So Kanda said OK. Because I was adviser to TRC [Tamil Representative Council]. So we had this meeting. There were about 100 people there. All key leaders of Indian organisations in their own right. So I just basically asked the question—do you want Indian representatives in Parliament? Under the current system, I explained to them, there was the possibility down the line that it could end up as an entirely Chinese Parliament. I was speaking with some authority from my experiences in Chong Boon. But Kanda went the other way round, asking them, telling them basically this is a political issue, we cannot have a view. And the whole meeting he conducted in Tamil. He knew that my Tamil was not strong. I can understand, so I said OK you carry on, I can follow, but I will give my replies in English. So Kanda took the table round saying no, this is political, we cannot have a view. But I wanted support from the community. So anyway, the way it was going, I turned it round the other way and asked them basically do you want Indians representing you? The response was—yes. Not only Indians, many felt strongly that Tamils had to be there. . . . So I said OK, if that's the case, this GRC is the option. So I was able to swing around the crowd, I had enough supporting me. So I got the statement from the community saying that they were in support. I read it in Parliament. So Kandasamy after the meeting told me, ya, I'm glad you got it done because I was playing the devil's advocate. I said OK, thank you very much.[66]

Representations from the Malay community to the Parliamentary Select Committee formed to consider public submissions on the GRC scheme were generally supportive, but there were also concerns within the community. During a public forum in 1988 organised by the Central Council of Malay Cultural Organisations, most participants criticised the scheme as they felt that it perpetuated a sense of Malay inferiority and would affect the credibility of Malay MPs, who would only get into Parliament on the coat-tails of the majority race.[67] One unnamed Malay community leader was quoted in the press as saying that having three MPs in a constituency might lead to "racial polarisation at the constituency level, reducing the Malay MPs to a parochial role as channels of Malay grievances instead of articulating the interests of the constituencies as a whole".[68] The rejoinder from the Party was that Malay MPs, far from being second class, actually had a harder job than others because a Malay MP would "have to look after his constituency as well as lead the Malay community".[69] On the whole, there was acceptance from the Malay ground of the notion that the GRC proposal was the way that the community could continue to have a voice in Parliament.[70] Important work was also done behind the scenes by the PAP's Malay Affairs Bureau, an organ of the HQ Executive Committee. The bureau—the core of which were the Party's Malay MPs and Party activists—was the key link to the Malay community. It met regularly with the Malay ground for dialogue and feedback during this period.[71] Individuals from the Malay community also came forward to make their views known on the issue. A group of friends (including journalists and civil servants) representing Taman Bacaan (the Malay Youth Library Association) made a written submission to the Select Committee in early 1988 which was broadly in support of the proposal.[72]

The PAP utilised the GRC system to its benefit by fielding high-flyers or individuals identified by the leadership to have office-holding potential, often fielded in GRCs with strong PAP support or as part of slates that were anchored by recognised PAP heavyweights. The 1988 election saw Mah Bow Tan, who had previously been defeated in Potong Pasir SMC by Chiam See Tong in 1984, fielded in Tampines GRC instead. Mah would later become a Cabinet minister.

In the era of GRCs, especially problematic for the Opposition was the shifting ground underneath their strongholds (or constituencies where they could count on a high percentage of bankable votes). In the 1988 election, Anson, which had previously elected J.B. Jeyaretnam in 1981 (in a by-election) and 1984, disappeared from the electoral map, partly absorbed into the new Tiong Bahru GRC. This pattern was to be repeated: the 1997 election saw Eunos GRC (which had seen close results in 1991 and 1988) split up into new GRCs. Cheng San GRC was also split up in 2001, after a Workers' Party (WP) team led by Jeyaretnam had obtained 45.2 per cent of the vote in 1997.[73]

An added challenge for the Opposition was how GRCs were to grow in size over time. The 1988 general election saw the Electoral Boundaries Review Committee announce 13 three-member GRCs, representing 39 of the 81 seats in Parliament. The maximum size of GRCs increased from three to four prior to the 1991 election, and then to six in time for the 1997 election. By the 2006 general election there were 14 GRCs, nine with five members and five with six members (for an average size of 5.4), with GRCs making up 75 of the 84 seats in Parliament.[74] This further challenged the logistical and recruiting abilities of Opposition parties. The PAP could attract credible candidates of high calibre boasting stellar academic and career qualifications, but the cash-strapped and fragmented Opposition would find it challenging to assemble a comparable slate of candidates. The reduced number of SMCs also reduced the odds of single charismatic Opposition candidates entering Parliament.

Different reasons were to be given in the 1990s for the enlargement of GRCs, leading to suggestions by some that the government had lost sight of the original reason for introducing GRCs in the first place—ensuring minority representation in Parliament.[75] The moves to enlarge GRCs in the 1990s meant that by 2006, the minimum required number of MPs from minority groups technically stood at 13, or 15 per cent of the total number of MPs. This was lower than the percentage of Singapore's population made up of minority races.[76] It should be observed, however, that the percentage of elected non-Chinese MPs in Parliament was actually to rise over time: from 20 per cent in 1988 to 27.4 per cent after the 2015 election (see Table 2.1).[77]

Table 2.1 GRCs and Ethnic Minority MPs (excludes NCMPs and NMPs)

Year	Single-member constituencies	3-member GRCs	4-member GRCs	5-member GRCs	6-member GRCs	Total GRCs	Elected seats in Parliament made up of GRCs	Average number of parliamentary seats per GRC	Number of ethnic minority MPs elected (% of MPs elected to Parliament)
1988	42	13	NIL	NIL	NIL	13	39/81	3	16 (20%)
1991	21	NIL	15	NIL	NIL	15	60/81	4	17 (21%)
1997	9	NIL	5	6	4	15	74/83	4.93	19 (23%)
2001	9	NIL	NIL	9	5	14	75/84	5.36	22 (26%)
2006	9	NIL	NIL	9	5	14	75/84	5.36	23 (27.4%)
2011	14	NIL	2	11	2	15	75/87	5	24 (27.5%)
2015	13	NIL	6	8	2	16	76/89	4.75	24 (27%)

Nominated Members of Parliament

On 24 September 1988, PM Lee wrote to all PAP MPs, noting that he had asked the Speaker to give all MPs, particularly new MPs, ample opportunities and latitude to speak in the first year of Parliament. He added:

> *You have to speak up and bring out the grapevine criticism in the coffee shops and hawker centres. It is damaging for the Government not to openly refute it with facts and argument. By bringing up apparently embarrassing issues, you help the Government openly state the facts and explain the reasons for our policies and so continue to hold the ground.*[78]

This preoccupation had a history to it. Former PAP MPs confirm that during the 1970s, when there had been no Opposition in Parliament, the whip was lifted regularly, with backbenchers repeatedly asked in caucus by PM Lee to speak out and even criticise policies, in order to reflect concerns from the ground and make a one-party Parliament palatable to the people.[79]

Getting backbenchers to speak up was one thing. However, the issue to Lee was about getting good ideas raised in Parliament, no matter one's affiliation. In September 1972, on the night the PAP comprehensively won the general election without losing a seat, Lee touched on this issue at the customary early-morning press conference. Given the occasion, he was in an unusually reflective mood:

> *I think the problem of getting an intelligent constructive opposition has got to be solved, and Singapore just hasn't got the kind of people who are coming into politics—are not likely ever to develop into a coherent, constructive, loyal opposition. So we are toying—I don't know; this is just, you know 20 past 2 in the early hours of the morning. We are just toying with the idea of getting some say, university seats—Nanyang and Singapore University graduates voting for one candidate and TTC (Teachers' Training College) plus the Polytechnic and the Ngee Ann College voting for another two or three so that they don't have to belong to the PAP, they don't have to be obliged to us. They can take us on—they are intelligent enough—I hope to point out where we are wrong.*[80]

Lee's tentative ideas in 1972 appear to have remained; certainly, some semblance of them was to come to fruition much later. As the 1980s were drawing a close, Goh and PM Lee appear to have formed the view that parliamentary debate with the Opposition had failed to produce genuinely constructive ideas for policymaking. They therefore began to think of ways to bring in more diverse, high-quality voices into Parliament, voices not tied to any one political party. This led to what was to become the NMP system.

On 27 March 1989, PM Lee wrote to 1DPM Goh, commenting on a Parliament which (after the 1988 general election) had only Chiam See Tong and Lee Siew Choh from the non-PAP ranks. He asked Goh to think of ways to bring in other voices to Parliament to represent professional and interest groups.[81] These individuals, he noted, could act as a foil for government ministries and raise the level of debate. 1DPM Goh, for his part, was already mulling ideas that would result in intelligent views and thence strengthen policymaking and had (not for the first time) anticipated Lee. His political secretary, Matthias Yao, had already drafted a proposal paper on "Functional Group Members of Parliament", which was considered by the leadership in May 1989.[82] The leadership also took the view that the existing state of play was not ideal: government MPs were subject to the whip, while Opposition MPs concentrated mostly on scoring political points. A mechanism to allow able Singaporeans (who might not be interested in standing for elections) to make real contributions and speak objectively would thus fill a gap inherent in the parliamentary system.

The problem was that many PAP MPs felt that this undermined their position. Backbenchers felt that people would see PAP MPs as people who were so ineffective that others who could speak frankly had to be brought in. While some MPs spoke in support of the constitutional amendment bill that would pave the way for nominated members of parliament when it was tabled in November 1989, an almost equal number spoke against.[83] One PAP MP, Philip Tan (Paya Lebar), went on a "bitter tirade" against the government, noting that the NMP proposal was an "insult to the intelligence, capability, depth and breadth of knowledge and courage of PAP MPs".[84] The government whip, Dr Lee Boon Yang, privately noted to 1DPM Goh in October 1989 that there were several MPs who were either undecided on the issue or opposed to the bill, including one—Dr Tan Cheng Bock—who intended to vote against the bill even if the whip was not lifted.[85] 1DPM Goh had to make strenuous attempts to assuage concerns and bring sceptical MPs round, making it clear during the debate on the second reading of the bill that there was no intention "to slight MPs".[86] The Select Committee examining the issue, which presented its findings on 15 March 1990, supported Goh's proposal of an amendment to the draft bill, giving each Parliament the discretion to appoint NMPs through a resolution adopted by each Parliament within six months of each first meeting following a general election.[87] This, together with Goh's argument that he was personally convinced the scheme was in the national interest, appears to have assuaged doubters within the Party, with all PAP MPs following the whip and supporting the bill when it passed at the third reading in March 1990.[88]

The mid- to late 1980s could thus be seen as altogether not an easy time for backbenchers. They had to speak up effectively against Opposition members. Often, they did so.[89] But at the same time, they had to be seen to be scrutinising government policy and speaking up for their constituents.[90] MPs interviewed for this book stressed that the overriding message of "not kicking the ball into your own goal" was continually reinforced by the Party leadership, discussed at Party caucuses, and reinforced by the Party whip. MPs were, of course, free to state their views but were expected to vote along the Party line if the whip was not lifted.[91] Chiam See Tong was able to take advantage of the situation by criticising PAP backbenchers, noting that some MPs voted for bills that they had initially opposed in parliamentary debate.[92]

PAP backbenchers needed latitude in order to be effective. The CEC in January 1987 decided that backbenchers were to be allowed more leeway in voting, except on matters of confidence. The CEC agreed, however, that in such cases backbenchers who disagreed with the policy were allowed to abstain from (and not vote against) the bill in question; and even then, prior approval had to be sought on the part of the government whip before abstaining.[93] Separately, PM Lee had himself suggested to the Party CEC that it was in the Party's interest to build up five or six backbenchers, credible figures in their own right, who would cut a figure with the public. Lee's view was that this would enable MPs with calibre who did not make it as office-holders still to have a key role rather than becoming quiescent over time. All this would make one-party dominance more palatable.[94]

The fact that these moves do not appear to have been seriously followed up on, despite endorsement by the Party leadership, is perhaps indicative of some of the internal contradictions in such thinking. In the post-1984 era, it was simply too problematic to attempt to provide for an internal opposition (which might have unpredictable results) while needing to close ranks against the real Opposition.

There were, in fact, already in place tested mechanisms for intra-Party differences to be resolved (or at least discussed) behind the scenes. The Party whip would occasionally bring together backbenchers and ministers so that the rationale for policies could be explained. In addition, there was the Party Caucus: a more formal affair that would often see a presentation on a given topic (usually an important one) by an office-holder. MPs would then discuss the issue at hand.[95] Another forum was the long-standing Tuesday Lunch at Parliament. This lunch, open to PAP MPs only, brought together backbenchers and ministers, functioning as an informal forum that allowed backbenchers to engage with office-holders on a variety of issues—even cases that had arisen from the MPs' meet-the-people sessions. Ministers could also take the opportunity to clarify points of policy.[96] All these were important avenues for settling differences behind the scenes and eased somewhat the backbenchers' task of defending government policy.[97] Not that MPs had much choice. Breaking ranks was seen as a serious matter, and disciplinary action could be taken behind the scenes if MPs did not vote with the Party. A case in point was the decision by Dr Toh Chin Chye (by then a backbencher) to abstain from a vote on the Housing and Development Board (HDB) (Amendment Bill) on 31 July 1986.[98] The *Straits Times* was moved to note: "The abstention is a unique and isolated instance of PAP parliamentarians breaking ranks since 13 of its Legislative Assemblymen abstained on a motion of no confidence in July 1961 and later started the Barisan Sosialis."[99] 1DPM Goh Chok Tong seemed inclined to downplay the issue, noting lightly, "Dr Toh is dribbling the ball in the wrong direction, but he has not yet kicked the ball into his own goal. So there is no need to sideline him."[100] In fact, Dr Toh was taken to task, as the various comments by Government Whip Lee Yiok Seng made clear at the time.[101]

Toh's intervention in Parliament should be set in its proper context. Some of the old guard veterans who were now backbenchers clearly felt that they should speak up freely to make their views known on a variety of issues.[102] Since they were near the end of their political careers, they had little to lose by making their points in as direct a fashion as possible in Parliament. In fairness, it should also be observed that these interventions were not simply sniping by those who had been eased out. Some had concerns that reflected ground sentiment, or which were in fact shared by other MPs.[103]

The PAP leadership did not in general take exception to comments from PAP MPs (either old or new) that were critical of policy, provided that these were reasoned, and provided that Party discipline was observed in voting. MPs interviewed for this book suggested that backbenchers had, for their part, to become more adept at framing their criticisms in a manner that did not damage the standing of the Party and did not give the Opposition the opportunity to further stoke fires over contentious issues.

Dr Lee Boon Yang, elected to the Jalan Besar seat in 1984, was appointed government whip in 1988. He recalled that there was still a great deal of vigorous debate in Parliament between PAP MPs and ministers, particularly during the annual budget debate, and also during time allotted for oral answers to questions.[104] Such encounters could be bruising, or lead to bruised feelings on the part of MPs, especially when (as often happened in the latter half of the 1980s) young PAP office-holders rebutted long-serving MPs.[105] Occasionally, a dressing-down would be given by a more senior figure, as was done by Senior Minister S. Rajaratnam to Jek Yeun Thong (who had been dropped from Cabinet in 1980) in March 1985.[106] But even then, rebuttal was usually calculated with a purpose. Rajaratnam's rebuttal of Jek was, by his own account, to help guide the younger leaders: it was "an opportunity to give a fatherly lecture to the newer MPs on the uses and abuses of criticism, the difference between constructive criticism and, what I call, 'fun and games' criticism."[107]

As we shall see, it was only after the 1991 general election, when the Opposition boasted four MPs, that the PAP could be said to have undergone a proper closing of ranks. But the movement to increase Party discipline was certainly ratcheted up after 1984. The ruling party formed the government, and the government would continue to make the hard decisions—even unpopular ones—to bring the country forward. MPs played a key role in this process. This was the message that was reiterated whenever criticism from backbenchers reached levels that Party leaders deemed unacceptable. In January 1989, 1DPM Goh Chok Tong commented on the issue during the debate on the President's Address to Parliament:

> Some Members seem to think that an MP's duty is to attack the Government, and to repeat the criticisms which they have heard others make. In other words, be humble towards the public, but truculent towards the Government. If this were so, the PAP would not have such difficulty finding good and suitable men to become Members of Parliament. To be an MP, you must have judgement, intelligence, character and courage. Reflecting public sentiment is part of an MP's role, but only a small part. As a Member of Parliament, an MP is a key digit in our political structure. Parliament has the sole power to make and unmake the Government, because in our system of Government, the Prime Minister can only remain PM so long as he enjoys the confidence of the majority of MPs.[108]

Senior Minister S. Rajaratnam, once again playing his customary role as a guide on the dos and don'ts of parliamentary debate, was also moved to remind MPs that they should "not be populists, but problem solvers". Rajaratnam commented on the role of Parliament: "It should be a classroom conducted by the Front and Back

Bench PAP MPs to educate the people on political realities, not a place for staging boxing matches."[109]

Backbenchers were by this stage wilting somewhat under the collective import of such admonishments. Some backbenchers began to wonder whether it was worth making any intervention at all. What was needed was a clear direction not just on the limits of speaking, but on what an MP could—and should—say. PM Lee called for a meeting of MPs (including office-holders) on 2 May 1989 to clarify the role of backbenchers in Parliament. At this meeting, the key issue Lee dealt with was how to achieve high-quality debate without acrimony. He made it clear that MPs and ministers had to have a high tolerance for verbal sparring and attacks against each other that could be unpleasant and even irritating. In Lee's view, there had to be a great deal of give and take. Some sense of what Lee intended can be glimpsed from a paper which he wrote and circulated to PAP MPs in advance of the meeting. It is worth quoting at length:

> We have an opposition so weak, that unless our own MPs play a critical role the public will vote for more opposition next time. Therefore immediately after the Barisan withdrew from Parliament in 1966, I have encouraged PAP MPs to take up the role of a critical but constructive opposition. They pressed for facts and explanations; they voiced dissatisfactions at specific policies or problems, thereby letting people know that their grievances, whether real or unfounded, are ventilated and Ministers given the chance to explain. So popular frustrations or grumbles in the coffee shops are diffused. In this way we took the steam out of frustrations and anger that could have built up. Thus we won clean sweeps in four successive General Elections—1969, 1972, 1976, 1980.

> . . . There have to be sharp exchanges between PAP MPs and Ministers from time to time. But remember the aim is to improve the PAP's overall standing and thus win the next election. We shall do that if we show that we have intelligent, critical, objective, and independent minded MPs, who are prepared to point out problems and allow a Minister who is in error to correct his position or to have a convincing explanation. But never knock down the PAP Government as such. Do not allege that a whole Cabinet is at fault when a Minister makes a mistake. Nor should MPs attack a particular government policy as evil and misguided in its inspiration. The people are not stupid. If they see PAP MPs make the PAP Government lose credibility and prestige, they will despise MPs and Government as foolish and incompetent.

> . . . our backbenchers have high potential. Let them not be inhibited by robust and sharp criticism by Ministers, nor should they be troubled when an individual Minister is upset, so long he alone has been attacked and discomforted. We are all on the same side. We want to show the people that they have a good parliament and a good government, one they should vote for again at the next elections. That is what it is all about.

> . . . *Individual Ministers and MPs may suffer setbacks, but the PAP Government as a whole must not. That is the trick of the trade and we have to master it. We need diverse styles for an interesting Parliament. Each MP has to find his right pitch and style.*[110]

PM Lee's thinking on this matter and how backbenchers should comport themselves went back decades. When MPs from the main opposition Party, the Barisan Sosialis, absented themselves from Parliament after Singapore became independent in August 1965, PM Lee asked the Speaker, until such time as the Barisan MPs turned up, or resigned, to allow a certain latitude:

> *My colleagues and I will try as scrupulously as we can to put forward all the pros and cons of every legislation and every policy in the hope thereby, of discharging the duties of the Opposition. But more so, I hope you will allow considerable latitude amongst the back-benchers on the Government side to take up more of their time to playing the role of the constructive critic. It is part of the technique of the open society that the wisdom of certain policies, of certain programmes is tested in the open argument.*[111]

This had borne fruit by the 1970s, with Lee observing in 1977: "if we do not bring out these differences of opinion, and if we had not done so successfully since 1965 when the Barisan Sosialis MPs walked out of this Chamber, I do not believe that in February, 1968, in September 1972, and again in December 1976, we could have been returned unanimously and completely."[112] Lee's efforts in this respect continued, with no opposition from MPs in Parliament during the decade of the 1970s. Lee on several occasions got the backbenchers together and told them that they had to ask questions in Parliament and play the role of a constructive opposition, and bring up issues simmering at the ground level. It did not matter to Lee if individual MPs or ministers suffered hits in debate; what was important was that the standing of the Party as a whole was not diminished.[113]

We now return to Lee's 1989 meeting with MPs. This went a considerable way towards clarifying the expected behaviour as well as the overall goal. The session also helped to boost the spirits of backbenchers. Letters to him from backbenchers after the meeting (in response to his request to them for feedback) made it clear they had found it morale-boosting. They now knew that they could criticise government policies within reason without being accused of disloyalty.[114]

For Lee, the Opposition was the target. And it was not enough for Opposition MPs to be bested in parliamentary debate: the people had to see this happen. Lee raised the issue with his colleagues of having parliamentary proceedings televised. He ultimately left the decision in the hands of the younger leaders and 1DPM Goh, but he pushed this point hard.[115] Others in Cabinet had reservations about the wisdom of the move. Rajaratnam wrote to Lee in January 1985, suggesting that television coverage of parliamentary proceedings be postponed, as it was not clear to him that the younger ministers could assert their dominance over Chiam See Tong and J.B. Jeyaretnam.[116] Lee replied:

> *If Goh Chok Tong cannot hold his own against Chiam or Jeyaretnam in Parliament, when he has sound policies to defend, then he cannot govern Singapore. To keep these encounters away from the viewers and only allow them to be written about will not hide the fact from the voters. The impression of a Chiam or Jeyaretnam dominating Chok Tong will spread quickly by word of mouth throughout Singapore. And that was not the impression Chok Tong created in his exchanges with Jeyaretnam from 1981–4. . . . I believe that Goh Chok Tong will eventually be seen to dominate the debates and the agenda in Parliament. And the other Ministers can more than hold their own. If Chok Tong cannot do this, then the MPs and other Ministers had better know it, and soon.[117]*

In the end, televised parliamentary proceedings did not show a PAP advantage over the Opposition in the way which was hoped; indeed, it may have helped the Opposition more than it did the PAP. Press reports could make sense out of thoughts and words expressed, but having these words actually seen, unrehearsed, under public scrutiny was a different matter. One letter writer to the *Straits Times* pointed out that "one's concept of parliamentary proceedings had always been one of a gathering of well-informed politicians with 'connected thoughts' and given to elegance in speech", but that on the government bench, "the image that came across forcibly was the brittleness of the new generation leaders".[118] All in all, the general feeling was that TV coverage had not been kind to most PAP MPs, especially backbenchers, whom the *Straits Times* described as being "blanketed by an anonymous uniformity". There was also sympathy for the Opposition members, especially given what was seen as the overly hardline attitude of the PAP MPs towards them.[119]

Government Parliamentary Committees

More needed to be done to deal with the growing feeling on the part of many back-benchers that they were disengaged from policy formulation. In a 13 May 1986 memo to PM Lee, 1DPM Goh surfaced a paper on government parliamentary committees (GPC) by Dr Hong Hai, an academic who was to be a PAP candidate in the 1988 general election.[120] Dr Hong Hai was part of Goh's extensive network of contacts whom Goh tapped on regularly for ideas, and who themselves could be asked to stand for election if found suitable. On the role of backbenchers, the paper commented:

> *Backbenchers in the Singapore parliament do not play a role that is commensurate with their numbers and abilities. Presumably they provide feedback to cabinet on problems at the grassroots, and maintain public relations in their constituencies. Their participation in the legislative and policy formation process appears to be perfunctory. In other words, they go little beyond delivering the votes in election year.[121]*

The paper went on to note that parliamentary committees could be an effective way by which ministers' decisions could take into account the views of their colleagues in Parliament and those of people who were directly affected by these decisions. The paper also suggested that the committees (which would themselves get feedback from other MPs and citizens) could comment on proposed legislation and suggest changes before a bill became final. The committees could also provide a formal channel by which the effectiveness of policy implementation could be evaluated:

> *The present practice of decisions being handed down from Cabinet, apparently with inadequate input from backbenchers, has undesirable consequences. A number of decisions had to be amended or withdrawn, for example, the graduate mother scheme. Some of these reversals could conceivably have been avoided if MPs outside Cabinet had a greater hand in evaluating proposed legislation. What we want is a system by which Cabinet is seen to be decisive but not high-handed.*[122]

PM Lee replied to 1DPM Goh the following day. Lee was initially sceptical and queried how far the idea would be taken: Would the proposed committees have the authority of US congressmen, who could block legislation?[123] By the time the GPC proposal was tabled at the Party CEC, changes had been made to the paper which made it clear that this would not happen.[124] The CEC agreed that they would have no power to compel persons to attend their proceedings and answer questions.[125] When the GPC idea was eventually aired publicly in February 1987, prior to their official formation, Goh was also clear on the limits: that GPCs would not be able to block bills, and that he would not allow situations where bills were "suffocated" by the time they had reached Parliament for consideration.[126]

The Institute of Policy Studies

1DPM Goh separately began to consider additional, extra-parliamentary institutions to obtain views that could feed into the policymaking process. His idea was a higher-level counterpart to the Feedback Unit. Goh employed his usual method of checking with trusted individuals on the feasibility of the proposal, and using them to further flesh out the idea.[127] The concept that eventually emerged from these consultations was for a closed-door, no-holds-barred forum where the intelligentsia, journalists, and academics (in particular) could speak up freely. This could be a vehicle which examined government policy and made suggestions that fed into it, particularly when it came to cross-cutting issues across ministries.[128]

The choice of the founding director for the Institute of Policy Studies (IPS) in 1988 was significant. Assoc. Prof. Chan Heng Chee was an academic who understood the workings of the Party—having authored a book on it—and who had been critical of aspects of policy in the past. She had, for example, defended the fundamental rights of citizens to speak up on matters of public policy, pointing out also the incongruity of attempts to clamp down on views, especially in the light post-1984 moves to invite feedback.[129] At the same time, however, some of her views were consonant with the thinking of 1DPM Goh. In a commentary for *Petir* in July 1987, Chan pointed out that the National Agenda had "a lively intellectual environment" as one of its objectives. Chan pointed out that for this to develop, "the political leadership must be prepared to widen the parameters of participation and adopt an encouraging style of discussions. It must develop a capacity to abide with alternative views, diverse views and unconventional views, so long as these views are not systematically directed at destroying racial harmony or dismantling the constitutional–legal order."[130]

Chan was already being drawn at this time into the process of widening the parameters for discussion. When leadership considered the proposal for the setting up of IPS in September 1987, it had before it a proposal paper written up by Chan.[131] The leadership decided that IPS should focus on imparting to the younger, educated Singaporeans important lessons on Singapore history, and also to stimulate lively discussions on Singapore's future and to harvest valuable ideas from such discussions.[132] This was the brief given to Chan Heng Chee.[133]

1DPM Goh's determination to make feedback more participatory and more useful meant that government was more prepared to consider the co-opting of outsiders critical of the Party. Goh for his part was determined that discussions did not degenerate into a free-for-all. Parameters were widened but kept within defined limits. Interviewed for this book, Chan Heng Chee stressed the difficulty of fostering genuine discussions during the first years of IPS, because the participants "did not know how much room there was" in debating issues. The government wanted to open up but was uncertain how far to do so.[134] What this meant was that IPS found it difficult to fulfil its key, original goal: providing alternative policy ideas to government. It became more useful instead as a think tank, and sounding board, that worked with government and examined aspects of policy.

Town Councils

The final major innovation in the 1980s we should consider is the town councils concept. This was first publicly floated by the MP for Kebun Baru , Lim Boon Heng, at an election rally on 13 December 1984.[135] The idea was publicly taken up and supported by Lee Hsien Loong and Goh Chok Tong. The idea as it was pitched was to let people decide on the look of their estates, and to hand power over to the community and local leaders.[136] People would be empowered to put into effect ideas that they might have about their immediate environment, which would give them a sense of belonging to their individual neighbourhoods. Local identities could be created.

This was how it was presented in 1984: as a response to calls by Singaporeans for a more participative democratic process.[137] But for the real origins of the idea, we need (as was so often the case with fundamental changes of the 1980s) to go back to an idea germinating in PM Lee's mind. Lee had paid a visit to Ang Mo Kio town on 21 October 1984 and had on the sidelines a conversation with Liu Thai Ker, the CEO of HDB. Liu highlighted during this conversation how residents were increasingly demanding better services and a better quality of life. PM Lee spent a few days mulling the issue and then wrote to Goh Chok Tong on 24 October 1984. PM Lee suggested grouping new towns to form "a kind of mayorate or a new town council or a secretariat". He added:

> *The new town councils could be given their own budget, raise more money if they want higher services, to look after the needs of the new towns. They will have to decide their own priorities. The objective would be to transfer from the HDB those areas where increasing demands for qualitative improvements are being made to these new town councils.*[138]

PM Lee also noted that this might remove some of the "immediate political pressures on HDB". This was a crucial point, and one that dovetailed with observations made in the 1984 general election post-mortem report, which minced no words when addressing the same subject:

> *There is one general policy direction [to] which we may aspire: that the government move away from providing the wide range of inessential services which it presently is responsible for. The reason is that the population does not translate absence of discomfort into a sense of positive well-being. For example, the HDB provides conservancy services to all the housing estates in Singapore. The 99% of the blocks which are well looked after do not even notice the efficient and unobtrusive attention they are receiving. However, the 1% who are not well maintained blame everything on the government. The net result is a job well done, but no votes gained, and even perhaps some lost.*[139]

The Party had concluded that the "omnipresence" of government agencies, and particularly of HDB, had created a blowback whose brunt had fallen on the PAP itself. HDB's control over housing estates was, in short, going to be increasingly politically costly for the PAP. The solution was to decentralise. A Town Council Committee comprising BG Lee Hsien Loong and eight other MPs was formed to look into the composition, scope and responsibilities of a body that could take over some of HDB's management powers over housing estates.[140] Three pilot town councils started functioning in Ang Mo Kio in September 1986, with the Town Councils Act (June 1988) seeing HDB hand over running of housing estates to town councils by 1991.[141]

From an early stage there was a recognition within the Party leadership that the town councils would force the Opposition to step up to the plate; this was, in fact, a key facet of how the concept came to be presented publicly (rather than emphasising relieving the pressure on HDB). A poorly run Opposition ward would reflect badly on the MP in charge, and this explains why there was a readiness from the beginning to hand over the management of HDB estates in Anson and Potong Pasir to Opposition members and to allow them to run the town councils there.[142] PM Lee in his 1988 eve of National Day message had made precisely this point:

> *If your MP is not honest, or not competent, you will know it soon enough. And if your estate is poorly run, repairs slow and lift maintenance poor, you will be*

inconvenienced and worse, the resale value of your flat will be affected. So you had better take a careful look at the person or the three persons, in a GRC, who seek to represent you. Your personal well-being will be at stake when you choose your MP.[143]

At the 1988 hustings, town councils were a key theme, with the PAP putting forward its candidates as being qualified and capable to run town councils. The implication was that Opposition candidates fell short of the mark. A key campaign theme was the inconvenience that running town councils was no simple matter, and residents would have to suffer if an MP with insufficient skills and calibre to see to the general well-being and maintenance of the estate was elected.[144] The intention was to make voters pause and think whether the Opposition could step up to the plate; but there was at the same time a realisation that Opposition MPs might indeed manage to do precisely this. In February 1985, when discussion on the issue was still at a very preliminary stage, PM Lee had written to Minister for National Development Teh Cheang Wan, commenting on the duties involved in running the town council. Lee had asked:

How can we make the task heavier and the responsibilities greater? The more the responsibilities, the more things can go wrong, for the voters. Of course it also means the opposition MPs have a bigger chance to demonstrate their competence, and make their cards stronger for the next elections. And this is as it should be.[145]

The PAP and Its Opposition, 1984–88

The prospect of two Opposition MPs in Parliament meant that PAP MPs had to step up and engage.[146] Flawed arguments had to be rebutted and exposed. Stalwarts in Cabinet felt just as strongly that younger MPs and ministers should be prepared to demolish the arguments of the Opposition. Senior Minister S. Rajaratnam's call for a more combative "knuckle-duster" style on the part of PAP politicians was a case in point.[147] There is some suggestion (supported by interviews with former MPs and ministers) that in Parliament there was an informal system of "markers" that operated during this period. The markers were assigned to shadow their opposite numbers, to destabilise them and generally to rebut them wherever possible. Prof. S. Jayakumar was the marker for Jeyaretnam; Chiam See Tong appears to have had different markers over time, including Chandra Das.[148]

The personal antipathy between PM Lee and Jeyaretnam ran deep.[149] Lee was clear that Jeyaretnam fell into the lowest category of politicians—"the riff-raff, fly-by-night type" who had to be destroyed politically.[150] Their mutual dislike was in full view on several occasions, most notably in the September 1986 hearings of the Committee of Privileges, which examined Jeyaretnam's allegations of executive interference in judicial appointments:

Jeyaretnam: So you think I have to be destroyed?

Lee: Politically, yes. You have to be debunked, exposed as a charlatan, as basically dishonest, as immoral and utterly opportunistic, unscrupulous, that you made any allegation so long as you are protected. But the moment you have to bear the consequences, you flinch and cringe.[151]

But could it have been different? An important undercurrent of thinking amongst some backbenchers at this time was that the Party leadership did not know properly how to react after the 1984 general election reverse. Some backbenchers (and indeed, some office-holders) took the view that life with the Opposition in Parliament could have been a great deal easier if more of a live-and-let-live spirit had been exercised.[152] Some sort of entente had been achieved—but with Chiam See Tong alone. Chiam would come to the Members' Room in Parliament and chat with PAP MPs over coffee. Jeyaretnam never did this.[153] The reality, perhaps, was that a more congenial atmosphere was impossible to achieve simply on account of the animosity between Jeyaretnam and PM Lee.

In 1983, Jeyaretnam (along with Workers' Party Chairman Wong Hong Toy) was charged with several offences, including making a false declaration in Workers' Party accounts. In 1984 Jeyaretnam and Wong were both acquitted by a District Court of all but one charge. The prosecution appealed the decision to the High Court. The High Court, presided by Chief Justice Wee Chong Jin, ordered a retrial at the District Court for some of the charges, allowed the prosecution's appeal in respect of two of the charges, and rejected Jeyaretnam's appeal against his conviction under the one charge. At the retrial, Jeyaretnam and Wong were found guilty on all charges. Both men appealed to the High Court against their conviction and sentence, which only allowed their appeal against their sentence and reduced their sentence to one month's imprisonment and a $5,000 fine. Jailed for one month and fined, Jeyaretnam was forced to vacate his parliamentary seat in 1986, a disqualification lasting until 1991.[154] A Law Society hearing also resulted in Jeyaretnam's disbarment from the legal profession.[155]

Jeyaretnam claimed that the charges against him were motivated by political animus and aimed at preventing him from being an MP.[156] At the hearings Committee of Privileges convened to examine Jeyaretnam's allegations of executive interference in judicial appointments (where his acrimonious exchange with PM Lee, given above, took place), his various allegations were found to be baseless and without merit, with the committee also finding Jeyaretnam guilty of abuse of parliamentary privilege.[157]

Jeyaretnam appealed to the United Kingdom's Privy Council against his disbarment from the legal profession. The Privy Council reversed the disbarment in 1988, noting that Jeyaretnam and Wong Hong Toy had suffered a "grievous injustice" and had been "fined, imprisoned and publicly disgraced for offences of which they are not guilty".[158] Following this, Jeyaretnam wrote to President Wee Kim Wee to ask that the convictions be removed. President Wee, on the advice of the Cabinet, refused to remove the convictions. While accepting the judgement of the Privy Council, the government expressly reiterated, on the basis of the contents of the Privy Council's decision and the attorney-general's advice, that the decision only allowed Jeyaretnam to resume his legal practice but did not affect his criminal convictions.[159]

Jeyaretnam's disqualification from Parliament until 1991 therefore stood. And although he was to make a parliamentary comeback as a non-constituency member of parliament in 1997, there were to be further legal troubles, resulting in bankruptcy and the loss of his NCMP seat in 2001.

Chiam See Tong, secretary-general of the SDP who was elected to the Potong Pasir seat in 1984, was a completely different matter. The leadership had a long-standing understanding of aspects of Chiam's persona, stretching back to his first outing as a candidate in 1976.[160] Chiam lacked Jeyaretnam's personal antagonism, being prepared also to give some credit to the PAP government on account of its achievements. The PAP's thinking was set out within a few days of the 1984 general election, with 1DPM-designate Goh suggesting that the government was prepared to cooperate with Chiam if he was a "loyal opposition".[161] The danger of the other kind of MP—in a series of remarks by PAP MPs clearly aimed at Jeyaretnam—was one who "opposed for the sake of opposing". As PAP Organising Secretary (Special Duties) Lau Ping Sum noted at the time:

> *If an opposition MP concentrates on only the negative aspects of government policies or continues to ridicule them, then I don't see his role as useful. . . . If his line of questioning is always to mock and is not based on facts and statistics, and if he does not offer better alternatives to a problem, then his presence in the House is pointless.[162]*

Other Developments, 1985–86

On 28 March 1985, C.V. Devan Nair, president of the republic, suddenly resigned. While Nair's resignation letter was read out to Parliament by Speaker Yeoh Ghim Seng, it fell to PM Lee to shed light and put the facts before the people and Parliament.[163] Nair's alcoholism, hitherto well hidden, had come to a head during a visit to Kuching, Sarawak, amid reports of confusion and erratic behaviour. A potential public embarrassment had been avoided only by Nair's physician personally bringing him back from Kuching. PM Lee, emotional at several points in his statement before Parliament, said that this was "an immense personal tragedy", also wishing Nair fortitude in his struggle against dependency.[164]

Nair and Lee and been political comrades for over 30 years. Nair's trade unionism and anti-colonial stance had brought him (besides time in detention) to the attention of Lee in 1951, and when the People's Action Party was formed on 21 November 1954, Nair was among its founding members.[165] Later Nair became an important figure for the PAP, when, having renounced his own Communist beliefs and broken with his associates, he stood with the PAP, leading the pro-PAP labour union NTUC from 1961 to 1965 (he was to lead it again from 1970 to 1981). Nair was a key figure behind the early modernisation of mindsets in Singapore's workforce, also helping to make the tripartite National Wages Council a success.[166]

Devan Nair's achievements had been subject to fulsome tribute in 1981, when PM Lee moved the motion proposing Nair, then MP for Anson, for the presidency.[167] Lee was also to note in his memoirs and elsewhere that Nair's subsequent behaviour could not erase his achievements.[168] From the ground, there were some murmurings of sympathy for Nair at the time of his resignation, and (for those who remembered his championing of workers' rights) also respect for what Nair had done in the past.[169]

From 1985, however, the relationship between Nair and Lee was to take on a deteriorating turn of rancour and acrimony.[170] One issue was the question of a pension, which Nair had requested but which he refused to accept given that the government made this conditional upon his undertaking treatment for alcoholism.[171] The issue rankled with Nair, who, after his initial cognisance of his own alcoholism, later claimed he had never had the problem.[172]

The government released a White Paper in June 1988 detailing his alcoholism, revealing all the details of events concerning Nair's resignation and releasing his medical records.[173] The White Paper shone light not only on Nair's alcoholism but also his bizarre behaviour in Kuching, as well as his association with a woman from Germany, details of which had not previously come to light.[174] It also laid bare that Nair had essentially had to resign, whereas what had been suggested by all concerned in 1985 was that Nair had voluntarily stepped down.[175]

Through the release of a lengthy open letter, Nair accused Lee of mounting a public exercise in the denigration of an old colleague.[176] He also accused the government through the release of the White Paper of seeking political revenge on him. Nair had after his resignation given a speech critical of the government, accusing it of muzzling dissenting voices.[177] Nair also spoke in support of former Solicitor-General Francis Seow, who had been detained in May 1988 under the Internal Security Act.[178] Seow was accused of colluding with an American diplomat in Singapore to encourage dissident lawyers and professionals to run for elections in opposition to the PAP. In an interview, Nair stated that Seow had not done anything wrong in seeking foreign support for his political plans because Lee had done the same in the past. This led to Lee bringing a libel suit against Nair (by then out of the country).[179]

Nair withdrew his statements, but this was simply the beginning.[180] Based in the United States and latterly Canada, Nair was in later years to become a staunch critic of Singapore's political system—and of Lee Kuan Yew in particular. Nair also claimed that he suspected Lee had had government doctors slip him hallucinatory drugs to make him appear befuddled. This led to another lawsuit, which Lee was to discontinue in 2004 only when two of Nair's sons stated that there was no basis for this allegation, further stating that Nair was no longer mentally competent to give evidence in court.[181] Nair was to pass on the following year.

Devan Nair had been an old comrade and friend of Lee. Teh Cheang Wan, the minister for national development who died suddenly on 14 November 1986, had been neither—but his passing deprived the Cabinet of an able minister, someone who had since the 1950s been intimately involved in the success story that was Singapore's public housing. What made headlines was the coroner's verdict of suicide through an overdose of amytal barbiturate. Teh, as it turned out, had been under investigation on two allegations of corruption by the Corrupt Practices Investigation Bureau (CPIB). The first concerned a case where the developer had been allowed to retain a portion of land that had been acquired by the government; and in the second, Teh had allegedly assisted another developer to purchase a piece of state land for private development. In each of these cases Teh was alleged to have received gratification of $400,000.[182] Just as had been the case in the Devan Nair affair, it fell to PM Lee to put the full facts before Parliament.[183] Throughout the investigation, which in its earlier phase was conducted discreetly by the CPIB and behind closed doors, Teh maintained his innocence, attempting at one point to get the CPIB to discontinue the case and also requesting a personal meeting with PM Lee to give his side of the story. Lee, having seen a summary of the evidence and being satisfied by the CPIB director that there were sufficient grounds, approved an investigation and declined to meet Teh until investigations were complete.[184] Teh's suicide came before he could be charged in court.

Chiam See Tong sought, and got, a public inquiry convened to look into the facts of the matter.[185] The commission conducted hearings from May to August 1987. Chiam cut a frustrated figure there—rebuffed in his request that certain individuals be procured for interview, and refused access to CPIB files he was interested in.[186] While making some material available, the commission noted that Chiam would not be allowed to go on a "fishing expedition" to prove his suspicions concerning the wrongdoing. Indeed, the commission's report was rather critical of Chiam, of his conduct and his seeming lack of preparation.[187]

Teh's suicide, a tragedy for his family, also deprived the government of an effective minister. But Teh's alleged corruption did not lead to blowback against the government. The commission noted that Teh might never have been found out if not for the CPIB's commitment to fearless investigation and its perseverance in checking every lead.[188] There was some sense that the public had been reassured by the impartiality shown by the CPIB.[189] PAP figures, for their part, underlined the point that the integrity of the system was not in question and remained intact—despite occasional mishaps, the PAP government had run, and kept on running, a clean and honest system.[190] Clean government featured in the PAP platform in the lead-up to the 1988 election campaign and indeed after it, with PM Lee, 1DPM Goh and others stressing the PAP's track record and its commitment to getting men and women of honesty and integrity to serve.[191] The point was further driven home through the passage in March 1989 of the Corruption (Confiscation of Benefits) Act. The Act went beyond existing laws, extending the definition of corruption benefits to any property or funds for which the person in question could not satisfactorily explain the provenance of.[192]

Chiam had sought an accounting and full disclosure but had not gone overboard. Enter into the frame J.B. Jeyaretnam. Jeyaretnam had been barred from contesting the 1988 general election, having been earlier convicted of misappropriating Party funds. But he could still campaign, and at a campaign rally in Bedok on 26 August 1988 he went too far, suggesting PM Lee had encouraged Teh to commit suicide, or that he took no action to prevent Teh's suicide when he had knowledge of it in order to avoid full investigations into the corruption allegation.[193] Lee sued for defamation. Jeyaretnam argued that his remarks constituted fair comment but lost the defamation suit and subsequent appeals (in series of court cases lasting until 1992). This was eventually to cost Jeyaretnam over $700,000 in all, including damages, costs and interest.[194]

The 1988 General Election

PM Lee had specifically directed that his successor be chosen by peers. When Goh Chok Tong was chosen, Lee accepted the choice. It was known and understood between Goh and Lee, however, that Lee's preference was for Dr Tony Tan. This was something that Lee had privately shared with Goh.[195] It did not affect their working relationship; both men continued to work well together on Party and policy matters after the succession was settled in the final days of 1984. Until 1988, Lee's comments on Goh and his team were, when he made them, generally positive. For example, Lee commented on the eve of his National Day broadcast on 8 August 1988 that foreign investors, having met the new team, were confident of Singapore's prospects.[196]

Settled Succession?

It was therefore all the more puzzling to Goh's colleagues in government (as well as the public) that Lee, a few days after his National Day broadcast, chose to embark on a series of pointed criticisms of the man anointed as his successor. The first instance was Lee's televised National Day Rally speech (on 14 August 1988), where, with unusual candour, he chose to make known his ranking of ministers after the 1980 and 1984 elections. In doing so, he revealed that Goh Chok Tong had been second behind Dr Tony Tan. Lee's 1980 assessment had Dr Tan heading the list on account of his decisiveness. Goh was second, with his flaw being that he listened too much and tried to please "too many people".[197] Lee continued in this vein at the Party rally on 21 August 1988 at the Singapore Conference Hall, making comments that were clearly aimed at Goh: "If people want smiling, congenial, affable, soft-approach, soft-touch leaders, they cannot at the same time demand of those leaders a certain steel in them to stand up to pressures . . . you can have a velvet glove . . . but if you have a spongy hand . . . that is no use."[198]

What was unknown to the public at the time was just how much PM Lee had thought out his remarks in advance, as well as subsequent ones he intended to make. On 22 August 1988, Lee was due to speak to a combined forum of students from the National University of Singapore and the Nanyang Technological Institute. Days before the talk, Lee had written to his ministers, circulating his planned remarks in advance:

> *On Sunday, I recounted how in 1980, I rated the five Ministers as potential leaders. It was deliberate. I knew people will query my present assessment of Goh Chok Tong. I will be speaking to NUS students on Monday, 22 August. I will be asked what I think of Goh Chok Tong as a leader now. Then I will give his strong and weak points. My assessment will therefore be credible. If I do not state his problems in communicating, I will sound like a salesman for my PAP successor.*[199]

Some of the ministers clearly felt that Goh had been undermined by PM Lee's comments and that he had gone far enough. Minister for Foreign Affairs and National Development S. Dhanabalan wrote to Lee:

> For better or for worse, the second generation of Ministers and Parliamentarians have chosen Goh Chok Tong to be their leader. You yourself said that you cannot nominate your successor. My view is that periodic school report card type of assessments of Goh Chok Tong do not help his credibility or acceptability as a political leader. The people will have to make their own judgement of him when he takes over. It would be better [if] you could avoid elaborating further on what you said at the National Day rally.[200]

Dhanabalan was not alone. Minister for Law and Home Affairs Prof. S. Jayakumar wrote to Lee:

> Everyone whom I have met was disappointed, critical and confused by your National Day Rally remarks on Chok Tong, Tony Tan, Teng Cheong and Dhanabalan. They could not understand why you did this; several felt it was unfair and unkind to Chok Tong. Some have interpreted it as laying the groundwork for changes in Cabinet line-up.[201]

Other ministers wrote to Lee suggesting that the parts dealing with Goh's strong points be strengthened. These suggestions were taken on board and used by Lee. Lee's view at this stage can be seen from his reply to S. Dhanabalan: the subject of his 1980 assessment could not be left hanging. Lee said that he had to state his 1988 assessment, noting also that DPM Goh preferred that he do this.[202]

At the 22 August 1988 forum with university students, Lee gave a long list of the qualities of the new guard and Goh Chok Tong, and listed instances where they had worked to combat problems together. Lee had some kind words for Goh, who he said was capable of making tough decisions and had first-class listening and interpersonal skills.[203] The praise was, however, overshadowed by remarks Lee made during the question-and-answer session when asked to elaborate on his assessment of the younger generation of leaders. Lee remarked that under Goh's leadership, the new guard's consensual approach meant that the decision-making process took longer. He also listed instances—such as how the Cabinet had handled the April 1988 rearrests of Marxist detainees—where he wished that the younger leaders had acted more decisively.[204] Lee also chose to repeat his comment made at the 21 August 1988 Party rally that the new leaders had a 60–40 chance of gelling into a team when faced with a crisis, capping this off by suggesting that Goh consult a psychiatrist, given his "wooden" demeanour and inability to communicate with the masses.[205]

Lee criticised Goh either implicitly or directly on three separate occasions in the space of a fortnight.[206] Those close to Goh were hurt and mystified.[207] Goh's ministerial colleagues, men who had chosen him to lead, by this stage felt it necessary to restore certainty. On the same day (21 August 1988) that PM Lee commented on Goh and his leadership style at the Party rally, Minister of Trade and Industry BG Lee and Minister for Education Dr Tony Tan commented on the issue, stating that Goh Chok Tong was the unanimous choice as leader and would be the next PM.[208] Other Party members chimed in in support, even venturing to disagree with Lee's assessment of Goh.[209] Goh's own approach was measured. He noted that he had told Lee in the past that he had no issue with Lee's frank assessment being made public, and that indeed it would be better if the public knew in advance what sort of leader they were getting. As an aspirant to the premiership, being scrutinised in this manner by Lee or the public was not something that troubled him.[210] But Goh also realised that he had to assert himself. The sting in Lee's remarks could hurt him politically.[211] In a pointed comment during a lunchtime rally at Fullerton Square on 1 September 1988, Goh mused that he might still be the "second choice" and that PM Lee's first choice and a possible "challenger" might be BG Lee, someone whom Goh said he had great respect for.[212] This was notwithstanding the fact that BG Lee had on separate occasions during the course of the affair been at pains to stress that he was not a challenger to Goh.[213]

By the hustings, there was still enough uncertainty in the air for Lee to decide that a clarification was required. At the 1 September 1988 lunchtime rally, Lee stated that the criticism of Goh was a "gambit"—and not a bad gambit, in his assessment—to make Goh come out of his shell and be less inhibited.[214] Goh had shown from his responses that he could be his "own man".[215] But was this really a ploy by Lee to goad Goh, make him come out of his shell, and become the more assertive leader Lee wanted? Goh recalled:

> He wanted to shake me up. He was nearing sixty-five and had said publicly that he would like to retire, like CEOs of MNCs, at that age. After the 1988 GE, he would have to hand over to me, if he still wanted to step down at sixty-five. He was obviously concerned about my ability to lead if I could not communicate well publicly. He had told me in private that he could not understand me—in private, I was animated and was able to put my points across clearly, but in public I was "wooden". He advised me to see a psychologist or psychiatrist. When PM Lee criticised me publicly, he was distancing himself from the choice of my colleagues. He did not want to be blamed by the public should I fail as a PM. He still preferred Tony Tan. . . . This was what he told me in private. He was honest and open with me. I had no problem with that and appreciated his honesty with me.[216]

It is possible that Lee was testing the waters on the issue of a possible change in political succession:

> [PM Lee] also could sense that the MPs preferred me. On the ground, Tony was still quite popular at that time, I would say very popular, if you were to put it to the ground, Tony and myself, he might have in an election beaten me. Put it to the cadres, I'm not so sure, because cadres you know, because cadres you got to spend time with them . . . [but] to the ground, Tony might in a straight election [have] beaten me. Or at least, there would be a fight. In the Party, of course,

I would have an advantage, because I spent time with the branch secretaries, visiting people, dialogue sessions. So I think [PM] was trying to change things. In other words, this is my public assessment, if there is a rejection of me by the Party members, by the MPs, then, well, Tony would have to serve.[217]

In 1988, as in 1984, PM Lee's preference was for Dr Tony Tan (who appears throughout to have been completely uninterested in the premiership). Goh's reaction in 1988 was simple and straightforward: even if personally stung by the public nature of Lee's criticism, he had no difficulty going back to his colleagues to ask whether the choice made in late 1984 should be considered anew. Which is precisely what happened. Goh asked the core group of ministers, the PG (Political Group), to have a rethink.[218] This time, however, there were no formal meetings to settle the matter; it was essentially a non-issue. As Goh was to make known on 1 September 1988, his Cabinet colleagues were fully behind him. "Don't waste time. We go for you," was the message given to Goh by Cabinet colleagues. Cabinet members he consulted were keen to move on to other issues, not least the coming general election.[219]

Lead-up, Campaign, Aftermath

A number of issues, some contentious, could have had an impact on the result of the 3 September 1988 polls. These included what became known as the 1987 Marxist Conspiracy (covered later in this chapter) and the resulting brush between the government and Catholic Church, the 1988 detention of Francis Seow under the Internal Security Act (ISA), and finally 1DPM Goh's own position as successor to PM Lee.[220]

The fact that these did not feature prominently as election issues is indicative of the extent to which the PAP succeeded in shaping discourse before and during the election campaign. The core issues were town councils and elected presidency, with debates on the latter proposal in different languages.[221] Attention was brought to bear on the topics that the PAP itself had decided would be on the table; voters were meant to understand these issues and know their choices affected their future. The mistakes of 1984 were not repeated. The simple slogan of "More Good Years" replaced the grand visions of a Singapore in the far-off future.

Seventy-one out of 82 seats were contested, with the Opposition mounting its strongest challenge (in terms of seats contested) since 1972. The biggest Opposition showing was from the WP, which fielded 32 candidates.[222] The SDP fielded 16 candidates. Besides Chiam, the SDP also fielded Ashleigh Seow (the son of Francis Seow) and, in what counted as something of a minor coup, former PAP MP Low Yong Nguan.[223] The SDP and WP finalised an electoral pact on 19 August, designed (on paper at least) to avoid the two parties being involved in three-cornered fights with the PAP.[224]

The internal PAP assessment was that the Party might lose as many as four seats.[225] The actual result—the PAP winning 80 of 81 seats, with a vote share of 63.2 per cent (down by 1.6 per cent from the 1984 general election)—clearly showed (to the evident surprise of some foreign commentators and publications) that the Party had been given a new mandate.[226] Media commentary at the time focused on how the electorate had behaved in a mature fashion by voting in Chiam in Potong Pasir but at the same time giving overwhelming support to the PAP.[227] The general sense was that there was no widespread backlash against the government on earlier issues such as the Marxist Conspiracy. The PAP failed to recapture the ground it lost in 1984 but managed to arrest the large swing against it from the previous election. There was to be no gloomy early morning press conference as there had been in 1984 (and as there was to be in 1991). PAP leaders instead at the press conference evinced some satisfaction at the result, with PM Lee describing it as a "solid majority" for the PAP, and with 1DPM Goh stating that this result gave him the confidence to confirm that he would take over as PM within two years.[228]

To have a realistic chance of winning a GRC, the Opposition had to find three credible—or credible-looking—candidates. And even then, arrayed against them would be a PAP slate of one or possibly more heavyweights, including office-holders. This scenario materialised in Eunos GRC, one battleground where arguably personality mattered more than national or even local issues.

Some explanation is in order as to why the Eunos contest was consequential beyond any ordinary constituency tussle. Francis Seow, who led the WP team there, was a well-known figure. A former solicitor-general (1967–71), Seow had entered private law practice in 1972 and was elected president of the Law Society in 1986. His tenure there coincided with clashes between the Law Society and the government on various issues. In Seow's view, it was the role of the Law Society to pass comment (and criticism) on new legislation, a position that brought the society into conflict with the government, especially on the issue of amendments to the Newspaper and Printing Presses Act, which came into force in September 1986.[229] The government's response to the Law Society's activism was the introduction of amendments to the Legal Profession Act that effectively barred the Law Society from commenting on legislation. A televised parliamentary select committee hearing on the proposed amendments, which saw testy and very direct exchanges between PM Lee and Seow, further brought Seow into the public eye, especially given the view of many watching at the time that Lee on that occasion had not got the better of Seow in their exchanges.[230] After less than a year at the helm of the Law Society, Seow was forced to step down as president in November 1986, following the introduction of legislation prohibiting the appointment or election of council members who had been struck off the rolls or suspended from practice for six months or more.[231] However, he continued to be a thorn in the side of the government on various issues.[232]

This was just the beginning. Investigations following the 1987 Marxist Conspiracy had surfaced the fact than an American diplomat at the US embassy in Singapore, E. Mason "Hank" Hendrickson, had been cultivating Singaporeans, including Seow, who had acted for some of the detainees. This might not in itself have been objectionable, but the investigations showed that Hendrickson had instigated Seow and others to stand for election as Opposition candidates. Hendrickson, who was expelled from Singapore, had from the government's point of view been meddling in Singapore's domestic politics. The public disclosures of Hendrickson's conduct on 8 May 1988 shed light on the detention under the Internal Security Act two days earlier of Seow, who was now shown to have been under American influence from 1987.[233] The government accused him of "colluding with foreign diplomats and officials to lead a group of opposition lawyers and professionals into Parliament"; in addition, Seow was alleged to have misused his status as legal counsel as a "cover for political propaganda and agitation".[234] Seow was held in detention for 72 days before being released on 16 July 1988—as the government had promised, in time to contest the general election.[235]

The PAP's attacks against the WP team during campaigning were personal to an unusual degree. Party leaders made it clear that Seow and the rest of his team (Dr Lee Siew Choh and Mohd Khalit bin Mohd Baboo) were not credible figures to begin with, and not fit to run the town council.[236] The Party machine cranked out lengthy pamphlets on Seow, who was made out to be an individual with a questionable private life and financial problems.[237] On the ground, WP supporters acted in an unrestrained manner; at the counting centre, some were worked up to such a degree that it took the riot squad to disperse them after they refused to leave; three individuals were arrested in the incident.[238]

The PAP team (Minister of State for Education Dr Tay Eng Soon, Chew Heng Ching and Zulkifli bin Mohammed) took the GRC by an extremely narrow margin, winning 50.89 per cent of the valid vote.[239] The press was moved to comment that the close result indicated a "moral blind eye" amongst the electorate.[240] The Party leadership saw things somewhat differently. Interviewed for this book, PM Lee Hsien Loong (who had chaired the Post-mortem Committee) acknowledged that some at the time may have thought that the campaign against Seow had been overdone. But in his view, it was the propaganda campaign against Seow which in fact saved Eunos for the PAP. In Lee's view, the campaign against Seow "encouraged PAP people and put Francis Seow on the defensive. If Francis Seow had come in, there would have been a different political outcome for Singapore, not just for the constituency . . . if he can win, something is wrong with Singapore."[241]

As we shall see in the following chapters, the leadership would not hesitate to expose the flaws of individual Opposition members, especially when convinced that such exposure was in the national interest, whether or not it might lead to a backlash against the Party itself.[242]

✣✣✣

Following the PAP's election victory, at the customary post-election press conference in the early hours of 4 September 1988, PM Lee said that the transition to the younger-generation leaders was complete and that Singapore's future now lay with them. Lee was now prepared to be "nudged" aside by his successor. Goh's response was that he believed he and his colleagues would be ready to "gently nudge" the prime minister out within two years.[243]

These were reassuring lines. Gone were the pre-election criticisms of Goh. As noted earlier, various ministers had privately urged Lee to desist from further comments that might be seen to undermine Goh, who had in any case received resounding backing from his colleagues.

Overall, the PAP seemed to have won a handsome victory in 1988. But the fact was that close to 40 per cent of the electorate had voted for the Opposition, and there were a number of close shaves.[244] These included the contests in Eunos GRC (50.89 per cent), Aljunied GRC (56.33 per cent), Bedok GRC (54.92 per cent), Bukit Batok (55.94 per cent), Bukit Gombak (53.46 per cent) and Paya Lebar (52.36 per cent). Based on comparison solely of constituencies contested in both 1984 and 1988, the PAP vote share slid 4 per cent. The PAP General Election Post-mortem Committee (chaired by BG Lee) focused on what this meant and what the longer-term trends were.[245]

The report noted that the Party had successfully controlled the agenda, with the two key issues—town councils and elected presidency—dominating most of the discussion. The Opposition was forced to attack these issues rather than introducing new ones to confuse the electorate.[246] But as BG Lee was to comment in his 15 December 1988 note to Assistant Secretary-General Goh summarising the report's findings, it was troubling that the PAP could not improve on its 1984 performance despite ideal conditions. BG Lee commented that this was the "confirmation of the long-term upward trend of anti-votes even in the absence of major issues directly affecting voters".[247] The post-mortem report also commented on this issue: "The trend towards Western voting patterns is likely to continue. Whatever our policies in the next five years, it is unlikely that this can be reversed. If better qualified, more credible and apparently honourable opposition candidates come out to challenge the PAP next time, they will be much harder to deal with."[248]

In his note to 1DPM Goh, BG Lee commented that the key aim of the PAP had to be to arrest this erosion and win back anti-votes. This should be done through continued consultation, driving home the consequences of voting for the Opposition, providing new outlets for dissenting views (such as through extending or modifying the NCMP scheme), inculcating communitarian values in the population and preventing further Westernisation in society.[249]

The 1988 post-mortem exercise (and the resulting report) was more sophisticated than its 1984 counterpart. The impression was that the Party was better informed as a result of the post-1984 groundwork and had developed better sensing mechanisms. The 1984 report had not attempted to desegregate voting patterns (and had in fact made the observation that it was difficult to identify which groups had supported the Party). The 1988 report did attempt some analysis—apparently through intelligence from Party branches, and straw polls on the ground—on who had voted for the Party and who had not.[250] The conclusion was that many professionals and younger, better-educated and upwardly mobile families living in new housing estates had not voted for the PAP. The post-mortem report also commented on the increasingly Westernised outlook and individualistic values of many within this group.

The ability to identify groups and trends in turn marked an evolution in thinking within the Party leadership in terms of how it perceived the electorate. If the policies that amounted to "helping everyone" could not work to swing the tide back to the PAP by 1988, when no major issues had arisen to cause unhappiness, then sharper differentiations had to be made between those who had supported the Party and those who had not. This thinking had two principal strands. First, voting for the Opposition would have to have consequences. This idea was not in itself new. In 1985 Minister for National Development Teh Cheang Wan had clarified in Parliament that on 21 March 1985 HDB's non-emergency maintenance services would be given first to constituencies with PAP MPs, with Opposition constituencies being served last.[251] This was surprising to some and shocking to others. An editorial in the *Straits Times* summed up the mood. It called on the government to reconsider, noting that the less favourable treatment given to non-PAP constituencies was essentially "an exercise in punitive politics" and that "the ripples of resentment could spread well beyond the boundaries of these two constituencies [Anson and Potong Pasir] and affect a broader spectrum of Singapore".[252] For present purposes, it should be observed that the PAP leadership's thinking on this matter was still embryonic in 1984–85; it was reinforced by the 1988 general election result, but even then the Party leadership could not decide on whether services should be withdrawn from Potong Pasir.[253] This thinking was only to harden into its fullest expression after the 1991 general election, through the withdrawal of services in Opposition wards and the HDB Upgrading Programme.

The Malay Community

A second strand of thinking was more immediate in nature. This was the PAP leadership's willingness in 1988 to sift through voting patterns not just in terms of education and class, but in terms of race. The 1988 general election post-mortem report noted that there had been a clear swing within the Malay ground against the PAP in the last days of campaigning. This was due in part to the televised debate in Malay on the elected president proposal, which had seen BG Lee Hsien Loong and Ahmad Mattar pitted against Mohd Jufrie Mahmood of the SDP and M. Taib Saffar of the WP. The PAP did not anticipate the hostile reaction to a non-Malay participating in a Malay discussion, or the even more hostile reaction to BG Lee playing a dominant role in the discussion. This, the report noted, had been "a disaster for the PAP".[254] There was a recognition, however, that Malay dissatisfaction had not been about the debate alone. There was a deeper underlying current of disquiet that linked back to earlier issues. These included the November 1986 visit of Israeli President Chaim Herzog, the issue (felt keenly by the Malay community, and raised from time to time) of Malays serving in the Singapore Armed Forces, and what seemed to be the continual questioning of the loyalty of the Malays. The 1988 general election post-mortem report concluded that the Malay community had felt hurt by these episodes and had not forgotten the hurt.

1DPM Goh had over the years paid particularly close attention to the Malay community's support for the Party. When the Party leadership had, three years previously, considered the 1984 general election post-mortem report, it was Goh who expressed concern at what he saw as the disassociation of Malay voters from the PAP.[255] Goh took up this issue again—this time publicly—soon after the 1988 election, noting that the "feel from the ground", straw polls, and feedback from PAP MPs had led the

PAP to believe that "it had lost a significant proportion of Malay votes".[256] Goh asked, "Should we not encourage open identification and commitment to the PAP, and extend more help to those who can help and support us?"[257]

Goh's comments occasioned surprise and a degree of bewilderment from within the Malay community, which felt unfairly singled out.[258] Many within the community disagreed with the assessment that Malay support for the PAP had fallen off.[259] Goh also stated that he was reconsidering the amount and type of assistance given to the Malay community, further raising ire within quarters of the community and some community organisations.[260] The subsequent history of the government's relations with the Malay community, including landmark events such as the revision of the policy on free education for Malays, have been covered in detail in other works.[261] It is worth noting here that this was a critical period when PAP Malay MPs came under pressure and were increasingly beleaguered. The dilemma that PAP Malay MPs increasingly found themselves in was summarised by the MP for Siglap, Abdullah Tarmugi, in a 1990 *Petir* commentary. As Tarmugi observed, Malay MPs had to serve "two constituencies": the constituents generally, and also the Malay community. The latter group scrutinised their MPs closely: "His lifestyle, behaviour, religious piety, even his command of his language are under scrutiny and taken as measures of his affinity with the community."[262] In a revealing passage, Tarmugi proceeded to summarise the issues in the Malay community, not leaving out the chief criticisms commonly made of PAP Malay MPs:

> *Stubborn social problems continue to plague the community. And while nation-building has moved up in priority and urgency, Malays feel increasingly alienated and distanced from the rest of Singapore. The brunt of the blame for this state of affairs, so they argue, falls on the government generally and on the Malay Members of Parliament in particular. In short, Malay MPs have failed in their task of leading the Malay community and of moving it to be on par with the other communities here. Because of this, the argument continues, the Malays have become sceptical over the role and effectiveness of Malay MPs or have even rejected them.[263]*

It was against this backdrop that a group of Malay–Muslim professionals (which was to become the Association of Muslim Professionals, or AMP, in 1991) organised a convention to discuss issues relating to the community on 6 and 7 October 1990. 1DPM Goh's personal inclination was to engage, and he accepted the invitation to attend the convention as guest of honour. The issue of how to treat the new group had been thoroughly discussed in advance by PM Lee, key ministers and the PAP Malay MPs. Goh's conciliatory approach towards the new group had to some extent been anticipated by PM Lee when Lee was guest of honour at the PAP Malay Affairs Bureau (MAB) dinner on 15 July 1990:

> *I therefore welcome the interest shown by a group of young Malay professionals who have come together to assess how to hasten progress. This is a positive*

development. The more leaders amongst the Malay intelligentsia spontaneously come forward, the better it is for the Malay community. We hope they can provide constructive and practical solutions to tackle problems faced by the Malay community.[264]

Goh had written to Lee a few days before the latter was due to speak, observing that he (Goh) had given his blessings to the Malay professionals for their forthcoming convention. Goh suggested that Lee could also signal support in his speech at the MAB dinner: "Whether we like it or not, this is a spontaneous grouping, and will grow, to either supplement MENDAKI or challenge it. Far better for us to bless it and influence it so that it will supplement the PAP Malay leadership."[265]

The PAP Malay MPs involved in these discussions accepted Lee's view that the existence of the group was not something that he could ignore entirely in his speech. But they were concerned and felt that the directions that might emanate from the forthcoming convention were unknown. The majority of them felt that it would be premature for Lee to declare support for the group. PAP Malay MPs had been stressing to leaders of the Malay–Muslim community for some time that the best way to help the Malay community was to work within the PAP government. Pledging support for an independent group would be seen as a departure from this line.[266] Already, there were sections of the Malay community which felt that Mendaki was too closely associated with the PAP, or even serving the PAP's interests.[267]

Lee's comments at the MAB dinner were not made public. Goh's remarks at the convention of Malay–Muslim professionals on 7 October 1990 were, on the other hand, widely reported. In essence, Goh agreed that there should be no issue for Malay-based groups outside of the PAP or Mendaki ambit attempting to uplift the community. The government would even be prepared to give support to any group that professionals chose to form for this purpose, provided that it did not work to undermine the government of the PAP Malay MPs, nor argue its points from a communal-based standpoint.[268] Sidek Saniff, one of two Malay PAP MPs attending the convention (the other being Othman Haron Eusofe), also urged unity when invited by the organisers to deliver brief remarks.[269]

Goh's willingness to discuss frankly some of the sensitive issues concerning the Malay community was generally well received by the community. However, a distinction should be drawn here between the reaction of the Malay community, on the one hand, and the Malay professionals who went on to form the AMP, on the other.

The AMP derived from Goh's remarks the sense that it could, in time, form a collective and alternative leadership for the Malay community independent of the PAP Malay MPs.[270] As the PAP Malay MPs saw in 1990, the AMP agenda inevitably meant a partial usurpation of the role and significance of the PAP Malay MPs themselves. Goh and the PAP leadership chose not to puncture these assumptions in 1990. But when these same issues resurfaced ten years later, at the second AMP convention, Goh—by then a more seasoned (and tougher) leader—was to take a much harder line on the issue and against the AMP.[271]

Practical Policymaking and Ethnicity

The point of the preceding excursus has been to illustrate how, as the 1980s wore on, the Party adopted an increasingly pragmatic attitude to the issue of race. The theme of a homogenous, "Singaporean" Singapore still being a considerable way off was to become more pronounced in political discourse. There was more discussion of sensitive issues touching on ethnicity (during for example the passage through Parliament in 1988 of amendments to the constitution and the Parliamentary Elections Act, which paved the way for the introduction of GRCs), but what came through most clearly from government leaders was that ethnic groups in Singapore were different, and that these differences could never be completely subsumed under a single Singaporean identity. As PM Lee noted at his January 1988 briefing to newspaper editors on the Team MPs concept, "I think we had better face it. To pretend we are all the same and we have all become Singaporeans, homogeneous, is to cheat ourselves."[272] On one of the final occasions that saw Lee addressing the people as premier, he returned to this topic:

> It's no use, it's futile kidding ourselves, deceiving ourselves. These are important things. So when Rajaratnam says, "Malaysian Malaysia, therefore you must have a Singaporean Singapore". I read him, I said, "Ah Raja is getting forgetful". When we said Malaysian Malaysia, if you tell the Malay that he will become a Malaysian, and he is no longer a Malay, he'll be very, very unhappy. He doesn't mind becoming a Malay Singaporean but he wants to remain a Malay, and identifiable as a Malay. And there are many Chinese who will be very upset if they can't identify their children as Chinese.[273]

The 1980s was thus the period when the PAP's philosophy began to deviate for good from the ideal, put forward most notably by S. Rajaratnam, of a Singaporean Singapore. Rajaratnam maintained to the end of his political career (and indeed beyond, as a private citizen) that evolving a Singaporean identity where race was purely secondary should be an integral part of nation-building. Ethnicity, he maintained, could in certain respects be a useful concept, especially in the effort to understand one's roots, but "this should in no way hamper the development of an overriding Singapore identity or the strengthening of a Singapore nationalism in the face of competing and even warring ethnic nationalisms".[274] Ultimately, though, it was Lee's pragmatic view that prevailed. The Singaporean ideal had to be circumscribed by the realities—the fact, for example, that the population was by no means homogeneous. Lee stressed on several occasions that communalism would always be present—full assimilation was not possible because getting Singaporeans of different races to marry and adopt one religion, the apotheosis of such a concept, was simply not possible. It was "impossible" to build a homogeneous society.[275]

The changes in the late 1980s did not simply extend to an increased willingness to talk about sensitive ethnic issues. The polity had to adjust itself to reality. Where necessary, solutions tailored to what the Party saw as the overall national interest (such as the GRC system) began to be adopted. This was not, of course, something that had its beginnings in the late 1980s. Some policies, notably the introduction of Special

Assistance Plan schools (1980) and the formation of Mendaki (1982), came before this. Ministers such as Rajaratnam, who uncompromisingly believed the multiracial ideal, were firmly opposed to ethnic-based self-help groups such as Mendaki, taking the view that this was communal backsliding and that it would divide Singapore. Lee, however, felt that approaching the problem by trying to reach out to the Malay community through the bureaucracy would not work. Too few would be reached. In Lee's view, ethnic self-help groups leveraging on the community and community leaders were the practical solution.[276]

Practical solutions to potentially sensitive ethnic issues was a central theme of policymaking in the PAP government from the 1980s. Given the growing recognition that the ethnic groups were ultimately distinct, calibrated policy interventions had from time to time to be introduced to maintain a balance between the ethnic groups in Singapore. By 1986, for example, the issue of Malay–Muslim pupils being overly represented in certain schools had become enough of an issue to be raised by Dr Ahmad Mattar, the environment minister and minister-in-charge of Muslim affairs, with the government accepting that their proportion should more or less keep with the overall proportion of Malays in the population.[277] It appears that this was an issue that had been identified as a problem, and one that the leadership felt it would be better for the Malay MPs to speak up on first. This was also the approach taken for the most important and wide-reaching policy to do with ethnicity, the Ethnic Integration Policy, which was introduced in 1989.

HDB had since 1976–77 implemented administrative measures controlling the ethnic distribution in each new housing block.[278] But the issue of the continuing efficacy of HDB's controls was not revisited until taken up by the high-level Ministerial Committee on Housing (which met from 1986 to 1987) in the course of a thoroughgoing review of housing policy.[279] The committee found that there was evidence of Malays regrouping into areas such as Eunos and Bedok by buying three-room flats in the resale market. Left unchecked, this would lead to the Malay population in these areas reaching close to 30 per cent by 2000.[280] This finding prompted 1DPM Goh to initiate discussions with the Malay MPs, who saw the dangers and were convinced that a regrouping should not be allowed to happen.[281] Sidek Saniff (parliamentary secretary in the Ministry of Trade and Industry) spoke on the issue during the Agenda for Action debate on 25 February 1988, asking 1DPM Goh to examine and clarify the issue.[282] In November 1988 the leadership approved the measures to adopt the proposed control limits for open market sales of resale flats, to bring the racial mix within the desired ceilings.[283]

Early on, the leadership understood that it would be difficult to keep secret measures for ethnic integration, and that it would be necessary to announce these measures openly to prevent misunderstanding. Effective communication was therefore crucial, especially given that some adverse reaction was expected. The decision was taken that public communications would be staged. Only after a public discussion on the importance of ethnic distribution in public housing estates would details of the new control policies be announced. This approach meant that the public could first understand the seriousness of the matter.[284] On this occasion (unlike the initial linking of GRCs to town councils), there were no strained attempts to nuance the issue nor to sugarcoat the message. Minister for National Development S. Dhanabalan first brought up for attention the emergence of ethnic enclaves in HDB estates in January 1989, making it known that there were moves in the offing to address the growing issue of communal clustering (or reclustering, as flat applicants tended to move back to where their ethnic roots were established) so as to maintain and foster social and racial cohesion.[285] When the Ethnic Integration Policy was implemented on 1 March 1989, establishing ethnic quotas for blocks and neighbourhoods in HDB estates, there was some degree of understanding, if not acceptance.

Still, dealing in a direct and open fashion with the issue of race was somewhat unsettling for many. Observers were not entirely sure that Singaporeans becoming more aware of ethnicity was necessarily a good thing.[286] Perhaps some of the uncertainty had to do with the fact that (as can now be seen with hindsight) the ideal of a Singaporean Singapore—one that downplayed the essence of ethnicity in favour of the unifying ideal of an identity transcending race—began to falter. Instead, what began to surface was an idea much more nuanced: that the differences between various races in the country could not, and indeed should not, be artificially subsumed within the construct of a national identity.

A key force in this conceptual remaking of the Singapore identity was BG George Yeo, who had been elected to Parliament in 1988. Yeo's thinking on the subject can be glimpsed in his early speeches and interviews as a politician:

> We went through a phase when we become very westernised, when we as a result of the colonial experience looked to the West for ideas, for insights, inspirations. But as Asia becomes more developed, and indeed over the last 10, 20 years, Asia has progressed tremendously, there is a sense that, look, we are ourselves drawn from an ancient civilisation, ancient cultures, and that we should not lightly discard those. It's part of the maturing process. As it were, we are passing the adolescent phase when we were easily swayed by fads and fetishes. And now we are going back to what is more permanent and more enduring, looking at our own history and finding in that history enough strength to take us into the future. . . . Our common experience as a nation is only a thin veneer upon our entire historical memory as a Chinese, as an Indian or a Malay. So that which is the veneer, we can lose very quickly. But that which is ancient, will remain with us much longer. And we have to blend the two. I think it is a high ideal of our society in Singapore that we accept that every Singaporean should have two parts in him or her. One which is drawn from his or her ancestral culture, and the other which is Singaporean. And we make no attempt to rub out the ancestral culture because that will be foolish indeed.[287]

This construct of what made a Singaporean was cosmopolitan, nuanced and arguably better suited to take Singapore into what became the globalised world of the 1990s. But it also had other implications. If one could not be bound by a single Singaporean identity, then what did tie the peoples of Singapore together? It is unsurprising, therefore, that the late 1980s and early 1990s was also a period when the government began to search for a common creed to bind the people together. This effort culminated in the National Ideology and Shared Values initiatives of 1988–91. But before we deal with these, it is first necessary to ask why the PAP leadership was prepared to go through these efforts in the first place. Broadly speaking, there appear to have been three reasons. First, there was the realisation of fundamental differences between the races in Singapore, as discussed earlier. The second was that nationally, there seemed to be an ongoing discernible drift from the values and mores the government deemed desirable. The third reason was shocks to the body politic such as the Marxist Conspiracy and (linked in some ways to it) increased religiosity. These need to be examined in turn.

The Marxist Conspiracy

In May and June 1987, the government used the Internal Security Act to detain 22 activists who were allegedly part of a "Marxist conspiracy" to topple the government. The government's case was that the detainees (a mixed group that included social activists, members of the Catholic Church, lawyers, and supporters of the Workers' Party) were controlled ultimately by London-based Tan Wah Piow.[288] Tan's chief conspirator in Singapore was, according to the government, one Vincent Cheng. Cheng was active in the Catholic Church and held the position of executive secretary of the Church's Justice and Peace Commission in Singapore. The story of these arrests (and the rearrests in 1988 of some of the individuals involved) is well known and will not be repeated here.[289] Those arrested seemed unlikely Communists. They were English-educated professionals, a world apart from the Chinese-educated Communists that Singapore had known in the 1950s and 1960s. Many expressed—or privately felt—doubts over whether those detained were indeed Communists or out to topple the state. Some of those who could not fully agree with the official version of events were at that time (or subsequently became) part of government. S. Dhanabalan (then the minister for foreign affairs and national development) was one. Bound by collective responsibility, he did not make public his doubts nor criticise his Cabinet colleagues at the time of the arrests. But the matter was for him a matter of conscience and was later revealed to have been the reason why he stepped down from the Cabinet in September 1992.[290]

Another was Tharman Shanmugaratnam. Tharman (who was to be elected to Parliament in 2001 as a PAP candidate and rose to become deputy prime minister and senior minister) had associated with Tan Wah Piow as a student in London and was part of Tan's study group; these links led to his being questioned by the Internal Security Department (ISD) during the period of the 1987 arrests.[291] Interviewed in 2001, Tharman, at that time senior minister of state for education and trade and industry, stated: "Although I had no access to state intelligence, from what I knew of them, most were social activists but not out to subvert the system."[292]

The issue continues to have the afterlife that it does—in the form of online commentaries, memoirs published by those who were detained, and gatherings in commemoration of the anniversary of the detentions—partly because of these doubts.[293]

The *Straits Times* noted in a retrospective on the issue 20 years after the arrests:

> *1987 may have cast longer shadows and caused deeper political changes than most people assume. Although the Government described its swoop as anti-Marxist, many critics read it as a much broader clampdown on political activism—and therefore as relevant today as it was 20 years ago. . . . What is not in doubt is that many of those who were arrested were doing social work to help the poor and migrant workers, in organisations linked to the Catholic Church. Their ultimate goals, however, were a matter of dispute.*[294]

The perspective of the government and the security services has been consistent. When the government moved in 1987, it was clear "that it was not acting against genuine social activists or members of the clergy, but only those who were covertly pursuing a subversive political agenda by hiding within the church organisations".[295] The government's view was that Communist Party of Malaya (CPM)-linked elements had begun (in response to a 1979 CPM directive calling for higher priority to be placed on penetrating and subverting open social and political organisations) to infiltrate various organisations in Singapore, including some linked to the Catholic Church.[296] ISD had from 1986 kept the leadership informed on trends it was detecting in the local religious scene. These included the mixing of religion with politics among some sections of the Catholic Church.[297] Old and new guard leaders had a continuing awareness that the Communist threat was not over. Speaking to Party cadres on 23 November 1986 at the PAP biennial conference, PM Lee singled out the threat of CPM metamorphosis, commenting on "those who were English-educated and who took after the British leftists and the radicals in the United States".[298] There was speculation in the press and the wider public as to whom—or what—Lee was referring to. The *Straits Times* came close to the mark in its assumption that PM Lee was not simply speaking of distant possibilities:

> *Mr Lee's concern is probably directed at those Singaporeans who, even though they do not call themselves communists, nevertheless share ideals similar to those of leftists, extreme socialists and Euro-communists. The warning appears to be a timely one. Younger Singaporeans are not facing their first trial in these difficult recessionary times. Being idealistic and inexperienced, it is natural for some of them to think that leftist approaches may provide solutions. Though recent reports suggest Euro-communism has lost some ground in the West, it remains a trap for the unwary.*[299]

In further remarks while addressing PAP cadres (remarks not publicly reported at the time), Lee added:

> *If any Euro-Communist group, Marxist, Radical or New Left types, think that they can take over in Singapore, it's a pipe dream. They will try. But they will be Trojan horses for the CPM. It may be different in another two generations if*

the present CPM groups have all died without leaving successors trained in their conspirational skills. Without the personal experience of how to run a guerrilla war, how to run an elimination squad, the Western orientated communists and Marxists will just be push-overs. For the next 30–40 years, there are young men now in their thirties, out on the border and in the jungles. They will not be stopped by any English-speaking Marxist types.

Each generation throws up its share of rebels or misfits, people who are against the system. In the 50s, 60s and 70s, the Chinese-educated communists in the CPM would absorb them. They will now build up the English-educated groups. The old University of Singapore had such groups in the Socialist Club. In the 50s and 60s, people under CPM influence like Dr Poh Soo Kai and Dr Lim Hock Siew led them. Since social and economic antagonisms in the 80s are not as acute as in the 60s, the numbers are less. But, there will always be some with the irresistible urge to stir things up. . . . We have to be vigilant and never let them grow out of hand.[300]

Matters were coming to a head even before 1987. Government officials had raised their concerns in private meetings with the archbishop in December 1985 and July 1986. In particular, there was unhappiness at the tenor of articles in Church publications such as the *Catholic News*, which was edited by Father Edgar D'Souza.[301] Senior officials, including Prof. S. Jayakumar (then the minister for home affairs) and BG Tan Chin Tiong (the permanent secretary at the Ministry for Home Affairs), had at these meetings also warned the archbishop that the Church was being made use of.[302]

At the time of the detentions, many speculated that the actual target was the Catholic Church itself, and that the arrests were a warning that the Church should stay out of social activism.[303] Critics pointed out that PM Lee himself was dismissive of what Vincent Cheng and Tan Wah Piow could achieve, with Lee dismissing Cheng's group as "stupid novices" and Tan as a "simpleton" during a critical 2 June 1987 meeting with the archbishop and Catholic Church leaders.[304] Ultimately, however, individual motivations (and who exactly was a committed Marxist) did not appear to have been the key calculation when action was taken. The government's action would be hard and drastic if the strands discovered were upon investigation found to go back to the CPM, the historical nemesis of the PAP. These connections—between Vincent Cheng, Tan Wah Piow and elements in the CPM—were indeed found. From ISD's perspective, anyone with even indirect connections to this axis would be under tremendous suspicion.[305] ISD's job was to deny the CPM an iota of room to operate or form networks in Singapore.

Religious Harmony

PM Lee repeatedly emphasised as events unfolded during the Marxist Conspiracy that the government did not want a confrontation with the Church.[306] But such a clash was barely—if at all—avoided. Near the beginning of the affair, the Catholic

Church had expressed its support for those detained, and held a special Mass and service for the detainees on 27 May 1987.[307] Lee's personal perspective was one of anger and irritation that members of the clergy had so willingly strayed into the political domain and were showing tendencies towards liberation theology. Only after the 2 June 1987 meeting with PM Lee and government officials did Archbishop Gregory Yong (having been shown the evidence gathered) state that he was satisfied that the government had a case against Vincent Cheng, and that the government's actions were not directed against the Church.[308] But to make things clear, government delimitation between the Church, acceptable social activism, and other activities deemed undesirable had to be made. Social services and charitable works provided by religious groups were encouraged and indeed welcomed, but there was beyond this a line that could not be crossed. This line was clearly identified by PM Lee in his 1987 National Day Rally speech:

> I urge that churchmen, lay preachers, priests, monks, Muslims theologians, all those who claim divine sanction or holy insights, take off your clerical robes before you take on anything economic or political. Take it off. Come out as a citizen or join a political party and it is your right to belabour the government. But you use a church or a religion and your pulpit for these purposes and there will be serious repercussions.[309]

The concern, however, was not simply that the events of 1987 had shown that Church activists and clergy could try to exploit religion for political purposes. A separate strand of security reporting in 1986 had alerted the leadership of aggressive proselytisation by Christian groups, which was part of a worldwide trend of rising religious fervour.[310] Following the 1987 National Day Rally, PM Lee requested that the Ministry of Community Development conduct a study on religion in Singapore.[311] This study, carried out by three academics from the National University of Singapore, was discussed by the leadership in January 1989, prior to its official release in February 1989 as a report titled "Religion and Religious Revivalism in Singapore".[312] This report confirmed that religious fervour was on the rise. The report noted that there had been substantial growth in the number of Christians over the decades, and that the charismatic churches in particular had made inroads: "Revivalism in Christianity is not only manifested in the growing number of its followers, but also in the increased fervent and zealous work they put into Christian activities."[313] The report observed that revivalism was not simply confined to the Christian faith and suggested that further study be done on the teaching of Religious Knowledge in schools in order to see whether this was accentuating religious differences.[314]

It was this last observation that was picked up on by the leadership. Goh Chok Tong summarised the concerns:

> We noticed a trend that the Religious Knowledge classes were actually dividing the students. Instead of getting them to understand each other's religion, young people will identify themselves as Christians, Muslims, and Buddhists and so

on. Of course, the Christians were aware that they were Christians and they were different from the Buddhists; and you could see that in schools, people were actually dividing themselves along religion. Not every student, but you find that there are classes of students. So, there was a discussion, you see. Well, if that is so, and we are convinced that that would be even more so in the future, then better scrap it.[315]

By March 1989 the leadership had decided to accept recommendations put up by the Ministry of Education (MOE): from 1990 Religious Knowledge would no longer be a compulsory subject, and it would be completely phased out by 1992.[316] That the decision was taken this early was not public knowledge. During the budget debate of March 1989, Minister for Education Dr Tony Tan informed Parliament that MOE was looking into the issue of religious instruction in schools, and that the key reason for revisiting the issue had been the conclusions of the report "Religion and Religious Revivalism in Singapore".[317] Subsequently, MOE consulted widely, holding over the course of 1989 meetings and dialogue sessions with educators, the GPC for Education, heads of religious organisations, community leaders, and the general public. Unsurprisingly, there was no consensus at these meetings.[318] In his 6 October 1989 parliamentary statement, Dr Tan summed up these sessions and announced that Religious Knowledge would be replaced with an expanded Civics programme. Dr Tan asked whether there had been any fundamental change in the circumstances since 1982, when Religious Knowledge had been made compulsory. He then chose to answer the question himself:

Unlike 1982, there is today a heightened consciousness of religious differences and a new fervour in the propagation of religious beliefs. This trend is world-wide and it embraces all faiths. It can be seen in the growth of Islamic fundamentalism, enhanced Christian evangelisation and resurgence of activity and interest among traditional religions such as Buddhism. Sir, if carried to extremes, this trend towards greater fervour in the propagation of religious beliefs can disrupt our traditional religious harmony and religious tolerance which are pre-requisites for life in Singapore. It is not possible for Government to ignore this new development. We must take cognizance of it and we must implement measures to ensure that it does not upset the present climate of religious tolerance in Singapore.[319]

The phasing out of Religious Knowledge was only the first step. It was becoming clear that more needed to be done to ensure the peaceful coexistence of religions in the country; more needed to be done also to lay out ground rules and to explain why they were needed. Even after the arrests and the attempted drawing of red lines by PM Lee and others, individuals within the religious establishment were still venturing into political terrain, and the religious themselves were still engaged in actions that could offend those of other faiths. This was made clear when in November 1989 ISD issued a security report titled "Religious Trends: A Security Perspective", which contained instances of aggressive proselytisation and the mixing of religion and politics. It showed, amongst other things, that Catholic priests continued to make political statements from their pulpits in the aftermath of the Marxist Conspiracy, as well as commenting on politics.[320] The report noted that some Protestant churches and groups had engaged in "aggressive and insensitive proselytization"; it also pointed to fault lines emanating from other (non-Christian) religions.[321]

Rather than proceed immediately with a bill on maintaining religious harmony—which had been the initial plan—the leadership decided to first issue a White Paper setting out the basic proposals that would subsequently be enshrined in legislation.[322] This White Paper, presented to Parliament on 26 December 1989, set out the penalties that would be meted out to anyone (individual or religious leader) causing enmity between religions, or anyone carrying out political activities under the guise of practising any religious belief.[323] The issuance of the White Paper also meant an occasion to get religious leaders to squarely confront the realities. On 22 November 1989 the government called for a meeting, held at the Ministry of Community Development, to discuss the White Paper and the ISD report (which was circulated at the meeting). A group of key religious leaders representing all faiths were in attendance, as were PM Lee and several government ministers.[324] During the meeting, religious leaders were generally supportive of the aims of the White Paper. But there were reservations expressed, particularly by representatives of some Christian denominations. Faced with these reservations, PM Lee took a harder line. He had taken care in his discussion during the meeting to show that the issue was not with one particular religion, pointing out that the ISD report had given instances of incendiary Muslim clergy preaching in mosques, and also noting that members of other religions, including Buddhism, had become more assertive.[325] But as the meeting wound down, Lee felt it necessary to make some pointed comments:

> [PM Lee declared that] the Singapore Government relied on its own moral authority to govern Singapore. The Government was one that dared to say what the law was and to uphold it. There must be recognition by the religious groups, particularly the Christians, that they could survive only with a strong secular Government. If they wanted to play to popular will, they would not survive. Christians had grown because the Government had allowed them to grow. They were putting themselves "in peril" if they did not understand the basis on which events had developed in Singapore. The Government could have governed Singapore differently if it had wanted to, by not attempting to bring all groups together in open accommodation and understanding of each other's conflicting desires.[326]

This was Lee's bottom line on the issue—as well as the government's final warning.

Shared Values and a National Ideology

The jolts to the body politic in 1987–88 had been stark reminders of the differences—religious and ethnic—within the nation. The leadership was increasingly concerned about rising evangelical zeal amongst religious groups and insensitivity between religions, especially in the matter of proselytisation. The issue was how to ensure that tensions between races and religions would not grow. Thoughts were beginning to coalesce on how to further bind Singaporeans and reinforce a common creed. There was, of course, a second set of concerns: that of Western mores and individualistic thinking permeating society. In internal Party discourse, the issue was being framed in very direct terms as being linked to the longer-term survival of the Party. In submitting the report of the 1988 General Election Post-mortem Committee to Assistant Secretary-General Goh Chok Tong, the head of the Post-mortem Committee, BG Lee Hsien Loong, had written that the PAP could not simply continue efforts at consultation and provide outlets for dissenting views. In order to ensure support in future elections, the Party would also have to emphasise "inculcating correct communitarian values in the population through the national ideology exercise, to prevent further Westernisation and deculturalisation of our society".[327] The report of the PAP Central Executive Committee—a document presented at the January 1989 Party conference—put the issue in equally direct terms for consideration of the PAP cadres:

> *The core values of diligence, thrift and placing community above self have brought prosperity and survival. It is necessary to formalize these values into shared values for all Singaporeans for two reasons—to immunize Singaporeans from the undesirable effects of Western influences and to bind Singaporeans together as a nation. The challenge facing us is how to preserve the cultural heritage of each of our communities, and uphold certain common values which will give us a unique sense of identity.*[328]

The National Ideology initiative (as it was at first known) was first publicly mooted by 1DPM Goh in a 28 October 1988 speech to the PAP Youth Wing.[329] In his remarks, Goh cast the initiative as an organised effort to counter the shift to individualism and the preoccupation with the self rather than with the community. This would "prevent our society from drifting aimlessly into the 21st Century". Goh was clear that between individualism and communitarianism, it was the latter which would ensure Singapore's competitiveness and survival.[330] His suggestion was that the values be formalised into a national ideology and then taught in schools, homes and workplaces "as our way of life. Then we will have a set of principles to bind our people together and guide them forward."

PM Lee was uneasy about the attempt to find, and codify, a national ideology. Interviewed by Taiwanese journalists on 8 March 1989, he made it clear that this was 1DPM Goh's idea and also elaborated on his reservations:

> *No, I'm not formulating it. My first Deputy Prime Minister mooted this and he feels the time has come to try and get some common shared belief defined between the races. I personally felt, when I read him, that he was being very bold, very brave because it's very difficult to do. You are dealing with different peoples and different cultures and different religions, and values are very deep and emotional*

factors in a person's life. But they are prepared to try. I wish to help them. But I would have hesitated.[331]

Goh felt that the effort was worth pushing through. At the opening of Parliament on 9 January 1989, President Wee Kim Wee listed four values to be enshrined in the national ideology: placing society above self, upholding the family as the basic block of society, resolving major issues through consensus instead of contention, and racial and religious tolerance and harmony.[332] These seemed unexceptionable. But there was considerable discomfort evinced by PAP MPs when discussing the national ideology during the Debate on President's Address.[333] Ethnic minority MPs were clear that the national ideology would not be—*could* not be—a mechanism to impose the values of the majority on minority groups. At the end of the debate, Abdullah Tarmugi (who had just been elected first deputy speaker) summed up by noting that while he could not say what the national ideology would be, he could "narrow the ground by asserting what it is not". It would not, according to Tarmugi, be a means by which the values of the majority were foisted on minority groups.[334] Tarmugi went to great lengths to assure younger Singaporeans that the national ideology and the communitarian values associated with it were "not meant to bury democracy in this country", and that the government was committed to the path of openness and consultation.[335] Much of this was clearly aimed at Chiam See Tong, who had in this debate claimed that national ideology, with its emphasis on Asian values and decrying of Western mores, was simply a ploy to reject Western-style democracy and perpetuate PAP rule.[336] But it is also possible to see in Tarmugi's remarks, and in remarks made by other MPs during the parliamentary debate, some sense of warning to Party leaders that the national ideology should not run counter to the stated path of consultation that 1DPM Goh had committed the government to. As Tarmugi pointed out, there had to be "a visible interplay of contending forces. In other words, openness, flexibility, a softer approach to govern should not rest only in commitment but should also be visible to the population."[337]

These doubts lingered. The parliamentary committee that had been set up to formulate the national ideology, headed by Trade and Industry Minister BG Lee Hsien Loong, was from the beginning in the position of having to make clear that this was not an exercise in keeping the population "cowed and submissive"; nor was it a means of foisting Confucian values onto minority groups in Singapore.[338] The charge of creeping Confucianism was difficult to dispel, partly because leaders such as 1DPM Goh, PM Lee and BG Lee clearly appreciated Confucianism's positive aspects. There was certainly considerable governmental support for the ideal of Confucianism in Singapore in the 1980s, with PM Lee favouring Confucian Studies as a bulwark against the creeping in of Western values.[339] However, by the late 1980s the leadership was by its own admission coming to see that the races in Singapore were very different. Encouraging Confucianism nationally was bound to face increasing resistance.[340]

Clearly some time was needed to give the Parliamentary Committee on the National Ideology time to think through the issue more deeply.[341] In 1989, IPS was commissioned to conduct a study to identify the basic values.[342] The ten months

(August 1989–May 1990) that the team took to research and publish its findings also gave the committee and the government as a whole the time it needed for a deeper consideration of the issues.[343]

Files show a fascinating interplay between leaders—new and old—involved in applying the finishing touches to the White Paper. BG George Yeo, acting minister for information and the arts, wrote to DPM Lee Hsien Loong on 17 December 1990 proposing that "social justice" or "humanitarianism" be included as one of the values:

> *My unease with the present formulation is that all 5 values are weighted in favour of the group over the individual. Although this is our present concern, we must not give the impression that the individual is secondary and this is in fact a common criticism against us: that in the name of the group we ride roughshod over the individual. On Shared Values, we are not just presenting a correction (not just the delta) but the long term position. The explanations in the White Paper are balanced but they will be quickly forgotten. The formulation itself must be balanced.*[344]

PM Lee was unconvinced and not a little dismissive, responding that support for social justice "would lead people to believe that there is an absolute standard of 'justice' to measure rewards and social positions. This will trap us into a serious bind".[345] Lee also objected to a subsequent proposal to change "social justice" to "fairness and compassion". Quoting the economist Friedrich Hayek, Lee noted: "If you want a thriving economy, do not start interfering with the 'extended order' which came about naturally by trying to redirect rewards." Lee suggested "charity", or if this was not acceptable, to use "compassion and mutual help" or "compassion and Community support".[346]

For all this, it is striking how the essence of the White Paper, when eventually presented to Parliament in January 1991, hardly deviated in substance from the values first identified by the government, and from President Wee's speech of January 1989. There was only one significant addition to the four original core values: "regard and community support for the individual" had made an appearance.[347] This (as we have seen) was the result of "fairness and compassion" and "social justice" being rejected in the leadership's internal deliberations. Fine-tuning continued even after the White Paper had been presented to Parliament. There was particular discussion on the proposed inclusion of "consensus instead of contention", which could be construed as an attempt to stifle contrary views.[348] This was all old hat to the *Straits Times*, which observed somewhat mordantly that the January 1991 parliamentary debate on shared values had been less than inspiring, with no real impact on Singaporeans.[349] If the end result disappointed, it also fell short of the expectations that Goh Chok Tong (by now the prime minister) himself had had. Interviewed for this book, Goh also pointed to the lack of push to implement the values of the White Paper—for example, getting them taught in schools. This was linked to the pushback that the government had faced over communitarian values; in the end, the final result had to be a set of values that "everybody would be happy with".[350]

The national ideology/shared values initiative ended, somewhat anticlimactically, in 1991. But PM Goh was to persist with the idea of binding Singaporeans closer and anchoring them to the country. Underlying Goh's thought was a set of deep ruminations on the future shape of the country and its values. There had to be more to Singapore, and Singaporeans, than simply material well-being. In his swearing-in speech as premier in 1990, Goh stated that one of his missions was to emphasise values and culture: "A country cannot be a piece of driftwood, carried along by the wind and tide. . . . Like a majestic tree, it needs to be firmly anchored by deep roots: a unique set of values to help it grow and thrive, and to distinguish it from other countries."[351]

Goh's government would return to this theme of "heartware" at various points in the 1990s and beyond—especially through the periodic revival of national conversations such as the Singapore 21 initiative of 1997–99 and Remaking Singapore in 2002–03. A useful template had been provided by the National Agenda effort of 1987–88. But while attempts would continue to be made to control the agenda and to shape the national mood going forward, it could be argued that the government after 1991 now knew where the limits where. From this point on, there would be a reluctance to attempt to shape values as directly as the national ideology/shared values initiative had attempted to do. It was one thing to embark on wide-ranging attempts at soliciting feedback and controlling the national discourse; it was another for the government to try to bind people and form one national ethos based on a set of communitarian (or Confucian) values. Singapore's growing maturity—which brought with it the recognition that the proverbial melting pot could not exist—had put paid to this idea. Having at various junctures pointed out how different Singaporeans actually were, it was perhaps asking too much to remake the whole.

The Goh Premiership: Inauspicious Beginnings

> *The bottom-line for the PAP is that, after spending so much time worrying about the needs and aspirations of the able—who are welcome anywhere in the world—it should now re-focus its attention on those who are unlikely to be welcome anywhere else but Singapore. It is those with nowhere else to go and increasingly perceiving that they have little to lose that the PAP has to contend with in the next lap. And these form a more substantial portion than those who agonise over the artistic integrity of films or are voluble about freedom of the press. Some of them gave their signal last Saturday. The party with the privilege to rule ignores that signal at its own peril.*[352]
>
> —*Straits Times* post-election commentary, 6 September 1991

The public front that was put out after the 1988 elections, when the new Cabinet line-up was announced, had it that PM Lee was prepared to step down at any time, with 1DPM Goh deciding that Lee would stay on for up to two years.[353] In reality, PM Lee had indicated to Goh during their private exchanges in 1988 that he felt Goh was not yet ready to take the reins of the premiership, with Lee deciding to carry on for two more years.[354] Goh was relieved, as he too felt that he needed more time. But two years later, in 1990, Lee requested that Goh take over, without asking whether Goh felt ready. Clearly, Lee felt that Goh had proved himself. Goh, too, felt more confident by then and agreed without hesitation.[355]

The premiership passed from Lee Kuan Yew to Goh Chok Tong on 27 November 1990 in exactly the way that both men wanted—with minimum fuss. Lee now took on the position of senior minister in Cabinet, also retaining the secretary-general position in the PAP's Central Executive Committee. In June, providing Parliament the timeframe for the handover, Goh observed baldly that there would be no departure from the fundamentals that had made for Singapore's success: the government would "continue to be hard-headed and tough-minded. It will not govern by popular polls."[356] But Goh also promised a society that would be "refined, more compassionate, kinder and gentler".[357] A different, more consultative style of governance was clearly in the offing.[358]

Goh wanted confirmation that the people did indeed want him and the style of leadership he represented. Soon after his surprise August 1991 announcement of early polls (well in advance of the expected 1993 date), Goh gave his reasons for calling the election. His position, Goh noted, had been inherited from former PM Lee: "I will not have the political strength until I face the people and win." Goh did not want to end up like other leaders who had similarly inherited positions and lacked the political clout to carry out policies as a result.[359]

Apart from an early personal endorsement from the people that Goh felt was the sine qua non of his premiership, there were other reasons for calling for the snap polls. It had been an unsettled, and unsettling, few years on the world stage, with events such as the collapse of Communism and the Iraq War. If, as was commonly believed, the world order was entering into a completely different era, then a message had to be sent that it was the PAP that would secure this future and take the nation into the 1990s.[360] The PAP vision was set out in "The Next Lap", which had been launched on 22 February 1991 and released as the Addendum to the Presidential Address.[361] The calling of an early general election was to seek a mandate to carry out this programme.[362]

Campaign and Results

Twelve new PAP candidates were fielded in the election, held on 31 August 1991. This was fewer than in 1988 (19 new faces), an indication that the normally exhaustive PAP talent search had not quite run its course and that the customary renewal would be on a smaller scale (see Appendix One, Table 1.4).

As with previous elections, late calls and last-minute switches had to be made for tactical reasons. Among those fielded with a higher profile was Lim Hng Kiang, former chief executive officer of the Housing and Development Board (and who had had a career in the Administrative Service and the Singapore Armed Forces). Expecting to be fielded in Kuo Chuan SMC, he was whisked the night before Nomination Day to Telok Blangah, a division within the larger Telok Blangah GRC.[363] The Party had made a late decision not to put up for re-election Dr Koh Lam Son, who since 1984 had been the MP for Telok Blangah SMC.[364]

Party activists at the Telok Blangah branch included some extremely vocal individuals who felt strongly about Lim being "parachuted" in to replace Dr Koh without any warning.[365] Koh was known to be a hard-working MP—popular on the ground and with his activists, who had been gearing up in the expectation of another campaign with him. Dr S. Vasoo, part of the PAP Tanjong Pagar team (and also chairman of the Tiong Bahru Town Council) knew some of the key activists. It took all of his personal skills, as well as an intervention by PM Goh, to convince the activists to accept the change—but not before an extremely heated meeting.[366] Eventually most of the branch activists came round, with most (but not all) electing to stay on with Lim and continuing to help out at the branch level, some for a good number of years.[367]

There had been similar episodes at other branches, in other elections. Activists did not in themselves—no matter how strong their feelings on such matters—have the power to effect a change in the MP. But mismanagement of the situation by the new entrant could lead to a situation where activists "downed tools" and simply stopped volunteering their time, which could affect cohesion at the branch and hamstring the MP's efforts at making connections with residents. This was avoided in Telok Blangah, where Lim subsequently worked hard to gain the trust of activists, avoiding (in particular) making the mistake of bringing in his own friends and associates to supplant established activists, which would have frayed relations further.[368]

Dr Tay Eng Soon, anchor minister of the PAP's team for Eunos GRC, had as we have seen played the star role in a last-minute switch in 1988. On that occasion, the stratagem had been devised earlier, with the likely strength of the WP's team in Eunos GRC in mind. Having prevailed in 1988 with his GRC teammates (Chew Heng Ching and Zulkifli bin Mohammed), Dr Tay and team (Sidek Saniff, Chew Heng Ching and Charles Chong) again faced a tough battle in 1991 in what was now a four-member GRC. Again, Eunos proved a flashpoint for personalities and (to the PAP leadership's mind, at least) issues. The PAP team won by a narrow 52.38 per cent against a Workers' Party team comprising Dr Lee Siew Choh, Wee Han Kim, Neo Choon Aik and Mohd Jufrie Mahmood. In his campaigning, Jufrie had accused the government of being "anti-religion" and also claimed that Sidek Saniff from the PAP slate had sold out on his moral and religious principles.[369] The PAP view was that Jufrie had indulged in extremist politics, with Party leaders taking particular exception to Jufrie's Islamic invocations at rallies, which the PAP felt were attempts to carry the Malay ground and gain political support.[370]

Immediately after the narrow PAP victory in the GRC, Dr Tay Eng Soon mused that the PAP warnings of communal politicking had not been taken seriously. The close result may have been a "weak signal" that "Singaporeans don't understand the danger of communal politics".[371] Tay's remarks were echoed by Goh in his post-election press conference. "I find it incomprehensible that on this basic issue, we should have won by only such a small margin," he said, adding that his conclusion was that voters there had not understood the gravity of what communal politics could portend for Singapore.[372]

The remarks by Goh and Tay were similar to the comments made by PAP leaders in the aftermath of the 1988 campaign in Eunos—in 1988, there was a sense of disbelief within the PAP that Francis Seow had come so close to winning, despite strenuous attempts by the PAP to "expose" him during the campaign. What the PAP leadership appears to have had difficulty realising was that the electorate could in fact overlook personal failings of any candidate, and even shrug off matters of alleged communal politics. This was particularly where the constituency in question was hotly contested and was seen as being the Opposition's best chance in that election. Besides this, people found it difficult to accept the charge of communal politics in 1991. The charge of racial politicking was, in fact, questioned by figures such as S. Rajaratnam (former DPM and senior minister) and prominent members of the Malay community, including the chief executive of Mendaki, Zainul Abidin Rasheed.[373]

Eunos may have been the flashpoint in 1991, but it was not where the real damage was done to the Party. Nationally, the Party's share of the vote declined to 61 per cent (from 63.2 per cent in 1988). Three single-member constituencies were lost: Hougang (to the WP's Low Thia Khiang), Nee Soon Central (to the SDP's Cheo Chai Chen) and Bukit Gombak (to SDP chairman Ling How Doong). In addition, SDP chief Chiam See Tong comfortably retained his Potong Pasir seat. The loss in Bukit Gombak meant the unseating of a PAP office-holder (Acting Minister for Community Development Seet Ai Mee) for the first time since 1963. There were also other marginal PAP wins in some SMCs.[374] The result was particularly pleasing for the SDP, which gained 48.02 per cent of the vote in the seats that it contested.[375]

Sombre reactions at post-election conferences were not exactly unknown in the PAP's history, but there were important differences in the early morning post-election analysis between 1984 and 1991. Goh had staked a great deal, personally, on the outcome of the 1991 election. The result was a personal setback to him. Goh commented at the press conference in the early hours of 1 September 1991 that he would need to change his style and there had been a rejection of his call for support for himself, his style and his policies.[376] Goh's reaction was, of course, an overreaction, if an understandable one. It did not take long for it to become clear that voters had been happy to give Goh the personal endorsement he asked for—77.25 per cent in Marine Parade GRC. Letters to the *Straits Times* Forum made it clear that there had been no rejection by the voters of Goh's style.[377] It became clear, in short, that things were not actually that bad. This was also apparent when comparing percentages of votes cast for the PAP in wards contested in both 1988 and 1991.[378] By this measure, the PAP vote share had declined only 2.2 per cent.

Some reasons for Opposition gains were clear. Chiam See Tong's by-election strategy (of allowing the PAP to be returned to power on Nomination Day) had worked. The people had reason to believe that they could now safely vote for Opposition candidates in order to have the best of both worlds—a PAP in government and an Opposition in Parliament. As the post-mortem report was to note, the PAP could not find a convincing counter to this argument. But Opposition tactics could not explain the result in its entirety. The question nagged away at Goh: Why? Even more than two months after the election, Goh would express his perplexity when addressing the PAP convention on 17 November 1991: "I cannot understand why Singaporeans are still so dissatisfied. Year after year, our lives become better in terms of standards, in terms of income. The votes go down. The more open and friendly we are, the better we do for Singaporeans, the worse for votes."[379]

The matter had to be investigated in depth.

Local Issues

Local issues affected the outcome in constituencies that the PAP lost. In Hougang SMC Low Thia Khiang, 35, had built on the credibility he had earned through his performance in the 1988 televised Mandarin debate on the elected president proposal, where he had left an impression by holding his own against BG Lee Hsien Loong. Even so, his defeat of the PAP's Tang Guan Seng had not been foreseen by the PAP's Elections Task Force, which had the internal codename Task Force 93. The task force, chaired by Foreign Affairs Minister Wong Kan Seng, had met regularly in the lead-up to the polls—and close to Polling Day itself, daily.[380] The task force's assessment even in late August was that Tang Guan Seng was not likely to lose in Hougang.[381] Interviewed for this book, Dr Lee Boon Yang (chairman of the task force's Candidates Liaison Committee) suggested that Low had chosen his target constituency with care. Low was even likely aware of ground disquiet in Hougang concerning Tang Guan Seng's perceived inaccessibility to residents.[382] Low, of course, also did much of his campaigning in dialect, making extremely well-received speeches in eloquent Teochew. For the first time in an election campaign since the 1960s, dialect was used successfully not just as the primary medium of campaigning but as a means to stir up emotions. The post-mortem report was to acknowledge that dialect and clan loyalties persisted and had been underestimated.[383]

There were other local issues. The most well-known was that of Acting Minister for Community Development Seet Ai Mee, whose notorious "hand-washing" (an incident that occurred during campaigning for the 1988 election) came back to haunt her in 1991.[384] Another local issue was the alleged failure by the town council in Nee Soon Central to provide burners for burning joss paper during the Seventh Moon period.[385] The incumbent PAP MP, Ng Pock Too, was unseated by the SDP's Cheo Chai Chen by a wafer-thin margin of 168 votes.[386]

Communication mattered. It was difficult to counter allegations or smears against candidates in 1991 because the PAP had decided to replace traditional rallies with dialogue sessions.[387] Dialogue sessions did not suffice for mobilising support or getting the word out through the coffeeshop grapevine. And where clarifications on local issues were attempted (as was the case with Goh Chok Tong speaking at an election rally about Seet Ai Mee just two days before the polls), these could also backfire and give the issue greater circulation.[388]

Local issues were present in the 1991 election, as they had been to some extent or other in previous GEs. They were not, however, core themes of the post-election soul-searching and did not feature prominently in the post-mortem report. There had been too many close shaves in other constituencies without local issues, near-losses in constituencies where MPs were generally recognised to be both popular and effective communicators. Clearly changes were taking place within the electorate that needed to be understood. While the importance of bread-and-butter and cost-of-living issues were recognised, the leadership needed a finer resolution if it hoped to plot the course of the nation through the 1990s.

From Election Reflections to Post-mortem

The Post-Election Debrief Committee was constituted quickly, with DPM Lee Hsien Loong at its head. But even as the report was being worked on, individuals within the PAP were weighing in with their own analyses. Wong Kan Seng, the chairman of Task Force 93, was interviewed by *Petir* in September 1991. Wong zeroed in on cost-of-living and "bread and butter" issues, as well as the effect of Chiam See Tong's by-election strategy.[389] The same issue of *Petir* featured an editorial by John Chen, chairman of the PAP's Publicity and Publications Committee (and MP for Hong Kah GRC), which expanded further on the reasons for the Opposition's success. Chen noted that some might have felt the need for an Opposition on account of disenchantment with certain government policies, the consequences of which were felt across the board and across all races. Chen noted that there were groups of people in the lower socio-economic category who were "struggling to make ends meet". Finally, Chen noted that some amongst the Chinese-educated felt alienated "as they feel their culture and traditions withering".[390]

Cost-of-living issues factored in every general election. But the point about the Chinese-educated was new, and it was this point that was taken up and further developed by others. MP for Leng Kee and First Organising Secretary Dr Ow Chin Hock was interviewed by *Shin Min Daily News* on 7 September 1991. Ow acknowledged that cost of living was an issue as well as the desire for an Opposition, but he also noted that the new consultative-style government had favoured the English-educated and taken the Chinese-educated and older voters for granted.[391] This was Ow's personal reading of the ground; he had also been informed by feedback and comments by Party activists and community leaders before, during and after the election.[392] What was unsaid, but which Ow felt, was that there had been the perception of a gradual shift to elitism. People without whose support the PAP would not have come to power—the lower-income Chinese- and dialect-speaking classes—had been alienated.[393]

Others associated with the Party shared this view and were prepared to make it known without pulling punches. Speaking on the Chinese current affairs programme *Focus*, Lee Khoon Choy, who had stepped down as senior minister of state and member of parliament in 1984, noted that the PAP candidates were largely English-speaking and unable to communicate in Mandarin or dialects and (according to him) had no rapport with the grassroots. Lee's criticism was that the PAP had distanced itself from the masses by taking an elitist approach. Given that PAP candidates could, according to Lee, only speak English, "the future is pessimistic".[394]

Ong Teng Cheong and the Chinese Ground

Present and former MPs who voiced their views were not speaking in a vacuum. The leadership was paying close attention, and some quarters were sympathetic to the reading given by Ow Chin Hock and (to an extent) Lee Khoon Choy. Ow had soon after his interview with *Shin Min Daily News* been contacted by DPM Ong Teng Cheong. Ow's recollection is that Ong had wanted to find out more on Ow's assessment and his reading of the election result.[395] Ong was also in the process of clarifying his own thinking for an important speech that he was shortly to give.

DPM Ong spoke on 16 September 1991 at the Chinese Press Club. Ong (agreeing with John Chen and Dr Ow Chin Hock) noted that there were those who thought an Opposition was necessary, those who could not improve their standard of living, and those who blamed the government regardless of issues. Ong elaborated on Ow Chin Hock's theme of the fortunes of the Chinese-educated. To Ong, this was the real issue—the disadvantaged and the struggling classes, who were to him predominantly the Chinese-educated.

> *They feel that the Government is greatly influenced by a small group of English educated who dare to criticise and dare to speak up, but has not taken the views of the Chinese educated seriously.*

> *The relaxation of censorship, in their view, is the result of the pressure from a small group of the English educated who want greater freedom. The Chinese educated are fearful that moral standards of the society will deteriorate. On the other hand, they feel that their concern and worries over the Chinese culture and language have not attracted due attention of the Government. They feel that although the Government keeps mentioning the importance of learning the mother tongue, it has not given serious attention and care to the use of the Chinese language and development of the Chinese culture.*

> *They also feel that because of the dominating role of the English language in the society, and because the English educated Singaporeans are holding all the key appointments, the Chinese educated Singaporeans do not have the opportunity to rise in society. And because of the difference in values and perceptions, they feel that they are unable to communicate with the elites in society.*

> *Cabinet members and senior civil servants are predominantly English educated technocrats. They could not understand the thinking and the views expressed by*

the Chinese educated Singaporeans. They also could not understand the problems of the lower middle income group and the ordinary folks.

The Chinese educated have often wondered if they are there only to be pushed around. Why can't they have the right to take part in policy decision-making? But they keep their grievances to themselves, and have become the neglected "silent majority". Indeed their unhappiness is not the result of recent developments. They have probably felt this way for a long time. The PAP will take a serious look at this particular issue in greater depth. The feeling of dislocation of the society among the Chinese-educated Singaporeans must be corrected at the earliest opportunity.[396]

In Ong's view, the Chinese-educated working class had different aspirations and objectives in life compared to the English-educated: "Through the use of votes in this election, they reminded the Government of their existence, their problems, their feelings and their concerns."

What was not known at the time was that Ong had shared his concerns, and the substance of his planned remarks, with other Party leaders (including PM Goh) in advance. Ong was encouraged to speak on the issue and to find a suitable venue to do so before the issue "got cold".[397] Unsurprisingly, then, PM Goh gave a measured response to Ong's remarks, acknowledging that Ong represented the conservative Chinese-educated ground, and had voiced in particular concerns of the lower-income Chinese community.

Other leaders absorbed the point about Chinese-educated and their aspirations. In October 1991, SM Lee made it a point to note publicly during his speaking engagements that the government knew that more reaching out needed to be done to the Chinese ground, and that not enough had been done to promote their language and culture.[398] Lee had, in fact, been concerned for some time and was particularly aware of the disenchantment within the Chinese community following the conversion of all vernacular schools to the English medium by 1987. In the late 1980s, Lee had engaged Dr Tony Tan, then the minister for education, extensively in discussions on the issue of Chinese-language education and language competency in schools. For example, Lee had written to Dr Tan in early 1989 concerning the idea of strengthening Chinese-language primary schools over the coming years. Lee resurfaced this idea— this time publicly—after the election in October 1991, suggesting that Chinese clan associations be allowed to run a number of primary schools.[399] PM Lee had separately (in 1990) requested that MOE undertake a review on the teaching of the Chinese language.[400] This led to the setting up of the Chinese Language Review Committee (CLRC) headed by DPM Ong in June 1991. It is clear, therefore, that significant steps were taken to meet the concerns of the Chinese ground—especially with respect to language and culture—before the 31 August 1991 election.[401]

Was this enough? Policy was one thing, emotional connection another. Towards the end of his premiership, PM Lee had tried to bring home the message to his Cabinet colleagues that on certain occasions Mandarin should (besides English) be used to communicate, and that exclusive use of English ran the risk of alienating sections of the

Party faithful who lacked English competence.[402] After the 1991 election, Lee reflected in public that the changing composition and educational profile of the Cabinet made it more difficult for the leadership to be aware of Chinese ground sentiments.[403] PM Goh took the point to heart, even acknowledging that PAP MPs might have to speak dialects to reach more Chinese, even if this would in some ways be a retrogressive step for the community.[404]

Goh's main point, however, was not about the Chinese ground. While acknowledging that DPM Ong's critique had been valid, Goh felt that the government had lost support from those who were in the lower economic strata, and that it was "coincidence" that many Chinese-speaking Singaporeans fell in this group. There were others in this group who were Malay- and English-speaking.[405] Others within the PAP leadership came to similar conclusions. Soon after the election, DPM Lee had written to PM Goh, enclosing a 3 September 1991 *Business Times* article titled "What the Voters Are Saying"—an article that was to be influential and debated extensively within the Party leadership.[406] The article noted that the election result was not about "woolly issues" such as PM Goh's style or "The Next Lap". The decline in support was really about bread-and-butter issues (these included the cost of cars, fees at independent schools, and rising hospital bills). DPM Lee gave PM Goh his own observations:

> *The real problem is the increasing gap between the elite of yuppies and professionals, and the working class Singaporeans who know that they themselves will never be that successful however hard they work, and neither will their children. . . . The PAP's argument has been that life in Singapore has improved for everyone, for those at the bottom as much as for those near the top. But this does not satisfy those who remain near the bottom. They want to see the first last and the last first. We knew that this was a simmering problem, which we tried to defuse. . . . But the balm has changed neither the reality, nor the perception.[407]*

Zeroing in on the real reasons for disquiet was DPM Lee's assignment as chairman of the Post-mortem Committee.[408] But Lee had occasion to write to PM Goh again in September, with a quite different concern. Lee had visited many of the PAP branches, especially in the marginal constituencies, in the course of his work. The mood was sullen and recriminatory. PAP activists had attacked car park charges, time-based phone charges, fees at independent schools, higher medical fees (resulting from the restructuring of government hospitals) and shophouse rentals as vehemently as any Opposition politician. Lee commented to Goh, "If our supporters feel like this, the mood of the uncommitted must be much worse." The mood was not helped, Lee observed, by media coverage after the election which reflected the souring of the mood after the elections (an issue which we shall return to). Lee suggested a line had to be drawn:

> *While we work out our long term position, I think we should respond to the immediate situation. Unless the Government takes a clear lead, popular opinion*

will continue to drift, lose perspective and get out of hand. It is totally untrue that
PAP policies have hurt the people, that we have wrongly biased our actions in
favour of the rich and privileged, and that everything we have done in education
healthcare and economics is wrong. The widespread improvement of standards of
living in Singapore is real and continuing, even if it is being taken for granted.
Life in Singapore is getting better, not worse, for nearly all Singaporeans.

. . . There is no need for the Government to take a harsher line in public than the
mellifluous rhetoric we have confined ourselves to for the last few months. But we
should stop the public soul searching and breast-beating, and proceed in a matter
of fact way with the business of governing Singapore. We and the public should
discuss the substance of what we need to do, not how nicely we propose to approach
our problems. Unless we continue to make progress and achieve economic growth,
we will only have less to distribute and more to quarrel over.[409]

The Party, and government, had to move on.

The PAP Convention, November 1991

Party leaders had by the time of the November 1991 PAP convention come to the general recognition that votes had been lost because of the wide swathe of the population left out of the nation's progress. DPM Ong himself was by this stage prepared to see the problem as being not solely confined to the Chinese-educated. At the opening of the convention, Ong noted that just as the PAP provided opportunities for the better-endowed to help create a better Singapore, ways must be found to look after the common man and the underclass, regardless of their ethnic origins: "This way, our party will then be able to continue to enjoy the support of the majority of Singaporeans."[410]

The team engaged in the post-mortem process had (per normal practice) sent copies of the post-election questionnaire to branches, as well as making branch visits for the Post-mortem Committee. Separately, Goh had asked MPs—especially from the constituencies that had seen close results—for their assessments and for views on how to recover lost ground. These MPs had in several cases sent in their own post-mortem reports. The reports and feedback kept coming back to the same bread-and-butter issue that had been highlighted to DPM Lee and his team on their branch visits. Other issues (such as Goh's style; or issues from recent years such as communalism, religion and politics; or the Maintenance of Religious Harmony Act) were conspicuous by their absence.[411] Also almost completely absent was the sense that government measures such as Edusave and MediFund had made much of an impact in alleviating some of the issues associated with the rising cost of living. There was, in fact, hardly any suggestion of gratitude.

Activists from City North District had submitted a paper for discussion at the convention. The paper repeated assertions that the Party was perceived as money-grabbing and elitist and echoed suggestions that the PAP was out of touch.[412] This elicited a strong response from Goh, who during his speech at the convention on 17 November chose to make a robust defence of PAP policies. Goh's view was that Singaporeans wanted more subsidies, but therein lay the road to economic and social disaster. In firmly rejecting subsidies and handouts, Goh said he would resign if he failed to convince Singaporeans of his point of view.[413]

What rankled with Goh and led to his robust defence of the PAP's economic philosophy at the convention was the idea that the PAP government was getting richer at the expense of the people. Here, Goh was actually taking issue with the wider criticism that had been floated by others, including Opposition MPs such as Low Thia Khiang. Low had exploited this point on the campaign trail, proclaiming at rallies "天顶一只 鹅，政府有钱，人民无" (In the sky there is a goose. The government has money, but not the people).[414] This catchphrase, implying that the government had exploited the people, was powerful and effective. It had more traction than the PAP's campaign line that surpluses should be returned and redistributed to the people, through means such as Edusave and MediFund.[415]

The theme of an extractive government resonated widely. A retired senior civil servant, Wong Yew Kwan, wrote a letter to the *Straits Times* Forum touching on the issue. Choosing his words carefully, Wong cited the philosopher Mencius' warning of the state which was jeopardised because "the King and the aristocracy of the day had forgotten about benevolence and righteousness and that, although they had already accumulated great wealth, they still went on scheming to gain more".[416] This was a theme that even the editor of the *Straits Times* felt moved to comment on, suggesting that the government find better ways to show that the country's reserves did indeed benefit the people.[417] After the election, PM Goh conceded that some of the previous government policies might have been relevant only to the upper tiers of society but that the government was now committed to "levelling up" and helping those who were not within the more affluent classes.[418] Surpluses had accumulated, and now the "pleasant problem" was how to allocate them to enhance the people's assets, such as through the refurbishing of public housing.[419]

The CEC met on 26 December 1991 to discuss this swirl of issues, to deliberate on the post-mortem report, and to discuss how to proceed in what seemed to be a changed Singapore. The report noted:

> Underlying long term trends in the structure and temperament of Singapore society are gradually eroding the PAP vote. If we had not called early elections, but continued with the policies of recent years and held elections in 1993 or 1994 as originally planned, the erosion would have gone further. The early elections have enabled us to detect the problem early and deal with it.[420]

"Dealing" with the problem meant that the people had to be appealed to in a way that would win them over.[421] Policies needed to be introduced that increased the value of people's assets. There was agreement that the government should redouble efforts at refurbishing and upgrading HDB flats and find ways to make the value of housing go up two to three times. This had to be done quickly, and results had to be seen.

In these discussions, economic pragmatism prevailed over pandering to populist sentiment. The CEC in discussing the post-mortem report agreed that more efforts had to be made not just to help children of poor families but to help and create hope for low-income groups (for example, upgrading neighbourhood schools rather than focusing on independent schools). Still, the overall direction would be to phase out subsidies, with people paying for goods and services at their true costs. The main problem, the report stated, was that the underlying sentiment tended in the opposite direction—since the perception existed that the government was rich, it should give subsidies, rather than trying to recover costs on its services. What this meant was that the ideas raised by the Party's detractors—of a rich and profiteering government—would become difficult to dispel. The impression held in some quarters of an extractive government would not go away—not in the 1990s, and not in the 2000s. It had not been an issue in 1988, but it was for the first time in 1991 and in every election after.

One final point in the post-mortem report the CEC took note of was to have reverberations through the 1990s and beyond. The report noted that there had to be some reward for those who supported the PAP, while those opposed to it had to pay some price. This (the report noted) had been discussed before, but it should now be followed up on, even though PAP supporters in Opposition wards disliked being penalised: "The gentle approach has failed repeatedly to win back Anson and Potong Pasir, and has contributed to the loss of fear and inhibition. This cannot continue. The PAP MPs now overwhelmingly support this approach, at least in principle."[422]

Closing Ranks

PM Goh's early morning press conference on 1 September 1991 gave a clear indication of what he thought the result portended. It was the start of a new phase in politics. There was now a "proper" Opposition in Parliament, with Chiam See Tong as its leader. Goh added that the PAP's role would be that of a conventional governing party in a conventional two-party situation: "The PAP's self-imposed opposition role is now over. In other words, PAP MPs have no further need to play opposition in Parliament. This role will be taken over by Mr Chiam and his opposition Members of Parliament."[423] These remarks are revealing in that they also show how Goh perceived the to and fro of parliamentary debate (sketched out earlier in this chapter) during the late 1980s. During this period backbench MPs had, notwithstanding the presence of Opposition MPs and NCMPs in Parliament, continued with a form of debate that was at times too robust and inquisitorial for Goh's liking. There was therefore to be a change in approach, now that the nation appeared to have entered into an era of a two-party system. Internal meetings were held where it was made clear that MPs were expected to tone down their criticism of policies, and that strong disagreements should be confined to internal Party debate.[424] Unsurprisingly, PAP MPs interviewed for this book concur that the real closing of ranks took place after the 1991 (and not 1988) general election.

PM Goh also wanted the institutions he had had a key role in creating to operate differently. Chief among them were GPCs and the Feedback Unit. His initial view (expressed in the heat of the election aftermath, during the 1 September 1991 early morning press conference) was that GPCs would be scrapped now that there was a larger Opposition in Parliament. Soon after he appears to have reconsidered, stating that GPCs would continue to function but not in an adversarial manner that would pit PAP backbenchers against their own government.[425]

The aftermath of the 1991 election had seen ground discontent simmering for an unusual length of time. PAP leaders felt that this had been fed by unhelpful (and unflattering) post-election media. These analyses recycled issues such as the cost of living and thwarted the PAP's attempts to regain the high ground.[426] The feeling began to develop within the Party leadership that ongoing efforts at dialogue and garnering feedback had also indirectly contributed to the post-election malaise. Some of PM Goh's thinking can be glimpsed in a 27 December 1991 memo to Chandra Das, chairman of the Feedback Unit Supervisory Panel:

> The Feedback Unit should begin to cut down on public dialogues with media reporting. This is to avoid old issues being aired and fanned and the public using such dialogues to multiply opinion to put pressure on government policies. Even the frequency of closed-door dialogues can be scaled down to prevent the development of vested interest pressure groups.[427]

When Chandra Das stepped down as chairman of the supervisory panel in March 1992, there was considerable speculation that it was because of the inability of the unit to communicate with the Chinese ground, or even because the unit had "wrongly" advised the government that the timing was right for an election.[428] Interviewed for this book, Chandra Das pointed out that there had been many dialogues (close to 50 per cent of the total) in Chinese, and that others on the panel (such as Yu-Foo Yee Shoon and John Chen) attending and chairing sessions were Chinese-educated.[429] But the fact that Chandra Das' replacement was Dr Ow Chin Hock said a great deal. Ow had been one of the first to identify the alienation of the Chinese ground in post-election analysis.[430] The tenor of Feedback Unit dialogue sessions shifted, with dialogue sessions conducted for the first time in dialect. Dialogues were held at community centres instead of the Community Development Ministry. The aim, stated by government officials, was to bring in the "silent majority" that hitherto had not had the means to convey their views effectively to the unit.[431]

These were useful signals to send. Additional signals were needed to show the Chinese-speaking conservative ground that their concerns had not been forgotten. Goh had commented after the election that DPM Ong's speech at the Chinese Press Club had been a sign to him and George Yeo (minister for information and the arts, regarded as a liberal):

> That section [the Chinese-educated lower-income] might have felt that I was moving too fast because I was trying to reach out to the yuppies, the professionals . . . opening up discussion on the liberalising of film classifications, establishing

the Singapore International Foundation, and so on. . . . These policies do not
quite appeal to the lower-income group whose main concerns are essentially
bread-and-butter issues like carpark charges.[432]

The implication was that the government had moved too fast for what was still primarily a society very Asian in its outlook. The issue that had been especially singled out in PAP dialogue sessions during the campaign had been Restricted (R)-rated movies, with many objecting to the introduction of this category of films, which had more risqué content than what had previously been allowed.[433] Doing away with the R classification was a convenient signal, with the age minimum for the new Restricted (Artistic) or R(A) category raised from 18 to 21—all this barely a week after the election result.[434]

George Yeo described this period as one where he was under significant pressure, held up by observers and the media as a liberal and a symbol of English-educated yuppies. Yeo was friendly with DPM Ong and did not believe that Ong's 16 September 1991 remarks were personally directed at him. At the same time, Yeo did not think that the reasons offered by Ong for the election reverse encapsulated what was happening in Singapore society. Yeo chose instead to look at the broad sweep of Singapore's development until the 2011 elections, and the inevitability of events as society matured. To him, the 1990s and the election in 1991 marked the beginnings of an important awakening:

> *I don't think that that was the main reason. It was Singapore's transformation.*
> *It is quite remarkable how a strong PAP Government lifted whole communities,*
> *relocated them and then tried to reform them after possessing their land and so*
> *on. In many of these places whether it was in Nee Soon or in Hougang, there*
> *remains considerable resentment, deep resentment. . . . It has been building up.*
> *I look at the Lee Kuan Yew era from that perspective. He created the country.*
> *He was dominant. He reprogrammed all of us—from dialects to Mandarin, de-*
> *emphasised clans and so on . . . and then achieved great unity of purpose so that*
> *we were able to do remarkable things and build new institutions. And then people*
> *got tired of the forced march. They said no, and now [after the 2011 election]*
> *there is this huge revolt against some of the old policies. In a sense, society must be*
> *rebuilt from the bottom up with much wider participation . . . this process began*
> *in the 1990s or even before.*[435]

March On

The 1991 election post-mortem report noted that the polls and the aftermath had been notable especially for the lack of fear: people believed that they could now pressurise the government and individual MPs. Even grassroots leaders, themselves under pressure, preferred to attack rather than defend government policies. If a balance was not restored, governing between elections would become increasingly difficult: "The public must learn that consultation does not mean weakness and should not encourage contempt. Otherwise they will believe that they can pressure the government, and lose the traditional respect for authority."[436]

Apart from the 1 September 1991 early morning press conference, PM Goh never gave a public hint that he was under pressure at this time. But concerns on how to govern in his own style, while maintaining the traditional respect his predecessor had had, must have weighed heavily. SM Lee had himself written to Goh on 16 September 1991, highlighting feedback from Chinese-educated MPs:

> *There is now absolutely no fear of the government and PAP MPs. The government is thought to be powerless to hurt anybody. . . . They [Chinese-educated MPs] believe that if the Chinese-educated do not hold the government in some awe, that spells trouble. It comes back to the problem of who will carry the big stick for you.*[437]

Goh's note in reply summed up his mood: "SM, I have to carry the big stick myself— quietly like Suharto."[438] Goh may well have been encouraged by the number of letters and notes written to him by MPs. Several ranged beyond the usual election analyses and were of a personal nature, encouraging Goh to stay the course. One in particular stands out. This was from Fong Sip Chee, the veteran PAP politician who in the course of his political career had suffered his own disappointments:

> *Dear Chok Tong*
>
> *I watched through the election results and your press conference. I share your anguish. Perhaps my only feeling is that of concern and disappointment. I do hope you will find time to read this letter.*
>
> *Do pardon me for taking the liberty as an old guard to offer a few words of counsel, for whatever they are worth. My view, and that which I gathered from many people is that, "Go on, we want you to be our PM." You should now stop talking about what the results meant to your premiership. Frankly, it was wrong of you in this instance to have staked your personal position on this issue. . . . The concentration on the dialogue sessions was a mistake. For whatever effects they were supposed to have brought about, media coverage, for instance, they were efforts trying to convince the already convinced, or converted. They left out the older voters who would not have participated in such exercises. They felt neglected. In bygone days, we said we would fight, and did fight for every vote. This time around, we neglected and ignored the old voters. To the older folks, the TV coverage meant: "Look what these young people are trying to decide what to do to us." My view is: have the dialogue sessions by all means, but do something to reach out to the older voters. On their own, the sessions were counter-productive.*[439]

Fong offered his own analysis and criticism. But his overall slant was positive, and quite different from those post-election critiques which had suggested a bleak future for the PAP. Unconsciously echoing SM Lee, Fong proffered his own advice:

> I remember handing you a copy of a Chinese classic as a token of my good wishes on your assumption of premiership. What happened is almost exactly what the article described. You are a gentleman, kind and honest. But you must carry the cane too, or people will climb all over you and take advantage of your kindness. I am sending you another copy. I hope you would read it over again. May I conclude by being as candid as you always have been. I say, "March on, Chok Tong. Let not this little setback deter you."[440]

The extracts enclosed by Fong were from a translation of a Chinese classic, the *Zuo Commentary*:

> When government is mild, the people despise it. When they despise it, severity must take its place. When the government is severe, the people are slaughtered. When this takes place, they must be dealt with mildly. Mildness serves to temper severity, and severity to regulate mildness; it is in this way that the administration of the government is brought to harmony.[441]

Goh would take heed.[442]

Notes

1   PAP Central Executive Committee Report October 1984–October 1986 (PAP archive).
2   *1984 General Election PAP Post-mortem Report* (PAP archive). The number of new voters in 1984 was 251,000, with the actual votes cast much lower on account of walkovers and spoilt votes. "251,000 Will Vote for First Time", *Straits Times*, 30 June 1984.
3   Minutes of PAP Central Executive Committee Meeting, 24 July 1986 (PAP archive); "Some Changes to Party Organisation", PAP internal paper (PAP archive). See also "Party Will Spend a Year Gathering Views", *Straits Times*, 22 Nov. 1986; and "Five Ways to Let Voters Have Say", *Straits Times*, 11 Dec. 1986.
4   "Party Manifesto" (note from BG Lee Hsien Loong to all PAP MPs, 31 Jan. 1987, PAP archive).
5   "PAP Reaches Out for Consensus", *Straits Times*, 19 Feb. 1987.
6   Ibid.
7   "The Men Who Came Up with the Concept", *Straits Times*, 12 Dec. 1984.
8   Exchange of letters between SG Lee Kuan Yew and Goh Chok Tong, 6 Dec. 1984 and 9 Jan. 1985 (PAP archive).
9   "Ailment in the Body Politic", *Straits Times*, 30 Dec. 1984.

10 *1984 General Election PAP Post-mortem Report.* Amongst the better-remembered facets of Vision 1999 was the goal to make Singapore reach the "Swiss standard" of living by 1999. "First Division Singapore", *Straits Times*, 12 Dec. 1984.

11 For a convenient summary of issues discussed under the Agenda, see "The National Agenda: The Outline—and a Host of Questions", *Petir*, Feb. 1987, pp. 8, 19–20; and May 1987 ("The National Agenda: Questions Part II"), pp. 21–2.

12 "People Now Looking Closely at National Problems: BG Lee", *Straits Times*, 20 Apr. 1987.

13 "View It as a 'Public Education Exercise'", *Straits Times*, 6 Apr. 1987. One-day "national education" courses specifically for grassroots leaders were also organised.

14 "Party Manifesto".

15 Ibid. The Manifesto Committee comprised BG Lee Hsien Loong (chairman), Dr Lee Boon Yang, Dr Ow Chin Hock, Abdullah Tarmugi, Wong Kan Seng, Tang Guan Seng, Goh Chee Wee, Dr Aline Wong, Yeo Cheow Tong, Yatiman Yusof and Dr Tan Cheng Bock. The fact that eight of the committee members were drawn from the group first voted in in 1984 was perhaps indicative of the Party's growing desire to communicate effectively with the younger generation. "Singaporeans to Have a Say on Their Future", *Petir*, Jan. 1987, p. 7.

16 "PAP Reaches Out for Consensus".

17 "House to Debate Agenda for Action", *Straits Times*, 20 Feb. 1988.

18 Chan Heng Chee, "The Structuring of the Political System", in *Management of Success*, ed. Kernial Singh Sandhu and Paul Wheatley (Singapore: Institute of Southeast Asian Studies, 1989), pp. 70–89, esp. 83.

19 "Young PAP Leaders Get Closer to the Ground", *Straits Times*, 4 Feb. 1986.

20 Speech by PM Lee Kuan Yew, Party convention, 23 Jan. 1988 (PAP archive).

21 *Agenda for Action: Goals and Challenges. Misc. 2 of 1988. Presented to Parliament by the First Deputy Prime Minister and Minister for Defence and Ordered by Parliament to lie upon the Table,* 15 Feb. 1988, available at https://www.nas.gov.sg/archivesonline/ government_records/record-details/3e92c6fb-7958-11e7-83df-0050568939ad (accessed 23 Jan. 2021).

22 "Six Ministers Head 'Action Teams'", *Straits Times*, 26 Feb. 1988; "Councils Have Six to Nine Months to Finish Work", *Straits Times*, 20 Apr. 1988.

23 An example is the 1989 report by the Advisory Council on Culture and the Arts led by 2DPM Ong Teng Cheong. See Bridget Welsh, James U.H. Chin, Arun Mahizhnan and Tan Tarn How (eds), *Impressions of the Goh Chok Tong Years in Singapore* (Singapore: NUS Press, 2009), pp. 425–35, esp. 428–9.

24 This was the third major series of walkabouts in the Party's history. The first began in 1962. The second was from 1982 to 1984.

25 "Tour by 4 Ministers Today Brings Walkabout Series to a Close", *Straits Times*, 20 Nov. 1988.

26 "Younger Ministers to Lead New Round of 'Few Frills' Walkabouts", *Straits Times*, 19 Feb. 1987.

27 "Feeling the Constituency's Pulse", *Straits Times*, 19 Apr. 1987.

28 "What the Results Mean", *Straits Times*, 23 Dec. 1984; "PM Replies to Voters' Signal", *Straits Times*, 24 Dec. 1984. For Lee's publicly expressed doubts in 1984 on the usefulness of one-man-one-vote, see "Can the One-Man-One-Vote System Continue to Work for Singapore?" (speech by PM Lee at the National Day Celebration at the Tanjong Pagar

Community Centre, 16 Aug. 1984): "The question is whether one-man-one-vote will continue to work in Singapore under different leaders. I believe it can, provided we can get sincere, honest and able men to run for elections, and also provided we make adjustments from time to time to meet the changing conditions of our society." *The Papers of Lee Kuan Yew, Vol. 9*, pp. 313–8, esp. 317.

29   Goh: "The Prime Minister has more experience than ourselves, so let him come up with modifications. He will not come up with proposals that will not be suited to Singapore. But our position is that whatever the proposals, he must convince us that they are for the better for all of us." "People Will Have the Final Say—Chok Tong", *Straits Times*, 1 Jan. 1985.

30   Goh Chok Tong, interview with the author, 22 June 2012.

31   For conventional accounts of the evolution of the institution of the elected presidency, see James Cotton, "Political Innovation in Singapore: The Presidency, the Leadership and the Party", in *Singapore Changes Guard: Social, Political and Economic Directions in the 1990s*, ed. Garry Rodan (New York: St. Martin's Press, 1993), pp. 3–33, esp. 8–9; and the various contributions in Kevin Y.L. Tan and Lam Peng Er (eds), *Managing Political Change in Singapore: The Elected Presidency* (London: Routledge, 1997).

32   A sense of this ongoing thinking can be gleaned from the interviews that the New Zealand academic Dr Raj Vasil had with government leaders, including S. Rajaratnam, in 1983. See Raj Vasil, *Governing Singapore* (Singapore: Mandarin, 1992), pp. 218–9.

33   "Introducing Safeguards to Protect Singaporeans", PM Lee Kuan Yew, National Day Rally Speech at the Singapore Conference Hall and Trade Union House, 19 Aug. 1984. *National Day Rally Speeches: 50 Years of Nationhood in Singapore 1966–2015*, pp. 118–9; "From the Politics of Poverty to the Politics of Progress", *Straits Times*, 20 Aug. 1984. See also "Elected President 'Ensures Security'", *Straits Times*, 26 Aug. 1984. Lee was here amplifying on comments made on 15 April 1984 (the first time he alluded publicly to the possibility of enhanced presidential powers with a blocking mechanism to prevent a future government squandering the nation's reserves). "24 Years of Hard Work Could Vanish in 25 Days", *Straits Times*, 16 Apr. 1984. See Hussin Mutalib, "Singapore's First Elected Presidency: The Political Motivations", in *Managing Political Change in Singapore*, ed. Tan and Lam, pp. 167–87, esp. 174.

34   *White Paper on Constitutional Amendments to Safeguard Financial Assets and the Integrity of the Public Services, Cmd. 10 of 1988.* Presented to Parliament on 29 July 1988, available at https://www.nas.gov.sg/archivesonline/government_records/record-details/ebace2d2-8133-11e7-83df-0050568939ad (accessed 23 Jan. 2021). Parliament on 12 August 1988 adopted after debate a motion supporting the principles set out in the White Paper as the basis for preparing a bill for an elected president. Singapore Parliamentary Debates, 12 Aug. 1988, cols 571–638; "No Referendum, Says Chok Tong", *Straits Times,* 13 Aug. 1988.

35   "Pang Boon Not Convinced System Should Be Changed", *Straits Times*, 13 Aug. 1988.

36   Singapore Parliamentary Debates, 12 Aug. 1988, col. 573.

37   Ibid., cols 573–4; "Pang Boon Not Convinced System Should Be Changed". Toh Chin Chye's intervention in this parliamentary debate was muted compared to Ong's but should also be seen as being directed against the possibility of Lee becoming president: "We

should not bulldoze this because we are committing future generations of Singapore to a scheme which may not be workable. I do not know how many Ministers have a great yen to be the President in future. They may not. They may want to leave the Istana." Singapore Parliamentary Debates, 12 Aug. 1988, cols 599–600.

38   Lee Kuan Yew, National Day Rally Speech at the Kallang Theatre, 14 Aug. 1988. *National Day Rally Speeches: 50 Years of Nationhood in Singapore*, p. 186; "Me Retire? Those Who Believe That Should Have Their Heads Examined", *Straits Times*, 15 Aug. 1988. In his memoirs, Lee acknowledged that "many believed I was preparing a position for myself after I stepped down as Prime Minister". But his views on the possibility of standing for the position were clear: he had "no interest in this high office as it would be too passive for my temperament". Lee Kuan Yew, *From Third World to First*, pp. 196–7.

39   *Safeguarding Financial Assets and the Integrity of the Public Services: The Constitution of the Republic of Singapore (Amendment No. 3) Bill, Cmd. 11 of 1990.* Presented to Parliament on 27 Aug. 1990, pp. 6–7, available at https://www.nas.gov.sg/archivesonline/government_records/record-details/ac86db7a-7aea-11e7-83df-0050568939ad (accessed 23 Jan. 2021). See also Kevin Y.L. Tan, "The Elected Presidency in Singapore: Constitution of the Republic of Singapore (Amendment) Act 1991", *Singapore Journal of Legal Studies* (July 1991): 179–94, esp. 182.

40   The select committee was chaired by the Speaker of Parliament, Tan Soo Khoon, and comprised key Cabinet ministers as well as the sole Opposition member of parliament, Chiam See Tong. *Report of the Select Committee on the Constitution of the Republic of Singapore (Amendment No. 3) Bill [Bill No. 23/90]. Parl. 9 of 1990.* Presented to Parliament on 18 Dec. 1990, available at https://www.nas.gov.sg/archivesonline/government_records/record-details/eba96b29-0537-11e8-a2a9-001a4a5ba61b (accessed 23 Jan. 2021).

41   *Report of the Select Committee on the Constitution of the Republic of Singapore (Amendment No. 3) Bill [Bill No. 23/90],* pp. iii–xii. Other clauses were broadened to apply to requiring the president's concurrence and approval for appointments to the Presidential Council on Religious Harmony, the Advisory Board constituted under the Internal Security Act, and chairmen and members/directors of the boards of key statutory boards/government companies. Additional changes were made to the financial aspects of the president's powers. These included provisions mandating that audited statements of the budgets, revenues and expenditure, as well as assets and liabilities of statutory boards and government companies, be submitted to the president, with similar controls imposed on the minister for finance regarding government budgets, while the requirement for presidential approval in the incurring of government debt was done away with (pp. xxxi–xxxviii). For full discussion of the provisions of the final bill, see Kevin Y.L. Tan, "The Elected Presidency in Singapore", pp. 179–94.

42   Speech by President Ong Teng Cheong at the swearing-in of the fifth president at the Istana on Wednesday, 1 Sept. 1993, available at https://www.nas.gov.sg/archivesonline/speeches/record-details/71dbf6ad-115d-11e3-83d5-0050568939ad (accessed 23 Jan. 2021). In standing for the elected presidency, Ong came up against Chua Kim Yeow, a former accountant-general and banker. Chua put negligible effort and resources into campaigning but managed to win 41.3% of the vote against Ong's 58.7%, in a sign that

many voters preferred a president without any ties to the ruling party. From the point of view of the leadership, a contest to decide Singapore's first elected president was preferable to none, with senior figures from the PAP (notably former DPM Dr Goh Keng Swee and Finance Minister Richard Hu) instrumental in persuading Chua to stand. See Chia Shi Teck, "Notes from the Margin: Reflections on the First Presidential Election, by a Former Nominated Member of Parliament", in *Managing Political Change in Singapore: The Elected Presidency*, ed. Tan and Lam, pp. 188–99, esp. 188; see also "Chua Kim Yeow, Singapore's First Local Accountant-General, Dies at Age of 90", *Straits Times*, 21 Aug. 2016.

43 Speech by President Ong Teng Cheong at the swearing-in of the fifth president at the Istana on Wednesday, 1 Sept. 1993; see "How I Will Do My Job: President Ong", *Straits Times*, 2 Sept. 1993.

44 After Devan Nair's sudden resignation in 1985, Lee (then PM) had sounded out Ong to see if he would be willing to take on the presidency. Ong, caught unprepared and considering himself too young, declined. 王鼎昌：走向总统府之路 [Ong Teng Cheong: Road to the Istana (*Lianhe Zaobao*, 1994)], p. 125. Cited in Huang Jianli, "The Head of State in Singapore: An Historical Perspective", in *Managing Political Change in Singapore: The Elected Presidency*, ed. Tan and Lam, p. 39n127.

45 "Elected President's Job Is to Be Strong, Not Popular—SM Lee", *Straits Times*, 2 Sept. 1993. In order to stand as a candidate for the 1993 presidential election, owing to criteria which had been introduced under the 1991 constitutional changes, Ong resigned from both his positions as second deputy prime minister and chairman of the PAP effective 16 August 1993. "Teng Cheong Quits Cabinet and His Party", *Straits Times,* 14 Aug. 1993; "DPM Ong's Resignation: Exchange of Letters", *Straits Times*, 14 Aug. 1993.

46 "'Vote MPs by Team' System Proposed", *Sunday Times*, 25 Jan. 1987; "Proposed Changes Won't Affect One-Man-One-Vote, Says MP", *Sunday Times*, 25 Jan. 1987.

47 Jon S.T. Quah, "Singapore in 1987: Political Reforms, Control, and Economic Recovery", *Southeast Asian Affairs* (1988): 235.

48 See "Team MPs Concept Can Ensure a Multi-racial House", *Straits Times*, 4 May 1987; and "For All Races to Ponder", *Straits Times*, 14 Apr. 1987.

49 PM Lee was making his points against the wider context of communal and religious differences not just in Singapore but in the region that complicated the task of nation-building. Lee Kuan Yew, National Day Rally Speech at the Kallang Theatre, 16 Aug. 1987. *National Day Rally Speeches: 50 Years of Nationhood in Singapore 1966–2015*, pp. 149–67, esp. 165–6. See also "Team MPs Proposal Can Ensure a Continued Multi-racial Parliament", *Straits Times*, 17 Aug. 1987.

50 See Edwin Lee, *Singapore: The Unexpected Nation* (Singapore: Institute of Southeast Asian Studies, 2008), pp. 499–500. As Edwin Lee notes, PM Lee appears to have been somewhat exasperated that the younger ministers had chosen the path of political correctness in linking the GRC concept to town councils.

51 "Idea Is Vague and May Backfire on the PAP", *Straits Times*, 12 Feb. 1987. See also Hussin Mutalib, *Parties and Politics: A Study of Opposition Parties and the PAP in Singapore* (2nd ed.) (Singapore: Marshall Cavendish, 2006), pp. 335–40.

52 "Team MPs: Cabinet Papers Released", *Straits Times*, 22 Jan. 1988.

53   At the time of the second reading of the Team MPs bill, PM Lee during a background briefing to newspaper editors noted that the first signs of race-based voting started to show in 1976. What Lee did not mention during the briefing, but what Party records show, is that his thinking on the subject went back even further. The idea of "twinning" constituencies makes a fleeting (but inconclusive) appearance in internal discussions in 1972. PM Lee had by this time already noticed that non-Chinese MPs had some difficulty rallying the ground in some areas. Lee wrote to MPs in September 1972, remarking that the recently concluded elections had seen chauvinistic appeals by some members of the Opposition. He noted that PAP Chinese MPs had helped minority PAP candidates by promising to pitch in and help in their wards. Lee wrote, "I propose that our non-Chinese MPs should choose a Chinese MP as his partner, or pair. Together, they can combine and look after the interests of both their constituents." Lee's idea was that the Chinese MP could help to bridge cultural and linguistic differences that the non-Chinese MP found more difficult to cross. The ethnic minority MP could in turn help handle non-Chinese residents. Lee further commented in his note to MPs: "And this will also help to calm down voters agitated by chauvinistic appeals. This problem is going to last for a long time. It may be another full generation, some 20–25 years, before we can have a population that talks a common language. Even then, there will be special difficulties, for there are the conservative who, for reasons of sentiment, prefer to deal direct with an MP of his own dialect or religion on personal problems, without the intervention of an interpreter." Letter from PM Lee Kuan Yew to all MPs, 26 Sept. 1972 (National Archives of Singapore), made available to the author.

54   "The Origins of the Team MPs Concept", *Straits Times*, 22 Jan. 1988; "PM Proposes Twin Constituencies Idea", *Straits Times*, 22 Jan. 1988; "Mattar Explains Why He Is against the Idea", *Straits Times*, 22 Jan. 1988; "I Can Understand Mattar's Reaction", *Straits Times*, 22 Jan. 1988; "Younger Ministers Have Reservations", *Straits Times*, 22 Jan. 1988.

55   "Team MPs: Cabinet Papers Released". The press coverage should be read in conjunction with the parliamentary proceedings, where amendments to the Parliamentary Elections Act (that would pave the way for GRCs) were debated, and where some of the history and evolution of thinking on the Team MP concept was given by PAP leaders. Singapore Parliamentary Debates, 11 Jan. 1988, cols 180–3. See also Jon S.T. Quah, "Singapore in 1988: Safeguarding the Future", in *Singapore 1989* (Information Division, Ministry of Communications and Information), pp. 3–4.

56   "I Can Understand Mattar's Reaction". When PM Lee had mooted what became the twinning idea in 1982, the Indian PAP MPs had not been supportive of the idea of having Indian MPs elected through this route. "Team MPs: Cabinet Papers Released".

57   S. Chandra Das, interview with the author, 16 Nov. 2012.

58   PM Lee was to remark on Chandra Das' close shave during the 1988 Select Committee hearings on the GRC proposal. *Report of the Select Committee on the Parliamentary Elections (Amendment) Bill [Bill No. 23/87] and the Constitution of the Republic of Singapore (Amendment No. 2) Bill [Bill No. 24/87], Parl. 3 of 1988. Presented to Parliament on 5 May 1988, Minutes of Evidence*, 9 Mar. 1988, cols 1368, 1392, available at https://www.nas.gov.sg/archivesonline/government_records/record-details/982b35cd- 0537-11e8-a2a9-001a4a5ba61b (accessed 23 Jan. 2021).

59   "MPs' Deft Performance Leaves No Room for Bruised Feelings", *Straits Times*, 12 Jan. 1988. The "that Indian man" comment was also cited 32 years later, by PM Lee Hsien Loong, while campaigning in May 2016 in support of Murali Pillai, who was contesting the Bukit Batok by-election against the SDP's Dr Chee Soon Juan. "PM Cautions against Exploiting Sentiments Based on Race", *Straits Times*, 1 May 2016.

60   "SDP's Ling Denies He Campaigned on Racial Lines", *Straits Times*, 20 Jan. 1988; "I Am Stating Bare Facts", *Straits Times*, 9 Feb. 1988.

61   *Straits Times* Forum letters: "Opposition Rejection Underlines Need for Team MPs", 19 Jan. 1988; "SDP a Multi-racial Party: Chiam", 26 Jan. 1988; "Does SDP Support Such a Policy?", 28 Jan. 1988; "Chiam Should Sack Ling if He's Not in Line", 29 Jan. 1988; "SDP Shows It Is Not Multi-racial", 29 Jan. 1988; "More Multi-racial than PAP", 9 Feb. 1988; "Chong Boon Residents Willing to Appear before SDP Inquiry", 13 Feb. 1988.

62   Memorandum from PM Lee to 1DPM Goh, 26 Jan. 1988 (National Archives of Singapore), made available to the author.

63   But not all. S. Dhanabalan remained opposed to the scheme. Alongside Abdullah Tarmugi, he was to be one of the last minority-race PAP candidates to stand in a single-member constituency (in Kallang in 1988, with Tarmugi standing in Siglap) until Michael Palmer successfully stood in Punggol East in the 2011 general election. With the passage of time, however, Dhanabalan came to believe that GRCs were necessary to ensure minority representation in Parliament: "The other policy I disagreed with him [Mr Lee] on was the Group Representation Constituency (GRC) system. I was against it because I was probably more of an idealist and not realistic enough. I felt that if the Chinese in my constituency did not want to elect me, then so be it, because I saw being Singaporean more important than anything else. I thought that if the Chinese Singaporean or the Indian Singaporean was not prepared to vote for someone of another race just because he was of a different race, then there was something basically wrong with our society." Dhanabalan was opposed, however, to how GRCs later evolved (from smaller slates of three MPs to as many as six). See "Remembering Lee Kuan Yew: A Leader Who Was Ruthless in Demanding Honesty", *Straits Times*, 24 Mar. 2015.

64   "Team MPs Ensure Racial Balance", *Straits Times*, 28 Sept. 1987.

65   G. Kandasamy (1921–99) was a lifelong trade unionist and influential member of the Tamil community. From 1978 to 1997 he was the president of the Tamil Representative Council.

66   S. Chandra Das, interview with the author, 16 Nov. 2012.

67   Mutalib, *Parties and Politics*, p. 216. See also "Sidek Speaks Up for Team MP Proposal", *Straits Times*, 12 Dec. 1987; and "Lengthy Debate with Chiam over 'Second-Class' MPs", *Straits Times*, 10 Mar. 1988.

68   "Team MPs—What Malay and Muslim Leaders Say", *Straits Times*, 11 Dec. 1987.

69   Abdullah Tarmugi, quoted in "Malay MP 'Not Second-Class'", *Straits Times*, 12 Dec. 1987.

70   Abdullah Tarmugi, interview with the author, 9 Mar. 2013.

71   Ibid. All important issues facing the Malay ground were debated in the bureau; indeed, as DPM Goh Chok Tong was to note in 1990, of all the Malay grassroots organisations, it was the Malay Affairs Bureau which was "closest to the Party and the national leadership". "The Role of the Malay Affairs Bureau—Goh Chok Tong", *Petir*, July 1990, p. 49. The

bureau was made up exclusively of PAP Malay MPs from 1984 to 1989. From 1989 onwards, PAP office-holders who were non-Malays, as well as Malay Party activists who were non-MPs, began to be inducted. "PAP Bureau Admits Two Non-Malay MPs", *Straits Times*, 13 Apr. 1989.

72   "How 13 Friends' Coffee Shop Chats Led to a Submission", *Straits Times*, 10 Mar. 1988. Two from this group of 13 were to become PAP MPs: Abdul Nasser Kamaruddin (in 1988) and Mohamad Maidin Bin Packer (in 1991). Maidin Packer, a journalist with *Berita Harian* at the time, had not originally been due to give evidence in person but due to a change of plans within his group eventually ended up doing so and acquitted himself well. Mohamad Maidin Bin Packer, Oral History Interview (in Malay), Accession Number 003180, Reel 4, at 42:30–56:48 (National Archives of Singapore), available at https://www.nas.gov.sg/archivesonline/oral_history_interviews/record-details/52112bc5-1161-11e3-83d5-0050568939ad (accessed 23 Jan. 2021). Another individual who gave evidence to the Select Committee and caught the eye of PAP leaders was Harun Ghani, a Malay community leader and specialist writer at the Curriculum Development Institute of Singapore (Ghani was at the time already a PAP member). Harun Abdul Ghani, Oral History Interview (in Malay), Reel 5, Accession Number 002853 (National Archives of Singapore), available at https://www.nas.gov.sg/archivesonline/oral_history_interviews/record-details/5178bbbe-1160-11e3-83d5-0050568939ad (accessed 23 Jan. 2021). See also "Call for GRCs in All Constituencies", *Straits Times*, 8 Mar. 1988.

73   "Tool to Strengthen PAP's Hand?", *Straits Times*, 2 Aug. 2008.

74   The larger the electoral division, the higher (generally speaking) the likelihood of the actual result following the trend of the popular vote nationwide (support for the PAP). For observations on "the law of large numbers", see Derek da Cunha, *The Price of Victory: The 1997 General Election and Beyond* (Singapore: Institute of Southeast Asian Studies, 1997), pp. 15, 23.

75   Kevin Y.L. Tan, *An Introduction to Singapore's Constitution* (Singapore: Talisman, 2005), pp. 57–8.

76   "GRCs: 20 Years On", *Straits Times*, 2 Aug. 2008.

77   While contesting parties in GRCs are required to field at least one member from a racial minority group, it does not follow that parties have the freedom to select within their multi-member slate a candidate from *any* racial minority background. The president, by an order in the *Gazette*, declares which GRCs require the minority candidate fielded to be Malay, and which GRC requires the minority candidate to be from the Indian/other minority category. In addition, three-fifths of the total number of GRCs are designated constituencies where at least one of the candidates in every group shall be a person belonging to the Malay community. See "Types of Electoral Divisions" (Elections Department of Singapore), available at https://www.eld.gov.sg/elections_type_electoral.html (accessed 2 Dec. 2020).

78   Letter from PM Lee Kuan Yew to all PAP MPs, 24 Sept. 1988 (PAP archive).

79   Personal communications with Tang See Chim (29 Jan. 2013) and Ng Kah Ting (12 Mar. 2013).

80   "No Intelligent, Constructive Opposition in Singapore", remarks by PM Lee, press conference at the Polytechnic after the results of the general election were announced

(3 Sept. 1972). *The Papers of Lee Kuan Yew: Speeches, Interviews and Dialogues, Vol. 6: 1973–1974* (Singapore: Cengage Learning Asia, 2012), pp. 138–9.

81   The preliminary airing of what became the NMP scheme began with Trade and Industry Minister BG Lee Hsien Loong floating the idea in Parliament on 18 January 1989 during the debate on the President's Opening Address to Parliament. "Non-partisan MP Mooted", *Straits Times*, 19 Jan. 1989; Singapore Parliamentary Debates, 19 Jan. 1989, col. 256.

82   "Non-constituency MPs", exchange of memoranda between PM Lee and 1DPM Goh Chok Tong, 27–28 Mar. 1989 (National Archives of Singapore), made available to the author.

83   "MPs Clearly Divided over Bill", *Straits Times*, 30 Nov. 1989.

84   "Dissenting Views Are Already Being Aired but Aren't Taken Seriously", *Straits Times*, 1 Dec. 1989.

85   12 Oct. 1989 Memorandum from the Government Whip, Dr Lee Boon Yang, to 1DPM Goh (National Archives of Singapore), made available to the author. (Dr Tan Cheng Bock spoke out against the bill at the second reading of the bill, on 29 November 1989, but eventually voted for the bill at the second and third reading stages.) Other MPs canvassed by Dr Lee Boon Yang saw further into the issue. In his note to 1DPM Goh, Dr Lee noted Dr Ong Chit Chung's reaction. Ong had commented to Dr Lee that the NMP idea would not hold back the tide insofar as the people's demand for an Opposition was concerned.

86   Singapore Parliamentary Debates, 30 Nov. 1989, col. 841. See also "A Bold Step to Build a Strong Government Based on Consensus", *Straits Times*, 5 Dec. 1989. The first two NMPs, Dr Maurice Choo and Leong Chee Whye, were sworn in on 22 November 1990.

87   *Report of the Select Committee on The Constitution of the Republic of Singapore (Amendment No. 2) Bill [Bill No. 41/89], p. iv; Minutes of Evidence*, 23 Jan. 1990, p. C14, available at https://sprs.parl.gov.sg/selectcommittee/ selectcommittee/ download?id=296&type=report (accessed 23 Jan. 2021).

88   "Overwhelming 'Aye' for NMP Bill", *Straits Times*, 30 Mar. 1990. Goh additionally promised to lift the whip over PAP MPs, enabling them to vote according to their conscience in such a resolution. Singapore Parliamentary Debates, 29 Mar. 1990, cols 1014, 1042. The practice of Parliament deciding by resolution whether it wished to have NMPs for the duration of that Parliament continued until 2010, when the requirement was abolished. NMPs have since the commencement of the Twelfth Parliament (October 2011) been a feature of every Parliament.

89   In Nov. 1985, for example, PM Lee wrote to S. Dhanabalan, leader of the House, concerning the recently concluded debate on Jeyaretnam's motion criticising the government for obstructing the development of the Opposition in Singapore: "By not winding up the debate quickly to get it over with, many PAP backbenchers spread their wings and made impromptu contributions. Some brought credit to themselves and to Parliament. This freedom from time constraints made for spontaneity in the exchanges. The Whip should compliment our MPs on their unplanned interventions." PM Lee Kuan Yew to S. Dhanabalan, 16 May 1985 (National Archives of Singapore), made available to the author.

90 On the tricky position that backbenchers found themselves in at this time, see Lim Boon Heng, "Speaking Up", *Petir*, Jan. 1989, p. 2.

91 "Government Whip on Need for Party Discipline" (interview with Government Whip Lee Yiok Seng), *Petir*, Aug. 1986, pp. 21–2. As Jek Yeun Thong noted following his critical comments on the NCMP Bill, "I will vote with the Government. This may sound like politics of hypocrisy. Well, this is the rule of the game of this House." Singapore Parliamentary Debates, 8 Mar. 1985, col. 473.

92 "Chiam on MPs Who Vote for What They Criticised", *Straits Times*, 2 Aug. 1986; "Braver to Stay and Fight than Quit in Protest—MP", *Straits Times*, 3 Aug. 1986.

93 Minutes of PAP Central Executive Committee Meeting, 8 Jan. 1987 (PAP archive). Documents in the PAP archive made available to the author indicate that this was simply one occasion of several where the idea of allowing the whip to be lifted on parliamentary voting was discussed. Suggestions had been made to this effect since the 1970s. Interestingly, despite the 1987 CEC decision, on only one occasion in parliamentary debate from 1987 to 1990 does the whip appear to have been lifted for voting—during the debate on measures to curb car usage in May 1989.

94 Minutes of PAP Central Executive Committee Meeting, 8 Jan. 1987 (PAP archive).

95 Caucuses became more regular after the 1988 general election (personal communications from multiple former PAP MPs who were backbenchers in the 1980s and 1990s).

96 In the late 1980s, up to 50–60 MPs and ministers would attend the Tuesday Lunch. The number was to dwindle over time. Lau Ping Sum, personal communication, 1 Mar. 2013.

97 "The Role of the Whip in Parliament", *Straits Times*, 25 Aug. 1986.

98 The amendment empowered HDB to repossess the flats of those responsible for throwing down "killer litter" from their flats.

99 "Role of the Whip in Parliament". The article added that the incident had shown there was a need for "frequent intra-party discussions and consultations towards consensus on issues that reflect the increasing complexity of life in Singapore".

100 "Role of the Whip in Parliament"; "No Tough Action Likely, Says Chok Tong", *Straits Times*, 18 Aug. 1986.

101 "Dr Toh to Be Asked Why He Abstained on Vote", *Straits Times*, 2 Aug. 1986; "Why Party Discipline Must Be Maintained", *Straits Times*, 25 Aug. 1986; "Government Whip on Need for Party Discipline", *Petir*, Aug. 1986, pp. 21–2, esp. 22.

102 On Toh's parliamentary interventions during his time as a backbencher and after, see Lee Kuan Yew, *From Third World to First*, pp. 742–3; and Lam Peng Er, "The Organisational Utility Men: Toh Chin Chye and Lim Kim San", in *Lee's Lieutenants*, pp. 42–79, esp. 62–6.

103 A case in point is the intervention of Jek Yeun Thong and other PAP MPs on the issue of Chinese language standards in schools during the parliamentary budget debate in March 1987. See "Right from the Heart", *Straits Times*, 21 Mar. 1987; and "Spirited Debate on Standard of Chinese", *Straits Times*, 21 Mar. 1987.

104 Dr Lee Boon Yang, interview with the author, 12 Mar. 2013.

105 One example was when during the budget debate of 1985, Dr Lee, in his capacity of parliamentary secretary to the minister for the environment, responded to the claim of the long-serving MP for Punggol, Ng Kah Ting, that cessation of the building of wet

markets and food centres would lead to higher costs by noting that this was "a simplistic conclusion which can only be arrived at by those who choose to ignore the obvious" (Singapore Parliamentary Debates, 27 Mar. 1985, cols 1547–8). Ng took offence, and it took considerable time and effort before Dr Lee was able to restore friendly and cordial relations with him. Dr Lee Boon Yang, interview with the author, 12 Mar. 2013; Ng Kah Ting, personal communication, 12 Mar. 2013.

106 On 5 March 1985 Jek Yeun Thong (a veteran PAP MP who had held ministerial positions, and who had been dropped from the Cabinet along with Dr Toh Chin Chye in 1980 as part of the renewal push) had delivered a wide-ranging speech dealing with, amongst other things, the negative aspects of the Pinyinisation effort, and on what he felt was the marked decline in the fortunes of the less well-off in Singapore over the decades (and particularly during the time that he had been away as high commissioner to the United Kingdom). Singapore Parliamentary Debates, 5 Mar. 1985, cols 235–47; "Politics Is Giving Hope to Common Man", *Straits Times*, 6 Mar. 1985. For the rebuttal by Rajaratnam, see Singapore Parliamentary Debates, 6 Mar. 1986, cols 313–26. See also "Raja Delivers a Sermon on Criticism", *Straits Times*, 7 Mar. 1985; and "Storm after Three Dry Days in the House", *Straits Times*, 7 Mar. 1985. At the 22 March 1985 Parliament sitting, PM Lee produced figures to show that Jek had been mistaken in arguing that workers' salaries had fallen disproportionately behind the salaries of MPs and ministers.
Lee asked the whip to request Jek to be present at the 22 March 1985 sitting, but Jek absented himself, by Lee's account, telling the Whip "he had no desire to be present". Singapore Parliamentary Debates, 22 Mar. 1985, col. 1213.

107 Singapore Parliamentary Debates, 6 Mar. 1985, col. 313.

108 Debate on President's Address, Singapore Parliamentary Debates, 20 Jan. 1989, cols 444–5. Also "Mission of MPs", *Petir*, Jan. 1989, p. 13. See also the comments of Thomas Bellows, "Singapore in 1989: Progress in a Search for Roots", *Asian Survey* 30, 2 (Feb. 1990): 201–9.

109 "Rajaratnam to MPs: Be Problem-Solvers, Not Populists", *Petir*, Jan. 1989, pp. 15–6, esp. 15. Clearly Rajaratnam wanted PAP MPs to reserve their belligerence for MPs from other parties. His aversion to "boxing matches" between PAP MPs in Parliament should be compared with his earlier 1985 call for a "knuckle-duster approach" by PAP MPs to the Opposition.

110 Lee Kuan Yew, "Critical Debating by PAP MPs", internal paper, 29 Apr. 1989 (PAP archive).

111 Speech made by the Prime Minister, Mr Lee Kuan Yew, when he moved the Motion of Thanks to the Yang Di-Pertuan Negara, for his Policy Speech on the Opening of Parliament on 14 December 1965. Singapore Parliamentary Debates, 14 Dec. 1965, cols 107–8. The Barisan boycotted Parliament on account of its opposition to what it (or at least the faction led by Barisan Chairman Dr Lee Siew Choh) saw as Singapore's "phoney independence". "Opposition MPs Boycott S'pore's First House Session", *Straits Times*, 6 Dec. 2015. Lee's preoccupation went back even further. Soon after the PAP's victory in the 1963 Legislative Assembly general election, Lee noted that "it would be useful if at these [Assembly] meetings criticism of our shortcomings either in policy or implementation were aired not only by the Opposition but also by our own backbenchers. It can serve a useful purpose in bringing public attention on how things are done, how they can be done better or why

an apparent ineptitude has in fact a rational and valid explanation." Speech by Prime Minister Lee Kuan Yew, On the Motion of Thanks to the Yang Di-Pertuan Negara, 9 Dec. 1963, at the Legislative Assembly. Singapore Legislative Assembly Debates, 9 Dec. 1963, col. 149. Lee added for good measure: "It is for this reason that I invite our own backbenchers to criticize the government in this chamber for what they consider to be its shortcomings, even though this may not be the practice elsewhere" (col. 150).

112 Speech by the Prime Minister, Mr Lee Kuan Yew, in Parliament on 23 Feb. 1977 during the Debate on the President's Address. Singapore Parliamentary Debates, 23 Feb. 1977, col. 407.

113 Ng Kah Ting, personal communication, 8 Nov. 2013.

114 Responses by MPs to PM Lee's letter to them (5 May 1989) requesting their feedback on the 2 May 1989 meeting (PAP archive).

115 PM Lee to SM S. Rajaratnam, Memo "TV in Parliament", 22 Jan. 1985 (National Archives of Singapore), made available to the author.

116 SM S. Rajaratnam to PM Lee, 18 Jan. 1985 (National Archives of Singapore), made available to the author.

117 PM Lee to SM S. Rajaratnam, Memo "TV in Parliament".

118 Philip Goh, "MPs Need to Polish Up Their Act", letter to Straits Times Forum, 4 May 1985.

119 "TV Makes It a People's Debate", Straits Times, 8 Apr. 1985; "More Have Better Idea of Parliament", Straits Times, 5 Apr. 1985; Old Singaporean, "Time to Really Listen", letter to Straits Times Forum, 8 Mar. 1985. See also Chan Heng Chee, "Singapore in 1985", Asian Survey 26, 2 (Feb. 1986): 158–67, esp. 163.

120 Assistant Secretary-General Goh Chok Tong to Secretary-General Lee Kuan Yew, 13 May 1986 (PAP archive). There is some suggestion that the idea was raised by Dr Hong Hai to Goh during the former's PAP recruitment tea session. See "Backbench with Front-line Impact: 30 Years On, Are GPCs Still Relevant?", Straits Times, 19 Nov. 2017.

121 "Parliamentary Committees" (PAP archive). The paper was reprinted with minor changes in the press. "How Parliamentary Panels Can Play a Greater Role", Straits Times, 17 Jan. 1987.

122 "Parliamentary Committees".

123 Secretary-General Lee Kuan Yew to Assistant Secretary-General Goh Chok Tong, 14 May 1986 (PAP archive).

124 The fact that Lee and Goh had allowed informal parliamentary groups (Goh's idea) looking at specific subjects to come into being and operate on an informal basis in 1986 would have given him the opportunity to assess GPCs' likely effectiveness as well as their remit. "MPs' Panels for Quality", Straits Times, 17 Jan. 1987.

125 Minutes of PAP Central Executive Committee Meeting, 8 Jan. 1987. PM Lee had himself warmed to the proposal by this stage, even suggesting that GPCs could eventually evolve into Select Committees. Lee also made the intriguing point that it did not matter if such Select Committees included members of the Opposition. The Party leadership does not appear to have subsequently returned to the topic of GPCs evolving into Select Committees.

126 "Panels No Extra Burden, Civil Servants Told", *Straits Times*, 14 Feb. 1987. For further details on the origins, subsequent evolutions and successes (as well as limitations) of GPCs, see the coverage in *Straits Times* (19 Nov. 2017) marking the 30th anniversary of GPCs.

127 Goh Chok Tong, interview with the author, 30 Nov. 2013.

128 See the *IPS 20th Anniversary Report*, Institute of Policy Studies, *Issuu*, 4 July 2011: 4–5. https://issuu.com/ips-singapore/docs/ips_20thann (accessed 9 Oct. 2019). For the public presentation of the concept, see "Think Tank Set Up in Singapore", *Straits Times*, 16 Jan. 1988; and "Think Tank Hopes to Have Impact on Policy-Making", *Straits Times*, 20 Jan. 1988.

129 Chan had also (in a somewhat forgotten letter to the *Straits Times*) defended the Law Society's right to comment on, and criticise, legislation. Chan Heng Chee, "Speaking Out to Protect Home and Political Legacy", letter to *Straits Times* Forum, 6 June 1986. This was in the wake of a clash between the government and the Law Society (led by its president, Francis Seow) on proposed amendments to the Newspapers and Printing Presses Act.

130 "A Lively Intellectual Environment", *Petir*, July 1987, p. 29.

131 Papers made available to the author on the origins of the Institute of Policy Studies (National Archives of Singapore), Ref 005/87, 30 Sept. 1987.

132 Ibid.

133 It was already known and resolved within the relevant circles in government that Chan Heng Chee would leave to take up the post of permanent representative to the United Nations (in New York) in February 1989. 1DPM Goh thought, nonetheless, that it was important to have someone who had a credible reputation as an independent (and occasionally critical) thinker be IPS' founding director, to underline that the government was open to listening to all views (papers made available to the author on the origins of the Institute of Policy Studies; Chan Heng Chee, personal communication, 5 Dec. 2020). When Chan Heng Chee left for New York in early 1989, IPS Deputy Director Associate Professor Jon Quah became acting director.

134 The government would not, for example, release data that might have allowed proposals aired within IPS discussions to be more fully thought out. Chan Heng Chee, interview with the author, 20 Nov. 2012.

135 "Vasoo Makes an Impact at Rally", *Straits Times*, 14 Dec. 1984.

136 "Chok Tong All for Town Councils", *Straits Times*, 19 Dec. 1984.

137 "How It All Started", *Petir*, June 1988, pp. 4–11.

138 "New Town Councils or Mayorates", memorandum from PM Lee Kuan Yew to Goh Chok Tong, 24 Oct. 1984 (National Archives of Singapore), made available to the author.

139 *1984 General Election PAP Post-mortem Report*.

140 "Will a Viable and Better Service Result?", *Straits Times*, 25 June 1985.

141 "Self Rule for HDB Estates", *Straits Times*, 16 Aug. 1986; "How It All Started".

142 "Anson to Be Among First Town Councils", *Straits Times*, 20 Apr. 1985.

143 "Elected Governments Only as Good as Those Who Choose Them", PM Lee Kuan Yew, Address on the Eve of National Day, 8 Aug. 1988. *The Papers of Lee Kuan Yew: Speeches,*

Interviews and Dialogues, Vol. 10: 1988–1990 (Singapore: Cengage Learning Asia, 2012), p. 125.

144 "Running Town Councils No Simple Matter: Dhana", *Straits Times*, 1 Sept. 1988; "Misery, if Wrong MPs Are in Charge of Town Councils", *Straits Times*, 15 Aug. 1988; "Getting down to Brass Tacks in This Election", *Straits Times*, 29 Aug. 1988.

145 PM Lee Kuan Yew to Minister (National Development) Teh Cheang Wan, 12 Feb. 1985 (National Archives of Singapore). The PAP would not hand over control of grassroots organisations under the PA (People's Association) to elected Opposition MPs but was prepared to allow them to be in charge of town councils (a double-edged sword, as PM Lee had observed). Both J.B. Jeyaretnam (Anson) and Chiam See Tong (Potong Pasir) were prepared to take on the challenge. Jeyaretnam made tentative moves in this direction but was disqualified from Parliament before the Town Councils Act was passed by Parliament (1988). See "Anson to Be Among First Town Councils", *Straits Times*, 20 Apr. 1985; "What the Housing Board Statement Said", *Straits Times*, 20 Apr. 1985. Chiam See Tong's Potong Pasir Town Council began operations in September 1989.

146 An NCMP seat was offered to M.P.D. Nair of the Workers' Party. Nair declined, following which the seat was offered to Tan Chee Kien, chairman of the Singapore United Front, who also declined. NCMPs were thus only to enter parliament following the 1988 election.

147 "Of Kid Gloves and Queensbury Rules", *Straits Times*, 29 July 1985; "Minister on Stronger Response to Opposition", *Straits Times*, 14 Aug. 1985.

148 Prof. S. Jayakumar, interview with the author, 29 Apr. 2013; interviews (2012–16) with other former PAP MPs, including backbenchers in the 1980s.

149 One episode that lingers in the memory of many MPs who were present took place on 26 March 1982. Chandra Das recalls: "I was new at the time. After the budget debates, we had a post-budget dinner. Eddie Barker [Law Minister E.W. Barker] was leader of the House. I was helping Eddie. This post-budget dinner really was to thank Parliamentary staff and MPs because they worked late nights . . . in those days we used to sit late at night. And this is the dinner meant for PAP MPs to socialise. We all used to contribute towards the costs. Eddie Barker, being the gentleman cricketer that he is, invited all MPs. Including JBJ [Jeyaretnam]. So I was seated at one table with Lee Kuan Yew. I was one of the organisers, so I was seated there. In walks JBJ. You could literally feel the crowd tense up. . . . PM went red. Then he told Ng Kah Ting, in Mandarin, to tell me to leave the table. He told me to leave the table because he was not going to speak in English—he was only going to speak in Mandarin. I was the only non-Mandarin speaker at the table. He was that angry. PM scolded Eddie Barker, 'You do not fraternize with your enemies.' Then JBJ sat . . . after a little while, JBJ also felt uncomfortable, and he left. After this, I sat with Eddie Barker and a few others, drinking with Eddie into the early hours. . . . [Eddie said], 'He scolded me in front of you young punks, I'm going to resign tomorrow.'" S. Chandra Das, interview with the author, 16 Nov. 2012. (Individuals familiar with the incident suggested when interviewed by the author that PM Lee subsequently apologised to Barker.)

150 *First Report of the Committee of Privileges: Complaints of Allegations of Executive Interference in the Judiciary. Parl. 3 of 1987*. Presented to Parliament 21 Jan. 1987, Minutes of Evidence, p. D502, available at https://www.nas.gov.sg/archivesonline/government_

records/record-details/f4cd4aa0-0537-11e8-a2a9-001a4a5ba61b (accessed 21 Jan. 2021).
See also "You've Demeaned Us: PM to Jeya", *Straits Times*, 13 Sept. 1986.

151 *First Report of the Committee of Privileges: Complaints of Allegations of Executive Interference in the Judiciary, Minutes of Evidence*, p. D508. The hearings were convened as a result of a complaint made against Jeyaretnam following his accusations in Parliament of executive interference in the judiciary.

152 Interviews with multiple former PAP MPs who were backbenchers in the 1980s. Goh Chok Tong recalled of the 1986 Budget Debate (which had seen brutal exchanges between Jeyaretnam and Lee): "Most of us felt very awkward. Mr Lee used very strong language, but all within Parliamentary rules. It was very personal, very insulting. And JBJ tried to insult back but he did not have the same vocabulary. In other words, it was intimidation. Take out the gloves, as Mr Lee would say. Either I destroy you or you destroy me. I wanted to get up and say, stop it. For us, it was not the way Parliament should be conducted. That was the way other countries ran their Parliament. I was not used to such a display." Peh Shing Huei, *Tall Order: The Goh Chok Tong Story, Vol. 1*, p. 114.

153 Interviews with multiple former PAP MPs who were backbenchers in the 1980s.

154 Jeyaretnam's fine of $5,000 was above the threshold triggering a disqualification from Parliament. His MP's office in Anson was demolished shortly after he began his prison sentence, a move which, to his supporters, showed the desire on the part of the authorities to obliterate the Opposition and all trace of Jeyaretnam. This was to linger long in the memory of the Workers' Party. As its 50th anniversary commemorative book (published in 2007) notes tersely, "The office was demolished and within 24 hours, the office site was reinstated to the original void deck, perhaps showing an urgency to leave no trail of the first opposition MP office in Singapore since independence." *The Workers' Party 50th Anniversary Commemorative Book* (Singapore: The Workers' Party, 2007), p. 25. See also Loke Hoe Yeong, *The First Wave: JBJ, Chiam & the Opposition in Singapore* (Singapore: Epigram Books, 2019), p. 54.

155 For the train of events, see Loke, *First Wave*, pp. 49–55.

156 Jeyaretnam had alleged that the executive had caused the transfer of Senior District Judge Michael Khoo from the Subordinate Courts to the Attorney-General's Chambers, and that this transfer had been effected because the executive had been displeased by Judge Khoo's 1984 acquittal of Jeyaretnam and Wong Hong Toy of all but one of the charges against them. "House Acts on Jeya's 'Smear'", *Straits Times*, 20 Mar. 1986; "PM Satisfied There's Nothing Improper", *Straits Times*, 22 Mar. 1986.

157 *First Report of the Committee of Privileges: Complaints of Allegations of Executive Interference in the Judiciary*, pp. 20–4.

158 See the Privy Council's decision in Joshua Benjamin Jeyaretnam v Law Society of Singapore [1989] 1 AC 608 at 631–32: "Their Lordships have to record their deep disquiet that by a series of misjudgements the solicitor and his co-defendant Wong have suffered a grievous injustice. They have been fined, imprisoned and publicly disgraced for offences of which they were not guilty. The solicitor, in addition, has been deprived of his seat in Parliament and disqualified for a year from practising his profession. Their Lordships' order restores him to the roll of advocates and solicitors of the Supreme Court of Singapore, but, because of the course taken by the criminal proceedings, their Lordships have no power to right the

other wrongs which the solicitor and Wong have suffered. Their only prospect of redress, their Lordships understand, will be by way of petition for pardon to the President of the Republic of Singapore."

159 "Criminal Convictions against Jeya Still Stand, Says Govt", *Straits Times*, 2 Dec. 1988.

160 "PAP MPs Look Forward to a Loyal Opposition", *Straits Times*, 5 Jan. 1985. As Lee Kuan Yew observed of Chiam, "We treated him differently, extending him respect and latitude. We hoped that if he expanded, those who opposed us could gravitate towards a non-subversion opposition." Lee Kuan Yew, *From Third World to First*, p. 147. For what Chiam understood by "loyal opposition", see "The Concept of a Loyal Opposition" in the SDP organ, *The Demokrat* (May 1993): "The Opposition has to remain loyal to the people of Singapore by fighting for an open and democratic process. Being loyal to the citizenry also means that the Opposition cannot afford to challenge the basic tenets upon which the society functions and which Singaporeans have come to cherish. These include inter-ethnic and -religious harmony, non-violent resolution of conflicts through open debate, and continued economic expansion of the country. Therefore, Singapore's Opposition must not only be competitive but also cooperative with the Government whenever it is necessary vis-à-vis these belief systems" (pp. 6–7). Chiam resigned as SDP secretary-general in May 1993, the same month that this *Demokrat* issue was published (as part of its internecine strife [that was to see him finally leave the SDP for the Singapore People's Party in 1996]), but it is possible to see in the *Demokrat* article an important—and telling—restatement of Chiam's principles at a time of turmoil within the SDP. Chiam's successor as leader of the SDP, Dr Chee Soon Juan, was to take on a far more confrontational approach.

161 The PAP leadership had been preoccupied with the idea of fostering a "loyal" constructive Opposition since the 1960s. As Thomas Bellows (who had access to the Party leadership) observed when it came to PAP leaders' thinking in the mid- to late 1960s, "the virtual collapse of an organised opposition in 1968 distressed a majority of the PAP Central Executive Committee. The belief persists among much of the leadership that: 1) a political system is distorted if a responsible and loyal opposition does not exist; and 2) a political system declines in stature without a vocal, moderately successful, and loyal opposition." Bellows, *People's Action Party of Singapore*, pp. 119–20. While there is the possibility that Bellows took too uncritically assurances on the part of the PAP leaders of the continued need for an Opposition, there seems to me to be a stronger case for arguing that it was the idea of PAP having a responsibility to nurture a loyal Opposition that began to diminish from the 1970s on. It is clear enough that the idea having opposing views ventilated—ground grievances and legitimate criticism—continued to be viewed as a priority by the PAP leadership. What assumed more importance over time, and certainly from mid- to late 1970, was that this could be done by PAP backbenchers, and if necessary by innovations in Parliament (the NMP and NCMP schemes come to mind).

162 "PAP MPs Look Forward to a Loyal Opposition".

163 "President Resigns", *Straits Times*, 29 Mar. 1985; Singapore Parliamentary Debates, 28 Mar. 1985, col. 1684.

164 "Day an Emotional PM Hushed the House", *Straits Times*, 29 Mar. 1985. By the account of those close to him, Devan's resignation was one event that shook Lee personally. "Between Close Friends", *Straits Times*, 27 Nov. 1990.

165 Lee Kuan Yew, *The Singapore Story: Memoirs of Lee Kuan Yew* (Singapore: Times Editions, 1998), pp. 159–60. For Nair's recollections of their first interactions, see Nair, Chengara Veetil Devan, Transcript of Oral History Interview, Accession Number 000049/26, Reel 12, p. 112, and Reel 13, pp. 126–8 (National Archives of Singapore), available at https://www.nas.gov.sg/archivesonline/oral_history_interviews/record-details/df0830cc-115d-11e3-83d5-0050568939ad (accessed 21 Jan. 2021).

166 Lee Kuan Yew, *From Third World to First*, pp. 109–10.

167 Singapore Parliamentary Debates, 23 Oct. 1981, cols 228–34.

168 Lee Kuan Yew, *From Third World to First*, p. 253.

169 "He Fought for a Better Life for Singaporeans", *Straits Times*, 12 Apr. 1985.

170 See Lee Kuan Yew, *From Third World to First*, pp. 250–3.

171 Government Statement Relating to Devan Nair's Pension, 4 Sept. 1985, available at https://www.nas.gov.sg/archivesonline/speeches/record-details/7390021e-115d-11e3-83d5-0050568939ad; *C.V. Devan Nair: Circumstances Relating to Resignation as President of the Republic of Singapore. Command 8 of 1988*. 29 June 1988, p. 2, available at https://www.nas.gov.sg/archivesonline/government_records/record-details/eb5e9aca-8133-11e7-83df-0050568939ad (accessed 21 Jan. 2021).

172 *C.V. Devan Nair: Circumstances Relating to Resignation as President of the Republic of Singapore*, p. 2.

173 Ibid. For Nair's response to the White Paper, see "Devan: Why Did Govt Deny Me Documents?", *Straits Times*, 15 July 1988.

174 "Govt White Paper Reveals Sordid Details about Devan Nair", *Business Times*, 30 June 1988; "Visits to German Woman Began after '84 Election", *Straits Times*, 1 July 1988; "Devan Nair's Sarawak Escapades", *Straits Times*, 1 July 1988.

175 The White Paper noted that the Cabinet after having discussed the issue had decided that Nair had to step down or else be removed from office, and that Nair had initially refused, agreeing only when told there would be a motion in Parliament for his removal. *C.V. Devan Nair: Circumstances Relating to Resignation as President of the Republic of Singapore*, p. 1.

176 "PM Seeking Political Revenge", *Straits Times*, 9 July 1988. For the open letter, see "PM's Act 'a Shameless Demolition Effort'", *Straits Times*, 9 July 1988.

177 "Devan Criticizes Govt's Political Style", *Straits Times*, 24 June 1987.

178 "Devan Alleges Abuse of ISA and Calls on PM to Resign", *Straits Times*, 24 May 1988.

179 "PM Lee Demands Retraction, Apology", *Business Times*, 24 May 1988; "PM Files Libel Suit against Devan Nair", *Straits Times*, 26 May 1988.

180 "Nair Withdraws Remarks He Made about SM", *Straits Times*, 20 Apr. 1993.

181 "Singapore Sage", *Globe and Mail*, 29 Mar. 1999; C.V. Devan Nair, "Point of No Return for Singapore", *Sydney Morning Herald*, 5 Apr. 1999; "SM Drops Suit against Ailing Devan", *Straits Times*, 6 July 2004.

182 "Graft Probe Led to Teh's Suicide", *Straits Times*, 21 Jan. 1987; *Report of the Commission of Inquiry on Investigations Concerning the Late Mr Teh Cheang Wan*

(Singapore: Singapore National Printers, 1987), p. 1, available at https://www.nas.
gov.sg/archivesonline/government_records/record-details/f1304836-8133-11e7-83df-
0050568939ad (accessed 21 Jan. 2021).

183 Singapore Parliamentary Debates, 26 Jan. 1987, cols 932–5.

184 Ibid., col. 933; Lee Kuan Yew, *From Third World to First*, pp. 187–8.

185 Singapore Parliamentary Debates, 4 Mar. 1987, cols 41–55. For Chiam's thinking during
     this period, see Loke, *First Wave*, pp. 55–68.

186 *Report of the Commission of Inquiry on Investigations Concerning the Late Mr Teh Cheang
     Wan*, pp. 47–8. See also "Why Panel Refused to Let Chiam See CPIB Files", *Straits Times*,
     3 Jan. 1988.

187 *Report of the Commission of Inquiry on Investigations Concerning the Late Mr Teh Cheang
     Wan*, esp. pp. 53–4.

188 Ibid., pp. 44, 55.

189 *The Journey: 60 Years of Fighting Corruption in Singapore* (Singapore: Corrupt Practices
     Investigation Bureau, 2012), pp. 54–5.

190 "Jaya: System's Integrity Intact", *Straits Times*, 14 Jan. 1988; "System Kept Clean and
     Honest Despite 'Mishaps'", *Straits Times*, 2 Sept. 1988. Zero tolerance for corruption had,
     of course, been the PAP's hallmark from the very beginning, but this aspect of governing
     had not been in the forefront of the news for some time. The last serious corruption case
     within the highest levels of government had been in 1974, when Wee Toon Boon, senior
     minister of state for environment, was charged with corruption in 1975 and sentenced to
     18 months' jail the following year after using his influence to help a businessman, being
     rewarded with a bungalow and other favours in return. "The Charges", *Straits Times*, 3
     July 1975; "Toon Boon: 18 Months' Jail after Appeal", *Straits Times*, 14 July 1976. In
     1979 Phey Yew Kok, NTUC president and PAP MP, was charged with misappropriating
     union funds. He skipped bail and spent 36 years on the run before turning himself in in
     2015. "Former NTUC Chairman and ex-MP Phey Yew Kok Sentenced to 60 Months'
     Jail", *Straits Times*, 22 Jan. 2016.

191 "PM to Voters: Don't Have Double Standards if You Want Honest Govt", *Straits Times*,
     15 Aug. 1988; "Clean Government Can Be Lost by Taking It for Granted", *Straits Times*,
     21 Dec. 1988.

192 "Bill to Confiscate Gains from Graft Passed", *Straits Times*, 4 Mar. 1989. The powers
     under the new law could be used against corruption offences committed before the bill
     came into operation. But separately, the government had already filed a suit against Teh
     Cheang Wan's estate for recovery of sums derived from corruption. "Government Files $1
     Million Suit against Teh's Estate", *Business Times*, 2 Mar. 1988.

193 "PM Lee Sues Jeya for Defamation", *Straits Times*, 3 Sept. 1988.

194 "Jeya's Appeal over Libel Suit Dismissed", *Straits Times*, 23 Feb. 1990; "Court Was
     Right to Rule that Jeya Had Defamed Mr Lee", *Straits Times*, 21 Feb. 1992; "Mr
     Lee's Defamation Suit: Jeyaretnam Loses Appeal", *Straits Times*, 19 Apr. 1992; "SM's
     Defamation Suit: Jeya Makes Final Payment of $124,500", *Straits Times*, 23 Mar. 1993.

195 Goh Chok Tong, interview with the author, 30 Nov. 2013. See also Lee, *Unexpected
     Nation*, pp. 475–8; and Yap et al., *Men in White*, pp. 424–8.

196 "Elected Governments Only as Good as Those Who Choose Them", PM Lee Kuan Yew, Address on the Eve of National Day, 8 Aug. 1988. *The Papers of Lee Kuan Yew, Vol. 10*, pp. 123–4.

197 PM Lee Kuan Yew, National Day Rally Speech at the Kallang Theatre, 14 Aug. 1988. *National Day Rally Speeches: 50 Years of Nationhood in Singapore 1966–2015*, pp. 188–9. Ong Teng Cheong ranked third, said Lee, on account of his lack of proficiency in English. "How PM Rates His Top Ministers", *Straits Times*, 15 Aug. 1988; "Support the New Team, PM Urges", *Straits Times*, 15 Aug. 1988.

198 "Now to Secure the Future: PM", *Straits Times*, 22 Aug. 1988; "Why PM Prefers the Robust Approach", *Straits Times*, 22 Aug. 1988.

199 Notes from PM Lee to Cabinet colleagues, 17 Aug. and 19 Aug. 1988 (National Archives of Singapore), made available to the author.

200 S. Dhanabalan to PM Lee Kuan Yew, 19 Aug. 1988 (National Archives of Singapore), made available to the author.

201 Prof. S. Jayakumar to PM Lee Kuan Yew, 18 Aug. 1988 (National Archives of Singapore), made available to the author.

202 PM Lee Kuan Yew to S. Dhanabalan, 19 Aug. 1988 (National Archives of Singapore), made available to the author.

203 "Prime Minister's Assessment of Goh Chok Tong", *Straits Times*, 24 Aug. 1988; "University Students Question PM on Election Issues", *Straits Times*, 24 Aug. 1988.

204 "Prime Minister's Assessment of Goh Chok Tong". On 18 April 1988, a number of individuals who had been detained by the government in May the previous year for their part in the Marxist Conspiracy released a joint statement stating that their confessions had been obtained through duress and torture. 1DPM Goh and his key colleagues deliberated that evening before taking the decision to have these individuals re-arrested the next day. PM Lee (who was out of Singapore at the time the joint statement was issued) evinced frustration at the delay, taking the view that the younger generation leaders were not decisive enough in a crisis. He felt that the individuals should have been immediately re-detained. Lee took out his frustration in particular with 1DPM Goh, who had been acting PM in Lee's absence. Allowing his frustration to spill over at a subsequent Cabinet meeting, Lee told Goh, "If Loong [Lee Hsien Loong] is not my son I would have asked him to take over from you now." (This was the recollection of Dr Ahmad Mattar, who describes being "embarrassed and infuriated" by PM Lee's comment. Peh Shing Huei, *Tall Order*, p. 205.) Looking back (and confirming Mattar's recollection), Goh observed that "not decisive enough" did not mean the younger leaders were indecisive. The consensual approach could mean slower decision making, but tough decisions could be, and were, taken by Goh and the younger leaders collectively in other instances. I am grateful to Goh Chok Tong for a personal communication (27 Sept. 2020).

205 "Prime Minister's Assessment of Goh Chok Tong"; Lee did, however, add that this was his conservative estimate.

206 The only aspect of his remarks Lee seems to have regretted was his revelation that he had suggested to Goh that he see a psychiatrist. Lee subsequently made an attempt—

too late—to request that the press not carry it (files made available to the author on the subject). PM Lee Kuan Yew, instructions to Press Secretary James Fu, 23 Aug. 1988. Ref. NAS BF 22/88 Vol. 2 (National Archives of Singapore; made available to the author).

207 Yap et al., *Men in White*, pp. 424–5. Those who were puzzled by Lee's comments included (by Goh's own account) Prof. S. Jayakumar, Dr Tony Tan and Dr Tan Cheng Bock. "PM Showed His Assessment to Chok Tong", *Straits Times*, 2 Sept. 1988.

208 "Chok Tong's Our Leader: BG Lee and Tony Tan", *Straits Times*, 22 Aug. 1988.

209 "To Each His Own", *Straits Times*, 25 Aug. 1988; "Support for Chok Tong's Consensus Style", *Straits Times*, 25 Aug. 1988.

210 "Take Me for What I Am", *Straits Times*, 24 Aug. 1988; "Chok Tong to Voters: Bear This in Mind", *Straits Times*, 26 Aug. 1988.

211 "PM Showed His Assessment to Chok Tong", *Straits Times*, 2 Sept. 1988; "Francis Seow Again Calls Deputy PM Names", *Straits Times*, 3 Sept. 1988.

212 "Thoughts on BG Lee the Challenger", *Straits Times*, 2 Sept. 1988.

213 "Chok Tong's Our Leader: BG Lee and Tony Tan", *Straits Times*, 22 Aug. 1988; "BG Lee Stresses PAP Teamwork", *Straits Times*, 4 Sept. 1988; "More Open Style of Government to Continue, Says BG Lee", *Straits Times*, 22 Aug. 1988. BG Lee used the occasion of the Party rally to make the point: the same forum that PM Lee had used to make some of his comments on 1DPM Goh.

214 "PM Gives Chok Tong Clear Vote of Confidence", *Straits Times*, 2 Sept. 1988.

215 Ibid.

216 Goh Chok Tong, personal communication, 30 Apr. 2013.

217 Goh Chok Tong, interview with the author, 30 Jan. 2013. See also Yap et al., *Men in White*, pp. 425–6.

218 Goh felt that this was the correct course, not just because of Lee's criticism. By 1988 BG Lee's calibre and leadership potential were clearly apparent, and he too could be considered as a possible leader. Goh Chok Tong, personal communication, 30 Apr. 2013. It should be noted, however, that then PM Lee was subsequently (in 1990) to make it clear that he had not wanted his son to succeed him (contrary to speculation in some quarters in 1988). "I've a Stake in Success of Chok Tong and Team: PM", *Straits Times*, 26 Nov. 1990.

219 "Thoughts on BG Lee the Challenger". Goh chose to emphasise during this rally speech that it was the ministers, and not PM Lee, who would decide the next leader. This was Goh's way of making the point to Lee that he (Lee) would not be blamed if Goh failed as PM. Goh Chok Tong, personal communication, 30 Apr. 2013.

220 The issue of PM Lee's public criticisms of 1DPM Goh has been dealt with further above; see also the treatment by Edwin Lee, *Unexpected Nation*, pp. 475–8.

221 The debates were the result of the PAP agreeing to take up the challenge thrown down by J.B. Jeyaretnam for the elected president proposal to be debated on television. "Have TV Debate on Elected President Proposal", *Straits Times*, 26 Aug. 1988; "PAP Willing to Debate Elected Presidency", *Straits Times*, 27 Aug. 1988. See also "From the Hustings into the Studio for a TV Debate", *Straits Times*, 31 Aug. 1988.

222 Before the election, WP absorbed members from two parties, Barisan Sosialis and Singapore United Front (SUF). "Two Opposition Parties to Merge", *Straits Times*, 11

Jan. 1988; "Ex-SUF Chief Joins WP with 7 Others", *Business Times*, 20 Aug. 1988. The Barisan (while later defunct) and the SUF did not, as some thought at the time, dissolve but continued on paper to exist, with the SUF later being renamed the Democratic Progressive Party. The PKMS (Pertubuhan Kebangsaan Melayu Singapura, or Singapore Malay National Organisation) also agreed to cooperate with the WP in the 1988 election, an arrangement which saw the PKMS adopting the WP manifesto, and an agreement not to compete where the other party was fielding candidates. See "PKMS to Team Up with Workers' Party for Polls", *Straits Times*, 18 June 1988.

223 The SDP had been strengthened by the entry into its ranks in February of a group of former WP members (led by Wong Hong Toy, who had quit as WP chairman in November 1987). "Wong Hong Toy Quits Workers' Party", *Business Times*, 5 Nov. 1987; "Ex-Workers' Party Chairman and Members Join SDP", *Straits Times*, 7 Feb. 1988. Wong had been disaffected by J.B. Jeyaretnam's style. Low Yong Nguan (who had held the Crawford seat for the PAP between 1968 and 1972) was part of this faction. Loke, *First Wave*, pp. 141–2.

224 According to the terms of the pact, SDP would contest in single-member constituencies, with the WP focusing on Group Representation Constituencies. "SDP and WP Form Electoral Pact", *Straits Times*, 20 Aug. 1988. However, this pact was not strictly adhered to as both the SDP and WP ended up contesting SMCs.

225 Multiple interviews (2012–13) with former PAP MPs and activists familiar with Party thinking at the time.

226 On the foreign commentary, see "US Media's View of the Singapore Elections", *Straits Times*, 12 Sept. 1988; and "Victory for PM's Style of Government, Say 2 Papers", *Straits Times*, 9 Sept. 1988.

227 "A Victory of the People", *Straits Times* Editorial, 5 Sept. 1988.

228 "Clear Mandate for New Guard"; "PAP Landslide", *Straits Times*, 9 Sept. 1988.

229 "Law Society on Collision Course", *Straits Times*, 14 June 1986.

230 *Report of the Select Committee on the Legal Profession (Amendment) Bill [Bill No.20/86]. Parl. 7 of 1986. Presented to Parliament on 16 Oct. 1986. Minutes of Evidence*, paras. 371–651 (pp. B60–B90); paras. 1162–1261 (pp. B163–B175), available at https://www.nas.gov.sg/archivesonline/government_records/record-details/fa9b0116-0537-11e8-a2a9-001a4a5ba61b (accessed 21 Jan. 2021). For a flavour of their exchanges, see "Lawyers Subject to the Control of Supreme Court Too", *Straits Times*, 10 Oct. 1986; and "PM Again Challenges Seow's Veracity", *Straits Times*, 11 Oct. 1986.

231 Seow had in 1973 been suspended from practice for a year following "grossly improper conduct" in what was known as the Gemini Chit Fund scandal. "Lawyer Francis Seow Suspended for One Year", *Straits Times*, 1 May 1973. See also "Tougher Laws if Necessary: PM".

232 See, for example, "Francis Seow Raps Law Society Silence on Human Rights", *Straits Times*, 4 July 1987.

233 "US Officials Egged Me On: Francis Seow", *Straits Times*, 21 May 1988; "Hendrickson Told Seow: You Are Best Man to Lead Opposition", *Straits Times*, 21 May 1988.

234 "How I Became Interested in Going into Politics", *Straits Times*, 21 May 1988.

235 "One Year Detention for Seow", *Straits Times*, 6 June 1988. For further reflections on the Hendrickson affair, see Lee, *Unexpected Nation*, pp. 469–75. For Seow's own account, see

Francis Seow, *To Catch a Tartar: A Dissident in Lee Kuan Yew's Prison* (New Haven: Yale University Southeast Asian Studies, 1995).

236   "Dr Tay's $10 Million Question", *Straits Times*, 27 Aug. 1988; "2 Eunos Candidates Reply to Dr Tay", *Straits Times*, 28 Aug. 1988.

237   On the letters and pamphlets to voters in Eunos, see "Open Letters on Francis Seow: Voters Must Know All the Details", *Straits Times*, 2 Sept. 1988; and "PM Calls Seow Financially Untrustworthy", *Straits Times*, 2 Sept. 1988. Mohd Khalit, the Malay candidate in the WP slate, was constantly referred to in the press as a "part-time comedian". "PAP Sweeps All 10 GRCs at Stake", *Straits Times*, 4 Sept. 1988.

238   "Younger Voters Have Got What They Wanted", *Straits Times*, 24 Sept. 1988. The presence of WP supporters outside the counting centre at East View Secondary School (with several hurling insults at the PAP candidates within) was menacing enough for the PAP candidates to elect to stay inside the counting centre until well into the early hours of the morning following polling (Zulkifli bin Mohammed, personal communication, 23 Oct. 2020). In another earlier incident at Bedok, WP supporters attacked a Singapore Broadcasting Corporation van after a WP rally. "Younger Voters Have Got What They Wanted".

239   The PAP leadership recognised the potential threat from the WP team and saw the need for a slate that could overcome the challenge. The story was put out that Dr Tay Eng Soon, seen as a heavyweight, would contest in Tanglin, a single-member constituency which had been vacated following the retirement of E.W. Barker. Tay's former constituency, River Valley, had ceased to exist, with its constituents now coming under Cairnhill or Tanglin. Tay's switch to contest Tanglin thus seemed plausible. On Nomination Day (24 August 1988), however, a (seeming) last-minute switch took place which saw Tay file his papers in Eunos instead, taking the place of Lew Syn Pau (who went to Tanglin, but who had seemed set to stand with Chew Heng Ching and Zulkifli bin Mohammed in Eunos). The move was premeditated. Tay had actually been closeted at a PAP branch not far from Eunos until almost midway through the nomination process before proceeding to the nomination centre. The Party leadership had wanted the element of surprise and also had not wanted the WP team in Eunos to have time to make its own last-minute changes (personal communications from MPs familiar with the game plan for Eunos on Nomination Day; see also "Dr Tay to Contest in Tanglin", *Straits Times*, 24 Aug. 1988; and "Dr Tay Keeps Them Waiting", *Straits Times*, 25 Aug. 1988.) Such was the secrecy that even the wives of Tay Eng Soon and Lew Syn Pau were kept in the dark. Lew Syn Pau, transcript of Oral History Interview, Accession Number 002385/11, Reel 8, pp. 110–1 (National Archives of Singapore), available at https://www.nas.gov.sg/archivesonline/oral_history_interviews/interview/002385 (accessed 23 Jan. 2021).

240   "Chok Tong's Task Ahead: Forging a Consensus", *Straits Times*, 9 Sept. 1988. Although the winning margin, 1.8% over the WP team (a difference of approximately 1,300 votes), was within the 2% threshold that allowed the WP team to request for a recount, Dr Lee Siew Choh when asked his intentions at the counting centre declined to do so, conceding to the PAP team (Zulkifli bin Mohammed, personal communication, 23 Oct. 2020).

241   PM Lee Hsien Loong, interview with the author, 19 Dec. 2014. See also "Seow Silent on 'Sue Us' Challenge by PAP", *Straits Times*, 2 Sept. 1988; "Open Letters on Francis Seow:

Voters Must Know All Details"; and "A Dramatic Show but Nothing More than a Con Job", *Straits Times*, 3 Sept. 1988.

242 There were to be recurrences in Eunos in 1991 (Mohd Jufrie), in Cheng San in 1997 (Tang Liang Hong), and in Aljunied in 2006 (James Gomez).

243 "Inside 2 Years, Says DPM Again", *Straits Times*, 5 Sept. 1988. Reference has also been made to the transcript of the 4 September 1988 post-election press conference, which was made available to the author (National Archives of Singapore).

244 "From Close Shaves to Straight Losses—How the Women Fared", *Straits Times*, 4 Sept. 1988.

245 The members of the Post-mortem Committee were: BG Lee Hsien Loong (chairman), Dr Yeo Ning Hong and Prof. S. Jayakumar (advisers), Wong Kan Seng (secretary), Lew Syn Pau (assistant secretary), Yeo Cheow Tong, BG George Yeo, Dr Seet Ai Mee, Dr Ow Chin Hock, S. Chandra Das, Dr Tan Cheng Bock, Abdullah Tarmugi, Chew Heng Ching, Ibrahim Othman and Dr Hong Hai.

246 The report also remarked on the emergence of Low Thia Khiang from the Workers' Party and his credible showing during the Mandarin-language TV debate on the elected president proposal: "Low Thia Khiang of WP spoke extremely well, and made a good impression on viewers. He will be a figure in future elections" (*1988 General Election PAP Post-mortem Report* [PAP archive]). Low joined the WP in 1982 and had served as its organising secretary. He had also been J.B. Jeyaretnam's election agent in Jeyaretnam's successful re-election bid for Anson in 1984. Low's reasons for joining the WP had to do with, first, his unhappy experiences as a student at Nanyang University, where he felt disadvantaged by government policies that hindered the progression and future prospects of students whose primary language was Chinese; and second, (when he later became a teacher) witnessing students from poorer backgrounds disadvantaged by what he felt was the unfair policy of streaming students at an early age based on their academic ability. "Workers' Party's Low Thia Khiang: 'Confronting Tigers' and Making History with Bold GRC Win", *Straits Times*, 5 Nov. 2017.

247 BG Lee Hsien Loong to Assistant Secretary-General Goh Chok Tong, 15 Dec. 1988 (PAP archive).

248 *1988 General Election PAP post-mortem Report*.

249 BG Lee Hsien Loong to Assistant Secretary-General Goh Chok Tong, 15 Dec. 1988 (PAP archive).

250 On the straw polls (which gave DPM Goh the sense that support from the Malay community had fallen), see "We Lost More Votes than We Won", *Straits Times*, 26 Sept. 1988.

251 Singapore Parliamentary Debates, 21 Mar. 1985, cols 1090–2, 1097–8; "Serve PAP Constituency First Policy", *Straits Times*, 22 Mar. 1985.

252 "Reconsider the Priority Decision", *Straits Times*, 23 Mar. 1985. An individual writing under the pseudonym "Demos" summed up the mood in writing to the *Straits Times* Forum on 29 March 1985: "The winning party is expected to get down to the job for which it is elected, that is looking after the welfare of all the people fairly and equally and not those in the PAP constituencies first, otherwise the next punitive move will be to discriminate against the voters in PAP wards who have refused to vote for the party."

253 As revealed by PM Goh in 1991: "PM's Shock Therapy for Election", *Straits Times*, 18 Nov. 1991.

254 *1988 General Election PAP Post-mortem Report.*

255 Minutes of PAP Central Executive Committee Meeting, 13 Aug. 1985 (PAP archive).

256 "Malays Must Decide Who Can Best Meet Their Needs", *Straits Times*, 11 Sept. 1988; "We Lost More Votes than We Won".

257 "We Lost More Votes than We Won". Goh was giving written replies to questions posed in the Malay-language *Berita Minggu*.

258 The puzzlement was shared by some of the PAP Malay MPs. Interviewed for this book, Abdullah Tarmugi commented: "We weren't too sure actually how Chok Tong arrived at that conclusion. I mean straw polls perhaps . . . well there was some unhappiness definitely. But not to the extent of any disenchantment with the government to the point of voting against the government" (Abdullah Tarmugi, interview with the author, 9 Mar. 2013).

259 "Govt Wants a Clear Signal of Malay Support for Its Plans", *Straits Times*, 30 Sept. 1988 (translation of "The Malays and the Government", *Berita Harian* Editorial, 28 Sept. 1988).

260 "4 More Malay Bodies Respond on Chok Tong's Comments", *Straits Times*, 1 Oct. 1988. See also "Malay Teachers' Union Writes Open Letter to Chok Tong", *Straits Times*, 11 Oct. 1988.

261 See, for example, Yang Razali Kassim, "Winning Over the Malay Community", in *Impressions of the Goh Chok Tong Years*, ed. Welsh et al., pp. 363–74, esp. 366–70.

262 Abdullah Tarmugi, "The Dilemma and the Promise: A Response to Criticisms of Malay MPs", *Petir*, Aug. 1990, pp. 5–9, esp. 7. Tarmugi was subsequently to serve as minister for community development; he was also minister in charge of Muslim affairs from 1992 to 2002.

263 Ibid., pp. 5–9, esp. 5.

264 PM Lee Kuan Yew, speech at PAP Malay Affairs Bureau dinner, 15 July 1990 (PAP archive).

265 1DPM Goh Chok Tong to PM Lee Kuan Yew, 11 July 1990 (National Archives of Singapore), made available to the author.

266 Letters from Zulkifli bin Mohammed (11 July 1990), Ibrahim Othman (10 July 1990), Ahmad Mattar (11 July 1990) and Abdullah Tarmugi (11 July 1990) to PM Lee Kuan Yew (National Archives of Singapore), made available to the author.

267 Zainul Abidin Rasheed, Transcript of Oral History Interview, Accession Number 2281/08, Reel 3, pp. 127–8 (National Archives of Singapore), available at https://www.nas.gov.sg/archivesonline/oral_history_interviews/record-details/e71785e8-1162-11e3-83d5-0050568939ad (accessed 24 Jan. 2021).

268 For Goh's speech at the convention and his comments on the dialogue there with Malay/Muslim professionals following his speech, see https://www.nas.gov.sg/archivesonline/speeches/record-details/f550b392-e1b2-11e4-a0fd-0050568939ad (accessed 19 Feb. 2021). See also "Look for Results, Not Miracles", *Straits Times*, 9 Oct. 1990; and "Community Will Be Polarised 'If Leaders Are Not United'", *Straits Times*, 8 Oct. 1990.

For further analysis, see Kassim, "Winning Over the Malay Community", pp. 363–74, esp. 368–70.

269 Sidek Saniff, "The Self-Made Man", in *We Also Served*, ed. Chiang Hai Ding and Rohan Kamis, p. 186. Sidek Saniff was senior parliamentary secretary (education) at the time. Other PAP Malay MPs had behind the scenes warned AMP contacts not to provoke a clash within the community. Mohamad Maidin bin Packer Mohd, Oral History Interview (in Malay), Reel 5, Accession Number 003180 (at 46:04/ 50:48), available at https://www.nas.gov.sg/archivesonline/oral_history_interviews/record-details/52112bc5-1161-11e3-83d5-0050568939ad (accessed 24 Jan. 2021).

270 It could also be observed that the absence of rebuttal from Goh or other PAP leaders at this early stage gave the AMP leadership reason to believe that their view on the recent history of the Malay community was not being seriously contested. The view was, in essence, that there had been problems brewing in the Malay community for decades, and that the PAP government had failed to heed calls to act. For an early articulation of the AMP point of view, see "Partners in Progress, Interview with AMP", *Petir*, Mar. 1991, pp. 23–7.

271 Lily Zubaidah Rahim, "A New Dawn in PAP-Malay Relations?", in *Impressions of the Goh Chok Tong Years*, ed. Welsh et al., pp. 354–5. See also Lee, *Unexpected Nation*, pp. 502–9.

272 "Team MPs: Cabinet Papers Released".

273 PM Lee Kuan Yew, National Day Rally Speech at the Kallang Theatre, 26 Aug. 1990. *National Day Rally Speeches: 50 Years of Nationhood in Singapore 1966–2015*, p. 229.

274 "Ethnic Counter Revolution", opening address by S. Rajaratnam at the Second Annual Singapore Tamil Youth Conference, 30 Dec. 1989. A. Mani and Malathi Bala (eds), *The Last Twenty Five Years 1965–1990* (Singapore: Singapore Tamil Youths' Club, 1991), p. 10; see also "Ethnic Conflicts Will Hot Up and Hinder Global Unity, Says Raja", *Straits Times*, 31 Dec. 1989. For the difference in views between Lee and Rajaratnam, see Lee, *Unexpected Nation*, pp. 619–21.

275 "Communist Threat Still There, but in New Forms—PM", *Straits Times*, 24 Nov. 1986.

276 Lee Kuan Yew, *From Third World to First*, p. 239.

277 "Govt Accepts That '20% or Less' Call", *Straits Times*, 30 Dec. 1986; "Limit Proportion of Malay Pupils in Each School, Muslim MPs Urge Ministry", *Straits Times*, 29 Dec. 1986.

278 Files on housing policy (Ref ND 311/4-165 Vol. 2) (National Archives of Singapore), made available to the author.

279 The Ministerial Committee on Public Housing (which met from May 1986 to November 1987) was chaired by 1DPM Goh. Several of the conclusions and recommendations of the committee were to have far-reaching implications and will be dealt with in chapter 3.

280 1DPM Goh Chok Tong to Minister (National Development) S. Dhanabalan, 26 Feb. 1988 (National Archives of Singapore), made available to the author.

281 1DPM Goh Chok Tong to Minister (National Development) S. Dhanabalan, 6 Feb. 1988 (National Archives of Singapore), made available to the author.

282 Singapore Parliamentary Debates, 25 Feb. 1988, cols 542, 585–6.

283 Files on housing policy (Ref ND 311/4-165 Vol. 2) (National Archives of Singapore), made available to the author. For the control limits, see "Racial Limits Set for HDB Estates", *Straits Times*, 17 Feb. 1989; and "Maximum for Blocks Set 3 Points Higher", *Straits Times*, 17 Feb. 1989.

284 Maidin Packer to 1DPM Goh Chok Tong, 6 Dec. 1988. This staged approach for public communications was suggested to Goh by Maidin Packer, political secretary to the minister for communications and information. Information in this paragraph is drawn from files on the Ministerial Committee on Public Housing (Ref. MND 311/13/29 Vol. 3) made available to the author (National Archives of Singapore). See also Lee Kuan Yew, *From Third World to First*, p. 237.

285 "Dhana: Clear, Open Policies Needed to Prevent Enclaves", *Straits Times*, 7 Jan. 1989; "Resettlement Decision Was the Right Move", *Straits Times*, 23 Jan. 1988.

286 Even the editor of the *Straits Times* could in January 1991 remark on the "disturbing phenomenon" of Singaporeans becoming more conscious of their race. "Too Soon to Say if 1990 Was a Watershed: Editor", *Straits Times*, 12 Jan. 1991.

287 BG George Yeo, interview with Singapore Broadcasting Corporation, *Friday Background* programme, telecast 1 Dec. 1989. Excerpted in "We Should Find Strength in Our History to Take Us into the Future", *Straits Times*, 8 Dec. 1989.

288 Of the 22 detained, four worked full-time in organisations affiliated with the Catholic Church. Others volunteered their time at organisations linked to the Church. On their identities and connections, see "Those Who Were Arrested", *Straits Times*, 27 May 1987; and "The 16 Who Were Arrested", *Straits Times*, 2 June 1987.

289 A great deal of ink has been spilt on the Marxist Conspiracy. My intention, rather than covering the issue in exhaustive detail, is to give a sense of the views and mindset of the PAP leadership during the period when the key events unfolded. Existing histories, and memoirs by those detained or otherwise involved (as well as in the Marxist Conspiracy's coda, the Hendrickson affair), have provided both sides to the story and should be consulted. See Lee Kuan Yew, *From Third World to First*, pp. 137–8; Yap et al., *Men in White*, pp. 435–44; C.M. Turnbull, *A History of Modern Singapore, 1819–2005*, 3rd ed. (Singapore: NUS Press, 2009), pp. 338–40; and Lee, *Unexpected Nation*, pp. 468–75. For the "other" side, see Teo Soh Lung, *Beyond the Blue Gate: Recollections of a Political Prisoner* (Petaling Jaya: Strategic Information and Research Development Centre, 2010); Seow, *To Catch a Tartar*; Tan Wah Piow, *Smokescreens & Mirrors: Tracing the "Marxist Conspiracy"* (Singapore: Function 8, 2012); and Chng Tuan Tze, Low Yit Leng and Teo Soh Lung (eds), *1987: Singapore's Marxist Conspiracy 30 Years On* (Singapore: Function 8, 2017).

290 Yap et al., *Men in White*, pp. 467–8. For Dhanabalan's thoughts on the affair, see "Remembering Lee Kuan Yew: A Leader Who Was Ruthless in Demanding Honesty", *Straits Times*, 24 Mar. 2015. See also Peh Shing Huei, *Tall Order*, pp. 269–70. I am grateful to S. Dhanabalan for a personal communication on the issue (14 May 2013).

291 Yap et al., *Men in White*, p. 505; Lee, *Unexpected Nation*, p. 643. See also Hong Lysa and Huang Jianli, *Scripting a National History: Singapore and Its Pasts* (Hong Kong: Hong Kong University Press, 2008), p. 145.

292 "Been There, Done That, and Thrived", *Straits Times*, 14 Dec. 2001. Law lecturer Walter Woon (who would become Singapore's attorney-general in 2008) commented in 1991, "As far as I am concerned, the government's case is still not proven. I would not say those fellows were Red, not from the stuff they presented. I think a lot of people have this skepticism." "Stand Up and Be Quoted", *Straits Times*, 6 July 1991.

293 One such gathering involving members of the public, social activists and some of the former detainees from 1987 took place on 19 May 2012 at Speakers' Corner, Hong Lim Park.

294 "The Legacy of 1987", *Straits Times*, 7 July 2007. In her account of the events of 1987–88, the historian C.M. Turnbull noted: "The alleged Marxist conspiracy and the Liberation Theology menace turned out to be myths, but the episode did reveal a strong undercurrent of dissatisfaction with some of the ruling party's basic policies, which attracted these disparate elements. At the time of independence the PAP had hoped the Christian churches would help nation-building by providing moral fibre and encouraging sacrifice for the good of society. But the Church in many respects was out of sympathy with the road to nationhood that the PAP had chosen, with its emphasis on tough self-reliant meritocracy, material achievement, entrepreneurship and profit-making." Turnbull, *History of Modern Singapore*, p. 339.

295 Parliamentary Speech on the Internal Security Act by DPM Teo Chee Hean (also Coordinating Minister for National Security and Minister for Home Affairs), 19 Oct. 2011 (Singapore Parliamentary Debates, 19 Oct. 2011, Debate on the President's Address).

296 Ibid.

297 Singapore Parliamentary Debates, 23 Feb. 90, col. 1149 (1DPM Goh Chok Tong's Speech during the Second Reading of the Maintenance of Religious Harmony Bill).

298 "Communist Threat Still There, but in New Forms—PM".

299 "Flirting with Communism", *Straits Times* Editorial, 25 Nov. 1986.

300 Secretary-General Lee Kuan Yew's Speech at the Biennial Party Conference, 23 Nov. 1986 (PAP archive).

301 "Government Displeasure with Church Began in 1985, Says Robertson", *Straits Times*, 12 Oct. 1989.

302 PM Lee also spoke to the Pope on the issue during the Pope's visit to Singapore in November 1986. "Why Should We Attack the Church when They Were Our Allies?", *Straits Times*, 24 Aug. 1988.

303 Another charge made by the government—that some of those detained had been tasked by Tan Wah Piow to infiltrate the Workers' Party and had succeeded in capturing the WP's organ, *The Hammer*—was disputed by J.B. Jeyaretnam and the WP, who saw them as activists with a social conscience. "Group Captured Control of WP Publication", *Straits Times*, 27 May 1987; "Anger and Courage", and "Desperate PAP" (editorial), *The Hammer*, Aug./Sept. 1987, pp. 1, 5.

304 Lee apparently said in his meeting with the archbishop that the detainees were "do-gooders, who wanted to help the poor and dispossessed". The minutes of this meeting were released to the court during the government's legal action against the *Far Eastern Economic Review* in 1989. "Istana Meeting with PM Left Priest 'Stunned and Worried'", *Straits Times*, 5 Oct. 1989.

305 When interviewed, Goh Chok Tong noted that he had shown S. Dhanabalan (who was uncomfortable with the arrests) evidence of the links that the security services had uncovered between those detained, Tan Wah Piow and ultimately the CPM. Goh Chok Tong, interview with the author, 30 Jan. 2013.

306 "ISA Is Crucial to Singapore—PM", *Straits Times*, 28 May 1988.

307 "Church 'Perturbed at Arrests and Statement'", *Straits Times*, 29 May 1987.

308 "Archbishop Accepted Evidence", *Straits Times*, 3 June 1987.

309 PM Lee Kuan Yew, National Day Rally Speech at the Kallang Theatre, 16 Aug. 1987. *National Day Rally Speeches: 50 Years of Nationhood in Singapore*, p. 163. PM Lee had also noted that "what we want our religious and para-religious groups to do is to give relief to the destitute, the disadvantaged, the disabled, to take part in activities which will foster communal fellowship" (p. 159). See also "The Challenges and Pitfalls—by PM", *Straits Times*, 17 Aug. 1987; and "Even the Pope Doesn't Tell the Govt What to Do", *Straits Times*, 17 Aug. 1987.

310 Singapore Parliamentary Debates, 23 Feb. 1990, col. 1148 (1DPM Goh Chok Tong's Speech at the Second Reading of the Maintenance of Religious Harmony Bill).

311 Information drawn from File ref MCD 132-06-33 V3 (National Archives of Singapore), made available to the author.

312 Eddie C.Y. Kuo, Jon S.T. Quah and Tong Chee Kiong, "Religion and Religious Revivalism in Singapore" (Singapore: Ministry of Community Development, 1988). For a summary of the findings, see "Religious Trends 'Need Careful Handling'", *Straits Times*, 19 Feb. 1989; and "Ministry Releases Final Reports on Religion", *Straits Times*, 31 Aug. 1989.

313 "Religion and Religious Revivalism in Singapore", pp. 4–5. The report noted that for "hard-core Christians", "Christianity is non-compromising. The tenets of the Bible are given a fundamentalist interpretation. Thus, their stance towards other religions is more confrontational. There is a 'sense of mission', a divine call to preach and convert adherents of other religions, be they Muslims or Hindus, to the 'true way'" (pp. 12–3).

314 Ibid., pp. 38–41. See also Jon S.T. Quah, *Public Administration Singapore-Style* (Bingley: Emerald Group Publishing, 2010), pp. 199–235; and Jason Tan, "The Rise and Fall of Religious Knowledge in Singapore Secondary Schools", *Journal of Curriculum Studies* 29, 5 (1997): 615–8.

315 Goh Chok Tong, interview with the author, 22 June 2012.

316 Files on the phasing out of Religious Knowledge made available to the author (Ref MOE C07-01-067 Vol. 6; National Archives of Singapore).

317 Singapore Parliamentary Debates, 20 Mar. 1989, cols 511–4.

318 "Crucial for Govt to Be Neutral in Religious Matters", *Straits Times*, 7 Oct. 1989. Resistance to the phasing out of Religious Knowledge was especially strong from the religious leaders. "GPC's Reasons for Scrapping Subject at Odds with Its Proposal", *Straits Times*, 13 Aug. 1989.

319 "Crucial for Govt to Be Neutral in Religious Matters"; Singapore Parliamentary Debates, 6 Oct. 1989, col. 578.

320 "Religious Trends: A Security Perspective", annex to White Paper on Maintenance of Religious Harmony, pp. 13–9, esp. 15–8. The statements included a sermon given by

one priest on the second anniversary of the ISA arrests, which included a comment that "the Minister for Home Affairs, Jayakumar, all Judges and ISD officers would face God's punishment" for detaining the individuals involved in the Marxist Conspiracy (p. 16). See also "ISD Report Cites Cases of Religious Tension", *Straits Times*, 30 Dec. 1989; and "Stopping the Over-zealous Before They Cause Strife", *Straits Times*, 30 Dec. 1989.

321 Government documents made available to the author make it clear that the release of the ISD report as an annex to the White Paper on Religious Harmony was on the direction of PM Lee himself. PM Lee Kuan Yew to Prof. S. Jayakumar, 21 Nov. 1989 (National Archives of Singapore), made available to the author.

322 "White Paper on Religion and Politics Ready in 2 Weeks", *Straits Times*, 30 Nov. 1989. Attempts were made as far back as late 1988 to sensitise religious leaders and the public to the continued dangers of mixing religion and politics, and to prepare the ground for legislation. PM Lee touched on the issue on 13 December 1988 during his speech at a Singapore Buddhist Federation religious observance function, warning that religious groups should not try to "define the socioeconomic agenda" nor try to mobilise the ground through "social action programmes", as this would lead other religious groups to do so too. "Tolerance of Each Other's Religion Is Vital in Singapore", PM Lee Kuan Yew, speech at the Singapore Buddhist Federation, 13 Dec. 1988. *Papers of Lee Kuan Yew, Vol. 10*, p. 175.

323 *White Paper on Maintenance of Religious Harmony, Cmd. 21 of 1989. Presented to Parliament on 26 Dec. 1989*, pp. 9–10. Available at https://www.nas.gov.sg/archivesonline/government_records/record-details/fc4424cf-7957-11e7-83df-0050568939ad (accessed 24 Aug. 2020).The Maintenance of Religious Harmony Act (MRHA) was eventually to be passed by Parliament in November 1990.

324 Besides PM Lee, the government ministers present were 1DPM Goh, 2DPM Ong Teng Cheong, S. Dhanabalan, Dr Tony Tan, Dr Ahmad Mattar, Prof. S. Jayakumar, Wong Kan Seng, BG Lee Hsien Loong and BG George Yeo.

325 As pointed out in "Religion and Religious Revivalism in Singapore", p. 6.

326 Notes of Meeting between PM and Religious Leaders at the Ministry of Community Development, 22 Nov. 1989 (National Archives of Singapore), made available to the author.

327 BG Lee Hsien Loong to Assistant Secretary-General Goh Chok Tong, 15 Dec. 1988; *1988 General Election PAP Post-mortem Report*.

328 *Report of the Central Executive Committee, January 1989–October 1990* (PAP archive).

329 "Our National Ethic", speech by Goh Chok Tong, First Deputy Prime Minister and Minister for Defence, at the PAP Youth Wing Charity Night, 28 Oct. 1988. The dinner also marked the second anniversary of the Youth Wing, available at https://www.nas.gov.sg/archivesonline/speeches/record-details/7157e523-115d-11e3-83d5-0050568939ad (accessed 24 Jan. 2021).

330 "A National Ideology: Govt's New Goal", *Straits Times*, 29 Oct. 1988. The Shared Values/National Ideology debate is also discussed in Michael Hill and Lian Kwen Fee, *The Politics of National Building and Citizenship in Singapore* (London: Routledge, 1995), pp. 210–9; and (in an interesting and somewhat critical fashion) John Clammer, "Deconstructing Values: The Establishment of a National Ideology and Its Implications for Singapore's

Political Future", in *Singapore Changes Guard: Social, Political and Economic Directions in the 1990s*, ed. Garry Rodan (New York: St. Martin's Press, 1993), pp. 34–51.

331   Lee Kuan Yew, interview with Clara Chou (*United Daily News*), Sheena Chang (*China Times*) and Ralph Ma Ning (Central News Agency), 8 Mar. 1989. *Papers of Lee Kuan Yew, Vol. 10*, pp. 203–4. See also Lee, *Unexpected Nation*, pp. 546–50. These were Lee's personal reservations at the time. Files made available to the author show that Lee subsequently wrote to Goh informing him that in his (Lee's) view, it was important that the National Ideology effort, once announced, had to be followed up on and brought to a conclusion.

332   "Government's Aim Is to Create a Better Life for All Singaporeans", *Straits Times*, 10 Jan. 1989.

333   "Society Before Self: Many Disturbed by This—Chay", *Straits Times*, 20 Jan. 1989.

334   "MP Cheered by Consensus on Racial Harmony", *Straits Times*, 21 Jan. 1989. Tarmugi's comments were telling. He was later to characterise the 1980s as a period when there were "manifestations of increased Chinese-ness in the environment" and that these were "widely perceived, as, at best, an insensitivity to Malay and minority feelings and, at worst, as an attempt to engulf Singapore society with the attributes and the will of the majority." Tarmugi, "The Dilemma and the Promise", p. 5.

335   Singapore Parliamentary Debates, 20 Jan. 1989, col. 450.

336   "BG Lee: No Intention to Stifle Individual", *Straits Times*, 18 Jan. 1989.

337   Singapore Parliamentary Debates, 20 Jan. 1989, col. 453.

338   BG Lee Hsien Loong, "The National Ideology: A Direction and Identity for Singapore", in *Speeches: A Bimonthly Selection of Ministerial Speeches* 13, 1 (1989): 37–8 (Singapore: Information Division, Ministry of Communications and Information), also available at https://www.nas.gov.sg/archivesonline/speeches/record-details/724e0042-115d-11e3-83d5-0050568939ad (accessed 18 Feb. 2021). See also "BG Lee Zeroes In on the Core Issues", *Straits Times*, 12 Jan. 1989; and "Parliamentary Panel to Identify Core Values", *Straits Times*, 4 Dec. 1988.

339   PM Lee had felt, when Religious Knowledge was first introduced, that the majority of Chinese parents would want their children to choose Confucian Ethics (as the subject was called), and not Buddhism Studies. PM Lee Kuan Yew, "Forging Confucian Values in the Young amidst Rapid Urban Changes", speech at the Chinese New Year Reception at the Istana, 7 Feb. 1982. *Papers of Lee Kuan Yew, Vol. 9*, p. 155. See also "To Each Family a Share of Singapore", *Straits Times*, 8 Feb. 1982. Lee was mistaken in his belief. In 1989, 18% of Chinese students chose Confucian Ethics, 44% chose Buddhist Studies, and 21% chose Bible Knowledge. Eddie C.Y. Kuo, "Confucianism as Political Discourse in Singapore: The Case of an Incomplete Revitalisation Movement", in *Confucian Traditions in East Asian Modernity: Moral Education and Economic Culture in Japan and the Four Mini-Dragons*, ed. Tu Wei-Ming (Cambridge: Harvard University Press, 1996), pp. 294–309, 391–4 (see p. 393n25 for the statistics on the take-up of Religious Knowledge subjects).

340   The White Paper went to great lengths to dispel the idea of creeping Confucianism: "Initially, non-Chinese Singaporeans were concerned that the Shared Values might become a subterfuge for imposing Chinese Confucian values on them. This was never

the Government's intention. The Government has never allowed the majority race to impose itself on the minority communities." *Shared Values. Cmd. 1 of 1991. Presented to Parliament by Command of the President of the Republic of Singapore. Ordered by Parliament to lie upon the Table: 2 January 1991*, p. 7. (Hereinafter cited as White Paper on Shared Values), available at https://www.nas.gov.sg/archivesonline/government_records/record-details/a472b486-7aea-11e7-83df-0050568939ad (accessed 24 Jan. 2021).

341 Perhaps in an indication of the uncertain train of development behind the eventual White Paper, the green paper for public discussion which was mooted as early as January 1989, and then announced again for likely release in 1990, never materialised. "Green Paper, Public Views to Be Sought on National Ideology", *Straits Times*, 21 Jan. 1989; "Green Paper on National Ideology May Be Out Next Year", *Straits Times*, 20 June 1989.

342 On 21 January 1989, DPM Goh announced that a discussion paper on shared values would be presented to Parliament. He disclosed that IPS had formed a study group, at the government's request, to examine the issue. (The IPS study was published in 1990: Jon S.T. Quah [ed.], *In Search of Singapore's National Values* [Singapore: Times Academic Press for the Institute of Policy Studies, 1990].)

343 A delegation led by BG (Res) George Yeo was sent to Jakarta to study Indonesia's state ideology, Pancasila. "From Here to Ideology", *Straits Times*, 31 July 1989.

344 BG (Res) George Yeo to DPM Lee Hsien Loong, 17 Dec. 1990 (National Archives of Singapore), made available to the author.

345 SM Lee Kuan Yew to DPM Lee Hsien Loong (cc Cabinet), 18 Dec. 1990 (National Archives of Singapore), made available to the author.

346 18 Dec. 1990 Exchange of Memoranda between SM Lee Kuan Yew and DPM Lee Hsien Loong cc Cabinet (National Archives of Singapore; made available to the author). DPM Lee agreed that "social justice" should not be included, noting that he had been reminded after meeting several MPs that "Social Justice" was a slogan of Liberation Theology. In the end, this point finally appeared as "regard and community support for the individual" in the White Paper (National Archives of Singapore), made available to the author.

347 *White Paper on Shared Values*, pp. 6–7; "Govt Proposes 5 Shared Values", *Straits Times*, 6 Jan. 1991.

348 DPM Lee Hsien Loong observed in a 14 January 1991 memo to the "Kitchen Cabinet" (a smaller group of Cabinet ministers responsible for critical portfolios that later came to be known internally as the Political Group or PG) that a recent Feedback Unit discussion had seen several speakers note that the value as it stood would suppress dissent. DPM Lee noted that it might be worthwhile to make a gesture to this group, which represented the more articulate and sceptical professionals. He proposed to note in Parliament that the government was open to suggestions on improving the phrasing (National Archives of Singapore, made available to the author). The final formula (proposed by Arthur Beng, MP for Fengshan) was "consensus, not conflict" instead of "consensus instead of contention". See "2 Shared Values Amended to Make Them More Acceptable", *Straits Times*, 16 Jan. 1991.

349 "Lack of Urgency about Need for Shared Values Makes for Grey Debate", *Straits Times*, 16 Jan. 1991.

350 Goh Chok Tong, interview with the author, 22 June 2012.

351 "PM Goh's Plan for Singapore", *Straits Times*, 29 Nov. 1990.

352 "PM Goh Should Re-think His By-election Pledge", *Straits Times*, 6 Sept. 1991.

353 "Chok Tong: Why I Decided PM Should Stay", *Straits Times*, 11 Sept. 1988.

354 Goh Chok Tong, personal communication, 29 Apr. 2013.

355 Ibid.; Peh Shing Huei, *Tall Order*, pp. 239, 249.

356 Singapore Parliamentary Debates, 13 June 1990, col. 232.

357 Ibid.

358 Yap et al., *Men in White*, pp. 448–9; Lee, *Unexpected Nation*, pp. 481–2.

359 "Why I Called for Polls Now", *Straits Times*, 18 Aug. 1991.

360 Goh Chok Tong, interview with the author, 30 Nov. 2013. This interpretation is also confirmed through author interviews (2012–16) with PAP leaders, including former Cabinet ministers.

361 *Singapore: The Next Lap* (Singapore: Times Editions, 1991). The Next Lap had its beginnings in 1989, the year the Long Term National Development Committee (comprising ministers of state) had been formed to put together a vision of a future Singapore. The Next Lap drew on earlier efforts such as Vision 1999 (1984), the Economic Committee (1986), Agenda for Action (1988), and the 1989 reports of the six advisory councils on various aspects of society. "Government Unveils Its Vision of a Future Singapore", *Straits Times*, 23 Feb. 1991; "Ready, Steady, Go", *Straits Times*, 24 Feb. 1991.

362 "PM Will Call Early General Election", *Straits Times*, 5 Aug. 1991. The Party Manifesto, released on 17 August 1991, drew heavily from The Next Lap. "A Personal Message to All Singaporeans", *Straits Times*, 18 Aug. 1991.

363 The Electoral Boundaries Review Committee had reconstituted the existing Tiong Bahru GRC, which would be renamed Tanjong Pagar GRC, and which would absorb Tanjong Pagar and Telok Blangah SMCs. *The Report of the Electoral Boundaries Review Committee, 1991. Cmd. 12 of 1991. Presented to Parliament by Command of the President of the Republic of Singapore. Ordered by Parliament to Lie Upon the Table: 8 August 1991*, p. 3, available at https://www.nas.gov.sg/archivesonline/government_records/record-details/a8a70f21-7aea-11e7-83df-0050568939ad (accessed 5 Apr. 2021).

364 Dr Koh, an obstetrician, had in December 1988 overseen a delivery where the mother died following post-childbirth complications. In May 1991 the state coroner found that these complications were unfortunate but unavoidable, and found no wrongdoing on the part of Dr Koh. "Misadventure Verdict On Death of Woman After Induced Labour", *Straits Times*, 19 May 1991. The Party leadership while taking note of the state coroner's finding that Dr Koh was not at fault, decided not to field him in the 1991 election given that civil proceedings (contemplated by the husband of the deceased) might prove a distraction to Dr Koh and to the Party. Goh Chok Tong, personal communication, 7 Apr. 2021.

365 Lim Hng Kiang, interview with the author, 30 Mar. 2021; Dr S. Vasoo, interview with the author, 3 Apr. 2021.

366 "I was initially rejected by the branch activists at Telok Blangah. It was a very uncomfortable feeling—that was a very tough night before Nomination Day. Fortunately Dr Vasoo was able to persuade the group." Lim Hng Kiang, interview with the author, 30 Mar. 2021. PM Goh subsequently hosted the branch activists to lunch in order to soothe

raw feelings and explain the Party's decision. Goh Chok Tong, personal communication, 7 Apr. 2021.

367 Lim Hng Kiang, interview with the author, 30 Mar. 2021.

368 Ibid.

369 "Communal Politics a Key Issue", *Straits Times*, 28 Aug. 1991. During the campaign there were also threats of a personal nature, purportedly from members of the Malay community, directed at Sidek Saniff, accusing him of disloyalty to Malays/Muslims. See Sidek Saniff, *Life Reflections at Eighty*, pp. 168–70.

370 "Kan Seng: Jufrie Used Islamic Phrases to Stir Muslim Sentiments", *Straits Times*, 6 Sept. 1991.

371 "Narrow Victory for Moderate Politics", *Straits Times*, 1 Sept. 1991.

372 "PAP Wins All but 4; Share of Votes Dips to 61%", *Straits Times*, 1 Sept. 1991. On the 1991 campaign in Eunos, see Bilveer Singh, *Whither PAP's Dominance? An Analysis of Singapore's 1991 General Elections* (Petaling Jaya: Pelanduk, 1992), pp. 79–83, 128–30.

373 Singh, *Whither PAP's Dominance?*, pp. 129–30. Zainul Abidin Rasheed, who was also the president of MUIS, the Islamic Religious Council of Singapore (and who was to become a PAP MP), took the view—which seems to have been the one held by the majority within the Malay/Muslim community—that there was nothing untoward about Jufrie's use of the phrases in question. Sidek Saniff, part of the PAP slate in Eunos GRC, had the same view as Zainal Abidin Rasheed. Sukmawati bte Haji Sirat, *Trends in Malay Political Leadership: The People's Action Party's Malay Political Leaders and the Integration of the Singapore Malays*, pp. 211–3. There are shades here of the PAP's overreaction against Tang Liang Hong during the December 1996 campaigning in Cheng San GRC (on which see chapter 3). See also S. Rajaratnam's insightful post-election commentary, "The Politics of Crying Wolf", *Straits Times*, 29 Sept. 1991.

374 Braddell Heights (52.27%), Bukit Batok (51.82%), Changi (53%) and Nee Soon South (52.76%).

375 Chiam was in January 1992 given the unofficial title of leader of the Opposition, which in practice meant he was given a certain precedence amongst opposition MPs. "Chiam Named Unofficial Leader of the Opposition", *Straits Times*, 7 Jan. 1992. A more official designation—coming with responsibilities, duties and privileges, as well as resources allocated to the role—would have to wait until July 2020, when WP Secretary-General Pritam Singh was appointed leader of the Opposition following the 10 July 2020 general election.

376 "Politics Here Can't Go On as Before: PM Goh", *Straits Times*, 1 Sept. 1991.

377 "Letter Writers to PM: Election Results Not a Rejection of 'Open' Style", *Straits Times*, 7 Sept. 1991.

378 The PAP had itself observed this prior to the polls. "BG Lee on What Constitutes 'Strong Endorsement'", *Straits Times*, 28 Aug. 1991.

379 "Some Reasons Why Good Deeds Cause Resentment, Not Love", *Straits Times*, 23 Nov. 1991.

380 Wong Kan Seng was to chair all campaign task forces from 1991 until 2011. The other members of the 1991 Task Force were: Dr Lee Boon Yang (secretary; also chairman,

Candidates Liaison Committee), Ahmad Mattar (chairman, Finance Committee), Yeo Cheow Tong (chairman, Feedback Committee), BG George Yeo (chairman, Ops Centre), Mah Bow Tan (chairman, Media Relations), Peter Sung (secretary, Mass Rally Committee) and Lim Boon Heng (chairman, Publicity and Information Committee). The task force held 14 meetings in all, but (in a sign of the lack of time the main Party machine had to prepare for the election) only three of these were held before the dissolution of Parliament on 14 August 1991.

381 PAP 1991 General Election Task Force, Minutes of 7th Meeting, 24 Aug. 1991 (PAP archive).

382 Dr Lee Boon Yang, interview with the author, 12 Mar. 2013. For Low's account (suggesting that Hougang was picked by chance and was not in any case his first choice), see his interview in Daniel Goh (ed.), *Walking with Singapore: The Workers' Party's 60th Anniversary* (Singapore: Workers' Party, 2017), p. 80.

383 It is also no accident that the PAP from this point on would deploy Teochew speakers to contest in Hougang: Heng Chee How (1997) and Eric Low (2001, 2006) against Low Thia Khiang; Desmond Choo (2011) against the WP's Yaw Shin Leong; and Lee Hong Chuang against the WP's Png Eng Huat (2015) and Dennis Tan (2020).

384 In 1988 Seet had washed her hands immediately after shaking the hand of a fishmonger (or pork seller), leading to the Opposition accusation that she was elitist and out of touch. "'Seet Ai Mee Is a Strong Woman with a Good Record'", *Straits Times*, 30 Aug. 1991. For Seet's point of view, see Tan Bee Bee, "Why Dr Seet Needed to Wash Her Hands", letter to *Straits Times* Forum, 5 Sept. 1991; "Ex-Minister Speaks Out, after 18 Years", *Straits Times*, 13 Aug. 2009; and "Welcome Home, Mum", *Petir*, July/Aug. 2009, pp. 29–30.

385 "The Many Issues that Split Nee Soon Central Residents", *Straits Times*, 13 Sept. 1991.

386 Cheo Chai Chen also had long-standing connections to the Nee Soon area that bolstered his credibility: his grandfather had been the foreman in business magnate and community leader Lim Nee Soon's rubber estate. Singh, *Whither PAP's Dominance?*, p. 106.

387 The PAP held rallies only in Eunos, Bukit Gombak and Ulu Pandan. Opposition rallies were far more numerous.

388 "'Seet Ai Mee Is a Strong Woman with a Good Record'".

389 "Fine-Tuning Feedback", *Petir*, Sept. 1991, pp. 6–9.

390 John Chen, "Reaching Out to All", *Petir*, Sept. 1991, pp. 4–5.

391 "欧进福吁请政府：别把华教者支持视为理所当然" [Ow Chin Hock implores the government: do not take the support of the Chinese-educated for granted], *Shin Min Daily News*, 8 Sept. 1991.

392 Dr Ow Chin Hock, personal communication, 14 Nov. 2012.

393 Ibid.

394 "李炯才在《大选的回顾》座谈会上说行动党竞选策略应用上有些失当" [Lee Khoon Choy at the talk on "review of the election": PAP deployed somewhat inappropriate election strategy], *Lianhe Zaobao,* 9 Sept. 1991.

395 Ow was together with a small number of other MPs invited to a lunch discussion with PM Goh on 15 September 1991, when Goh was attempting to make his own

preliminary post-election soundings. Dr Ow Chin Hock, personal communication, 14 Nov. 12.

396 Speech by Ong Teng Cheong, Deputy Prime Minister, at the Chinese Press Club talk at New Park Hotel on 16 September 1991. Available at https://www.nas.gov.sg/ archivesonline/speeches/record-details/726054b8-115d-11e3-83d5-0050568939ad (accessed 6 Aug. 2021). The main points from the talk were carried in "Teng Cheong Lists Four Groups of Opposition Voters", *Straits Times*, 17 Sept. 1991. For good measure, Ong also reiterated his main points in a 17 September 1991 interview with the *Straits Times*. "Govt Cannot Cater Solely to Needs of English-Educated, Says Teng Cheong", *Straits Times*, 18 Sept. 1991.

397 Goh Chok Tong, personal communication, 17 May 2014; *1991 General Election PAP Post-mortem Report* (PAP archive).

398 "A Matter of Language", *Petir*, Oct. 1991, pp. 13–5.

399 Information drawn from government files made available to the author on Chinese language policy (Ref MOE Education Plan 17.10.88-28.9.94, National Archives of Singapore).

400 Information drawn from government files made available to the author on Chinese language policy (Ref MOE Education Plan 17.10.88-28.9.94, National Archives of Singapore).

401 The report of the CLRC was submitted in April 1992 and represented the most extensive review to date of the teaching and learning of Chinese in schools. The review made recommendations not just on language learning but also on steps to improve the morale and career development of Chinese language teachers. See Lee, *Unexpected Nation*, pp. 513–22. On the political considerations and ground sensitivities underlying language instruction at this time, see S. Gopinathan, "Language Policy Changes 1979–1992: Politics and Pedagogy", in *Language, Society and Education in Singapore: Issues and Trends*, 2nd ed., ed. S. Gopinathan, Anne Pakir, Ho Wah Kam and Vanithamani Saravanan (Singapore: Times Academic Press, 1998), pp. 19–44, esp. 37–44.

402 PM Lee Kuan Yew to 1DPM Goh Chok Tong, 10 Mar. 1990 (National Archives of Singapore), made available to the author.

403 "Ministers' Reading Habits May Be Why They Lost Touch", *Straits Times*, 23 Sept. 1991; "More Attention for the Chinese Silent Majority", *Straits Times*, 23 Sept. 1991.

404 "The Dialect Dilemma", *Straits Times*, 14 Dec. 1991.

405 "Government Will Find New Ways to Sell Policies", *Straits Times*, 23 Sept. 1991. While sympathetic to some of DPM Ong's views, other Party leaders do not appear to have fully subscribed to the view that it was primarily a loss of votes amongst the Chinese-speaking working class that led to the 1991 election setback. Wong Kan Seng, chairman of the 1991 Elections Task Force, observed that it was actually during the 1997 election that the "Chinese issue" reared its head more substantially in the shape of Tang Liang Hong and the campaign in Cheng San. Wong Kan Seng, interview with the author, 16 Apr. 2013.

406 The article was penned by Agnes Chen, the executive editor of *Singapore Business*.

407 DPM Lee Hsien Loong to PM Goh Chok Tong, 3 Sept. 1991 (PAP archive); "What the Voters Are Saying", *Business Times*, 3 Sept. 1991.

408 The Post-mortem Committee comprised BG Lee, BG George Yeo, M. Maidin, Dr Yeo Ning Hong, Wong Kan Seng, Dr Ong Chit Chung, Dr Hong Hai, Yeo Cheow Tong, Ch'ng Jit Koon, Lim Boon Heng, Matthias Yao, Dr Lee Boon Yang, Abdullah Tarmugi and Tang Guan Seng. Four new MPs were secretaries for the visits to selected Party branches: Dr Ker Sin Tze, Lim Hng Kiang, Ho Peng Kee and Koo Tsai Kee.

409 DPM and Minister (Trade and Industry) Lee Hsien Loong to PM Goh Chok Tong, 30 Sept. 1991 (National Archives of Singapore), made available to the author.

410 "Help the Common Man Achieve His Goal", *Straits Times*, 17 Nov. 1991.

411 *1991 General Election PAP Post-mortem Report.*

412 "Paper on PAP Philosophy Draws Most Debate", *Straits Times*, 18 Nov. 1991. The paper clearly touched a raw nerve with Goh; but the irony is that Party leaders had in fact been encouraging Party activists to form study groups that examined issues and presented quality feedback in a constructive manner. "Form Study Groups, PAP Activists Urged", *Straits Times*, 29 Apr. 1990.

413 "Government Will Be Firm and Fair to All", *Straits Times*, 18 Nov. 1991; "Find a New PM if You Want More Subsidies", *Straits Times*, 18 Nov. 1991.

414 Low's remarks, originally made in Teochew, lose something of their flavour when rendered into Mandarin and English. But the effectiveness of this rallying call was pinpointed by several former PAP MPs and ministers interviewed for this book. I am grateful to Lau Ping Sum for a personal communication on the subject.

415 "Money Back to the People", *Straits Times*, 20 Aug. 1991.

416 Wong Yew Kuan, "Mencius Says: Govern with Benevolence and Righteousness", letter to *Straits Times* Forum, 21 Nov. 1991.

417 "False Image of a 'Greedy Govt' Needs to Be Corrected—Fast", *Straits Times*, 30 Nov. 1991.

418 "PM: I Want to Be the People's Choice", *Straits Times*, 31 Aug. 1991.

419 "Govt Will Be Firm and Fair to All", *Straits Times*, 18 Nov. 1991.

420 *1991 General Election PAP Post-mortem Report.*

421 There was Party criticism in the lead-up to the hustings that "The Next Lap", while attractive to the English-educated, did not resonate with the ground, partly because in Chinese translation the slogan became "A New Starting Point" (implying having to start all over again). This led to the revival of the 1988 slogan "More Good Years" for use in the 1991 campaign in the form of "Go for More Good Years" (Party files on the aftermath of the 1991 election, made available to the author).

422 *1991 General Election PAP Post-mortem Report.*

423 "Politics Here Can't Go On as Before". The post-mortem report noted that while what Goh had said at the press conference was necessary, "It showed the PAP wounded and at bay, weak rather than resolute. It would have been better for the press conference to have ended on a positive note, calling on the people to rally around the government so that it could govern effectively. This triggered an almost visceral response from voters, and contributed to the catharsis which followed." *1991 General Election PAP Post-mortem Report.*

424 "GPC Chairmen to Discuss New Role", *Straits Times*, 13 Nov. 1991; "7 New GPC Chairmen Named", *Straits Times*, 2 Nov. 1991.

425 "7 New GPC Chairmen Named".

426 Party leaders felt that the press had gone to town in its post-election coverage. Commentary (especially in the Chinese press) focused on the Opposition wards, on the defeated PAP candidates and the alleged wrongs of the PAP. Gossip was occasionally reported as fact. The Chinese press even carried advertisements congratulating Opposition candidates who won. The sense was that the press was testing the limits of the new relationship. *1991 General Election PAP Post-mortem Report.*

427 PM Goh Chok Tong to Chandra Das, 27 Dec. 1991 (National Archives of Singapore), made available to the author.

428 "Feedback Unit: The Task Ahead", *Straits Times*, 14 Mar. 1992.

429 S. Chandra Das, interview with the author, 16 Nov. 2012.

430 The brief given to Ow by PM Goh was to reach out to the Chinese ground. Dr Ow Chin Hock, personal communication, 2 Nov. 2012.

431 "民意组将倾听沉默一群心声" [The Feedback Unit will listen to the silent majority], *Lianhe Zaobao*, 18 Sept. 1991.

432 "Government Will Find New Ways to Sell Policies", *Straits Times*, 23 Sept. 1991.

433 "R-Rating Will Only Be Given to Artistic Films", *Straits Times*, 5 Sept. 1991.

434 "New Rules for R-Rated Films Welcome by Most", *Straits Times*, 8 Sept. 1991. Yeo noted that in post-election discussions within the leadership, he had pushed for the new R(A) classification, in order to make the point that the policy of gradual relaxation of censorship had not been abandoned altogether. George Yeo, interview with the author, 19 Sept. 2012.

435 George Yeo, interview with the author, 11 Oct. 2012.

436 *1991 General Election PAP Post-mortem Report.*

437 SM Lee Kuan Yew to PM Goh Chok Tong, 16 Sept. 1991 (National Archives of Singapore), made available to the author.

438 Lee would have known what Goh meant by this reply. Lee had, in fact, on an earlier occasion (at the 18 November 1990 Party conference) contrasted Indonesian President Suharto and Goh. On this occasion, Lee had commented that although Goh would never be a great orator, he could quietly lead the nation to success just as Suharto had done. (Excerpted in "Preserving Singapore's Unique Political Culture", *Straits Times*, 26 Nov. 1990.)

439 Fong Sip Chee to PM Goh Chok Tong, 2 Sept. 1991 (PAP archive).

440 Ibid.

441 *The Zuo Commentary on the Spring and Autumn Annals*, trans. James Legge (Hong Kong: Hong Kong University Press, 1960), pp. 684–5.

442 Arthur Fong, Fong Sip Chee's son (who was also to serve as a PAP MP from 2001 to 2015), recalled: "[My father] took a long time to write that letter. He sat there looking at it for a long time. . . . His ashtray was full of cigarettes. Finally he faxed the letter, sat back, and gave a big sigh" (Arthur Fong, interview with the author, 9 Nov. 2012). Fong Sip Chee would succumb to cancer a little over a year later, on 5 December 1992, aged 54.

Chapter 3

1992–97: The Mandate

When snap polls were announced in 1991, Workers' Party Secretary-General J.B. Jeyaretnam complained that PM Goh's calling of the election was no more than a ploy to keep him out of Parliament, given that his disqualification from serving in Parliament (the result of his 1986 criminal conviction) still had a few months left to run.[1] Goh's response was that Jeyaretnam had only himself to blame for his predicament. Goh did, however, say that he would call for by-elections 12 to 18 months after the 1991 general election. This would, Goh noted, bring fresh blood into government, as the timing of the 1991 polls meant that the PAP had not been able to find all the candidates it wanted.[2]

It is clear that Goh's personal disappointment at the 1991 election result had not prevented some clear-headed thinking about future battles. The Party machine from the 1991 election was not allowed to fall dormant. As noted in chapter 2, an internal Party task force, Task Force 93, had overseen the Party machinery's preparations for the 1991 elections. Its successor, known as Task Force 97, was convened by Goh in December 1991. The brief given to Task Force 97 was to take charge of the machinery for the coming by-elections as well as the next general election. The task force, which first met in January 1992, was again chaired by Wong Kan Seng. It had an extraordinary longevity even by PAP standards, continuing to meet at intervals throughout 1992–96.[3]

Goh and his PAP colleagues in Marine Parade Group Representation Constituency (GRC)—Matthias Yao, Lim Chee Onn and Othman Haron Eusofe—resigned as MPs on 1 December 1992. Nomination Day was 9 December 1992, with Polling Day for the by-election falling on 19 December 1992. As expected, and as Goh had promised, the by-election was the chance for the PAP to surface new blood. Lim Chee Onn stepped down to make way for ex-Navy Chief Cdre Teo Chee Hean, aged 37.[4] The expected challenge of Jeyaretnam and the Workers' Party did not materialise. The WP team (Jeyaretnam, Jufrie Mahmood and Tan Bin Seng) turned up at the nomination centre, apparently waiting in vain for a fourth who never turned up.[5] Whether or not the Workers' Party had in fact intended to contest and mount a serious challenge, the actual turn of events brought some relief within the PAP leadership. It was the Jeyaretnam–Jufrie axis that had given it the most cause for concern. The Party leadership began from this point to believe that Jeyaretnam would be much diminished even if he attempted a political comeback.[6]

This left the stage to the Singapore Democratic Party (SDP), the National Solidarity Party and the Singapore Justice Party. It quickly became clear that the last two would not seriously figure in the contest. The SDP, however, was a different matter. A great deal of attention was on the SDP's new find, Dr Chee Soon Juan, 30, a trained neuropsychologist and a National University of Singapore (NUS) lecturer. Chee was clearly intelligent, well-spoken and articulate. The fact that SDP Secretary-General Chiam See Tong had been able to tempt Chee into the Opposition ranks was itself seen as something of a breakthrough, given that Chee had the kind of credentials the public tended to expect from PAP candidates. Perhaps, as the press mused, Chee's decision to stand would "start others of similar background thinking the hitherto unthinkable and challenge the PAP Government".[7]

Early on in the campaign in Marine Parade, there was concern within the PAP leadership. The SDP appeared well prepared, organised, and was able to attract large crowds at its rallies (there were approximately 15,000 people on the night of its 13 December 1992 rally). The SDP campaign themes played heavily on the cost of living, the additional thrust being that PAP policies benefited the rich at the expense of the poor. There was a personal element too, with Dr Chee Soon Juan noting how Cdre Teo Chee Hean was the privileged son of a banker, a scholarship holder who lived in a bungalow, and thus not someone who could relate to the poor. PM Goh and other PAP leaders were able to rebut this angle of attack simply by pointing to Goh himself, who had progressed from a house with no electricity to private housing—this was and should be counted as a Singapore success story.[8]

The personal element extended to the SDP posing questions about PM Goh's leadership. Chiam's argument was that PM Goh was dispensable, since (Chiam claimed) others such as Dr Tony Tan, BG George Yeo or S. Dhanabalan could take over. Party leaders came out quickly to say this was "foolish talk". Dr Tony Tan stressed that PM Goh had been the choice of all second-generation leaders, including himself. In the uncertain economic global climate, Tan said, the nation had better stick with known and trusted leaders.[9]

The Party leadership decided that point-by-point rebuttals were not enough, and that more needed to be done to snap the SDP's momentum. PM Goh decided to shock the electorate with the stark possibility of a PAP defeat. At a press conference on 16 December 1992, Goh spelled out the high stakes involved—if he lost his seat, he would have lost the moral authority to continue leading the Party. There would have to be a new PAP secretary-general and a new prime minister. Goh even raised the possibility of the government resigning in the event of a by-election defeat in Marine Parade; there might have to be a new general election to let people decide whether they still wanted a PAP government.[10] SM Lee also joined the fray in campaigning later on, speaking at a rally and raising the possibility of PM Goh losing or being returned with a severely reduced majority. This would, he noted, deprive Goh of the moral authority with the public, foreign investors and other governments.[11] Lee was now protective of Goh, even to the extent of holding an umbrella over Goh and himself on a rain-soaked election platform. Lee's interventions mattered, as they amounted to important and visible signs of his belief in Goh.[12]

Earlier, at the Party CEC meeting of 2 December 1992, SM Lee had proposed Goh for the position of secretary-general, a nomination accepted unanimously.[13] The news was communicated to the press a day later.[14] The fact that it was the outgoing secretary-general who had proposed the change was a point Lee himself was able to deploy while campaigning in Marine Parade in support of Goh, making it known that he had stepped down because he had full confidence in Goh's abilities.[15] There were other reasons, too, for the public signalling of trust in Goh's leadership. DPM Lee Hsien Loong had been diagnosed with intermediate-grade malignant lymphoma in October 1992. SM Lee's calculation in the handover and the public announcement of it was done so as to signal confidence in PM Goh, in the wake of the rumour and speculation that had followed the announcement of DPM Lee's illness.[16]

The way that the PAP conducted the campaign in Marine Parade showed that important lessons had been learned from 1991. An Intelligence Committee headed by Dr Tay Eng Soon ran a network which covered Opposition activities and gathered ground feedback (this extended to monitoring betting odds all over Singapore). The PAP "coffeeshop" network was run by fluent—and multiple—dialect speaker Chin Harn Tong. This was the grapevine through which the Party connected to local residents and other key groups, such as taxi drivers, to propagate its views and counter Opposition views and rumour-mongering. Issues that were catching fire could be quickly spotted using such networks, and just as quickly dealt with and countered. The PAP post-mortem team—headed by Chairman of the HQ Elections Committee George Yeo—was to ascribe a great deal of importance to such networks, particularly given that the Opposition agenda was propagated through similar means.[17] The need to maintain informal networks at the coffeeshop level might seem natural and indeed obvious, but it had not figured as prominently in previous PAP post-election thinking. It was arguably only after experiencing the hard lessons of 1991, where rumours had played a significant part in the losses of Bukit Gombak and Nee Soon Central, that the PAP began to pay more attention to the issue. The need to further improve such networks also figured heavily in the PAP's 1992 by-election post-mortem analysis. These efforts were (as we shall see) to play a part in winning back Bukit Gombak and Nee Soon Central in 1997.

It was not networks alone which made for a comfortable victory in the Marine Parade by-election. The PAP went back to straightforward, old-style campaigning, using dialect and different languages, expressing its ideas in emotive terms to the masses at rallies, and debunking Opposition arguments in the process. PM Goh himself held forth in his first ever campaign speech in Hokkien for no less than 20 minutes at a rally on 12 December 1992.[18] The PAP post-mortem concluded that PM Goh's use of Hokkien in campaigning (the first time he had used the dialect during elections) helped to win over, and create a real connection with, the Chinese ground. In another critical observation, the post-mortem report also assessed that the SDP began to lose its momentum and strategic discipline as the campaign wore on. It had been a mistake, the report concluded, for the SDP to have chosen to go canvassing house to house when it should have held more rallies.[19]

The end result was a comfortable win for the PAP, which took 72.94 per cent of the vote. Chiam left disappointed with the SDP's 24.5 per cent, after having earlier predicted a vote share of at least 40 per cent.[20] On the whole, voters in Marine Parade did not buy Chiam See Tong's argument that Goh was expendable. There was strong support—as well as a feeling of personal connection—for Goh, especially on his home turf of the Marine Parade division within the GRC, where he had been MP since 1976. Goh had got the mandate he wanted, while the media consensus was that the SDP had not made inroads in its aim to be the main Opposition party in a two-party system.[21]

The internal Party assessment was marked by circumspection rather than jubilation. There was some sense that the by-election had removed some of the pessimism that settled over the PAP after the 1991 general election. But when the CEC discussed the 1992 by-election in early January 1993, there was also the recognition that while the SDP might have suffered something of a setback, the issues it had raised were likely to remain present through the rest of the decade and beyond. The SDP had in its own way further developed themes that it had used in 1991—the idea of the PAP as a party for the rich, of a growing elitism, and of rising costs. In its own way, the SDP had done enough to keep these issues alive and to set the stage for an ongoing debate throughout the rest of the 1990s. As the by-election analysis noted with some prescience: "Class and economic issues will become more important at the next GE. As competition separates the strong from the weak, we can expect the opposition—both SDP and WP—to play up class divisions in our society."[22]

No Place for Old Certitudes

The 1990s is remembered by many as a time of economic growth and rising affluence, and of the quickening of Singapore's embrace of globalisation.[23] It was also a time when thinking and decisions of the PAP government in the 1980s began to have an impact. These should be revisited, as they form a prelude to the economic and social directions taken in the 1990s.

Following the 1984 general election, there was the strong sense within the Party leadership that the government was a ready target for the people to take aim at; what loomed particularly large was the perceived inflexibility of the bureaucracy, which the people generally tended to equate with the PAP. The 1984 general election post-mortem report had noted:

> *Because government policies have been so successful, the government has become omnipresent in the lives of the people. Other examples are car parks, hawker licences, taxi licenses, and so on. Wherever possible, we should hive off these responsibilities to the free market and private enterprise, and move the government out of the front line. Government should do less, rather than more, for the people.*[24]

Government agencies holding too much power—or even the mere perception of it—was becoming a political liability. But the larger point was that Party longevity would be affected if some form of de-bureaucratization was not attempted.[25] Some aspects of the PAP government's response have been discussed earlier. The formation of town councils, for example, was a result of the thinking within the Party leadership that some responsibilities that were previously the province of government agencies should be devolved.[26]

The thinking began to extend to favouring a smaller government role in business and enterprise. The leadership had in fact been mulling over the issue of allowing the market to operate with fewer restrictions since the early 1980s.[27] The pace now began to quicken. On 8 February 1985, 1DPM Goh commented (at a dialogue with community leaders) that private initiatives to create wealth should be encouraged, and that the government would move further away from the concept of a welfare state. Singaporeans had an urge to achieve, something that could be unleashed only through privatisation and more enterprise.[28] Government leaders were, in fact, by early 1985 increasingly commenting on the need to reduce unnecessary government regulations and allow freer private enterprise. Where government participation was not essential, it would divest or reduce its role. These pronouncements were clearly coordinated. Goh's theme was elaborated on by Finance Minister Dr Tony Tan, who in his budget speech on 8 March 1985 noted that the time had come in Singapore's economic development for large-scale government intervention in the economy to be no longer needed. It was now time, Dr Tan observed, for the private sector, and not the government, to drive growth.[29]

The issues of privatisation and free enterprise, therefore, were linked to Singapore's continued survival—to use Goh's apt analogy, the second stage of the rocket had to be ignited, lest the first stage come to an end and the entire rocket fall.[30] This thinking was further reinforced by the deliberations of two critical committees examining the future course of Singapore's economic development. The first was the Economic Committee. Chaired by then Minister of State for Trade and Industry BG Lee Hsien Loong, it was convened in April 1985 to examine the causes of Singapore's worst recession since independence, and to chart future directions for the economy.[31] The main conclusions and recommendations of the Economic Committee—a larger role for the private sector, wage reform, and reductions in employers' Central Provident Fund (CPF) contributions—are well known.[32] What is less known is that there existed in parallel an internal Ministerial Economic Committee. This committee, headed by 1DPM Goh and comprising the key ministers involved in economic decision-making, provided the main discussion forum where the leadership, without other observers present, could wrestle with the fundamental issue of Singapore's future growth model. The behind-the-scenes discussions of the Ministerial Economic Committee were to shape the deliberations of the Economic Committee (which had external participation, particularly in the form of private sector participation from industry); it was also these internal discussions that were to leave an imprint on the entire range of government policymaking in the years to come. Consider the following extract from the October 1985 Ministerial Economic Committee meeting:

> *Dr [Tony] Tan [minister for trade and industry] said that the aspect of loosening up government controls to allow private enterprise to flourish and become more profitable, was ticklish. In his opinion, it represented a major U-turn in government philosophy. We had always governed on the basis that the government*

knew best. In major fields of activity, controls had so far been initiated and directed by the government. Mr Goh [Chok Tong] remarked that while this might be true of social policies, it was not so in the field of business. It was not his intention to remove all government controls.

. . . Mr Ong [Teng Cheong] felt that there was a need to define the type of controls we wanted to loosen. Mr Goh replied that we should ease controls which stood in the way of market-pricing of government goods and services, like prices of Housing and Development Board (HDB) flats. BG Lee added that the intention was to loosen indirect controls by government through price-setting. Mr Dhanabalan remarked that market-prices would allocate government goods and services such as HDB shops, to those who could or were prepared to pay market prices. Dr Tan commented that this would indeed be setting a new direction in economic policy.[33]

It was not felt just that the government should loosen controls over the private sector. The market, and market pricing, should have a greater role too.[34]

There were also external factors that came to play a major role in shaping the thinking of the second-generation PAP leadership, and in convincing them that the chosen path was the right one. An important—and often overlooked—event was the dismantling of the Soviet Union beginning in the late 1980s and the subsequent collapse of the Russian economy. This left an imprint on the psyche of the PAP. In July 1989, 2DPM and NTUC Secretary-General Ong Teng Cheong led a delegation of unionists to the Soviet Union at the invitation of the All-Union Central Committee of Trade Unions. His remarks upon his return capture the essence of PAP thinking on the correctness of Singapore's economic model:

The countries in the free world have achieved significant economic progress over the past 30–40 years. One of the key ingredients that spurs individuals, corporations or even states to do better economically is the incentive to accumulate part of the wealth they created. Conversely, they will have to pay a price for failure. . . . Such a system induces keen competition, and in an open economy like Singapore's, only the fittest will survive. We have not only survived under such a system, but we have even prospered . . . we must congratulate ourselves that the PAP Government had defeated the communists in the 1960s, and so made it possible for Singapore to grow and prosper uninterrupted for the last 24 years. We must preserve the present economic system in Singapore. We must remain an open and free economy.[35]

The internal process of the PAP's ideological vindication had begun even as Communism was still unravelling. By the early 1990s, this thinking had been reinforced. It is perhaps best exemplified by the writings and speeches of George Yeo, who arguably (although he never made the claim himself) had taken on the mantle of S. Rajaratnam as chief PAP ideologue. Yeo's speeches at this time shed some light on the uncertainties of the post-Cold War situation, and what the PAP leadership felt was the correct recipe for economic and social development. His 1991 commentary on the PAP and the updating of its values deserves extended quotation and consideration:

> We are at a great turning point in post-war history. The older certitudes are gone. The Cold War has ended. Communism is in crisis. New poles have appeared in Western Europe and in Japan. But no one can be sure what the shape of the new world will be.
>
> . . . The logic of the market is irresistible. With the revolution in information and communication technology, no society can be closed. Governments which resist the market will be defeated by it. It is the market which has subverted the control of central authorities in the Soviet Union and China. Operating as efficient a market economy as possible in Singapore is therefore central to everything else . . . we live in a world where capital and labour are both mobile.

Yeo then tackles socialism:

> Carried to its extreme, however, the market undermines itself. This is so because in any competition there are winners and losers. If the losers lose time and again and feel they have little to gain from the system, despair will set in. The losers and those who empathise with them will then work to subvert the system . . . thus, to enable the market to function efficiently, competition must be tempered by cooperation and compassion.
>
> Socialism is not dead. It is being transformed by failure . . . the fact is socialism is an ideal which will never go away because it springs from altruism that is in the very nature of man. Altruism prompts re-distribution and re-distribution is necessary to hold a group together.

Yeo separately considers state socialism: socialism which uses state power to effect massive redistribution. In Yeo's view, this system weakens the work ethic and "takes the sense of altruism out of the redistributive process":

> The PAP can either drop the term "socialism" or re-interpret it. We should not drop socialism, because we are still committed to the altruism and compassion which helped give birth to the Party. What socialism should mean for us is not state welfarism, which has failed in so many countries, but community support for one another and selective state intervention to help equalise opportunities. State welfarism must fail because it goes against the market. Capital and talent will migrate to escape its clutches. Community support, in contrast, is voluntary. It soothes the hurt of competition, reducing the resentment which competition causes.[36]

The cold hand of the market, therefore, would be tempered by the altruistic touch of government intervention applied selectively to those in need. This was the course that had been set. It is noteworthy that one of the first moves introduced by Goh Chok Tong—within three weeks of his becoming prime minister—was the introduction of Edusave, which was funded by government surpluses. Goh, who personally credited a bursary given to him when a student as being instrumental in enabling him to finish his studies, believed strongly that education gave the less fortunate an opportunity to level up.[37] When Goh spoke about the scheme, he noted that he wanted to give everybody a chance to appear at the same starting line, regardless of financial background. The aim was "to temper our meritocratic, free market system with compassion and equal opportunities".[38]

The overall message was clear. Rather than across-the-board welfarism, government policy would be to use targeted schemes to protect the interests of the disadvantaged groups and level the playing field.

Events in the wider world had strengthened the belief within the PAP leadership that the vision described above had been vindicated. But this did not automatically mean that the people accepted this. Indeed, the period from the late 1980s onwards (and particularly after the 1991 election) could be seen as a time when the Party faced a significant pushback from the ground—a reaction on issues connected to the cost of living and to the government's privatisation drive. Simply put, the perception had arisen that the government's market-oriented policies had led to difficulties for the people, and a price spiral.

A new MP, Assoc. Prof. Koo Tsai Kee, trenchantly summarised the PAP view in 1991 in his maiden parliamentary speech:

> *Unfortunately, at exactly the same time when Singaporeans should tighten the embrace of the market, they have developed a fear for it. Why? Because the market has been wrongly diagnosed as the source that drives up the cost of living. When in fact the opposite is true. Market oriented policies have brought us success, jobs and affluence. The rising cost of living is only a side effect of the rising standard of living. . . . At a time when significant parts of the world were fixated with command economies and its social cousins, we had a headstart by implementing market reforms. The rest of the world is now charging ahead, while our people appear to be hesitant. Now that Marxism has been lowered into the grave, market-oriented economics have found universal embrace.*[39]

The PAP government would not, and could not, reverse course; nor could it heed calls for more welfarism, just at the juncture in history where the correctness of its own economic decisions had been proved. PM Goh noted in a May 1992 speech to Party activists that former Communist regimes wanted to learn from Singapore and were "feverishly trying to free prices in the economies, to let them reflect market supply and demand . . . it would be supreme irony that just when communist countries, both former and present, are cutting down on subsidies that Singapore should increase subsidies".[40] Goh continued:

> *The wealth gap is not determined by the Government. It is determined by the difference in a person's ability, performance and prudent habit. It is a gap determined by the market and the people themselves. It is not wise for the Government to artificially try to close the gap. The countries which have tried have ended up in bankruptcy. Examples are the former communist countries in the Soviet Union and Eastern Europe. Communist countries do not believe in the individuals owning assets. . . . The result for the individual is no incentive to work, dependence on the state, no drive and initiative, envy for others who are better off.*[41]

The PAP government had stated its case as clearly as it could. But not all were convinced. One sociologist commenting in 1992 was to note with some perspicacity:

> *Yet, exactly how "levelling up" can be achieved is not made clear. Even with billion-dollar schemes, like Edusave, to maximise the potential of Singaporean children, and MediFund to help the poor pay hospital bills, which the government insists are "not entitlements", the basic idea to help people help themselves remains unchanged. Meanwhile, the efficiencies of the free market approach are re-embraced to justify the government's privatisation plans, which caused much public alarm in the "restructuring" of government hospitals and the creation of independent schools. As class cleavages become more obvious and less tolerable, the fundamental question is whether the government's communitarian welfare strategy can forestall the emergence of class contradictions inherent with the development of a capitalist economy.*[42]

The Party would have to continue grappling with these issues for the rest of the decade and beyond.

Issues and Challenges

The real challenge to PAP economic policy in the early to mid-1990s came from the SDP, which began to increasingly focus on the cost-of-living issue. A diverse array of rising fees and charges—parking, TV licences and taxi fares—were among the issues singled out. The SDP also pointed to fee increases at independent schools, and rising charges at restructured hospitals, to support its claim that the government was only interested in making profits.[43] The message—sharpened and deployed on the campaign trail in 1991—was that all this was a great burden on the working classes.[44] This was to develop into a more general attack on class and elitism, and charges of a calculative, profiteering government.

From 1993 onwards, a driving force behind these arguments was Dr Chee Soon Juan. For Chee, the unsuccessful run in Marine Parade in 1992 was just the beginning; from that year until the middle of the decade he was arguably in his pomp. Chee's preferred mode in expounding his point of view was letters (often very lengthy ones) to the *Straits Times*, which chose to print these in full. No Opposition figure had been given a platform of this order by the media in the recent past.

Chee's principal respondent was the PAP second organising secretary, Matthias Yao, who took on Chee in an extended exchange of letters in the *Straits Times* from 1993 to 1994. As Yao noted, the PAP could not make living standards of the less successful equal to those of the successful—no country could do this. Yao implied that Chee's attacks on independent schools, and on the trappings of the well-to-do (like golf courses), essentially amounted to engaging in the politics of envy.[45] Chee denied these charges, arguing that the government had a particular duty to look after the poor; the SDP did not (he said) begrudge the rich what they had worked hard for.[46]

Yao was unable to best Chee in their robust early exchanges; and indeed Chee in making his points probably emerged with some credit, at least in their initial parries. The equation was to change after Chee was sacked in April 1993 by NUS for misusing research funds. He then went on hunger strike to clear his name (although, as the PAP pointed out, he sustained himself daily with servings of glucose). Chee was also the defendant in a defamation lawsuit brought against him by his immediate superior in NUS, PAP MP Dr S. Vasoo. Chee in February 1994 abandoned his defence, essentially admitting he had defamed Vasoo.[47] The PAP now had added ammunition to undermine Chee, with the debate between Chee and Yao becoming increasingly acrimonious. This was especially after Chee in May 1994 published his personal vision of Singapore, *Dare to Change*, which was adopted by the SDP as its platform.[48] Following DPM Lee Hsien Loong's July 1994 criticism of *Dare to Change* as no more than a rehash of Western liberal ideas, Chee called for a public debate on the ideas. The PAP had no intention of giving Chee more airtime; its challenge to Opposition MPs, particularly the SDP ones, was that they should debate these issues in Parliament.[49] And the very specific challenge to Chee—conveyed by Matthias Yao through the press again—was that he had been exposed as someone who lacked integrity for political leadership, and Chee could sue Yao if he liked for saying so.[50]

Chee was by this time (mid-1994) engaged in an expanded letter-writing campaign that saw him taking on all comers—not just Matthias Yao but also members of the public, his former boss at NUS, Dr Vasoo, and other PAP politicians.[51] In Chee's view, the PAP was becoming "more and more irrational as it feels increasingly threatened because it knows that the SDP is determined to challenge its authoritarian style and constructive alternatives".[52] At the end of his long-running war of words with Chee in 1994, Matthias Yao (in response to a challenge thrown down by Chee) requested that PM Goh ask the Electoral Boundaries Review Committee to redraw the constituency boundaries to allow a straight fight between Chee and Yao at the next election.[53]

The PAP clearly felt that it was important to discredit Dr Chee personally, to undermine his platform, and to show the people that he had behaved dishonourably. Matthias Yao's letters to the *Straits Times*, engaging Chee and rebutting his points, had been carefully crafted and thought out by the PAP leadership with this in mind.[54] All this would help to show that the SDP did not present a real alternative to the PAP.

But until 1994, these efforts had only been partly successful. An informal survey was carried out by the *Straits Times* in September that year, near the end of the long-running war of words and exchange of letters between Chee and Yao. The survey found several people inclining to the view that Chee, if not quite the person completely lacking in integrity that the PAP said he was, was perhaps flawed in some way. But even then, there were some within this group who felt that Chee's ideas should have been addressed by the PAP.[55]

Chee's real undoing—when he began to miscalculate, and to bring the SDP in directions which the majority of the people could not accept—will be covered later in this chapter.

Costs, Expectations, Aspirations (I)

> *The challenge for the Government is to bridge two worlds: the public domain where the impersonal logic of facts and figures holds sway, and the private realities of flesh-and-blood people. What compounds Mr Goh's problem is that, during the early years of Singapore's modernisation, high growth rates and a low baseline made the fruits of development tangible to everyone. Now, rising public expectations—particularly among the already affluent—engendered by high growth are coinciding with the more modest rates reflective of a maturing economy. This creates a double bind for the Government as it tries to keep individuals' attention focused on the overall picture. How can it do so?* [56]

The PAP leadership was by this point coming to the realisation that something had to be done to counter the rising tide of dissatisfaction on the cost-of-living issue. In his 16 August 1992 National Day Rally speech, PM Goh noted that the preoccupation with costs was threatening to distract Singaporeans from the real issues (such as economic growth and competing with other newly industrialising economies).[57] Goh announced the setting up of the Cost Review Committee (CRC) chaired by Senior Minister of State (Trade and Industry) Lim Boon Heng. The committee, Goh said, would review the impact of cost increases on different income groups, and on businesses.

The thinking of the leadership up to this point had been elucidated in a number of dialogue sessions and talks given by Party leaders, all aimed at tackling the cost-of-living issue by Party leaders. In essence, material well-being had bred higher expectations. While living standards had increased over the years as wages rose, Singaporeans' aspirations had risen even faster, causing some to feel that they could not afford their new lifestyles.[58] Statistically, PAP leaders viewed the case as watertight: the fact was that real incomes had increased and inflation was under control. Education and healthcare, which people appeared to worry about the most, formed only a small part of household expenditure.[59]

Why, then, was the CRC necessary at all? While the diagnosis above may have been clear-cut to the leadership, it was not so to the people. Goh, in announcing the convening of the CRC and in giving its remit, placed special weight on the CRC's role in determining why the public perceived the increases to be worse than they were. The committee would also recommend ways to convince people that the increases were proper and had been checked. It was also important, Goh noted, to dismiss the notion that the government was attempting to disguise actual inflation or price rises through "cooking" figures.[60] The point, then, was not just to show that there had been no price spiral, but also that there had been no obfuscation on the part of the government.

An attempt was made to make the CRC representative of a broad array of views. Besides PAP MPs, its composition included academics, leaders from the business sector, labour leaders and journalists.[61] Chiam See Tong and other SDP MPs declined to serve on the CRC, despite repeated invitations. The SDP MPs cited their busy schedules, but other reasons were also proffered. The SDP felt that because government ministers had, even before the first sitting of the CRC, commented that the whole cost issue had arisen on account of the high expectations of the people, the issue had been prejudged and so SDP participation would be to no purpose.[62] Yet another sticking point was how many from the SDP should serve on the CRC, and whether non-MPs from the SDP could serve.[63] There were some signs of disappointment and even anger at the SDP decision not to participate. Many remembered how the SDP had campaigned in 1991 on the issue of rising costs, and felt that the SDP MPs had been elected precisely to voice the concerns of the people on this issue. Some observers felt that there was some loss of credibility with the SDP decision not to participate in the CRC.[64]

It is instructive to contrast the SDP stance with that of Low Thia Khiang, the sole Workers' Party MP in Parliament, who took a constructive position, agreeing to serve on the CRC.[65] Some of Low's suggestions were included in the Terms of Reference for the committee; he even extracted an assurance that his opinions, if different, would ultimately be included in the final report.[66]

The CRC (which met 19 times over ten months) published its report on 27 September 1993, with Parliament debating the motion to accept its recommendations on 13–14 October 1993.[67] Low abstained from the actual vote on 14 October but was again able to make his mark through his involvement in the debate, engaging S. Dhanabalan (minister for trade and industry) and Dr Richard Hu (minister for finance) on issues such as the Consumer Price Index and the proposed Goods and Services Tax (GST), topics which the CRC had tackled.[68] The three SDP MPs were, in contrast, absent for large parts of the debate on 14 October 2013 and did not vote.

While the CRC's findings were largely consonant with the PAP view of matters, the whitewash that the SDP had suggested might transpire did not materialise. The final report acknowledged that Singaporeans had been paying more for higher-quality goods and services, and that there had indeed been steep increases in the cost of healthcare, housing, education and transport in the preceding years (the CRC in its deliberations and fact finding paid particularly close attention to the issue of housing and housing costs—an issue we shall return to). The report called for the timing of fee increases to be staged better by government agencies. This would avoid the "bunching phenomenon" of fee increases in 1989–91.[69] The CRC also recommended the compilation and publishing of separate Consumer Price Indexes for different income groups, to give a more accurate sense of different inflation rates faced by households with different consumption patterns.[70]

The *Straits Times* was to characterise 1993 as "the year the Government took the bull by the horns". This was a reference to attempts to tackle cost issues—not just through the CRC but through the parliamentary debate on the GST, as well as the issuing of a White Paper on Affordable Health Care.[71] These interventions did not put matters to rest, with widespread ground concerns continuing to simmer. The CRC report did serve a purpose, however. It brought fully into public discourse a point that PAP leaders had been making for some time: that there was a need to temper expectations even as Singaporeans became more affluent.

Minister for Trade and Industry S. Dhanabalan summarised the issue on 14 October 1993, before Parliament voted to endorse the report:

> There is nothing wrong with rising aspirations, but we must be clear that when people complain about rising cost, it is not because the same lifestyle that they enjoyed cheaply in the past costs more today. That is not what they are complaining about. It is really because the higher standard of living which they now enjoy cost more than their old, simpler standard of living which they have left behind. That's what they are complaining about. Furthermore, they fear that what they aspire for the future, which is even higher than what they enjoy now, would remain out of their reach. That is their fear. So it's not as if costs are going up and they can't afford to maintain the present lifestyle or the lifestyle that they used to enjoy. They are complaining about something quite different.[72]

A final observation should be made on the findings of the 1993 CRC. The report noted that there was nothing wrong with graduates having aspirations of the good life. This would motivate Singaporeans to work hard.[73] But the committee felt that "the Singaporean notion of what constitutes the 'good life' would need to change in the years to come", with CRC members unanimously agreeing that these aspirations would in the coming years have to be moderated and channelled into other areas, especially non-material ones.[74] But this was an extremely difficult proposition for many. As one *Straits Times* poll showed, there was a feeling that since Singaporeans had been fed the notion over the years of aspiring to life in a fully developed nation (with its attendant trappings), it was unfair, and probably even unrealistic, to now tell them that they had to moderate their expectations.[75]

The effort to educate people on realistic aspirations went beyond the conclusion of the parliamentary debate in October 1993. The PAP would spend the better part of the rest of the decade engaged in this argument, with cost concerns continuing to dominate the political agenda. The CRC was reconvened in July 1996 in order to examine claims made by the PKMS (Pertubuhan Kebangsaan Melayu Singapura; Singapore Malay National Organisation) and the SDP (in a report jointly issued by these two parties in June 1996) that the Department of Statistics had "massaged" data to derive a low inflation rate as shown by the Consumer Price Index.[76] The report accused the PAP government of raising costs deliberately "to control the purse string of Singaporeans and make them ever more dependent on the Government for their livelihood".[77]

The undoubted highlight of the reconvened CRC occurred when the SDP–PKMS team, including Dr Chee Soon Juan, met with the CRC panel on 6 August 1996.[78] The meeting lasted close to three hours before the SDP–PKMS team was asked to leave. It was, from the CRC's point of view, highly unsatisfactory. The SDP–PKMS team proved unwilling or unable to say on what basis they had said that price rises constituted the major component of increases in household spending.[79] The tactics used by the SDP–PKMS team—best described as evasive or perhaps obfuscatory—should be compared with the SDP performance at the hearing of the Select Committee examining healthcare costs (and in particular, subsidies given at government clinics and hospitals) on 8 July 1996. The SDP had put up a performance there which was possibly even poorer than its CRC cameo. SDP Chairman Ling How Doong was forced to concede at the Select Committee hearing that the SDP had been mistaken on its earlier claim (made in March 1996) that public healthcare was "hardly subsidised at all"; he agreed in committee that government subsidies were, in fact, "substantial".[80]

The 1996 CRC submitted its report to PM Goh on 24 October 1996, with Parliament (minus the SDP MPs, who chose to be absent) debating the report and endorsing its conclusions on 7 November 1996. The report noted that costs had indeed risen for healthcare, education, transport and housing, even as heavy government subsidies had kept these generally affordable. Thirty-five specific recommendations were made on how to keep costs down.[81] But cost increases were not "phenomenal", as the SDP–PKMS report had claimed, nor could the allegation of a "statistical massage of the numbers" be supported. In addition, the CRC found that while household spending had risen substantially in previous years, only a small fraction of this had been due to price rises. The bulk was due to Singaporeans buying better-quality goods and services.[82] It was, essentially, more comfortable but costlier lifestyles that were at the root of the issue.[83]

The PAP point of view had been summed up by PM Goh in his 18 August 1996 National Day Rally speech:

> *Spending more does not necessarily mean that things are getting more expensive. In Singapore, where growth rates have been high but inflation rates low, it means that standards of living are going up. The question we must ask is how much of our extra spending is because prices have gone up, and how much because people are buying more items, and better items.*[84]

PM Goh insisted that the specific recommendations of the 1996 CRC were not made on the initiative of the Opposition, and that these measures would in any case have been adopted.[85] But the SDP, despite its failures and ineptitude in the 1996 CRC and Health Select Committee hearings, played a role in ensuring that the concerns on costs were never fully dispelled. Another player in the counternarrative was the Workers'

Party's Low Thia Khiang, who had declined the invitation to participate in the 1996 CRC but was the only Opposition MP in the House when the report was debated. Continuing on from his campaign theme in 1991, and from his contributions to the CRC in 1993, Low highlighted the need for the government to lighten the burden of cost increases on the people.[86] Low had, in fact, developed his argument further—and it was in some ways a persuasive one. His basic point was that it was unfair of the CRC to imply that people were to blame for rising costs; the people should not be blamed for pursuing a better standard of living.[87]

Costs, Expectations, Aspirations (II)

The 1993 and 1996 CRCs investigated in depth issues such as cost of education, transport, healthcare and housing. While there was a degree of public disquiet on all these issues, the depth of feeling on housing outweighed the rest. Housing was the issue that the government had to tackle.

Upgrading, Assets

We have already seen that some of the seeds of the thinking behind allowing HDB flat prices to rise to market levels were present in discussions of the 1985 Economic Committee.[88] It was the subsequent internal Ministerial Committee on Housing (1986–87) chaired by 1DPM Goh Chok Tong that refined this thinking.[89] The policy recommendations of this committee (which met from May 1986 to November 1987, and reported internally to the leadership) were to have lasting implications through the 1990s. The committee's key recommendation was that there should be a move towards allowing market forces to determine flat prices. Instead of the government setting the prices of HDB flats, the prices should be determined by flat applicants based on what they were willing and able to pay; in the longer term, prices of all HDB flats should be better adjusted to better reflect the construction cost and economic value of land. Other recommendations were to have downstream implications. These included having the private sector play a bigger role in housing development, slowing down the HDB building programme (with future building to be based on actual demand), and rejuvenating older estates to bring them closer to the standard of newer ones.[90]

The recommendations of the committee were endorsed by the leadership in early March 1988. S. Dhanabalan, the minister for national development, then gave a broad indication as to future directions in housing in Parliament on 16–17 March 1988 when the budget estimates for his ministry were being debated. Dhanabalan was careful in what he said: while HDB pricing policy would be brought closer to the market, there would be no immediate, sweeping across-the-board price increases for flats. At the same time, the government would ensure that Singaporeans would be able to afford at least basic (three-room) flats. The overall thrust, however, was clear: over time subsidies would be decreased, although flats would continue to be sold at subsidised prices to ensure affordability.[91]

The government was separately attempting to provide for those who wanted to upgrade to private property. As the 1980s drew to a close, the leadership decided that the government would go some way at least in satisfying this desire, held by the more affluent Singaporeans. In March 1989, 1DPM Goh wrote to S. Dhanabalan on the issue:

> We have encouraged Singaporeans to aspire to a middle class life. The basic criterion is home-ownership. With growing affluence, it is a quality of home-ownership that counts more and more. We pride ourselves in being able to house 85% of the population in public housing estates. The question is: what's next for Singaporeans to aim for in home ownership? Can we increase the percentage of upper middle-class home owners (i.e., landed property owners)?
>
> Will middle class Singaporeans be satisfied with HDB upgrading the common areas of housing estates, making them approximate condominiums? Or will they not aspire for ownership of a private home rather than a HDB flat? Should we not try to increase the percentage of private home ownership? What should be the ultimate percentage of private home ownership—20% or even 30%? How should land be distributed between high rise and landed properties? Can our able young afford private homes at current prices? By how much have private residential property prices gone up in the last 1–2 years? Will they go up beyond the reach of most? Should we not now release land for more private residential property development in order to reach our higher percentage of private home ownership? Do we have enough land for this purpose?[92]

The final issue germane to the thinking of the PAP government on housing was upgrading, which had been conceived by the 1986–87 Ministerial Committee on Housing. The Main Upgrading Programme for HDB estates was announced by S. Dhanabalan in July 1989.[93] The government was clear why upgrading was being offered—estates should be given distinctiveness and quality, and the quality of older estates should be brought up to a level that matched HDB's newest projects. The government also acknowledged that the scheme would go some way to meeting Singaporeans' aspirations of a better quality of life.[94]

There were, of course, political considerations too. S. Dhanabalan later recalled that the leadership had begun to realise by the late 1980s that older estates had become run-down. In addition, the workmanship of older flats left a great deal to be desired, especially compared to the flats being built in newer estates. The leadership felt that there would be resentment if improvements were not made.[95] One concern of the leadership was to make sure the upgrading scheme would be big enough to make an impact: the government could afford to be generous, especially given that the scheme was a way to redistribute government surpluses not required to build long-term reserves. The Ministry of National Development was directed to work out the programme costs for the entire stock of 370,000 flats, and tasked also with working out a new schedule that would see more flats upgraded per year.[96]

Housing, of course, was a core plank of the social compact that had for decades tied the people to the PAP government. The Main Upgrading Scheme was the means by which the PAP government reinforced the stake that people had in the roof over their heads, as well as adding value to it. In April 1992, with the Main Upgrading Scheme already well under way, Minister of State for National Development Lim Hng Kiang shed light on government thinking on the subject:

> To meet the aspirations of a middle-class home owning society, the Government has successfully launched the demonstration phase of the upgrading programme. The objective of the heavily subsidised upgrading programme is to upgrade the older HDB flats to the latest standards in fittings and finishes. The programme will enhance the value of old flats, while the massive public housing programme and the home ownership drive has given the majority of Singaporeans a stake in the nation. The upgrading programme is thus, in a sense, an "extension" of the home-ownership scheme.[97]

The government was thus trying to do several things from the late 1980s. It realised many would increasingly desire private property, and was beginning to think through how some of these aspirations could be met, for those who could afford it. The government had also moved on the HDB front. It was determined to allow market forces greater play in determining flat prices, while continuing to guarantee HDB dwellers at least a basic roof over their heads. This was a roof which could, thanks to upgrading, in time become an appreciating asset.[98]

~???~

HDB flat prices (including resale prices) rose, with the price of a four-room resale flat rising from $96,000 in 1992 to over $260,000 in 1996.[99] By 1995, concerns were beginning to be widespread that HDB might not be building enough to meet demand, and that flats might be becoming too expensive.[100] Pressure on the government had increased. Part of the remit of the reconvened CRC in 1996 was to examine the issue.

The CRC quickly pinpointed the underlying reasons. Rising land costs and better finishings in new flats had led to higher HDB flat prices.[101] The rising prices of resale flats were a result of a slew of liberalising measures introduced since 1989 that resulted in prices moving closer to the private housing market.[102] In addition, a scaled-down HDB building programme (which, as we have seen, was the result of thinking that dated back to the 1986–87 Ministerial Committee on Housing) meant that the queue for new flats lengthened. Average waiting time for a new flat was now three to five years.[103] This may have played a role in increasing the demand for resale flats (which rose 60 per cent from 1993 to 1994) and private housing.[104]

Technically, the government had the facts on its side when attempting to address public concerns on affordability. Flats were on the whole still affordable, with the government continuing to heavily subsidise flats it sold. An index on the affordability of housing worked out by the *Straits Times* with academics and property analysts showed that in 1983, the prices of flats were on average 26 and 37 times (for four- and five-room flats, respectively) the average household monthly income; the figures were 23 and 38 times the average household monthly income in 1996. Prices had gone up, but these were matched by rises in workers' incomes—enabling them to meet higher mortgages.[105]

We turn now to the wider (and in many respects more significant) observations made by the 1996 CRC. The CRC report noted that the critical issue was not so much one of flat affordability or getting a roof over one's head, but upgrading. Even younger Singaporeans buying HDB flats for the first time were increasingly opting for larger flats.[106] The CRC report noted that this raised serious questions. HDB had been set up to provide affordable public housing for the masses. Was it in danger of being pushed by rising public expectations to move beyond its original intended role? Who should receive government subsidies, and for what sort of housing? The CRC report noted (with the then-ongoing property boom in mind) that "unless these issues are kept clearly in mind, Singaporeans could risk urging on the Government to provide solutions which, while seemingly popular in the short term, might ultimately cost the nation dearly".[107]

By the mid-1990s, it was clear that a nation of upgraders had been created. HDB dwellers had become increasingly willing, and able, to sell their flats for large capital gains and upgrade either to a bigger flat or to private property. Upgrading had become not just acceptable but a positive aspiration, replacing the goal of the earlier generation which had simply been to live in HDB housing.[108] Many upgraders did make good, able to ride out price rises as they benefited from capital gains by selling existing properties.[109] But at the same time, there was frustration amongst others (particularly young professionals) that the Singapore dream of owning private property was rapidly fading away. While announcing property curbs on 14 May 1996, DPM Lee acknowledged that young couples and professionals "feel resentment or even despair that private properties seem to be receding permanently beyond their reach".[110] DPM Lee said that while the government could guarantee everybody in Singapore an HDB flat, and attempt to ensure an adequate supply of private property, it was "not possible for us to guarantee everyone a private property. No Government in the world can do that."[111]

Society had become more complex and more difficult to manage. A cycle of upgrading that had been created had in turn shaped a certain mindset. People were becoming more demanding, aspirations more insistent. Dr Augustine Tan, an economics professor and former PAP MP, was blunt when weighing in on the subject of the Singapore Dream. Commenting on how many yuppies desired to display a certain affluent lifestyle, he observed: "Yuppies should be realistic and not mistake fantasy for dream. Expectations that exceed one's capacity to earn can only lead to the frustrations of envy, covetousness and lust, and cause otherwise rational, well-educated young people to accept the blandishments of the politics of envy and populism which can only be destructive to Singapore."[112]

Rising prices all round—including in the private housing market—continued to bite, despite increased HDB supply and government land sales for private housing.

The leadership had to act. On 14 May 1996 a surprise series of targeted interventions were announced, aimed at deflating a bubble caused by speculative activities that had been developing in the private property market.[113] The bubble was not peculiar to Singapore: it was in evidence also in countries such as Hong Kong, Malaysia and Thailand. Property exposure in these countries had risen to high levels and was linked to excessive consumption and speculative activity—key factors in the subsequent Asian Financial Crisis.[114]

In Singapore, the 1996 measures worked quickly to cool the property market—the private property price index eased by about 16 per cent between the peak in Q2 1996 and Q4 1997. Subsequently, in April 1997, curbs were introduced also in the HDB market, with some of the key measures aimed at staunching the number of upgraders (especially those applying for a second, new, subsidised flat).[115]

Lee Kuan Yew, writing about this period in his memoirs with events fresh in his mind, saw the lead-up to this as a sequence where the government yielded to popular pressure:

> I should have known that it does not pay to yield to popular pressure beyond our capacity to deliver. Yet I was party to a similar mistake in the early 1990s. As property prices rose, everybody wanted to make a profit on the sale of their old flat and then upgrade to a new one, the biggest they could afford. Instead of choking off demand by charging a levy to reduce their windfall profits, I agreed that we accommodate the voters by increasing the number of flats built. That aggravated the real estate bubble and made it more painful when the currency crisis struck in 1997. Had we choked off the demand earlier, in 1995, we would have been immensely better off.[116]

From Lee's point of view, policy mistakes had been made. But there is another important undercurrent, which was the lens through which key leaders came to look back on this period. The region was seeing rapidly rising asset prices, in housing and the stock market, with easy and rising levels of debt. This resulting asset and debt bubble was to burst, in the shape of the Asian Financial Crisis beginning July 1997. Singapore was not immune to these regional forces, but with its anti-speculation measures in 1996, the leadership began to steer a course that eventually saw Singapore avoiding the worst of the bubble that resulted in the crisis that severely affected several of its neighbours. Teo Chee Hean, a young minister at the time being put through various portfolios, recalled:

> The leadership was concerned that the HDB market had taken on a life of its own. Collectively, we came to a decision that there had to be policy measures to tame the market. The aim was not to prevent price rises per se if these were driven by market fundamentals. All around the region asset prices and debt to finance this had been rising rapidly. We had a responsibility to consider the wider effect of this on the economy, especially systemic risks to the banking system. Bank assets were being based more and more on housing loans for property whose price was rising

rapidly. Individual buyers and borrowers were overextended too. If the property market crashed, it would affect the banking system and have severe repercussions throughout the economy. The market was buoyant at the time we introduced the 1996 cooling measures—we therefore knew we would be roundly condemned by investors and homeowners who wanted to see their property prices continue to rise. But we had to do what was right, and none too soon. The Asian Financial Crisis struck in July 1997, bringing asset prices in the region crashing down. The contraction in Singapore we saw in 1997–98 would have been much more severe if not for the cooling measures we took in 1996. Our ability to weather the Financial Crisis relatively unscathed, with our reputation and attractiveness to investors enhanced and economic fundamentals intact, was noted all round and by key institutions such as the IMF. These fundamentals would have been severely weakened if we had not taken steps early in 1996.[117]

Forging Cohesion: The Grassroots

Grassroots leaders, a large proportion of whom are Chinese-educated or dialect-speaking, are in a position to explain policies, especially unpopular ones, in jargon-free language, avoiding the cold and seemingly uncaring character of bureaucratic rationalisations of costs, benefits and the national interest. As an important communicative link between the government and the people, the grassroots sector is the human face of an administrative state that often demands sacrifices from ordinary Singaporeans in the interest of nation-building, but that also needs the continued electoral support and mandate of the people to go on doing this legitimately. Through the activities and services that it organises, particularly those aimed at promoting social and political education, the grassroots sector influences Singaporeans in more subtle ways, as a tool of socialisation taking its cue from values defined by a still highly paternalistic government.[118]

One of the core aspects of the Party's political programme as the 1990s progressed would be strengthening the bond between the people and the PAP. As PM Goh noted in an important speech to PAP activists on 24 May 1992, this bond was a "virtuous circle". But it could become a "vicious circle" in future if voters hurt the relationship by voting against the government because of narrow, self-serving interests:

Some voters are seized with an unhealthy "serve me or else" attitude. Such a voter complains easily and loudly over small issues. He often proclaims his support for the PAP, for the Government, for the MP, but he threatens them in the same breath to get things done for him. He is demanding, insisting that the law must make an exception of his case. He fails or refuses to see that he is part of a larger society and that he must live within the laws and norms that regulate the smooth functioning of that society.[119]

With such people, Goh observed, the good that the government had done was forgotten, while the pain caused by a single policy or administrative measure was remembered. He noted, "If more and more voters behave this way, there will be a musical chair government because every policy and administrative measure must affect somebody."[120]

The thinking was not entirely new; critical appraisals of the electorate (particularly concerning the rising tide of individualistic behaviour that ignored the common good) had featured to some degree in every PAP general election post-mortem and subsequent internal Party discussion since 1984. Historically, the Party had relied—especially in the interregnum between the elections—on the use of non-Party bodies—Grassroots Organisations (GROs)—to sense the mood of the people, and to educate and mobilise them. These bodies included the People's Association (PA), Residents' Committees (RCs), Citizens' Consultative Committees (CCCs) and Community Centre Management Committees (CCMCs).[121] Over time, other bodies were added which augmented the apparatus (the Feedback Unit being one). There were clear signs from the early 1990s of attempts to galvanise this network, with the changes to the Feedback Unit following the 1991 general election being a case in point. The PAP's 1991 general election post-mortem had, in fact, concluded that the bond with the people needed to be strengthened through education, persuasion and organisation, and for this to happen, grassroots organisations had to be strengthened.[122] We will now consider the mechanics of how the PAP in the 1990s tackled the problem of winning the people over and explaining policies at the grassroots level.

The clarion call, one made often by ministers in the early 1990s, was of revitalisation. One of the key challenges set for the PA in 1993 by Wong Kan Seng, its deputy chairman, was to energise a new generation to work with the government to tackle problems, just as their parents' generation had done. The PA's challenge, Wong said, was to consolidate its grassroots network and reach out to the community.[123]

Wong's comments were a harbinger of changes. A mid-1993 reorganisation meant that all GROs came under the PA (previously, CCCs and RCs were under the Ministry of Community Development, while the PA looked after community centres and CCMCs).[124] The organisations themselves remained essentially unchanged in structure, but the move made it easier to bring them together for the purposes of administration and control—and for political education.[125] The PA and the National Community Organisations Council organised the first Triennial Conference for Grassroots Organisations in April and May 1994 with the theme of "Bonding People and Government: The Role of Grassroots Organisations". In his keynote address to the conference on 29 April 1994, PM Goh Chok Tong took pains to justify the government's policies on market pricing and on cutting down on subsidies.[126] The conference adopted 61 recommendations which had been raised by the workgroups under it. The recommendations, which had been put together by various workgroups, were in themselves unremarkable, with many dealing with how the grassroots could explain national issues to rally support. What was new was how the grassroots organisations themselves—the RCs, CCCs, CCMCs, and also in this case the Women's

Executive Committees (WECs), Youth Executive Committees (YECs) and Senior Citizens' Executive Committees (SCECs)—had been brought together as workgroups at the district level earlier, from October 1993 to January 1994, to discuss these issues. The recommendations were then submitted to the district CCCs for finalisation and consideration at the conference.

Consolidation was only the prelude. There was a pronounced movement to reconnect with the ground, and particularly with the Chinese ground, in the years immediately following the 1991 general election. The PAP in its internal post-mortem after the 1991 general election had recognised that the SDP had made inroads by cultivating groups on the ground (hawker associations being one). According to the post-mortem report, the government's market-oriented economic policies had affected, and even demoralised, many of the PAP's supporters. Some grassroots leaders, under pressure, had even attacked the PAP's policies.[127] It is unsurprising that government leaders—including PM Goh and Dr Ow Chin Hock (chairman of the Feedback Unit Supervisory Panel)—were to subsequently publicly say that the difficulties in getting people to accept the need for market-oriented policies was the chief obstacle in government-to-people communication. The difficulties, Goh observed, had led to the increasing perception that the government was uncaring.[128]

There was also the realisation that attempts to convince the people and educate them about government policies could not simply take place within the cozy confines of dialogue sessions with MPs. In order for useful feedback to be provided, conversations had also to take place in more informal settings.[129] Dr Ow Chin Hock announced in April 1994 (in what was a change of direction for the Feedback Unit) that the Feedback Unit would reach out to the "silent majority" by holding dialogues in neighbourhoods (including community centres) rather than at the Ministry of Community Development building.[130] The move was necessitated partly, Ow observed, by the fact that people had become more sceptical about giving feedback to the government: the level of feedback given to the unit had stagnated over the previous two years.

Reaching out to the "silent majority" appears to have been a major aim of the government in the first half of the decade, with channels other than the Feedback Unit increasingly active. Even in 1992, the *Straits Times* could note in its analysis of the CCCs that they were "now the main channel for the government", contributing 65 per cent of all feedback. The Feedback Unit and letters from the public made up the remainder.[131] These were seen as positive developments. Ch'ng Jit Koon, senior minister of state for community development, observed in 1992 that while feedback to the Feedback Unit tended to come from the "vocal minority" or from the "personally aggrieved", "feedback from CCCs covers the silent majority, and forms a welcome ballast to the weight of the vocal minority".[132]

Grassroots leaders for their part were being asked to do considerably more. This was not a straightforward proposition. Convincing the people was hard enough; doing so with insufficient knowledge of the government's policy rationale made things much more difficult. A major survey by the Ministry of Community Development (MCD) of grassroots leaders, conducted in 1992, showed that many leaders felt they did not have enough information on government policies.[133] This lack of information could easily translate to a lack of understanding and was of course doubly problematic from the government's point of view: the grassroots leaders, besides not being able to explain to the people, might not themselves be convinced. The *Straits Times* in describing one Feedback Unit dialogue session in 1994 remarked on the grouses of these leaders, who were presumably PAP supporters: "They did not have enough information on the policies; worse, they themselves could not understand them—which might well be a code word for saying that they, too, did not like these polices."[134]

The problem was recognised, and efforts were made by the government in this respect. As the decade wore on, there was an increase in the number of dialogues for MPs to explain issues and policies; ministers also began to visit grassroots events regularly.[135] The National Community Leadership Institute developed orientation programmes to cover government policies and current issues.[136]

Consolidation was one thing. But actual reinvigoration could not take place without renewal; and this posed greater difficulty for a variety of reasons. Increasingly, questions were being asked about how grassroots organisations could relate to the new generation of Singaporeans. Many observers felt that there was the danger of obsolescence.

The RCs, for example, had faced an increasing problem with manpower and recruitment since the late 1980s.[137] It was becoming more difficult to persuade young people to join the grassroots, with statistics showing that the number of RC members in their 20s was on the decline.[138] Renewal was not simply a numbers game. If it had been, the trend would have seemed to be a healthy one. RC membership, for example, had actually grown from 1990 to 1993.[139] But it was recognised that there were several inactive members hidden within the figures and much more was needed in order to replenish the ranks.[140]

The problem of renewal was not specific to RCs: there was an equally pressing and in some ways more complex set of problems at work in the area of CCC/CCMC renewal. In the 1960s, many CCC members had been respected community leaders, or individuals drawn from the Mandarin- or dialect-speaking merchant classes. More than a few were known quantities within their communities: figures who could disseminate news or inform the people about government plans. But the move into government housing, and the dissolution of traditional village and community bonds, had meant that the role of headman or leader had been eroded.[141] Rising education levels and (particularly from the 1990s) the growth of the mass media meant that people could seek information elsewhere and make up their own minds without having to resort to the grassroots.[142] The core of the original leadership of the CCCs was ageing and did not have the same links to the younger generation.

There was from the mid-1980s a movement to induct English-speaking, tertiary-educated professionals into the CCCs. In 2005 Lee Kuan Yew (by then minister mentor) reflected on this period:

> *I would say those [the 1980s] were years of consolidation as we developed more sophistication in the way which volunteers were appointed, monitored and renewed. It was a time when we felt we had to bring in young people. It was*

a difficult period especially in the late 1980s, as we moved from the Chinese-educated who were accustomed to this community work, to the English-educated who did not have this tradition. . . . There was quite a problem recruiting them. It was only after we got young MPs bringing in their friends who were professionals, accountants, lawyers, doctors, whatever, that the gaps were filled, as the older generation of Chinese-educated faded away.[143]

The figures tell the story of leadership transition. Eighty per cent of CCC members in the 1960s were businessmen (which usually meant in practice members of the Chinese-educated merchant classes). Ninety per cent of CCC members during this period were Chinese-educated.[144] By the mid-1980s, only 30 per cent of CCC members were businessmen, and only 45 per cent were Chinese-educated (51 per cent were English-educated).[145] By the early 1990s, the balance had shifted even further. In 1992, for example, 55.5 per cent of the 2,000 CCC members were English-educated holding jobs in the professional or managerial class. The figure for Chinese-educated CCC members had dipped to 40.8 per cent.[146]

Resettlement from kampongs (villages) to new HDB towns was a key issue in the 1970s, with many of the grassroots volunteers tasked with explaining government policies on the issue being traditional leaders from the area. They were able to relate to the ground as they had command of Chinese dialects. But the issues faced by the people began to change by the 1980s, and problems that young, educated couples faced were in many cases best dealt with by a newer generation of grassroots leaders who were themselves professionals fluent (or at least conversant) in English.[147]

Replacing the pioneer generation of grassroots leaders with younger, educated professionals was not easily done.[148] Many from the older group were either entrenched or had made themselves and their counsel well-nigh indispensable. Some of the newer prospective entrants were leery of becoming involved in grassroots work because they feared being politicised or associating with what were seen as political bodies.[149] There was also the issue of how the new generation of grassroots leaders (many of whom tended to be more proficient in and more comfortable with English) connected with the people. Even though the use of English as a means of communication was increasing, at this stage, large numbers of people living in the housing estates continued to rely on their respective mother tongues (Mandarin, Malay and Tamil) or Chinese dialects over the use of English as their preferred medium of communication.[150]

A full examination of the difficulties and details of grassroots renewal lies outside the scope of this book. But there are two points that should be borne in mind. First, renewal in the GROs mirrored the process that was even then ongoing within the PAP. The Party had to continually refresh and re-energise itself with younger, better-educated recruits; so too with the grassroots.[151] The second point is that strengthening the GROs, and making them better platforms for communication and feedback, was a work in progress in the 1990s. Even in the following decade, ministers would periodically highlight the continuing need for grassroots renewal.[152] But it was in the 1990s that the attempts at bureaucratisation and professionalisation began to pick up steam. From 1996 onwards, grassroots bodies had their performance evaluated by the

PA, with special recognition accorded to those which surpassed the standards set. And at the level of Community Development Councils (dealt with below), the government began from 1996 to bring in a corps of professional managers, including administrative officers from the civil service.[153]

⁂

We now return to the specific challenges that the 1990s brought for the PAP government. As we have seen, these included dealing with costs, expectations and the attendant public unhappiness. Strengthening the grassroots and feedback processes could do only so much. In their public statements, PAP leaders began to evince increasing concern about the direction that society was headed in. More needed to be done to build unity and cohesion. The idea began to be enunciated that some sort of ballast for society was required—a system that could maintain cohesion and values that were at risk. Speaking at a student forum on 18 July 1996, Senior Minister of State for Health and Education Dr Aline Wong commented on the need to emphasise the non-material aspects of life. The challenge in the 21st century would be to develop personal, family and community relationships that would counterbalance the "everyone for himself, grabbing mentality that seems to have gripped so many among the general population".[154]

This theme was taken up and developed further by PM Goh in his 18 August 1996 National Day Rally speech. Goh addressed the issue squarely: he noted that upgraders who disdained HDB housing and who distanced themselves from the majority would make for a class-conscious Singapore and would weaken the social fabric.[155] Goh also tackled the issue of emotional bonding among Singaporeans. His solution, announced during his speech, was the introduction of Community Development Councils (CDCs). The country would be divided into ten to 15 CDC districts, made up of a combination of GRCs and single-member constituencies. Each CDC, headed by a mayor, would be a community that would look after the welfare of its residents. CDCs would also manage applications for various funds from the needy. But more important, CDCs would revive the old community spirit of mutual help, build social cohesion, and bring the goal of a civic society closer to realisation.[156]

The issue of social cohesion was a pressing one. As Singapore progressed economically, the bonds holding Singaporeans together became increasingly important. Hard infrastructure was taken care of by town councils; there was now a parallel need for social infrastructure (CCCs, CCMCs and RCs) to be coordinated by one body. This body would also seed activism from the ground up with Singaporeans rendering community self-help through a localised form of participative government.[157]

There were, of course, other considerations. The longer-term intention was for there to be devolution of power to the CDCs. As time passed, more responsibilities (especially in the area of social assistance) would be taken over by the CDCs, which would evolve into a form of local government.[158] CDCs would be the focal point and local administrator of social services and schemes, while ministries would be the policymakers, regulators and national planners.[159]

To the Opposition members, the introduction of CDCs was nothing less than a partisan move aimed at politicising welfare services and entrenching PAP control. In the view of the SDP's Chiam See Tong, the "bonding" aspect of CDCs was simply "bonding people with the PAP".[160] The National Solidarity Party's statement on the issue was (in a similar vein) that CDCs were "old wine in new bottles", representing nothing more than the revamping of existing GROs. Setting up the CDCs was, according to the National Solidarity Party, an indication that GROs were unable to play the role of "uniting and serving the people", due to their having degenerated into "subordinate organisations" of the ruling party, "thereby arousing the disgust of the people".[161]

The PAP had, of course, anticipated this type of argument and was having none of it. The countering line used was that CDCs were apolitical bodies with an important social mission—fostering social cohesion through their activities at the ground level.[162] The CDC scheme, the PAP claimed, would be politically neutral— Opposition wards would receive the same services from CDCs as PAP wards did.[163] But there was undeniably a strong exclusionary element. The Opposition pointed out that Opposition MPs were denied roles in CDCs.[164] It had also been made clear that CDC funds would not be given to Opposition MPs to disburse. In Opposition-held wards, the purse strings would be controlled by others, such as the PAP adviser or second adviser to grassroots organisations (often seen as the shadow MP).[165]

All these arguments, for and against, were hardly new. The Opposition had for some time now been pointing out that their MPs were not appointed advisers to the grassroots organisations in constituencies which they had won. Instead, the PAP candidate defeated at the election (or a new face the Party intended to field in the coming election) would be placed in this position.[166] During the Second Reading of the People's Association (Amendment) Bill in 1996 (which paved the way for the introduction of CDCs), Opposition MPs raised objections to PA's practice of appointing PAP MPs the adviser or (in the case of prospective candidates) second adviser in Opposition-held wards, effectively freezing out the Opposition. Chiam See Tong lamented the position he was in, in vivid terms:

> In fact, the PA has elevated a defeated PAP candidate at the polls to a higher status than the elected Opposition MP at Potong Pasir. The defeated PAP candidate is given all the facilities to win back the seat. He has been given special facilities such as a room in the void deck to hold meetings and to hold his meet-the-people sessions. That room is fully air-conditioned and fully equipped with computers and other clerical aids. On the other hand, the elected Opposition MP has to work from a table that is placed in the open void deck, no different from a fortune-teller plying his trade on a five-foot way.[167]

It is worth recounting here some of the history. J.B. Jeyaretnam's victory in the Anson by-election (31 October 1981) raised certain long-dormant issues, given that there had been no Opposition MPs in Parliament from 1968. The rule that the elected MP had to be the adviser to the various grassroots organisations (GROs) in the constituency appears to have changed at around the time of Jeyaretnam's win in Anson, with the rule change meaning that the adviser would be chosen by the Prime Minister's Office. The PMO's position was that Jeyaretnam was "not expected to work for the success of the government's social policies", whereas advisers were chosen "for their commitment to government policies".[168] This remained the PAP government's position despite questioning of the rationale by Opposition MPs through the years.[169]

Behind the scenes, at an important internal PAP meeting that took place on 17 November 1981 at Parliament House—shortly after Jeyaretnam took Anson. Goh Chok Tong recalled what transpired many years later, in 2004:

> *Secretary-General Lee called a meeting of PAP MPs to discuss how to handle the new situation. Specifically, he wanted to know whether we should hand over the Anson community centre and the other grassroots organisations and facilities to J.B. Jeyaretnam. Should we follow Queensberry rules and hand everything over to the opposition except our party branch or should we use them to fight the opposition? Some MPs, especially the new ones, felt that we should act gentlemanly and hand over the government-related grassroots organisations to the opposition. The majority, however, were against handing over what we had built up. So we dug in and fought to recapture Anson.*[170]

Issues concerning the role of the PA and the appointment of advisers to GROs continued to be argued out between the PAP and the Opposition, not altogether without rancour, at various points in the 1990s. During a parliamentary debate concerning amendments to the People's Association Act on 18 January 1993, Chiam See Tong claimed that the PA's real aim was to promote the interest of the ruling party. This elicited a forthright response from the foreign affairs minister and deputy chairman of the PA, Wong Kan Seng: "I make no apology for the fact that the PA is a unique creation of the PAP government." Pointing out that the PA was set up to mobilise the people to support government policies, Wong noted that it was "quite difficult to envisage an instance where opposition MPs in their capacity as advisers to CCs help to carry out government policies. After all, their job is to oppose the Government."[171] This summed up the PAP position: the Opposition could hardly be counted on to promote the cause of the government, and thus had no place in grassroots bodies.

The PAP maintained that grassroots bodies such as the CCCs (and now, by extension, the CDCs) were non-partisan and non-political. They could be pro-government but were not pro-Party. Naturally, this was a distinction that blurred in practice. As one MP, Lew Syn Pau, noted in 1992, "Any party which comes into power will use the grassroots organisations to help gain support for its programmes."[172] It was this that was the real bone of contention between the PAP government and the Opposition: other issues (such as the disbursing and control of funds, and the position of the adviser to the GROs in Opposition wards) were merely side arguments to the main issue.

The close links between the PAP, the PA and GROs were well-established, and had in fact been commented on by academics for almost as long as the PAP had been a subject of academic study.[173] Close scrutiny by the PAP government over GRO membership was also not new. Only those who were recommended by the adviser could be appointed to key positions in the CCC and CCMC, and only then could they be screened by the PA and government agencies.[174] A 1992 study of CCCs by the *Straits Times* noted that as many as one-third of CCC members were also PAP members.[175] One CCC chairman interviewed by the *Straits Times* noted that he expected his CCC members to join the PAP and required an explanation if faced with a refusal.[176]

In the context of renewal efforts in the 1990s, the line continued to be held in terms of how the GROs stood regarding their relationship with the PAP. The Opposition might periodically highlight the perceived unfairness of the system, but in practice the extensive co-mingling between the PAP and GROs continued, as did the exclusion of the Opposition. It is difficult, however, to accept the notion that various moves on the ground in the 1990s (such as the creation of the CDCs) had solely to do with the aim of entrenching control, although this was certainly one aspect. The type of emotional bonding, activism and mutual self-help that PM Goh and other leaders repeatedly highlighted during the late 1990s and during the debate on CDCs was something which appears to have been a deep and abiding concern.[177] It made an appearance repeatedly in various forms, and in various places, throughout the 1990s. We have already had occasion to note that a major gathering of GROs took place in April 1994, where PM Goh Chok Tong, in his capacity as PA chairman, spoke on the need for the GROs to understand and explain government policy, particularly on market pricing, subsidies and costs. The second such triennial conference, held on 19 October 1997, saw Goh and Wong Kan Seng addressing issues of cohesion, building emotional bonds, and the need for GROs to explain issues (such as foreign talent) which, if left to fester, could threaten cohesion.[178]

These were concerns articulated in very similar terms within Party circles. Consider, for example, this excerpt from the Report of the PAP Central Executive Committee for January 1995–November 1996, presented to cadres at the Party conference on 17 November 1996:

> *Emotional bonding between Singaporeans is a key task ahead for the future. It will determine whether Singapore will remain cohesive and flourish in the next century.*
>
> *Singapore cannot afford to weaken its social cohesion, as had happened in the West where the social and family responsibilities have been pushed to the Government. We must continue to build a society where the successful are generous in their help for the disadvantaged, and where the recipients look upon such assistance not as right but with appreciation. The less fortunate should support the able and successful, and take them as inspiration to achieve higher goals. Community leaders must renew their commitment and work for the benefit of their communities, while the members should give them all the support they need.*

The bonding between the Government and the people is critical in this relationship. Mutual trust and understanding must be maintained so that we can take quick decisions to respond to global, regional and domestic changes without protracted argument. In times of national or international crisis, the bonding is even more important as it will determine whether Singapore will remain strong in the face of adversity or crumble at the slightest threat.[179]

As the 1990s progressed, the PAP government was to increasingly appreciate that more needed to be done to counter feelings of rootlessness, alienation and anomie. "Heartware" had to be (re)built, and the efforts had to go beyond strengthening feedback mechanisms or the grassroots. New approaches would be tried. These would include co-opting the populace in national discussions (the Singapore 21 initiative in 1997 and Remaking Singapore in 2002–03), and in allowing, in a limited form, the growth of civil society. These will be considered in chapter 4.

Coffeeshops and Carrots

For democracy to work, there must be a clear understanding that you cannot elect "A" and ask "B" to provide for you. You cannot expect the PAP to lay golden eggs for you when you are helping to weaken it. If you want more golden eggs, you must nurture and support it.

—PM Goh Chok Tong, speech to Party activists, 24 May 1992[180]

The PAP in the 1990s saw no high-signature reform or restructuring to parallel the initiatives spearheaded by Goh Chok Tong in the mid-1980s. No major new Party bodies were created, although there were incremental efforts at renewal and reinforcement of existing structures (to be dealt with later in this chapter). It would thus be tempting to infer that the Party had hit some sort of organisational plateau or even a stagnation. The reality, however, was quite different. The leadership was for the greater part of the 1990s preoccupied with issues directly relevant to the Party's long-term future. These included: improving the public image of the PAP, attempting to understand the aspirations of the people, and (closely related to the latter) an investigation on how to win back the ground that had been lost in 1991. A great deal of the Party thinking on these matters was done behind the scenes, by work in committee.[181]

In February 1995, following discussions with MPs, the Party CEC directed that three committees should be formed to monitor the mood on the ground and recommend new measures to win the hearts and minds of the people. These were the "A" or "Aspirations" Committee, the "G" or "Ground" Committee, and the "O" or "Opposition" Committee. They were chaired, respectively, by Heng Chiang Meng (MP from the Cheng San GRC), Dr Ow Chin Hock (MP for Leng Kee and OS [Special Duties]) and Dr Ong Chit Chung (MP for Bukit Batok). The reports of these committees were submitted to the CEC by August 1995. Several of the conclusions of these committees reinforced conclusions which the Party leadership had already come to. The report of the "A" Committee, for example, focused on cost-of-living issues, especially pertaining to housing. It concluded that as Singaporeans achieved more, they had also come to expect more, and that these issues would become more difficult to manage as education levels rose.[182]

It is significant that the reports of all three committees dealt extensively with the issue of the PAP's public image. The committees highlighted that the PAP had the image of being elitist, aloof and uncaring, and noted that its seeming disregard for the people's feelings had caused the loss of support. The prospect was also raised of the young turning against a patronising style of government. The report of the "G" Committee was particularly blunt:

> *The Party is criticised as being autocratic, arrogant, secretive, and defensive. It has also a harsh and unsympathetic image. Despite what it has done, many still regard the PAP government as uncaring and not doing enough for the less fortunate. The Party needs to build on its positive image and ameliorate the impact of the negative [image]. It must pay more attention to explanation of policies. The Party must place more emphasis on political considerations, human feelings and emotions in carrying out its work. Policies must not only appeal to the mind, but also to the heart. . . . The Party must appear more caring, compassionate and approachable. It must not be seen as lacking in humility and high handed and top down in approach.[183]*

Observations that the PAP needed to project a more caring image, and that ministers and MPs should have more personal contact with the ground (something raised by all three committees), were not new. These themes were developed with particular urgency by the "O" Committee. Dr Ong Chit Chung's committee had a wide remit. It had been tasked to study all aspects of the Opposition, as well as to anticipate and analyse the issues that would be raised against the government.

The report made almost as much of the PAP's weaknesses as it did of the Opposition's. Two of the most important points will be highlighted here. First, there was (the report noted) the perception that few PAP candidates were good in grassroots work, genuinely interested in politics, or interested in meeting people and serving them. Few had the ability to truly mobilise the people. There had to be a balance in the slate of candidates presented at elections, with more candidates fielded who were genuinely keen on grassroots work. And these candidates had to be put through longer attachments of on-the-ground training and assessment.

This was a complaint that had been circulating within PAP branches (as we have seen) since the 1980s. But the "O" Committee report went further, in a second set of observations:

> *We have lost the art of propaganda; our machinery is geared towards providing services, information and news, but not in making propaganda. People do not*

know that we agonise for them, care deeply for them, ensure their security, protect their interests, and do everything possible to upgrade their living standards. There is no chorus on the ground singing praises of the government. After a while, the people take things for granted, and the Government appears to be distant and cold to them.[184]

The report went on to comment on the need to influence, monitor, plant and direct coffeeshop talk: "We have hardly any influence on coffeeshop talk. This is a very important political battle ground and we must seize the initiative, and not be at the mercy of Opposition propagandists."

The "O" Committee had arrived at conclusions that the Party leadership did not dispute. In fact, these suggestions were integral to the operation to win back the Opposition-held constituencies that had already been ongoing for some time.

✦✦✦✦

In the period before the 1997 general election, the PAP maintained a low-key presence in the Opposition-held wards of Potong Pasir, Nee Soon Central, Bukit Gombak and Hougang. Branch offices were still open, but meet-the-people sessions had been officially discontinued. Some effort was made to maintain visibility. The second adviser (essentially the shadow PAP MP) and branch activists would frequent coffeeshops. But the PAP branches took care not to maintain an overly high profile. Grassroots bodies such as the CCCs and RCs did not cooperate with Opposition MPs.[185] A balancing act was being attempted—the direction from Party HQ to the branches in Opposition wards was to try to find ways to help only known supporters of the Party (rather than all who called on the branch). The reasoning was simple: people could not have their bread buttered on both sides and believe that there was no cost to voting Opposition.[186] They had elected an Opposition MP, and it was the latter who should help his constituents, rather than the PAP man.

The seemingly hands-off approach belied the fact that the Party leadership had begun to plan for the next general election at an early stage. A key player here was the chairman of Task Force 97 and Second Assistant Secretary-General of the Party Wong Kan Seng. From 1993 onwards, Wong visited the PAP branches in Opposition-held wards on several occasions, where he met with PAP activists, branch members and advisers. The purpose of these visits was to get a feel of the PAP's standing in the constituency, and to hear suggestions on what could be done to regain the constituency for the Party. These visits were also an opportunity for two-way communication between the Party leadership and PAP branch activists. There was some scepticism on the part of Party activists that the low-key approach in Opposition wards was the correct strategy. This was particularly in wards where the margin of the loss in 1991 had been small. Only 168 votes, for example, had separated the SDP's successful candidate, Cheo Chai Chen, from the PAP's Ng Pock Too in Nee Soon Central in 1991. Some

PAP activists took the view that working harder, and reaching out more, was the way to win back this and other wards. Wong Kan Seng's response during his engagements with the branches was simple: in Potong Pasir (and before that, in Anson), the PAP had lost despite working harder. Residents had to appreciate that there was a cost to voting for the Opposition. The Opposition MP was officially the man in charge. If the Opposition MP could not do things for residents, then residents should change the MP by using their vote. Wong agreed that the PAP branch could organise some activities, but there should be no major initiatives as this would benefit the residents even though the majority had not voted for the PAP.[187] In making these points, Wong was reflecting the conclusions which the PAP leadership and the majority of MPs had come to during the post-mortem following the 1991 general election.

These visits were important morale boosters, with Wong and his small team from PAP HQ urging activists and grassroots leaders to continue the fight and prepare for the next general election. PAP activists for their part welcomed the visits and were gratified that PAP HQ had shown concern and cared about the feedback from the ground. But some constituencies' activists felt more left out, and had become more cynical, than others. In Potong Pasir, for example, several activists were convinced that PAP HQ's intention was not to mount an overly strong challenge to the SDP's Chiam See Tong. The PAP leadership (so the theory ran) was willing to allow Potong Pasir to continue being under the Opposition, so as to enhance Singapore's credentials of being a multiparty democracy. Wong's visit to the Potong Pasir branch and his dialogue with activists was an attempt to dispel this feeling.[188]

The importance of personal contact and relationships was a theme that consistently ran through these meetings between the branches and representatives from PAP HQ. Branch activists stressed to Wong and other HQ representatives that the likely candidate for the next election who was to be (or had been) sent to the branch had to be able to strike up a rapport with residents. Wong's own visits and fact-finding were also an opportunity to confirm that the leadership had made the right choices in this regard.

Ong Ah Heng and Ang Mong Seng, the second advisers in Nee Soon Central and Bukit Gombak respectively, were to succeed in ousting the SDP incumbents at the 1997 general election.[189] Studying how they did so is instructive. Both were known as "coffeeshop MPs", after the amount of time they spent building relationships with residents at the *kopitiams* (coffeeshops) both before and after being elected. Ong in particular took relationship building to a level that in some ways harked back to the days when politicians needed to know and cultivate those at the fringes of the law:

> When I first went to Nee Soon Central, it was important for me to spend time at the coffeeshops. These kopitiams often had secret society members. Ang Soon Tong was the main society. There was also Tiong Yee Tong and Hai Lok San. I had some of my contacts introduce me to the leader of Ang Soon Thong. Initially they were quite friendly, but had their reservations about me because I was new. They

made inquiries with their contacts in Anson and Tanjong Pagar about me as a person. Only when they were confident that I would not betray their trust did they become friendly and saw me as someone they could surface their concerns with. From 1992 to 1997, I established good relationships with a very important source of ground information.

Most of the residents in Nee Soon were resettled kampong folks, of Taoist faith. Religion was important for them, particularly the issue of incense paper burning. This was an offering to their gods. They appealed for my help to facilitate this practice. Gradually, I got to know these folks well. I spoke in their language and understood their concerns, especially bread-and-butter livelihood issues about the cost of living. They considered me as their friend, and when they see me, they would shout "Ong-eh! Want to have a cup of coffee?" which I suspect is why people call me a Kopitiam MP.[190]

Ong's efforts in getting to know the underworld and his cordial relationship with its denizens led to him being called other things as well—including "the gangster MP", a tag which still persists in some quarters to this day. But Ong took this in his stride. In every ward, Ong reasoned, there were influential non-grassroots leaders who could give real, unadorned feedback. Ong reasoned that if Nee Soon Central was to be won back for the Party, these men had to be sought out and cultivated in informal settings.[191] Trust could then be gained over frank exchanges of views. This approach was to pay off in spades in the 1997 general election.

Ang Mong Seng had initially been second adviser to the Hougang GROs for a short period in 1996, before moving over to Bukit Gombak at the end of that year.[192] He did not have the luxury of almost five years on the ground that Ong Ah Heng had had. But Ang simply took his election battle plan for Hougang and used it for Bukit Gombak. The plan was simple: sparing no effort to connect with the ground and knowing what residents' issues were. Ang insisted on getting to know residents personally—this could not be done solely at the coffeeshops given that time was clearly running out before the election.

In the face of doubts even from his branch activists, Ang succeeded in covering the entire ward in three months through a punishing schedule of block tours. This involved block visits to HDB flats as well as private residences in the ward three nights every week, with more time spent at coffeeshops on the weekends (followed again by block visits on weekend afternoons).[193] Through the course of the year leading up to the 1997 general election, Ang was careful how he and PAP branch members behaved. No negative remarks or smears were allowed against the SDP MP in Bukit Gombak, Ling How Doong. Like Ong Ah Heng, Ang knew that in winning back Opposition ground, it was important to show sincerity and humility.[194]

Both Ong Ah Heng and Ang Mong Seng were of humble origins.[195] Both were long-serving PAP branch members: Ong since 1964, and Ang since 1978.[196] Both men had long-standing involvement in the community and GROs.[197] Both men were

Nantah graduates.[198] They did not boast stellar qualifications that might to observers have marked them out for higher office. But they were heavyweights of a different type—the type of grassroots mobiliser which various committees of MPs (including the "O" Committee in 1995, and others before it) had been calling for. The right men had been chosen for the job.[199]

One further observation should be made about the PAP's attempt to recapture Opposition ground during the 1990s. The Party was attempting to shed the image of being uncaring and aloof. But at the same time, it was increasingly taking steps that many saw as punitive on swathes of the electorate, particularly those in Opposition wards. The argument which had been developing within PAP circles—starting from the leadership and then percolating down to the MPs—was that those who had voted for the PAP had to be privileged in some ways above those who had not. It was the 1991 general election result and the subsequent discussions within the Party that put the seal on this thinking. From 1992, the votes-for-upgrading strategy became fully crystallised. PM Goh spelled this out on 12 April 1992, when he made known that this would be the PAP's election strategy for the next two elections, as well as for the coming by-elections that he had promised.[200] At around this time, elaborating on this strategy and the rationale behind it in a speech to Party activists, Goh observed:

> On a national basis we cannot deny voters in opposition wards the benefits of national programmes like Edusave, MediFund and the HDB upgrading programme. We fought the general elections on the basis of The Next Lap, which included these programmes. The majority of Singaporeans supported The Next Lap. So these programmes will be applied nationally. But it is perfectly legitimate to serve the constituencies which voted for the programme first, as against another which did not. Can you imagine how silly I would have sounded had I said that where two constituencies had equal claims on the HDB upgrading Programme, the ward which voted against the Government programme would be served first?[201]

As PM Goh noted in his speech, the message had to be brought home in a very direct and personal way: "The voter must feel that he is better off if he chooses the right party and worse off if he votes the wrong one."[202]

Upgrading was not the only tactic used. Following the 1991 election, the PAP Community Foundation (PCF) began to reduce the number of places in PCF kindergartens located in Opposition wards. Three hundred places were cut by July 1992. The reductions did not go as far as the 50 per cent cut that had initially been threatened, but they were still deep enough to be felt.[203] The resulting unhappiness on the ground was an issue brought up by activists at every PAP branch in Opposition territory during the 1993 visits by Task Force 97 Chairman Wong Kan Seng.[204] But by this time, PAP MPs had begun to accept the idea that while some residents might be angry at the PAP for using these tactics, they had to be brought to understand the price of voting for the Opposition.[205] The pain involved might range from a scaled-down PCF intake and bus services cut down in the ward, to seeing covered walkways in the neighbouring (PAP) precinct while the Opposition area had none.[206]

During the 1990s, this strategy—particularly its upgrading facet—was to face sustained criticism from the Opposition, neutral observers and the man on the street. In April 1992 the *Straits Times* interviewed a range of individuals (members of the public, academics, lawyers and other professionals) and conducted a poll on the subject. Most polled took the view that the PAP had erred in politicising HDB upgrading. There were three main objections. The first was that the PAP had conflated Party interests with its duties as a government, which it was now abdicating through the upgrading strategy. The second argument was that upgrading was funded by the body of taxpayers and should not be used as a carrot—or threat—to support the political strategy of a Party. And finally, some felt that the upgrading strategy went against previous attempts to build cohesion and consensus.[207]

PAP leaders robustly defended their approach. On 19 April 1992, Labour Minister Dr Lee Boon Yang took on the issue while speaking at a grassroots event. Dr Lee, clearly with the recent poll results from the *Straits Times* in mind, noted that it was the policy of the PAP government to upgrade HDB estates. The Party should therefore be supported at the ballot box if people agreed with the policy:

> It is naive, intellectually dishonest, and irresponsible to advocate a view that voters can act emotionally or irresponsibly at elections and not expect to have to live with the consequences. . . . The danger of such mental seduction is to encourage more voters into assuming that it is their privilege to vote against the PAP and yet expect that their lives, hopes and aspirations will not be affected.[208]

Far from the upgrading carrot being a case of bribery (only "mindless" people could call it that, Dr Lee said), there was an extremely logical system at work from the PAP's point of view. People were naïve to think that they could vote against the Party and then expect the same quality of life as if they had supported it. Dr Lee commented that this was the surest way to a freak election result—Singaporeans might throw out the PAP unwittingly, even though most might want it to form the government.

In sum, then, the Party leadership—supported increasingly by its MPs—had no qualms in using the machinery of the government to support the Party. Upgrading was one aspect of this. There were others: the arm of government was used to show that the PAP MP-in-waiting would be more effective than the incumbent Opposition MP. Men who were to be fielded in Opposition wards in the 1997 general election were using their coffeeshop networks to sense what people were unhappy about, and were trying to show that they could make a difference.[209] In WP-held Hougang, for example, Ang Mong Seng (the former second adviser to Hougang grassroots organisations, and fielded in Bukit Gombak in the election) appealed successfully to the relevant ministries for a small heavy vehicle park to be built.[210] As we shall see when dealing with the 1997 general election and its aftermath, the PAP saw this as the correct and logical strategy to pursue. But what the Party could not do was to put the issue conclusively to rest.

Ripples of unhappiness over the votes-for-upgrading strategy would continue right through the 1990s into the following decade. The Party could answer the question on why it had chosen this course. But it was considerably more difficult to answer the question as to whether the PAP now had a different standing in the eyes of the people, and whether the conduct of politics had become a negative art. In April 1992, during the initial phase of the upgrading strategy controversy, Leslie Fong, editor of the *Straits Times*, wrote that he could understand why the PAP "felt compelled to grasp the nettle". But at the same time, he wondered about the "long-term repercussions the strategy might have on the political culture here. Would it prove divisive?"[211]

Co-opting, Renewing, Adapting

The PAP is willing to experiment but intends to maintain a high degree of centralised control.

—*Straits Times*, 27 April 1993[212]

Some sense of the thinking behind Party selection and renewal in the 1980s has been provided in previous chapters, with processes becoming more formalised as time passed. Systematisation of processes, however, did not mean that talentspotting and induction had become less challenging. Recruitment of MPs and finding "good people" was in fact becoming increasingly problematic. The CEC was concerned enough by November 1990 to direct the formation of two committees comprising MPs to look into issues pertaining to the MPs' roles and recruitment and (separately) the Party's image. The reports of these committees (essentially study groups made up largely of backbenchers) were considered by the CEC in April 1991. Both committees concluded that the Party would find it increasingly difficult to attract the right persons with the commitment, verve and stamina to serve as backbench MPs:

> *Professionals also consider a backbench role as a waste of time, as the backbencher has in their view no meaningful input on policies; a tedious chore, with the endless rounds of functions; a tiresome task to win support on the ground, especially with the lack of staff support, the perpetual demands of fund raising, more and more frequent parliamentary sittings, myriad other committee meetings to attend and the additional burdens like Town Council work. Amongst professionals, there is little prestige and significance in being a backbench MP.*[213]

The reports from 1991 reflected the difficulties that backbench MPs faced. The points find echoes in the reports of similar internal committees which reported in the mid-1980s.[214] All these reports reflected some frustration at the perceived lack of a meaningful role for backbenchers in shaping government policies—people did not want to become MPs because they did not think that they could make a real difference. The 1990–91 committees (like their predecessors) also noted that ministers had to take

MPs and their suggestions seriously, and that the government should lift the whip on some bills to allow MPs to vote freely.[215]

But not all recommendations represented recycled thinking. The 1991 reports injected a new sense of urgency into the intra-Party debate on recruitment, and highlighted the pressing need for a diversification of the recruitment base:

> *The committee has also noted that there are talented people who may be willing to enter politics but are not sought after by the Party. These people may not have a university degree but are successful in their own fields, be they in business, arts or social welfare services. There are also successful women who are single, assertive and with grassroots appeal who should be considered. Party leaders must therefore select MP candidates from a wider range of professions and interests. These people will give the Party a better balance and will help improve its image.*[216]

Singapore's own success, the conducive economic environment, and the lack of compelling causes had contributed to the reluctance of successful Singaporeans to make the necessary sacrifices and enter politics:

> *Young people, in particular, who are doing well in their career are only likely to be persuaded to take on a second job as an MP and make the consequential sacrifices, if they believe that at the end of the day, they can come away feeling that they have achieved something, or that they can register a plus in their CV. Active steps must therefore be taken to help form this perception and that a sense of personal satisfaction will follow.*[217]

These were issues that were to trouble the PAP in the 1990s: the difficulty in ensuring a more diverse base, the unwillingness of people to make sacrifices, and the sense that there was no "achievement" in the career of an MP. And these did not simply apply to the recruitment of potential MPs, but to renewal of the Party as a whole. The Party had to continually ensure that existing Party bodies were kept invigorated, especially those which depended on an element of mass participation, or mass support.

Young PAP

After the 1992 by-election victory, there was the sense within the Party leadership that some breathing room had been won, and that there was now the opportunity to turn to issues such as strengthening the PAP's base through recruiting newer, younger members.[218] But it was at the same time becoming apparent that the downward slide in recruitment and renewal efforts needed to be arrested. After reaching a membership peak of 2,000 in 1989, the numbers of Youth Wing members had halved by 1993. The Youth Wing's problems were apparent enough for the *Straits Times* to run a full-length feature on the subject in February 1993. Current and former members interviewed by the *Straits Times* evinced some frustration that following the high-profile publicity and buzz of the launch in 1986, most Youth Wing branches were dormant, with the Wing itself appearing to lack a clear vision going forward.[219] Among the complaints from members were that the activities it organised (such as political talks and social activities) did not appear to have a long-term planning basis; the lack of clear direction meant that the Youth Wing had drifted from the original purpose of getting the youth involved in the political issues of running a country.[220] In addition, although half a dozen MPs had come through the Youth Wing ranks, young, ambitious members did not believe that joining the wing would necessarily enhance their political prospects.[221] For many who wanted to move up quickly through the ranks, the structure and processes of the Party were an impediment: seen as autocratic, opaque and ossified.[222]

Something had to be done. As the *Straits Times* noted, there was going to be a political cost if the PAP failed to connect with and meet the aspirations of the younger generation.[223] The Party had even before this (in 1992) embarked on a review of the Youth Wing led by its then Chairman BG George Yeo. In March 1993 the CEC approved an entire raft of changes that Yeo had proposed.[224] Some of the changes were cosmetic, others more far reaching. The CEC decided to relaunch the Youth Wing as Young PAP (YP) with a new logo. The qualifying maximum age limit was raised to 40 years. There would be provisions for membership for affiliate members, together with a stepped-up recruitment drive.[225] An International Relations section was also established to promote relations with political parties in other countries. A Policy Studies Group was formed to examine current issues and present the views of younger Singaporeans to the relevant authorities. Finally, in an attempt to give a sense of participation and a taste of politics, district- and branch-level elections were introduced for YP members who would be elected by their peers.[226]

These moves, when announced in April 1993, were greeted with a degree of caution or even scepticism by Youth Wing members. One member interviewed by the *Straits Times* noted that the mission statement outlined by BG Yeo for the YP was not that much different from that of the Youth Wing when it had first been launched.[227] It is important, however, to consider not just the details of the revamp, but also what these changes can tell us about the thinking of the Party leadership at the time. It was certainly true (as subsequent media commentary noted) that young members had to be aware of issues and also convey aspirations of their peers to Party leaders.[228] But the process worked both ways. The CEC in considering the issue of the revamp of the Youth Wing had agreed it was imperative that the Party should identify what waves were sweeping along the youth and to tap into these. If the new Young PAP could identify such causes and adopt them, it would attract the young to associate themselves with the Party.[229] Some sense of this two-way process was reflected in the speech given by BG Yeo at a closed-door talk to Party activists on 25 April 1993 (where the changes to the Youth Wing were first aired). Yeo acknowledged that the YP should occasionally differ with the Party leadership, even as it took on the job of selling the Party's policies and giving feedback to the Party leadership from the ground.[230]

There was thus a very rational set of calculations at work behind the major changes. These represented genuine attempts to meet the expectations from Youth Wing members, but also were designed to reinforce the process of co-opting the younger generation. And this could only be done if co-opting brought with it the sense of meaningful participation. An example was the formation of the Policy Studies Group (PSG) under YP, to analyse policy alternatives and make recommendations to the main party. The forum did succeed in becoming a generator of policy ideas. By the second half of the 1990s, the PSG was actively channelling ideas to ministers and was being invited to sit in on parliamentary select committees to debate parliamentary bills.[231] The PSG subsequently spawned PSTs (Policy Study Teams)—smaller, more focused groups providing feedback from young Singaporeans to government parliamentary committees. PST meetings saw members propose ideas and debate on issues. The PSG and PST were not simply more avenues to collect feedback. Issues were discussed and thrashed out, with the discussions leading participants to have a better understanding of issues.[232] Similarly, the reintroduction of overseas study trips was aimed at building ties with YP's counterparts, but also brought home to YP members the geographical and socio-economic realities, and perhaps even reinforced the sense of how fortunate Singaporeans were.[233]

The reboot of the Youth Wing was an ongoing process. The process of gathering feedback and exchanging views on how to make YP more effective continued through informal dialogue sessions between the YP leadership and stakeholders, including the branches. There were many other operational aspects which cannot be considered here in full. It can be said, however, that the process of entrenching YP and ensuring its continued appeal went through the 1990s and beyond. The YP's own fate was also tied to the periodic PAP reorganisations (one of which, the Refreshing PAP initiative from 2002, will be considered later).[234]

It was also apparent even during the process of revamping the Youth Wing in 1993 that the Party leadership had the final, absolute say over all changes.[235] As BG Yeo made clear in his talk to activists on 25 April 1993, YP was simply the "net" to bring in "new combatants"; it was the Party itself that always had to be in the vanguard.[236] Every aspect of change was carefully managed; those refinements (such as direct elections within YP) which represented moves into uncharted territory were those which were pondered the longest.[237] Ultimately, giving a sense of meaningful participation had to be balanced with the need for control.

Party HQ and the Branches

When considering the proposed changes to the Youth Wing in early 1993, there had been the broader recognition within the leadership of the changes taking place in Singapore society. A better-educated people had wider choices and expected to be able to participate more effectively in the political process.[238] More avenues for participation thus had to be offered within the Party. In 1992, a year before the revamp of the Youth Wing took place, a HQ branch of YP was formed. This was partly to absorb Youth Wing members who had not yet decided which branch to join.[239] But the HQ branch was also designed to cater to young professionals, especially graduates, who might find the activities and environment of HQ membership altogether more salubrious than doing routine branch work.[240] The Women's Wing followed suit in establishing an

HQ branch in January 1997. The move was aimed at recruiting and tapping the views of professional women who were interested in politics but may not have the time or inclination to join regular PAP branches.[241] Like the HQ branch of its YP counterpart, the Women's Wing HQ branch held seminars on political and current affairs.

Two types of affiliate membership were also created. The first (created in 1993 during the revamp of the Youth Wing) was to cater to individuals who were keen to participate in Young PAP activities but not yet ready to become full, card-carrying PAP members. This class of affiliate membership would, the Party leadership felt, also be useful for involving those who because of their jobs could not join the PAP in the Party's activities.

The second group of affiliate members were known as "Friends of the PAP". The creation of this class of membership was first discussed by the CEC in 1994, with the scheme finalised towards the end of 1995.[242] Friends of the PAP were individuals who were prominent in other fields (especially business). They were, for the most part, known to the Party and supportive of it. The considerations of the leadership in creating this group were partly fiscal: it was envisaged that the Friends might make donations to the Party. But the move should also be seen as part of the Party's efforts to build contacts and influence among key personalities in the private sector. The total number of Friends was kept small.[243] Two MPs involved from an early stage in organising the group of Friends (and who were its earliest chairmen) were S. Chandra Das and Heng Chiang Meng, both MPs from Cheng San GRC and prominent personalities in the business world.

Since its formation in 1985, the HQ Executive Committee (HQ Exco) had increasingly taken on the operational work of running the Party. In the 1990s it began to range further in terms of coordinating the relationship with the branches and ensuring that the overall Party structure was sound.[244] In 1994, HQ Exco tightened procedures for the appointment of branch chairmen and Branch Executive Committee members. Branch chairmen now had to be MPs and be appointed by HQ Exco. The new arrangement meant that branch chairmen were now required to propose office-bearers and committee members for the Branch Executive Committee, with these nominations being subject to the approval of an Appointments Committee established under HQ Exco.[245]

Separately, by 1999 there was a basic system of key performance indicators in place by which branches were measured. This was a simple scoring system that gave an indication of the activity levels of the branches. The measures used included recruitment of new members, the level of feedback from the branch, and whether branch accounts were properly kept. Other variables were subsequently added, including, for example, the regularity of submissions of statistics from meet-the-people sessions.[246] There was no overall ranking of branches but a system of "banding". Branches were alerted which band they fell into based on their performance.[247]

HQ Exco also began from 1993 to tackle the long-term issue of how branches could be organised more effectively within the GRC framework. Eventually, in 1998, the CEC adopted HQ Exco's proposal that GRC Standing Committees (GSCs) be created.[248] These would comprise the MPs in each GRC, in addition to a small number of key activists from each branch. This group would make up the GSC Executive Committee, with other subcommittees formed if deemed necessary. The two most important aspects of the GSCs were consistency and coordination. The leadership was increasingly coming to realise (especially after the 1997 general election) that political work had to be carried out systematically at the GRC level between and during elections by the same core group of activists. Hitherto, many GRCs had functioned, in the words of Matthias Yao (the second organising secretary at the time), as "a Federation of Single-Member Constituencies".[249] The GSC framework would enable the problems in the GRCs to be viewed holistically and identified earlier. Closer understanding, better teamwork, and tighter coordination among the branches could thence be achieved, especially through the initiation of political activities at the GRC level.[250]

General Membership

In the years approaching the turn of the millennium, the Party was managing to recruit close to 1,000 new members annually.[251] By 2000, total membership was approximately 27,300, a significant rise over the figure of 17,500 in 1990.[252] The figure would reach approximately 34,000 in 2005, of whom just under 20 per cent were also YP members.[253]

The overall numbers were healthy, but they told only part of the story. Forty per cent of the ordinary membership (approximately 7,000 members) was aged 51 and above in 1990. The figure was 42 per cent in 1995, 49 per cent in 2000, and even reached 56 per cent (18,600 members) in 2005. In 1990, 11 per cent of the total PAP membership was aged 30 and under. This figure was 8 per cent in 1995, and declined further to 5 per cent in 2000 (it remained at 5 per cent in 2005). The overall figure for members aged 30 and under in 2005 was approximately 1,800, almost unchanged from the figure for 1990. The average age of Party members was 48 in 1990, 49 in 1995, 51 in 2000, and 53 in 2005.

The picture that begins to emerge is that the Party was finding it less than easy to rejuvenate itself, even as overall membership numbers increased. Throughout the 1990s, study groups of MPs were periodically formed to examine the issue of rejuvenation of the Party base. The studies showed that while the Party was taking in younger and better-educated members, there was still a large base of older—and ageing—members. In 1990, 39 per cent of members had only primary education, while 12 per cent had tertiary qualifications. The figures in 1995 were 35 per cent and 14 per cent; in 2000, 32 per cent and 16 per cent. By 2005, the figures were 27 per cent and 22 per cent.[254] The base was certainly becoming better educated, but, for various reasons, not all the new members taken in were of the younger, educated profile that the Party leadership had wanted.[255] As overall membership rose, it is telling that absolute numbers of those members who held only primary school level qualifications also rose throughout the period 1990–2005. This figure began to decline only after 2005.[256]

There are two points that should be considered here in assessing the makeup of the Party's membership base. First, rejuvenation was important, but there was at both the HQ and branch levels the recognition that recruiting efforts could not focus solely on younger professionals. The Party still needed to have broad-based recruitment in order to retain its appeal to all groups. On 22 November 1999, during a speech to mark the 45th anniversary of the PAP, PM Goh described the three types of members the Party was looking for. The first was a group of professionals, academics and senior executives who could refine national policies. The second was "muscle people"—Party activists and branch officials who could reach out to voters. The last group was "messengers and opinion multipliers"—Party members who (like muscle people) could reach out to the broad mass of people.[257]

Second, the drive to bring in younger, better-educated members also depended to a large extent on the efforts of the branches and on the stance of the MP in question.[258] Some PAP MPs were keen, once elected, to bring in their own associates to the branch. Others made it a point to retain incumbent (and long-standing) branch staff for some time, effecting over time a sensitive transition that also allowed for institutional knowledge to be retained.[259]

As the old generation of branch officials left the scene, a new breed of younger, educated activists slowly began to emerge, just as it had done for the GROs. The length of time they stayed varied greatly and often depended on the "fit" with the branch in question. It can be said, however, that the era of branch members serving for decades began to be in eclipse by the late 1990s. Branch members and long-serving grassroots leaders with ties to the community stretching back decades were becoming the exception. Those who took their places, however diligent, did not have the same networks (at least not immediately), might not have the same antennae for ground feedback, and would not have the same familiarity with the MP that had characterised the relationship between the previous generation of MPs and branch activists. The renewal thus had implications that could not be easily measured, and whose effects were not, perhaps, immediately felt in the 1990s. But these issues—in particular, the quality of feedback and the giving of it—were always present below the surface and would make their appearance again in the 2000s.

Cadres

The 1990s revamp of the Youth Wing, and the creation of new bodies such as the PSG and the GSC, could perhaps be described as a combination of pragmatic adaptation and the incremental consolidation of existing structures. The sense of this pragmatism and willingness to adapt was present in other discussions within the Party leadership in the early 1990s. An example of this was the issue of strengthening the cadre base. In September 1992, when the issue was discussed at the CEC, the secretary-general, SM Lee, noted that the existing cadre system had been conditioned by the Communist threat. Lee suggested that now that the threat had faded, a different approach could be adopted in the appointment of cadres. Lee pointed to the selection system of the Chinese Communist Party, which saw Party members with capability and potential systematically assessed and tracked throughout their careers. A core base of cadres was thus created which could be drawn on when higher positions needed to be filled. Lee suggested that the PAP study the feasibility of setting up a similar system.[260] He suggested that the net be cast as wide as possible: since the talent pool within the Party's membership ranks was limited, the tracking system should also include potential candidates for elections who were not yet members of the Party.[261]

A team led by Organising Secretary Dr Lee Boon Yang was tasked to review the cadre system. The committee made several recommendations, many of which were accepted. Among them was the recommendation that the process of developing cadres and tracking potential should be overseen by a new body, a Cadre Membership Committee under HQ Exco. The committee would monitor existing as well as potential cadres, organise training sessions, and schedule discussions with Party leaders.[262]

In its report, the committee acknowledged the advantage of preserving secrecy over the identities of cadres: it made it difficult for factionalism to develop, or for anyone to destabilise the Party by lobbying cadres before a CEC election. But the committee noted that the need for secrecy had become less imperative, observing that cadres not knowing each other hindered the fostering of camaraderie. It suggested that the identities of cadres could be made known within branches.[263] The Party leadership, however, preferred a more gradual approach. It did not agree to the disclosure of the identities of cadre members. Nor did the leadership agree with a key proposal by the committee—that there should be a fixed-term cadre membership. The view was that those who had been loyal to the Party for a long period of time might feel slighted at being pushed out; the leadership suggested instead that the new Cadre Membership Committee review the present list of cadres and put those who were inactive into a reserve list.[264]

The Party had approximately 1,300 cadre members in 1995. The figure rose to approximately 1,600 in 2000 and 1,800 in 2005. The changing profile of the cadre base mirrored that of the general membership. A total of 62 per cent of cadre members in 1995 were over the age of 50. The figure was 70 per cent in 2000 and hit 74 per cent in 2005.[265] This could be seen partly as a result of the reluctance of the Party leadership to employ radical measures to replenish cadre ranks (such as the decision not to use fixed-term membership). But it is also perhaps indicative of the Party's continued (and historical) caution in awarding cadre membership. Members had to have done a length of time within the branches (usually five years' service) and be known to the MP before becoming eligible for consideration. Only a minuscule number of Party members under the age of 30 were cadres, something which remained unchanged throughout the 1990s and early 2000s.

Cadre promotion was taken seriously, with promotion exercises becoming after 1995 an annual (instead of biennial) affair. The procedure was for branch chairmen (in practice the MPs) to nominate members—usually no more than two per branch—whose contributions made them deserving of cadre membership. For the better part of the 1990s, the Cadre Promotion Committee was headed by Wong Kan Seng in his capacity as second assistant secretary-general, usually assisted (as overall secretary) by the second organising secretary, Matthias Yao. Three subcommittees (each with its own chairman and secretary) did the work of interviewing candidates and reporting back to the main committee. For most of the 1990s, the number of nominees from the branches interviewed by the subcommittees was approximately 100. The percentages of candidates found suitable for cadre membership (those graded "A" to "C") ranged from 75 per cent to 85 per cent during this period.

This seemingly high percentage belies the fact that candidates in the highest category—those graded "A" and judged to be potentially of MP material—were few and far between. In most years during the 1990s and early 2000s, the number of such candidates was in the low single digits, and in some years there were none at all. This was not that much different from the situation in the late 1980s, as we have seen. In the 1990s, those who came before the cadre promotion subcommittees with university degrees never comprised much more than 25–30 per cent of the overall pool of those put forward. For most years, by far the largest group of nominees was those with only secondary-level education (usually in excess of 50 per cent, and sometimes well in excess of it). The rate of success for the latter group was usually over 60 per cent; this rate was for most of the decade only slightly inferior to the success rate for those who had university degrees.

But over time the educational profile of the cadre base did slowly change, in line with the changes in general membership. Twelve per cent of cadres had only primary education in 1995. The figure was 9 per cent in 2000 and 5 per cent in 2005. Thirty-six per cent of cadre members in 1995 had tertiary qualifications. The figure was 39 per cent in 2000 and 45 per cent in 2005.

Towards the end of the 1990s, attempts began to be made to diversify the cadre base. Some individuals (particularly those from the Friends of the PAP list) began to be considered by the main committee headed by Wong Kan Seng for cadre membership at the HQ level; there were also occasionally nominations from the Women's and Youth Wings. Overall, though, the transformation envisaged by SM Lee—that the cadre base could become the key source from which leaders were drawn—was not to be realised.

Candidates

The Party leadership was mindful of the sentiment of branches—that there should be some candidates fielded who had worked their way up from the level of branch activists. There is some suggestion that thought had been given in the early 1990s to instituting more formal mechanisms through which PAP branches could nominate their members to stand.[266] However, major changes did not materialise. The procedure with regard to nominations from the branches was to continue to retain something of an ad hoc nature in the 1990s. MPs were encouraged to put forward the names of community leaders and branch activists in the ward whom they could vouch for. But the overall chances of a branch activist or community leader getting through all the rounds of tea sessions and MP selection interviews were not high.[267]

Dr Lee Boon Yang was from 1993 to 2001 the first organising secretary of the Party and was intimately involved in the recruiting process.[268] Lee's job was to pop the question to individuals found suitable (after the first two stages of tea sessions) as to whether they would be prepared to go through the formal interview process. Lee noted that in the 1990s, out of every ten individuals he approached, only two or three would agree to go through the formal interview process. The majority of those agreeing to let their names go forward were individuals with substantial grassroots or branch experience, and who had been noticed because of this involvement.[269]

What began to change in the 1990s was the success rate of the Party's recruiting apparatus in drawing in successful individuals from outside the Party who had the potential to hold higher office:

> *Most of them said no. Most of them cited family commitments and their personal lack of interest in active participation in politics. They would say while they have an interest in current affairs, they don't really want to get involved in politics. They were quite clear about what they wanted to make of their career, what they wanted to make of their life. Political participation was just not part of the landscape for them. Only a few of them could be persuaded to serve. Many were highly successful professionals . . . many of them said no. Many of these people went on to become very successful, very wealthy individuals, after turning down the invitation. Some became wealthy beyond imagination. There were quite a number of these people. Excellent and very capable people. Not just IQ wise but EQ wise. The kind of people who have a certain charisma and who could generate loyalty and also support. They turned me down when we invited them back after the various tea sessions to pop the question to them to say would they come in or not. A flat no. Not interested in politics.*[270]

The problem ran deeper than simply getting people to come forward to serve; it extended to replenishing the slowly diminishing talent pool within the Cabinet. In the 1990s, several ministers left the Cabinet. These were S. Dhanabalan, Dr Yeo Ning Hong, Dr Ahmad Mattar, Ong Teng Cheong and Dr Tony Tan.[271] From late 1992 onwards, government leaders began to discuss openly, and urgently, the problem of finding individuals to take their places. At the Party conference on 15 November 1992, PM Goh (in remarks which were carried by the media) told Party cadres that renewal and finding individuals of ministerial calibre was his top priority. Goh remarked that the Cabinet was ageing (with an average age of 50.3 years), also noting that three ministers were shouldering double portfolios.[272]

There was a clear link between the decision to air the talent/renewal issue and the fact that on 16 November 1992 (just a day after Goh's remarks), it was made public that the two DPMs, BG Lee Hsien Loong and Ong Teng Cheong, were suffering from cancer. Some commentators speculated at the time that the possibility of losing BG Lee to illness showed up the fear that there was not enough leadership at the top level.[273] But there was more to it than that. There was also the sense that recruitment of the very top tier of talent—potential ministers—had not been altogether successful in the 1990s. As SM Lee pointed out in Parliament in 2000, most of the leaders at that time had been selected as MPs before he had stepped down as PM in 1990. Since that time, only three had made it to minister of state—Peter Chen, Lim Swee Say and David Lim.[274]

Why exactly was it becoming so difficult to get people to stand (or be considered) as candidates? Three factors were at work here. The first had been highlighted (as we have seen) by the various Party committees set up as early as the late 1980s, to examine recruitment and the roles of MPs. In essence, there was the recognition that the role of the backbench MP was thankless and onerous and contained little reward. The job was unattractive, especially to professionals. A second, related point was that it had become increasingly clear as the 1990s progressed that successful people—on track to become wealthy or influential (or both)—had no need to interact with the political sphere or to become involved in politics.[275]

There is a further point that should be considered. An argument that began to develop in the 1990s was that the Party had only itself to blame for its failure to attract qualified candidates. The people (so the argument ran) had in former times spoken of the Party with respect and affection and expected politics under the PAP to be clean. The PAP had, however, chosen to employ harsh tactics at election time, and this had turned off idealistic Singaporeans, who chose to contribute to the nation in other ways. As one *Straits Times* journalist noted while expounding this argument, the PAP "had to look deeper to see where the malaise lies" when it bemoaned the lack of candidates coming forward, adding that "three decades of depoliticisation have brought about a society that today looks on politics either as a vocation best left to those of a masochistic-messianic bent, willing to subject themselves to a holy order of sorts, or a dirty word for selfish individuals looking after their own interests".[276]

The Party leadership did not place weight on theories of the latter kind, however interesting or persuasive they might seem on paper. The issues of renewal, and making up the losses to Cabinet, were from the late 1980s acquiring an urgency that demanded practical but potentially unpopular solutions.

Ministerial Pay

> *That period of revolutionary change that threw up people with deep convictions and overpowering motivations is over. This is a fact.*
>
> —SM Lee Kuan Yew, 30 June 2000[277]

> *If we do not pay Ministers adequately, we will get inadequate Ministers. If you pay peanuts, you will get monkeys for your Ministers. The people will suffer, not the monkeys.*
>
> —PM Goh Chok Tong, 3 December 1993[278]

The leadership, and SM Lee in particular, had over time become convinced that the pay for ministers had to be competitive with salaries in the private sector if men with exceptional ability were to be recruited into the leadership ranks.[279] In March 1989, new salary packages for top civil servants and political appointment holders were introduced. During the parliamentary debate on the issue, government leaders, with 1DPM Goh at the forefront, enunciated some of the principles that had come to represent the core of the PAP government's thinking on attracting top talent. Pay for top civil servants and ministers would not lead the private sector but had to keep pace with it. This was in order to mitigate some of the sacrifice (and opportunity cost) that talented people made when they chose politics. The new package at least gave the leadership a better chance of recruiting people who might otherwise have been content pursuing careers in the private sector.[280] And there was an increasing acceptance that the age which had seen men coming forward to do the job out of a sense of duty, or idealism, had passed. Idealism was important, but it would not suffice to bring in the right people.[281] The overall message—one reiterated by PM Lee to the people in his 1990 eve of National Day message—was that the people should not try to get, nor expect, a government on the cheap.[282] From here on in, the job had to be made attractive enough for people of genuine calibre to consider doing it, and the consequences of not attracting the best men into politics would be devastating for the country.

If the 1989 revisions had been an attempt to settle the issue of ministerial pay once and for all, it did not work. From 1989 to 1993, salaries in the civil service rose modestly. But salaries in the private sector (especially those of the top earners at senior management level) rose much faster—faster than the leadership had expected. By late 1993, the leadership had decided that something had to be done to keep the salaries of top-tier administrative officers and political appointment holders competitive. A new round of salary revisions (which saw ministers' salaries going up by 25–30 per cent) was introduced and debated in Parliament. The arguments used by PM Goh when defending the revisions were the same as those used in 1989: the prosperity of the nation depended on an honest and competent Cabinet. Goh acknowledged that there was a political cost to raising salaries. Besides unhappiness on the part of the people, the issue would likely be exploited by the Opposition, but this (Goh said) had to be weighed against greater cost if the country did not have a Cabinet of exceptional integrity and ability.[283]

A critical intervention was made by SM Lee in Parliament on 14 January 1994 (during the debate on the president's address at the opening of the parliamentary session). In defending the latest round of pay increases and highlighting the imperative need to get the brightest into government, Lee made the suggestion that there should be a formula to determine ministerial salaries.[284] This formula would essentially peg the pay of ministers to a percentage of the remuneration enjoyed by top earners in the private sector.[285] With this formula, there would be no need to justify a pay revision every three to four years.

Behind the scenes, Lee was also at work convincing his colleagues, including PM Goh, of the usefulness of the formula and having it implemented expeditiously. During the course of the subsequent drafting of the White Paper on the subject, Lee more than once made known that an overly cautious approach would not suffice. His argument was simple: there would be major opportunities and huge rewards over the next decade for talented people in the private sector. A benchmark therefore had to be set for the long term that comprehensively tackled the issue of salaries for ministers and top civil servants. Settling for the status quo or half measures would mean that the issue would be reopened again after a year or two. Lee wrote to PM Goh on 2 February 1994 on the subject:

> *We have already stirred up the waters, so let us get it over with in one go. To leave it to next year, is to have the arguments all over again. The people who are against it can only be won over by successful policies that bring them benefits. I am convinced that realistic rewards are very necessary to get Singapore through the next 1–2 decades of high rewards in booming East Asia.*[286]

The White Paper on Competitive Salaries for Competent and Honest Government was tabled in Parliament on 21 October 1994. The White Paper proposed a formula that would see ministerial salaries as well as salaries of senior civil servants linked to the top earners in six professions (banking, law, accountancy, engineering, local manufacturing firms and MNCs), and made recommendations on the exact formula for the pegging of salaries.[287] Parliament debated the White Paper from 31 October until 3 November 1994, when it was endorsed. In summing up during parliamentary debate, PM Goh announced that he would appoint an independent panel to verify the figures used in the White Paper. This independent panel would also consider the appropriateness of the prime minister's salary. Goh explained that leaving this issue to an independent would enable him to argue with greater moral conviction and authority what ministers and civil servants should be paid.[288]

A Salaries Benchmark Committee (headed by Michael Fam, the executive chairman of Fraser & Neave, and comprising respected figures from the corporate sector) was set up in November 1994 to study the accuracy of the figures in the White Paper and to recommend the PM's salary. The report of the committee, made public in January 1995, verified the data and calculations used in the White Paper and found these to be satisfactory. The report also endorsed the proposal within the White Paper that the prime minister's salary be set at twice that of the most junior minister ("Staff Grade I") in the Cabinet (or about $2.4 million yearly).[289] The committee recommended that ministers would take a one-third "discount" to reflect public service, while the top civil servants should be paid the full salary for this grade.[290] These would not be effected immediately. Ministerial salaries would be raised to 60 per cent of the new benchmarks in three years, and to the two-thirds level in an unspecified "longer term".[291] Following the government's acceptance of the report, PM Goh announced that he would forgo any salary rise for himself for a period of five years to "give him greater authority to implement the revised salaries for ministers because he will not benefit from it".[292]

Goh's emphasis on moral authority throughout the debate on the White Paper, and later in accepting the findings of the Salaries Benchmark Committee, was significant. This was something he felt deeply, noting as he did in his response to the Salaries Benchmark Committee that monetary reward "could not be the principal motivating factor for anyone wanting to be Prime Minister. Indeed, the Prime Minister must be motivated by a deep sense of responsibility towards his fellow citizens and the passion to further their interests."[293]

But however much PM Goh tried to keep the moral high ground for government through his personal example, it was to prove difficult to sell the idea to the people, both then and in the years to come. Even during the parliamentary debate on the subject in October 1994, Dr Ow Chin Hock, chairman of the Feedback Unit Supervisory Panel, noted that the ground reactions to the proposals in the White Paper were uniformly poor. Participants in sessions organised by the unit were unhappy at being asked to accept the principle of high pay for ministers at a time when they felt squeezed by rising COEs and GST (which had been introduced in 1994 at a rate of 3 per cent).[294] Ow also noted that people felt that ministers should be motivated by noble ideals and the desire to serve. This was a point of view held by many. One letter to the *Straits Times* Forum on 24 July 1996 summarised the general sentiment:

> *[The changes] have transformed the office of political leadership from a noble calling into a highly paid bureaucratic job. It will also erode the high respect which our people have of our leaders as exemplified by our past and present crop of leaders. . . . Leaders who do not recognise their special obligation and duty to society, which has invested so much in them and helped them attain a high status and position, and need to be rewarded handsomely by very high salaries are no longer extraordinary leaders.*[295]

The government was on the defensive. But as we shall see, it saw itself as partly vindicated by the result of the 1997 general election, which was a strong mandate for the PAP and was an improvement over the result of the 1991 election. PAP leaders thus saw themselves as being on firmer ground when resisting calls for ministers to take pay cuts, or when rejecting the idea (periodically raised) of an independent panel to review ministerial salaries.[296]

Not all calls for the government to set an example could be dismissed, especially during periods of general austerity. During the Asian Financial Crisis in 1998 there were calls from various quarters, including Workers' Party Non-Constituency Member of Parliament (NCMP) J.B. Jeyaretnam, for ministers to share the hardships of the people and take a pay cut. But PAP leaders were at first quick to dismiss such calls, with Minister without Portfolio Lim Boon Heng noting that this was "not the time for symbolism and rhetoric, what is more important is substance".[297] It could hardly escape attention, then, that there was subsequently a move by the government to lead in wage restraint, with a pay freeze and a suspension of the planned upward wage adjustment for top civil servants and ministers.[298]

The government may have believed that it would be politically unwise to proceed when austerity was the general watchword. The 1998 pay freeze may have been appreciated by the people, but there was a mixed reaction from observers and the media. One argument was that since a formula had been devised and defended, it should have been adhered to, and planned increases should have been kept to. Doing otherwise could be "a tacit admission that the formula has failed".[299]

There could also never be a good time to restore earlier pay cuts for ministers and top civil servants. In 2000 the cuts from 1998 were restored, partly to keep pace with rising private sector benchmarks.[300] The public was not won over, asking how these rises could be justified at a time when the earlier cuts in employer CPF contributions had not yet been restored.[301]

In defending the government's proposals in Parliament on 1 November 1994, SM Lee had said that he was prepared "to put my experience and my judgment against all the arguments that doubters can muster. In five to ten years, when it works and Singapore has a good government, this formula will be accepted as conventional wisdom".[302] In this, Lee was mistaken. The issue festered on right through the 1990s and beyond. The *Straits Times* was to observe in 1998 that ministerial salaries had "moved from being a periodic issue to a recurring one . . . since 1994, it has become an issue lurking below the public consciousness".[303] This unhappiness was linked to the fact that from the late 1990s onwards private sector pay for top executives began to rise appreciably, thereby affecting the benchmark. As the *Straits Times* noted in 2000, "A ministerial pay salary pegged to a runaway pay for top executives that defies economic growth trends is guaranteed to become a definite political liability."[304]

The problem went beyond simple political costs. It was clear that the issue had had a role in fundamentally changing the relationship between the people and the government. Gone for good was the idea of a noble breed of idealistic, self-sacrificing politicians prepared to toil for the benefit of people and nation. PAP leaders in explaining the ministerial pay emphasised—especially from 1994 onwards—that the government was unlikely to get individuals of the right calibre to enter politics simply by appealing to their idealism and self-sacrifice, without providing an adequate level of remuneration. Concomitantly, what began to be entrenched from 1994 onwards was the idea on the part of the people that politicians were paid, and paid extremely large sums, to do a job. The hard figures themselves gave cause for incomprehension and indeed some bewilderment, especially within the lower socio-economic classes. One long-serving grassroots leader (who had served since the 1960s) reflected the views of many:

> It was a big issue. . . . The people start to think—I give you such a high salary, you should do things for me. You are not serving the country. I paid for you to do it. If you cannot work for me to my satisfaction, I want to sack you. To me, I could understand. Certain people, you must pay them well. But not the general public. Last time, I also told our MPs. I told them, "you don't say how many millions . . . some people, they don't even know what is a thousand. Once you tell them million, how can they understand?"[305]

This was a fundamental change to the social compact. The people, seeing these salaries, also became far more demanding, more sensitive, and less tolerant of shortcomings.

The element of public service had been diminished within this compact, and some moral authority was lost. The relationship between rulers and ruled became much more transactional.

So, too, in some ways did the relationship change between the PAP MPs and the grassroots activists. Lim Sah Soon had been involved in the formation of RCs and later became the chief liaison officer of the RC Central Secretariat under the Prime Minister's Office. He was to end his career in public service in 1994, as the deputy executive director of the People's Association.[306] Lim recalled:

> The moment the government started to up ministers' pay, there was a spiral effect. In the old days, people believed that the MP made a sacrifice for the nation. So there was the principle of equal misery—they were more than willing to help the MP and make sacrifices themselves. But now the MP or minister lost some of the moral authority to tell the grassroots leaders to make sacrifices. People started to say, since you are paid market price, why should I do all these things to help you? Even those who were willing—their families, their spouse—would ask them, the minister gets big pay, what do you get? And then after the ministerial pay rises, they start asking for perks. In the old days, they would feel shy about asking. It is a pity—the volunteerism began to dissipate. The new generation of grassroots— many will look at the opportunity cost. They will still volunteer service, but they will start calculating—many began to want more tangible rewards.[307]

The real extent to which the mindsets of the new generation of grassroots leaders emerging in the 1990s changed as a result of this issue is a subject beyond the scope of this book. But on the subject of ministerial pay, this much can be said. The PAP government had attempted—just as it had done for costs and aspirations—to put out logical, reasoned explanations. It was well aware that the issue would inevitably feature in Opposition campaigning in the next election, and it therefore sought to shift the ground, explaining its position through various dialogue sessions. On paper, the government had sound arguments which should have gone a considerable way towards addressing people's concerns. But yet again, while the Party could debate with ironclad logic, it could not reach into, nor win, the emotional side of the debate.

The SDP Implodes

The ministerial salaries issue could, or perhaps should, have had a major influence on the result of the next general election. In the event, the PAP actually managed to improve on the 1991 result at the ballot box on 2 January 1997. This should not, however, be taken as a sign that all had been forgotten by then. The issue of pay still simmered, but the Opposition had not generated heat over it—nor on other hot-button issues—to the extent that observers expected. A key reason for this was decline and internal division within what was at that time (in the mid-1990s) the main Opposition party, the SDP. The SDP's descent was so calamitous, and played out in such public view, that some time needs to be spent on the issue, as it had an important bearing on the 1997 election result.

In May 1993 SDP Secretary-General Chiam See Tong had attempted to get the SDP CEC to censure Dr Chee Soon Juan (by then the assistant secretary-general of the SDP) for going on a hunger strike in April to protest his sacking from NUS. Chiam's failure to convince the CEC led to his resignation, with Chee becoming acting secretary-general. In August, Chiam was sacked from the Party following a disciplinary hearing investigating Chiam's public attacks on the Party leadership. Chiam challenged his expulsion, obtaining a court order against the SDP freezing the SDP's expulsion of him. Chiam subsequently won a suit against the CEC in December 1993, which led to him being reinstated as an SDP member.[308]

There were several strands to this—one was friction and personality differences between Chiam and other members of the SDP CEC. Related to this was the emergence of new power bases within the SDP, with a growing number, including SDP Chairman Ling How Doong, favouring the more confrontational approach to the PAP government espoused by Chee Soon Juan. There was also a power struggle between Chee and Chiam, with the suggestion from Chiam that Chee, his protégé, had attempted to wrest power from Chiam, eventually ousting him.[309]

The second part of the affair began on 28 August 1993, when 27 SDP cadres—essentially part of a pro-Chiam faction purged from the SDP earlier that month—convened, elected their own CEC, approved a vote of no confidence in the SDP CEC, and reinstated Chiam to the Party membership roll.[310] On 31 August 1993, the SDP leadership led by Ling How Doong obtained an interim injunction preventing the breakaway faction from representing itself as the SDP CEC, also filing a suit requesting that the court declare the 28 August 1993 election null and void (which the High Court subsequently did).[311] The High Court in April 1994 reaffirmed the status of the anti-Chiam faction as the properly elected CEC.[312] The counter from the pro-Chiam group came in July 1994, when a breakaway SDP group led by Chiam's supporters filed an application to register a new political party—the Singapore People's Party. This was to be Chiam's vehicle for the next general election.[313]

But Chiam remained an SDP member in the meantime. At the SDP Party conference on 14 January 1995, there was a showdown between Chiam's supporters and Chairman Ling How Doong. Both sides moved resolutions against the other. Chiam attempted to censure Chee for going on a hunger strike to further his own political agenda. Another of Chiam's motions represented an attempt to prevent Chee from holding office in the SDP if he did not take legal action to clear his name.[314] But Chiam was comprehensively outnumbered and outmanoeuvred at the conference, which saw the SDP electing a new CEC that included Ling How Doong as chairman and Chee Soon Juan as secretary-general. The conference also passed a resolution calling on Chiam to resign from the SDP immediately.[315]

The Ling How Doong–Chee Soon Juan group might appear to have been the victors. But as the media noted, there were many—even within the SDP—who were uncomfortable with Chee's confrontational style, his aggressive trumpeting of

Western-style democracy, and his forging links with foreign NGOs which supported these causes.[316] As the *Straits Times* noted on 11 February 1995:

> *Some members [of the SDP] are beginning to find him a trifle too Western, introducing ideas and concepts alien to the party. There is much concern that the party has changed from what many perceived to be a constructive opposition committed to nation-building to one that was confrontational, taking on the Government at every turn.*[317]

By 1995, the confrontational approach was in full view. At a press conference on 27 July 1994 Chee blasted the government's policy on Myanmar, accusing the government of "doing business" with a regime which had plundered the nation and placed Aung San Su Kyi under house arrest.[318] During the height of the Flor Contemplacion affair in April and May 1995, the SDP issued statements that were seen as critical of the handling of the case by the Singapore government and judiciary.[319]

By this stage, the PAP was beginning to find its range against Chee. PAP leaders began to ask the SDP to explain why it supported the Western liberal media and human rights groups in attacks against Singapore.[320] And the Party was presented with a golden opportunity to ram this message home in September 1995, when matters came to a head.

PM Goh's alma mater, Williams College, had decided to confer on Goh an honorary doctorate as a distinguished alumnus. A Williams College professor of political science, Dr George Crane, protested against this, ostensibly on account of Singapore's human rights record, and together with like-minded students organised an alternative panel discussion at the same time as the main convocation where the doctorate was conferred upon Goh on 16 September 1995. Dr Chee Soon Juan, together with Francis Seow (by then in exile in the United States) and former NUS lecturer-turned-Singapore-critic Christopher Lingle, were among those invited to attend this discussion.[321]

In his remarks at the alternative panel, Chee was careful to state that he did not oppose Williams College's award of the doctorate to Goh, also making some attempt to distance himself from the views of some of Singapore's more outspoken critics.[322] But for the PAP, Chee had gone too far simply by being present at Williams, and had not gone far enough in his defence of Singapore. Chee had failed to refute the attacks on the Singapore judiciary made by Francis Seow during the panel, even appearing to voice some agreement with these attacks.[323] Chee had (in the words of the press secretary to PM Goh) shown that he was "a willing stooge of American media and human rights groups who want to intervene in Singapore domestic politics".[324] Dr Ow Chin Hock, the PAP organising secretary (special duties), pointed out on 21 September 1995 that while Chee had congratulated Goh on the award of the doctorate, he had taken part in a panel discussion which opposed the conferment.[325] This led to further debates in the press (with Chee as respondent) on what exactly Chee had said at Williams College, what his intent had been, and whether he had been disloyal.[326] Chee insisted that he had not gone to oppose the award to Goh, and even suggested that the SDP had played a part in dispelling misconceptions about Singapore (as well as giving the PAP credit where it was due).[327]

Chee's assertions in his defence were generally disbelieved. On 3 November 1995 Parliament passed a motion of censure against the SDP, expressing regret at the SDP's attendance at Williams College and at its alleged support for Francis Seow's attacks against the Singapore judiciary. The parliamentary debate also gave Chiam See Tong the opportunity to twist the knife. Chiam (who supported the motion of censure) said that he would not have gone to Williams College if he was still in charge of the SDP, adding that Chee was a "megalomaniac" who "wants the centrestage all the time".[328] Chiam's devastating indictment of the SDP's leadership, his personal attack against Chee, and his robust defence of the Singapore judiciary attracted an unprecedented level of House approval for a speech by an Opposition member. All this was particularly humiliating for the unofficial leader of the Opposition in Parliament, SDP Chairman Ling How Doong, who was forced (in a generally poor performance) to concede that Chee had been wrong not to rebut Francis Seow.

We have remarked earlier that the SDP had tried, even in the midst of its difficulties, to put out a platform on various issues, including issuing occasional reports on topical issues which also contained policy suggestions.[329] Until 1994–95, the PAP had not been wholly successful in persuading the people to reject the SDP vision. Williams College was the turning point. After this episode, the feeling on the ground was one of disappointment (and anger, even) that Chee appeared to have gone to Williams to oppose, or perhaps even to ridicule, Singapore's prime minister. Chiam See Tong had himself observed during his parliamentary intervention on 3 November 1995 that Opposition members had to be "patriotic Singaporeans" and could not "go around the world denouncing Singapore".[330] The PAP was determined to milk this for propaganda to the fullest extent possible. In November 1995, *Petir* issued a special supplement aimed at exposing Chee Soon Juan and the SDP. The supplement detailed the Williams College incident and highlighted criticism of Chee made by Chiam and others, suggesting that Chee was a stooge of Western human rights groups. It was also released to the media, and was distributed in SDP wards and in areas where the SDP was expected to contest at the next general election.[331]

More generally, it was becoming clear that the SDP was not going to be able to make substantive policy recommendations. It was hamstrung by the underwhelming performance of its MPs in parliamentary debate, as well as by their lack of preparation (and occasional lack of decorum).[332] The SDP was also absent from key debates in Parliament. During the parliamentary debate on land transport in January 1996, Ling How Doong was absent—he was with Chee Soon Juan in the Philippines, meeting with the Philippines Liberal Party. PAP MPs charged that Ling should have stayed to debate the issue.[333] SDP MPs were also absent from Parliament on 7 November 1996, when the CRC report was endorsed. The three SDP MPs were at the High Court, where the libel case filed by Chiam against the SDP CEC was being heard.

The refutation of the substance of the SDP's arguments on cost-of-living issues has already been detailed earlier in this chapter. Where the SDP did try to stand its ground and argue out its points, it came disastrously unstuck. Its appearances before the Health Care Select Committee in July 1996, detailed in part earlier in this chapter, are a case in point. SDP members appearing before the committee were obfuscatory, argumentative and ill-prepared. Crucially, figures presented by the SDP and defended by its officials during the hearings were found to be false. As a result, on 27 August 1996, Health Minister George Yeo lodged a formal complaint against the SDP for contempt of Parliament. On 22 November 1996, the Committee of Privileges found Chee Soon Juan and three of his SDP colleagues guilty of presenting false data to the Select Committee. They were fined for perjury, wilfully giving false answers, and misconducting themselves.[334]

What had the SDP achieved by 1997? It had certainly succeeded in drawing a great deal of attention to itself, mostly for the wrong reasons. Dr Chee Soon Juan had become one of the best-known Opposition figures in the nation—something of an achievement for an individual who did not hold a parliamentary seat. But Chee's rise to prominence was tied to the SDP's decline. The early promise from 1991—that the SDP might develop into something representing a genuine alternative to the PAP—had all but disappeared by the time of the polls in January 1997.

The 1997 General Election

Besides the strife that the SDP found itself in, the WP was also far from being in good health. J.B. Jeyaretnam was re-elected as secretary-general of the Party in March 1994, but there were signs of friction within. In June 1993 Dr Lee Siew Choh quit the WP, citing problems with Jeyaretnam. There were also beginning to be signs of a strain in the relationship between Jeyaretnam and the one WP Member of Parliament, Low Thia Khiang.[335] More damagingly, the WP was faced with serious legal troubles. Eleven committee members of Tamil Language Week (as well as, separately, five PAP MPs) had sued the WP for libel over remarks in an August 1995 article in the *Hammer*, the Party organ of the WP.[336]

The Prelude

The Opposition had been hamstrung by changes to GRCs. On 1 October 1996, PM Goh introduced a bill in Parliament seeking to amend the Parliamentary Elections Act. This bill, which passed on 28 October 1996, enlarged the size of GRCs to incorporate a maximum of six MPs (instead of the earlier four); it also reduced the number of single-member constituencies to a minimum of eight. The government's position was that the changes would "facilitate" the formation of the recently announced CDCs, and that enlarging the GRCs would help in fostering community ties.[337]

Opposition MPs roundly condemned these changes, arguing that they were a ploy designed to perpetuate PAP rule and counter the Opposition's "by-election effect". Unknown candidates would now find it easier to enter Parliament on the coattails of well-known figures.[338] The PAP response was to point out that it was the Opposition's fault that they could not find good men to contest a GRC.[339]

That the Opposition had been put at a disadvantage was further evidenced by the redrawing of electoral boundaries by the Electoral Boundaries Review Committee. The committee, which issued its report on 21 November 1996, left intact in its recommendations the four constituencies in Opposition hands. It did, however, recommend that four of the constituencies which had been won by the PAP in close fights in 1991 (Bukit Batok, Braddell Heights, Changi and Nee Soon South) should be absorbed into GRCs.[340]

What were the election issues? Besides ministerial salaries, it was clear that bread-and-butter issues and the cost of living would (as always) figure prominently in the campaign. But there was an important difference from 1991. The PAP government had from 1991 to 1996 made strenuous attempts to bring the issue of costs out into the open through the CRC mechanism, Select Committees, and dialogue sessions. In addition, more tangible ways to help those who most felt the pinch had been attempted. The budget introduced in February 1996 had been widely seen as an election budget, with "goodies" aimed at HDB-dwelling heartlanders. These included MediSave top-ups, and rebates from service, utility and conservancy charges.

Despite these moves, many of the rank-and-file PAP MPs were not exactly optimistic in the months leading up to the election. Party caucuses that were held in the lead-up to the polls, where MPs shared their own prognostications, were tinged with gloom. Many MPs felt that GE results would be marginally worse than in 1991, with a decline in PAP vote share in the region of 3–5 per cent. Only a very few thought the PAP would do marginally better.[341] Some MPs were worried about what they saw as the cynicism of the young, and unhappiness (despite government efforts to engage and explain) over ministerial salaries, healthcare costs, and the cost of living. MPs were convinced that all this would be exploited by the Opposition during the hustings. Some MPs even wrote to PM Goh in the lead-up to the polls, noting that the likely drop in support had nothing to do with the government's ongoing programmes or with Goh's leadership—the sense amongst MPs was that these counted in the PAP's favour.[342] Goh, however, was quietly confident that the PAP would do better than in 1991, exhorting his MPs at these meetings to work the ground thoroughly in the time left before the election.[343]

The Campaign

The PAP was returned to power on Nomination Day, 23 December 1996. Only 36 seats were contested, four fewer than in 1991. In what was likely a reflection of the fact that PM Goh had not had time to go through a full renewal process in the snap polls of 1991, 18 MPs stood down, making for the biggest renewal since 1984. The 24 new candidates introduced by the PAP boasted impressive credentials (see Appendix One, Table 3.1). All the new faces were graduates. Sixteen had gone on to do postgraduate studies. Eight were scholarship holders, and three were holders of the President's Scholarship. It was also a slate that was impressive in its balance and diversity. Ten were from the private sector and ten from the public sector (four had experience in both). Four were academics, three were journalists, and four were trade unionists. It was also noteworthy that of the 17 ethnic Chinese candidates, six were Chinese-educated. These included a community leader from the Chinese Development Assistance Council, a former Chinese newspaper editor, and a Chinese-language inspector from the Education Ministry.[344] As usual, a number of the candidates lacked meaningful substantial branch or grassroots experience. Eleven were appointed to grassroots positions as second advisers only in 1996. But even those who lacked deep grassroots experience cultivated the ground assiduously in the time that was available. This was a factor which the Party post-mortem report credited with swinging support over to the PAP.

The Party manifesto, "Singapore 21: Make It Our Best Home", was introduced by PM Goh at the Party conference on 17 November 1996. Key planks were improvements in housing, education and transport. The goals encapsulated within it included the creation (and sharing) of wealth, investing in the young, caring for the old, and building ties among the people.[345] It was a solid, if unremarkable, manifesto. But here the PAP appears to have learnt an important lesson from the experience of The Next Lap and the 1991 election. The new, and more important, facet of the PAP manifesto was the pledge to fight the 36 seats as a "local government election", pitting candidates' ward improvement plans against what the Opposition had to offer. PAP MPs drew up and presented to the public their detailed programmes for the constituency for the coming years—improving works, the Main Upgrading Plans and Interim Upgrading Plans. Some of these programmes were visions which were grand and eye-catching in scope, such as (the grandest of them all) Punggol 21. Punggol 21, which targeted Cheng San voters, was meant to be the model for new estates into the next millennium. It offered waterfront housing, a mix of housing types, and recreational facilities.[346]

PAP MPs were convinced later that it was the tactic of fighting "local elections" (rather than the politics of fear which the Opposition complained about) that swung votes in their favour.[347] Allied to this, it had been made crystal clear that if people voted for the PAP MP (especially those battling Opposition incumbents), the machinery of government would move in their favour. Much was promised; most of the payoff (particularly in terms of municipal improvements) came only after PAP had actually been voted in. Post-election articles in the PAP organ, *Petir*, catalogued the long list of improvements made by government agencies at the request of the PAP MP—essentially, a catalogue of election promises that had been fulfilled. These included the introduction of the Interim Upgrading Programme; the conversion of a medical centre to a polyclinic; and the construction of linkways, a new indoor sports hall and a new community club.[348]

There was some coverage at Opposition rallies on this approach, and whether it was fair for the PAP to use what were seen as public funds for upgrading PAP precincts. The PAP leaders had no compunction in explaining that the PAP was the government, and it was the government which decided these matters.[349] But the issue threatened to escalate. Late in the campaign, the Party was concerned enough about allegations of unfairness to send out an open letter to Singaporeans explaining the issue in simple terms. It was not (as was commonly believed) that Opposition wards would not get the upgrades, but that resources were limited, and the PAP had the right to prioritise.[350]

Cheng San

The most bitterly fought battle was in the "Quiet Hill"—Cheng San—where J.B. Jeyaretnam sprang a surprise by contesting. His WP team there also comprised WP Chairman Tan Bin Seng, Abdul Rahim Osman, Huang Seow Kwang and the lawyer Tang Liang Hong. They faced a PAP team made up of Lee Yock Suan (minister for education), Michael Lim, Yeo Guat Kwang, Zainul Abidin Rasheed and Heng Chiang Meng.

Early in the campaign, PAP leaders seemed confident that Jeyaretnam had made a miscalculation by coming to Cheng San to contest.[351] But it became apparent that the PAP had a very real fight on its hands. Centre stage in this drama was taken by Tang Liang Hong.[352] Tang was a relative unknown but was a familiar face in some Chinese cultural circles. He was also known to a number of Chinese-educated PAP MPs through these circles. Some of these MPs had in 1992 written in to the speaker of Parliament, Tan Soo Khoon, expressing reservations about Tang and recommending against his being made a nominated member of parliament on account of his extreme views. This and other disclosures of Tang's alleged Chinese chauvinism were made on 26 December 1996 by PM Goh.[353] The attacks on Tang were designed to show Cheng San voters that he was a "dangerous character" with extreme views on Chinese language and culture—someone not fit to be an MP.[354] Chinese-educated PAP MPs came in to cement the criticism.[355] Tang threatened to sue if these comments were not withdrawn, whereupon PM Goh and SM Lee (who had been amongst the chief critics) promptly invited Tang to proceed with legal action against them.[356]

As campaigning progressed, the PAP view was that Tang was showing more of himself. Tang had, for example, claimed at a 29 December 1996 rally that the PAP would not allow mosques in constituencies that had voted for the Opposition. This, to the PAP, was Tang dissembling and trying to reach out to the minorities (in this case, to the Malay community).[357] After the election, PM Goh was to contrast Tang Liang Hong with PAP MPs Ong Ah Heng and Ang Mong Seng. The latter two could speak Mandarin and dialect and had a rapport with the Chinese heartlanders. But at the same time, they understood that minority groups did not want to be dominated by the Chinese and wanted their own space. This understanding had enabled them to win minority votes, without which they could not have won back Nee Soon Central and Bukit Gombak.[358]

It was clear that Tang was far more than a nuisance: he had made the WP team a credible threat to the PAP in Cheng San.[359] By 30 December 1996, the assessment of the PAP Elections Task Force (which by this stage met nightly) was that the PAP could win with 53–55 per cent of the vote. But by the following night, the assessment was that the odds of a PAP win were down to 50 per cent. The WP was well organised and appeared to be fighting Cheng San and Hougang as one campaign, with its supporters criss-crossing the constituencies.[360]

The PAP felt it was necessary to take a tough line and to persuade the ground that Tang was not fit for Parliament.[361] Late in the campaign, on 30 December 1996, PM Goh made it known that the battle was now a personal one between him and Tang, declaring also that he was personally entering into the battle for Cheng San. Cheng San thus acquired a national significance, with Goh putting himself firmly against Tang and the chauvinist views he was said to represent. Lee Yock Suan, the education minister and the ranking PAP member in the PAP slate for Cheng San, was almost completely overshadowed in the last days of the campaign. Instead, the heavyweights such as Goh, SM Lee and the two DPMs (Lee Hsien Loong and Dr Tony Tan) came to the fore, dominating the last two days before polling through rally speeches and walkabouts. The message was pointed. SM Lee warned that "if they [the PAP team in Cheng San] lose, the Government is diminished", and that there would be "grave consequences for Singapore, all around, including Cheng San".[362]

As PM Goh revealed after the election, Cheng San's electorate was 90 per cent Chinese, and most of it Chinese-educated. Goh revealed that the PAP's own straw polls revealed that when the PAP exposed Tang and his past, the Chinese ground in Cheng San had shifted against the PAP, while minority opinion inclined to the Party.[363] Goh, in other words, was pointing out that the PAP had (unlike Tang) played a principled game, keeping its commitment to multiracialism even though there might be a political cost.

The Result

The victory when it came was resounding. The Party took 34 of the 36 seats contested (and all the GRCs), and 65 per cent of the valid votes, up from 61 per cent in the 1991 general election. The result represented the PAP's best showing since 1980. In Cheng San GRC, the Party won 54.82 per cent of the valid votes.[364] The victories by Ang Mong Seng (65.14 per cent) and Ong Ah Heng (61.33 per cent) in Bukit Gombak and Nee Soon Central respectively against SDP opposition were significant.[365] The swing against Ling How Doong in Bukit Gombak was 22.9 per cent, while Cheo Chai Chen in Nee Soon Central experienced a swing against him of 11.6 per cent. This was the first time since independence that the PAP had succeeded in wresting back an Opposition-held constituency. It also meant that the SDP, which had won three seats in 1991, had now been completely shut out of Parliament. None of its 12 candidates were successful. This was deeply dispiriting for the SDP, which in 1991 had won 48.02 per cent of the vote share in the wards it had contested. This declined to 33.1 per cent in 1997.

In Nee Soon Central and Bukit Gombak, the PAP candidates had worked the ground hard and had shown the electorate what they could do for them (and what the government would do for them). This certainly helped sway voters. But the wide margin of these defeats is perhaps a reflection of the SDP's prolonged disarray. This effect was seen also in the re-election of Chiam See Tong in Potong Pasir. Chiam had crossed over to the Singapore People's Party just before the polls. Chiam had had his own legal wrangles with the SDP, and his party was new and not well established.

His victory (with a vote share of 55.15 per cent over the PAP's Andy Gan) was 14.49 percentage points down from his return in 1991.

Another keenly watched battle, in MacPherson, turned out to be an anticlimax, with the PAP's Matthias Yao polling 65.14 per cent against Chee Soon Juan. As we have seen, MacPherson had been carved out of Marine Parade GRC to allow Yao to take on the challenge issued to him by Chee. The Party leadership had considered the challenge carefully. Both PM Goh and Yao himself were aware that a heated election battle was likely as Chee would have his supporters. But both were confident of the ground and did not think a defeat was possible, even at the time when the challenge was issued in 1994 (when the SDP, and Chee himself, were arguably more credible in the eyes of the public).[366] By 1997, Yao was confident that he had established a good rapport with residents in MacPherson. During the campaign Yao was given full support from Party HQ and activists—including those from adjacent Marine Parade GRC, which was uncontested. Yao held two rallies and visited every block, pressing for a strong result.[367] Chee's behaviour, on the other hand, was puzzling to some observers. He seemed to lose momentum as the campaign wore on, and appeared to have ceased serious campaigning by 31 December 1996, the night of the SDP's final rally in MacPherson. It might have been, as Yao speculated, that Chee misread the ground and was confident that he was on the way to victory. But if this indeed were the case, then Chee had seriously miscalculated.[368]

The biggest (and only) winner in the Opposition camp was the Workers' Party incumbent in Hougang, Low Thia Khiang, who took 58.02 per cent of the valid votes in defeating the PAP's Heng Chee How. Low was the only successful WP candidate out of the 14 fielded, and his margin of victory bettered his 1991 result (52.82 per cent).

The Analysis

> *The defining moment was the 1997 General Election. As you know, I was handed the premiership by Lee Kuan Yew when he stepped aside in 1990—though, of course, I had been selected by my own peers. The following year, I called an election just to show that I'm my own man. Of course, I was re-elected, but the votes for the party came to about 61%, which was slightly lower than the previous election. But then in 1997, I was able to reverse the trend and increase the percentage of support by 4% and also recover two seats from the four which we'd lost in 1991. So it was a defining moment, because I felt that I had bonded with the people. I'd shown I was a Prime Minister in my own right, not a Prime Minister because I'd been given it on a silver platter.*[369]
>
> —PM Goh Chok Tong, 25 November 1999

The result was a tremendous personal vindication for Goh. This sense of having been proved right permeated the Party, too. There was no soul-searching as there had been in 1991—simply the feeling that the Party had pursued the correct policies and had used the right election tactics. Looking back on the polls while speaking at the Party convention on 11 January 1998, PM Goh singled out the key reasons for the decisive victory. Upgrading had been the single most important factor in the swing to the PAP and was "decisive in tipping the floating voters in our favour".[370] Other factors included rewarding people directly through other programmes (to be implemented after the PAP victory) and defusing thorny issues (both policy and local matters) well in advance of the elections.

Goh's remarks were a summary of the internal Party analysis, which also singled out upgrading as the single most important factor. In some wards where there were large numbers of undecided voters, upgrading may have tipped the balance, leading to a swing that may have been as large as 5–10 per cent in favour of the PAP, especially in areas where flats were very old. More generally, the PAP's "local government" strategy, which focused attention on issues that mattered to residents (municipal services, and the availability of services such as polyclinics and PCF kindergartens), also played a role. The PAP had also benefited from the fact that potential issues that could have adversely affected the vote had been addressed in some depth before the election. These included healthcare costs and ministerial salaries. The media also played a role. For example, extensive coverage of the debates and deliberations of the Select Committee examining healthcare subsidies helped in ameliorating public dissatisfaction.[371]

In the internal analysis, the Opposition's lack of success was put down to the fact that Chee Soon Juan had been effectively discredited, and to the tarnishing of the SDP's image following its internal schisms.[372] The post-mortem report did note, however, the public perception that there had been a campaign of character assassination directed against Tang Liang Hong. This had not been seen solely amongst the Chinese-educated: even many English-educated (the report noted) felt Tang had been victimised. There had been a groundswell of sympathetic support for Tang, with the post-mortem committee even suggesting that a serious reverse might have occurred if the campaign had gone beyond 2 January 1997.[373]

The PAP felt that upgrading, and presenting detailed improvement plans, worked well as an election tactic. In the post-election glow of early 1997, little serious consideration appears to have been given to the limitations of this approach. Andy Gan had promised Potong Pasir voters an MRT station if they voted him in. But this had not worked against Chiam See Tong.[374] There had been the implied threat that Potong Pasir would become, in Gan's words, "tired and jaded" as other wards were upgraded.[375] This had not worked either. Many in Potong Pasir were sympathetic to Chiam, seeing him as a decent man who had run the constituency well in the face of considerable difficulties against the PAP juggernaut.[376] The same could be said of Low Thia Khiang, who was (as we have seen) in an even stronger position after the 1997 election. Like Chiam, he was commonly perceived to have done a good job in his constituency and in Parliament. Low had even been the recipient of praise from PAP leaders on several occasions.[377]

There appears to have been an acknowledgement that established Opposition figures with a good track record would prove difficult to dislodge, even when PAP carrots were offered to voters. The topic was indirectly addressed by PM Goh at the 1998 Party convention. In making it clear that the Party should aim to repeat its 1997 performance at the next general election, Goh said that he aimed to recapture Potong Pasir, but only to "restrain the support level" for Low Thia Khiang in Hougang. Goh said that Low would take over from Chiam See Tong and Jeyaretnam as the leader of the Opposition, and that dislodging him from Hougang would be difficult as Singaporeans "still like to see some Opposition MPs". But Goh was also clear that the PAP need not be overly concerned. Low was "no threat to the PAP and he will fulfil the role of Chiam".[378]

The PAP post-mortem report suggested that Opposition candidates could be grouped into two broad types. There were more passionate and extreme figures such as Jeyaretnam, Tang Liang Hong and Chee Soon Juan, and—on the other hand—an emerging group of less confrontational, "cleaner" types. The report noted that a minor party such as the National Solidarity Party could boast such people (who included professionals such as doctors) among their ranks. Some in the post-mortem committee felt that in the long run a credible, moderate party would pose the bigger challenge.[379]

But this is as far as the over-the-horizon analysis went. The possibility of a longer-term threat had been raised and briefly acknowledged, but no one within the Party could say, in 1997–98, whence this threat might come.

The Aftermath

The 1997 general election had been a bruising affair. Claim and counterclaim between Tang Liang Hong and PAP leaders had resulted (shortly before voting) in PM Goh and SM Lee, together with six other PAP leaders, suing Tang for saying they had committed a criminal offence and for calling them liars.[380] Shortly after the election Tang fled to Malaysia, apparently (by his own account) because he feared for his safety. SM Lee, PM Goh and other senior PAP figures had separately filed suits against Jeyaretnam, alleging that he had defamed them at an election rally.[381]

Speaking at the early morning post-election conference on 3 January 1997, PM Goh repeated (in what had become a PAP mantra for this election) that allowing people to see the concrete programmes materialise as a result of voting for the Party was key to the victory. But it was telling that even at this early stage, questions were raised by those present on whether the PAP appealing to the immediate interests of voters could be good for Singapore in the long term. Goh himself had had to acknowledge at the press conference that voters would want "more and more".[382] Chiam See Tong was quick to highlight this subsequently: the people had been swayed by upgrading, but eventually this would not suffice, and the PAP would be forced to come up with more and more "material incentive" in order to satisfy voters.[383]

The factors that PM Goh had credited as being key to victory were precisely what made commentators (and indeed the people themselves) uncomfortable. It also gave ample opportunity for Opposition figures to accuse the PAP of engaging in pork-barrel politics and (in the case of upgrading) to restate the charge that the PAP was using public funds to secure votes at the ballot box.[384] All in all, it was hard to avoid the impression that upgrading had been used as bait, and also punitively, in a manner that discriminated against voters in Opposition wards.[385]

In Low Thia Khiang's post-election analysis, this made some voters afraid to vote against the PAP.[386] The Opposition also buttressed its charge that the election had been conducted in an atmosphere of fear by pointing to the new system of decentralised vote counting, which enabled the government to ascertain voting preferences down to precinct levels of 5,000 voters. Low's observation was that voters had in effect been made even more fearful, realising that the PAP had a microscopic view of the voting patterns of each district. This data would also (according to Low) allow the government to redraw electoral boundaries more precisely, to the detriment of the Opposition's chances in future elections.[387]

The Opposition marshalled all this to develop one of its key themes in Parliament over the next few years—while the government talked about cohesion at the ground level, its election tactics and strategy had been forces working against this. During the 2 June 1997 debate on the President's address, Low claimed that PAP tactics had divided the nation and that the strategy "had caused Singapore to start to unravel".[388] Chiam See Tong (not for the first time displaying a good feel for the telling analogy) noted that the government was alienating the people—it was as if all Singaporeans were in one boat but PAP supporters were in first class, with Opposition supporters confined not even to third class but "in the bottom or in the hull of the ship".[389]

In the wake of the PAP's earlier 1991 victory, a senior *Straits Times* journalist commented that while the PAP deserved to win elections and run the country, it had hindered the Opposition to the extent that its triumph had become a case of *sheng zhi bu wu* (you win but you don't win fair).[390] This sense weighed even more heavily in the aftermath of the 1997 polls—there was something of a sour aftertaste, and a palpable sense of rifts and division. The Party knew that it needed to make efforts to heal some of these rifts.[391] The Chinese-educated ground, which had seen the fate which had befallen Tang Liang Hong, needed to be placated. Steps were taken in this direction. Following the election, the PAP set up a liaison group of Mandarin-speaking MPs led by Parliamentary Secretary Chan Soo Sen, to pay regular visits to Chinese community groups.[392]

The situation was different from the aftermath of the 1991 victory in other respects. The PAP had for the first time to deal with opinions—in some cases cogently expressed and argued—that represented the initial stirrings of civil society's engagement with the political sphere. Two members of a civil society group, the Roundtable, wrote a commentary on the election published in the *Straits Times* on 10 January 1997. The writers, Simon Tay and Zulkifli Baharudin, expressed concern over how the PAP had won the 1997 election. The PAP, the writers noted, had traditionally tried to appeal to as many people as possible. It should therefore move beyond tactics which made distinctions between PAP and Opposition wards, and indeed move beyond inducements, seeking instead to appeal to the hearts and minds of Singaporeans.[393]

The response (in the form of an article and a letter in the *Straits Times*) came from Minister without Portfolio Lim Boon Heng. Lim argued that the Opposition had nothing fresh to offer and could not offer a meaningful alternative to the PAP's

Singapore 21 programme: this was the real reason for the PAP's victory. Lim also defended the PAP against the charge of pork-barrel politics, observing that promising to look after interests of supporters was something practised in other countries too. Lim adopted an open tone of engagement, noting that he welcomed further debate with the Opposition or "nonpartisan" groups such as the Roundtable.[394] But he also had this to say: "The civil society which Mr Zulkifli talks about requires more than public debate. Participation in community affairs is not just talking about what should be done, and then leaving the Government to do it. A civil society means people themselves doing things for the community. This means actual community and social work."

The implication was that this type of activism—work in the community that improved the lives of others—was better, and altogether more constructive, than what Lim described dismissively as "armchair debates before and after an election campaign".[395] The comments represented an important articulation of the PAP government's stance in dealing with activism in the civic space, and were clearly aimed not just at the Roundtable but at any would-be entrant into the space of civil society. We now turn to an examination of this space in society and the PAP's attempts to control this space and actors within it—increasingly important elements in the body politic as the decade drew to a close, and as the next began.

Notes

1   On the events leading to Jeyaretnam's disqualification, see chapter 2, pp. 90–1.

2   "PM Goh Spring By-election Surprise", *Straits Times*, 18 Aug. 1991; "Snap Polls a Disgraceful and Desperate Ploy to Keep Me Out Again: Jeya", *Straits Times*, 16 Aug. 1991.

3   Documents on Task Force 97 (PAP archive), made available to the author.

4   "By-Election in Marine Parade GRC on Dec 19", *Straits Times*, 3 Dec. 1992; "PM Calls By-election in His Own Ward", *Business Times*, 3 Dec. 1992; "Former Navy Chief Is New Man in PAP Slate", *Straits Times*, 9 Dec. 1992.

5   It appears that the Workers' Party's (unnamed) fourth candidate pulled out. A last-minute substitute, WP Chairman John Gan, arrived at the nomination centre seven minutes too late to file his papers. "The Beginning of the End of WP Leader Jeyaretnam?", *Straits Times*, 12 Dec. 1992; "My Government Will Go if I Lose—PM Goh", *Straits Times*, 17 Dec. 1992. A recent account has raised the possibility that this was something of a ruse and that J.B. Jeyaretnam had from the outset decided not to contest the Marine Parade by-election. Loke, *First Wave*, pp. 207–9.

6   *1992 Marine Parade By-election PAP Post-mortem Report* (PAP archive).

7   "Why Four-Cornered Fight Is Good for Opposition and Singapore", *Sunday Times*, 13 Dec. 1992.

8   "Family Background No Bearing on Ability to Serve Country: PM", *Straits Times*, 17 Dec. 1992.

9   "Tony Tan: Do You Want a Change of Leaders *Now*?", *Straits Times*, 16 Dec. 1992.

10   "My Government Will Go if I Lose—PM Goh".

11   "Lee Tells Voters: Give Goh a Strong Mandate", *Straits Times*, 18 Dec. 1992.

12   Post-election surveys by the *Straits Times* suggested that rally speeches made late in the campaign by SM Lee were one of the factors that influenced the result. Others included PM Goh's personal popularity, and Marine Parade residents' wanting to vote for the status quo. "Residents Were Voting for PM and the Status Quo", *Straits Times*, 23 Dec. 1992.

13   This passing of the torch from Lee, who had headed the Party since its founding in 1954, was marked simply by the CEC "placing on record its deepest appreciation to SM Lee Kuan Yew for his lasting contribution to the Party". The Party record gives no sense of the handover being marked by ceremony, nor of either SM Lee or PM Goh dwelling on the moment. Somewhat typically, SM Lee at the CEC meeting in question, after proposing PM Goh for the secretary-generalship, simply highlighted the importance of renewal, emphasising to the CEC that Cdre Teo Chee Hean, who was about to be fielded in the Marine Parade by-election, was in his assessment clearly of ministerial calibre. Minutes of PAP Central Executive Committee Meeting, 2 Dec. 1992 (PAP archive).

14   "PM Goh Takes Over as PAP Secretary-General", *Straits Times*, 4 Dec. 1992.

15   "Lee Tells Voters: Give Goh a Strong Mandate".

16   Personal communications with PM Lee Hsien Loong and Goh Chok Tong.

17   *1992 Marine Parade By-election PAP Post-mortem Report.*

18   "Chok Tong Leads the Charge—in Hokkien", *Straits Times*, 12 Dec. 1992.

19   *1992 Marine Parade By-election PAP Post-mortem Report.*

20   "SDP Had Expected at Least 40% of Votes: Chiam", *Straits Times*, 21 Dec. 1992.

21   "SDP an Alternative Party? It Has a Long Way to Go", *Straits Times*, 22 Dec. 1992.

22   *1992 Marine Parade By-election PAP Post-mortem Report.*

23   For some sense of this rising affluence, see *General Household Survey 1995—Release 1: Socio-Demographic and Economic Characteristics* (Singapore: Department of Statistics, Ministry of Trade and Industry, 1996), p. 28. The period 1990–95 saw an average growth in real monthly income of 7.6%.

24   *1984 General Election PAP Post-mortem Report* (PAP archive).

25   Chan Heng Chee, "The Structuring of the Political System", in *Management of Success,* ed. Singh and Wheatley, pp. 84–5.

26   *1984 General Election PAP Post-mortem Report.*

27   Dr Tony Tan, interview with the author, 11 July 2013.

28   "Govt Plans Fewer Curbs", *Sunday Times*, 10 Feb. 1995. See also Chan Heng Chee, "Singapore in 1985: Managing Political Transition and Economic Recession", in *Asian Survey* 26, 2, *A Survey of Asia in 1985: Part II* (Feb. 1986): 158–67, esp. 160.

29   Singapore Parliamentary Debates, 8 Mar. 1985, cols 479–82; "Government to Play Smaller Role in Business", *Straits Times*, 9 Mar. 1985; "Private Sector's Role Now to Lead Nation into New Economic Era", *Straits Times*, 9 Mar. 1985.

30   "Govt Plans Fewer Curbs", *Sunday Times*, 10 Feb. 1995.

31   This chapter does not attempt to offer a full analysis of the causes of the 1985 recession; this has been attempted elsewhere. See, for example, Lim Chong Yah, "From High Growth Rates to Recession", in *Management of Success*, ed. Singh and Wheatley, pp. 201–17, esp. 208ff; and Lee, *Unexpected Nation*, pp. 464–7, 560–1.

32 *Report of the Economic Committee—The Singapore Economy: New Directions* (Ministry of Trade and Industry, Feb. 1986). For a sense of the inner workings of the Economic Committee, and the interplay between the key personalities involved, see "How the Team of Seven Got the Economy Back on Track", *Straits Times*, 23 Aug. 1988.

33 Notes of 85(4) meeting (10 Oct. 1985) of the Ministerial Economic Committee (National Archives of Singapore), made available to the author.

34 For some sense of the role that younger-generation ministers had in bringing this thinking into the highest levels of decision-making, see Peh Shing Huei, *Tall Order: The Goh Chok Tong Story, Vol. 1*, pp. 126–7. The Economic Committee observed that the wider question of the government's role in promoting economic development had to be rethought: while the government would continue to provide basic infrastructure, education and defence, as well as providing for general areas of economic activity, exploiting business opportunities and identifying best ones to take up had to be left to the private sector (*Report of the Economic Committee*, pp. 16–7, 83). There were important moves in economic policy with far-reaching implications that owe their origins to this and to the thinking outlined above. An example is the Public Sector Divestment Committee (PSDC), set up in 1986, to explore and make recommendations on the privatisation of Government-Linked Companies (GLCs) and Statutory Boards. A key principle was the withdrawal from commercial activities which need no longer be undertaken by the public sector. For discussion, see Ng Chee Yuen, "Privatization in Singapore: Divestment with Control", *ASEAN Economic Bulletin* (Mar. 1989): 290–318.

35 "The Price of Subsidies" (speech by Ong Teng Cheong at National Day celebrations in Punggol Constituency, 6 Aug. 1989), *Petir*, July 1989, pp. 12–3. Other articles in the same issue by Charles Chong and Lim Boon Heng (also in the delegation) have similar musings on the Soviet system, the failures of its economic model, and in particular the lack of incentives to work hard.

36 George Yeo, "Beyond the Horizon", *Petir*, Oct. 1991, pp. 44–51; originally published in the PAP Youth Wing's Fifth Anniversary Commemorative Book, *PAP Youth in Action 1986–1991*.

37 For Edusave, see, Jason Tan and S. Gopinathan, "An Innovation in Educational Financing", *CHANGE: Transformations in Education* 2, 2 (Nov. 1999): 66–79. For Goh's personal interest, see Bridget Welsh, James U.H. Chin, Arun Mahizhnan and Tan Tarn How, "Introduction: A Redefined Singapore", in *Impressions of the Goh Chok Tong Years*, ed. Welsh et al., pp. 1–23, esp. 6.

38 "Edusave: Tempering Meritocracy for a More Caring Society", *Straits Times*, 18 Dec. 1990.

39 Singapore Parliamentary Debates, 13 Jan. 1992, cols 99–100. See also "Support Market-Oriented Policies", *Petir*, Jan. 1992, pp. 29–31, esp. 30.

40 "Pressing Ahead with Our Political Programme", *Petir*, June 1992, pp. 5–11, esp. 9 (Goh Chok Tong, speech to Party activists, 24 May 1992).

41 Ibid., pp. 5–11, esp. 9–10.

42 Liew Kim Siong, "State Welfarism and Affluent Singaporeans", *Straits Times*, 26 June 1992.

43 See, for example, "SDP Slams Rise in Hospital Fees", *Straits Times*, 7 June 1990; and "SDP Voices Concern over Proposed Increases in Independent School Fees", *Straits Times*, 12

Sept. 1990. The SDP had also, in April 1991, called for public inquiry into the cost of university education following the government announcement of fee increases. "SDP Calls for Public Inquiry into Costs", *Straits Times*, 25 Apr. 1991.

44   SDP candidates with a command of Mandarin were particularly effective in bringing this message home on the campaign trail. "SDP Highlights Rising Cost of Living", *Straits Times*, 28 Aug. 1991.

45   2OS Matthias Yao, "Under the PAP, Even the Poor Are Better Off Today", letter to *Straits Times* Forum, 5 Mar. 1993.

46   A sampling of Chee's letters: "Leasing Not the Same as Ownership of Property", *Straits Times*, 17 Feb. 1993; "Govt Must Ensure Poor in S'pore Not Disadvantaged", *Straits Times*, 2 Mar. 1993; "PAP's Politics of Make-Believe", *Straits Times*, 17 Mar. 1993. This was part of the exchange with PAP Second Organising Secretary Matthias Yao. For Yao's key ripostes, see "SDP Promoting Politics of Envy to Attract Votes", *Straits Times*, 20 Feb. 1993; "Under the PAP, Even the Poor Are Better Off Today"; and "SDP Should Publish Its Own Ideas to Improve Singapore Since It Aspires to Govern", *Straits Times*, 20 Mar. 1993.

47   Parliament had debated Chee's sacking in April 1993. Chee subsequently made statements to the press which Dr S. Vasoo felt were defamatory, and he filed suit the same month. For a summary, see "Chee Abandons His Defence in Defamation Suit", *Straits Times*, 18 Feb. 1994.

48   Chee Soon Juan, *Dare to Change: An Alternative Vision for Singapore* (Singapore: Singapore Democratic Party, 1994). Chee was to publish a second book, *Singapore, My Home Too* (Singapore: Melodies Press), in August 1995.

49   See, for example, "Why Didn't the 3 SDP MPs Debate These Issues in Parliament?", *Straits Times*, 2 Aug. 1995.

50   For the key 1994 exchanges between Chee and Yao, see "Points Made in Dare to Change Backed Up by Research, Analyses and Historical Data", *Straits Times*, 28 July 1994; "Dr Chee Fails First Prerequisite for a Political Leader—Integrity", *Straits Times*, 2 Aug. 1994; "Sue Me, Clear Your Name if My Charges Are False", *Straits Times*, 11 Aug. 1994; "Matthias to Chee: Sue Me to Redeem Your Honour", *Straits Times*, 20 Aug. 1994; "Chee: Why I Will Not Sue Matthias Yao", *Straits Times*, 24 Aug. 1994; "Will Yao Allow Me Fair Access to MacPherson Constituents?", *Straits Times*, 3 Oct. 1994; "Yao to Chee: Will You or Will You Not Stand against Me?", *Straits Times*, 9 Oct. 1994; and "Why PAP Is Afraid to Debate SDP Publicly on Important Issues", *Straits Times*, 18 Oct. 1994.

51   Chee's critics raised various issues concerning his motives—especially his dalliances with foreign NGOs and his perceived attacks on Singapore (dealt with later in this chapter).

52   "Let S'poreans Read My Book and Decide: Chee", *Straits Times*, 13 Sept. 1994.

53   "Stand with Me in a One-to-One Contest at the Next Elections", *Straits Times*, 16 Aug. 1994; "Will Chee Declare Publicly that He Will Contest in MacPherson?", *Straits Times*, 17 Sept. 1994; "Equal Fight Possible in MacPherson: SDP Chief", *Straits Times*, 17 Sept. 1994.

54   SM Lee had a key role in the crafting of Yao's replies to Chee Soon Juan that were carried in the *Straits Times*, although he was at pains to check that Yao was at all times comfortable with the tenor and phrasing of the replies. Matthias Yao, interview with the author, 22 Aug. 2013.

55 "Matthias Yao–Chee Debate: And the Winner Is . . . ", *Straits Times*, 24 Sept. 1994.

56 "When the Big Picture Counts", *Straits Times*, 21 Aug. 1992.

57 PM Goh Chok Tong, National Day Rally Speech at the Kallang Theatre, 16 Aug. 1992. *National Day Rally Speeches: 50 Years of Nationhood in Singapore*, pp. 264–6.

58 See, for example, "Aspiring to a Better Life May Not Be a Totally Good Thing", *Straits Times*, 24 Oct. 1992; and also "Costs of Living and Medical Costs", *Petir*, Oct. 1992, pp. 4–25 (talk by DPM Lee Hsien Loong to Party activists, Sept. 1992). As the *Petir* editorial for that issue noted, "even as we become more affluent and more of our material needs are met, our aspirations of a better life are racing ahead". "The Root of Costly Talk: Rising Expectations and Misconceptions", *Petir* (Editorial), Oct. 1992, pp. 2–3, esp. 2.

59 According to the Department of Statistics 1987–88 Household Expenditure Survey, education and healthcare made up 5% and 2% respectively of average household expenditure, figures which were confirmed by a more recent Singapore Institute of Labour Studies study in 1992. See "Costs of Living and Medical Costs", *Petir*, Oct. 1992, pp. 4–31, esp. 8–9.

60 "Govt to Set Up Panel on Cost Increases", *Straits Times*, 17 Aug. 1992.

61 The composition of the 1992–93 CRC: Senior Minister of State (trade and industry) Lim Boon Heng (chairman), PAP MP for Leng Kee Dr Ow Chin Hock (deputy chairman; Ow was also Feedback Unit chief and National University of Singapore economics lecturer), Low Thia Khiang (WP MP for Hougang), Nominated MP Chia Shi Teck, Dr Lee Tsao Yuan (deputy director of the Institute of Policy Studies), Dr Chia Siow Yue (an economist at the National University of Singapore), Dr Chiew Seen Kong (sociologist at National University of Singapore), Madam Halimah Yacob (board member of the Consumers' Association of Singapore), Nithiah Nandan (general secretary of the PUB Daily-Rated Employees Union), Victor Pang (NTUC vice-president), Freddy Lam (managing director of Solid Gold Jewelry), Stephen Lee (president of the Singapore National Employers' Federation president), David Wong (lawyer and chairman of Bedok Citizens' Consultative Committee), Tan Poh Hong (vice-chairman of Changkat CCC), Lim Jim Koon (*Lianhe Zaobao* journalist) and Warren Fernandez (*Straits Times* journalist).

62 "Boon Heng Invites Ling, but SDP MP Rejects Offer", *Straits Times*, 15 Oct. 2002; "Ling Rejects Cost Panel's Invitation", *Business Times*, 15 Oct. 1992.

63 "Cost Review Committee: SDP Has a Duty to Care", *Sunday Times*, 1 Nov. 1992.

64 "SDP MPs 'Should Have Joined Cost Review Panel'", *Straits Times*, 21 Oct. 1992. *Lianhe Zaobao* published letters it had received criticising the SDP for its stance. "SDP MPs under Fire from Zaobao Readers", *Straits Times*, 20 Nov. 1992.

65 Low was singled out for praise by the PAP in Parliament when the report was debated on 13 October 1993 for agreeing, in contrast to SDP MPs. Singapore Parliamentary Debates, 13 Oct. 1993, cols 682–3, 716.

66 "Cost Review Panel Accepts Hougang MP's Three Proposals", *Straits Times*, 3 Oct. 1992. The final CRC report did indeed contain Low's detailed, dissenting minority report, which saw Low provide his own take on GST, the computation of the CPI (Consumer Price Index), housing and other issues. *Report of the Cost Review Committee* (Ministry of Trade and Industry, Sept. 1993), pp. 177–229, available at https://www.

nas.gov.sg/archivesonline/government_records/record-details/3b0739f8-7958-11e7-83df-0050568939ad (accessed 2 Mar. 2021).

67 For a summary of the CRC's recommendations (and the government's response), see "Govt 'Yes' to All but Five CRC Proposals", *Straits Times*, 15 Oct. 1993.

68 Low's contention (also included in his "minority report" section of the final CRC report) was that the proposed introduction of GST would serve as a "money-making machine" for the government and would cause a price spiral affecting especially low-income people. This was rejected by the CRC report and by Finance Minister Richard Hu in Parliament. Singapore Parliamentary Debates, 14 Oct. 1993, cols 814–6, and (on the CPI) cols 827–32. See also *Report of the Cost Review Committee* (Sept. 1993), pp. 97–8, 168–9, 211–7.

69 *Report of the Cost Review Committee* (Sept. 1993), p. 122.

70 Ibid., p. 1. The government accepted this recommendation. "Govt 'Yes' to All but Five CRC Proposals".

71 "1993: The Year the Government Took the Bull by the Horns", *Straits Times*, 25 Dec. 1993.

72 Singapore Parliamentary Debates, 14 Oct. 1993, col. 840; "Rising Cost of Living: The Myth—and the Facts", *Straits Times*, 15 Oct. 1993. Dhanabalan's view was identical to the message that PAP leaders had been conveying at dialogue sessions, Party events and other forums since the early 1990s. Speaking to cadres during the 15 November 1992 Party conference, Senior Minister of State for Trade and Industry Lim Boon Heng (who was to chair the 1993 CRC) noted that while people might feel anxiety over increased costs, assets had in fact appreciated. Lim said that the perception gap between what the Consumer Price Index showed and what Singaporeans felt about the cost of living arose from lifestyle changes; for example, the widespread unhappiness over higher housing prices had arisen because Singaporeans chased ever bigger dreams to own bigger homes. "Government Sold Short in Living Costs Debate—Boon Heng", *Business Times*, 11 Dec. 1992; for extended excerpts, see "Putting Cost of Living in the Proper Perspective", *Petir*, Nov.–Dec. 1992, pp. 64–9.

73 This was a point periodically echoed by PM Goh and other PAP leaders. In a speech at his Marine Parade constituency on 27 August 1994, Goh had said that he was "not too perturbed by the high expectation. It is precisely this eagerness to achieve which drives Singaporeans forward. I will really be worried if Singaporeans lose their drive, slacken and wait for the durians to fall." PM Goh Chok Tong, speech at Marine Parade National Day Dinner, 27 Aug. 1994, available at https://www.nas.gov.sg/archivesonline/speeches/record-details/73cb8d43-115d-11e3-83d5-0050568939ad (accessed 3 May 2021). See also "Low Income S'poreans Gain from $20,000 a Year in State Benefits", *Straits Times*, 28 Aug. 1994.

74 *Report of the Cost Review Committee* (Sept. 1993), pp. 124–5. For a summary of the CRC's deliberations and findings, see "A Costly Consensus", *Straits Times*, 1 Oct. 1993.

75 See "Hard for S'poreans to Lower Expectations of 'The Good Life'", *Straits Times*, 3 Oct. 1993; and "Boon Heng Defends Cost Review Findings", *Straits Times*, 14 Oct. 1993.

76 *The SDP-PKMS Cost of Living Report 1996* (Singapore: Singapore Democratic Party; Pertubuhan Kebangsaan Melayu Singapura, 1996); "State True Increase in Costs: BG Lee", *Straits Times*, 1 July 1996. The SDP again declined to serve on the panel. The

invitation had been for one SDP MP to serve, but the SDP wanted the three members of the SDP–PKMS research team involved in the report, including SDP Secretary-General Chee Soon Juan, to participate.

77 "SDP–PKMS Allegations Absurd, Says BG Lee", *Straits Times*, 29 June 1996.

78 The 1996 CRC was again chaired by labour chief Lim Boon Heng (by then also minister without portfolio). Its membership was largely the same as the 1992–93 CRC, except that it did not feature Low Thia Khiang and Chiew Seen Kong.

79 "Cost Review Panel Calls Off 'Fruitless' Talks with SDP", *Straits Times*, 7 Aug. 1996. The view of the SDP–PKMS team was that the CRC had not wanted to grapple seriously with the substance of the SDP–PKMS report but had wanted to "politicize" matters. "Chee— Hearing a Great Disappointment", *Straits Times*, 7 Aug. 1996.

80 *Report of the Select Committee on Verification of Health Care Subsidy of Government Polyclinics and Public Hospitals, Parl. 5 of 1996. Presented to Parliament on 30 Sept. 1996,* Minutes of Evidence, 15 July 1996, p. viii, pp. C46–C47, C50. The Select Committee was convened to examine assertions made by SDP MP Ling How Doong and carried an article in the SDP organ, *The New Democrat*, that suggested that public healthcare costs were subsidised by the government only to a minimal extent. See "The Truth about Health Care Costs", *The New Democrat* 1 (1996): 5; "Healthcare Subsidies Exist, Ling Concedes", *Straits Times*, 9 July 1996; and "Another SDP Debacle, but Are Voters Watching?", *Straits Times*, 14 July 1996. Incorrect figures and data were presented by the SDP at the Select Committee hearing, something which was to cost it politically. The SDP's defence was that it had made valid arguments at both the CRC and Health Select Committee hearings but had been portrayed in an unflattering light by biased media reporting. "Biased Reporting by Local Media", *New Democrat* 3 (1996): 1; "SDP Makes PAP Apologise", *The New Democrat* 4 (1996): 1–2.

81 *Report of the Cost Review Committee* (Ministry of Trade and Industry, Nov. 1996), pp. 1–12, available at https://www.nas.gov.sg/archivesonline/government_records/record-details/c5ad6737-73d7-11e7-83df-0050568939ad (accessed 2 Mar. 2021). The 1996 CRC also established that the price of basic food items had hardly changed since 1988. See "Little Change in Prices of Basic Food Items since '88", *Straits Times*, 8 Aug. 1996; and "Cost Panel Suggests 35 Steps to Help S'poreans", *Straits Times*, 2 Nov. 1996.

82 "Spending Rise: Higher Prices Played Small Part", *Straits Times*, 7 Aug. 1996; "Little Change in Prices of Basic Food Items since '88".

83 See "The Price of the Politics of Costs", *Straits Times*, 5 Nov. 1996.

84 "Social Stratification and Commitment", PM Goh Chok Tong, National Day Rally Speech at the Kallang Theatre, 18 Aug. 1996. *National Day Rally Speeches: 50 Years of Nationhood in Singapore*, p. 334. As DPM BG Lee Hsien Loong separately remarked in the same month (in what was a revealing comment), the aim of the CRC was "to explain, show and persuade them [the people]—not just intellectually, but emotionally—that lives are getting better". "Why CRC Dissected Chee's Claims", *Straits Times*, 20 Aug. 1996.

85 "PM Hits Out at Chee for Not Defending S'pore", *Straits Times*, 4 Nov. 1996.

86 Singapore Parliamentary Debates, 7 Nov. 1996, col. 887.

87 Ibid., cols 885–7; "Unfair to Blame Rising Costs on People, Says Opposition MP", *Straits Times*, 8 Nov. 1996.

88 See pp. 172–3.

89 Among the key members of the Ministerial Committee on Housing were BG Lee (then acting minister for trade and industry), Teh Cheang Wan (minister for national development) and S. Dhanabalan (minister for foreign affairs). In December 1986 Dhanabalan was appointed minister for national development following Teh's suicide.

90 Information on government thinking in this paragraph is drawn from files on the Ministerial Committee on Housing made available to the author (Ref MND 311/13/29 Vol. 3; National Archives of Singapore). The existence and work of the Ministerial Committee on Public Housing was alluded to by National Development Minister S. Dhanabalan when discussing future directions on housing policy in Parliament on 16 March 1988. Singapore Parliamentary Debates, 16 Mar. 1988, col. 832; "HDB Will Focus on Building Flats", *Straits Times*, 17 Mar. 1988.

91 Singapore Parliamentary Debates, 17 Mar. 1988, cols 886–7. See also "Dhana Explains the Policy behind Pricing of HDB Flats", *Straits Times*, 17 Mar. 1988; and "Goal Still Is Full Home Ownership for All", *Straits Times*, 18 Mar. 1988.

92 "Middle Class Society and Release of Land for Private Residential Development", note from 1DPM Goh to Minister (National Development) S. Dhanabalan, 20 Mar. 1989. Goh concluded by requesting that the Ministry of National Development study the issue of how the class of private property owners (both high-rise and landed) could be enlarged (National Archives of Singapore, Ref ND 3/3-7 PT A, made available to the author).

93 "Housing Board to Transform Its Estates", *Straits Times*, 12 July 1989.

94 Ibid.

95 S. Dhanabalan, interview with the author, 14 May 2013.

96 1DPM Goh Chok Tong to Minister (National Development) S. Dhanabalan, 3 Aug. 1989 (National Archives of Singapore), made available to the author.

97 Lim Hng Kiang, talk at Bakit Batok Community Centre Current Affairs Club, 21 Apr. 1992. Excerpted in "Sharing the Country's Wealth", *Petir*, May 1992, pp. 44–7, esp. 46.

98 Preliminary discussions on housing as an "appreciating asset" had taken place during the meetings of the Ministerial Committee on Housing in 1987, with details and approach to the upgrading scheme discussed by the leadership until just before Dhanabalan's announcement on the Main Upgrading Programme in July 1989. A key point was that people had to understand and value what was being done for them. PM Lee Kuan Yew wrote to his ministers on the subject: "No item is worth investing in unless it is valued by Singaporeans. In other words, invest only if it increases the market value because owners and buyers value it. We will only know what upgrading items are valued by testing the market. To help test the market, we must require the owner to pay at least 5% or 10% of the cost. Otherwise we will spend money on upgrading items which are not valued by owners and prospective buyers." "Upgrading of HDB Flats", note from PM Lee to ministers, 14 Aug. 1989 (Ref PM 0043/70 vol2, *Refurbishing of HDB Flats 12.8.89–14.8.89*, National Archives of Singapore), made available to the author.

99 *Report of the Cost Review Committee* (Nov. 1996), p. 64.

100 "Issues Surrounding HDB Flats Get an Airing, Once Again", *Straits Times*, 23 Mar. 1995.

101 *Report of the Cost Review Committee* (Nov. 1996), pp. 56–7.

102 Ibid., p. 64. These measures, most of which were mentioned in the CRC report, included: allowing PRs to buy HDB flats and allowing private property owners to buy resale HDB flats (1989), allowing Singaporeans who were single and older than 35 to buy one- to three-room flats outside the central area (1991), allowing the use of CPF funds for properties with at least 60 years remaining on the lease (1992; previously, the unexpired lease had to be at least 75 years), and relaxing rules for mortgage financing for resale flats—financing terms were brought closer to market practice by granting financing up to 80% of the current valuation of the flat (1993). For an analysis of these moves, see "Government to Reduce Restrictions on Resale of HDB Flats", *Business Times*, 31 Aug. 1993; and "HDB Upgraders Give Property Prices a Big Push", *Straits Times*, 15 June 1996.

103 It was the 1986–87 Ministerial Committee on Housing that had recommended slowing down the building programme to maintain an appreciable waiting time for flats, and basing the HDB's future building programme on actual demand. Ministerial Committee on Housing files (Ref MND 311/13/29 Vol. 3) (National Archives of Singapore), made available to the author.

104 It is also likely that the resale transaction increases were due to the change in mortgage financing policy (which had improved liquidity), backed by strong economic growth.

105 "HDB Flats More Affordable Now", *Straits Times*, 30 May 1996.

106 The percentage of first-timers opting to buy five-room flats and executive flats increased from 47% in 1992 to 65% in 1995. *Report of the Cost Review Committee* (Nov. 1996), p. 59.

107 Ibid., p. 128.

108 The idea of a mindset shift is supported by data from MPs' meet-the-people sessions collected and analysed by PAP Organising Secretary (Special Duties) Dr Ow Chin Hock. From 1990 to 1995, housing-related issues constituted 33% of all cases. Of these, only a small number were from tenants wanting to buy flats. The majority were people who wanted to upgrade to bigger flats with more rooms, or who were more insistent on the location of their flats. "How We Look after Concerns", *Petir*, Mar.–Apr. 1997, p. 20.

109 "HDB Flats More Affordable Now".

110 See "Govt's Aim to Curb Property Speculation and Cool Market Frenzy", *Straits Times*, 16 May 1996; and "Cooling the Private Property Pie", *Straits Times*, 20 May 1996.

111 "Govt Acts to Cool Private Home Market", *Straits Times*, 15 May 1996. The government was through the mid-1990s (and particularly in 1995–96) making repeated public assurances that the supply of private homes was on a stable footing, that enough land had been set aside to build private homes (in the order of 100,000 units over a five-year period), and that the long-term goal was to raise the proportion of private housing from 14% in 1996 to 25%. See "Govt Earmarks Enough Land for Building 100,000 Private Homes", *Straits Times*, 1 Feb. 1996.

112 "Housing Aspirations Must Be Rooted in Reality", *Straits Times*, 2 July 1996.

113 The measures included taxing capital gains from property sales if the sale was within three years of purchase; new stamp duties payable on the full value of the property on every sale and subsale of the property, with a new stamp duty imposed on those selling their properties within three years of purchase; and tighter loan conditions—housing loans were limited to 80% of the value of the property, including the use of CPF funds. For details, see "Surprise Curb on Property Speculation", *Business Times*, 15 May 1996.

114 For the regional context, see Linda Lim, "Free Market Fancies: Hong Kong, Singapore, and the Asian Financial Crisis", in *The Politics of the Asian Economic Crisis*, ed. T.J. Pempel (Ithaca: Cornell University Press, 1999), pp. 101–15, esp. 110–2; and also Charles Collyns and Abdelhak Senhadji, "Lending Booms, Real Estate Bubbles and the Asian Crisis", IMF Working Paper WP/02/20 (Jan. 2002).

115 "HDB Loans: Now Two Bites of Cherry Only", *Straits Times*, 13 Apr. 1997.

116 Lee Kuan Yew, *From Third World to First*, p. 121.

117 Teo Chee Hean, personal communication, 15 Dec. 2017. For the IMF's view, see "IMF Gives Singapore Policies the Thumbs Up", *Straits Times*, 10 July 2000.

118 Kenneth Paul Tan and Andrew Sze-Sian Tan, "Democracy and the Grassroots Sector in Singapore", *Space and Polity* 7, 1 (2003): 3–20, esp. 8.

119 "Pressing Ahead with Our Political Programme", *Petir*, June 1992, pp. 5–11, esp. 5.

120 Ibid. See also "PM Spells Out PAP's Main Goals", *Straits Times*, 15 June 1992; and "To Win the 'Serve-Me-or-Else' Voter", *Straits Times*, 15 June 1992.

121 For useful treatments of these organisations (especially in the context of how they were used by the PAP government), see Seah Chee Meow, "Grassroots Political Participation in Singapore", in *People's Action Party 1954–1979* (Singapore: Central Executive Committee, People's Action Party, 1979), pp. 276–81; and Ch'ng Jit Koon, "The Role of Grassroots Organisations", in *People's Action Party 1954–1984* (Singapore: Central Executive Committee, People's Action Party, 1984), pp. 180–9. For background on these bodies, including their history and evolution, see Seah Chee Meow, "Parapolitical Institutions", in *Government and Politics of Singapore*, ed. Jon Quah, Chan Heng Chee and Seah Chee Meow (Singapore: Oxford University Press, 1985), pp. 173–94; and M. Shamsul Haque, "A Grassroots Approach to Decentralization in Singapore", *Asian Journal of Political Science* 4, 1 (1996): 64–84, esp. 65–71.

122 *1991 General Election PAP Post-mortem Report*.

123 "Younger S'poreans 'Must Work as a Team'", *Straits Times*, 2 Jan. 1993. Similarly, RCs at this time were periodically prompted by government ministers to play a bigger role in terms of strengthening the partnership between government and people, providing useful feedback to government, and helping it better understand the needs and aspirations of the people. See "RCs Urged to Play More Effective Feedback Role", *Straits Times*, 22 Dec. 1991.

124 "RCs and CCCs Now Come under PA's Wing", *Straits Times*, 27 July 1993.

125 Having one grassroots movement, and one body overseeing the myriad organisations within the movement, was the brainchild of Wong Kan Seng. His appointment as deputy chairman of the People's Association in 1992 set the wheels in motion, although the idea itself had been discussed earlier. See *We Are One: The People's Association Journey 1960–2010* (Singapore: People's Association, 2010), p. 26.

126 Speech by PM Goh Chok Tong, at the Triennial Conference "Bonding People and Government: The Role of Grassroots Organisations", 29 Apr. 1994, available at https://www.nas.gov.sg/ archivesonline/speeches/record-details/73ca30d1-115d-11e3-83d5-0050568939ad (accessed 2 May 2021). See *Report on the First Triennial Conference for Grassroots Organisations. Bonding People and Government: The Role of Grassroots Organisations. 29 April 1994–15 May 1994* (Singapore: People's Association, 1994), pp. 11–5.

127 *1991 General Election PAP Post-mortem Report*.

128 "Feedback Unit's Work Being Reviewed by Panel", *Straits Times*, 20 Apr. 1994; "Grassroots Leaders Suggest Ways to Streamline Work", *Straits Times*, 16 May 1994.

129 "Report on RCs Outlines the Challenges Ahead", *Straits Times*, 17 July 1990.

130 "Feedback Unit's Work Being Reviewed by Panel". Ow noted that through this move, he hoped to draw in groups from the community and work more closely with grassroots organisations. This initiative was part of a review of the Feedback Unit, undertaken by a committee under the Ministry of Community Development chaired by Senior Minister of State Ch'ng Jit Koon.

131 "CCCs at the Crossroads", *Straits Times*, 25 July 1992.

132 Ibid.

133 "Government Seeking Ways to Strengthen the Role of Grassroots Leaders", *Straits Times*, 10 May 1992.

134 "More to Be Done Before a General Election", *Straits Times*, 19 June 1994. See also "Hard to Explain Government Policies to the People, Say Leaders", *Straits Times*, 9 June 1994.

135 No fewer than 661 such dialogue sessions were held between January 1995 and September 1997. "PM Goh to Address Grassroots Leaders", *Sunday Times*, 19 Oct. 1997.

136 Ibid.

137 A study team comprising officials from the Ministry of Community Development and RC members, which reviewed the progress of RCs since the scheme began in 1978, had in 1990 named the manpower shortage and the problem of inactive members as one of the key areas which needed to be dealt with in the 1990s. "Report on RCs Outlines Challenges Ahead", *Straits Times*, 17 July 1990.

138 "RCs Crying Out for Young Members and Women to Join", *Straits Times*, 8 May 1994.

139 Membership across RCs grew from 8,590 in 1990 to 9,687 in 1993. "Challenging Time for the Grassroots Movement", *Straits Times*, 14 May 1994.

140 "Report on RCs Outlines the Challenges Ahead"; "RCs Need 10,000 New Members over the Next 5 Years", *Straits Times*, 25 Nov. 1992.

141 This began to happen from the 1970s. See "How Grassroots Leaders Can Help Mobilise S'poreans for Next Lap" (speech by SM Lee Kuan Yew at the CCC National Tribute Dinner, 4 Oct. 1991), *Straits Times*, 5 Oct. 1991.

142 See "CCCs at the Crossroads".

143 Leong Ching, *Citizens, Conversations & Collaborations: Chronicles of the Citizens' Consultative Committee* (Singapore: People's Association, 2005), p. 21.

144 "More English-Educated Professionals Are Moving into the CCCs", *Straits Times*, 1 Aug. 1992. In the 1960s and 1970s, many of the Chinese-educated grassroots leaders were village heads, well-known in the area, who might be fluent in one or more of the Chinese dialects (but often, not in Mandarin). See Dr Lau Teik Soon, Transcript of Oral History Interview, Accession No.187/130, Reel 19, p. 170 (National Archives of Singapore). Lau was a PAP MP from 1976 to 1996.

145 "More English-Educated Professionals Are Moving into the CCCs".

146 Ibid. The renewal process was to advance even further in subsequent years. In 2005, 29% of CCC members were tertiary educated and 70% were professionals, managers, executives and businessmen. A total of 71% were English-educated. *Citizens, Conversations & Collaborations*, p. 21.

147   Lau Teik Soon, author interview, 27 Oct. 2020. For a good account of this transition, see
        Dr Lau Teik Soon, Transcript of Oral History Interview, Reel 19, pp. 172–3.

148   This was a problem which had been foreseen by commentators writing earlier: see
        Seah, "Parapolitical Institutions", p. 189. See also Haque, "Grassroots Approach to
        Decentralization": 64–84, esp. 75–6.

149   Haque, "Grassroots Approach to Decentralization": 64–84, esp. 81n33 (relying on an
        interview with PAP MP Dr S. Vasoo).

150   Literacy in English in 1990 in the overall population was 65% in 1990 (the figure for
        1980 was 56%). The proportion of households speaking English at home rose from 12%
        in 1980 to 20% in 1990. Chinese dialects were the preferred means of communication
        for 36.7% of households in 1990 (compared to 59.5% in 1980). Department of Statistics
        Singapore, *Census of Population 1990: Advance Data Release* (Singapore: SNP Publishers,
        1991), pp. 17–8. The changes in dialect use should, of course, be put down to the
        government's heavy emphasis on the use of Mandarin for the ethnic Chinese population
        and its active discouraging of dialect use.

151   On the conceptual link between renewal in the PAP and in the grassroots, see the remarks
        of SM Goh Chok Tong in 2005: "We understood the importance of political self-renewal,
        and sure that same concept must apply to grassroots organisations. I found that most of
        the CCC members were getting on in years. As a result, we were not attracting younger
        people, because the key positions were filled by older people." *Citizens, Conversations &
        Collaborations*, p. 27. Goh was referring to the renewal in the 2000s, but his comments are
        relevant to earlier renewal efforts.

152   Several of the key moves by the PA in the context of renewal were to come in the 2000s.
        Chief among these was the introduction of the compulsory retirement age (set at 65)
        for holders of key CCC and CCMC posts (2002). In 2003 further guidelines were
        introduced that limited the tenure of RC and NC (Neighbourhood Committee) chairmen
        to three consecutive terms, or six years. Easing out was done sensitively and in a way
        that recognised the contributions of grassroots leaders and allowed their institutional
        knowledge to be tapped. A case in point was the introduction of the honorary chairman
        and immediate past chairman titles for retired CCC and CCMC chairmen, and the
        Grassroots Senior Scheme, in 2002 and 2004 respectively. These moves also made it easier
        for young blood to advance through to grassroots leadership positions. See "Greener
        Grassroots", *Straits Times*, 19 Apr. 2003; and *Citizens, Conversations & Collaborations*, pp.
        27–8.

153   Kenneth Paul Tan and Andrew Sze-Sian Tan, "Democracy and the Grassroots Sector": 18.

154   "S'pore Needs Value System to Hold People Together", *Straits Times*, 19 July 1996.

155   "Social Stratification and Commitment", PM Goh Chok Tong, National Day Rally
        Speech at the Kallang Theatre, 18 Aug. 1996. *National Day Rally Speeches: 50 Years of
        Nationhood in Singapore*, pp. 330–1. Goh's message was remarkably similar to what SM
        Lee had said in a speech a month before (on 19 July 1996) to unionists: "The social
        glue which holds a society together is the crucial factor which decides whether a society
        endures, overcomes its problems and provides a satisfying life for all. To strengthen
        this social glue, we must resist the present tendency of the successful to seek status and
        snobbishness, and to disassociate themselves from the less successful in where they live and

where their children go to school. If all the successful want to move out of HDB flats or out of HDB areas for private condos, they unwittingly accentuate social stratification. We should not carry this segregation too far. For Singapore to succeed, our society must be cohesive and our system must be fair and must cater to all, based on merit, not on money or social status." "Pegging Ministers' Pay to That of the Top Earners in the Private Sector", Speech by SM Lee Kuan Yew to the National Trades Union Congress at the Singapore Conference Hall and Trade Union House, 19 July 1996. *The Papers of Lee Kuan Yew: Speeches, Interviews and Dialogues, Vol. 12: 1994–1997* (Singapore: Cengage Learning Asia, 2013), pp. 377–8.

156 PM Goh Chok Tong, National Day Rally speech, 18 Aug. 1996. *National Day Rally Speeches: 50 Years of Nationhood in Singapore*, pp. 333–4. See also "Mayors 'Can Do More for Residents than MPs'", *Straits Times*, 20 Aug. 1996; and "Mayors and the CDCs; Election Strategy or Radical Political Change?", *Straits Times*, 24 Aug. 1996. In introducing the concept, Goh noted that the more able and successful should help the less able and the less well-off, as they used to do and were respected for doing. Those who received help would naturally (according to Goh) respect the successful instead of resenting their success.

157 "Establishment, Objectives and Functions of Community Development Councils", People's Association information paper, 22 Aug. 1996 (Ref MCD 22-03-42 Community Development Councils v2) (National Archives of Singapore), made available to the author.

158 "Well-Placed to Respond to Community Needs", *Straits Times*, 24 Mar. 2000; "CDCs to Take Over Local Matters", *Straits Times*, 16 Mar. 2000.

159 Information drawn from File Ref MCD 22-03-42C : Inter Ministry Task Force (IMTF) on Enhancing the Role of CDCs and the Mayors; *Minutes of IMTF 16 Aug 99* (National Archives of Singapore), made available to the author.

160 "Mayors and the CDCs". See also "Give CDCs a Chance to Succeed", *Straits Times*, 8 Apr. 2000.

161 "Mayors and the CDCs".

162 "Soo Sen on Why Opposition MPs Are Not for CDCs", *Straits Times*, 28 Apr. 1997.

163 "Up to Nine CDCs to Be Set Up by End of the Year", *Straits Times*, 22 Mar. 1997.

164 In the CDCs covering the Opposition-held constituencies of Potong Pasir and Hougang, the PAP appointed as chairmen the defeated PAP candidates from the 1997 election, Heng Chee How and Andy Gan. "9 CDCs for Singapore", *Straits Times*, 3 Aug. 1997.

165 "Chok Tong Lists Schemes Which Will Be Managed by CDCs", *Straits Times*, 24 Dec. 1996; "Town Councils and CDCs 'Will Evolve as One Entity Eventually'", *Straits Times*, 29 Oct. 1996.

166 A particularly sore point with Opposition MPs in the 1990s (and the subject of lengthy debates in Parliament) was the use of funds controlled by the Community Improvement Projects Committee (CIPC). Applications to the CIPC had to be vetted by the CCC, which in practice meant that no application from an Opposition MP succeeded. Where CIPC funds were disbursed in Opposition wards, they were given not to the Opposition-controlled town councils, but to the CCCs in the ward. See

"Funds for Community Improvement Projects: It's Hardball Politics", *Straits Times*, 2 Sept. 1995; and "Money from Govt Fund to Improve Two Opposition Held Wards", *Straits Times*, 2 Sept. 1995.

167 Singapore Parliamentary Debates, 10 Oct. 1996, col. 653; "People's Association Gets More Functions under New Bill", *Straits Times*, 11 Oct. 1996. (The "defeated candidate" in question was Andy Gan, Adviser to Potong Pasir GROs, whom Chiam had bested in the 1991 election and would defeat again in Potong Pasir in 1997.) Opposition MPs had also been hamstrung by the HDB rule change in November 1991, which stopped political parties using void deck premises as offices. In practice, PAP MPs were not seriously disadvantaged, as they could use PCF (PAP Community Foundation) kindergarten premises to meet their constituents. See "Opposition MP Says His Request for Permanent Office Was Turned Down", *Straits Times*, 13 Nov. 1991; "About 40 MPs Have to Vacate Void-Deck Offices by Sept '92", *Straits Times*, 17 Nov. 1991; and "Opposition MPs: New Void Deck Rule Favours PAP", *Straits Times*, 6 Dec. 1991.

168 Statement from the Prime Minister's Office: Appointment of Adviser to CCC, CCMCs and RCs in Anson, 23 Dec. 1981, available at https://www.nas.gov.sg/archivesonline/speeches/record- details/738202a3-115d-11e3-83d5-0050568939ad (accessed 26 Feb. 2021).

169 Statement from the Prime Minister's Office: Appointment of Adviser to CCC, CCMCs and RCs in Anson, 23 Dec. 1981.

170 "PAP's History through SM Goh's Eyes", Goh Chok Tong, speech at Party Conference, *Petir*, Nov.–Dec. 2004, pp. 28–47, esp. 40–1. In the immediate aftermath of the Anson result, it appears that several PAP MPs felt that Jeyaretnam should be made adviser, but by the 17 November 1981 meeting views had hardened, with only five MPs (almost all of them newer MPs) supporting the proposal that Jeyaretnam be appointed adviser. Many of the older MPs at the meeting took the view that nothing should be done, that the grassroots apparatus had been built up since the 1960s by the old guard in the PAP, and that any concessions on the issue might help Jeyaretnam further entrench himself in Anson. This more hardline group appears to have been in the majority. At the meeting, PM Lee chastised those in favour of appointing Jeyaretnam as adviser for their political naiveté. What the MPs did not know, but what PM Lee had earlier consulted members of the younger generation of ministers (Goh Chok Tong, S. Dhanabalan, Lim Chee Onn and Dr Tony Tan) and come to consensus on, was that no concessions on the issue would be made to Jeyaretnam. Documents from File "31 Oct 1981 Anson By-election Defeat—PM's Meeting with MPs and MP's Reports/Assessments" (PAP archive). I am grateful to various former PAP MPs, including Lau Ping Sum and Tang See Chim, for sharing their recollections of the 17 November 1981 meeting. See also Peh Shing Huei, *Tall Order*, p. 109.

171 Singapore Parliamentary Debates, 18 Jan. 1993, cols 390–1; "People's Association 'Not PAP's Propaganda Arm'", *Straits Times*, 19 Jan. 1993. Wong was to restate the argument in almost identical terms when Chiam raised the issue again during the 1995 budget debates. See "PAP and Opposition Lock Horns over Govt Grassroots Policy", *Straits Times*, 24 Mar. 1995.

172 "CCCs at the Crossroads".

173 Commenting on the appointment of CCMC members (but at the same time acknowledging that this was also applicable to CCC members), Chan Heng Chee had observed as early as 1976 that "the role of the MC members is to act as the co-opted functionaries of the governing party through which it would widen its support network and increase its capacity to influence and penetrate into each neighbourhood sector". Chan Heng Chee, *The Dynamics of One Party Dominance: The PAP at the Grassroots* (Singapore: Singapore University Press, 1976), p. 158.

174 On the vetting process, see Chan, *Dynamics of One Party Dominance,* p. 158; Haque, "Grassroots Approach to Decentralization": 64–84, esp. 67–9; and "CCCs at the Crossroads".

175 The advisers to the CCCs in the four Opposition-held wards were either the defeated PAP candidates from the 1991 election (Andy Gan, Ng Pock Tock and Tang Guan Seng) or, in one case, a sitting PAP MP (Dr Wang Kai Yuen, whose Bukit Timah constituency was close to Bukit Gombak, which had seen Dr Seet Ai Mee defeated by the SDP's Ling How Doong in 1991). "CCCs at the Crossroads".

176 The PAP's Andy Gan, who stood unsuccessfully against the SDP's Chiam See Tong in the 1991 general election (and who was adviser to the Potong Pasir GROs), told the *Straits Times* that known Opposition supporters would be asked to leave GROs in Potong Pasir. "CCCs at the Crossroads".

177 The government introduced other measures in the latter half of the 1990s to raise the level of community spirit. An example of this was the introduction of Neighbourhood Committees (NCs) in 1998—essentially, RC equivalents for private housing estates. When NCs were first mooted, it was made known that their aim was to promote neighbourliness and cohesiveness—and also to be a bridge between residents and government. See "3 Private Groups Eye NC Status", *Straits Times*, 2 May 1998.

178 *Report on the Second Triennial Conference for Grassroots Organisations. "Grassroots 21: Stronger Community Bonds"* (Singapore: People's Association, 1997), pp. 12–8.

179 *Report of the Central Executive Committee Jan. 1995–Nov. 1996* (PAP archive).

180 "To Win the 'Serve-Me-or-Else' Voter", *Straits Times*, 15 June 1992; "Pressing Ahead with Our Political Programme", pp. 5–11, esp. 7.

181 Numerous committees comprising MPs were set up in the 1990s to investigate particular issues, or to suggest improvements within the Party. A description of the workings and conclusions of only the most important is given in what follows.

182 In their reports, the "A" and "G" Committees went so far as to suggest that there should be a rethinking of the asset appreciation policy—the MPs felt that the policy was not widely appreciated and had played a part in reinforcing the culture of rising expectations.

183 *Report of the "G" Committee*, 14 Aug. 1995 (PAP archive).

184 *Report of the "O" Committee*, 28 July 1995 (PAP archive).

185 "The PAP in Opposition", *Straits Times*, 13 Mar. 1993.

186 Ibid.

187 "Visit by 2ASG to Opposition Wards (1993)" (PAP archive), made available to the author.

188 Notes of Meeting, Wong Kan Seng at Potong Pasir Branch, 28 July 1993, file "Visit by 2ASG to Opposition Wards (1993)" (PAP archive).

189 Ong Ah Heng was appointed second adviser to the Yishun Central GROs in 1992. Ang Mong Seng was appointed second adviser to the Bukit Gombak GROs in December 1995, following the death of Ho Yew Ming, the previous second adviser, in October that year. Ang had earlier, from May to December 1995, been second adviser to the Hougang SMC GROs. His replacement as second adviser to the Hougang SMC GROs was Heng Chee How, a former superintendent with the Singapore Police Force.

190 Ong Ah Heng, interview with the author, 16 May 2013.

191 Ibid.

192 It is possible that the Party's original intention—before circumstances intervened—had been to field Ang (a Teochew speaker) in Hougang against Low Thia Khiang of the Workers' Party, whose Teochew oratory had been seen by many as a key factor in his victory in the 1991 general election. I am grateful to Ang Mong Seng for clarification on this point.

193 Ang also credited the time he had spent at PCF kindergartens in Bukit Gombak as another reason for his success in the 1997 election. Ang made a point as far as possible to celebrate the birthdays of all children at the kindergarten (which in practice meant getting to know the parents who would attend these celebrations). Ang Mong Seng, interview with the author, 20 May 2013.

194 Ibid. For Ang's own account of the winning back of Bukit Gombak, see "Ang Mong Seng: How I Recaptured Bukit Gombak", *Straits Times*, 26 Mar. 2011.

195 Ang Mong Seng grew up in the Jurong area. His father's leadership abilities (which left a deep impression on the son) led him to assume the unofficial title of *kepala*, or local village leader, also acting as a bridge between residents and government. Ong Ah Heng grew up in a kampong house in the Jalan Kayu area. His father was a subcontractor and his mother a cleaner. "The GE: New Faces", *Straits Times*, 16 Oct. 1996. I am grateful to Ang Mong Seng and Ong Ah Heng for supplying additional biographical information.

196 Ang joined the Party as a branch member in 1978 and rose to become branch secretary at the Boon Lay branch, a position he held from 1985 to 1996. Ong Ah Heng also had extensive experience serving in various PAP branches. "The GE: New Faces".

197 Ong Ah Heng had strong labour credentials: he was the assistant secretary-general of NTUC. Ang Mong Seng had extensive experience as an RC and CCC member and had served for several years in the HDB, before becoming general manager of the Sembawang Town Council (1991–96).

198 Nantah, or Nanyang University, was the Chinese-medium university merged by the government with the University of Singapore to form the National University of Singapore in 1980.

199 Despite the outstanding grassroots and branch experience that both men had, it is noteworthy that the Party allowed no shortcuts in the key stages of the selection process. Both men had to go through interviews with the Secretary-General's Committee and (the final stage) with the Party CEC before the decision was taken to field them. I am grateful to Ang Mong Seng and Ong Ah Heng for personal communications on the subject.

200 "Vote Will Decide Upgrading Priority", *Straits Times*, 13 Apr. 1992.

201 "Pressing Ahead with Our Political Programme", PM Goh Chok Tong, speech to Party activists, 24 May 1992, *Petir*, June 1992, pp. 7–8.

202 "Pressing Ahead with Our Political Programme", p. 7. While various facets of this strategy were fully fleshed out by the PAP government only in the 1990s, some sense of what was to come can be glimpsed from occasional statements by ministers in the previous decade. National Development Minister Teh Cheang Wan, for example, stated in Parliament in March 1985 that Anson and Potong Pasir (which were in the hands of opposition MPs J.B. Jeyaretnam and Chiam See Tong) would be served last by HDB when it came to a variety of services. Singapore Parliamentary Debates, 21 Mar. 1985, cols 1090–2. The Opposition MPs in the house challenged this as a threat and as discriminating against constituencies which had voted to have an Opposition MP (cols 1090, 1097). The *Hammer*, the Workers' Party organ, decried this as an "abuse of power . . . such undemocratic and blatant tactics to threaten the electorate who dared to vote for the opposition should be condemned". "Vengeance—The HDB Way", *Hammer*, June/July 1985, p. 2.

203 "PCF Kindergarten Places to Be Cut by 300 in Opposition Wards", *Straits Times*, 11 July 1992.

204 Wong's reply—that there had to be a cost to voting for the Opposition—has been noted earlier, p. 199.

205 For a sense of the views of PAP MPs, see "PAP Wards Upgraded First: Mixed Reaction", *Straits Times*, 14 Apr. 1992.

206 Among the specific recommendations of Dr Ong Chit Chung's 1995 "O" Committee was the denial of improvement works to Opposition wards.

207 "Polls Plan 'Fails to Distinguish between Party's Interests and Govt's Duties'", *Straits Times*, 17 Apr. 1992; "Upgrading 'Not the Only Issue Voters Will Consider'", *Straits Times*, 17 Apr. 1992.

208 Dr Lee Boon Yang, speech at the opening of the Kallang McNair Residents' Committee Centre, 19 Apr. 1992; for a sense of his remarks, see "Boon Yang Defends PAP's 'Votes-for-Upgrading' Strategy", *Straits Times*, 20 Apr. 1992.

209 Ang Mong Seng, interview with the author, 20 May 2013.

210 "New Parking Area Eases Woes of Heavy-Vehicle Owners in Hougang", *Straits Times*, 20 Oct. 1996.

211 "Think, Before Crying Foul over Vote-Linked Upgrading", *Straits Times*, 25 Apr. 1992.

212 "Changes May Signal Start of More Dynamic PAP Youth Wing", *Straits Times*, 27 Apr. 1993.

213 *Enhancing the Roles and Effectiveness of PAP MPs*, internal report, 28 Feb. 1991 (PAP archive). The study group behind the report comprised Dr Tan Cheng Bock (chairman), Yeo Cheow Tong, Chng Hee Kok, Heng Chiang Meng, Yu-Foo Yee Shoon, Zulkifli bin Mohammed and Dr Ong Chit Chung (secretary).

214 Many of the specific recommendations essentially revived older suggestions. For example, MPs proposed that exit management should be carried out in a more sensitive manner. Retiring MPs should be assisted in finding jobs elsewhere, in order to avoid giving the impression that they had somehow done wrong, or failed as an MP. *Recruitment of MPs, the Party's & MPs' Image*, internal report, 1991 (PAP archive). The committee members

responsible for this report were Dr Tay Eng Soon (chairman), Dr Aline Wong, Abdullah Tarmugi, Chandra Das, Dr Arthur Beng, Matthias Yao, Dr John Chen (secretary) and Davinder Singh (secretary).

215 But here, the response from the Party CEC was that the whip would only be lifted for matters of conscience. It was a confirmation of how the leadership assessed the changing landscape after the 1991 general election. There was no longer a need for a vocal PAP Opposition in Parliament.

216 *Recruitment of MPs, the Party's & MPs' Image.*

217 Ibid.

218 *1992 Marine Parade By-election PAP Post-mortem Report* (PAP archive).

219 "Decline of the PAP Youth Wing", *Straits Times*, 27 Feb. 1993.

220 "New Committees to Boost Youth Wing's Image a Timely Move", *Straits Times*, 13 June 1992.

221 It was clear that the leadership would also continue to bring in non-Party members to stand as MPs. "Will Decline of PAP Youth Wing Portend Hollowing of Party?", *Sunday Times*, 14 Mar. 1993.

222 Many Party branches were dominated by long-standing Party members who did not necessarily welcome the newcomers from the Youth Wing; this contributed in turn to the Young Wing committees in many branches being functionally dormant. "Decline of the PAP Youth Wing".

223 Ibid.

224 BG George Yeo, note titled "Young PAP", 27 Mar. 1993 (Minutes of PAP Central Executive Committee Meeting, 31 Mar. 1993) (PAP archive).

225 For the changes, see "PAP Youth Wing Revamped in Bid to Renew Party Ranks", *Straits Times*, 26 Apr. 1993. The provision for affiliate or HQ membership was announced as part of the package of changes to the Youth Wing in April 1993 but, as explained further below, had actually been introduced in 1992.

226 For extended excerpts of BG Yeo's 25 April 1993 speech to Party activists detailing these changes, see "Young PAP—Recasting the Net", *Petir*, May–June 1993, pp. 10–29.

227 "Members of Young PAP Greet the New Order with Cautious Optimism", *Straits Times*, 29 May 1993.

228 "Youths Must Convey Aspirations to Party Leaders", *Straits Times*, 10 July 1994.

229 Minutes of PAP Central Executive Committee Meeting, 31 Mar. 1993.

230 Yeo also left open the possibility that the YP could over time shape the direction of the Party itself: "And if we are right in our views and correctly express the views of a younger generation, then eventually we will help to redirect the central tendency of the Party's position." "Young PAP—Recasting the Net", pp. 10–29, esp. 25.

231 "People on the Move", *Petir*, May–June 1996, p. 71.

232 "Policy Studies Group: A Dragnet for Ideas", *Petir*, Nov.–Dec. 1998, pp. 62–3.

233 "BG Yeo to Young PAP: Listen to the Hearts and Minds of S'poreans", *Straits Times*, 10 July 1994. The revival of study trips by YP began with a visit in December 1993 to Malaysia, where BG Yeo and a delegation of 35 YP members met youth leaders and government ministers from UMNO, the United Malays National Organisation (the main party within the ruling coalition). A similar visit followed in July 1994 to touch base with

the youth wing of Indonesia's Golkar Party. These were efforts at fostering goodwill and friendship with neighbouring countries but also to find out about the programmes and set-up of YP's overseas counterparts. "Call for Closer Ties between Umno Youth and Young PAP", *Straits Times*, 9 Dec. 1993; "Young PAP to Meet Golkar Youth Wing in Indonesia", *Straits Times*, 8 June 1994.

234 Some of the bodies that had been created under the YP, such as the PSG and PSTs, would in fact no longer be extant in the 2000s—they had evolved into still different bodies. These will be considered in subsequent chapters.

235 "Changes May Signal Start of More Dynamic PAP Youth Wing", *Straits Times*, 27 Apr. 1993.

236 "Young PAP—Recasting the Net", pp. 10–29, esp. 29.

237 BG George Yeo had mentioned the possibility of direct elections for YP positions in April 1993, but the issue was still under study in 1994. "Young PAP Studying Direct Election Systems", *Straits Times*, 23 Apr. 1994.

238 Minutes of PAP Central Executive Committee Meeting, 31 Mar. 1993.

239 "Young PAP—Recasting the Net", pp. 10–29, esp. 23–4.

240 Especially, as BG Yeo suggested, when they might not be immediately welcomed by long-standing branch members. "Young PAP—Recasting the Net", pp. 10–29, esp. 23.

241 "New PAP Women's Wing Branch Woos High-Profile Professionals", *Straits Times*, 19 July 1997.

242 "Fundraising for PAP HQ", tabled at PAP Central Executive Committee meeting, 8 Feb. 1995 (PAP archive).

243 Cultivating and maintaining contact with the Friends of the PAP was an ongoing process, done through annual dinners and golf tournaments. The Friends of the PAP Committee chaired by Heng Chiang Meng also continually identified suitable individuals who might be considered Friends of the PAP. Over time, a separate group of Mandarin-speaking Friends was also created (at the suggestion of PM Goh) as it was felt that this was a constituency that also had to be cultivated.

244 Important changes were usually referred to the CEC for approval. In practice, there were few, if any, disagreements. From December 1992, the chairman of the HQ Exco was DPM BG Lee Hsien Loong, who succeeded PM Goh Chok Tong, himself newly elevated to the post of secretary-general of the Party. BG Lee had also succeeded Goh in another position: as first assistant secretary-general.

245 In the case of a ward without a PAP member of parliament, the HQ Exco would designate a suitable person to be branch chairman.

246 Party documents on the subject of branch performance made available to the author (PAP archive).

247 The moves to introduce performance indicators were successful in the sense that branches, and the MPs who headed them, were keen to end up in a good "band"—and to avoid falling into the band of poor performers. Branch accounts and statistics on meet-the-people session cases began to be submitted to HQ with greater promptitude. Lau Ping Sum, personal communication, 7 Aug. 2013.

248 Although the final decision was to create GSCs, other possibilities were discussed at earlier stages between the HQ Exco and the district chairmen, before being discarded.

One idea was the creation of a "super" GRC branch. The proposal was not taken further because district chairmen were uncomfortable with the idea of such a super GRC branch—especially if it meant the end of individual branches, which people had become used to. "GRC Organisation for the General Election", internal paper, 15 Oct. 1997 (PAP archive).

249 Matthias Yao, interview with the author, 22 Aug. 2013.

250 As GRCs became more established, the MPs (led by the senior MP or minister in the GRC) were able to improve coordination independently of the GSC mechanism, which eventually fell into disuse (Ibid.).

251 "Look Out for the Third Generation Leaders", *Straits Times*, 23 Jan. 1999.

252 But the actual strength was less than this, as it included those who did not renew their membership or ceased to be active. The Party's publicly acknowledged strength of 15,000 members at the turn of the millennium is probably a truer reflection of its actual (and active) numbers (Ibid.).

253 Unless otherwise stated, all membership data given in this section is from files concerning recruitment and renewal from the PAP archive made available to the author.

254 The YP base was through the 1990s and 2000s better-educated than the PAP's membership. In 2005, 55% of YP members had tertiary education compared to 22% in the Party itself.

255 Some branches in the 1990s appear to have made particular efforts to induct senior citizens into the PAP. The main sources were market committees, old community groups and senior citizen groups. This type of recruitment was done on an ad hoc basis and sometimes had the purpose of counteracting Opposition influence (sometimes within these same groups) on the ground. A small number of branches did this as they were overly anxious to fulfil the performance indicator of membership recruitment, without paying heed to the directive that younger members be recruited. Lau Ping Sum, personal communication, 7 Aug. 2013.

256 There were approximately 9,300 members with primary school qualifications in 2005. This number had declined to 7,100 by 2010.

257 "PAP to Recruit More Members", *Straits Times*, 22 Nov. 1999.

258 The branches, faced with the target set by the HQ Exco of 50 new members a year, could not afford to focus their recruiting efforts on younger professionals alone. Most branches in the 1990s never reached this target.

259 One point which was always to set the branches apart from the GROs was the issue of perks for PAP branch members. This was an issue which the Party periodically attempted to grapple with in the 1990s. Various membership committees suggested that some form of perks be introduced for branch members, akin to what key members of GROs received. But the Party leadership did not waver from the view that Party members had to serve out of a sense of dedication to the Party (interviews with multiple former PAP MPs and branch officials, 2013–16).

260 The leadership had around this time also been discussing how it would be useful to study the way political parties elsewhere had created, and modified, power structures which attracted those who were interested in politics. Minutes of PAP Central Executive Committee Meeting, 31 Mar. 1993 (PAP archive).

261 Minutes of PAP Central Executive Committee Meeting, 10 Sept. 1992 (PAP archive).

262 The Cadre Membership Committee became part of the Membership and Cadre Appointment Committee in the HQ Exco.

263 *Cadre Review Committee Report, 9 Jan. 1993*, Minutes of PAP Central Executive Committee Meeting, 21 Jan. 1993 (PAP archive).

264 Minutes of PAP Central Executive Committee Meeting, 21 Jan. 1993.

265 Unless otherwise indicated, data in this section on cadres is drawn from relevant Party files made available to the author.

266 The creation of such mechanisms was mooted by PM Goh in his address to cadres at the Party conference on 15 November 1991. "PAP Scours Its Party Branches for Activists Who Are MP Material", *Straits Times*, 30 May 1992.

267 This was so apparent that branch activists had no qualms making the observation to the media (Ibid.). It should be noted, though, that some MPs and ministers had a better "hit" rate than others. Dr Yeo Ning Hong, for example, put forward the names of three community leaders in his Kim Seng ward—Peh Chin Hua, Choo Wee Khiang and Dr Ker Sin Tze. All passed the selection process and became MPs.

268 The candidate selection process in the 1990s functioned much as it did the previous decade (outlined in chapter 1). Tea sessions hosted by various Ministers would be held. Those thought to have potential would then be invited to go through the three-stage interview process (which culminated in an interview with the Party CEC). The various interview panels saw changes in personnel as the years passed. Lim Kim San stepped down in the early 1990s from the chairmanship of the committee which represented the first formal interviewing stage after the tea sessions. His place as chairman was taken by Dr Yeo Ning Hong, who was in turn succeeded by Prof. S. Jayakumar (with the committee becoming known as the "J" Committee by the mid-1990s). The second interviewing stage was chaired by the Party Secretary-General (after 1992, Goh Chok Tong), also known internally as "PM's Committee". Other ministers sat in this committee, with SM Lee Kuan Yew also occasionally sitting in. It was this committee that would decide if an individual ought to be fielded. Often, this committee might post the individual to a constituency in advance of the election in order for the individual to have a hands-on feel of ground level work (which meant that feedback on the individual from sitting MPs observing the newcomer could be fed back to the committee). Other issues discussed within this committee included whether the individual had office-holder potential. The final round with the Party CEC, which usually came much later, nearer the election, was meant to formally endorsem the candidate (although as shown in chapter 1, not all who reached this stage were fielded).

269 Dr Lee Boon Yang, interview with the author, 28 Mar. 2013. It should not, however, be assumed that this was invariably the case.

270 Ibid. DPM Lee Hsien Loong, who chaired the second round of the PAP interview process for a time in the 1990s, could remark in 2000 that more people than ever were declining invitations to be considered as candidates. "PAP Finding It Harder to Get New Blood", *Straits Times*, 23 Sept. 2000.

271 Dr Ahmad Mattar and Dr Yeo Ning Hong left the Cabinet in June 1993 and July 1994 respectively. S. Dhanabalan returned to the Cabinet in December 1992 as minister for

trade and industry (three months after leaving), and then left again for a second time in January 1994. DPM Ong Teng Cheong left Cabinet (resigning also from his position as PAP chairman) in August 1993 to contest for the elected presidency. Dr Tony Tan left the Cabinet in December 1991 but returned as DPM and defence minister in August 1995. He continued to serve in the Cabinet until 2005.

272   The three ministers were Dr Richard Hu (finance and national development), Prof. S. Jayakumar (law and home affairs) and Yeo Cheow Tong (health and community development). For Goh's remarks, see "Finding Ministers Is Top Priority", *Business Times*, 16 Nov. 1992; and "Why the Urgent Need to Find New Pillars for the Cabinet—PM", *Straits Times,* 13 Dec. 1992.

273   D. Mauzy, "Leadership Succession in Singapore: The Best Laid Plans . . . ", *Asian Survey* 33, 12 (Dec. 1993): 1163–74, esp. 1173.

274   "Fact of Life Today: Govt No Longer Has Pick of Scholars", *Straits Times*, 1 July 2000.

275   This point was made in an insightful commentary by the *Straits Times* journalist Asad Latif, "Fishing for Talent? Cast the Net Wider", *Straits Times*, 4 Dec. 2000.

276   "Lack of Candidates More to Do with the Party" (Commentary by Chua Lee Hoong), *Straits Times*, 6 Dec. 2000.

277   Singapore Parliamentary Debates, 30 June 2000, col. 582. See also "Fact of Life Today".

278   Singapore Parliamentary Debates, 3 Dec. 1993, cols 1263–4.

279   There is no suggestion that those ministers who left Cabinet in the 1990s did so for pecuniary opportunities outside of politics. Dr Tony Tan left to take up the chairmanship of OCBC Bank, a long-held personal as well as family aspiration, while S. Dhanabalan's reservations about the government's treatment of the Marxist conspirators in 1987 were strong enough for him to leave the Cabinet. See Yap et al., *Men in White*, pp. 466–8.

280   "Market Rates for Civil Servants", *Straits Times*, 18 Mar. 1989; "New Pay Package for Ministers Unveiled", *Straits Times*, 24 Mar. 1989.

281   This was a point made by government ministers at several junctures during the 1989 debate. "BG Lee on Fair Basis of Determining Salaries", *Straits Times*, 24 Mar. 1989. The "idealism" argument was championed by SDP MP Chiam See Tong during the March 1989 debate. "PM on the Scholar Who Got Away", *Straits Times*, 25 Mar. 1989.

282   "The Prime Mnister's National Day Message: A Good Government Does Not Come Cheap", *Straits Times*, 9 Aug. 1990.

283   "Cabinet Posts Harder to Fill if Pay Not Competitive", *Straits Times*, 4 Dec. 1993.

284   See Lee Kuan Yew, *From Third World to First*, pp. 194–6.

285   Singapore Parliamentary Debates, 14 Jan. 2013, cols 168–9. See "SM Lee: Formula Needed to Link Minister's Pay to Private Sector", *Business Times*, 14–15 Jan. 1994; and "Old Guard Move by the Times, Not Monetary Rewards", *Straits Times*, 15 Jan. 1994.

286   "PM's and Ministerial Salaries", note from SM Lee Kuan Yew to PM Goh Chok Tong, 2 Feb. 1994 (National Archives of Singapore), made available to the author.

287   *White Paper: Competitive Salaries for Competent and Honest Government. Cmd. 13 of 1994. Presented to Parliament by Command of The President of the Republic of Singapore. Ordered by Parliament to lie upon the Table: 21st October 1994* (Singapore: Prime

Minister's Office, 1994), pp. 7–12, available at https://www.nas.gov.sg/archivesonline/
government_records/record-details/a0bef428-730e-11e7-83df-0050568939ad (accessed 3
Mar. 2021).

288 Singapore Parliamentary Debates, 3 Nov. 1994, col. 875.

289 "White Paper Data on Salaries Verified, Benchmarks Appropriate", *Straits Times*, 13 Jan.
1995.

290 Ibid.

291 Ibid.

292 "PM Goh to Forgo Salary Rises for Five Years", *Straits Times*, 14 Jan. 1995.

293 "White Paper Data on Salaries Verified".

294 "High Negative Reaction and Feedback Session", *Straits Times*, 1 Nov. 1994.

295 Wong Wee Nam and Patrick Kee, "Wage Restraint: Ministers' Moral Responsibility to
Show the Way", letter to *Straits Times* Forum, 24 July 1996.

296 The call for such a panel was made by NCMP J.B. Jeyaretnam in October 1997. "Pay
Issue Was Settled in 1994 and at Polls", *Straits Times*, 8 Oct. 1997.

297 "WP Wants Ministerial Pay Cut", *Straits Times*, 21 Jan. 1998. For Jeyaretnam's motion for
a voluntary pay reduction of 25% on the part of political appointment holders and MPs,
and his debate with DPM Lee Hsien Loong on the subject, see Singapore Parliamentary
Debates, 19 Feb. 1998, cols 378–404.

298 "Pay Freeze for Ministers and Top Civil Servants", *Straits Times*, 20 Feb. 1998.

299 "Whither Pay? To Slow Down, Freeze or Cut?", *Straits Times*, 14 Mar. 1998.

300 "Pay Cuts of Ministers to Be Restored", *Straits Times*, 24 Nov. 1999.

301 "Pay Rise for Ministers: 'Too Much, Too Early'", *Straits Times*, 6 July 2000.

302 Singapore Parliamentary Debates, 1 Nov. 1994, col. 825. See "Political Entrepreneurs
Needed for Success", *Straits Times*, 2 Nov. 1994. Lee was at various points in the 1990s to
reiterate the point and assert that he would eventually be proven right. See, for example,
"It's an Emotional Problem, Says SM Lee", *Straits Times*, 20 July 1996.

303 "Whither Pay?".

304 "Ministers' Pay: That Million $ Question", *Straits Times*, 20 May 2000.

305 Koh Lian Huat (vice-chairman, Tampines East CCC), interview with the author, 12 Aug.
2013. Like many senior grassroots figures within the parapolitical apparatus, Koh was
also a long-serving PAP activist and branch member, having joined the Party in 1966.
PAP Pioneers: 50 Ordinary Stories (Singapore: PAP Seniors Group Executive Committee,
2015), p. 49.

306 Lim was at the time of the transfer the director of social defence and community relations
at MCD.

307 Lim Sah Soon, interview with the author, 21 Aug. 2013.

308 For a useful blow-by-blow account of the Chee/Chiam affair and its aftermath, see Bilveer
Singh, "Singapore: Change amidst Continuity", *Southeast Asian Affairs* (1994): 267–84.
For the *Straits Times*' coverage of the affair (which included accounts by insiders keen to
put across their side of the story), see "Chiam Quit After CEC Vetoed Censure Move",
Straits Times, 26 June 1993; "Chiam's Resignation—A Move That Shocked SDP and
Outsiders", *Straits Times*, 26 June 1993; "SDP Kicks Chiam Out", *Straits Times*, 21 Aug.

1993; "SDP—The Insight Story", *Straits Times*, 28 Aug. 1993; and "The Sacking of Chiam See Tong", *Straits Times*, 28 Aug. 1993. Loke Hoe Yeong's account while sympathetic to Chiam is also essential reading. Loke, *First Wave*, pp. 213–88.

309 "Chee Challenge to Quit His SDP Post", *Straits Times*, 3 July 1993.

310 "SDP Cadres Elect Chiam Chairman of Party's 'New CEC'", *Straits Times*, 29 Aug. 1993.

311 For a chronology and summary of issues up to this point, see "SDP's 'New CEC' Decides Not to Fight Legality Suit", *Straits Times*, 7 Jan. 1994.

312 "High Court Throws Out Bid to Oust SDP Leaders", *Straits Times*, 8 Apr. 1994.

313 "Breakaway SDP Group Registering New Party", *Straits Times*, 6 July 1994.

314 In February 1994, Chee abandoned his defence in the libel suit brought against him by his former boss at NUS, Dr S. Vasoo, essentially admitting he had defamed Vasoo.

315 "SDP Factions Prepare for Clash at Party Conference", *Straits Times*, 11 Jan. 1995; "SDP Elects New Central Executive Committee", *Sunday Times*, 15 Jan. 1995; "SDP Passes Resolution Calling on Chiam to Quit", *Straits Times*, 16 Jan. 1995.

316 By this time, Chee was already well on his way to becoming a regular at international human rights forums and seminars. Chee had led an SDP team attending a meeting for human rights NGOs in Bangkok in July 1994. He was also attending programmes and delivering talks farther afield, such as in the United States, at the invitation of NGOs and universities there. See, for example, "SDP Officials to Attend Manila Gathering", *Straits Times*, 29 Oct. 1994.

317 "SDP: The Appearance and the Reality", *Straits Times*, 11 Feb. 1995.

318 "SDP Calls on Govt to Sever All Links with Myanmar", *Straits Times*, 28 July 1994. Myanmar was to prove something of a pet topic with Chee. In November 1996, he called on the government to address allegations made in a documentary (which Chee had featured in) by the Australian Special Broadcasting Service aired in October 1996 that the Singapore Government Investment Corporation was linked through its investments to the Myanmar drug lord Lo Hsin Han and his companies. The government issued a press statement rebutting the allegations, accusing Chee of again siding with foreign interests to attack or undermine the country. "Chee 'Joins Foreigners in Attacking S'pore for the Third Time'", *Sunday Times*, 3 Nov. 1996.

319 "SDP Urges Singapore and Manila to Show Restraint", *Straits Times*, 11 Apr. 1995; "SDP Sec-Gen's Critical Letter Cited in Manila Paper", *Straits Times*, 22 Apr. 1995. Contemplacion, a Filipino domestic worker in Singapore, had been hanged in March 1995 for the murders of another Filipino domestic worker, Della Marga, and the child under Marga's care. The SDP was, following its interventions, in turn criticised by PAP MPs in Parliament, with the SDP accused of not backing Singapore when it should have. For this, and the SDP's defence of its actions, see "Chee: SDP Never Questioned Govt's Handling of Case", *Straits Times*, 31 May 1995; and "SDP Accused of Not Backing Singapore in Trying Times", *Straits Times*, 31 May 1995.

320 "SDP Asked Why It 'Sides with Human Rights Groups'", *Straits Times*, 24 July 1995.

321 For a blow-by-blow account of the Williams College episode, including its context and aftermath, see Asad Latif, "The Internationalisation of Singapore Politics", *Southeast Asian Affairs* (1996): 321–36. See also S.R. Nathan, *An Unexpected Journey: The Path to the Presidency* (Singapore: Editions Didier Millet, 2011), pp. 595–8.

322 "S'pore 'Faces Problems Entrenching Democracy'", *Straits Times*, 18 Sept. 1995.

323 "Cheats and Liars Are Not Honourable Opponents", *Straits Times*, 21 Sept. 1995.

324 "'Chee Shows He's a Willing Stooge'", *Straits Times*, 10 Sept. 1995.

325 "Cheats and Liars Are Not Honourable Opponents".

326 "What Dr Chee Said at Williams", *Straits Times*, 3 Nov. 1995.

327 At the panel discussion, Chee had attempted a partial refutation of the views of William Safire, the *New York Times* columnist who had in May 1995 published a piece critical of the Singapore government. "S'pore 'Faces Problems Entrenching Democracy'", *Straits Times*, 18 Sept. 1995. See also "SDP Has Never Been, and Will Never Be, Used by Anyone", *Straits Times*, 27 Sept. 1995.

328 Singapore Parliamentary Debates, 3 Nov. 1995, cols 279–82. See also "Move against Support for Attacks on Judiciary", *Straits Times*, 4 Nov. 1995.

329 See, for example, "Economy Not Doing That Well: SDP Report", *Straits Times*, 9 May 1995.

330 "Move against Support for Attacks on Judiciary".

331 *Petir* (supplement), Nov. 1995; see "*Petir* Details Censure in Parliament", *Straits Times*, 28 Nov. 1995.

332 See, for example, "Ling Should Have Been More Prepared on a Matter of Life and Death", *Straits Times*, 20 Mar. 1992.

333 "SDP Gives Three Reasons Why It Missed Land Transport Debate", *Straits Times*, 24 Jan. 1996.

334 "Committee of Privileges Report", *Straits Times*, 23 Nov. 1996.

335 "Workers' Party Holds Election amidst Signs of Discontent", *Sunday Times*, 7 Mar. 1994.

336 The offending article had suggested that the organisers of Tamil Language Week were, amongst other things, government stooges. "The Tamil Language Week—A Drama Enacted to the Written Ruling", *Hammer*, Aug. 1995 (in Tamil). A November 1998 High Court ruling awarded damages to the organisers of Tamil Language Week. Jeyaretnam's difficulties in paying, together with the suit brought against him by PAP leaders following his remarks at an election rally in Cheng San, set in train a sequence which led to his bankruptcy and the loss of his NCMP seat in 2001.

337 "Political Ploy? GRCs Can Help Bond the Community", *Sunday Times*, 13 Oct. 1996.

338 "Govt Ruining Our Chances: Opposition", *Straits Times*, 2 Oct. 1996; "How the Various Parties See the Amendments—Govt Ruining Our Chances—Opposition", *Straits Times*, 2 Oct. 1996; "Opposition MPs Lash Out against Amendments", *Straits Times*, 29 Oct. 1996.

339 "Few Good Men? Blame Yourself, Opposition Told", *Straits Times*, 23 Nov. 1996.

340 See Derek da Cunha, *The Price of Victory: The 1997 Singapore General Election and Beyond* (Singapore: Institute of Southeast Asian Studies, 1997), pp. 9–15.

341 Notes of meeting with MPs, 3 Sept. 1996, from file "Task Force 97 (Dec. 1991–Dec. 1996)" (PAP archive).

342 Documents in file "Task Force 97 (Dec. 1991–Dec. 1996)".

343 Notes of meeting with MPs, 3 Sept. 1996, from file "Task Force 97 (Dec. 1991–Dec. 1996)".

344 "Minorities Represented Well in Slate of New Faces", *Straits Times,* 18 Nov. 1996.

345 "PAP's Programme Outlines Five Key Roles", *Straits Times*, 25 Nov. 1996.

346 For a summary of these plans, see "On the Drawing Board", *Straits Times*, 1 Jan. 1997.

347 "Our Concrete Plans Did the Trick, Say PAP MPs", *Business Times*, 3 Jan. 1997.

348 "Ang Mong Seng in Bukit Gombak", *Petir*, July–Aug. 1997, pp. 54–6; "Improvements to Nee Soon Central since Ong Ah Heng Became MP", *Petir*, Sept.–Oct. 1997, pp. 42–3.

349 "PAP Not Unfair in Using Public Funds for Upgrading: PM", *Straits Times*, 28 Dec. 1996.

350 "Upgrading: PAP Sends out Open Letter to Singaporeans", *Straits Times*, 29 Dec. 1996.

351 "WP Chief Losing His Touch, Says SM Lee", *Straits Times*, 24 Dec. 1996.

352 When introduced as a candidate, Tang was already facing a defamation suit brought against him by SM Lee and DPM Lee Hsien Loong for comments he had made in a magazine (Hong Kong-based *Yazhou Zhoukan*) about the purchases of property by the Lee family in what had become known as the HPL saga. "WP Introduces Lawyer Ahead of Nomination Day", *Straits Times,* 22 Dec. 1996.

353 Tang had apparently implied at a dinner two years before that there were too many English-educated and Christians in the Cabinet. "WP's Tang Has 'Extreme Views'", *Business Times*, 27 Dec. 1996. See also "No Breach of Confidentiality, Says PM", *Straits Times*, 20 Nov. 1997. For Tang, his motivations and the campaign in Cheng San, see also Lee, *Unexpected Nation*, pp. 522–8.

354 "Yock Suan: Polls Always about Giving Power to Voters", *Straits Times*, 28 Dec. 1996.

355 "PAP Focuses on Tang Liang Hong Threat", *Straits Times*, 29 Dec. 1996. A summary of the views and episodes which the PAP felt showed Tang in his true colours: At a Feedback Unit session in July 1995, he had noted that the Cabinet was dominated by English-educated Christians—suggesting that the policies made by these people might not benefit the majority. In a seminar organised by alumni of Hwa Chong (a junior college with strong and long-standing connections to the Chinese community) in late 1996, he had asked why the Chinese-educated were "the ones carrying the sedan chair", noting that it was the Chinese-educated who should be the ones sitting on the chair. He had also in an April 1996 letter to the Chinese press lamented that Chinese-educated were abandoning their traditional religion in favour of "other" religions.

356 "Sue Us, PM Goh and SM Lee Tell WP's Tang Liang Hong", *Business Times*, 30 Dec. 1996.

357 "Tang Using a 'Dangerous Mix' of Politics and Religion to Woo Malays, Indians", *Straits Times*, 1 Jan. 1997.

358 "How they Won . . . When They Could Not", *Sunday Times*, 5 Jan. 1997.

359 Tellingly, when Goh was asked about the Democratic Progressive Party's Tan Soo Phuan, who also had strong views on the Chinese language, the response was, "He's a nobody." "Tang Using a 'Dangerous Mix' of Politics and Religion to Woo Malays, Indians".

360 Minutes of task force meetings, file "Task Force 97 (Dec. 1991–Dec. 1996)" (PAP archive). The task force's assessments relied on feedback and intelligence from branch activists.

361 As Polling Day (2 January 1997) approached, the PAP distributed open letters in all four national languages to Cheng San voters highlighting Tang's extremist views and calling

for the rejection of his chauvinistic politics. "Three PAP Open Letters Question WP Leadership", *Straits Times*, 31 Dec. 1996; "PAP Issues Three Letters on Tang", *Straits Times*, 1 Jan. 1997. The PAP's pamphleteering efforts in this election were prolific and not confined to Tang Liang Hong. Pamphlets were circulated attacking Chee Soon Juan as well, while yet others dealt with upgrading, healthcare and other issues such as cost of living. These efforts should be contrasted with the reliance on dialogue sessions in 1991. All in all, the propaganda battle was waged more effectively in 1997.

362 "DPMs Join in Battle for Cheng San", *Straits Times*, 1 Jan. 1997.

363 "Sticking with Multiracialism in a Chinese Ward", *Business Times*, 4 Jan. 1997. The issue was not as clear-cut as Goh suggested. The internal postmortem noted that even sections of the English-educated ground were not convinced by the case against Tang. See p. 228. Heng Chiang Meng, whose Jalan Kayu division of Cheng San GRC had traditionally not been PAP-supporting (it had been seen as something of a hotbed of Barisan Sosialis activity from the 1960s, with embers of anti-establishment sentiment flickering even decades on), felt that the middle- /lower-middle-class HDB dwellers and individuals who had been resettled from farms in Jalan Kayu had by his time been brought around and were supportive of the PAP, but that during the campaign, a third group—middle-class professionals from the Seletar Hills area—disagreed with how the PAP had taken on Tang. Heng Chiang Meng, interview with the author, 3 Nov. 2020.

364 The highly charged atmosphere just outside the Bishan Institute of Technical Education (the main counting centre for Cheng San GRC), where supporters of both sides had gathered, was not soon forgotten by those present. When it became clear in the early hours of the morning that the PAP team had prevailed, anger mixed with disappointment on the part of WP supporters seemed about to spill over. Zainul Abidin Rasheed recalls : "The WP supporters were really upset. They thought they had won. JBJ [J.B. Jeyaretnam] was not supposed to be up on stage meant for winners, but he did, glaring all the while. When I spoke, I first thanked our supporters. Then fearing that the WP supporters would cause a stir if not riot, as they were shouting and heckling the PAP candidates when they spoke, I decided I thought I should try to calm them down by speaking to them directly: 'Now, dear WP supporters, look, we have had a hard nine days of campaigning and the voters have decided, so let's please accept the results, and work together, after all we are Singaporeans.' These were more or less the words I used. This appeal for unity appears to have had some effect with much of the heckling and shouting dying down" (Zainul Abidin Rasheed, personal communication, 27 Oct. 2010; see also "Calming Down Cheng San Hecklers", *Straits Times*, 6 June 1997). J.B. Jeyaretnam, writing later, described the scene and his feelings : "The intense passion of those who wanted us to win gathered at the final counting centre on the night of 2nd January still haunts me. It was a cry coming straight from their hearts repeated incessantly. I was very very upset, not so much for myself or for the Workers' Party, but for the hundreds assembled on the field." Jeyaretnam ascribed the PAP victory to "intimidation and bribery" of the voters. J.B. Jeyaretnam, *The Hatchet Man of Singapore* (Singapore: Jeya Publishers, 2003), pp. 9–10.

365 The contest in Bukit Gombak had a third player: Syed Farid Wajidi from the Singapore People's Party, who did not seriously figure, polling 6.44% of the vote.

366 It was, in fact, PM Goh who suggested to Yao that he take up the challenge, saying that he would not send Yao into a battle he felt Yao could lose. Matthias Yao, interview with the author, 22 Aug. 2013.

367 "Matthias Yao Says after Home Visits: I'm Confident", *Straits Times*, 2 Jan. 1997.

368 Matthias Yao, interview with the author, 22 Aug. 2013. Among the several reasons for Chee's defeat, Yao intriguingly singled out the possibility that older voters (and there were many in MacPherson) did not like the way that Chee supposedly ousted Chiam from the SDP.

369 "Finally, Being His Own Man: Goh Chok Tong on Singapore, Asia—and Himself", PM Goh Chok Tong, interview with *Asiaweek*, 25 Nov. 1999. Quoted in "Introduction: A Redefined Singapore", in *Impressions of the Goh Chok Tong Years*, ed. Welsh et al., pp. 1–23, esp. 7.

370 PM Goh Chok Tong, speech at Party convention, 11 Jan. 1998. "How to Win an Election: Four Major Lessons from GE 97", *Petir*, Jan.–Feb. 1998, pp. 8–9.

371 *1997 General Election PAP Post-mortem Report.*

372 To PAP leaders, the SDP's reverse also showed that its style of confrontational politics was out of place in Singapore. PM Goh asserted in the customary early morning post-election press conference that the election result was a rejection of liberal democracy as seen in the West. "PM Goh on Reasons for Large Swing to Party: PAP's Concrete Programmes the Key", *Straits Times*, 4 Jan. 1997. There was also a certain degree of head-scratching (which no doubt gave the PAP leadership added satisfaction) on the part of the foreign press as to why the democratically inclined SDP, which had early on promised much, had failed so badly. See, for example, "Pondering the Elections, Why Did the Singapore Democratic Party Lose?", *Asiaweek*, 7 Feb. 1997.

373 *1997 General Election PAP Post-mortem Report.*

374 "PAP's Andy Gan Promises MRT Station if He Wins", *Straits Times*, 24 Dec. 1996.

375 "Potong Pasir Estates Growing Jaded and in a Sad State, Andy Gan", *Straits Times*, 14 Aug. 1995.

376 "Few Complaints Raised in Straw Poll of Potong Pasir Residents", *Straits Times*, 20 Aug. 1995.

377 Much to the annoyance of PAP activists in Hougang, who felt that it made the job of dislodging Low that much harder. The activists had made their view—that no PAP leader should commend Low—clear to the Party leadership (personal communications from multiple Party sources connected to PAP's Hougang branch in the 1990s).

378 "Five Goals for GE 2002", *Petir*, Jan.–Feb. 1997, pp. 10–1, esp. 11.

379 *1997 General Election PAP Post-mortem Report.*

380 "PAP Leaders Take Legal Action against Tang", *Straits Times*, 1 Jan. 1997.

381 Jeyaretnam had at an election rally publicly referred to the police reports made by Tang Liang Hong against PAP leaders. The police reports had Tang alleging that the PAP leadership had defamed him during the campaign by labelling him as a chauvinist.

382 "Our Concrete Plans Did the Trick", *Business Times*, 3 Jan. 1997; "Big Swing to PAP", *Straits Times*, 3 Jan. 1997.

383 "Upgrading Tactic Means More Material Bait Later", *Straits Times*, 6 Jan. 1997.

384 "Upgrade Yourselves, Not Your Flats: WP", *Straits Times*, 2 Jan. 1997.

385 There were also other episodes that led to the Opposition crying foul. PM Goh, BG Lee Hsien Loong and Dr Tony Tan were seen inside a polling station in Cheng San as votes were cast, in apparent contravention of clauses in the Parliamentary Elections Act that prohibited waiting or loitering near polling stations. The WP felt that the presence could have influenced voters within polling stations. The complaint was dismissed by the police based on advice by the public prosecutor, a decision which baffled the WP, with J.B. Jeyaretnam calling the law "an ass". For the incident, see "WP Lodges Police Report Against Ministers' Presence", *Straits Times*, 7 Jan. 1997; "WP Asks Public Prosecutor to Explain Stand on PAP Men at Polling Stations", *Straits Times*, 15 July 1997; and "Waiting, Loitering in Poll Station Not an Offence: A-G", *Straits Times*, 31 July 1997. Memories of the incident lingered on and are periodically resurfaced by current and former Opposition figures, as an example of an inherent unfairness in the system, or specifically to call for an independent electoral commission. See, for example, Jeanette Chong-Aruldoss, "Inside, Outside . . . Upside Down!", *Online Citizen*, 3 Feb. 2014, available at https://www.theonlinecitizen.com/2014/02/03/inside-outside-upside-down/ (accessed 5 Mar. 2021).

386 Low made these remarks during a 28 January 1997 NUS dialogue on the future of the Opposition, which he had attended with Chiam See Tong. "Chiam, Low Disagree on Mood of Electorate", *Straits Times*, 29 Jan. 1997.

387 "Opposition Hits Out at Linking Upgrading to Precinct-Level Support", *Straits Times*, 2 Jan. 1997; "Chiam, Low, Disagree on Mood of Electorate". PM Goh had reasoned those precincts with greater support for the PAP (within constituencies which had voted for the PAP) should get upgraded first, and that this method would enable parties (and not just the PAP) to ascertain precinct-level support. "MPs Can Tell Support at Each Counting Place", *Straits Times*, 1 Jan. 1997; "Precincts' Vote Support to Decide Upgrading Priority", *Business Times*, 1 Jan. 1997.

388 Singapore Parliamentary Debates, 2 June 1997, cols 136–7; "Opposition Accuses PAP of Dividing the Nation", *Straits Times*, 3 June 1997.

389 Singapore Parliamentary Debates, 3 Aug. 1998, cols 866–7; "Opposition Says Govt Causing Rift", *Straits Times*, 4 Aug. 1998.

390 "You Win but You Don't Win Fair", *Sunday Times*, 29 Dec. 1991. The journalist had been careful to note that the PAP moves were within its legal rights, but wrote that the Party should remind itself: *gong dao zi zai ren xin* (justice is in the hearts of the people).

391 "Time to Close the Cracks after GE", *Straits Times*, 6 Feb. 1997. See Da Cunha, *Price of Victory*, pp. 105–10.

392 The Chinese Community Liaison Group is led at the time of writing (November 2020) by Minister for Culture, Community and Youth Edwin Tong.

393 "PAP Must Go Beyond Package Politics to Win the People's Hearts and Minds", *Straits Times*, 10 Jan. 1997.

394 "Voters Choose PAP's Comprehensive Programme", *Straits Times*, 17 Jan. 1997.

395 Lim Boon Heng, "It Takes More than Public Debates to Create a Civil Society", letter to *Straits Times* Forum, 29 Jan. 1997.

Chapter 4

1997–2001: Banyan—Bonsai—Tembusu?

By the early 1990s, there was the sense within the leadership that the government had to move quickly in order that Singapore not be left behind in the global revolution beginning to sweep across multiple fields. A key milestone and an important signifier of change was the merging in 1990 of parts of the Ministry of Community Development and the Ministry of Communications and Information, creating the Ministry of Information and the Arts (MITA), headed by Brigadier General (BG) (Res) George Yeo. Other changes quickly followed. The National Arts Council and the National Heritage Board were formed in 1991 and 1993 respectively. In May 1991 the government appointed the Censorship Review Committee, chaired by Ambassador-at-Large Tommy Koh. The committee was notable for the diverse composition of its membership, with journalists, actors and educators among its members, and for the wide range of views canvassed. It submitted its findings in September 1992.[1] While the report's recommendations did not represent radical departures, the report itself was widely seen as signalling a more relaxed attitude.[2] These moves were part of the beginnings of Singapore's transformation. What followed included improved government funding for the arts, new performance venues (planned in the 1990s, realised in the 2000s) and, from 1996, an arts festival.

This transformation had pragmatism in its thrust. It was partly a drive to ensure that Singapore remained relevant.[3] In December 1990, Yeo (just two weeks into the job as acting minister for information and the arts) commented on the ministry's mission. He observed that culture was integral to the state—Singapore could not become a "hub city of the world" without such artistic and cultural development. The mission of the ministry was to help inform, educate and entertain Singaporeans and make Singapore a hub city of the world: one that was economically dynamic, socially cohesive and culturally vibrant.[4]

There were additional considerations, some of which had been percolating within the Party for some time. Not least was the sense that Singapore had to change to keep pace with the needs and aspirations of its people. As far back as the 1986 Party conference, the Central Executive Committee (CEC) report circulated to cadres had included a telling paragraph in the section looking forward to the future and the PAP's Vision 1999:

> *Social and cultural development must advance in parallel with economic success.*
> *It is empty to talk about cultural sophistication when the population is not yet*

properly fed, clothed or housed; but it is equally incomplete to have a population
whose material needs are well met but who see no higher goals in life. Now that
most Singaporeans' basic needs are met, we should devote more attention to
artistic and cultural pursuits, and to creating an environment which brings out
the innovative and creative spirit in our people.[5]

The 1986 CEC report was the work of the younger generation of leaders and bore in particular the imprint of then-1DPM Goh Chok Tong's thinking. The recognition of changing circumstances had been part of internal Party discourse for some time, present—in embryonic form—as far back as the soul-searching following the 1984 general election.[6] Lee Kuan Yew himself appears to have been coming to the realisation that a gradual broad-based opening up of Singapore society was needed if the nation was to continue to flourish.[7] Writing privately to Goh in November 1991, SM Lee had commented on the subject:

After 31 years of my systematic demolishing of wrong-headed wisdom and soft-
headed ideas, PAP ideas became accepted wisdom. But it is time for a change,
or to use a metaphor, to re-pot the Bonsai, which is Singapore. A root-bound
bonsai has to have its roots loosened up, cut and re-potted. But it must be
carefully and skilfully done. I discovered, when the Istana curator tried it on
two bonsais given to me by the Taiwanese leaders, the bonsai died because he
lacked the skills.[8]

This, then, was the direction in which Party and government would move—not just in the area of cultural liberalisation, but in the spheres of politics and civil society, too. On 20 June 1991, BG (Res) George Yeo delivered a landmark speech on civil society and the role of the state on the occasion of the NUS Society's Inaugural Lecture. This speech laid down an important marker as to how the state (and by implication the Party) had to evolve to allow space for diverse views and for civil society actors:

For our civic institutions to grow, the state must withdraw a little and provide
more space for local initiative. If the state is overpowering and intrudes into every
sphere of community life, the result will be disastrous. . . . The problem now is
that under a banyan tree very little else can grow. When state institutions are too
pervasive, civic institutions cannot thrive. Therefore it is necessary to prune the
banyan tree so that other plants can also grow.[9]

Yeo chose his words with care, observing during the question and answer session that there would always be limits, and that a strong centre would always be necessary: "The ship of state needs certain controls so that we can navigate and change directions quickly."[10] But this aspect tends to have been forgotten. The "banyan tree" speech grew in the retelling, discussed and cited by many—erroneously—as the starting point of the Party's post-Lee Kuan Yew liberalisation, delivered by a young minister with liberal—if not the most liberal—inclinations in the Cabinet.[11]

George Yeo was to be associated, somewhat illogically, with the 1991 election reverse, perceived in some quarters to have been one of the "liberals" not in sync with the needs of the heartlanders. Yeo felt himself scapegoated—not so much in Cabinet but in the wider court of public opinion and speculation.[12] The experience of the 1991 election was to prove salutary for him. Throughout the 1990s, MITA would tread carefully in the area of restrictions in the arts and media, even as MITA and associated agencies embarked on a longer-term vision to transform Singapore to where it could now aspire to the first rank of global cities.[13]

The overall thrust of opening up remained, but those expecting a radical sea change were thus to be disappointed in the face of government recalibrations. In the years immediately after the 1991 general election, the promise held up by PM Goh of a more open era seemed to have faded somewhat. Especially strong was the sense in the air that the government would not pander to the demands of a minority of liberal intellectuals. The limits of openness were nowhere better in evidence than in cases where artistic expression was deemed to have transgressed into political commentary. On 31 December 1993, two performance artists—Josef Ng and Shannon Tham— were brought to book. Ng had created and performed performance pieces which were broadly in support of the gay community, and which were construed as protests against earlier cases of alleged police entrapment against homosexuals. Tham's offence was a protest against the press reporting of the arts festival (organised by two groups, The Artists' Village and Fifth Passage), in which Ng and Tham were taking part. The government view was that these performances—which included Ng snipping off his pubic hair—had exceeded the limits of decency. The details of these incidents need not concern us here.[14] What is more important is the government's response. The National Arts Council condemned the acts as "vulgar and distasteful".[15] Restrictions were also imposed on performance art and forum theatre.[16]

The concerns went beyond matters of taste. The government in explaining these decisions reasoned that performance art or scriptless performances "may be exploited to agitate the audiences on volatile social issues or to propagate the beliefs and messages of deviant social or religious groups, or as a means of subversion".[17] While the performances undoubtedly were meant to make a point, whether or not they were capable of (or intended to) subvert anyone or propagate any belief is a question that was asked by many at the time. The incident, however, provides a useful insight into the mindset of government leaders at around this time—and this was not an isolated case. On 5 February 1994, the *Straits Times* ran an article highlighting (somewhat sensationally) that two well-known figures in the local drama scene from the group the Necessary Stage had "trained in Marxist workshops", with the insinuation that the two individuals had ulterior motives in attending the workshop, or might be used as pawns by a wider network.[18] Many rallied to the defence of the two, including the chairman of the National Arts Council, Prof. Tommy Koh.[19] In Parliament, George Yeo acknowledged the somewhat overblown nature of the reporting by the *Straits Times* but also noted that the coverage

did focus public attention on a potential problem which we should be mindful of.

It is not good for the arts in Singapore to become politicised. While art, especially theatre, cannot avoid commenting on social and political conditions of society, in Singapore art should not be used to promote particular political causes, and certainly not in a covert way. Otherwise, the Government will be forced to treat and regulate such performances as a form of political activity.[20]

The year 1994 came to be seen as marking a clampdown of sorts on political and artistic expression. The management committee of the National University of Singapore Society (NUSS) aborted the publication of the mid-year issue of its journal *Commentary*, on the grounds the contents (which included articles on forum theatre and performance art) were likely to annoy the government.[21] This was widely seen as an act of self-censorship and led to the en masse resignation of the journal's four editors. One article in the journal (later republished in the *Straits Times*) by the well-known intellectual and playwright Tan Tarn How summarised the effect of what had happened within the arts community in 1994. Tan observed the increasing alarm in the community: "You should have felt the alarm in the arts community, and felt it mounting as in falling-domino-like manner one thing touched off another . . . to the artists, it very much looked like the whole establishment apparatus has fallen on them."[22]

"Rebuttal Is Not Retribution"

The incident that was to cast the longest shadow over the rest of the 1990s was what became known as the Catherine Lim affair. Lim, a well-known local author, had published two commentaries in September and November 1994 in the *Straits Times* on the subject of Goh's government and his style. In the first, Lim had written about how people were yearning for more than just an efficient government that could deliver the goods. The absence of an "affective" dimension in the relationship between Party and people had alienated the people from the leaders. This was not an outright attack on the government. In fact, Lim had taken some pains to cite a new openness, as well as concern for the disadvantaged (and also developing the arts), as evidence that steps were being taken to narrow the divide.[23]

It was Lim's second commentary, on 20 November 1994, that raised the ire of PM Goh and other leaders. Lim observed of the ministerial salaries debate:

It is a chilling thought that in the writing of future history books, the date of the passing of the White Paper will draw a precise line of demarcation separating the old leadership of Singapore, motivated by raw guts, nerve and passion, from the new leadership motivated by the opulence of a lifestyle equal to that of the top company executives in the country.[24]

Lim also made other cutting observations. PM Goh, Lim wrote, was shedding the consultative approach which he had promised, having decided that the older, more authoritarian style of Lee was best suited to face the challenges of the 1990s. In addressing the issue of ministerial pay, Lim observed:

> *To many concerned Singaporeans, the issue is symptomatic of a much larger problem—the growing alienation of the people by the Goh Chok Tong Government. It seems to confirm an increasing fear that the consultative, consensual approach which the Government had promised and by which it had wanted to be distinctively defined is being abandoned in favour of the authoritarian style of its predecessors. Of late, the voice has become sterner, the stand harder.*[25]

At the time of publication of Lim's second commentary, PM Goh was away in New Zealand. SM Lee wrote to PM Goh (still overseas) on 24 November 1994, summing up the mood of the key ministers: they were unanimous in the view that Goh should reply to Lim and assert his authority. The two main points ministers felt should be rebutted were Lim's suggestion that PM Goh was not fully in charge, and also her insinuation that unlike the old guard, the new generation was motivated by pay. In discussing the proposed reply, Lee stressed that Goh could not allow the people to see him as defensive or soft.[26]

Goh concurred. His reply to Catherine Lim came in the form of a 3 December 1994 letter from his press secretary, Chan Heng Wing, published by the press the following day.[27] While the letter bore Chan's name, its main authors were Goh, SM Lee and DPM Lee Hsien Loong. The letter pointed out Goh welcomed diverse views but would not hesitate to rebut fallacious arguments. Chan also addressed the suggestion that it was SM Lee, and not PM Goh, who was really in charge:

> *The Prime Minister does not expect the Senior Minister to undergo a personality change because he is no longer Prime Minister. But he does expect, and has received, loyal support for his decisions, on the few occasions when Senior Minister has disagreed with him.*[28]

The sharp rebuttal was rounded off by a challenge to Lim to enter politics and take responsibility for her views. Speaking to reporters a day later, PM Goh said that Lim had "gone beyond the pale" in implying that Goh had allowed himself to be overwhelmed by his predecessor.[29] Goh also emphasised the point that had been made by his press secretary: "If a person wants to set the agenda for Singapore by commenting regularly on politics, our view has been, and it is my view too, that the person should do this in the political arena."[30]

There followed a private exchange of letters between PM Goh and Lim, which saw Lim (who averred that she had no intention of entering politics) apologising for the distress her articles had caused.[31] Lim stated in her apology that she had the greatest respect for Goh's government. Goh's 13 December 1994 reply (parts of which were published) gave reasons for the tenor of the rebuttal:

> *Had I not sharply refuted you on these points, your article would have undermined respect for me and my office. No one reading your articles would have concluded*

*that you had the greatest respect and regard for my government. Although you
have clarified that you do not intend to enter politics, your article would encourage
others to seek political influence from outside the political arena. I have to set out
the out-of-bounds markers clearly, so that everyone knows the limits of openness
and consultation. They do not include demolishing the respect for and standing of
the Prime Minister and his government by systematic contempt and denigration
in the media.*[32]

A mid-December poll of politicians, professionals and academics conducted by the
Straits Times saw views evenly split on the matter. Many respondents felt that Lim had
been within her rights to pen her commentaries, just as the government had the right
to respond robustly. But many were critical of the stand that those seeking to comment
on politics had to openly enter the political fray.[33] Numerous letters to the press also
posed the same question.[34]

The *Straits Times* had in fact written to PM Goh in advance of its December poll
on the issue, seeking clarifications on the limits of expression and making reference in
its questions to the "trimming back of the Banyan Tree". SM Lee wrote to Goh on 12
December 1994, observing that Goh had himself never used this phrase—it was the
press attempting (Lee felt) to set the agenda. Lee's view was that press coverage of the
issue was muddying the waters, and that a further clarification was necessary in order
to put the issue to rest and to definitively state the government's point of view:

*You should make clear that this is not a matter for a free-for-all run by the
newspapers with the results settled by what the newspapers choose to highlight. The
agenda and the limits are settled by those in the political arena, not academics,
professionals and all and sundry, i.e. those journalists choose to play up.*[35]

A second letter from Press Secretary Chan Heng Wing appeared in the press on 29
December 1994, elaborating on the government's point of view. Chan cited the 1991
election results, noting that Goh's kinder, gentler style had been rebuffed—this was a
sign that people simply wanted a good government that produced results. The larger
concern was that elements in society might be attempting to take advantage of Goh's
"softer" style to engage in a type of political activism, agenda-setting and commentary
that might undermine the government.[36] Chan observed that journalists, writers and
theatre groups had been "pushing back the limits" of Goh's openness by lobbying their
private causes and having "the last word" on political issues, like the US media. If the
government allowed critics and lobbyists to pile on the pressure, it would lose control:
"The result will not be more freedom but confusion, conflict and decline."[37] Chan
noted that Goh had placed Out of Bounds (OB) markers to define the limits, but these
would evolve: indeed, many sensitive issues not aired publicly 10 to 20 years ago were
now being discussed. But, said Chan, "there will always be some limits to openness
and consultation". Chan's letter has been quoted in detail, as (taken together with his 3
December 1994 letter) it gives perhaps the best direct insight into the evolution of PM

Goh's thinking in the aftermath of the 1991 election. Goh had clearly taken on board the advice that while he should not alter his consensual style, he had to show that he could govern firmly and respond to criticism.[38]

What captured public attention was not the lengthy explanations offered for the tough response to Lim and other critics, nor the concerns over the denigration of government, nor even Goh's promise of future flexibility. Rather, it was the suggestion that individuals making criticisms of government would be forced to join a political party. Goh appears to have realised that this was something which the government could not force. When queried on the issue in Parliament on 23 January 1995 by nominated as well as Opposition MPs, Goh did, however, make it clear that those who wanted to set the political agenda would be treated by the government as having entered the political arena:

> You can criticise us, and we would treat you as though you have entered the political arena. If you do not wish to do so, you want to hide in sanctuaries to criticise the Government, to attack the Government, we say, even though you do not want to join a party, we would treat you as though you have entered the political arena. I think that is fair. Because you cannot just criticise without expecting us to reply to you in the same manner which you have attacked us. If you land a blow on our jaw, you must expect a counter-blow on the solar plexus.[39]

Goh also refused to cede ground on the issue of the limits and tenor of debate. It was the government, he said, that would decide on the strength of any rebuttal, and this would vary according to the tone and the motive of the person giving the criticism (which Goh freely acknowledged could be subjective). Intellectuals who wished to participate in political debate need not fear punishment, but "they must expect a rebuttal where we disagree with them. A rebuttal is not a retribution."[40]

George Yeo touched on the subject of citizens taking on politicians as equals in 1995. His message was simple: citizens had to remember their place in society before engaging in political debate. Ministers and MPs could be criticised, but only in a way which "doesn't tear the social fabric".[41] Yeo said a distinction had to be made between the "junior" and "senior" in the debate—only within such a framework could a discussion be held. Yeo's comments are now chiefly remembered for his use of a memorable Hokkien phrase, *boh tua, boh suay*—literally, "no big, no small"—in this context meaning disrespect for authority, which on a broader level was taken to mean that members of the public had to know their place when referring to those in power.

Unsurprisingly, there was a feeling—particularly in civil society and arts circles—by 1994 that "the days of a consultative, consensus-seeking government are over".[42] A key point, repeatedly singled out by commentators, was the vexed question of OB markers. It was undeniable that the undefined parameters of these markers had something of a chilling effect within the entire spectrum of discourse, running from political commentary to the arts. The government line from 1991 right through to the Catherine Lim affair (and beyond) had been consistent: there was the promise of slowly pushing back OB markers, but there was a concomitant refusal to define them and an insistence that the drawing of lines to denote acceptable limits was the government's own prerogative.[43]

Within the Party itself, though, there was the recognition that the longer-term process of opening up, and the acceptance of criticism—even in the political sphere— had to continue. The response to critical commentary against the government after the Catherine Lim affair from actors other than Opposition parties is illustrative. Where criticism was viewed as being of the type that did not fall within the class that denigrated (or undermined) the government or PM Goh himself, more leeway— sometimes considerably more—could be given. Or, the criticism might be ignored entirely. A case in point was a series of observations made by Nominated Member of Parliament (NMP) Walter Woon during his address at a 29 October 1994 dialogue session organised in response to the episode by Young PAP. Woon made several remarks critical of the PAP, noting that the PAP was "fixated" on vote share when it should be attempting to aim for respect and trust.[44] Woon, whose comments attracted no rebuttal from PAP leaders, also commented that the rising demand for an Opposition meant an inevitable slide in the PAP's vote share.

And what of Catherine Lim herself? Despite having to apologise to Goh in 1994, Lim continued to expound her themes of disaffection and alienation between the people and the Party. In a commentary penned in 2000, Lim observed that government–people relations continued to be soured by the issue of ministerial pay, despite people having warmed to the style of PM Goh. Lim also claimed (in comments perhaps as hard-hitting as those she had made in 1994, but less personally directed against PM Goh) that the PAP government's manipulative strategy was of encouraging feedback, then ignoring it. These comments elicited a reasoned rebuttal from the government, but on this occasion there was no suggestion that Lim had overstepped the mark.[45]

It is noteworthy that at exactly the same time (December 1994) as the Catherine Lim affair was being played out, the first "political" civil society group, the Roundtable, was registered. The Roundtable was made up of businessmen, lawyers, journalists and academics. Raymond Lim, a well-regarded economist with a stellar academic record and Rhodes Scholarship to boot, was elected its founding president.[46] At the Roundtable's inaugural press conference on 28 December 1993, Lim commented that the purpose of the new group was to function as an alternative problem-solving centre (and a more independent one than government-linked think tanks such as the Institute of Policy Studies [IPS]), given Singaporeans' penchant to look to the state for solutions to most issues.[47] Lim was careful to avoid giving the impression that the Roundtable was in any way in opposition to the PAP government; nor would the Roundtable become a political party.

The Roundtable was registered in the same month as the Socratic Circle, another group of professionals who had come together to form a non-partisan forum to discuss social and political issues.[48] Its founding members too stressed that the group was not a political party, although some of the ten founding members had been active in student politics and members of the NUS Democratic Socialist Club.[49]

A considerable amount of scrutiny was brought to bear on these two groups before their registration was allowed.[50] The Registry of Societies' (ROS) view was that such groups had to restrict their activities to only their members. The Roundtable had had to change its constitution in order to comply, limiting its activities to members only, while the Socratic Circle had been forced to accede to the ROS' demand that a phrase in its constitution which referred to reaching out to and educating the general populace be removed. The ROS had also refused to allow members of political parties as members or even associate members, as it was felt that this would compromise the neutrality of these bodies.[51]

The Post-1997 Situation: No "Big Bang"

We have already seen how the 1997 general election had been a bruising affair. There has been criticism (not just from the Opposition but also from civil society groups) that the PAP had not played fair during the campaign, and that the manner of its victory had been at odds with the inclusive rhetoric of PM Goh and government leaders. The high ground had to be regained. Something was needed in order to move forward and to refocus national attention on core challenges that the country faced (a theme that was to be employed in the aftermath of all general elections from 1997 onwards). PM Goh tackled the issue in an important set of remarks in Parliament during the debate on the President's Address in June 1997:

> *Affluence and prosperity cannot be the only glue holding us together. If Singaporeans are just economic animals, materialistic with no sense of belonging, they will be like migratory birds, seeking their fortunes in other lands when the season changes. They will have no cause to fight for, no community to live for, no country to defend or die for, only the pragmatic desire to get on and get rich. If it ever comes to this, Singapore will not survive as a sovereign nation.*

> *. . . We need a new vision for Singapore, an ideal, a fresh mindset. We need to move beyond material progress, to a society which places people at its very centre. Singapore 21 is my team's vision for the future of Singapore, a Singapore where people make the difference, where each citizen is valued, a Singapore which is Our Best Home, an ideal home which we all help to build. Singapore 21 is about what the people of Singapore want to make of this country. More than a house, Singapore must be a home. The Government can provide the conditions for security and economic growth. But in the end, it is people who give feeling, a human touch, a sense of pride and achievement, the warmth. So beyond developing physical infrastructure and hardware, we need to develop our social infrastructure and software. . . . We need to go beyond economic and material needs, and reorient society to meet the intellectual, emotional, spiritual, cultural and social needs of our people.[52]*

Goh's speech was a wide-ranging one, covering external economic competition, cohesiveness and social problems in Singapore. His key argument was that it was "heartware", and not individual prosperity, that would bond Singaporeans and help them overcome future challenges. Goh also addressed the issue of civil society, noting that people had to "participate actively and become involved in community and national issues"—this was how they would "build ties among themselves and bond to the country". Goh acknowledged that Singapore's political life had to evolve in the direction of greater participation by the people, but the corollary was that the people had to dispense with the mindset that "only a few leaders at the top" were responsible for solving national problems. The people had instead to shoulder more responsibilities and give more to the country than what they took from it. For its part, the government, Goh conceded, would be prepared on some issues to "take a back seat" and allow some free play to develop.[53]

The theme of unity and coherence as a bulwark against the challenges to come was further developed in PM Goh's 24 August 1997 National Day Rally speech. This was in several respects a landmark speech—perhaps the defining National Day Rally speech that Goh was to deliver in the 1990s. The speech was an attempt to shore up aspects of the compact between government and people. Goh devoted a great deal of this speech to explaining the need for foreign talent and immigrants who could contribute to Singapore, a topic which was already beginning to be discussed openly, to some disquiet. There was also a striking emphasis on the need to relook processes to re-examine fundamentals in all aspects of government and society. Goh noted that failure to update government would mean that "we will find ourselves locked into outdated and irrelevant practices and dogmas. Eventually the system will become arthritic, seize up and collapse. This is what happened to the former Soviet Union after 70 years of Communism. It must never happen to us." Goh used this point as a lead-in to announce the setting up of a new committee, Singapore 21 (S21), which would "identify new ideas to make Singapore the place of choice to live a fulfilling life, to make a good living and raise a happy family".[54]

Goh was clearly drawing inspiration for Singapore 21 not just from his parliamentary speech of 5 June 1997, but also from the PAP manifesto for the 1997 election, "Singapore 21: Make It Our Best Home".[55] In emphasising the need to build social cohesion to face the challenges of the new century to come, Goh was also recycling themes he had touched on on the campaign trail in November and December 1996. This was not the first time that an election manifesto had had a continued afterlife in this way. Vision 1999 from the 1984 election had, as we have seen, directly fed into Agenda for Action of 1987–88.

There were, however, important differences from the situation in the 1980s. In the background, the machinery of government had become more sophisticated in thinking about what the future held—a point that should be considered here. In 1995, the Scenario Planning Office (SPO) had been set up under the Prime Minister's Office (PMO). The first major SPO product, the 1997 National Scenarios, was extremely influential in policymaking circles. As one commentator noted:

> *The 1997 iteration (which had a 20-year perspective) postulated two possible futures: "Hotel Singapore" on the one hand, in which the economic imperative will reign supreme and where the price of commercial success and global cosmopolitanism was paid in terms of increased atomism and a sense of anomie and dislocation. The second scenario, "A Home Divided," painted a future in which the singular national narrative would splinter, giving way to a plethora of irreconcilable stories that are centred on different loci of identities—ethnic, religious, special interests, ideology, all of which potentially challenging [sic] the national identity.*[56]

These scenarios also pointed to the risks of ignoring issues such as the building of social bonds, especially at a time when fissures in society (the divide between the professional elite and the lower-educated, for example) were becoming increasingly apparent.

The ideas generated by ministries during the course of the 1997 Scenarios project, and the developing of a strategic agenda at the national level, also fed into the envisioning and overall strategising of the Singapore 21 exercise. The leadership came to realise that in the face of these putative challenges, there should be a process to send a powerful message that all Singaporeans needed to contribute towards making Singapore a cosmopolitan city and "Best Home".[57]

But how was this to be done? Singapore 21 could not simply be an exhortation to Singaporeans to grasp opportunities and to progress. If by 1997 the myriad challenges facing the nation had become more complex than in the decade before, the populace had become increasingly mature and questioning in outlook too. Civil society—non-existent in the mid-1980s—was also beginning to be a presence.[58] Criticism from organisations (other than Opposition parties) on the Party's dominance over the political landscape, almost unknown in the 1980s, had become more pronounced. The process of bringing various constituencies on board would have to be carefully managed.[59]

An important and early step in post-1997 engagement took place in May 1998, when IPS organised a conference on the state of civil society in Singapore. This conference, "Civil Society: Harnessing State–Society Synergies", was an opportunity for a stocktaking of sorts to be done on how far civil society had come since BG (Res) George Yeo's landmark 1991 "banyan tree" speech. The conference is now chiefly remembered for BG Yeo's keynote speech—his first major speech on the subject of civil society since 1991. Yeo stated that he thought the "monopoly power of the state" would become weaker. But this did not mean that emergent civil society would be given untrammelled freedom. Yeo called on civil society groups to act in the national interest, or what he called "the Singapore idea".[60] But the general implication was that more space would be given to civil society groups, even as these groups were expected to support and work with the government.[61] Summing up discussions at the press conference, one of the co-chairmen of the conference, Ambassador-at-Large Prof. Tommy Koh, characterised the Goh Chok Tong era as the era of the "Tembusu Tree"—the canopy was now smaller than the banyan tree of the Lee Kuan Yew era, allowing trees below to grow.[62]

It was also apparent that there was still a considerable amount of scepticism about the government's engagement efforts, and that this had to be tackled before the S21 vision could be taken forward. Conference discussants highlighted the usual issues, including OB markers and the climate of fear that held people back from speaking out. As the *Straits Times* noted in its survey of the papers presented at the conference, "an undergrowth of frustration, suspicion, scepticism and distrust still exists".[63] This was perhaps unsurprising, given the setbacks faced by civil society groups, government rebukes of individuals like Catherine Lim, and measures taken against artistic expression detailed earlier in this chapter.[64] At stake was the question of whether the government's intention was really to promote its own concept of civil society all the while maintaining ultimate control.[65] This distrust naturally extended to the government's Singapore 21 initiative, with the issue being how closely the government intended to manage the feedback process.[66]

Scepticism (together with a dose of apathy) was not confined to civil society. A survey conducted by the Feedback Unit in March and April 1998 (at the request of the S21 Subcommittee looking into issues relating to consultation) found that while 80 per cent of the 1,000-plus respondents were confident that the government could run the country, only 22 per cent agreed that the government consulted people on its policies. Forty-one per cent of respondents took the view that there was no freedom of speech in Singapore. In addition, only 28 per cent of respondents agreed with the view that the government was able to accept criticism. Tellingly, better-educated and younger Singaporeans tended to feel less satisfied (across the range of responses) and less able to connect with the government.[67]

Clearly, there was work to be done by the S21 Committee. The main committee comprised ten members of parliament, who in turn co-chaired five subject committees.[68] The 66 members of these subcommittees came from all spheres. What made S21 different from previous editions (such as The Next Lap or Agenda for Action) was how much further down the reach of the subcommittees went. Singapore's future, and the coming challenges, were discussed with approximately 6,000 citizens across the entire spectrum of society, through over 80 forums in a year-long process.[69]

The Singapore 21 report was made up chiefly of the five subject reports submitted to the committee, representing the distillation by the subcommittees of key themes, or rallying calls, to help the country face future challenges.[70] The recommendations embedded within the S21 subject committee reports were not radical. Some ground that was by now well-worn was covered, including a call for OB markers in public debate to be spelt out more clearly. Other recommendations were laudable but unremarkable—especially those calling for improving social cohesion and strengthening communities and families (including help for the aged).[71] One PAP MP, Dr Ong Chit Chung, was even moved to remark during the parliamentary debate on the report that "no one in his right mind would oppose S21. No one would want to oppose the clear-cut, wholesome, motherhood statements. To oppose would be like turning against what is good."[72] What was important to the government, however, was not so much outcome but process. Noteworthy was the sheer extent of inclusiveness, and the pains taken to make the effort a ground-up exercise, with public input making up a significant proportion of the finished product.[73] In unveiling the Singapore 21 vision on 24 April 1999, PM Goh took pains to stress that this was not an "official" vision that the government had come up with, but one that had in effect been drafted by the people, a people who now wanted emotional and social fulfilment. The vision of the people, Goh noted, went beyond economic and material needs to make Singapore a home.[74]

S21 was the antecessor of future consultation exercises of the 2000s. Like later efforts, an important internal calculation was that the S21 exercise should function as an effort to educate Singaporeans and to inject a healthy dose of reality into their aspirations.[75] An example was the emphasis on mobilising the people and active citizenry, which was an important aspect of the S21 process. The chairman of the main S21 committee, Teo Chee Hean, said that of the five main S21 themes, the one which required the most work was in fact, "Active citizens", which he gave the lowest attainment level (2 out of 10).[76] Teo said that only a small number of Singaporeans volunteered, compared to other countries.[77] As part of its work, the S21 committee conducted a survey to measure citizen involvement. Eighty-five per cent of the respondents said that they would prefer not to be directly involved in the community. Only 15 per cent said they would like to be involved in making decisions or in initiating change.[78] It is unsurprising, therefore, that when Parliament endorsed the S21 report on 6 May 1999, government leaders emphasised that the parliamentary debate was not the end of the process, but the beginning of a considerable amount of work to be done to achieve the vision.[79]

There is also the question of what the government had learnt from the various discussions in the S21 process, and from the exercise as a whole. There was the overwhelming sense that the people wanted a bigger role in national discussions. They wanted to be consulted before policies were implemented, and wanted the sense that this input mattered rather than disappearing into a black box. In 1998, academic and NMP Dr Lee Tsao Yuan (in one of her perceptive observations in Parliament) pointed to a "disequilibrium situation", noting that demand for public consultation had outpaced the supply of feedback channels in the 1990s. She noted that most Singaporeans now had their basic needs met, leading them to look to "higher order needs", such as a greater sense of participation and belonging. In addition, globalisation, and access to information and the Internet, meant that Singaporeans were better informed and had views on various issues.[80] This analysis was not a new one. In March 1997, when Dr John Chen (minister of state for communications and national development) took over from Dr Ow Chin Hock as chairman of the Feedback Supervisory Unit, he had commented to the *Straits Times*, "We are seeing a society that is becoming more complex and information-driven. New things, new policies keep coming up, usually spurred by technology. So it is good to get as many people as possible to contribute ideas."[81]

It was clear that the government would face mounting frustration if it did not act to improve existing consultative channels, cast a wider feedback net, and allow more space for discussion. In June 1997, Parliament passed the constitutional amendment bill increasing the maximum number of nominated MPs from six to nine.[82] In the same month changes were effected also in the Feedback Unit, which formed 17 new groups comprising approximately 500 members in all. Each group tackled a hot-button issue, such as the cost of living, housing, or education. The groups were meant to be autonomous, free to choose the issues they wanted to debate.[83] The subgroups themselves adopted an innovative, decentralised meeting format: they were free to convene anywhere, at a frequency of their own choosing. In a significant first, two of the 17 groups were overseas ones, in Beijing and London.[84] The unit, which as early as 1995 had already provided a channel to allow people to submit Internet feedback, also stepped up its virtual presence in response to an increasing volume of online feedback.[85]

These were additional signs that the government was prepared to be more flexible in managing the feedback loop and in broadening space for discussion. Just as select individuals who were well known in civil society (and who had not always seen eye to eye with the PAP) had been involved in or even co-chaired S21 subject committees, similar individuals were invited to head the Feedback Unit's groups. These included individuals from the Roundtable: Zulkifli Baharudin (also a nominated MP), who headed the Media Feedback group; and Viswa Sadasivan, who headed the Political Matters group. The suggestions made, while not radical, did occasionally push the envelope. In 1998, for example, the Political Matters group made a call for a more independent press and for more balanced coverage of parliamentary sessions.[86]

The developments in the Feedback Unit certainly meant discussions that were more freewheeling in nature from 1997 onwards. Content was not, of course, completely left to individual whim. Refinements from 1998 saw the feedback groups working with relevant ministries, which suggested themes that the groups could discuss.[87] In June 1998, when the Feedback Unit held its first conference to bring together its various groups, there was a conscious alignment of the papers presented by the groups with the "five dilemmas" of S21, with many of the feedback groups themselves spending most of 1998–99 seeking public feedback on the S21 themes.[88]

The leadership was becoming concerned with how the "active citizenship" component had bred the expectation of significant political liberalisation. There seemed in the aftermath of S21 to be the growing idea not just that the government would consult people, but that this consultation would mean policy changes should be debated (especially in Parliament) before being made.[89] The second, related idea was that civil society should be allowed to grow and truly complement the state. As NMP Simon Tay put it during the parliamentary debate on the S21 report on 6 May 1999:

> *Our desired society is not one in which Government is strong and people are weak. Nor in calling for an active people sector, is it a desire to see Government weak and the people strong. The two are not always and necessarily in conflict. Our desired society lies in the growth of an active people sector, participating in community and national issues, as an independent entity. When I say "independent", I do not mean one that is determined to oppose, nor do I mean one that is beholden to obey. I mean, one that is free to agree and cooperate, or to disagree and make counter arguments. With such an independence, we have to see that the two can come together and truly cooperate.*[90]

"Independence" suggested to PAP leaders a separate power centre; it went beyond what they were comfortable with. It was necessary, from the government's perspective, to manage and tone down expectations. This can be seen in the careful management of the feedback process and also the circumspect tending of the S21 initiative; indeed, by the conclusion of the latter, the government had become almost downbeat. In their interventions in Parliament during the S21 debate PM Goh and SM Lee preferred to downplay expectations, making it clear that S21 was a continuing vision. Goh said that a "strong dose of realism" was necessary and that he had to put the debate "in perspective". Harking back to aspects of Singapore's past (in particular racial riots and communal tensions), Goh said that while Singaporeans should strive to create a Singaporean "tribe", this would not be done through "nice-sounding slogans and motherhood statements".[91] Both Goh and Lee stressed that achieving the S21 vision would take years, with Lee adding for good measure (in a direct rebuttal of Simon Tay) that it was not likely that civil society would "throw up another leadership".[92]

Interest groups, or even NMPs, would have limited ability to dictate the course of politics and governance—not far from the premise originally put forward by PM Goh in his 1994 rebuttal to Catherine Lim. Real political power lay in the hands of the party in government. Goh touched on this theme on several occasions in the immediate aftermath of the S21 report being endorsed. Speaking during the debate on the president's address at the opening of Parliament on 13 October 1999, Goh made it clear that while he was in favour of consultation, he would not be conceding power to any group: "While Singaporeans will have more space for political debate, it does not mean that the Government is vacating the arena. Anyone who wants a policy changed, or to set the national agenda, must expect a debate with the Government." Those without a hidden agenda need not fear reprisals, he added, but those intending to undermine the government would expect "an extremely robust" response.[93]

∗∗∗

It is worth pausing here to consider a separate issue that has occasioned much comment: President Ong Teng Cheong's relationship with the government in the 1990s, which came to wider public attention in 1999, at the point of Ong stepping down.

Ong, an architect by training, had entered politics in 1972 when fielded as the PAP candidate for Kim Keat. By 1978 he was minister for communications and three years later was appointed minister for labour. In 1981 he was also elected PAP chairman. He was appointed minister without portfolio and took over the position of NTUC secretary-general from Lim Chee Onn in 1983. A core member of the second-generation leadership, he was also appointed 2DPM after the 1984 election.

Ong was highly regarded by Lee Kuan Yew, who saw in him a fair, patient and decisive mind.[94] One aspect of this decisiveness was an independent mind that could on occasion mean breaking with the usual collegial decision-making found within the Cabinet. In 1986 Ong, in his capacity as NTUC secretary-general, sanctioned a brief strike—the first in Singapore in eight years—involving workers of an American company, with the root cause being the management's anti-union practices and unfair dismissals of workers. Ong, convinced that the workers were in the right, sanctioned the strike without keeping his Cabinet colleagues informed, incurring the displeasure of Lee Kuan Yew and at least one other member of Cabinet (Dr Tony Tan, trade and industry minister).[95]

PM Lee first sounded out Ong to see whether he could take over the presidency following the resignation of Devan Nair in 1985.[96] Ong demurred then, but became Singapore's first elected president in September 1993 after prevailing over former Accountant-General Chua Kim Yeow.

Ong's attitude going into the job was to discharge his duty—which he saw as being the custodian of Singapore's reserves—to the letter.[97] But trying over the course of his presidency to get to grips with the various issues that would in his view have enabled him to do this was not simple. Frustration spilled over at a 16 July 1999 press conference called by Ong to announce that he would not stand for re-election as president. At the press conference, Ong described a "long list" of problems he had encountered in trying to protect past reserves. These included the definition of reserves and what physical assets the government had.[98] Ong also criticised the attitude of public servants his office had had to deal with: he felt that they should feel it their duty to cooperate with the president to protect past reserves. Clearly he felt that some had not had this attitude: "I suspect that they consider the Elected President a nuisance—checking on them or looking over their shoulder." Ong's "unpleasant encounters" included one involving a statutory board where he had to withhold approval of its budget.[99]

The criticism that public servants and government bodies (amongst other points raised) had not been cooperating with the President's Office necessitated a reply. This came in the form of parliamentary statements on 17 August by Minister for Finance Dr Richard Hu and PM Goh.[100] The government's factual record when it came to some instances that Ong recollected showed that where lack of cooperation had been cited, assistance and cooperation had in fact been given. Other issues had arisen due to differences of opinion on the accounting of the government's physical assets, and yet others could be put down to difficulties that would naturally arise in the new relationship between the elected president and the government. On several of these issues that had been made out as contentious, accommodation with the government had in fact been reached.[101] Goh was pained and saddened, as well as puzzled, that some of these clarifications were needed and that these issues had been dragged out into the open, especially when Ong was very recently bereaved. Ong's wife, First Lady Ong Siew May, had passed away of cancer on 30 July 1999.

One issue PM Goh had to tackle squarely was that of President Ong's health. Ong had been suffering from lymphoma for several years, but at the 16 July press conference he made it a point to say at the outset that his health was good. However, on the basis of Ong's most recent medical reports (Goh revealed this evidently reluctantly when faced with persistent questioning, including from PAP MPs), which showed that Ong's cancer had worsened to become high-grade lymphoma, Cabinet unanimously decided that it could not support Ong's re-election if he decided to once again stand.[102] Whether or not to seek re-election, Ong had made known to

Goh, was solely Ong's own decision, but Goh's account naturally led to questions (which Goh declined to be drawn on) as to whether Ong had raised the various issues at his press conference in pique, given the stand taken by Cabinet on any potential re-election bid.

Even in disagreement, the points made by Ong in 1999 and the replies by government had been characterised by correctness—and the appearance of it. Goh had been punctilious in his dealings with Ong and had shown (though not perhaps to Ong's satisfaction) that government servants had not been disrespectful to Ong personally nor to the office of the president. Ong's conduct had been impeccable, and there were no personal failings on his part.[103] In Parliament, Goh paid tribute to Ong's "significant contributions", noting that he had remained independent notwithstanding his past links; Goh added that he had helped iron out ambiguities in the powers of the new office.[104]

Goh had had to be especially firm on one additional point in Parliament. Following Ong's press conference, there had been talk on the ground as well as by academic commentators on the role of the president, talk which in Goh's view had given rise to confusion concerning the president's role.[105] Goh made it clear that the president exercised limited custodial powers (over the reserves, and the power to block certain public appointments), not executive powers: "Singapore does not have an executive President, because Parliament did not create one."[106]

MPs wanted clarification on whether the elected president was after all a check and balance against the government. SM Lee, the originator of the elected presidency concept, was clear on this point: the president was no counterfoil to the government; those who assumed otherwise were wrong.[107] With the passage of time, Lee was to be even more direct—he felt that Ong had tried to "carve out an active role for the president" because he wanted a "powerful presidency".[108]

Lee had been responsible for advancing Ong's political career in the 1970s and 1980s, and he knew well Ong's various qualities, as noted above. One of Ong's other qualities that stood out was a streak of what could be described as a combination of rectitude and probity. This came into play when it came to how Ong viewed his role as president. Those who worked closely with him observed that Ong viewed it as his job to test out the government—almost as if it had gone bad.[109]

It is doubtful that Ong had any sort of hidden agenda, but it is likely that he felt it was his duty to perform a certain role as president that was fixed in his mind. The envisioning of his role, if it was to be fulfilled, required more powers than what the government was comfortable with. Speaking after his presidency in 2000, Ong (who was to pass away of cancer in February 2002) tersely observed (in giving his take that he had felt stonewalled by the civil service), "I had a job to do, whether the government liked it or not."[110]

Ong's presidency came to an end not as either he or his many friends in government would have wanted—marked by disagreements with government and at a point of his own life where he had experienced deep personal grief. Perhaps there was at this time additional regret, too, from Ong's point of view, that he was not supported by ministers who had been his political comrades, and who could not support his standing for the presidency again if he had been inclined to. There was also regret (that was not to abate even after the passage of years) on the part of PM Goh: perhaps things could have been different if he had reached out directly to Ong to resolve disagreements, rather than allowing the public service to deal with the issues Ong faced while president.[111]

ٔ؎؎؎

We now return to the issue of managing of space for political debate. Wholesale change was not on the cards, but the creation of small, managed arenas was. In early 1999 there had been a raft of commentaries and letters (some from the Roundtable) calling for free speech venues to be set up.[112] Some of the calls had also extended to arguments for a relaxation of the Public Entertainments Act, which required that individuals speaking in public first apply for a permit. These calls coincided with the period when SDP Chairman Dr Chee Soon Juan had given public talks without a permit. Public opinion was not generally in favour of Chee, but there had been some questioning as to whether existing laws on speech and assembly were too strict, and whether there should at least be areas of Singapore sectioned off as free speech venues.[113] SM Lee, commenting on Chee's actions in an interview with the *New York Times* columnist William Safire in January 1999, had himself mooted the possibility of Singapore introducing its own version of London's Hyde Park Corner.[114] PM Goh, however, had made known in interviews in 1999 that he did not think Singapore was ready for untrammelled freedom of speech—people might choose to make incendiary speeches on religion, for example.[115] Goh's initial thinking at the time (shared by most of his colleagues) was that setting up a Speakers' Corner then would be seen as conceding to Chee, who might choose to claim victory in his fight to give Singaporeans more political space.[116] But Goh announced he had changed his mind in March 2000, a mere six months after he had discounted the idea.[117] SM Lee had privately made it known to Goh and other ministers that in his view the idea was worth trying.[118] Lee's input informed a wider reconsideration of the issue, although it was not the clincher. The internal discussion within the leadership focused on how after the S21 process, an increasingly educated people expected more leeway to be active in discussing issues of the day. A key consideration was the belief that allowing a free speech venue would be a highly visible signal of government preparedness to walk the talk of an active citizenry. At the same time, however, the leadership did not feel that allowing such a venue should be presented as a great breakthrough in terms of government liberalisation. There were doubts—which proved to be valid—as to whether such a venue would lead to any significant contribution to the national debate, given that one-way oratory would not allow for thorough and serious debate of political issues. The final consensus was to proceed, bearing in mind that allowing a Speakers' Corner was emblematic rather than substantive—useful more than anything else as a sign that Singapore did not have an oppressive system.[119]

The leadership also appears to have been persuaded by the fact that the small arena of Hong Lim Park (close to the Central Business District) chosen as the venue for

Speakers' Corner could be managed—by location as well as by law. On 10 December 2000, Think Centre (an independent research centre set up in July 1999 by the political activist James Gomez) and Open Singapore Centre (an NGO set up in March 1999 by J.B. Jeyaretnam and Dr Chee Soon Juan) organised an event at Speakers' Corner to mark International Human Rights Day, a rally that was deemed to have been illegal assembly. The organisers were given a warning by the police, with the government making it clear that Speakers' Corner was subject to Singapore's laws on illegal assembly.[120] In the aftermath, Think Centre and Open Singapore Centre were gazetted as political associations under the Political Donations Act and were barred from receiving foreign funding.[121] The Act, introduced in February 2001, prohibited donations to political parties and civil organisations deemed to be political associations whose activities wholly or mainly related to politics in Singapore. Civil society leaders wrote to the government expressing fears that the Act could retard the growth of civil society in Singapore.[122] The government, however, remained unmoved, simply stating that the bill would not stunt civil society, and that civil society groups could not be left out of the bill lest they be made use of by foreign powers.[123]

The government's legislative moves were held by observers to have contributed to a "chilling effect" on civil society, which had held out hopes of political change following the setting up of Speakers' Corner and pledges of a more consensual approach in the wake of the S21 process.[124] But in the view of PM Goh and his colleagues there had been progress, albeit of the incremental type. In an interview in March 2000, Goh had noted that the government would consult more, but that there would be "no Big Bang".[125] The message was repeated for good measure in Goh's National Day Rally speech on 20 August 2001. Goh noted that the government had allowed freer expression of divergent political views, citing Speakers' Corner and the formation of the Roundtable and Think Centre as examples. But if the government thought that what they said would hurt Singapore, it would rebut them—forcefully, if necessary. According to Goh, this should not be seen as the government smothering free speech. Some people wanted even greater freedom, Goh acknowledged, but he preferred "to ease up slowly rather than open up with a big bang". The Soviet Union had collapsed with a big bang after its leader Mikhail Gorbachev introduced political openness through glasnost: "We should, therefore, pump the air into the political balloon slowly. I don't intend to change my name to 'Goh Ba Chev'!"[126]

The issue of Speakers' Corner shows clearly how any opening up had to be on the government's own terms. It also shows the government's response to organisations with a more overtly confrontational stance that began emerging around the turn of the millennium. Distinctions were drawn between civil society organisations that were either neutral or contributed positively in some fashion, and organisations that were antagonistic to the government or aligned with Opposition parties. Think Centre, for example, was singled out by PM Goh as being openly critical of the government in its coverage of issues, with Goh taking care to distinguish it from the Roundtable, which the government did not see as an opponent.[127] From the latter half of the 1990s, the government had to differentiate its responses to activism, on the one hand, and dissent. With activism, there appears to have evolved (certainly after the S21 process) a more calibrated approach, one that embodied an increased sense of willingness to allow greater space. For example, a short-lived but influential network of individuals affiliated to various civil society organisations, known as The Working Committee, operated without government interference from 1998 to 1999. Perhaps, as some of its members mused, the price of taking action against such groups was "higher than in the past".[128] This was, in fact, very close to what government leaders were beginning to state in public. DPM Lee Hsien Loong, speaking at a Singapore 21 Forum on 16 June 2000, noted that in dealing with challenges that came from outside the Opposition parties, the government had to make a judgement call. Too harsh a response would end up alienating the people and losing support.[129]

During the Singapore 21 Forum, DPM Lee also commented on the progress that had been made from the government's point of view. The OB markers were now extremely wide, and even sensitive issues could be discussed openly and rationally. All this, he said, represented an enormous step forward. In giving examples, Lee alluded to the 1999–2000 controversy surrounding what the Malay-Muslim community felt was the government's attempt to phase out madrasah education, in the context of the wider move towards nationwide compulsory education. The Singapore Islamic Scholars and Religious Teachers Association (PERGAS) took the lead in confronting the government on the issue, with tension defused only by PM Goh's personal intervention and assurances that madrasah students would not be forced into the secular school system.[130]

The Association of Muslim Professionals (AMP) went in some ways further than PERGAS. It used the madrasah issue to restate its position that there should be a collective leadership for the Malay community which went beyond what PAP Malay MPs could offer. In suggesting that PAP Malay MPs had been found wanting, the AMP had certainly been encouraged by the openness of the Goh era, and by S21's call for active citizenship. But the government response on this occasion was more aggressive, going head to head with the AMP and facing it down. At the AMP's Second National Convention on 5 November 2000, PM Goh bluntly told the AMP leadership that the organisation was straying into the political arena with its collective leadership proposal, which in the view of the government had the effect of undermining the standing and role of PAP MPs.[131]

✣✣✣

Ultimately, the PAP government retained the commanding heights. Civil society activists hoping for freewheeling debates of the type seen in the West, where NGOs could raise any issue and be almost co-equal with the government, remained disappointed with the government's exhortations to be "constructive" or to contribute within a consensual framework of nation-building while observing OB markers.[132] It can be observed, however, that the nature of the response to increased activism in the post-S21 period depended on a number of factors—not least, the origins and intent of activism. The government was quite prepared to be flexible (and even cede ground to some extent) on certain issues.[133] But there remained deeply entrenched suspicions of the type of action that used pressure tactics in an effort to secure political change, questioned the PAP's standing and fitness to lead, or was seen to be aligned with the Opposition cause.[134] It also fell to the government to decide what was a civil society group and a political association. It would not allow one disguised as the other. The situation in and around 2001, when some individuals from civil society resigned from their organisations to join political parties, suited the Party and in a sense vindicated its approach. Those who wanted to effect political change could not do so from the periphery: they had to join the fray.[135] But to civil society activists, the glass remained half full. Singapore Internet Community's (Sintercom's) Dr Tan Chong Kee characterised civil society in 2001 as being in a cycle "of formation and dissolution, activism and caution, confidence and fear".[136]

S21, and the efforts by civil society actors to carve more space that paralleled it, represented only beginnings. They did not achieve the full sum of what their originators had intended. There would be further S21-like iterations by the government in the new millennium. Civil society, for its part, would continue to play a role in the transformation of Singapore society, beyond the snapshot that has been provided above for the late 1990s and early 2000s, and beyond the parameters that had been set by the government. This transformation would in turn be fuelled by developments in the virtual world. Neither the first Internet pioneers like Tan Chong Kee, nor the government itself, could have foreseen the role that the Internet and new media would play in the shaping of post-millennial Singapore. We turn now to these developments, and to the government's response.

Aspects of Control: The New Media

The government was by 1993–94 beginning to grapple with a multiplicity of control and regulatory issues in broadcasting and IT, especially in the area of converging telecommunications. There was the recognition that Singapore could be a global hub only if it permitted some of these technologies. The difficulty was deciding how to gear up for impending challenges, which included managing technologies and platforms that had been unknown just a few years before.[137] These included the impending launch of multichannel cable TV in mid-1995, and also the more thorny issue of regulation of the Internet in Singapore, which by 1994 was beginning to attract users in ever-increasing numbers.[138]

The passage of the Singapore Broadcasting Authority Bill through Parliament in August 1994 marked an important point in the government's attempt to grapple with these issues. The major thrusts of the bill were provisions for the privatisation of the Singapore Broadcasting Corporation, and for the establishing of the Singapore Broadcasting Authority (SBA) as a statutory board to regulate and at the same time promote the broadcasting industry. The bill also included some other sweeping provisions, such as broadening the definition of broadcasting to include programme transmission to all or part of the public regardless of means used.[139] While BG George Yeo in his Second Reading Speech on the bill on 26 August 1994 stated that "computer information services" would not be regulated, as the government did not want to hinder the growth of these networks, he rejected the argument that the government should abandon attempts at regulation simply because it had become more difficult to control the flow of information.[140] Yeo returned to the issue of regulation and control during the budget debates in March 1995. Referring to the potential negative influences of cable TV and the Internet, Yeo observed that Singapore had no choice but to accept changes that the information revolution had brought about. But he was clear that some controls (such as laws on libel and sedition) would, and could, be successfully applied to the Internet realm.[141] Yeo went further in suggesting that other measures would be considered:

> No, [can we say] "we don't want CableVision, we don't want Internet, we don't want regionalisation, we don't encourage foreigners in our midst"? We cannot. We want at the same time for the windows to be opened and, at the same time, for the flies to be gotten rid of. I do not think we can get rid of all the flies. But I think if we apply ourselves and if we are assiduous in our efforts, and if we have many fly swatters at hand, I think there are many things we can do to keep the flies off our plates. That we can do.[142]

The calculations were soon to evolve, even as the Internet did. There was the increasing realisation that the Internet would become an important part of the mass media. Political and religious groups worldwide were beginning to use it to propagate their causes, and foreign newspapers were publishing on the World Wide Web. It was therefore all the more important for the government to retain some semblance of control. A basic framework to regulate the mass media in cyberspace was needed. The chosen approach was to have a broad regulation with the provision for future tightening. Once that was in place, the internal calculation of the leadership was that this framework could be tightened, loosened and refined over time in the same way the regulations governing newspapers had evolved.[143] The leadership wanted to avoid giving the public the impression of a repressive approach, with the decision taken at an early stage that political parties would be allowed on the Internet. The rationale was to avoid accusations that the government was attempting to exert overarching control, and to avoid moves that might drive political websites onto the less easily regulated parts of the Internet.[144]

The government on 5 March 1996 announced a regulatory framework for the Internet. This would block easy access to undesirable content, including material that undermined political stability and religious harmony in Singapore. Local Internet service operators and content providers would be licensed by the SBA through a "class licence" mechanism, effectively bringing them under the government regulatory ambit without their having to apply. Individual users acting in their personal capacity would be excluded from the licensing, but content providers—including political parties, and those discussing matters of religion or political affairs—would have to register separately with the SBA.[145] Giving details, BG George Yeo attempted to downplay the import of these moves, likening the regulations to "a kind of an anti-pollution measure in cyberspace", designed to bring a certain responsibility and accountability to online discussions.[146] Yeo stressed that regulations were not aimed at curbing growth of the Internet, nor were they meant to curb anti-PAP discussion.

Viewed through a wider lens, government was unwilling to run the risk of the political process degenerating into a free-for-all through the use of new media—or the new use of old media. In 1996 the SDP had applied for a licence to sell a political videotape. The government promptly announced a ban on such media. In explaining the government's position, BG George Yeo explained that politics had to be a "rational discussion and a good exchange of ideas". Yeo said that such videos would sensationalise issues, not allow for effective rebuttal of errors, and could lead to politics turning into a contest between "advertising agencies".[147] In February 1998 Parliament passed changes to the Films Act banning the making, distribution and exhibition of political films. BG George Yeo, as well as the PAP MPs who spoke in favour of the amendments, equated the use of such material with the debasement of the political process, as such films could be used to distort issues and sway voters.[148]

Opposition parties, of course, saw all these moves in a very different light. The regulations were seen (in the case of the Class Licence Scheme) as a form of control that "may help buttress the PAP's total domination of Singapore's politics for a few more years" and would "act to the detriment of the welfare of Singapore as a whole" (SDP Secretary-General Dr Chee Soon Juan) or as "a violation of democracy" (National Solidarity Party Secretary-General Yip Yew Weng).[149] The view in the Singaporean quarters of cyberspace was similarly negative, particularly when the SBA moved to operationalise the Class Licence Scheme. Discussions on the main Singapore-related newsgroup, soc.culture.singapore, and postings on the Sintercom feedback page, were generally critical of the regulations, with calls for a petition to be sent to the SBA in protest.[150] The detailed guidelines which accompanied the Class Licence Scheme came in for particularly harsh online judgement. These seemed to many to spell out, vaguely (almost too vaguely) OB markers online. Undesirable material included "contents which tend to bring the government into hatred or contempt, or which excite disaffection against the government" and "contents which undermine the public confidence in the administration of justice". There was therefore a concern, voiced by journalists, Opposition politicians, and letter-writers to the *Straits Times* Forum, that all this was less a move to protect the interests of the nation than it was a ploy to prevent criticism of the PAP government online.[151] This was especially given that it was now clearer which of the existing websites would need to register (upon notification by SBA). The websites in question were not just those run by political parties (the YP and National Solidarity Party websites) but also those operated by the Socratic Circle and Sintercom.[152]

It is worth pausing for a moment here to note that the PAP had itself been an early mover into cyberspace. The Young PAP's Internet Committee was operating online by late 1994.[153] Unlike later PAP Internet teams, the first incarnation in the 1990s operated almost in a guerrilla fashion, taking informal guidance from YP Chief George Yeo, but out of the arc of central Party control.[154] A key preoccupation of the committee members was to correct distortions and misrepresentations of Singapore and the Party online.[155] Writing in the Party organ *Petir*, Harold Fock, the chairman of the Young PAP Internet Committee, observed:

> *Unlike magazines and newspapers where the editor has control over the "forum" page, the s.c.s [soc.culture.singapore] newsgroup has no such moderator. He can write anything, criticise any policy and insult anyone. In that sense, Internet is like a road full of debris and uncontrolled traffic, users can ride it with the best or worst of intentions. Presently, there are quite a few individuals who spread falsehoods about Singapore and the PAP. Other destructive behaviour include [sic] impersonating our President and PAP leaders. We need to respond decisively, convincingly and stylishly. We have a duty to combat misinformation and make a stand for the PAP.[156]*

Speaking in February 1995, BG George Yeo observed, "if we do nothing about it [misrepresentations and distorted information] and leave cyberspace to all those with axes to grind, there will only be ourselves to blame." Yeo also noted the inevitability of political debates being conducted on the Internet: "We must have our battalions there all ready to engage in that debate."[157] One area that received particular attention from the Young PAP Internet Committee was the discussion group soc.culture.singapore. This corner of cyberspace was an early hive of Singapore-related discussion, with thousands of messages posted between 1994 and 1995. Most of the postings were civil. From time to time there were, however, heated debates (some amounting to flame wars) on a gamut of issues. These ranged from the Flor Contemplacion case and PM Goh's trip to Williams College and the subsequent parliamentary censure of SDP Secretary-General Dr Chee Soon Juan over his conduct there, to the Michael Fay affair and the death penalty for drug trafficking.[158]

On soc.culture.singapore, individual postings could be critical of the government, but the overall tone of the newsgroup cannot be said to have been virulently anti-PAP. There was, however, a measure of resentment at the Young PAP's presence online and the interventions by the Young PAP team. Interviewed by the *Straits Times*, Harold Fock gave some sense of how difficult the job was, alluding to the "flaming" that the Young PAP members intervening in discussions were subject to.[159]

One receives the impression that the sheer impossibility of positively influencing (still less controlling) discourse on the Internet during those heady, freewheeling years of 1994–95 played a part in the government's moves to regulate the Internet in Singapore through the Class Licence provisions introduced in July 1996. It is noteworthy, however, that in 1996 some leeway was given to websites or discussion groups which fell in the no man's land between general and political commentary. No attempt seems to have been made to bring soc.culture.singapore under the Class Licence provisions.[160] Sintercom, which had been in operation since October 1994, was able to escape registration (after prolonged negotiations with the authorities), although this was to prove temporary.[161]

There were additional considerations. Even at this stage, the leadership was concerned about the impact that online political discussions might have on electoral politics. The initial trigger for MITA's push to regulate political discussion on the Internet appears to have been the launch of the Socratic Circle's Internet homepage in 1995, and its subsequent invitation to the public to contribute views on the coming general election on the website.[162] This was seen by the authorities as a circumvention of the Socratic Circle's constitution, which prohibited non-members from participating in the group's activities (which, as we have seen, had been a condition imposed on the Socratic Circle at the time of its registration in 1994). The ROS instructed the group to keep political discussions online to within its membership.

In the event, online commentary did not feature prominently during the 1997 general election.[163] Only from the 2001 general election was the Internet to be more than a negligible presence.[164] Before the polls, in August 2001, amendments to the Parliamentary Elections Act (PEA) were introduced that had the effect of regulating political discussion on the Internet during the campaign period. Despite attempts to make this appear a step in the right direction—for the first time, the government was explicitly allowing a measure of Internet campaigning by political parties—many were against the new regulations. Opposition MPs were upset by what they saw as an unnecessarily restrictive "positive list"—a list of items of permitted types of election advertising on the Internet. Any item not on the positive list was disallowed. There was also concern over the broad definition of "election advertising" in the PEA (Amendment) Bill which, it seemed to some, would catch out individuals expressing their personal views in a private capacity over media such as email.[165] Even some PAP MPs asked for confirmation that the intention was not to stifle political comment.[166] As the *Straits Times* was moved to note in an editorial, it would have been more enabling—and liberating—to state what was expressly prohibited rather than what was permitted.[167]

The amendments meant that non-party websites were prohibited from carrying election advertising during the campaigning period. In addition, such websites were, shortly before the PEA (Amendment) Bill passed in Parliament, asked to register, and gazetted as "non-party political websites". The gazetted sites included Sintercom (in what amounted to the end of its 1996 reprieve) and the political think tank Think Centre. Tan Chong Kee shut down Sintercom in protest in August 2001. Also in protest, Think Centre closed down its online discussion group, Speakers' Corner Online, citing its inability to control what people would post, and its reluctance to start censoring messages.[168]

Minister for Information and the Arts Lee Yock Suan gave a sense of how the PAP viewed the issue in his address to Parliament during the Second Reading of the PEA (Amendment) Bill on 13 August 2001:

> *[A] free-for-all Internet campaigning environment without rules is not advisable. The Internet is a double-edged sword. Whilst it facilitates discussion and communication, the seriousness of political debates may be cluttered by noise, mischief or frivolities during the election period. Worse, the anonymity in the Internet opens a door for surreptitious elements to mislead, distract and confuse the public. On the Internet, once a false story or rumour is started,*

it is like water that has been spilt. It is almost impossible to remedy matters, especially in the limited period of an election campaign. The Government has always maintained that politics should be based on factual and objective presentation of issues, and reasoned debate. Regulations are therefore necessary to protect the integrity of our electoral process, and guide responsible use of the Internet during the elections.[169]

While Party leaders had, post-S21, been keen to acknowledge that public opinion and the civil society movement had to be increasingly engaged with, there was clearly the feeling that strict markers should be placed over online political discourse during the election period. A reading of the evidence suggests that this desire for control was premised on the belief held by the leadership that an election campaign had to be kept to a straight fight between parties. The growing incursions made by civil society into the online space, through websites such as Sintercom or even discussion corners such as that hosted by Think Centre, might introduce unpredictable outcomes into this hitherto stable process, especially given the growing realisation that the Internet had huge potential as a medium to communicate, convince and influence opinion.

⁓ഃഃ⁓

The *Straits Times* interviewed BG (NS) George Yeo in May 1999, when he relinquished the information and the arts (MITA) portfolio. As the *Straits Times* observed, MITA had done a great deal in the arts and cultural scenes, but Yeo in some respects had been more hardline than people expected, one who could wield (as Yeo himself acknowledged) both carrot and stick. He had defended the ban on satellite dishes and tabled legislation to ban political videos. In addition, there had been no liberalisation of laws governing the press.[170]

Yeo would have been the first to acknowledge, however, that media policy was not decided by the MITA minister alone. On sensitive issues, all Cabinet members gave their views, with the prime minister ultimately making the decision on key issues. During the 1990s, when Singapore was changing in so many ways, the voice of Senior Minister (SM) Lee Kuan Yew was particularly influential in internal deliberations. Interviewed by the author, Yeo observed that during the 1990s Lee closely followed issues connected with the media, not simply to understand new trends but to see whether the younger generation of leaders were politically sensitive enough to understand the limits of opening up.[171]

In September 1995 Lee was interviewed by Nathan Gardels of the Global Viewpoint Network. Towards the end of the interview, Lee gave his view on how Singapore had to react to the quickening pace of developments in technology and the media. His thinking is an appropriate summing-up of the PAP philosophy when it came to change at this time:

Gardels: America's most prominent futurist said to me "I used to think of Lee Kuan Yew as a man of the future, now I think of him as a man of the past. You can't try to control information flows in this day and age." Bill Gates has said Singapore wants to have its cake and eat it too. They want to be wired into cyberspace, but keep control over the information that affects their local culture. But no place is an island anymore, not even Singapore. If you get the Internet, you will get Madonna's lewd lyrics and Bill Safire calling you a dictator. Are you a man of the past, or a man of the future? Can you have your cake and eat it too?

Lee: I accept two fundamental truths: First, in an age when technology is changing so fast, if we don't change fast we'll be left behind and become irrelevant. So we have to change—fast.

Second, how you nurture the children of the next generation has not changed, whatever the state of technology. From small tribes, to clans, to nations, the father-mother-son-daughter relationship has not changed. If children lose respect for their elders and disregard the sanctity of the family, the whole society will be imperilled and will disintegrate. There is no substitute for parental love, no substitute for good neighbourliness, no substitute for authority in those who have to govern. If the media is always putting down and pulling down the leaders, if they act on the basis that no leader deserves to be taken at face value but must be demolished by impugning his motives and character, and that no one knows better than media pundits, then you will have confusion and eventually disintegration. Their attacks may make good news copy and increase sales, but will make it difficult for the society to work.

Good governance, even today, requires a balance between competing claims by upholding fundamental truths, that there is right and wrong, good and evil, that government must bring good to the largest number of people and not allow lobbies and interest groups to triumph because of superior funding or organisation. We cannot abandon society to whatever the media or Internet sends our way, good or bad. If everyone gets pornography on a satellite dish the size of a saucer, then the governments of the world have to do something about it, or we will destroy our young and with it human civilisation.

Without maintaining a rational balance between competing interests, no society has a future.[172]

The leadership of the PAP was thus determined to maintain what it saw as the basic integrity of the political process, even in the face of rapid technological developments from the mid-1990s onwards. Speaking to cadres at the 3 December 2000 Party conference, DPM BG Lee Hsien Loong commented that the government had to manage debate "actively and skilfully, guide the debate without stifling it, allow free play of ideas without losing the initiative or letting wrong ideas take root".[173] Attempts to manage the debate (particularly in the face of technological developments) did not end at the millennium—there were to be further moves, as we shall see, in the lead-up to the 2006 general election. These will be dealt with in the next chapter. But one observation should be made here. Seen with hindsight, the 1990s was the last decade when the government was able to definitively control the discourse and set OB markers. Up till the turn of the millennium, Party leaders could make calculations on how much to control (and how much leeway to give). But with the times, the people and technology all changing, control increasingly had its limits. By the second half of the decade of the 2000s, technology and the aspirations of the people would edge ahead of efforts to regulate the new media. From then on limits could be set, but they could just as often be tested and breached.

The Pangs of Transformation

By 1998–99, there was the palpable sense in the air that the transformation envisaged earlier in the decade was well under way, one that would see Singapore become a world-class knowledge economy, a magnet for talent, a creative and artistic hub, and, as PM Goh noted in his 1999 National Day Rally speech, a home even as the nation embraced globalisation.[174] A crucial plank here was the reshaping of the economy, with an increasing emphasis towards liberalisation and less government intervention in key sectors. Key markers included the liberalisation of the telecommunications market in 2000, and the shake-up of the banking sector.[175]

This transformation was taking place at a testing time, with the Asian Financial Crisis having had a profound effect on many regional economies. Singapore, however, had emerged comparatively unscathed, with government leaders being clear (both in their public pronouncements and in internal Party discourse) that this crisis presented a window of opportunity to prepare to face the challenges of the new millennium. Speaking to cadres at the 24 January 1999 Party conference, BG Lee, who was the PAP's first assistant secretary-general, summed up the thinking of the leadership when he noted that Singapore should use the crisis to transcend the limitations of the region and build capabilities. Lee noted that Singapore could "turn adversity to advantage" as it was "not preoccupied with pressing immediate problems" and could focus resources and attention on longer-term issues.[176]

Planning for the future could be done only if Singapore continued to have sound economic fundamentals, and if discipline and competitiveness were maintained in the midst of regional turmoil. Tellingly, the theme for the 11 January 1998 Party convention was "Staying Competitive". Three teams made up of PAP activists presented reports on this issue at the convention, after studying the issue for four months. The reports were titled "Continuing to Get Our Economic Fundamentals Right", "Upgrading Human Resources" and "Enhancing Social Cohesion".[177] The first needs no elaboration. But the latter two themes were also to figure prominently in speeches by government leaders around the millennium and should be considered here. In his 2000 National Day Rally speech, PM Goh touched on what was needed in order for Singapore to stay ahead of the competition. The nation and its people had to be more versatile and adaptive, ready even to "think and act like revolutionaries".[178] But Goh acknowledged that some painful adjustments would be needed in order to make the jump to a knowledge economy. There were many who would not benefit from globalisation to the same extent as those with higher skill and education levels. A key prong of the government response to this was increasing resources being put into skills development, retraining and lifelong learning.[179] This would hopefully lead to fewer workers being caught in the low-skill, low-wage trap.

It was also increasingly apparent that inequality was rising, and that at the bottom, numbers of people were finding it harder to make ends meet. In February 2001, data from the Department of Statistics (DOS) 2000 census (the first since 1990) was released. The advance release, titled "A Decade of Progress", lent support to the idea of a Singapore that had prospered over the previous ten years. Median household income from work grew by an average of 4.6 per cent over this period.[180] However, the overall census data also revealed trends that were less positive both for their impact on the less well-off and in terms of what they portended overall. As *Straits Times* Assistant News Editor Chua Mui Hoong observed, the DOS figures showed that the top 10 per cent of households earned 36 times what the bottom 10 per cent did, up from 16 times in 1990. The trend accelerated as time passed, with the top 10 per cent experiencing an 8.8 per cent rise in income from 1999 to 2000 alone. Those in the bottom 20 per cent saw their incomes drop during this period.[181]

These difficulties, experienced not just by the poor but by many in the middle classes, were exacerbated by the economic downturns of 1998 (linked to the Asian Financial Crisis) and 2001 (which, pre-9/11, had the dot.com bust as a key underlying factor). The government made it clear that while it would help those in need, particularly the indigent, the forces of globalisation should be embraced, not resisted. In his 23 February 2001 Budget statement, Finance Minister Dr Richard Hu gave a succinct exposition of the government's perspective:

> While we make these adjustments to anticipate and embrace global trends and changes, we must continue to be mindful of our local context: those who can run faster should pave the way for the rest; however, those who may be unwittingly left behind must not be left with no help. The government realises that realignments of our economy have often meant displacement of jobs, or even disappearance of industries, but for every door closed, we have opened many others, leading to greater opportunities. We understand that it is not easy for workers to continually learn new skills and work in a new environment, or for enterprises to quickly change direction and pursue business prospects in new areas. It takes a great deal of courage to embrace changes, and take the steps to walk through new doors of opportunity. The transition often entails adjustments which are sometimes painful. But we want to help. We want to lessen the hardship for those who find it difficult to adapt to the changes. But change we must. And at the end of the day, we have to ensure that every Singaporean has a place in the Singapore of the new millennium.[182]

The plain fact was that some would succeed in the new, knowledge-based economy, while there were others who would lag behind.[183] In the aftermath of the release of the 2000 census data, Irene Ng, a senior political correspondent with the *Straits Times* (who would in 2001 successfully contest the general election on the PAP ticket), was moved to comment that it was disturbing how "this country seems set to change from a bastion of the middle class in the last decade to a gulf of inequality in this decade". Ng also wondered what would happen if the trend was left unchecked: "The danger goes beyond weakening the ties that bind this society. If some groups do not feel like they are reaping the benefits of economic growth but feel, instead, that they are disproportionately burdened by the costs of economic growth, they will support policies that ultimately sacrifice economic growth."[184]

The dangers of fissures developing in society had already been seen by PAP leaders. The concern with cohesion was noticeable in messaging from key leaders as the new millennium approached. PM Goh, in his 1999 National Day Rally speech, had made a distinction between "cosmopolitans", English-speaking professional types who had skills that were marketable worldwide, and "heartlanders"—those who had to make a living in Singapore, particularly in blue-collar professions. Goh noted that Singapore society would fall apart if these two groups ceased to identify with each other.[185] Official surveys at the time suggested that the issue highlighted by PM Goh could indeed portend larger divisions within society.[186]

A balancing act was at work—preserving principles of self-reliance and hard work, but also giving the sense to those in the lower socio-economic rungs that the government could temper ideology with some flexibility and was prepared to help. PM Goh had made it a point to state in his 2000 National Day Rally speech that "there would be no social cohesion if the lower-income perceive that society is not willing to give them a helping hand to improve their lives. Or they fall so far down that they cannot afford even basic amenities." The National Day Rally speech was used also to announce a slew of off-budget measures to help the needy and the elderly. These included MediShield insurance coverage for Singaporeans 61 and above (with the government footing the bill for basic MediShield premiums for two years), enhancements to the Eldercare Fund (a healthcare endowment scheme for the elderly), and Central Provident Fund (CPF) top-ups (above and beyond those that had been announced earlier in the year by the finance minister), with those earning less than $1,200 getting the greatest amount.[187]

It was not handouts but redistribution (especially to the most needy) that underpinned the government's philosophy in alleviating hardship.[188] An example was the New Singapore Share scheme, introduced by Goh in his 2001 National Day Rally speech. New Singapore Shares functioned essentially as bonds, providing a guaranteed minimum 3 per cent return per year, with extra dividends declared in the years that saw positive GDP growth. The allotment of shares to Singaporeans depended on housing and income type: the least well-off adult citizens received the largest amount of shares, half of which could immediately be exchanged for cash. The redistributive aspects of government assistance were visible also in other measures introduced as part of the 2001 budget. The existing scheme of household utilities rebates was extended, with $350 given to households living in one- to three-room Housing and Development Board (HDB) flats, $300 to households living in four-room flats, and $250 (the least) to households in five-room flats. Rebates on HDB service and conservancy charges and rentals granted over past years to Singaporeans living in rented and owner-occupied HDB flats were also extended and increased, with households living in one-room flats receiving the largest rebate.[189]

To some, these measures would never be enough. Singapore People's Party (SPP) leader Chiam See Tong had, for example, called on the government to draw on past reserves to tide Singapore through the difficult period. PM Goh's biting response was that this would amount to slowly "killing the goose" that gave Singapore the golden eggs.[190] Opposition parties were to use the plight of the needy as a key part of their platform in the 2001 general election.[191] But the PAP leadership was convinced that it had gone about things the right way and had shown that it would help those in need. In January 2001, PM Goh (who had been posed questions by *Straits Times* readers) was asked which policy he felt the most proud of. His response was revealing:

> *I would say giving a human, compassionate face to the PAP Government. The PAP has always been caring for poorer people, for the disabled, for the less fortunate, but the emphasis has always been also for economic growth, on hard decision. I thought I was able to give it a more human touch, to give people a sense that we care for you, not just in terms of statistics or in terms of the programmes which people can tap, but the sense that we do care for you.[192]*

The 2001 General Election

As the millennium neared, there was the marked sense in internal Party discourse that the PAP government had pursued the correct course in every major area; its prudence and circumspection had meant that Singapore emerged from the regional crisis intact (and indeed enhanced).[193] Self-belief, which had been somewhat lacking in the uncertain years after 1991 when the Opposition appeared to have gained ground, had now returned. In 1999, interviewed for the *Petir* special issue marking the 45th anniversary of the founding of the PAP, PM Goh could say:

> *The PAP has over the last 45 years built itself up as the only institution that is capable of holding the country together. . . . PAP is not just a Party that dominates the political scene and wins elections and governs. The values of the Party have become national values, and these national values are in turn attributes which help the country to be held together.[194]*

The Party's confidence and successes were viewed as assets that should be showcased openly, to demonstrate ability and competence in advance of the next election. The CEC took the unusual step of releasing to the press its report presented at the December 2000 Party conference. This document, which served as an open report card to cadres, was very positive when it came to the Party's achievements. These included building cohesion and introducing measures to combat the effects of the regional crisis. Also touched on were measures to help those in need (including the CPF and MediSave top-ups for the less well-off and senior citizens). But in a clear message that the people should continue to support the Party, which had delivered stability in uncertain times, the CEC report also sounded a warning of continued uncertainty in the medium term for the region.[195] The warnings were more prescient than the Party leadership realised.

Even close to the beginning of September 2001, there were some signs that the government was planning for a 2002 general election (polls being required by August 2002). But the 9/11 attacks changed all this. Speaking to the media the day that polls were announced for 3 November 2001, PM Goh was clear that the attacks had persuaded him to bring forward the date: he wanted to get the polls out of the way and then deal with the "big problems" of likely recession and job losses.[196] The general election may to Goh have been something to be gone through before dealing with pressing issues, but the election itself was undeniably becoming one with big-picture characteristics. As the *Straits Times* noted, the character of the polls had been changed completely by events, with the election being "a casualty of the war on terrorism. . . . When the world is on such a knife-edge, when there is so much uncertainty about the future, and so much danger of the region undergoing another catastrophic upheaval, minds will begin to concentrate on the important and the urgent."[197]

The widely felt need for certainty, security and stability was also heavily in evidence in the Party manifesto, unveiled on 19 October 2001 as "A People United: Secure Future, Better Life". The manifesto emphasised unity and resilience, positing that neither the economic crisis nor ethnic and religious issues (which had been thrown into sharp relief by 9/11) could divide Singaporeans.[198] Featuring most prominently were undertakings in terms of enhancing citizens' well-being and economic security in the face of grave crisis. The PAP promised, if returned, to introduce a new social compact that would see the country's wealth shared through programmes such as New Singapore Shares and the upgrading of housing estates. There would also be a new economic strategy to upgrade and revitalise the economy.[199] PM Goh, in a sombre open letter to the people, which accompanied the PAP manifesto, stated that he understood people's concerns about their jobs and future. He asked voters to place their trust in the PAP, which would take Singapore safely through the prolonged economic downturn.[200] In a sense, the PAP was reaching deep down into its own playbook in assuring that the Party would tide the people over in tough economic circumstances. SM Lee made a comparison with the 1968 election, when the Party had won with 87 per cent of the votes in the seven contested seats. That year, Lee recalled, "everything looked bleak". The economy was not doing well, Singapore faced confrontation with Indonesia, and the British had announced the withdrawal of their forces from Singapore: "It looked like Singapore would not survive."[201]

The press noted that it was something of a gamble going into an election when the economic prognosis was one of almost unmitigated gloom. The government estimate for fourth-quarter performance in 2001 was –7 per cent, with overall economic growth for the year forecast to be –2.2 per cent. The sense of pessimism was seen also in polls and dialogue sessions conducted by the Feedback Unit just prior to the election being called. Nearly 60 per cent of those polled feared losing their livelihoods. The difficulties facing jobseekers, the costs of living and business, and other problems facing small and medium enterprises were also brought up.[202] But what was significant in these opinion polls—which should be considered a pre-election testing of the waters—was the overwhelming sense that the people had confidence in the government, with nine of every ten taking the view that the government would lead the nation out of the crisis.

The government, for its part, was careful to show that this feedback was taken seriously, with the Feedback Unit chief, Dr John Chen, making it clear that the views given had played a role in the shaping of the second off-budget package for 2001. This huge package, worth $11.3 billion, was announced by DPM Lee Hsien Loong on 12 October 2001, mere days before the election was called. It had something for everyone, with (besides the New Singapore Shares scheme, already announced earlier by PM Goh) tax rebates, schemes to assist businesses, skills training for workers, and various forms of help for the unemployed and lower-income workers in the form of an economic downturn relief scheme, which saw aid being disbursed through Citizens' Consultative Committees.[203]

State of the Party

The 2001 election was the PAP's largest renewal exercise since 1984 (see Appendix One, Table 4.1). Twenty-three MPs retired, and 25 new candidates were introduced (a further two, Heng Chee How and Andy Gan, had been unsuccessful candidates in 1997). To the surprise of many, there were no SAF Scholars in the slate, and only two of the 25 were from the public sector.[204] The PAP leadership had been at pains to stress well in advance of the polls that it had put together an exceptionally diverse slate of new candidates.[205] There were three single women, where there had been none in 1997.[206] There was also one tudung-wearing Malay-Muslim woman (Halimah Yacob, the first woman candidate from the Malay community since 1959) and the first Indian woman candidate since 1965 (Indranee Rajah). A more flexible thinking in selection was at work.[207]

It was clear that the search for candidates over the previous four years had been a major exercise. The Party had realised that an infusion of new talent was needed, partly to connect with younger voters (a point which will be considered later) and especially for political renewal at the top.[208] The media made much of the group which came to be known as the "Super Seven", individuals who seemed to hold the promise of being more than backbenchers, and who it was commonly thought—correctly, as it turned out—would be elevated to junior ministerial positions after the election. It was the biggest infusion of new talent at the top since the 1984 election (which saw five new MPs subsequently becoming full ministers). Those elevated immediately after the 2001 election were Tharman Shanmugaratnam (managing director, Monetary Authority of Singapore), Khaw Boon Wan (permanent secretary, Ministry of Trade and Industry), Raymond Lim (managing director, Temasek Holdings), Dr Vivian Balakrishnan

(CEO, Singapore General Hospital), Dr Ng Eng Hen (a cancer specialist in private practice), Dr Balaji Sadasivan (a neurosurgeon in private practice), and Cedric Foo (a senior executive at Singapore Airlines).[209] What was especially striking was that most of those elevated did not come from the usual recruiting grounds of the upper echelons of the civil service. Two of these individuals—Balakrishnan and Lim (founding president of the Roundtable)—were known to have been critical of the government. A third, Tharman, had been linked in the past with left-wing student politics in the UK and had been called in for questioning during the 1987 Marxist Conspiracy. He had also previously fallen foul of the law—convicted and fined in 1994 in a case relating to a breach of the Official Secrets Act.[210]

State of the Opposition

Parliament was dissolved on 18 October 2001, just one day after the Electoral Boundaries Review Committee submitted its report to the Prime Minister's Office. Polling Day was 3 November 2001, nine days (the legal minimum campaign time) after Nomination Day on 25 October 2001. The Opposition, put on the back foot, cried foul, claiming that inadequate preparation time had been given.[211] Areas that the Opposition had spent time cultivating had as a result of the recommendations of the electoral boundaries now been redrawn (or, in some cases, vanished altogether).[212] In addition, the scrapping of four-member Group Representation Constituencies (GRCs) meant that Opposition parties now had to muster credible candidates to contest in five- or six-member GRCs.[213] There were now nine five-member GRCs and five six-member GRCs. GRCs accounted for almost 90 per cent of all elected seats.

Opposition complaints of underhand tactics extended much further than this. Already hampered in fundraising by the 2000 introduction of the Political Donations Act (which limited anonymous donations to political parties to not more than $5,000), the Opposition also chafed at the raising of the election deposit to $13,000, meaning that $65,000 was needed to contest a five-man GRC, with the sum forfeited if the team did not poll at least one-eighth of the votes in the GRC. The Opposition view was that the high sum circumscribed the right of people to participate in politics.[214]

Unsurprisingly, the PAP was returned to power on Nomination Day, 25 October 2001, unopposed in 55 of the 84 seats—the largest number of walkovers since 1968. The Opposition was able to put up a contest in just four GRCs, the fewest since 1988.[215]

The Opposition parties themselves were in the process of transition and reorganisation. In June 2001, several of them (the SPP, National Solidarity Party, Singapore Malay National Organisation and Singapore Justice Party) registered under one banner as the Singapore Democratic Alliance (SDA), designed to be a united front in the coming general election. The SDA's prime architect and founding chairman, the SPP's Chiam See Tong, was given sweeping—some said dictatorial—powers under the SDA's constitution.[216] This went some way to explaining why the WP and SDP declined to be part of the SDA, although the public explanation proffered by the respective leaders, Low Thia Khiang and Dr Chee Soon Juan, was a preference for focusing on building the strength of their own parties.[217]

Given the personal history between Chiam and Dr Chee, the SDP's decision to stay out of Chiam's alliance was to be expected. The calculations of the new WP secretary-general, Low Thia Khiang, were less personal and perhaps guided more by the imperative of ensuring that the WP took its first steps of the post-Jeyaretnam era without distractions. Low had been chosen by cadres as the WP secretary-general in May 2001, replacing Jeyaretnam, who chose not to put his name forward for the position. Jeyaretnam subsequently resigned from the WP in October 2001.[218] There had been friction between Jeyaretnam and some members of the WP, including Low, partly on account of what Jeyaretnam saw as a lack of support from the WP in his attempts to hold a fundraising drive to pay off debts arising from his legal troubles.[219] Declared a bankrupt in February 2001, Jeyaretnam lost his non-constituency MP (NCMP) seat in July that year, ruling him out of the electoral contest.[220]

Mindful of how the PAP had successfully neutralised its by-election strategy by fighting "local elections" in 1997, the Opposition chose to play a slightly different card: that of the spectre of PAP dominance. One-party rule, Opposition voices noted in campaigning, was dangerous. SDA leader Chiam See Tong was especially keen to emphasise to voters that they should deny the PAP a two-thirds majority in Parliament. In an emotional rally at Jalan Besar on 2 November 2001, the day before polling, Chiam called for a stronger check on the PAP government and said that there would be "total darkness for Singapore" if the PAP were to obtain a clean sweep.[221] This theme of checks and balances was also taken up by WP leader Low Thia Khiang. Low (in a theme which resonated, and which he was to steadily develop over coming elections) asserted that the PAP could not be a check on itself. Only the Opposition could fulfil this role: "Don't give the PAP a blank cheque. You have to decide, do it now or you run the risk of not having the opposition to provide the check and balance. The decision is yours."[222]

The key Opposition players—the SDA, WP and SDP—also chose in their own ways to focus on those who had been left out of economic success, or who faced hard times during the recession. The WP made much of "the New Poor": the unemployed, people in low-paying jobs, and other disadvantaged groups including the disabled, the infirm and the elderly. Beyond the catchy slogan, however, the WP was light on concrete measures to help these groups of people.[223]

The SDP's plan, on the other hand, went some way beyond a mere outline. Its economic plan for Singapore, unveiled by Dr Chee Soon Juan on 23 October 2001, consisted of three major planks. First, it wanted a minimum wage introduced. Second, the SDP proposed positive job discrimination in favour of Singaporeans, with jobs to be made available to foreigners only if a suitable Singaporean could not be found. Foreigners should also be retrenched first in the event of layoffs. Finally, the SDP proposed the introduction of retrenchment entitlements, suggesting that the government compensate retrenched workers the full amount of the last drawn salary for six months.[224] PAP leaders were quick to state that the SDP economic plan was flawed and would, if implemented, have ruinous outcomes.[225] Still, the coherence of several facets of the SDP platform came through, with even the press noting that it had at least came up with alternative economic proposals.[226]

One single, catastrophic incident utterly extinguished any hopes of positive gains that the SDP might have entertained. On 28 October 2001, while on the campaign trail at Hong Kah West hawker centre in Jurong East, Dr Chee was interviewed by media, holding forth on the subject of the government's reluctance to help local workers but seeming willingness to remit money overseas for various purposes. His particular bugbear (for which he was lecturing reporters on their failure to report) was Singapore's rescue package ($17 billion, but not lent in the end) to Indonesia during the Asian Financial Crisis. Spotting PM Goh a short distance away, Chee, already somewhat agitated, proceeded to approach him, verbally haranguing him on the issue. Chee repeated the attack against Goh at an election rally at Nee Soon Central the same evening, broadening it to include SM Lee as well. Goh and Lee took legal action, with their lawyers stating that Chee had made the libellous allegation that the loan was made to Indonesia without the knowledge of Parliament and the public—that Goh and Lee had in effect misled both. Chee offered an initial apology for the offence to PM Goh. But he failed to offer compensation and subsequently withdrew his apology, which led to his being sued again. In 2005 the High Court would order Chee to pay damages to Goh and Lee. Chee's inability to pay led to his bankruptcy.

Dr Chee's baffling behaviour defies easy explanation. It is possible that his personal history with PM Goh, and his experiences prior to 2001, played a part. After a sojourn in Australia following the 1997 general election, Chee had on his return been giving public talks in 1998–99 without a permit. Charged in court, he stated that he was within his constitutional rights. He refused to pay the fine and went to jail. Some commentators observed that Chee may have been trying to play "the politics of martyrdom".[227] If so, it was a miscalculation. The people were not ready for the politics of martyrdom. There was some sense, supported by press surveys at the time, of public interest in some of the issues raised by Chee, even though he was not seen as too credible a figure.[228] But Chee's impetuosity meant that his issues, and the SDP's economic plan, had become irrelevant at a stroke. The majority of the people— save diehard Opposition supporters—would not even consider the party's platform and ideas if they were not convinced that the candidate was a serious figure. It was a major calamity for Chee personally, and for the SDP's electoral chances, which he had effectively torpedoed.[229]

The Result

> But why won't the opposition stand to gain from an election in a recession? Because of two quintessentially Singaporean traits: they are pragmatic, and they are kiasu. When it comes to the crunch, at a time when their jobs and incomes are at stake, they will vote with their hearts and minds in their pockets.
>
> —*Business Times*, 26 October 2001[230]

The victory when it came was a landslide. The PAP secured all but two of the 27 contested seats, with 75.3 per cent of the valid votes. This was the PAP's third-highest return from the general elections it had contested, after the 86.7 per cent showing in 1968 and 77.7 per cent in 1980. In Potong Pasir, Chiam See Tong's vote share dipped to 52.43 per cent (from 55.15 per cent in 1997), with him polling 8,107 votes to Sitoh Yih Pin's 7,356—a win by only 751 votes. This was Chiam's poorest performance since he became an MP. In Hougang, Low Thia Khiang's vote share also dipped—to 54.98 per cent (12,070 votes)—against the PAP's Eric Low (9,882 votes), a drop from 58.02 per cent in 1997.

The PAP also easily brushed aside the challenges from the SDA and SPP in the four contested GRCs. In these contests, the PAP teams garnered on average 76.83 per cent, a 10.23 percentage point improvement over the 66.6 per cent average in GRCs in the 1997 polls. The best-performing Opposition GRC performance came from the SDA team in Tampines, but even here the SDA was able to take just 26.66 per cent of the vote. In Jalan Besar GRC, ground the SDP had been cultivating for the previous two years, the PAP team (consisting of Manpower Minister Lee Boon Yang, Dr Lily Neo, Dr Yaacob Ibrahim, Loh Meng See and Heng Chee How) took 74.49 per cent of the vote, improving on its 1997 margin by nearly seven percentage points. It won 68,309 of the valid votes against the SDA's 23,391. And, in a victory which must have been sweet if not unexpected, the PAP team in Jurong (NTUC chief and Minister without Portfolio Lim Boon Heng, Tharman Shanmugaratnam, Halimah Yacob, Yu-Foo Yee Shoon and Dr Ong Chit Chung) won against the SDP team (Chee Soon Juan, his sister Chee Siok Chin, Gandhi Ambalam, Mohamed Isa Abdul Aziz and Vincent Yeo) with 79.75 per cent of the vote. The 20.25 per cent polled by Chee and his team was far worse than his 34.86 per cent (albeit standing alone in MacPherson, an SMC) in 1997.

The overwhelming nature of the victory belies the fact that there were isolated hotspots. In Nee Soon East SMC, Senior Minister of State for Law and Home Affairs Assoc. Prof. Ho Peng Kee won with 73.68 per cent of the vote, defeating Dr Poh Lee Guan, the assistant secretary-general of the Workers' Party. Dr Poh, a training consultant, had family links to the area. His linguistic skills, including a mastery of Hokkien (a facility Ho did not possess), were out in full force during the campaign.[231] It was not language, however, but temple politics on which the campaign almost turned. PAP election post-mortems had warned over the years that temple and Seventh Moon groups should be treated carefully, as these were influential and opinion multipliers during elections.[232] On this occasion, which was Associate Prof. Ho's first contested election since his entry into politics in 1991, earlier warnings were not remembered. During the campaign period, organisers of the Hungry Ghost Festival alleged that they had been asked for donations by grassroots leaders when applying for permits to hold celebrations in the seventh lunar month. Organisers charged that certain grassroots figures had delayed approval of permits and also blocked access to the MP until these donations (which were sometimes given voluntarily by organisers, after the festival) were made.[233] The situation was defused only when SM Lee, on hearing of the complaints, personally met the organisers on 1 November 2001.[234] This helped to smooth matters and swung the odds back to the PAP, after the bookies had made it nearly even running between the two candidates earlier in the campaign.[235] After the rumblings had been quelled, Lee referred enigmatically to "subterranean forces at work, a reality in every society". What was not revealed at the time, but which perhaps goes some way to explaining why higher-level intervention was needed, was that the PAP had received ground intelligence from its activists suggesting that elements from the Workers' Party, and possibly Dr Poh Lee Guan himself, may have had connections to some of the temple groups in question.[236]

The time and attention paid by the PAP to the campaign in Nee Soon East gives us some inkling as to the PAP's evolving threat perception of Low Thia Khiang and the Workers' Party. The PAP had by 2001 come to accept that Hougang would take far longer to win back than Potong Pasir, with PM Goh even stating during the campaign that Low Thia Khiang as the incumbent would beat Eric Low. Potong Pasir, on the other hand, was likened to a tree whose ripening fruit was there for the plucking.[237] After the election, Goh revealed that Eric Low and Sitoh Yih Pin had been sent to Hougang and Potong Pasir in order to "block" Opposition forces. Goh said that if people sensed that Hougang and Potong Pasir would be won by the PAP, Opposition forces would move to other wards and create fresh support there. Goh's reasoning, which he was happy to share publicly, was also that the PAP felt it necessary to give the Opposition hope—so there would be no need to go elsewhere to create new Opposition strongholds.[238] Whether all this was political smoke and mirrors on the part of Goh, or whether it had an element of post-facto rationalisation, is difficult to tell. But it is worth considering these points together with another nugget that Goh threw in: he subsequently revealed that he had made it a point to praise the SDA candidate Steve Chia (he "tried to speak sensibly" and was "more like a PAP candidate"), because Goh preferred Steve Chia as an NCMP to the WP's Dr Poh Lee Guan. Goh said his fear was that Poh as an NCMP would join forces with Low Thia Khiang and create an "opposition enclave" in the north.[239] This shows that although the WP ran a small campaign in 2001, the PAP saw Low Thia Khiang as entrenched enough to have wider ambitions over the longer term. This was to be proved correct.

The upgrading carrot had also failed to shift Low Thia Khiang and Chiam See Tong, although the PAP had attempted to refine its 1997 tactics. PM Goh promised on the campaign trail that even if Hougang and Potong Pasir could not be won, upgrading would be considered for individual precincts within these constituencies, which had seen over 50 per cent (or even 45 per cent) votes for the PAP.[240] This was tempting—if double-edged—bait, but the voters in Opposition-held wards refused to succumb en masse. This must partly be put down to the track record of the incumbents. By common consent, Low Thia Khiang and Chiam See Tong had done well in maintaining their estates, given the limited resources available to them. Earlier PAP predictions that Hougang and Potong Pasir would turn into slums had been proven wrong. Property values in these constituencies had also not been greatly affected by the fact that the estates were maintained by Opposition-run town councils.[241] In the end, both Chiam See Tong and Low Thia Khiang suffered some loss of votes over the 1997 result, but they prevailed. The PAP threats of denial of upgrading, and the withholding of services traditionally dispensed from the Party branch (to prevent constituents from getting the "best of both worlds", as we have seen), all had failed to have the desired effect. On upgrading, the PAP had been fought to a stalemate. Although the issue would feature again in the 2006 election, the beginnings of the decline of the upgrading carrot as an effective tool should be traced to 2001.

The Party's success in defusing some of the tensions in its relationship with the Malay-Muslim community should also be considered. Within some quarters of the community, issues concerning madrasah education, the wearing of the tudung, and government disagreements with PERGAS and the AMP still rankled.[242] But PAP leaders were to make it known after the campaign that they were in no doubt the community had voted overwhelmingly for the Party.[243] Several factors played a part. Following the AMP's failed collective leadership proposal in 2000, PAP Malay MPs had stepped up and embarked on a series of moves with the clear design of showing that there was no need for an alternative Malay leadership. The MPs pushed initiatives that would lead to the betterment of the community, particularly its less-well-off members.[244] More attempts were also made by the MPs to engage the Malay ground through dialogues. These were complemented by face-to-face sessions involving the most senior leaders within the Party—in particular, SM Lee. These frank discussions touched on the AMP's collective leadership proposal, the role of the Malays in the SAF, and the pace of integration of the Malay community into the mainstream. Meetings like this did not lead to decisive breakthroughs, but they did serve to an extent to bridge the gap of understanding and perception.[245]

The nature of the response from the government to anxieties within the Malay-Muslim community following 9/11 was also a plus. The terror attacks had put the community in the spotlight; it felt exposed and increasingly misunderstood. Malay-Muslim PAP MPs, past and present, took leading roles in condemning terrorism and distancing the Malay community from such acts.[246] They featured in dialogues with the Malay ground and were prominent in cross-community attempts to bridge the interracial and inter-religious divide.[247] During the campaign, Malay-Muslim MPs helped out in SMCs (or in GRC divisions with a high concentration of Malay voters), especially where the PAP candidate was from another race.[248] All these efforts paid off. Just as it had done with the electorate as a whole, the PAP had marked success in making itself out to be the Malay community's best bet.[249]

The final factor was the quality of the four new Malay PAP candidates—Halimah Yacob, Ahmad Khalis, Dr Maliki Osman and Zainudin Nordin. PAP leaders made it a point to state on the campaign trail that able Malays were coming forward to join the PAP, and that the four selected were the equal of other PAP MPs. This showed that Malays could succeed in a meritocracy.[250] It also helped (as the PAP post-mortem was to note) that among the new Malay candidates were individuals who had credentials that might appeal to the more conservative elements in the Malay-Muslim community.[251]

The Aftermath

The PAP had known for some time that a handsome victory was in the offing. As far back as the 3 December 2000 Party conference, PM Goh had been confident enough to state plainly that the Opposition posed little threat—it had too few new faces, and the "old jaded opposition figures" were still there.[252] But no one concerned—the public, the media, the Opposition, nor even the PAP—had foreseen a victory of such crushing proportions in the 2001 general election. The margin, however, was not something on which the PAP leadership chose to dwell overmuch, with the Party's post-election deliberations marked by heavy realism and scant exultation. What was present was the sense of getting on with the business of governance in a testing time. For PM Goh personally, the result was a mandate to proceed with his timetable for political renewal. In the customary early morning post-election press conference, held in the early hours of 4 November 2001, Goh made it known that his top priority was to have a smooth transition to the ministerial team of the future by the next general election.[253]

There was also the recognition that a victory of the order of what had been achieved in 2001 would not happen again. PM Goh said at the Party convention (held three weeks after the polls) that anything above 65 per cent would be regarded as a strong mandate at the next election.[254] A few days earlier, DPM and Party Chairman Dr Tony Tan had warned that the Opposition would recover, with the election result due mainly to a "confluence of factors" that would not come together in the future. This confluence included the external global and security situation, the trust that the people had placed in the Party, and finally the Opposition's "unfocused, poorly-organised campaign with few credible candidates".[255] When the CEC met to consider the election post-mortem report in late March 2002, it was this external confluence of factors that was singled out as being key to the upsurge of votes. Other points highlighted were Goh's personal popularity and the economic rescue package (and New Singapore Shares in particular).[256]

Per past practice, the post-mortem report contained observations on what could have been done better. Almost inevitably, the Party manifesto came in for criticism. Despite attempts made to jazz up the manifesto, it had on the whole failed to make an impact with the public and the press. A better and more impactful way of putting across the Party's programme was needed, the post-mortem committee observed, in the form of a more informal document, boiled down to a very few digestible messages.

The post-mortem committee also made technical observations relating to how the workings of PAP HQ could be better coordinated with the needs of candidates on the ground. These suggestions (which were not entirely new) related to the beefing up of HQ machinery and the deployment to contested wards of support teams led by MPs not facing a contest. These suggestions, which appear to have originated mainly from newer MPs who had faced a contest, occasioned a pointed internal intervention from the experienced campaigner Wong Kan Seng, who had chaired the PAP General Elections Task Force (just as he had done in 1991 and 1997). Wong noted that the Party had had the luxury of many uncontested wards in 2001, allowing a redistribution of manpower. Wong's main concern was what he saw as a dependency mentality, with some MPs appearing to have expected a great deal of help from Party HQ. Future elections might not be like 2001, Wong observed. Many more—or even all—wards might be contested:

> *Our candidates must learn to fight elections with whatever resources they can muster themselves. I remember when I was a candidate in single member constituency in 1984, there was not so much support from the HQ, other than the handbook for the candidates, posters and stickers distributed by the HQ. We depended on our own manpower on the ground to run the campaign, including organising our own rallies!* [257]

༈

It is time now to turn to a wider consideration of what the huge victory actually meant for the PAP's future direction. The post-mortem had singled out the discussion and thrashing out of contentious issues with the people in advance as a key reason for electoral success. An example was ministerial pay, which had failed to catch fire as an Opposition campaign issue in 2001.[258] The post-mortem report had been silent on whether these and other issues had been settled definitively. (But as we shall see, the issue of ministerial salaries would in fact resurface through the rest of the decade and beyond, particularly when issues of political accountability were raised.) Other aspects of the Opposition's platform, including the criticism that the PAP government was not doing enough to help the needy, were to come up again, repeatedly, as society became increasingly affluent and the wealth gap more pronounced.

There were also other seemingly niggling issues that were to acquire a much deeper significance as the decade wore on. One was population. In July 2001 the Ministry of National Development unveiled a new Concept Plan with a population projection of 5.5 million. There was some concern, as many remembered that the 1991 Concept Plan had envisaged a long-term figure of 4 million. Addressing these concerns in Parliament on 13 March 2001 during the budget debate, Minister for National Development Mah Bow Tan acknowledged the concerns and attempted to allay them, giving assurances that the 5.5 million figure was a long-term projection, to be used as a planning parameter for the next 40 to 50 years. But he also acknowledged (in a reference to the 1991 Concept Plan) that earlier projections had been wrong.[259]

The related issue of foreign talent was to prove the thorniest of all. There had been a huge effort to sensitise the citizenry to the importance of attracting and retaining global talent. The point had been made by the prime minister in every National Day Rally speech between 1997 and 2001, such was its importance in the eyes of PAP leaders. It had also featured prominently in the S21 process.[260] But top-down efforts to persuade had run up against a growing sense of discomfort on the part of the people.[261] Concerns over competition for jobs had been exacerbated during the uncertain years of the Asian Financial Crisis and its aftermath. The government's response as the elections neared was to make minor concessions and to restate why the gates could not be closed. On 12 October 2001, DPM Lee announced in Parliament (together with the other measures to tackle the downturn) the tightening of criteria for the admission of certain categories of foreign workers in order to afford locals a degree of "protection". The minimum salary for the highest category of work pass, the employment pass, was raised from \$2,000 to \$2,500.[262] In the course of this sitting, Lee stressed the fundamental point that Singapore would suffer the consequences of a failure to attract top talent—making foreigners leave would hurt Singaporeans, who would stand to lose jobs if companies were forced to close because they could not find workers.[263]

During the 12 October 2011 parliamentary sitting, DPM Lee crossed swords with WP chief Low Thia Khiang over foreign talent. Low agreed that foreign talent was needed to some degree, but he argued that the policy should be implemented in a manner that did not alienate Singaporeans, and that Singaporeans could do some of the jobs foreigners had been brought in for.[264] A week later, when polls had been announced, the government again went on the offensive on the issue, with DPM Lee making it clear that the government would vigorously defend its position if the Opposition made foreign talent a campaign issue: "Singaporeans first" was a catchy slogan, but it would do harm to the country.[265]

Fighting what was very much a rear-guard action in 2001, the Opposition was in no position to attempt to land a knockout blow on these and other issues on which the PAP had staked so much. But things could only look up for the Opposition from its 2001 nadir. Its slow regrouping involved the recruitment of committed and credible people, and also the refining of its own arguments and political platform—including on some of the issues discussed in this chapter. These arguments would be deployed to increasing effect as the decade wore on. On critical, slowly simmering issues of policy, the government had held the ground in 2001 but did not carry it. The Party would never again have as easy a ride as it did in 2001.

Notes

1   *Censorship Review Committee Report 1992* (Ministry of Communications and the Arts, 1992), esp. pp. 12–5, 41. Available at https://eresources.nlb.gov.sg/printheritage/detail/e634b8b0-b986-4c14-9016-b8dcfe12dd6b.aspx (accessed 9 Aug. 2021).

2   The Censorship Review Committee recommended that theatre groups with proven track records need not have their scripts vetted (they were instead meant to self-regulate their scripts). Soon after the release of the report, a political satire by the journalist Tan Tarn How was passed uncut, and this was seen "as one of the first fruits of a new way of pruning". "Prudent Pruning", *Straits Times*, 7 Dec. 1992. In another significant move, a number of films that would ordinarily have been banned or cut were allowed at the 1993 Singapore International Film Festival. "Guidelines Relaxed so 22 Festival Films Passed in Full", *Sunday Times*, 18 Apr. 1993.

3   The present chapter does not propose to offer a detailed survey of the momentous changes that took place in Singapore in the arts and cultural scenes during the 1990s. For an introduction to these issues, see Kwok Kian Woon and Low Kee Hong, "Cultural Policy and the City-State: Singapore and the 'New Asian Renaissance'", in *Global Culture:*

Media, Arts, Policy, and Globalization, ed. Diana Crane, Nobuko Kawashima and Ken'ichi Kawasaki (New York: Routledge, 2002), pp. 151–68; Chua Beng Huat, "Liberalising Culture", in *Impressions of the Goh Chok Tong Years*, ed. Welsh et al., pp. 436–43, esp. 438–42; Tan Tarn How, "To the Market", in *Impressions of the Goh Chok Tong Years*, ed. Welsh et al., pp. 425–35, esp. 428–30; and Karl Hack, "Remaking Singapore 1990–2004: From Disciplinarian Development to Bureaucratic Proxy Democracy", in *Singapore from Temasek to the 21st Century*, ed. Karl Hack and Jean-Louis Margolin (with Karine Delaye) (Singapore: NUS Press, 2010), pp. 345–83, esp. 354–60.

4   "New Ministry Will Draw on Outsiders", *Straits Times*, 14 Dec. 1990. See also "Get Ready to Compete in League of Cities", *Straits Times*, 21 Aug. 1992.

5   *Report of the Central Executive Committee, October 1984–October 1986* (PAP archive). Parts of the report were—unusually—released to the press, in a sign perhaps of how the Party even at this stage was cognisant of the need to change, and the need to show itself as being in tune with the aspirations of the people. See "Do More to Get People behind the Party, PAP Cadres Told", *Straits Times*, 22 Nov. 1986.

6   See for example chapter 1, p.14.

7   Goh Chok Tong, interview with the author, 22 June 2012.

8   SM Lee Kuan Yew to PM Goh Chok Tong, 15 Nov. 1991 (National Archives of Singapore), made available to the author.

9   G. Yeo, "Civic Society: Between the Family and the State", *Speeches '91: A Bimonthly Selection of Ministerial Speeches* 15, 3 (1991): 82. See also "Lively Civic Society Needed to Develop a Soul for S'pore", *Straits Times*, 21 June 1991.

10   "Govt 'Will Always Have to Balance Pressures'", *Straits Times*, 22 June 1991. This should be read together with Yeo's comment to reporters in June 1991 that the newly formed Censorship Review Committee would have to strike a "sensible" balance in recommending changes to censorship rules. "Censorship Review Panel Must Strike Balance", *Straits Times*, 13 June 1991.

11   In his December 1990 interview, Yeo chose to quote Mencius' observation that governing a country was like frying a small fish—it should be done very lightly. "New Ministry Will Draw on Outsiders". Yeo was to repeat this quotation in his 1991 "banyan tree" speech.

12   George Yeo, interview with the author, 11 Oct. 2012.

13   George Yeo acknowledged that in the early years of the Goh Chok Tong premiership, "it was really tough for Cabinet to discuss the pull and push of how to evolve and open up" (Ibid.).

14   Ng was charged with committing an obscene act in public. Iris Tan, a founder member of one of the groups involved, 5th Passage, was prosecuted for providing public entertainment without a licence. See Gary Rodan, "State-Society Relations and Political Opposition in Singapore", in *Political Oppositions in Industrialising Asia*, ed. Gary Rodan (London: Routledge, 1996), pp. 111–2.

15   "'Art' Acts at Parkway Parade Vulgar and Distasteful: NAC", *Straits Times*, 5 Jan. 1994. George Yeo recalled: "Josef Ng snipped off his pubic hair in public. . . . Tommy Koh was chairman of NAC. I said if you don't act, I will have to act as this has crossed the Out-of-

Bounds or OB marker. I said you do not know where it is, but when it happens you will know where it is—and you too have a stake in this, and that established the point" (George Yeo, interview with the author, 11 Oct. 2012).

16 See "What Led to Govt Action", *Straits Times*, 23 Jan. 1994. The licensing procedure for scriptless performances was tightened, with scripts now having to be submitted to the authorities in advance. Official funding for performance art and forum theatre was discontinued; it was restored only in 2003. "NAC Lifts Rule on Scriptless Art Forms", *Straits Times*, 28 Nov. 2003.

17 Joint press statement by the Ministry of Home Affairs and Ministry of Information and the Arts, 21 Jan. 1994, quoted in "Govt Acts against 5th Passage over Performance Art", *Straits Times*, 22 Jan. 1994.

18 The two individuals were Alvin Tan (founder and artistic director of the theatre group) and Haresh Sharma (the group's resident playwright). "Two Pioneers of Forum Theatre Trained at Marxist Workshops", *Straits Times*, 5 Feb. 1994. See also Alvin Tan, "Forum Theatre: A Limited Mirror", in *Building Social Space in Singapore: The Working Committee's Initiative in Civil Society Activism*, ed. Constance Singam, Tan Chong Kee, Tisa Ng and Leon Perera (Singapore: Select Publishing, 2002), pp. 73–80.

19 Prof. Tommy Koh, "Necessary Stage Still Has NAC's Support", letter to *Straits Times* Forum, 7 Feb. 1994.

20 Singapore Parliamentary Debates, 23 Jan. 1994, col. 375.

21 "NUS Society Scraps Mid-year Issue of Journal", *Straits Times*, 29 Oct. 1994; "No Clear Explanation for Scrapping *Commentary*", *Straits Times*, 10 Nov. 1994.

22 "Far-Reaching Stricture on the Arts", *Straits Times*, 13 Nov. 1994.

23 "The PAP and the People—A Great Affective Divide", *Straits Times*, 3 Sept. 1994.

24 "One Government, Two Styles", *Sunday Times*, 20 Nov. 1994.

25 Lim had cited the scuttling of the issue of NUSS' *Commentary* by the NUSS management committee as a sign of "sensitivity" to the signals of a harder style being adopted by the government, but she also clearly had some of the other recent strictures on the arts in mind.

26 SM Lee Kuan Yew to PM Goh Chok Tong, 24 Nov. 1994 (National Archives of Singapore), made available to the author. SM Lee had initially suggested replying himself, but the majority of younger ministers favoured a reply by PM Goh or his press secretary.

27 Chan Heng Wing, "PM Goh Remains Committed to Consultation and Consensus Politics", letter to *Sunday Times*, 4 Dec. 1994.

28 Ibid. This part of the letter had been a suggestion from SM Lee to PM Goh, with SM Lee noting in his 24 November 1994 letter to Goh, "This line is totally credible because it is consistent with the facts."

29 "PM: No Erosion of My Authority Allowed", *Straits Times*, 5 Dec. 1994.

30 Ibid.

31 "Catherine Lim: I'm Not Interested in Politics", *Straits Times*, 6 Dec. 1994.

32 "PM Tells Dr Lim Why He Responded to Commentary", *Straits Times*, 17 Dec. 1994. The quotation above relies on the complete text of Goh's letter to Lim, which was made available to the author.

33 "Politics for Politicians Only?", *Straits Times*, 17 Dec. 1994.

34 See, for example, Chia Hern Keng, "Why the Need to Join a Party to Air Views?", and Chang Pei, "Govt Should Heed Points", letters to *Straits Times* Forum, 7 Dec. 1994.

35 SM Lee Kuan Yew to PM Goh Chok Tong, 12 Dec. 1994 (National Archives of Singapore), made available to the author.

36 Chan Heng Wing, "There Are Limits to Openness", letter to *Straits Times* Forum, 29 Dec. 1994. The letter also noted that "a gentler, more open political style does not mean allowing crudity and obscenity to pass off as avant garde theatre, or ignoring political criticism which masquerades as artistic expression".

37 "Process of Openness Best Achieved Gradually", *Straits Times*, 29 Dec. 1994.

38 See chapter 2, pp. 130–1.

39 Singapore Parliamentary Debates, 23 Jan. 1995, cols 1017–9; "PM: Debate Welcomed but Govt Will Rebut Malicious Arguments", *Straits Times*, 24 Jan. 1995.

40 Singapore Parliamentary Debates, 23 Jan. 1995, col. 1021. For Goh's own reflections on the Catherine Lim Affair, see Peh Shing Huei, *Standing Tall: The Goh Chok Tong Years*, Vol. 2 (Singapore: World Scientific, 2021), pp. 86–95, 97–9, 303–4.

41 "Debate Yes, But Do Not Take On Those in Authority as 'Equals'", *Straits Times*, 20 Feb. 1995.

42 "Hard to Believe PM Has Made U-Turn in Open Govt Promise", *Sunday Times*, 20 Nov. 1994.

43 "More Freedom for Journalists but Govt 'Will Still Set the Boundaries'", *Straits Times*, 27 Oct. 1991. See also "Where One Should Draw the Line in Art", *Straits Times*, 16 Mar. 1994. The term "Out-of-Bounds (or OB) markers" appears first to have been used by Information and the Arts Minister BG George Yeo in conversations with then Chairman of the National Arts Council Prof. Tommy Koh, sometime in 1991 or just prior. The term acquired greater currency when the gist was recounted by Prof. Koh at an October 1991 seminar on the role of the press organised by IPS and the Singapore Press Club. "Pushing Back Out-of-Bounds Markers for the S'pore Press", *Straits Times*, 22 Nov. 1991.

44 "PAP 'Should Stop Being Fixated with Vote Percentage'", *Straits Times*, 30 Oct. 1994.

45 "PAP and the People: A Return of Disaffection?", *Straits Times*, 26 Aug. 2000. Lim had claimed in this piece that the ministerial pay rises in 2000 had undermined the vision and spirit of the recently concluded Singapore 21 initiative. For the PAP rebuttal, see the letter by Minister of State for Defence and Information and the Arts David Lim, in *Straits Times* Forum, 31 Aug. 2000 ("Dissent Reflects a Society Alive to S21"). Lim's reply was that the government's decision to have open consultation and discussion on the issue of ministerial pay was in fact in the spirit of S21. This was to prove a running debate, with Catherine Lim continuing to press her points on the widening of the "Great Affective Divide" through articles, letters and speeches. See, for example, "Views Aired, but Is the Government Really Listening?", *Straits Times*, 15 Dec. 2002. The Party's response throughout was the same: what people were interested in was whether the government could make a difference in their daily lives, and that the PAP's track record would be judged at the polls. "That Divide: Same Debate, Same Answer", *Straits Times*, 16 Dec. 2002.

46 "Second Citizen's Think Tank Gets Official Go-Ahead", *Straits Times*, 6 Jan. 1995.

47   "New Think-Tank Plans to Offer Non-partisan Views", *Straits Times*, 29 Dec. 1993.

48   "Professionals Form Club to Discuss Political Issues", *Straits Times*, 11 Sept. 1993; "Second Citizen's Think Tank Gets Official Go-Ahead".

49   "Professionals Form Club to Discuss Political Issues"; "Socratic Circle Seeks to Improve Society by Improving Individuals", *Straits Times*, 22 Oct. 1994.

50   The Roundtable was registered in December 1994, a full year after the submission of its application to the ROS. Similarly, the Socratic Circle was formed in September 1993 and received ROS approval in September 1994.

51   Those members of the Socratic Circle who were also members of political parties had had to resign from the parties in order to remain members of the Socratic Circle. "Socratic Circle Seeks to Improve Society by Improving Individuals".

52   Singapore Parliamentary Debates, 5 June 1997, col. 405.

53   Ibid., cols 409–10.

54   "Global City, Best Home", PM Goh Chok Tong, National Day Rally Speech at the Kallang Theatre, 24 Aug. 1997. *National Day Rally Speeches: 50 Years of Nationhood in Singapore*, pp. 351–67, esp. 366.

55   See "PM: Trust Me and My Team to Deliver Again", *Straits Times*, 20 Nov. 1996.

56   Adrian Kuah, "Foresight and Policy: Thinking about Singapore's Futures", in *Social Space* 2013/2014 (No. 6), ed. Tan Chi Chiu (Singapore: Lien Centre for Social Innovation), p. 106. See also Neo Boon Siong and Geraldine Chen, *Dynamic Governance: Embedding Culture, Capabilities and Change in Singapore* (Singapore: World Scientific, 2007), p. 209.

57   Documents on the Singapore 21 exercise (Ref PM Comm/S/13 Singapore 21 Committee) (National Archives of Singapore), made available to the author.

58   The discussion of the PAP government's stance on civil society offered in this chapter is not intended as a comprehensive treatment of the issue. For civil society in the Goh era, see Gillian Koh, "Pruning the Banyan Tree? Civil Society in Goh's Singapore", in *Impressions of the Goh Chok Tong Years*, ed. Welsh et al., pp. 93–106 (and the references cited therein). Also useful reading for the 1990s are the contributions in the volume which grew out of the May 1998 IPS conference on civil society. Gillian Koh and Ooi Giok Ling (eds), *State-Society Relations in Singapore* (Singapore: Institute of Policy Studies and Oxford University Press, 2000).

59   Documents on the Singapore 21 exercise (Ref PM Comm/S/13 Singapore 21 Committee) (National Archives of Singapore), made available to the author.

60   BG George Yeo, speech at the IPS conference "Civil Society: Harnessing State-Society Synergies", 6 May 1998, available at https://www.nas.gov.sg/archivesonline/speeches/record-details/752a36c9-115d-11e3-83d5-0050568939ad (accessed 3 May 2021). See also George Yeo, "Worldwide Web: Strengthening the Singapore Network", in *State-Society Relations in Singapore*, ed. Koh and Ooi, pp. 18–26, esp. 19.

61   "IPS Conference on Civil Society: BG Yeo Sends 'Strong Signal' to Civic Groups", *Straits Times*, 8 May 1998.

62   "IPS Conference on Civil Society: More Space in Tembusu Tree Era", *Straits Times*, 8 May 1998; "What Plants Will Grow under the Tembusu Tree?", *Straits Times*, 9 May 1998.

63   "What Plants Will Grow under the Tembusu Tree?". Other forums held around the same time threw out similar sentiments. See "Room for Civil Society to Grow Here, Say Speakers", *Straits Times*, 18 Mar. 1998.

64   See the Roundtable response to BG Yeo's 6 May 1998 speech at the IPS conference on civil society. "Barriers to a Web Society", *Sunday Times*, 17 May 1998.

65   See Derek da Cunha, "Singapore in 1998: Managing Expectations, Shoring-Up National Morale", *Southeast Asian Affairs* (1999): 275–6.

66   The IPS conference was also a testing ground of sorts for S21. The S21 committee chairman, Education Minister Teo Chee Hean, together with several members of the S21 committee, took part in a closed-door dialogue session with approximately 150 of the participants immediately following the conference.

67   "8 in 10 Have Faith in Govt", *Straits Times*, 20 June 1998; "More Say in Policies, Please", *Straits Times*, 20 June 1998.

68   All but two of the subject committee heads were PAP MPs (the other two, Dr Lee Tsao Yuan and Simon Tay, were NMPs). For the full composition of subject committees, see "The Singapore 21 Committee", *Petir*, Nov.–Dec. 1997, pp. 28–9. Opposition members were excluded from participating in the committees, leading to charges from Chiam See Tong that the S21 exercise was simply an instrument of PAP legitimisation. See "Panel to Get Views of as Many People as Possible", *Straits Times*, 20 Oct. 1997; and "S21—PAP or Public Agenda?", *Straits Times*, 5 May 1999.

69   "A Quiet Revolution in the Making?", *Straits Times*, 28 Apr. 1999.

70   *Singapore 21: Together, We Make the Difference* (Singapore: Singapore 21 Committee, 1999). The five themes were "Every Singaporean matters", "Strong families: Our foundation and our future", "Opportunities for all", "The Singapore heartbeat", and "Active citizens: Making a difference to society".

71   For a summary of recommendations, see "Balancing Needs of Old and Young: S21 Report", *Straits Times*, 1 May 1999.

72   Singapore Parliamentary Debates, 6 May 1999, col. 1598.

73   As PM Goh remarked (in what was probably an attempt to show that the newer generation of leaders did things differently), he would have run the whole exercise differently, preferring instead to ask Cabinet to come up with a vision and decide on it there and then. "A Quiet Revolution in the Making?".

74   "People's Vision of New Singapore", *Sunday Times*, 25 Apr. 1999.

75   S21 Committee Chairman Teo Chee Hean had intentionally framed themes to be tackled by the five subcommittees not just as a series of "wants" by the people, but as a series of dilemmas. The intention was that even as they brought their ideas to the table, citizens would see in the course of their contributions the limitations, tradeoffs and choices that Singapore faced. Teo Chee Hean, interview with the author, 12 July 2013. (The five dilemmas were Internationalisation/Regionalisation vs Singapore as Home, Less Stressful Life vs Retaining the Drive, Attracting Foreign Talent vs Looking after Singaporeans, Needs of Senior Citizens vs Aspirations of the Young, and Consultation and Consensus vs Decisiveness and Quick Action.)

76   "Can Singaporeans Shake Off Passivity?", *Straits Times*, 12 June 1999.

77   Ibid.

78   "The Young and Educated More Vocal", *Straits Times*, 25 Aug. 1998; "Are We a Nation of Armchair Critics?", *Straits Times*, 7 Sept. 1998. This was, of course, not a new concern: it was one that had been enunciated in public by key leaders, in increasingly direct fashion, as the 1990s wore on. In his 18 August 1996 National Day Rally speech, PM Goh (who devoted a good deal of time in the speech to issues relating to community bonding and social cohesion) pointedly noted that many post-independence Singaporeans, having benefited from the fortitude and vision of the founding generation, were too absorbed with their own "promotions, houses and holidays". "Social Stratification and Commitment", PM Goh Chok Tong, National Day Rally Speech at the Kallang Theatre, 18 Aug. 1996. *National Day Rally Speeches: 50 Years of Nationhood in Singapore*, p. 330.

79   Minister of State for Defence David Lim (widely viewed at the time as an up-and-coming member of the new, third generation of leaders) was appointed to head the S21 facilitation committee, which was to lead the S21 follow-up efforts to strengthen and sustain the process of active citizenship. "New Team to Oversee S21 Vision", *Straits Times*, 7 May 1999.

80   Singapore Parliamentary Debates, 1 June 1998, cols 124–6; "NMP Calls for Debate on All Major Policies", *Straits Times*, 3 June 1998.

81   "Singapore Benefits if People Can Send Signals to Govt Early", *Straits Times*, 20 Sept. 1997.

82   "House Votes to Add Three More NMPs, Raising Total to Nine", *Business Times*, 6 June 1997.

83   "17 Feedback Groups Formed to Discuss National Issues", *Sunday Times*, 31 Aug. 1997; "New Feedback Groups: Govt 'Realises Need for Expression'", *Straits Times*, 14 Sept. 1997.

84   "Newly Set-Up Group Will Provide Overseas Perspective", *Straits Times*, 31 Aug. 1997.

85   By 1998, Feedback Unit Chairman John Chen was receiving 250 to 300 pieces of unsolicited feedback a month (more than half via email). "Feedback Unit Wants to Expand", *Straits Times*, 14 May 1999. See also *Building Bridges: The Story of the Feedback Unit* (Feedback Unit, Ministry of Community Development and Sports, 2004), p. 51.

86   "Consultation Need Not Mean Indecision", *Straits Times*, 20 June 1998.

87   "First Annual Feedback Unit Meet", *Straits Times*, 11 June 1998.

88   Ibid.

89   This suggestion was made on several occasions in the late 1990s, particularly by NMPs. See Singapore Parliamentary Debates, 1 June 1998, cols 124–6, and 6 Sept. 1999, col. 2306.

90   Singapore Parliamentary Debates, 6 May 1999, col. 1267.

91   "S'pore Is Not a Nation Yet", *Straits Times*, 6 May 1999; "Will a Singapore Tribe Emerge?", *Straits Times*, 6 May 1999.

92   Singapore Parliamentary Debates, 6 May 1999, cols 1619–29, 1646–55. See also Simon S.C. Tay, "Island in the World: Globalization and Singapore's Transformation", *Southeast Asian Affairs* (2001): 289.

93   Singapore Parliamentary Debates, 13 Oct. 1999, col. 354. "'Let Ideas Bloom' Says PM", *Straits Times*, 14 Oct. 1999. In another parliamentary intervention at this time, Goh had commented that "meaningful" political participation meant joining a political party and

those who wanted to be part of the decision-making process had to be prepared to do so. Singapore Parliamentary Debates, 6 Sept. 1999, col. 2381. See "Allowing Diversity without Undermining Government", *Sunday Times*, 12 Sept. 1999.

94   *National Day Rally Speeches: 50 Years of Nationhood in Singapore 1966–2015*, p. 188.

95   "I Had a Job to Do", *Asiaweek*, interview with Ong Teng Cheong, 10 Mar. 2000, Vol. 26 No. 9, available at https://web.archive.org/web/20010210092142/http://www.asiaweek.com/asiaweek/magazine/2000/0310/nat.singapore.ongiv.html (accessed 13 Apr. 2021); "Workers Strike over 'Anti-Union Moves' by Firm", *Straits Times*, 3 Jan. 1986. For confirmation that PM Lee was unaware of Ong's move in sanctioning the strike, I am grateful to ESM Goh Chok Tong for a personal communication (20 Apr. 2021). Another issue where Ong differed from some Cabinet colleagues, and was prepared to back himself in the face of strong opposition from them, was whether to build a Mass Rapid Transit (MRT) system. Ong was a proponent of the MRT from an early stage, but other Cabinet members, including DPM Goh Keng Swee and Trade and Industry Minister Dr Tony Tan, were initially against the concept for various reasons, including cost. Eventually, Ong's view prevailed. See Tisa Ng and Lily Tan, *Ong Teng Cheong: Planner, Politician, President* (Singapore: Editions Didier Millet, 2005), pp. 43–55; and "Ong Teng Cheong Pushed for Building MRT in S'pore Despite It Being a Controversial Idea", *Mothership.sg*, 8 Dec. 2017, available at https://mothership.sg/2017/11/ong-teng-cheong-pushed-for-building-mrt-in-spore-despite-it-being-a-controversial-idea/ (accessed 18 Apr. 2021).

96   For Lee's approach to Ong, see chapter 2.

97   "How I Will Do My Job: President Ong", *Straits Times*, 2 Sept. 1993.

98   "'I Had a Long List of Problems'", *Straits Times*, 17 July 1999. Another, more involved, issue had to do with the treatment of Net Investment Income (NII). Under the Constitution, the president's custodial powers were over "reserves which were not accumulated during the current term of office of the Government". The position taken by the government (having consulted the attorney-general) was that NII was accumulated during the current term of office of the government (current income), falling outside of the president's custodial powers. President Ong made clear his disappointment that the government declined his offer to unlock past reserves to finance its package of fiscal measures in the face of the 1998 recession, with Ong claiming that the government had not needed presidential assent as it had changed its treatment of NII to count as current reserves. This was later shown by Finance Minister Dr Richard Hu to have been a mistake on the part of Ong. Singapore Parliamentary debates, 17 Aug. 1999, cols 2027–9."Outstanding Issue—'And This Was One of Them'—NII", *Straits Times*, 17 July 1999.

99   "Public Officers 'Need Change of Mindset'", *Straits Times*, 17 July 1999.

100 "Issues Raised by President Ong Teng Cheong at this Press Conference on 16th July 1999" (Statements by the Prime Minister and Minister for Finance), available at https://www.mof.gov.sg/docs/default-source/default-document-library/policies/reserves/what-is-the-president's-role-in-safeguarding-the-reserves/issues-raised-by-president-ong-teng-cheong.pdf (accessed 15 Apr. 2021) (Singapore Parliamentary Debates, 17 Aug. 1999, cols 2018–43).

101 "Dr Hu: Problems Were Neither Fundamental nor Intractable", *Business Times*, 18 Aug. 1999. Ong had himself acknowledged in his 16 July press conference that many of the issues had indeed been resolved, with the White Paper that had been tabled in July 1999 setting out the understandings (particularly when it came to transactions involving the reserves) between the president and government, that would ensure (on paper at least) a harmonious working relationship. *White Paper on the Principles for Determining and Safeguarding the Accumulated Reserves of the Government and the Fifth Schedule Statutory Boards and Government Companies*, available at https://www.nas.gov.sg/archivesonline/ government_records/record-details/12ec06c2-4a32-11e7-9199-0050568939ad (accessed 1 May 2020).

102 "Why Govt Could Not Support President's Re-election", *Straits Times*, 18 Aug. 1999.

103 The manner in which the government rebutted Ong's charges was not the same as how it responded to, and subsequently took on, former president Devan Nair (who after his resignation was to become a critic of the government in the 1990s).

104 "PM: Only Issue Was President Ong's Health", *Business Times,* 18 Aug. 1999. These were points that Goh came back to at the farewell reception for Ong on 30 August, where he alluded to the difficulties in the relationship between president and government, noting too that the positions put forward by both sides had crystallised not just issues of dispute but also the powers and role of the elected president. Speech by Prime Minister Goh Chok Tong at the Farewell Reception for President Ong Teng Cheong on Monday, 30 Aug. 1999, at the Istana at 6.30pm, available at https://www.nas.gov.sg/archivesonline/speeches/ record-details/7564da7c-115d-11e3-83d5-0050568939ad (accessed 19 Apr. 2021).

105 Constitutional law expert and academic Dr Kevin Tan had argued in an interview published on 30 July in the *Straits Times* that it was confusing to have a president who was both a figurehead and an executive president. "Presidency 'a Confusing Institution'", *Straits Times*, 30 July 1999.

106 "Elected President's Powers Are Custodial, not Executive", *Straits Times*, 18 Aug. 1999.

107 Singapore Parliamentary Debates, 17 Aug. 1999, cols 2064–8; "MPs Raise Questions about Presidency", *Straits Times*, 19 Aug. 1999.

108 "What Makes a Good President?", *Straits Times*, 10 June 2011.

109 Some of this comes through clearly in the memories of Ong's principal private secretary at the time, Lim-Yeo Siok Peng: "He felt it very strongly that being the first elected President, you know, he was elected for a purpose. And that purpose was to test the system. . . . He says, I must try to behave as if the Government is a rogue government. As if. I must treat the Government as if it is a rogue Government, not that it is, but as if it is. So that we can see if the system works out, and really can protect the past reserves. And so similarly if we need the second key, does it work? So he was very very keen on testing out all those things." Lim-Yeo Siok Peng, transcript of oral history interview (for *Ong Teng Cheong: Planner, Politician, President*), Accession Number E000016, Reel/Disc 4, p. 1, available at https://www.nas.gov.sg/archivesonline/oral_history_interviews/record-details/ d18dcfab-1161-11e3-83d5-0050568939ad?keywords=Siok%20Peng&keywords-type=all (accessed 18 Apr. 2021). PAP MP S. Chandra Das, who was a close associate of Ong, was to observe after Ong's passing, "If there was a weakness in him, it was that he saw things in black or white, there were no grey areas. You were either with him or against him. He

was not vindictive, and would try to win you over by argument, but if he could not, he left you alone, and he would go ahead on his own steam." *Ong Teng Cheong: Planner, Politician, President*, p. 143.

110 "I Had a Job to Do".

111 "吴作栋：政治没有万无一失" [Goh Chok Tong: politics is not foolproof], *Lianhe Zaobao*, 26 May 2019. Goh had made the same comment—that he should have reached out to Ong directly—in Parliament in August 1999 (Singapore Parliamentary Debates, 17 Aug. 1999, cols 2045–6), but the 2019 interview is notable in that it was given to the Chinese press (Ong's links to the Chinese ground were strong, and the ground retained a very favourable impression of Ong and his presidency), where Goh described the conflict as the real regret of his political career. See also Peh, *Standing Tall: The Goh Chok Tong Years*, Vol. 2, pp.164–72, 180–2.

112 Cherian George and Zulkifli Baharudin (from the Roundtable), "The Case for Free-Speech Venues", *Straits Times*, 20 Jan. 1999; Zulkifli Baharudin and Kevin Tan (from the Roundtable), "Free Speech Venues an Incremental Step", letter to *Straits Times* Forum, 3 Feb. 1999; Jason Lim Swee Kay, "Avenue for Public Discussion Needed", letter to *Straits Times* Forum, 5 Feb. 1999. For the government position, see the letters in reply: Casimir Rozario (director, public affairs, Ministry of Home Affairs), "Free Speech Venues May Threaten Order", letter to *Straits Times* Forum, 28 Jan. 1999; and "No Lack of Avenues to Express Views", letter to *Straits Times* Forum, 12 Feb. 1999.

113 See "What's Chee Up to Now? . . . And What Is He Fighting For?", *Straits Times*, 26 Feb. 1999.

114 SM Lee Kuan Yew, interview with William Safire, 31 Jan. 1999. *The Papers of Lee Kuan Yew: Speeches, Interviews and Dialogues, Vol. 13: 1997–1999* (Singapore: Cengage Learning Asia, 2013), pp. 372–3.

115 "S'pore 'Not Ready for Speakers' Corner'", *Straits Times*, 12 Sept. 1999.

116 Correspondence on the origins of Speakers' Corner (Ref "Speakers' Corner 10.2.99") (National Archives of Singapore), made available to the author.

117 "Speakers' Corner Details in a Few Months", *Straits Times*, 20 Mar. 2000; "Speakers' Corner—Govt Is Sincere", *Straits Times*, 26 Apr. 2000.

118 Correspondence on the origins of Speakers' Corner (Ref "Speakers' Corner 10.2.99") (National Archives of Singapore), made available to the author.

119 Ibid.

120 "Opposition MPs Question Decision to Ban Marathon", *Straits Times*, 23 Feb. 2001; "Police Warning for Speakers' Corner Event Organisers", *Straits Times*, 28 Mar. 2001.

121 "2 Civil Groups Gazetted as Political Associations", *Straits Times*, 31 Mar. 2001.

122 "Call to Change Wording of Political Donations Bill", *Straits Times*, 20 May 2000.

123 "Politics Here Is for Singaporeans Only", *Straits Times*, 23 May 2000.

124 Tay, "Island in the World", p. 291. See also "Is a Clenched Fist a Protest?", *Straits Times*, 6 Mar. 2001.

125 "Getting Ready to Take a More Relaxed Approach", *Financial Times*, 13 Mar. 2000; "No Big Bang but Singapore Will Move with the Times", *Straits Times*, 18 Mar. 2000.

126 "New Singapore", PM Goh Chok Tong, National Day Rally Speech at the University Cultural Centre, 19 Aug. 2001. *National Day Rally Speeches: 50 Years of Nationhood in*

Singapore, p. 450. See also "Government Will Respond to Opponents", *Straits Times*, 20 Aug. 2001.

127 "Think Centre 'Not Govt's Opponent'", *Straits Times*, 21 Aug. 2001.

128 Koh, "Pruning the Banyan Tree?", pp. 93–106, esp. 98; Constance Singam, Tan Chong Kee, Tisa Ng and Leon Perera (eds), *Building Social Space in Singapore: The Working Committee's Initiative in Civil Society Activism* (Singapore: Select Publishing, 2002), p. 162.

129 "Come Join in the Debate: BG Lee", *Straits Times*, 17 Jan. 2000.

130 Madrasahs were instead given eight years from 2000 to achieve minimum levels (benchmarked to standards in government schools) in the secular subjects they offered. See Lee, *Unexpected Nation*, pp. 505–7; Koh, "Pruning the Banyan Tree?", pp. 100–1; and Lily Zubaidah Rahim, "A New Dawn in PAP–Malay Relations?", in *Impressions of the Goh Chok Tong Years*, ed. Welsh et al., pp. 355–8.

131 See Lee, *Unexpected Nation*, pp. 507–9; Rahim, "A New Dawn in PAP–Malay Relations?", pp. 354–5.

132 Especially those who felt that fierce debates could actually be constructive. "Contest of Ideas Critical, Says NMP", *Straits Times*, 6 Mar. 2000.

133 The Nature Society of Singapore had, for example, since the late 1990s been pursuing advocacy on issues relating to the conservation of areas important for their biodiversity and other green spaces, with some success. See Karyn Wang, "Moving from Survival to Sustainability in the Environment", in *Impressions of the Goh Chok Tong Years*, ed. Welsh et al., pp. 293–4.

134 "NGOs Should Cooperate, Not Confront", *Straits Times*, 27 Feb. 2000.

135 Raymond Lim from the Roundtable joined the PAP in 2001. James Gomez and Yaw Shin Leong joined the Workers' Party in July 2001 and became part of its Central Executive Council. All resigned from the civil society organisations that they had been members of in order to join political parties and contest elections. "Former Think Centre Leaders Now with WP", *Straits Times*, 21 Aug. 2001.

136 Quoted in "Revisiting the Banyan Tree: Civil Society 10 Years On", *Straits Times*, 30 June 2001.

137 The idea that Singapore had to take steps to become a leading hub into the next century, and take advantage of new technologies to do so, was prominent in the speeches of government leaders in the mid-1990s. On 27 April 1995, Information and the Arts Minister George Yeo commented, "Geography will matter less in the future. We must therefore think of new ways to retain our position as a hub. Over the next 20 to 30 years, we must make sure that we have the new infrastructure to remain a junction for goods, services, people, information and ideas. If we succeed, we will be one of a number of great cities in the Pacific Century. If we fail, other hubs will displace us and we will be relegated to a backwater." Brigadier-General (NS) George Yeo, speech at the launch of Singapore Technologies Teleport, 27 Apr. 1995, available at http://www.nas.gov.sg/archivesonline/data/pdfdoc/yybg19950427s.pdf (accessed 21 Jan. 2021).

138 By March 1995 there were 26,000 Singaporeans on the Internet, with the number growing by 1,000 a month. "26,000 S'poreans Using Internet Now", *Straits Times*, 18 Mar. 1995.

139 Singapore Parliamentary Debates, 26 Aug. 1994, col. 564.

140 Ibid., cols 564–70. See also "Government to Continue Its Tight Control over Broadcasting", *Straits Times*, 27 Aug. 1994; and "Broadcast Laws Exclude Computer Networks for Now", *Straits Times*, 2 Sept. 1994.

141 Singapore Parliamentary Debates, 17 Mar. 1995, col. 647.

142 Ibid., col. 644. See "S'pore Must Open Windows but Swat the Flies—BG Yeo", *Straits Times*, 18 Mar. 1995.

143 Documents (1996) from files (Ref MITA B01.018.13) concerning the thinking of the leadership on Internet regulation made available to the author (National Archives of Singapore).

144 Ibid.

145 "Govt Proposes Regulatory Framework for Internet", *Business Times*, 6 Mar. 1996; "SBA to Monitor Websites for Objectionable Material", *Straits Times*, 6 Mar. 1996.

146 "Govt Proposes Regulatory Framework for Internet".

147 "Using Videotapes Will Debase Politics—BG Yeo", *Straits Times*, 28 July 1996. See also "Govt Says 'No' to Party Political Videotapes", *Straits Times*, 27 July 1996.

148 "Tougher Porn Penalties, No to Party Political Films", *Straits Times*, 28 Feb. 1998.

149 "How Political Groups See the Move", *Straits Times*, 6 Mar. 1996.

150 See "Postings of New SBA Rules Flood the Net", *Straits Times*, 17 July 1996; and "Cyberspace—Issues Are Here on Earth", *Sunday Times*, 21 July 1996. The Class Licence Scheme took effect on 15 July 1996.

151 "New Rules Easy to Follow Say Some Internet Providers", *Straits Times*, 13 July 1996; "Internet OB Markers Should Protect Nation", *Straits Times*, 5 Aug. 1996. See also letters to *Straits Times* Forum: "Broad Phrasing of Guidelines Open to Wide Interpretation" (Harish Pillay, 13 July 1996); and "How Does One Query SBA's Net Guidelines?" (Au Wai Ping, 17 July 1996).

152 "Scheme Affects 2 Groups—Content, Access Providers", *Straits Times*, 12 July 1996.

153 The Young PAP launched its website in August 1995 (in what was possibly the first official online platform of any political party in Asia), but the beginnings of the PAP's Internet Team should be traced earlier, to 1994 (I am grateful to Harold Fock for a personal communication on the issue). See "Young PAP Can Now Be Found on Internet", *Straits Times*, 15 Aug. 1995. Subsequently, in 1997, a discussion forum, Young PAP Network, was set up on the YP website, taking in views, suggestions, and feedback to the government. "Young Singaporeans Can Now Air Their Views on Young PAP Website", *Straits Times*, 27 July 1997.

154 Harold Fock, interview with the author, 21 Jan. 2014.

155 "Young PAP Makes a Stand on Behalf of S'pore on Internet", *Straits Times*, 8 Apr. 1995.

156 "Why We Need to Go into Cyberspace", *Petir*, May–June 1995, pp. 55–6, esp. 55. See also "Young PAP Makes a Stand on Behalf of S'pore on Internet".

157 "S'pore Bulletin Board on the Internet Soon", *Straits Times*, 20 Feb. 1995. Yeo was reflecting conclusions that the Party leadership had already arrived at. The PAP's "O" or Opposition Committee, one of three committees that reported internally to the CEC in mid-1995, had highlighted the need to use propaganda more effectively, and the need for new channels in addition to *Petir*. One solution, noted the report, was to participate

actively on the Internet to educate the people on the Party's point of view, as well as on its role and contributions. *Report of the "O" Committee*, 28 July 1995 (PAP archive).

158 "Internet Abuzz with 'Talk' of Maid's Hanging", *Straits Times*, 5 Apr. 1995; "Crane Triggers off Debate on SDP Censure on Internet", *Straits Times*, 28 Nov. 1995.

159 "Young PAP Makes a Stand on Behalf of S'pore on Internet". George Yeo was to remark later, in 1998, that Young PAP members attempting to comment on soc.culture.singapore had complained that they were "hated" there. "Full Alert as Asian Storm Rages", *Petir*, July–Aug. 1998, pp. 22–9, esp. 25.

160 During the 5 March 1996 press conference announcing the class licence regulations, George Yeo had made a distinction between political websites and newsgroups. Yeo said that discussions on newsgroups "is like graffiti. We can clean it up now, but it will come back later. And it is also unlikely to create a major public impact." Yeo added, "We are not that concerned with newsgroups because most of them are dominated by rumours and frivolous discussion. We are only concentrating on broadcasting with large impact" (from the transcript of the press conference made available to the author; for the proceedings of the press conference, see "Govt Proposes Regulatory Framework for Internet"; and "SBA to Monitor Websites for Objectionable Material", *Straits Times*, 6 Mar. 1996).

161 On Sintercom, see Cherian George, *The Air-conditioned Nation: Essays on the Politics of Comfort and Control, 1990–2000* (Singapore: Landmark Books, 2000), pp. 133–8; and Singam et al. (eds), *Building Social Space in Singapore*, pp. 107–18.

162 Documents (1996) from files (Ref MITA B01.018.13) concerning the thinking of the leadership on Internet regulation made available to the author (National Archives of Singapore).

163 During the 1997 general election, Sintercom appears to have been the only reasonably active non-political party website, reporting rally speeches and election results. But there was no campaigning by political parties online as the SBA took the view that since the Parliamentary Elections Act was silent on the issue of online campaigning, parties would be contravening the Act by putting election advertising online. Shortly after Nomination Day on 23 December 1996, the SBA directed the SDP and NSP to remove biodata of their candidates from their websites. "No Biodata on the Web, Parties Told", *Straits Times*, 29 Dec. 1996.

164 For a survey of online activity by political parties during the 2001 election, see R. Kluver, "Political Culture and Information Technology in the 2001 Singapore General Election", *Political Communication* 21, 4: 435–58.

165 The government subsequently clarified that this was not the intention. "Bill Not Meant to Regulate Private Correspondence", *Straits Times*, 14 Aug. 2001.

166 Ibid.; "MPs Split over Net Campaigning Rules", *Straits Times*, 14 Aug. 2001.

167 "To Nurture or Confine?", *Straits Times*, 15 Aug. 2001.

168 See "Think Centre Shuts Web Forum", *Straits Times*, 17 Aug. 2001; "Sintercom Founder Fades Out of Cyberspace", *Straits Times*, 22 Aug. 2001; and Tan Chong Kee, "Impact of Technology in Enabling Discussion and Interaction", in *Building Social Space in Singapore: The Working Committee's Initiative in Civil Society Activism*, ed. Singam et al., pp. 117–8.

169 Singapore Parliamentary Debates, 13 Aug. 2001, cols 1985–6. See also "Others Ban Straw-Polls Results Too", *Straits Times*, 14 Aug. 2001.

170 "BG Yeo's Eight Years at MITA", *Sunday Times*, 30 May 1999.

171 George Yeo, interview with the author, 11 Oct. 2012.

172 SM Lee Kuan Yew, interview with Nathan Gardels of Global Viewpoint, 26 Sept. 1995; *The Papers of Lee Kuan Yew: Speeches, Interviews and Dialogues, Vol. 12: 1994–1997* (Singapore: Cengage Learning Asia, 2013), pp. 196–7.

173 "PAP to Field at Least 12 New Candidates", *Straits Times*, 5 Dec. 2000.

174 "First-World Economy, World-Class Home: Setting Fresh Goals", PM Goh Chok Tong, National Day Rally Speech at the Kallang Theatre, 22 Aug. 1999. *National Day Rally Speeches: 50 Years of Nationhood in Singapore 1966–2015*, pp. 391, 410.

175 See Lee Kuan Yew, *From Third World to First*, pp. 98–101; Mauzy and Milne, *Singapore Politics under the People's Action Party*, pp. 71–81.

176 "1999 Will Be a Tough Year", *Petir*, Jan.–Feb. 1999, pp. 18–9, esp. 19.

177 "How to Maintain Singapore's Competitive Edge", *Petir*, Jan.–Feb. 1998, p. 15.

178 "Transforming Singapore", PM Goh Chok Tong, National Day Rally speech at the Kallang Theatre, 20 Aug. 2000. *National Day Rally Speeches: 50 Years of Nationhood in Singapore*, p. 414.

179 Ibid., pp. 419–21.

180 *Census of Population 2000: Advance Data Release No. 9—A Decade of Progress* (Department of Statistics, 2001), p. 6; "Making 2010 Better than 2000", *Straits Times*, 21 Feb. 2001.

181 "Mind the Widening Income Gap", *Straits Times*, 11 Feb. 2001. See *Singapore Census of Population 2000: Advance Data Release No. 7—Household Income Growth and Distribution*, available at https://www.nas.gov.sg/archivesonline/speeches/record-details/7797c138-115d-11e3-83d5-0050568939ad (accessed 15 Apr. 2021).

182 Singapore Parliamentary Debates, 23 Feb. 2001, col. 34.

183 "Mind the Widening Income Gap", *Straits Times*, 11 Feb. 2001. See also "Making 2010 Better than 2000".

184 "This Tale of Two Cities Calls Out for Reconciliation", *Straits Times*, 22 Feb. 2001.

185 "First-World Economy, World-Class Home: Setting Fresh Goals", PM Goh Chok Tong, National Day Rally Speech at the Kallang Theatre, 22 Aug. 1999. *National Day Rally Speeches: 50 Years of Nationhood in Singapore*, p. 408. It is noteworthy that Goh chose to restate the need for cohesion just a few months later in his year-end message: "We must embrace change, ride the new economic wave, innovate and create new wealth . . . . Singapore needs to be a cohesive society, and not just so many individuals who can feel at home anywhere in the world." "'A Great Start to the New Year' Says PM", *Straits Times*, 1 Jan. 2000.

186 Following Goh's comments, the Feedback Unit conducted a poll of approximately 1,000 individuals, the results of which suggested that there was indeed a social barrier dividing "cosmopolitans" and "heartlanders". Of those polled, 55% agreed that a social barrier existed, with 83% saying more should be done to bring people together; 28% said heartlanders were envious of cosmopolitans, while 27% said cosmopolitans looked down on heartlanders. The one bright spot: 59% saw themselves as a mix between the two. "Break Down the Social Barrier and Bring People Together", *Straits Times*, 5 Jan. 2000.

187 PM Goh Chok Tong, National Day Rally speech, 20 Aug. 2000. *National Day Rally Speeches: 50 Years of Nationhood in Singapore*, pp. 427–9. See also "$2b in CPF Top-ups, with the Poor Getting More", *Straits Times*, 21 Aug. 2000.

188 In his 20 August 2000 National Day Rally speech, PM Goh stressed that he was against measures that would artificially raise the earnings of lower-income Singaporeans. This, he said, would "reduce the incentive for them to take the responsibility of improving their lot and that of their children". PM Goh Chok Tong, National Day Rally speech, 20 Aug. 2000. *National Day Rally Speeches: 50 Years of Nationhood in Singapore*, p. 427.

189 Singapore Parliamentary Debates, 23 Feb. 2001, cols 50–2. See also "Govt Cuts Personal Income Tax to 5%", *Straits Times*, 26 Feb. 2000.

190 "New Singapore", PM Goh Chok Tong, National Day Rally Speech at the University Cultural Centre, 19 Aug. 2001. *National Day Rally Speeches: 50 Years of Nationhood in Singapore*, p. 451. See "Hands off the Golden Goose", *Straits Times*, 20 Aug. 2001.

191 See Lee, *Unexpected Nation*, pp. 578–9.

192 "Facing Changes, Changing Faces", *Straits Times*, 24 Jan. 2001.

193 A *Petir* editorial noted in 1999 (even when the effects of the Asian Financial Crisis were still being felt regionally): "The PAP Government has steered the nation along a prudent, transparent and careful path, and we have emerged from the crisis with our reputation enhanced." "Preparing for the Future", *Petir*, Mar.–Apr. 1999, p. 2.

194 "PAP: An Institution that Holds the Country Together", *Petir*, Nov.–Dec. 1999 Special Issue, pp. 56–9, esp. 56.

195 "Confidential Report: Made Public", *Straits Times*, 4 Dec. 2000.

196 "PM Goh: Why I Brought the Election Forward to Nov. 3", *Business Times*, 19 Oct. 2001.

197 "It's Time for a Big-Picture GE Like No Other", *Straits Times*, 13 Oct. 2001. The *Straits Times* commentary, by Political Editor Han Fook Kwang, added for good measure, "These are serious times requiring a serious GE with serious issues from serious men and women who dare to want to lead in this dark period."

198 "A People United: Secure Future, Better Life" (PAP manifesto, 2001), p. 5. This theme of unity in crisis was reiterated at the time in speeches by key leaders. See, for example, "Youths Facing First Real Crisis: BG Lee", *Straits Times*, 8 Oct. 2001.

199 "A People United", pp. 11, 13. See also "Economic Plan Part of PAP Manifesto", *Straits Times*, 20 Oct. 2001.

200 "PAP Opts for a Sombre Slogan: A People United", *Straits Times*, 20 Oct. 2001.

201 "Recession Will Benefit the PAP, Not the Opposition", *Business Times*, 26 Oct. 2001; "SM: Be Prepared for a Bumpy Ride", *Straits Times*, 3 Nov. 2001.

202 "Anxious S'poreans Await Government Aid", *Straits Times*, 12 Oct. 2001; "Most Polled Say Govt Can Pull Singapore through Slump", *Business Times*, 12 Oct. 2001.

203 For the full package, see "Help Across the Board", *Straits Times*, 13 Oct. 2001; and "New $20m Relief Scheme for Families of Unemployed", *Straits Times*, 13 Oct. 2001.

204 "What, No SAF Scholars in New PAP Line-up?", *Straits Times*, 24 Oct. 2001. Only four individuals from the 2001 batch (Gan Kim Yong, Khaw Boon Wan, Raymond Lim and Dr Vivian Balakrishnan) had held government scholarships, as opposed to eight in 1997.

205 "New PAP Faces: Most from Private Sector", *Straits Times*, 25 Dec. 2000.

206 The three single women were the journalists Irene Ng, financial consultant Penny Low and lawyer Indranee Rajah. PM Goh made it known that earlier failures to get single women to stand on the Party ticket were not on account of a want of effort by the Party. See "PAP Looking at Singles, Divorcees Too", *Straits Times*, 24 Jan. 2001.

207 Ibid. Feedback from within the Party probably played a role too in making the 2001 slate as diverse as it was. Senior Minister of State for Education and MP for Changkat Dr Aline Wong on the occasion of the tenth anniversary of the PAP Women's Wing delivered a hard-hitting critique of the Party's attitude to women. Wong (who was to step down as an MP in 2001) spoke about the "slow progress women have been making both inside and outside the Party" and called on the Party to include single women and married non-working women among their candidates. "Wanted: Women in Politics", *Petir*, July–Aug. 1999, pp. 70–1; "Spore Women Want to Surge Ahead", *Straits Times*, 11 July 1999.

208 There was some suggestion in the press that the process of renewal had after 1997 become "unstuck", given the fact that very few from the 1997 batch progressed to senior appointments. "Why the PAP Isn't Playing It So Safe", *Straits Times*, 24 Nov. 2001. There was some truth to this. At the time of the 2001 polls, only two candidates from the 1997 batch had progressed to senior political appointments. Lim Swee Say was acting minister for the environment in 2001, while David Lim was minister of state for defence, as well as for information and the arts. A third individual from the 1997 slate, Peter Chen, was appointed senior minister of state for education and trade and industry but stepped down in 2001.

209 Interviews conducted by the author with some of the "Super Seven" suggest that while some had the impression that they might eventually be more than MPs, they were surprised at being appointed to junior ministerial positions immediately after the polls, having thought that some time might first be spent on the back benches. For his part, Goh Chok Tong observed: "Generally as a practice, we would throw many of the potential ministerial office-holders into the deep end of the pool. The sooner we can discover their strengths and weaknesses, the more time we will save." Goh Chok Tong, personal communication, 17 May 2014.

210 In 1992, Tharman, then director of Monetary Authority of Singapore's Economics Department, had brought to a meeting a report containing flash estimates of Singapore's 1992 second-quarter growth rate. The figures were allegedly sighted by another individual, with the information subsequently passing to journalists at the *Business Times*, which printed the information. The subsequent court case saw Tharman acquitted of the charge of communicating confidential data, but he was found guilty on a lesser charge of negligence and fined $1,500.

211 See "Ward Changes Unfair, Say Party Leaders", *Straits Times*, 18 Oct. 2001; "Dash to the Polls", *Straits Times*, 19 Oct. 2001; and "Opposition Complains about Short Notice", *Straits Times*, 19 Oct. 2001.

212 Cheng San GRC, which had seen the Workers' Party mount a very strong challenge in 1997, was erased from the electoral map. Some single-member constituencies where the Opposition had spent time working the ground also ceased to exist. See "Ward Changes Unfair, Say Party Leaders".

213 According to the PAP, this problem could be put down entirely to the inability of the Opposition to attract good people. "Can't Find Five Men?", *Straits Times*, 18 Oct. 2001.

214 "$13,000: Opposition Slams Poll Deposit", *Straits Times*, 20 Oct. 2001. The government's rejoinder was that this was to discourage individuals from contesting frivolously, and that in any case, the move should not have been a surprise as the deposit followed a fixed formula prescribed by the Parliamentary Elections Act (8% of an MP's allowance for the preceding year).

215 Six GRCs had been contested in 1997, five in 1991, and ten in 1988. In 2001 the team that the Workers' Party attempted to field in Aljunied GRC was disqualified owing to an administrative oversight: the space in the form that should have been filled with the name of the contested ward was inadvertently left blank. See "PAP Sweeps 55 Seats", *Straits Times*, 26 Oct. 2001; and "WP Could Have Avoided Debacle in Aljunied: PM", *Straits Times*, 27 Oct. 2001.

216 Under the SDA constitution, Chiam would retain the SDA chairmanship for two general elections. In addition, he would have the power to veto decisions made by the SDA council and executive committee, and have the power to appoint SDA officials to boot. See "WP and SDP 'Did Not Respond to Alliance'", *Straits Times*, 29 July 2001.

217 "WP, SDP to Stay Out of Alliance", *Straits Times*, 3 Aug. 2001.

218 See "Is the Election Outcome a Foregone Conclusion?", *Straits Times*, 26 May 2001; and "Thia Khiang Is New WP Chief", *Straits Times*, 28 May 2001.

219 Jeyaretnam pinned the failure of the WP to help him raise funds squarely on Low. See Jeyaretnam, Joshua Benjamin, Transcript of Oral History Interview, Accession No. 002932/23, CD 12, pp. 190–1 (National Archives of Singapore), available at https://www.nas.gov.sg/archivesonline/oral_history_interviews/record-details/467b2c9a-1161-11e3-83d5-0050568939ad (accessed 26 Jan. 2021).

220 The legal troubles of Jeyaretnam and the Workers' Party (which ultimately led to Jeyaretnam's 2001 bankruptcy) stemmed from two separate cases. The first was Jeyaretnam's remarks at a 1 January 1997 election rally, which were found by the courts to have been libellous against PM Goh and other PAP leaders. The second was legal action for defamation relating to an article in a 1995 issue of the *Hammer*, the publication of the Workers' Party. In the latter case, there were two sets of plaintiffs—the organisers of the 1995 Tamil Language Week, and a group of PAP MPs. Jeyaretnam's final appeals were dismissed in 2001, resulting in bankruptcy, expulsion from Parliament, and debarment from contesting the 2001 elections. See chapter 3; and Mauzy and Milne, *Singapore Politics under the People's Action Party*, pp. 134–5.

221 "Chiam—Don't Snuff Light Out of Opposition in Singapore", *Straits Times*, 3 Nov. 2001.

222 "Election—Opposition Will Provide Check and Balance in Parliament—WP", *Channel NewsAsia*, 2 Nov. 2001.

223 "No Ideas from Opposition on Long-Term Challenges", *Business Times*, 25 Oct. 2001. For the SDA manifesto, which included a repeat of Chiam's earlier call for drawing on Singapore's reserves to help ordinary Singaporeans cope with the recession, see "Alliance Promises More Help for Needy", *Straits Times*, 24 Oct. 2001.

224 The SDP had in addition to this revived its 1990s theme of high healthcare costs, proposing increased healthcare subsidies. For the SDP platform, see "Minimum Wage

for Workers and Pay for Jobless", *Straits Times*, 24 Oct. 2001; and "Give Money to Retrenched Workers", *Sunday Times*, 28 Oct. 2001.

225 "SDP's Plan 'Causes Higher Unemployment'", *Straits Times*, 29 Oct. 2001.

226 "GE 2001—It's Economics versus Politics", *Business Times*, 3 Nov. 2001.

227 See "Chee Goes Ahead with Second Public Talk", *Straits Times*, 6 Jan. 1999.

228 A 1999 *Straits Times* straw poll found that nine in ten people did not respect Chee: they questioned whether he was fighting a cause for Singaporeans or an opportunist trying to become a political martyr. At the same time, those polled were interested in the issues of freedom and democracy he touted, with the majority taking the view that Chee should have been given the permit for his public talks. "What's Chee Up to Now? . . . And What Is He Fighting For?", *Straits Times*, 26 Feb. 1999.

229 "How SDP Faltered after Chee's Misstep", *Straits Times*, 8 Nov. 2001.

230 "Recession Will Benefit the PAP, Not the Opposition", *Business Times*, 26 Oct. 2001. The Hokkien term *kiasu* can be translated as "afraid of losing out".

231 "'I Have Passion and Conviction'", *Sunday Times*, 28 Oct. 2001; "Ho Peng Kee Trounces Rival in 'Keen' Contest", *Sunday Times*, 4 Nov. 2001.

232 The Hungry Ghost Festival, celebrated by many Chinese (generally those with Taoist beliefs) in the seventh lunar month, is associated with the belief that prayers and offerings are required during the seventh month to appease the spirits of ancestors. Events taking place during the month are commonly held at Taoist temples and open-air precincts in the heartlands, with celebrants generally comprising local Chinese Taoists, Buddhists, businessmen with links to the local community, and members of clan associations. Volunteer organising committees for these events are informally known as Seventh Moon groups.

233 "Festival Permit Only after Donations?", *Straits Times*, 8 Nov. 2001.

234 "SM Lends a Hand in Nee Soon East", *Straits Times*, 2 Nov. 2001.

235 "Odds Now in Favour of Prof. Ho in Nee Soon East", *Straits Times*, 3 Nov. 2001.

236 *2001 General Election PAP Post-mortem Report* (PAP archive).

237 "Should the PAP Have Split into Two?", *Straits Times*, 17 Nov. 1999; "WP Could Have Avoided Debacle in Aljunied: PM".

238 "Why PM Talked Down His Men", *Straits Times*, 27 Nov. 2001.

239 "Because He Wanted Prof Low's Rival as NCMP", *Straits Times*, 27 Nov. 2001; "A Tougher GE Ahead, Says SG Goh", *Petir*, Jan.–Feb. 2002, pp. 6–8, esp. 8. PAP leaders occasionally chose to bestow a "halo" on Opposition MPs for their own reasons, but this almost never went down well with the PAP MP unlucky enough to have to face the beneficiary of the praise. In this case, Assoc. Prof. Low Seow Chay, the PAP incumbent in Choa Chu Kang, acknowledged PM Goh's "hidden agenda" in praising Steve Chia but was also moved to comment to reporters while on the campaign trail, "it's not very fair for me that the Prime Minister tries to campaign for my opponent". "PAP's Low Seow Chay Rues 'Hidden Agenda'", *Business Times*, 30 Oct. 2001.

240 "Defeated—but Promises Will Be Kept", *Straits Times*, 5 Nov. 2001; "Hougang Voters Wanted Me, and Upgrading—Low", *Straits Times*, 5 Nov. 2001.

241 See "Hougang—Eight Years Later", *Straits Times*, 30 Oct. 1999; "Opposition Has Capability—Chiam", *Straits Times*, 2 Nov. 2001.

242 For a useful treatment of the various issues between the government and the Malay community in 2000–01, see Gillian Koh and Ooi Giok Ling, "Singapore: A Home, a Nation?", *Southeast Asian Affairs* (2002): 257–63.

243 "Malay/Muslim Backing Vital to Win", *Sunday Times*, 4 Nov. 2001; "BG Lee Glad Jurong GRC Voters Rejected 'Opposition Theatrics'", *Straits Times*, 5 Nov. 2001.

244 See "Plan to Help Poor Malay-Muslims", *Today*, 13 Dec. 2000.

245 See "Malay MPs to Reach Out More to Community", *Straits Times*, 10 Nov. 2000; "Looking on Bright Side of Reality Checks", *Sunday Times*, 11 Mar. 2001; "We Are Not Unchanging Immoveables—SM", *Sunday Times*, 11 Mar. 2001.

246 "Malay MPs Slam Sept. 11 Attacks", *Straits Times*, 3 Oct. 2001.

247 "Muslims Must Reach Out to Others", *Straits Times*, 21 Oct. 2001.

248 See "Malay MPs Slam Sept. 11 Attacks"; "Muslims Distancing Themselves from Attacks", *Sunday Times*, 7 Oct. 2001; "Malays in Singapore 'Very Rational' Today", *Straits Times*, 11 Oct. 2001; and "See Islam in Perspective", *Straits Times*, 11 Oct. 2001.

249 The (largely unarticulated) sense that the economic downturn could hurt the community more than others may also have contributed to more of the Malay-Muslim vote going to the PAP. I am grateful to Abdullah Tarmugi for a personal communication on the state of the Malay-Muslim ground at the time of the 2001 elections.

250 See "Able Newcomers Prove Meritocracy Works—BG Lee", *Straits Times*, 29 Oct. 2001. Two of the new Malay candidates fielded in 2001—Halimah Yacob and Dr Maliki Osman—were known to have grown up in very humble circumstances. As a child, Halimah assisted her widowed mother, an illegal pushcart vendor, sell food while attempting to escape the attentions of police inspectors. Maliki was the eighth of nine children born to a bus conductor and a housewife. On the campaign trail, Maliki recalled that the family one-room HDB flat was so cramped that he spent "a significant part of my life sleeping on the cement corridor floor". "Once Poor, She Wants to Help Others Make It", *Straits Times*, 19 Oct. 2001; "Lecturer's Top Concern Is Health of Family Unit", *Straits Times*, 20 Oct. 2001.

251 Ahmad Khalis, a practicing lawyer, was also a madrasah supervisor and was known to have sent his two daughters to madrasahs for their education. He was also a long-time volunteer and general secretary of the Muhammadiyah Association, a Muslim welfare organization. The fielding of Halimah, a tudung-wearing unionist, was also seen as a striking choice. Some commentators noted that it was "a surprising but effective gesture for the Party to admit her in spite of the Party and Government's preference for a secular bearing among those associated with it". Koh and Ooi, "Singapore: A Home, a Nation?", p. 263.

252 "2007 Polls Will Be Crucial for PAP—PM Goh", *Business Times*, 6 Dec. 2000.

253 To emphasise his point, Goh was flanked by younger ministers as well as up-and-coming MPs who would be elevated to junior ministerial appointments later that month. "PM's Goal—Ensure Good Team by 2007", *Straits Times*, 4 Nov. 2001.

254 "PAP Targets Opposition Seats, Big Win in 2007", *Straits Times*, 27 Nov. 2001.

255 "PAP's Highest Award for Ex-Ministers", *Straits Times*, 25 Nov. 2001; "PAP Must

Press on with Self-Renewal", *Petir*, Jan.–Feb. 2002, p. 26. DPM Tan even suggested that by 2007 the PAP could be faced with an Opposition that might challenge the PAP in all seats.

256 The members of the post-mortem committee were Teo Chee Hean (chairman), Lim Hwee Hua (secretary), Dr Lee Boon Yang, Dr Yaacob Ibrahim, Indranee Rajah, Lim Hng Kiang, Raymond Lim, Lim Swee Say, David Lim, Irene Ng and Seng Han Thong.

257 Wong Kan Seng, addendum to *2001 General Election PAP Post-mortem Report* (PAP archive).

258 Ministerial pay had resurfaced as a hot-button issue in mid-2000 when another round of salary increases for top civil servants and ministers was announced. But the increases were partly reversed in 2001 in tandem with the economic slowdown. Just before the 2001 polls, the government announced a wage-reduction package in the civil service. Political appointment holders and the most senior civil servants took the biggest cut, with a 10% reduction of their salaries. Singapore Parliamentary Debates, 12 Oct. 2001, cols 2290–1; "Civil Service Cuts", *Straits Times*, 13 Oct. 2001; see also Mauzy and Milne, *Singapore Politics under the People's Action Party*, pp. 61–2.

259 Singapore Parliamentary Debates, 13 Mar. 2001, cols 945–73; "Comfy Fit for 5.5 Million in S'pore", *Straits Times*, 14 Mar. 2001.

260 Attracting Foreign Talent versus Looking after Singaporeans had been one of S21's key dilemmas. As the S21 Subject Committee (co-chaired by David Lim and Seng Hang Thong) addressing the issue noted piquantly in its report, "foreign talent does not just help to enlarge our economic pie but also make our pie tastier and more diverse in flavour. They introduce the *croissant* to supplement our *roti prata*." "Summary of the Deliberations of the Subject Committee on 'Attracting Talent vs Looking after Singaporeans'" (Singapore: Singapore 21 Committee, 1999), p. 3.

261 In a 1999 survey carried out as part of the S21 process, a quarter of those polled thought the government treated foreigners better than Singaporeans, while 55.2% felt that Permanent Residents had the same privileges as citizens. "Balancing Needs of Old and Young".

262 In addition, the qualifying standards for work permit holders whose permits attracted a "low levy" were raised, to ensure that a greater proportion of them had higher education levels. Singapore Parliamentary Debates, 12 Oct. 2001, cols 2282–3; "Stricter Criteria for Hiring Foreign Talent", *Straits Times*, 13 Oct. 2001.

263 The message that foreigners were necessary for Singapore to sustain its competitiveness and prosperity was rammed home as the polls drew closer. The Ministry of Trade and Industry produced figures to show the contribution of foreign workers to Singapore's GDP. "Foreigners Boosted Economy by 37 Per Cent", *Straits Times*, 1 Nov. 2001.

264 Singapore Parliamentary Debates, 12 Oct. 2001, cols 2329, 2398–9, 2405–8.

265 "Looming Clash over Foreign Talent", *Straits Times*, 24 Oct. 2001.

Chapter 5

Holding the Ground:
The PAP Within and Without, 2002–06

So comprehensive was the PAP's 2001 election victory that questions started to be asked in certain quarters about the nature of the win, what it portended for the political process, and to what extent (given the number of walkovers) the PAP actually had the mandate of the people. On 10 November 2001, the *Straits Times* published a letter written by leading members of the Roundtable. The letter, much more direct compared to a similar intervention the civil society group had made in the aftermath of the 1997 election, noted that elections in Singapore were "fast becoming almost a non-event" and made much of the fact that only 33 per cent of the eligible voters actually cast their votes. The PAP government had almost "legislated the Opposition into oblivion" (a reference to enlarged GRCs, the redrawing of electoral boundaries, and higher election deposits), with ministers and MPs returned unopposed in GRCs lacking moral authority and the political mandate of the majority. The letter concluded by asking whether it could be good in the long run, whether "the absence of competition over time might well lead to a flabby party led by those who enjoyed walkovers and continue to stay in power by making the field even less level for a diminishing opposition".[1]

The response came on 22 November 2001 in the form of a letter to the Straits Times from Press Secretary to the Prime Minister, Ong Keng Yong. Ong questioned those who claimed that the PAP government "lacked moral authority and political mandate", noting that in the 1997 Asian Financial Crisis and in the then-ongoing economic and security-related crisis, the PAP government had proved its worth, with Singaporeans overwhelmingly prepared to entrust leading the country through the crisis to the PAP, which would again have to face the electorate five years down the line. Ong rounded off by arguing (in response to the Roundtable's arguments for a credible Opposition) that it was up to the Opposition to up its game—no one could force the Opposition to put up GRC teams to ensure a contest. It was the PAP that scoured the island to get the best and most diverse slate of new talent:

> *The Roundtable should encourage such people to come forward and represent the interests of the people. If they are good, the PAP will offer them places in government. Instead of being in the wilderness for two or more terms, trying to build up a credible alternative, they can join the PAP and change its policies from within. This is how the PAP has stayed relevant in a fast-changing Singapore*

that is part of an ever-different world. This is why a credible opposition has not
emerged in Singapore.[2]

All in all, the reply was civil in tone and indeed more muted than might have been
expected. There were no jibes at "armchair critics", which had been part of the
government's response to the Roundtable's post-election intervention in 1997. This
may have been on account of the fact that the concerns expressed had not been just
from civil society, but from individual members of the public evincing views similar
to the Roundtable's.[3]

Some of the points raised were being considered at the same time within the Party.
The 2001 general election post-mortem report had noted that younger voters especially
might not want the impression of being taken for granted, and would increasingly
place weight on the issue of fairness and the need to have a genuine Opposition. The
report had commented that in future, there would be some merit in allowing some
time for the Opposition to react to the new electoral boundaries.[4] These observations
carried some weight, given that the chairman of the post-mortem committee, Teo
Chee Hean, had chaired the S21 committee and was widely seen as a minister in touch
with the aspirations of the young. But Teo and his post-mortem team were not alone
in musing about what the election result really meant. During the campaign, SM Lee
had expressed the concern that 18 new PAP MPs had benefited from "walkovers" in
constituencies where there were no Opposition candidates, denying them a "fight".[5]
Lee professed himself "uneasy" about Tanjong Pagar GRC's third walkover since it
was formed in 1991 (and with only one of his team having experienced a contest in
the past). Lee's concern was that the small number of seats contested meant that the
percentage vote of support for the PAP was not an accurate indicator of support for the
Party. Lee said that before he left the scene, he would try to contrive a way to expose
MPs "if not to a real baptism of fire, at least to a simulated one".[6]

Lee did not elaborate on what he had in mind. But similar sentiments had been
brewing elsewhere. During the campaign, PM Goh had proposed the setting up of
a People's Action Forum in the event of a PAP clean sweep at the polls. This would
essentially be a group of 20 PAP MPs that functioned like a constructive Opposition,
surfacing alternative ideas on policy and free to challenge the government, making for
better parliamentary debate. Goh's idea was to have the whip lifted over this group
for all issues except constitutional bills. In fact, Goh went even further, tentatively
floating the idea of a "shadow PM", with Government Parliamentary Committee
(GPC) chairmen to become shadow ministers.[7]

Goh's proposal—a sketch of how the PAP could still be checked from within even
if was unencumbered by an Opposition presence in Parliament—was a counter to
Opposition calls to deny the PAP precisely this clean sweep. In the event, however,
the People's Action Forum idea was shelved after discussion with PAP MPs. Wong
Kan Seng, the leader of the House and PAP second assistant secretary-general, made
it known in March 2002 that MPs had felt that having a group of MPs with a free
vote would be divisive and would degrade the value of votes coming from PAP MPs
not selected to be in the proposed forum. Instead, a new proposal was surfaced: the

whip would be lifted for all matters of conscience, remaining only for matters affecting national security, the budget, the constitution and no-confidence motions. PAP MPs could in addition make requests on a case-by-case basis to the PAP whip, Dr Lee Boon Yang, for it to be lifted.[8]

The Opposition, if not quite pushed to oblivion, seemed at the time to have been put so firmly into eclipse that it was difficult to see how it could represent a credible check on the government. It made sense, therefore, to allow some empowerment of the backbenchers, not unlike the type of leeway that had been afforded them in the 1970s. This would provide an answer to the post-election criticism (which had come not just from the Opposition but from academic commentators) that backbenchers had very little real say, did not provide enough fresh ideas, and could not truly reflect the concerns of the people given the conformity forced upon them by the Party whip.[9]

But what did the backbenchers themselves make of all this?

Niceties of Debate

On 3 April 2002, Tan Soo Khoon, freed from the role of Speaker and making his first speech in 13 years, delivered one of the most remarkable (and on the backbenches, well-received) parliamentary speeches seen in years. Castigating the PAP's leadership, Tan argued that people were cynical about the parliamentary process because of the perception that the government did not really listen, and pushed through legislation without enough consultation. Tan offered ideas: ministers should be more receptive to criticism and should credit MPs for suggestions that were taken up. More bills should be sent to select committees to obtain the views of the public before being passed by Parliament. Tan argued that the recent move to lift the whip was insufficient, as he still had to get permission to disagree. Tan said that there was no need for the whip at all (if the leadership was serious about freeing up MPs), except for issues that were absolutely critical, especially given the PAP's overwhelming parliamentary majority.[10]

Tan's performance was unscripted in that it clearly took the front bench (which conspicuously remained silent while other MPs gave a hearty round of applause) by surprise. Rebutting Tan in Parliament two days later, PM Goh rejected the idea that the Party whip should be removed altogether. Goh's arguments were similar to those proffered in the past by Party leaders when underlining the need for overall discipline. He argued that voters chose MPs on the basis of party platform. MPs, he said, could not be "too sanguine" in assuming that the unity and cohesion of the PAP would last forever: "No one can tell what the state of the Party will be like in the future, or how some MPs will behave once they think that the ministers are beholden to them because they can vote against the ministers freely."[11]

Goh's warning was apposite, given that the parliamentary sitting on that very day had seen PAP MPs vigorously—even heatedly—debating each other (with the whip lifted) on whether NMPs should be allowed in the House. SDA Chairman Chiam See Tong was even moved to remark that the session had been "completely different" from previous debates he had seen, and that seeing PAP MPs arguing issues in this manner was "a very, very rare thing" in the House.

The Party leadership from here on in would consent to the lifting of the whip on other issues. In November 2002, Parliament debated a motion on the review of upper secondary and junior college education. There was an extended but amicable debate, ending with unanimous support.[12] The whip was lifted also in January 2004, for the debate on the move to expand the scope of the Human Organ Transplant Act. All the 12 MPs who spoke, including Chiam See Tong, supported the move.[13]

In a way, therein lay the problem. As Opposition MPs pointed out, while it was good that the Party saw fit to lift the whip with a view to encouraging debate, it should also be lifted for contentious issues, not simply on matters where there was broad support at the outset (or where ultimate agreement was likely in any case). As the press observed, the government had in reality little to lose by allowing PAP MPs to debate and vote freely on the latter type of issue, whereas it had refused to lift the whip for an issue like the debate on the transport fare hikes in July 2002.[14]

The parliamentary debate on the hikes took place on 9 and 10 July 2002. Three motions on the issue were moved over the days. The first, and most important, was moved by Tan Soo Khoon.[15] Tan urged the Public Transport Council to review the fare increases; he also asked the government to ensure that there would be no unreasonable price increases in public services during the economic downturn.[16] A dominant theme during the debate—which proved to be a passionate one—was how Singaporeans were finding it difficult to make ends meet, whereas the public transport companies continued to be profitable. It was a sensitive and strained time. Several speakers made reference to the negative sentiment over economic prospects, and widespread coffeeshop talk of hardship and job losses. The Workers' Party's Low Thia Khiang was for his part able to use the motion to strike some blows of his own:

> *DPM Lee has just said recently that Singapore is in a stage of economic transition where the days of high growth and high employment rate have passed. At this time, when our economy is going into a transition, the ordinary people are affected the most. Although we are not a welfare state, the Government should not neglect the welfare of the people. The Government must try to help them to alleviate their burden, and public transport policy is one of the items that the Government should look into. We should question the PAP Government on its profit-driven policy through privatisation in providing public services. We are pursuing a market economy, but when the environment changes, when the gap between the rich and the poor has widened, when the poor get poorer and the rich get richer, the contradictions surrounding these changes would become more and more acute. This round of fare hike has generated a strong dissent among the people, and this is not just a momentary reflex. The policy of allowing the public transport service to be operated by private companies whose objective is to make profits needs to be re-examined.[17]*

Low's comments (which were similar in many ways to those expressed by PAP backbenchers during the debate) are worth quoting, given the recurrence of his themes through the rest of the decade. But on this occasion, the PAP backbench revolt needed no assistance. It was clearly (as MPs themselves noted during the course of the debate) a planned and organised intervention that had specific objectives: to reflect ground sentiment, to deliver a rebuke to transport operators, and to demand more transparency in the workings of the Public Transport Council.[18] Tan's motion was eventually passed, but not before amendments were made which in effect diluted it (the final motion lacked the original call for the Public Transport Council to review its decision to raise fares).[19]

A storm in a teacup? The Party leadership clearly felt that a line had to be drawn. It subsequently emerged that after the debate, Goh had, during a Party caucus on 16 July 2002, given the backbench a severe dressing-down. His stern injunction contained a reminder of the "OB markers" for PAP MPs. MPs should not play to the gallery; nor should they score "own goals". Backbenchers should also not expect to be treated with kid gloves if they were targeting the front bench. At this caucus Tan Soo Khoon apologised to DPM Lee for certain remarks made during the parliamentary debate, which had clearly been construed by the Party leadership to mean that Lee and the Public Transport Council had misled the public on the issue of whether there would in fact be an increase in public transport fares in 2002.[20] Tan (who denied that he had been told to apologise) repeated this apology in Parliament on 22 July 2002.[21]

Many PAP backbenchers had expressed their views passionately and occasionally fiercely during the parliamentary debate. But this can only partly account for the discomfort on the part of the Party leadership. More important was something that had been seen and remarked upon by independent commentators at the time: PAP backbenchers were doing the work of the Opposition better than the Opposition itself.[22] Chiam See Tong, in supporting the motion, had even found himself in the position of commending the views of PAP MPs Tan Soo Khoon and Dr Tan Cheng Bock.[23]

The whole transport fare hike debate seemed to end with Tan Soo Khoon's apology, and (as the press commented) with a whimper.[24] But the reverberations were felt for a considerable length of time. There had been some sense after the 2001 general election (and especially when PM Goh had broached the idea of a shadow cabinet and the People's Action Forum) that the PAP would start to evolve more democratic processes through debates within and without Parliament.[25] Clearly this was never realised, and any movement in this direction was shorn off in July 2002, in the course of the PAP's self-analysis after the fare hikes debate.

Public sentiment, expressed for example through letters to the press, seemed to support the view that the whip should have been lifted for the debate, given that the issue did not pertain to extremely sensitive matters such as public security or race. Scepticism of the parliamentary process was fuelled also by the fact that the parliamentary debate on the fee hikes only took place a week after the fare rises had actually taken effect. There was, in short, the palpable sense of the wider public being unhappy at not having a genuine outlet to express their views. This was to dominate the national agenda for several months. It came through particularly strongly in dialogue sessions held by the Feedback Unit, swamping in effect all other issues through the rest of 2002. Dr Wang Kai Yuen, chairman of the Feedback Unit Supervisory Panel, noted that while the government used the Feedback Unit as a listening ear, the people expected it to function as a "collaboration between equals".[26]

This was not a view shared by government leaders. Responding to comments that the government had not listened to feedback on the issue of fare hikes, PM Goh stressed that Singaporeans first had to understand the nature of the feedback loop. The government would consider all views, and the important thing in the parliamentary debate was that MPs had in fact spoken frankly, in a reflection of their being in tune with ground sentiment. But Goh also said that the final decision had to be taken for the good of the nation: "The Government, like a good doctor, must apply its own knowledge and experience, consult experts, take in feedback, and then prescribe what, in its considered opinion, is the best treatment."[27]

PM Goh's clampdown on dissenting backbenchers in July 2002 should be put down to the simple fact that the debate had got out of hand. The idea that backbenchers had inadvertently contributed to an undermining of the relationship between the PAP government and the public was something that particularly rankled: any suggestion of this would be dealt with, with little regard for niceties. Some of this can be seen from the parliamentary debate in September 2003, following a cut in employers' Central Provident Fund (CPF) contribution rates. During this debate, the word "betrayal" had been used by Low Thia Khiang and PAP MP Dr Amy Khor as a reflection of public sentiment (given the general expectation that the overall CPF contribution rate would be restored to its original level of 40 per cent).[28] Low was dealt with in a straightforward fashion: Goh chastised him for fanning discontent without making constructive suggestions. Goh gave a nod to the fact that Dr Khor had in fact overall been supportive of the changes, but he also had a steel-edged word of advice: "I advise PAP MPs not to unwittingly erode the trust between the people and the Government. . . . PAP MPs should be careful not to broadcast such strong words, when there was no betrayal. They must not sing the same tune as opposition MPs. Instead, they should stand their ground and debunk this betrayal nonsense."[29]

Goh had been extremely direct in issuing his rebukes. However, the PAP's tough treatment of its MPs went no further than the debating floor of Parliament and closed-door caucus discussion. Of the backbenchers who spoke in support of Tan Soo Khoon's motion on the public transport fare hikes in July 2002, several were at or near the beginning of their careers. Some of them would become prominent while continuing to retain their reputation for being independent speakers and thinkers. Examples included Inderjit Singh, Halimah Yacob and Dr Amy Khor, with the latter two going on to subsequently hold political office.[30]

Those PAP MPs who wanted to speak up would do so, even without any attempt to organise them. The identities of the more vocal PAP MPs were well known. Besides those named above, these backbenchers included Dr Tan Cheng Bock, Dr Wang Kai Yuen and Tan Soo Khoon himself, who according to the *Straits Times* was "an icon of the kind of MP Singaporeans would like to see".[31] It was outspoken backbenchers like these who were popular on the ground but who were inevitably castigated when deemed by the Party leadership to have crossed the line. A well-known example of such a situation was Dr Tan Cheng Bock's call during the March 1999 budget debate for restraint in bringing in foreign talent. Tan asked that the government "think Singaporeans first", especially given the depressed regional climate.[32] This call was subsequently supported by several MPs, who took the view that skilled foreigners were welcome but that the criteria should be tightened to make sure that only deserving foreigners got in.[33] However, this elicited a robust response from Second Trade and Industry Minister George Yeo, who rejected what he said was Tan's emotional line of attack. Singapore, Yeo said, could ill afford to send a message that it was abandoning its welcome of foreign talent simply on account of the tough economic situation.[34]

What could perhaps be taken away from these parliamentary debates was confirmation that organised attempts on the part of the leadership to stimulate intra-Party debate did not work. The simple fact was that with an Opposition presence in the House, however small, an overly critical PAP backbench could easily provide ready fodder for government critics. As PM Goh said after the transport hike debate, MPs had done their job if they reflected ground feedback. What Goh did not say, but which could be inferred, was that MPs ran the risk of being taken to task—sometimes very publicly—if they chose aggressive lines of questioning on the wisdom of policy. Especially telling were Goh's remarks in November 2001 in raising the People's Action Forum idea. Goh had said he was confident that "as a Government, I have enough control over my own backbenchers, that nothing will go wrong. You can then generate debate in Parliament."[35] Enforcing discipline over the backbenchers was of vital importance, even in a period when the Opposition had been decimated.

One also receives the impression that the Party leadership, while recognising the importance of parliamentary debate, was not overly keen to extend its boundaries. In October 2004 parliamentary procedures were changed, putting a limit to the number of questions MPs could raise during question time.[36] This is not to say that the leadership had completely discounted the idea of Parliament as a forum for genuine insight and policy-related suggestions. There were, in fact, moves at this time that showed a leadership well aware of the need for quality debate. The nomination process for NMPs was refined in 2002, with more groups from social and community service organisations, tertiary education institutions, and media, art and sports organisations being roped into the consultation process to surface NMPs.[37] Separately, GPCs were in 2002 enlarged and reorganised into ten groups to tackle issues in specific ministries. For the first time, office-holders (at the level of senior parliamentary secretary) were inducted into GPCs. The new GPCs were now to have more regular contact with the relevant ministries, in addition to being given more research resources and staff support.[38]

Outside of Parliament, too, moves were made at this time that represented attempts to broaden and decentralise the process of garnering views. Dr Wang Kai Yuen, the Bukit Timah MP known for speaking frankly, had in March 2002 taken over from Dr John Chen as chairman of the Feedback Unit Supervisory Panel. In an effort to make the reach of the unit more representative, Wang announced in May 2002 the setting up of a People's Forum, made up of approximately 5,000 members of the public. The group would be broadly representative of the population in terms of age, gender and religion.[39] Wang also announced that the existing Feedback Unit tea sessions would be reconfigured, henceforth being no-holds-barred discussions on any topic (rather than specific issues).

Not that freewheeling discussions within the Feedback Unit were entirely unknown. The unit's Political Matters and Media Feedback Group, chaired by Viswa Sadasivan, a well-known political commentator not tied to any political party, was already well known as a forum for exceptionally frank discussion. The group had in September 2002 released a report urging the government to make the electoral system more transparent. The content was eyebrow-raising and even read, as the press put it, "like a wish-list of the Opposition parties".[40] It must be counted as significant that a major October 2002 reorganisation of the Feedback Unit, which saw a streamlining of the total number of subgroups from 17 to eight, saw not just the Political Matters Group survive the cull, but also the reappointment of Sadasivan as chairman of this subgroup.[41] This could perhaps be put down to the careful manner in the way the group used to make its recommendations. The points made in its September 2002 report were cast as representing legitimate ground sentiments—many rules were seen as less than fair. If changes were not made, the bond between government and people would weaken.[42] The absence of a tough reply from government was perhaps a reflection of its expanding (but gradual) readiness to allow the expression of political sentiment that it did not necessarily agree with.

The Millennial Sense

In September 2003 a highly-respected retired permanent secretary and former head of civil service, Ngiam Tong Dow, gave an interview to the *Straits Times*. Ngiam's comments (made at a time when the national mood was still pessimistic, with the economic gloom only slowly lifting) were widely remarked on, dealing in the main with issues concerning Singapore's long-term future and its prospects under the PAP government. Ngiam suggested that Singapore should open up politically, and criticised the PAP's tactic of placing scholars in the civil service, thereby (he said) retaining the PAP government's monopoly on talent. This, Ngiam commented, would be a recipe for political atrophy. It was better to allow an alternative leadership to emerge:

> Unless SM [Lee] allows serious political challenges to emerge from the alternative elite out there, the incumbent elite will just coast along. At the first sign of a grassroots revolt, they will probably collapse just like the incumbent Progressive Party to the left-wing PAP onslaught in the late 1950s. I think our leaders have to accept that Singapore is larger than the PAP.[43]

Ngiam's views were of course not shared by the Party, but it is worth observing that as the millennium approached, and in the years approaching the half-centenary of the Party, a degree of introspection had begun to creep into Party discourse when it came to issues of political longevity.[44] Lee Kuan Yew himself had at a 6 September 1999 parliamentary sitting ruminated on the issue in terms not altogether dissimilar to Ngiam's, noting that if the PAP allowed itself to become "soft and flabby", a leaner and shrewder team could displace it, just as the PAP had taken only a few years from its formation to win power.[45]

Lee was not alone in casting his mind forward. Close to the new millennium, there were several opportunities for the Party leadership to take stock of what had been achieved, and to survey future challenges. Key amongst them was the 1999 celebration of the PAP's 45th anniversary. Interviews given by Party leaders at this time are informative of these leaders' attitude to some of the questions above, and to the idea of one-party dominance. PM Goh revealed that the leadership had on several occasions discussed whether it would be "better to split the PAP ourselves for Singapore's good". According to Goh, the leadership had considered a scenario where two factions might agree on basics but disagree on policies, timing and implementation. The two factions could then contest elections on the basis of personality and the ability to articulate ideas. But ultimately, Goh said, there had been agreement that what was needed was one strong team and getting more good people to join the PAP, rather than two sides contending for support. There was no point factionalising the Cabinet artificially when all concerned agreed on the basics: Singapore, Goh stated, would not benefit.[46]

Exactly how long the plan to split the Party had been on the drawing board (and how intensively it was discussed) is unclear. But the idea of political competition—within and without—had exercised the minds of some within the Party leadership for some time. Speaking to students from Nanyang Technological University in February 2000, SM Lee touched on the issue of a two-party system. He said, "to have a two-party system, you must have real alternatives—alternative policy, alternative philosophy—and the men and women to propound them and execute them if they get into office". In Lee's view, Singapore, unlike other countries, lacked the critical mass to generate alternative ideas.[47]

The sense of introspection was most marked from around 1999 to 2004. The culmination was the year-long series of events in 2004 marking the 50th anniversary of the Party. Party leaders in their speeches evidenced a clear sense (clearer than what had been seen in 1999–2000) that the Party would thrive and lead the people for the foreseeable future. Speaking at one of the centrepiece events, the PAP's 50th anniversary dinner, SM Goh stated plainly that it was the PAP that was the force that was going to get the job done for Singaporeans:

> *It is a quiet national movement of people who believe in Singapore and are willing to contribute to make Singapore succeed. . . . Without the PAP, the history of Singapore would be totally different. I do not see another group of men and women who can do a better job of looking after Singapore than the PAP.*[48]

The various events in 2004 celebrating the Party's 50th anniversary had a fair dose of nostalgia, but sentiment of the overly saccharine sort was absent. Laced throughout was the idea that the Party had to remain young, co-opt the best, and have the best ideas. Goh himself was clear that in order to retain the popular mandate, the PAP had to remain young and continue to connect directly with the people: "If success gets into our heads and we begin to lose touch with the people, that will be our downfall."[49]

The post-millennial moment was not simply about introspection within the Party. The depressed economic climate (combined with the increasingly felt economic might of countries like India and China), sporadic jolts such as the loss of major shipping carriers to Malaysia, and larger, looming spectres such as radical Islamism had combined to create a national mood that was decidedly pessimistic. This was a malaise lasting well into 2003–04. Government leaders made no secret of their concern that Singaporeans might be losing their confidence amidst the economic gloom and retrenchments.[50] The message from the PAP leadership was that the people should snap out of the gloom, and that better things (and better economic news) would come. Attempts by the government to rouse the people culminated in PM Goh's National Day Rally speech on 18 August 2002. Goh highlighted recent media reports and letters to the media that had quoted some young people as saying they felt no sense of belonging and, rather than fighting for Singapore, would run off at the drop of a hat. Goh took issue with "fair-weather Singaporeans who, having benefited from Singapore, will pack their bags and take flight when our country runs into a little storm. . . . Look yourself in the mirror and ask: Am I a stayer or quitter? Am I a fair-weather Singaporean or an all-weather Singaporean?"[51]

The post-rally reaction to Goh's "quitter" comment was mostly negative.[52] The deeply felt, emotional reaction on the part of the people (evinced, for example, through dialogue sessions conducted by the Feedback Unit) betrayed a sense of hurt and incomprehension. The reaction, however, largely ignored the nuances of PM Goh's exhortation. What had been glossed over was Goh's attempt to give an uplifting message even as he threw down a challenge to the young—to rise and face the challenges head-on, just as Singaporeans had done in difficult circumstances in 1965: "Today it's the turn of our young to be tested. This baptism of fire will temper your generation. . . . I'm confident that you have what it takes to secure your place under the sun."

During this period, government leaders were in fact making it a habit in their public statements and engagements to hearken back to the difficult days of the 1960s, asking the youth whether they had gone soft or would rise to the challenge to make a better Singapore.[53] But internally, the leadership realised that exhortations alone would not be enough. It appears to have come to the conclusion, beginning from around the turn of the millennium, that co-opting the post-independence generation was essential to the fortunes of both the nation and the Party. Two major initiatives were set in train across both fronts in order to achieve this.

Betwixt Remaking and Refreshing

Refreshing PAP

At the Party conference on 3 December 2000, Deputy Prime Minister and PAP Assistant Secretary-General BG Lee Hsien Loong told cadres that the Party's goals and programmes had to be relevant to the new generation of Singaporeans. DPM

Lee emphasised the need for the Party to ensure that in this new, information-rich environment, its message still got through.[54] What was wanted, according to Lee, was "not just good men and women, but people representing a wide range of views, including those who disagree with the party on certain issues, but care about the country and want to contribute. The test is not conformity. . . . We hope we will influence their views, and they will also influence our policies."[55] Speaking to Young PAP members at an event just a few days after the Party conference, YP Chairman Lim Swee Say said that the Party wanted to develop greater political awareness amongst young people, "so they will come forward to contribute and contest ideas".[56]

Lim Swee Say had in October 1999 been tasked by the CEC to help the Party think afresh about its future. This included making a systematic study of the mood of the younger generation and exploring, inter alia, what could be done to make them more willing to join, identify with and support the Party. Lim's task group, which began its work in February 2000, comprised approximately 40 core YP members (who in turn consulted close to 200 YP members at the district and branch levels). The task group's paper, "Capturing Interest and Winning Loyalties of the Younger Generation", was tabled before the CEC in October 2000.[57] Observations were made about the lack of mechanisms within the Party to bring members closer together, and how there was no compelling reason for young people to join the Party. In addition, the paper observed that the younger generation had different expectations and wanted to see a faster pace of change in the social and political spheres. They also wanted to see a higher level of mutual trust and respect between the government and the people. The key recommendations were as follows:

- Turning YP into a more active and open platform for young Singaporeans to debate economic and social issues. People would then find it worthwhile to join the Party. YP would also strive to expand its membership base.
- Making more use of technology (especially the Internet) within the Party and in communications with the public.
- PAP office-holders adopting a more active profile in various National Education seminars conducted at the pre-university level. The intention was to help the younger generation better understand the process of nation-building. This would also give them a chance to listen to and interact directly with government leaders.

When the CEC approved the proposals in Lim's paper (which formed part of what came to be known as the YP21 initiative, discussed further below) in October 2000, there was agreement that YP should present itself as a platform for younger Singaporeans to express their views and come up with constructive ideas to deal with major long-term issues. YP had to actively present and advocate Party principles and policy positions in the Internet arena to engage the younger Internet-savvy generation.[58]

The conclusions and recommendations of the task group's paper might seem unremarkable, but there was within the Party a deeply felt concern at the price that would be paid if the Party failed to connect with the younger generation. In announcing the YP21 initiative during the 3 December 2000 Party conference, Lim Swee Say signalled some of the urgency:

> *There is a growing gap between the young and the old in abilities, values and aspirations. The danger was that the different generations would pull in different directions. We should align the mindset between the young and the old to increase our national cohesion and resilience. The challenge for Singapore was to strengthen our "heartware". The young should be given not just an economic stake in our future, but also an emotional stake. This could be brought about through consultation, consensus building, involvement and participation in policy formulation . . . the vision [of YP21] was to increase political awareness and encourage the young to contribute more ideas. It was hoped that the process would nurture some young Singaporeans to become political leaders to serve Singapore.*[59]

There were equally important developments taking place in parallel. During the 3 December 2000 Party conference, PM Goh outlined the vision of the Party for the new millennium. The Party needed to anticipate developments in the next decade, understand shifts taking place in society, and decide on changes to make Singapore an even better home for all. Goh said that this would inform the election manifesto. He said he had asked Education Minister Rear-Admiral (NS) Teo Chee Hean to consult Party members and MPs and work out this vision, which he suggested be themed "The Future Society".[60]

There was fresh impetus after the 2001 election. In December that year, PM Goh tasked the YP Executive Committee (Exco) to submit a paper detailing how YP could be remade to remain relevant to young Singaporeans. Titled "Remaking and Reshaping PAP and YPAP", the paper was considered by the CEC in March 2002. It made points that were similar to those covered in the YP21 paper of October 2000. First, young people were better informed and would demand more involvement in decision-making and push for a climate of open consultation and consensus-building. Second, although the Party had sound policies, it needed to update the form and tone of communication to better explain policy and relate policy changes to the ground. YP also had to be given more room and flexibility to voice its views and position on policy and issues, even if some of these might not necessarily be in line with the PAP's position. The paper concluded by noting that the PAP and YP could attract the interest and commitment of young Singaporeans only by moving from a hierarchical structure to an inclusive and dynamic network, one that had a participative and consensus-building culture.[61]

Party leaders were clear that the PAP was prepared to let its younger activists and MPs influence the Party, and national policy, in order to keep abreast of the aspirations of young Singaporeans. "Let's make use of our new people," noted DPM Lee in a March 2002 interview, "and their ideas and their inputs, and then see how the party and our policies can adjust".[62] The importance of this point should not be underestimated. The Party at the turn of the millennium had come to embrace the idea that Party longevity could be ensured only if people with different political views and philosophies (but of proven integrity and ability) were brought into the Party. As Minister Mentor (MM) Lee Kuan Yew was to note in 2004, differences in views would then be in the form of intra-Party arguments on alternative policies and different futures, which was in fact preferable: "If we do not have these arguments within the party, they will surface as inter-party competition."[63]

By 2002, some of these themes were beginning to spill out into wider Party discourse. The CEC report presented to cadres at the December 2002 Party conference noted that it was a key challenge for the PAP to renew and remake itself, especially with younger voters becoming increasingly vocal, and with their expectations of the government rising. Discussions and dialogues at the 2002 Party conference tackled this and addressed the sense that there needed to be more debate within the Party.[64] It was at the 2002 Party conference that PM Goh, also the Party secretary-general, announced the setting up of the Refreshing PAP Committee to look into how to reinvigorate the Party and to ensure it would continue to win the support of the people.[65] The Refreshing PAP team was chaired by RADM Teo Chee Hean. This was a logical and unsurprising choice, given Teo's experience in marshalling the S21 process, his work on the Future Society concept, and his having overseen the post-mortem for the 2001 election. Teo was to be assisted by National Development Minister Mah Bow Tan (deputy chairman). The team itself was a young one, with six of its nine members elected as MPs only in 2001.[66]

The terms of reference given to the committee were broadly defined. The first was to reinvigorate the PAP so as to enable it to continue to win the support of the people and lead the country. The second was to update the Party objectives, constitution, organisation, programmes and activities so that all Singaporeans (particularly the young) would want to identify with the Party. Throughout 2003, the Refreshing PAP Committee consulted widely with Party members and interested Singaporeans through a series of dialogue sessions with the five districts, YP and the Women's Wing. This was, significantly, also the first internal revamp of the Party that had actively sought the views of civil society activists.

The leadership considered the report of the Refreshing PAP Committee in September 2003, with the key recommendations presented at the Party convention on 9 November:[67]

- Local elections: The committee recommended that some members of the district committees and HQ Exco be elected. Each district committee would have ten elected members drawn from about 50 to 90 members from their respective branches and one elected member each from their respective sections of YP and the Women's Wing. The district committee chairman and two vice-chairmen would be elected from among the MPs/branch chairmen in that district. The elected members of the five district committees would elect two members into the Party HQ Exco.
- Changes in YP and the Women's Wing: YP district chairmen and vice-chairmen would be elected from among the branch YP chairmen

(instead of being appointed by the PAP district chairmen). The district chairmen and vice-chairmen would also become YP Executive Committee members. (Hence, ten of the 24 YP Executive Committee positions would be elected.[68]) More YP activities would be organised at the district level, in an attempt to grow a critical mass of members. In addition, the Women's Wing would attempt to reach out more to professionals.

- Policy forum: A policy forum would be set up. This would be an avenue for two-way consultation between the Party leadership and the rank and file. Party members would use this platform to express views and comment on policies. The forum would comprise 188 members, consisting of two representatives from each of the 84 branches and ten each from YP and the Women's Wing. Two MPs would be appointed as advisors to the forum. Forum members would select a chairman and ten other members to form the Joint Forum Council (JFC) for a one-year term, with the council overseeing the forum and setting the agenda for the year.[69]

The aim of all these changes, as Party leaders made clear at the convention, was to make the Party more "ground up"; foster (especially through limited elections and the Policy Forum) a greater sense of involvement, ownership and participation in Party activities; and provide feedback and ideas to help understand and shape Party policy. All this would in turn help the Party keep itself relevant to Singapore and in tune with the aspirations of Singaporeans.[70]

The final recommendations owed a great deal to the Refreshing PAP Committee's engagements with younger Party members. Many within this segment had become cynical, and did not see themselves as making a difference. The issue of making membership meaningful came up at all the consultation sessions that the committee had. This declining sense of worth was attributed to the lack of recognition of younger members as Party members and their inability to influence policymaking. Younger Party members wanted greater participation in the political process—first within the Party and ultimately in society. Another finding related to the depoliticisation of the Party was that the PAP's influence was so pervasive and embedded in grassroots organisations that the Party's image and identity had been subsumed, and indeed integrated, into these entities. The need and motivation for people to join a political party had therefore been negated. The Refreshing PAP Committee acknowledged the validity of these points. As the final report submitted to the CEC noted, "the political instincts and musculature of our members can atrophy through disuse".[71]

When the Refreshing PAP report was presented at the November 2003 Party conference, there was the palpable sense of the PAP breaking away from the old way of doing things, connecting with the aspirations of the young, and bringing in fresh minds to offer new ideas. But there was also scepticism from certain quarters as to what the entire initiative had actually achieved. One of the more outspoken PAP MPs,

Inderjit Singh, queried whether the proposed Policy Forum would be distinguished from existing feedback and outreach efforts.[72]

Ideas on engaging the young, and encouraging a freer flow of ideas, were hardly new. Many of the observations from these discussions had suggested themselves in the S21 process. There was therefore some scepticism within the Party when it came to the PAP's refreshing. Some activists had wanted a more wide-ranging review of the Party, one that would lead to more decision-making authority given to the body of MPs (rather than just ministers).[73] There were also activists who felt that the democratisation of Party processes, and the limited introduction of elections for certain posts, had not gone far enough. This point had come up during the course of the Refreshing PAP Committee submitting its findings at the November 2003 Party convention. One activist suggested that the pool of positions to be contested should be larger, and that key officials in the YP Exco (for example, the deputy chairman, secretary and treasurer) should be elected. The idea was that this would allow activists to learn about electioneering; it would also help to debunk the notion that those chosen were simply handpicked in an opaque process. Party leaders, including YP Chairman Lim Swee Say and PM Goh, while not rejecting these suggestions outright, responded that change had to be evolutionary.[74]

On the face of it, it might seem that the Refreshing PAP initiative stopped well short of promoting substantial changes within the Party. Perhaps this had to do with the mindset of key leaders, which was that no major overhaul was necessary. But rather than viewing the Refreshing PAP initiative in isolation, it is more helpful to see it together with other changes to the Party that were already taking place. In particular, efforts to rejuvenate YP under YP21 (launched in December 2000) should be considered briefly:

- A YP Forum would be set up, distinct from the main PAP Policy Forum. This would see YP members and friends of the PAP debate topical issues amongst themselves and with political leaders.
- "YP Community" (an initiative to enlarge the pool of politically aware activists and opinion leaders).
- From 2001, there would be new YP Action Groups (YPAG), which were essentially special interest groups. Some catered, for example, to those keen to help the underprivileged. Others were more topical and discussion-based, focusing on themes such as religious harmony, manpower, or education. Separately, many of these centred on social activities. For example, YPAG Active Lifestyle focused on social or sporting activities.
- The setting up of an online discussion forum, YP Net.[75]

These were in part deliberate moves to strengthen the Party, away from formal recruitment channels. There was increasing recognition within the Party that while established mechanisms should not be dispensed with, there had to be less structured interactions and settings that would enable interested people to find out more, and interact with others of like mind.[76] Non-members were, for example, asked to attend YPAG activities and YP Policy Forum meetings. From this starting point, some would be invited to other events, such as talks and dialogues with ministers (which were ramped up at the district and branch levels from 2001). Of these, some might be invited to join the Party later.[77]

YP's increased activity from 2001 was manifested also in more aggressive recruitment efforts. YP branches and the HQ General Branch stepped up their membership drive, holding more dialogue sessions and recruiting new members. YP membership nearly doubled from about 3,100 in 2000 to 6,103 in 2004.[78] Membership of the General Branch increased from 150 to approximately 500 by 2002.[79] Efforts were made to bring YP members into the branches rather than keeping them at the HQ General Branch, where they were confined to discussing policy issues.[80] There were also moves— important ones—to ensure that renewal at the branch level remained on track. From the early 2000s, increasing numbers of younger branch secretaries and assistant branch secretaries began to be brought in.[81] The CEC for a time considered introducing age limits for Branch Exco officials (similar to what had been done for grassroots organisations). But the option eventually preferred was, from the early 2000s, to regularly remind the branches that 25 per cent of branch committee members should be renewed after each election, with better-educated and younger members being the preferred replacements.[82]

Naturally, progress was uneven, with some branches more assiduous than others in attracting younger activists. Many young activists found themselves grappling with the issue of credibility, particularly when inducted into branches with large numbers of veteran members.[83] Some MPs, mindful of the sensitivities, wisely chose to introduce these Young Turks in a gradual fashion. Rather than taking over the work of veteran activists immediately, some of the younger inductees were first given work that suited their (often professional) temperament, such as the discussion of the branch's progress, and the work plan for the following year.[84]

More members in YP also meant an increasingly diverse make-up. In the first half of the decade, blue-collar, non-tertiary-educated workers formed the fastest-growing group in YP. The move to recruit more non-graduates was a deliberate move by YP to make itself more representative of the population, and to dispel notions of elitism.[85] A separate trend, which became more pronounced as the decade wore on, was that of entrepreneurs and businessmen joining the PAP. Many of these individuals professed themselves keen to serve the community, and did indeed contribute their time at the branches. But it was also apparent, as several of the individuals in question acknowledged themselves, that serving in this fashion was also a way of making contacts, networking and sharing knowledge.[86]

Documents made available to the author concerning YP's revamp in 2002 make it clear that even at the stage where the larger initiative that would become Refreshing PAP was already being considered, there was the acceptance that the PAP and YP could only attract the interest and commitment of young Singaporeans by making several major shifts.[87] First, there had to be a move from passive to proactive membership, from a centrally driven culture to a participative and consensus-building one. It was also realised that the Party had to facilitate the remaking of YP by continuing to give it more freedom and autonomy to speak up on policy matters, so that YP could better reflect the ideas and sentiments of the younger generation (and draw more of them into the Party). Regeneration of the membership base was another key issue that was considered. But the goal was not simply inducting new blood: those absorbed needed to have the chance to engage and interact with other Party members and the leadership, through the Party's political education platforms. In sum, these were quite deliberate moves to increase diversity, but they were calibrated in a manner designed to ensure strengthened unity and not contention within the Party.[88]

Reasons of space preclude detailed examinations of each and every new initiative rolled out during these years. Efforts to revamp YP were a continuing process, with an afterlife that eclipsed even Refreshing PAP. In April 2005 a new group, YPAP Women, was formed. The move arose out of discussions between female Young PAP members (marshalled by Irene Ng, an MP for Tampines GRC) and YP Chairman Dr Vivian Balakrishnan in 2004.[89] The new group was aimed at women professionals in the Party aged 17 to 40 and was in part a response to the feeling in some quarters that the main Party was still too patriarchal, and the feeling that the Women's Wing was too staid and only for middle-aged women.[90] The point, as Balakrishnan noted, was to have a political platform that would tap on the energy and talents of young women, and to do so in a manner that would engage them directly, on their wavelength.[91]

The effort to engage the younger generation also involved the rebranding of YP in a manner designed to show that the Party could keep up with the times. Some of these attempts appeared to be deliberate efforts to go against the staid image of the Party. In October 2003, for example, YP celebrated its 17th anniversary at a well-known local nightspot, Zouk. The celebrations were marked by a fashion show that featured YP members modelling the Party's all-white uniform, and culminated in YP Chairman Lim Swee Say and Deputy Chairman Vivian Balakrishnan climbing onto the bar together with other YP leaders.[92]

The main leadership, as well as that of YP, was well aware that efforts to connect in this vein made the Party vulnerable to accusations that it was artificially trying to be trendy. Speaking in September 2006 to YP members, Dr Vivian Balakrishnan, minister for community development, youth and sports (and by then YP Chairman) tackled the perception head on, cautioning that updating the PAP was not just about trying to be "hip". The main issue, he said, was trying to be "real". This meant, in addition to sincerity and commitment, having a "constant stream of fresh faces with new ideas" that would keep the Party attractive. Balakrishnan noted that the PAP had been in power for so long that it was in danger of being seen as "old, stale and more of the same". If new ways were not found to win over the young, the PAP would lose the battle for the hearts and minds of the next generation: "So our greatest imperative now is to reach out to people who may be different from us, who may disagree with us, but who share a commitment to building a better future, and to bring them into the party and to say, we have a space for you."[93]

ᒼᔭᔭᔑᔭ

It will be recalled that the Refreshing PAP Committee had made recommendations relating to the introduction, in a limited manner, of democratic elections for positions in district committees and the HQ Exco, as well as for key YP positions at the district level (with the successful candidates then being appointed to the YP Exco). When, in May 2003, the interim recommendations from the Refreshing PAP Committee were sent to Party leaders for consideration, there was some debate on why intra-Party elections should be allowed at all. One senior Party figure was moved to comment internally:

> Insofar as the party believes in democracy, then local elections would lend weight to it and confer greater legitimacy to local party leaders, as their peers would have freely chosen them. But we should bear in mind, that in effect, we are changing the established practice of the party and must be prepared that it may have a life of its own. It may not be possible to be just a little pregnant. Before we introduce glasnost for local party positions, we needed to make a considered decision in why we are introducing greater political competition at the local level, how far we are prepared to go and whether this is a process that we can effectively manage.[94]

As we have seen, however, the decision eventually taken was to allow limited elections: the benefits outweighed the risks. Younger activists would be given a greater sense of participation within the Party and would in the process have their political instincts honed. These elections, once introduced, were keenly contested. In February 2004, YP held its first ever internal election to choose its 14th Exco. Thirty candidates contested the positions of chairmen and deputy chairmen of the five districts, with 150 delegates representing 5,000 YP members voting for their choices. The ten candidates were elected (with the other YP Exco positions filled by non-elected appointees). Subsequently, in July 2004, two Party members were the first to be elected (by approximately 60 elected members from the five districts) into the PAP HQ Exco.[95] The elections for HQ Exco positions were real contests: in some editions, runoffs were needed to separate candidates who were tied.[96]

What has been described above is merely a snapshot of the Party at one important moment. Various subgroups and subcommittees (such as the YP Action Groups) could pop up, metamorphose over time into something else, or else die down altogether. Over time, many of the processes described evolved. So too with intra-Party democracy, which proved overall to be a plus.[97] The calculation within the Party leadership was that the process of elections was something that could be managed and would have beneficial outcomes. This was largely borne out. The outgoing YP district chairmen from 2004 (who were for the most part in their early 40s) continued to provide guidance to their successors. The other, appointed, members were key members of the previous Exco (and all holding concurrent appointments at branch and district level) who were judged by the Party leadership to have the potential to contribute significantly in the next term.[98] It is worth noting, too, that there were people who, in coming through this process, were noticed by the Party leadership and later fielded in general elections.[99]

A final word on Refreshing PAP and associated initiatives. Senior Party leaders such as PM Goh and SM Lee left much of the actual concept and execution to the younger generation. But this does not mean that their guidance was not sought. When sought, it was rarely ignored. Dr Vivian Balakrishnan had been put at the head of a small team within the Refreshing PAP effort to recast the Party's values in a manner that would resonate with the younger generation. Before presenting the "refreshed values" at the November 2003 Party convention, Balakrishnan thought it wise to consult SM Lee, who alone of all active Party leaders had been present at the beginnings of the Party. Balakrishnan set out the four PAP values that the Party had consistently manifested and which were now being formally proposed: a Party that was honest, multiracial, meritocratic and self-reliant. What, actually, Balakrishnan asked, should be at the core of this? Lee's reply (now ensconced at the centre of the schema making up the PAP's values and attributes) consisted of five words: "a fair and just society."[100]

Chart 5.1 Party Values and Attributes

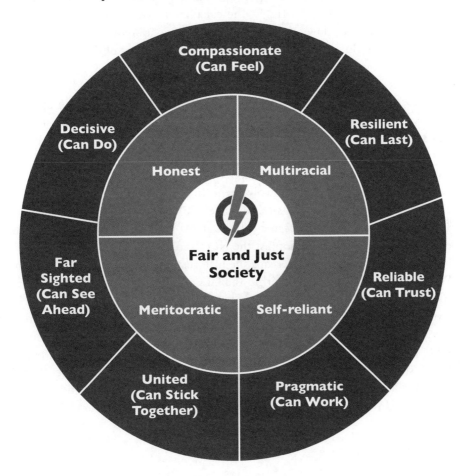

The Central Executive Committee, c. 2000–06

The sensitive realm of the CEC was not immune to some of the changes taking place. In 2000, non-MPs were for the first time allowed to have a role in the drawing up of the list of candidates to be put up for CEC election at the Party conference (in what amounted to the first major changes to the process since the 1950s). The CEC and caucus of MPs would put up a slate of 16 nominees. Branch secretaries who were cadre members, and five cadres each from YP and the Women's Wing, would put up the other two names. (Previously, all 18 names had been put up by the outgoing CEC and the Party caucus of MPs.[101]) There were additional changes in 2004 that took effect at the Party conference in November that year. The CEC approved the further widening of the participation of cadres in the process of nominating candidates. The two new groups brought in now were cadre branch committee members (with one to be nominated by each branch chairman) and elected district committee members.[102]

The role of the cadres could be said to have expanded, given their greater say in the nomination process. However, care was taken in these changes. Although select cadres were from 2000 given a say in the drawing up of the list of candidates put up for election to the CEC, votes from this bloc of non-MPs (YP and Women's Wing cadres, and branch secretaries) were given less relative weightage (a fixed percentage) compared to the votes cast by MPs.[103] The calculation within the CEC was that if further moves were made down the line to widen participation by non-MP cadres, this fixed percentage would mean no diminution of the total weight of the MPs' votes.[104]

Expanding the pool of cadres involved in drawing up the list for CEC nominations was a very limited move. There is no sign that more radical steps (such as direct elections to the CEC, or tinkering with the system that allowed the CEC to co-opt up to four additional members into the CEC following the Party conference) were considered.[105] Nor does there appear to have been any agitation for this on the part of the cadre pool. But (as some within the Party leadership had foreseen) the introduction of limited intra-Party democracy had whetted the appetite of those who had taken part, leading to occasional calls for even greater involvement. In 2006, the two activists elected into the HQ Exco called for more seats to be made available in the HQ Exco for elected representatives. There had even been a call (in 2004) to allow Party activists a chance to be elected into the CEC and not just the HQ Exco.[106]

These calls were to no avail. Perhaps the historical memory of the 1957 putsch by the Party's left wing still lingered within the CEC. This might explain the reluctance to tinker too radically with the fundamental processes for electing the Party leadership. But even in this aspect, there was the recognition that change might eventually be required. In 2002 the CEC discussed the possibility that over a longer-term horizon, the CEC could comprise a quarter to even a third of younger leaders—leaders who might not share the views of the main leadership. Incorporating them, the reasoning went, would keep the Party in touch with the younger generation, and new ideas evolving from this group would keep the Party relevant to the younger electorate.[107]

There were also important changes in the composition of the CEC in the first half of the decade; changes signalling its rejuvenation. Younger leaders began to enter the CEC ranks. Two senior ministers of state and members of the "Super Seven" from the 2001 batch, Tharman Shanmugaratnam and Khaw Boon Wan, were in 2002 co-opted into the CEC after polling the next highest number of votes (after those elected in directly).[108] But it was the December 2004 changes in office-holding appointments within the CEC that were historic, amounting to the most important transition within the CEC since Lee Kuan Yew relinquished the secretary-general position in 1992.[109] SM Goh Chok Tong relinquished the secretary-generalship of the Party (but remained a CEC member), with PM Lee Hsien Loong succeeding. Two Party stalwarts, Dr Tony Tan (chairman) and Prof. S. Jayakumar (vice-chairman), stepped down from the CEC, having chosen not to offer themselves for re-election at the 7 November 2004 Party conference. They were succeeded respectively by Lim Boon Heng and Dr Yaacob Ibrahim.[110] At this Party conference, Tharman Shanmugaratnam, Khaw Boon Wan and Lim Hwee Hua were voted in: all had previously been co-opted. To the leadership, the rise of the younger generation was a validation of the confidence placed earlier in their abilities.[111] The changes (and the direct election into the CEC of some of the younger leaders) were also a sign that the Party rank and file were increasingly accepting the credentials of the fast-rising generation of younger leaders.[112]

Remaking Singapore

If we look ahead, I think what we should watch out for is not to become fossilised, that is, to be resistant to new ideas and new arguments, not to accept people with different points of view, or to believe that we are always right. I think that this is the downfall of many societies and many political parties. We have to reflect from time to time on the direction we are taking, re-examine ourselves to see whether our policies are still relevant.

—Party Chairman Dr Tony Tan, November 1999[113]

The PAP does not need remaking. But it can do with some refreshing.

—PM Goh Chok Tong, Party conference, 1 December 2002[114]

The germ of the idea to "remake" the nation for the long term, with a particular emphasis on reaching out to the younger generation, was already present, as we have seen, from around 2000–01. Party leaders were already beginning to engage the young in an effort to make them understand that recent as well as ongoing challenges in fact provided a window to look far into the future.[115]

The Remaking Singapore Committee (RSC) was first publicly mooted by PM Goh in his New Year message to Singaporeans on 31 December 2001 and was formally constituted in February 2002, chaired by Dr Vivian Balakrishnan. The RSC was touted as the social and political counterpart of the Economic Review Committee (ERC; also set up in December 2001, and discussed later in this chapter). It was a canny choice to have Balakrishnan, a former critic of the government, leading the RSC. He was seen as being in touch with the younger generation and their aspirations—and it was precisely this vein that had to be tapped. As PM Goh said, the remaking of Singapore went beyond economics: "The third generation of post-independence Singaporeans has different aspirations and expectations from the founder and second generations . . . how do we help them in their quest to realise their dreams?"[116]

While the RSC ostensibly tackled aspirations, it was in fact intimately bound into issues relating to economics and the survival of Singapore. Interviewed for this book, Dr Vivian Balakrishnan pinpointed the three main reasons why the RSC was thought necessary. It seemed likely that the final conclusions of the ERC would contain a dose of bitter medicine (as it proved to be, particularly in its recommendations on wage restraint and the speedy implementation of GST rises). Second, the implication of the events of 9/11, and the subsequent arrests of Singaporean cell members of the Jemaah Islamiah (an al-Qaeda affiliate), had shown that fault lines of race and religion were always present. Social harmony could not be taken for granted. A final point was the sense of heightened political awareness, brought on by the increasingly pervasive role of the Internet and the growth of civil society. It was, Balakrishnan noted, a testing period: some mechanism was needed to instil cohesion and give Singaporeans the sense that they were all in the same boat.[117]

Of course, questions could be—and were—raised about why another committee was needed not long after the S21 report had been endorsed by Parliament in 1999. Some wondered whether the RSC would simply end up as a talk-shop. Cynical observers noted that the RSC was simply a means to assess the new generation of political leaders while at the same time inducting them into the real world of politics.[118] In introducing the RSC, Balakrishnan stated that the committee would, when compared to its predecessor (S21), be more of an "action group" and more focused on the "practical"; the RSC aimed to produce results more meaty than "airy-fairy motherhood statements".[119] Also heavily implicit in the RSC process as a whole was the idea of mobilising Singaporeans themselves to better their future. Singaporeans could not come to the government for help at every instance—they needed to shed a sense of entitlement and take the initiative to better their own lives.[120]

The RSC comprised five subcommittees, each tasked with examining issues beyond the "5Cs"—what were commonly seen to be the main aspirations of Singaporeans (credit card, condominium, car, country club, career). Members of the RSC itself ranged from ministers of state and members of parliament to members of the public from the private sector, voluntary organisations and tertiary institutions. Other groups involved included think tanks and business associations.[121] Many Singapore-linked overseas organisations (Singapore clubs, business associations, and student associations from various countries) submitted substantial formal proposals through the Singapore International Foundation. Dialogue sessions, focus group discussions and conferences were organised by grassroots organisations, the Feedback Unit, ethnic self-help groups, voluntary welfare organisations and educational institutions. Notable in particular was the attempt to garner online comments and suggestions—an online forum was set up for feedback and debate, overseen by Dr Tan Chong Kee, former editor of Sintercom.[122]

After 17 months of work, involving some 10,000 people and 65 dialogue sessions, the final report was presented to PM Goh in July 2003.[123] The government was to accede to 60 of the total of 74 proposals. There were, however, suggestions that were not accepted. Examples included the proposal for a five-day workweek and the withdrawal of CPF funds by the jobless. Ministers rejected these two suggestions publicly even before the report had been formally submitted to PM Goh.[124] Besides leading to disappointment amongst those who had participated in the discussions as well as in the wider public sphere, questions were raised as to what clout the RSC actually had. The impression many received was that views had been heard and then quickly dismissed without even meriting serious consideration.[125] There was also the feeling that while the government seemed willing to implement changes in the realm of social policy, on political matters nothing much seemed to have moved.[126] The suggestion that more clarity be given to OB markers was not taken up, while other suggestions in the RSC's report in the sphere of politics were left in the "Proposals without Consensus" annex.[127]

The RSC had stopped well short of remaking Singapore. So what good had it really brought, and what lessons had been learnt? In the view of the minister in charge, Vivian Balakrishnan, the RSC captured the key changes that needed to be made and pointed the way for future change. He observed that the inclusion of the annex, in effect a minority report of sorts (a feature absent from the earlier S21 report), was a recognition that diversity and divergent views had—had to have—a legitimate role in national discourse.[128]

The RSC's free-flowing discussions were also to prove a useful template for future national consultations. The policymaker, the member of parliament and the typical "heartlander" were put together in the same room in the course of RSC discussions.[129] These conversations helped people from different segments of society understand points of view that were not their own (these types of sub-discussion, found useful, were to feature prominently within a later initiative, Our Singapore Conversation [OSC; 2012–13]). The government had also learnt something about managing expectations and the necessity of setting parameters, so that the public would not have unrealistic hopes as to the outcome. Finally, something was also learnt about the uses of holding back from rejecting outright suggestions while they were still under discussion. This too would be taken on board in the course of the OSC.

The sense of an opening up in Singapore went far beyond the RSC. Singapore's efforts to build a creative economy were by the early 2000s yielding results, some of which were startlingly visible. In October 2002 a major performing arts venue—the Esplanade Theatres on the Bay—opened, at a cost of over $600 million. Views on the actual edifice were mixed, but there was the sense that it represented Singapore's increasingly assured arrival on the world stage. It was anticipated that Singapore's new emphasis on the creative cluster would have positive spin-off effects on tourism and hospitality. It is no accident that the idea of a creative infrastructure—increasingly seen as critical to future growth strategies—was to feature prominently in the report of the Economic Review Committee.[130]

The sense of a quickening within the cultural and arts scenes in the early 2000s was visible elsewhere. Singapore from 2003 saw the relaxation of rules in several spheres, which was in keeping with its growing reputation as a cosmopolitan city, one where cultural and artistic pursuits could flourish. Official funding support for performance art and forum theatre, discontinued in 1994, was restored in 2003, following the recommendations of the 2003 Censorship Review Committee.[131] A risqué (but ostensibly tasteful) topless cabaret act from Paris, Crazy Horse, was allowed to open in Singapore in late 2005.[132] Publications previously deemed undesirable, such as *Cosmopolitan*, were also allowed into Singapore (albeit shrink-wrapped). The numerous moves made around this time went beyond a liberalisation in the arts. The public sector ban on employing openly gay individuals had been dropped by mid-2003.[133] There was the sense of the beginning of a measured, inclusive opening up of society. In accepting most of the Censorship Review Committee's recommendations, the government observed that norms of governance had to change, even as society evolved:

> *Exposure to a wide array of content and communication channels had increased expectations for greater space and wider access in segments of our society. As we brace ourselves for the emerging economy where ideas, creativity and innovation are key economic and social imperatives, we must learn to accommodate this diversity and aspirations to nurture a more vibrant society.*[134]

Succession

PM Goh took great pains to effect a smooth transition, making it plain from an early stage that DPM Lee Hsien Loong was his (as well as his Cabinet colleagues') clear choice as the next prime minister. He was also clear, however, that the reins of premiership would be handed over only when the country had recovered from the effects of the economic crises.[135] Notwithstanding the fact that DPM Lee was the obvious choice, Goh had (in consultation with select CEC members) put in place a process for the nomination and confirmation of his successor. There were three separate meetings of ministers and MPs to settle the issue of the succession. Ministers first came to a consensus (22 May 2004) before the choice was presented to the caucus of PAP MPs (28 May).[136] At this meeting, MPs were invited to suggest alternative names. There were, unsurprisingly, none, with MPs unanimously supporting the choice of DPM Lee. The last step was a simple endorsement by the CEC (29 May).[137]

By his own account, Goh had instituted this process and hoped to entrench the tradition (especially the role now given to MPs) because the choice, while clear in 2004, might not be so straightforward in future successions.[138] And although Goh did not say so, it is conceivable that he had in mind his own position in 1988, when, despite his having been chosen by his peers, it had (as we have seen) not been altogether clear whether he enjoyed the complete confidence of then PM Lee Kuan Yew.[139] Goh's process of involving the rank and file as well as the leadership seemed to have the aim of entrenching a process that might have the effect of removing as much uncertainty as possible (if indeed there were doubts) in future leadership transitions.

Through the last years of his premiership, PM Goh had made it a point to give positive and public affirmations to his successor. Where Goh did offer advice in public, it was (as Goh said in his 17 August 2003 National Day Rally speech) that DPM Lee should "let his softer side show". In his unusually frank remarks, Goh noted that some Singaporeans, having got used to his own "gentler" style, were apprehensive of the coming handover as they were not comfortable with Lee's public persona, which was seen as no-nonsense and uncompromising.[140]

Goh's pointed comments did not pass unheeded. Well in advance of his accession, Lee had made attempts to project himself as a leader who, if not quite the same as Goh, was committed to the "kinder and gentler" Singapore that Goh had built. Lee had also been at pains to sketch out the kind of Singapore he wanted: a dynamic economy with a vibrant and more open society, where changes in the political, cultural and arts scenes would continue at a steady (but not destabilising) pace.[141] Lee's clearest declaration of his vision for Singapore came during his widely remarked upon 6 January 2004 address at the Harvard Club. Lee stated that the government was committed to the path of greater openness and consultation—he had "no doubt that our society must open up further". Critics, Lee added for good measure, would not necessarily be viewed as adversaries—unless they attempted to undermine the government.[142]

The transition had been achieved seamlessly and without fuss, as had been intended, but absent was some of the staid predictability that had usually characterised political transitions in Singapore. By the time of the actual handover of power, in August 2004, positive expectation had turned into something akin to ebullience. During his 12 August 2004 swearing-in speech, PM Lee paid tribute to Goh's "softer touch", which he acknowledged had transformed Singapore and made it more vibrant and cohesive.[143] Lee (perhaps taking Goh's advice) also showed his personal side and won plaudits for speaking from the heart, promising (again) a more open and inclusive Singapore, where people "should feel free to express diverse views, pursue unconventional ideas, or simply be different".[144] But Lee also threw down a challenge to Singaporeans, and in particular the post-independence generation: "Do not wait to be invited to tea but step forward to make a difference to yourselves, to your fellow citizens and to Singapore."[145] The exhortation was to be repeated several days later during Lee's first National Day Rally speech, on 22 August 2004. But this time, the emotive appeal was accompanied by the announcement of symbolic but significant changes, which gave the appearance to many of being the initial instalment in what might be a series of concrete liberalising measures. The measures included doing away with the requirement for licences for indoor political talks. Performances and exhibitions were also added to the list of activities exempted from licensing requirements at Speakers' Corner. Separately, Lee also announced that the government would embrace proposals that it had long resisted. In what amounted to either a U-turn or delayed acceptance of recommendations made by the Remaking Singapore Committee, Lee announced the introduction of a five-day workweek for government, and the equalisation of medical benefits across the sexes for government employees.[146]

A wide cross-section of the public had been invited (in what was a first) to witness the handover ceremony at the Istana, in a sign that Singapore's leadership and PM

Lee especially wanted all Singaporeans, especially the post-independence generation, involved in shaping Singapore's next lap.[147] It had not gone unnoticed, too, that in August, as part of Cabinet reorganisation, Dr Vivian Balakrishnan had been promoted to full (acting) minister and given the helm of the newly named Ministry for Community Development, Youth and Sports ("Youth" having been previously absent from the old MCDS). Balakrishnan, chairman of the RSC and the youngest minister in Cabinet, was generally held to be the right person for the job of connecting with Singapore's youth, not least because of his reputation of being a plain speaker and someone who had formerly been critical of aspects of PAP policy.[148]

Just two days after PM Lee's swearing-in, Balakrishnan announced that three MPs from the post-1965 (P65) generation would be fanning out to get feedback from Singaporean students and working adults.[149] Networking groups such as Contact Singapore would also be used to reach out to overseas Singaporeans.[150] The message, which was a continuation of themes raised during the Remaking Singapore process, was that the government would continue its commitment to openness and was prepared to become more unstructured in taking in views from the people. Balakrishnan also threw down the gauntlet, making it clear, as PM Lee had done, that the young for their part had to step up to the plate and take responsibility for shaping Singapore's future—the job of nation-building could not be shirked nor left to others.[151]

The mild euphoria that had developed was, of course, unsustainable. PM Lee had started his premiership with a great deal of inclusive rhetoric, and over the next months he proceeded to outline a vision of a PAP-led Singapore as a "land of opportunity", with each person treated fairly, rewarded according to their effort and ability, and allowed to realise their full potential. Policy refinements in 2005 were to support these thrusts, with enhancements to MediFund to help the disadvantaged and needy.[152] As some observers had already pointed out, however, talk of a major political liberalisation was overblown.[153] From the government perspective, the way forward, and its pace, had been clearly marked out. PM Lee had been consistent throughout his political career on this point, noting in 2002 that political space should be opened in "gradual, successive increments: and not in the form of a 'cathartic revolution' . . . I think it's better not to have a revolution. It's very dangerous."[154] Still, so great had been the expectation, that the failure of a major political liberalisation to materialise was something of an anticlimax, in part dissipating the national "honeymoon" accorded to PM Lee after his accession. By 2005, it was crystal clear that Lee's administration had inherited the political conservatism of its forebears and that room to push the political boundaries, and protest against existing strictures, would be extremely limited.

A handful of instances suffice to illustrate this. In 2005 a young filmmaker, Martyn See, was investigated by the police under the Films Act (which prohibited the making of any "political" film) for a short film on SDP leader Chee Soon Juan. The case garnered widespread local and international attention, partly because of See's regular updates on the course of the investigation on his blog, and partly because See appeared to have been caught by critical clauses in the Act that were generally held to be ambiguous, sweeping and vague. This led to the perception, especially in the international community, that a draconian law had been used to bring an Opposition-sympathising filmmaker to book. The government's case was not helped by Minister Mentor Lee Kuan Yew remarking in an interview with *Time* magazine that "if you had asked me, I would have said to hell with it. But the censor, the enforcer, he will continue until he is told the law has changed. And it will change."[155] See was eventually given a stern warning by the police after being under investigation for over a year.

International opprobrium had not mattered to the authorities in the case of Martyn See; it also mattered little during another controversy that nearly came to overshadow the International Monetary Fund (IMF) and World Bank meetings held in Singapore in September 2006. The government initially refused to admit into the country 27 NGO activists accredited by both the IMF and the World Bank. Both institutions accused the government of breaching a prior agreement by failing to allow the protestors into the country.[156] Separately, the government also refused to waive its ban on outdoor protests during the meetings. Activists from NGOs were permitted to stage their protest only in a special cordoned-off area within the convention centre.

Political challenges, or anything resembling civil disobedience, continued to be tackled in an uncompromising fashion. During the IMF-World Bank meetings, SDP Chairman Dr Chee Soon Juan, together with a small number of supporters, attempted to march to Parliament House and then to Suntec Centre, the site of the meetings. The resulting standoff was captured by international media, memorably showing Chee ring-fenced by police.[157] Chee was by his own account protesting against Singapore's repressive laws against expression and freedom of assembly. His actions did not attract a great deal of notice locally, perhaps because the public had grown accustomed to them.

Despite some important refinements in social (and, as we shall see, economic) policy after the leadership transition, critical areas in political discourse and action remained comparatively untouched. The media watchdog Reporters without Borders ranked Singapore 140th out of 167 countries in its 2005 Press Freedom Index (below countries such as Sudan and Afghanistan), leading to some debate within Singapore on whether this was a matter for concern. Government leaders downplayed the significance of the poor ranking, suggesting that the results were filtered through the prism of the Western liberal establishment; older arguments that a freewheeling Western-type press would not be in Singapore's interest were also rehashed.[158]

One academic observer, surveying all this, was moved to comment on the paradox of "selective globalisation", which saw Singapore fully embracing many of the outward forms of globalisation but being locally particular and conservative in other respects:

> *The fact that Singapore's survival as a nation-state depends on its status as a global city means that the government has little choice but to constantly shift gears between the national and the global when it comes to policymaking, thus compelling it to send mixed signals to this international community. Casinos are allowed but satellite dishes are not, topless cabaret shows are permitted but civil disobedience is not, and the list goes on. These discrepancies are at the heart of the*

dilemma facing Singapore at the dawn of the 21st century—globalizing at one's own pace and terms may be prudent for a small nation-state, but how much of this prudence can an aspiring global city afford?[159]

One would be tempted to draw parallels with other points in time where hoped-for political thaws had not quite proved what they seemed to be. Examples might include the accession of Goh Chok Tong to the premiership and the "Banyan Tree" moment (1990–91), or the period in the late 1990s that saw the fruition of the S21 process. There were, however, important differences. An increasingly vocal and educated population, with access to and use of new media, was beginning to make for greater scrutiny of the government and its policies. It was also beginning to make for increased contestation in political discourse at various levels. Seen with hindsight, there began to be from this point an accretion of issues chipping away at the government's aura of infallibility and efficiency.

Seeds of Discontent, 2003–06

A nondescript MRT station in the northeast of Singapore, Buangkok, was to become the locus of a standoff involving residents, the rail operator and the government in 2003. The station, which was situated along the new North East Line operated by SBS Transit, had been initially slated to open in 2003 but remained closed, much to the displeasure of local residents. The government's logic was simple: the low number of residents living in the station's vicinity did not warrant its opening. Repeated appeals by the PAP MP for Punggol South, Charles Chong, were to no avail. On 28 August 2005, in what was to become something of a minor *cause célèbre* known as the White Elephant saga, eight cardboard cut-outs of white elephants were found lining a road to greet Dr Vivian Balakrishnan (minister for community development, youth and sports) on his visit to the area. While Balakrishnan took the show in good spirit, a police report was lodged by a member of the public. Eventually, a grassroots leader known to be closely associated with the MP, Sunny Leow, received a stern warning from the police for the offence of public display without a permit, although he was widely believed to have taken the blame for what was a collective action. Discontent was not confined to grassroots leaders and those who wanted the station open; the critical mood took hold in the court of public opinion as well, which held that the protest (if it had been that) had been a light-hearted one and that the authorities had overreacted and come down with a sledgehammer.[160]

This was not all. With the opening of the North East Line, bus services running along the same route had been cut in July and August 2003. There was an angry and emotional reaction from affected residents, who now felt worse off.[161] During a heated debate in Parliament on the issue, Transport Minister Yeo Cheow Tong acknowledged that SBS Transit had "made mistakes" in the way it had communicated with residents and grassroots activists.[162] Inevitably, though, there was a palpable sense of grievance directed at the government, which had upheld the argument that the cuts in bus services were essential so as not to duplicate services or waste resources.[163] The discontent began to ebb only in late 2005, when (in a change of heart, due at least in part no doubt to the fact that elections were due) it was announced that Buangkok station would open by early 2006.[164]

The affair emphasised that despite rhetoric on increased public consultation, appeals to the government—even if brokered by the MP—could rarely make an impact when coming up squarely against the prevailing economic wisdom or planning orthodoxy. In such cases, the MP himself would—as he did here—come in for scrutiny, with his constituents wondering about his worth and effectiveness. It is also worth noting that PM Lee had made calls—for example, at the November 2005 Party convention— for members who thought differently and "who are loyal but not always obedient" to step forward.[165] Clearly, the White Elephant saga showed that both qualities were still expected from the Party faithful in large measure.

The discontent ran deeper than simply being about the running of an MRT line. The Buangkok/North East Line affair rebounded on the government in terms of questions being raised about the wisdom of a particular slice of its economic policy: specifically, whether it had miscalculated in forcing competition between rail operators. PAP MPs asked in Parliament why SBS Transit was allowed to run the line given the huge losses (it had clearly failed to forecast the shortfall in passenger numbers along the line), and whether having a single operator, Singapore Mass Rapid Transit (SMRT), would enable better economies of scale.[166] The issue of whether there was a conflict of interest (with SBS Transit being allowed to run both bus and train services in the same area) was also posed.[167] As we shall see, dissatisfaction over aspects of planning and economic policy was something that the PAP government was to face with increasing regularity.

There were other rumblings, all unconnected but which taken together could be seen as illustrative of a diminution of trust between the government and the people. A seemingly innocuous question was tabled in Parliament by NCMP Steve Chia on 11 November 2003, on the question of "White Horses", sons of influential Singaporeans who were commonly thought (at least by a large segment of the population) to get special treatment during their full-time National Service (NS). Minister of State for Defence Cedric Foo replied that there had indeed been such a category, but it had been abolished in 2000.[168] However, the rationale given for the existence of the system—that it was to identify sons of influential persons specifically to ensure that they received no preferential treatment or special privileges—attracted widespread incredulity and a degree of derision.[169] Many, especially those who had gone through NS, found it difficult to believe the official position that the system prevented abuse and that equity was scrupulously adhered to in NS training.[170] The affair attracted a great deal of commentary online (most of it critical of what was seen as government obfuscation) and in the form of letters written to the press.[171] It did not help—and probably exacerbated matters—that the White Horse saga had been preceded by another much-talked-about military-related issue: training deaths in the SAF. The most well known of these concerned the death of Second Sergeant (2SG) Hu Enhuai, who died on 21 August 2003 during a Combat Survival Training course conducted by the School of Commando Training. The picture that emerged of lax controls and failure to follow proper procedures did not reflect well on the Ministry of Defence, notwithstanding the fact that there had been efforts to be transparent and ensure that those responsible were dealt with.[172]

Similar themes of the failure of controls and a lack of transparency featured also in what became known as the National Kidney Foundation (NKF) affair. An April 2004 *Straits Times* article on the NKF included the claim that a plumber had been asked to install (among other items) a gold-plated tap in the washroom of the NKF CEO, T.T. Durai.[173] The NKF took the view that this suggested public funds had been misused, and it demanded a retraction and apology, suing for defamation when this was not forthcoming. In court in July 2005, Durai wilted under withering cross-examination by the lawyer for Singapore Press Holdings, Davinder Singh (a PAP MP), and withdrew the lawsuit on the second day of the trial.

The brief trial riveted the public not so much on account of its sudden denouement, but because of sensational revelations made during proceedings. These included the news that Durai's total compensation package, which amounted to $1.8 million from 2002 to 2004, had included (besides his monthly salary of $25,000) annual bonuses of ten to 12 months' pay. As part of his perks, Durai also had personal use of eight chauffeured cars. Further revelations were found in the December 2005 report prepared by an independent auditor. The report painted a picture of poor corporate governance and found that in 2003, only 10 cents of every dollar raised were used for dialysis costs—far less than the NKF had claimed. Instances of corporate malpractice were also highlighted. Durai was arrested and charged with corruption in April 2006.[174]

The independent report also faulted the government for lax oversight, something for which the government accepted responsibility.[175] But more important was the judgement in the court of public opinion. The sensational revelations at the trial had led to a feeling of betrayal. NKF donors and the general public felt that Durai and his associates had enriched themselves from the NKF's coffers, monies that should have gone to deserving NKF patients. In certain quarters, the political blowback extended even deeper. Some—especially in the online world, where commentary could be freewheeling, anonymous, and quite often both—attempted to somehow link wrongdoing in the NKF with the government. It had always been a central plank of the government's argument (on, for example, ministerial salaries) that high salaries prevented corruption, but this had not been the case with the NKF.[176]

There was an additional element in the affair—one the government could have done without. The NKF patron, Tan Choo Leng (the wife of Senior Minister Goh), had made a careless and ill-advised remark about Durai's pay when queried by the press: "For a person who runs a big million-dollar charitable organisation, with a few hundred million in reserves, S$600,000 a year is peanuts." This comment became a target (when it naturally went viral) for anger, as well as widespread and imaginative Internet parody. Many netizens also observed that there were several Singaporeans who would not make that amount of money in a lifetime. The impression had been reinforced in certain quarters of the public, in both the online and real worlds, that the government was becoming out of touch with the difficulties experienced by ordinary Singaporeans.

The NKF affair was notable in that it showed a more opinionated public and pointed to an increasingly contested public discourse. The Internet had played a key role in the rising tide of awareness. Its use had stoked discussion (and unhappiness) and in some cases had forced the government to either go on the defensive or, in some cases, to be more open.[177] Hot-button issues could be, and were, discussed intensively over the Internet, with a maelstrom of online comment and anger (or lampooning) capable of being whipped up in a short amount of time. Despite assertions that people would be held responsible for online activity and comment just as in the real world, when it came to criticism of the government and its policies generally—particularly on issues that went viral—the government could do little.[178] Of course, not all issues that went viral were critical of the authorities. But the overall trend was clear: increasing use of new media had brought additional scrutiny and pressure to bear on the government.[179]

ჯჯჯ

The preceding discussion has not sought to make explicit connections between this confection of controversies, but to illustrate the increasing post-millennial willingness on the part of the people to take on and criticise the government on various matters. The issue was not simply increased contestation. More and more, people were coming to demand a say in the direction of the country, and on key issues pertaining to the national interest. One example will suffice to illustrate this. It had become clear by March 2004 that the government was considering allowing casinos into the country, after a decades-long ban.[180] The actual decision to proceed with the casinos (to be built within larger integrated resorts) was made by the Cabinet on 9 April 2005, with PM Lee making the decision known in Parliament on 18 April 2005.[181] In the lead-up to the decision being made, PM Lee had rejected calls for a public referendum on the issue, stating that the decision on whether to have a casino was "not an issue of national survival" nor an issue of "conscience or fundamental principle". He also set aside calls from his own MPs (several of whom had urged caution on the issue, or expressed outright objections) for a full parliamentary debate on the issue, one that would see the whip lifted to allow MPs to vote freely.[182]

The public perception was that mass opinion (which itself appeared polarised) had been ignored with no real consultation, and that Parliament (which had met to consider, but not vote on, the issue from 18 to 21 April 2005) had simply acted as a rubber stamp.[183] The leadership recognised the depth of public feeling and the emotion that the debate had generated. In attempting to put a positive spin on the heated views expressed by the public, PM Lee preferred to see the reaction as a form of "active citizenry"—views expressed by people who cared for society. But his bottom line was this: ultimately, the elected government had been entrusted by citizens to decide on issues. This, Lee stated, "was a responsibility it would not abdicate. It would listen, consult and take them into consideration before arriving at a decision."[184]

The whys and wherefores of the casino debate have been treated at length elsewhere.[185] For present purposes, two strands are worth pondering. One was the government's argument that on issues of national significance, it would consult the people where it could, but ultimately would itself decide what was best for Singapore. After the decision was made, arguing further would have very limited usefulness. The government, and the people, had to move on.[186] The casino debate, however, could with hindsight be seen as a very visible point where this approach became markedly less easy to maintain. In what was obviously becoming an increasingly contested political space, it would become more difficult to shape public discourse and control the length to which issues were debated, especially on very controversial issues. The passionate and occasionally vociferous nature of public debate had also spurred some commentators to note that the rules of engagement for debate were changing. Previously, a certain deference to political leaders was expected. Now, however, Singaporeans (who after all had been told that they had to be involved in the making, or remaking, of their country) felt little need for deference in taking up issues, and even less fear.[187] There was the concomitant feeling that the old social compact was fading, with a tendency on the part of the people to trust the government less.[188]

The second point to be considered relates to the overall perceptions of how Singapore society was developing. Parts of the casino debate had more than a whiff of elitism and class divides. Early on in the saga, there had been the suggestion that the government would only allow Singaporeans who passed a certain income threshold to gamble at the casinos. Although this idea was subsequently dropped, Trade and Industry Minister George Yeo's comment early on in the saga—"If you are not of a certain economic class, you should not even think of going there"—was not forgotten.[189]

The sense of a growing elitism was an issue that cropped up with increasing regularity. In October 2006, an 18-year-old student from the prestigious Raffles Junior College, Wee Shu Min (daughter of a newly-minted PAP MP, Wee Siew Kim), penned on her personal blog a scathing attack on another individual, a 35-year-old professional who had expressed fears on his own blog about future job security as an older worker in the wake of competition from foreign workers. Wee's exceptionally splenetic comments included a description of her target being "one of the many wretched, under-motivated, over-assuming leeches in our country" and concluded with a call for him to "get out of my elite, uncaring face". Her comments on her blog (which she subsequently shut down) were widely—and inevitably—seen as elitist and lacking in empathy, and led to a storm of comments online and in the mainstream press. In his daughter's defence, Wee Siew Kim stated that he supported Shu Min's point in principle and that "people cannot take the brutal truth". His defensive and half-hearted initial apology, which appeared to condone what his daughter had said, inflamed matters further. Only two days later did Wee Siew Kim (who was to last only one term as MP) tender a full apology to those offended by his daughter's comments.[190]

All this could only feed the increasing perception of a growing divide between the haves and the have-nots in society, those born with all the natural advantages and those without these trappings. In certain quarters, the idea was beginning to take root that segments of the affluent social and political elites, besides having a relatively easy ride through the system, were increasingly out of touch.[191] As PAP MP Sin Boon

Ann was to observe in Parliament in November 2006, in a reference to the Wee Shu Min affair, "The perception exists that Singapore is a society that is bifurcated between elites and the commoners, the scholars and the Normal stream . . . and the rich and the poor."[192]

Sin Boon Ann was not referring simply to class envy at work. Questions were increasingly being asked about the nature of Singapore's meritocracy; there was increased scrutiny of the economic model that had served the nation well over previous decades. Some of these themes were to become more prominent later on, and are discussed in the pages that follow. Of those who had views or concerns even at this stage, some chose to make vitriolic comments on the internet and left it at that. Others felt the need to be involved in more meaningful and direct ways. Sylvia Lim, a law lecturer and former police inspector, joined the Workers' Party (WP) in 2001, soon after the general election, and quickly rose to become WP chairman in 2003. Lim cited as a motivating factor for her decision to join the WP her unease at the large number of walkovers in 2001.[193] But pressed on why she chose not to join the PAP given her qualifications, Lim commented, "I don't agree with some of PAP's elitist policies."[194]

Aspects of Economic Policy

> *Singapore is going through a testing time. Since the financial crisis in 1997, we have been through one painful wringer after another. It's like going through a squashing machine. Each time as we were recovering, a new disaster sets us back.*
>
> —Lee Kuan Yew, dialogue with unionists, 23 July 2003[195]

During the 2001 election campaign, the PAP had promised a new economic plan: fresh strategies that would upgrade and revitalise the economy, in the wake of new challenges.[196] In his early morning press conference after the election victory on 4 November 2001, Prime Minister Goh Chok Tong announced the establishment of an economic committee that would formulate the blueprint.[197] The Economic Review Committee (ERC), formally established on 3 December 2001, was chaired by DPM and Finance Minister Lee Hsien Loong, who had also chaired the 1985 Economic Committee. The ERC included established figures such as George Yeo (trade and industry minister), DPM Dr Tony Tan, and also new faces Tharman Shanmugaratnam, Khaw Boon Wan and Raymond Lim.[198] Seven subcommittees and numerous working groups studied various aspects of the Singapore economy. These subgroups in turn took in contributions from a large number of people, numbering over 1,000 in all.[199]

Many of the ERC report's core recommendations (released on 6 February 2003) pertained to maintaining competitiveness.[200] Recommendations were made also on promoting exportable services, encouraging entrepreneurship, and developing human capital.[201] Underpinning all this was the belief that these longer-term strategies would within 15 years make Singapore a leading global city, a hub of talent and enterprise. The new, remade Singapore would be a creative and entrepreneurial nation with a dynamic workforce, with vibrant local companies complementing multinational corporations. It would be a truly globalised economy, linked to all the major economies and emerging regions.[202]

DPM Lee, also the finance minister, gave the official government response to (and acceptance of) the ERC recommendations in his Budget Statement on 28 February 2003. There was a pronounced emphasis on reducing business costs, in line with ERC recommendations. The headline-grabbing announcements: a two-year freeze on the employer's contribution towards CPF, and the raising of Goods and Services Tax (GST) from 3 to 5 per cent.[203]

The ERC's place in Singapore's economic history should not be underestimated.[204] It did not exist simply to tide the nation through immediate difficulties. To the leadership, it represented nothing less than the successor to the 1985 Economic Committee, which itself had been set up on the back of another recession, and which had laid the basis for more than a decade of growth. Just as the recipes prescribed by the Economic Committee had worked to put Singapore back on competitive ground (and had in effect been the blueprint for economic success until the end of the 1990s), the ERC report was a similar attempt to fundamentally rethink Singapore's growth strategies and to chart the way forward over what would clearly be an intense global competition and knowledge-driven growth. Major new competitors were emerging, and old sources of growth (especially manufacturing) could no longer be relied on to drive Singapore's economy. Other engines, such as services, had to be developed. Singapore thus had to move to new sources of capability and competitiveness, and in the process take painful measures (including those involving CPF and GST) in order to be more flexible in a rapidly changing environment.[205]

The 2003 budget and the ERC report that informed it were the products of considerable effort and thought. But not all were satisfied, and some saw the report itself as something of an anticlimax. Part of the problem was that Singaporeans had already become familiar with some of the key proposals, which had been publicly telegraphed in preceding months.[206] But more importantly, the long-term feel-good vision painted by the ERC in terms of what Singapore could in time be jarred with the gloom-ridden mood on the ground. Singapore would not be declared free from Severe Acute Respiratory Syndrome (SARS) until 31 May 2003. The general malaise was compounded by what by this time was felt to be the inevitability of a downturn that would follow a US-led invasion of Iraq (which materialised on 20 March 2003). Questions were also being asked as to whether Singapore could continue to outshine competition as well as face down new, more nimble rivals. In 2000 and 2002, the world's largest container shipping operators, Maersk and Evergreen, moved the bulk of their traffic from the Port of Singapore Authority (PSA) to Johor's Port of Tanjong Pelapas in Malaysia. These moves were put down by observers to the cost of operations in Singapore (with the government's land use policy coming in for particular criticism during the 2003 budget debate) and a degree of bureaucratic inflexibility.[207] At the PSA, one in seven workers were to lose their jobs in 2003. Another brand name synonymous with the Singapore success story, Singapore Airlines, shed close to 500 jobs that year. The unemployment rate in 2003 hit 4 per cent, with just over 16,000 workers retrenched.[208] During the budget debate in March 2003 one MP, Dr Wang Kai Yuen (whose words carried particular weight given his position as chief of the Feedback Unit), warned that confidence had dipped to unprecedentedly low levels, with the budget not having gone far enough in addressing the fears of the people over the economy and job creation: "Based on this Budget statement, there is a mismatch between people's expectations and the ability of the Government to deliver."[209]

There were sustained attempts to dispel the gloom. During the period 2002–03, when the sense of pessimism seemed to hang most heavily, leaders took pains to meet different cross-sections of society, to lift their spirits and convey the sense that troubled times would not last. These included intra-Party meetings, dialogues with workers and unionists to explain the global shifts taking place (as well as the need for measures such as cost-cutting and bringing in foreign workers), and also meetings with students to highlight the importance of the next generation remaining cohesive and committed to Singapore.[210] It was also at this time (in mid-2003) that constituency visits and walkabouts were revived, to allow the younger ministers to get a feel of the ground.[211]

These engagements were necessary to explain tough and potentially unpopular decisions being taken. The government continued with its plan to raise the GST from 3 to 5 per cent but decided to phase in the hike in two stages (1 percentage point each in 2003 and 2004), partly because of the economic conditions and also as it was cognisant of widespread public dismay over the issue.[212] But what proved to be a real jolt was PM Goh's announcement in his 17 August 2003 National Day Rally speech that in order to save jobs and make Singaporean workers competitive, CPF contribution rates would not after all be restored over the long term to the full 40 per cent when conditions permitted, but might in fact shrink to as low as 30 per cent.[213]

The 2003 budget, and the ERC report that had preceded it, largely refrained from making specific promises on doling out aid to those faced with genuine difficulty.[214] The woes of the jobless were best addressed, according to the ERC, by continuing education and training, with the government accepting the ERC recommendation to set up a statutory board to coordinate these efforts. But the absence of targeted aid schemes meant that whispers as to how much the government cared for those in need could grow.[215] There were, as both PAP and Opposition MPs observed during the budget debate, people struggling to make ends meet in the HDB heartlands.[216] From the government's point of view, however, help had been given. The 2003 budget had included the extension of rebates on service and conservancy charges and utilities charges for HDB dwellers. There were additional rebates for those paying service and conservancy charges, with these moves costing the government just over $100 million. Separately, approximately $1 billion worth of Economic Restructuring Shares had been distributed to Singaporeans in January 2003 to tide them through the current economic downturn and offset the increase in the GST. As DPM Lee observed in his defence of the budget, which had for the third time in consecutive years posted a deficit, the government was trying its best to work with Singaporeans to create wealth for Singapore, but it was "not Santa Claus".[217]

The gloom began to lift in 2004. The economy rebounded strongly, growing 8.3 per cent. Unemployment fell to below 4 per cent for the first time since 2001, with foreign trade expanding by 22 per cent over 2003. It was, however, increasingly apparent that even as Singapore recovered, disparities were becoming more pronounced. Those who had skills, or who had otherwise been able to ride the global wave, continued to thrive. One study in 2005 concluded that of all countries surveyed, Singapore had posted the biggest leap in the number of millionaires (with nearly 50,000 in 2004, a rise of 22.4 per cent over the previous year).[218] But the less well-off and lower-skilled were lagging further behind, in part victims of structural unemployment and the migration of their jobs to lower-cost locations, a phenomenon which the ERC had indicated would likely be a permanent feature of the landscape.[219] Government data released in 2005—which became a hot topic of discussion—showed that the monthly incomes of the poorest 20 per cent of households fell by 3.2 per cent a year between 1998 and 2003.[220] The average household income of those living in one- and two-room HDB flats dropped for the first time in 35 years.[221]

Overall, incomes had risen faster than living costs, as government leaders were at pains to point out. But the situation was different from the 1990s, when the government could argue more convincingly that it was people's aspirations and expectations that had led to the perception of rising costs. Now, as even PAP MPs observed, statistics told only part of the story. The cost of key components of the overall basket such as education and healthcare had risen appreciably.[222] There also began at this point to be increasing talk of the difficulties faced by the "sandwiched middle-class", the group that did not receive the subsidies and rebates given to the poor, but which had been hit by cost increases. Healthcare was especially singled out, with some beginning to make the argument that the older generation were unable to retire with any peace of mind.[223]

During the January 2005 parliamentary debate on the President's Address, several MPs again rose to tell of their own experiences dealing with constituents who could not make ends meet.[224] On this occasion, PM Lee announced a major, billion-dollar government assistance package targeted at the needy and the unemployed. The centrepiece was the Community Care Endowment Fund (ComCare), a new fund managed by CDCs that would disburse assistance to needy and deserving families. The kitty for ComCare—$500 million to begin with, eventually to be raised to $1 billion—was significant.[225] Half of this was channelled towards ensuring that children from low-income families would receive assistance for education: a move to help them break out of the poverty trap and to ensure that their starting points, as far as possible, were levelled up.[226] In announcing details of this and other schemes in his February 2005 Budget Statement, PM Lee once again outlined the government's thinking on the parameters for assistance. Lee acknowledged the problems faced by those who were in difficulty but spoke of avoiding "tempting but ultimately self-defeating strategies. . . . We must not breed a culture of entitlement, encouraging Singaporeans to seek Government support as a matter of right, whether or not they need it."[227] PM Lee's references to an entitlement mentality were in part jabs at the Opposition, and in particular the WP's Low Thia Khiang, who during the debate on the President's

Address the previous month had argued that a comprehensive social safety net should be put in place.[228]

The government was, in fact, beginning to move—but in ways of its own choosing. An Inter-Ministerial Committee headed by Manpower Minister Dr Ng Eng Hen had spent six months looking at ways to help low-wage workers. A central thrust of the recommendations, announced in January 2006, was Workfare, which became a core plank of the $2.6 billion "Progress Package" unveiled by PM Lee as part of the budget in February 2006. The Workfare Bonus was given to low-wage workers above the age of 40 earning $1,500 a month or less who had worked a minimum period of six months the previous year.[229] In accepting the thrust of the committee's recommendations, PM Lee noted that through Workfare, "individuals are encouraged to work and achieve self-sufficiency for themselves and their families. It is a sustainable approach that reaffirms our work ethic."[230]

There was an increasing certainty at top policymaking levels when it came to the link between growth and rising inequality. More redistribution was needed.[231] The 2006 budget was noticeable for a decided tilt towards sharing surpluses with the lower-income groups. PM Lee announced a new Growth Dividend Scheme, to be given out in cash to all adult citizens. Unlike previous sharing schemes such as Economic Restructuring Shares and New Singapore Shares, Growth Dividends saw the less well-off receiving more.[232] Separately, a slew of schemes to help low-wage workers were announced. These included funding for retraining and upgrading, as well as job recreation programmes. There was also an emphasis on levelling-up opportunities, with schools being given "Opportunity Funds" to pay for enrichment activities. The maximum household income to qualify for the Edusave merit bursary was raised from $3,000 to $4,000. Childcare and student care subsidies were also increased.[233]

In what was something of a first, Opposition members criticised the government for overspending on the needy, characterising the budget as nothing more than an election ploy to win votes. Even some PAP MPs wondered whether the government was being overly generous, and whether the Progress Package might lead to the development of a crutch mentality. PM Lee (also the finance minister) was adamant that the Progress Package was not a pre-election sweetener: "This Budget is different because it recognises that the world has changed and growth will no longer deliver the same opportunities to every individual. Going forward, we will work systemically to ensure that no Singaporean is left behind as we forge ahead."[234] Put more starkly, the Progress Package was, in the words of PAP MP Dr Amy Khor, "designed to arrest the simmering tensions that arise from a widening income gap that could tear our social fabric apart".[235]

᷾ꝫꝫꝫ᷾

Singapore by 2006 was well on its way to becoming what the ERC and other reports before it had predicted: a cosmopolitan, global city and a hub for international talent. But increasingly, questions were being asked about this transformation: at what cost had it come? During the 2005 parliamentary debate on the casino issue, for example, some PAP MPs had stated that they felt economic benefits had trumped the argument to preserve Singapore's existing clean image, with one arguing that the entire issue was (despite arguments to the contrary by government leaders) simply about "money versus values".[236] It is this period that would later be pinpointed by some commentators as a time when the government made a sharp tilt in privileging growth above all other concerns.[237]

Interviews for this book conducted with government leaders provide something of a corrective to this. The nadir of 2003—when the economic downturn was compounded by the appearance of SARS (which nationally was to infect 238 individuals and claim 33 lives)—left a deep imprint on the minds of the leadership. There was a renewed, urgent determination that growth had to be prioritised. New approaches, or even ones that had been examined and discarded before, had to be looked at afresh, going beyond even what had been recommended by the ERC. As early as 2003 the government had set up an internal committee headed by Minister of State for Trade and Industry Dr Vivian Balakrishnan to examine the possibility of Singapore allowing a casino, even though the suggestion had not made it into the final ERC report submitted in February that year.[238] Balakrishnan recalled: "The feeling was that we had to look for every opportunity for growth including upending orthodox wisdom by saying no to casinos. That's how keenly we felt this need to get growth."[239]

Growth apart, it is tempting to see this as a period when the government could have done more by way of anticipating levels of public dissatisfaction that were to peak around the time of the 2011 election. Some of the decisions taken in the first half of the decade (on GST and CPF, for example) were undoubtedly tough— and for the people, painful. But at the same time, there had been major shifts in thinking when it came to those who were struggling or at the lower end of the socio-economic spectrum. Workfare, for example, represented a significant deviation from earlier thinking, incorporating as it did a carefully thought-out element of giving direct assistance without too many additional bureaucratic strings attached. When Workfare was still at the planning stage, officials from various ministries had carried out interviews with those who stood to benefit from the scheme. The conclusion was that the workers themselves did not want handouts. What they needed was help with daily needs and (critically) the ability to save for their future healthcare and retirement needs.[240]

What the government decided not to do should also be considered. In internal discussions, officials rejected no-strings-attached ideas of a minimum wage as well as unemployment benefits. Officials concluded that choosing these options would not improve the lives of low-wage workers in a sustainable way (while recognising at the same time that these were popular options that had been the preferred route in other countries). In rejecting these options, officials embarked on a path deemed harder but ultimately more useful: actively raising workers' skills (and improving career pathways) to enable them to command a better wage. It was no accident that Workfare marked the start of a strong training infrastructure. The government was now willing to provide assistance that included training allowances, with this help extending even to the unemployed, provided that they were willing to commit to training.[241]

Could more have been done by way of redistribution and transfers to the less well-off? Tharman Shanmugaratnam, who from his 2001 entry into politics was to hold several key ministerial portfolios, shed light on government thinking during the first half decade:

> *You have to focus on the most important things at any time and get it done. We were facing a critical need for new sources of growth and competitiveness, so as to create jobs. We had gone through a series of downturns in quick succession—the Asian financial crisis, followed by the global dot-com bubble burst, then 9/11, and again when SARS hit the region. We were also facing very sharp competition not just from countries immediately around us but from China, and renewed from amongst the developed countries. I think it was reasonable for government to focus on making sure that you had new sources of growth. It was not that redistribution was unimportant, but there was a pretty serious issue of whether you would continue to grow as an economy and do reasonably well, and continued weak growth would have been even tougher on jobs and wages for the lower segments of the workforce. So that was a reasonable judgement. We focused on what were the most important issues at the time.[242]*

Foreign Workers and Immigrants

> *Singapore will become the most open and cosmopolitan city in Asia, and one of the best places to live and work. In another decade and a half, Singapore will connect China, India and Southeast Asia, and beyond. We will become an Asian centre of choice for global talent, attracting skilled technicians, managers, entrepreneurs and creative people from all over the world.*
>
> —*Report of the Economic Review Committee*, 2003[243]

Developing Singaporean talent was important, noted the ERC report, but the indigenous pool was by itself too small to meet the needs of an increasingly sophisticated and globalised economy. Singapore therefore had to continue welcoming foreign talent as well as keeping foreign worker policies flexible enough to allow companies to employ the numbers they needed (which would in turn help to keep down their overall costs).[244]

At the higher, Employment Pass (EP) level (which was generally meant for professionals, executives and managers), the broad principles governing inflows had been agreed internally within government by 1998.[245] "Talent" was defined as foreigners who could provide the base for Singapore to transition into a knowledge economy. The emphasis was on quality and not numbers. But by the early 2000s, there was an increasing recognition within the leadership (informed not just by the ERC but also by various internal committees examining talent and population issues) that Singapore might lose out in the war for talent. These reports pointed to the fact that educated and qualified foreigners had an increasing number of options. Singapore lacked buzz, especially in the eyes of global talent, who saw the country as a place bound by many rules and rigidities. In addition, China's rise and the relocation of businesses there meant that Singapore might have to content itself with a smaller share of the international investment pie.[246] If Singapore faced the prospect of an ebbing appeal, then bringing in international talent capital had to be the next line of defence, and it was thus vital that Singapore redouble its efforts in the quest for this talent.

There were concerns also on the wider population front. The total fertility rate had been dropping steadily since the 1970s, falling to 1.6 in 2000, with the number of births well short of what was needed to sustain the population.[247] New incentives were announced in 2000 to encourage procreation, and to relieve some of the financial burden associated with child-raising. The Marriage and Parenthood Package, which came into effect in 2001, had as its key features a cash "Baby Bonus" and a Child Development Co-Savings Scheme under which the government would open and put money into an account for any couple when they had their second or third child. The funds could be used to defray the cost of childcare fees. The overall package of benefits was to be enhanced in 2004, 2008 and 2013.[248] But the overall impact of the package and its later editions was limited: overall total fertility rate was to decline to 1.24 in 2005 (and further, to 1.15, in 2010).

Upping the inflow of suitable foreigners, and their subsequent naturalisation, was increasingly seen as critical to growing the population and sustaining an economically viable Singapore. From 2004, the criteria for evaluating applications for Permanent Residency (PR) and citizenship was broadened, with the revised framework taking into account, amongst other factors, a wider set of attributes, including the potential to contribute to Singapore in the future. The residential requirement for PR or citizenship applicants deemed well qualified was also shortened. The EP framework was also reviewed along similar lines at this time to take into account broader attributes (again, with consideration given to the longer-term potential to contribute to Singapore), in line with the fresh thrust of attracting global talent to augment the Singapore population base. In the following years, new strategies and schemes were rolled out with the aim of facilitating the entry of top-end talent. These included granting more dependent privileges to a wider range of foreigners working in Singapore, which was recognised as being an important determinant in the final decision made to settle.[249]

All levels of work pass (including the mid-skilled S Pass, introduced in 2004, and the Work Permit or R Pass catering to semi-skilled and lower-skilled foreign workers who did not qualify for any of the higher work passes) came under various forms of administrative control by the Ministry of Manpower. One such control was the Foreign Worker Levy, a pricing mechanism applied to each foreign worker and payable by the employer, which varied across industry sectors. But the key control mechanism for low-skilled and semi-skilled jobs was the Dependency Ratio Ceiling (DRC), the maximum permitted ratio of foreign workers to the total workforce that a company was allowed to hire (at the S Pass and Work Permit levels). A company's access to foreign workers was therefore based on the size of its local workforce, in theory preventing over-reliance on foreigners at the expense of local employment. Sectors where local recruitment had been shown to be difficult due to the unattractive nature of the work were allowed a more generous DRC. After 2004 the general trend was to accord increasingly greater flexibility to companies when it came to the DRC. By January 2008, for example, the S Pass DRC (which stood at 5 per cent in 2004) had reached 25 per cent. There was also from 2004 onwards a general trend towards greater flexibility in country "source" access, as the labour market tightened.[250] From 2004 onwards, there were significant inflows of foreign workers: close to 49,800 in 2005, 85,100 in 2006, 144,500 in 2007, and 156,900 in 2008.[251] Almost 300,000 PR applications were approved across this five-year period, with a peak of 79,200 in 2008.[252]

When queried on foreign talent at the point when the ERC was established in December 2001, the ERC's chairman, DPM Lee, had simply said that "some other part of the Government" would be looking at social and political implications of the issue.[253] In 2001, such a reaction was understandable: the focus was on reshaping Singapore's economy to face future challenges. But the leadership was well aware of the political downside when taking critical decisions on talent inflow and naturalisation. Large-scale immigration could be a social stressor, and there would be opposition from the citizen base concerned especially about competition for jobs and (for their children) schools. The alternative, however, was the certainty of a diminishing, greying and less vigorous Singapore. There could be no U-turn.[254] There was at this time though the recognition that persuasion was going to be a problem for a considerable length of time to come. After 2004, there was a noticeable intensification on the part of the leadership to convince Singaporeans that the country had to remain open to foreign talent, not just to stay ahead of the competition but also in order to ameliorate the effects of the sharply declining birth rate.[255] PM Lee, in his 2006 National Day Rally speech, gave a broad hint that the definition of foreign talent had been widened and that Singapore was not looking at netting only high-income, high-skilled foreigners. Lee, in giving examples of those from humble origins who had made good in Singapore, stressed the need for Singaporeans to welcome newcomers: "We must look for all kinds of talent. It's not just numbers. We're looking for people with ability, with drive, with initiative and ideas and not just one kind of initiative and ideas, graduates, or professionals or bankers and lawyers, but all kinds."[256]

Convincing people was an uphill task despite evidence that most Singaporeans understood the basic argument for having foreign talent. A 2001 Gallup poll showed that 80 per cent of Singaporeans thought that the foreign talent in Singapore had contributed to the nation's success. But the percentage that believed in the necessity of having foreign workers had fallen to 64 per cent (down from 72 per cent in 1997).[257] People were not entirely convinced that foreign workers were committed to the Singapore cause. In another survey, conducted the same year by professors at the

National University of Singapore (NUS), seven in ten locals evinced the view that foreigners were in Singapore only for the economic benefits and had no commitment to the nation.[258]

The government had made the intellectual argument for foreign talent as best it could. The leadership knew full well that pushback on the foreign talent policy should be expected. It may not, however, have calculated how deep the resentment would eventually prove to be. This would play out over subsequent years.

The 2006 General Election

PM Goh had successfully executed his plan to have a new ministerial team in place before the next general election. Younger ministers had moved up. Some had been battle-hardened by SARS (with ministers such as Lim Hng Kiang, Khaw Boon Wan and Dr Vivian Balakrishnan all part of the Ministerial SARS Combat Unit). Others, such as Tharman Shanmugaratnam and Raymond Lim, had played important roles in the ERC.[259] Within the election machinery, DPM Wong Kan Seng, the Party's first assistant secretary-general, coordinated the main election committee. But apart from Wong, it was for the most part members of the younger team in charge.[260]

The slate presented for election was exceptionally young and diverse, the result of the PAP recruitment machinery making "special efforts" in this respect, according to Defence Minister Teo Chee Hean, who was now in charge of the PAP's recruitment of new candidates.[261] Among the 24 new candidates the average age was 40.3 years, slightly younger than the average age of 41.1 years in the 2001 election. Half the new candidates were aged under 40 (see Appendix One, Table 5.2).[262] Half of the new slate of 24 were from the post-1965 generation.[263] This was not surprising. The Party had long expressed a wish to reach out to voters born after Independence. Those born after 1965 by now made up more than half of Singaporeans, and approximately 40 per cent of the electorate.[264] The Party had also put forward a much more gender-balanced slate than in any previous election, with seven new women candidates. When taken with the ten already in Parliament, women made up more than a quarter of the total number of candidates presented for election.

The Class of 2006 had just a few individuals who could be counted as the scholar or Mandarin type. More in evidence were candidates who could speak their mind—or even occasionally disagree with PAP policies.[265] Some, such as Denise Phua, Zaqy Mohamad and Lim Wee Kiak, had a strong track record of social service or grassroots work. Phua in particular was held up as the type of candidate the PAP sought: she had on her own initiative taken up the case for enhanced (and mainstream) education for special needs children, after finding out about her son's autism. She had her own mind and could disagree with aspects of policy.[266] There was a noticeable smattering of the type of candidates the PAP particularly prized: "bicultural" individuals who were equally at home in English and Mandarin—Lee Yi Shyan, Grace Fu and Baey Yam Keng.[267] Some candidates had come up the hard way. Liang Eng Hwa had failed O Level English, eventually gone to polytechnic, and then (after four years as a regular in the army) obtained a university degree in commerce. There was also a sprinkling of candidates who had risen through the PAP ranks. One of them, Lim Biow Chuan, had been the branch secretary at Jalan Kayu since 2003.

There were 14 GRCs (nine with five MPs each, and five with six MPs each) and nine SMCs—the same as in 2001. The changes to boundaries made by the Electoral Boundaries Review Committee (whose report was published on 3 March 2006) were on the whole minor, making it the first time since 1984 that there were no major changes to the electoral map (and the first which had seen no GRCs disappear).[268] Even Aljunied GRC, where the WP had been walking the ground for four years and was seen as a likely election hotspot, was left largely intact.[269] As the press commented at the time, the fact that minimal changes were preferred and that there was a gap of over two months between the publishing of the report and the polls on 6 May 2006 was likely an attempt to arrest cynicism about the political process. PM Lee had himself acknowledged just before the polls that it was a matter for concern if young people felt the political process to be unfair.[270]

New Media

Eyes were on the government also to see how it would choose to recognise, or regulate, the emerging new media. Here, too, minimal changes were preferred—but the reaction was to be quite different.

In the period leading up to the election, a series of government announcements and clarifications reinforced the earlier position taken in 2001. It was made clear that while non-Party websites and blogs could comment on politics during the campaign period, those that went beyond mere dabbling in politics to blatantly endorse one party or "persistently propagate, promote or circulate political issues relating to Singapore" would have to register with the Media Development Authority. In other words, private individuals could not cross the line into supporting one candidate or party during the campaign period, as this would transgress into the realm of Internet advertising.[271]

Predictably, there was concern from the Internet community. More parties now had websites, and there had been a proliferation of websites and blogs run by individuals that expressed views on political matters either directly or tangentially. It was unclear where exactly the government drew the line in terms of when commentary became "election advertising": this has been skirted in official explanations. Many held that the government's stance had contributed to a chilling effect. But the real talking point was the government stand that podcasts and videocasts of a political nature would be prohibited, as they were not part of the "positive list" in the Parliamentary Elections (Election Advertising) Regulations. The government's view, as explained by Dr Lee Boon Yang, minister for information, communications and the arts, was that allowing podcasts and videocasts would turn political campaigning into "info-tainment", "where the line between fact and fiction gets blurred, and people get worked up emotionally without understanding the substantive issues".[272]

The ban on podcasts was slammed by the Opposition, with the SDP and WP having to scrap their plans to use the medium during campaigning.[273] The wider public also appeared unconvinced, with some evincing the view that an active and engaged citizenry engaged in political discourse was the wellspring for a mature society.[274] There was also the issue of how watertight enforcement could be. Many websites and blogs were anonymous, and enforcing the government's intent was not going to be a straightforward affair. Prior to the polls, Dr Lee Boon Yang had acknowledged that regulation would not be straightforward, but the point was to "set a certain standard and help maintain order and accountability in the way political issues are discussed over the Internet".[275]

In the event, there was scant evidence of government policing of the online space during the election period when it came to private websites and blogs. Videocasts or video clips of Opposition rallies were put up by several websites, with no government action taken. There was also in general a lively online election discourse on numerous blogs and websites.[276] This was perhaps to be expected, given the increasing ease of use of many aspects of new media. What was perhaps less foreseeable (as we shall see) was the form taken by some of new media's most memorable scene-stealers of the 2006 campaign: satire and sheer visual, viral impact.

Battle of the Manifestos

Policing anonymous blogs and websites was difficult. Political parties, of course, were a different matter, and their online offerings could be regulated without much difficulty.[277] What the election advertising rules meant was that much of the campaigning by political parties took place outside of cyberspace, along very conventional lines.

The PAP manifesto "Staying Together, Moving Ahead" was unveiled on 15 April 2006, the product of a team led by Raymond Lim (minister in the Prime Minister's Office).[278] Lessons had clearly been learnt: the brief manifesto was glossy, heavy on visuals, and short on the type of wordiness that had characterised previous editions.[279] Parts of the manifesto were clearly influenced by the ERC and RSC reports. Growth strategies to keep Singapore going were highlighted (the government would create more opportunities through investments and encourage entrepreneurship, as well as investing in education). Looking after less well-off Singaporeans and the elderly, and providing affordable healthcare, were also addressed.[280] According to WP leader Low Thia Khiang, the PAP manifesto said nothing new, had no new ideas, and was full of "motherhood statements".[281] Low's criticisms were to be expected, especially given that the WP's 52-page manifesto, "You Have a Choice", unveiled much earlier on 14 January 2006, had itself come in for sustained attacks by PAP leaders. The WP's manifesto represented the most coherent Opposition statement of policy and intent for some time. Careful thought had clearly gone into the effort, and concrete suggestions had been made. These included scrapping the elected presidency, doing away with PAP-linked grassroots organisations, abolishing ethnic quotas for HDB flats, increasing subsidies (and running budget deficits) to help the disadvantaged, nationalising public transport, and allowing those in financial trouble to dip into their Central Provident Fund accounts.[282] PAP leaders had been quick to label the WP proposals "time bombs" or "poisons" that would destroy the nation, with Low Thia Khiang being invited to back down and rethink his party's manifesto.[283] Low politely declined, with the WP also issuing a detailed point-by-point rebuttal to the PAP's criticisms.[284]

The lines taken by the PAP say something about its threat perception and its recognition that the WP was making itself into a force to be reckoned with.[285] The WP was beginning to look and act like a credible political party, with the press commenting that it might finally be emerging from the J.B. Jeyaretnam era.[286] By Low Thia Khiang's own account, the WP was also increasingly placing a stress on renewal and connecting with young voters.[287] Since 2001, half the members appointed to the WP CEC had been from the younger generation, including Sylvia Lim, who became chairman in 2003.[288]

The WP's discipline and organisation had improved too. Quietly, the WP had been working the ground in its chosen areas (which included the GRCs of Aljunied, East Coast, Ang Mo Kio and Sembawang) for some time, stepping up its efforts from mid-2005, when it seemed that polls might be drawing near.[289] The WP approach to cultivating the ground was a low-key one that eschewed high-profile constituency tours in public areas. Instead, small groups of activists and potential candidates would canvass door to door.[290] Such was the WP's standing that in a late December 2005 meeting to coordinate Opposition strategy, it could reserve four GRCs—Aljunied, East Coast, Ang Mo Kio and Sembawang—in part because of the groundwork done earlier in these areas.[291] The Opposition was also able to come to an agreement to avoid three-cornered fights. The fact that these understandings were reached relatively early was something of a first.

The general impression that the WP had made significant progress in attracting credible and qualified individuals to the fold was confirmed when its new candidates began to be unveiled during the approach to Nomination Day (27 April 2006).[292] Of the 20 WP candidates, 15 were new faces (in 2001 the WP fielded only two candidates—Low Thia Khiang and Dr Poh Lee Guan). Fifteen of the total slate were graduates, and 11 were from the post-1965 generation. There were also several bicultural candidates who lost little, if anything, in comparison to the bicultural candidates fielded by the PAP.[293] The WP even had the temerity to challenge PM Lee on his own home turf, Ang Mo Kio GRC, with a young and untested team.[294]

The SDP had found itself (just like in 2001) caught in a net largely of its own making. Articles addressing the NKF saga, published in the February 2006 issue of the SDP organ the *New Democrat*, drew certain parallels between the running of the old NKF and the government. This led to a lawsuit by PM Lee and MM Lee against SDP Chairman Dr Chee Soon Juan, the rest of the SDP CEC, and the printing company that had published the newsletter, for alleging that the PAP leaders knew about the NKF's problems but covered them up.[295] The SDP at first refused to apologise and continued to sell the newsletter, but ultimately all its leaders save Dr Chee Soon Juan and his sister Chee Siok Chin backed down and apologised.[296] In September 2006 the High Court was to rule that the siblings had defamed PM Lee and MM Lee through the articles, which implied (inter alia) government mismanagement and that the Lees were unfit for office.[297]

The entire SDP campaign had elements of farce and sheer theatricality that rivalled or even outdid its 2001 foray. There appeared to be internal rifts within the leadership, with the suggestion that senior party leaders, including Chairman Ling How Doong, were unhappy with the confrontational stance of Dr Chee. At the same time, senior SDP figures (especially the Chees) were having to make public assurances—largely unconvincing—that the SDP leadership (which had seen resignations in the wake of the *New Democrat* apology fiasco) and its election challenge were not falling apart.[298] For his part, Dr Chee was bankrupt and unable to stand for election or take part in election activities. But he proved irrepressible nonetheless. There were dramas at SDP rallies, as he variously tried (on one occasion) to mount the rally stage, or to address groups of supporters at the sidelines. After one rally, Dr Chee, his sister, and other SDP members and supporters sealed their mouths with adhesive tape with the letters "NKF". All these actions led to police warnings and probes.[299]

Potong Pasir and Hougang

PM Lee entrusted SM Goh Chok Tong with the "special responsibility" of assisting Eric Low and Sitoh Yih Pin to win back Hougang and Potong Pasir. Some analysts thought that this was an astute move—an attempt, it seemed, to tie down Low Thia Khiang and Chiam See Tong and limit the attention they could devote to their parties' wider campaigns.[300] The carrots dangled by Goh before residents of these constituencies were not insignificant. In a repeat of an offer that had been made to Hougang residents in 2001, Goh announced that precincts offering strong (60 per cent or more) support to the PAP would receive upgrading.[301] Potong Pasir, too, was not disregarded. Sitoh Yih Pin, the adviser to the Potong Pasir grassroots organisations, had continued to be active there after having lost to the SDA's Chiam See Tong in 2001 by just 751 votes. The services he provided to residents included serving abalone porridge and shark's fin soup on special occasions (either free, or at low prices), as well as organising activities and outings.[302] But the real centrepiece of Sitoh's campaign promises in 2006 was a lift-upgrading programme covering all 62 of Potong Pasir's HDB blocks, which would eventually see lifts upgraded and stopping on every floor. All this was contingent, of course, on his winning.[303]

Promises on upgrading were not exactly new. What was new was a series of direct PAP attacks against the SDA chairman and incumbent in Potong Pasir, Chiam See Tong, who was clearly seen as the more vulnerable of the two Opposition MPs. Chiam had attempted to match the PAP's promise of constituency-wide lift upgrading that would see lift landings on every floor of all HDB blocks, but Sitoh Yih Pin and SM Goh insisted that Chiam's town council did not have sufficient funds to deliver on his pledge.[304] The second prong of the attack, speared in by SM Goh, was much more personal. Chiam was, according to Goh, an MP who could not match the energy (nor ideas) of his younger opponent (aged 29), who had the vigour to run the town council and serve residents.[305] Goh was careful not to take an overly ageist stance against Chiam, but his message was unmistakable: Chiam had had his time, and now it was up.

Direct and personal interventions by PAP heavyweights into the electoral fights of their candidates were also not new. SM Goh, when PM, had been involved (though to a lesser degree) in the attempts to take back Potong Pasir and Hougang in the 2001 polls. And the Party's own post-1997 election analysis suggested that multiple interventions by PAP leaders in Cheng San had been crucial in swinging the result the PAP's way. The fact was, however, that taking a personal line in the heat of electoral battle was rarely completely successful, and so it proved in 2006.[306] In the case of HDB lift upgrading in Potong Pasir, Chiam was widely and sympathetically perceived as attempting to play a lone hand with what funds he had available to him, whereas Sitoh had the backing of the entire government for his upgrading plan.[307] When it came to SM Goh's attempts to usher Chiam into retirement, Chiam gained sympathy—and likely votes—from those who saw him as the victim in an unequal match-up. Goh's intervention may in the end have helped not just Chiam but also Low Thia Khiang, who was in any case clearly on a firmer footing in Hougang. As one Hougang resident observed when interviewed by the press, "I want to see what [PAP candidate] Eric Low can do as an individual, without the backing of so many PAP Ministers."[308]

Aspects of the Campaign

The WP manifesto had been thorough—dense, even—but the WP did not make the mistake of simply regurgitating it at rallies. Instead, it chose a few simple and salient messages that would resonate. The rising cost of living (especially transport and medical costs) was repeatedly highlighted.[309] The WP's accusation (against which the government strenuously defended itself) was that not enough had been done to help the people cope.[310] Besides stressing the difficulties faced by ordinary people, the manifesto had specific new areas aimed at the concerns of those in the middle and lower-middle classes. In particular, the WP highlighted healthcare costs and the proposed introduction of means testing for those using the public health system, suggesting that this would lead to further cost increases post-election.[311]

These were telling punches. PAP leaders on the campaign trail found themselves in the position of spending a great deal of time rebutting Opposition arguments, especially on the allegations of government callousness in the face of rising costs and job losses. The PAP response was that the key factor in rising costs was globalisation—something the government could not slow. However, targeted help could, and would, be given, especially for the lower-income group.[312] On means testing, the PAP's response was that the WP was indulging in rumour-mongering and being misleading.[313] It was made clear that the government (which had earlier said that means testing would be implemented in 2007 or 2008) would first consult widely and implement the measure only if it could be done fairly. Reassurances were also given that even if it was implemented, Singaporeans would still not have to worry about not being able to pay their medical bills.[314]

Sniping at living costs was a tried and tested campaign tactic. But in other respects, aspects of WP campaigning were becoming more conceptual and sophisticated. Just before Nomination Day, MM Lee commented that Singapore would not have a First

World parliament if it did not have a First World opposition. Low Thia Khiang's rejoinder was to make the theme of a First World government and parliament one of the WP's core campaign planks.[315] Part of this riposte (with the WP citing the lack of civil and political rights, the PAP government's use of the estate-upgrading carrot, and the lack of independent checks on the government) was that the PAP government itself could not be counted as a First World one.[316]

In WP rallies and political broadcasts, Low Thia Khiang and other WP candidates made much of the idea that the party could fulfil Singaporeans' desire for a check on the PAP. The PAP would thereby be made more accountable to the people, especially with a strong Opposition voice in Parliament.[317] It would be a mistake, the WP reasoned aloud, for the people to give the PAP a huge mandate; this would allow the government to do what it liked after the election.[318]

Savvy WP marketing was coupled with clever tactical strokes. For the first time, on 5 May 2006, the WP chose to conclude its rally (at an overflowing Serangoon North Stadium in Aljunied GRC) with a recitation of the National Pledge.[319] This appears in large part to have had to do with refuting the idea that Opposition members were somehow disloyal to the country or "troublemakers".[320] It may also have been linked to PM Lee's throwaway and ill-advised remark during a lunchtime rally on 3 May 2006 that if there were many Opposition members in Parliament, he would have to "spend all my time thinking: What is the right way to fix them, what's the right way to buy my own supporters over."[321] The WP was quick to deny—even mock—the suggestion that PM Lee's task of governing the country would be made that much more difficult if more Opposition members were elected.[322]

Aljunied and GomezGate

Whenever the opportunity presented itself, the WP had taken its campaign to the level of "national" issues. This struck a chord with many voters; the PAP's strong municipal track record remained therefore largely undiscussed, and it was in the position of having to do a lot more explaining than it would have liked.[323] There were concerns particularly when it came to Aljunied GRC, where the PAP team led by Foreign Minister George Yeo faced off against what was widely regarded as the WP's strongest team, led by its chairman, Sylvia Lim, a law lecturer.[324] The PAP was well aware in advance that a tough fight could be expected. The estate-upgrading plan for Aljunied (worth $160 million) was the first of all such plans to be unveiled, in October 2005. The PAP team in Aljunied also spent a good deal of time during the campaign reminding residents of its track record and promising more improvements.[325] The word on the street, however, was that while the PAP team had the incumbent's advantage, it would be pushed by the WP team (which, following the WP playbook, focused on national issues), and victory was by no means a foregone conclusion.

What happened next was a sequence of events that became the most talked-about issue in the 2006 election, and one which the PAP was to try to exploit to the hilt. James Gomez, a WP candidate officially unveiled on 25 April 2006, had turned up at the Elections Department (ELD) the following day to collect his minority candidate certificate, which he claimed to have submitted an application for two days earlier.[326] When told that there was no trace of this form, Gomez stood his ground, insisted that the form in question had been submitted, and appeared to warn ELD officials of unspecified consequences. Security camera footage from the ELD subsequently emerged, showing that Gomez on his 24 April 2006 visit to the Elections Department had in fact taken the form and left without submitting it. Caught out, Gomez apologised for his apparent oversight. The PAP (after a short initial period when it seemed content to accept Gomez's explanation) decided to take the line that there were sinister overtones. Gomez's explanations and apology were brushed aside, with PAP leaders demanding that he come clean on what had actually happened. According to MM Lee, Gomez was a "liar", who until showed up by security footage had been attempting to cast doubt on the integrity of ELD officials: he might even have stage-managed the entire incident in order to make it seem as if the ELD was trying to deprive him of the right to seek election as a minority candidate in a GRC where he might be needed.[327] The attack was widened by the PAP and linked to the question of the WP's accountability and transparency, especially given that Low Thia Khiang had earlier said that the WP's candidates met high standards of character.[328] The integrity of the system was at stake (according to the PAP), and matters could not be so simple as accepting Gomez's proffered apology.[329]

There was indeed some evidence to suggest that Gomez (who was to be fielded in the WP team in Aljunied GRC) had not simply been forgetful as he had initially claimed. In unguarded comments to two acquaintances, including a PAP MP, Gomez said that the whole incident and his actions had been a "wayang" or ruse to throw people off the scent as to where he would actually contest.[330] But even as the PAP used this and other evidence to press its attack well into the campaign period, the public was beginning to lose interest. Press polls suggested that many of those still following the issue inclined to the WP's explanation (which it doggedly maintained throughout) that an innocent mistake had been made and all concerned should move on.[331] The growing consensus was that the PAP's attacks and attempts to tarnish the WP (especially its slate in Aljunied) were in danger of backfiring, with even the press suggesting that it was better after a certain point to return to the real issues on the ground.[332]

The general perception that the PAP was making a mountain out of the proverbial molehill was compounded by a podcast created at the height of the affair by a well-known local blogger, Lee Kin Mun, known popularly by his moniker of Mr Brown. The satirical effort, which was essentially a parody of the government's overreaction to the Gomez affair, featured an exchange between a bak chor mee (minced meat noodles) hawker and his customer, one "Jeff Lopez", with the hawker smugly and insistently demanding an explanation after having proved to "Lopez" through footage from a closed-circuit television camera that he had placed a wrong order.[333] The podcast poked fun at the PAP and mocked its stand that "GomezGate" was about wider issues of integrity. The podcast also insistently declaimed its "persistently non-political" nature, in all likelihood also a jab at the ambiguity of the election advertising regulations. Mr Brown's creation was not just very funny; it was influential, quickly going viral and being downloaded by over 100,000 people. Parody had trumped serious politics, with Mr Brown more successfully painting a picture of overreaction than the WP explanations had done.

The PAP had to refocus. This happened late—very late, only two days before the polls—with a concerted attempt to return to the main theme of what the Party could do for the people.[334] (Separately, a full reckoning on the Gomez affair was promised, after the election.[335]) The change of tack was necessary, as the PAP sense on the ground appeared to have detected a shift against the Party in Aljunied. George Yeo held a press conference on 5 May 2006 with his fellow team members, where he acknowledged that "the picture got a little bit confused" and that too much time had been spent on the Gomez affair.[336] Yeo also used the occasion to release a letter, sent to every single one of the 75,000 households in the GRC, spelling out what the PAP team had done for the GRC and what its future plans were.

The PAP Analysis—and Beyond It

The PAP took 66.6 per cent of the popular vote, up from the 65 per cent in 1997, 61 per cent in 1991, and 63.2 per cent in 1988. (In the anomalous 2001 election the PAP had taken 75.3 per cent of the vote, a performance that its leaders at the time had acknowledged would not be repeatable.) In the seven contested GRCs, the PAP won 67.63 per cent of the vote. This was down from the 76.8 per cent in 2001 but above its returns in 1997 and 1991 (66.56 per cent and 62.49 per cent respectively).

Unsurprisingly, the WP was the best-performing Opposition party, with 38.4 per cent of the vote where it contested. Its "A" GRC team in Aljunied took 43.91 per cent of the vote, making it the best-performing Opposition GRC team. Low Thia Khiang took 62.74 per cent in Hougang (his best-ever result), improving on his 2001 result by seven percentage points and easily beating the PAP's Eric Low. The PAP team retained Ang Mo Kio GRC with 66.14 per cent of votes against the WP's "suicide squad", in a result that was not as good as PM Lee and his team had hoped for.

None of the other Opposition parties could be said to have made significant headway, although Chiam See Tong's coming through in Potong Pasir (with 55.82 per cent of the votes against Sitoh Yih Pin) was notable. Chiam's Singapore Democratic Alliance took 32.5 per cent of the vote in its contested seats.[337] The SDP, which contested one GRC and one single-member seat, was the biggest loser. In Sembawang, its team fared the worst of all parties contesting GRCs (23.3 per cent) against the PAP team led by Health Minister Khaw Boon Wan (a margin of just over 90,000 votes). The SDP chairman, Ling How Doong, was the worst-performing Opposition politician, taking in just 22.81 per cent of the vote in the single-member constituency of Bukit Panjang.

From the PAP's point of view, it was a very satisfactory result: a strong mandate, and a creditable performance for PM Lee leading his first election campaign.[338] There was no soul-searching of the type that had characterised the aftermath of then PM Goh's first campaign in 1991. Not that there was any complacency in evidence: the post-election rallying call was that the PAP would immediately begin to prepare for the next election.[339] This was something done routinely after most elections. But in this case the call was more insistent than usual, with one eye clearly on the possibility that the Opposition might continue to build strength. The PAP had been unable to contain Low Thia Khiang from breaking out of Hougang, which had been an issue of concern even in 2001.[340] The general sense was that WP influence had seeped from Hougang (which was essentially a single-seat enclave within Aljunied GRC).[341] There were, perhaps, the beginnings also of something even more than this. The WP team contesting East Coast GRC (with four of its five candidates fighting their first electoral battles) had put up an unexpectedly strong showing against a PAP team anchored by Deputy Prime Minister and Minister for Law Prof. S. Jayakumar, becoming in the process the second- highest scoring Opposition team in a GRC.[342]

PM Lee acknowledged with perspicacity that the next election would be much tougher: "My concern is not so much this election, but the next one. By 2011, the world will have changed, and so will Singapore."[343] This was something that commentators and the press had already latched onto: the idea that it was not the 2006 election that might prove to be a watershed, but the one after it, when (presumably) more senior PAP heavyweights would have retired, and when the post-Independence generation would make up more than half the electorate for the first time.[344] That tougher battles almost certainly lay ahead was also the conclusion of the Party's post-election internal analysis. In previous elections, branches (and HQ) needing help could tap on the pool of uncontested candidates and supporters. But this pool, the analysis concluded, would likely shrink in future. Branches had to build up resources to fight campaigns on their own, with MPs having to start early to build a cadre of dependable activists.[345]

Separately, there was also the realisation that the growing disapproval of PAP tactics such as its votes-for-upgrading strategy could not be ignored.[346] Government leaders (including National Development Minister Mah Bow Tan) restated the established PAP principle that the upgrading scheme was one of the PAP's key programmes and funded out of budget surpluses generated by the PAP government. All wards would get upgrading, but limited resources meant that other things being equal, PAP constituencies would be the first recipients.[347] Mah's explanations may have been important from the government's point of view to set the record straight, but his points were in reality the embers of the PAP's argument. The Party had attempted to hold the line on upgrading since 1992, but now a serious rethink had to be done. Future battles, as SM Goh observed soon after the election, could not be fought using old strategies.[348] PM Lee had himself acknowledged, at the traditional post-results press conference in the early hours of 7 May 2006, that change was needed. Dislodging the Opposition MPs would involve "not just offering them something better, but overcoming this natural loyalty voters had to their MP".[349]

It was also clear that the PAP would have to evolve in other ways, particularly in its approach to the new media. The 2006 election was the first one where the Internet had really mattered—not so much in terms of the offerings of party websites (which were anodyne), but in the content of the numerous politically inclined blogs and websites. This was complemented by the development of technology. Digital cameras and mobile phones that could record and transmit video images and video content were now far more prevalent, as were websites that could host and distribute such material. This confluence meant that in 2006, many online discussions clearly went far beyond the allowed limits (the "persistent propagation") of political discussion set out by the relevant regulations, the breaching of which would have warranted registration with the authorities. Given that these limits were flouted insouciantly or perhaps ignorantly, on such a wide scale, the inevitable conclusion—but one never enunciated publicly as such by PAP leaders—was that a great part of online political commentary was developing in a way which was beginning to elude the reach of the law.

It was probably a recognition of this that led some PAP leaders after the polls to suggest that policies governing the Internet would evolve. Minister for Information, Communications and the Arts Dr Lee Boon Yang promised that a "lighter touch" approach would be in place by the next election. But at the same time, Dr Lee defended the basic tenets of government regulation, noting, "There are many people who use their websites and blogs to put out malicious and false information in order to further their own agendas." But Lee's underlying message was consistent with the earlier government insistence that there could not be a free-for-all; nor should online content be allowed to obfuscate the real issues at hand. Dr Lee observed that Mr Brown's podcast on the Gomez affair had been "clever and funny", although he added "humorous creations are fun but may not contribute to a better understanding of deep-seated issues".[350]

There were also suggestions that online political discussions and related offerings on unofficial blogs or websites were more interesting than what could be found in the mainstream media, which at times appeared to be struggling to keep up. Besides Mr Brown's intervention in the James Gomez saga, there was another less humorous intervention, one that in some ways had just as much of an impact, highlighting as it did the potential of citizen journalism. A photograph of a 30 April 2006 WP rally at Hougang taken by a well-known blogger, Alex Au, went viral online, in part because it showed a huge crowd, numbering in the tens of thousands.[351] It took several days (until 5 May 2006) for the *Straits Times* to publish the image, leading to online speculation that the mainstream media was deliberately suppressing information or images showing mass attendance at Opposition rallies. Unsurprisingly, when the *Straits Times* ran a poll on readers' preferences (between print and online media) in September 2006, several respondents evinced cynicism of the mainstream media, which in their view was bound to report positively on the government given that it was government controlled. Many preferred to ignore the mainstream media entirely, with some also expressing a preference for online media given the greater freedom of expression to be found there.[352]

After the 2001 election, the PAP post-mortem report had noted that the Internet had hardly been exploited, and that this would not be the case in the future.[353] On paper, the right Party structures to address these issues were in place by 2006. The Internet Subcommittee (which came under the HQ Exco) had been revamped and renamed the New Media Committee in May 2004, with Dr Ng Eng Hen appointed as its head in December that year. Three subgroups (each with a distinct role) were formed under the New Media Committee in preparation for the general election. Politically active blogs and websites were followed closely, and with their impact assessed. Monthly new media reports were submitted to the chairman of the New Media Committee, Dr Ng Eng Hen.[354] But notwithstanding these developments, the PAP's online efforts both before and during the campaign period (when the stricter regime dictated by the "positive list" applied) did not appear to be markedly better than the attempts of other parties. The PAP still appeared to be feeling its way forward. Its overall strategy for campaigning online and grappling with online political content on blogs and websites (given that the tenor of much of this was not favourable to the PAP) was still not fully formed. The 2006 post-mortem report was to comment that a genuine cyberspace strategy and presence had to be developed by the next election.[355]

It did not take long for the Party to begin recognising openly that it would have to up its game when it came to the new media. In his 20 August 2006 National Day Rally speech, PM Lee made it a point to underline this: "We will use the new media, multimedia, podcast, broadcast: all these things which you get in the Internet, or somebody sends to you by e-mail, I think our ministries, our agencies have to experiment, have to try it out."[356] By this time, cautious attempts were already being made to turn the PAP's rudimentary online presence into one that would resonate with the Internet generation. In August 2006, soon after PM Lee's rally speech, Foreign Minister George Yeo had begun blogging (albeit without a website of his own).[357] And in October, the 12 new PAP MPs born after 1965 launched www.p65.sg. This was a blog site that would show their "personal, non-political side", but the MPs involved also acknowledged that the blog represented a move to connect with the ground.[358]

Informal polls by the press after the election found that among the top reasons voters went with the Opposition was the idea that PAP candidates seemed unapproachable and out of touch with the concerns of ordinary folk.[359] This was an issue taken up in the PAP's election post-mortem: the poor perception of the Party in some quarters, and the need to work on improving the Party's public image. One conclusion was that it would be useful in future for potential candidates to start working the ground earlier if possible. This would allow them to understand the constituency better, be more familiar with issues, and have time to get to know the residents and grassroots leaders in advance of the next election.[360]

These were, of course, commendable ideas, but they were not fixes for the overall problem. The idea of the PAP being uncaring and out of touch, present in some quarters in 2006, was to become much more pronounced by the time of the 2011 election.[361]

"The Mood of the Times"

Low Thia Khiang's 2001 appeal to voters—not to allow the Opposition to be extinguished—had on the 2006 campaign trail been honed further, into the idea of the Opposition being a check on the PAP. The WP had divined the growing public mood. Surveys carried out both before and after the election by the press and think tanks suggested an increased desire for a credible Opposition to act as just a check: an Opposition that could give alternative views, and even concrete solutions.[362]

A week after the polls, George Yeo gave his own assessment as to why Aljunied GRC had seen a close fight. One reason, he said, was the Gomez saga. But in addition, Yeo noted, "Many Singaporeans would not want an outcome where the PAP won all eighty-four seats. They don't think it's healthy."[363] This was a key point touched on in the PAP's 2006 election post-mortem.[364] It noted that people were increasingly coming to believe that good government was a given, and indeed part of the natural order of things. Given this, in the minds of the people, stability and progress would not be affected by a less dominant PAP; it was good for the PAP to share power with the opposition, the press and other civil society groups. As the internal analysis noted, even a party facing severe problems like the SDP could garner about 23 per cent of the votes where it contested. The SDA with its crop of fresh faces could obtain 32 per cent.

In the post-election ruminations in public by senior leaders, there was what amounted to an acknowledgement that the Party would have to make deep shifts in order to maintain its supremacy. It would have to work even harder to understand (and to a degree accept) the aspirations and desires of the younger generation. Clearly, it would be a challenging task.

One encounter before the election highlighted the generational gap—an encounter that was to become one of the most widely talked about issues in the lead-up to the polls. This was MM Lee's 12 April 2006 televised dialogue with ten young journalists and undergraduates. The dialogue saw a wide variety of topics raised, ranging from why MM Lee did not retire or withdraw fully from politics, to the perceived politics of fear in Singapore.[365] Jarring to many watching was the fact that large parts of the dialogue were conducted in the form of testy exchanges. There seemed to be a yawning gap in understanding. One of the journalists involved commented after the forum, "I would like to say that what my generation wants is not just the reminder that we are the lucky beneficiaries of successful PAP policies, but also a greater sense of ownership, a sense that we are treated like citizens able to exercise rational judgement when it comes to choosing our politicians."[366] Another journalist, Ken Kwek (widely seen to have been the most abrasive of those involved), said:

> We the post-65ers stand on the precipice of the present and the future, and believe that politics is not only about the basics of life, but a balance between material sustenance and the ideals of an inclusive society. Looking into the eyes of Mr Lee Kuan Yew, the veritable mentor of modern Singapore, I felt both admiration and distance, respect and indignation.[367]

The question of whether the young journalists had in fact overstepped the line and not shown due respect to MM Lee divided opinion (and to some extent divided generations).[368] The internal Party analysis suggested that this was illustrative of how the younger, educated generation resented the PAP's dominant control and wanted the Party to allow other centres of influence and power to emerge. In MM Lee's own view, however, these "radical English-educated young" represented only a small segment of the youth and would in time come to think differently, realising "that a large majority of Singaporeans are steeped in their respective Asian cultures, whose core values will not be easily displaced".[369]

Some Party leaders were concerned. Dr Vivian Balakrishnan, YP chairman, said that he felt "an acute sense of discomfort" watching the forum, noting that the exchanges appeared to point to a gulf "between what the young people think they want or need, and what the party has actually delivered".[370] PM Lee himself weighed in, expressing the view that while the group engaging MM Lee was not representative of most other young Singaporeans, it was nonetheless a matter of concern if young Singaporeans had these views, and especially if they thought that the political process was unfair.[371]

It was not unheard of for members of the younger generation standing up in public to challenge Party leaders and even MM Lee. A year earlier, at a 31 January 2005 forum with university students, an NUS honours student, Jamie Han, had engaged MM Lee in an exchange that saw Han singling out for criticism (inter alia) the Internal Security Act and newspaper laws. Han was careful in his criticism not to launch a full-on broadside, but he did observe pointedly: "The truth of the matter is this: No matter how enlightened a despot is, ultimately he'll turn into a tyrant if there are no checks and balances in place." Han's comments were greeted with a measure of applause from the 1,500 students gathered.[372] At this forum MM Lee talked about the earlier generation, one that "knew that I fought for them". This generation, Lee averred, knew that he was no despot.[373] He also stressed the track record of the PAP in tackling crises such as the 1997 Asian Financial Crisis and SARS: "This is not an ordinary country. You have two election terms of a dud, lousy, incompetent government and you will set Singapore back so badly, it may take you decades to recover, and maybe never. If you dismantle the organisation that brought us here, don't believe it will come back."[374]

Dominant strands of the leadership's thinking at this time can be discerned here: still strong was the belief that the PAP was the institution that would continue to lead the country, even as the nation and people matured (and even, as noted earlier, with the Party leadership knowing full well that with tougher electoral fights ahead).

The final word should perhaps be left to Lee Hsien Loong. In 1999, in an interview given to mark the 45th anniversary of the Party, then-DPM Lee was asked about the possibility of a two-party system emerging in Singapore. His response was telling and perhaps even prophetic:

> *I doubt that we'll have a two-party system. We are not likely to end up with two equally plausible parties, unless something very drastic has changed. But if you ask what Parliament will look like in ten, fifteen years' time, I do not know. Will the PAP still be dominant? Will there be stronger opposition, or at least more opposition? Will the country split due to divisive issues? That depends. It depends on the leaders the PAP throws up, as well as the mood of the times.*[375]

Notes

1   Lam Peng Er, Harish Pillay and Chandra Mohan Nair, "Lack of Competition Will Hurt PAP and Nation", letter to *Straits Times* Forum, 10 Nov. 2001. The letter suggested, amongst other things, the establishing of an independent commission to look at the boundaries issue, smaller GRCs, more SMCs, and a longer campaign period to debate national issues.

2   Ong Keng Yong, "GRCs Have Many Virtues over Single Seats", letter to *Straits Times* Forum, 22 Nov. 2001. See also "Election Rules 'Make for Stable Govt'", *Straits Times*, 22 Nov. 2001.

3   See, for example, "给全国大选提些意见" [Giving some suggestions on the national electoral system], letter from Lim Kim Bock to *Lianhe Zaobao*, 17 Nov. 2001.

4   *2001 General Election PAP Post-mortem Report* (PAP archive).

5   "Walkovers Deny New MPs a Fight, Says SM Lee", *Straits Times*, 26 Oct. 2001.

6   Ibid.

7   "PM Goh Plans Alternative PAP Voice in Parliament", *Straits Times*, 3 Nov. 2001; "Party Whip to Be Lifted Partially for 20 MPs", *Straits Times*, 7 Nov. 2001; "Lifting Party Whip a Good Idea: PAP MPs", *Straits Times*, 8 Nov. 2001; "What PM Goh's Shadow Cabinet Is All About", *Straits Times*, 8 Nov. 2001.

8   "PAP Eases Up to Let MPs Debate More Freely", *Straits Times*, 21 Mar. 2002; "PAP Whip to Be Lifted for All MPs at Times", *Business Times*, 21 Mar. 2002.

9   See, for example, the commentary by Ho Khai Leong, a political science lecturer at NUS: "Building an Effective Shadow Cabinet", *Straits Times*, 8 Nov. 2001.

10   Tan went so far as to suggest that on important issues, even ministers should be allowed to state individual views, without compromising the principle of collective responsibility and confidentiality in Cabinet. See Singapore Parliamentary Debates, 3 Apr. 2002, cols 279–92; "Soo Khoon Lights Up the House", *Straits Times*, 4 Apr. 2002; and "Why Are People Cynical about Politics? Are We Missing Something?", *Straits Times*, 4 Apr. 2002.

11   Singapore Parliamentary Debates, 5 Apr. 2002, cols 542–5; "Not in People's Interest to Lift Whip", *Straits Times*, 6 Apr. 2002.

12   "PAP MPs to Vote Freely on School Reforms", *Straits Times*, 17 Nov. 2002; "Now, if Only We Could Convince the Parents", *Straits Times*, 28 Nov. 2002.

13   "Despite Worries, MPs Back Broader Organ Act", *Straits Times*, 6 Jan. 2004.

14   "A Powerful Influence if They Say 'Aye'", *Straits Times*, 23 Nov. 2002.

15   Other backbenchers also sponsored the motion: Dr Tan Cheng Bock, Leong Horn Kee, Dr Wang Kai Yuen, Chay Wai Chuen and Dr Amy Khor.

16   Singapore Parliamentary Debates, 9 July 2002, cols 200–14.

17   Ibid., cols 230–1.

18   Singapore Parliamentary Debates, 10 July 2002, cols 404–5.

19   The final motion did, however, call on the Public Transport Council when reviewing requests for fare increases, "to take into consideration relevant factors such as the state of the economy, the employment situation, the affordability of commuters and the viability of the transport operators". Singapore Parliamentary Debates, 10 July 2002, cols 404–6, 416.

20   See Singapore Parliamentary Debates, 9 July 2002, cols 215–6.

21   "What Really Happened at Transport Fare Hike Debate", *Straits Times*, 24 Aug. 2002.

22   "What Does Recent Political Sound and Fury Signify?", *Straits Times*, 27 July 2002.

23   Singapore Parliamentary Debates, 9 July 2002, col. 220.

24   "What Does Recent Political Sound and Fury Signify?"

25   Ibid.

26   Singapore Parliamentary Debates, 9 July 2002, col. 235 (for Wang's intervention during the parliamentary debate); "Giving Feedback—Stay with It or Quit?", *Straits Times*, 7 Sept. 2002.

27   "PM to People: Snap Out of the Gloom", *Straits Times*, 22 July 2002; "Govt Listens, but Also Does What's Best", *Straits Times*, 19 Aug. 2002.

28   Singapore Parliamentary Debates, 1 Sept. 2003, cols 2964, 2966.

29   "Betrayal", *Straits Times*, 3 Sept. 2003.

30   Another PAP backbencher who had been critical of the way the public transport fare hikes had been handled (but who did not explicitly support the call for a review of the fare hikes) was Gan Kim Yong. Singapore Parliamentary Debates, 9 July 2002, cols 286–90. Gan would go on to become acting minister for manpower (2008; appointed full minister in 2009) and later minister for health (2011).

31   "Hats Off to Ex-Speaker and Responsive Ministers", *Straits Times*, 24 May 2002.

32   Singapore Parliamentary Debates, 8 Mar. 1999, col. 103; "Parliament—'Let's Think of Our Own First' Call", *Straits Times*, 9 Mar. 1999.

33   "Parliament—Welcome Foreigners, but Tend to Citizens Too", *Straits Times*, 16 Mar. 1999. Tan received support from several MPs, including Dr Wang Kai Yuen, Chay Wai Chuen and the SDA's Chiam See Tong. See Singapore Parliamentary Debates, 15 Mar. 1999, cols 724, 725, 728.

34   Singapore Parliamentary Debates, 11 Mar. 1999, col. 574, and 12 Mar. 1999, cols 582–3; "Don't Send 'Wrong Signals' to Foreigners", *Straits Times*, 12 Mar. 1999.

35   "Party Whip to Be Lifted Partially for 20 PAP MPs".

36   "Non-PAP MPs Query Limits on Questions", *Straits Times*, 23 Oct. 2004. This change dismayed some MPs, who perceived it as an attempt to limit the rights of MPs to query ministers. It even came in for criticism from the former speaker, Tan Soo Khoon. Tan had in 2000 (while still speaker) extended the period for MPs to direct questions to ministers from one hour to one and a half hours: "I wasn't happy that many questions were passed over and that MPs were being deprived of the opportunity to ask questions." "Speaking His Mind", *Straits Times*, 17 Mar. 2002.

37   "NMPs to Come from Wider Pool", *Straits Times*, 21 Mar. 2002.

38   "New Line-up for Parliament GPCs", *Straits Times*, 16 Mar. 2002.

39   "Feedback Polls to Represent Views Better", *Straits Times*, 3 May 2002.

40   The report suggested that the electoral system in Singapore fell well short of accepted best practices, pointing, for example, to the redrawing of electoral boundaries at short notice, sudden changes in election rules prior to polling, and the perceived lack of independence of the Elections Department and the Electoral Boundaries Review Committee. See "Feedback Group Calls for Better Political Governance", *Straits Times*, 17 Sept. 2002. See also "Panel Calls for More Fairness in Politics", *Business Times*, 17 Sept. 2002.

41   "Number of Feedback Groups Slashed from 17 to 8", *Straits Times*, 3 Nov. 2002.

42   I am grateful to Viswa Sadasivan for a personal communication (13 Aug. 2016) on the matter.

43   "S'pore 'Bigger than PAP'", *Straits Times*, 28 Sept. 2003.

44   In his 1999 National Day Rally speech, PM Goh quoted the American political scientist Samuel Huntington, who in 1996 had commented, "The honesty and efficiency that Senior Minister Lee has brought to Singapore are likely to follow him to his grave." Goh insisted that Singapore would flourish in the new millennium, stating that it had to continue to have high standards of government, and self-renewal within the PAP: the answer to Huntingdon lay in what Singapore would do and achieve in the next decades. "First-World Economy, World-Class Home: Setting Fresh Goals", PM Goh Chok Tong, National Day Rally Speech at the Kallang Theatre, 22 Aug. 1999. *National Day Rally Speeches: 50 Years of Nationhood in Singapore 1966–2015*, pp. 408–9, 410.

45   Singapore Parliamentary Debates, 6 Sept. 2099, cols 2354–5. See also "Will the PAP Become Obsolete?", *Straits Times*, 11 Sept. 1999.

46   "Secretary-General Goh Chok Tong: PAP an Institution that Holds the Country Together", *Petir*, Nov.–Dec. 1999 (PAP 45th Anniversary Special Issue), p. 59. See also "Should the PAP Have Split into Two?", *Straits Times*, 17 Nov. 1999; and *For People through Action by Party* (PAP 45th Anniversary Celebrations Editorial Committee, 1999), p. 142.

47   "How will Singapore Compete in a Global Economy?", speech to Nanyang Technological University and National University of Singapore students, 15 Feb. 2000. *The Papers of Lee Kuan Yew: Speeches, Interviews and Dialogues, Vol. 14: 1999–2000*, pp. 163–84, esp. 182. See also "PAP May Field NMPs in Next Polls", *Straits Times*, 16 Feb. 2000. Lee said that finding talent was so difficult that some of the younger leaders in the Party were seriously considering asking some of the nominated members of parliament to stand as its MPs—an intriguing possibility that never appears to have been seriously pursued.

48   Speech by Secretary-General Goh Chok Tong at the PAP 50th Anniversary Dinner on 23 October 2004, at Suntec International Convention & Exhibition Centre, available at https://www.nas.gov.sg/archivesonline/data/pdfdoc/20041023_0001.pdf (accessed 21 Jan. 2021). See also "PAP Is 50 Years Old but It Still Has Appeal, Says SM Goh", *Straits Times*, 24 Oct. 2004.

49   "PAP Is 50 Years Old but It Still Has Appeal, Says SM Goh".

50   See, for example, "PM Wants to Boost Singaporeans' Morale", *Straits Times,* 20 May 2002; and "PM to People: Snap Out of Gloom", *Straits Times*, 22 July 2002.

51   "Remaking Singapore: Changing Mindsets", PM Goh Chok Tong, National Day Rally Speech at the University Cultural Centre, 18 August 2002. *National Day Rally Speeches: 50 Years of Nationhood in Singapore*, pp. 473–4.

52   "'Quitter' Label Rankles with Feedback Group", *Straits Times,* 22 Aug. 2002; "Stayers versus Quitters: Nailing Down the Real Issues", *Straits Times*, 24 Aug. 2002.

53   During an 18 February 2003 dialogue with undergraduates, SM Lee Kuan Yew issued a similar challenge, asking those present whether they had grown soft in an overly comfortable environment: "Do you have the guts and gumption that your parents and grandparents displayed when they faced the stark choice of either working together to

make Singapore succeed, or face the humiliation of failure, wishing we had never been ousted from Malaysia? Amid the comfort and affluence of present-day Singapore, do you feel that urge to stay ahead of the pack in order to maintain our lead?" "What Has the Future in Store for Your Generation?", Speech to National University of Singapore, Nanyang Technological University and Singapore Management University students, 18 February 2003. *The Papers of Lee Kuan Yew: Speeches, Interviews and Dialogues, Vol. 15: 2001–2003*, p. 384. See also "SM Lee Presents Young S'poreans with Stark Choice", *Straits Times*, 19 Feb. 2003.

54 "Reaching Out to All Singaporeans", *Petir*, Dec. 2000 (Party Conference Special), pp. 10–1.

55 Ibid., p. 11. Earlier, during the Party's 45th anniversary celebrations in 1999, PM Goh had already pointed out that the ability of Party members to shape the thinking of leaders on policies was important—far more important a privilege than material perks. "Secretary-General Goh Chok Tong: We're Different Because of Core Values", *Petir*, Jan.–Feb. 2000, p. 39.

56 "Young Should Speak Up on Issues, Says DPM", *Straits Times*, 9 Dec. 2000.

57 Minutes of PAP Central Executive Committee Meeting, 6 Oct. 1999 (PAP archive).

58 "Capturing Interest and Winning Loyalties of the Younger Generation" (23 Oct. 2000) (PAP archive); Minutes of PAP Central Executive Committee Meeting, 25 Oct. 2000 (PAP archive).

59 Minutes of Party Conference, 3 Dec. 2000 (PAP archive).

60 "New Millennium, New Vision", speech by Secretary-General Goh Chok Tong at the PAP Party Conference, 3 Dec. 2000, *Petir*, Dec. 2000 (Party Conference Special), pp. 2–3.

61 "Remaking and Reshaping PAP and YPAP" (5 Mar. 2002), tabled at 28 March 2002 CEC meeting (PAP archive).

62 "Opening Up Political Space Gradually Better: DPM", *Business Times*, 10 Feb. 2002. DPM Lee had in the same interview highlighted the case of Tharman Shanmugaratnam, noting how he had been a left-wing student dissident in London: "We have changed somewhat, he has changed somewhat."

63 "MM Lee: PAP Must Recruit People of Ability, Integrity", *Business Times*, 22 Nov. 2004. Just as the PAP had used its 45th anniversary in 1999 to pause and reflect on what had been achieved (and how this achievement should continue), 2004, the 50th year since the Party had been founded, was also a year of reflection. Speaking at the 50th anniversary celebration of the PAP at Victoria Concert Hall (at the same place and on the same day that the PAP had its inaugural meeting half a century before), Minister Mentor Lee noted that the PAP "must from time to time re-examine all its assumptions and policies. However successful they may have been in the past, they may not be relevant for the future. . . . We must have that clear-headedness, to analyse Singapore's challenges, and to debate them within the PAP, in Parliament with other parties, and work out solutions."

64 "PAP Pays Tribute to Party Faithful", *Petir*, Nov.–Dec. 2002, p. 25.

65 Speech by PAP Secretary-General Goh Chok Tong at the Ordinary Party Conference on Sunday, 1 December 2002, at Kallang Theatre, available at https://www.nas.gov.

sg/archivesonline/speeches/record-details/703d492c-d5d7-11e8-ab1b-001a4a5ba61b (accessed 22 Jan. 2021).

66   They were Khaw Boon Wan, Tharman Shanmugaratnam, Dr Ng Eng Hen, Dr Vivian Balakrishnan, Raymond Lim and Dr Amy Khor. The three other members (Lim Hwee Hua, Lim Swee Say and Dr Yaacob Ibrahim) had entered Parliament in 1997. Wong Kan Seng acted as adviser to the team.

67   The main recommendations were subsequently released to the media. See "PAP Refreshes Core Values to Foster Greater Involvement", *Business Times*, 10 Nov. 2003. For detailed treatment, see "Refreshing PAP", *Petir*, Nov.–Dec. 2003, pp. 6–24.

68   For the recommendations in full, see "Refreshing PAP", pp. 8–15.

69   The Policy Forum was launched in April 2004. The first Joint Forum Council chairperson was the lawyer and Fengshan Branch member (and from 2006 member of parliament for Sembawang GRC) Ellen Lee.

70   Speech by PAP Secretary-General Goh Chok Tong at the Ordinary Party Conference on Sunday, 1 December 2002, at the Kallang Theatre; see also "Refreshing, but Is Change What the PAP Really Needs?", *Straits Times*, 21 Dec. 2002.

71   *Refreshing PAP Report*, 8 Sept. 2003 (PAP archive).

72   See "Backbenchers' Bite: When Feedback Is Not Enough—By MP Inderjit Singh", *Petir*, Nov.–Dec. 2003, p. 52. These same concerns were raised even at the inaugural Policy Forum meeting in April 2004. See "PAP Members Want Forum with More Bite", *Straits Times*, 25 Apr. 2004.

73   "Refreshing, but Is Change What the PAP Really Needs?".

74   "Top-Down or Bottom-Up?", *Petir*, Nov.–Dec. 2003, p. 21.

75   "Shaping Young Leaders in S'pore", *Straits Times*, 4 Dec. 2000. YP Net, which was to boast 2,600 registered members by 2005, was hosted on the main YP website, which had been revamped and relaunched in February 2003. Besides facilitating discussion, YP Net was used as the medium of exchange for the greater part of the YP21 initiatives. See "Offensive Posting Removed from Young PAP Internet Forum", *Straits Times*, 11 Nov. 2005; and Edwin Pang, "Refreshing the Young PAP", in *Renaissance Singapore? Economy, Culture and Politics*, ed. Kenneth Paul Tan (Singapore: NUS Press, 2007), pp. 231–8, esp. 233–4.

76   Pang, "Refreshing the Young PAP", pp. 231–8, esp. 234.

77   "Refreshing, but Is Change What the PAP Really Needs?".

78   "Young PAP Has Got Recruitment Down to a Tea", *Straits Times*, 16 Sept. 2005.

79   Documents on Young PAP made available to the author (PAP archive).

80   For example, in 2000 YP Chairman Lim Swee Say began an experiment in his Buona Vista ward, inducting five YP members from the General Branch. This group had by 2004 grown to 50, with the majority in their 20s. "She's the Youngest PAP Member", *Straits Times*, 19 Dec. 2004. See also "Young PAP Has Got Recruitment Down to a Tea".

81   "32, and Heading a PAP Branch Office", *Straits Times*, 21 Mar. 2005.

82   I am grateful to Lau Ping Sum for a personal communication on the issue of branch renewal in the early 2000s.

83   See "Renewing the Branches", *Petir*, Nov.–Dec. 2003, pp. 18–9.

84   "She's the Youngest PAP Member".

85 "Changing Face of the Young PAP", *Straits Times*, 11 July 2004.

86 "Young PAP Draws Young Entrepreneurs", *Straits Times*, 11 June 2005; "Why Join a Political Party? Keep It Purely about Politics. Period", *Straits Times*, 17 June 2005.

87 "Remaking and Reshaping PAP and YP", paper drafted by chairman and Exco of YP, tabled at 28 March 2002 CEC meeting; Minutes of PAP Central Executive Committee Meeting, 28 Mar. 2002 (PAP archive).

88 One of the first initiatives by the new YP chairman, Dr Vivian Balakrishnan (who took over from Lim Swee Say in March 2004), was the launching of the Young PAP "School"—essentially a series of courses (which involved lectures and seminars, as well as outdoor components) held at different places and aimed at inculcating core values and a sense of the Party's organisation and history (as well as getting new Party members to gel). See "Back to School for YP Leaders", *Petir*, July–Aug. 2004, pp. 72–5; and "A School for Tomorrow's Leaders", *Straits Times*, 1 Aug. 2004.

89 Irene Ng, personal communication, 22 July 2015.

90 See "Young PAP Women Formed: Official Launch of New Group Targeting Young Women Set for April 26", *Today*, 14 Mar. 2005; "PAP to Set Up New Youth Wing for Women", *Straits Times*, 14 Mar. 2005; and "Squaring Up to the Challenge", *Straits Times*, 22 May 2005. The initial membership base drew from the approximately 2,400 women who were already members of YP.

91 "Young PAP Women Formed". Zouk was also the venue chosen when activists (together with PM Lee and YP Chairman Vivian Balakrishnan) celebrated the 50th anniversary of the Party and the 18th anniversary of YP on 23 September 2004. "People! Action! Party!", *Straits Times*, 24 Sept. 2004.

92 "Bar-top Speaking", *Straits Times*, 26 Oct. 2003; "Bar-top Action", *Petir*, Nov.–Dec. 2003, pp. 32–3. The YP leadership's mounting of the bar was surely a nod to the July 2003 lifting of the ban on bar-top dancing, which itself had been taken by many as a sign of Singapore's loosening up.

93 "Vivian: PAP Must Engage Young or Lose a Generation", *Straits Times*, 3 Sept. 2006. Somewhat ominously, Balakrishnan observed that if YP approached the young wrongly, "we will turn that generation off, and then we will sow the seeds of our destruction".

94 Refreshing PAP Committee, minutes of third meeting, 29 Apr. 2003 (PAP archive).

95 "Two New Faces in HQ Exco", *Petir*, July–Aug. 2004, pp. 62–3. The two elected for a two-year term were Dr Teng Su Ching, an academic (and vice-chairman of the Yuhua Branch of the PAP Community Foundation), and Frederick Ho, a union executive (and also Young PAP treasurer).

96 In the September 2006 elections for HQ Exco positions, a second round of voting had to be conducted to separate Patrick Tay (branch secretary at Bedok) and Low Peng Kit (branch secretary and CCC chairman at Yew Tee), with Tay eventually besting Low. Tay and Wong Mun Chiang, branch secretary at Hong Kah North and a former YP district chairman, were the two successful candidates (of the 11 who stood). "Neck and Neck Battle in HQ Exco Vote", *Petir*, Nov.–Dec. 2006, pp. 14–5.

97 The limited number of elected positions within Party bodies was to expand over time. One example: in 2008 the position of YP organising secretary became an elected one, with the successful candidate voted in by both the incoming and outgoing YP Exco.

Another change in 2008 saw the region (defined as a GRC with attached SMCs) becoming the main operational unit, in place of the district. The 14 regional YP chairmen (whom the YP branch chairmen now reported to) were chosen by YP delegates through either consensus in caucus, or by secret ballot. They then held office in the YP Exco. District representatives still remained in the YP Exco, but this became an administrative appointment without any seniority over the regional chairmen.

98   "Appointment of Exco of the Young PAP", tabled at 29 May 2004 CEC meeting (PAP archive).

99   Examples included Liang Eng Hwa (YP Exco member from 2000 to 2006) and Muhammad Faishal Ibrahaim (2004–06), both fielded in the 2006 election.

100 Dr Vivian Balakrishnan, interview with the author, 14 May 2014. For the Party values and attributes, see https://www.pap.org.sg/ABOUT/Content (accessed 27 Apr. 2020).

101 "Activists Get More Say in Picking PAP Leaders", *Straits Times*, 1 Dec. 2000.

102 "SM Goh Steps Down as SG", *Petir*, Nov.–Dec. 2004, p. 15.

103 "Wider Participation by Key Cadres in the Nomination of Candidates for CEC Election", tabled at 16 September 2004 CEC meeting (PAP archive).

104 Ibid.

105 The CEC usually co-opted the 13th and 14th highest vote-garnering nominees at the Party conference, over time also adopting the general practice of co-opting the next four unsuccessful candidates with the most votes. But this was by no means an invariable rule—in practice the further co-opted names depended more on who the Party secretary-general felt could make a contribution. As noted earlier in chapter 1, there were also occasions where the CEC co-opted individuals (usually those seen to have strong links to the ground) who had not even featured in the final shortlist. An example is Sitoh Yih Pin, co-opted into the 34th and 35th CECs, who had not featured in the final shortlist of 18. (Author interviews with Party sources familiar with the conduct of elections into the CEC.)

106 "Two New Faces in HQ Exco", p. 62; "Behind the Scenes", *Petir*, Nov.–Dec. 2006, p. 15.

107 Minutes of PAP Central Executive Committee Meeting, 9 Oct. 2002 (PAP archive).

108 "New Faces Join PAP Leadership at Party Conference", *Straits Times*, 2 Dec. 2002. Subsequently co-opted in January 2003 were National Development Minister Mah Bow Tan and MPs Lim Hwee Hua, Dr Wang Kai Yuen and Hawazi Daipi. "Two Non-MPs Sit In", *Straits Times*, 22 Jan. 2003.

109 Major changes within the CEC had been widely anticipated by all concerned, with Party Chairman Dr Tony Tan noting just before the November 2004 Party conference that the PAP had to undergo "generational change" in order to stay relevant and in tune with the concerns and aspirations of younger voters. "PAP Leadership to Stay in Tune with Young", *Straits Times*, 7 Nov. 2004.

110 In other movements, Home Affairs Minister Wong Kan Seng, formerly second assistant secretary-general, became first assistant secretary-general. The new second assistant secretary-general was Defence Minister Teo Chee Hean. Minister for National Development Mah Bow Tan, who had been co-opted after he received the 13th highest number of votes at the Party conference, was elected Party treasurer. Also co-opted after gaining the 14th highest number of votes was YP Chairman Dr Vivian Balakrishnan.

The four others co-opted subsequently by the CEC were Dr Ng Eng Hen, Assoc. Prof. Ho Peng Kee, Halimah Yacob and Dr Teo Ho Pin. See "PAP Leadership Changes Complete", *Straits Times*, 3 Dec. 2004; and "CEC Elects Office-bearers", *Petir*, Jan.–Feb. 2005, pp. 28–9.

111 Khaw and Tharman were two of the three acting ministers who had in August 2004 been promoted to full ministership in PM Lee's first Cabinet. Before this, they had high-profile roles and had clearly acquitted themselves well. In 2003 Khaw (senior minister of state for transport, and for information, communications and the arts) headed (from April) the Severe Acute Respiratory Syndrome (SARS) Ministerial Combat Unit, and he was promoted to acting health minister in August. Tharman (then senior minister of state for trade and industry, and for education) had chaired a critical subcommittee (examining policies related to taxation, CPF and wages) of the Economic Review Committee (2001–03).

112 Lim Hwee Hua's election into CEC was particularly notable as she was the first woman to be voted in directly since Chan Choy Siong's election into the seventh CEC in August 1961.

113 "Gearing Up for a Knowledge-Based Economy" (interview with Dr Tony Tan), *Petir*, Nov.–Dec. 1999, pp. 50–3, esp. 53.

114 Speech by PAP Secretary-General Goh Chok Tong at the Ordinary Party Conference on Sunday, 1 December 2002, at Kallang Theatre.

115 Speaking at a forum with undergraduates on 15 October 2001, SM Lee noted that riding out short-term difficulties was not the issue; the key question was how to remake Singapore for the next 10 to 20 years. Singapore had to "re-examine every policy assumption and test its validity in the new international context". "Remaking Singapore for the New Age", speech to National University of Singapore, Nanyang Technlogical University and Singapore Management University students for the NUS Students' Union Senior Minister Forum 2001, 15 October 2001. *The Papers of Lee Kuan Yew, Vol. 15,* p. 203. See also "SM: We Have to Remake Singapore", *Straits Times*, 16 Oct. 2001. The challenge of "remaking" was alluded to also in PAP political broadcasts in late October 2001. "Let's Unite to Secure the Future", *Straits Times*, 28 Oct. 2001.

116 "Will It Be Real Make or a Mere Makeover?", *Straits Times*, 12 Jan. 2002.

117 Dr Vivian Balakrishnan, interview with the author, 14 May 2014. As one commentator observed: "These 'remaking' exercises for the economy and the nation more generally, though consultative in a somewhat limited way, are nevertheless important as platforms for a 'visionary' politics. If nothing else, they simulate a 'national' effort where technically this would be impossible. They decompress latent pressures for radical democratization, generate a widespread sense of stake in and belonging to the country, and give the new generation of PAP leaders a chance to inspire the people with charisma and high-mindedness instead of the technocratic expertise that had bought them the party ticket. . . . The national life cycle of Singapore must be sustained by a perpetual sense of crisis that leads not to despair, but to collective hope and self-renewal." Kenneth Paul Tan, "Crisis, Self-Reflection, and Rebirth in Singapore's National Life Cycle", *Southeast Asian Affairs* (2003): 253–4.

118 "Remaking Citizens to Be Fit for Democracy", *Straits Times*, 9 July 2003.

119 "New Committee to Focus on Details", *Straits Times*, 15 Feb. 2002; "New Team to Take S'pore beyond 5Cs", *Straits Times*, 15 Feb. 2002.

120 "Remake S'pore? Start with Yourself First", *Straits Times*, 12 June 2003.

121 The five subcommittees were Beyond Club: Ethnic and Religious Cohesion (chairman Dr Vivian Balakrishnan, co-chairman Lim Hwee Hua); Beyond Credit Card: Income Distribution, Safety Nets, Sports and Arts (chairman Dr Ng Eng Hen, co-chairman S. Iswaran); Beyond Careers: New Roads to Success (chairman Cedric Foo, co-chairman Hawazi Daipi); Beyond Condo: Sense of Ownership and Belonging (chairman Raymond Lim, co-chairman Sin Boon Ann); and Beyond Cars: Balancing Physical Development Needs in Our Small Island (chairman Dr Balaji Sadasivan, co-chairman Ong Kian Min).

122 "New E-forum Welcomes Frank Debate of Policies", *Straits Times*, 6 June 2002. The website and various dialogue sessions were also conducted in different languages to allow people who were more comfortable in their mother tongue (i.e., Tamil, Malay, Mandarin) to be engaged as well.

123 *The Report of the Remaking Singapore Committee: Changing Mindsets, Deepening Relationships* (Singapore: Remaking Singapore Committee, 2003), available at https://eresources.nlb.gov.sg/webarchives/wayback/20070115030050/http://www.remakingsingapore.gov.sg/Full Version of Remake Sg.pdf (accessed 8 June 2020).

124 "BG Yeo Turns Down Five-Day Work Week Idea", *Straits Times*, 17 June 2003; "5 1/2-Day Work Week Stays", *Straits Times*, 23 June 2003; "Not Time for Jobless to Dip into CPF—DPM Lee", *Straits Times*, 30 June 2003.

125 "After Months of Talk, What Next?", *Straits Times*, 5 July 2003.

126 "Remaking Singapore—Slow Lane for Politics?", *Straits Times*, 17 Apr. 2004.

127 These included suggestions on the relaxation of defamation laws, liberalising the legal regime governing the mass media, and bringing clarity to the changes in electoral boundaries through amending the Parliamentary Elections Act. "Report of the Remaking Singapore Committee", pp. 45, 84–9; see also "Remaking Singapore—Slow Lane for Politics?".

128 Dr Vivian Balakrishnan, interview with the author, 14 May 2014. Some of the RSC suggestions rejected in 2003 (including instituting a five-day workweek) were subsequently adopted. The RSC subgroup on education made a call for streaming (the channelling of students into different classes based on academic ability) in the education system to be scrapped, a suggestion which did not make it into the main body of the final report (the critique on streaming had been diluted and placed in the "Proposals Without Consensus" annex). Streaming at the primary level was, in fact, refined in 2004 with the merger of the EM1 and EM2 streams (EM meaning "English as a mother tongue"; EM1 students would study English and their mother tongue at first-language level). The system was further refined by the scrapping of EM3 (essentially meaning the end of streaming in primary schools) and the introduction of subject-based banding starting with the 2008 Primary Five cohort.

129 Some critics also commented that while the topics (beyond 5Cs) were understood by the middle class, those who were less well-off were unaware and uninterested in these topics when they were preoccupied with trying to make ends meet. The media also reported examples where some of the older and illiterate people were found to not

know about the whole project at all, and therefore left out in the discussions. The OSC initiative was to drill much further downwards in terms of drawing in those from the lower middle classes in discussions.

130 See Tan, "Crisis, Self-Reflection, and Rebirth": 241–58, esp. 249–50.

131 "NAC Lifts Rule on Scriptless Art Forms", *Straits Times*, 28 Nov. 2003. The mandatory security deposit (of $10,000) for scriptless performances was also removed. The Ministry of Information and th Arts, MITA, also agreed with the CRC recommendation that scripts for plays be exempt from pre-vetting where the content was not considered sensitive.

132 "Crazy Horse Cabaret Chooses S'pore Asia Home", *Straits Times*, 19 May 2005. Allowing in such entertainment may have been less of a straightforward decision than it now appears. For an allusion by Lee Kuan Yew to the fact that the Cabinet was split on the issue, see *The Papers of Lee Kuan Yew: Speeches, Interviews and Dialogues, Vol. 17: 2006–2008*, p. 267.

133 "Big Step Forward for Gay Cause", *Straits Times*, 9 July 2003.

134 "Working Together towards a Responsible and Vibrant Society", MITA's response to recommendations of the CRC, 8 Sept. 2003, available at https://www.nas.gov.sg/archivesonline/speeches/record-details/77756b8a-115d-11e3-83d5-0050568939ad (accessed 22 Jan. 2021).

135 "DPM Lee to Be My Successor—PM Goh", *Channel NewsAsia*, 13 Jan. 2001; "Succession: DPM Lee a Clear Choice", *Straits Times*, 18 Aug. 2003; "Next PM? Consensus Is Hsien Loong", *Straits Times*, 23 Aug. 2003.

136 The 22 May 2004 meeting was a lunch hosted by then Home Affairs Minister Wong Kan Seng at the Istana. Recalling this meeting several years later, in 2018 (at a time when the issue of succession to PM Lee was being publicly aired), Lim Boon Heng told the *Straits Times*: "It was a short meeting, because the choice was clear. As DPM under Mr Goh, Mr Lee Hsien Loong was doing a lot of heavy lifting." One minister put forward Lee Hsien Loong's name during the lunch, and "the rest of us agreed". "Selection Process for Fourth PM May Have Echoes of 1984", *Straits Times*, 5 Jan. 2018.

137 "Next PM—the MPs' Choice?", *Straits Times*, 14 Feb. 2004; "Choosing the Next PM", *Petir*, May–June 2004, pp. 6–7; "Choosing a Leader—MPs' Role Is Still Evolving", *Straits Times*, 1 June 2004; "MPs Endorse DPM Lee as Next PM", *Straits Times*, 1 June 2004. The 22 May 2004 meeting of ministers (not unlike the gathering on 30 December 1984 which decided on Goh as the future premier) involved mainly younger ministers who would form the core of Lee's team.

138 Goh highlighted the importance of MPs getting involved in the process of choosing the next premier: "The confidence of MPs is important. I want to put in place a process so that, in future, if there is a contest for the position, there's a process to follow." "Choosing the Next PM", *Petir*, May–June 2004, p. 7; "Choosing a Leader: MP's Role Still Evolving", *Straits Times*, 1 June 2004.

139 It is noteworthy that during the caucus meeting of PAP MPs on 28 May 2004, Goh made it a point to state that he would not stand for the position of secretary-general at the November 2004 Party conference (even though, as everyone present would have known, the actual appointments in the CEC were decided typically some weeks after

the conference). "Different Views, but Same Purpose", *Petir*, May–June 2004, p. 8. It is tempting to make the comparison with Goh's own position from November 1990 to December 1992, when he was PM but did not hold the secretary-generalship (which had been retained by SM Lee Kuan Yew).

140 "Best Man . . .", *Straits Times*, 18 Aug. 2003.

141 "Let's Shape Our Future Together", PM Lee Hsien Loong, swearing-in speech, 12 Aug. 2004, available at https://www.nas.gov.sg/archivesonline/speeches/record-details/7851c88b-115d-11e3-83d5-0050568939ad (accessed 22 Jan. 2021). See also "DPM's Vision for Singapore", *Straits Times*, 12 Oct. 2003.

142 "DPM Promises a More Open Singapore", *Straits Times*, 7 Jan. 2004.

143 For Lee's remarks, see "Building a Civic Society", speech by DPM Lee Hsien Loong at the Harvard Club of Singapore's 35th Anniversary, 6 Jan. 2004. https://web.archive.org/web/20101229193738/http:/unpan1.un.org/intradoc/groups/public/documents/APCITY/UNPAN015426.pdf, accessed 3 May 2021. See also "Join Me to Write This Next Chapter", *Straits Times*, 13 Aug. 2004.

144 Ibid.

145 "Working Hand in Hand . . . to Write the Singapore Story", *Straits Times*, 14 Aug. 2004.

146 PM Lee Hsien Loong, National Day Rally Speech at the University Cultural Centre, 22 Aug. 2004. *National Day Rally Speeches: 50 Years of Nationhood in Singapore*, pp. 504, 529. See also "A Step Forward, a Level Higher", *Straits Times*, 24 Aug. 2004.

147 "Handover: Invitation to Public a Signal", *Straits Times*, 26 July 2004.

148 "Vivian's the Man to Connect with Young", *Straits Times*, 11 Aug. 2004.

149 The P65 MPs involved were MCYS Parliamentary Secretary (and Sembawang GRC MP) Mohamad Maliki Osman, Tanjong Pagar GRC MP Chong Weng Chiew and Pasir Ris–Punggol GRC MP Penny Low. "Govt Wants Youth Views to Chart Future", *Sunday Times*, 15 Aug. 2004.

150 "Vivian's the Man to Connect with Young"; "Govt Wants Youth Views to Chart Future", *Straits Times*, 15 Aug. 2004.

151 "Vivian's the Man to Connect with Young".

152 See, for example, "Make Small S'pore 'A Great Nation'", *Straits Times*, 6 Dec. 2004; and "PM Lee Offers Lifelines to Old, Needy, and Jobless", *Straits Times*, 20 Jan. 2005.

153 "Political Watchers See No Radical Shift", *Straits Times*, 14 Jan. 2004.

154 "Govt to Open Up Political Space Gradually". Lee had for good measure told PAP cadres at the Party conference on 8 November 2004 that while the PAP government had to give people more space, strong government was not obsolete: "We still need a strong and capable government, enjoying strong support from Singaporeans and able to act on their behalf." "Singapore Still Needs a Strong Govt: PM Lee", *Straits Times*, 9 Nov. 2004.

155 Lee Kuan Yew, interview with *Time* magazine, 27 Sept. 2005; *The Papers of Lee Kuan Yew: Speeches, Interviews and Dialogues, Vol. 16: 2004–2006*, p. 427. On Martyn See, see Kenneth Paul Tan, *Cinema and Television in Singapore: Resistance in One Dimension* (Leiden: Brill Academic Publishing, 2008), pp. 265–8. As Tan notes, the film became "a spectacle of political repression in Singapore, and has achieved audiences and a 'success' that are well beyond what the film's own merits probably deserve" (p. 268).

156 "World Bank Accuses S'pore of Breaching Formal Agreement", *Straits Times*, 14 Sept. 2006. Despite a partial climb-down that saw the government allowing 22 of the 27 into the country, Paul Wolfowitz, president of the World Bank, criticised the government's "authoritarian" actions for causing "enormous damage", stating that "a lot of that damage has been done to Singapore, and it's self-inflicted". "Singapore Rebuked for Ban at Meeting", *Washington Post*, 16 Sept. 2006.

157 For a treatment of the affair, see Ho Khai Leong, "Singapore: Campaigning for the Future", *Southeast Asian Affairs* (2007): 301–2.

158 "Take a Hard Look at Bad Press on Freedom", *Straits Times*, 28 Oct. 2005; "How Free Should a Free Press Be?", *Straits Times*, 1 Nov. 2005.

159 Terence Chong, "Globalising on Its Own Terms", *Southeast Asian Affairs* (2006): 280.

160 "Residents Shocked at 'White Elephant' Police Probe", *Straits Times*, 3 Sept. 2005; "Police Explain Probe into 'White Elephants'", *Straits Times*, 8 Sept. 2005.

161 "Bus Services Parallel to NEL Cut—Operators and Commuters Unhappy", *Straits Times*, 23 July 2003; "SBS Transit Pledges to Look into Grievances", *Straits Times*, 8 Aug. 2003.

162 "SBS Transit 'Made Mistakes' over Buangkok Station", *Straits Times*, 15 Aug. 2003.

163 "Govt Backs Bus Route Changes along NEL", *Straits Times*, 6 Aug. 2003.

164 "It's Confirmed: Buangkok Station Opens in Jan", *Straits Times*, 12 Nov. 2005.

165 "New PAP Members Speak Their Mind", *Straits Times*, 7 Nov. 2005.

166 Singapore Parliamentary Debates, 14 Aug. 2003, cols 2385–6; "SBS Transit 'Made Mistakes' over Buangkok Station".

167 Singapore Parliamentary Debates, 14 Aug. 2003, col. 2381.

168 Singapore Parliamentary Debates, 11 Nov. 2003, col. 3443; "No 'White Horse' Label in NS since 2000", *Straits Times*, 12 Nov. 2003.

169 "Minister Tells More about 'White Horses'", *Straits Times*, 19 Nov. 2003.

170 "The White Horse Credo", *Today*, 22 Nov. 2003.

171 "Hot Threads", *Straits Times*, 16 Nov. 2003. See also Michael Loh, "A Flawed System?", letter to *Today*, 20 Nov. 2003.

172 2SG Hu's death was reported in a bland Ministry of Defence statement the same day. A national serviceman and friend of the deceased put up an online posting on a military-related forum detailing what had actually transpired. 2SG Hu, it emerged, had died after being "dunked" in water, an unauthorised training procedure which had seen several others suffer near-drowning in the same exercise. This was subsequently confirmed in Parliament by Defence Minister Teo Chee Hean. Repercussions were immediate: the chief commando officer was removed from his post, and other instructors were suspended or relieved of their positions. In 2005 four commandos were found guilty and jailed for causing the death of 2SG Hu. Singapore Parliamentary Debates, 16 Oct. 2003, cols 3161–200; "Course Suspended, Training Safety Procedures under Review", *Straits Times*, 17 Oct. 2003; "2 Commandos' Jail Terms Upped", *Straits Times*, 8 July 2005.

173 "NKF: Controversially Ahead of Its Time?", *Straits Times*, 19 Apr. 2004 (the article that started the entire cascade of events).

174 Civil and criminal suits were filed by the newly appointed NKF board and the public prosecutor against Durai and three other former board members (including the board chairman, Richard Yong). Durai was convicted in both suits and jailed. The other board members implicated were given fines or (in the case of Yong, who fled Singapore before being extradited) a jail term.

175 "Health Ministry Accepts Partial Blame for the Mess", *Straits Times*, 22 Dec. 2005.

176 An example of such an online commentary is "The Political Parallels to the NKF Scandal", a December 2005 post by Alex Au, a blogger known to be critical of many aspects of government policy, available at https://web.archive.org/web/20060117144046/http:/ www.yawningbread.org/arch_2005/yax-527.htm (accessed 22 Jan. 2021).

177 In the wake of the death of 2SG Hu Enhuai, DPM Lee had told reporters that the government would be transparent: "Nobody should be left in any doubt that there is a cover-up or that Mindef will be kind to its own people. . . . If we did not tell the truth, then people will start believing what is on the Internet uncritically." "The Internet: The New Political Ward?", *Straits Times*, 29 Nov. 2003.

178 The authorities did on occasion step in and take action when lines were crossed. In 2005 three individuals were convicted under the Sedition Act for inflammatory online postings against Malays and Muslims. "Support for Racist Blogger's 'Malay Immersion'", *Straits Times*, 3 Dec. 2005.

179 As one PAP MP was to remark in 2007, summing up a practice that had become increasingly prevalent, "I get lots of e-mail from youth, which are cc'ed to the President, PM and all the MPs. . . . I'm not sure they are well thought through." "Internet Users Learning Netiquette the Hard Way", *Straits Times*, 25 July 2007.

180 "Why the Casino Rethink", *Straits Times*, 14 Mar. 2004. The reasons for the change of heart will be discussed later in this chapter.

181 "How Ministers Were Won Over to the IRs", *Straits Times*, 19 Apr. 2005.

182 "MPs: Put Casino Issue to the Vote", *Straits Times*, 2 Mar. 2005; "19 Bids to Build Casino Resort", *Straits Times*, 3 Mar. 2005.

183 A petition against the casinos had garnered close to 30,000 signatures by April 2005. "Man behind Casino Petition", *Straits Times*, 24 Apr. 2005.

184 Singapore Parliamentary Debates, 2 Mar. 2005, col. 1182.

185 See, for example, Derek da Cunha, *Singapore Places Its Bets* (Singapore: Straits Times Press, 2010), pp. 44–60.

186 "Casino: Not Fruitful to Keep Arguing, Says PM", *Straits Times*, 27 Apr. 2005.

187 See, for example, "The Responsibility Imposed by Free Speech" (commentary by NUS law professor Thio Li-Ann), *Straits Times*, 28 Apr. 2005.

188 "Is the Social Compact Changing?", *Straits Times*, 22 Nov. 2003; "Torn between Two Instincts—More or Less Govt", *Straits Times*, 29 Nov. 2003.

189 "If Your Chips Are Down, You're Out", *Straits Times*, 17 Mar. 2004.

190 See "Teen Blogger Counselled for Her 'Elitist' Remarks", *Straits Times*, 24 Oct. 2006; "Wee Siew Kim Apologises for Remarks", *Straits Times*, 26 Oct. 2006; and "Time to Learn that Sorry Isn't the Hardest Word to Say", *Straits Times*, 28 Oct. 2006.

191 See "Why the Elite Envy?", *Straits Times*, 9 Dec. 2006. Concerns about elitism notably spilled into the public domain in the case of the pianist Melvyn Tan. Tan, a talented

pianist when young, had elected not to serve National Service but instead to continue his musical studies in London, later renouncing his Singapore citizenship. In November 2005 Tan (by then a renowned performer) returned to Singapore to visit his aged parents after paying a fine of $3,000 (a sum he professed not to remember in a media interview). There was debate in the media and an outcry in online circles. The fine was viewed by many as being too paltry a sum, with the attendant perception (incorrect, as it turned out) that the punishment for others evading National Service would have been much more severe. See "Did Pianist Melvyn Tan Get Off Too Lightly?", *Straits Times*, 20 Nov. 2005; and "Revealed for First Time: Why Melvyn Tan Was Fined $3,000", *Straits Times*, 17 Jan. 2006.

192 *Singapore Parliamentary Debates*, 8 Nov. 2006, col. 124.

193 "WP Grooming New Faces Ahead of Next Election", *Straits Times*, 26 Oct. 2002; "A Passion for Politics . . . and the Underdog", *Straits Times*, 11 June 2003.

194 "A Passion for Politics . . . and the Underdog".

195 "How and Why This Economic Downturn Is Different", Address at a Dialogue Session with National Trades Union Congress Leaders, 23 July 2003. *The Papers of Lee Kuan Yew: Speeches, Interviews and Dialogues, Vol. 15: 2001–2003*, p. 443.

196 "A People United: Secure Future, Better Life", PAP 2001 election manifesto (Singapore: Times Printers, 2001), pp. 11, 13. See also "Economic Plan Part of PAP Manifesto", *Straits Times*, 20 Oct. 2001; and "Fresh Talent to Tackle Economy Issues", *Straits Times*, 2 Nov. 2001.

197 "Getting Down to Work Right Away", *Straits Times*, 4 Nov. 2001.

198 The subcommittees and their chairmen were: Subcommittee on Policies Related to Taxation, the CPF system, Wages and Land (Tharman Shanmugaratnam); Subcommittee on Promoting Entrepreneurship, and the Growth and Internationalisation of Singapore Based Companies (Raymond Lim); Subcommittee on Enhancing Human Capital (Dr Ng Eng Hen); Subcommittee on the Manufacturing Sector (Johan van Splunter); Subcommittee on Service Industries (Khaw Boon Wan); Subcommittee on Domestic Enterprises (Stephen Lee); and Subcommittee on Dealing with the Impact of Economic Restructuring (Heng Chee How).

199 These included government agencies and private companies, as well as Singaporeans and expatriates based both locally and abroad.

200 The government had already slashed direct taxes in the 2002 budget (an interim proposal made by the ERC), bringing down corporate and personal tax rates.

201 *Report of the Economic Review Committee: New Challenges, Fresh Goals—Towards a Dynamic Global City* (Singapore: Ministry of Trade and Industry, Feb. 2003), available at https://www.nas.gov.sg/archivesonline/government_records/record-details/9a3e288d-da9c-11e6-bb26-0050568939ad (accessed 22 Jan. 2021).

202 "Report of the Economic Review Committee", pp. 5–7.

203 For a summary of the budget, see "A Budget to Revitalise the Economy", *Business Times*, 3 Mar. 2003.

204 Tharman Shanmugaratnam, interview with the author, 7 May 2014.

205 "Report of the Economic Review Committee", pp. 9–10.

206 "ERC—a Work in Progress?", *Straits Times*, 15 Nov. 2002.

207 "Govt Policy Blamed for PSA Woes", *Business Times*, 12 Mar. 2003.

208 "Execs, Professionals Again Biggest Retrenched Group", *Business Times*, 13 Mar. 2004.

209 Singapore Parliamentary Debates, 11 Mar. 2003, col. 304; "Budget Reveals a Troubling Gap", *Straits Times*, 12 Mar. 2003.

210 See "S'pore Can Get on Top of SARS—SM", *Straits Times*, 12 May 2003; "Work in Progress", *Straits Times*, 7 June 2003; and "SM's Dialogue with Union Leaders", *Straits Times*, 24 July 2003.

211 These visits, which were to continue monthly until the next general election, were meticulously planned. As revealed by the coordinator for the walkabouts, Chan Soo Sen (minister of state in the Prime Minister's Office and also minister of state for community development and sports), the MP for the area would first draw up a plan for the visit. Chan would then visit the constituency twice, first to hear the MP's plan and then for a trial run. After the actual ministerial visit, the People's Association (PA), HDB and town council would submit a report on the issues raised, the mood on the ground and lessons learnt to the minister, the PA and Chan. "New Round of Visits by Younger Ministers", *Straits Times*, 9 July 2003.

212 "1 Per Cent GST Hike to Go Ahead", *Straits Times*, 29 Aug. 2003; "Report of the Economic Review Committee", p. 74.

213 "From the Valley to the Highlands", PM Goh Chok Tong, National Day Rally Speech at the University Cultural Centre, 17 August 2003. *National Day Rally Speeches: 50 Years of Nationhood in Singapore*, pp. 486–7. For a sense of the internal discussions—and disagreements—within the Party on the CPF cuts, see "Slaughtering the Most Sacred Cow", *Straits Times*, 23 Aug. 2003.

214 On the issue of helping the needy, the ERC report had confined itself to general observations on widening the social safety net, tapping on grassroots leaders and Voluntary Welfare Organisations, and rationalising various help schemes. "Report of the Economic Review Committee", pp. 188–9. See also "Get Relevant or Get Retrenched", *Business Times*, 23 Nov. 2002; "Widen Safety Net but Tighten Aid Terms of Jobless—ERC Panel", *Business Times*, 23 Nov. 2002.

215 See, for example, Lim Boon Heng, "Don't Feel Let Down, the Govt Does Care", *Straits Times*, 8 Mar. 2003. Lim, minister in the Prime Minister's Office and secretary-general of the National Trades Union Congress, had originally written this comment in the 7 March 2003 issue of *NTUC News* in response to earlier press reporting on the budget: "Workers Let Down by Lack of Aid", *Sunday Times*, 2 Mar. 2003.

216 "Help Them! They're Older, Jobless and Have Low Skills", *Straits Times*, 13 Mar. 2003.

217 "Budget Tight, but Help Has Been Given", *Sunday Times*, 2 Mar. 2003.

218 "Singapore's Millionaire Ranks Swell to Almost 50,000", *Business Times*, 11 June 2005. The survey, conducted by Merrill Lynch and Capgemini, defined millionaires as those with financial assets worth over US$1 million, excluding primary residential property.

219 "There is No Magic Cure as Lower-End Jobs Vanish", *Straits Times*, 15 Feb. 2003.

220 The average income of all households rose by 1.1% a year during the same period, while the top 20% of households saw their annual income grow 2.2% a year (2003 Household Expenditure Survey; see "Govt Mindful of Growing Income Gap", *Straits Times*, 27 June 2005).

221 Data from 2003 HDB Household Survey. See "Another Survey Shows Income Gap Widening", *Straits Times*, 21 June 2005.

222 Incomes rose 5.9% from 1998 to 2003, while the overall Consumer Price Index rose 2.5%. But during this period, education costs rose 8.9% and healthcare costs by 11.1%—both faster than incomes. "The S'pore Struggle: Glowing Stats Don't Tell the Full Story", *Straits Times*, 20 Jan. 2005.

223 See, for example, Ling Chien Yien, "Why S'poreans Complain about the Cost of Living", *Straits Times*, 4 Feb. 2005 (letter originally published in *Lianhe Zaobao*, 28 Jan. 2005).

224 See "The S'pore Struggle". Statistics kept by the PAP of attendance at meet-the-people sessions shed some light. Its MPs saw 105,083 cases in 2002, 110,210 in 2003, 120,450 in 2004, and 128,529 in 2005. "More Seek Out MPs as Elections Close In", *Straits Times*, 5 Apr. 2006.

225 See "PM Lee Offers Lifelines to Old, Needy and Jobless"; and "ComCare Fund to Target Children, Elderly and Needy", *Straits Times*, 24 Jan. 2005. Other measures announced by PM Lee included more money being injected into MediFund (aimed at helping the poor and elderly defray the cost of medical bills), the setting up of a new tripartite committee to help older workers, and a new programme to redesign jobs, targeted at unemployed or retrenched workers.

226 "Half of ComCare Fund to Aid Needy Kids", *Straits Times*, 12 Mar. 2005. It is worth noting that even before the ComCare Fund was established in 2005, government momentum to assist the socially disadvantaged had been building, in the form of targeted schemes. Pre-2005 social assistance schemes broadly came under the umbrella of the Community Assistance Fund (CAF) set up in 2001. The fund covered a number of social assistance programmes. These included the Work Assistance Programme, which provided short-term financial and employment assistance for those who were unemployed; the Rent and Utilities Scheme, which provided assistance to low-income families in rental and utility arrears to upgrade themselves with appropriate supportive assistance and counselling; the Public Assistance and Special Grant Schemes, which provided long-term assistance for those who were permanently unable to work due to old age, illness or permanent disability; and childcare subsidies for the low-income through the centre-based Financial Assistance for Childcare Scheme.

227 Singapore Parliamentary Debates, 18 Feb. 2005, col. 660–1; "Something for Everyone", *Straits Times*, 19 Feb. 2005.

228 Singapore Parliamentary Debates, 17 Jan. 2005, cols 121–2.

229 See "More Precise Way to Give Bottom 20% a Helping Hand", *Straits Times*, 13 Jan. 2006.

230 "Moving Forward Together", *Straits Times*, 13 Jan. 2006.

231 Interviews with officials responsible for the Workfare scheme, 14 July 2014.

232 Singapore Parliamentary Debates, 17 Feb. 2006, cols 62–4.

233 See "Government to Share Over 2.6B in Surpluses", *Petir*, Mar.–Apr. 2006, pp. 14–5.

234 Singapore Parliamentary Debates, 1 Mar. 2006, col. 503.

235 Singapore Parliamentary Debates, 27 Feb. 2006, col. 183.

236 "MP Takes Issue with Casino Remarks", *Straits Times*, 18 Jan. 2005.

237 See, for example, the essays in Donald Low and Sudhir Thomas Vadaketh (eds), *Hard Choices: Challenging the Singapore Consensus* (Singapore: NUS Press, 2014), especially Donald Low, Yeoh Lam Keong, Tan Kim Song and Manu Bhaskaran, "Economic Myths in the Great Population Debate", pp. 40–7; and Donald Low, "What Went Wrong for the PAP in 2011?", pp. 168–77, esp. 169–72.

238 One of the ERC subcommittees had made a preliminary recommendation in favour of Singapore having casinos, but the main ERC committee, chaired by PM Lee, rejected the idea. "A Work in Progress?", *Business Times*, 16 Nov. 2002.

239 Dr Vivian Balakrishnan, interview with the author, 14 May 2014.

240 Interviews with officials responsible for the Workfare scheme, 14 July 2014.

241 Ibid.

242 Tharman Shanmugaratnam, interview with the author, 7 May 2014.

243 *Report of the Economic Review Committee*, p. 5.

244 Ibid., pp. 14, 173–4.

245 Ministry of Manpower files (Ref "The International Talent Challenge", 2000) on the challenge of attracting international talent (National Archives of Singapore), made available to the author.

246 Ibid.

247 For the key data, see *Population Trends 2013* (Department of Statistics, Ministry of Trade and Industry, Singapore), pp. 22–3; and Saw Swee Hock, *The Population of Singapore*, 3rd ed. (Singapore: Institute of Southeast Asian Studies, 2012), pp. 177–80, 184.

248 For a summary of the scheme and its enhancements, which should be considered within the broader framework of the introduction of family-friendly measures in the 2000s, see Saw, *Population of Singapore*, pp. 222–49.

249 Ministry of Manpower files on the evolution of the workpass framework (National Archives of Singapore), made available to the author.

250 The relaxation was particularly in the services and manufacturing industry, as well as in specific subsectors that had traditionally had problems attracting local workers. One facet of this was the general move to allow, over time, increasing numbers of workers from Mainland China, particularly in the manufacturing sector (effected through a relaxation of the dependency ratio). Eventually, in 2007, Mainland Chinese nationals were allowed in also as an approved source for the services sector. Ministry of Manpower files on the evolution of the workpass framework (National Archives of Singapore), made available to the author.

251 *Labour Market Report 2013* (Singapore: Manpower Research and Statistics Department, Ministry of Manpower), p. 10.

252 Data provided to the author by the National Population and Talent Division. Close to half of new PRs were drawn from the foreign worker pool in Singapore. Other groups contributing to the PR inflow included dependents and spouses of Singaporeans, PRs, and foreign workers, as well as international students.

253 "Separate Economics and Politics No More", *Straits Times*, 5 Dec. 2001.

254 In 2001, faced with the prospect of weak economic growth and rising unemployment, there was preliminary discussion involving key leaders on whether to require employers attempting to hire lower-level, or Q1, EP holders (at the lower range of the salary

threshold of $2,000), to first try to find Singaporeans to fill their vacancies. The conclusion reached was that this would send a signal that Singapore was turning away from its consistently held open policy on foreign talent. Exchange of correspondence between PM Goh Chok Tong and DPM Lee Hsien Loong, Aug.–Sept. 2001 (National Archives of Singapore), made available to the author.

255 See, for example, "Foreign Talent Critical to S'pore: DPM", *Straits Times*, 6 Aug. 2006.

256 PM Lee Hsien Loong, National Day Rally Speech at the University Cultural Centre, 20 Aug. 2006. *National Day Rally Speeches: 50 Years of Nationhood in Singapore*, p. 570. See also "S'pore Needs More Talented Foreigners Like Mustafa's Managing Director", *Straits Times*, 21 Aug. 2006; and "Welcome Newcomers with a Big Heart", *Straits Times*, 21 Aug. 2006.

257 The poll also revealed a concern that foreign workers might in future take jobs away from Singaporeans. About 68% of respondents believed foreign talent would compete for jobs with future generations of Singaporeans, up from 60% previously. "4 in 5 Think Foreign Talent Has Helped", *Straits Times*, 20 Oct. 2001.

258 "Expats Here to Stay? S'poreans Don't Buy It", *Straits Times*, 19 Feb. 2004.

259 Four members of the 2001 "Super Seven" were full ministers by 2006: Khaw Boon Wan (health), Tharman Shanmugaratnam (education), Dr Vivian Balakrishnan (community development, youth and sports), and Dr Ng Eng Hen (manpower).

260 The key roles were campaign publicity (Khaw Boon Wan), the PAP manifesto (Raymond Lim), reaching out to the young (Vivian Balakrishnan), and political broadcasts (Tharman Shanmugaratnam). By this point, younger ministers were also involved in the critical rounds of the interview process for new candidates. These included Dr Yaacob Ibrahim, Dr Ng Eng Hen and Tharman Shanmugaratnam. "Younger Team Driving PAP Campaign", *Straits Times*, 25 Apr. 2006.

261 Teo was assisted by Lim Swee Say. "Teo Chee Hean Heads PAP's Recruitment Drive", *Straits Times*, 30 Dec. 2004.

262 See "More than Half of PAP's New Faces Born after 1965", *Straits Times*, 23 Mar. 2006; and "How the PAP Keeps It Fresh", *Straits Times*, 14 Apr. 2006.

263 In 2001 only two of the PAP candidates introduced came from the post-Independence generation: Penny Low (age 37) and Dr Chong Weng Chiew (age 34).

264 "Race Is On to Win Young Voters' Hearts", *Straits Times*, 8 Apr. 2006.

265 See "PAP Begins Introducing 'New Breed' of Candidates", *Straits Times*, 24 Mar. 2006.

266 "New PAP Members Speak Their Mind", *Straits Times*, 7 Nov. 2005.

267 "Bipolar Views on Biculturalism", *Straits Times*, 8 Apr. 2006.

268 Only 11 of the 23 electoral divisions had their boundaries tweaked, in contrast to 2001, when 19 of the 23 electoral divisions saw changes. "Few Major Changes to Electoral Boundaries", *Straits Times*, 4 Mar. 2006.

269 The boundaries of Aljunied GRC were expanded to incorporate 28,000 more voters from the middle-class Serangoon Gardens area, which was formerly part of Marine Parade GRC. The biggest changes were, in fact, with the SMCs. Bukit Timah and Ayer Rajah SMCs were merged into the renamed Holland–Bukit Timah GRC and West Coast GRC, respectively. Two new single seats were created: Bukit Panjang and Yio Chu Kang.

270 "Minimal Changes Help to Arrest Political Cynicism", *Straits Times*, 4 Mar. 2006. As we have seen, this was something that the 2001 internal Party post-mortem had also commented on.

271 "Political Podcasts, Videocasts Not Allowed during Election", *Straits Times*, 4 Apr. 2006.

272 "New Media, Same Rules", *Straits Times*, 15 Apr. 2006.

273 "Opposition Parties Slam Podcast Ban Rule", *Straits Times*, 5 Apr. 2006.

274 See, for example, Edmund Lim Wei Kiat, "Encourage, Not Curb, Views on Political Issues", letter to *Straits Times* Forum, 6 Apr. 2006.

275 "New Media, Same Rules".

276 Video clips of rallies were, for example, to be found on websites (without a readily identifiable owner) such as SG Rally and Singapore Election Rally Videos. "'Citizen Reporting' Despite Ban on Podcasts", *Straits Times*, 4 May 2006. See also "Net Was Abuzz with Politics", *Straits Times*, 9 May 2006.

277 The SDP was directed by the Elections Department on 25 April 2006 to remove a podcast from its website. The SDP complied apparently without demur. "Party Removes All Podcasts from Website", *Straits Times*, 26 Apr. 2006.

278 The simplicity of the final product belies the effort that went into it. Lim's team (which included MPs Irene Ng, Arthur Fong, Dr Mohamad Maliki Osman and Gan Kim Yong) had since 2004 sought feedback on people's concerns from the Party rank and file (with over 200 people polled from the branches and the YP/Women's Wing) as well as (unusually) members of the public not linked to the Party. The findings from the feedback sessions, including the engagements with members of the public, were discussed in five closed-door PAP Policy Forum sessions with ministers. The conclusions of these discussions formed the core of the manifesto. "Many Had a Hand in Crafting Manifesto", *Straits Times*, 16 Apr. 2006.

279 "Staying Together, Moving Ahead" (People's Action Party, 2006), available at https://web.archive.org/web/20060508021145/http://www.pap.org.sg/uploads/ap/587/documents/papmanifesto06_english.pdf (accessed 7 July 2020).

280 Ibid. See also "PM: This Election Is about the Future", *Sunday Times*, 16 Apr. 2006; and "Staying Together, Moving Ahead", *Sunday Times*, 16 Apr. 2006.

281 "PAP Manifesto Full of Motherhood Statements: WP", *Straits Times*, 20 Apr. 2006.

282 "You Have a Choice" (Workers' Party, 2006), available at https://issuu.com/wpsg/docs/wp_manifesto_2006 (accessed 7 July 2020). See also *The Workers' Party 50th Anniversary Commemorative Book* (Singapore: Workers' Party, 2007), pp. 103–5.

283 "Govt Warns of 'Time Bombs' in Workers' Party Manifesto", *Straits Times*, 22 Jan. 2006; "Khaw Likens WP's Four Proposals to Poisons", *Straits Times*, 25 Jan. 2006; "PAP Disappointed with WP's Response", *Straits Times*, 24 Jan. 2006.

284 "Reconsider WP Manifesto? Thanks but No, Says Low", *Straits Times*, 23 Jan. 2006; "Revise Manifesto? WP Chief Says No Again", *Straits Times*, 24 Jan. 2006; "WP Leader Tackles 'Time Bomb' Criticisms", *Straits Times*, 27 Jan. 2006.

285 "PAP MPs Expect Tougher Contest at Next Election", *Straits Times*, 21 Dec. 2005.

286 "Will Workers' Party Succeed in Writing a New Chapter?" *Straits Times*, 2 May 2006.

287 The WP had started a new youth wing in August 2005. "Fresh Faces in Workers' Party", *Straits Times*, 9 Sept. 2005.

288 For renewal in the WP, see *The Workers' Party 50th Anniversary Commemorative Book*, p. 129; also "2 New Faces on WP Executive Panel", *Straits Times*, 31 May 2005; "The Outspoken One", *Straits Times*, 9 Sept. 2005; and "Making Way for the New Face of the WP", *Straits Times*, 10 June 2006.

289 "Opposition Adopts Low-Key Approach", *Straits Times*, 22 Apr. 2006.

290 "WP Strategy: Focus on House-to-House Visits Away from Media Spotlight", *Straits Times*, 16 Apr. 2006.

291 "Opposition Guns for 57 Seats after Reaching Electoral Pact", *Straits Times*, 11 Mar. 2006; "The Night of the Opposition Huddle", *Sunday Times*, 12 Mar. 2006. The WP was also to stake its claim to contest the SMCs of Hougang (with WP Secretary-General Low Thia Khiang the incumbent MP), Joo Chiat and Nee Soon East. Subsequent rearrangements between the WP and SDP saw the WP ceding ground to the SDP when it came to which party contested Sembawang GRC. As part of the arrangement, the WP also fielded a candidate in Nee Soon Central SMC, a ward where the SDP had earlier staked a claim. "Sembawang GRC Won't See Three-Way Contest", *Straits Times*, 13 Apr. 2006.

292 For the first time since 1988, the Opposition was able to prevent the PAP from being returned to power on Nomination Day. Forty-seven of the 84 parliamentary seats were contested. This was an increase from the 29 candidates put up by the Opposition in the 2001 election. In 2006 only 37 seats went to the PAP in walkovers (all in GRCs).

293 The WP's bicultural candidates were Goh Meng Seng (businessman), Yaw Shin Leong (business analyst), Lee Wai Leng (businesswoman) and Lian Chin Way (regional business manager). "Workers' Party Shows New Professional Face", *Straits Times*, 27 Apr. 2006.

294 "When the Young Ones Take On the PM", *Straits Times*, 29 Apr. 2006.

295 "MM Acts against Chee for Suggesting He Is Corrupt", *Straits Times*, 22 Apr. 2006.

296 "SDP Not Saying Sorry, Will Still Contest Election", *Straits Times*, 26 Apr. 2006; "Four More SDP Leaders to Say Sorry", *Straits Times*, 1 May 2006.

297 "Chees Defamed PM and MM, Court Finds", *Straits Times*, 13 Sept. 2006; "Chees' Defence was Deficient, Says Judge", *Straits Times*, 8 Dec. 2006.

298 "SDP: The Inside Story", *Straits Times*, 29 Apr. 2006; "SDP's Team in Sembawang 'Is Not Falling Apart'", *Straits Times*, 2 May 2006; "Two SDP Leaders Resign as Party's Fate Hangs in Balance", *Straits Times*, 19 May 2006.

299 "Clear Signs of Disarray at SDP Rally", *Straits Times*, 3 May 2006; "SDP Team in Sembawang Tries to Get Campaign Going Again", *Straits Times*, 5 May 2006.

300 "Good Move for SM to Provide Extra Firepower, Say MPs, Experts", *Straits Times*, 21 Mar. 2006.

301 "Eric Low Expects Boost from SM's Upgrading Offer", *Straits Times*, 11 Apr. 2006. In the 2001 polls, Goh's offer, made to precincts in both Hougang and Potong Pasir, had been set at a lower threshold of 45% in Hougang and 50% in Potong Pasir. No precinct qualified in Hougang, while in Potong Pasir only Sennett Estate did. Separately, another offer made by Goh in 2006 (which had echoes of a similar suggestion made on the 2001 campaign trail) was to lift the Party whip for Eric Low and possibly also Sitoh Yih Pin if they were elected to Parliament, enabling them to function as an "Opposition" of

sorts in Parliament, thus giving voters the "best of both worlds", according to Goh. "PAP's Man in Hougang Could Play Opposition Role in House", *Straits Times*, 27 Mar. 2006; "Will Sparing the Whip Win PAP Worry Wards?", *Today*, 27 Mar. 2006.

302 "PAP's Sitoh Has 10-Year Facelift Plan for Potong Pasir", *Straits Times*, 5 Feb. 2006.

303 "Sitoh Unveils $80m Upgrading Plan", *Straits Times*, 5 May 2006.

304 Ibid.; "Mr Candidate, Can We Have Lifts that Stop on Every Floor?", *Straits Times*, 4 May 2006.

305 "Chiam Running Out of Steam and Time, Says SM", *Straits Times*, 3 May 2006; "Chiam Should Make Way for New Blood: SM", *Straits Times*, 5 May 2006.

306 For the PAP's personal line of attack against the WP's James Gomez, which was also to achieve limited success, see the section in this chapter on the campaign in Aljunied and GomezGate.

307 This was even though the doubts aired publicly by SM Goh and Sitoh Yih Pin (as well as other PAP MPs) about Chiam's ability to fully fund his proposed lift upgrading programme were not without some justification and had been based on the close scrutiny of the town council accounts in question. "Chiam Won't Have Enough Funds for Lift Upgrade: PAP MPs", *Straits Times*, 26 Apr. 2006; "Enough Funds for Upgrading, SDA Chief Insists", *Straits Times*, 6 May 2006.

308 "Eric Low Expects Boost from SM's Upgrading Offer", *Straits Times*, 11 Apr. 2006.

309 This was a continuation of a theme taken up at the 2001 polls, but it was also a canny move, in that surveys carried out by the mainstream press had shown the cost of living to be the key concern on the part of the electorate and younger Singaporeans. One *Straits Times* survey conducted in March 2005 of over 400 Singaporeans aged between 21 and 34 pinpointed living costs as the key concern, followed by jobs and housing. 89% of respondents said issues relating to costs would influence their vote, compared to 4% who said issues relating to political freedom would. "Living Costs, Jobs Are Top Concerns of Young Voters", *Straits Times*, 17 Mar. 2006.

310 "PM Lee: We Are Tackling Rising Costs", *Straits Times*, 1 May 2006; "WP Puts Spotlight on Cost of Living", *Straits Times*, 2 May 2006.

311 "Workers' Party Takes Aim at Health Care Costs", *Straits Times*, 1 May 2006.

312 "PM Lee: We Are Tackling Rising Costs".

313 "PM Accuses WP of Inciting Insecurity", *Straits Times*, 5 May 2006.

314 "S'poreans Need Not Worry about Medical Bills: Khaw", *Straits Times*, 6 May 2006.

315 "Workers' Party to Campaign on First World Govt", *Straits Times*, 26 Apr. 2006.

316 "No First World Parliament? It's PAP's Fault: Opposition", *Straits Times*, 24 Apr. 2006; "PAP Not a First World Govt, Says WP Chief", *Straits Times*, 25 Apr. 2006; "PM Raps WP for Picking Up Tossed 'Hand Grenade'", *Straits Times*, 28 Apr. 2006.

317 "All-Out Bid to Deny PAP a Clean Sweep", *Straits Times*, 6 May 2006; "Let Us Provide the Check in Parliament: WP's Low", *Business Times*, 6 May 2006.

318 See, for example, "Will Workers' Party Succeed in Writing a New Chapter?", *Straits Times*, 2 May 2006; and "People's Action Party", *Business Times*, 5 May 2006.

319 "All-Out Bid to Deny PAP a Clean Sweep"; "Support WP and Help Its Renewal", *Straits Times*, 6 May 2006.

320 The idea that the Opposition were troublemakers appears to have been ignited by a remark at a rally by PAP MP Irene Ng (Tampines GRC) on 3 May 2006. Ng had suggested that a minister from the PAP would be more likely to listen to a PAP MP than "an Opposition MP out to make trouble". Low Thia Khiang demanded an apology, which proved not to be forthcoming. "Irene Ng Won't Say Sorry to Low for Remark", *Straits Times*, 6 May 2006.

321 "Flirting with the Other Suitor?", *Straits Times*, 5 May 2006. Lee's point had been that a large Opposition presence in the House would distract him from thinking of long-term issues, and that it was in the nation's interests for the PAP to remain dominant. Such was the negative feedback, however, that he felt it necessary to make an apology for using a "strong, sharp" word to convey his point. "Apology for Using 'Strong, Sharp' Word", *Straits Times*, 6 May 2006.

322 "WP Attacks PM over Comments on Opposition", *Straits Times*, 5 May 2006; "Govt Needs to Be Accountable to Voters, Says Sylvia", *Straits Times*, 6 May 2006; "Support WP and Help Its Renewal", *Straits Times*, 6 May 2006.

323 "5 Factors that Stirred the Ground", *Straits Times*, 20 May 2006.

324 The PAP team in Aljunied consisted of George Yeo, Lim Hwee Hua (minister of state for finance and transport), Zainul Abidin Rasheed (minister of state for foreign affairs and mayor of Northeast District), Yeo Guat Kwang and Cynthia Phua (the last two both senior NTUC officials, with Phua also the Aljunied Town Council chairman). They faced a WP team comprising Sylvia Lim, Tan Wui-Hua (financial controller), James Gomez (analyst with a think tank), Goh Meng Seng and Mohammed Rahizan Yaacob (the last two both businessmen).

325 "Expect Good Fight in Election Hot Spot", *Straits Times*, 5 May 2006.

326 One minority certificate was required from each GRC slate wishing to stand for election. Despite his snafu and lack of a certificate, Gomez and the WP's Aljunied slate were able to stand as there was already another WP member of the team, Mohammed Rahizan Yaacob, with a minority certificate.

327 "PM: Come Clean, Gomez: I'm Sorry", *Straits Times*, 30 Apr. 2006; "Gomez Lied, Facts Show That Clearly: Kan Seng", *Straits Times*, 3 May 2006; "MM: Gomez a Liar Who Planned to Damage Govt", *Straits Times*, 3 May 2006.

328 "An Issue that Cries Out for Explanation", *Straits Times*, 1 May 2006.

329 "Low Thia Khiang: It's an Innocent Mistake", *Straits Times*, 30 Apr. 2006.

330 "Gomez Lied, Facts Show That Clearly: Kan Seng"; "'Gomez Laughed, but I Didn't Think He Was Joking'", *Straits Times*, 3 May 2006; "'Gomez Told Me It Was Just Another Wayang'", *Straits Times*, 3 May 2006.

331 "Expect Good Fight in Election Hotspot".

332 "Gomez Blundered but Let's Move On, Say Some Voters", *Straits Times*, 2 May 2006; "Quietly Does It on Gomez Saga; There Are Other Concerns Too", *Straits Times*, 4 May 2006. At a lunchtime rally on 5 May 2006, PM Lee in reference to the Gomez affair acknowledged that there were people who saw the PAP reaction as "overkill, typical PAP, we hit too hard, sledgehammer". "The Difference Two Weeks Make", *Straits Times*, 6 May 2006.

333 "Browncast: The Persistently Non-political Podcast No. 6", 1 May 2006, available at http://www.mrbrown.com/blog/2006/05/browncast_the_p.html (accessed 22 Jan. 2021).

334 "PAP Puts Aside Gomez Case and Returns to Key Issue", *Straits Times*, 5 May 2006.

335 After the election Gomez was prevented from leaving the country and placed under police investigation for criminal intimidation, giving false information and using threatening words. The public prosecutor was satisfied at the completion of investigations that Gomez had committed the offence of using threatening words against a public servant, but took into account the circumstances and Gomez's clean record, letting him off with a stern warning. "Gomez Let Off with a 'Stern Warning'", *Straits Times*, 13 May 2006.

336 "George Yeo's Team Reaches Out to Voters with Detailed Plans", *Straits Times*, 6 May 2006.

337 The SDA contested three GRCs (Pasir Ris–Punggol, Jalan Besar and Tampines) and four single seats (Choa Chu Kang, Potong Pasir, MacPherson and Yio Chu Kang).

338 "It's a Very Strong Mandate", *Straits Times*, 7 May 2006.

339 MM Lee, in remarks to residents and supporters after he led the PAP team in Tanjong Pagar GRC on its victory parade, noted of the WP, "They can grow bigger, they can grow cleaner, they can grow stronger. Then we'll have a bigger fight next time. We are not standing still. We are going to keep clean, we're going to deliver, we're going to get better men and we'll fight." "'We're Going to Get Better Men and We'll Fight'", *Straits Times*, 9 May 2006.

340 Interviewed for this book, Low's adversary in Hougang, Eric Low, acknowledged his opponent's mastery of the ground situation in the constituency. Because applications had to be made to the town council for the use of void decks for funerals, Low Thia Khiang would invariably be the first to know if a constituent had passed away. A wreath and banner bearing the WP's hammer would arrive with extraordinary promptitude. Eric Low tried to compete for some time, even sending out an activist on a bicycle to look out for funerals, but conceded that the WP was usually too quick. Eric Low's countertactic was to focus on children, who at the age of six months would receive a gift from the PAP Community Development Council. As Eric Low remarked, "He looked after the dead, I looked after the living." Eric Low, interview with the author, 11 Feb. 2014.

341 The *Straits Times* suggested that support for the PAP had taken a hit especially in the areas of Aljunied GRC that immediately bordered Hougang (in particular, Hougang Avenue 3). As George Yeo pointed out, Hougang and Aljunied were "connected organically. . . . Many families have friends and relatives on both sides. Residents cross the boundary every day to shop, take buses and the MRT." "5 Factors that Stirred the Ground".

342 It still had to be counted a comfortable victory by the PAP team in East Coast GRC, which collected 66,931 votes (63.86%) against the WP's 37,873.

343 "Battle Begins Now for Next Polls, Says PM", *Straits Times*, 23 July 2006.

344 See, for example, "Why the Next Election Will Be Crucial One to Watch", *Straits Times*, 20 May 2006.

345 *2006 General Election PAP Post-mortem Report* (PAP archive).

346 "Desire for Opposition an Unstoppable Tide?", *Straits Times*, 13 May 2006. There were also suggestions that some voters, particularly older ones, preferred not to have upgrading

in their precincts, given the inconvenience and cost. One 63-year-old Hougang voter, interviewed by the press, summed up the feeling: "If the PAP wins, the upgrading will be very large-scale, very *ma fan* [troublesome] and I will have to pay. I'm already 63 years old, but I can still climb the stairs." "Factors in Their Favour", *Straits Times*, 5 May 2006.

347 "Upgrading for All Wards, but PAP Ones First", *Straits Times*, 11 June 2006; "Upgrading Is a Unique Programme by Govt", *Straits Times*, 17 June 2006.

348 "PAP Needs to Change Tack in Next Polls: SM", *Straits Times*, 4 June 2006.

349 See "PAP Will Have to Review Ways to Win Opposition Wards: PM", *Straits Times*, 8 May 2006; also "Three Different Styles in PAP Campaign", *Straits Times*, 8 May 2006. SM Goh notably said that the results in Hougang and Potong Pasir reflected well on the voters, who were loyal to the Opposition incumbents rather than "chasing after every goodie" offered to them.

350 "Blogs and Podcasts May Get More Leeway at Next GE", *Straits Times*, 1 June 2006; "Net Spoof Too Funny for Serious Politics", *Straits Times*, 1 June 2006.

351 For the striking photograph and the blog entry, see "On Hougang Field" (May 2006), available at https://web.archive.org/web/20060927151105/http:/www.yawningbread.org/arch_2006/yax-581.htm (accessed 7 May 2020).

352 "Your Insights", *Straits Times*, 9 Sept. 2006.

353 *2001 General Election PAP Post-mortem Report* (PAP archive).

354 *Report of the Central Executive Committee, January 2005–November 2006* (PAP archive).

355 *2006 General Election PAP Post-mortem Report* (PAP archive).

356 PM Lee Hsien Loong, National Day Rally Speech at the University Cultural Centre, 20 Aug. 2006. *National Day Rally Speeches: 50 Years of Nationhood in Singapore*, p. 576.

357 Yeo's online musings were hosted on blogs belonging to his contacts. "George Yeo Gets Personal Online", *Straits Times*, 13 Oct. 2006.

358 "PAP MPs Launch Blog Site to Connect with Young Netizens", *Straits Times*, 5 Oct. 2006.

359 "Desire for Opposition an Unstoppable Tide?"; "They Vote Opposition but Want PAP in Power", *Straits Times*, 13 May 2006.

360 *2006 General Election PAP Post-mortem Report.*

361 It is possible that the problem of perception was linked to the passing from the scene of PAP veterans who had standing on the ground. MPs such as Dr Tan Cheng Bock and Dr Wang Kai Yuen, who stepped down to make way for new candidates in 2006, were generally seen as being amongst the more approachable PAP MPs. They had vast institutional knowledge too, and knew how to campaign and win election fights. Some aspects of this knowledge could, of course, be passed down and shared with younger MPs, but other aspects, such as rapport with the ground, were not so easily transmitted. See "How to Win Polls? MP Shares Tips from 'Secret' File", *Straits Times*, 14 Mar. 2006.

362 For the polls and surveys, see "Living Costs, Jobs Are Top Concerns of Young Voters", *Straits Times*, 17 Mar. 2006; "Race Is On to Win Young Voters' Hearts"; "Engage Political Rivals on Issues, Don't Just Dismiss Them", *Straits Times*, 8 May 2006; "Desire for Opposition an Unstoppable Tide?"; "The Young and the Restless (but Not Reckless)", *Straits Times*, 12 May 2006; "They Vote Opposition but Want PAP in Power"; "Bread-

and-Butter Issues 'Not the Main Concern' of Voters", *Straits Times*, 3 June 2006; "GE 2006: The Other Answers to What Voters Care About", *Straits Times*, 3 June 2006; and "PAP Needs to Change Tack in Next Polls: SM", *Straits Times*, 4 June 2006.

363 "George Yeo: Two Reasons for Close Fight in Aljunied", *Straits Times*, 15 May 2006.

364 The post-mortem committee (a 17-strong group of MPs led by Dr Ng Eng Hen) submitted its report to the CEC in September 2006. It was an unusual and extremely thorough effort, based on submissions from all GRCs and SMCs in response to a specially designed questionnaire. In addition, the post-mortem committee had met with activists from all contested constituencies, as well as retired MPs (Party sources).

365 For the proceedings, see "Getting Good Candidates to Run", *Straits Times*, 13 Apr. 2006; "MM Lee: There Are Things I Can Do", *Straits Times*, 13 Apr. 2006; and "Who Is Afraid of Voting against PAP?", *Straits Times*, 13 Apr. 2006.

366 "Shielding Us Will Not Make Us Stronger in Times of Crisis", *Straits Times*, 13 Apr. 2006.

367 "Admiration and Distance, Respect and Indignation", *Straits Times*, 13 Apr. 2006.

368 "Three Questions from Dialogue", *Straits Times*, 20 Apr. 2006.

369 "Not All Young People Think Like Those at Forum, Says MM", *Straits Times*, 20 Apr. 2006.

370 "TV Forum with Youth Exposes Gulf: Vivian", *Sunday Times*, 16 Apr. 2006.

371 "Youth's View of Political Process 'Is of Concern'", *Straits Times*, 25 Apr. 2006.

372 "How to Rein In a 'Despot'? Form a Party", *Straits Times*, 1 Feb. 2005.

373 Ibid.; "Lively Exchanges", *Straits Times*, 2 Feb. 2005.

374 "How to Rein In a 'Despot'?"; "Lively Exchanges".

375 "Two Party System? Not Likely, Says BG Lee", *Straits Times*, 16 Nov. 1999.

Chapter 6

2007–11: Inflexion

I'm confident that our policies will bear fruit. By the next election, in 2011, we will be ready to present our report card to Singaporeans. Then, judge us on our performance: Whether the economy has grown, whether people have better jobs, better lives, whether we live in a harmonious society.

—PM Lee Hsien Loong, address to Party cadres, 3 December 2006[1]

Following the 2006 election, a notable undercurrent of government messaging was that Singaporeans should close ranks—seen by some as an implicit acknowledgement of the divisions that had opened up during the campaign. The tone was set at the opening of Parliament on 2 November 2006, when President S.R. Nathan traced the government's policy contours over the coming term. Needy Singaporeans would be helped more, building on earlier measures such as ComCare and Workfare. But President Nathan also highlighted the dangers of "well-intentioned" welfare schemes that had caused economies elsewhere to stagnate, draining the motivation and work ethic of the people. It was the role of every citizen to contribute to society, and in particular to help the less successful. This was the key to maintaining social cohesion and building an inclusive society.[2]

Elaboration was not long in coming. In his 3 December 2006 speech to cadres at the PAP conference, PM Lee provided an important scene setting to what he saw as priorities for his first full term in office. Meritocracy, Lee observed, did not mean that people should forget the debt that they owed to society. Those who were successful owed something to the system which had given them opportunities, and ought to give others a helping hand.[3] Lee also stressed that it was crucial (and increasingly difficult) to ensure that all less well-to-do but talented Singaporeans could move up, even if equal outcomes for all could not be assured.[4] Implicit in PM Lee's remarks was recognition of the risk that the PAP government itself might become associated with uncaring elitism and privilege.[5]

Lee's preoccupation with meritocracy should be read in conjunction with then-ongoing soul-searching (partly played out in the media) about social mobility. Some were openly suggesting that the meritocracy that had served the nation well in earlier years had taken an unintended turn, and that opportunities were perhaps not as evenly distributed as they once had been.[6] There had, for example, been observations made about how Public Service Commission Scholars were increasingly drawn from families in the more affluent classes.[7] This, commentators observed, was simply one facet of a mix which, if left unchecked, would fuel class envy and threaten to undermine the narrative of social mobility and meritocracy—part of the government's founding compact with the people.[8]

Another, related concern was the growing wealth gap and the difficulties faced by those at the bottom of the socio-economic ladder. While the top decile of households had over the first half of the decade seen appreciable income growth, those at the bottom deciles had seen negative income growth.[9] The budget debate in Parliament in February–March 2007 was to see an airing of this issue, with Second Minister for Finance Tharman Shanmugaratnam observing that "over the last five years, lower-income households have seen little growth in their incomes. In fact, in real terms, the lowest 20% of households have seen their incomes per capita decline from 2000 to 2005. . . . Nonetheless, household incomes at the top end are pulling away faster."[10] Inequality had also become an increasingly noticed, and commented-on, topic. The Gini coefficient for households (excluding government transfers) rose from 0.442 in 2000 to 0.468 in 2006.[11] The strong economy had also brought with it inflation, which by 2007 was becoming another increasingly debated topic. Inflation was to reach 6.6 per cent in 2008, a 25-year high.[12] Particularly affected were the prices of food and transport. MPs reported more people coming to them with requests for financial assistance.[13]

Some commentators were arguing that there would be social repercussions if income inequality and stagnating social mobility remained unaddressed. The argument (as one respected government economist forcefully observed) was that leaving lower-income individuals to struggle for subsistence would lead to a growing sense of social injustice, which in turn could have detrimental effects on social cohesion:

> With long-term wage stagnation, this wide poverty gap will not easily be whittled away. If wages continue to stagnate, there is a limit to poverty alleviation through working longer and harder, or driving the unemployment rate lower. An underclass of our own may well be emerging.

> In the long run, this malign combination of median wage stagnation, low wage decline and rising inequality is potentially poisonous for the social compact underpinning globalisation and the bedrock of our virtuous cycle of strong governance.

> If the broad median faces medium- to long-term wage stagnation and rising income inequality, the credibility of tough policies—wage discipline, raising the Goods and Service Tax or public sector wages, further deregulation that demand sacrifice or pain in anticipation of future economic betterment—will be undermined and there could be increasing difficulty in garnering acceptance. Many will feel that their basic stake in the common enterprise of prosperity has

been eroded. What is left will be the bitter, zero-sum politics of envy and dead-end populism.[14]

On costs, government officials and leaders acknowledged the pinch of rising prices (especially food prices) but stressed that Singapore would not follow the example of other countries whose governments had artificially kept down the prices of staples. The government would help, but through indirect means such as subsidies in education and in public housing, and through (for example) periodic Central Provident Fund (CPF) top-ups.[15] In his response to President Nathan's 2 November 2006 speech at the opening of Parliament, PM Lee pledged to "tilt the playing field" to help lower-income Singaporeans affected by globalisation, and in a manner that would give such individuals a lasting boost.[16] The 2007 budget (which saw details announced of a new permanent scheme, the Workfare Income Supplement [WIS], to replace the one-off Workfare Bonus) was lauded by several PAP backbenchers as one of the most generous to date.[17]

But even within Party ranks, there were murmurings on whether more could be done, and whether help was reaching those truly in need. There was clearly a growing tension between, on the one hand, the government's stated aim of preserving the ethic of self-reliance, and on the other, the sense that more people were falling through the cracks. The government's logic on the issue can be summed up in comments made by Minister for Community Development, Youth and Sports Dr Vivian Balakrishnan during the March 2007 budget debate:

> *Please do not run away with the misconception that Singapore is a cold, heartless place where, because we are so strict on criteria and entitlements, people are starving, freezing and denied the dignities of life. All I am asking Members is just to bear these principles in mind. Entitlements will always be low, i.e., the person has to ask you for help and not bang on your table for help. We will always need the many-helping-hands model, not because the Government is broke. We can always do more and we can always raise GST further. But that is not the tone of the society that we are trying to create. We are saying that, yes, there will always be problems in society and it cannot be only the Government to do it because, if you want the Government to do it all, it means higher taxes and a large bureaucracy. As we can see in many other countries who have created elaborate welfare-states based on the best of intentions and the softest of hearts, such systems ultimately failed, they are not efficient and they are going to run out of money. We will see that happen in our lifetime, but we will make sure that that does not happen in Singapore.*[18]

Balakrishnan's comments above are less well remembered than his exchange on the same occasion with PAP MP Dr Lily Neo (Jalan Besar GRC). Neo was not satisfied with the rise in the public assistance (PA) quantum for the most vulnerable by approximately $30 per month, arguing that an effective increase of a dollar a day was not going to help her most needy constituents, some of whom skipped one meal a day in order to live out the month on their PA.[19] When Neo pressed Balakrishnan on whether it was too much to ask for PA recipients to be entitled to three meals a day, it was the minister's reply—"How much do you want? Do you want three meals in a hawker centre, food court or restaurant?"—that caught the imagination—and incurred the ire—of many, particularly online commentators.[20]

Some elements within the Party, particularly at the backbench and activist level, were hinting that the PAP's socialist credentials were being eroded, or even usurped, by others. During the 2 November 2008 Young PAP (YP) convention, for example, there was discussion on whether the Party had strayed from its socialist roots, with one activist pointing out that the Workers' Party was now seen as more socialist— the Party could not win hearts and minds by always insisting that people had to be self-reliant.[21] Outside the Party, there was also an increasingly enunciated sense that the government's "Many Helping Hands" approach over-emphasised self-reliance and pushed official channels of help too far to the margins, to be made available only in extremis.

The issue was germane to the Party's compact with the people, and it was to have a a bearing on the 2011 general election. It is therefore necessary at this point to delve a little deeper in an attempt to disentangle several strands: what the government did to strengthen social safety nets, what the effect of these measures was, and what went on in the realm of public perception.

Support Measures

The period 2001–05 had seen considerable efforts on the part of the government to enhance assistance for those who needed it. Funding for assistance schemes during this period increased by 300 per cent, from $15.6 million to $49.6 million.[22] The largest component of this increase went towards better supporting children from low-income families.[23] These increases were on top of existing programmes that helped lower-income individuals in specific ways, such as HDB's Special Housing Assistance Programme (introduced in 2000) and Ministry of Manpower and Workforce Development Agency's skills upgrading and job redesign programmes. In response to the economic slowdown, the government also offered assistance such as rebates on rent and utilities for HDB flats, Economic Restructuring Shares, and the 2006 Progress Package. The final layer of social security was provided by CPF and the 3Ms (MediSave, MediShield, and MediFund).[24]

Two major additional milestones, touched on earlier, should again be mentioned. The first was Workfare, which was born out of the recognition that (partly on account of globalisation-related trends) more help had to be given to low-income workers in order to help them achieve greater income and job security as well as social mobility. As noted above, the one-off Workfare Bonus Scheme (introduced in 2006) was in 2007 replaced by the permanent WIS, which would become a long-term feature of the social safety net.[25] The beneficiaries—older, low-wage workers—received wage supplements in the form of cash and CPF to help them provide for their daily needs and save for their retirement and healthcare needs (only if they continued to work), and also received subsidies such as training and childcare grants. Unchanged was the core principle underlying the original Workfare Bonus: dispensing help without eroding the will to work.

The second milestone was ComCare, introduced in 2005. ComCare underwent a significant expansion over time, with its initial $250 million endowment fund reaching $1.7 billion by 2013. ComCare expenditure was steadily ramped up during the decade. In 2005, the first year of the scheme, ComCare expenditure was $23 million. This was to reach $45 million in the 2008–09 financial year, and $71 million in 2011–12.[26] The number of individuals receiving help from ComCare schemes (including Public Assistance) was approximately 18,100 in 2005, 22,300 in 2008, and 27,500 in 2011. As ComCare evolved, new schemes were introduced, with more emphasis placed on flexibility, allowing the CDCs (which administered many of the ComCare schemes at the time) to give more help where it was needed. For example, in recognition that there would be a group of low-income persons who were temporarily unable to work due to long-term illness or caregiving needs, a new interim welfare assistance scheme—ComCare Transitions—was introduced in 2008. This scheme provided interim assistance to those who were temporarily unemployed and did not qualify for public assistance.[27]

Government help efforts during this period were also marked by an emphasis on supporting families with children, especially lower-income families. In 2008, the rates and coverage of the childcare and pre-school assistance schemes were expanded. The Kindergarten Financial Assistance Scheme, a scheme under the ComCare umbrella, was extended that year to cover nursery programmes; subsidies for another ComCare scheme, the Centre-Based Financial Assistance Scheme for Childcare, were also increased to help mothers from lower-income families take on full-time employment.[28]

There were refinements in government thinking even on Public Assistance, an issue that had seen Dr Vivian Balakrishnan robustly holding the line against Dr Lily Neo (and other PAP MPs) in March 2007. It had been made clear at the time of the 2007 upward revision that there would be no further increases in the immediate future.[29] As it turned out, less than a year later, in March 2008, PA rates were increased again (by 14 per cent to 19 per cent).[30]

These refinements were precisely that: modifications to the existing social assistance superstructure that remained largely unchanged in its essentials and principles, even as more help was given. With the possible exception of Workfare, the changes in social assistance policy during the decade up to 2008, while significant, could best be described as evolutionary rather than revolutionary. The suite of social support programmes was expanded and made available to a larger group of beneficiaries, but the government continued to hold the line when it came to eschewing universal, non-conditional entitlements. The basic underpinnings of policy had not changed. Government and people would avoid a welfarist mindset, with the people being self-reliant, and with the government for its part providing incentives for people to work hard and build up their own assets through savings.[31] As Dr Vivian Balakrishnan said during the 2005 budget debate, "The social safety net must be more like a trampoline, springy enough to help people bounce back and take advantage of opportunities for a better life so that they do not need to rely solely on the Government."[32]

Self-reliance was key. But for those who needed more help, or who were unable to help themselves, social safety nets were available. Support was provided by voluntary welfare organisations (many themselves funded by the government), religious groups, and grassroots organisations working together to provide social assistance to the needy. In its original form, this "Many Helping Hands" framework was intended to foster shared responsibility, community involvement and active volunteerism.[33] This relatively decentralised system of administering help was meant also to enable flexibility, and to be more effective than direct government intervention. There was an important place for volunteerism within this framework, which would see more fortunate members of society help their less well-off fellow citizens.

Through the 1990s and into the next decade, there was increasing government emphasis on the point that within the context of Many Helping Hands, the government would step in to help only when other avenues had been exhausted, and that this had to be so, lest people modify their behaviour and rely too much on the resources of the state.[34] If individual self-reliance failed, it was the family that had to be the next line of support. Needy individuals without—or with insufficient—family support could then turn to the network of voluntary welfare organisations and charities.[35]

Unsurprisingly, the question therefore began to be asked in some quarters soon after the turn of the millennium, when it had become clear that some (especially the poor and the lower-middle-income) were being left behind in the socio-economic stakes, whether the social safety net was truly effective, and whether the government had in effect begun to abdicate some of its responsibilities. Workers' Party chief Low Thia Khiang, in particular, was able to score effective points with his arguments: the government should help those truly in need and should not be overly concerned that giving help to the genuinely deserving would breed a welfare mentality. Low argued that failure to act, and failure to tackle the rich–poor divide, would lead to social divisions in Singapore.[36] Even PAP backbenchers urged a re-examination of fundamental principles, calling for more clarity on the role that the government could play—with the attendant suggestion that the government could do more.[37] For their part, government leaders stressed that the Many Helping Hands model was not a means (as some critics charged) through which the government saved money, pointing to the sizeable funding and top-ups to various social assistance programmes.[38]

The system was designed to disburse assistance in a manner which saw to the needs of the genuinely needy. But beyond this, there was from the middle of the first decade of the millennium an increasing amount of commentary on how, despite the wide variety of aid schemes, people continued to fall through the cracks.[39] Here, it should be observed that while Many Helping Hands had an extensive reach in theory, it could—and did—run into implementation issues at the ground level. Some commentators, while giving credit to the help that the government offered and to the multiplicity of aid schemes, pointed out that it could be difficult to navigate government bureaucracy, with help dispensed (and information held) by different agencies.[40] Many of the schemes were themselves compartmentalised: different agencies oversaw schemes for (for example) housing, healthcare, employment, and children's education. The eligibility criteria and benefits of the numerous social assistance schemes varied widely. Potential recipients often had to visit multiple agencies. In short, navigating the pathways of help that could be on offer was not a straightforward process. The government by the latter half of the decade was beginning to address the issue of navigability, taking steps to make help schemes more visible and organised. In January 2008, for example, the Ministry of Community Development, Youth and Sports (MCYS) launched ComCare Call. The hotline essentially functioned as a one-stop solution that would allow the genuinely needy to have a first point of access to the various social assistance programmes on offer.[41]

There were several other issues around this time which, when taken together, led some to form the impression that the government could do more or—at worst—was uncaring. The government had waited until soon after the 2006 general election (and well in advance of the next polls) to deliver unpalatable news. A case in point was the 2007 GST hike, which was poorly received even though strenuous efforts were made to explain the necessity of the rise, and to stress that help would be given to those who needed it most (specifically, in the form of GST offsets).[42] Similarly unenthusiastic was the reception to the 2007 announcement that the age at which individuals would be allowed to draw down on their CPF savings would go up from 62 to 65 by 2018, even though the government's calculus was logical: Singaporeans needed to work longer in order to have adequate retirement savings.[43]

But public discontent was most apparent in April 2007, when, once again, the review and upward revisions to ministerial salaries came up for debate. The revisions, the first since 2000 and aimed at addressing the widening discrepancy between the private sector benchmark and salaries for top civil servants and political office-holders, meant that the prime minister's annual salary would now be pegged at just above $3 million, while that of the other ministers would rise to $1.6 million.[44] In Parliament, the familiar arguments were wheeled out: Singapore needed the best people, with the existing system having worked to surface leaders, including ushering in a leadership that had capably steered Singapore through SARS and the Asian Financial Crisis.[45] In PM Lee's view the government had to act quickly, as private sector compensation had surged ahead since the 2000 revisions. Not acting would have meant the government ran the risk of losing more talented people.[46]

Timing was the crux of the issue. Raising ministerial pay was being discussed at the precise moment when a great deal of attention was focused on the difficulties faced by those left behind—in the same month, in fact, which saw MPs pointing out that the increases in public assistance were not sufficient to make a genuine difference. As one political scientist (Ho Khai Leong) observed, "in a year when we are trying to bridge the gap between the rich and the poor and when MPs have been debating about how to help the poor, it is certainly an inappropriate time to raise the issue—unless there is an urgent need to do so".[47] Workers' Party Chairman Sylvia Lim attacked the government for its insensitivity, noting that the pay revisions were being considered when the general public felt a great deal of anxiety about the GST hike and rising fees in polyclinics and hospitals: "Practically in the same breath, Singaporeans are told to be happy with a few dollars more a month under Workfare, while their leaders' salaries need to go up from $100,000 monthly to as much as $180,000."[48]

From the point of view of the PAP leadership, there could never be a good time to introduce an upward ministerial salary revision. But this was enormously difficult to explain in a completely satisfactory manner to the ground. The realisation that most had not been persuaded, and the fact that ground discontent surpassed what had been seen in 2000, were points hoisted in by the leadership. PM Lee elected to hold his own salary at the then-current level of $2.5 million, donating the increase to charity for the next five years, in order to retain "moral standing to defend this policy [of high ministers' salaries] with Singaporeans".

The gesture was of limited effect, and rumblings of discontent continued to bubble near the surface. This was noticeable for example during the 2008 budget debate, when it emerged that the government had (in the wake of a rebounding economy) found itself with a surplus of $6.4 billion against what had been a projected deficit of $700 million.[49] One MP, Dr Amy Khor (chairman of REACH, the former Feedback Unit), noted that some Singaporeans felt that the government was being *kiam siep* (Hokkien for tight-fisted) in sharing a mere $1.8 billion of a $6.4 billion surplus.[50] Government leaders were again forced to come out to defend earlier, painful measures, such as the 2007 GST hike, while also having to go into painstaking detail as to how surpluses shared with the people.[51]

Various incidents served to reinforce the view, increasingly held by those critical of the government, that not enough was being done to help the genuinely needy. In October 2006 an unemployed individual, Tan Jee Suan, committed suicide by throwing himself in the path of an oncoming MRT train. According to media reports, Tan (who had two young sons and a polio-stricken wife) owed money in utilities, HDB housing loan payments and school fees, with the family having difficulty even affording three meals a day.[52] Various facts disclosed by the media about the family and Tan's last hours prompted an outpouring of public sympathy, with over $500,000 donated to the family.[53] In the aftermath, MPs (including PAP MPs) came forward to share their experiences of encounters with others in need—some with stories almost as desperate as that of Tan Jee Suan. Particularly noticeable was the call made by several MPs that more flexibility and compassion be given by government departments and other agencies (such as HDB, utilities providers or the Community Development Councils) when it came to the less well-off needing help or not being able to meet their financial obligations. Some chose to venture further, questioning why, given the multitude of social assistance schemes in place, some Singaporeans still seemed unable to get the help they needed.[54]

Another issue which began to rear its head increasingly after the midpoint of the decade was accountability. The civil service pay revisions (which included revisions to ministerial salaries) was one factor, but there were other issues, seemingly mere pinpricks when taken individually, that contributed. In January 2009 a senior civil servant, Tan Yong Soon (permanent secretary of the Ministry for the Environment and Water Resources), contributed a feature to the press that described a five-week sojourn in Paris (involving Tan, his wife and his son) to attend culinary courses at Le Cordon Bleu cooking school.[55] The article attracted a near-immediate negative backlash, particularly online, especially when it became known how much the course would have cost (several months' wages for the average Singaporean) and also on account of the language used by Tan in the article, which smacked of elitism or hubris.[56] Real-world consequences were not long in coming: Tan was reprimanded by the minister in charge of the civil service, Teo Chee Hean, for "showing a lack of sensitivity" in writing about his experiences, especially at a time when the economic outlook had turned gloomy and when many Singaporeans faced financial hardship.[57]

All these unconnected episodes added up. The impression was being reinforced that the government was losing its compassion for—and connection to—the people. And in the case of Tan Yong Soon, even though the official response was that what the permanent secretary had done in his own time was his affair (his transgression had been to publicise his experiences at a time of economic hardship), there was inevitably a backlash against the bureaucracy, which was seen by some as overpaid at the top and out of touch.[58]

Accountability had earlier been at the forefront when, on 27 February 2008, a ranking member of the Jemaah Islamiah terror group, Mas Selamat Kastari, escaped from the custody of the Internal Security Department (ISD). The resulting Committee of Inquiry report, details of which were disclosed by DPM (and Home Affairs Minister) Wong Kan Seng in Parliament on 21 April 2008, identified critical factors (a combination of lapses, negligence and faulty procedures) that allowed the escape. Several ISD officers were disciplined, with two of them (including the superintendent of the detention facility where Mas Selamat Kastari had been held) being sacked.[59] But even prior to the release of the committee's findings, there had been calls for the government to bear full responsibility at the top for the incident, and (particularly in online discussion) for the resignation of DPM Wong. Wong had apologised in Parliament the day after the escape, but his apology was seen by critics as sidestepping responsibility and lacking contrition.[60]

The issue came to a head on 21–22 April 2008, when the leadership addressed in Parliament the overarching question of overall government responsibility. Low Thia Khiang, the Workers' Party chief, asked point blank for an apology from the government. PM Lee's reply was that the apology given by Wong Kan Seng on 28 February, which had been on behalf of the government, sufficed.[61] Low went further, tying the issue of accountability directly to ministerial pay:

> *Does the Prime Minister agree that this is not a question of a witch-hunt as to who should be directly responsible? It is a question of accountability of the Government and at what level and what responsibility a Minister should take. I think we will remember that, when we debated the Ministers' salaries in this House, we were talking about pitching the Ministers' pay to the corporate world or the private sector. But in the corporate world, when something goes wrong, heads roll, and it includes the CEO, whereas here, when something goes wrong, we are talking about honest mistakes. So, I think a lot of people, including myself, cannot*

reconcile the principle on which the Government applied in looking at the salaries of the Ministers, pitching them to the corporate world vis-a-vis when it comes to accountability and responsibility.[62]

PM Lee's reply was as follows:

I have explained where lines have to be drawn. Even the Member has not suggested that I should resign because I appointed Mr Wong Kan Seng, and Mr Wong Kan Seng was a Minister, and a soldier under him let this happen. A line has to be drawn somewhere. We have to see this in perspective. Even in the private sector, you have to see things in perspective. A company turns turtle, the CEO leaves. Problems happen in the company, CEOs have to stay to sort them out. Companies which change CEOs every two months or every two years do not prosper. So I have to make a judgment who is responsible at what level, and I have discussed this with the DPM, and I agree with his judgment and I have confidence in him. The DPM was here, the Member yesterday had full opportunity to question him. If there are any questions which he found unsatisfactorily answered, he could have pursued the matter. If there are any questions which showed that the DPM was not up to this, that he was to blame, he gave the wrong instructions, he told people not to grille up the window, he suggested that we did not need so much fencing and therefore this happened, he should have raised it. Nothing happened. Today, the Member comes around and throws a general cloud and says, "You are well paid, you should resign." Let me ask the Member whether he thinks the DPM ought to resign because of this. No answer. So, I think that settles the point.[63]

Having raised the issues of accountability and the personal responsibility to be borne by DPM Wong, Low Thia Khiang was unwilling to press home his points when faced by a prime minister—firm and not without a hint of menace—coming to the defence of a key lieutenant. But neither Lee's rebuttal of Low, nor DPM Wong's 28 February 2008 apology, nor for that matter Mas Selamat's recapture (by the Malaysian authorities in Johor in April 2009) sufficed to put the issue to rest. The issue lived on in fierce online criticism against the government (and inevitably parody, given the circumstances of Mas Selamat's escape during an ostensible lavatory break). The affair was also to become one facet of an important apology by PM Lee while on the election campaign trail in May 2011.

⁂

The leadership was well aware of the gathering clouds in public sentiment. In April 2007, when the upward salary revisions of top civil servants and political office-holders were discussed, PM Lee made it known that the government was aware that Singaporeans were "sour on this issue", and would address the underlying issues that had led to dissatisfaction.[64] One of the issues, Lee acknowledged, was growing anxiety over rising healthcare costs. We now turn to an examination of this and other issues affecting the national mood at this time.

Healthcare

The healthcare consumer price index increased 16.4 per cent from 2006–11.[65] Key contributors to this were rising fees at public hospitals and polyclinics, as well as fees for private healthcare patients. The government stated that these rises, which began to kick in in earnest in 2006–07, were unavoidable—and indeed necessary—on account of inflation, wage increases and drug pricing.[66] Health Minister Khaw Boon Wan had in March 2007 promised to "weave in such adjustments gradually, compassionately and pragmatically".[67] But at a time when the government was still generating healthy budget surpluses, there were calls to go beyond existing relief mechanisms (such as the MediSave top-ups given to individuals above the age of 51) and for real help to be afforded to those who had genuine difficulty in coping with rising healthcare costs.[68]

There were, as some commentators were beginning to point out, gaps in the 3M framework. Many Singaporeans did not meet the MediSave Minimum Sum (MMS, the amount of savings that had to be held in their MediSave accounts when they reached the age of 55).[69] This meant that they had less MediSave to help defray their healthcare costs in retirement. MediShield was useful in that it covered catastrophic big-ticket health events. But it had limitations. It was not universal, and elderly persons above the maximum coverage age (which stood at 85 in 2006) were excluded.[70] Changes in MediShield in 2005 meant an increase in premiums (of between $1.50 and $11.25 a month), with higher deductibles. These, taken together with the doubling of claim limits, were made to return MediShield to its original intent: covering large hospital bills for the minority that would have to at some point foot such bills.[71] But one effect of the changes was that more patients with relatively small hospitalisation bills found themselves having to pay for a larger portion of their bill through MediSave or other savings.[72]

Increasing numbers (spanning the low-wage to the middle class) caring for the elderly or infirm within their families were beginning to feel the squeeze. Due to an ageing population, smaller family sizes, and rising healthcare costs, it was becoming increasingly necessary to depend on one's own MediSave for healthcare on a personal basis, with less available from the extended kin to tap into.[73]

There were several other issues, all linked to affordability. One was the rising MediShield premiums, which left some individuals unable to pay the premiums from their MediSave balances and having to leave the scheme.[74] Individuals with relatively little by way of savings and MediSave balances were beginning to ask if they would have enough to see out their twilight years, especially given the fact that the costs of healthcare, and private insurance plans, escalated as one aged. This was especially for the older generation who had a shorter runway from when MediSave started in 1984, and hence lower MediSave balances. Unsurprisingly, there was an increasing amount of commentary that the healthcare financing arrangements were not satisfactory in the long term, and that systematic reforms were needed.[75]

From the government's point of view, a great deal was being done. There were occasions during the decade when the government came out forcefully to rebut what it viewed as erroneous attacks on the 3Ms and the healthcare system as a whole. In essence, the official view had it that healthcare costs and insurance premiums had been kept affordable through careful planning. A combination of government subsidies, compulsory savings, and risk pooling had kept the healthcare financing model stable and bills affordable, with mechanisms to deal with huge "outlier bills".[76]

It was true (as officialdom acknowledged), that government healthcare expenditure had been historically low when compared to OECD countries and other developed Asian economies.[77] For the second half of the decade, government expenditure on healthcare was between 0.8 per cent and 1.3 per cent of GDP. But these indicators were moving in the first decade of the millennium. Between 2002 and 2011, when overall healthcare spending increased by an average of 9 per cent per annum, government healthcare spending grew more quickly—in excess of 11 per cent per annum.[78]

There were some efforts—innovative for their time—to communicate policy thinking directly to the public, through, for example, the Ministry of Health (MOH) Facebook page and Health Minister Khaw Boon Wan's blog. But what appears to have been insufficiently understood by the authorities during this period was the growing wellspring of discontent over an area that was somewhat subjective: the rising perception that healthcare was becoming increasingly difficult to afford.[79] This was coupled with the sentiment that there was no peace of mind on healthcare matters.[80]

As we shall see, these points were germane to what the government was later to glean from the Our Singapore Conversation (OSC) initiative of 2012–13, and other feedback channels. The year 2013 was to see the announcement of a thorough review of the healthcare financing model: one that would see a rise in government healthcare spending as a proportion of total healthcare spending (even as the financing model itself would remain sustainable).[81] The changes were designed to give greater reassurance and peace of mind to Singaporeans. They would cover not just the poor; the middle-income group would be a major beneficiary as well.[82]

Housing

The series of economic downturns beginning in the late 1990s had downstream implications not just on wages and jobs, but also the housing market. Between 2000 and 2006, HDB pulled back the supply of new flats being built in the light of the large number of unsold flats.[83] But by 2007, with economic recovery and an accelerating foreign worker inflow, the prices of both Build-to-Order (BTO) flats and flats on the HDB resale market were beginning to see dramatic upswings. Average selling prices of three- and four-room BTO flats rose markedly in 2011.[84] The resale price index, which had been nearly stagnant before 2006, experienced an even more dramatic rise. From the end of 2006 through 2011, this index rose more than 84 per cent.[85] The median resale prices of three- and four-room flats in non-mature estates in 2006 were $153,000 and $222,000 respectively; these prices in 2011 were $305,000 and $395,000.[86] For most of those who increasingly found themselves being priced out of the HDB resale market, private property was not an alternative: private home prices in 2010 (for example) were to see a 17.6 per cent year-on-year rise.

By 2007, there was widespread concern about the overheating property market. The government announced that there would be an increased supply of HDB flats, with key leaders maintaining that the government was committed to making public housing affordable for Singaporeans.[87] From 2007, there were also moves to curb excess speculation, in the wake of public unhappiness given the perception that some (including foreigners) were speculating and making profits from the sale of property.[88] In addition, from 2010, more land was made available for the building of executive condominiums (ECs) to cater to the "sandwich" class of middle-income families who did not qualify for subsidised HDB flats.[89] But the effects of undersupply were at the same time hitting home. In 2007 and 2008, the new supply of residential housing flats (BTO flats and flats under the Design, Build and Sell Scheme [DBSS]) was less than 16,000 in total, even as these two years alone—2007 and 2008—saw close to 142,800 new PR and 37,900 new citizenship applications approved.[90]

Although plans to ramp up flat supply were announced in the first half of 2008, these did not materialise later that year, likely due to weak sentiment during the global financial crisis.[91] Supply saw a significant ramping up only after 2010 (see Table 6.1).

This shortage hit in particular younger, first-time entrants into the housing market, who found the high housing prices unpalatable.[92] With high BTO application rates, many of those eligible for BTO HDB flats felt that only the extremely lucky would be successful at the first application. Moreover, some also felt that the wait time from flat booking to key collection was overly long.[93] Those just ahead in the socio-economic stakes also faced difficulty. Couples with a combined monthly income of over $10,000 (above the maximum income threshold to purchase an EC unit from the developer) found themselves having to look at the resale or private property markets, which were

Table 6.1. HDB Flat Supply, 2007–12[*]

Year	Build-to-Order	Design, Build and Sell Scheme
2007	5,900	-
2008	7,800	1,800
2009	8,900	1,600
2010	16,100	-
2011	25,200	3,600
2012	27,100	1,100

* Figures in the table have been compiled from official statistics and information in the public domain. The figures do not include flats offered under other HDB sales modes such as the Sale of Balance Flats (SBF) exercise and open booking of flats.

in any case at record levels.[94] By mid-2010, resale flat prices were almost 18 per cent above the previous peak of the last quarter of 1996 and were beginning to reach eye-popping proportions in the more popular estates.[95] And in many cases, would-be buyers of resale flats were also hit by the pinch of higher cash premiums—known as cash-over-valuation, or COV—demanded by sellers, which had hit $30,000 by the second quarter of 2010.[96] The EC and DBSS schemes were meant to meet the aspirations of the middle class. However, questions were increasingly being raised about the prices of ECs and DBSS flats, and BTO showpieces such as the Pinnacle@Duxton.[97]

The state of affairs left the government perhaps the most vulnerable it had been on the issue of providing affordable housing since HDB's beginnings. Opposition politicians and critics claimed that the government was squarely to blame for pricing so many out of the housing market, noting especially that HDB flat prices were rising far quicker than median incomes.[98] The government, forced on the back foot, found recourse in disclosing figures which, in its view, showed that HDB new flat prices remained within reach for all concerned. The debt servicing ratio, which was the proportion of household monthly income that went into paying mortgages, averaged (for first-time buyers of new HDB flats in non-mature estates) 23 per cent in 2010. As the government pointed out, this was below the 30–35 per cent mark, which was recognised internationally as the threshold of housing affordability.[99]

Key moves to cool the property market began in 2010. These included introducing a seller's stamp duty (SSD) on all residential private properties sold within one year from the date of purchase, lowering the loan-to-value limit to 80 per cent for all housing loans provided by financial institutions regulated by the Monetary Authority of Singapore, tightening HDB mortgage financing terms, disallowing private residential property owners from buying a resale HDB flat without disposal of their private property, and increasing the Minimum Occupation Period (MOP) for non-subsidised resale HDB flats to five years.[100]

The intent of all these moves (as members of the leadership made clear at the time) was to emphasise that HDB flats were to live in, and not to be purchased speculatively.[101] It should be noted, however, that the initial set of measures failed to have sufficient effect. The medicine had to be applied again in repeated doses, and with increasing force.[102] Additional moves, which spanned 2011 to 2013, included the introduction of an additional buyer's stamp duty (introduced in 2011 and raised in 2013), the introduction (2013) of the total debt servicing ratio threshold for property loans extended by financial institutions, and controls on permanent residents (PRs) using HDB resale flats as an investment vehicle. The most notable of the moves concerning PRs was the August 2013 measure requiring PRs to wait three years after obtaining PR status before they could purchase an HDB resale flat.[103]

Viewed in totality, the multiple rounds of cooling measures from 2009 to 2013 brought to an end the idea of housing as an asset that was simultaneously appreciating and affordable.[104] The conundrum of asset appreciation meant that many of those who had benefited also stood to lose in some way. Many were happy to see the value of their flats increase, but they wanted housing to continue to be affordable as they cashed out and sought to move to other housing. The older generation, which had an interest in maintaining the value of their housing asset, were at the same time concerned about their children not being able to afford a home.

For present purposes, we should note that the leadership was acutely aware that housing would be a politically costly issue if not addressed.[105] There were various attempts to explain the government's perspectives—what it was doing, and what the fundamentals were that the government intended to keep to. A case in point was the publication in February 2011 (three months before the general election) of a collection of commentaries on the housing issue by Minister for National Development Mah Bow Tan, where the minister tackled a range of issues from housing supply (addressing in particular the issue of whether HDB was building enough new flats) to affordability.[106]

As we shall see, these were to prove insufficient to put a salve on the growing discontent. Increasingly, it was the Opposition's narrative—that of a populace finding it ever more difficult to make ends meet—that was finding resonance among sections of the population and radiating into the overall national mood.

Problems of Success

We have already examined the thinking behind the post-2000 liberalisation of foreign workforce inflows.[107] The government made painstaking and repeated attempts to explain its thinking and policy rationale. A distinction was made between non-resident foreign workers (mostly transients, who would not remain in Singapore over the long term) and others, including PRs, who the government hoped would stay in Singapore over the longer term, sink roots in the country, and potentially enrich the citizen pool. This was desirable given that fertility rates remained dismal despite incentives targeting Singaporeans to encourage procreation.[108]

Notwithstanding these explanations, there was increasing unease within the citizen core as the decade drew to a close. In the period leading up to the global financial crisis, with the economy healthy and job creation at record highs, government data showed that there were years when the local share of the total number of new jobs created was eclipsed by the foreigners' share.[109] The official approach was to provide reassurance, with data advanced to show that locals (citizens and permanent residents) had benefited from overall job creation, and that there were limits to the growth of the indigenous workforce.[110] Still, surveys showed that while there might be a general acceptance of the principle that foreigners had a role to play in the economy, many citizens retained significant reservations. Very few felt that either they, or Singapore, were unequivocally better off as a result of the presence of foreigners.[111]

Part of the issue was the sheer speed and magnitude of the influx. By 2009, one in three people (36 per cent) in Singapore was a foreigner, compared to one in four (26 per cent) in 2000. From 2004 to 2009, the non-resident population grew from about 750,000 to 1.25 million. The official logic was straightforward: allowing in foreign workers, especially at a time when the economy was doing well (2004–07), meant that the nation as a whole gained. If an attempt had been made to choke off this inflow, the argument continued, Singaporeans would have been worse off.[112] As government leaders noted, the foreign worker inflow had been progressively tightened from 2009, when the economy hit headwinds caused by the global financial crisis.[113] Immigration policy had also been tightened: the number of permanent residency applications approved hit a peak in 2008 (79,200), but this number was 59,500 in 2009 and 29,200 in 2010.[114] Assurances were given that the framework would be tightened further to raise the quality of new immigrants.[115] In addition, in what was clearly an attempt to assuage growing resentment within the citizen base, the government announced that existing differentiations between citizens, PRs and foreigners would be "made sharper over time to reflect the responsibilities of citizenship".[116] These included moves to raise school fees for PRs and foreigners (from January 2011).[117] When taken together with revisions to healthcare subsidies announced in 2010 (which saw the fee gap between citizens and PRs widen), it was clear, all in, that a conscious and deliberate statement had been made: there could now be no doubt Singaporeans would come first.[118]

The machinery of government was also beginning to evolve. The ministerial National Population Committee (NPC) had been formed in August 2004, chaired by then-Deputy Prime Minister and Minister for Home Affairs Wong Kan Seng.[119] The NPC's remit ranged from supporting marriage and parenthood, to promoting and attracting skilled migrant workers.[120] Over time, a more integrated and holistic approach in dealing with population and immigration issues became visible. A full-time National Population Secretariat (NPS) in the Prime Minister's Office was formed in June 2006 to support the work of the NPC, replacing the earlier part-time secretariat based in the MCYS. The NPS was itself replaced by the National Population and Talent Division (NPTD) in January 2011.[121] In April 2009 the National Integration Council was formed, with the aim of building bonds and enhancing trust between Singaporeans and immigrants, and helping immigrants assimilate in Singapore society. The council was chaired at the ministerial level—by Community Development, Youth and Sports Minister Dr Vivian Balakrishnan—a sign of the importance the government attached to these issues.[122]

※※※

The top-level revamp of the official apparatus would mean, over the longer term, an enhanced ability to think through the many issues pertaining to the inflow of foreigners. But in the meantime, anti-foreigner feeling continued to simmer in various quarters, in some cases as a result of long-standing, ground-level issues. Residents in Joo Chiat, for example, had since 2004 banded together in opposing sleaze (in the form of massage parlours, pubs, and hotels offering hourly rates, all of which attracted sex workers, many of them foreign). Residents succeeded in obtaining additional police enforcement and a moratorium on new pubs. But the sex workers remained, with residents continuing to air their grievances well into 2010.[123] The government observed that sleaze in the stretch of road in question had gone down considerably over time, but its failure to do more meant that it came in for criticism not just from residents but also from the Workers' Party, which was clearly sizing up its chances if it were to contest there in the coming election (which it duly did).[124]

Elsewhere, in the comfortably middle-class area of Serangoon Gardens, unhappiness in 2008 against a planned dormitory housing 1,500 foreign workers in the heart of the estate was again squarely directed against the government. Over 1,400 residents, angry at being presented what seemed to be a fait accompli, submitted a signed petition to the government against the dormitory. They were not appeased when seemingly minor concessions were made after face-to-face dialogue and consultation. The government went ahead with the project.[125]

There is some suggestion, therefore, that visceral opposition to the presence of foreigners, and the subsequent blowback against the government, should not be put down just to the sheer numbers brought in over a relatively short space of time, but linked also to their coming in in a manner which put them in close and persistent proximity with locals. Germane to this was the increasing sense that public transport had become overcrowded. Government leaders had as early as 2006–07 acknowledged the need to alleviate this, promising also that land transport would be subject to a major review.[126] But alongside this, the early lessons learnt from the North East Line—which had operated at a loss and under capacity for several years since it began operations in 2003—exercised, it appears, a concomitant hold on policymakers. There was a reluctance to build ahead of demand. The concrete announcements on improvements (the introduction of new rail lines, additional trains, the upgrading of the MRT signalling system to speed up waiting times) came late, in 2010. Work on these measures, which would take several years to see a significant effect, began only in 2011.[127]

The issue of public transport was to prove a serious political liability in the general election of 2011. But in the years immediately preceding the election, the official position was simply that while transport and other issues (such as housing) would be seen to, the people had to recognise that these were the inevitable consequences of allowing foreigners into the country. Giving his take on PM Lee's 29 August 2010 National Day Rally speech (which had seen PM Lee touching on the influx of foreigners, public transport congestion, and shortage of public housing), SM Goh Chok Tong commented that Singaporeans who complained about issues such as crowded trains and public housing should realise that "We are in fact quite fortunate. These are problems created by our success." He added that it was important for people to put these things into perspective and not complain too much.[128] This did not go down entirely well. One member of the public commented, "Mr Goh must have missed the point. If you created the problems, then solve them."[129]

The impression one receives (especially in surveying the period 2006–11) is that the general public wanted—expected—the government to be successful not just in solving some of the problems associated with rapid growth, but in anticipating them as well.

It is useful at this juncture to examine what key leaders were later to say about this period, when time had passed and perspectives been gained. In interviews for this book with the principal actors, there was an acknowledgement that some of the key issues addressed comprehensively after the 2011 general election should have been tackled differently or tackled earlier. PM Lee, when interviewed in 2014, expressed the following view:

> *I think in retrospect that it is easy to say, we should have been building up our infrastructure a lot faster—that we should have got more trains running, we should have built more HDB flats. At the time we thought we were doing the right thing, pacing it, measuring it out, building it when we needed it and not spending resources until we needed to spend them. It turned out that things did not pan out the way we expected. I think that we have to plan in future less conservatively and try to be less precise in our prognostications. . . . So that is why when we talk about population planning and infrastructure and looking forward to 2030, we said 6.9 million. We are not planning to have, we do not want, 6.9 million as a target, but I want to have infrastructure, I want to have facilities, I want to get myself ready.*[130]

But was the pace at which critical policies of growth were pushed through an issue? PM Lee remarked:

> *Today, if you ask me I would say yes, I would have shifted the trade-off point and slowed down both immigrants as well as workers and tightened up faster. But if we had made a different trade-off, I think you would have seen the pain turn up somewhere else, and in particular, a slower economy and less vibrancy, lift and opportunities. You would have had angst appearing for that reason also, which is what has happened with the developed countries.*[131]

The Economy, 2008–11

The effects of the worst global economic decline in 60 years associated with the United States' subprime mortgage crisis began to be felt in Singapore by late 2008. In the third quarter of that year, Singapore fell into its first recession since 2002. GDP growth for 2008 slowed to 1.9 per cent, with the figure declining further in 2009 to 0.1 per cent.[132]

Extraordinary and urgent measures were needed to restore confidence and to help those hit by the recession. The 2009 budget announcement, symbolically brought forward to January, was indeed out of the ordinary in several respects. At its core was the $20.5 billion Resilience Package. The package had within it schemes that were innovative and indeed unprecedented, especially when it came to helping businesses retain workers. The centrepiece was the $4.5 billion Jobs Credit Scheme. The scheme paid 12 per cent of the first $2,500 of each local worker's wage bill to the company in four instalments annually. Given directly to companies in the form of cash grants, the subsidy (equivalent to a 9 percentage point cut in employers' CPF contributions) proved very popular, especially with companies already struggling to find credit.[133] It also made local workers less expensive than before to retain, and in some cases less expensive than foreign workers.[134] Another important facet of the Resilience Package was the Skills Programme for Upgrading and Resilience. The programme absorbed up to 90 per cent of course fees for workers choosing to upgrade their skills at local polytechnics and universities.

All these measures came at a cost. The $43.6 billion budget featured a deficit of $8.7 billion. Past government prudence and policy measures meant that Singapore was amply resourced to fight the crisis and help businesses and households.[135] A key measure was the introduction of the Net Investment Returns framework. This move, linked to long-term needs and not specifically introduced to combat the downturn, involved constitutional amendments (which came into force in 2009) that allowed the government to spend up to 50 per cent of the expected long-term real rate of returns on assets invested by the Monetary Authority of Singapore and the Government Investment Corporation of Singapore.[136] This significantly expanded the amount the government could extract from past investment returns. Contributions from Net Investment Returns in FY2009, at $7.7 billion, were significantly higher than the Net Investment Income Contribution (the existing component) of $3.7 billion in FY2008.[137] Rather than emulating other countries which spent part of their GDP servicing debt, Singapore had placed itself in a position where its reserves could generate a steady stream of income for public expenditure, in areas such as knowledge and innovation, infrastructure, and social expenditure.[138]

Parts of the budget were extraordinary, as Finance Minister Tharman Shanmugaratnam observed. These had to be funded by extraordinary means—either borrowing, or drawing down on Singapore's reserves.[139] The decision was taken to fund the measures from past reserves—the first time that the use of the "presidential second key" had been requested to unlock access to these reserves. The government's reasoning was that the global financial crisis was precisely the type of situation that justified a draw on the reserves.[140]

Government messaging in early 2009, when it looked like Singapore might experience a painful, prolonged downturn, was not confined to highlighting big-ticket items seen in the Resilience Package. In their speeches and public statements, key leaders reinforced the idea that Singaporeans had the resilience and mettle to survive no matter how severe the conditions, and that the nation would emerge stronger for the experience.[141] In addition, those who did fall behind during tough times— in particular, needy families, lower-income households, and those needing help with education—would receive a special helping hand.[142]

In the end, though, the crisis did not quite fulfil the gloomiest prognostications put forward by the more pessimistic commentators. Interviewed by the author, PM Lee was clear as to the reasons; and as to the unintended side effect of the government's quick action, he said:

> *The response to the global financial crisis was the Resilience Package and especially Jobs Credit. . . . We decided to have a big package, but rather than dribble it out, we decided to have an early budget in January 2009. It was spectacularly successful. We were also spectacularly lucky. We did not have that dramatic*

squeeze on workers. The numbers of retrenchments were not huge. The result was politically not to the government's advantage, because people did not feel it. They did not feel the shock; they did not give credit for the cure. Without the Resilience Package and Jobs Credit, you would have had quite a different trajectory. But this went almost completely unnoticed.[143]

۶۶۶۶

Even as the immediate needs of the people and businesses were seen to, the leadership knew it had to look even further ahead, for this was a crisis not to be wasted. Finance Minister Tharman Shanmugaratnam noted when presenting the budget, "We should take the opportunity of this downturn to build up our capabilities and infrastructure, and position Singapore for its next phase of growth."[144]

The result of this thinking was the setting up of the Economic Strategies Committee (ESC), established in May 2009, to come up with, as PM Lee put it, "new creative ways to grow the economy for the long term".[145] It was the first major review of the economy since the Economic Review Committee (ERC; 2001–03). Like the ERC, the ESC (chaired by Finance Minister Tharman Shanmugaratnam) drew its membership from both the public and private sectors.

The ESC, which issued its report in February 2010, had at its core a set of recommendations charting out Singapore's future roadmap as a maturing economy— an economy that could no longer use earlier growth strategies to propel itself. The report stated at the outset that skills, innovation and productivity had to be the drivers of growth.[146] Particular attention was paid to the latter. The ESC envisaged productivity improvements in time accounting for two-thirds of GDP growth, as opposed to just one-fifth previously. The focus on productivity was understandable: as the report observed, the healthy GDP growth of 5 per cent per year over the previous decade had come from labour input into the economy. This was not sustainable.[147] Productivity, then, was an integral part (and indeed the flip side) of the foreign worker equation. The ESC report stated that the Singapore economy needed to avoid being too dependent on foreign workers over the longer term, and that dependence on foreign workers should not be allowed to grow significantly beyond then-existing levels (approximately one-third of the total workforce). Companies could to some extent be weaned off unhealthy overdependence on foreign workers through a progressive increase in foreign worker levies.[148] But in the new reality envisaged by the ESC, growth would come mainly from productivity gains now that labour input was not to be as prominent a factor as it previously had been.

Many of the major ESC thrusts—productivity, deepening skills and human capital (with a particular emphasis on continuing education and training)—were taken up by the government in the 2010 budget. These included the setting up of a National Productivity and Continuing Education Council, and the launch of a Productivity and Innovation Credit scheme that allowed companies to claim generous tax deductions for certain activities.[149]

Also prominent in the ESC report was the acknowledgement and emphasis that future growth had to be inclusive and broad-based: all citizens had to be able to share in the nation's prosperity.[150] The ESC report announced a revamp of the Workforce Income Supplement (WIS). The details of the revisions, when announced during the 2010 budget debate, were significant: the kitty would boast an additional $100 million annually, with up to 400,000 low-wage workers (approximately 100,000 more than previously) benefiting through stronger incentives (in the form of higher WIS payout quanta) to stay in continuous employment.[151]

The changes were the result of serious behind-the-scenes thinking on WIS and the low-wage worker issue. Those responsible for conceiving the scheme and for the comprehensive review undertaken in 2010 had concluded that the fundamental design of WIS was sound. Internal studies suggested that a net total of 30,000 employees were added to the citizen workforce in 2007 and 2008 as a result of WIS (when taken together with the 2007 changes in the CPF contribution rate).[152] The internal conclusion, however, was that WIS did not directly lift low-wage workers out of their low-wage condition. In the three years since the introduction of the scheme, the bottom 30 per cent of workers continued to experience real wage stagnation, with the bottom 20 per cent experiencing declines even when economic conditions were good. This was the key reason for extending WIS eligibility, with benefits under the 2010 review extended up to around the 30th income percentile. WIS would also now be complemented by the Workfare Training Support scheme (announced in the 2010 budget), which provided subsidies for lower-wage workers (especially those without secondary education) attending training courses, together with generous absentee payroll funding for employers who allowed their workers to attend these courses. The point, of course, was to improve the employability of these workers and to place them, post-training, in positions where they might be able to earn more.

Growth had to be inclusive for all Singaporeans: to create this environment, workers had to be in a continuous cycle of training and improvement (with attendant returns in terms of better remuneration when workers moved up the skills ladder). But companies would have the incentive to hire these workers only if the foreign worker supply—particularly low-skilled foreign labour supply—was managed. Hence, the ESC report (as noted above) stated that foreign workers would be limited to a third of the workforce. This was a political message, inserted deliberately, to show Singaporeans that some effort had been made to have a cap on foreign workers, and that Singapore would not be going down the road of other countries, such as Dubai, where expatriate workers formed the majority of the workforce.[153]

It was the targets set by the ESC—and not just those aimed at limiting foreign workers—that were especially noteworthy. The ESC report did not just make a vague emphasis on productivity: a hard target was set of productivity growth of 2–3 per cent per annum on average. This, if achieved, would raise productivity by a third over the coming decade. It was, however, a challenging task, as the ESC report noted, being more than double the 1 per cent growth achieved over the prior ten years.[154] Implied in this target was a commitment to real income growth, a commitment made explicit in Finance Minister Tharman Shanmugaratnam's 2011 budget speech:

> We must grow incomes for all Singaporeans. We aim to raise incomes by 30% in real terms over this decade. However, we can only achieve this if we grow our economy, upgrade our businesses and invest in raising skills, craftsmanship and the quality of service in every job. That is the only way we can improve incomes and living standards, including for those at the lower end of the income ladder.[155]

Looking back, Tharman shed light on the thinking of the leadership at this time on the ESC, income growth and improving the lives of Singaporeans:

> The earlier ERC had been needed because the world was changing. We had at that time to develop new verticals—new industries, new sources of growth, and new ways of addressing demands in Asia and elsewhere. The ESC, on the other hand, came about not so much because the world was changing, but because we had changed, we were running up against real constraints as a small country.
>
> The ESC was concerned not with generating new demand, but with overcoming our own constraints—labour constraints because we couldn't keep bringing in foreigners at the rate that we were doing before, constraints of land, and to some extent even future constraints on energy.
>
> We had to not just change the way we grow: we had to refocus on the prospects for the middle end of the workforce and the lower end. We were thinking a lot more about how economic growth translates into jobs and wages or all, and thinking more about choosing industries to grow based on their ability to benefit Singaporeans who could be employed in them.
>
> We had of course always been concerned about income growth for all, and in the earlier decades GDP growth and income growth more or less went together. But as the economy matured, the disparities become more important. Not everyone saw incomes growing at the same rate. Even before the ESC, the leadership had intensively discussed how we reduce disparities, and achieve broad-based income growth as the key objective of growth rather than GDP growth per se. And that meant thinking very hard about productivity too, because broad-based income growth can only be sustained on the basis of productivity improvements.
>
> We became a lot more focused on what was happening to the average Singaporean, what was happening to median households, and also what was happening at the lower end. Particularly the bottom 20 per cent. All this was an important shift, but an evolution rather than a sudden break in thinking. The key was going for quality growth, based on productivity, rather than labour force increases, and going for growth that would benefit the average Singaporean, and the lower

income Singaporean, because that would no longer come automatically with overall economic growth.[156]

From the government's point of view, some deep thinking had presaged and gone into the ESC. But for some, this was not enough. One PAP MP, Inderjit Singh, took the line that the earlier pace of growth should have been moderated, and that the government's failure to do this, and embracing of what he termed a "grow at all costs" strategy in the earlier part of the decade, had led to problems that the ESC now had to address.[157]

The ESC report did not dwell overmuch on what, if anything, had gone wrong in the past, nor what should have been done better. It is perhaps for this reason that some observers felt that the report itself disappointed.[158] However, behind the scenes a considerable amount of soul-searching had been going on in internal policy circles, long before the ESC report was actually presented. In what amounted to an "internal phase" of the ESC before it became a public committee, at the end of 2008 senior civil servants were tasked to red team the existing economic model (including examining alternative growth paths). From a very early stage, the various teams were given leeway to revisit the very fundamentals of the Singapore "go for growth" model. The critical questions, intensively discussed (both internally at the staff level, and with the political leadership) included what kind of growth Singapore had to aim for, what the objectives of growth were in the first instance.[159]

Embedded within the outcome of these discussions, and informing the subsequent ESC deliberations, was a fresh appreciation that the ultimate objective of growth lay in increasing sustained opportunities for Singaporeans, and continuously improving their standard of living (or that of their children). All Singaporeans had to be able to participate actively and meaningfully within the new model for growth. While some citizens might not immediately reap tangible fruits, it was important for all, and especially those in the lower income strata, to retain hope for the future. In ensuring opportunities for all Singaporeans, the new growth model had to address aspirational needs, cushioning the disutility arising from the income gap through provision of hope for intergenerational mobility, or directly alleviating the income gap via ensuring that these opportunities also created good jobs—dignified, and well-paying relative to Singapore's standard of living.

There was a tacit recognition, too, that keeping Singaporeans engaged was inextricably tied to social cohesion and rootedness. Singapore had to remain market-driven, but sustainable growth was possible only with a strong social fabric where aspirational needs were taken into account. New measures and socio-economic indicators would be needed to help judge the true cost of growth and its impact on citizens, as well as to answer the question of whether quality growth was indeed being achieved. These would supplement traditional economic measures of growth, which, it was now accepted, were unable to fully capture what was truly important.

The ESC process did not propose a radical break with the past. But when considered together with the thought processes underpinning it, a fundamental refocusing emerged that was just as significant as any of the national-level economic committees that had preceded it. Under the refined model for economic growth that ultimately emerged from the thinking and deliberations, the national objectives of growth were broader and more ambitious than they had ever been.[160]

Some of this was visible in PM Lee's 2010 National Day message. In the course of acknowledging the "valid concerns" of the man on the street over the foreign worker issue, Lee noted that the inflow would be controlled: "We will only bring in people who can contribute to Singapore, and work harder to integrate them into our society. And we will make clear that citizens come first. After all, we are doing this for the sake of Singaporeans."[161]

Online Strategy

In the early part of the decade, Minister of State for Information and the Arts David Lim, who chaired the PAP Internet Committee, commented that the Party believed the Internet, with its anonymity, lent itself to "less meaningful and thoughtful" discussions than desired, and "political discourse is probably best done face to face". This was reflective of the government's and the PAP's own approach. As Lim noted, the PAP did not want its website to be a place "to vent emotions or to let go certain ideas and expressions".[162] This was essentially government policy during the first half of the decade: new media was kept at a safe distance, and neither the government nor Party generally ventured into that arena to combat criticism.

Younger Singaporeans were starting not just to spend more time in the online world, but to rely on this space for news and information during key moments such as elections.[163] New media had also in the PAP's 2006 election post-mortem been identified as an area that had to be focused on—specifically, the need to develop a cyberspace strategy and presence. In addition, the Party, and Young PAP (YP) in particular, had also taken note of the masterful use of the new media and social media platforms that had a role in propelling Barack Obama to the US presidency in 2008.[164] This had left an imprint. The PAP had to deepen its engagement with new media and build capabilities.[165] The Party had, as PM Lee was to observe in 2008, to deepen its online engagement particularly with younger Singaporeans "in a serious way, but in a way which people can accept and that will resonate with them, on our websites and on many other places in cyberspace".[166]

In 2009 the YP website was revamped to include new sections and features, with its first Facebook post having come out in September the previous year. Two new subcommittees operating under the PAP's New Media Committee (chaired by Manpower Minister Ng Eng Hen) played key roles in the stepped-up online drive. The first, in charge of overall strategy, was co-headed by Minister of State (Education) Lui Tuck Yew and Hong Kah GRC MP Zaqy Mohamad. The second, known as the "new media capabilities group", was chaired by Tanjong Pagar GRC MP Baey Yam Keng and Bishan–Toa Payoh GRC MP Josephine Teo.[167] The latter subcommittee had members who went online and anonymously rebutted anti-government and anti-PAP views on Internet forums and blogs.[168] This aspect of the Party's foray into the online world was described by the *Straits Times* as the PAP's "quiet counter-insurgency against its online critics".[169] The Party saw it differently: since many ordinary citizens were venting their frustrations online, reasonable countervailing views (especially when there were untruths and distortions involved) could be put forward—not in an attempt to neutralise negative voices, but to provide a corrective where necessary.[170] There was, however, some degree of discomfort among members of the public: the feeling in some quarters was that rebutting criticism of the Party and the government through anonymous postings would be counterproductive, lack credibility, and not be that much different from the (mostly) anonymous criticisms themselves.[171]

The Party's initiatives in this space did not simply consist of rebuttals by online teams operating in guerrilla fashion. In November 2008 the Party launched its revamped website (a revamped YP website was to follow in 2009), with its content refreshed by branch activists' reports on events.[172] The branches themselves during the period 2008–09 set up their own new media committees, with branch activists tasked to build and maintain branch websites and social media pages.[173]

Even as the Party was from 2006 to 2010 feeling out the prospects and possibilities of online engagement, individual MPs were experimenting to find their metier with regard to social media. By early 2009, about 25 PAP MPs were on Facebook, with the number increasing to 53 (out of 80 PAP MPs in all) by October 2010. Those with a Facebook presence included ministers such as DPMs Wong Kan Seng and Teo Chee Hean, and Ministers George Yeo, Dr Yaacob Ibrahim, Mah Bow Tan, Dr Vivian Balakrishnan, and Lim Hwee Hua.[174] The general consensus among MPs was that an online presence facilitated communication and interaction with constituents.[175] Facebook (in particular) allowed for a certain degree of two-way communication, and matters (such as feedback on municipal affairs) could be raised for immediate attention. But MPs were also rapidly becoming aware that the mere fact of a social media presence raised expectations on the part of constituents that their needs would be quickly seen to. Within the MPs' ranks, too, there was the realisation that while a social media presence could complement the hard yards on the ground, it could not replace walkabouts or face-to-face interactions. Nor was social media the ideal means to have in-depth discussions on substantive issues of policy. When such attempts were made in the online space, what could—and did—sometimes occur were heated, unfocused discussions that could spiral out of the control of any moderator.

This particularly affected YP's online platforms. The Young PAP leadership had made it clear that it was intent on playing the lead role in connecting with the younger, Internet-savvy generation, an effort that would also serve the purpose of explaining government policy (as well as the standpoint of the Party).[176] YP had at first no less than three Facebook pages. Besides engaging the youth, these were found useful for recruitment and for the mobilisation of volunteers.[177] Two of these pages—YP Community and YP Network—were essentially run and maintained by volunteer activists, without moderation from Party HQ, to discuss issues relating to Singapore and its politics. This could—and did—lead to problems, with the YP pages becoming a magnet for anti-PAP rants and, inevitably, trolls. In one instance in early 2010, known as the "Eric How" episode, a netizen put up an inflammatory post on the YP Network page denigrating lower-income Singaporeans. This led to police reports by real-life Eric Hows against an alleged online impersonator—and also questions over why YP took as long as three weeks to distance itself from the comments.[178] In another incident the same year, netizens on YP Network alleged that a YP member had taken advantage of his position as a grassroots volunteer to gain business for his company.[179] Following these episodes, YP Network and YP Community were closed in March 2010, leaving just the main YP Facebook page, overseen directly by the YP leadership.[180]

These difficulties could easily be put down—as they were by the YP leadership—to the initial period of "experimentation", feeling out what worked and what did not, with lessons learnt along the way that would help to refine online strategy.[181] But as some observers of new media noted, the online engagement attempts by the YP during this period appeared to be characterised by a lack of conceptualisation and deep thinking.[182] Critics could also point to particular aspects of online engagement that withered. An example was the P65 blog, set up in October 2006 by 12 young PAP MPs born after Singapore's independence, with the intention of reaching out to the younger generation. The blog, which suffered from poor readership, had become all but defunct by late 2008, the young MPs who had shown themselves to be more Net savvy migrating to platforms such as Facebook.[183]

Leveraging on new media was not the same as embracing it. What the Party had learnt across this period was that—inevitably—it preferred arenas where most facets of the discussion could be controlled, over online spaces that allowed for untrammelled discussion. The latter could lead in turn to untoward ramifications (as can be seen from the incidents on YP Network).[184] The experiences over this period also appear to have confirmed to the Party leadership that while new media could be used to propagate news, the time had not yet come to conduct serious discussions of policy in the online space. Even on the revamped PAP and Young PAP websites, there was very little room for policy discussion or vigorous debate.

It is easy in assessing the experimentation of 2006–10 to overlook the overall progress made. By 2010 some of the wariness of new media, visible in the earlier years of the decade, had been shed. Numerous ministerial dialogues (and even the Party convention that year) featured real-time updates via Twitter and other social media tools, while videos of key speeches were also quickly put up online. By 2010, too, the once static Party website could boast regular updates of activities, as well as videos produced by activists.[185] It had gone some way to answering calls by activists and MPs (particularly backbenchers) to use new media more creatively to communicate the PAP's vision.[186]

The PAP's attempts to up its game in the online engagement stakes had, of course, a great deal to do with the likely impact of the Internet and social media in the next election, but also, as the decade progressed, with the changing nature of the Internet itself. By December 2010, Singapore had just shy of 2.5 million Facebook users—just over four years after Facebook's public launch in September 2006.[187] Locally, websites purveying local news and commentary were becoming increasingly influential. All were to some degree critical of the government, but they ran the entire gamut: from the satirical and sometimes scurrilous Wayang Party (reconstituted as the Temasek Review in 2009) to the Online Citizen (founded in December 2006). Individual bloggers such as Mr Brown were also increasingly seen as important barometers of public opinion.[188] By 2010 many of the main Opposition parties also had a substantial—and, compared to the PAP, much more regularly refreshed—presence on various social media platforms (Facebook, Twitter, YouTube).[189] The Opposition had clearly realised that the Internet was a low-cost medium to speak to the electorate directly, to bypass traditional media, and to recruit a support base.[190]

It should also be observed that the online engagement efforts to match moves by the Opposition went beyond the Party: government machinery as a whole was engaging citizens online. REACH (formerly the Feedback Unit) had a Facebook presence from June 2008. Most observers agreed that these changes were made not just to get government messages across. Society was itself changing—not simply on account of the pervasiveness of new media (and the increasing ease with which one could bypass existing regulations), but also partly on account of the evolving of mores and attitudes of an increasingly wired younger generation. It was with this generation that connections had to be made, in terms that it could understand, and through media it was familiar with. Clearly, the government had to show that it was cognisant of these winds and was prepared to amend aspects of the regulatory regime that governed what was permissible.

In April 2007 a high-level Advisory Council on the Impact of New Media on Society (AIMS) was formed by the Ministry of Information, Communications and the Arts to make recommendations relating to new media. The AIMS report, partly the product of a large-scale consultation exercise with the public, industry players, bloggers, and other interested groups, was issued in December 2008.[191]

The government accepted 17 out of AIMS' 26 recommendations. Among the recommendations accepted was one that essentially amounted to a partial lifting of the proscription on party political films. The government effected this suggestion through an amendment to the Films Act in March 2009, with political parties now able to make and circulate political videos (those deemed factual, objective, and unsensational) under certain conditions.[192] The government acknowledged that a complete ban on political films could not work. The *Straits Times* commented that "the ban, in place since 1998, has been looking increasingly archaic and unenforceable, given the speed and ease with which today's digital natives upload and share videos of all forms on the Internet".[193]

Another significant, and related, AIMS recommendation taken up by the government was extending the list of online political activities that were explicitly allowed by law during an election period. Election advertising regulations governing new media use by political parties during election campaigning were relaxed in March 2011. The number of items on the "positive list" (items expressly allowed) during the campaigning period was more than doubled. Political parties, candidates and members of the public were allowed to use podcasts, vodcasts, blogs and other new media tools when engaging in "election advertising". Effectively recognising the reality of what had happened in 2006, campaigning on social media was for the first time explicitly allowed, and the ban on political podcasts and videocasts was lifted.[194]

Of course, the government's responses to reports like AIMS were opportunities for it to clarify its stand on critical issues. A case in point was the suggestion in the AIMS report that the government broaden the scope of its online engagement and engage voices outside of official government platforms.[195] The government in response agreed to re-evaluate the effectiveness of its online citizen engagement, but also noted that citizens would be engaged on national issues through the official REACH portal, and not through other Web platforms such as blogs.[196]

Should more have been done? Even during this period, PAP MPs would occasionally comment publicly or in print about how the government could, or should, have leveraged on new media in communicating policies and their rationale to the public.[197] It is here that the Party—and government—may have missed a trick, with lingering wariness of new media meaning that it was not yet seen as a suitable tool to communicate when it came to important matters of policy.

Several important policies and initiatives were introduced during this period. These were issues where the government was convinced it had got its formulation—as well as calculations—right, but where the intricacies (as well as benefits to Singaporeans) were sometimes not easily explainable to the average individual. On the whole, traditional formats such as dialogue sessions were still preferred. Examples included explaining the details of schemes like the Workfare Income Supplement, to why changes in the CPF scheme were necessary (the changes in question concerned CPF Life, a compulsory annuity scheme mooted in 2007 and introduced two years later, which the government deemed necessary since increasing longevity and simple demographics meant that individuals had to work longer and draw down on their CPF later in life).[198] Another case in point was distance-based fares for public transport, introduced in 2010, which (contrary to widespread perception) saw most commuters paying less. Many—not just the remaining one third of commuters who paid more—sensed unfairness in the changes.[199] But here, as with the major policy points, official communication remained firmly entrenched in tried and tested channels.

The overriding impression as the decade passed its midpoint was of a cautious willingness to open up, underpinned by an innate degree of conservatism in terms of how government perceived new media and its independent actors. Nowhere was this better evidenced than in an episode in 2006 that came to be known as the Mr Brown saga. Lee Kin Mun, a popular and influential blogger seen by many as representing the views of ordinary, middle-class Singaporeans, penned an article (as part of a regular series of columns in the *Today* newspaper) that was critical of various aspects of contemporary Singapore society, pointing the blame at the government for issues relating to cost of living.[200] The content, couched in language both sarcastic and witty, irked the government, which issued a strong rebuttal calling his article "polemics dressed up as analysis . . . calculated to encourage cynicism and despondency, which can only make things worse, not better, for those he professes to sympathise with".[201] Mr Brown's (Lee's online moniker) column was suspended by the newspaper, with the government accusing him (in echoes of the Catherine Lim saga 12 years earlier) of presenting himself as a non-political observer, while in reality crossing the line into partisan political involvement through undermining the government's standing with the electorate. The government response might seem to have embedded within it a message to the mainstream media itself: it should not get involved in telegraphing critical views that had new media origins (or, in this case, that came from a new media actor).[202]

※※※

The times, and the people, were changing. Dissent, activism and critical comment were all becoming enmeshed—often with new media as a catalyst—in a manner that was difficult to turn back. It was around this time—in the second half of the decade—that people were beginning to speak for their causes (or ventilate their grievances) in a manner that saw little of the deference (and still less fear) of the past, and in a manner that the government had in any case increasingly make a modicum of accommodation for. In 2008, for example, a group of bloggers staged a protest at Speakers' Corner against transport fare hikes; the protest was possible only because effective September that year there had been a rule change allowing protests at Hong Lim Park, where Speakers' Corner was located.[203]

This was not a blanket opening up. Certain sensitivities remained. Issues touching on race and religion remained out of bounds at Speakers' Corner. But in other arenas, it was increasingly possible to debate with candour issues formerly considered sensitive. In October 2007, for example, there was a contentious (and at points heated) debate in Parliament on the issue of decriminalising homosexual acts between consenting adults, during the (successful) passage of an Amendment Bill that legalised private, consensual anal and oral sex between heterosexual adults. Part of the debate concerned a public petition signed by over 2,000 individuals, which called for the repeal of the relevant part of the penal code (S377A, which criminalised sexual intercourse between men).[204] In the end, PM Lee weighed in, acknowledging the "legal untidiness and ambiguity" but giving reasons why S377A had to remain.[205]

The fact that such open debate had taken place at all was arguably more noteworthy than the quashing of the hopes of the gay community. The Workers' Party chief, Low Thia Khiang, could in 2007 point to the government's handling of the S377A debate as a sign of a more relaxed and open political atmosphere: "You don't see very strong reactions from the Government towards criticisms and citizen initiatives. . . . The environment has changed compared to when I just joined politics in the early 80s. . . . People are more vocal and people are more comfortable to air their views in public. So I think it is an improvement."[206]

There was also another noteworthy type of speaking up. This had to do in the main with discomfort over Singapore's trajectory (or the pace of it) and, perhaps, nostalgia for what had seemingly been lost. One of the most talked-about, and certainly eloquent, speeches during the whole of the Eleventh Parliament (November 2006–April 2011) was the one made by Nominated Member of Parliament Viswa Sadasivan. Sadasivan, making his maiden parliamentary speech on 18 August 2009, moved a motion for the House to reaffirm its commitment to the nation-building ideals enshrined in the National Pledge. In his 50-minute speech Sadasivan ranged widely over many issues, spending time in particular on the importance of rootedness, patriotism, and citizenry. To Sadasivan, resilience and rootedness had diminished, partly as a result of widening disparities in society and also government policies, including its welcome of foreign talent.[207] Sadasivan's motion (and implication that governmental course corrections were needed) provoked over the next two days a healthy debate in the House concerning what had and had not been achieved in the course of Singapore's history since the drafting of the Pledge in 1965. Minister Mentor Lee Kuan Yew, in his last major speech in Parliament, found it necessary to respond with a rebuttal, taking aim particularly, it seems, at the parts of Sadasivan's argument that suggested Singapore should move beyond race and see all as equal:

> *MM Lee: Sir, I had not intended to intervene in any debate. But I was doing physiotherapy just now and reading the newspapers and I thought I should bring the House back to earth. Mr Rajaratnam had great virtues in the midst of despondency after a series of race riots when we were thrown out during Independence. And our Malays in Singapore were apprehensive that now that we were the majority, we would in turn treat them the way a Malay majority treated us. He drafted these words and rose above the present. He was a great idealist. It came to me; I trimmed out the unachievable and the Pledge, as it stands, is his work after I have trimmed it. Was it an ideology? No, it is an aspiration. Will we achieve it? I do not know. We will have to keep on trying. Are we a nation? In transition. [Lee then moved an amendment to make it clear that while the nation had made progress in achieving the tenets of the pledge, these were not ideology but "aspirations". Using examples from the past, Lee showed that notwithstanding progress made in nation-building, achieving the ideals set out in the pledge was a continued work in progress given fundamental differences between races and religions.]*

> *. . . So the basis on which the Nominated Member has placed his arguments is false and flawed. It is completely untrue. It has got no basis whatsoever. And I thought to myself, perhaps I should bring this House back to earth and remind everybody what is our starting point, what is our base, and if we do not recognise where we started from, and that these are our foundations, we will fail.*

> *. . . So I think it is dangerous to allow such highfalutin ideas to go undemolished and mislead Singapore. We are here today, we have this building, we have all these facilities. All around us is evidence of our accountability. Without being accountable, we would not have been re-elected and there would be no Singapore of today.[208]*

MM Lee's response was not an outright rejection of the motion (which eventually passed with amendments the following day), but a forceful restatement of the point that the equality of men was an aspiration, as were the values enshrined in the pledge. Progress would be made, in MM Lee's view, "by a realistic step-by-step forward approach".

Sadasivan's *cri de coeur* and MM Lee's response remained for some time a much-discussed episode in Singapore's cyberspace, even if it did not quite (as some Internet commentary had it) "shake the foundations of the PAP facade to the core".[209] It should be observed in this connection that segments of the youth were also beginning to find their voice, speaking frankly in a manner that was occasionally discomfiting to the political leadership. Leading up to the 2011 general election, there were signs that government leaders were concerned that the youth did not really "get it"—the sacrifices that had been made to ensure Singapore's survival, and the fragility underlying the nation's continued existence. Speaking to undergraduates from Nanyang Technological University at a forum on 29 October 2010, Senior Minister Goh Chok Tong said he was of the view that some young Singaporeans "simply yearn for liberal Western-style democracies without considering whether these will produce a good and effective government".[210]

At this forum, one student stood up and engaged SM Goh, noting that when he was young he felt proud to be a Singaporean, but "with all the changes in policies and the influx of foreign talent, I really don't know what I'm defending anymore". Citing a sentiment he said was widely held by males serving National Service who had to compete with foreigners for jobs, the young man said, "I feel that there is a dilution of the Singapore spirit in youth. . . . We don't really feel comfortable in our country any more."

In response, Goh said, "This is one early sign of danger. . . . If this is happening, it is very serious."[211]

Parliamentary Innovation

On one particular area—a sense of cynicism and disengagement from politics—the government had already begun to move. By 2008, key government leaders were speaking about the need for the political system to evolve to meet the changing demands of a new electorate. The liberalisation that had taken place thus far (allowing outdoor demonstrations at Speakers' Corner, the relaxation of what was permissible election advertising material online) had gone only so far. Was more change in the offing? Even if so, the Party leadership was keen to manage expectations, with PM Lee stating at the Party conference in late 2008 that Singapore was better off with one clean, strong political party—the PAP—in charge, rather than having the politics of contention and division.[212]

Incremental political change was, of course, what the PAP excelled at. In his address at the opening of Parliament on 18 May 2009, President S.R. Nathan called for Singapore politics to evolve in a manner that responded to demands for change by a younger electorate. Responding, PM Lee acknowledged that the time was right for the political system to change in a way that met the aspirations of the people.[213] He unveiled several changes to the electoral and parliamentary system. The upper limit for the number of non-constituency MPs (NCMPs, the "best loser" Opposition MPs) would be raised from six to nine—essentially a guarantee of a minimum of nine Opposition members in Parliament after the next general election.[214] The Nominated Member of Parliament (NMP) scheme (which allowed for nine NMPs) was also tweaked. The Parliamentary Special Select Committee that had hitherto invited nominations from six groups (business and industry; the professions; the labour movement; social and community organisations; the media, arts, and sports; as well as tertiary education institutions) would broaden its scope to include an additional group from the people sector. PM Lee said that this would be to "give civil society a voice in Parliament and encourage civil society to grow and to mature further".[215] The effect of these changes meant that Parliament would have at least 18 members not from the PAP. PM Lee also announced that the GRC system would be tweaked, with new terms of reference given to the Election Boundaries Review Committee, to make it clear that there should be more smaller GRCs, fewer six-member GRCs, with the new average size of GRCs not to exceed five (as opposed to the then-current figure of 5.4). The number of single-member constituencies would also go up, from nine to at least 12.[216]

The purpose of these changes, according to PM Lee, was not to engineer having more Opposition MPs in Parliament, nor to have more seats contested. The point was to encourage a wider range of views in Parliament—having more alternative voices would "generate more robust debate, improve policy formulation, expose PAP MPs to the cut and thrust of debate (and) demonstrate what the opposition can and cannot do".[217] But this did not stop some observers from drawing their own conclusions. One was that parliamentary discussion had to be shown as relevant given that political discussion had increasingly moved into cyberspace. The other was that the near-complete parliamentary dominance held by the PAP had led to cynicism, especially within that part of the electorate that did not support the Party. The changes made might therefore, some surmised, be a way to quench the thirst for an Opposition by guaranteeing their continued presence in Parliament. Such an assurance would in theory remove the impetus to vote them in.[218]

One further and important change should be considered here. This was the provision for a "cooling-off day"—the day before Polling Day—during which no electoral campaigning (both in the real and virtual worlds) would be allowed. The key reason given by PM Lee when mooting the idea in November 2009 was that before voting, the public had to have time for calm, sober reflection after the hurly-burly of the election campaign.[219] In arguing for the change, PM Lee acknowledged it would be difficult to bring the entire spectrum of new media to heel and obey the new rule.[220] But notwithstanding this, some surmised that the cooling-off idea might have owed something to the possibility of last-minute rumour or innuendo having an effect on the overall vote or in particular hotspots. As the writer and occasional government critic Catherine Lim noted:

The PAP realises that in the coming General Election, emotions could actually become the rogue factor in the political equation. . . . For, the electorate will include a large number of new, young voters who belong to the noisy, rumbustious world of the Internet, where emotions rather than cool reason prevail. The Opposition is sure to make opportunistic use of this new force.[221]

As could be expected, the suggestion of a cooling-off day (passed by Parliament in April 2010 through constitutional amendments and amendments to the Parliamentary Elections Act, at the same time as the changes in the NCMP system) did not sit well with Opposition politicians, who felt that these moves seriously disadvantaged the Opposition cause but not that of the PAP, given that the PAP could simply put out messages during the cooling-off day if it had to using the mainstream media or government machinery.[222]

Leadership and Succession

The initial public reaction after the 2006 general election to the efforts of the P65 MPs to reach out and connect with the ground had been decidedly mixed. In 2007, 12 P65 MPs performed a hip-hop dance routine for the Chingay Parade. This was seen variously as an overblown attempt to show "street-cred" or, at worst, overt publicity-seeking.[223] The more general criticism—one extending well beyond the P65 MPs' attempts to dance—was while hype had been generated, Young PAP and its MPs had not changed much in terms of genuine substance.[224]

What the criticism failed to take into account were other more low-key (and arguably more genuine) attempts by YP after 2006 to connect with the younger demographic. The P65 team conducted numerous small dialogue sessions with key subgroups (including students, younger professionals, and parents). In 2007, monthly information sessions by P65 MPs were started for individuals keen to find out more about the Party—these well-attended sessions saw many attendees either volunteering their time to assist, or else progressing to full membership.[225]

The pace of work quickened after Senior Parliamentary Secretary Teo Ser Luck took over from Dr Vivian Balakrishnan as YP chairman in 2008.[226] Other groups that YP had hitherto not cultivated in an organised fashion were now tapped on. In 2010, YP started a programme for teenagers aged between 15 and 17 who had shown an interest in politics. These youths were involved by YP in MPs' meet-the-people sessions and community projects, with some also attached to Party branches. The programme was started on account of an increase in the number of these teenagers attending YP's outreach sessions. The idea was to develop the interest of these individuals in politics, with the possibility of their becoming full members of the Party when they turned 18.[227]

All these measures paid off when it came to numbers. In 2009 more than 1,000 young Singaporeans joined YP. YP officials felt this was the result of YP going beyond its old image as an extension of the Party and representing itself as an organisation which served the community. Forty-five per cent of new recruits were women, and approximately 55 per cent were aged under 30.[228] Even as recruitment remained healthy, other initiatives within YP sprouted to deal with the influx. These cannot here be considered in full, but broadly speaking they involved leadership camps, team bonding and fostering esprit de corps. Some of these came under the broad umbrella of the YP "School".[229]

Internal processes pertaining to competition for positions within YP were also tweaked. The year 2008 marked the first time that the majority of YP Exco members were elected, when nearly 200 YP members from 14 regions gathered at the elections in August that year to select one individual from each region to represent them.[230] The entire 31-member exco elected and appointed that year was (from the chairman down) from the P65 generation.

In a further 2009 restructuring, exco members were tasked to head subcommittees (YP Media, Political Discussions, YP School, YP Network, YP Empower) and functional teams (YP International Relations, YP Community, YP Communications).

In 2010, for the first time, candidates vying for elected posts of regional chairmen on the YP Exco were allowed a campaigning period of three weeks.[231] The move to a more competitive process would, according to YP officials, attract a wider pool of talent, with some officials acknowledging that elected politicians could emerge from this pool.[232]

YP's changes—in particular the move from appointed to more elected exco members—were mirrored in the wider Party. By 2010, all of the council positions on the PAP Policy Forum were elected save for chairman and vice-chairman. There had been similar changes—albeit at a slower pace—within the HQ Exco, which stood just below the CEC in the hierarchy of Party organisations. In September 2008, Party members voted to decide which four district members (double the number of slots available in 2006) would represent them in the HQ Exco. In addition, one representative each from YP, the Women's Wing and the Policy Forum were appointed by Party leaders, bringing the total number of elected representatives in the HQ Exco to seven.[233] Younger political office-holders such as Grace Fu, Lui Tuck Yew and Lee Yi Shyan were at the same time increasingly taking over the key non-elected (appointed) positions within the HQ Exco, which saw them helm important subcommittees overseeing issues ranging from publicity to new media and external relations.[234]

Changes aimed at promoting the younger generation of leaders were taking place also at the CEC level (though without, it should be noted, the enhanced competition for places that had been seen in organs such as YP and the HQ Exco). From 2004, there was an increasing trend of younger leaders being either directly appointed or co-opted into the CEC. As early as the 28th CEC (elected in 2004), four of the "Super Seven" from 2001 were CEC members (Tharman Shanmugaratnam, Dr Ng Eng Hen, Khaw Boon Wan and Dr Vivian Balakrishnan). Among the other younger leaders who began to feature in the CEC from 2002 (although not necessarily as fixtures) were Lim Hwee Hua and Gan Kim Yong (see Appendix Two).

All this was, of course, tied into the fact that the wheels were turning to rejuvenate ministerial ranks. In the May 2008 Cabinet reshuffle, Gan Kim Yong, previously minister of state for manpower, became acting manpower minister. K. Shanmugam took over the Law Ministry portfolio of Prof. S. Jayakumar—unusually, direct from the backbenches, without serving first as a junior minister. Four ministers of state (Lim Hwee Hua, S. Iswaran, Grace Fu and Lui Tuck Yew) were promoted to senior minister of state. In 2009 both Gan Kim Yong and Lim Hwee Hua were made full minister, with Lui Tuck Yew also being appointed acting minister. Lim Hwee Hua's appointment as minister in the Prime Minister's Office was especially significant, as this marked the first time in history that a woman had become a member of the Cabinet.[235]

PM Lee and other key figures (notably Minister for Manpower & Second Minister for Defence Dr Ng Eng Hen, who had in 2007 taken over responsibility for the recruitment and talent search effort from then Defence Minister Teo Chee Hean) had been very clear in their public statements that the top priority for the Party was to find men and women of MP calibre, as well as those with the right qualities to serve as ministers. Their comments acquired a particular urgency as the decade wound down, suggesting that finding the right people was proving a difficult task. As PM Lee put it, these were "not revolutionary times", with few Singaporeans willing to step forward on account of a fervent cause or ideology.[236] The Cabinet "worried obsessively", according to Lee, about finding the next generation of leaders.[237] Despite the difficulties, however, there seemed to be a measure of confidence that overall, the core of the fourth-generation leadership would be in place by the time of the next general election.

GE 2011: The Build-up

Party leaders were prepared to acknowledge, late into 2010 and in early 2011, that the PAP would face a considerably tougher fight compared to the previous election.[238] Senior Minister Goh Chok Tong commented, one day before Parliament was dissolved (19 April 2011), that "the ground may not be as sweet" for the PAP, citing issues that might prey on voters' minds, including the rising cost of living.[239] This sensing of the ground mood was the reason why the Party leadership had been particularly active, especially from 2010, in pointing out what had been done for the people. PM Lee's 29 August 2010 National Day Rally speech had an extended defence of the government's immigration policy and the need to remain open to talent, and also separately covered tangible measures to ease MRT congestion, even as he acknowledged the many complaints on both sets of issues. Throughout that year there were several attempts to highlight how the government had been doing more, and had a range of mechanisms, to help needy Singaporeans.[240]

Discourse of a similar nature was ongoing within internal Party circles. Highly unusually, at the Party conference in November 2010 no MP took to the floor to speak, with rank-and-file activists instead dominating proceedings. Four of the six who spoke were to be fielded in the general election, with their remarks to cadres exhibiting an emphasis on helping the poor.[241] In his own address at the conference, PM Lee spent time covering government schemes such as Workfare and ComCare, stressing that there was help for those needing it.[242]

Even more was to come. The 2011 budget had as its centrepiece a "Grow and Share" package worth $3.2 billion (this included, amongst other things, special one-off Growth Dividends and CPF MediSave top-ups, a Workfare Special Bonus and utilities rebates) that were meant to see the surpluses shared with the people—with the poor and the middle class benefiting more. Separately, the government committed another $3.4 billion to enhance the well-being and care of the elderly.

The 2011 general election was to see several firsts. These included the largest number of voters ever—2.2 million, up from 2.1 million in 2006; and the largest number of first-time voters—200,000. An estimated 600,000 of the electorate were younger voters between the ages of 21 and 35 (the largest number ever in this age bracket).

The PAP fielded its youngest crop of candidates since 1991, with a median age of 38.5 (see Appendix One, Table 6.2).[243] From the Party's point of view, the slate of new candidates presented was not just any ordinary one: an "extra effort" had been made to find individuals and future leaders who could take Singapore to 2020 and beyond. Only one in ten individuals had made the final cut in a talent-spotting and interview process (that included nearly 200 "tea sessions" to which more than 260 individuals were invited) that had begun at the end of 2006.[244] Dr Ng Eng Hen noted when wrapping up the introductions of new PAP candidates that the 2011 slate had the highest number of potential office-holders compared to any previous election. Among the 24 presented were two high-profile generals from the army, Major-General Chan Chun Sing and Brigadier-General Tan Chuan-Jin. There were also several former senior civil servants: Heng Swee Keat, Ong Ye Kung, Lawrence Wong and Sim Ann. All had recently resigned or retired from their former jobs in the government or military.[245] As the press remarked, this was no simple renewal exercise. The outlines of the team (mentored by the existing leadership) likely to eventually take Singapore into the next lap was now coming into sharper focus.[246]

Inevitably, as part of renewal, several experienced politicians stepped down or retired. These included Senior Minister S. Jayakumar (seven terms), Speaker of Parliament Abdullah Tarmugi (six terms), former Ministers Dr Lee Boon Yang and Yeo Cheow Tong (both with six terms) and Party Chairman Lim Boon Heng (seven terms). MPs known for their strong relationship with the ground also stepped down, including Ang Mong Seng and Chan Soo Sen. Somewhat predictably, questions were asked about whether the PAP's new finds would be able to fill the shoes of the outgoing MPs.[247] It may not have been a coincidence that several of the candidates, when introduced to the public, displayed a certain keenness to stress ordinary upbringings, struggles in childhood or other adversities. Perhaps, as the *Straits Times* mused:

> *This narrative of struggle seems to have been adopted by the new candidates in the PAP camp—perhaps to chip away at the notion that the folks in white are all high-fliers who have had it easy all their lives. . . . Could this be an attempt to counter perceptions of elitism in the PAP?*[248]

Some candidates had struggle embedded deeper in their family lines. The press made much of the fact that Ong Ye Kung and Dr Janil Puthucheary (another prospective PAP candidate) were both sons of former Barisan Sosialis members. Ong Ye Kung's father, Ong Lian Teng, had been elected MP at the 1963 general election before resigning his seat in 1966 with other Barisan members. Janil Puthucheary's father, Dominic, had been a founding member of the PAP who had later defected to (and helped set up) the Barisan, and had been detained in Operation Coldstore in 1963.[249] Dominic Puthucheary supported his son's decision to stand for election, while Ong Ye Kung sat out the 2006 elections even though he had been invited to stand, out of respect for his father and despite his father having given his blessings.[250] Even former Barisan members interviewed said that there should be no objection if offspring of Barisan members joined the PAP to serve the country.[251]

The scale of the challenge to the PAP became clear only on Nomination Day, 27 April 2011. Eighty-two of the 87 seats were contested.[252] The strongest challenge from the Opposition, at least numerically, was from the National Solidarity Party (24 candidates) and the Workers' Party (23 candidates). The only GRC to see a walkover was Tanjong Pagar (there had been six GRC walkovers in 2006). All 12 single-member constituencies (SMCs) were contested.[253]

The most eye-catching developments were the decisions of the chiefs of the WP and Singapore People's Party (SPP), Low Thia Khiang and Chiam See Tong, to leave their respective strongholds of Hougang and Potong Pasir in order to contest the GRCs of Aljunied and Bishan–Toa Payoh. But also noteworthy was the PAP decision to field Michael Palmer in Punggol East SMC. Palmer, an Eurasian, was the first minority candidate to be fielded by the PAP in an SMC since 1988.[254]

Early on, there were some signs that the PAP machinery was perhaps not as well oiled or meticulous as had formerly been the case. One new PAP candidate, unionist Steve Tan, who had been formally introduced to the public and originally been slated to run as part of the Tampines GRC team, withdrew his name from consideration just one day before Nomination Day, after allegations surfaced concerning his personal life. Tan's last-minute replacement in Tampines was Baey Yam Keng, who had originally been due to continue in Tanjong Pagar GRC, which he had been elected to in 2006. Baey's replacement in Tanjong Pagar was orthopaedic surgeon Dr Chia Shi-Lu. Chia was dubbed by some online commentators an "overnight MP", given Tanjong Pagar's status as an uncontested GRC. The moniker also reflected a degree of derision on the part of sceptics of the GRC system, since Chia had not been formally introduced to the public and was an almost completely unknown quantity, yet had become an instant MP (so the critics felt) riding on the coattails of others in the GRC.[255]

Perhaps recognising how this would be a different kind of election, one where new media might have an important—perhaps even defining—role, the Party had for the first time given some training to its new candidates on how to handle new media (in addition to traditional media).[256] Still, online scrutiny, criticism, and vitriol heaped on certain individuals, particularly the PAP's new finds, were at levels that would have taken many by surprise. Despite having to withdraw his likely candidacy, the

PAP's Steve Tan did not fare the worst. There were a great deal of negative comments, especially online, directed at the somewhat folksy speaking style of Chan Chun Sing.[257] In Chan's case, the scrutiny and online flaming were perhaps amplified by the fact that he was widely seen as a likely office-holder.

The online attacks extended to other PAP candidates. Malaysian-born Dr Janil Puthucheary, who had become a Singapore citizen at the age of 35, chose (perhaps unwisely) to answer criticisms concerning his not having served National Service (NS) with the comment that he had been doing public service as a paediatrician: "I've spent the last 10 years saving kids' lives."[258] This led to his being flamed further online, and also provoked unfavourable comparisons with the WP's star find, the Taiwanese-born Chen Show Mao, who had moved to Singapore when still a child and who volunteered to serve his NS before he became a Singapore citizen in 1986.[259]

Online scrutiny meant that the personal lives and personal details of individual candidates could be ruthlessly picked apart and discussed in the online arena—a space where a mixture of fact, rumour, supposition and outright fabrication congealed. The candidate who came in for the most severe treatment was the PAP's youngest candidate, 27-year-old business consultant Tin Pei Ling, standing in Marine Parade GRC. Tin was to become something of a lightning rod for criticism against the PAP. Images from her social media account showing her posing with a shopping bag from a well-known brand name were widely circulated, and held up as evidence of alleged frivolity and unsuitability for politics. A viral video of Tin acting as emcee at a PAP event showed her at a seeming loss for words. This, taken together with other statements (for example, her saying that she could not find a policy that she disagreed with) was further adduced by critics to support the argument that Tin was a political lightweight, out of her depth, and someone who had to be defended by senior figures within the Party.[260] To the critics, the unfairness of the GRC system would be fully evidenced if Tin were to "sneak into Parliament" on the shoulders of heavyweights in the Party, such as SM Goh Chok Tong, the anchor minister in Marine Parade.[261] There were also unfavourable comparisons with Nicole Seah from the National Solidarity Party (NSP), part of the NSP team standing in Marine Parade GRC, who cut a poised, convincing and eloquent figure on the campaign trail.[262] There was even an online petition calling for Tin to be fielded in a single-member constituency in order to prove her mettle.[263]

The Party was firm in its decision to field Tin. Goh Chok Tong said, having watched her deal with the maelstrom of criticism, that she had been found to be "tough enough" for the challenge—someone Goh wanted on his team.[264] Goh later recalled that PAP grassroots leaders who worked with Tin on the campaign trail gave very positive reports. She had the ability in particular to bond with the many older residents in the MacPherson division of Marine Parade:

> PM asked me about her. I knew she would do well because MacPherson, being a very old estate, the grandmothers, the old aunties, the old uncles, they like her. So when they saw her, they will say, Miss Tin, you know, or in Chinese they will say, Pei Ling, Pei Ling, come, come. And they would hold her hand and so on.

And I said, OK, being an old precinct, they will support her. I was aware that some of my colleagues were not so confident. They said, would we lose. No, I said, we won't lose. I gave my feedback to PM. I felt strongly that once you have chosen somebody on the basis of merit, you stand by her. In the counting of votes in the divisions, her results were the same as the others.[265]

The PAP–WP Dynamic

The years after the 2006 general election were marked by what could be described as a ratcheting up of the stakes between the PAP and WP. From the PAP's point of view, the overall performance of the Opposition MPs in Parliament had been disappointing. PAP leaders said that the WP had been content to remain in its comfort zone without offering concrete new ideas. WP chief Low Thia Khiang was singled out by PM Lee for his reluctance to debate the PAP on core policies: "He seems more keen on catching the Government on its shortcomings, so as to embarrass the Government."[266]

For his part, WP chief Low Thia Khiang stated that it was the people, after all, who had in 2006 decided that they wanted a PAP government. Low saw the WP's role as that of a "watchdog", acting as a check on the PAP government and prodding it to respond to the needs of the people (as well as to deliver on its promises).[267] The PAP retort to the "watchdog" argument was that the WP's refusal to state up front that it had aspirations of forming the government at some point in the future meant that Singaporeans were not being offered a "real choice", and that the WP therefore could not be taken seriously.[268] But Low had no qualms in stating, in the years preceding the 2011 general election, that the WP would not be ready to challenge the PAP in the near term: "A political party needs to reach a certain stage before it can offer alternative policies, that is, at a stage where it is capable of replacing that government. And WP still has a very long way to go before reaching this stage."[269] Instead, Low was keen to show that the WP would be a "responsible" Opposition party, one that could offer meaningful alternative views in a manner that would not be obstructionist to Singapore's governance and success.[270]

Low did not simply envisage the WP remaining completely in the PAP's slipstream. At the WP's 50th anniversary dinner in November 2007, Low set out the aim to make a breakthrough by winning a GRC at the next general election:

In my view, as long as the opposition is unable to secure a breakthrough in a GRC, the opposition remains a marginal player and at risk of extinction one day. . . . Any talk of checks and balances and alternative government would be just talk, let alone the dream of seeing an opposition party winning an election and taking over the government like in mature Western democracies.[271]

The WP used two key catchphrases to good effect in the lead-up to the 2011 election. The first was that of the need for a "First World Parliament" (drawn from the title of its election manifesto) in Singapore. The PAP made energetic attempts to rebut this vision, questioning its meaning and validity and challenging the WP to expound on this vision.[272] The WP simply maintained that this was a Parliament with a significant number of elected Opposition members, and a Parliament that was accountable to the people.

The second catchphrase, which became a core plank of the WP campaign and an oft-used analogy by Low Thia Khiang, was that the Opposition would be a responsible co-driver to the PAP government, one that would be prepared to reprimand the driver if he veered off track. Low's co-driver analogy was challenged in particular (in what was to become a running battle of co-driver or co-pilot analogies) by Home Affairs and Law Minister K. Shanmugam, who observed, "That is only possible if the co-pilot and pilot work as one team, with 100 per cent trust—not if one is slapping the other."[273]

The WP seemed, as the campaign progressed, able to fend off the persistent attacks by the PAP on the validity of its vision (as well as its slogans), partly because of the hold that the "co-driver" analogy was to take in the imagination of swathes of the electorate. At one rally, Low elaborated on this job of the "co-driver":

> [His job is] to slap the driver when he drives off-course or when he falls asleep or drives dangerously. . . . He supports and advises the driver from time to time and to make sure that he is alert and well enough to complete the journey. . . . When the bus driver falls asleep and drives towards a ravine, would you go behind him and only ask him "uncle why are you sleeping? Can wake up or not? The bus is going to drop down you know?" Slap him lah![274]

A second prong of the PAP attack also came up somewhat short. This was the questioning of the motivations of the WP's star catch, accomplished corporate lawyer Chen Show Mao. Dr Ng Eng Hen, the PAP organising secretary, wrote to the *Straits Times* Forum page criticising the WP for not answering directly why Chen was choosing to enter politics now, after having spent most of the previous three decades away from Singapore. Ng also questioned Chen's ability to identify with the aspirations of Singaporeans.[275] In the minds of independent political observers, the PAP saw Chen as a possible threat, given his undeniably impressive resume and stellar academic credentials (a Rhodes Scholar who boasted degrees from Oxford, Harvard and Stanford). The fact that the Taiwan-born Chen voluntarily served National Service even when not yet a citizen meant that the questioning of his motivations did not diminish him in the eyes of most. Chen was also effectively defended by Low Thia Khiang and WP Chairman Sylvia Lim, with Lim asking in a retort to Ng: "By again raising the question of Show Mao being outside Singapore for a long time, is the People's Action Party signalling to Singaporeans that the return of a successful Singaporean is not welcome? Or is his loyalty being questioned simply because he is with WP?"[276] Perhaps realizing that this line of questioning ran the risk of backfiring, the PAP leadership declared itself more or less satisfied, especially when Low Thia Khiang declared that he too had had initial doubts about Chen, only to have them dispelled when checks and due diligence had been done.[277]

There was a third prong of attack the PAP used against the WP: the charge of "messy" accounts in the Hougang Town Council. Lim Hwee Hua, a minister in the Prime Minister's Office, spoke on the campaign trail of the "troubling" lack of clarity in the accounts for the Town Council. Low Thia Khiang's vehement response included an invitation to the PAP to report him to the Corrupt Practices Investigation Bureau if it had proof of wrongdoing, calling this charge a "personal attack" aimed at discrediting him, and a ruse to "hoodwink the voters" during the critical election period.[278] In the event, the matter did not have any discernible impact on the results at either Hougang SMC or Aljunied GRC. But this issue—that of accounts and more generally the competence of the Opposition to run town councils—was to linger and impact the results of the 2015 general election.

⁂

One of the first chances the electorate had to weigh up the issues—as well as some of the key personalities—came during a televised debate on 2 April 2011 involving PAP and Opposition figures. There were credible performances by the SDP's Dr Vincent Wijeysingha and the WP's Gerald Giam, and a poor showing by Lina Chiam, the wife of SPP leader Chiam See Tong. Lina Chiam's performance almost certainly was a contributing factor to her loss in Potong Pasir (which Chiam See Tong had left in order to stand in a GRC) to the PAP's Sitoh Yih Pin at the polls. In his remarks at the debate, Finance Minister Tharman Shanmugaratnam said that a strong Opposition was good for the PAP and Singapore.[279] This was somewhat at variance with the line that PAP leaders had used in the past: that the PAP would be weakened by a two-party system and that talented Singaporeans aspiring to serve the country should join the PAP.[280]

Tharman's remarks seemed to suggest to some that the era of direct PAP attacks against Opposition figures (and occasionally vice versa) might be replaced by, if not more civilised debate all round, at least a type of electioneering that might see debates on the substance of policy at the forefront. Indeed, SM Goh had in the lead-up to Nomination Day called for a more gentlemanly form of debate: "Go for a clean fight in the upcoming contest in the election, no personal attacks, no rude language. . . . Singapore is a gracious, generous community and the contest should be about which party voters trust to secure you and your children a better future."[281]

Members of the public, too, evinced similar hopes. Letters to the media expressed the desire for a clean and smear-free campaign.[282] Preference for this type of debate seemed to be fuelled by the apparent maturing of the Opposition, manifested most visibly in the intriguing mix of Opposition candidates coming to the fore—men and women like Vincent Wijeysingha, Gerald Giam, Chen Show Mao and several others who were clearly far more inclined to debate issues of policy with far less rancour than had been the case with previous Opposition figures. Several of these individuals could boast stellar academic and professional accomplishments that compared well with those of their PAP rivals. Opposition parties had clearly met with some success in finding (and persuading) a new breed of professional, highly educated individuals to join their cause. The National Solidarity Party's husband-and-wife duo of Tony Tan and Hazel Poa were both former Public Service Commission government scholarship holders. Poa was to be the first former government administrative officer (along with the SPP's Benjamin Pwee, also a former government scholarship holder) to run in an election against the PAP government; her husband, Tony Tan, was a Singapore Armed Forces Merit Scholarship holder who had attained the rank of major.[283] Another Opposition candidate, the SDP's Tan Jee Say, a private investor, had in the 1980s been the principal private secretary to Goh Chok Tong when Goh was the deputy prime minister, before leaving public service to enter the world of fund management.

While the arrival of well-credentialled professionals prepared to throw in their lot with the Opposition certainly boosted individual parties, it was not entirely clear whether the Opposition as a whole was in better shape than it had been in previous elections. The Workers' Party in particular had clearly built itself into a force to be reckoned with, with political observers agreeing that it would pose a stern challenge to the PAP GRC team in Aljunied. Its discipline and cohesion meant that any internal disagreements were kept well out of sight of the media. There was, however, a great deal of infighting in the smaller Opposition parties. In the SDA, Chiam See Tong had a serious falling-out his with protégé Desmond Lim. This was the result, among other issues it appeared, of widespread resistance within most of the parties that made up the SDA to Chiam's idea of allowing Reform Party, helmed by Kenneth Jeyaretnam, to join the SDA.[284] In late February 2011, SDA leaders relieved Chiam of his duties as SDA chairman; two days later, Chiam pulled his Singapore People's Party out of the SDA.[285] Desmond Lim for his part quit the SPP the same month, rejoining the Singapore Justice Party (SJP) as its secretary-general and also becoming secretary-general of the SDA, which now had only two parties left in the alliance: the Singapore Malay National Organisation (PKMS) and the SJP itself.[286]

Kenneth Jeyaretnam's Reform Party (RP) had had similarly mixed fortunes.[287] It was hit by a series of resignations in February 2011 (these included several members of its CEC, including RP Chairman Tan Tee Seng). There appeared to be differences in viewpoints with Jeyaretnam and dissatisfaction with his leadership style.[288] The exodus was to reach as many as 20, with some of the more qualified or charismatic individuals wooed and snapped up by other Opposition parties. These included Hazel Poa and Tony Tan as well as the telegenic and articulate Nicole Seah, who was to feature prominently in the campaign. All three went to the NSP.

The SDP had, with a modicum of success, been trying to profile itself through its policy suggestions (most notably its call for a minimum wage to help low-wage workers cope with the cost of living, an idea it repeated in its economic manifesto released in November 2010).[289] As it did so, it was arguably succeeding to a degree in distancing itself from the abrasive style of Dr Chee Soon Juan, a style that the electorate had traditionally associated with civil disobedience, and which the people as a whole were uncomfortable with.[290] Chee himself appeared on the campaign trail to have mellowed his style, giving thoughtful comments on various topical issues. He was, however, unable to contest the election due to his status as an undischarged bankrupt.[291]

The Opposition parties met in the lead-up to the election in an effort to resolve overlapping claims over single-member constituencies and GRCs. The initial multiparty horse-trading meetings in early March 2011 appeared to have resolved some but not all of the outstanding issues, with the press openly speculating about outstanding disagreements and the possibility of multiple three-cornered fights.[292] Smaller, bilateral meetings appear to have subsequently taken place away from the glare of the media. On Nomination Day, only one constituency—Punggol East SMC—saw a three-cornered fight, with the PAP's Michael Palmer facing off against the WP's Lee Li Lian and the SDA's Desmond Lim.

Voter Sentiment

The PAP manifesto, "Securing Our Future Together", released on 17 April 2011, was the result of an extensive collection of views from the ground—putting it together had involved engaging Party activists, unionists, and average Singaporeans. These views, centred on what a future Singapore should be like, were distilled at the Party leadership level to produce a document that was "simply written and easily read". The key themes of the glossy, image-rich manifesto included growing the economy and finding ways to ensure that every citizen shared in the progress of the nation.[293] Although key hot-button issues were indirectly tackled in other sections—promises were made with regard to affordable and high-quality flats, as well as the MRT network features—these were not in-depth, detailed treatments. And there were few details in terms of how the government intended to tackle issues such as the cost of living, which looked set to feature strongly in the coming election.[294] Surveys carried out by the media just before the election showed the importance of bread-and-butter issues in the minds of voters.[295] This received some support from a small but significant survey carried out during the campaigning period by a respected Malaysian polling firm, the Merdeka Center. Of those polled, 42.9 per cent said that inflation and cost of living were their key concerns (concerns that ranked far ahead of other factors).[296]

As with previous elections, the manifesto simply set what the PAP hoped would be the mood music. Tackling head-on key lightning-rod issues had to be done elsewhere. An example was housing. The WP had blamed the government's asset enhancement policies for the high prices of HDB flats, and offered alternative proposals in its election manifesto, launched on 9 April 2016.[297] Mah Bow Tan, the national development minister, called the Workers' Party proposals to lower the price of new HDB flats "dangerous", singling out in particular the suggestion to lower flat prices by paying less for state land. This, he claimed, would amount to an "illegal raid" on Singapore's reserves.[298] In defending the existing policy, Mah stressed that the government would "continue to ensure that HDB flats will be both a home and an asset for successive generations".[299] The WP stuck to its guns, however, and the housing issue became a subject of protracted debate on the campaign trail between the two parties. Low

Thia Khiang was able to score points by doggedly sticking to the theme of housing affordability, pointing out escalating property costs and warning of the financial burden on the younger generation, who would be "mortgaging their future if they spend their whole lives paying for the housing mortgage".[300]

The PAP's guns were not trained solely on the WP. The SDP could not be ignored completely. Its suite of alternative policy proposals seemed to resonate, at least more so than in any previous election. Its campaign was helped not just by Dr Chee Soon Juan's more muted style. It had intelligent and coherent candidates, and a good new media strategy (including the most regularly updated website).[301]

In Holland–Bukit Timah GRC, the "A" team of the SDP (Ang Yong Guan, Michelle Lee, Tan Jee Say and Dr Vincent Wijeysingha) against the PAP incumbents (Christopher de Souza, Liang Eng Hwa, Sim Ann and Dr Vivian Balakrishnan, the anchor minister) became embroiled in a spat that appeared more personal than political. The issue in question was first raised on 24 April 2011, three days before Nomination Day, by Dr Balakrishnan in an interview with the *Straits Times*. Balakrishnan said that the SDP was suppressing a video "which raised some very awkward questions about the agenda and motivations of the SDP candidates".[302] Since the comment at first caused widespread puzzlement, it was followed up with a clarificatory statement by all PAP candidates in the Holland–Bukit Timah GRC slate asking whether the SDP harboured a "gay agenda". At the heart of the issue was a video posted online (which featured, amongst other things, Dr Wijeysingha participating in a gay rights forum). The PAP team was clear that Dr Wijeysingha's sexual orientation was not the issue; the issue was whether he and the SDP would pursue the gay cause in the political arena. In response, Dr Chee Soon Juan stated that no such agenda existed, and that the individuals on the SDP team had stepped forward for no other reason than to serve Singaporeans. Chee also called the PAP statement on the matter personal attacks and "smear tactics".[303]

The reaction to the PAP questioning of Dr Wijeysingha's motives was decidedly mixed, and overwhelmingly negative online.[304] Some observers speculated that this was nothing more than a tactic used by the PAP in order to put the SDP on the defensive, and perhaps to pre-emptively divert attention from PAP vulnerabilities. These included the public criticism over the fact that Singapore's hosting of the Youth Olympic Games (YOG) in 2010 (overseen by Minister Vivian Balakrishnan) had seen the government spend some $387 million, more than three times the original budget.[305]

In addition, the contest in Holland-Bukit Timah GRC looked to be shaping up to be a close one, with some speculating that the high proportion of middle-class and upper-middle-class voters in the GRC might be more amenable to the SDP's political liberalism and its alternative economic platform.[306] This gay smear was, according to some commentators, bound to have some effect on the electorate in the GRC and make them think twice about voting for the SDP, especially given that many residents of the GRC were thought to be socially and religiously conservative.

At any rate, the point had been made. By the time Nomination Day came, Dr Balakrishnan clearly felt that while the questions he had posed with his team were legitimate ones, they had been answered by Chee Soon Juan and there was no need for the matter to be raised again during the campaign.[307] The calculation may have been that drawing out the matter would have risked a real-world (and not just online) backlash against the PAP. Balakrishnan may also have been taking a lead from the Party leadership. Asked by the media on Nomination Day about smear tactics, PM Lee (without directly commenting on the video) set out his view and what was presumably the Party line:

> *This should be a clean fight. I mean we are fighting on serious matters concerning the lives of Singaporeans and we should focus our minds on. . . . Character is not irrelevant. The quality of a candidate is not irrelevant but this is not a matter of personal attacks on people, this is a matter of trying to decide who are qualified to represent the voters and if there is something which is relevant to that and it has to be brought out, well, it has to be properly brought out and discussed.*[308]

PM Lee's injunction concerning a clean fight was well received, but this was followed by a curious statement from Senior Minister Goh Chok Tong, which, while not actually a smear, struck a somewhat discordant note. This was Goh's frank appraisal of the man who had once been his principal private secretary, the SDP's Tan Jee Say. Tan, in Goh's view, had been able and hard-working but not good enough to be a permanent secretary.[309] This, together with incidents like the Vincent Wijeysingha saga, led to accusations not just from the Opposition but also from sections of the public that the PAP had chosen to hit below the belt.[310] There was the wider impression, too, that the PAP was running a campaign that was not as coordinated or disciplined as previous ones. SM Goh, for example, said to the media on 2 May 2011 that losing Foreign Minister George Yeo in Aljunied would be a huge loss—an obvious point, but he added for good measure, and somewhat inexplicably, "What mistake has he made? Ask yourselves. You can take a minister, you can criticise him for not delivering perhaps on housing, on transport. Like Wong Kan Seng can say vote him out because he let Mas Selamat escape. So George Yeo, what has he done to deserve this?"[311]

The May 2006 general election had seen blogs and podcasts play a noticeable but on the whole limited role. In 2011 social media came to the fore, with Facebook and to a lesser extent Twitter playing roles in disseminating information, news and gossip. The effect of the development of the social media space was liberating to individuals, with for the first time in the election political matters discussed in a completely open and fearless vein. The overall effect of social media was to ensure that issues (such as Tin Pei Ling, or MM Lee's "repent" comment, which we will presently come to) kept circulating, even when the media and PAP politicians attempted to move on. The overall effect was that a significant part of framing the discourse of key issues, usually done either by PAP heavyweights or by the mainstream media, had now passed out of their hands into a volatile and unpredictable online space.[312] On the whole, this space was characterised by an unforgiving, largely anti-PAP tenor, which almost became the default. There was no genuine sense of there being any middle ground, with very few voices of moderation. The key platforms that had come online, or else grown in popularity since the 2006 general election, seemed firmly in the thrall of anti-PAP voices.[313] Few prominent figures in the Singapore social media space evinced support for the PAP; when one of them, Wendy Cheng—a well-known blogger (but not known for blogging on serious sociopolitical issues) better known under her moniker Xiaxue came out during and soon after the campaign period with posts supportive of the PAP (and in particular George Yeo and the PAP's Aljunied team), she came under sustained attack by others in the Singapore online community.[314]

﹋

The increased number of SMCs (12—up from nine previously) had triggered something of an Opposition scramble that saw various parties staking claims. Realising that a number of close contests were probably in the offing in the SMCs, the PAP tasked MPs who were very well-known quantities to stand in these constituencies. These were individuals who, in many cases, had previously polled strongly in divisions within GRCs that had now been carved out to form SMCs. These included Dr Lam Pin Min (Sengkang West SMC, formerly part of Aljunied GRC), Heng Chee How (Whampoa SMC, formerly part of Jalan Besar GRC), Lim Biow Chuan (Mountbatten SMC, formerly part of Marine Parade GRC), Cedric Foo (Pioneer SMC, formerly part of West Coast GRC), Michael Palmer (Punggol East SMC, formerly part of Pasir Ris–Punggol GRC), and Grace Fu (Yuhua SMC, formerly part of Jurong GRC).[315] These individuals had, of course, the incumbent's advantage. But others now fielded in SMCs had been specifically redeployed. The popular and durable (five-term) backbencher Charles Chong, formerly in the Pasir Ris–Punggol GRC, was fielded in Joo Chiat SMC, where a strong Opposition showing was expected. Chong had been used as a "troubleshooter" before, leaving Sembawang GRC in the 1991 general election to contest in the Eunos GRC against a WP team helmed by Dr Lee Siew Choh, in what turned out to be a close victory for the PAP.[316]

Besides the SMCs, some GRCs were shaping up to be hotspots. In the white heat of the campaigning, Party activists and candidates canvassing on the ground encountered at numerous turns a sullen, visceral mood of resentment, the depths of which were fully understood only during the course of the campaign. Of course, some of this had been sensed in advance. PM Lee recalled:

> *Just before the actual campaign, I did two forums on television called "Question Time with the Prime Minister", one in English and one in Chinese. Small groups of about a dozen people each. I had done the same in 2006. In 2006 it went off swimmingly, but this time the people who came were very querulous, both the Chinese as well as the English group. I had met them beforehand, we had a chat, and they were completely equable and amenable during the chat. This was just to get to know one another. But when they went on television, the tone totally changed and they said "My people want me to ask these questions", and it was quite a hostile pitch. Some of them were retirees, some of them were PMEs. We*

*did not handpick them. They were very vocal, and I did not like the feel. So I
suppose that was a sign; it was not a very good feel.*[317]

Looking back on this, as well as the campaign that followed, PM Lee was clear that
to him the issue was not so much the percentage that the Party ended up with. The
surprise to him was the feeling on the ground:

> *So it looked as if it was a calm situation, but by the end of the election campaign
> that was no longer the position. Did we mis-sense or did the position change and
> we could not catch up? My inclination is it was a combination of both, because I
> think that the nine days makes a big difference. So that is part of it. . . . I think
> we were taken aback by the mood. You must expect a drift from time to time on
> the percentage. It is a more open and more contested environment. So I would
> not have been astonished if you had told me beforehand that we will end with
> 60 per cent of the votes, but what surprised me was the harshness of the tone, the
> generational divide in the attitudes, and the degree to which the things people
> were unhappy with could escalate in a short period of time.*[318]

The attention of the press and commentators was trained particularly on Aljunied
GRC, where the PAP team received a generally civil but cool reception while walking
the ground. George Yeo (foreign minister), Zainul Abidin Rasheed (senior minister
of state for foreign affairs), Lim Hwee Hua (minister in the Prime Minister's Office),
Ong Ye Kung (seen by many as a certain appointee to the ranks of office-holders
if elected), and Cynthia Phua were in the fight of their political lives against the
WP "A" team of Low Thia Khiang, Sylvia Lim, Pritam Singh, Chen Show Mao and
Muhamad Faisal Manap. The likelihood that the GRC would again see a serious
contest had been discussed at the Party level soon after the 2006 general election.
Consider the following from the Party organ *Petir*, an account of the 11 November
2007 PAP convention:

> *Besides national issues, party-level issues were raised too. At least two people
> brought up the matter of winning Aljunied GRC at the next election. One
> member praised Mr George Yeo, the Party's heavyweight MP for Aljunied GRC,
> but noted that as he was also the foreign minister, he was often not in town. Mr
> Lee [prime minister and Party secretary-general Lee Hsien Loong] responded that
> despite his busy schedule, Mr Yeo made time to visit his constituency. As for the
> Workers' Party, most of their Aljunied team have dropped out of sight, said Mr
> Lee, a point he made at the Central Singapore CDC dialogue a few weeks earlier.
> The "A" in the WP's A-team stood for AWOL (absent without official leave), he
> added, eliciting laughter. Mr Lim [Lim Boon Heng, the Party chairman] assured
> that he is not worried about losing Aljunied at the next elections because the
> GRC's MPs work harder than the average MP. "Maybe those of you who think
> you're safe should work harder," he said.*[319]

This may have been the perception in 2007. But the WP had, in fact, been continuously active and walking the ground in the aftermath of the 2006 election.[320] The WP had also looked closely at the reasons for its loss in the GRC in 2006. It had come to the conclusion that the lack of support from minorities, and particularly from the Malay community, had been a key contributing factor. Attempts were made to broaden the WP's multiracial appeal, and serious efforts were made—with partial success—to attract Malays to join the WP.[321]

Low Thia Khiang had stirred the imagination of Opposition supporters, and many undecided voters, in his attempt to break out from his Hougang stronghold. And, as often was the case, Low had ready an apt—and colourful—turn of phrase to match the occasion. Quoting a well-known Chinese proverb, he commented to the press, "We know there is a tiger on the mountain, but we are moving towards that mountain" [明知山有虎，偏向虎山行].[322] This was not just a one-man show: convincing voices had now been added to the roster in Aljunied, and in Pritam Singh the WP had found an excellent public speaker.

The WP rallies in Aljunied were extremely well attended. And unlike in 2006, the press reported the scale of these rallies. The PAP did not seem unduly concerned—it had seen huge rallies before, and its stock line was that many there were not necessarily supporters of the Opposition but merely curious. The PAP team in Aljunied did not have glaring weaknesses. Its town council had performed well in tending to residents' municipal needs. There were, however, question marks that were exploited by the WP team, or by netizens. One was Foreign Minister George Yeo's frequent absences from the GRC and the country.[323] Other points—not so much ignited by the WP but more in the vein of coffeeshop talk—that went viral on the ground during the campaign concerned the feisty and outspoken MP for the Paya Lebar division of Aljunied GRC (and also the chairman of the Aljunied Town Council), Cynthia Phua. Late in the hustings, Phua, who had the reputation of being an extremely hard-working MP but very direct in her dealings with residents, apologised for ruffling feathers in her quest to "get things done" in Aljunied GRC.[324] Also not forgotten was the 2008 furore involving the proposed dormitory to be built for foreign workers in the middle of the comfortably middle-class Serangoon Gardens estate. Lim Hwee Hua, the MP for the division (which fell within Aljunied), worked tirelessly with the authorities to allay residents' concerns over the proposal to repurpose an unused school building into the dormitory. She may have convinced some residents, but not others. This episode— essentially a case of not-in-my-backyard syndrome on the part of some residents—was to cost Lim votes in 2011.[325]

A final issue that played into the Aljunied result should be considered here. This concerned comments made by MM Lee on the Malay community in a book that had been published in 2011, *Hard Truths*. In this book, which had at its core interviews of Lee conducted by a team of journalists, Lee made a series of extremely direct comments about the Malay community, and the state of its integration with Singapore society.[326] MM Lee's views led to discontent within quarters of the Malay-Muslim community, with the likely impact of these comments certainly recognised by the rest of the PAP leadership. PM Lee (as well as other PAP figures) stated that these were not views they held, and that Singapore Malays were in fact better integrated than MM Lee had suggested.[327] But some of the damage could not be undone.[328]

The PAP team in Aljunied could promise an attractive suite of upgrading and improvement services, all coming under their local manifesto, "Kuay Teow Hot and Nice".[329] Naturally, they were keen at rallies to showcase this programme and to show up the WP's lack of any equivalent plan. But the WP team doggedly refused to be drawn in on local issues despite repeated challenges for it to show how it would improve the lives of residents of the GRC. Instead, the WP kept to its theme of a "First World Parliament". There were also attacks against the GRC system, which Low Thia Khiang said served the interests of the PAP and blocked Opposition politicians from entering Parliament. "Let me tell you, if no opposition is able to break through the GRC, you will be forever shackled by the system. The PAP will continue to govern, and to bully you without having to account to you all," he said at the party's first rally in Aljunied GRC.[330] Low was thus recycling his earlier theme from 2006: the idea that the light of the Opposition should not be extinguished, this time allowing people to get the impression that if the WP bid in Aljunied failed, there was the real possibility that the Opposition might be completely shut out of Parliament. Responding, the PAP team accused the WP of "playing with the lives" of Aljunied voters and using them as a "springboard" to gain power, without caring overmuch about the residents themselves.[331] Still, the point that a PAP victory might portend the near-destruction of the Opposition as a national force for the future was something that preyed on the minds of Aljunied voters. The contest had thus been transformed into something far bigger than control of the GRC itself.

Ong Ye Kung reflected on this:

> There is a huge cost to domination. When Low Thia Khiang suggested that 87–0 was a real possibility, this stirred something powerful in people's minds, and this had perhaps more of an impact than Mr Lee Kuan Yew's "repent" remark. An affluent society breeds expectation and a stronger desire for opposition. The people want the PAP in power but also want an Opposition. So Aljunied turned into a microcosm of this—people got the idea that these five seats, where the WP had fielded its best team, should go to the WP, especially as Low had vacated Hougang and there was no guarantee that the Opposition might win there.[332]

The PAP leadership recognised this risk, of course. In what could be seen as ameliorative attempts, various key figures talked up the potential of individual Aljunied team members. PM Lee promised to appoint Zainul Abidin Rasheed Speaker of Parliament if he was re-elected, with SM Goh Chok Tong observing that George Yeo was "too important a person for the Cabinet to lose". Goh went further, also noting that Aljunied voters could get a "win-win" outcome by electing the PAP team in Aljunied: George Yeo would remain an office-holder, with Low Thia Khiang still able to enter Parliament through the NCMP route.[333] These blandishments did not seem to have much of an effect. In any case, the WP was able to come out with effective counters, pointing out that Zainul Abidin Rasheed could still be Speaker of Parliament without being an elected MP, and—not entirely tongue in cheek—that George Yeo could still run for the elected presidency if the PAP lost Aljunied.[334]

Perhaps the most talked-about campaign utterance, and one with a very pronounced bearing on the Aljunied result, came from MM Lee. Commenting on the close contest in the GRC on 30 April 2011, he said that "it would not be the end of the world" if Aljunied went with the Workers' Party, adding for good measure—somewhat ominously—that "if Aljunied decides to go that way [vote WP], well Aljunied has five years to live and repent".[335] Predictably, there was an immediate backlash. In the words of George Yeo, speaking five days later at his final rally speech on 5 May 2011, Lee's remarks had "created greater anger, greater resentment in many people".[336]

The issue of resentment from the people—not just in reaction to MM Lee's remarks but tied to some policy missteps and miscalculations—had to be tackled. At his lunchtime rally on 3 May at Boat Quay, PM Lee made an unprecedented apology, notable for its humility in tone, for the government's mistakes. His comments tackled issues on two broad fronts. The first was the apology itself, encompassing an acknowledgement of the depth of feeling against the PAP from a wide swathe of the electorate, and a promise that the PAP government was working to fix the issues:

> No government is perfect. We can have our best intentions, make our best efforts, but from time to time, mistakes will happen. We will make mistakes. We made a mistake when we let Mas Selamat run away. We made a mistake when Orchard Road got flooded. And there are other mistakes which we have made from time to time, and I'm sure occasionally will happen again—I hope not too often. But when it happens, then we should acknowledge it, we should apologise, take responsibility, put things right, if we have to discipline somebody we will do that, and we must learn from the lessons, and never make the same mistake again.
>
> So we didn't get it perfect, and I appreciate and I sympathise with Singaporeans when they tell me and they tell the government repeatedly that this is impacting us, affecting us—do something about it. Well, we're sorry we didn't get it exactly right, but I hope you'll understand and bear with us, because we're trying our best to fix the problems—building twenty-two thousand flats this year, opening one new MRT line or extension line every year for the next seven years, investing in our people, in our future, coming back on course, continuing to make progress.[337]

The second aspect of PM Lee's remarks was an attempt to assuage those who had been hurt (or, in Aljunied, swayed to the WP) by MM Lee's words. Here, PM Lee explicitly referenced the difference in the way MM Lee did things from the younger generation of leaders:

> We've had a PAP government in Singapore now for more than fifty years, since 1959. Our ideals, our passion hasn't changed. But our policies have been updated, our approach has shifted, our style has changed. You know MM's style. He tells

it like it is. When he tells you something, you know exactly what he is thinking and what he is talking about—straight from the shoulder—no ifs, no buts, solid hard talk.

You know—I think you have gotten used to our style. We understand the hard truths, we understand what we need to do, but we cannot do it and we don't try to do it MM's style. We do it our way; we spend some time to talk, to explain, to persuade, to understand the difficulties and the hesitations, to overcome some of these working problems, so that we can go in the right strategic direction.

. . . So give us time, I think we know what we are doing, we will work with Singaporeans in our own way to deliver results. So MM understands that. But MM is MM, and whether it is ordinary times, whether it's election time, you can be sure it's still the same MM. But this is the PAP government—me, my team, and we are taking it forward—same strategic direction, but doing it our way. So I hope voters will understand and will support what we are doing.[338]

PM Lee's apology attracted a great deal of comment and, as might have been expected, criticism from Opposition figures, who questioned the motives behind the apology, hinting that nothing within the PAP would really change. WP leaders in particular argued that the apology would never have been forthcoming without a strong Opposition to challenge the PAP, and that an effective Opposition presence in Parliament was required to ensure that the PAP would continue to listen to the people.[339]

Why was it necessary, and what had the PM actually intended? He explained his thinking in 2014:

MM Lee said that the people of Aljunied will repent if they vote for the Opposition. That unfortunately caused a lot of unhappiness. So one of the things I had to do for the rally was to do some repair job on that. I had to say MM is MM—he has his views and he sticks to his ways. We have a different style, and we operate like this.

On the apology itself: people read a lot more into it than I had intended. It was not meant to be a deep bow or a mea culpa. But the fact was there were policy shortcomings or side effects which had an impact on people. Not everything has worked out well. That is a fact, and I think we had to acknowledge it. I went down to Aljunied GRC to campaign for George Yeo, and when we went round, the ground was cold. After that we sat down at a coffee shop with George and his team and he said well, it is very difficult. His own branch member, an old Malay member, had come to him in tears and said, "Can't you do something? Can't you change something?" A certain mood had taken hold; the feeling was that all these things had happened and the government are not taking responsibility. I decided that if I am going to say that there are problems, I might as well say for the problems we are responsible, we apologise for them. And that was as far as it was meant to go. I did not expect it to have

*an enormous bang, but I suppose it had been so long since we actually explicitly
said sorry for anything. It changed the mood. I do not know how much it
changed the votes, but it changed the mood, and I could have stabilised the
national position in the last few days.*[340]

There were no illusions, however, that the apology had turned the tide against the WP
in Aljunied.[341] The WP seemed to have succeeded in framing the issues and had made
almost no mistakes. The PAP seemed to have been unable to break through, to ignite
its own campaign, and score telling points of its own. In the last days of the campaign
(and particularly on the final campaigning day itself), the PAP anchor in Aljunied,
George Yeo, went further than he or any PAP candidate had gone before in any election
in promising a rethink of how the PAP governed. In a short video uploaded online on 3
May 2011, Yeo acknowledged that many young Singaporeans "think the Government
is arrogant and high-handed". He pledged, "I will be your voice in Government. I will
listen to what you have to say. . . . In whatever way I can, I will speak up for you in
Government and in Cabinet."[342] Yeo was to further acknowledge on 5 May (the last
day of campaigning) in an interview that there was "considerable resentment against
the Government and its policies, and some of them run deep".[343] Yeo said that he had
noted the "cry from the heart" among Singaporeans. The PAP had to listen harder
to the people's grievances, and not be "too quick to defend, to explain or to justify".
Finally, Yeo pledged that his Aljunied team would, if re-elected, be the voices of reform
in Cabinet and Parliament.[344]

Result

Just 15 minutes into the counting of the votes on Polling Day, 7 May 2011, Ong Ye
Kung could tell that the battle was lost. Kaki Bukit, the ward Ong was contesting
within Aljunied GRC, had long been thought to be the division within the GRC least
likely to be affected by the WP "breakout effect" from Hougang, which had until 2011
been held by Low Thia Khiang. With the votes in Kaki Bukit polling even with the
Opposition, he knew that the PAP team was headed for defeat.[345] At almost the same
time, George Yeo, the lynchpin of the PAP team in Aljunied, also arrived at the same
conclusion. Yeo was mentally prepared, having in fact been privately forewarned by a
professional pollster that the PAP team would garner 43–47 per cent of the vote.[346]

For his part, Low Thia Khiang, almost always cool and rational, had not been
entirely sure whether the greatest gamble of his life would pay off in Aljunied, choosing
on Polling Day to prepare both victory and concession speeches.[347] In the end, the
latter proved unnecessary. The WP took the GRC, winning 54.72 per cent of the vote
there, the first time a GRC had fallen into Opposition hands. The PAP saw a drop of
10.8 percentage points over the 2006 result in Aljunied, a difference of 12,433 votes.
The Aljunied defeat meant that at one fell swoop the Party lost three office-holders:
George Yeo, Zainul Abidin Rasheed, and Lim Hwee Hua (the sole female minister in
Cabinet). In addition, the new candidate in the PAP's Aljunied slate, Ong Ye Kung,
who would certainly have joined the ranks of the leadership if elected, was now in the

political wilderness. In his victory speech at Hougang Stadium on 8 May 2016, Low declared to euphoric supporters—indeed some quarters of those present were in near-delirium—that they had made history: "Your votes tell the government that what you want is a home and not just a house. Your votes tell the world that Singapore is not just an economic success to you. Singapore is our home." Low added for good measure, "Your votes tell the world you want Singapore to mature as a democracy, that you want to tell the government that you want a more responsive, inclusive, transparent, accountable government."[348]

Nationally, the PAP garnered 60.14 per cent of the total votes (its worst performance since independence in 1965), winning 81 out of 87 seats. For the first time since 1966, Parliament would have six elected Opposition members (eclipsing the Opposition's previous record—four seats in the 1991 polls). All would be from the WP. Overall, the WP was clearly the main beneficiary of the nationwide swing against the PAP. Its overall vote share where it contested climbed from 38.43 per cent in 2006 to 47.03 per cent, well above the average of 36.53 per cent for the other five Opposition parties.[349] The WP's second-strongest GRC team, its "B" team in East Coast GRC, took 45.17 per cent of the vote against a PAP team that included two full ministers (Raymond Lim and Lim Swee Say). Even the WP team in Moulmein–Kallang GRC (seen by observers as its weakest GRC team) managed 41.45 per cent of the vote. Victory for Low Thia Khiang in Aljunied was made sweeter by the fact that his chosen replacement in the Hougang SMC, Yaw Shin Leong, was able to easily defeat the PAP's Desmond Choo with 64.8 per cent of the vote, improving even on Low's own winning margin from 2006 (62.7 per cent). Elsewhere, the WP candidate in Joo Chiat SMC, Yee Jenn Jong, lost by a mere 382 votes against the PAP's Charles Chong (who took 51.02 per cent of the vote, with the SMC seeing a 14 percentage point fall in support for the PAP from 2006).[350]

Some key GRCs saw the PAP polling lower than its national average. These included Bishan–Toa Payoh (56.93 per cent) and Tampines (57.22 per cent). The anchor ministers for Bishan–Toa Payoh and Tampines, Deputy Prime Minister Wong Kan Seng and Minister for National Development Mah Bow Tan, had helmed ministries or overseen issues linked to serious levels of public dissatisfaction. DPM Wong, whose team defeated an SPP team led by Opposition veteran Chiam See Tong (in his first foray into a GRC), remained linked in the minds of many with the 2008 escape of the terrorist Mas Selamat Kastari, while Mah's tenure as national development minister had seen rising unhappiness over the cost of housing. East Coast GRC also saw a below-par PAP showing—54.83 per cent against the WP's "B" team. The PAP team there was anchored by Minister in the Prime Minister's Office Lim Swee Say, but the slate also had another minister overseeing hot-button issues, in this case Minister for Transport Raymond Lim.

The margins in several other SMCs and GRCs were noteworthy. Nicole Seah, the seeming political ingénue, turned out to be the standout of an unheralded NSP team that took to the field against the PAP's Marine Parade GRC team, led by Senior Minister Goh Chok Tong (and which also could boast a likely office-holder, former army general Tan Chuan-Jin). Seah's 90,000 "likes" on her Facebook account surpassed even those of MM Lee, making her (by social media measures, at least) the most popular Singaporean politician. But more important, Seah's star turn meant that the NSP team scored a very respectable 43.36 per cent, or a hefty 59,833 votes versus the PAP's 78,182. SM Goh acknowledged the below-par showing by the PAP team: "I was expecting, to be frank, a slightly better result . . . it's a new situation. There is a sea change in the political landscape."[351]

A few other PAP candidates had a somewhat easier time. The best performing of these, Dr Amy Khor, scored 70.61 per cent in Hong Kah North against Sin Kek Tong from the SPP. The Ang Mo Kio GRC team, led by PM Lee, took 69.33 per cent of the vote against a Reform Party team. In doing so, this PAP team actually improved on its 2006 performance by just over 3 percentage points—the only PAP GRC team to improve on its 2006 previous outing.[352] The PAP team in Jurong GRC, led by Finance Minister Tharman Shanmugaratnam, also performed credibly, with 66.96 per cent of the vote against an NSP team.

Two single-member constituencies saw recounts that eventually went the way of the PAP by the narrowest of margins. One was Charles Chong's victory in Joo Chiat, mentioned above. The other saw Lina Chiam, standing in Singapore's longest-surviving Opposition bastion, Potong Pasir, losing to the PAP's Sitoh Yih Pin by a mere 114 votes (49.64 per cent versus 50.36 per cent). Knowledgeable observers agreed that Sitoh's low-key approach and personal campaign strategy were key factors in the win. Sitoh insisted on keeping PAP heavyweights away from the constituency, and avoiding dangling huge infrastructural carrots as enticements. It was also known before the election that he had declined PAP offers to let him contest in a Group Representation Constituency team.[353] Sitoh's efforts and his commitment to stay the course (this was his third tilt at Potong Pasir) swayed voters.

Opposition parties such as the SDA and RP were in general unable to match the significant inroads made by the WP.[354] Some mention, however, should be made of the SDP. Holland–Bukit Timah GRC, where the SDP fielded its strongest team, turned out in the end not to be such a close fight as some had predicted, with the SDP team taking only 39.9 per cent of the vote. Overall, the SDP's vote share of 36.8 per cent in the constituencies it contested was a creditable 13.6 per cent jump over what it had obtained in 2006, which some observers put down to a moderation of its confrontational image. In general, though (and away from Holland–Bukit Timah GRC, which was made up of largely middle-class and well-to-do households), the SDP suffered from a lack of heartland (in particular, Chinese-speaking) support.[355]

The PAP had suffered its most serious electoral reverse since 1984, and, perhaps for the first time since 1991, there was some sense in the offing of beginnings towards a two-party system. Certainly, the Workers' Party would now be a force in the next Parliament, given its stellar electoral performance. Besides its six elected MPs, it also had two non-constituency MP slots to fill.

In taking questions from the press during the customary early morning post-election press conference, PM Lee evinced the sense that there might be a way for the PAP and the Opposition to have a constructive relationship, one that would not hinder the policymaking process or cause political gridlock.[356] Lee also called for national unity and acknowledged that the PAP needed to do some "soul searching":

> *While voters have given the PAP a strong mandate, many voters, including some of those who voted for us, have also clearly expressed their significant concerns, both on the issues and on our approach to government. We hear all your voices, whether it's expressed in person or over the Internet. The PAP will analyse the results of the elections, learn from what has emerged in this General Election, put right what is wrong, improve what can be made better, and also improve ourselves to serve Singaporeans better. . . . It's time for healing and for acceptance of the people's decisions, not just for the PAP but for all Singaporeans. The political contest goes on in every country in one form or other. But in Singapore, we must make sure it's harnessed for the good to make Singapore stronger and never to divide us.[357]*

PM Lee in his comments did not go as far as George Yeo, who in some of his last campaign remarks (as well as just after the polls) had come close to suggesting a serious emotional disconnect between the PAP and the ground, and a pressing need for the PAP to transform itself.[358] But what was clear from PM Lee's remarks was that the Party would learn, engage and attempt to find ways to forge national unity. The coming months would see intense soul-searching within the PAP and would constitute a critical phase in the future course of the Party.

Very few could have foreseen, however, that the nadir of the PAP's fortunes had not yet come, and that the Party would receive further serious setbacks—only partly of its own making—over the next two years. Only then would the tide begin to turn.

Notes

1   "Priority: Securing Home Base", *Straits Times*, 5 Dec. 2006.

2   President S.R. Nathan, address at the opening of Parliament, 2 Nov. 2006. Singapore Parliamentary Debates, 2 Nov. 2006.

3   "Priority: Securing Home Base".

4   "Meritocracy, Singapore Style", *Straits Times*, 4 Dec. 2006.

5   As we have seen, there were murmurings along precisely these lines after the 2006 election. See for example chapter 5, pp. 352–3 and 388–9n191.

6   "How Meritocracy Can Breed Intellectual Elitism", *Straits Times*, 10 Nov. 2006. A critique of the evolving nature of meritocracy in Singapore at this time can be found in Kenneth Paul Tan, "Meritocracy and Elitism in a Global City: Ideological Shifts in Singapore", *International Political Science Review* 29, 1 (2008): 7–27.

7   As the *Straits Times* noted, in the previous five years one in three students awarded scholarships came from households that had an income of more than $10,000 a month (such households made up just 13% of the total). Awardees coming from households

earning less than $2,000 a month made up only 7% of scholarship winners. "Why the Elite Envy?", *Straits Times*, 9 Dec. 2006.

8   Ibid. Reflections on elitism inevitably meant broader ruminations on Singapore's meritocratic model. One senior journalist was moved to comment around this time on a "creeping, merit based elitism. . . . Rather than assume the elitist position that Singapore's meritocratic system is so well-oiled that those who don't succeed deserve to fail, we should be taking a more rigorous look at how our much-vaunted meritocratic system may be failing those who deserve to succeed." "How Meritocracy Can Breed Intellectual Elitism".

9   Between 2000 and 2005, the average monthly household income for the top 10% of resident employed households grew by 13.4%. But household income for the bottom decile of resident employed households decreased by 9%. See "Average Monthly Household Income from Work (Including Employer CPF Contributions) among Resident Employed Households by Deciles, 2000–2020 (Table 14A)" (Department of Statistics), available at https://www.tablebuilder.singstat.gov.sg/publicfacing/createSpecialTable. action?refId=17262 (accessed 5 Mar. 2021).

10   Singapore Parliamentary Debates, 15 Feb. 2007, col. 1401.

11   It peaked at 0.48 in 2007. For the Gini coefficient during this period, see "Income Growth, Mobility and Inequality Trends in Singapore", Ministry of Finance Occasional Paper, Aug. 2015, available at https://www.mof.gov.sg/Portals/0/Feature%20Articles/ Income%20Growth,%20Distribution%20and%20Mobility%20Trends%20in%20 Singapore.pdf; and (for 2006 and 2007) "Household Income Grew amidst Strong Economic Performance", Department of Statistics press release, 13 Feb. 2008, available at https://www.nas.gov.sg/archivesonline/speeches/record-details/7f0a3c1b-115d-11e3-83d5-0050568939ad (accessed 6 Mar. 2021).

12   "PM: Let's Tackle Cost Fears Together", *Straits Times*, 4 Feb. 2008; "Economic Growth Key to Dealing with Rising Costs: PM", *Straits Times*, 9 Feb. 2008. For inflation data, see "T6. Percent Change in Consumer Price Index (CPI) over Corresponding Period of Previous Year, 2019 as Base Year, Annual" (Department of Statistics, n.d.), available at https://www.singstat.gov.sg/-/media/files/publications/economy/excel/cpimar20.xlsx (accessed 30 Apr. 2020).

13   "We Can Barely Stay Afloat, Say Low-Income Folk", *Sunday Times*, 2 Dec. 2007. The PAP's own figures showed a rising trend in terms of individuals coming to seek MPs' help. In the mid-1980s, when records were first kept, there were about 35,000 cases a year; in 2006 there were over 157,000. "Meet-the-People Sessions Get More Complex", *Petir*, Mar.–Apr. 2007, p. 11.

14   Yeoh Lam Keong, "Rethinking a New Social Compact for Singapore", *Ethos* 3 (2007): 7–12, available at https://www.csc.gov.sg/articles/rethinking-a-new-social-compact-for-singapore (accessed 7 Jan. 2020).

15   "Spore Way to Fight Rising Cost of Living Works: PM", *Straits Times*, 12 Nov. 2007.

16   Singapore Parliamentary Debates, 13 Nov. 2007, col. 692.

17   "MPs Laud Budget as 'Creative, Generous'", *Straits Times*, 28 Feb. 2007. The budget had also seen a restoration of the CPF employer's contribution rate by 1.5 percentage points, a cut in corporate tax, and an offset package to take the sting out of the hike in GST from 5% to 7%.

18   Singapore Parliamentary Debates, 9 Mar. 2007, col. 3514.

19   The actual increase in public assistance was 10–14%. Neo was supported by other PAP
     MPs, including Sin Boon Ann, who commented, "the fact remains that we come across
     people who are indeed hungry, people who are left out, basically fall through the cracks".
     Singapore Parliamentary Debates, 9 Mar. 2007, col. 3515. See also "Exchange Pits Head
     against Heart", *Straits Times*, 10 Mar. 2007.

20   Singapore Parliamentary Debates, 9 Mar. 2007, col. 3536. For online reaction, see, for
     example, Siew Kum Hong, "How Many Portions of Help, Sir?", 31 Mar. 2007, available
     at http://siewkumhong.blogspot.sg/2007/03/how-many-portions-of-help-sir.html
     (accessed 26 Jan. 2021). The minister's other comment—that the system was set up with
     a certain amount of "healthy tension", with help available for those who genuinely needed
     it and were prepared to look for it—went relatively unnoticed. Singapore Parliamentary
     Debates, 9 Mar. 2007, cols 3536–7. Neo's own point—that more help for those at the
     bottom was not necessarily at odds with the principles of responsibility or self-reliance
     (and still less a call for mass welfarism)—was something on which she was to cross swords
     with Balakrishnan again in later years. "From the Gallery: Women in the House Make
     Themselves Heard", *Straits Times*, 9 Mar. 2011.

21   "But Is It Socialist Enough?", *Straits Times*, 3 Nov. 2008.

22   Singapore Parliamentary Debates, 10 Nov. 2006, col. 488.

23   Ibid., col. 489.

24   For a description of the social safety net at this time from the government point of view,
     see "Improving the Lives of Low-Income and Vulnerable Families in Singapore", Ministry
     of Social and Family Development Occasional Paper, Nov. 2018, pp. 6–7, available at
     https://www.msf.gov.sg/publications/Documents/Improving%20the%20lives%20of%20
     low-income%20and%20vulnerable%20families%20in%20Singapore.pdf (accessed 10
     Jan. 2020).

25   For a full exposition, see Jacqueline Poh, "Workfare: The Fourth Pillar of Social Security in
     Singapore", *Ethos* 3 (Oct. 2007), available at https://www.csc.gov.sg/articles/workfare-the-
     fourth-pillar-of-social-security-in-singapore (accessed 21 Jan. 2021).

26   *ComCare Annual Report for Financial Year 2012* (Singapore: Ministry of Social and Family
     Development, 2013), p. 19, available at https://www.msf.gov.sg/publications/Documents/
     ComCare%20Annual%20Report%202012%20(1).pdf (accessed 10 Jan. 2020).

27   Under the scheme, individuals requiring help were given assistance to cover rental,
     utilities, service and conservancy charges, and medical expenses for up to 12 months. This
     period could be extended upon review.

28   To expand the coverage of both schemes, a new subsidy tier was established for families
     earning between $1,501 and $1,800.

29   "$290? Aid for Needy Adds Up to $2000", *Straits Times*, 13 Apr. 2007.

30   A key reason for the 2008 revisions was the recognition that with smaller family sizes
     and rising living and healthcare costs, more families—especially low-wage earners—were
     finding it difficult to care for their ageing parents. The 2008 revisions in the criteria
     for PA meant the inclusion of elderly whose children had household incomes below
     $1,000 and were supporting their own children. Previously, only the destitute who were
     unable to work and who had no family support were eligible for PA. See "More Help

for the Needy", MCYS Media Release, 5 Mar. 2008. Available at https://www.nas.gov.
sg/archivesonline/speeches/record-details/7f2dc00d-115d-11e3-83d5-0050568939ad
(accessed 15 Aug. 2021).

31   As PM Lee noted at the launch of ComCare, "we must avoid a welfare mentality in
     Singapore. It is important therefore that we stress mutual responsibility on the part of the
     Government and the individual needing help." Speech by Mr Lee Hsien Loong, Prime
     Minister and Minister for Finance, at the launch of ComCare, 28 June 2005, 3.30pm
     at the NTUC Auditorium, available at https://www.nas.gov.sg/archivesonline/data/
     pdfdoc/20050628996.htm (accessed 21 Jan. 2021).

32   Singapore Parliamentary Debates, 10 Mar. 2005, col. 2413.

33   The principle had been present in the PAP government's national agenda-setting
     efforts since the early 1990s. See, for example, *The Next Lap* (Singapore: Government
     of Singapore, 1991), pp. 117–30. "Many Helping Hands" also featured in President
     Wee Kim Wee's speech at the opening of Parliament in 1991. Singapore Parliamentary
     Debates, 22 Feb. 1991, col. 11.

34   See Lim Xiuhui, "Security with Self-Reliance: The Argument for the Singapore Model",
     Ethos 3 (Oct. 2007), available at https://www.csc.gov.sg/articles/security-with-self-reliance-
     the-argument-for-the-singapore-model (accessed 21 Jan. 2021).

35   See, for example, *Report of the Inter-Ministerial Committee on the Ageing Population*
     (Ministry of Community Development, 1999), p. 176: "As a society, we will be
     inhumane if senior citizens are not cared for by anyone. However, to be in line with
     the other principles, the State's involvement should be a last resort, and should not be
     above the minimal level in case it discourages personal responsibility, family support and
     volunteerism."

36   Singapore Parliamentary Debates, 8 Nov. 2006, col. 135. "WP's Low Urges Govt Not to
     Be Fearful of Helping Poor", *Straits Times*, 9 Nov. 2006.

37   See Singapore Parliamentary Debates, 8 Nov. 2006, col. 237. There was also increasing
     evidence that it was not just the poor who needed help. Analysis in 2008 from the
     PAP Policy Forum's council established that HDB four-room flat dwellers made up a
     disproportionately large number of hardship cases (38%) at PAP meet-the-people (MPS)
     sessions. The council's analysis of the data (spanning all MPS sessions over the previous
     five years) showed that the second most numerous group were those who lived in five-
     room flats (30%). These cases were spread across a range of issues: jobs, welfare and
     assistance matters, and difficulties in paying utility bills. "Money Problems: Hardest Hit
     Live in 4-Room Flats", *Petir*, July–Aug. 2008, p. 18.

38   Singapore Parliamentary Debates, 10 Nov. 2006, cols 489–91.

39   "Help for the Poor: So Close, yet So Far", *Straits Times*, 7 May 2007.

40   See "Many Helping Hands, but Who Has the Overview?", *Straits Times*, 2 June 2007;
     and "Bring the 'Many Helping Hands' Together" and "NMP Urges Better Coordination
     among Agencies Serving the Elderly", *Today*, 18 Nov. 2008. As Nominated Member of
     Parliament Assoc. Prof. Kalyani Mehta pointed out (with reference to services for the
     elderly), "The delivery of services is fragmented, piece meal and not easy to navigate by
     end-users. . . . There's an urgent need to standardise and centralise the services so that the
     public can use them without experiencing the 'passing-the-parcel' syndrome."

41 "Need Any Kind of Aid? Call New Helpline First", *Straits Times*, 10 Jan. 2008.

42 The GST rise was defended by the government during the 2007 budget debate, with it being made clear that Singapore could not live beyond its means: revenues were declining, with the government having to fund the new Workfare Income Supplement (WIS) scheme ($400 million a year), $300 million a year for continuous education and training, and a further $300 million a year in healthcare for the next five years. Besides these, as Second Finance Minister Tharman Shanmugaratnam observed, additional sources of revenue had to be found to pay for major future investments, including R&D, rejuvenating housing estates, and infrastructure such as new MRT lines. Singapore Parliamentary Debates, 1 Mar. 2007, cols 2169–71; "More Funds Needed to Pay for the Future", *Straits Times*, 2 Mar. 2007.

43 The news was first delivered by PM Lee during his National Day Rally speech on 19 August 2007. This headline overshadowed the news on other changes to CPF: first, the interest rate would go up by 1 percentage point on the first $60,000 of each worker's CPF; and second, the compulsory purchase of an annuity would be introduced to guard against "longevity risk". "City of Possibilities, Home for All", PM Lee Hsien Loong, National Day Rally Speech at the University Cultural Centre, 19 Aug. 2007. *National Day Rally Speeches: 50 Years of Nationhood in Singapore,* pp. 599–600.

44 "Public Service: New Round of Pay Hikes, New Round of Debates", *Straits Times*, 24 Mar. 2007.

45 Singapore Parliamentary Debates, 11 Apr. 2007, col. 479; "Pay Good Salaries to Ensure Good Governance", *Straits Times*, 12 Apr. 2007.

46 Singapore Parliamentary Debates, 11 Apr. 2007, cols 460–6. See also "It's Not Just about Pay, It's about Securing Bright Future", *Straits Times*, 12 Apr. 2007; and "Urgent Need to Narrow Pay Gap Now", *Straits Times*, 12 Apr. 2007.

47 "The Timing: Why Now?", *Straits Times*, 24 Mar. 2007.

48 Ibid.

49 "Robust Economy, Property Market Lead to $6.4 Surplus", *Straits Times*, 16 Feb. 2008.

50 Singapore Parliamentary Debates, 25 Feb. 2008, col. 590. See also "The Finance Minister Is Not the God of Fortune", *Straits Times*, 26 Feb. 2008.

51 These included $1.6 billion to top up endowment funds for workers, the poor and the elderly; $800 million to the Lifelong Learning Fund; $400 million to the Eldercare Fund; and $200 million each to MediFund and the ComCare Fund. Separately, another $1.8 billion went back to the people as part of a wide-ranging surplus-sharing package. Singapore Parliamentary Debates, 15 Feb. 2008, cols 365–416.

52 "Buy Mum, and Brother Chicken Rice", *New Paper*, 20 Oct. 2006.

53 Tan had only $16 in his wallet at the time of his suicide. One of his last acts on the day he died was to give some of his remaining money to his youngest son for the family's dinner and transport fares, asking the son also to care for his mother. Tan's wife did not even have the bus fare to go and view her husband's body: the policeman who told her of her husband's death gave her $5 to make the trip. All these details, first reported in the print media, were widely discussed online. "Buy Mum, and Brother Chicken Rice"; "Unnatural Death", *New Paper*, 23 Oct. 2006. For online commentary, see "Your Views: What Can We Do to Try to Prevent Another Singaporean from Being Driven to Desperation because

He or She Cannot Pay Bills?", *Singapore Media Watch*, 29 Oct. 2006, available at http://mediawatchsg.blogspot.sg/2006/10/your-views-what-can-we-do-to-try-to.html (accessed 26 Jan. 2021).

54 "Time to Weave a Stronger Net", *Straits Times*, 30 Oct. 2006; "MP Calls for More Help for Those Who Fall between the Cracks", *Straits Times*, 10 Nov. 2006. The South-West Community Development Council had, according to media reports, given Tan financial assistance for a time, but this help had subsequently been discontinued.

55 "Cooking Up the Holiday Spirit", *Straits Times*, 6 Jan. 2009.

56 "Taking five weeks' leave from work is not as difficult as one thinks. Most times, when you are at the top, you think you are indispensable. But if you are a good leader who has built up a good team, it is possible to go away for five weeks or even longer." "Cooking Up the Holiday Spirit". For an example of the online reaction, see Mr Brown, "Singapore Gahmen Becomes Famous Overseas for Its French Cooking Skills", 14 Jan. 2009, available at http://www.mrbrown.com/blog/2009/01/singapore-gahmen-becomes-famous-overseas-for-its-french-cooking-skills.html (accessed 26 Jan. 2021). Mr Brown is the online name of the well-known Singapore blogger Lee Kin Mun.

57 "Perm Sec's Article Showed a Lack of Sensitivity", *Straits Times*, 20 Jan. 2009.

58 This point was made, for example, by NMP Siew Kum Hong, who in raising the Tan Yong Soon affair in Parliament made the link to ministerial pay. Singapore Parliamentary Debates, 19 Jan. 2009, cols 1052–4.

59 "Detention Centre Superintendent Gets the Sack", *Straits Times*, 27 May 2008.

60 Singapore Parliamentary Debates, 28 Feb. 2008, col. 1147.

61 Singapore Parliamentary Debates, 22 Apr. 2008, col. 2643.

62 Ibid., cols 2643–57.

63 Ibid.

64 "Urgent Need to Narrow Pay Gap Now", *Straits Times*, 12 Apr. 2007.

65 Calculated from Healthcare Consumer Price Index, available at https://data.gov.sg/dataset/consumer-price-indices-general-and-healthcare (accessed 6 Jan. 2020).

66 For details, see "Hospital Fee Hike: Subsidised Patients to Pay a Few Dollars More", *Straits Times*, 16 Mar. 2007; and "New Fee Hikes at Public Hospitals and Polyclinics", *Straits Times*, 29 May 2007.

67 "Hospital Fee Hike: Subsidised Patients to Pay a Few Dollars More".

68 "Bonanza Budget Furthers Strategic Aims", *Straits Times*, 16 Feb. 2008.

69 The percentage of active CPF members (excluding pensioners) meeting the MMS at age 55 was 59.4% in 2007, and 58.9% in 2011. *CPF Board Annual Report 2011*, p. 35 (see also chart at p. 35), available at https://www.nas.gov.sg/archivesonline/government_records/record-details/49f796a0-d636-11e5-b8bb-0050568939ad (accessed 26 Jan. 2021). It should be observed that many of those who did not meet the MMS were of the generation who were halfway through their working lives when MediSave started. These individuals not meeting the MMS could still make MediSave withdrawals to pay for MediSave-approved treatments, up to the prevailing withdrawal limit for the treatment in question.

70 In 2006, 77% of the resident population (2.76 million individuals of the 3.58 million resident population) were covered by MediShield. This gradually increased to about 94% in 2013 as the maximum coverage age was lifted. *CPF Board Annual Report 2013*, p. 29, available at https://www.nas.gov.sg/archivesonline/government_records/record-details/7b64d258-d635-11e5-b8bb-0050568939ad (accessed 26 Jan. 2021).

71 "Premiums for MediShield Up with Better Cover", *Straits Times*, 27 Jan. 2005.

72 MediShield coverage for smaller subsidised bills fell following the 2005 reforms, but MediShield coverage increased for larger bills. See Yeo Yi Lin, "Update on MediShield Reform: Early Results", MOH Information Paper 2006/013, available at https://www.moh.gov.sg/docs/librariesprovider5/resources-statistics/information-papers/op_on_msh_reform_update_on_early_results_1nov.pdf (accessed 9 Oct. 2018). For commentary, see M.G. Asher and A. Nandy, "Health Financing in Singapore: A Case for Systemic Reforms", *International Social Security Review* 59: 90; and Stanley Jeremiah, "MediSave, MediShield . . . Medi-Crisis?", *Today*, 5–6 Jan. 2008. From 2009 to 2011, the average coverage of class B2/C hospitalisations by MediSave and MediShield was above 90%. See *Singapore Public Sector Outcomes Review 2014* (Singapore: Ministry of Finance, Aug. 2014), p. 16, available at https://www.mof.gov.sg/docs/librariesprovider2/past-editions/spor_2014.pdf (accessed 26 Jan. 2021).

73 For details of MediSave withdrawals by patients and their family members for medical treatment in 2010, see "Payment of Medical Bills Using MediSave Account Monies", *CPF Trends* (July 2011; archived by CPF Board).

74 See, for example, "MediShield Premium a Tremendous Increase", *Straits Times*, 20 Dec. 2004; "Hike in MediShield Premiums Too Drastic", *Straits Times*, 5 Feb. 2008; and "Rising MediShield Premiums Depleting Seniors' Medisave Accounts", *Today*, 26 Mar. 2013.

75 Asher and Nandy, "Health Financing in Singapore": 75–92, esp. 90; Jeremiah, "MediSave, MediShield . . . Medi-Crisis?".

76 "MOH Response: We Can Be Proud of 3Ms", *Today*, 7 Jan. 2008. This was a response to Stanley Jeremiah, "MediSave, MediShield . . . Medi-Crisis?", and his "Make Medical Cover Compulsory", *Today*, 5–6 and 7 Jan. 2008. Jeremiah, a Singapore Insurance Institute council member, had questioned the viability of the 3M system, arguing (amongst other things) for a form of universal health coverage. Jeremiah also observed that the number of aid applications under MediFund was growing at a significantly faster rate than the payout to successful applicants—meaning that there was "decreasing support when one is faced with increasing cost". Jeremiah further observed that the number of people whose applications for MediFund were rejected was 201 in 2005, but 6,500 in 2006. MOH clarified that 98% of all MediFund applications were in fact approved. "MOH Response: We Can Be Proud of 3Ms", available at https://www.moh.gov.sg/news-highlights/details/medisave-medishield-medi-crisis (accessed 1 Apr. 2020).

77 See Bhaskaran et al., "Inequality and the Need for a New Social Compact", in *Singapore Perspectives 2012: Singapore Inclusive: Bridging Divides*, ed. Kang Soon Hock and Leong Chan-Hoong (Singapore: World Scientific, 2013), pp. 174–5 (and Figure 8). See also M.K. Lim, "Shifting the Burden of Health Care Finance: A Case Study of Public–Private Partnership in Singapore", *Health Policy* 69 (2004): 83–4.

78   See the reply from the health minister to Parliamentary Question 515 from Gerald Giam, "Healthcare Financing Sources".

79   See the reply from the health minister to Parliamentary Question 515 from Gerald Giam, "Healthcare Financing Sources", Ministry of Health, available at https://www.moh.gov. sg/news-highlights/details/healthcare-financing-sources (accessed 6 Jan. 2020).

80   A survey conducted by the media company Mindshare in 2012 revealed that 72% of Singaporeans felt that they "cannot afford to get sick these days due to the high medical costs". "Singapore's Emigration Conundrum", *Business Times*, 6 Oct. 2012.

81   "Our Singapore Conversation on Healthcare", Ministry of Health Press Release, 1 July 2013.

82   "6 More Hospitals, Lower Medical Bills", *Straits Times*, 13 Mar. 2013. These changes were part of a much wider revamping of healthcare provisions and MediShield that had affordability and peace of mind at its core. Relevant here is the Committee of Supply Speech by Health Minister Gan Kim Yong during the 2013 budget debate. Singapore Parliamentary Debates, 12 Mar. 2013 (Gan Kim Yong, Minister for Health); see also PM Lee Hsien Loong, National Day Rally Speech at the Institute of Technical Education, 18 Aug. 2013. *National Day Rally Speeches: 50 Years of Nationhood in Singapore 1966–2015*, pp. 730–3.

83   Between 2002 and 2006, BTO flat supply was in the range of just 1,000 and 3,000 flats annually, due to the large existing unsold supply of up to 31,000 flats during this period.

84   BTO flat prices had historically been pegged to their market value (what they would have fetched on the resale market) and discounted with a market subsidy. New flat prices were delinked from the resale market in May 2011, after the general election that year.

85   See "Resale Statistics", HDB, available at https://www.hdb.gov.sg/residential/buying-a-flat/resale/getting-started/resale-statistics (accessed 26 Jan. 2021); and "HDB Resale Price Index", available at https://data.gov.sg/dataset/hdb-resale-price-index (accessed 26 Jan. 2021).

86   HDB data made available to the author.

87   See, for example, "Keeping Watchful Eye on Property Market", *Straits Times*, 30 Oct. 2007.

88   These included the withdrawal of the Stamp Duty concession in December 2006, new collective sales rules to tame the en bloc market in October 2007, and the removal of the Deferred Payment Scheme from property purchases in October 2007. For details on these moves, see "Amendments to En Bloc Sale Legislation Take Effect on 4 Oct 2007", Ministry of Law press release, 3 Oct. 2007, available at https://app.mlaw.gov.sg/news/press-releases/amendments-to-en-bloc-sale-legislation-take-effect-on-4-oct-2007; and "First Reading of the Land Titles (Strata) (Amendment) Bill by DPM S. Jayakumar, 27 Aug. 2007" (Ministry of Law, 27 Aug. 2007), available at https://www.mlaw.gov.sg/news/speeches/first-reading-of-the-land-titles-strata-amendment-bill-by-dpm-s-jayakumar-27-aug-2007 (accessed 26 Jan. 2021).

89   In 2010 MND reintroduced ECs into the government land sales programme, after a period when it had stopped selling land for EC development.

90   *2014 Population in Brief* (National Population and Talent Division), p. 13, available at https://github.com/isomerpages/isomerpages-stratgroup/raw/master/images/PublicationImages/population-in-brief-2014.pdf (accessed 6 Jan. 2020).

91 During his COS speech in February 2008, then Minister for National Development Mah Bow Tan said that HDB had been stepping up its BTO launches and would continue doing so, starting with 4,500 BTO units in the first half of 2008. However, the supply in the second half of 2008 was a much lower 3,300 units, when the crisis struck.

92 There is a strong suggestion that those upwardly mobile, younger couples whose combined income disqualified them from BTO flats (thence forcing them to look at purchasing flats on the resale market) were hard hit. See "Redefining Affordability of Homes", *Straits Times*, 14 July 2011.

93 The BTO application rate in 2010 was 5.3 times, meaning that there were 5.3 applicants balloting for each flat available. The overall BTO application rates for 2007, 2008, and 2009 were 4.7, 3.6, and 4.1 times respectively.

94 The government resisted calls during this period to raise the income threshold. The one major concession to buyers within the sandwich class was the policy change in 2010 which allowed couples with a monthly household income exceeding $8,000 and up to $10,000 to buy DBSS flats—previously, this group had been unable to buy new DBSS flats, and their only resort was to buy ECs or unsubsidised resale flats on the open market.

95 "Resale HDB Flat Prices Hit New High", *Straits Times*, 24 July 2010.

96 Ibid.

97 "How Affordable Are HDB Flats?", *Straits Times*, 25 Oct. 2008.

98 See, for example, "Are Homes Affordable?", *Straits Times*, 27 Sept. 2009.

99 "Redefining Affordability of Homes", *Straits Times*, 14 July 2011. See also "New HDB Flats Still Affordable: Mah", *Straits Times*, 27 Apr. 2010.

100 Previously, the MOP had been one or 2.5 years, depending on whether a concessionary loan had been taken out with HDB. For these and other key measures imposed at the same time, see "Measures to Ensure a Stable and Sustainable Property Market", Monetary Authority of Singapore media release, 19 Feb. 2010, available at https://www.mas.gov.sg/news/media-releases/2010/measures-to-ensure-a-stable-and-sustainable-property-market (accessed 4 Apr. 2020); and "More Help for First-Time Home Buyers", HDB press release, 30 Aug. 2010, available at https://www20.hdb.gov.sg/fi10/fi10296p.nsf/PressReleases/895204e2295bdc394825778e007fa919?OpenDocument&Click= (accessed 26 Jan. 2021).

101 "Homes Are for Keeps, Not Speculation", *Straits Times*, 22 Feb. 2010; "HDB Revises Policies to Stamp Out Speculation", *Business Times*, 6 Mar. 2010.

102 The February 2010 imposition of SSD on properties bought and sold within a year of acquisition was a case in point. Six months later, in August, the government further announced that SSD would be payable on residential properties which were acquired (or purchased) on or after 30 August 2010 and disposed of (or sold) within three years of acquisition. This was further extended from three to four years in January 2011, based on higher rates. Another example was the loan-to-value limit for housing loans granted by financial institutions. This was lowered from 90% to 80% in February 2010, and then to 70% in August that year, and to 60% in January 2011 (where the purchasing individual had one or more outstanding housing loans at the time of the new housing purchase). The MOP for non-subsidised resale flats, which was set at three years in March 2010, was

increased to five years in August that year; at the same time, concurrent ownership of both HDB flats and private residential properties within the MOP was disallowed.

103   For these moves, see "Additional Buyer's Stamp Duty for a Stable and Sustainable Property Market", Monetary Authority of Singapore media release, 7 Dec. 2011, available at https://www.mas.gov.sg/news/media-releases/2011/absd-for-a-stable-and-sustainable-property-market; "MAS Restricts Loan Tenure for Residential Properties", Monetary Authority of Singapore media release, 5 Oct. 2012, available at https://www.mas.gov.sg/news/media-releases/2012/mas-restricts-loan-tenure-for-residential-properties; and "More Help, Stronger Support, Better Homes", HDB press release, 27 Aug. 2013, available at https://www20.hdb.gov.sg/fi10/fi10296p.nsf/PressReleases/2311677DFDF53AC248257BD40032F6A4?OpenDocument. Two further sets of cooling measures introduced in 2013 were structural in nature but had a cooling effect on the property market. See "Additional Measures to Ensure a Stable and Sustainable Property Market", Monetary Authority of Singapore media release, 11 Jan. 2013, available at https://www.mas.gov.sg/news/media-releases/2013/additional-measures-to-ensure-a-stable-and-sustainable-property-market; and "MAS Introduces Debt Servicing Framework for Property Loans", Monetary Authority of Singapore media release, 28 June 2013, available at https://www.mas.gov.sg/news/media-releases/2013/mas-introduces-debt-servicing-framework-for-property-loans (all sources accessed 26 Jan. 2021).

104 See the remarks of Donald Low, "Rethinking Singapore's Housing Policies", *IPS Commons*, 3 June 2013, available at http://www.ipscommons.sg/rethinking-singapores-housing-policies/ (accessed 26 Jan. 2021).

105 Dr Amy Khor, interview with the author, 2 Dec. 2014. Amy Khor was chairman of the Feedback Unit from 2006 (when it was renamed REACH) to 2015.

106 *Reflections on Housing a Nation: A Collection of Commentaries by Mah Bow Tan* (Singapore: Ministry of National Development, 2011), available at https://www.mnd.gov.sg/Reflections%20on%20Housing%20a%20Nation/Reflections%20on%20Housing%20a%20Nation.pdf (accessed 26 Jan. 2021). The commentaries originally appeared in *Today* newspaper from September to December 2010.

107 See chapter 5, pp. 359–61.

108 DPM Wong Kan Seng, speech on population at Committee of Supply Debate, 4 Mar. 2010. Singapore Parliamentary Debates, 4 Mar. 2010, col. 2938.

109 In January 2008, it was reported that six of every 10 jobs created in 2007 went to foreigners. Of the 236,600 new jobs created that year, 144,500 (61%) went to foreigners, with 92,100 (39%) going to "locals" (Singapore citizens and PRs). The local share of total new jobs in 2006 had been 52%. "Employment Situation in Fourth Quarter 2007", Ministry of Manpower press release, 31 Jan. 2008, available at http://www.nas.gov.sg/archivesonline/data/pdfdoc/20080131998.pdf (accessed 26 Jan. 2021). See also "6 in 10 Jobs Go to Foreigners", *Straits Times*, 31 Jan. 2008.

110 Of the 360,700 jobs created between 2004 and 2006, 141,700 (39.3%) went to Singapore citizens, 62,500 (17.3%) to PRs, and 156,500 (43.4%) to foreigners. "Singapore Citizens Benefit from Record Employment Creation, Securing Good Quality Jobs", Ministry of Manpower press release, 29 Feb. 2008, available at http://www.mom.

gov.sg/newsroom/press-releases/2008/singapore-citizens-benefit-from-record-employment-creation-securing-good-quality-jobs (accessed 26 Jan. 2021).

111 A survey conducted in February 2009 by the Institute of Policy Studies is illustrative. Of the Singapore residents surveyed, 4% said they believed they were better off given the presence of foreigners. When asked about the overall impact of foreigners, 34% stated Singapore was better off as a result. "Findings of Survey Conducted by the Institute of Policy Studies", Institute of Policy Studies presentation, Feb. 2009, available at https://lkyspp.nus.edu.sg/docs/default-source/ips/pops-1_slides_0209.pdf (accessed 26 Jan. 2021). Among the participants at a Young PAP forum on immigration in mid-2007, 72% saw foreigners as a threat when it came to jobs (although 54% believed that foreigners were a boon for industries Singapore was promoting, which the forum organiser admitted "sound contradicting"). Two-thirds of the participants wanted a citizenship examination for new immigrants. "YP Tackles Old Issues with New Format", *Petir*, July–Aug. 2007, pp. 20–3.

112 See, for example, DPM and Minister for Home Affairs Wong Kan Seng, speech on population at Committee of Supply Debate, 4 Mar. 2010. Singapore Parliamentary Debates, 4 Mar. 2010, col. 2932.

113 "Services Sector Feels Pinch of Foreign Worker Controls", *Straits Times*, 28 Aug. 2009.

114 The number of citizenship applications approved also peaked in 2008: approximately 20,500, versus 19,900 in 2009 and 18,800 in 2010. For the data, see Population in Brief: 2009 (National Population Secretariat and agencies, 2009), p.13. Available at https://github.com/isomerpages/isomerpages-stratgroup/raw/master/images/PublicationImages/population-in-brief-2009.pdf; Population in Brief: 2010 (National Population Secretariat and agencies, 2010) p.12, available at https://github.com/isomerpages/isomerpages-stratgroup/raw/master/images/PublicationImages/population-in-brief-2010.pdf, and Population in Brief: 2011 (National Population and Talent Division and agencies, 2011), p.14. Available at https://github.com/isomerpages/isomerpages-stratgroup/raw/master/images/PublicationImages/population-in-brief-2011.pdf (all sources accessed 14 Aug. 2021).

115 DPM and Minister for Home Affairs Wong Kan Seng, speech on population at Committee of Supply Debate, 4 Mar. 2010. Singapore Parliamentary Debates, 4 Mar. 2010, col. 2942.

116 PM Lee Hsien Loong, speech at the NTU Students' Union Ministerial Forum, 15 Sept. 2009, available at https://www.pmo.gov.sg/Newsroom/transcript-prime-minister-lee-hsien-loongs-speech-ntu-students-union-ministerial-forum (accessed 8 Feb. 2021).

117 As part of these moves to give Singaporeans an edge over PRs and foreigners in the local school system, citizens were from 2010 given an additional ballot in primary school registration (two instead of one), meaning that the Singaporean child would have a higher chance of securing a place in the school of choice during the balloting process. "Measures to Further Differentiate Citizens, Permanent Residents and International Students in Education", Ministry of Education press release, 20 Dec. 2009.

118 See "Citizen–PR Distinction Has Sharpened: MM", *Straits Times*, 19 Feb. 2010. These moves were by no means kneejerk reactions. PM Lee had stressed as early as 2006 (during the Party conference held in December) that Singaporeans would always come first in

the government's priorities, even then noting that while the government had not hitherto made great distinctions between Singaporeans and others, changes were in the offing. "Singaporeans 'Always Come First'", *Straits Times*, 4 Dec. 2006. Education and healthcare were specifically singled out by PM Lee as areas that would see sharper differentiations.

119 See Saw Swee Hock, *The Population of Singapore*, 3rd ed. (Singapore: Institute of Southeast Asian Studies, 2012), pp. 328–30.

120 National Population Secretariat interview with Wong Kan Seng, minister in charge of population issues, 16 Aug. 2006, available at https://www.strategygroup.gov.sg/media-centre/press-releases/media-interview-with-dpm-wong-kan-seng-on-population-challenge-for-singapore (accessed 26 Jan. 2021).

121 The NPTD's key function was "to formulate, coordinate and review whole of Government policies related to population and talent. It will focus on achieving a sustainable population profile." The NPTD assumed larger responsibilities than its predecessor, the National Population Secretariat, overseeing overall population management, promoting marriage and parenthood, and taking on functions (including talent attraction and retention, as well as integration) that previously lay within the purview of other ministries. Keynote address by DPM and Coordinating Minister for National Security Wong Kan Seng, at the Singapore Perspectives 2011 Conference, 17 Jan. 2011, available at https://lkyspp.nus.edu.sg/docs/default-source/ips/singapore- perspectives-2011-keynote-address-by-mr-wong-kan-seng.pdf (accessed 26 Jan. 2021).

122 "High-Powered Team to Help Immigrants Fit In", *Straits Times*, 27 Apr. 2009. There were also at this time important moves to look at the effect—and impact—of the influx of low-skilled migrant workers, who made up the largest part of the foreign worker inflow. In 2008 an Inter-Ministerial Committee (IMC) chaired by Deputy Prime Minister and Minister for Finance Tharman Shanmugaratnam was set up, with a focus on managing and meeting the needs of lower-skilled migrant workers, while keeping in mind the potential impact on local communities. For the IMC, see "Ministry of Manpower Introduces the Foreign Employee Dormitories Bill 2014, Annex A: Background on the IMC on FW Management and FW Housing Landscape", Ministry of Manpower press release, 4 Nov. 2014, available at http://www.mom.gov.sg/newsroom/press-releases/2014/ministry-of-manpower-introduces-the-foreign-employee-dormitories-bill-2014 (accessed 26 Jan. 2021).

123 "Where Issues Go Beyond the Basics", *Straits Times*, 8 Oct. 2010.

124 Ibid.

125 "Residents Air Dorm Fears to Their MPs", *Straits Times*, 4 Sept. 2008. Lim Hwee Hua, MP for the area (a division of Aljunied GRC) was to be one of the casualties in the 2011 general election, when the PAP slate for the GRC was toppled by the team from the Workers' Party.

126 "PM Signals Tough Measures Ahead", *Straits Times*, 30 Oct. 2007; "PM Sets 2008 Agenda in 3 Areas", *Straits Times*, 1 Jan. 2008.

127 "New Trains to Ease MRT Crush Next May", *Straits Times*, 3 Sept. 2010.

128 "SM: We're Victims of Our Own Success", *Sunday Times*, 5 Sept. 2010.

129 Another member of the public : "I don't think these are just complaints. There is genuine unhappiness among the large middle class and if you suppress them, there will be social tension." "Gripes Are 'Expression of Concern'", *Straits Times*, 8 Sept. 2010.

130 PM Lee Hsien Loong, interview with the author, 19 Dec. 2014.

131 Ibid.

132 World Bank, "GDP Growth (Annual %)—Singapore", n.d., available at https://data.worldbank.org/indicator/NY.GDP.MKTP.KD.ZG?end=2018&locations=SG (accessed 20 Oct. 2020).

133 J. Pflug, "Extraordinary Times, Fundamental Principles: The 2009 Budget and the Ministry of Finance's Approach to Countercyclical Economic Strategy", *Ethos* 6 (1 July 2009): 20–6, available at https://www.csc.gov.sg/articles/extraordinary-times-fundamental-principles-the-2009-budget-and-the-ministry-of-finance's-approach-to-countercyclical-economic-strategy (accessed 26 Jan. 2021).

134 The scheme, meant to last for one year, was extended for another six months, albeit with reduced quarterly payouts of 6% in January 2010 and 3% in March 2010 (compared to 12% at the beginning of the scheme) of the first $2,500 of the monthly wages of affected workers. While there was no way of verifying the direct impact of the Jobs Credit Scheme, some estimates suggest that the scheme may have saved approximately 30,000 jobs in 2009 alone. See "Measuring Its Effectiveness", *Straits Times*, 16 Feb. 2009.

135 "Keeping Jobs, Building for the Future", Ministry of Finance press release, 22 Jan. 2009, available at https://www.mof.gov.sg/news-publications/press-releases/Keeping-Jobs-Building-for-the-Future (accessed 26 Jan. 2021).

136 Temasek was included in the Net Investment Returns framework in 2015. For details on the changes and the introduction of the Net Investment Returns Contribution, see "How Do Singaporeans Benefit from Our Reserves?" Ministry of Finance, n.d., available at https://www.mof.gov.sg/policies/reserves/how-do-singaporeans-benefit-from-our-reserves (accessed 26 Jan. 2021).

137 "Keeping Jobs, Building for the Future", Budget Speech delivered in Parliament by Minister for Finance Tharman Shanmugaratnam. Singapore Parliamentary Debates, 22 Jan. 2009, col. 1309, available at https://www.nas.gov.sg/archivesonline/speeches/record-details/8008b212-115d-11e3-83d5-0050568939ad (accessed 26 Jan. 2021).

138 "How Do Singaporeans Benefit from Our Reserves?"

139 Singapore Parliamentary Debates, 22 Jan. 2009, col. 1305.

140 Ibid., cols 1307–8. Earlier, in October 2008, a similar request to the president had been made for approval to draw on past reserves when the government moved to guarantee all bank deposits in Singapore. However, this was technically only a potential draw on reserves and was never put into effect.

141 See, for example, "S'poreans Have What It Takes to Bounce Back", *Straits Times*, 7 Feb. 2009.

142 "PM Vows Help for All Needy", *Straits Times*, 2 Feb. 2009. For the measures in the budget designed to help the less well-off (including rebates on income tax and service and conservancy charges), see Singapore Parliamentary Debates, 22 Jan. 2009, cols 1293–4.

143 PM Lee Hsien Loong, interview with the author, 19 Dec. 2014.

144 Singapore Parliamentary Debates, 22 Jan. 2009, col. 1267.

145 "Panel to Prepare for Long Term Growth", *Straits Times*, 28 May 2009.

146 *Report of the Economic Strategies Committee: High Skilled People, Innovative Economy, Distinctive Global City* (Singapore: Economic Strategies Committee, Feb. 2010), pp.

6–7, 82, available at https://web.archive.org/web/20170319192204/http://www.mof.gov.sg/Portals/0/MOF%20For/Businesses/ESC%20Recommendations/ESC%20Main%20Report.pdf (accessed 26 Jan. 2021).

147 Ibid., p. 5.

148 Ibid., pp. 6–7, 82.

149 For a dissection, see Faizal bin Yahya, "Singapore in 2010: Rebounding from Economic Slump, Managing Tensions between a Global City and a Fledgling Nation State", *Southeast Asian Affairs* (2011): 258–60.

150 *Report of the Economic Strategies Committee*, pp. 1, 12.

151 Ibid., p. 16. The income cap for WIS eligibility was increased to $1,700 from $1,500, allowing greater eligibility. For details (including details of the increased payouts), see the factsheet "Workfare Income Supplement", Ministry of Manpower, 11 Mar. 2010, accompanying the Manpower Minister's 11 Mar 2010 budget speech, available at https://www.mom.gov.sg/~/media/mom/documents/speeches/2010/factsheet%20-%20wis%20(110310).pdf (accessed 26 Jan. 2021).

152 WIS also ameliorated, to a degree, problems in retirement adequacy. A 35-year-old worker earning $1,000 a month could expect to have an additional 10% in his CPF retirement account by age 65 as a result of WIS (internal government study [Ref WIS review C002.240.0013.V1] made available to the author, 2009).

153 PM Lee Hsien Loong, interview with the author, 19 Dec. 2014.

154 *Report of the Economic Strategies Committee*, p. i.

155 Singapore Parliamentary Debates, 18 Feb. 2011, col. 2641.

156 Tharman Shanmugaratnam, interview with the author, 7 May 2014.

157 "I was once told when I argued against that, that 'the grow at all costs' policy was intentional and the Government will deal with the impact when it happens. Well, the impact has happened and the outcome has been negative in some areas. I wish the policymakers had been willing to listen and slow down a little. . . . I am sure when the idea of the need for a much larger population was conceived, it was not intended to happen overnight so there must have been an error of judgment by the implementers." "Don't Duck Those Hard Questions", *Straits Times*, 3 Mar. 2010.

158 Ibid.

159 Interviews with senior government officials involved in the Economic Strategies Committee, 2017.

160 These reflections and those in the previous two paragraphs are drawn from interviews with senior government officials involved in the Economic Strategies Committee (2017).

161 "PM's Goal: All to Enjoy Fruits of Growth", *Straits Times*, 9 Aug. 2010.

162 Quoted in "Have You 'Poked' Your MP Today?", *Straits Times*, 20 Feb. 2010.

163 An Institute of Policy Studies (IPS) study conducted in 2006 found that younger and better-educated Singaporeans relied on information from the Internet when deciding their vote. "PAP Moves to Counter Criticism of Party, Govt in Cyberspace", *Straits Times*, 3 Feb. 2007.

164 "Does the Internet Matter?", *Straits Times*, 7 Nov. 2008; "Young PAP Chiefs Plug In", *Straits Times*, 12 Dec. 2008.

165 This was especially important since (as commentators were pointing out) other parties were aggressively exploiting new media to get their message across. "Have You 'Poked' Your MP Today?".

166 "Engaging the Pop Culture Generation", *Straits Times*, 21 Nov. 2008.

167 "PAP Moves to Counter Criticism of Party, Govt in Cyberspace"; "On Track Online for GE Campaign", *Petir*, May–June 2011, pp. 37–9.

168 "PAP Moves to Counter Criticism of Party, Govt in Cyberspace".

169 Ibid.

170 Baey Yam Keng, interview with the author, 30 Oct. 2015.

171 "PAP Cyber-rebuttals May Be Counterproductive", *Straits Times*, 7 Feb. 2007.

172 "PAP Aims to Click with Young Online", *Straits Times*, 16 Nov. 2008; "From Static to Dynamic", *Petir*, Nov.–Dec. 2008, pp. 16–7.

173 "On Track Online for GE campaign", p. 38.

174 "Do 'Friends' and 'Fans' Equate to Votes?", *Straits Times*, 30 Oct. 2010. Some politicians evinced a particular savviness with new media. George Yeo, for example (an early adopter of blogging in 2006 and Facebook in 2008), was known not just to personally manage his Facebook page, but also to make efforts to become personally acquainted with his Facebook "friends" (even occasionally inviting them to join his jogging sessions).

175 "More PAP MPs on Facebook", *Straits Times*, 20 Feb. 2010.

176 "Young PAP Chiefs Plug In", *Straits Times*, 12 Dec. 2008.

177 "Young PAP Attracting Members via Facebook", *Straits Times*, 17 May 2009.

178 "YP to Close 2 Facebook Pages", *Straits Times*, 18 Mar. 2010.

179 Ibid.

180 Ibid.

181 Ibid.

182 Ibid.; "The PAP's New Media Experiment", *Straits Times*, 11 June 2010.

183 "Young PAP Chiefs Plug In".

184 "Do 'Friends' and 'Fans' Equate to Votes?". As Zaqy Mohamad, YP vice-chairman and head of its new media operations, observed in relation to the closure of YP Network and YP Community, comments by any individual activist would inevitably be taken as representing the whole party. "The PAP's New Media Experiment".

185 "Have you 'Poked' Your MP Today?".

186 "New Times, New Moves", *Petir*, May–June 2008, p. 39.

187 "The Battle for Eyeballs Is On", *Straits Times*, 4 Dec. 2010.

188 As one commentator noted, looking back on the period leading up to the 2011 general election, "Online information and views were widely recirculated via social media platforms such as Facebook, YouTube, and Twitter, as well as face-to-face chatter. The Internet became an important extension of Singapore's civil society, where intellectual leadership roles were taken up by articulate and charismatic netizens, who had fewer mainstream perspectives and were often supportive of opposition candidates." Kenneth Paul Tan, "Singapore in 2011: A 'New Normal' in Politics?", *Asian Survey* 52, 1 (2012): 224.

189 The SDP had made some of the earlier running, with a website featuring near-daily updates, as well as translations into Malay, Tamil and Chinese of selected articles featured

on its website. But other parties, too, notably the Workers' Party and the Reform Party, also had websites with innovative (and interactive) features, and content sharing across multiple platforms. "Political Parties Enhance Their Websites", *Straits Times*, 30 Apr. 2009; "The Battle for Eyeballs Is On".

190　For internal PAP dialogue and debate about the Opposition's use of new media (with some parties refreshing their online content much more regularly compared to the PAP's website), see "YP Sets Up Page on Facebook", *Petir*, Sept.–Oct. 2008, pp. 24–5. The Reform Party in particular was known to recruit the bulk of its supporters through social media. "The Battle for Eyeballs Is On".

191　*Engaging New Media, Challenging Old Assumptions: A Report by the Advisory Council on the Impact of New Media on Society (AIMS)* (Singapore: Dec. 2008), available at https://www.mci.gov.sg/~/media/mcicorp/doc/aimsreportdec08engagingnewmediachallengingoldassumptions.pdf?la=en (accessed 26 Jan. 2021).

192　"Films Act Amended", *Straits Times*, 24 Mar. 2009.

193　"Reel Knots in Changes to Films Act", *Straits Times*, 27 Mar. 2009.

194　"Green Light for New Media Use at GE", *Straits Times*, 15 Mar. 2011.

195　"Engaging New Media, Challenging Old Assumptions", p. 13.

196　As the *Straits Times* was moved to note, "Some bloggers have questioned its decision to concentrate resources on the official feedback unit Reach, but if the Government cannot interact effectively with netizens through e-mail, blogs and discussion boards hosted on its own turf, then what more can it do elsewhere in cyberspace?" "Green Light on Grey Areas", *Straits Times*, 16 Jan. 2009.

197　"The need to stay relevant in our methods of engagement cannot be underestimated. Surely we can do more than the usual karaoke sessions and lucky draws to up the participation rate at our events for the ground. Surely in a world of blogs, podcasts and vodcasts, we can be more gung-ho and adopt new media tools creatively to communicate what we stand for, our dreams and plans, and ask for better ideas?" Denise Phua (MP for Jalan Besar GRC), "New Times, New Moves", p. 39.

198　For the Workfare Income Supplement, see "S'pore Way to Fight Rising Cost of Living Works: PM", *Straits Times*, 12 Nov. 2007. For the changes to the CPF system, see "Coming Up with the Right Brew on CPF", *Straits Times*, 8 Dec. 2007. Both issues saw important acknowledgements by PM Lee and PAP MPs that communicating the fine print should have been done better. "PM Throws 5 Minute Challenge at Policymakers", *Straits Times*, 14 Nov. 2007.

199　"The Return of Politics", *Straits Times*, 24 May 2011.

200　"S'poreans Are Fed, Up with Progress!", *Today*, 30 June 2006.

201　K. Bhavani (press secretary to the minister for information, communications and the arts), "Distorting the Truth, Mr Brown?", letter to *Today*, 3 July 2006. The somewhat curious challenge contained in the letter—for Mr Brown (the online moniker of Lee Kin Mun) to "come out from behind his pseudonym to defend his views openly"—was taken by some netizens to show up the government's lack of understanding of the Singapore blogosphere and its opinion shapers, given that Mr Brown's real name was well known and in the public domain.

202 For an analysis of the Mr Brown episode, see Terence Lee and Cornelius Kan, "Blogospheric Pressures in Singapore: Internet Discourses and the 2006 General Election", *Continuum: Journal of Media & Cultural Studies* 23, 6 (Dec. 2009): 879–80.

203 "Ban on Outdoor Demos Eased from Monday", *Straits Times*, 26 Aug. 2008; "Bloggers Speak Out against Public Transport Fare Hike", *Straits Times*, 14 Sept. 2008.

204 For a summary of the debate, see "When the Government Chooses to Follow, Not Lead", *Straits Times*, 23 Oct. 2007.

205 These included the fact that many, including those with deep religious convictions, remained fundamentally opposed to homosexuality. "PM Lee: Why Singapore 'Must Leave Section 377A Alone'", *Straits Times*, 13 Oct. 2007.

206 "Greater Openness Here Now, Says WP Chief", *Straits Times*, 1 Nov. 2007.

207 Singapore Parliamentary Debates, 18 Aug. 2009, cols 1007–43.

208 Singapore Parliamentary Debates, 19 Aug. 2009, col. 1145 (19 Aug. 2009). See "MM Rebuts NMP's Notion of Race Equality", *Straits Times*, 20 Aug. 2009. For the Pledge, its origins, and purpose, see "National Pledge", https://www.nhb.gov.sg/what-we-do/our-work/community-engagement/education/resources/national-symbols/national-pledge (accessed 13 Aug. 2021).

209 Ng E-Jay, "NMP Viswa Sadasivan: Did He Just Shake the Foundations of the PAP Facade to the Very Core? (Part One)", 20 Aug. 2009, available at https://web.archive.org/web/20160331144905/http:/www.sgpolitics.net/?p=3553 (accessed 21 Jan. 2021). I am grateful to Viswa Sadasivan for a personal communication on the issue of his 18 August 2009 parliamentary speech.

210 "A Watershed Election for Youth", *Straits Times*, 30 Oct. 2010.

211 "A Disempowered Generation?", *Straits Times*, 30 Oct. 2010.

212 "Two-Party System Cannot Work Here, Says PM Lee", *Straits Times*, 18 Nov. 2008.

213 "A System in Sync with Aspirations of S'poreans", *Straits Times*, 28 May 2009.

214 In GRCs that produced NCMPs, the number of NCMP nominees was to be capped at two.

215 "Nominated MPs to Be a Permanent Feature", *Straits Times*, 28 May 2009. The requirement (which had existed since the NMP scheme was introduced) that Parliament would after each election pass a motion resolving that there should be NMPs for that term was also done away with.

216 For the changes, see "A System in Sync with Aspirations of S'poreans". The average size of GRCs was to fall further in the 2015 elections (4.7). The 2015 election also saw more four-member GRCs (six, as opposed to just two in 2011) and one more SMC (13) than there had been in 2011.

217 "Creating a Buzz in Parliament", *Straits Times*, 29 May 2009.

218 Ibid.

219 "24 Hours to Cool Off Before Polling Day", *Straits Times*, 1 Dec. 2009.

220 When the changes were promulgated, there was an exemption that covered the transmission of personal political views by individuals through new media. "24 Hours to Cool Off Before Polling Day". For the government's rationale behind the introduction of a cooling-off day, see the speech by Minister for Law K. Shanmugam during the second reading of the Parliamentary Elections (Amendment) Bill. Singapore Parliamentary Debates, 27 Apr. 2010, cols 238–9.

221 Catherine Lim, "Surprised by 'Cooling Off' Idea", letter to *Straits Times* Forum, 13 Jan. 2010.

222 "Should Media Also Cool Off?", *Straits Times*, 28 Apr. 2010.

223 "Political Virgins No More", *Straits Times*, 18 May 2007; "P65 MPs Get into Their Stride", *Straits Times*, 21 Sept. 2007.

224 As one commentator and academic (Terence Chong, from the Institute of Southeast Asian Studies) put it, "The post-65 branding is about repackaging and marketing an old product to younger consumers. Upon opening up the new package, these consumers have realised that the product has not changed." "P65 MPs Get into Their Stride".

225 "YP Woos New Citizens and the Young Overseas", *Straits Times*, 5 Jan. 2008.

226 The handover, which took place at the Young PAP convention on 2 November 2008, was marked by a transition of leadership positions within YP that had a certain significance: for the first time, YP's entire leadership (numbering 31 in all) was made up of individuals from the post-1965 generation.

227 "YUP, Teens Can Take Part in PAP Activities", *Straits Times*, 5 July 2010. Youths were also beginning to figure more prominently in other Party bodies. In 2010 the PAP Policy Forum (the main avenue for Party members to participate in active discussion on matters of national policy, often face to face with government ministers) saw no less than three undergraduates elected to its 12-member council. All three were active in various Party branches. "3 Students Elected to PAP Forum Council", *Straits Times*, 11 Apr. 2010.

228 "Young PAP Gets Over 1000 New Members", *Straits Times*, 4 Feb. 2010.

229 "New Tack at Camp a Winner", *Petir*, Nov.–Dec. 2009, p. 26; "Meet the Principal", *Petir*, Mar.–Apr. 2010, p. 19. For the YP School, see chapter 5.

230 The actual selection of each regional representative was done either by caucus (when the majority within each region could agree on the representative) or by a show of hands, or by secret ballot. See "14 Elected to YP Exco", *Petir*, Sept.–Oct. 2008, p. 26. The selection of regional chairmen became a fully elected process in 2011, partly in a bid to identify talent at the branch level that could step up to larger responsibilities. "YP turns 25", *Petir*, Nov.–Dec. 2011, pp. 17–9, esp. 18.

231 Previously, candidates were limited to introducing themselves and giving a two-minute speech on the day of the election itself. When elections were introduced for YP Exco positions in 2004, these had been for five district chairman positions. In 2008 these districts were subdivided into 14 regions.

232 "Young PAP Elections to Have Campaign Period", *Straits Times*, 15 Sept. 2010. This was no idle hope. Trainee oncologist Dr Tan Wu Meng, elected in 2008 as the first YP organising secretary (a post itself created to give non-MPs more leadership opportunities), would become an elected MP in 2015. Others who were members of the YP Exco before becoming MPs included Yeo Guat Kwang (1997), Liang Eng Hwa (2006), Assoc. Prof. Muhammad Faishal Ibrahim (2011), Vikram Nair (2011) and Desmond Choo (2015).

233 "14 Elected to YP Exco". The YP, Women's Wing and Policy Forum appointees to the HQ Exco had all earlier been elected to their positions in the respective Party bodies.

234 "Three New Faces in PAP Central Committee", *Straits Times*, 20 Dec. 2008.

235 For the movements, see "Highest Number of Senior Ministers of State", *Straits Times*, 30 Mar. 2008; and "Cabinet Comings and Goings", *Straits Times*, 1 Apr. 2009.

236 "Wanted: Singapore's Fourth PM", *Straits Times*, 18 Apr. 2008. See also "PAP Aims for Good Mix of Candidates", *Straits Times*, 4 Apr. 2009.

237 "Becoming the Top Man", *Straits Times*, 6 Oct. 2007. See also "In Search of 4th-Generation Leaders", *Straits Times*, 6 Oct. 2007.

238 Detailed and useful treatments of the 2011 general election may be found in Derek da Cunha, *Breakthrough: Roadmap for Singapore's Political Future* (Singapore: Straits Times Press, 2012); and Kevin Y.L. Tan and Terence Lee (eds), *Voting in Change: Politics of Singapore's 2011 General Election* (Singapore: Ethos Books, 2011). Catherine Lim's *A Watershed Election: Singapore's GE 2011* (Singapore: Marshall Cavendish, 2011) is more in the vein of an exuberant and impressionistic exercise in political *schadenfreude* than it is a serious analysis.

239 "Rising Costs a Likely Issue: SM", *Straits Times*, 19 Apr. 2011. Some mention should also be made of the fact that this was the first election where pre-election polls turned out to be both attention-grabbing and accurate. One survey, conducted by the Australia-based research firm UMR Research on 3–5 May 2011, predicted that the PAP's vote share would go down from 67% to 61%. Not published in Singapore (in order, it appears, to avoid running afoul of Singapore laws prohibiting the publication of opinion polls during the election period), the survey was being cited and discussed in the international media before Polling Day. Those surveyed were generally positive on the direction in which the country was heading, but there was unhappiness over a wide range of issues, including the cost of living, housing affordability and government accountability. See "Research Firm Almost Spot-On in Vote-Swing Prediction", *Straits Times*, 14 May 2011; and "Factbox: Main Issues in Singapore's 2011 General Election", *Reuters*, 6 May 2011.

240 "No Shortage of Schemes to Help Needy Singaporeans", *Straits Times*, 29 Nov. 2010; "Workfare Better than Minimum Wage: PM", *Straits Times*, 29 Nov. 2010.

241 "Taking the Floor", *Straits Times*, 29 Nov. 2010. The four were Foo Mee Har, Gan Thiam Poh, Vikram Nair and Desmond Choo.

242 "Workfare Better than Minimum Wage: PM"; "No Shortage of Schemes to Help Needy Singaporeans".

243 "Under-40s Make Up Half of PAP New Faces", *Straits Times*, 22 Mar. 2011.

244 "Nothing Left to Chance in PAP Selection Process: Ng Eng Hen", *Straits Times*, 1 Mar. 2011.

245 "Record Number of Potential Office Holders on PAP Slate", *Straits Times*, 15 Apr. 2011.

246 "The PAP's 4G Leadership Taking Shape", *Straits Times*, 15 Mar. 2011.

247 "Need to Look Beyond Chinese-Educated Candidates", *Straits Times*, 24 Mar. 2011.

248 "Wearing Failure Like a Badge of Honour", *Straits Times*, 21 Apr. 2011.

249 "Their Dads Were Once PAP Adversaries", *Straits Times*, 22 Mar. 2011.

250 George Yeo, who was to stand with Ong Ye Kung in Aljunied GRC, advised Ong that it would be best to state publicly, in advance of the election, his position on the issue of his father's membership in the Barisan Sosialis, and his initial reluctance to support his son joining the PAP. Ong took this advice and spoke about his father's point of view in an interview with *Lianhe Zaobao* ("老左的儿子 王乙康：父亲解放了我" [Son of a leftist Ong Ye Kung: my father freed me], 10 Apr. 2011). I am grateful to George Yeo and Ong Ye Kung for personal communications on this issue.

251 "Positive Reaction to PAP Fielding Sons of Ex-Leftists", *Straits Times*, 23 Mar. 2011.

252 At the previous general election, in 2006, Opposition parties had contested 47 of the 84 seats.

253 A mixed Opposition team intending to run in Tanjong Pagar GRC was 35 seconds too late in filing the required nomination papers. See Ko Siew Huey, "TOC Exclusive: 35 Seconds Too Late—What Happened?", *Online Citizen*, 28 Apr. 2011.

254 The 1988 election had seen the PAP field two minority candidates in SMCs: S. Dhanabalan (in Kallang, where he triumphed against A.L. Sundram of the Workers' Party) and Abdullah Tarmugi (in Siglap, where he beat Chong Tung Shang, also of the Workers' Party).

255 "11th-Hour Pullout Sees Quick PAP Reshuffle", *Straits Times*, 28 Apr. 2011; "Why Tan Withdrew", *Straits Times*, 28 Apr. 2011.

256 "PAP Training Potential New Faces for Media Debut", *Straits Times*, 24 Feb. 2011.

257 For the infamous *kee chiu* (Hokkien for "hands up") incident, which took place on 17 April 2011 during the course of Chan's remarks at the Young PAP's 25th anniversary celebration, and which attracted derision from some netizens, see "Chan Chun Sing: Heartlander with Eye on Big Picture", *Straits Times*, 23 Nov. 2018.

258 "New PAP Faces Stunned by Online Vitriol", *Straits Times*, 31 Mar. 2011.

259 See "PAP's Janil Puthucheary, 'I Did Not Do NS . . . Those Are the Facts'", *Online Citizen*, 15 Apr. 2011, available at https://www.theonlinecitizen.com/2011/04/15/paps-janil-puthucheary-i-did-not-do-ns-those-are-the-facts/ (accessed 26 Jan. 2021).

260 "I Have No Reason Whatsoever to Worry about Tin Pei Ling", *Straits Times*, 19 Apr. 2011.

261 Tan Siong Kuan, "Gen Y in GE 2011: Wrong to Let Young Candidate Sneak In", letter to *Straits Times* Forum, 5 Apr. 2011.

262 "Social Media: The New Voice of the GE", *Straits Times*, 15 May 2011.

263 "I Take Valid Criticisms Seriously: Tin Pei Ling", *Straits Times*, 18 Apr. 2011. Tin's detractors also alleged that she was fielded on account of the fact that her husband, Ng How Yue, was principal private secretary to PM Lee.

264 "I Have No Reason Whatsoever to Worry about Tin Pei Ling".

265 Goh Chok Tong, interview with the author, 22 June 2012.

266 "Leading and Lightening up in the YouTube Age", *Straits Times*, 16 Apr. 2008 (extract translated from an interview originally given by PM Lee to *Lianhe Zaobao*, "对新媒体条例可能放宽" [Possible relaxation of new media regulations], 13 Apr. 2008).

267 "My Role That of Watchdog: WP Chief", *Straits Times*, 19 Apr. 2008.

268 "Keep Low 'on His Toes' in Hougang", *Straits Times*, 27 July 2008.

269 "Greater Openness Here Now, Says WP Chief", *Straits Times*, 1 Nov. 2007.

270 The PAP counter to this is encapsulated in a *Petir* editorial in 2008, where Dr Ng Eng Hen (the Party organising secretary [special duties]) commented, "to simply criticise or make opportunistic snipes without offering solutions or, worse, to fudge on national issues instead of taking a clear stand, does little to raise the standard of political debate or the reputation of the Workers' Party as a responsible opposition". "Credible Opposition: Taking a Clear Stand", *Petir*, May–June 2008, pp. 6–7. See also "PAP Raps WP for Ill-Timed Silence and Double-Talk", *Straits Times*, 20 June 2008.

271 "WP Chief Sets Target of Winning GRC in Next Election", *Straits Times*, 4 Nov. 2007.

272 "WP Should Justify Its Slogan: Shanmugam", *Straits Times*, 21 Apr. 2011; "Shanmugam to Workers' Party: Reveal Your Real Aim", *Straits Times*, 23 Apr. 2011. Senior Minister Goh derided the WP's vision as *koyok* (Malay for "quack remedy"). "WP 'Selling Koyok' with Vision of First World Parliament", *Straits Times*, 1 May 2011.

273 "Low's 'Co-pilot' Theory Cannot Fly", *Straits Times*, 2 May 2011.

274 "PCF, PA Give Ruling Party Unfair Edge", *Straits Times*, 1 May 2011. For the full comments, see "Low Thia Khiang's English Speech at the Workers' Party Rally at Bedok Stadium" (30 Apr. 2011), YouTube, https://www.youtube.com/watch?v=wRHRXpRt2lo (accessed 1 Apr. 2020).

275 "GE 2011: PAP Salvo Targets Workers' Party 'Star' Chen", *Straits Times*, 19 Apr. 2011.

276 Sylvia Lim, "WP Defends Chen, Questions PAP's Motive", letter to *Straits Times* Forum, 20 Apr. 2011.

277 "Personal Attacks on WP's Chen Will 'Backfire': Analysts", *Straits Times*, 20 Apr. 2011; "Low Satisfied with Chen's Background", *Straits Times*, 21 Apr. 2011; "Minister Welcomes Low's Remarks on Chen Show Mao", *Straits Times*, 22 Apr. 2011.

278 "Punggol East SMC: Low Calls PAP's Town Council Allegations a Personal Attack", *Straits Times*, 4 May 2011.

279 Shanmugaratnam did add, however, "Every independent international observer knows that Singapore wouldn't be where it is if not for its leadership team and if not for the PAP." "Strong Opposition Good for PAP: Tharman", *Straits Times*, 3 Apr. 2011.

280 "Why Singapore's Political System Works", *Straits Times*, 21 Nov. 2008; "Low: Joining Opposition Is No Loss", *Straits Times*, 7 Apr. 2011.

281 "GE: SM Goh Urges 'Clean Fight' in GRC Contest", *Channel NewsAsia*, 21 Apr. 2011.

282 "Tough on Ideas, Civil on Opponents?", *Straits Times*, 29 Apr. 2011.

283 Benjamin Pwee had been branch leader in the PAP Youth Wing and was the son of a long-time PAP grassroots leader. "GE 2011; PAP Profile, but Likely Opposition Candidate", *Straits Times*, 9 Apr. 2011. Another former scholarship holder was Jimmy Lee from the SPP, who contested as part of Chiam See Tong's slate in the Bishan–Toa Payoh GRC. Lee had studied computer science at Cornell University on a scholarship from the Defence Science and Technology Agency.

284 The SDA had already been diminished in 2007 when the National Solidarity Party pulled out of the grouping.

285 "Show Cause Letter Widens Rift in SDA", *Straits Times*, 11 Feb. 2011; "Chiam's Former Protégé Quits SPP, Rejoins SJP", *Straits Times*, 4 Mar. 2011.

286 "Chiam's Former Protégé Quits SPP, Rejoins SJP".

287 The Reform Party had been formed by veteran Opposition politician J.B. Jeyaretnam in July 2008, but he passed away in September that year. The chairmanship of the Party passed to Ng Teck Siong, and then to Jeyaretnam's son Kenneth in April 2009.

288 "Reform Party Chairman Quits", *Straits Times*, 26 Feb. 2011.

289 Other SDP policy recommendations included a call for the minimum tax rate for top earners to be raised and the resultant tax revenue to be used to fund social programmes, and a "Singaporeans First" policy in the job market that would mandate that employers could hire foreigners only if they could prove that they were unable to recruit a

Singaporean for the job in question. See "Rebranding the SDP", *Straits Times*, 20 Nov. 2010; and "Opposition Parties Finalising Their Manifestos", *Straits Times*, 10 Dec. 2010.

290 As the SDP's own organ was to observe, "Since the last General Elections (GE) 2006, many people have remarked that the SDP has undergone a transformation. And they are right. We have jettisoned the old-school opposition politics and embraced a reenergized approach that has won much support over the years." *New Democrat* 1 (2011): 1.

291 Chee was declared a bankrupt in February 2006 for failing to pay $500,000 in damages to Senior Minister Goh Chok Tong and Minister Mentor Lee Kuan Yew for defaming them during the 2001 general election. He and other SDP figures were involved in a series of convictions for taking part in illegal protests and assemblies from the midpoint of the decade, leading to further fines and jail terms (including for Chee, who also ran afoul of the law for attempting to leave the country without a permit despite being a bankrupt). For a flavour, see "SDP Trio Declared Bankrupt", *Straits Times*, 18 Aug. 2007; "Five SDP Supporters, Members Stage March", *Straits Times*, 17 Sept. 2007; "Chee Ignored Warning Curb on Bankrupts", *Straits Times*, 25 Sept. 2007; "5 SDP Members Arrested for Staging Illegal Protest Outside Istana", *Straits Times*, 9 Oct. 2007; "SDP Holds Illegal Protest against Rising Consumer Prices, 12 Held", *Straits Times*, 16 Mar. 2008; "Chee, 5 Others Charged with Illegal Assembly", *Straits Times*, 22 Aug. 2008.

292 "Opposition Parties Still Locked in Debate", *Straits Times*, 6 Mar. 2011.

293 "Securing Our Future Together" (PAP 2011 general election manifesto). See also "PAP Aims to Build on Its Successes with Manifesto", *Straits Times*, 18 Apr. 2011.

294 As usual, redrawing of constituency boundaries before the election led to Opposition charges of gerrymandering by the PAP government. The changes left only two GRCs and two SMCs completely intact. There would now be 12 SMCs and 15 GRCs at stake, up from nine and 14 respectively. The total number of MPs would rise from 84 to 87. For details, see "Major Changes to Electoral Map", *Straits Times*, 25 Feb. 2011. For a flavour of the Opposition charges, see "Opposition Accuses PAP of Gerrymandering", *Straits Times*, 25 Feb. 2011; and "'No Evidence' of Unfair Edge for PAP", *Straits Times*, 26 Feb. 2011. There is no indication that the Opposition charges of unfairness (dismissed as usual by the PAP) played significantly on the minds of the electorate.

295 "Survey of Young Voters: Cost of Living Is Top Concern of Gen Y", *Straits Times*, 16 Apr. 2011.

296 "Merdeka Center's Poll of Singaporeans during the GE Campaign Point to Increasingly Engaged and Diverse Electorate—Survey", Merdeka Center news release, 27 May 2011, available at https://merdeka.org/v2/download/news-release-28-may-2011-merdeka-centers-poll-of-singaporeans-during-the-ge-campaign-point-to-increasingly-engaged-and-diverse-electorate/ (accessed 26 Jan. 2021). Of those surveyed, 13.1% said that affordable healthcare was the key concern, while 12.3% placed affordable housing at the top of their list. See Bridget Welsh, "Does Difference Matter? Particular and National Political Identities in Singapore's 2011 General Election", in *Voting in Change: Politics of Singapore's 2011 General Election*, ed. Kevin Y.L. Tan and Terence Lee, pp. 95–6 (and Table 2, p. 96). A separate, and comparatively little-noticed survey, carried out on 3–4 May 2011 by the Singapore market research firm Blackbox Research, similarly found that the cost of living was the top issue on the minds of Singaporeans polled (55% ranked this as the key

voting issue, with housing prices separately singled out by 22% of those polled as a key sub-issue). See "Singapore General Election 2011, Independent Data Release Special: A Survey of Campaign Impressions Amongst Singaporean Voters", Blackbox Research, May 2011, available at http://www.blackbox.com.sg/wp-content/uploads/2011/05/Blackbox_GEGraphs_May-2011.pdf (graph 6) (accessed 26 Jan. 2021).

297 "Towards a First World Parliament" (Workers' Party 2011 general election manifesto), available at https://www.scribd.com/doc/52644250/Workers-Party-Manifesto-2011 (accessed 8 Jan. 2020).

298 "WP's Proposals Dangerous: Mah", *Straits Times*, 21 Apr. 2001, Mah's point was that "when the Government takes state land for public housing, it has to pay the full value of the land back into the reserves. This value is determined not by the Government 'as it pleases'."

299 Ibid.

300 "Low Continues War of Words over Housing", *Straits Times*, 29 Apr. 2011.

301 The SDP's performance in the 2011 general election—36.8% of votes where it contested and vastly improved on its 2001 and 2006 performances—should be put down to Chee Soon Juan's more moderate stance and the Party's own policy platform. But its savviness with new media may also have played a part. See Cherian George, "Internet Politics: Shouting Down the PAP", in *Voting in Change: Politics of Singapore's 2011 General Election*, ed. Kevin Y.L. Tan and Terence Lee, p. 151. As George observes, this new media effort "was part of a determined effort to bypass the largely unsympathetic media, reach out directly to Singaporeans, and cultivate the image of a serious, professional outfit".

302 "'Strange Bedfellows' in SDP Team", *Sunday Times*, 24 Apr. 2011.

303 "PAP and SDP Square Off over 'Smear Tactics'", *Straits Times*, 26 Apr. 2011.

304 See Da Cunha, *Breakthrough: Roadmap for Singapore's Political Future*, pp. 80–1.

305 Balakrishnan explained at an election rally that the miscalculation of the initial budget had been partly on account of the fact that it was the first time the YOG had ever been organised and there was no other model that the organising team could use for reference. This notwithstanding, the government "did not overspend, or waste, or squander money that was properly budgeted" for the YOG. "4th May Speech at People's Action Party Rally for Holland–Bukit Timah GRC" (Dr Vivian Balakrishnan), 5 May 2011, available at http://vivian.balakrishnan.sg/2011/05/05/4th-may-speech-at-peoples-action-party-rally-for-holland-bukit-timah-grc/ (accessed 26 Jan. 2021).

306 "Fight in 'Rich Man's GRC' Heats Up", *Straits Times*, 6 May 2011.

307 "Objection Raised but Rivals Stay Cordial", *Straits Times*, 28 Apr. 2011.

308 "Tough on Ideas, Civil on Opponents?".

309 "Tan Jee Say's Move 'Not Wise': SM Goh", *Straits Times*, 1 May 2011. Tan Jee Say's riposte—undoubtedly more effective than Goh's initial comments—was, "I have given five of my best years in my career to Mr Goh, and I do not expect such comments from him. I wish he had not gone down to the personal level." "Tan Jee Say Saddened by SM Goh's Comments", *Channel NewsAsia*, 1 May 2011; "SDP Tan Jee Say Rebutted against SM Goh 'Personal Attack'—1 May 2011", MediaCorp Channel 5 news report, available at https://www.youtube.com/watch?v=h-jelKjkxLY (accessed 22 Oct. 2020).

310 See, for example, "Walk the Talk and Fight Fairly", *Straits Times*, 5 May 2011. The line of questioning that was over the longer term the most potent involved comments by the PAP's Lim Hwee Hua that seemed to suggest that the accounts of Low Thia Khiang's Hougang Town Council might not be completely in order. Low Thia Khiang characterised this as a "personal attack" against him. However, the issue of financial probity in matters relating to town council accounts was in the years to follow to develop into something much bigger, engulfing the WP-run Aljunied–Hougang Town Council and playing a part in the WP's near-loss of Aljunied GRC in the 2015 general election. See "Accounts Query 'Wasn't Meant as a Personal Attack'", *Straits Times*, 5 May 2011.

311 Transcript of Senior Minister Goh Chok Tong's Media Interview on 2 May 2011 at 6pm, available at https://www.nas.gov.sg/archivesonline/speeches/record-details/7ab659e6-d5d7-11e8-ab1b-001a4a5ba61b (accessed 26 Jan. 2021).

312 As one commentator, a long-time student of media and the Internet in Singapore, observed, "Another key function of the new media was to enable members of the public to surface and keep alive issues that mattered to them, even those that the politicians and professional media did not care for." George, "Internet Politics: Shouting Down the PAP", pp. 146–59, esp. 151–2.

313 For a sense of the Twittersphere and the febrile social media space generally during this period, see T.T. Sreekumar and Shoba Vadrevu, "Subpolitics and Democracy: The Role of New Media in the 2011 General Elections in Singapore", *Science, Technology & Society* 18, 2 (July 2013): 231–49.

314 The backlash was so vitriolic that advertisers had to pull their content from Cheng's blog in order not to themselves fall victim. "Singapore Politics Have Been Changed Forever—By Social Media", *Business Insider (Singapore)*, 24 May 2011. See also "Blogger Xiaxue: I Will Not Change", *New Paper*, 27 Mar. 2012. The posts by Cheng ("What the Fuck, Singaporeans?", 3 May 2011, available at http://xiaxue.blogspot.sg/2011/05/what-fuck-singaporeans.html; "Vote Wisely", 4 May 2011, available at http://xiaxue.blogspot.sg/2011/05/vote-wisely.html; and "Aftermath", 11 May 2011, http://xiaxue.blogspot.sg/2011/05/aftermath.html) are no longer accessible but have been saved by other netizens (see, e.g., https://xiaxueforyou.blogspot.com/, accessed 22 Oct. 2020).

315 The decision to field Palmer was notable as it was the first time that the PAP had fielded a minority in an SMC since 1988. But this was not a sign, as PM Lee noted, that the Party believed the electorate had lost the propensity to vote along ethnic lines. "GRC 'A Good Start for Potential PM'", *Straits Times*, 6 Apr. 2011.

316 "Wooing Hearts and Minds on the Campaign Trail", *Straits Times*, 26 Mar. 2011. Chong would in fact be used in this manner again, at the 2015 general election, where he narrowly defeated the WP's Lee Li Lian in Punggol East.

317 PM Lee Hsien Loong, interview with the author, 19 Dec. 2014. The English forum was telecast on 12 April 2011 and the Mandarin forum on 16 April 2011. See "Squaring the Emotions and Logic in the Foreigner Debate", *Business Times*, 13 Apr. 2011.

318 PM Lee Hsien Loong, interview with the author, 19 Dec. 2014.

319 "Town Hall Format at Party Convention", *Petir*, Jan.–Feb. 2008, p. 12.

320 From the WP slate that contested in Aljunied in 2006, only one—the Party's chairman, Sylvia Lim—was to contest again in the GRC in 2011. Lim was, in fact, a continuous

presence on the ground in the intervening period. On the PAP's part, besides the MPs walking the ground, a team led by heavyweight ministers from the CEC made weekly visits to all branches in the lead-up to the 2006 election (to check on activists' preparation and get a feel of what the hot-button issues were) and in the 18 months that followed. The frequency of these visits dropped thereafter, but then picked up again as the 2011 election approached. "Has the Opposition Gone Awol?", *Straits Times*, 17 Nov. 2007; "PAP Leaders Set Up Branch Visits", *Straits Times*, 14 Dec. 2010.

321 "WP Forms 'Action Plan' to Attract More Malays", *Straits Times*, 3 Feb. 2007.

322 "Battle Royale", *Straits Times*, 28 Apr. 2011. Low's remarks were made at a WP press conference on Nomination Day, 27 April 2011. "WP's Low: 'There Is a Tiger in the Mountain'", *TODAYonline* Youtube Channel, 27 Apr. 2011, available at https://www.youtube.com/watch?v=TEm7K5nkC2A (at 1:12-1:20). George Yeo's response—"Do we look like tigers? We are rather mild, friendly people" (see https://www.youtube.com/watch?v=BWOiUVB7UM0, at 1:25-1:32)—led to an uproarious moment at a later WP rally on 29 April when Low proceeded (in Mandarin) to painstakingly "explain" the meaning behind his metaphor. "WP Serangoon Rally (29 Apr 2011)", https://www.youtube.com/watch?v=NI9C9cZNrDM (at 1:47-2:55) (all links accessed 13 Apr. 2021).

323 This had been an issue with residents as far back as the 2006 election campaign. "Aljunied GRC: Projects Spur Transformation", *Straits Times*, 5 May 2007.

324 "Aljunied Voters 'Chips in Game of High Stakes'", *Straits Times*, 4 May 2011. For one of the incidents that may have counted against Phua, see "Teen Arrested for Violence in MP's Office", *New Paper*, 8 May 2009. For an example of the commentary in the blogosphere on this, see Gilbert Koh (aka Mr Wang), "PAP's Cynthia Phua and Her Most Famous Moment as an Aljunied MP", 3 May 2011, http://mrwangsaysso.blogspot.sg/2011/05/paps-cynthia-phua-and-her-most-famous.html (accessed 22 Oct. 2020).

325 For Lim's own analysis, see "On Winning Back Aljunied and Lessons from Politics", *Straits Times*, 12 May 2011. Serangoon and Paya Lebar (the divisions of Aljunied GRC helmed by Lim Hwee Hua and Cynthia Phua respectively) were the divisions that saw the lowest support for the PAP team in the election. "Reasons behind Aljunied Swing", *Straits Times*, 8 May 2011.

326 "'Very Sad' if the Comment Cost Votes", *Straits Times*, 1 May 2011.

327 Ibid.; "Muslims Have Done Much to Integrate: PM", *Straits Times*, 31 Jan. 2011. For MM Lee's subsequent retraction of these comments, see "Muslim Leaders Welcome MM Lee's Clarification", *Straits Times*, 9 Mar. 2011.

328 Zainul Abidin Rasheed, part of the PAP team ousted from Aljunied, was to comment soon after the election, "You need only ask the Malays and Muslims in Singapore—many were hurt by those remarks and remain so." "Many Were Hurt by MM Lee's Remarks", *Today*, 13 May 2011. I am grateful for a personal communication from Zainul Abidin Rasheed on this issue and on the Aljunied campaign in 2011.

329 "PAP Out and About", *Straits Times*, 6 Mar. 2011. Kuay teow (or kway teow) is a popular flat noodle dish usually made with rice flour with origins in Chinese cuisine found (typically, but not exclusively) in hawker centres.

330 "Low Attacks GRC System for Serving PAP, Not the People", *Straits Times*, 30 Apr. 2011.

331 "WP 'Using Residents as Springboard'", *Straits Times*, 1 May 2011.

332 Ong Ye Kung, interview with the author, 2 Jan. 2013.

333 "Zainul to Be Speaker if Re-elected", *Straits Times*, 24 Apr. 2011; "George Yeo Too Important for Cabinet to Lose: SM Goh", *Today*, 3 May 2011.

334 "Many Voters Still Undecided: George Yeo", *Straits Times*, 3 May 2011. It was not a constitutional stipulation that the Speaker of Parliament had to be drawn from the ranks of elected MPs. "WP Offers 'Win-Win' Option: Zainul Loses, but Can Still Be Speaker", *Straits Times*, 5 May 2011.

335 "Aljunied Is the Only Hot Seat", *Straits Times*, 1 May 2011. Lee was, in fact, ramming home a message he had made just the night before, after a visit to Tampines: "If they [the voters in Aljunied] choose the opposition, then I say, good luck to them. They have five years to ruminate and to regret what they did. And I have no doubts they will regret it. . . . It may well happen that they win, in which case the people of Aljunied live with the results. . . . The only way people learn is when they have to pay a price. From time to time we may lose, and the voters pay the price." "MM: Critical Choice for Aljunied Voters", *Straits Times*, 30 Apr. 2011.

336 "PAP's George Yeo at Aljunied GRC rally, May 5 (Part 2)", *Todayonline* YouTube Channel, available at https://www.youtube.com/watch?v=34yLiRUC5rg, at 7:16-7:22 (accessed 14 Aug. 2021). For these remarks, see also Asad-ul Iqbal Latif and Lee Huay Leng (eds), George Yeo on *Bonsai, Banyan,* and the *Tao* (Singapore: World Scientific, 2015), p. 194. George Yeo was later to reveal that following the PAP election post-mortem in 2011, MM Lee, having realised the effect that his "repent" remark had had on the electorate, emailed the defeated PAP Aljunied GRC team to convey his apologies. "杨荣文：加入与退出政坛-全因建国总 理一句话" [George Yeo: Entering and Leaving Politics All because of a Remark from Founding PM], *Lianhe Zaobao*, 24 Mar. 2015.

337 "PM Says Sorry", *Straits Times*, 4 May 2011.

338 "PM: We'll Make the System Better", *My Paper*, 4 May 2011. See also "Transcript of PM Lee's Apology", *Singapolitics*, 5 May 2011, available at https://web.archive.org/web/20110713072637/http://www.sgpolitics.net/?p=6756 (accessed 26 Jan. 2021). Notwithstanding his "repent" remark, MM Lee was deeply involved in the PAP's campaign in Aljunied, keeping in touch every night with the candidates in order to stay abreast of developments and proffer advice. He was also, after the election, the prime mover behind a closed-door dinner to thank the defeated PAP MPs. Zainul Abidin Rasheed, personal communication, 22 June 2016.

339 "Opposition's Reaction: It's Not Enough", *Straits Times*, 5 May 2011.

340 PM Lee Hsien Loong, interview with the author, 19 Dec. 2014. George Yeo, speaking soon after the election, acknowledged his own role in the PM's apology: "I told him that there was deep resentment which had to be acknowledged, not just cursorily but in detail, and it was not just a question about policies, it was not just the minds we were addressing, we had to address their hearts too. He listened very hard, he paused and later he told me that it was because of that conversation that he took that position at Boat Quay." "George Yeo Pledges to Help Transform PAP", *Straits Times*, 11 May 2011.

341 Comments after the PM's apology by PAP candidates standing in Aljunied suggesting the contrary should perhaps be read as morale-boosting attempts at sustaining the campaign effort, rather than definitive prognostications. See, for example, "Ground 'Shifting' in PAP Team's Favour", *Straits Times*, 5 May 2011.

342 George Yeo, "A Personal Message to My Young Singaporean Friends", YouTube, https://www.youtube.com/watch?feature=player_embedded&v=zQ87v52GeIg#t=0s (accessed 22 Oct. 2020). Separately, on 4 May 2011 the PAP team sent a letter, hand-delivered, to every one of the 58,000 households in Aljunied, detailing the PAP's plans for the GRC. "Letter Hand Delivered to 58,000 Homes", *Straits Times*, 5 May 2011.

343 "PM Asks for Strong Mandate to Serve", *Straits Times*, 6 May 2011. Lim Hwee Hua, pushed into political retirement by the Aljunied defeat, acknowledged soon after the election that it was only during the campaign that "we began to fully appreciate the extent of the unhappiness and resentment towards the Government". "'It Is a Surprise for Us that the Resentment Is So Deep': Minister Lim Hwee Hua Says PAP Needs to Seriously Look at Transforming Itself", *Today*, 12 May 2011.

344 "PM Asks for Strong Mandate to Serve". The theme of internal PAP rethinking and reform was touched on also by Yeo in his final campaign speech, on the evening of 5 May 2011. Acknowledging that there was resentment against the Party because it was "too arrogant and high-handed", Yeo spoke of the need for a "transformation" if the PAP wanted to engage the new generation of Singaporeans. He added, "In your hearts, you know that Singapore needs the PAP. That without the PAP, there is no Singapore." Latif and Lee, *George Yeo on Bonsai, Banyan, and the Tao*, p. 196.

345 "15 Minutes into Counting, He Knew PAP Lost Aljunied", *Straits Times*, 10 May 2011. I am also grateful to Minister Ong Ye Kung for a personal communication on the subject.

346 Yeo had kept this prediction to himself, not wanting to demoralise his running mates. See Latif and Lee, *George Yeo on Bonsai, Banyan, and the Tao*, p. 2.

347 "Anguish and Agony Paved Low's Road to Victory", *Straits Times*, 21 May 2011.

348 "A Night to Remember in Hougang", *Straits Times*, 8 May 2011; "Workers' Party Low Thia Khiang Victory Speech", *AsiaOne*, 8 May 2011.

349 Author's calculations, using figures (valid votes cast) from ELD website.

350 Non-constituency MP places were offered to the WP "best losers" in East Coast GRC and Joo Chiat SMC. These went to Gerald Giam (East Coast GRC) and Yee Jenn Jong (Joo Chiat).

351 "Architect of a Kinder, Gentler Nation", *Straits Times*, 15 May 2011.

352 This comparison is based on GRCs contested in both 2006 and 2011, and which survived boundary redrawing exercises more or less intact into the 2011 election.

353 "PAP's Sitoh Hopes to Be 3rd Time Lucky in Potong Pasir", *Straits Times*, 4 Apr. 2011.

354 "What Signals Did 2 Million Voters Send in GE 2011?", *Straits Times*, 14 May 2011.

355 "Lack of Heartland Support Cost SDP Votes", *Straits Times*, 9 May 2011.

356 "81-6", *Straits Times*, 8 May 2011.

357 "PM Lee: Serve Responsibly and Humbly", *AsiaOne*, 8 May 2011; "PAP to Adapt to New Electorate: PM", *Straits Times*, 9 May 2011.

358 "George Yeo Pledges to Help Transform PAP".

Chapter 7

New Normal: Rethinking, Reform, Revival

This general election has proven to be a little scary in the sense that many of us misjudged the mood of the population. There was nearly a swing which may result in something which all of us did not want. It nearly happened in this election.

—Goh Chok Tong, 31 December 1984[1]

After a 12.9 per cent vote swing against it in 1984, the PAP moved quickly both in its internal rejuvenation and in its follow-up in the political and policy realms. Likewise in 2011. One week after the election, Minister Mentor Lee Kuan Yew and Senior Minister Goh Chok Tong announced their stepping down from the Cabinet. The two senior politicians (who would remain as MPs), having "studied the new political situation and thought how it can affect the future", decided that it was time for "a fresh clean slate".[2] PM Lee, after accepting their resignations, appointed Goh to the positions of emeritus senior minister (an honorary title) and senior adviser to the Monetary Authority of Singapore (MAS), while Lee Kuan Yew (who relinquished the title of minister mentor) became senior adviser to the Government of Singapore Investment Corporation (GIC).[3]

This was accompanied by a radical Cabinet reshuffle—a set of changes that PM Lee himself described as "epochal". The reshuffle saw Wong Kan Seng, Raymond Lim and Mah Bow Tan left out. All three had returned below par results in their Group Representation Constituencies; all three had also helmed ministries that were linked to issues of serious public dissatisfaction. The reshuffle was, according to PM Lee, a chance to have a "fresh slate after a watershed election", with the appointment of newly elected MPs to office-holding positions reflecting "the urgency of leadership succession". To emphasise the point, Lee said that he had set himself the deadline of 2020 to hand over to the fourth-generation leadership: "I wanted a fresh start and that's why I'm calling for radical change."[4]

The new Cabinet with 15 ministers was leaner than its predecessor (21).[5] Other aspects of the reshuffle were noteworthy. New ministers were put at the helm of 11 of the 14 ministries; Finance Minister Tharman Shanmugaratnam was also promoted to deputy prime minister. An unusually large number of new MPs (seven in all) were appointed to political office.[6] Equally unusually, two of them were immediately asked to head ministries. Heng Swee Keat, the former managing director of the MAS, became education minister, while Major-General (NS) Chan Chun Sing, the former Army chief, was appointed acting minister for community development, youth and sports.

The PAP Central Executive Committee (CEC) also saw change just two weeks after the new Cabinet was announced (see Appendix Two). National Development Minister Khaw Boon Wan took over the chairmanship of the Party from Lim Boon Heng, who retired from politics shortly before the election. Deputy Prime Ministers Teo Chee Hean and Tharman Shanmugaratnam now took on the positions of first and second assistant secretary-general, respectively. Prime Minister Lee Hsien Loong remained as the Party's secretary-general. Further CEC changes, indicative of the Party's push to renewal, were to follow in October 2011, when Lee Kuan Yew, Goh Chok Tong, Lim Boon Heng, Wong Kan Seng, George Yeo and Lim Hwee Hua (the last two on the losing PAP Aljunied slate) resigned from the CEC. Among those elected the following month to fill the vacant positions were three office-holders who had been elected in the 2011 ballot (Education Minister Heng Swee Keat; Acting Minister for Community Development, Youth and Sports Chan Chun Sing; and Minister of State for National Development and Manpower Tan Chuan-Jin).[7]

The way in which the vacant slots were filled bears comment. Rather than simply following the normal practice of co-opting members into the CEC, a three-stage process of voting took place before the final six were selected. The first round of voting was done on 20 October 2011, when MPs arrived at a shortlist of 12 names from a list of all MPs. Shortly after this, Party cadres (whose ranks included non-MPs such as branch secretaries and individuals representing the Women's Wing and Young PAP) shortlisted another list of 12 names (again, all serving MPs). Then (in another departure from the normal process used in CEC elections) the highest-polling dozen from these two sessions were once again put to a vote by MPs in order to make a final list of six.[8] Party sources suggested to the media that this drawn-out method was employed in order to give a greater voice to the rank and file, with this also appearing to be the reason why MPs were apparently told to select four office-holders and two backbenchers to make the final list.[9] The backbenchers elected into the CEC were both second-term MPs: Denise Phua (known for her outspoken views, and particularly her advocacy of individuals with special needs) and Seah Kian Peng, the deputy Speaker of Parliament who was also CEO of NTUC FairPrice, a co-operative tied to the labour movement.

Post-mortem

Serious rethinking on issues where the government had previously held its ground was set in motion very soon after the election. The first major announcement made by PM Lee after unveiling his new Cabinet concerned the appointment of a committee headed by Gerard Ee, the widely respected chairman of the National Kidney Foundation (and well known for his work in the charity sector), to review politicians' salaries.[10] The Party had lost votes in 2011 on account of the issue, and there appeared to be recognition on the part of the Party leadership that the effort to persuade Singaporeans intellectually over several years on the matter had not been successful. The committee's findings, published as a White Paper and endorsed by Parliament in January 2012, contained a new formula pegging ministerial salaries to the median income of the top 1,000 earners who were Singaporean citizens, with a 40 per cent discount to reflect the ethos of political service. (The formula used before this had pegged ministerial salaries to two-thirds of the income of the top four earners in six professional occupations in the private sector.) The new formula meant a 37 per cent salary cut for entry-level ministers and a 36 per cent cut for the prime minister.[11]

The adverse election result had occurred despite the PAP government steering the economy out of the deepest recession since independence. New Party Chairman Khaw Boon Wan was put in charge of the PAP's Election Post-mortem Committee, aimed at finding out why.[12] The post-mortem committee was tellingly in its 2011 incarnation also known internally as the transformation committee: its mandate went beyond analysis of the election result to issues pertaining to reinventing the Party and ensuring that it remained relevant to a new generation.

Immediately after the election, the committee began visits to the 87 Party branches. All branches had been asked to compile individual reports on learning lessons from the polls. MPs were told that these reports should reflect honestly the views on the ground, on both local and national issues.[13] In many cases, discussions at the branch level when the post-mortem committee made its rounds were extremely spirited.[14] One charge—picked up by the media—had it that PAP activists themselves at the ground level had "shielded" MPs by filtering out unpalatable feedback (such as criticisms on matters of policy). It is possible that some activists behaved this way; for his part, PM Lee stated that grassroots leaders and volunteers provided honest feedback, but "we may not have picked up and interpreted it correctly".[15] Some MPs went further, taking the view that "filtering" had not been as much a problem as the policies themselves. Inderjit Singh, PAP MP for Kebun Baru in Ang Mo Kio GRC (an individual known for being particularly independent-minded amongst PAP backbenchers) commented when interviewed by the author:

> There was the view—and some ministers felt this—we failed to communicate policies properly and the people therefore did not understand enough. I told them that this was not the problem—the problem was that we needed a rethink in policies. I told them if in the next five years you want to win back their support, it is not a matter of explaining policies, it's to do what is right, people's lives improve . . . they will support you.[16]

Dr Amy Khor, chairman of REACH, recalled:

> After the 2011 elections, some quite senior PAP leaders asked whether we really understood the people's angst on issues of social disamenity, the sense of being crowded out by foreigners . . . why is it that we didn't seem to react to it more proactively. One of the lessons that we should learn is that if so many people on the ground and all the MPs keep telling we should be doing things differently, there must be some truth in it, you can't be brushing it away. It is not simply

government knows best and telling people what to do . . . we must be sincere about
addressing concerns through engagement and communication. Most people are
quite rational and reasonable. If enough people say something about an issue, then
the government should sit up and listen—not about populism, it is about studying
where the problem really lies.[17]

One PAP heavyweight who had lost in some ways the most, George Yeo, suggested that the adverse election result had not come about because of a lack of feedback channels. Rather, the time had simply come to "shake the box. . . . Because whatever system you set up, after a while, it becomes so predictable that it doesn't capture all the feedback that it needs to have. So a certain shaking of the box is required from time to time, and this is such a time."[18] Yeo did not specify what exactly this entailed, but subsequent moves by the PAP government in terms of new ways of engaging the people (notably the Our Singapore Conversation initiative, which shall be dealt with presently) suggest that the PAP leadership was itself in the course of reaching similar conclusions.

When, at the end of the post-mortem exercise, Khaw Boon Wan chose to speak candidly about the reasons for the Party's poor showing, imperfections in feedback mechanisms did not feature prominently. Khaw instead identified several issues:

(1) Policy shortcomings on the part of the government (including housing, immigration, transport, and issues pertaining to the cost of living) that could not be resolved by the time of the election

(2) An increased receptiveness for Opposition voices partly tied to the arrival on the scene of younger voters who could be influenced by new media

(3) A more effective Opposition that had fielded better-qualified candidates than previously

(4) Shifts in demographics: There were more young voters, who were influenced not just by what they read on the Internet, but also by a certain mood for political change

(5) The digital age: People were easily connected on the Internet, with anti-establishment sentiment also spilling over into the physical world

(6) The perception that the PAP had become disconnected from the people (itself tied to the failure to explain and win acceptance for unpopular policies)

(7) Campaign coordination on the ground that left something to be desired. In some branches, campaign strategy on physical development did not gain good traction with voters[19]

Khaw's remarks were very frank—more than was apparent. His public-facing critical appraisal of the PAP's shortcomings had, in fact, given the essence (albeit in somewhat distilled form) of the PAP's internal post-mortem conclusions.

Within internal post-mortem discussions, there was the recognition that some major policies not been handled well: a certain policy may have been calculated, but in some cases attendant consequences had not been fully foreseen.[20] Regarding foreign workers, for example, the policy of allowing in greater numbers had been adopted to take advantage of favourable global conditions and grow the economy. This contributed to income growth for Singaporeans, even among the lower-income groups. But this significant influx of foreigners created social frictions and unhappiness, with infrastructure bottlenecks in housing and transportation exacerbating the problem. Old emotive issues such as ministerial salaries could be raked up again because of the feeling that the PAP was not doing enough to improve the lives of the people. This fuelled the perception that the Party was elitist, disconnected from the people, and unsympathetic to ground realities. There was agreement, too, that the result reflected longer-term challenges in the political landscape and fundamental forces likely to persist in the years ahead, such as the conditions of the globalised economy (with the widening income divide contributing to negative sentiment on the ground).

The Party had also misread ground aspirations. Campaign strategy at the branch level had to a large degree focused on multimillion estate upgrading plans. This had little traction with voters, with Opposition parties much more successfully playing up national hot-button issues appealing to the idea of having alternative voices in Parliament. The post-mortem noted the credibility in particular of the WP and the strength of its "First World Parliament" theme, reinforced by a simple yet powerful message: to reject an 87–0 outcome. With the Opposition message resonating so strongly with voters, credible Opposition candidates (and in particular credible WP candidates) did well wherever they stood. PAP activists sensed support levels slipping away, but late in the day it was not easy to mount effective countermeasures to the Opposition campaign. It was recognised too, internally, that branches did not get sufficient support from PAP HQ, which was stretched. In the past, when there were walkovers in several constituencies the Party had been able to get by with a thinly resourced HQ, with candidates from uncontested constituencies helping out in HQ. But in 2011, and in all likelihood the elections to come, virtually all of the MPs and their branch activists would be busy fighting their own battles.

The post-mortem committee concluded that without a fundamental overhaul and reinvention, the Party would lose more ground, with the attendant possibility of another significant slide and the PAP at some point in the future being out of government. The recommendations were in many ways self-evident. The PAP government had to be prepared to relook all policies, and be prepared to rethink what was best for the country and for Singaporeans. The Party had to find ways to enhance the well-being of Singaporeans—not just those in the lower-income group, but also in the broad middle. This would require significant resources, and it had to be done without turning populist, and without compromising the spirit of good long-term policies.

The post-mortem discussions had noted that the PAP had to improve presentation and communication of policies. Programmes had to be presented in a way that resonated with the people, particularly the younger generation.[21] This meant an increased engagement with new media—an arena where untruths and distortions could spread rapidly, with negative online sentiments spilling over into the physical world.[22] The post-mortem noted shortcomings of the earlier approach, which had been not to engage anti-government websites and social media presences (so as not to give credibility to them). Ignoring half-truths and untruths spread by cynics and anti-government voices had entailed ceding the Internet space to the Opposition.[23] The PAP could no longer afford to be absent from this space. It had to master this medium and also find ways (and the right people) to generate content that captured the national mood and debunked false allegations.[24]

⁕ঞ⁂

The PAP's internal self-reflection did not end with the completion of the post-mortem; for that matter, the post-mortem had not marked the beginning of such reflection. Independent of the workings of the post-mortem committee, Party leaders were from mid-2011 beginning to stress that the PAP needed to find better ways to engage and re-establish its emotional connection with the ground. A second, and not altogether unrelated, theme that would receive more emphasis in the years to come was the idea that PAP MPs and activists were there to serve the people.[25] Some of this manifested itself in terms of changes to how MPs interacted with their residents, with many MPs evincing a humbler (or service-oriented) approach to dealing with residents and addressing their issues. Some MPs began to deepen engagement with residents and interest groups—doing so in smaller groups, and more frequently. In walking—and working—the ground, PAP MPs, activists, and likely candidates for the next election eschewed conspicuous trappings of ceremony, with communication and contact becoming more personal and taking on much more of the tenor of "servant leadership", a phrase in currency at this time within Party discourse.[26]

Tan Chuan-Jin remarked on these developments:

> *Engagement isn't just engagement for its own sake. Over time, form and ceremony can actually separate you from the people you serve. Maybe in the earlier years there was a need for the outward form. Now there began to be an active effort to streamline. MPs began to go around with smaller entourages—because large groups actually create barriers. If you are a real grassroots type, an activist mixing with the residents, then you genuinely build a relationship. If you are spending all your time hanging around the MP, what sort of feedback is the MP going to get? Grassroots will start to lose that real contact—and in a few cases they might simply be surfacing their own issues. This can lead to blind spots in feedback.[27]*

Chan Chun Sing recalled:

> *Direct and sincere contact in smaller groups was an important part of the new playbook. The mark of success is not how big your event is—how many people come—it's really the real intimate connections. House visits: what counts is not*

> *how many houses you covered, but how many families you've touched. So with this kind of orientation, slowly but surely we began to see a new generation of Party activists who are much more focused on connection rather than simply contact.*[28]

The optics were changing, certainly, in terms of a much more personal form of engagement on the part of MPs. This was not simply enhanced outreach to residents.[29] A thoroughgoing change was in the making—not just in the way interaction was done, but in whom it was done with. Consequently, the PAP's feedback loop began to improve; so too did its overall sense-making. Chan Chun Sing observed:

> *Yes there were at this time intense efforts to connect with the ground—house visits, meet-the-people sessions and so on. But after 2011, we thoroughly reviewed our approach of reaching out to the known stakeholders. We wanted really to reach out to a more diverse segment of the population, in a targeted fashion. Some of these new stakeholders were disparate groups the Party would not formerly have thought of reaching out to. We had to communicate with them and understand how they felt. One example is how the Chinese Community Liaison Group went far beyond its usual outreach to engage those beyond the conventional traditional clans and religious groups to engage others and bring them into the fold. That is the art of political persuasion—you have a vision and mission you want to convince people, even relatively unknown groups, of your good intentions to bring the country to the next level.*[30]

After the 2011 election, there was an effort to reach out to and induct people with some standing in the community and influence on the ground.[31] New links were made in ways that prefigured the Our Singapore Conversation (OSC) initiative that was to get under way in 2012. Tan Chuan-Jin commented:

> *Many of us did outreach to all sorts of groups—animal welfare groups, heritage, nature groups. We even established relations with online presences that were on the whole not friendly to the PAP. In some of these cases—many of them, in fact—their politics remained where it is, but at least we had a basis to talk and a working relationship. Trust was key. Some felt, "I do not agree with you, but I am prepared to follow you because I trust you have my best interest at heart." Some felt this way because of the feeling that the PAP was competent and had the ability and also values to take the country forward. Of course, others never felt this trust, and we have to accept that. But at least now there was an avenue to connect if they wished—previously, for some there was none.*[32]

Feedback and engagement sessions were used not just to understand the aspirations of the people and groups, but to explain policies. More care was taken, compared to the pre-2011 situation, not to assume that the public would automatically understand the intellectual arguments for these policies.[33] And if individuals and groups could be won over, then this represented an opportunity not just for outreach but also for widening the Party base (including inducting new ordinary Party members, cadres and even potential MPs).[34]

The culmination of the post-2011 PAP post-mortem process came most visibly during the Party convention on 27 November 2011. In his speech, PM Lee, the Party secretary-general, said that in the face of new realities, the PAP would correct policy shortcomings, such as in housing, and do more to take care of not just the elderly and the needy, but the middle-income group too. It would overhaul its outreach strategy and consult Singaporeans more actively. Activists and MPs, Lee said, would be more empowered to reflect people's views, while ministers would work harder to build political support for tough policies. The Party would also beef up its recruitment machinery, identifying and testing out potential election candidates earlier, drawing as it did so from a more diverse talent pool.[35]

But the most important remarks PM Lee made came when he discussed the past, present and new phases of the Party's struggle. Lee provided important clues about the Party's rethinking—especially about how it saw itself against the broad currents of its own history. Noting that the Party had in the past transformed Singaporeans' lives and garnered broad-based support through successful policies, Lee observed that the 2011 general election marked the start of a third phase, where he hoped the PAP would carry the ground ("politics"), even as it pursued hard-headed governance ("policies"). If it succeeded in achieving this balance, the PAP would have used its general election setback as an opportunity to find a new equilibrium.[36]

PM Lee stressed not just the ability to persuade but also an openness to be persuaded (especially when it came to the younger generation). "As they work with us, they change—and we change," he observed.[37] He concluded: "I pledge to Singapore, a new PAP."[38]

The Game Plan

As the PAP post-mortem process wound down, its leaders were increasingly willing to talk publicly not just about shifts in thinking within the Party, but also more broadly about substantive changes of policy, extending also to reflections on what kind of society the government and people should aspire to. In an important speech in Parliament in October 2011, during the debate on the president's address at the opening of Parliament, PM Lee dwelt at length on the need to preserve social mobility in a maturing and stratifying society, as well as the stresses that income inequality could bring to Singapore. To ensure that Singapore went some way to remaining egalitarian in the face of this, Lee said that changes would be made in the education system, especially to support the disadvantaged and those who did not have a head start in life. More generally, Lee promised more social assistance to preserve opportunities for the less advantaged to rise up, with the government also enhancing opportunities for education and training.[39]

In his speech, PM Lee said that he had asked for the high-level committee to be set up after the general election in May to examine these issues. Chaired by Deputy Prime Minister Tharman Shanmugaratnam, the committee was comprehensively reviewing social policies in a holistic, multi-agency manner. This, as PM Lee made clear, was simply an inter-agency exercise—he called it a "national mobilisation".[40] The existence of the committee in question—known internally as the Social Policy Review Committee—had been alluded to before, with PM Lee in June 2011 noting that the government would undertake a "soul searching" review of its policies and approaches.[41]

This, then, represented the start of the PAP government's post-2011 policy roadmap. The government moved to come to grips with voter dissatisfaction. One area where the government moved relatively quickly to relieve pressure on various pain points was healthcare. The government announced in August 2011 moves that benefited low- to middle-income patients. These included increasing subsidies for select high-cost drugs. In addition, it was announced that MediFund (a scheme which supported the most needy Singaporeans) would be expanded to include non-residential intermediate and long-term care services, with the aim of supporting individuals ageing in place within the community.[42] One important announcement (made by PM Lee in his 2011 National Day Rally speech) was the expansion and enhancement of the Primary Care Partnership Scheme, which was aimed at making private outpatient primary care affordable. The changes, which took effect from January 2012, were to see this scheme replaced by the Community Health Assist Scheme. The enhancements included lowering the qualifying age and raising the income criteria, which meant that more Singaporeans could receive subsidies for healthcare services (including dental treatment and treatment for some chronic conditions) at clinics near their homes. The aim was to provide accessible and affordable primary care services to more Singaporeans.[43]

There were other moves that could be effected relatively quickly. In the area of housing, for example, government leaders were by mid-2011 acknowledging that rising home prices was a major factor in the adverse election result, promising that the supply/demand mismatch would be resolved within four years.[44] Decisive action was taken to ramp up the building of new HDB flats, in order to increase supply and reduce waiting times for Singaporeans. There were also further efforts to cool the property market, with four more rounds of property cooling measures from the end of 2012. Separately, in December 2011, tweaks were announced in the HDB Interim Rental Housing scheme, essentially a temporary subsidised housing scheme designed to provide short-term assistance to needy families who faced a transition in housing arrangements. The changes included increasing HDB's oversight of the operators to better meet the families' needs, and refinements in matching families who had to live together.[45] In addition, in January 2013 the Parenthood Provisional Housing Scheme (PPHS) was launched to provide temporary housing for couples. Under this scheme, married couples with children buying an HDB flat for the first time would get to rent homes from HDB while waiting for their flats to be built.[46] All these moves had the effect of relieving some of the immediate pressure on those who needed help. The overall point was that the government was showing some flexibility and going some way towards assuaging ground feeling in some quarters, which had it that the machinery of bureaucracy was unthinkingly inflexible.

But not all issues could be seen to immediately, with some continuing to rumble on after the 2011 general election. A stark reminder of issues with public transportation and infrastructure was to come in the form of massive MRT disruptions on the North South Line at the end of 2011: a five-hour disruption on 15 December followed by a seven-hour disruption on 17 December (affecting 221,000 commuters in all).[47] The incident on 15 December was particularly acute, as many passengers were literally kept in the dark and had to walk along the underground rail tunnels to reach the nearest station. These service disruptions were the most severe since the MRT started operating in 1987. PM Lee Hsien Loong announced the formation of a Committee of Inquiry (COI) to get to the bottom of the matter. But the announcement in itself could not ameliorate the fact that the episodes were a blow to the government's efforts to encourage Singaporeans to use the public transport system. The disruptions were also for their sheer scale serious dents in the government's claim, made in the lead-up to the election and on the campaign trail, that things would start to look up in terms of remedying deficiencies in public infrastructure.

There had already been other jolts. Flash floods—the result of unusually intense torrential rain—had been increasingly regular occurrences since 2010. Notable instances included flooding in the Orchard Road area in June 2010 and December 2011. These two episodes caused millions of dollars' worth of damage. Although preliminary drainage improvement and other mitigating measures had been ongoing since 2010, online chatter had it that the government had not come to grips with the problem, even after PM Lee's apology to the people on the campaign trail in May 2011 (which had included an apology for the 2010 flooding episode) and even though an inter-agency committee had been formed in 2011 to examine the issue. There was some degree of finger pointing, too, in the aftermath of the 2011 incident, with landlords and retailers taking the view that the additional mitigating measures should have been taken by the government; the Public Utilities Board, on the other hand, appeared more keen (initially, at least) to engage in technical semantics.[48]

Next, on 26–27 November 2012, came an illegal strike staged by 171 bus drivers from SMRT, a public transport provider. The strike, which involved drivers from China, had at its root issues pertaining to poor dormitory living conditions and grievances over pay disparities compared to SMRT's other bus drivers (including those from Malaysia). At its heart this was an SMRT matter, with the internal investigation concluding that the company's supervisors should have been more sensitive to drivers' complaints. But the issue did have some degree of blowback for the government, given that this was the first industrial strike since 1986. It seemed that the normalcy the PAP government had provided was no longer something that could be taken for granted.[49]

Again upsetting the sense of social normalcy was a major riot—the first in over 40 years—that took place in the Little India area on the evening of 8 December 2013. The trigger was a fatal accident involving an inebriated construction worker from India. Approximately 300 rioters (some of them intoxicated) gathered, damaging several emergency and police vehicles and setting an ambulance on fire.[50] Dozens of police and civil defence officers were injured, and damage to the tune of half a million dollars was caused. Only when officers from the Police Special Operations Command were deployed was the situation brought under control. In the aftermath, 25 individuals were charged in court, 57 foreign workers repatriated and over 200 warned.

A Committee of Inquiry (COI) led by a retired Supreme Court judge was set up to examine the causes of the riot and make recommendations. The COI found that on the whole the response on the part of the police was commendable, but there had been specific lapses, particularly during the earlier phases of the riot. There was also the need to improve communications and incident response protocols.[51] Although the COI was emphatic that the riot was not linked to any form of discrimination and did not affect Singapore's ethnic harmony, subsequent debate and discussion (particularly in the online realm) linked the incident to ongoing ethnic tensions within Singapore, with some of the discussions revealing in themselves a xenophobic strand, especially when it came to the issue of overcrowding.[52] Not entirely unexpectedly, some in the online arena took the view that the incident was the consequence of the government's manpower policies and over-reliance on foreign migrant workers.

There were also other issues that impacted the Party in a somewhat direct manner. One example was the presidential election held on 27 August 2011—the first contested presidential election since 1993. Those contesting in 2011 were Dr Tony Tan (former deputy prime minister and, until December 2004, PAP chairman), Dr Tan Cheng Bock (a former PAP backbencher with a reputation for speaking his mind), Tan Kin Lian (former CEO of NTUC Income, the largest local insurance cooperative), and Tan Jee Say (who, it will be recalled, had contested in the general election under the SDP ticket).[53]

Strictly speaking, this election was not a party political matter at all, since all candidates were required to be non-partisan and could not be a member of any political party.[54] Notwithstanding this, Dr Tony Tan was widely seen as the candidate favoured by the PAP and by the leadership, despite not being formally endorsed.

Dr Tan Cheng Bock had been a PAP MP from 1980 to 2006. He had enjoyed broad-based grassroots support as an MP and, notwithstanding his longevity in the Party, had enjoyed a reputation as something of a contrarian both within and without. He said that "many" former PAP MPs were helping with his campaign behind the scenes, and that he had strong support from the rank-and-file grassroots Party members.[55] Tan also claimed that many PAP members openly told him that he had their support, despite their being told by PAP leaders not to support him. These claims appear to have had some currency with the ground—at any rate, they appear to have been widely believed.[56]

Dr Tony Tan's winning percentage of 35.2 per cent of the vote (a hair ahead of Dr Tan Cheng Bock's 34.85 per cent) was perceived by commentators as a vote by a large base of people against the Party. Questions were even asked about the internal cohesion within the PAP itself. Dr Tan Cheng Bock in his concession remarks stated as a fact that the results showed the Party was split "exactly right down the middle" (something denied by PAP MPs), adding for good measure that many from the PAP grassroots had ignored Party leaders' advice not to support him.[57] Also of note was Tan Jee Say's vote share of 25.04 per cent. This was indicative, it appeared, of sizeable lingering ground resentment against the PAP and its policies. Tan Jee Say's support levels may have had something to do with the fact that his campaign had an activist tinge to it: he was campaigning by his own account for a presidency that provided "checks and balances on the Government"—a role that politicised the office of the president. His interpretation of the presidential role was sharply dissonant from that of the government's view, which held that the president had to act within the role and limits prescribed by the constitution. In this reading the president's role was more custodial in nature, with the responsibility to ensure that Singapore's reserves were safeguarded, but apart from this role the president had to act on the advice of the Cabinet.[58] This, the more limited (but also realistic) reading of the role of the president, was put forward by the government and was the line taken by Dr Tony Tan and Dr Tan Cheng Bock.

The overall sense from the politicised presidential election was that of a febrile ground that had yet to settle after the 2011 general election. For the PAP, there were to be more setbacks. A by-election for the Hougang Single-Member Constituency was held in May 2012 because of the expulsion of the sitting MP, Yaw Shin Leong from the Workers' Party. Yaw, a protégé of Workers' Party chief Low Thia Khiang (and hand-picked by Low to stand in the Hougang seat in the 2011 election), had been expelled by the Party for refusing to explain his alleged involvement in extramarital affairs. There was strong criticism by PAP leaders against the Workers' Party leadership for their handling of the issue, with PAP Chairman Khaw Boon Wan stating that Hougang voters had been misled by the WP.[59] Notwithstanding this, the candidate picked by the Workers' Party to fill Yaw's shoes, Png Eng Huat, prevailed in the by-election (held on 26 May 2012) against the clean-cut and likeable PAP candidate Desmond Choo (contesting for the second time in Hougang) with 62.08 per cent of valid votes cast.

More was to come. PAP MP and Speaker of Parliament Michael Palmer (who had had the responsibility of declaring the Hougang seat vacant months earlier), a married man, resigned from the Party in December 2012 after taking responsibility for his part in an extra-marital affair. A by-election for the seat he vacated, Punggol East, was held on 26 January 2013. The by-election saw Lee Li Lian from the Workers' Party soundly defeat the PAP's Dr Koh Poh Koon with 54.5 per cent of the vote against Koh's 43.7 per cent.[60] Koh was widely seen to have dented his own chances through remarks on the campaign trail which seemed to suggest that he was somewhat out of touch with ordinary people.[61]

Rather than choosing to bask in what had been an easy victory, WP chief Low Thia Khiang seemed to downplay the WP win. Low re-emphasised the standard WP line: it was there to provide checks and balances on the PAP government. Low averred that the WP had no ambitions whatsoever to take over government. Instead, the WP would assist "whenever we can" alongside the "competent" PAP government in improving policies and Singaporeans' lives.[62] All this was somewhat ironic. Low and the WP had campaigned in Punggol East on a platform that the PAP had lost its way, but post-election, he took the view that people had to give the PAP government time for its policies to work.[63] Low was, of course, trying to temper public expectations of the WP, and in doing so to downplay the idea (present in commentary in the online world and in the press) that this was the harbinger of a possible freak result in a future general election. It was all in a very shrewd performance and tactically clever.

Punggol East represented in the post-2011 period a high-water mark of the WP—not that anyone could have known it at the time. The PAP government seemed very much on the back foot. A mere three days after the by-election came the release by the National Population and Talent Division of a White Paper, *A Sustainable Population for a Dynamic Singapore*, better known as the Population White Paper. A cursory reading of the White Paper suggested that planners would allow the total population to increase by 6.9 million by 2030 and that Singaporeans would make up not much more than half this number.[64] Predictably, the ground reaction (which largely ignored the fact that the headline 6.9 million figure was a planning parameter and not an end goal) was extremely negative, with Singaporeans pointing to the overcrowding, social tension, and competition for jobs and housing that would result. Some of the reaction verged on unthinking xenophobia; another part was somewhat more rational, pointing out that talk of 6.9 million was premature, given the government had not been successful in ramping up infrastructure to cope with the influx of immigrants that had already come in in recent years. The general sense held by many who took umbrage at the White Paper was that the government seemed still set on pursuing courses of action that were unpopular, and was failing on its promise to listen more to the people. This sense was especially pronounced given that the White Paper came in the midst of the most important national consultation exercise for years, the Our Singapore Conversation (OSC) exercise (dealt with later in this chapter). As one former NMP commented, "The most damaging thing to happen is that most Singaporeans will now feel there has been a break of trust because of how the White Paper was initially presented. It gave the strong impression that the PAP did not hear them."[65] Even the *Straits Times* was moved to comment, "As an exercise in public communication or political messaging, the White Paper on Population left much to be desired."[66]

The online backlash against the White Paper was severe enough to spill over into real-world action. A series of protests (planned and organised by a mix of civil society and Opposition interests) were organised at Speakers' Corner at Hong Lim Park, with attendance ranging from several hundred to (on 16 February 2013) a few thousand. Opposition came also from respected academics and intellectuals who said the White Paper lacked depth and analytical rigour, failing to take into account academic scholarship and comparative examples of other countries facing similar challenges.[67] There was criticism, too, at the perceived insensitivity of some of the assertions in the paper, with one footnote suggesting that nursing was a "low-skilled job" that was "hard to offshore". This necessitated apologies from both DPM Teo Chee Hean (minister in charge of population issues) and PM Lee himself.[68]

Parliament saw five days of intense debate on the White Paper. MPs from the Workers' Party contended that continued dependence on immigration and on foreign workers would dilute the core Singapore citizenry, and that the key to Singapore's continued growth and prosperity lay in improvements to productivity and growth in the local labour force, as well as getting to the root of demographic challenges such as the total fertility rate. Not all of this was at variance with what some PAP backbenchers proposed during the debate. But the Workers' Party went much further and proposed that there should be zero growth in the foreign labour force for the remainder of the decade.[69]

During the parliamentary debate, even PAP MPs expressing some support for the motion to endorse the White Paper voiced concerns about the lack of communication and the speed with which Parliament was being asked to decide on such a weighty matter, especially when problems in housing and infrastructure had not yet been fully dealt with. MPs (and not just Opposition MPs) spoke about what it meant to be Singaporean and what a "Singaporean Core" was.[70]

PM Lee promised a review of the plans within the White Paper before the end of the decade, and also said that in his view the population in 2030 would be "significantly below" 6.9 million.[71] Speaking on a range of topics, PM Lee (picking up on concerns that had been expressed within the House during the debate) pledged that Singaporeans would not be "overwhelmed" by a flood of foreigners. He sought also to assure Singaporeans that their interests were at the centre of all the government's plans, with economic growth and population policies simply the means to improving citizens' well-being.[72]

An amendment to the original motion was proposed early on during the second day of the parliamentary debate by PAP MP Liang Eng Hwa. The amended motion made it clear that the figures given in the White Paper were a planning parameter and not a target; the amendment also explicitly stated that the White Paper "supports maintaining a strong Singaporean core by encouraging more Singaporeans to get married and have children, supplemented by a calibrated pace of immigration to prevent the citizen population from shrinking".[73] This amended motion was passed by the House on 8 February 2013. All Opposition MPs and NCMPs voted against the paper.[74] Support was not unanimous within the PAP. Even in supporting the amended motion, a number of PAP MPs were somewhat critical of aspects of the paper, and especially the way that it had been presented. Opposition was most direct from Inderjit Singh, PAP MP for Kebun Baru division in Ang Mo Kio GRC. He had spoken for several years in and out of Parliament on issues pertaining to immigration and infrastructure. During the debate, Singh asked the government (not for the first time in his political career) to abandon the "instant tree mentality" of growing the population to counter declining birth rates.[75] Rather than defying the whip (which had not been lifted), he chose to make his opposition to the White Paper clear by walking out of the parliamentary debate on the paper before the vote was taken, a plan that he had confided to a very select handful of close parliamentary colleagues.[76] Singh's opposition was personal—he did not instigate other PAP MPs to vote against the White Paper—but he was nevertheless on the receiving end of a stern reprimand behind the scenes.[77]

Could, or should, anything have been done differently when it came to the presentation of the White Paper? DPM Teo Chee Hean, the minister in charge of the National Population and Talent Division, was to reflect soon after the passage of the White Paper through Parliament:

Yes, communication could have been done better. But the issue could not have been avoided.

The White Paper had set up a scenario of where we might be in future. It set out a reality that we have to face. Within the next 15 years we are going to move from a situation where one tenth of the population—300,000 people—are over 65, to 900,000 people. This is an ageing transition that no other country in the world has encountered before. The speed at which this is happening is something that we had to prepare for. Even if we had the monetary means to look after ourselves and our aged, who is going to do it physically, and who is going to keep the economy energised? It's a real issue which we have to confront.

The government was planning for infrastructure, housing and economic develop-ment. If we did not have a planning basis in terms of roughly where we are going, what do we tell investors? It's therefore a question we had to face.[78]

PM Lee later reflected on key facets of the White Paper affair. One was pre-existing negative ground sentiment on the issue of foreign workers generally, something that the government thought had been managed until the 2011 election. However, the issue ignited during the 2011 election campaign and remained combustible for a considerable period after:

The numbers of foreigners had gone up, and there had been rumblings. We did what we thought we needed to do to tackle the rumblings, including with the unions. In terms of actual impact on persons adversely affected, actually there was not a lot to worry about. I mean, that you do not like the feel is one thing, but did you lose your job? No. Are you worse off? No. If you did not have the foreigners, chances are many people would have been worse off. So before the elections, in January 2011, we made an assessment, and our sense was that the foreigners matter had quieted down but it could be stirred up again in an election. Unfortunately, this is what happened. Earlier, we got rumblings on the Internet, but on the ground, at large, there was not a very strong animosity or anger over the matter. After 2011, the ground mood had queered and it in fact became much more of a problem.[79]

After the election, the government put in place measures from July 2011 to raise the bar for the entry of foreign workers, both at the mid-skill level (where requirements were put in place for better education qualifications) and at the higher Employment Pass level (which saw salary thresholds raised). There were further rounds of tightening announced from 2012 to 2013.[80] Government leaders said on numerous occasions that they understood Singaporeans' anxieties, and that rules governing foreigners' entry would be tightened to ensure that Singapore could grow sustainably.[81] But (these statements usually continued) enough foreign workers had to be brought in to complement Singaporeans and ensure that the economy could grow. Failure to get the balance right would ultimately hurt Singaporeans.[82]

Still, there remained the sense on the ground that Singapore was changing too quickly, in ways not altogether welcome, on account of the influx.[83] While this sense had existed before 2011, developing fault lines and tensions in society had now come into sharper focus. This put national cohesion in jeopardy and was a topic that government leaders had to address increasingly frequently.[84] The White Paper brought many of these issues to a head, and also saw the surfacing of latent issues such as xenophobia. But in the final analysis, from the PAP government's point of view, the ire of many segments of the population could not mean backtracking or paralysis.

In PM Lee's view, while timing and communication mattered when it came to the Population White Paper, there was a more important issue—the mandate to lead:

> *I felt that we had to continue to govern. If after Punggol East we still did not do anything, then we are scared and might as well not be in government. So we had to govern—we had to continue with the white paper. I think ideally it would have been good if we could have taken more time to do it. The issue was that it would have been quite inconvenient because we had a lot on the agenda, and if we had moved it, a lot of things would have been bumped off our political calendar. Unfortunately, we did not really have time after Punggol East to socialise people to what the contents of the white paper were.*[85]

In the end, buffeted as the PAP government was by these winds, the business of governing had to be got on with.

※※※

A combination of adverse by-election results and the groundswell of resentment arising from the Population White Paper might on the face of it seem to have brought the Party to something of a nadir. But in fact, seeds of revival had already been planted some time before these setbacks.

In August 2012, PM Lee had announced the start of Our Singapore Conversation, a form of national dialogue. The initiative was to be led by Education Minister Heng Swee Keat. In terms of scale, OSC dwarfed previous efforts (National Agenda/Agenda for Action, 1985–88; S21, 1997–99; and Remaking Singapore, 2002–03), reaching all told an estimated 47,000 individuals through over 660 dialogue sessions. The process itself was markedly more informal, and devolved, than its predecessors. It also drew on learning points from earlier exercises. DPM Teo Chee Hean recalled:

> *Society evolves. At each phase, you have to bring people together, examine what is it we are all trying to achieve together, and then move forward again. So too with the Singapore Conversation—a process of discovering for ourselves*

where we want to go. Many of the OSC issues were there in S21. But every new generation has to examine the issues for itself—so every now and again, we have to go through such an exercise. I suggested to Heng Swee Keat that he could look at how the S21 issues were framed as a series of five dilemmas. Because that's the reality of life—a series of trade-offs. It's not just a series of wants, but choices we have to make.[86]

Despite the setback of its timing clashing head-on with opposition to the Population White Paper in February 2013, the OSC proved to be a valuable exercise in several respects. It helped the government refresh its understanding of the concerns and aspirations of the people, and served as a mechanism to surface issues that had gathered further momentum since the 2011 election. It is important to note, too, that this was part of a wider sense-making effort that was beginning to change the dynamics of engagement—an effort that had been ongoing since the 2011 election post-mortem. The OSC was the most visible reflection of this.

Many ordinary Singaporeans involved in the dialogue sessions found it a useful thought exercise to come up against the sometimes very different views of their fellow citizens; this socialisation helped all concerned understand better (even if not all were convinced) the trade-offs involved in Singapore's growth trajectory moving forward. Singaporeans involved took in the fact that there could be other ordinary, equally rational citizens sitting down with them at the various OSC dialogue sessions who could have views that were very different from their own.[87] This was also a big learning point for the government itself—the realisation that understanding and leveraging on diversity was going to be critical for the future coherence of the Singapore polity. The minister in charge of the OSC, Heng Swee Keat, recalled:

The OSC was very important in that it helped Singaporeans to understand other Singaporeans. Through sitting down with their fellow citizens, they began to understand how diverse our society had become. The elderly would have a very different set of concerns from those with young kids, and of course there were those with different political views, views on LGBT issues, those with different personal circumstances and so on.

The challenge is to see how to turn this diversity into a strength—our earlier period was defined very much in terms of racial diversity. Now increasingly there is a diversity in terms of views. We experienced this in the OSC. Dealing with this and turning it into a source of strength will be an important part of our future. Only when we have platforms for this sort of interactions—to say that we have differences but we have things in common—can we contemplate a deeper interweaving of aspirations into something that is coherent—the sense that you and I can pursue together—we can go on the same boat together, and this will meet our needs. This sense of togetherness will be critical.[88]

Layered onto the OSC initiative were (as we have seen) redoubled efforts at the ground level when it came to PAP MPs' engagement with their constituents. The latter could perhaps be called (as it indeed was by Party insiders) the "retail" aspect of politics—shaking hands and house visits were facets. There was the feeling within the heart of the PAP leadership, however (even as the OSC progressed and MPs worked the ground) that some things were not quite right at the level above this: national-level communication.[89]

Prior to 2011, a master plan for overall government communications did not exist. When it came to individual ministries, communications on aspects of policy were put out in announcements often seen by the public as bland, or somewhat turgid, or both. There was insufficient coordination when it came to which messages should come first and which themes should be prioritised. The main message could be—and often was—lost. The danger in policy messages being seen as hard to decipher or overly technical was that this could feed into a lack of trust, an emotional divide, and the perception of an elitist and distant government, even if government itself thought it was doing what was right for country and people.

The broad rethinking of government communications drew in several ministers, including at the beginning K. Shanmugam and Chan Chun Sing. At the core of the effort lay attempts to identify and flesh out important themes that ministers would communicate in a series of speeches over a period of time at pre-identified events. A second and closely linked line of effort was gaining a better understanding of what the key concerns were on the ground and within various groups an effort that coincided with the OSC but also went beyond it. Once these concerns had been identified and discussed internally, "retail" aspects could come in—meeting the groups themselves. These included (inter alia) clans, unions, educators, workers in particular sectors, the intelligentsia, or even particular ethnic groups. All these were seen as important influence nodes. Time was also spent talking to students at universities, as fighting for hearts and minds of young people in particular was judged important. Many of these engagements took place not in large auditorium-style gatherings that involved hundreds of people, but with smaller numbers, as personal engagements made for higher-quality interactions. As more ministers (including junior ministers) and MPs were roped in, the entire effort became a broad exercise that saw ministers and MPs engaging groups, hearing their concerns, explaining the need for certain policies, and giving government thinking behind certain issues, including thorny ones such as having a sustainable population.

Some of the other issues surfaced in these engagements, and those that came under the OSC, pertained to education and housing. But there was a particular and persistent strand of OSC feedback centring on healthcare costs and retirement adequacy. By the end of the OSC in August 2013, Heng Swee Keat was clear that these concerns had been heard, and that substantive government responses—that would give patients, the elderly and their families assurance and greater peace of mind—were in the works.[90] As a whole, the leadership had by this point concluded that that these issues surfaced indeed weighed on the minds of many. PM Lee decided to go for universal healthcare coverage.

On 18 August 2013, during a landmark National Day Rally speech setting out a new direction forward for the government, community and people, PM Lee announced a swathe of changes to expand social safety nets. These included the introduction of two major schemes. The first was the Pioneer Generation Package (PGP), and the second was the new universal medical insurance scheme MediShield Life, which would replace the existing MediShield. Some consideration should be given to these moves here, which both had "assurance" as key leitmotifs.

MediShield Life was essentially a basic universal health insurance plan, based on risk-pooling, that provided lifetime coverage for all Singapore residents. It provided better coverage and higher payouts (particularly for large hospital bills as well as selected outpatient treatments involving large outlays such as dialysis and chemotherapy) compared to MediShield, the older scheme it replaced. The new scheme was an important part of the government's overall aim of improving healthcare affordability, with the government shouldering a higher share of national healthcare spending.

The PGP, on the other hand, was aimed at older Singaporeans. The package, conceived to honour their contributions to nation-building, provided the Pioneer Generation with greater assurance regarding healthcare costs in their old age.[91] A total of 450,000 citizens aged 65 and above stood to benefit from the generous suite of healthcare benefits at the core of the package, which the government undertook to fund to the tune of $8 billion.[92]

The government set up the Pioneer Generation Office (PGO) in 2014, almost on the fly in a start-up fashion. Instead of making a major announcement and crediting funds directly into the account of beneficiaries (which would have been in keeping with what was done for some earlier assistance schemes), there was a marked changed in approach. There was no assumption (as there had been with earlier policies) that the people would automatically grasp the details of the package. There was a massive campaign (spearheaded by the PGO) at the ground level to communicate details of the PGP. In addition to house-to-house visits to explain details directly to seniors, the intense ground engagement included road shows in constituencies and dialogue sessions, and the use of volunteers who were known as Pioneer Generation Ambassadors.[93] The wide reach meant that large swathes of society—not just seniors—grasped the policy and its implementation.

A key differentiating facet between the PGP and many other government help schemes lay in how the PGP disregarded what assets (including housing) recipients owned: help was being given regardless of where the recipients lived. This had an effect particularly on eligible seniors living in private estates who felt left out of existing schemes that gave help on a means-tested basis. In addition, the younger generation, many of whom felt that they had until that point felt the pressure of caring for their ageing parents, now sensed that some of this burden was finally being taken off their shoulders.[94]

Trust rose: more people, the PAP leadership assessed, were again beginning to feel that government was working for them.

The impact of other policy decisions was also beginning to be felt at this time. By the third quarter of 2013, prices for both public and private housing had begun to drop, after two years of heightened housing construction and four rounds of cooling measures, with the market on its way to a soft landing. By 2013, HDB had largely cleared the backlog of first-time HDB buyers. The vast majority of young couples who applied for a Build-to-Order flat in non-mature estates were able to book a flat within their first or second try. In addition, affordable housing was made more accessible to upper-middle-class Singaporeans through raising the income ceiling for both subsidised HDB flats and ECs, first in 2011 and again in 2015.

Flexibility on part of HDB as well as the Ministry of National Development (MND), already more in evidence from 2011, continued. The Multi-Generation Priority Scheme was introduced in March 2012 to help married children and parents live near each other. This scheme accorded priority allocation to married children and their parents when they jointly applied for flats in the same Build-to-Order (BTO) project. Several other measures were introduced in 2013. The Parenthood Priority Scheme (PPS), introduced in January 2013, which saw first-time buyers with young children given priority allocation for BTO flats, was itself extended in March to first-time buyers expecting a child.[95] The quota of two- and three-room BTO flats in non-mature estates was doubled for second-time buyers, following earlier increases in 2012.[96] There was greater support for the elderly to right-size, with HDB reserving studio apartments for eligible elderly applicants under the Studio Apartment Priority Scheme. This benefited elderly individuals who were downsizing and wanted to continue to live near their current flat or private property, or near their married children.[97]

Beginnings

PM Lee's National Day Rally speech in 2013 was not simply a vehicle to mark the ushering in of MediShield Life and the PGP, as important as they were.[98] The speech was brought to a new venue, the Institute of Technical Education College Central, a move made to signal change, and to underscore the government's commitment to invest in every Singaporean. Lee also spoke about the "new way forward" for Singapore, which was at a turning point, with a more diverse and vocal populace and contested political landscape and a maturing economy.

This sense continued into the PAP convention, held on 8 December 2013, which was themed "Our New Way Forward: A Call to Action". In his speech at this event, PM Lee spoke directly and personally about the Party's future. The Party would, Lee said, "rededicate ourselves to our core purpose: To continue taking Singapore forward and improving Singaporeans' lives".[99] Prior to the convention, key branches—the PAP Policy Forum, Women's Wing and Young PAP—had embarked on a series of dialogues with activists, seeking views on the PAP's way forward. The PAP Policy Forum played a key role in coordinating these dialogues and from this input assembling a resolution tabled at the convention. In its opening lines, the resolution stated: "We, members of the People's Action Party, dedicate ourselves to upholding our democratic socialist ideals, serving our nation and improving Singaporeans' lives." The resolution additionally highlighted the PAP's resolve to uphold "an Open and Compassionate Meritocracy, where everyone has the opportunity to fulfil his or her potential". Also stated within was the aim "to build a Fair and Just Society, which shares the benefits of progress with all Singaporeans", as well as developing "a Democracy of Deeds, and nurture a sense of collective responsibility and community action. We strive for a society where citizenship embodies a duty to one another and our community."[100] Finally, in an echo of PM Lee, the resolution pledged the PAP anew to its cause: "to build a better Singapore, for Singaporeans and with Singaporeans."

These ideals and the resolution itself did not simply emanate from the type of pre-convention dialogues involving activists that usually preceded the event. The thinking ran much deeper. As Heng Swee Keat noted:

> The 2011 election result had the effect of getting many of us to think hard in terms of what the PAP is about—what should be retained, what changed? Many of us went back to the history of the Party. In our earlier years, what resonated so well with the people was this sense that whatever the government does, it is for the well-being of Singaporeans and Singapore. So, that had to be front and centre. Even in our very earliest years, the PAP talked of a fair and just society. But in the modern era, we face issues like global inequalities. Singapore being a very globalised competitive economy—how do you balance all this? How do we redistribute? We had many internal discussions within the Party and leadership on what the right balance was and what sort of Singapore we wanted to build. Did we want a Singapore where disparities grow wider? The answer was no—we had better find ways to strengthen social cohesion and our sense of togetherness—these are what will hold our society together.[101]

Prominent in the resolution was mention of the PAP's democratic socialist ideals. Lawrence Wong, then the minister for culture, community and youth, who had the key role in drafting the new resolution, had observed first-hand how activists in engagement sessions had asked what the PAP actually stood for in the present age, when Singapore was a mature society. It was therefore the right moment in time to have a clearer statement on what the PAP stood for.[102]

> In the resolution—one of the first few lines on upholding the democratic socialist ideals of the Party arose from the whole engagement process we had, including with our own activists. One of the questions many activists were asking at the time was, what does the Party stand for? What is our cause? There was soul-searching, and we had our own engagements with our Party activists. In fact, the Party's values are relevant and do not change—but the way we apply these values continue to evolve and change. We are a Party of change—the values do not change, but the circumstances do change, the external environment changes. Globalisation is changing our society. Naturally the application of these values will have to adapt and change. That's why policies have to evolve. One of the strong themes that came out from the PAP conversation was that the Party should uphold its values. It was very important to help crystallise what we stood for and to get our own activists to understand better the whole aim

and objectives of the Party. We stand for our democratic socialist ideals and a
compassionate meritocracy and a fair and just society, and we ensure that every
Singaporean shares in the success of the nation, so that no one is left behind.[103]

The spirit of the 2013 resolution, and some of its most striking passages, were enshrined in changes to Article 2 of the PAP constitution (concerning Party objectives) that were effected at the Party conference in December 2014, the first changes to the Party constitution since 1982.

Compassionate meritocracy (a new phrase that had featured in the 2013 resolution) featured the sixth Party objective within the revised constitution: "to strengthen an open and compassionate meritocracy, with opportunities for Singaporeans to develop skills in diverse fields, active support for those who start off with less, and ladders to success at every stage of life". Party Chairman Khaw Boon Wan had presaged these changes during his speech at a November 2014 awards ceremony marking the 60th anniversary of the Party:

Meritocracy is still something we value and uphold. But as our society becomes
more settled, with widening income distributions, extreme meritocracy may
favour those with means. This can undermine social mobility and lead to
stratification in society. So we must change our approach. . . . We need to
develop an open and compassionate meritocracy—one with opportunities for
Singaporeans to develop skills in diverse fields, active support for those who start
off with less, and ladders to success at every stage of one's life, and not just focused
narrowly on success in school.[104]

The seventh Party objective in the revised constitution ran as follows: "to develop a democracy of deeds, where citizenship embodies both rights and duties, and nurtures a sense of collective responsibility and community action". Khaw Boon Wan commented that a fair and just society could not be conceived solely in transactional terms. It had, in Khaw's words, to "involve the community—to engage the human spirit, to provide personal fulfilment and to strengthen collective well-being. It must strengthen the culture of responsibility for one another."[105]

The intention in all this was that even as the PAP changed, and even as the government did more for the people, the people would also have to step up. As PM Lee observed:

We are in great danger of people taking the attitude that it is the government's
job to solve all our problems. If there is a problem, I look for the government. My
participation, my job is to criticise, my job is to talk, give feedback, but your job
is to make sense of it and make it happen. I think that is a bad basis on which to
build a nation.[106]

The period 2013–14 marked not just turning a corner, but also some sense of the Party as a whole recovering its bearings.[107] In doing so, the Party recast its relationship with the people within the prism of its own self-reflection, emerging with a clearer picture of what the social compact ought to be.

⁓ϡ ϡ⁓

The period 2011–13 had seen a national effort of consensual discussion, fleshing out the aspirations of Singaporeans, and—as the culmination, most visibly through the OSC and the revision of the PAP constitution—pointing the way forward in terms of where nation and society should go.

Striking as they were, these efforts did have parallels in earlier history. There was, for example, the Remaking Singapore process (2002–03) and Refreshing PAP (which spanned the same period). But these were done from a position of strength, after the PAP's crushing victory in the 2001 general election. The parallel with the National Agenda/Action for Action initiative of 1985–88 is more apt, coming (for the most part) as it did after the 1984 general election reverse. It is worth pausing to ponder the parallels.

The Agenda for Action, presented to Parliament by 1DPM Goh Chok Tong in February 1988, was the result of forums and discussions on the National Agenda at the grassroots level involving the people in the years preceding.[108] The 1988 document had a direct lineage from the PAP's 1984 manifesto (which saw the PAP outlining its Vision 1999), with an important deliberative stop at the January 1988 Party convention (which had seen the final draft endorsed). The Agenda for Action was seen by the PAP government as a consensus with the people.[109] In both 1985–88 and 2011–13, it was younger Party leaders who were at the forefront of the process.[110]

The differences between the Agenda for Action and the OSC also bear comment. The Agenda had a brief mention of the importance of a compassionate society and of supporting those unable to care for themselves—the infirm, disabled and destitute. It also gave a nod to the idea that the fruits of progress would be shared, with every Singaporean getting a fair share according to his contribution. Otherwise, however, much of the document was taken up with the exigencies of growth. The OSC report said much more about those left behind, the elderly, and those with special needs. There were also broadened definitions of success, and more space for diversity of views and people with different interests and niches in life. The overall emphasis was on a tempered, compassionate meritocracy.

Counternarratives

The Pioneer Generation Package, MediShield Life, and other policy moves and refinements were well received by the public. Naturally, there was talk on the ground and by the Opposition that all these schemes, and changes in policy thinking, had arisen on account of a PAP reaction to the 2011 election setback. After the MediShield Life Review Committee issued its recommendations, the WP put out a statement noting that many of the suggested enhancements that went into MediShield Life had in fact been articulated by WP MPs in Parliament (as well as by Singaporeans) over the years.[111] This in turn provoked a robust response from the PAP. It was necessary, from the PAP's point of view, to show that changes in policy had not been made as kneejerk reactions to the 2011 electoral reverse. It was important, too, not to give too much credence to the notion that it was the WP speaking up in Parliament since 2011 that had pushed the government to do more—this might lead to the impression on the part of the people that more Opposition members were a good thing. Senior Minister of State (Education and Law) Indranee Rajah, for example, stated that the WP had been "vague" and "quick to claim credit". MediShield Life and other changes, Indranee said, far from coming out of WP interventions in Parliament, had actually germinated through the feedback process on the ground, and in particular the OSC.[112]

Other senior figures were to weigh in. As DPM Tharman observed in August 2015 in a lecture at the Economic Society of Singapore, most of the main currents that had led to major policy shifts owed their origins to government predating 2011:

> And I recognise of course, there's some political cunning, saying this all came about because of GE 2011. I'm sorry, it didn't. The world did not start in 2011. We made very clear our intentions and motivations well before 2011, made clear that it was a multi-year strategy, and step by step, starting with the kids, through working life, and into the senior years, we have been moving towards a more inclusive society. We intend to continue on this journey, learning from experience and improving where we can. But this is a far more important agenda than a reaction to 2011.[113]

Tharman observed that the government's shift to the left in social and economic policies began well before 2011, with government transfers to the bottom one-fifth of the population seeing an uptick since 2005. Major departures in orthodox policymaking had included the groundbreaking Workfare policy—"a major break in our thinking"—which began topping up the wages of low-income earners from 2007.[114]

In other areas of policy, the relevant agencies had been drawing up plans prior to 2011. The Ministry of Health had, for example, been examining measures to expand capacity, with work on new hospitals commencing before 2011; in addition, there had been major moves to push care out from the hospitals into the community through the regional health systems. During this period, the ministry began expanding nursing home capacity and tried to conceptualise new primary care models. This thinking carried on after 2011, receiving a public unveiling in the form of the Healthcare 2020 Masterplan, first introduced during the 2012 budget debates.[115]

The to and fro in Parliament played out over 2011–15 between the PAP and the WP should not be seen solely as attempts by the PAP to set the record straight on the genesis of policy changes: there was far more to it than this. Locking horns with the WP should be viewed against the wider backdrop of the PAP's strategy of keeping the WP off-balance. On 28 May 2014 there was a memorable—and in parts heated—exchange between PM Lee and WP chief Low Thia Khiang. PM Lee had said it was "striking" that the WP leader's response to the address had nothing on the substance of the government's programme, "no critiques, no suggestions, no alternatives, nothing". Lee challenged the WP to state its direction and to "explain to Singaporeans what you stand for. . . . And what you stand for cannot be what the PAP is doing and a little better. That means you have no stand. Whatever the PAP's standing, ask them to do better. That's easy, I can do that too. But where do you stand?"[116]

Accusing the WP of not nailing its colours to the mast, and flip-flopping on issues (such as immigration), was part of the PAP critique developing especially from 2014 to 2015: that the WP MPs had put up a substandard performance in Parliament.[117] Such attacks were to become more pronounced as the next general election drew near. On the campaign trail in September 2015, PM Lee was to remark in response to a question about the belief that good governance could mean having more than one party in Parliament, "so, you voted for a tiger in the chamber and you got your mouse in the House. . . . But when they [the WP] come to Parliament, none of those issues are raised because they know in Parliament, if they raised those issues face-to-face, in debate, they will be pinned down, and the fallacies and the insincerities and the untruths will be exposed."[118]

Future PAP, Future Singapore

DPM Tharman's widely noted 2015 speech at the Economic Society of Singapore saw him sketching out the government's fresh approaches on three fronts: raising real incomes, tackling income inequality, and maintaining social mobility.[119] Observers in certain quarters commented that the PAP's keenness to restate its democratic socialist credentials had been accompanied by a pronounced shift to the left. Earlier, in 2013, Tharman had given his own take on this shift, and how the leadership approached social policy:

> If I compare our thinking in Cabinet, or the weight of thinking in Cabinet, when I first entered politics about 11 years ago, I would say the weight of thinking was centrist but there were two flanks on either side of it. There were some who were a little right-of-centre, and there were some a little left-of-centre. Now I would say the weight of thinking is left-of-centre. You still get diversity of views in Cabinet, but the centre of gravity is left-of-centre.[120]

Some mused about the long-term costs (as well as fiscal sustainability) about this shift, especially given that funding promised infrastructure, as well as schemes like the Pioneer Generation Package, meant that the government was in some years running budgetary deficits.[121] A few went even further, criticising the PAP for introducing populist moves to win back the ground. PAP leaders, however, stated that the government had no intention of becoming more populist, and that the fundamentals underpinning the social compact—such as encouraging self-reliance—still remained.[122]

PM Lee later reflected:

Our democratic socialist party values run deep, we have not changed that. You can think of us as left of centre. But the world has also changed: globally, the centre has moved left in terms of received thinking. The circumstances have changed. I think that it is necessary that we calibrate our position. If we keep our old formula in a new society, that would really become a much more right wing position than it was where we were.

If you asked me about my own position, I think my own position has changed; my attitudes have softened. Ten years ago I would have been very unhappy to go and make all these subsidies and grants and concessions to people, and feeling that we ought to do more. Firstly, you think it is a slippery slope. Secondly, you do not really believe that it will solve the problem. But after all these years, I have come to the conclusion that sometimes you cannot solve the problem, but you have to be seen to be doing something about it, whether it is very effective or not. It is a gesture to show that you are not completely out of touch. So we have done that. In terms of substance, I do think we have to do more. The dispensation we had before, where we say "What we will provide for you and your family are the opportunities for you to work hard and do well" will not work for a significant number of people, and we have to balance out that part of it.[123]

Former Foreign Minister George Yeo recalled:

After 2011 there was much better provision of infrastructure and much greater redistribution. These moves in the earlier days would have been considered heretical. But these could be done now because we had accumulated the resources to reallocate. We are in a strong financial position. Our taxes are still not too heavy, we have that luxury for the time being—but we can't assume that will be forever. We are ageing. Future commitments will be heavier. A point may come where we are no longer in the happy position of having all these resources to dish out. Then it becomes a real hard trade-off—taxing to redistribute, versus staying competitive and attracting investments . . . we've got to find this balance eventually. But calculating such trade-offs is part of the PAP's honed instincts.

There's also a sense—which arises out of Singapore's condition—that if we are not centralised, we will lose coherence and efficiency. Being small is a disadvantage, but being small enables us to react quickly to threats and opportunities. If we are small yet inflexible, our survival is imperilled. Our institutional arrangements must allow for a fairly high centralisation of power—that's very much the instinct and belief of the PAP. How do we stay centralised while being responsive to increasingly diverse needs on the ground? It is the key challenge. There are forces at work beyond our control, like technology and globalisation, which are fragmenting human society. How all this plays out in the coming years will define Singapore's future. Trust between government and people is critical and has to be rebuilt.[124]

As George Yeo suggested, and as the OSC showed, the Singapore of the future would be populated by a diversity of interests clamouring for attention and recognition. PM Lee had this to say on this subject:

> I think we have to take a somewhat detached perspective. We have to be responsive to groups, which have special interests, and are concerned with those special interests, but at the same time we should not be captured by them. LGBT groups have concerns which they are pressing the government, some more vocally than others, but they are not the only groups. The conservative groups are also pressing the government, some more vocally than others. There are other areas where there are special interest groups. There are pet lovers, animal lovers, there are nature groups, there are groups of people who are enthusiasts for some sport or activity, there are people who have a particular passion about some issue, some cause, maybe foreign workers, maybe the disabled. I think in a normal society and normal democracy, all these will have their place. People will speak and form and mobilise and will lobby. That is par. But the government has to be in touch with them, make friends with as many of them as possible, but at the end they must stand back and say, now what is in the national interest? How far can I accommodate you without compromising the national interest? And we have to make that judgement.[125]

If the PAP has ultimate responsibility for the political judgements that take Singapore forward, where does this leave the idea of having national conversations or having a consensus with the people? The view of the leadership is clear: governance must go hand in hand with a strengthening of the national consensus. DPM Tharman observed when interviewed in 2014:

> At the end of the day, it is the government that has to make decisions. And that remains our method. We are elected, we are responsible, we must listen, but we will be the ones who are accountable for the results, and people will decide whether we've done the right thing or not. We intend to lead, and not just to be carried by the flow.
>
> But there is something else that is as important, which is the role the PAP must play in the national discussion. It is not just a matter of having a national conversation, having all views aired, and then you collect them and decide what the sensible course of action is. The way that discussions are conducted, whether they end up with views and feelings becoming more polarised or whether the centre ends up stronger, is a critical feature of national life. It can easily become polarising. Look around the world. That polarisation can very easily happen in Singapore. The PAP has to be the party which is not just about its own beliefs, but about leading, coaxing and urging towards a strong consensus in the discussion. Not just being an arbiter. And certainly not just waiting on the sidelines. We must never be that way.[126]

Lessons of Victory

The PAP's efforts, policy- and engagement-wise, were to pay off in the general election on 11 September 2015, which it won with a resounding 69.9 per cent of the vote. This—the most keenly contested election since independence, with 181 candidates vying for 89 seats—was the PAP's best electoral showing since 2001. The 9.8 per cent improvement over 2011 confounded critics and even many neutral observers who had expected the Opposition to build on its gains of 2011. There were several noteworthy results in SMC and GRC battlegrounds. In Punggol East, the WP incumbent, Lee Li Lian (who had won the seat in the 2013 by-election there), was unable to withstand the challenge from veteran PAP MP Charles Chong. There was also an extremely close—and surprising—result in Aljunied GRC. The WP team there, helmed by party chief Low Thia Khiang, clung on with a slim margin of 50.95 per cent, down from 54.7 per cent in 2011, against an unheralded PAP team with no star names—and only after an early-morning recount.[127]

The result also surprised many within the Party. Within the top tier of the PAP, knowledgeable individuals (including experienced hands at predicting election results) varied in their pre-election prognostications. Several had internally forecast a small range around the 2011 result. Several senior PAP figures, including Party leaders, felt that the loss of one or more GRCs (besides Aljunied) was possible, or even likely, with East Coast and Marine Parade GRCs felt to be particularly at risk.[128]

PM Lee shared his view:

> Our honest take internally was that if we held steady, it was an achievement bearing in mind that there is a demographic shift taking place every five years—loyal elderly people passing from the scene and younger cohorts who we knew far less about in terms of their loyalties coming in. That alone meant a secular drift down—so if you hold steady it's an achievement, because you are resisting that drift.[129]

In short, no one saw 69.9 per cent coming.

Opposition missteps played into the result. There had since 2014 been concerns raised over apparent lapses in accounting and governance at the WP-run Aljunied–Hougang–Punggol East Town Council (AHPETC). An audit of AHPETC accounts for 2012–13 carried out by the auditor-general concluded in February 2015 that there had been "major lapses".[130] The WP maintained that the problems had been the result of "human error", also claiming (when the issue was aired in the lead-up to the campaigning period) that agencies such as the Ministry of National Development were attempting to politicise the issue and discredit AHPETC.[131] Unsurprisingly, PAP MPs sought to extract maximum leverage on the issue, pushing for transparency and accountability.[132]

Following the election, some senior WP figures were prepared to concede—privately—that the AHPETC issue might have swayed some voters against the WP.[133] This was hindsight, but on the campaign trail there was little sign overall that the issue had forced the WP on the defensive. Indeed, the WP campaigned with a certain swagger. There had been signs on the campaign trail that the Opposition (particularly the

WP) felt an easy ride was in store, expecting to make more inroads into PAP-held GRCs and SMCs. This perceived arrogance, combined with the fact that all seats were contested, seemed to weigh on the minds of the electorate.[134] On the campaign trail on 7 September 2015, Khaw Boon Wan, PAP chairman and national development minister, spoke of the possibility of a freak result, observing, "We cannot be sure of a PAP government on September 12. There probably will be but there is no guarantee. And we notice some opposition candidates have spoken of wanting to take over the government."[135]

Was this simply a PAP scaremongering tactic? It might perhaps be more accurate to say that the PAP leadership felt it incumbent to point out to the electorate (especially the younger segment) that an Opposition that was on paper stronger than it had ever been was now contesting all seats, and to point out at the same time the full ramifications. The people could then decide for themselves. Heng Swee Keat remarked:

> People knew that this was now a very serious business. All seats were contested. This was a very important factor. It wasn't any longer simply about electing Opposition for the sake of checking the government—which was an appealing prospect to some. The possibility of a freak election result was no longer just something quite remote. There would be important ramifications on how our country is governed, how things are run. Making this observation was not simply a PAP tactic. The people themselves were attuned to this. We could sense that voters were much more sensitive to the seriousness of the election, and the seriousness of governing.[136]

Some ministers went even further. Ong Ye Kung recalled:

> I thought—I might be in the minority view—we were closer to a change in government than many of us were prepared to admit. It could actually have been quite close. The momentum after 2011 all the way up till early 2015 was, I think, severely against the government. And we were looking at a strong possibility of losing two or three more GRCs, and maybe a quarter or a third of the seats at the impending GE. I think the trajectory was pointing in that direction. And I think the Opposition still campaigned on that assumption. Which turned out to be a mistake. To me, if the election had been held in January 2015, the PAP could have lost a third or a quarter of the seats, which would have totally undermined the effectiveness of the government. With the government's effectiveness clipped, the stage would be set for the Opposition to challenge for the mandate to govern at the following GE.[137]

In its own internal post-election discussions, no one factor was held to be the clincher when it came to the overwhelming nature of the result. There was the recognition that the election had been in many ways anomalous, one that had seen in its lead-up events that clearly had a bearing on the result, but which would not be repeated. The first was SG50: a carefully choreographed year-long series of events, celebrations and ceremonies that marked the 50th year of Singapore's independence. SG50 inevitably had an impact, reminding the people as it did about the achievements of the PAP and its track record of over 50 years in office (a tenure that pre-dated independence). The narrative acquired added poignancy following the death of Lee Kuan Yew, Singapore's modern founding father and first prime minister, on 23 March 2015. Following his passing, a seven-day period of national mourning was declared. Before the state funeral held on 29 March 2015, huge numbers of people—well over a million—paid their respects at the lying-in-state at Parliament House, as well as various other designated community sites.[138] Many paying their respects were from the generation that had grown up during Lee's premiership. But there were also many from the younger generation, who had during the period of mourning discovered (through media documentaries and newspapers) much more about Lee and his crucial role in the Singapore story. For many in this generation, Lee's passing was an awakening and a reminder of how far the nation had come.[139]

The effect of Lee's passing and the SG50 factor were obvious. There were other less visible (but still critical) areas that moved the needle when it came to percentages.

In the aftermath of the 2011 election, there had been deliberate moves to build up the Party machinery and the apparatus at HQ in order to fight elections. Progress had been made by way of putting in place a dedicated team overseeing the key functions of communication, intelligence, plans and operations during elections—a task made more pressing given the realisation that future elections would see most or all wards contested, leaving few MPs free to perform auxiliary support roles.[140]

The Party amply resourced its candidates. PAP candidates spent $5.3 million during the campaign, while the expenses of the eight Opposition parties contesting these seats totalled $1.8 million. A great deal of this was in conventional real-world expenditure: posters, banners, advertising collaterals and printing of materials.[141] However, 2015 was the first election that saw significant investments by the PAP in terms of social media engagement. This included funds allocated to the development of the PAP's mobile app, website development and support, as well as Facebook ads and Twitter engagement. The Party also hired a public relations consultant whose brief was "influencer engagement", which in plainspeak meant generating ad hoc content for the PAP's Facebook page.[142] One study on social media use during the election was to show that 70 per cent of voters used Facebook for election information, compared with just 22 per cent in 2011. Social media users were prepared to "like" pro-PAP content, with the PAP Facebook page becoming the most liked of all the parties, overtaking the WP, which had been the most liked in 2011.[143] This was a crude measure by some standards, but perhaps indicative of the PAP's newfound all-around comfort level and savviness—especially compared with 2011—in dealing with social media.[144]

If the PAP's new media strategy was more coherent and effective than it had been in 2011, its fan base was also much more in evidence than previously. In 2015, it was far easier to find postings and discussion threads in support of the PAP. There were also by 2015 websites and Facebook pages (not linked officially to the Party) set up with the main purpose of supporting PAP policies and attacking the Opposition.[145] All this when taken together played a major role ensuring that Opposition issues did not catch fire in the 2015 general election as they had in 2011.[146]

The issue of the hard yards on the ground since 2011 by PAP MPs and activists has been discussed earlier in this chapter, but bears mentioning again. Various MPs had their own ways of engagement and rebuilding trust with the people. Mohamad Maliki bin Osman, MP in East Coast GRC (in the division of Siglap) was convinced that trust-building meant that the Party had to be present, seen and felt in the lives of people.

> *The first 2–3 years post 2011 saw intense engagement on the ground—we were out on house visits 3 times a week together with dialogue sessions over the weekends. We organised the division into very micro units and called the approach "micro engagement". Every street, every HDB block, every condominium unit was covered. For private estates, we ended up walking down the streets and grouping every street into "clusters". Every cluster, each of not more than 100 units, was to us a small micro community. We ended up with detailed mapping of all clusters, and we made every effort to visit every household. Through the house visits, we understand the profile of every household—we knew what the concerns were, including emerging concerns. We would analyse the profile and observe for emerging trends—elderly, young people, children—and we respond with programmes that relate to that profile. That allows us to engage them directly in future when we do other forms of engagement. Following the house visits, we would proceed with dialogue sessions—we called them "In-conversations" or chit-chat sessions with each micro community. We did one block at a time—the numbers ranged from 20 to 80 people. There is no point having huge events without a personal connection. These sessions were about telling them who we are, that we are here to serve them. We wanted to know their concerns, how we can make their lives better, and what aspects of government policy they are unhappy about and shared other government policies they weren't aware of that were relevant to them. They could say absolutely anything. We gathered all this feedback and tried our best to respond. We followed up with the relevant agencies and put in place a monitoring system where after three months following the dialogue, we would provide an update to the residents on the issues raised and status of responses. This was a concerted and sincere effort, and in some cases we tried to raise funds and worked with community partners to bring in visible projects to show we were responding to some of their needs. Where issues raised were localised, we engaged the residents and formed task forces to find solutions.*[147]

The efforts by Dr Maliki, his activists and branch members might seem extraordinary, but they should be taken here as indicative of the work put in on the ground by PAP MPs across the board in the years 2011–15. The efforts of some of these MPs, each with their own systems of engagement, were explicitly recognised by PM Lee Hsien Loong at the December 2015 Party convention, following the election victory that year.[148]

The Party leadership surveyed its victory with scant exultation; instead, what dominated was a sober sense of realism. The winning margin, while large, had not meant a complete rout of the Opposition—especially a credible Opposition. Overall, the WP's vote share in the wards it contested slipped 6.8 points to 39.8 per cent, compared with 46.6 per cent in the 2011 general election. This was an appreciable slide, but still not the 9.8 percentage point nationwide swing against the Opposition. Already, within the PAP, there was a sense of looking forward to the future, with a mindfulness of the battles to come. Ong Ye Kung reflected on the post-election sense within the Party:

> *The result saw the WP vote share slide, but not by as much as the other parties. Just 6.8 per cent. And this in the SG50 year, and which saw Mr Lee's passing. I think the underlying desire for the people to have an effective Opposition is not going to go away. And we have to recognise that. We also needed to realise that the lessons of victory are as important as the lessons of defeat. It is good to be mindful we got here because we are humble, we are servant leaders, we have policies that benefited the people, and they can feel this is a government that cares. But I would have to say post-2015, there was no complacency amongst all our activists, volunteers. They don't have the attitude where they say we won big therefore we can push our weight around. . . . I don't see that. They knew 2015 was hard fought. The next round will be very hard fought too.*[149]

PAP leaders were prepared to reflect in public—and in rather generous terms—when it came to the road ahead for the Opposition. Just two days after the election, DPM Tharman observed to reporters that the Opposition played a critical role in advancing the country, commenting also that the Opposition should reflect on the result: "We need a more reflective attitude after each election, and on how the opposition can continue to play a constructive and positive role in Singapore politics, as they must."[150]

Three months after the election, DPM Tharman shed light on why these comments were necessary:

> *Firstly, we all had a feeling that we needed some humility after this very significant swing in our favour. A second reason is that we have to get a good measure of the longer-term direction in Singapore politics. And we must be stewards in this whole process. Not just participants in the fray. PAP is actually larger than Party politics in reality. It is what founded Singapore, it is what made Singapore, and it is what has to see through the evolution of Singapore's political space. And I think some of us in the leadership have to give Singaporeans the sense that we are guiding Singapore through its future in a way that isn't just about the PAP but about the maturing of the political space. We want to see that maturing of this political space. We think it's good for the PAP and good for Singapore.*[151]

Giving his own analysis of the election result at the Party convention in December 2015, PM Lee noted key factors included improvements in the precise areas of policy and infrastructure (housing, transport, immigration and healthcare) that had cost the Party votes in 2011, as well as the hard work by PAP MPs and activists over the previous four years. PM Lee acknowledged, too, the SG50 effect: the celebration of Singapore's 50th year of independence had strengthened the sense of national identity and benefited the Party.[152] PM Lee also highlighted one other factor that had had a bearing on the election result—Lee Kuan Yew's passing. The national mourning had had a profound effect on the nation and "left a deep mark on all of us".[153]

Lee Kuan Yew's last major public appearance had been on 7 November 2014, when, clearly frail, he attended the commemorative event marking the 60th anniversary celebrations of the PAP. Fittingly, this took place at the Victoria Memorial Hall, where it had begun for the Party all those decades ago. Fittingly, too, present with Lee were a few of his old comrades-in-arms (including Ong Pang Boon, Jek Yeun Thong and Chan Chee Seng), together with other pioneer activists who also had been there at the creation. At this event, Party Secretary-General Lee Hsien Loong rededicated the marker that commemorated the founding of the PAP, a marker his father had previously unveiled ten years before at the 50th anniversary of the Party, but which had been temporarily stored away. Lee Hsien Loong made clear that the symbolic act of rededication stood for those present committing themselves anew to the Party and to Singapore:

> *Singapore needs good leadership, and the PAP has the duty and the responsibility to provide this leadership for Singapore. We are a national party that represents Singaporeans from all walks of life. We must always be one. We have a team of Ministers and MPs, national leaders and ground activists, of mobilisers and organisers. Committed to Singapore, capable of taking the country forward.*
>
> *The PAP cannot decline this responsibility, much less can it shirk this responsibility. If we fail, Singapore is in deep trouble, and we must not fail.*[154]

Notes

1   "My Two Goals—by the Striker".
2   "Lee Kuan Yew Steps Down", *Straits Times*, 15 May 2011. The change was initiated by a brief phone call between MM Lee and SM Goh. MM Lee rang Goh, and the two discussed the need to press on with renewal in the ranks of the Cabinet. Neither man hesitated (ESM Goh Chok Tong, personal communication). There are marked similarities to the PAP leadership deciding to press on with renewal after the 1984 election result.
3   "PM's New Cabinet: Radical Reshuffle", *Straits Times*, 19 May 2011.
4   Ibid.
5   After a previous electoral setback, in 1984, there had been a similar (but smaller-scale) streamlining, with the Cabinet downsized from 14 to 12.
6   They were new Members of Parliament Heng Swee Keat, Chan Chun Sing, Tan Chuan-Jin, Lawrence Wong and Sim Ann, as well as backbenchers Halimah Yacob and Josephine Teo.
7   "Khaw Boon Wan Is New PAP Chairman", *Straits Times*, 2 June 2011; "PAP Unveils 6 New Committee Members", *Straits Times*, 10 Nov. 2011. Another office-holder elected

into the CEC was Grace Fu, senior minister of state with two portfolios (information, communications and the arts; and environment and water resources), and also chairman of the PAP Women's Wing.

8   The six from the final list put to MPs who were not chosen were Lui Tuck Yew (minister for transport), Lawrence Wong (minister of state for defence and education), Josephine Teo (minister of state for finance and transport), Halimah Yacob (minister of state for community development, youth and sports), Michael Palmer (Speaker of Parliament), and Charles Chong (deputy speaker and, like Palmer, a backbencher). "PAP Cadres Shortlist 12 MPs for Six Vacated Exec Spots", *Straits Times*, 28 Oct. 2011; "PAP Unveils 6 New Committee Members".

9   See also "PAP Unveils 6 New Committee Members".

10   Significantly, this announcement was made immediately after the Cabinet swearing-in ceremony, on 21 May 2011. "Ministerial Pay to Be Reviewed", *Straits Times*, 22 May 2011.

11   *Salaries for a Capable and Committed Government. Cmd. 1 of 2012. 10 January 2012* (Prime Minister's Office), available at https://www.nas.gov.sg/archivesonline/government_records/record-details/e5fd8a9c-d634-11e5-b8bb-0050568939ad (accessed 27 Jan. 2021).

12   The post-mortem committee was made up of Khaw Boon Wan (chairman), Lawrence Wong (secretary), Chan Chun Sing, Heng Swee Keat, Janil Puthucheary, Dr Amy Khor, Assoc. Prof Muhammad Faishal Ibrahim, Ong Ye Kung, Indranee Rajah, Sim Ann, Tan Chuan-Jin, Teo Ser Luck and Zaqy Mohamad.

13   "PAP Takes Hard Look at Election Showing", *Straits Times*, 15 June 2011.

14   Interviews (2013–17) with multiple PAP activists and MPs, including those present at branch-level post-mortem discussions.

15   "A Closer Ear to the Ground", *Straits Times*, 2 June 2011.

16   Inderjit Singh, interview with the author, 9 Feb. 2017.

17   Dr Amy Khor, interview with the author, 2 Dec. 2014.

18   "George Yeo Pledges to Help Transform PAP", *Straits Times*, 11 May 2011.

19   "GE 2011: What Went Wrong", *Straits Times*, 28 Nov. 2011; "Strategies, Shortcomings & Solutions", *Petir*, Jan.–Feb. 2012, pp. 16–8.

20   In the following paragraphs dealing with internal deliberations and conclusions, I have relied on documents from the PAP archive made available to him pertaining to the 2011 election post-mortem, as well as on interviews with members of the post-mortem committee.

21   The young had clearly shifted in terms of how they kept track of current and political events. One survey carried out by the *Straits Times* in March 2011 showed that the Internet was the top source for 36.3% of the young (against 35.3% who chose newspapers). In the equivalent survey in 2006, 88% said they relied on newspapers, 87% on TV, 12% on news websites, and only 5% on blogs and forums. "Survey of Young Voters: Cost of Living Is Top Concern of Gen Y", *Straits Times*, 16 Apr. 2011.

22   Although all PAP constituencies had some form of online presence during the 2011 campaign, the actual new media operations were left to the discretion of the candidate and the branch activists. There was also overlap—between, for example, the Facebook page of a constituency, run by the People's Association, and the Facebook page of the PAP branch

in that constituency, run by activists. The weaknesses in the decentralised strategy were acknowledged by Zaqy Mohamad, an MP for Hong Kah GRC and new media facilitator for the PAP: "We did not spend enough effort clarifying things that are wrong, which is a problem because if a misconception is left to be repeated long and often enough, people will believe it." "PAP Set to Launch Constituency Websites", *Straits Times*, 18 Mar. 2011; "Social Media: The New Voice of GE", *Straits Times*, 15 May 2011.

23   "My own honest view is that we made no impact in the new media in GE [General Election] 2011 despite the best efforts [*sic*] that the people we have, whom we thought are good at new media. . . . And because there was unhappiness, there were a lot of people who voiced their views and positions on the internet and some of which became viral." Lim Boon Heng, Transcript of Oral History Interview, Accession No. 002288/6, Disc 6, p. 102 (National Archives of Singapore), available at https://www. nas.gov.sg/archivesonline/oral_history_interviews/record-details/e7062f9c-1162-11e3-83d5-0050568939ad (accessed 27 Jan. 2021). Lim, a 31-year veteran PAP MP, NTUC secretary-general (1993–2006), minister in the Prime Minister's Office (2001–11), and PAP chairman from December 2004 until June 2011, retired from politics before the 2011 election as part of the PAP's renewal.

24   In one *Petir* editorial written during the phase when the post-mortem was being deliberated, PM Lee observed that simply being on social media platforms was not enough—what was important was "being on the same wavelength as netizens and resonating with the Internet generation". Lee Hsien Loong, "The Road Ahead", *Petir* editorial, July–Aug. 2011, pp. 6–7.

25   The theme itself was not entirely new and, in fact, had been enunciated by Party leaders, including PM Lee, before the 2011 election. In his rally speech during the Young PAP's 25th anniversary celebration on 17 April 2011 (where the PAP's 2011 general election manifesto was also launched), PM Lee observed, "Never forget we're servants of the people, not their masters. Always maintain a sense of humility and service. Never lord it over the people we're looking after and serving." "PAP Banks on the Future with New Line-up", *Straits Times*, 18 Apr. 2011.

26   See, for example, "No Fanfare when PAP MPs Meet Residents", *Straits Times*, 19 June 2011. Changes included curtailing practices that had existed for some time, such as asking residents at constituency functions to stand and applaud at the MP's arrival, and gathering residents together at the venue for an event long before the MP was due to arrive (the practices were often not originally put in place by the MP, but by grassroots leaders keen to ensure a good reception for the MP).

27   Tan Chuan-Jin, interview with the author, 24 June 2016. At the time of the interview Tan Chuan-Jin was minister for social and family development.

28   Chan Chun Sing, interview with the author, 12 July 2016. At the time of the interview Chan Chun Sing was minister in the Prime Minister's Office and NTUC secretary-general.

29   For a useful snapshot of the hard yards put in on the ground even before efforts were enhanced from 2011, see Meredith L. Weiss, *The Roots of Resilience: Party Machines and Grassroots Politics in Singapore and Malaysia* (Singapore: NUS Press, 2020), pp. 194–5.

30   Ibid. For some sense of the ground-level engagement and outreach done from 2011 specifically in constituencies that the Party was determined to either win back or hold onto in the face of what promised to be a strong Opposition effort at the next election, see "In PAP's Fight for Votes, a Formidable Weapon: Boots on the Ground", *Today*, 19 Sept. 2015.

31   Worth noting are parallels with the situation after the 1984 general election, when there was a similar organised, intensified effort by the PAP to reach out to groups both within and outside of the mainstream. Then, as in 2011, some of the energy derived from the fact that at the individual level, PAP MPs were concerned and perhaps even fearful of what the future might bring, wanting to play their part to ensure that there would be no repeat in the next general election. "Certainly, after 2011 there was a step up in activity— MPs raised their game. In some ways this was an unrecognised strength of the PAP. But in some ways, the sense of fear had led to a step up in activity; 2011 instilled fear. I could see it in individual MPs. Some were genuinely worried about how they are going to do in 2015" (Tharman Shanmugaratnam, interview with the author, 18 Dec. 2015). For outreach and engagement efforts after 1984, see the treatment in chapter 1.

32   Tan Chuan-Jin, interview with the author, 24 June 2016.

33   See "PAP Sets Out How to Reinvent Party", *Straits Times*, 10 Sept. 2011. It is worth noting that later on, at least some Opposition figures in their analysis of the 2015 general election result were to place a great deal of weight on the fact that PAP MPs worked the ground harder, suggesting also that Opposition members themselves might have underestimated this factor. See "毕丹星谈败选因素与反思：反对党低估耕耘基层重要性" [Pritam Singh on factors of the election defeat and personal reflections: opposition underestimated the importance of grassroots engagement], *Lianhe Wanbao*, 7 Aug. 2016.

34   Interviews with senior Party officials involved in Party recruitment, 2011–13.

35   "PAP Begins Search for New Candidates", *Straits Times*, 29 Nov. 2011.

36   "Time for New PAP Story", *Straits Times*, 5 Dec. 2011.

37   "PM: I Pledge a New PAP", *Straits Times*, 28 Nov. 2011; "Politics Must Take a Bigger Role Now", *Petir*, Jan.–Feb. 2012, pp. 14–5.

38   "PM: I Pledge a New PAP".

39   Singapore Parliamentary Debates, 20 Oct. 2011 (Lee Hsien Loong).

40   Ibid., p. 383.

41   "Resolving Policy Dilemmas", *Straits Times*, 11 June 2011.

42   "More Health Care Help for the Elderly", *Straits Times*, 15 Aug. 2011; "Thumbs Up for Subsidised Health Scheme", *Straits Times*, 18 Aug. 2011.

43   "More Singaporeans to Benefit from Subsidized GP Care from Today", *Straits Times*, 15 Jan. 2012.

44   "Rising Home Prices Hit PAP's Vote Share: Mr Lee", *Straits Times*, 14 Aug. 2011. At the ground level, high HDB prices and long waiting times had not simply been a grievance held by would-be first-time buyers. Many elderly people were worried about their children not being able to afford their first home. Some of the loss of votes amongst the elderly was in the PAP post-mortem deliberations put down to this factor (author interviews with Party activists with direct involvement in the post-2011 election post-mortem).

45   "Tweaks to Interim Rental Scheme", *Straits Times*, 31 Dec. 2011.

46   The PPHS was expanded in April 2013 to all first-time married couples, including those without children. In September 2013, eligibility was further broadened to include married couples comprising a first-timer and a second-timer, divorced or widowed parents with children, and engaged couples. "Childless Couples Can Apply to Rent From Pool of 900 Available Subsidised Flats", *Straits Times*, 8 Apr. 2013; "Temporary Housing Scheme Extended to More Groups", *TODAY*, 19 Sept. 2013.

47   *Report of the Committee of Inquiry into the Disruption of MRT Train Services on 15 and 17 December 2011*, Ministry of Transport, 3 July 2012, available at https://www.mot.gov.sg/news/COI%20report%20-%20Executive%20Summary.pdf (accessed 27 Jan. 2021).

48   See "Floods Again? Shops Seek Answers", *Straits Times*, 25 Dec. 2011; "Troubled Waters over Liat Towers", *Straits Times*, 28 Dec. 2011; and "Who Pays for Flood Damage?", *Straits Times*, 28 Dec. 2011.

49   See "Firms Must Reflect on Employment Practices", *Straits Times*, 2 Dec. 2012; "How the Illegal Strike Unfolded", *Straits Times*, 2 Dec. 2012; and "SMRT Told to Take Greater Care with HR Matters", *Straits Times*, 2 Dec. 2012.

50   Approximately 80 individuals were actively involved in the rioting. A sizeable figure (approximately 200 individuals) were found to have had a passive involvement in events. *Report of the Committee of Inquiry into the Little India Riot on 8 December 2013* (Ministry of Home Affairs, 27 June 2014), p. 57n8, available at https://www.mha.gov.sg/docs/default-source/press-releases/little-india-riot-coi-report---2014-06-27.pdf (accessed 27 Jan. 2021).

51   Ibid., pp. 53–4, 58.

52   Ibid., p. 46.

53   George Yeo seriously considered declaring his candidacy, notwithstanding his own doubts about whether he had the temperament for the job. He had encouragement from his supporters (both within and without the PAP), and also the benefit of a "guerrilla marketing" campaign initiated by a group of younger supporters (something that would probably have also stood him in good stead in the Aljunied contest). Yeo bowed out only when it became clear that Dr Tony Tan was willing to run and that he had the support of the PAP. *George Yeo on Bonsai, Banyan and the Tao*, pp. 2–3; "In George They Trust", *Straits Times*, 5 May 2011; "Supporters Collect Presidency Forms for George Yeo", *Straits Times*, 7 June 2011.

54   To meet the eligibility criteria, prior to the presidential election Dr Tony Tan and Dr Tan Cheng Bock resigned from the PAP. Tan Jee Say resigned from the SDP.

55   It appears that just over a dozen former PAP MPs assisted Dr Tan Cheng Bock in his presidential bid, either financially or through active involvement in his campaign (author's estimates and assessment, based on interviews with current and former PAP MPs).

56   "Many Ex-MPs Helping Me: Tan Cheng Bock", *Straits Times*, 23 Aug. 2011.

57   "There's Definitely a Division in the PAP: Tan Cheng Bock", *Straits Times*, 29 Aug. 2011.

58   "On the Roles of President and the Parliament", *Straits Times*, 17 Aug. 2011. For the government's explication of the role of the president, see "Law Minister Debunks Notions on What President Can Say", *Straits Times*, 6 Aug. 2011.

59   "Come Clean with the People, WP: Khaw", *Today*, 16 Feb. 2012.

60   Kenneth Jeyaretnam from the Reform Party and Desmond Lim from the Singapore Democratic Alliance also contested but polled an insignificant number of votes.

61   "PAP Doctor Diagnoses His Election Defeat", *AsiaOne*, 16 Dec. 2013.

62   For Low's reaction and the analysis, see "Don't Take Result as Sign of Future Trend: Low", *Today*, 28 Jan. 2013; "Why Workers' Party Is Talking Down Its Victory", *Straits Times*, 29 Jan. 2013; and "S'pore the Real Winner in Punggol East By-election", *Straits Times*, 3 Feb. 2013.

63   "Don't Take Result as Sign of Future Trend: Low".

64   *A Sustainable Population for a Dynamic Singapore: Population White Paper* (National Population and Talent Division, Jan. 2013), pp. 46–9, available at https://www.strategygroup.gov.sg/media-centre/population-white-paper-a-sustainable-population-for-a-dynamic-singapore (accessed 27 Jan. 2021).

65   "Let's Get Over That Emotional Hump", *Straits Times*, 9 Feb. 2013.

66   "Population White Paper: Let's Get Over That Emotional Hump", *Straits Times*, 10 Feb. 2013.

67   See, for example, "Fury over 6.9 Million Population Target for Singapore", *Yahoo*, 30 Jan. 2013; and Donald Low, Yeoh Lam Keong, Tan Kim Song and Manu Bhaskaran, "Economics Myths in the Great Population Debate", *IPS Commons*, 8 Feb. 2013, available at http://www.ipscommons.sg/economics-myths-in-the-great-population-debate/ (accessed 27 Jan. 2021).

68   "Govt Will Learn from White Paper Experience", *Straits Times*, 12 Feb. 2013.

69   Singapore Parliamentary Debates, 4 Feb. 2013 (Sylvia Lim); and 5 Feb. 2013 (Gerald Giam).

70   See, for example, Singapore Parliamentary Debates, 4 Feb. 2013 (Christopher de Souza).

71   Singapore Parliamentary Debates, 8 Feb. 2013 (Lee Hsien Loong).

72   Ibid. See "Discussions on Issue of Population 'Will Go On'", *Straits Times*, 9 Feb. 2013; "Population-Plan Review Nearer 2020: PM", *Straits Times*, 9 Feb. 2013; and "The Right Policies to Ensure Success", *Straits Times*, 9 Feb. 2013.

73   Singapore Parliamentary Debates, 5 Feb. 2013 (Liang Eng Hwa).

74   NMPs Faizah Jamal, Janice Koh and Laurence Lien voted against the motion. Another, Assoc. Prof Eugene Tan, abstained.

75   Singapore Parliamentary Debates, 5 Feb. 2013 (Inderjit Singh).

76   Inderjit Singh, interview with the author, 9 Feb. 2017.

77   Ibid.

78   Teo Chee Hean, interview with the author, 12 July 2013.

79   PM Lee Hsien Loong, interview with the author, 19 Dec. 2014.

80   For these moves, see "Higher Bar, Better Treatment", *Straits Times*, 29 Dec. 2011; "New Year, New Policies, New Measures", *Straits Times*, 2 Jan. 2012; and "S Pass Quotas to Be Cut, Criteria Tightened", *Straits Times*, 26 Feb. 2013. From September 2012, there were stricter rules in place when it came to skilled foreign workers bringing in their families to Singapore. "Stricter Rules on Passes for Foreign Workers' Families", *Straits Times*, 10 July 2012. As observed in chapter 6, the beginnings of the tightening on foreign worker inflows (as well as on immigration policy generally) predated the 2011 election and can be traced to 2009.

81 In early 2013 the government mooted the idea of a fair employment framework. This was aimed at strengthening the Singapore core within the workforce and ensuring that Singaporeans were considered fairly for jobs. This framework (which covered higher-level jobs at the Employment Pass level) was to come into force in August 2014. See "Don't Rush into New Framework on Fair Employment Practices, Say Stakeholders", *Straits Times*, 27 Feb. 2013; and "Firms to Consider Singaporeans Fairly for Jobs", Ministry of Manpower press release, 23 Sept. 2013, available at http://www.mom. gov.sg/newsroom/press-releases/2013/firms-to-consider-singaporeans-fairly-for-jobs (accessed 27 Jan. 2021).

82 See, for example, "Inflow of Foreign Manpower Needs to Be Calibrated to S'pore's Interest: Tan Chuan-Jin", *Straits Times*, 16 Aug. 2012.

83 "The Real Fear: Being Pushed Out of Home", *Straits Times*, 9 Sept. 2012.

84 "PM Lee Flags Two Worries", *Straits Times*, 5 Apr. 2012.

85 PM Lee Hsien Loong, interview with the author, 19 Dec. 2014.

86 Teo Chee Hean, interview with the author, 12 July 2013.

87 See *Reflections of Our Singapore Conversation*, Our Singapore Conversation Secretariat, Aug. 2013, p. 2, available at https://www.reach.gov.sg/-/media/reach/old-reach/ oursingaporeconversation/oursingaporeconversationreflection.ashx (accessed 27 Jan. 2021). In order to ensure that as many as possible could connect with the stories, a deliberate decision was made to put out this publication in a readable, eye-catching newsletter-style format (including online), and not as an extended report, even at the risk of not doing justice to the full volume of discussions. Heng Swee Keat, interview with the author, 6 Apr. 2017.

88 Heng Swee Keat, interview with the author, 6 Apr. 2017. At the time of the interview Heng Swee Keat was minister for finance.

89 What is described in this section of the chapter stems from interviews with multiple ministers involved in the overall shaping of government communications from 2012 onwards. The steps taken should be seen as an effort in some ways distinct from (but pursuant to) the post-mortem discussions that took place immediately following the 2011 general election.

90 "Policy Changes Coming Up: Heng Swee Keat", *Straits Times*, 10 Aug. 2013.

91 "Tribute to Pioneer Generation", *Straits Times*, 10 Feb. 2014; "Civil Service Must Pay Attention to Areas of Governance", *Channel NewsAsia*, 25 Mar. 2014. For retrospective recognition by government leaders of the role played by Pioneer Generation ambassadors in face-to-face communication, see "Govt Aims to Explain Policies More Clearly to Affected Groups", *Today*, 18 Apr. 2016. An equally concerted push was made to communicate the finer points of MediShield Life in an easy-to-understand manner. "MediShield Life: What's Your View? Tell REACH", *Channel NewsAsia*, 27 June 2014.

92 "Full S$8b for Pioneer Generation Package to Be Set Aside in Budget", *Today*, 22 Feb. 2014.

93 Pioneer Generation ambassadors personally went door to door explaining details of the package, in different languages. From 2015, ambassadors were also trained to explain details of other schemes such as MediShield Life. See Lai Szu Hao, "Communicating to Our Pioneer Generation", *Ethos* 15, 14 June 2016.

94   Dr Mohamad Maliki bin Osman, interview with the author, 25 Oct. 2017. In the
      period 2011 to 2014, Dr Maliki (in addition to holding senior parliamentary secretary
      and minister of state positions) was mayor of South East District, which encompassed
      East Coast and Marine Parade GRCs, as well as Joo Chiat, Mountbatten and Potong
      Pasir SMCs. His success in ground-level engagement with residents in East Coast GRC
      (discussed further below in this chapter) led to his being asked to come on board to assist
      the Pioneer Generation Office to develop its training program for volunteers and Pioneer
      Generation ambassadors to better connect and engage with individuals in dialogue
      sessions (Dr Mohamad Maliki bin Osman, interview with the author, 25 Oct. 2017).

95   For these moves, see "New Priority Scheme for Flats Attracts Families", *Straits Times*, 14
      Feb. 2013, and "More Couples to Get Help with New Homes", *Straits Times*, 9 Mar. 2013.

96   Quotas for BTO flats in non-mature estates for second-timers were raised from 5% to
      15% in 2012. The quotas were then doubled from 15% to 30% for two- and three-room
      flats in non-mature estates in 2013.

97   See "Bumper Launch to Meet Diverse Housing Needs", Housing & Development Board
      press release, 30 May 2013, available at http://www20.hdb.gov.sg/fi10/fi10296p.nsf/
      PressReleases/2B6DE2EB72C9056548257B7B000333F7?OpenDocument (accessed
      28 Jan. 2021). In addition, the Parenthood Provisional Housing Scheme was expanded.
      Married couples without children buying an HDB flat for the first time would now be
      eligible to rent homes from HDB while waiting for their flats to be built. Previously, only
      married couples with a child no older than 16 would have been eligible. "More Couples to
      Get Help with New Homes".

98   The schemes were implemented at different times on account of their complexity. The
      Pioneer Generation Package was unveiled progressively from mid-2014 (a key milestone
      being PM Lee's launch of the Pioneer Generation Card on 1 August 2014), while
      MediShield Life saw its official rollout in November 2015.

99   PM Lee Hsien Loong, speech at Party Convention 2013, available at https://www.pap.
      org.sg/conference-convention/party-convention-2013-speech-by-pm-lee-hsien-loong/
      (accessed 28 Jan. 2021).

100   "People's Action Party Resolution 2013", available at https://www.pap.org.sg/news/
      peoples-action-party-resolution-2013/ (accessed 28 Jan. 2021); "Addendum to PAP
      Resolution 2013", available at https://www.pap.org.sg/news/addendum-to-pap-resolution-
      2013/?doing_wp_cron=1611800205.7827069759368896484375 (accessed 28 Jan.
      2021). "Democracy of deeds" was a phrase coined by S. Rajaratnam (then Singapore's
      foreign minister) in 1971. For the original context of Rajaratnam's words, see Irene Ng,
      "Has S. Rajaratnam's 'Democracy of Deeds' Gone Beyond Words?", *Straits Times*, 14 Aug.
      2016; and "Revisiting S. Rajaratnam's Democracy of Deeds", *Commentary* 25 (2016;
      National University of Singapore Society), pp. 11–20, available at https://www.nuss.org.
      sg/publication/1465553438_commentary2016_VOL25.pdf (accessed 28 Jan. 2021).

101   Heng Swee Keat, interview with the author, 6 Apr. 2017.

102   Wong had earlier (in 2011) observed that there was a need to coherently articulate what
      the Party stood for as its sense of purpose had been diluted: "Part of it is that the party
      has been in existence for so many years. People after a while tend to forget what it stands
      for. . . . So it is useful to go back and revisit some of these fundamentals from time to

time." "Galvanise S'poreans through Strong Ideals", *Straits Times*, 21 May 2011. See also "To Be a Fair, Just Society that Is Also Sustainable", *Straits Times*, 14 Dec. 2013.

103   Lawrence Wong, interview with the author, 13 May 2016.

104   "PAP's Success over Past 60 Years Based on Values, People: Khaw", *Channel NewsAsia*, 22 Nov. 2014.

105   "Update to PAP Constitution Timely: Khaw Boon Wan", *Straits Times*, 8 Dec. 2014.

106   PM Lee Hsien Loong, interview with the author, 19 Dec. 2014.

107   It is worth noting that from this point on (2013), PAP leaders seemed much more willing to reassert a theme that had been present for decades in the PAP's discourse and self-reflection: that the PAP aspired to be much more than an ordinary party and was in fact a national institution. This idea was present, for example, at the 2014 Party conference. Party Chairman Khaw Boon Wan said during his speech at this event, "we the PAP must continue to be a national movement dedicated to representing and serving all Singaporeans. Our Party must seem to encompass all strata of society. Whether worker or employer, whether Malay, Chinese, Indian or Eurasian, whether young or old, all must feel that our Party cares about them, and will look after their interests." "PAP's Vision for Singapore: A Nation of Opportunity", Party Chairman Khaw Boon Wan, speech at PAP Party conference, 7 Dec. 2014, available at https://www.pap.org.sg/news/paps-vision-for-singapore-a-nation-of-opportunity (accessed 29 Jan. 2021; full speech archived at PAP HQ). Compare 1DPM Goh's remarks while presenting the PAP's Agenda for Action in 1988: "[The PAP] is a key institution in our body politic. It is the organization that has to, first, have the vision, then the ability to achieve national consensus, and finally turn that vision into reality. So we have to have a vision, attract able people to join so that we can, together, turn our vision, our role, into a meaningful programme for the people." "Agenda to Be the Basis of Future Govt Policies", *Straits Times*, 26 Jan. 1988.

108   *Agenda for Action: Goals and Challenges. Misc. 2 of 1988. Presented to Parliament by the First Deputy Prime Minister and Minister for Defence and Ordered by Parliament to lie upon the Table,* 15 Feb. 1988.

109   "Agenda to Be the Basis of Future Govt Policies", *Straits Times*, 26 Jan. 1988.

110   PM Lee Kuan Yew said to Party members at the 1988 PAP convention where the Agenda for Action was adopted, aiming his remarks at the younger generation, "You have to define the kind of society you want not only for yourselves and your children; you have to decide what kind of people you want Singaporeans to become." "In Pursuit of New Goals and Ways", *Straits Times*, 24 Jan. 1988. When presenting the agenda to Parliament in February 1988, Goh was clear that Parliament was asked to endorse the agenda as this captured the goals of the younger leaders and also the hopes and fears of the younger people, with younger leaders wanting to forge consensus with the people before the transition from old to new guard had been completed. Singaporeans would have a chance to get to know the younger leaders and have a sense of what Singapore would be like under the next generation of leaders, who were the primary authors of the agenda. "Groundwork Will Enable Younger Leaders to Embark on New Chapter", *Straits Times*, 26 Feb. 1988.

111   "WP's Statement on MediShield Life Review Committee's Recommendations", Workers' Party, n.d., available at http://www.wp.sg/wps-statement-on-medishield-life-review-committees-recommendations-2/ (accessed 28 Jan. 2021). Subsequently, on the campaign

trail in early September 2015, the WP listed on its website several policy changes ("government policy U-turns") made after 2011, which the WP said corresponded closely with points in its manifesto proposals in 2011: "The government made several key policy reversals since GE2011. This shows that a competitive political system with a significant opposition party presence in Parliament fosters a government that is more responsive to the needs and aspirations of Singaporeans." "The Workers' Party in Parliament, 2011–2015", Workers' Party, n.d., available at http://www.wp.sg/wp-in-parliament-3/ (accessed 28 Jan. 2021). See also "Workers' Party Cites Differences Its MPs Have Made", *Straits Times*, 3 Sept. 2015.

112 "Indranee Slams WP for Claiming Credit for MediShield Life Recommendations", *Today*, 10 June 2014.

113 "The Relentless Effort that Goes into Keeping Singapore Inclusive", *Straits Times*, 19 Aug. 2015.

114 "Govt Made Shift Well Before 2011 Election: Tharman", *Straits Times*, 15 Aug. 2015.

115 "Healthcare for the Future", *Straits Times*, 7 Mar. 2012.

116 "Heated Debate between PM Lee and WP's Low in Parliament", *Today*, 29 May 2014; "PM Lee Questions WP's Stand on the Big Issues", *Straits Times*, 29 May 2014.

117 On immigration, see "PAP and WP Argue over Immigration Issue", *Straits Times*, 2 June 2014.

118 "It's the Quality that Counts, Not the Quantity", *Straits Times*, 2 Sept. 2015.

119 "Govt Made Shift Well Before 2011 Election: Tharman".

120 "Cabinet: More Left-of-Centre Now, Helping the Lower-Income", *Straits Times*, 19 Apr. 2013.

121 The budget deficit in FY2014 was $100 million (partly on account of the government funding the Pioneer Generation Package), with the deficit for FY2015 at $4.9 billion.

122 "Cabinet: More Left-of-Centre Now, Helping the Lower Income".

123 PM Lee Hsien Loong, interview with the author, 1 Dec. 2015.

124 George Yeo, interview with the author, 22 July 2016.

125 PM Lee Hsien Loong, interview with the author, 1 Dec. 2015.

126 Tharman Shanmugaratnam, interview with the author, 7 May 2014.

127 For a snapshot of the key results, see "PAP Wins in 15 of 16 GRCs; Workers' Party Retains Aljunied GRC", *Straits Times*, 12 Sept. 2015. For deeper analyses, see the various contributions in Terence Lee and Kevin Y.L. Tan (eds), *Change in Voting: Singapore's 2015 General Election* (Singapore: Ethos Books, 2015).

128 Interviews with senior Party officials, 2016–17. In the end, these two GRCs were retained comfortably: 60.73% (East Coast) and 64.07% (Marine Parade).

129 PM Lee Hsien Loong, interview with the author, 1 Dec. 2015.

130 "AHPETC Findings: MND to Call for Stronger Legislative Framework for Town Councils", *Straits Times*, 9 Feb. 2015.

131 "Workers' Party Blames Human Error for Wrong Figure in Report", *Straits Times*, 27 Jan. 2015; "WP Hits Back at MND, Denying It Overpaid", *Straits Times*, 30 Aug. 2015.

132 The PAP distributed fliers in March 2015 to residents in Aljunied, claiming improper governance and urging residents to question their WP MPs about the lack of transparency. "PAP Activists Give out Fliers on Problems at AHPETC", *Straits Times*, 15 Mar. 2015.

133 "Workers' Party Trying to Move Forward", *Straits Times*, 11 Oct. 2015.

134 For useful post-election analyses, see "GE2015: 7 Takeaways from IPS Post-Election Conference that Explain PAP's Performance", *Straits Times*, 4 Nov. 2015; and "After the High of GE2011, a Reality Check for the Workers' Party", *Today*, 7 Nov. 2015.

135 "No Guarantee PAP Will Be in Government after Polls: Khaw Boon Wan", *Straits Times*, 8 Sept. 2015. Also a factor were viral WhatsApp messages of indeterminate origin and authenticity, widely shared, showing "bookies' odds", with the messages suggesting the PAP losing many seats (or key GRCs) to the Opposition. Many observers came to believe that these messages—and consequent fears on the part of the electorate of a PAP loss in the election—played a major part in the PAP's handsome victory. "They Are All 'Buay Zun'", *AsiaOne*, 22 Sept. 2015.

136 Heng Swee Keat, interview with the author. For post-election reflections by the PAP leadership on the crucial support from young Singaporeans, see "PM's Press Conference; Support from All Quarters, Especially the Young: PM", *Straits Times*, 12 Sept. 2015.

137 Ong Ye Kung, interview with the author, 10 June 2016. At the time of the interview, Ong Ye Kung was acting minister for education (higher education and skills) and senior minister of state for defence.

138 "Parliament House Queue Closes at 8pm, More than 1.2m Pay Last Respects to Mr Lee Kuan Yew", *Straits Times*, 28 Mar. 2015.

139 For a sense of the cross-generational impact of Lee's passing, see "Parliament House Queue Closes at 8pm, More than 1.2m Pay Last Respects to Mr Lee Kuan Yew".

140 Another area where there had been improvements since 2011 was political education, where serious efforts had been made to reinstil activists with a sense of purpose (personal communications from sources within the Party overseeing political education).

141 "GE2015 Spending: PAP Candidates Spent $5.3m while the Eight Opposition Parties' Expenses Totalled $1.8m", *Straits Times*, 29 Oct. 2015. Overall, spending by political parties in the 2015 election was approximately 30% more than the total figure ($5.5 million) in 2011.

142 "GE2015 Spending: PAP Candidates Spent $5.3m".

143 By Polling Day, the PAP's number of likes was 164,000, over three times the WP's. "Whispers, Not Shouts: A Re-reading of the Social Media Space", *Straits Times*, 4 Dec. 2015.

144 From 2013 to 2015, the PAP outperformed (in terms of number of posts on its home page) all other Opposition parties. There were between 200 and 450 posts a month during this period, with posts peaking during key events such as National Day and the mourning for Lee Kuan Yew. The PAP's closest "competitor", the WP, struggled to hit 100 posts per month in the same time frame. "GE2015: 7 Takeaways from IPS Post-Election Conference that Explain PAP's Performance".

145 The best known of these, the Facebook page "Fabrications about the PAP", had been founded by an individual supportive of the PAP in September 2011.

146 There were now also, for the first time, more balanced websites catering to the broad political middle ground. These served intelligent political commentary to an audience comprising those who were not necessarily dyed-in-the-wool supporters of any party, and those who did not want to get involved in the name-calling and diatribes that by this

time had come to colour much of political discourse in the Singapore online space. This was therefore the first election in the digital age where the (largely) silent majority could read and express reasonable views online. For analysis, see "Whispers, Not Shouts".

147 Dr Mohamad Maliki bin Osman, interview with the author, 25 Oct. 2017.

148 Speech by PAP Secretary-General Lee Hsien Loong at the People's Action Party Convention, Sunday, 6 Dec. 2015, available at https://www.pap.org.sg/conference-convention/lets-shape-our-future-together-pap-secretary-general-lee-hsien-loong/ (accessed 29 Jan. 2021).

149 Ong Ye Kung, interview with the author, 10 June 2016.

150 "GE 2015: Opposition Can Continue to Contribute to Singapore, Says DPM Tharman", *Straits Times*, 14 Sept. 2015.

151 Tharman Shanmugaratnam, interview with the author, 18 Dec. 2015.

152 "PAP's Hard Work, Policy Changes, and Jubilee Year Won GE2015, Says PM Lee", *Straits Times*, 6 Dec. 2015. There was also within the Party leadership the sense that the overwhelming mandate handed to the PAP was partly on account of the electorate's recognition of global uncertainties, and the need for capable hands at the till. As Tharman Shanmugaratnam observed: "The vote in the GE is a vote for stability and for steady progress in an uncertain world. Singaporeans have their eyes open. We spend a lot of our time talking about domestic issues but they are not unaware of the fact that we live in a very, very small country, in a world that can change very quickly. It is a vote of confidence in Singapore, in an uncertain world." "Vote in GE2015 Was One for Stability, Progress in Uncertain World: DPM Tharman", *Channel NewsAsia*, 13 Sept. 2015. One sociologist who had co-led a major survey of the electorate observed that while Singaporeans "still embraced democracy as an abstract idea", the election had seen "a flight to security and bread-and-butter issues" on account of greater risk and uncertainty globally. "Shift towards PAP among the Better-Off", *Straits Times*, 5 Nov. 2015.

153 Speech by PAP Secretary-General Lee Hsien Loong at the People's Action Party Convention, Sunday, 6 Dec. 2015.

154 "PAP Will Always Be on the Side of Singapore and of Singaporeans", Secretary-General Lee Hsien Loong, speech at PAP 60th anniversary commemorative event at Victoria Concert Hall, 7 Nov. 2014, available at https://www.pap.org.sg/news/pap-will-always-be-on-the-side-of-singapore-and-of-singaporeans/ (accessed 29 Jan. 2021).

Chapter 8

"Strange Dilemma": 2020 and Beyond

This book was nearly complete at the time of the 2020 general election, held on 10 July—during the worldwide COVID-19 pandemic, which did not leave Singapore unscathed. The full import of the result (the PAP winning 83 seats and 61.2 per cent of the popular vote, down from 69.9 per cent in 2015) will take time to sink in among all concerned—parties, people and observers. The following pages do not attempt a detailed analysis; it is a perilous business for the historian to attempt to make sense of events just gone by, and in some ways still unfolding (the derailing of the PAP's carefully laid plans for leadership succession being a case in point). Instead, there is a preliminary discussion of the 2020 election and impressions of episodes occurring in the lead-up, with (in conclusion, and in the light of recent events) a revisitation of some of the themes laid out in preceding chapters.

The result might seem to be a return to "normal", given that the PAP's victory in the 2015 election was against the backdrop of the passing of Singapore's modern founding father, Lee Kuan Yew, and also took place in the course of nationwide, often euphoric, celebrations of Singapore's 50th year of independence. The accompanying feel-good factor, which worked in favour of the Party in 2015, had faded by 2020.

Besides retaining Aljunied GRC (59.95 per cent) and Hougang SMC (61.21 per cent) with bigger margins than in 2015 (50.96 and 57.66 per cent respectively), the WP also (in a major surprise) triumphed in the newly-created Sengkang GRC, where its young team took with 52.12 per cent of the vote, against a PAP team anchored by a Cabinet minister: Labour chief Ng Chee Meng. Overall, the WP's garnering of over 50 per cent of the total vote within the four GRCs and two SMCs it contested against the PAP underlined its exceptional performance.[1] It achieved this while fielding only 21 candidates, down from 28 in 2015. The WP was also able to make these gains whilst in an ongoing renewal process. Pritam Singh (aged 41 at the time) had in April 2018 succeeded Low Thia Khiang as WP secretary-general; and just before the election, three WP MPs—Low himself, Png Eng Huat and Chen Show Mao—stepped down, in a tightly choreographed renewal process not altogether unlike that which the PAP has become known for.

Also putting up a creditable performance was the Progress Singapore Party (PSP), set up and led by former PAP MP and presidential candidate Dr Tan Cheng Bock. Dr Tan led what the media termed the PSP's "A" team in West Coast GRC, where it performed well in defeat, taking 48.32 per cent of the vote against a PAP team led by Minister for Communications and Information S. Iswaran.[2]

Although unsuccessful in winning any seats, the PSP's "premium" (it boasted an average vote share of 40.85 per cent where it contested) was in no small part down to Dr Tan's own personal appeal.[3] But the party was also able to field besides Dr Tan 23 other credible candidates, with their overall performance and the PSP's level of organisation belying the fact that it had been formed only in 2019.[4]

Build-up

The most significant political issue in the years before the election—one that had a bearing on the future of both country and Party—was Singapore's leadership transition. PM Lee Hsien Loong had in 2012 made known his intention to hand over the premiership to his successor by the time he turned 70, in 2022.[5] Naturally, this meant settling on the successor in question well before then, given the need to allow the chosen individual a clear runway (and period as DPM to understudy the PM); a runway afforded to both Lee himself (1990–2004) and Goh Chok Tong (1985–90). It was possibly with this urgency in mind that in December 2017, with no clear successor yet identified from amongst the possible contenders, ESM Goh wrote in a pointed Facebook post that the succession issue was "one urgent challenge I would like to see settled", noting his own hope that the cohort of fourth-generation (4G) leaders could settle it within the next six to nine months.[6] For good measure, Goh also observed that Singapore was different from many other countries when it came to settling political succession: "We normally don't want to fight for the post. And they're not fighting for the post, but they have to decide who should lead them. That's the difference in politics between us and other countries."[7]

Goh's message was put out "on purpose to elicit a response" from the 4G leaders. In this he succeeded—but the response itself was perhaps lacking in the clarity Goh (and an expectant public) craved. On 4 January 2018, 16 "younger ministers" issued a brief statement noting that they were aware and "conscious of our responsibility", and that they would settle the issue of the next leader "in good time". The message (in what seemed something of a riposte to Goh's point about infighting elsewhere) also highlighted "political stability" as a hallmark of Singapore's succession system, promising "smooth leadership succession". Overall, the intention seemed to be to show unity on the part of the group of younger leaders who would play the key role in selecting Singapore's next leader. The well-placed source (likely closely associated with the group and familiar with its thinking), who parsed the statement for the media, stressed that the group was "cohesive" and would reach consensus easily when it came to picking the next PM.[8]

PM Lee's response to ESM Goh's comment was more significant—not simply for what he said but in terms of what could be read into what was *not* said. In stating that Goh's envisaged timeline would not be met, Lee seemed to implicitly acknowledge public anxiety on the issue: "The team is taking shape. The dynamics amongst them, they are working it out. They are learning to work together. . . . Also, they need a bit of time for Singaporeans to get a feel of them—not just to be known as public figures, but to be responsible for significant policies . . . carrying them, justifying them, defending them, adapting them, making them work, and showing that they deserve to lead."[9] PM Lee seemed to be suggesting that matters had not been straightforward when it came to identifying a successor, notwithstanding how well-credentialed the contenders were. What he also seemed to be making an allusion to was the possibility that the younger team of leaders had not gelled effectively or as quickly as expected, and that the public had not yet warmed to them.

The major pieces of the puzzle fell into place in late 2018. In November, following the Party Conference and the election of a new slate of office-holders into the CEC, Finance Minister Heng Swee Keat was named the PAP's first assistant secretary-general in its 35th Central Executive Committee (CEC). This was followed closely by statements by PM Lee and by the younger-generation PAP leaders that their leader would be Heng.[10] In April 2019 he was appointed DPM, with the two existing DPMs, Tharman Shanmugaratnam and Teo Chee Hean, appointed senior ministers in the Cabinet. A group of younger PAP MPs and political office-holders—30 in all—endorsed the appointments, and also (in a significant nod to the progress of the leadership transition) thanked their senior colleagues for the guidance they had been given.[11]

The outline of how the succession would pan out now became clearer and even (it seemed at the time) final: at some point Heng would take over the premiership working closely with other members of the 4G leadership such as Chan Chun Sing and Ong Ye Kung.[12] A former Singapore Police Force scholar who had risen through the ranks of the Administrative Service, Heng had served in various positions, including that of principal private secretary to then-Senior Minister Lee Kuan Yew from 1997 to 2000, and subsequently permanent secretary at the Ministry of Trade and Industry (2001–05) and managing director of the Monetary Authority of Singapore (2005–11).[13] Heng's ascent was not altogether unexpected by observers, but it was made remarkable by his recovery from a serious stroke that felled him at a Cabinet meeting in May 2016—only immediate attention and emergency surgery averted a more serious outcome.[14]

Leadership transition at the top, only Singapore's third since independence, was assuredly newsworthy. These developments had to contend with news of a quite different kind: what seemed to be a family spat, which, if it had concerned an ordinary family, would never have made the headlines.

But the matter—to popularly become known as the Lee family feud—concerned the offspring of Lee Kuan Yew.

Controversy

In June 2017 the two younger siblings of PM Lee, Lee Hsien Yang and Dr Lee Wei Ling, issued a strongly worded statement accusing their brother of misusing his position to drive his "personal agenda".[15] On the face of it, what seemed to be driving the spat was a difference of opinion concerning the Lee family home at 38 Oxley Road. The two siblings accused their brother of deliberately attempting to subvert Lee Kuan Yew's wish in his will that the house be demolished after his death (should Dr Lee Wei Ling no longer want to live in the house). They had also been angered to learn about the existence of a ministerial committee, led by DPM Teo Chee Hean, examining the fate of 38 Oxley Road, which they suggested would simply do PM Lee's bidding.[16] Linked to this was the accusation that PM Lee intended to preserve the house to cement his own political credibility, which was tied to his being the son of Lee Kuan Yew. The statement did not spare the next generation, with the two siblings claiming that PM Lee and his wife, Ho Ching (CEO of Temasek Holdings, the state-owned investment company), harboured political ambitions for their son, Li Hongyi.[17]

Following his siblings' statement, PM Lee issued a public statement of his own detailing his concerns on the preparation of Lee Kuan Yew's final will.[18] He also apologised to Singaporeans, given that the public airing of these issues had "affected Singapore's reputation and Singaporeans' confidence in the Government".[19] The culmination of the first phase of the affair came in July 2017, with PM Lee giving a ministerial statement on 38 Oxley Road and rebutting allegations of abuse of power. This was followed by a two-day parliamentary debate on the issue.[20] Workers' Party chief Low Thia Khiang observed that the episode had led to an "ugly media circus" and had also led to the government and people being distracted from "far more important issues". Perhaps his most telling point was his call on PM Lee to settle the dispute in court, observing that individuals who had made less serious allegations against Singapore's leaders had been sued for libel. In not suing his siblings, PM Lee and the government risked, Low averred, "giving the impression that it is afraid of what the Lee siblings might say or reveal", and that this would "taint the trust Singaporeans have placed on the Government and compromise the high standards that the Government prides itself on achieving and aspires to maintain".[21] PM Lee had made it known in the course of his statement, however, that his preference was to not sue his siblings over their allegations. His reasoning was that legal action would "further besmirch" his late parents' names and create further "distraction and distress" for Singaporeans.[22]

Speaking during the parliamentary debate, ESM Goh Chok Tong voiced what many Singaporeans likely felt when he gave his own conclusions:

> *Neither money nor the house is the real issue. The dispute over 38 Oxley Road is only a fig leaf for the deep cracks within the family, cracks which perhaps started decades ago. What then is the agenda of PM's accusers? Are they whistleblowing in a noble effort to save Singapore, or waging a personal vendetta without any care for the damage done to Singapore? I have kept my ears open. From what Lee Hsien Yang and his wife are freely telling many others, it is clear that their goal is to bring Lee Hsien Loong down as PM, regardless of the huge collateral damage suffered by the Government and Singaporeans.[23]*

If this—bringing down PM Lee—had indeed been one of the aims held by Lee Hsien Yang and his wife, Lee Suet Fern, it was not realised. The affair had tarnished the legacy of Lee Kuan Yew, and of Singapore itself, as PM Lee acknowledged. But in the minds of the public, what seemed uppermost was puzzlement as to the root cause of the spat. There was no indication of a diminution of public support for PM Lee, or for the government, and the issue was to have no bearing on the result of the 2020 general election. As we shall see, a quite different set of circumstances was at play when it came to the decline in support for the PAP in the coming election.

It seemed for a time after the events of June–July 2017 that there might be a ceasefire between the parties involved. The fate of the house and the allegations levelled receded from the newspapers, and (for a time) claim and counterclaim (and the attendant revelations and accusations) seemed to tail off somewhat. But developments that were to come ensured, if nothing else, that the family rupture endured and would likely be permanent. In November 2020 the Court of Three Judges (the highest disciplinary body for the legal profession) found Lee Suet Fern guilty of misconduct in her preparation and execution of Lee Kuan Yew's last will (which contained the crucial clause providing for the demolition of 38 Oxley Road immediately after his death, should Lee Wei Ling choose not to live there).[24] The court found that she "blindly followed the directions of her husband, a significant beneficiary under the very will whose execution she helped to rush through".[25] Another development was Lee Hsien Yang and Lee Suet Fern's son, Li Shengwu, a gifted Harvard economist, being found in contempt of court and guilty of scandalising the judiciary in July 2020. Li had made a private Facebook post (which leaked into the public domain) in connection with the Oxley affair stating that the Singapore government "is very litigious and has a pliant court system".[26] Li, after earlier electing to no longer take part in the court case, subsequently decided to pay the fine imposed "to buy some peace and quiet" but refused to admit any guilt in the matter.[27]

Reserved Presidency

The Oxley affair, and the tensions underlying it, had been likely brewing for years, if not decades. An equally public controversy that had been gestating only since 2016 was to earn the government considerably more opprobrium, and from a larger swathe of the public. In January that year, during the opening of Parliament, PM Lee stated that he would appoint a Constitutional Commission chaired by the chief justice to study various aspects of the elected presidency. Besides reviewing the qualifying criteria of the elected president, PM Lee observed that a mechanism should be considered to ensure that minorities could be periodically elected, especially if there was a situation where there had not been a particular minority occupying the office of president for some time. The Constitutional Commission, which submitted its findings in August 2016, recommended that if any of Singapore's officially recognised ethnic groups had not occupied the president's office for five consecutive terms, the next presidential election should be reserved for that group.[28] The government White Paper that followed endorsed this suggestion and other key main recommendations made by the commission.[29] The Constitution of the Republic of Singapore (Amendment) Bill passed on 9 November, with PM Lee announcing that the 2017 presidential election would be reserved for candidates from the Malay community.

On 14 September 2017, Halimah Yacob became president by walkover. Singapore's first female president, Halimah was in many respects a role model in her own right (she had faced adversity and straitened circumstances in childhood following the early death of her father, something throughout her career she been careful not to overplay). As a tudung-wearing woman from Singapore's Malay minority, her elevation showcased Singapore's multicultural make-up.[30] Halimah, who had resigned her PAP membership and stepped down as an MP in order to contest the election, met the eligibility criteria on account of the fact that the position she had held until August— Speaker of Parliament (which she had also relinquished)—was one of those expressly designated by the public sector requirement of the part of the constitution that laid out the criteria for presidential candidates.[31] Other individuals had put their names forward, the most notable of them being the businessmen Mohamed Salleh Marican and Farid Khan. However, they failed to obtain Certificates of Eligibility from the Presidential Elections Committee. Their companies did not have least $500 million in shareholders' equity, a point where the criteria had been made more stringent following a recommendation by the Constitutional Commission.[32]

The PAP government had incurred a political cost, as it knew it would, and as PM Lee foresaw. He said that reserving the elected presidency for minority candidates from time to time was likely to have a political cost in the short term, but the move was a necessary safeguard for the country's long-term good. Lee observed that despite the progress made over decades, Singapore was not a post-racial country, and it was therefore harder for a member of a minority race to become president in an open, unreserved election.[33] "Guard-rails" such as the reserved presidency were therefore needed.[34] But many seemed to believe that the government deliberately took measures to block former PAP MP Dr Tan Cheng Bock, who came very close to victory in the 2011 presidential election, and who, it seemed, had planned to contest again. Dr Tan filed a constitutional challenge in May 2017 to determine whether it was correct to set the 2017 presidential election as the first election reserved for a minority group.[35] His challenge was dismissed by the High Court (an appeal was also dismissed in August), however, with the courts finding that it was for Parliament to specify the first term of office of the president.[36]

Dr Tan's objection was a technical one but won him renewed sympathy (after his near victory in 2011), with a great deal of acerbic online commentary from netizens suggesting that the government was somehow afraid of the possibility of his becoming president. Others—including most notably Sylvia Lim from the Workers' Party— were extremely critical over how the government made it seem at the beginning that counting under the hiatus-triggered model from President Wee Kim Wee was done on the basis of the advice from the Attorney-General's Chambers (advice that was never made public), when it later became clear in the course of the court proceedings initiated by Dr Tan that when to start the count was in fact a policy decision made by the government alone.[37]

The other issue—a much more emotive one and one that the government seemed less prepared for—had to do with race and identity. Halimah Yacob's father was Indian-Muslim. Salleh Marican (whose Indian-Muslim father had come to Singapore from India) was criticised by some for not being fluent in Malay. Farid Khan's father was from Pakistan. There were doubts expressed in some quarters as to whether they were

"Malay enough". Commentary favourable to the idea of a reserved presidency suggested that people should not be too fixated on the idea of what made the archetypal "Malay", nor cleave to an overly narrow definition of Malayness, also pointing out that all three potential candidates had received Community Certificates from the Community Committee, which confirmed they belonged to the Malay community.[38] But if this was the case, there was the sense that the government had opened the proverbial can of worms, including the question as to why a reserved election for Malays was necessary if the definition of "Malay" was so broad.[39]

Meritocracy

Salleh Marican and Farid Khan were successful businessmen, without any party affiliations, who appeared to many neutral observers to want genuinely—like Halimah—to contribute to the community. When Halimah was declared president, a number of Singaporeans began using the hashtag #notmypresident in their social media posts, and there was a protest drawing hundreds of Singaporeans at Hong Lim Park. A dominant strand of feeling, held not just by those at the protest but by a wider section of the public, was that the government did not trust voters.[40] There was some sense too among younger Singaporeans and netizens that a reserved presidency was not necessary and that it went against Singapore's meritocratic principles.[41]

The issue had reverberations beyond the presidency itself, touching on succession to the premiership. Many who felt that the reserved presidency was a backward step in terms of meritocracy, as well as other neutral observers, seemed to take the view that if the very best candidate were to be chosen to succeed PM Lee, it should be DPM Tharman Shanmugaratnam. Tharman was well-liked across all races, and respected internationally. He had stated in 2015 that he was not interested in the top job.[42] When a Blackbox poll commissioned by Yahoo Singapore in September the following year showed that he was the top choice of many Singaporeans (69 per cent of close to 900 individuals polled), he felt it necessary to come out more forcefully—categorically—to restate his lack of interest.[43] In making these comments, he also made clear that he supported the principle of choosing Singapore's next leader from the pool of 4G leaders. But there was clearly a section of the public—especially the young and educated—who were mystified and felt that if the best man had to do the job, then Tharman merited serious consideration.

In rejecting the notion of his becoming premier, Tharman had in 2015 observed that it was "inevitable" that someone from a minority race would become PM at some point, given Singapore's open and meritocratic system.[44] But other PAP leaders, looking at national circumstances as they then stood, had their own perspectives. In a university forum in March 2019, Heng Swee Keat—by this time deputy prime minister and the clear choice of the PAP leadership to be premier—was put on the spot with a question by an audience member, Asst Prof. Walid Jumblatt. Jumblatt, articulating the sense of unease that many Singaporeans, particularly from the younger generation, seemed to be feeling, observed that many Singaporeans seemed to prefer Tharman for the top job. Heng's reply was that while many in the audience (mainly students) might feel that

Singapore was ready for a minority PM, his experience walking the ground suggested to him that others—including those from the older generation (and presumably from the Chinese majority)—were not yet ready for such an eventuality.[45] In connection with the Yahoo-commissioned poll, Jumblatt also asked if the government was sending out contradictory messages by reserving the 2017 presidential election for candidates from the Malay community while stating that Singapore was not ready for a prime minister from a minority race. In denying the contradiction, Heng stressed, "It is precisely because we need to place this emphasis institutionally that we recognise that we have not arrived. It is important for us to ensure that we have that safeguard."[46] In this—that Singapore had not yet arrived—Heng was saying much the same as PM Lee had. But to some at least, this seemed to go down the wrong way.

⁕⁘⁕

Protagonists in the two major episodes detailed above—the fate of the Oxley house and the reserved presidency—were to become linked in interesting ways. Perhaps galvanised by his defeat in court, Dr Tan Cheng Bock formed the Progress Singapore Party in March 2019. In explaining his move, Dr Tan said that he saw "the foundations of good governance eroding. Specifically, there is an erosion of transparency, independence and accountability. . . . Yet these are the three foundations for creating trust between the Government and the people. . . . This means a robust system of checks and balances."[47] Underlining the rupture in the Lee family, Lee Hsien Yang joined the PSP in early 2020 and was very publicly presented with his PSP membership card in June, in a meeting with Dr Tan at Tiong Bahru Market (within the boundaries of Tanjong Pagar GRC, where Lee Kuan Yew had served as MP). Lee Hsien Yang stated in an online message on the same day that the PAP had lost its way: "The current government is distinctly different from when LKY [Lee Kuan Yew] was PM and subsequently MM."[48] In this, Lee came very close—the messages may even have been synchronised—to what Dr Tan had been saying, and which he was to amplify on the campaign trail, that the PAP had lost its way.[49] As Inderjit Singh, a former PAP MP, observed when asked by the media for his views, "When people see LKY's son switching camp to the opposition, this may create doubts . . . that the PAP of the present is not the same as the PAP of the past."[50]

"Drifting Along"

Impossible as it is to tell precisely how many voters were swayed by these lines of attack when casting their ballot in the 2020 general election, it is clear that the lines in themselves were damaging to the PAP. This was all the more so given that the electorate likely weighed these assertions—concerning the decline of Party and government—together with various other episodes that had accelerated the fading of SG50's afterglow, and which themselves impacted the reservoir of trust between government and people.

- In 2015 lapses in infection control in Singapore General Hospital (SGH) led to an outbreak of hepatitis C. Eight deaths were linked to the outbreak, with SGH faulted by an independent review committee for being slow to recognise the extent of the outbreak and report it to the Health Ministry.[51]

- In March 2016 two Singapore Mass Rapid Transit (SMRT) trainees were killed after being hit by an oncoming train in an area where inspections were being carried out. Investigations found that critical safety protocols had not been followed.[52] Another incident, involving major disruption but fortunately no injury or loss of life, took place in October 2017 when a section of tunnel flooded between Bishan and Braddell stations, causing major disruption. Investigations revealed that the team responsible had failed to carry out preventive maintenance and had falsified maintenance records.[53]

- A major cyberattack, and the most serious data breach in Singapore's history, saw an Advanced Persistent Threat (APT) group (emanating from an unnamed state actor) breaching the electronic medical records system of SingHealth (Singapore's largest healthcare provider) in June 2018, in what became known as the SingHealth/IHiS breach. Through exploiting weaknesses in Integrated Health Information Systems (IHiS), the central IT agency responsible for Singapore's healthcare sector, the APT group exfiltrated the details of 1.5 million patients, and PM Lee's own data was repeatedly targeted. The committee of inquiry investigating the SingHealth/IHiS breach found lax controls and a culture of complacency at both organisations, with financial penalties imposed on both.[54] SingHealth and IHiS were private companies; criticism nonetheless came to bear on government as confidential information of Singaporeans had been targeted.

- Lax controls were also partly to blame when it came to the leak online of the confidential information (which had taken place as early as 2016) of 16,600 people from Singapore's HIV (human immunodeficiency virus) registry. The individual responsible for the leak, Mikhy Farrera-Brochez, an American and a convicted fraudster, had been the partner of Ler Teck Siang, a Singaporean doctor who had previously been head of MOH's National Public Health Unit.[55] In this case, some of the public criticisms also arose from the fact that even though the leak had taken place as early as 2016, public acknowledgement from official sources of what had happened was not forthcoming until January 2019.

- Keppel Offshore & Marine (Keppel O&M), a government-linked company, was found to have made corrupt payments (amounting

to US$55 million) for several years to Brazilian officials in return
for securing contracts from Brazilian oil firms. In 2017 it was fined
US$422 million (as part of a global settlement involving authorities in
the United States, Brazil and Singapore). Keppel O&M was served a
conditional warning by the Corrupt Practices Investigation Bureau in
Singapore, in lieu of prosecution for corruption offences punishable
under the Prevention of Corruption Act. There were murmurs that the
penalty was insufficient, given that the affair had tarnished Singapore's
reputation for being nearly corruption-free.[56]

The above represents a selection of episodes that gave rise to public dissatisfaction.[57]
All of the incidents and episodes described were different, and did not relate in a direct
sense to failings within the PAP or within the top echelons of government. But there
were common strands which did in fact have political ramifications. One was the
perception of the formation of a culture of complacency; another was the sense of a
sense of degradation of institutions and things not being done correctly; and finally,
the idea that those at the top were not held accountable when things went wrong.
Put together, these disparate incidents contributed to a diminishing of the standing
of the government and, more corrosively, chipped away at the trust between the PAP
government and the people.[58]

A February 2019 *Lianhe Zaobao* editorial addressed some of these episodes and
others, including a spate of training deaths in the Singapore Armed Forces (SAF) and
the deteriorating quality of the national postal service (SingPost). The editorial writers
suggested these were "not accidental" and that at the root, many people had—without
realising it—become stuck in a mindset of "drifting along", and that their attitude
towards dealing with people had collectively degraded. Muddling through had become
deeply rooted, and this had dented public confidence.[59]

Earlier commentary had presaged this. In a carefully phrased December 2017 op-
ed in *Lianhe Zaobao* (pointed and noteworthy enough to be translated and reprinted in
the *Straits Times*), a former PAP MP, Goh Choon Kang, wrote about the loss of trust
between the elites and the masses, linking his observations to the political longevity
of those who ruled. Goh was referring mainly to Western societies, but he did warn
against Singapore going the way of those Western democracies where the ruling elites
had lost touch with the masses:

> *They feel that their achievements today are based solely on their own capabilities
> and talent within the meritocracy implemented by society. They bask in their own
> successes, sing their own praises and no longer have the slightest empathy for the
> people, with the political parties fighting for power but unable to understand and
> sympathise with the public feeling.*[60]

Goh warned that the PAP might become too comfortable and might therefore not be
able to sense and correct problems in time.

In bringing Goh's piece to wider attention and attempting to analyse some of the issues, a senior *Straits Times* journalist, Chua Mui Hoong, observed:

> *Trust is a valuable commodity. It takes two to trust. A government that asks its people to trust it more, must be deserving of that trust. Trust is not a natural legacy a new generation inherits from its elders. . . . I think the political elite has to start addressing the reality: trust has been chipped away in some quarters, although hopefully it is not pervasive; or deep-seated, and can be repaired.*[61]

Some sort of reply was clearly needed. It came in the form of a commentary by Finance Minister Heng Swee Keat published in the *Straits Times* and *Lianhe Zaobao* on 9 February 2019. Heng acknowledged past failures but pointed to independent committees of inquiries that had been convened, with their findings made public and individuals responsible for lapses being disciplined where needed:

> *We will not flinch from taking a hard look at ourselves each time there is a failure, and doing whatever is necessary to put things right. But I reject the suggestion by some that the political leadership has allowed the whole system to go slack. And worse still, that we have gone soft on ourselves and the public service, failing to hold senior people accountable when things go wrong.*[62]

It was a forceful statement, but perhaps not sufficient to erase the lapses that had occurred in the years leading up. The same could be said of the standout item from the 2019 budget, the Merdeka Generation Package, introduced to honour and thank the generation born between 1950 and 1959 for their contributions to nation-building.[63] The scheme, which targeted those who had just missed out on the Pioneer Generation Package (which benefited individuals born in 1949 or earlier), benefited approximately 500,000 Singaporeans. The package included MediSave top-ups and subsidies for MediShield Life premiums, as well as special subsidies for common illnesses, chronic conditions and dental procedures under the Community Health Assist Scheme.[64]

These were generous measures, and they were welcomed by those who stood to benefit directly; but they did not on their own provide a sufficient salve on the ground. Some sense of the mood can be discerned from events that took place within a few days in October 2018, when WP Secretary-General Pritam Singh, Sylvia Lim (WP chairman) and Low Thia Khiang (former WP secretary-general) put out an online appeal for funds to pay for legal expenses following lawsuits brought against Aljunied-Hougang and Pasir Ris-Punggol Town Councils. At the heart of the matter was the claim that the three (together with two other town councillors) had breached their fiduciary duties and made improper payments to FM Solutions & Services, the managing agent of Aljunied-Hougang Town Council. In their appeal, the trio raised the possibility of bankruptcy if they lost the suits and were unable to repay monies owed (which in turn would have meant disqualification from Parliament). The response from the public and well-wishers was swift: over a million dollars raised in under 72 hours.[65]

GE2020: Lead-up and Campaign

The first case of COVID-19 in Singapore was confirmed on 23 January 2020. In the face of an uptick in cases, the government declared a "circuit breaker" (essentially a near-lockdown) beginning 7 April. This measure, which likely avoided a massive outbreak within the community, was to last until 1 June. That Singapore's overall death toll was kept very low can be credited to a world-class healthcare system and the lessons learnt from SARS, including thinking through, post-SARS, what the next pandemic might look like and putting in place foundations to deal with the various possible eventualities.[66]

The total amount allocated in the unprecedented four budgets to deal with the fallout from the pandemic was $93 billion, of which $52 billion was approved to be drawn from the reserves. The largest component, in the form of the Jobs Support Scheme, went to subsidising wage costs. Without this support, many companies might have had to fold, leaving thousands of workers out of jobs.[67]

Some parts of the scorecard were less positive. The government had not paid sufficient attention to the dangers of an outbreak in foreign worker dormitories, where workers—over 300,000 in all—were housed in overcrowded and often unhygienic conditions.[68] The first dormitories were declared isolation areas in April 2020, but by then an average of 1,000 cases a day were being recorded in the dormitories, dwarfing the number of cases being recorded in the community.[69] This prompted a degree of national soul-searching in terms of the conditions in which these workers were housed, and took some of the shine off what some observers had initially called Singapore's "success story" in fighting COVID.[70]

There were calls also for accountability, with netizens in particular calling for Josephine Teo, the manpower minister, to take responsibility and apologise to foreign workers for both the outbreak in dormitories and for the poor living conditions they faced. Her somewhat defensive response when asked in Parliament whether she would apologise—that the issue of an apology had never been raised by the workers themselves—was seen by many as a less than satisfactory response.[71]

The economic fallout (a contraction of 6.7 per cent in the first half of the year) and concerns over livelihoods (approximately 147,500 jobs lost in the first half of the year, with the overall unemployment rate rising to 2.9 per cent in June) were overlain by global malaise as a consequence of the pandemic—experts could come to no consensus on how long it would last, when "normalcy" could return.[72] There was regional uncertainty, too, including in Singapore's nearest neighbours. Indonesia's officials reported that COVID-19 numbers heading into June were under 25,773—trailing, it seemed, the number for Singapore (34,366)—but this seemed to be partly a result of underreporting and a lack of diagnostic capability; the real toll appeared to be much higher.[73] In Malaysia there was political upheaval, with a new premier, Muhyiddin Yassin, taking over in February from veteran Mahathir Mohamad (following Mahathir's unexpected resignation), but not before what seemed to be a level of factional intrigue and behind-the-scenes manoeuvring unusual even by the standards of Malaysian politics.

There seemed no good time for PM Lee to call an election. "Phase Two", which began on 19 June, saw the calibrated resumption of most activities, with social gatherings in small groups allowed, retail businesses allowed to reopen, and dining in at restaurants (perhaps the thing Singaporeans had missed the most) once again permitted. But in the wider scheme of things, there was no guarantee that the local situation would improve quickly in terms of the course that the pandemic took, even as moves were made to improve the situation in dormitories and to continue encouraging the general populace to adopt social distancing and other measures. Similarly, there was no certainty that the economic situation would improve—indeed, it seemed reasonably clear in the middle of 2020 that the corner had not yet been turned. Perhaps it was on account of the possibility that things might in fact get worse that an election was called sooner rather than later.[74] And when Parliament was dissolved on 23 June (triggering the 2020 general election, with Polling Day on 10 July), the PAP leadership, perhaps in tacit recognition of the issues and anxieties that had been percolating on the ground—discussed above—gave little sense that they expected the election would see a "flight to safety" of the type seen in 2001.[75]

Opposition parties objected to the idea of holding an election during a pandemic, with Dr Tan Cheng Bock particularly vocal, arguing that this would increase health risks and suggesting that a caretaker government could be formed if elections could not be held by the latest date that the constitution allowed—April 2021.[76] There is no suggestion that this was considered seriously by the leadership, which dismissed the idea as unconstitutional.[77]

Themes: Social Media and Online Campaigning

Pre-emptive salvos by PAP figures and supporters did not quite find their range.[78]

One foray came in the form of an article by Senior Parliamentary Secretary (Foreign Affairs) and MP for Jurong GRC Dr Tan Wu Meng, published on the PAP website on 19 June (shortly before the dissolution of Parliament). Dr Tan criticised the writer and poet Alfian Sa'at, noting that Alfian had constantly maligned Singapore, and gave illustrative examples from the writer's previous work to substantiate his argument that Alfian was unpatriotic. Dr Tan's real target was WP leader Pritam Singh, who, defending Alfian, had spoken in Parliament of "loving critics" of Singapore.[79] Dr Tan (who, it seemed to observers, was engaging in an attempt to undermine Pritam Singh by associating him with Alfian's views) asked Singh to reconsider his support of Alfian.[80]

Some observers were puzzled over why Alfian (whose writings were often critical of the PAP government and of Lee Kuan Yew, but who had never been seen as a political figure) had been dragged into the political fray in this way.[81] Other aspects of the article that attracted criticism included what some saw as racial overtones that smacked of condescension or majoritarian arrogance.[82] This, to some at least, was gutter politics, and the politics of division.[83] But senior PAP figures such as Minister for Law and Home Affairs K. Shanmugam defended Dr Tan, pointing out that he had simply been setting out facts when asking where Pritam Singh stood on Alfian Sa'at's views.[84] Shanmugam also referred to PAP MPs and ministers being subject to personal attacks—in his view there was a double standard at work. "These people [those unhappy with the criticisms of Alfian Sa'at and Pritam Singh] who now rise up to complain about Dr Tan Wu Meng never breathed a word about that [attacks against PAP figures]."[85]

Dr Tan Wu Meng's critique of Alfian and Pritam Singh was frontal; its origins (the Party brains trust), reasonably certain. The Party, it seemed, was prepared to take the gloves off and engage in a more direct, combative style with detractors. In this, and implicit in the comments by Minister Shanmugam, was a rejection of the view (held by many, including those in the middle ground) that the PAP should play fair—very fair—and (by implication) receive attacks from all comers calmly and with equanimity.

There were other episodes that had been more indirect in terms of identifying an originating hand, but which had exhibited a similar style. The previous month, Global Times Singapore (GTS), a site on Facebook managed by individuals supportive of the PAP, trained its sights on a mixed group of Singaporeans—including writers, academics and scholars (many of them known to be critical of the government)—who had written in outlets such as Hong Kong's *South China Morning Post* (SCMP). GTS suggested that they were working as proxies for China, and working too for a weakened PAP. GTS further insinuated that Cherian George, a Singaporean academic based in Hong Kong, was close to the centre of this nexus, pointing to the position held by his wife, the former *Straits Times* journalist Zuraidah Ibrahim, then deputy executive editor of the SCMP. GTS included within this faction—puzzlingly—former PAP MP Inderjit Singh, who had previously written an op-ed for the SCMP.[86]

GTS was seen by many as being part of the unofficial PAP "Internet Brigade", although there were no overt links to the Party, and no figure from the Party defended GTS' comments.[87] The GTS line of attack did, however, share commonalities with Dr Tan Wu Meng's criticisms of Alfian Sa'at—not least the implication that there was a class of individuals who in disagreeing with the PAP government and its policies were somehow disloyal or unpatriotic. The category of netizens ordinarily critical of the government certainly seemed to make this connection. But within more moderate quarters of public opinion, there seemed also to be some discomfiture, as all this was taking place at a time when the government was also calling for unity and societal resilience in the face of the global pandemic.[88]

❧

The PAP manifesto "Our Lives, Our Jobs, Our Future" ticked the necessary boxes. Besides facing down COVID-19 and addressing jobs and the economy, there were also messages concerning the government's long-term plans for healthcare (and care for the elderly) as well as a vision of sustainability and co-creating Singapore's future designed to find traction with the younger generation.[89]

Senior figures retired and did not contest, including former PM Goh Chok Tong and Lim Swee Say (who in the course of his career held several Cabinet positions). The Party put forward as part of its renewal well-credentialled new faces—including the first woman general from the SAF, Gan Siow Huang.[90] There were, however, criticisms of some likely PAP candidates in the lead-up to Nomination Day, 30 June. One prospective candidate, Ivan Lim, who had seemed set to be fielded in Jurong GRC, faced online criticisms of his past behaviour and character, of his allegedly overbearing and arrogant attitude during national service and at his employer, Keppel Offshore & Marine.[91] In the face of a torrent of criticism (which included specific instances of his conduct posted online by individuals claiming to be personally acquainted with him), Lim chose to withdraw his candidacy before Nomination Day.[92] PM Lee, in accepting his withdrawal, noted in his letter to Lim, "Ideally, there would have been a fair and deliberate consideration of these allegations. . . . Unfortunately, the nature of the campaign is such that we do not have time for a thorough investigation. The allegations spread like wildfire online, eclipsing the serious life and death issues we must grapple with."[93] Lim's political career was over before it had begun, destroyed in a mere four days in a trial by public inquisition conducted almost wholly through social media.

DPM Heng Swee Keat was expected to stand again in Tampines GRC (where he had served since 2011) but in a major surprise was moved to East Coast GRC, where he replaced Lim Swee Say as anchor minister for the GRC. Heng's fumble in his Nomination Day speech when announcing his plans for East Coast GRC were widely mocked by netizens and spawned various memes.[94] Some netizens, though, felt that the joke was carried too far at Heng's expense, and that the belittling of Heng had exposed more than anything else Singaporeans' lack of compassion, plus a forgetfulness of Heng's contributions.[95]

COVID-19 had forced the Elections Department and the parties themselves to make major changes. Public rallies were replaced by online e-rallies, complemented by official party political broadcasts and constituency-level political broadcasts on television.[96] Major parties had also thought through other ways to get their messages across. The PAP's *Straight Talk* series, broadcast online, approached various issues (including policies and the rationale for them) in an informal manner. There was in the latter format (which also featured moderated discussions) a conversational style and the conscious avoiding of jargon. The WP had its daily *Hammer Show*, where it put across its messages in simple, digestible form. Its main format was that of an immersive talk show, showcasing WP figures discussing pressing issues of the day, that was interspersed with videos of WP figures giving brief prepared speeches. The WP's all-around strong online game was capped off by its agility on social media channels and messaging platforms of more recent vintage (including Instagram Stories) that were immersive, and which were pegged at the younger generation.[97]

There were also live TV debates (one in English and one in Mandarin). In the English debate the WP's star find, 44-year-old Economics Associate Professor Jamus Lim (part of the WP team standing in Sengkang GRC), was the talking point on account of his persuasive arguments put forward with eloquence and intelligence, and also for the amiable way he came across.[98] Lim's exchanges with the PAP representative, Foreign Minister Dr Vivian Balakrishnan (who also put on a strong performance), were characterised by and large not by rancour but by civility, with Balakrishnan giving the WP manifesto a backhanded compliment: he noted that the PAP could have written the WP manifesto, "And that's why people have called the Workers' Party 'PAP-lite' or 'PAP-like'." Balakrishnan added for good measure that the WP took reference from PAP's position on most issues but then took half a step to the left.[99] The WP was certainly not hurt, and probably even gained something by these helpful comparisons.[100]

Especially resonant was the WP position that the PAP should not be handed a "blank cheque". This was first raised during the campaign by Assoc. Prof. Jamus Lim, who in using the analogy also spoke persuasively on two related points: how the PAP would in any case likely end up with a strong mandate, and how the PAP did not have a monopoly on the best ideas to bring society forward.[101] The "blank cheque" was not an entirely new concept—it had been used in January by Pritam Singh while addressing WP members.[102] During the campaign Pritam Singh again took up the theme, emphasising that the PAP would certainly end up with a strong mandate, and what the WP sought to deny it was a "supermajority"—a denial that would force the PAP into a position where it could not simply enact major constitutional changes (such as changes to the elected presidency). Instead, it would have to explain planned changes.[103]

Not giving the PAP a blank cheque extended also to other issues such as the planned hike from 7 per cent to 9 per cent of the Goods and Services Tax (GST). Given the impact of COVID-19, the government had in February 2020 announced that GST would not be raised in 2021, but it was still expected at some point by 2025.[104] The WP's consistent position—repeated by its candidates during the campaign—was that it opposed the GST hike altogether, another message that resonated, given the overall sense of belt-tightening in an election held during a pandemic.[105]

WP candidates portrayed themselves in the flesh, as well as in the online world, in a manner that suggested authenticity without the pretence of it. The PAP did put forward new candidates who came from humble upbringings or who had unconventional backgrounds (or for whom success did not come automatically). While some of its candidates came across in a genuine, unforced manner, the overall portrayal seemed to lack the naturalness that the WP had, and indeed seemed on occasion rehearsed and orchestrated. This was partly in evidence in Sengkang, a new GRC, where the WP had been working the ground for some time and won 52.12 per cent of the vote against a PAP team with three office-holders (Labour chief Ng Chee Meng, Senior Parliamentary Secretary for Health and Home Affairs Amrin Amin, Senior Minister of State for Transport and Health Dr Lam Pin Min, contesting together with lawyer Raymond Lye), two of whom (Amrin Amin and Ng Chee Meng) were fairly new to the area.[106] Many of the 120,000 voters in the GRC were young couples living in HDB estates.[107] They found the young (average age 35) WP slate (Raeesah Khan, Jamus Lim, the equity research analyst Louis Chua and the lawyer He Ting Ru, all of whom had young children) more relatable and diverse than the PAP's all-male team.[108] Sengkang voters also seem to have found the WP team possibly more empathetic too, in that several of their proposals struck a chord with a focus on introducing either more amenities (such as coffee shops) or ways to ease the stresses on young families.[109]

Protection from Online Falsehoods and Manipulation Act

This was the first election in Singapore that had been held since the mainstreaming of fake news and disinformation within the global sociopolitical lexicon. Compared to 2015, the PAP government had a strengthened hand when it came to powers to correct falsehoods, given the passage of the Protection from Online Falsehoods and Manipulation Act (POFMA) that came into effect in October 2019. POFMA gave the government the power to compel individuals who had published false statements to publish a "correction notice" stating that the statement was false. It also gave the government the power to compel Internet platforms (such as Facebook) to put up a targeted correction notice (for example, next to where a particular piece of false information could be found on the platform) stating the information or news was false, and linking to (if need be) the government's rebuttal or corrective.[110]

From the government's point of view, POFMA was needed to combat the types of falsehoods that went against the public interest or could undermine public confidence in government. It was needed given what had happened in other countries, which had become victims of subversion and organised disinformation campaigns—exacerbated, as key ministers were keen to point out, by the failure of social media platforms to address the problem effectively.[111]

At the time when the bill was being debated in Parliament in 2019, the government seemed to have convinced most observers about the need to legislate on the issue. The case seemed to be further strengthened by the use of POFMA's Correction Direction to correct COVID-19 related misinformation.[112] But the law had in fact first been used (in November 2019) against an Opposition politician—Brad Bowyer from the PSP—and several subsequent uses (including those during the election period) were against Opposition politicians, or against news portals that had carried comments by Opposition politicians.[113] The criticism was that the government was using POFMA as a tool to silence the Opposition; even observers who were not political players (and who had indeed been broadly supportive when the bill was first mooted) expressed reservations, given that some of the cases were not exactly clear-cut and seemed to be more a matter of an individual expressing an opinion rather than the false statement of facts going against the public interest that POFMA seemed originally designed to catch.[114]

The government might have been in possession of data that could show a statement to be true or false, but POFMA's critics observed that the playing field was stacked against those with less information, leaving individuals—including Opposition figures—to make inferences and informed guesses that could be caught under POFMA. This in turn led to observations concerning unfairness and information asymmetry.[115] The asymmetry could be addressed, the argument ran, by releasing more data, or by clarifications from the relevant agency, rather than using the hammer blow of the hand of the law, which had the effect of chilling discourse. Even before the election there had been calls for an independent body that might review in the first instance the alleged falsehood and make decisions on remedial action required, if any.[116]

And then there were statements and innuendo that might have enough of a kernel to give individuals pause and muddy the waters on an issue. In some instances, their reach was amplified rather than being negated by a government rebuttal or the invocation of POFMA.

During the live television debate on 1 July 2020, SDP chief Dr Chee Soon Juan raised the issue of Singapore's eventual target population, insinuating that the PAP planned to substantially increase the population and suggesting, falsely, that DPM Heng Swee Keat had "toyed with the idea" of Singapore's population reaching 10 million.[117] An immediate and sharp rebuttal by Dr Vivian Balakrishnan was followed by the PAP putting out a statement the following day accusing Dr Chee of conjuring "a bogey out of thin air to befuddle, frighten and divide Singaporeans".[118] For good measure, in a Facebook post DPM Heng categorically denied that the government planned to raise the population to 10 million.[119] SDP was, however, able to extract mileage by stating that an assurance had been extracted from the PAP that the population would not rise to 10 million thanks to the pressure exerted by Dr Chee, pointing out too that it had been raising the issue of population for a considerable time, and that the government had not come out earlier to clarify matters.[120]

The issue of foreigners had featured heavily in the 2011 hustings, resurfacing during the furore over the 2013 Population White Paper. The SDP was preying on old fears—primal fears even—that many Singaporeans had concerning being swamped by foreigners. These feelings were especially acute during the pandemic, with fears over livelihoods and jobs compounded by a regular stream of news of retrenchments. The government's POFMA Office issued directions to various websites and Facebook pages requiring corrections to be made where there were suggestions that the government had considered raising Singapore's population to 10 million by 2030.[121] The issue did not abate, however, and became tied in with other concerns, including the perception that the government had been too liberal in signing agreements with other countries—agreements that according to government detractors made it too easy for foreign professionals to the right to seek employment in Singapore.[122] Besides jobs, the foreign worker issue commingled with concerns over bread-and-butter issues and anxiety over what lay in the future—concerns that came up to some degree in every election, but which in 2020 amplified exponentially on account of COVID-19.

In the backdrop was the online aspect of discourse. Some of this (notably party campaigning and outreach) was civil and conducted transparently. A second, less regulated, strand included election commentary by Internet figures, political commentators and sociopolitical websites that were known quantities and usually critical of the government. There were also individuals, websites, and social media presences and platforms that gave rise to a profusion of a mixture of rumours and false news (some parlayed into seemingly real nuggets over instant messaging services) relating to the pandemic. Finally, there was activity by unofficial Internet brigades (PAP supporters such as GTS, others that supported the Opposition line, and individuals of similar persuasions), many behaving in a baiting, troll-like manner. It was these latter groups especially that contributed to an online atmosphere that was the most toxic of any election. During the campaigning period, claims and counterclaims on various issues came thick and fast, as did police reports lodged on account of imagined offences. There were even threats of physical harm.[123] Polarising content in the online echo chambers of social media seemed to drown out presences in the middle ground favouring balance and civility. Whether one was internet-savvy or comparatively uninitiated, it was not altogether a simple matter to disengage from the vitriol, given how much news and information provision, as well as its consumption, had moved online during the pandemic.

Where required, major platforms such as Facebook complied with take-down notices (for example, orders to remove unauthorised paid online election advertising deemed to contravene the Parliamentary Elections Act) and Targeted Correction Directions issued under POFMA.[124] As the campaigning period neared, Facebook in the course of its own election integrity efforts removed the accounts of those administering the pro-PAP "Fabrications about the PAP", effectively disabling the page. Just before Polling Day, it also removed the page of Critical Spectator, run by an individual of Polish origin residing in Singapore, also a staunch supporter of the PAP government. Facebook took these steps on account of inauthentic behaviour by these presences, and violation of its community standards.[125]

Fairness and Authenticity

Discontent over foreigners and concerns over jobs were issues that could have been anticipated. But the 2020 election saw a different vein of discontent: the stirrings of a type of sentiment that was altogether newer, more difficult to grapple with, and indicative of developing trends within segments of the electorate.

Raeesah Khan, 26, daughter of the 2017 presidential aspirant Farid Khan and part of the WP team contesting in Sengkang GRC, had made social media posts before the election that appeared to suggest bias and racism against minorities on the part of the authorities (and especially, it seemed, the judiciary and the police). The first post, from February 2018, concerned a ruling by the Court of Appeal reaffirming an earlier decision that had seen the leaders of City Harvest Church, who had been found guilty of criminal breach of trust (CBT), sentenced to jail terms ranging from several months to three and a half years. The Attorney-General's Chambers had unsuccessfully argued for the original, longer sentences (under a different section of the Penal Code governing CBT) to be reinstated.[126] Khan had in her Facebook post commented that Singapore "jails minorities mercilessly, harasses mosque leaders but let's [*sic*] corrupt church leaders who stole SG50 million free. Who did they pay?" A second post, from May 2020 (in relation to a news item concerning foreigners in a well-known area, Robertson Quay, filmed ignoring safe distancing measures), saw Khan commenting on the enforcement of safe distancing measures during the pandemic, suggesting that law enforcement "discriminates against its citizens" and that "rich Chinese or white people" were given more favourable treatment.[127]

These posts were resurfaced by netizens during the campaigning period, with police reports made against Khan. The Attorney-General's Chambers advised the police that an offence of promoting enmity between different groups on grounds of race or religion had been disclosed.[128] The PAP was not, of course, about to let the issue slide, suggesting that Khan's posts were a "serious matter which goes to the fundamental principles on which our country has been built".[129]

This could have been a serious blow not just for the WP Sengkang team but for the WP itself and its new leader, Pritam Singh. In the event, the WP was able to defuse the matter in a manner that seemed unscripted, polished and personal at the same time. In an unscheduled doorstop interview, Khan (flanked by Pritam Singh and party Chairman Sylvia Lim, with her Sengkang GRC WP team members standing close by) apologised for her posts, acknowledging that her brief remarks had been "insensitive" and agreeing that she had to be held "accountable" for her "improper remarks", promising to cooperate in any police investigation. Khan, who said she was "passionate" about minority issues, said she did not mean to cause social divisions with her comments but wanted to raise awareness about the concerns of minorities. Pritam Singh, in giving his own take, said he had not been aware of Khan's posts but stated that he would have been "disappointed" if WP candidates tried to sanitise their past. They had to be "authentic to the public".[130]

Despite the seriousness of Khan's accusations against the authorities, the WP emerged unscathed, and the episode may even have strengthened the prospects of the WP Sengkang team.[131] There were clear signs that some younger voters, including those in Sengkang and those familiar with Khan's interest in social justice and activism (she was the founder of an empowerment group for marginalised women and children), were put off by what they felt to be unfair character assassination and the use of old-school, hardball PAP tactics.[132] An online hashtag in support of Khan, #IStandWithRaeesah, trended on social media. In apparent retaliation against the racism charge levelled at Khan, police reports were made against DPM Heng Swee Keat for saying in 2019 that Singapore was not yet ready for a non-Chinese prime minister.[133]

Fourteen years earlier, in 2006, Low Thia Khiang defended the WP candidate James Gomez from PAP charges of lying and dishonesty with what limited cards he had, suggesting that an innocent mistake had been made, when PAP figures asked why the WP had chosen to back an untruthful candidate who had stage-managed an incident at the Elections Department.[134] Despite Gomez apologising for what he said was a mistake without malicious intent, the PAP continued its attacks, deciding to drop the matter (as in 2020) only when it became clear that to press further might be counterproductive. In 2020 Pritam Singh acknowledged that Raeesah Khan had erred. Here, though, there was the additional, critical issue of the views and mindsets of the younger generation. Even in acknowledging mistakes, both Singh and Khan seemed in tune with this generation, large segments of which clearly felt very differently compared to the older generation when it came to speaking openly on issues concerning race. The PAP as much as acknowledged this when, after its loss in Sengkang GRC, Law and Home Affairs Minister K. Shanmugam was to comment that the younger generation had quite a different take on race relations, and that this was deserving of attention.[135]

Perceptions on race-related issues were not the only reason why the PAP lost Sengkang GRC. There were additional undercurrents in the voting trend picked up by the media, which interviewed Sengkang voters after the election. Many young voters valued diversity in political discourse and having alternative voices in Parliament.[136] This was reflective of something broader—and with implications for the PAP beyond simply having lost another GRC. In remarks during the customary post-election press conference held in the early hours of 11 July, PM Lee addressed the issue:

> The results show also a clear desire for a diversity of voices in Parliament. Singaporeans want the PAP to form the government, but they and especially the younger voters also want to see more Opposition presence in Parliament. . . .

> On the question of segments of the population and the youth vote . . . I would say that there are different generations have different life experiences and that the young people have very significantly different life aspirations and priorities compared to the older generations and that this will have to be reflected in our political process and in the government policies because in the end the government policies must be to achieve the aspirations of every generation of Singaporeans.[137]

Two GRCs and one SMC lost to the Opposition (all to the Workers' Party) made for the worst result (in terms of seats lost) for the PAP since independence.[138] At the press conference, PM Lee said that the PAP had been given a "clear mandate" but that the PAP's percentage of the popular vote (61.2 per cent) was not as high as he had hoped for.[139] In recognition of the gains made by the WP, which now had ten of the 93 seats in Parliament, Lee (in a major surprise) made it known that he had called WP chief Pritam Singh and offered him the designation of "Leader of the Opposition", with support and resources to perform his duties.[140]

There was no grandstanding from WP leaders despite the gains made. Pritam Singh noted that even as the PAP did its soul-searching, the WP would also work hard and give serious consideration to the way forward.[141] Singh's predecessor, Low Thia Khiang, had been known for his down-to-earth ways and for his ability to connect with heartlanders, especially the Chinese-educated. Singh gave a similarly down-to-earth impression, but his relatability was of a different hue—an excellent speaker in English, he had in the past made it a point to attempt to connect with the ground using rudimentary Mandarin as well.[142]

Confluence

The voters' desire for the PAP to remain in charge, while wanting at the same time more alternative voices in Parliament, was something the PAP would have to live with. As PM Lee observed in his remarks at the PAP Party Conference in November:

the unequivocal signal from voters was that they wanted the PAP to form the government, and to see Singapore through the challenges ahead. Even many who voted for the opposition, did so fully expecting that the PAP Government would be returned to power, and Singapore would continue to be in good hands. This voting behaviour did not arise because people wanted the PAP out. On the contrary and paradoxically, people voted like this because they believed that the PAP is the only party that could win and govern Singapore. The outcome is already certain; so no need to make extra sure. It is a strange dilemma that we face. But that is how it is.[143]

There was deeper reflection, too. A major part of the PAP election post-mortem had to do with the basic recognition that a confluence of factors had led to the decline in support for the PAP, without any one particular factor being privileged.[144]

The discontent evidenced in 2020 was not the same as had been apparent after 2011. Many of the "fixes" that were needed after 2011 were policy moves—improving transport, addressing the issue of waiting times for HDB flats, further calibrating workpass quotas and the inflow of foreigners, and addressing concerns on healthcare and retirement adequacy (culminating in the Pioneer Generation Package and MediShield Life). Some of the issues—concerns over the numbers of foreigners in Singapore and the fear of locals being displaced, for example—did make a reappearance, but on the whole, the 2020 election distinguished itself from 2011 in that there seemed to be the stirrings of something else—these stirrings of a different type of dissatisfaction.

In the paragraphs that follow, some broad lines (drawing in part on interviews with activists, MPs and ministers) of the PAP post-mortem thinking are traced.

Generations

An older generation of Singaporeans is passing from the scene, as the Party leadership as well as the rank and file know all too well. The Party does not necessarily bank on unswerving loyalty from this segment: even as its members diminish, this demographic will want assurance that the Party will continue to see to their needs. Still, many from this older generation have a strong emotional relationship with the PAP: they might from time to time disagree with its policies, but what might be termed emotional resonance often still leads them to vote for the Party.[145]

And then there are those in the age bracket below. PAP ministers made it known in the aftermath of the election that the Party had suffered a drop in support from the sandwiched middle class—those in the age range of 40 to their early 60s. This group had been particularly affected by the impact of COVID-19. Many from this group, breadwinners for their families, felt economic hardship and anxiety.[146] There was also the sense on the part of middle-aged and older workers of being displaced—through competition with foreign workers, or through technological change.[147]

Government assistance schemes were designed to support individuals, employees and business owners during the pandemic, but there was friction and unhappiness that came with having to deal with bureaucracy, especially from individuals who in the course of their ordinary lives would have had little interaction with government agencies. At the level of either individuals or business owners, they now had to navigate their way through a thicket of schemes and understand eligibility criteria.[148] For their part, the government agencies tasked with managing assistance schemes were doing so on a massive, unprecedented scale. There were frictions and slip-ups, and the overall big picture in terms of what help was available and how it could be accessed was not communicated as well as it could have been, given that the key agencies were overloaded.[149] Many owners of small and medium enterprises felt this. Businesses relying on foreign workers were particularly affected—the government was trying to bring down the number of foreign workers infected with the virus, but in the execution of plans there was a great deal of friction and anger, with business owners writing in and querying the need for tough measures, when the foreign workers they needed to keep their businesses running as viable enterprises were simply not to be had or confined to dormitories.[150] Other businesses (such as restaurants and bars) had their operations curtailed (or forced into near-cessation during the circuit breaker).

The hit was at the personal level too. During the circuit breaker, individuals were distressed at not being able to visit their aged parents. In addition, ways of working had been turned on their head, and for many, WFH (the nearly universally understood acronym for "working from home") brought additional stress. From a public health perspective the government had goals in mind—reducing the overall risk of COVID-19 infections, and reducing the risk to vulnerable groups—but the moves unsettled social and family structures and came with a social and emotional cost, and incurred resentment. And with the pain, there were many who felt that the PAP government was being opportunistic in calling for an election. To the PAP leadership this was perhaps to be expected, but it was also a misreading: there was global uncertainty related to the pandemic, and the very real possibility that things might get worse.[151]

For all the groups and individuals who were negatively affected personally or professionally by the government's pandemic management measures, the idea of "no blank cheque" resonated—one's vote could make for change, sending a message that within the overall handling of the pandemic there were things that could have been done better.[152]

What has been sketched out above reflects the issues and sentiments uncovered in the PAP's election post-mortem—but the general outlines were known in advance. Feedback from activists and ground intelligence meant that MPs on the ground were, going into the hustings, under no illusion that GE2020 would be a flight to safety on the part of the electorate. Layered onto this, and what the post-mortem pointed to as being especially significant, is the issue of the broader trajectory in terms of where Singaporeans—especially younger Singaporeans—are heading in terms of their worldview when it comes to politics, plurality and contestability.

Younger Voters

The feeling at all levels—Party activists, MPs and ministers—from an early stage after the election was that the young did not abandon the PAP en masse.[153] Younger voters looked closely at the candidates themselves and were prepared to give their vote to credible figures, as well as those with whom they felt a connection (especially those who had walked the ground for some time). There were SMCs with a relatively high proportion of younger voters where PAP candidates fared well.[154]

Increasingly, however, those in the young generation are asking deeper, tougher questions. Born from the 1980s onwards, their lived experience is quite different from that of their parents or grandparents. Many from the older generation had very little to begin with—uplifted from kampong to HDB flat, they could see and touch progress in tangible forms. This made for a strong emotional connection to the Party.

The younger generation, however, grew up in Singapore with relative affluence as the baseline—as an expectation—rather than the goal to strive for. Ministers, MPs and activists interviewed by the author suggest that overall, the younger generation's emotional relationship with the PAP is very different from that of their parents or grandparents.

This is a particular challenge for the PAP. As PM Lee observed at the 11 July post-election press conference:

> *Different generations have different life experiences and the young people have very significantly different life aspirations and priorities compared to the older generation and (that) this will have to be reflected in our political process and in the government policies, because in the end the government policies must be to achieve the aspirations of every generation of Singaporeans. At the same time, we also hope that new generations of Singaporeans look critically . . . but with an open mind at what the previous generations have done to examine what is relevant, what continues to make sense for them in a new environment and to learn from these experiences hard-won by their parents and grandparents so that they don't have to learn them all over again and pay a high price which has already been paid . . . the generations have to work together in order to achieve that and not have a disconnect and find ourselves with no historical memory.[155]*

The PAP makes its first appearance to many in the younger generation in the history books they study. They associate the PAP with dominance.[156] They know what the PAP has done to bring Singapore to its present success—they credit the Party to a degree, but to many, the credit is due especially to the older generation of leaders such as Lee Kuan Yew, Goh Chok Tong and PM Lee Hsien Loong, who brought Singapore to the present point.[157] They are now being asked to vote into Parliament a new set of PAP MPs and future leaders—who have yet in their view to earn their stripes. At the same time, they are seeing the emergence of credible Opposition candidates who promise to hold the PAP to account in Parliament and who connect as well as, or in some cases better than, new PAP candidates.

Some of this seems to have been foreseen. Lee Kuan Yew, interviewed by the author in 2011 after the election that year, observed:

> *A generation now believes that the system is in place and anybody can run it. I happen to believe the contrary because I built the system and I know that without more than very ordinary men in charge this will be a very ordinary country . . . I think it's about what the younger generation think. And the younger generation is prepared to take risks and say, let's try the Opposition. Put the PAP under pressure and see who performs better. How it progresses from there depends on the reactions of the government and the Opposition.*[158]

·ᢌᢌᢌᢌ·

The task of taking the PAP forward will not now fall on Heng Swee Keat, who had been appointed first assistant secretary-general in 2018, DPM in 2019, and coordinating minister for economic policies after the 2020 election, and who had seemed set to be Singapore's fourth premier.

During the 2020 campaign, in his speech at the PAP's signature Fullerton Rally, PM Lee said that he was "determined to hand over Singapore, intact and in good working order, to the next team".[159] He repeated this undertaking at the PAP Party Conference in November.[160] These words were widely remarked on by observers, who saw in this the implication that PM Lee had thought again about the succession timeline given earlier (that he would step down as PM at some point after the election, and before he turned 70 in February 2022). Senior figures from the PAP establishment also called at around this time for the PM to stay on and see Singapore through the pandemic.[161]

There had been rethinking on the part of key individuals, and not just about the timeline for succession. On 8 April 2021, at a specially called press conference, DPM Heng announced that he would step aside as head of the PAP 4G leadership, and from consideration for the premiership (he would, however, remain as PAP first assistant secretary-general and DPM). In his letter to PM Lee, Heng (who would turn 60 later, on 15 April) thanked PM Lee for his commitment to stay on until the crisis had passed. Heng wrote that he would be close to his mid-60s by then, leaving him "too short a runway" for the top job. The huge challenges ahead should, Heng wrote, be tackled by someone younger.[162]

The letters between PM Lee and DPM Heng, as well as their statements at the press conference, were carefully phrased, signifying mutual respect and understanding. In PM Lee's exchange of letters with DPM Heng, and in his remarks at the press conference, there was no sense of trying to persuade DPM Heng to stay on: Lee said that he understood and respected Heng's decision, and praised Heng's selflessness. So too with the statement issued on the same day (8 April) by the PAP 4G leadership: they accepted Heng's decision, noting that he did so with Singapore's interest at heart.

At the press conference, PM Lee said that Heng spoke to him "about the succession issue" after the February 2021 budget debate, but what exactly had transpired behind the scenes was the subject of much speculation.[163] None of the principals showed further inclination to delve further into the whys and wherefores. For his part, Heng was clear that the election, its result, and his own performance on the campaign trail had no bearing on his decision.[164]

The 4G leaders requested PM Lee to stay on as prime minister until they chose a new successor (to which PM Lee agreed). The 4G team acknowledged the likely anxieties that Singaporeans would have about the "unexpected turn of events" and sought Singaporeans' understanding as they chose another leader.[165] There was no disguising that this development had upset succession planning and a timeline for renewal that had been in place for a considerable time. One retired former minister, Dr Yaacob Ibrahim, enunciating a view held by many, especially in the professional classes, observed that the 4G leaders had had enough time to size each other up and decide who the next leader should be, and that the choice (of who would take Heng's place as the next PM-designate) should have been made "yesterday".[166] The developments also caused a degree of consternation—bewilderment even—within the PAP rank and file.[167] There was anxiety too on the part of ordinary Singaporeans: the majority of those polled by the media suggested that the new leader should be chosen sooner rather than later.[168]

PM Lee had said earlier on several occasions that he had no intention of staying on longer than necessary. But now, he was certainly going to remain PM beyond the age of 70, something he had hoped not to do, and possibly (no one conclusively ruled this out) even leading the PAP into the next election. He would not be drawn in as to what the actual timeline for a new successor might look like—longer than a few months, he suggested, appearing hopeful at the same time that the choice might be made before the next election.

The Challenge Ahead

Readers will forgive the author if in this final summing up, in the course of offering assessments of how the Party intends to move forward, some personal reflections are also set out—reflections that have come from several years of close study of the Party and its people.

The Leader

A major Cabinet reshuffle two weeks after Heng Swee Keat's announcement saw Heng (as had been signalled earlier by PM Lee on 8 April) relinquish the Finance portfolio while retaining the positions of DPM and Coordinating Minister for Economic Policies. Heng's replacement at the Finance Ministry was Education Minister Lawrence Wong. Other key members of the 4G leadership also moved to new roles (Chan Chun Sing from Trade and Industry to Education, Ong Ye Kung from Transport to Health).[169] No clues were offered as to who the next prime minister might be.

In 2018, when asked about the next leader and what role he should play in the next election, PM Lee observed:

> *He will have to pull his weight and . . . show that he deserves to be what his peers*
> *and his colleagues in Cabinet think that he can do . . . this is necessary. If you're*
> *unable to win elections, you cannot be the leader. You can be a great thinker, you*
> *can be a great planner, but you have to be in politics.*[170]

Besides technocratic excellence and acumen, then, the next prime minister and leader of the PAP will have to be able to campaign, canvass, and move the people. He will also have to have the qualities to best a strengthening Opposition in debate in and out of Parliament—an Opposition whose leader is able to match the most eloquent of the PAP's MPs and ministers in debate and unafraid to cross swords with PM Lee.[171]

The next prime minister will need to have intellect and charisma, but at the same time will lead in an era when he will likely be first amongst equals. One retired minister observed after the 2020 election:

> *We had an extraordinary run—either out of luck or destiny—we had Lee Kuan*
> *Yew, Goh Chok Tong, Lee Hsien Loong. We cannot expect or hope for a repeat—*
> *we need to transit to a different mode. The leadership of future generations will*
> *depend more on institutions, values and processes. We will still need excellent*
> *people, but we may not have one exceptional individual leader in charge of a team*
> *reporting to him. We may need more teams of leaders bringing us forward and*
> *navigating the complex issues likely to arise for the next 50 years.*[172]

It is this mode of consensual and combinatory leadership that will have to take Singapore forward. Lee Kuan Yew, who towered above almost all of his colleagues, recognised this, observing when interviewed by the author in 2011 that "every team has a different mix, but the total result of the mix is performance, in performance and persuading people to a course of action and delivering in that course of action".[173]

The Party's People

The concept of holistic renewal is deeply embedded within the Party. It knows that if it is to thrive, replenishment of the ranks cannot simply be at the leadership level. The Party will need to convince candidates with genuine ability to stand (many of whom will not become office-holders), supported by a strong network of volunteers and activists (who must also be refreshed).[174]

But as previous chapters have shown, inducting quality candidates into the Party has been problematic for decades, with the task likely becoming even more difficult in the coming years. Part of this stems from the demands on MPs: a swathe (large, and growing) of the electorate wants MPs to work for them, while at the same time desiring empathy, authenticity and relatability in the individual they elect. Some MPs interviewed by the author, especially well-known for putting in the hard yards and spending considerable time on the ground, have spoken of a type of "emotional availability" that they increasingly sense constituents desire in their MPs. MPs cannot merely be present, and even visibly walking the ground is not enough. The sense of fullheartedness and empathy, and being actively interested in the lives of residents, must be shown at all times. Any sense of being perfunctory in interactions is going to come with a cost, and MPs must increasingly be seen and felt to be working directly for the interests of constituents in very tangible ways.[175]

Many individuals considering heeding the call to stand for election accept that a certain amount of grassroots politics (meet-the-people sessions, walkabouts and block visits for example) is part of the package. Now, however, they have to learn how to project themselves both in the flesh and on social media. They can be directly targeted, too, on social media by critics, with some of the character assassination being of a very personal nature. This has a knock-on impact not just on the candidate but on his or her family. All these factors will now be weighed by candidates asked to stand. Many will decide that the role is not a fit for them. Some former ministers, interviewed by the author, suggest that if they were to be asked now to join the political fray as a PAP candidate, they might not have responded the same way as they did earlier.[176]

Toxic personal attacks may deter some from agreeing to stand as candidates. But the overall, critical challenge—perhaps *the* critical challenge—for the Party is talent. There will continue to be able people from the private sector as well as senior civil servants (including senior officers from the armed forces) willing to serve, but the Party may find that these taps will in future run less reliably than they formerly did. It will be important to find and nurture new clusters of talent, but it is not immediately apparent where these are. And where there are reservoirs of individuals found—individuals committed to making a difference in society—it may well increasingly be the case in the future that major Opposition parties such as the WP are attempting to tap these as well.

What type of person should the Party be looking for? SM Teo Chee Hean, who has been in politics since 1992, explained:

> It is ideal if you can find a person who is a persuader and a mobiliser and who is also able to think through the problems of the future. It is not easy to find such a person. Persuaders and mobilisers can be good on the stump. But you also need a person who can be good on the ground, not just people who turn up and make a good speech.

> We have many loyal activists at the branches who believe in what the PAP does— which is that it is a sincere party which works for the interests of the people. Many of them are motivated by this belief and serve with no great expectation of becoming members of parliament and so on. They just want to serve. That's a strength and an asset. I think the issue really is, can the MPs and the candidates spend more time before they get put up for election; can we "grow" them up within our branches so that they grow with us? The more time they have with the branches, the more time they spend working with the ground, the better. That's always true. But I think it's also important for the Party to cast its net wide. For every election you have people who have served for a long time as activists. You can find a number of such people today in our ranks. We always look for them,

and we hope to find more of them. But at the same time, we need to reach beyond the Party to look at the whole of Singapore, to bring in people who share the same ideals and the same beliefs.177

PM Lee commented:

We need a range. I need people from the private sector, I need people who know how the government works, I need people who have ground experience in the branches and constituencies. I need people who have political aptitude and skills. It does not mean experience necessarily, but just that kind of temperament, mindset and personality, so that they analyse problems that way, and if they are on stage they can project and have an impact.

It will be harder and harder to attract good people. For MPs I think we can get quite good people, but as it becomes less certain that you will stand in constituencies and win, the hurdle becomes higher. The hurdle is also higher because of the nastiness of the stuff thrown at you, particularly on social media. That is one minus. The other minus is that for ministers: first, the financial sacrifice is greater. Secondly, the uncertainty is also much greater, as you cannot be sure that you will come in and become a minister of state or a minister. You have to stand for elections; but it is a viable career. But I am not sure if that will continue to be the case in the future. So to get somebody who is midway through his professional life and to make a drastic change, which is mostly irreversible, is challenging. To get somebody later in life, who has already mostly proven himself, and say now you come in and try, and hope to replicate that success in government, is also not easy. But if we do not find the right people, the next team will be weaker, and if the team is weaker, it becomes even harder to maintain political dominance. It is a very serious problem.[178]

End of Dominance

Lee Kuan Yew pondered the most—and the furthest—when it came to the PAP's political longevity. Writing in 2008, he observed in an unpublished manuscript:

It does not seem likely that the opposition can field a First Division team of candidates to form a shadow government and challenge the PAP in the next General Election. That could change in future if the PAP slips by allowing sleaze and corruption to creep in. That would be the beginning of the end for the PAP. Next, the PAP could lose its dynamism because its leaders are not talented and dynamic enough as in previous generations. Then talented men and women of integrity outside the PAP must come forward to offer themselves as alternatives, otherwise the Singapore Story will unravel.

What is certain is that Singapore needs a First Division government, the best that Singapore can put together. This is the best way to organise ourselves as a society and a government. Only with such a government can we widen our economic and political space abroad and maximise our potential. Mediocrity in leaders will lose Singapore its brand name it has gained for itself.[179]

Elsewhere, Lee was even more stark, stating that the day would eventually come—either on account of a decline in the PAP's quality, or the Opposition fielding a team equal to the PAP—when the electorate would decide to vote the Opposition into power.[180]

Others within the Party have seen this possibility, but through the prism of the normal development of societies. Tharman Shanmugaratnam observed:

I believe it is not possible to resist a longer-term secular drift down in the PAP's share. It will happen in any maturing society. We should hope to achieve a new equilibrium eventually, and avoid a continuous spiral down. The PAP vote share might be somewhere slightly above 50 per cent, which is still unusually high by any standard. It will probably happen within a few elections from now. But we need to manage the process, avoid a destabilising decline and a loss of confidence by Singaporeans in their future. If you resist it completely you risk a sudden break. So how do we stay a little above the normal fray, so people think of the PAP really as stewards of Singapore's political as well as economic future? If it does come to a situation where we feel we really are at risk of losing because you've got a very capable Opposition in place, we would have an interest in them being as responsible as possible. Not taking positions that put Singapore's future at risk externally or even domestically. You'd have an interest in them having the right instincts and the right measure of things.[181]

Singapore politics changed permanently after 2020, but this is not to say that the leadership in its post-mortem has come to some sort of fatalistic appraisal concerning the irreversible tide of PAP decline. Nor do most PAP leaders think that the task has fallen on the PAP to ease Singapore into a two-party system featuring a strong Opposition.[182] As Chan Chun Sing (interviewed in 2016) maintained:

The Party is here to defy the odds of history and to make sure we can keep ourselves as a going concern—we have to work very hard to make sure we keep going in that way. In Singapore our circumstances are unique. It is for the PAP to lose rather than Opposition to win. Anybody who wants to run Singapore must gain the trust of the people. Singaporeans by and large are practical people—they look for people whom they can trust to deliver results and pull the country together. I don't think it's inevitable. Number one: can we continue to attract good people— the right people with the right values—who are in there for the larger good? Number two: having got good people in, can we keep our unity and cohesion in increasingly challenging global circumstances? We have been exceptionally fortunate up till this point to have been able to get in people and get the team to gel together. The new generation will have to bond together as a team in a much shorter time than Lee Kuan Yew's generation. That will be our challenge. Not so much a new leader, but to groom a team of leaders who can support each other in a more complex environment.[183]

What there *is* near-uniform recognition of within the leadership is that the PAP stands now near the end of an era in which the country had a single dominant party. The people, clearly, do not want a complete wipeout of the Opposition—they would not tolerate it.

Interviews with activists, MPs and ministers suggest that the PAP is gearing up and prepared to fight for the hearts and minds of an electorate that increasingly seems to want a sizeable Opposition presence in Parliament.[184] The Party is also gearing up for the challenge of an Opposition that at some stage will not be content with a handful of seats but will want more—more even than the denial of the PAP's "supermajority" in Parliament, notwithstanding the position taken by Pritam Singh, leader of the Opposition and chief of the Workers' Party (which poses the most formidable challenge), that the WP still has "many, many more miles to go".[185]

The thinking, as far as can be discerned in interviews and informal interactions with activists and MPs, is not solely about a binary future where the PAP and WP jostle. There is also interest, but not apprehension, in the moves of other parties such as the SDP and the PSP. If the PSP can build, consolidate its organisational machinery, and step out of Dr Tan Cheng Bock's shadow, then it might emerge in time as a significant player, and not just in areas in the west of Singapore, where it currently has more support.[186]

Some of the most visible, surface-level changes to the PAP's playbook may well be seen on the campaign trail in future elections. Desmond Lee, minister in charge of the PAP post-mortem effort, remarked that "the rallies are in your phone—you can have a rally every day by playing and replaying messages and themes. The 2020 GE though was almost entirely conducted on social media. People looking for answers and alternatives—they had it in their pocket all the time."[187] In 2020, as in 2011, the PAP tried to ensure that issues advantageous to the Party were front and centre of its campaign messaging, but the big picture (jobs and livelihoods in 2020, for example) was overshadowed by other issues, with the PAP's own rebuttals of points raised by the Opposition also seeming to have the effect of pushing its overarching narrative further into the background.[188] Even as future elections are likely to see a return to normalcy (with real-world rallies returning), more risks will be taken, with younger activists likely to have more say particularly when it comes to the crafting of messages and outreach using social media.[189] There will likely be further thinking, too, on what many observers saw as the negative style of campaigning.[190] It is unlikely, however, that the PAP in and out of the election cycle will simply adopt a gentler style. Calling out what it sees as Opposition mistakes and distilling hard truths that might seem unpalatable (but necessary for the electorate to hear) has simply not been part of the PAP's playbook. It is part of its DNA.

A National Consensus

The PAP's need to find and field people of ability will be all the more pressing in a future where the government will need to handle an ever-increasing plurality of views and interests with political dexterity.

Commentators who have been critical of the Party for some time suggest that this effort is beyond the Party. The argument runs as follows: the PAP, having been entrenched and incumbent for such a long time, has passed its zenith—it has ossified, has no new ideas (and is not open to them), and is probably incapable of reforming itself in a manner that can win over and motivate the people.[191]

The Party that the present writer has spent the past ten years studying, by interviewing leaders and interacting with activists and MPs past and present, is in fact more dynamic than many observers (and critics) think—it goes through periodic processes of rethinking and reinvention, some public and others internal. This has always been so, and the Party embarks on one such process now, far larger and more ambitious than the 2020 general election post-mortem.

One aspect eclipses the Party itself and is tethered to the narrative of stewardship of the nation, especially in the face of external headwinds. While this theme did not have as much traction as hoped in the 2020 general election, the leadership has not strayed from its conviction that it is its mission to chart a course that would safely steer Singapore in a very challenging global environment—one that it believes the nation can prosper in.

Heng Swee Keat observed in 2017:

> *We are in very uncharted waters. The consensus for globalisation lasted for quite a long while—partly because everyone benefited. Staying relevant to the world will be critical to our prosperity—we need to keep encouraging Singaporeans to build links all around us—the fact is we are a small island.*
>
> *At the same time, cities are going through changes that we may not have fully anticipated. One change carries with it a string of other changes. Economic and technological shifts are going to unleash new forces in the coming years with a huge impact on how we live and work. These will all be very significant for us—no less than what happened in the early years of independence. We have to ensure that our people are sufficiently equipped to deal with these changes.[192]*

The second, crucial aspect is internal. COVID-19 presents the crisis of a generation, and the leadership recognises that there are opportunities for a reset and rethinking on several fronts. Members of the 4G leadership have suggested that moves will be made in the direction of reinforcing Singapore's social safety nets, particularly to protect the disadvantaged.[193] A related facet is strengthening cohesion and social mobility—with the overall vision of making for a fairer and more equal society.[194] As informed and respected observers have noted, this is tied into what younger Singaporeans seem to want—coupled a sense of sustainability and environmental consciousness.[195]

The more urgent task now, it seems (if public pronouncements by 4G ministers are a guide), is redoubling efforts at forging national consensus at a time when there is greater diversity in sociopolitical discourse than ever before.[196] A future that sees politics more sharply contested leads to manifold dangers, from the PAP's point of view—with instability, or societal fissures, becoming more likely. 4G ministers clearly want to guard against polarised politics of the type seen elsewhere. As Heng Swee Keat observed after the 2020 election, "We must take an inclusive approach to serve all Singaporeans, and not pit one group against another. If our unity is lost, Singapore will stumble."[197]

This space, which will be closely watched, will likely see the PAP seeking to be more inclusive as it engages the electorate—especially segments that disagree with the PAP and its policies—within the framework of an outreach and communications approach that is itself likely to be more agile.

As one 4G minister observed:

> The way we exercise power has to change into something more like benevolent servant leadership. More and more Singaporeans want to understand why we are deciding things in a certain way—no matter how thoroughly ministers and civil servants have done homework behind the scenes. Singaporeans are beginning to question a lot more and are not taking things for granted. This is healthy and the result of educational investment over the years. But this also means that government must learn to work with the people and respect the people all the more—so we are working all the more with people and NGOs, and side by side with civil society on issues that we would have simply decided on our own in the past. We need a robust civil society. So you have a system where government has a close bond with people, VWOs, workers. This is the best bulwark against despotism and corruption of future government.[198]

Exactly what policy calibrations will be made in the direction of a more equal, cohesive and sustainable society will become clearer in the years to come. It is certain that hard calls will need to be made in the policymaking realm, at least some of which will be painful politically, and which will involve potentially tricky trade-offs. The same member of the 4G leadership emphasised in this context the need to have a "strategic reserve":

> Political capital has to be built up. It has to be built up cerebrally and emotionally. Personally. Not just doing the right thing, which is a given—being seen to be doing the right thing. We do need to build on the political capital that the earlier generation of leaders had, and the trust that the people reposed in them, in order

to win acceptance for the Party and for its policies. Otherwise we will be quite normal as a democracy.[199]

What might seem new in some respects is in fact old—foundational, for a party in power for 62 years since 1959 and victorious over 15 general elections. In the words of the PAP's first secretary-general and founding father of modern Singapore, Lee Kuan Yew, if there was one factor—one above all the others—behind the PAP's success, it was "trust in the ability of the PAP to deliver what it promises".[200] It was also his conviction that this was something that could not be wasted: "The next generation of PAP leaders will inherit this trust. They must not betray it. They cannot afford to squander it."[201]

If the Party retains and builds on its inheritance, its future—Singapore's future—will likely remain within its own hands.

Notes

1   *2020 Parliamentary General Election Results* (Elections Department Singapore), available at https://www.eld.gov.sg/finalresults2020.html (accessed 7 Apr. 2021). See also "Workers' Party Won 50.49% Votes in 6 Constituencies It Contested in against PAP", *Mothership*, 12 July 2020, available at https://mothership.sg/2020/07/workers-party-vote-share-ge2020/ (accessed 23 Apr. 2021). In 2011, the WP won 47.03% of the vote where it contested. The figure for 2015 (in an election year where the tide swung towards the PAP) was 39.75% (author's calculations based on ELD data).

2   The PAP team in West Coast GRC was strengthened by the last-minute addition of Minister for Social and Family Development Desmond Lee (who moved over from the adjacent Jurong GRC), a move that (in keeping with the PAP's practice when it came to tactical changes) became public only on Nomination Day. "Singapore GE2020: PAP's Desmond Lee Joins West Coast GRC Slate in Fight against Tan Cheng Bock's PSP", *Straits Times*, 30 July 2020.

3   As a PAP MP, Dr Tan Cheng Bock had been MP for Ayer Rajah Single Member Constituency for 26 years, from 1980 to 2006. Following his retirement as a PAP MP, Ayer Rajah was absorbed into West Coast GRC. As a medical GP practising in different parts of western Singapore for over 40 years, Dr Tan developed close bonds with his patients and strong grassroots links with constituents. See "Former Presidential Candidate Tan Cheng Bock Retiring from Medicine after 50 Years", *Straits Times*, 31 Dec. 2018.

4   The Singapore Democratic Party (SDP), a much more established party, had a vote share of 38.28% where it contested (author's calculations). Dr Tan Cheng Bock's draw was especially strong in the Ayer Rajah area, where he had been MP, and also in areas where he had formerly practised as a GP. He also drew on his long-standing contacts within the PAP to strengthen his PSP team and its organisation. Several PAP cadres are known to have left the PAP in order to join the PSP. See "Exclusive: Revealed—the People behind Tan Cheng Bock's Proposed New Party and Its Election Plans", *Today*, 8 Feb. 2019.

5   "Remain PM after 70? 'I Hope Not': Prime Minister Lee Hsien Loong, 60, Who Has Held His Post for Eight Years, Would Prefer Not to Retain It beyond 10 More Years", *AsiaOne*, 30 Sept. 2012 (originally published in the *Straits Times*), available at https://www.asiaone.com/print/News/Latest%2BNews/Singapore/Story/A1Story20120928-374401.html (accessed 16 Apr. 2021). PM Lee was to restate this timeline of stepping down from the premiership before he turned 70 on other occasions. See, for example, "CNBC Transcript: Lee Hsien Loong, Prime Minister of Singapore ", *CNBC*, 19 Oct. 2017.

6   Goh Chok Tong, post on MParader Facebook page, 31 Dec. 2017. Available at https://www.facebook.com/ MParader/posts/1954247007951289 (accessed 31 Mar. 2021). See also "ESM Goh Chok Tong Says Settling 4G Leadership an Urgent Challenge, Hopes Next PM Can Be Designated 'Before 2018 Ends'", *Straits Times*, 31 Dec. 2017.

7   "Facebook Post Meant to Nudge 4G Leaders to Act: ESM Goh Chok Tong", *Straits Times*, 7 Jan. 2018.

8   "16 'Younger Ministers' Sign Statement", *Straits Times*, 5 Jan. 2018. For the text of the statement, see "Some Observations from Ong Ye Kung ST Interview and 4G leaders' Statement on Succession", *Mothership*, 4 Jan. 2018, available at https://mothership.sg/2018/01/some-observations-from-ong-ye-kung-st-interview-about-4g-leaders-statement-on-succession/ (accessed 14 Apr. 2021).

9   "PM Lee: No New DPM to Be Appointed during Cabinet Reshuffle; Choosing Next PM Will Take 'A Little Bit Longer'", *Straits Times*, 2 Feb. 2018.

10   "Heng Swee Keat Picked as PAP's First Assistant Secretary-General, Indicating He Will Be Next PM", *Straits Times*, 23 Nov. 2018; "Statement by Younger Political Office-Holders", *Straits Times*, 24 Nov. 2018. PM Lee remained as secretary-general in the CEC, with Gan Kim Yong as the new chairman. See also PM Lee Hsien Loong, statement on new Party CEC, 23 Nov. 2018, available at https://www.facebook.com/pap.sg/posts/2302324019778985 (accessed 12 Apr. 2021); and "PAP's 35th Central Executive Committee", 23 Nov. 2018, available at https://www.pap.org.sg/news/paps-35th-cec/ (accessed 12 Apr. 2021).

11   "Younger Political Office-Holders Rally behind Heng Swee Keat and Chan Chun Sing as PAP's First and Second Assistant Secretaries-General", *Straits Times*, 23 Nov. 2018.

12   Trade and Industry Minister Chan Chun Sing was appointed second assistant secretary-general in November 2018. At the time of taking over the position of first assistant secretary-general, Heng Swee Keat made it known that he had asked Chan to act as his deputy. "Heng Swee Keat Picked as 4G leader, with Chan Chun Sing as Deputy", *Straits Times*, 24 Nov. 2018.

13   Lee had written that Heng "was the best Principal Private Secretary I ever had. The only pity is that he is not of a big bulk, which makes a difference in a mass rally. But he has one of the finest minds among the civil servants I have worked with." Lee Kuan Yew, *One Man's View of the World* (Singapore: Straits Times Press, 2013), p. 209.

14   "Finance Minister Heng Swee Keat Undergoes Surgery after Sudden Stroke during Cabinet Meeting, Remains in ICU", *Straits Times*, 19 Oct. 2016.

15   For the statement, see "What Has Happened to Lee Kuan Yew's Values?", *Online Citizen*, 14 June 2017, available at https://www.theonlinecitizen.com/wp-content/

uploads/2017/06/What-Has-Happened-To-Lee-Kuan-Yews-Values.pdf (accessed 23 Apr. 2021); original statement on Lee Hsien Yang's Facebook page no longer publicly accessible.

16   For a summary of the issues, see "Increasingly Anxious, Singaporeans Look to Parliament to Provide Answers on Damaging Oxley Road Saga", *Today*, 30 June 2017.

17   "What Has Happened to Lee Kuan Yew's Values?"

18   For the statement, see "PM Lee Hsien Loong Releases Summary of Statutory Declarations to Ministerial Committee Looking into Options for Oxley Road House", *Straits Times*, 16 June 2017.

19   "PM Lee Hsien Loong Apologises for Damage to Singapore Caused by Family Dispute", *Straits Times*, 20 June 2017.

20   Singapore Parliamentary Debates, 3 July 2017 (Lee Hsien Loong).

21   Singapore Parliamentary Debates, 3 July 2017 (Low Thia Khiang); "WP Chief Slams 'Ugly Media Circus', Wants Issue Settled in Court", *Today*, 3 July 2017. See also the interventions made during the course of the debate by Pritam Singh of the Workers' Party: "But it is the allegations of abuse of power that have to be decisively addressed, otherwise an odour will linger, one that will have severe and significant repercussions for Singapore's reputation. I do not believe a Parliamentary debate like the one we are having today will put the matter to rest, even as I hope I am wrong." Singapore Parliamentary Debates, 3 July 2017 (Pritam Singh).

22   Singapore Parliamentary Debates, 3 July 2017 (Lee Hsien Loong).

23   Singapore Parliamentary Debates, 4 July 2017 (Goh Chok Tong); "ESM Goh Chok Tong's Full Speech in Parliament (July 4, 2017)", *Today*, 4 July 2017.

24   "Lee Suet Fern Suspended for 15 Months", *Straits Times*, 21 Nov. 2020. The demolition clause provided for Lee Wei Ling to live in the house after Lee Kuan Yew's death if she chose to, with the house to be demolished immediately after she moved out. A second part of the demolition clause showed that Lee Kuan Yew recognised that 38 Oxley Road might not be demolished (in the event, for example, of changes in the law). In such an eventuality, Lee's final will stated that it was his wish that the house never be opened to others except his children, their families and their descendants. "Oxley Road Dispute: Two Parts to Demolition Clause in Lee Kuan Yew's Will, Says Indranee", *Straits Times*, 24 June 2017.

25   "Lee Suet Fern Suspended for 15 Months". For the chain of events in the preparation of the will, see "Events Involving Lee Hsien Yang in Preparation and Execution of Lee Kuan Yew's Will 'Troubling': Court", *Straits Times*, 21 Nov. 2020.

26   "Li Shengwu Fined S$15,000 for Scandalising Judiciary in 2017 Facebook Post", *Today*, 29 July 2020.

27   Li Shengwu, Facebook, 11 Aug. 2020, available at https://www.facebook.com/li.shengwu01/posts/10158737911423523 (accessed 28 Apr. 2021). See also "Li Shengwu Does Not Admit Guilt but Will Pay $15,000 Fine for Contempt of Court", *Straits Times*, 11 Aug. 2020.

28   *Report of the Constitutional Commission 2016*, pp. 95–7, available at https://www.gov.sg/-/media/gov/elected-presidency/report-of-the-constitutional-commission-2016.pdf (accessed 27 Mar. 2021). For the purposes of the elected presidency, Eurasians are considered part

of the "Indians and other minorities" group (the other ethnic groups being Chinese and Malay). For a summary of the recommendations, see "Constitutional Commission Report Released; Key Changes Proposed to Elected Presidency", *Straits Times*, 8 Sept. 2016.

29   *White Paper on the Review of Specific Aspects of the Elected Presidency, Cmd. 7 of 2016*, 15 Sept. 2016 (Prime Minister's Office), available at https://www.nas.gov.sg/archivesonline/government_records/record-details/1fd8053f-8632-11e6-9af5-0050568939ad (accessed 27 Mar. 2021); for a summary, see "Elected Presidency White Paper: Key Points at a Glance", *Straits Times*, 15 Sept. 2016.

30   For Halimah's upbringing and childhood, see "Halimah Yacob on Valuable Lessons from Her Early Struggles", *Straits Times*, 11 Aug. 2017.

31   *Constitution of the Republic of Singapore* (1999 Rev. Ed.), art. 19(3)(a), available at https://sso.agc.gov.sg/Act/CONS1963?&ProvIds=pr19-&ViewType=Advance&Phrase=General+Law&WiAl=1 (accessed 21 Mar. 2021).

32   "Salleh Marican 'Sad and Disappointed' with PEC Decision", *Today*, 11 Sept. 2017; "Farid Khan Explains Why Presidential Bid Was Rejected", *Straits Times*, 16 Sept. 2017. Candidates from the private sector must have served as the most senior executive of their company for a minimum of three years, with the company needing to have at least $500 million in shareholders' equity. The previous criteria stipulated that the candidate had to be a chairman or CEO of a company with at least $100 million in paid-up capital. *White Paper on the Review of Specific Aspects of the Elected Presidency*, pp. 10–3.

33   Before Halimah Yacob's elevation to the presidency, Singapore's last Malay president had been Yusof Ishak. The latter served as Yang di-Pertuan Negara, or head of state, from December 1959 to August 1965. When Singapore gained independence in August 1965, he became president, a role in which he served until his death in 1970.

34   PM Lee Hsien Loong, remarks at the PA Kopi Talk at Ci Yuan CC, 23 Sept. 2017, available at https://www.pmo.gov.sg/newsroom/pm-lee-hsien-loong-pa-kopitalk-ci-yuan-cc (accessed 27 Mar. 2021). See also "Reserved Presidential Election Was Right Thing to Do: PM Lee Hsien Loong", *Straits Times*, 29 Sept. 2017.

35   The crucial point of contention was this: the government had counted the five terms starting with Wee Kim Wee (1985–93), who was in office when the elected presidency took effect in 1991 and was the first to be vested with its powers. Dr Tan's contention was that the count should start with Ong Teng Cheong (1993–99), Singapore's first elected president. If Dr Tan's interpretation was correct, that would mean that four terms, not five, had passed under the elected presidency when Singapore had not had a Malay president (with the presidents coming after Ong Teng Cheong being S.R. Nathan [two terms] and Dr Tony Tan). If this interpretation had prevailed, the 2017 presidential election would be an open election. Ultimately, the Court of Appeal ruled that determining when the hiatus-triggered reserved election mechanism was engaged was solely for Parliament to decide. See "Law Allows Parliament to Count Wee Kim Wee's Term in Triggering Reserved Presidential Election: High Court", *Straits Times*, 7 July 2017.

36   "Apex Court Unanimously Dismisses Tan Cheng Bock's Appeal on Reserved Presidential Election", *Straits Times*, 23 Aug. 2017.

37   "The government should have told Parliament directly that counting from President Wee was its decision, and defended the decision on the merits. Instead, it chose to distract and

confuse. The government's inconsistent explanations would further fuel the suspicions of Singaporeans about the real intention behind the legislative changes that resulted in this year's Presidential Election being a closed one." Sylvia Lim, speech delivered in Parliament, 3 Oct. 2017, available at https://www2.wp.sg/counting-from-president-wee-kim-wee-or-president-ong-teng-cheong-for-reserved-presidential-election-policy-decision-or-legal-question-speech-by-sylvia-lim/ (accessed 9 Mar. 2021); Singapore Parliamentary Debates, 3 Oct. 2017 (Sylvia Lim).

38   The relevant part of Singapore's Constitution (Article 19B) which determines the evaluation of the Community Committee's Malay subcommittee states that a "person belonging to the Malay community" means "any person, whether of the Malay race or otherwise, who considers himself to be a member of the Malay community and who is generally accepted as a member of the Malay community by that community". Also relevant here are Sections 8E-8L of the Presidential Elections Act. The relevant parts of the Constitution and the Presidential Elections Act can be consulted at https://sso.agc.gov.sg/Act/CONS1963 and https://sso.agc.gov.sg/Act/PrEA1991.

39   Internet commentary from netizens as well as platforms usually critical of the government pointed out the discrepancy between the broad definition of "Malay" as it pertained to criteria for presidential candidates, and (on the other hand) how Malay self-help organisations such as Mendaki rejected requests for assistance from Indian-Muslims (who were not classed as "Malay"). See "Definition of a 'Malay Person' Opens Up a Can of Worms about Mendaki and Apparent Double Standards", *Online Citizen*, 24 July 2017, available at https://www.theonlinecitizen.com/2017/07/24/definition-of-a-malay-person-opens-up-a-can-of-worms-about-mendaki-and-apparent-double-standards/ (accessed 30 Mar. 2021).

40   "Hundreds Take Part in Silent Protest against Reserved Election at Hong Lim Park", *Straits Times*, 16 Sept. 2017.

41   "Readers Shout Down ST's Article Criticising Questions over 'Malayness' of Would-Be Presidential Candidates", *Online Citizen*, 21 July 2017, available at https://www.theonlinecitizen.com/2017/07/21/readers-shout-down-sts-article-to-criticise-malayness-of-would-be-presidential-candidates/ (accessed 30 Mar. 2021).

42   "'Matter of Time' before S'pore Has Non-Chinese PM", *Straits Times*, 4 July 2015.

43   "DPM Tharman Rules Himself Out as Next Prime Minister: 'I Am Not the Man for PM'", *Straits Times*, 28 Sept. 2016; "Most Singaporeans Would Choose Tharman as the Next Prime Minister: Survey", *Yahoo! News*, 26 Sept. 2016, available at https://sg.news.yahoo.com/most-singaporeans-would-choose-tharman-1523976433713206.html (accessed 4 Apr. 2021). In the poll, members of the fourth-generation leadership who featured included Heng Swee Keat (25%) and Chan Chun Sing (24%).

44   "'Matter of Time' Before S'pore Has Non-Chinese PM", *Straits Times*, 4 July 2015.

45   "Older Generation of S'poreans Not Ready for Non-Chinese PM: Heng Swee Keat", *Today*, 29 Mar. 2019.

46   Ibid.

47   "Tan Cheng Bock Says New Party Will Be 'Unifying Alternative' for Singapore", *Channel NewsAsia*, 26 July 2019.

48   Lee Hsien Yang also added for good measure: "It is possible to be loyal Singaporeans, to be proud of what has been accomplished in the past, to recite with pride, 'we the citizens of Singapore', to love Singapore and yet to not vote PAP." Progress Singapore Party, "A Message from Mr Lee Hsien Yang to All Singaporeans", Facebook, 24 June 2020, available at https://www.facebook.com/progresssingaporepartyofficial/videos/1731900436976261 (accessed 30 Mar. 2021). Lee Hsien Yang professed himself sympathetic to the ideals espoused by Dr Tan and the PSP, but he kept the public and media on tenterhooks as to whether he would actually contest the election as a candidate—in the end he did not—though he did campaign on behalf of the PSP.

49   See, for example, "PSP's Tan Cheng Bock: I'm Contesting This GE Because PAP Has Lost Its Way", *Mothership*, 2 July 2020, available at https://mothership.sg/2020/07/psp-tan-cheng-bock-pap-lost-its-way/ (accessed 26 Apr. 2021).

50   "Singapore PM's Brother Thrusts First-Family Row into Politics", *Reuters*, 29 June 2020.

51   "SGH's Lapses Led to Hepatitis C Outbreak Earlier This Year: Independent Review Committee", *Straits Times*, 19 Jan. 2016; "4 MOH and 12 SGH Staff Disciplined for Role in Hepatitis C Outbreak in Hospital", *Straits Times*, 17 Mar. 2016.

52   "Engineer Who Led SMRT Trainees onto Tracks in 2016 Fatal Rail Accident Jailed for 4 Weeks", *Straits Times*, 12 Mar. 2018.

53   "Investigation Findings on Flooding of MRT Tunnels between Bishan and Braddell Stations from 7–8 October 2017", Land Transport Authority, 5 Dec. 2017, available at https://www.lta.gov.sg/content/ltagov/en/newsroom/2017/12/2/investigation-findings-on-flooding-of-mrt-tunnels-between-bishan-and-braddell-stations-from-7--8-october-2017.html (accessed 27 Mar. 2021).

54   "Probe Report on SingHealth Data Breach Points to Basic Failings", *Straits Times*, 10 Jan. 2019; individuals at IHiS were also disciplined, fined or sacked. See "IHiS Sacks 2 Employees, Slaps Financial Penalty on CEO over Lapses in SingHealth Cyber Attack", *Straits Times*, 15 Jan. 2019.

55   Ler had access to Singapore's HIV registry in the course of his work duties. See "Data of 14,200 People with HIV Leaked Online by US Fraudster Who Was Deported from Singapore", *Straits Times*, 30 Jan. 2019; "Data Leak: MOH Knew Only in 2016 that Brochez Had Access to HIV Information", *Straits Times*, 13 Feb. 2019.

56   "Former Key Keppel Execs Arrested in Corruption Probe", *Straits Times*, 2 Feb. 2018.

57   There were other episodes that caused unhappiness amongst specific groups. One was the sudden decision by the Land Transport Authority (LTA) in November 2019 (following a spate of accidents that in some cases had led to injuries and even fatalities) to ban e-scooters from footpaths. The move, announced on 4 November and taking effect the next day, had an immediate impact on the surprised owners of e-scooters, particularly the large number of riders who used the devices (which were not allowed on roads) for food delivery services (the delivery services were themselves through software apps, which had become a popular means through which Singaporeans ordered their meals). An additional source of unhappiness was that many riders had earlier incurred costs in buying e-scooters that were compliant with the LTA-required fire safety standard. The move was welcomed by pedestrians, but what affected food delivery riders felt most was

the impression of a lack of coordination and forward planning by government agencies that affected what was in many cases their sole source of income. Also unimpressed were e-scooter retailers who were left with inventory they could not sell. See "E-scooter Ban on Footpaths: 5 Things You Need to Know", *Channel NewsAsia*, 4 Nov. 2019; and "E-scooters Banned on Footpaths: Food Delivery Riders Meet Shanmugam to Voice Concerns over New Rule", *Straits Times*, 8 Nov. 2019.

58   These and other episodes are detailed and discussed in Bilveer Singh, *Is the People's Action Party Here to Stay? Analysing the Resilience of the One-Party Dominant State in Singapore* (Singapore: World Scientific, 2019), pp. 166–71.

59   "社论：纠正过失恢复公众信心" [Editorial: correcting past lapses and restoring public confidence], *Lianhe Zaobao*, 1 Feb. 2019. See also "Comment: Openly Discussing Public Service Lapses Will Force Both PAP & Opposition to Do Better", *Mothership*, 19 Sept. 2020, available at https://mothership.sg/2020/09/singapore-public-pap-trust-issues/ (accessed 30 Apr. 2021).

60   "The Loss of Trust between the Elite and the Masses", *Straits Times*, 13 Dec. 2017. Originally published as "吴俊刚：信任是如何失去的?" [Goh Choon Kang: how is trust lost?], *Lianhe Zaobao*, 6 Dec. 2017.

61   "Has Trust in the Government Been Eroded? It's Time to Talk Frankly", *Straits Times*, 1 Feb. 2018.

62   Heng Swee Keat, "Singapore's Government Has Not Gone Slack", *Straits Times*, 9 Feb. 2019; "王瑞杰：再难也要守好业" [Heng Swee Keat: even if more difficult now, we must keep it going] , *Lianhe Zaobao*, 9 Feb. 2019. See Singh, *Is the People's Action Party Here to Stay?*, p. 169.

63   "Merdeka" means "independent" or "free" in Malay.

64   "Merdeka Generation Package", available at https://www.singaporebudget.gov.sg/budget_2019/budget-measures/merdeka-generation-package (accessed 27 Mar. 2021). Also part of the 2019 budget was a $1.1 billion Bicentennial Bonus (commemorating the 200th anniversary of the modern foundation of Singapore). Benefits included GST vouchers for lower-income Singaporeans and a personal income tax rebate.

65   "Workers' Party MPs End Fund-Raising Appeal as Public Donations Cross Million-Dollar Mark", *Straits Times*, 28 Oct. 2018. For a summary of developments in the legal travails of the WP MPs until the end of 2019, see Khairulanwar Zaini, "Singapore in 2019: In Holding Pattern", *Southeast Asian Affairs* (2020): 297–9.

66   The 330-bed National Centre for Infectious Diseases officially opened in September 2019.

67   "Four Budgets Projected to Help Avert $23.4 Billion in Economic Losses", *Straits Times*, 5 June 2020.

68   This was despite warnings from some quarters, including organisations concerned with the welfare of foreign workers. See, for example, "Straits Times Forum: Employers' Practices Leave Foreign Workers Vulnerable to Infection", Transient Workers Count Too (TWC2), available at https://twc2.org.sg/2020/03/23/straits-times-forum-employers-practices-leave-foreign-workers-vulnerable-to-infection/ (accessed 27 Mar. 2021).

69   By the end of 2020 nearly half of all foreign workers housed in dormitories had contracted COVID-19, with two deaths among this group. "Nearly Half of Migrant Workers in Dormitories Have Had Covid-19", *Straits Times*, 15 Dec. 2020; "Measures to Contain the COVID-19 Outbreak in Migrant Worker Dormitories", Minister of Manpower press release, 14 Dec. 2020, available at https://www.mom.gov.sg/newsroom/press-releases/2020/1214-measures-to-contain-the-covid-19-outbreak-in-migrant-worker-dormitories (accessed 2 Apr. 2021).

70   "Covid-19 Singapore: A 'Pandemic of Inequality' Exposed", *BBC News*, 18 Sept. 2020.

71   "Even if Josephine Teo Doesn't Want to Apologise to Migrant Workers, She Should Apologise to Singaporeans", *Online Citizen*, 6 May 2020, available at https://www.theonlinecitizen.com/2020/05/06/even-if-josephine-teo-doesnt-want-to-apologise-to-migrant-workers-she-should-apologise-to-singaporeans/ (accessed 14 Apr. 2021).

72   For the economic and employment situation, see "Singapore Sees Worst-Ever Quarterly Fall in Employment in Q2 as Retrenchments Double: MOM Data", *Straits Times*, 1 Sept. 2020.

73   "Virus Deaths May Be Three Times Official Tally in Indonesia", *Bloomberg*, 29 May 2020. For the Indonesia and Singapore case numbers, data from the World Health Organisation is useful: https://covid19.who.int/region/searo/country/id and https://covid19.who.int/region/wpro/country/sg (accessed 22 Apr. 2021).

74   "GE2020: PAP Govt Seizes 'First Window of Opportunity' to Hold Polls amid Concerns of Next Covid-19 Wave, Say Experts", *Today*, 24 June 2020.

75   It will be recalled that the 2001 election had seen the PAP romp home with 75.3% of the vote in an election held soon after the 9/11 terrorist attacks and amid signs of a global economic recession.

76   "Singapore GE: Tan Cheng Bock Urges Govt Not to Hold GE During Covid-19 Pandemic; Suggests Caretaker Govt if Polls Cannot Be Held by April 2021", *Straits Times*, 23 June 2020.

77   "Singapore GE: Tan Cheng Bock Defends Proposal to Delay Election by Having President Form Caretaker Government", *Straits Times*, 23 June 2020.

78   For a detailed examination of the lead-up, campaign, results and implications, see Bilveer Singh, Walid Jumblatt Abdullah and Felix Tan, *Unmasking Singapore's 2020 General Elections: Covid-19 and the Evolving Political Landscape* (Singapore: World Scientific, 2021); and the various contributions in Kevin Y.L. Tan and Terence Lee (eds), *Voting in a Time of Change* (Singapore: Ethos Books, 2021).

79   Dr Tan Wu Meng, "Mr Pritam Singh Supports Alfian Sa'at", statement on PAP website, 19 June 2020, available at https://www.pap.org.sg/news/opinion-news/mr-pritam-singh-supports-alfian-saat/ (accessed 14 Apr. 2021).

80   "Mr Pritam Singh Supports Alfian Sa'at".

81   After an earlier contretemps involving Alfian Sa'at and the establishment in late 2019, Sa'at was defended by influential figures (including those seen by most as above the political fray). Ambassador-at-Large Tommy Koh saw Sa'at (like Pritam Singh later) as a "loving critic" of Singapore. Tommy Koh, Facebook, 8 Oct. 2019, available at https://www.facebook.com/tommy.koh.752/posts/2323712111179729 (accessed 14 Apr. 2021).

82 Dr Tan's statement observed that Sa'at "grew up in Singapore. Singapore gave him his education and he earns a living here. An education and a living that is denied to many minorities in the region." For online criticism of this and other aspects of Dr Tan's article, see "PAP MP Tan Wu Meng Receives Backlash for Criticism of WP Chief Pritam Singh's Comments on 'Citizens Who Are Loving Critics'", *Online Citizen*, 21 June 2020, available at https://www.theonlinecitizen.com/2020/06/21/pap-mp-tan-wu-meng-receives-backlash-for-criticism-of-wp-chief-pritam-singhs-comments-on-citizens-who-are-loving-critics/ (accessed 14 Apr. 2021).

83 Pritam Singh's response to Dr Tan Wu Meng: "Dr Tan's questions, cloaked as innocent ones, were politically motivated to divide Singaporeans into those who are for or against— not Singapore—but the PAP, and to paint the WP in negative light." "Response to TWM Article", Pritam Singh, Facebook, 21 June 2020, available at https://www.facebook.com/pritam.eunos/posts/3226700714018886 (accessed 27 Mar. 2021). See also "PAP MP Tan Wu Meng's Comments on Alfian Sa'at 'Politically Motivated', Says WP Chief Pritam Singh", *Channel NewsAsia*, 22 June 2020.

84 "Tan Wu Meng's Opinion Piece on Pritam Singh Was 'Serious' and 'Thoughtful': Shanmugam", *Channel NewsAsia*, 21 June 2020.

85 "Legitimate to Question WP Chief Pritam Singh's Support for Playwright Alfian Sa'at, Says Shanmugam on Post by MP Tan Wu Meng", *Straits Times*, 21 June 2020.

86 The Global Times Singapore Facebook posts: "South China Morning Post Has a Clear China Agenda", 6 May 2020, available at https://www.facebook.com/GlobalTimesSingapore/photos/a.106460314058414/255257585845352/?type=3&theater; and "The South Morning China Post's Agenda, and Singapore's Motley Crew of Stooges Are Happy to Help", 10 May 2020, available at https://www.facebook.com/GlobalTimesSingapore/posts/258331475537963 (both accessed 31 Mar. 2021). By GTS' account the latter was a contribution from a "concerned Singaporean".

87 When individuals sympathetic to the PAP began to set up their own online presences with the aim of defending the PAP and its policies (and also with the aim of calling out what they saw as anti-Singapore behaviour and rebutting falsehoods against the PAP government), the PAP's reaction was measured. PAP figures in its New Media committee were reported as welcoming the creation of such presences but suggested that an arms-length relationship existed between the Party and the creators of such sites. "Netizens Set Up Page to Defend PAP", *Straits Times*, 16 Sept. 2011.

88 Dr Anne Lee Tzu Pheng, a noted poet, observed, after Alfian Sa'at had (in the earlier, 2019 episode) come in for criticism from Education Minister Ong Ye Kung: "Unfortunately, it seems it is all too common to find that unless one overtly expresses love and praise of country, anything that voices distaste, doubt and dissent tends to be labelled unpatriotic." "Arts Community Supports Alfian Sa'at after Poem Quoted in Parliament", *New Paper*, 9 Oct. 2019. The view taken by Cherian George, one of GTS' main targets, was that sites such as GTS were engaging in toxic and inauthentic behaviour in the way they went after critics of the PAP government, and that this type of behaviour should be regulated (and indeed should have been regulated under the Protection from Online Falsehoods and Manipulation Act [POFMA], which had become law in 2019). Cherian George, "Time

for a Code of Conduct", 10 May 2020, available at https://www.airconditionednation. com/2020/05/10/online-politics/?fbclid=IwAR0hE3u2ShzDUClcGeoje73duAx7vIUoB8iYe 9a5QhXqXgsTiLmRkfy98Lc (accessed 2 Apr. 2021). See also his "GE2020: Why Singapore May Lose, Whatever the Final Score", *Academia.sg*, 7 July 2020, available at https://www. academia.sg/academic-views/ge2020-why-singapore-may-lose/ (accessed 2 Apr. 2021), reprinted in Cherian George and Donald Low, *PAP v. PAP: The Party's Struggle to Adapt to a Changing Singapore* (Singapore: Self-published, 2020), pp. 16–21.

89   PAP 2020 general election manifesto, *Our Lives, Our Jobs, Our Future*, available at https:// www.pap.org.sg/manifesto/ (accessed 27 Mar. 2021).

90   Another female PAP candidate, Poh Li San, had been an air force helicopter pilot, reaching the rank of major, as well as an aide-de-camp to the president.

91   For a brief factual account of the Ivan Lim saga, see Bertha Henson, *GE2020: Fair or Foul?* (Singapore: Epigram Books, 2020), pp. 39–42.

92   Some of the main criticisms are available at "GE 2020: How the Ivan Lim Scandal Sparked a 'Trial by Internet'", *Vulcan Post*, June 2020, available at https://vulcanpost.com/703144/ge-2020-ivan-lim-scandal-trial-by-internet/ (accessed 14 Apr. 2021).

93   "Singapore GE 2020: PAP New Face Ivan Lim Withdraws from Election Following Allegations about His Past Behaviour", *Straits Times*, 28 June 2020.

94   "GE2020: PAP, WP Candidates for East Coast GRC Address Supporters on Nomination Day", *Channel NewsAsia* YouTube Channel, 30 June 2020, available at https://www.youtube. com/watch?v=-pg_v1KzTXQ&t=179s (at 2:04–2:32) (accessed 27 Apr. 2021). For (critical) online commentary, see "Heng Swee Keat's Speech Fumble Makes Him the Subject of Internet Memes", *Independent*, 2 July 2020, available at https://theindependent.sg/ heng-swee-keats-speech-fumble-makes-him-the-subject-of-internet-memes/ (accessed 14 Apr. 2021).

95   "Netizen Defends DPM Heng over 'East Coast Plan', Asks S'poreans For Compassion", *MustShareNews*, 4 July 2020, available at https://mustsharenews.com/dpm-heng-east-coast-plan/ (accessed 14 Apr. 2021). The WP had been working the ground in East Coast GRC for a number of years; in the end, the PAP team anchored by Heng came in at 53.4% (the result in 2015, also against a WP team, was 60.7%).

96   "Singapore GE2020: New Constituency Political Broadcasts to Air from July 3 to 7", *Straits Times*, 25 June 2020.

97   For discussion, see "Commentary: How the Workers' Party Won Big This General Election", *Channel NewsAsia*, 14 July 2020. There was recognition of the pressing need for the PAP to up its online engagement and communicate better in the virtual world by senior PAP figures after the election; this was feedback that surfaced as part of its post-mortem. "PAP Leaders Call on Activists to Find New Ways to Win Hearts and Minds, while 'Vigorously' Defending Party's Beliefs", *Today*, 8 Nov. 2020. National Development Minister Lawrence Wong observed just days after the election that the PAP despite producing a great deal of online content in its campaigning did not fare well when it came to connecting with voters over platforms such as Instagram or Telegram. "GE2020: Middle-Aged Voters, Not Youths, Accounted for National Vote Swing against PAP, Says Lawrence Wong", *Today*, 18 July 2020.

98   "Singapore Votes 2020: The Political Debate", *Channel NewsAsia* YouTube Channel, 1 July 2020, available at https://www.youtube.com/watch?v=8uOdz-Weivo (accessed 2 Apr. 2021).

99   "Singapore GE2020: WP Has Done the Math on Its Proposals, Says Jamus Lim in Live TV Debate", *Straits Times*, 2 July 2020.

100 Comparisons that, going by some of the online reaction, critics of the PAP felt were condescending, and which to them epitomised Balakrishnan's underlying attitude to Jamus Lim. See "Jamus Lim Warms the Cockles of Viewers' Hearts for his GE2020 Debate Performance", *Mothership*, 1 July 2020, available at https://mothership.sg/2020/07/jamus-lim-warms-the-cockles-of-viewers-hearts-for-his-ge2020-debate-performance/ (accessed 2 Apr. 2021).

101 "Singapore GE2020: WP Wants to Deny PAP a Blank Cheque, Says Jamus Lim", *Straits Times*, 2 July 2020.

102 "Members' Forum 2019: Secretary-General's Speech—One WP", speech by WP Secretary-General Pritam Singh, 19 Jan. 2020, available at https://www.wp.sg/members-forum-2019-secretary-generals-speech-one-wp/ (accessed 22 Apr. 2021).

103 "Singapore GE2020: PAP Can Carry Out Its Agenda Even if It Loses Supermajority, Says WP Chief Pritam Singh", *Straits Times*, 3 July 2020. The "no blank cheque" analogy was singled out by senior PAP figures soon after the election as one key reason for the WP's strong election showing. "GE2020: Middle-Aged Voters, Not Youths, Accounted for National Vote Swing against PAP, Says Lawrence Wong".

104 "Singapore Budget 2020: GST Hike Will Not Take Place in 2021; $6b Assurance Package to Cushion Impact of Hike", *Straits Times*, 18 Feb. 2020.

105 The WP proposed that GST be held to 7%, with the additional fiscal needs of government to be met through other sources of revenue. *Make Your Vote Count, The Workers' Party Manifesto 2020*, p. 23, available at https://d3bnzwrhehvhbjiwmja.s3-ap-southeast-1.amazonaws.com/The+Workers+Party+Manifesto+2020.pdf (accessed 22 Apr. 2021). See also "GST: To Raise, Suspend or Exempt?", *Straits Times*, 5 July 2020.

106 "Singapore GE2020: How Workers' Party Won over Sengkang", *Straits Times*, 12 July 2020. Sengkang GRC incorporated what had previously been Sengkang West and Punggol East SMCs, as well as parts of Pasir Ris-Punggol GRC. Some of these areas had seen the WP maintain a presence for some time. Punggol East SMC had been held by the WP's Lee Li Lian from 2013 to 2015. See "Singapore GE: New Sengkang GRC to Be Formed; Includes Single-Seat Wards of Punggol East and Sengkang West", *Straits Times*, 13 Mar. 2020.

107 Over 65% of residents in the GRC were aged below 45. "GE2020: Sengkang Residents Give Reasons They Plumped for WP, Including a Better Connection with Its Candidates", *Today*, 12 July 2020.

108 The PAP's Sengkang team had an average age of 49 (author's calculations).

109 For discussion and analysis, see "WP's Sengkang GRC Team Are Young Parents, Pushing for Easier Childcare Access, More Coffee Shops", *Mothership*, 4 July 2020, available at https://mothership.sg/2020/07/wp-sengkang-team/ (accessed 14 Apr. 2021); "PAP Lost the Youth Vote in Sengkang GRC", *Mothership*, 12 July 2020, available at https://

mothership.sg/2020/07/pap-lost-sengkang-grc-why/ (accessed 14 Apr. 2021); and
"GE2020: Sengkang Residents Give Reasons They Plumped for WP".

110 For a short primer on POFMA, see "Explainer: How Online News Sites Can Be Compelled
to Correct, Take Down Fake News", *Today*, 2 Apr. 2019. A longer treatment of Singapore's
approach to combating fake news and disinformation can be found in Shashi Jayakumar,
Benjamin Ang and Nur Diyanah Anwar, "Fake News and Disinformation: Singapore
Perspectives", in *Disinformation and Fake News*, ed. Shashi Jayakumar, Benjamin Ang and
Nur Diyanah Anwar (Singapore: Palgrave Macmillan, 2020), pp. 137–58.

111 For the government's point of view, and for its overall rationale for legislating on the issue,
see "Second Reading Speech by Minister for Law, K Shanmugam on the Protection from
Online Falsehoods and Manipulation Bill", 7 May 2019, available at https://www.mlaw.gov.
sg/news/parliamentary-speeches/second-reading-speech-by-minister-for-law-k-shanmugam-
on-the-protection-from-online-falsehoods-and-manipulation-bill (accessed 31 Mar. 2021).

112 "In Focus: Has POFMA Been Effective? A Look at the Fake News Law, 1 Year since It
Kicked In", *Channel NewsAsia*, 3 Oct. 2020; "Pofma Invoked against Website that Claimed
Cover-up on Coronavirus Case Numbers", *Straits Times*, 19 Apr. 2020.

113 For Bowyer's statements and the Correction Direction issued, see "POFMA Office Directs
Brad Bowyer to Correct Facebook Post in First Use of 'Fake News' Law", *Channel NewsAsia*,
26 Nov. 2019. For other uses of POFMA that related to comments or statements made by
Opposition politicians, see, for example, "Pofma Correction Directions Issued to Peoples
Voice Party's Facebook Page and Lim Tean's YouTube Channel", *Straits Times*, 2 July 2020;
and "Singapore GE2020: Correction Notices to News Portals an Inappropriate Use of
Pofma, Says SDP's Paul Tambyah", *Straits Times*, 7 July 2020.

114 "News Analysis: Fake-News Laws—What Do the First Two Cases Tell Us?", *Today*, 5 Dec.
2019. For a general summary of POFMA uses from October 2019 to early 2020, see
Khairulanwar Zaini, "Singapore in 2019: In Holding Pattern", pp. 304–5. A discussion of
POFMA's use during the election period can be found in Henson, *GE2020: Fair or Foul?*,
pp. 135–41.

115 There were also calls for the government to release more data in order for constructive
suggestions (on matters of policy, for example) to be put forward. "Set Stage for More
Constructive National Dialogue", letter to *Straits Times* Forum from Ang Ah Lay, *Straits
Times*, 1 Sept. 2020.

116 See "In Focus: Has POFMA Been Effective?". The suggestion of an ombudsman
or independent body had been raised in March 2018 at the public hearings of the
Parliamentary Select Committee examining the issue of disinformation and online
falsehoods. *Report of the Select Committee on Deliberate Online Falsehoods—Causes,
Consequences and Countermeasures. Parl 15 of 2018. Presented to Parliament on 19 September
2018*, pp. 87–8, 105, available at https://sprs.parl.gov.sg/selectcommittee/selectcommittee/
download?id=1&type=subReport (accessed 31 Mar. 2021).

117 "Singapore GE2020: 10 Million Population Claim by SDP", *Straits Times*, 5 July 2020.
The 10 million figure was raised as a possibility not by Heng but by former HDB Chief
Executive Liu Thai Ker, who suggested in 2015 that when it came to planning parameters
for the very long term (the year 2100), 10 million should not be ruled out if Singapore was
to remain a viable city.

118 "PAP Press Statement on SDP's False Population Claims", People's Action Party, 2 July 2020, available at https://www.pap.org.sg/news/ge2020-news/pap-press-statement-on-sdps-false-population-claims/ (accessed 14 Apr. 2021). See also "PAP Press Statement on Comments Made Regarding the 10 Million Population Falsehood", 3 July 2020, available at https://www.pap.org.sg/news/ge2020-news/pap-press-statement-on-comments-made-regarding-the-10-million-population-falsehood/ (accessed 14 Apr. 2021); and "Singapore GE2020: PAP Calls Out SDP's Chee Soon Juan for Misleading Singaporeans over 10m Population Figure", *Straits Times*, 3 July 2020.

119 Heng Swee Keat, Facebook, 2 July 2020, available at https://www.facebook.com/hengsweekeat/posts/3133213056717198 (accessed 1 Apr. 2021).

120 For the SDP's defence, see also "GE2020: PAP Should Raise Concerns on 10 Million Population Figure with the Straits Times, Says SDP", *Today*, 3 July 2020. See also Henson, *GE2020: Fair or Foul?*, p. 136.

121 "Pofma Correction Directions Issued to 4 Facebook Pages, 1 Website", *Straits Times*, 5 July 2020. The SDP, while complying with the Correction Direction on its Facebook page, deftly appended a note below disputing the validity of the government's reasoning. "Alternate Authority for the Minister for National Development Instructs POFMA Office to Issue Correction Directions and Targeted Correction Direction", POFMA Office media release, available at https://www.pofmaoffice.gov.sg/documents/media-releases/2020/July/pofma-pr-mnd-04jul2020-01.pdf (accessed 1 Apr. 2021); "10 Million Population", Singapore Democratic Party press release, 3 July 2020, available at https://www.facebook.com/yoursdp/posts/10159188889418455 (accessed 1 Apr. 2021).

122 As informed observers pointed out, many of these fears were overblown given that the rights given to foreign nationals when it came to seeking employment in Singapore were not unfettered. See "Singapore GE2020: The Long View on Ceca and Other Free Trade Agreements", *Straits Times*, 19 July 2020.

123 For examples, see "Singapore GE2020: Police Reports Made against DPM Heng for Remarks on Non-Chinese PM; AGC Says No Offence Committed", *Straits Times*, 8 July 2020; and "Police Report Made after Online Commenter Allegedly Threatens Person Who Called Out PAP Candidate Ivan Lim", *Mothership*, 28 June 2020, available at https://mothership.sg/2020/06/bryant-wong-police-report/ (accessed 14 Apr. 2021).

124 "Singapore GE 2020: IMDA Issues Notice to Facebook to Remove New Naratif's Unauthorized Paid Online Election Ad", *Straits Times*, 3 July 2020.

125 "Facebook Removes Fabrications about the PAP Admin Accounts for Violating Policies", *Channel NewsAsia*, 28 June 2020; "Facebook Removes Critical Spectator Admin Accounts for Violating Policies", *Channel NewsAsia*, 8 July 2020; "Facebook Takes Down Critical Spectator Page for Violating Its Policies", *Straits Times*, 9 July 2020.

126 "City Harvest Case: Apex Court Dismisses Bid for Longer Sentences for Kong Hee, Former Church Leaders", *Straits Times*, 2 Feb. 2018; "City Harvest Case: 5 Highlights from the Court of Appeal's Judgment", *Straits Times*, 1 Feb. 2018.

127 For the posts, see "Police Investigating WP Candidate Raeesah Khan for Social Media Posts Which Allegedly Promote Enmity between Different Groups", *Today*, 5 July 2020.

128 "Police Statement on Reports Lodged against a Candidate Contesting in the General Election 2020", Singapore Police Force, 5 July 2020, available at https://www.police.gov.sg/media-room/news/20200705_police_statement_cid (accessed 14 Apr. 2021).

129 "The Workers' Party's Position on Sengkang Candidate Ms Raeesah Khan", People's Action Party, 6 July 2020, available at https://www.pap.org.sg/news/the-workers-partys-position-on-sengkang-candidate-ms-raeesah-khan/ (accessed 14 Apr. 2021); "Singapore GE2020: WP Should State Stand on Raeesah Khan's Posts, Says PAP", *Straits Times*, 7 July 2020.

130 See "WP's Raeesah Khan Apologises for Insensitive Remarks", *Straits Times* YouTube Channel, 6 July 2020, available at https://www.youtube.com/watch?v=WBm-wD0IsTg (accessed 14 Apr. 2021). See also "Singapore GE2020: WP Candidate Raeesah Khan Apologises for 'Insensitive' Remarks in Posts", *Straits Times*, 6 July 2020. Pritam Singh (who during the doorstop interview invited questions from reporters by name) carefully steered away from any discussion of a possible smear campaign (when seemingly invited by one or two questions by reporters to go down that path) against the WP or its Sengkang team.

131 Khan was in the end given a stern warning by the police in September. "Workers' Party MP Raeesah Khan Given Stern Warning over Posts", *Straits Times*, 18 Sept. 2020.

132 *Unmasking Singapore's 2020 General Elections*, pp. 150–1.

133 "Singapore GE2020: Police Reports Made against DPM Heng for Remarks on Non-Chinese PM; AGC Says No Offence Committed", *Straits Times*, 8 July 2020. The police on consulting the Attorney-General's Chambers clarified that "Mr Heng's remarks, in the context they were made, do not evidence any intent to wound anyone's racial feelings or promote enmity between different races". Singapore Police Force statement, 7 July 2020, available at https://www.police.gov.sg/media-room/news/20200707_police_statement_others (accessed 14 Apr. 2021).

134 See the treatment of this episode in chapter 5.

135 "Singapore GE2020: Shanmugam Gives Take on Race Relations, PAP Loss in Sengkang", *Straits Times*, 12 July 2020. Shanmugam observed, "I think the older generation of Singaporeans takes one approach to how issues of race and religion are discussed, and they have a framework within the law. But it's also clear that the younger generation takes a different approach. . . . And I think we need to find a way in which those aspirations and viewpoints can be dealt with, because the younger generation of Singaporeans are going to be in charge of Singapore, and their views on how these things ought to be discussed need to get a substantial degree of attention too."

136 "GE2020: Sengkang Residents Give Reasons They Plumped for WP".

137 "PM Lee Hsien Loong on GE2020 Results: 'We Have a Clear Mandate'", *Channel NewsAsia* YouTube Channel, 11 July 2020, available at https://www.youtube.com/watch?v=BlhusR7McMg (at 2:51–3:05 and 13:19–13:56) (accessed 11 Apr. 2021).

138 Even where it was unsuccessful, in East Coast and Marine Parade GRCs for example, the WP succeeded in clawing back a substantial amount of ground that had been lost in 2015. In East Coast, the WP's 46.61% was an improvement of 7.34%, while its Marine Parade result (42.26%) was an improvement of 6.33%. Interesting snippets of the WP's approach to campaigning on the ground in Marine Parade can be found in Yee

Jenn Jong, *Journey in Blue: A Peek into the Workers' Party of Singapore* (Singapore: World Scientific, 2021).

139 PM Lee opened his remarks by addressing and apologising for an expected (and unwelcome) issue that arose on Polling Day itself—long queues at many polling stations (mainly caused by extra precautions necessitated by COVID-19) that forced the Elections Department to extend voting hours by two hours until 10pm. This move was lambasted by some Opposition politicians, including Dr Tan Cheng Bock, who called it a "highly irregular" move that "compromised the integrity of the process". It is difficult to tell how much the extension of voting hours affected the parties' vote shares, but if nothing else the issue contributed in some minds to the impression that the normally well-oiled machinery of the PAP government was not working as well as it should. "Singapore GE2020: Voting Hours Extended to 10pm, Opposition Parties Criticise Move", *Straits Times*, 10 July 2020.

140 Besides a salary and staff support, privileges included a seat directly opposite PM Lee in Parliament, and more speaking time in debates on par with office-holders. "Leader of the Opposition—a Double-Edged Sword", *Straits Times*, 20 July 2020; "Parliament Sets out Duties and Privileges of Leader of the Opposition Pritam Singh", *Straits Times*, 29 July 2020. SDP chief Chiam See Tong was given the unofficial title of leader of the Opposition in 1992, following the gains the SDP had made in the 1991 election. "Chiam Named Unofficial Leader of the Opposition", *Straits Times*, 7 Jan. 1992. Although the WP was after the 2011 election in a stronger position than the SDP had been 20 years before, WP chief Low Thia Khiang indicated that he would not accept a similar designation (no offer was made by the PAP in 2011, although it appears by then that the leader of the largest opposition party in Parliament was automatically recognised, informally, as unofficial leader of the Opposition); "Low Won't Be Unofficial Leader of Opposition", *Straits Times*, 8 Sept. 2011.

141 "GE2020: WP Will Also Be 'Soul Searching' as PAP 'Tries Its Hardest' to Take Back Lost Wards—Pritam Singh", *Yahoo! News*, 12 July 2020, available at https://sg.yahoo.com/news/ge-2020-wp-will-also-be-soul-searching-as-pap-tries-its-hardest-to-take-back-lost-wards-pritam-singh-144029323.html (accessed 14 Apr. 2021).

142 "WP's Pritam Singh Speaking in Mandarin", *Straits Times* YouTube Channel, 3 Sept. 2015, available at https://www.youtube.com/watch?v=AV2oe6zbnYQ (accessed 14 Apr. 2021). Like Low, Singh had had his struggles in the Singapore education system (his difficulties had occurred at an earlier stage compared to Low) but had made good. See "From Quiet, Shy Boy to Leader of the Opposition: Pritam Singh's School Teacher Reflects on His Growth", *Mothership*, 13 July 2020, available at https://mothership.sg/2020/07/pritam-singh-teacher/ (accessed 14 Apr. 2021).

143 Secretary-General Lee Hsien Loong: 36th Ordinary Party Conference Speech, 8 Nov. 2020, available at https://www.pap.org.sg/news/secretary-general-lee-hsien-loong-36th-ordinary-party-conference-speech/ (accessed 23 Apr. 2021).

144 Desmond Lee, interview with the author, 3 Feb. 2021.

145 Several MPs, ministers and activists interviewed by the author made this observation.

146 "GE2020: Middle-Aged Voters, Not Youths, Accounted for National Vote Swing against PAP, Says Lawrence Wong".

147   Credible post-election surveys seemed to confirm some of this. A survey carried out by
       the Institute of Policy Studies (IPS) suggested that the PAP suffered the sharpest drop
       (13 percentage points) in credibility (from the 2015 election) among voters aged 40–49.
       The survey suggested that the issues that had spiked in importance from 2015 were
       jobs, cost of living, and the need for diverse views in Parliament. *POPS (10)—IPS Post-
       Election Survey 2020*, survey by the Institute of Policy Studies, https://lkyspp.nus.edu.
       sg/docs/default-source/ips/pops10_ge2020-survey_061020.pdf (accessed 27 Apr. 2021).
       See also "IPS Post-GE2020 Survey: PAP Still Seen as Most Credible Party but Has Lost
       Ground from 2015", *Straits Times*, 1 Oct. 2020; "IPS Post-GE2020 Survey: Jobs, Political
       Diversity Important to S'pore Voters; Decline in PAP's Perceived Credibility Seen in All
       Age Groups", *Straits Times*, 1 Oct. 2020.
148   See "Coronavirus: Call for Improvements to Help Schemes", *Straits Times*, 19 Apr. 2020.
149   Desmond Lee, interview with the author, 3 Feb. 2021. Desmond Lee was at the time of
       the interview minister for national development.
150   Desmond Lee, interview with the author, 3 Feb. 2021.
151   Ibid.
152   Approximately nine out of ten voters surveyed by IPS said that the government's handling
       of the pandemic was either "important" or "very important", with the issue being one
       of the top three in voters' minds. "IPS Post-GE2020 Survey: Jobs, Political Diversity
       Important to S'pore Voters".
153   Author post-election interviews with ministers, MPs and PAP activists. See also "GE2020:
       Middle-Aged Voters, Not Youths, Accounted for National Vote Swing against PAP, Says
       Lawrence Wong".
154   An example is Punggol West SMC, where the PAP's Sun Xueling, 41, triumphed over
       the WP's Tan Chen Chen, 38, with close to 61% of the vote. Sun's creative approach to
       digital outreach had seen some of her walkabouts on the ground livestreamed; but as Party
       activists lamented after the election when interviewed by the media, other candidates
       elsewhere eschewed such methods. "The Big Read: What Went Wrong for the People's
       Action Party, in the Eyes of Party Insiders", *Today*, 18 July 2020.
155   "'We Have a Clear Mandate'" (at 13:30–14:50).
156   The dominance also entails association in the minds of younger voters with incidents
       and policies of the past, and, in particular, tough actions taken in terms of law and order.
       Many of the events and policies are from decades past, but younger voters remember
       these, from the Party's point of view, sometimes without the necessary context (that hard
       decisions had to be made in order to ensure Singapore's survival and then continued
       progress). Viewing past actions and policies without the context and using this lens
       to inform present perceptions is, in the view of one PAP minister, "historical baggage
       continuously being repackaged". Desmond Lee, interview with the author, 3 Feb. 2021.
157   In an interview for this book held after the 2011 general election, Lee Kuan Yew, speaking
       of the earlier generation, observed, "we transformed their lives from squatters to high
       rise—then we improved their standards of living . . . we stayed in power because they
       trusted us and had confidence in us". Lee Kuan Yew, interview with the author, 28 Dec.
       2011.
158   Ibid.

159 "Singapore GE2020: A Pledge to See Nation through Covid-19 Crisis, Hand Over Singapore Intact", *Straits Times*, 7 July 2020. In the rally, held online on account of the pandemic and restrictions imposed by the Elections Department, PM Lee said that he would see Singapore through the crisis together with senior colleagues (Senior Ministers Teo Chee Hean and Tharman Shanmugaratnam) and 4G leaders.

160 Secretary-General Lee Hsien Loong: 36th Ordinary Party Conference Speech, 8 Nov. 2020.

161 In a book published in November, former DPM and SM Prof. S. Jayakumar had observed that given the pandemic, it was not an appropriate time to talk of succession: "In my view, however capable the 4G leaders, we should not change horses in midstream"; S. Jayakumar, *Governing: A Singapore Perspective* (Singapore: Straits Times Press, 2020), p. 140. These remarks were widely commented on and carried by the media: "PM's Succession Timeline May Hinge on Covid-19 Situation: Jayakumar", *Straits Times*, 7 Nov. 2020. Observers were quick to point out, too, that ESM Goh Chok Tong (who retired before the 2020 election), in appearing to also suggest that PM Lee should stay on until the crisis had passed, used the same analogy—not changing horses in midstream—a few days later in a Facebook post. Goh Chok Tong, post on MParader Facebook page, 9 Nov. 2020, available at https://www.facebook.com/MParader/posts/4925993167443310 (accessed 27 Apr. 2021).

162 "Letter Exchange between PM Lee Hsien Loong and DPM Heng Swee Keat", 8 Apr. 2021, available at https://www.pmo.gov.sg/Newsroom/Letter-exchange-between-PM-Lee-Hsien-Loong-and-DPM-Heng-Swee-Keat (accessed 27 Apr. 2021).

163 Transcript of remarks by PM Lee Hsien Loong at the Press Conference on Leadership Transition, Istana, 8 Apr. 2021, available at https://www.pmo.gov.sg/Newsroom/Transcript-remarks-Lee-Hsien-Loong-Press-Conference-8-April (accessed 1 May 2021).

164 Heng's insistence that there was no link could not, of course, quell media speculation which suggested that notwithstanding his technocratic excellence, he had been found wanting in other respects. See "Singapore Faces Biggest-Ever Succession Planning Challenge", *Bloomberg*, 12 Apr. 2021, https://www.bloomberg.com/news/articles/2021-04-11/inside-singapore-s-unusually-shaky-leadership-transition (accessed 28 Apr. 2021).

165 "Statement from the 4G Team on DPM Heng Swee Keat's Decision to Stand Aside as Leader of the 4G Team on 8 April 2021", available at https://www.pmo.gov.sg/Newsroom/Statement-4G-Team-8-Apr (accessed 30 Apr. 2021).

166 "Ex-Minister Yaacob Ibrahim: Next 4G Leader Should Be Chosen 'Yesterday', but They'll Likely Need More Time", *Mothership*, 1 May 2021, available at https://mothership.sg/2021/05/yaacob-ibrahim-on-4g-new-leader/ (accessed 2 May 2021).

167 "PAP Leaders Meet Ex-MPs, Party Activists", *Straits Times*, 10 Apr. 2021.

168 "8 in 10 Polled Feel PAP Should Pick Its 4G Leader in Next 2 Years", *Straits Times*, 10 Apr. 2021.

169 "PM Lee Announces Cabinet Reshuffle: Lawrence Wong to Be Finance Minister, Ong Ye Kung to Take Over Health and Chan Chun Sing to Helm Education", *Straits Times*, 24 Apr. 2021.

170 "PM Lee: No New DPM to Be Appointed during Cabinet Reshuffle".

171 "Parliament: PM Lee, Pritam Singh Cross Swords over 'Free Rider' Election Tactics", *Straits Times*, 2 Sept. 2020.

172 Lim Hng Kiang, interview with the author, 30 Mar. 2021. Lim held several ministerial portfolios from 1995 to 2018. He stepped down as MP in 2020, not contesting the election that year.

173 Lee Kuan Yew, interview with the author, 28 Dec. 2011.

174 As Lee Kuan Yew observed in 1979: "The Party must likewise renew itself at every level, from branch members to branch committees, from cadres to the Central Executive. To keep the organisation vigorous, the Party has to recruit young men and women with idealism and enthusiasm. They must be activists, keen to work for the good of their fellow citizens, not for selfish or personal gain, but for the satisfaction of ensuring a better life for all. Unless enough capable and active young Singaporeans realise that some people have to come forward to attend to the needs and interests of society, to take on this responsibility, whatever has been achieved may well be lost by neglect." *People's Action Party 1954–1979. Petir 25th Anniversary Issue*, p. 43.

175 Author interviews with multiple PAP MPs after the 2020 general election.

176 Author interviews with multiple former PAP office-holders, 2020–21.

177 Teo Chee Hean, interview with the author, 12 July 2013.

178 PM Lee Hsien Loong, interview with the author, 19 Dec. 2014.

179 Lee Kuan Yew, "The Crucial Factor", unpublished draft chapter from planned continuation of memoirs (2008), made available to the author (National Archives of Singapore).

180 Han Fook Kwang et al. (eds), *Lee Kuan Yew: Hard Truths to Keep Singapore Going* (Singapore: Straits Times Press, 2011), p. 68.

181 Tharman Shanmugaratnam, interview with the author, 18 Dec. 2015.

182 The view of ministers just before the 2011 election was: "If voters elect more opposition MPs, so be it. But we do not believe that helping to build an opposition, to buy insurance in case the PAP fails, will work. Instead it will lead to more party politicking and distraction from long-term issues." Han et al., *Lee Kuan Yew: Hard Truths to Keep Singapore Going*, p. 62.

183 Chan Chun Sing, interview with the author, 12 July 2016.

184 Author interviews with multiple activists, MPs and ministers after the 2020 general election. For a sense of the Party girding itself for the struggle, see "PAP Leaders Call on Activists to Find New Ways to Win Hearts and Minds".

185 For the statement by Pritam Singh, made during the course of a—at times heated—clash with PM Lee in Parliament, see "Parliament: PM Lee, Pritam Singh Cross Swords". Former DPM and SM Prof. S. Jayakumar wrote to a serving Cabinet minister after the election, "At the next GE—their [the WP's] aim will be to prevent PAP having a two-thirds majority. Further down the road, we should not rule out them (in concert with other opposition parties) trying to prevent PAP winning a majority of seats. They will do so if they have enough winnable candidates. As I see it, the camel has gotten its nose into the PAP tent. It will want to occupy the whole tent in 2, 3 or 4 elections down the road." S. Jayakumar, *Governing: A Singapore Perspective*, p. 182.

186 In a sign that seemed to suggest that the PSP took renewal and succession seriously, Dr Tan Cheng Bock, 80, unexpectedly stepped down as secretary-general of the PSP in March 2021,

taking up the post of party chairman, which will see him, it appears, assume the role of mentor and elder statesman within the PSP. His replacement as secretary-general was Francis Yuen, 71, the PSP's assistant secretary-general. "Not Stepping Aside but 'Changing Gear', Says PSP Founder Tan Cheng Bock", *Straits Times*, 3 Apr. 2021.

187   Desmond Lee, interview with the author, 3 Feb. 2021.

188   See "The Big Read: What Went Wrong for the People's Action Party, in the Eyes of Party Insiders", *Today*, 18 July 2020.

189   Ibid.

190   For an allusion to this by a member of the 4G leadership, see "GE2020: Middle-Aged Voters, Not Youths, Accounted for National Vote Swing against PAP, Says Lawrence Wong".

191   Summaries of this argument (and variations of it) may be found in in Kenneth Paul Tan, "Singapore's GE2020: The Real Watershed Election?", 11 Sept. 2020, available at https://www.youtube.com/watch?v=M43KVVjzPlU (accessed 30 Apr. 2021); and "PAP v PAP: "The PAP Can Do Better on the Policy Side if It Gets Its Politics Right", *Online Citizen*, 12 Nov. 2020, available at https://www.theonlinecitizen.com/2020/11/12/pap-v-pap-the-pap-can-do-better-on-the-policy-side-if-it-gets-its-politics-right/ (accessed 30 Apr. 2021). See also the various essays in George and Low, *PAP v. PAP*.

192   Heng Swee Keat, interview with the author, 6 Apr. 2017.

193   See, for example, the speech by Minister for Education Lawrence Wong at the IPS Singapore Perspectives Conference 2021, 25 Jan. 2021, available at https://www.moe.gov.sg/news/speeches/20210125-speech-by-mr-lawrence-wong-minister-for-education-at-the-ips-singapore-perspectives-conference-2021 (accessed 2 May 2021).

194   "Lawrence Wong Outlines 'Resetting' for a Fairer, Greener, More United Singapore", *Straits Times*, 25 Jan. 2021.

195   "Singapore GE2020: Young Voters and Women Power", op-ed by Prof. Tommy Koh, *Straits Times*, 17 July 2020.

196   "Lawrence Wong Outlines 'Resetting' for a Fairer, Greener, More United Singapore". For observations on the national consensus, see also First Assistant Secretary-General Heng Swee Keat's speech at 36th Ordinary Party Conference, 8 Nov. 2020, available at https://www.pap.org.sg/news/1st-assistant-secretary-general-heng-swee-keats-speech-at-36th-ordinary-party-conference/ (accessed 2 May 2021).

197   First Assistant Secretary-General Heng Swee Keat's speech at 36th Ordinary Party Conference, 8 Nov. 2020. See also "PAP Leaders Call on Activists to Find New Ways to Win Hearts and Minds".

198   Author interview with 4G minister, Feb. 2021.

199   Ibid. The "strategic reserve" theme and variations of it are echoed in other author interviews with 4G ministers.

200   Lee Kuan Yew, interview with the author, 28 Dec. 2011.

201   Lee Kuan Yew, "What of the Past Is Relevant to the Future"? *People's Action Party 1954–1979. Petir 25th Anniversary Issue*, p. 38. Lee was referring in 1979 to the PAP's second-generation leaders, but his words could be taken to have a wider applicability given how often he was to return to this theme.

APPENDIX ONE: PAP CANDIDATES INTRODUCED AT GENERAL ELECTIONS, 1984–2015

Table 1.2 1984 General Election – PAP Candidates Information

Note: For the columns "Party / Community / Volunteer / Board Experience" and "Career", positions held at the time of being fielded are given at the top. For both columns, previous experience (or positions no longer held) is given in italics. Comprehensiveness has not been the object: I attempted instead to provide a representative selection of past experience.

Where discrepancies exist between Party records and information given in press reports, the former is used. Where possible, I have verified details directly with the MPs and former MPs.

Individuals from minority races contesting in a GRC require a community certificate from either the Malay Community Committee or the Indian and Other Minorities Communities Committee. "Race" for these individuals is given (as the case may be) as "Malay", "Indian", "Other (Eurasian)", or "Other (Sikh)".

Name	Age and Ethnicity	Constituency	Educational and Professional Qualifications	Party / Community / Volunteer / Board Experience	Career
Abdullah B. Tarmugi	Age: 39 Javanese	Siglap	Raffles Institution; University of Singapore (Bachelor of Social Sciences (Sociology) (Honours)); Commonwealth Scholarship – University of London (Post-graduate Diploma in Urban Studies (Merit))	Member, Mendaki; Member, Central Council of Malay Cultural Organisations; Member, Advisory Council on Community Relations in Defence (ACCORD); Volunteer Counsellor, Singapore Anti-Narcotics Association	Associate News Editor, *Straits Times*; *Senior Statistician and Planning Analyst, Research-Statistics Unit, Ministry of National Development*
Aline K. Wong	Age: 43 Chinese	Changkat	St Paul's Co-educational College (Hong Kong); University of Hong Kong (Bachelor of Arts (Honours)); University of California (Master of Arts; PhD in Sociology)		Associate Professor, Department of Sociology, National University of Singapore; *Head of Research (Research and Planning Department);* *Housing and Development Board (on secondment from the National University of Singapore);* *Lecturer, Chinese University of Hong Kong*

Table I.2 1984 General Election – PAP Candidates Information (cont'd)

Name	Age and Ethnicity	Constituency	Educational and Professional Qualifications	Party / Community / Volunteer / Board Experience	Career
Arthur Beng Kian Lam	Age: 35 Chinese	Fengshan	Anglo-Chinese School; University of Singapore (Bachelor of Medicine, Bachelor of Surgery, Distinction in Social Medicine and Public Health)	Vice-Chairman, PAP Anson Branch; Chairman, Ayer Rajah Community Services Project Committee	General Practitioner in private practice; *Medical Officer, Ministry of Health*
Chew Heng Ching	Age: 33 Chinese	Kaki Bukit	Tanglin Technical School; Raffles Institution; Colombo Plan Scholarship – University of Newcastle, Australia (Bachelor of Engineering (Industrial Engineering) (Honours); Bachelor of Arts (Economics))	Volunteer community work in Chong Boon constituency	Group Planning and Development Manager, Boustead Group; *Assistant Vice-President (Corporate Planning), Development Bank of Singapore;* *Public-sector experience in the Ministries of Finance and Trade and Industry*
Chng Hee Kok	Age: 35 Chinese	Radin Mas	Anglo-Chinese Secondary School; University of Singapore (Bachelor of Engineering (Honours)); National University of Singapore (Master of Business Administration) Program for Executive Development at IMD – Lausanne Switzerland	Involved in various community activities since 1982, including Meet-the-People Sessions at the PAP Leng Kee Branch	Managing Director, Dainovo Business Development Pte Ltd; *Previously employed in a Swiss trading firm and the Ministry of Defence*

(cont'd overleaf)

Table 1.2 1984 General Election – PAP Candidates Information (cont'd)

Name	Age and Ethnicity	Constituency	Educational and Professional Qualifications	Party / Community / Volunteer / Board Experience	Career
Dixie Tan-Lee Mo Chun	Age: 48 Chinese	Ulu Pandan	Victoria Institution (Malaysia); University of Singapore (Bachelor of Medicine, Bachelor of Surgery); National University of Singapore (Master of Medicine (Internal Medicine); Academy of Medicine, Singapore (Fellow); Royal Australasian College of Physicians (Fellow)	Founder-President, Association for Educationally Sub-normal Children; Founder-President, The Quota Club of Singapore	Medical Practitioner in private practice
Goh Choon Kang	Age: 35 Chinese	Braddell Heights	Tuan Mong High School; Nanyang University (Bachelor of Arts (Honours))	President, Singapore National Union of Journalists; Director, Confederation of ASEAN Journalists; Part-time Tutor, Department of Government and Public Administration, Nanyang University	Editorial and Specialist Writer, *Lianhe Zaobao;* *Extensive journalistic experience (Shin Min Daily News and Nanyang Siang Pau)*
Heng Chiang Meng	Age: 39 Chinese	Jalan Kayu	Raffles Institution; University of Singapore (Bachelor of Business Administration (Honours))	Member, Kim Seng CCC Board director, Economic Development Board	Executive Director, International Bank of Singapore (on secondment from Overseas Union Bank); *Extensive work experience in the banking sector, including stints at Citibank, Overseas Union Bank and the Monetary Authority of Singapore (MAS);* *Previous employment at the National Theatre Trust and Department of Civil Aviation*

Table 1.2 1984 General Election – PAP Candidates Information (cont'd)

Name	Age and Ethnicity	Constituency	Educational and Professional Qualifications	Party / Community / Volunteer / Board Experience	Career
Ho Tat Kin	Age: 40 Chinese	Boon Teck	Gan Eng Seng Secondary School; University of Singapore (Bachelor of Science (Physics) (Honours)); University of Stirling (Master of Science; PhD in Science)	Exco Member, PAP Buona Vista Branch; Member, Buona Vista CCC; Secretary, Buona Vista CCC; Member, Buona Vista CCMC; Member, Kampong Bugis CCMC; Volunteer Officer, People's Defence Force	Deputy Director, Japan-Singapore Institute of Software Technology; Assistant Registrar, Singapore Polytechnic; Specialist Science Adviser, Ministry of Education; Teacher, Raffles Institution
Ibrahim Othman	Age: 35 Malay	Tanah Merah	Monk's Hill Secondary School; Teachers' Training College (Certificate in Education); University of London (Bachelor of Arts (Malay Studies) (Sociology) (Honours); Diploma in Administration Management))	Subcommittee Member and Coordinator, Mendaki tuition centres; Member, Schools Council; Member, Education Sub-Committee for Darul Ihsan Orphanage; Member, Education Sub-Committee for Al-Mutaqqin Mosque; Deputy-President, Singapore Malay Teachers' Union; Member, National Cadet Corps Council; Member, Kebun Baru CCC	Principal, Mayflower Secondary School; Vice-Principal, Bartley Secondary School; Teacher, Queensway Secondary School; Teacher, Whitley Primary School

(cont'd overleaf)

Table 1.2 1984 General Election – PAP Candidates Information (cont'd)

Name	Age and Ethnicity	Constituency	Educational and Professional Qualifications	Party / Community / Volunteer / Board Experience	Career
Koh Lam Son	Age: 37 Chinese	Telok Blangah	St Joseph's Institution; University of Bristol (Bachelor of Medicine, Bachelor of Surgery); Royal College of Surgeons, Edinburgh (Fellow); Royal College of Obstetricians and Gynaecologists (Member)	Member, PAP River Valley Branch; Charter President, Lions Club Raffles City; Chairman, River Valley CCC	Gynaecologist in private practice; *Specialist Doctor, Toa Payoh Hospital*
Lee Boon Yang	Age: 37 Chinese	Jalan Besar	Montfort Secondary School; Colombo Plan Scholarship – University of Queensland (Bachelor of Veterinary Science (Honours))		Senior Manager (Projects and Development), Primary Industries Enterprise Pte Ltd; *Assistant Regional Director, US Feedgrains Council;* *Senior Primary Production Officer, Pig and Poultry Research and Training Institute, Primary Production Department*

Table 1.2 1984 General Election – PAP Candidates Information (cont'd)

Name	Age and Ethnicity	Constituency	Educational and Professional Qualifications	Party / Community / Volunteer / Board Experience	Career
Lee Hsien Loong	Age: 32 Chinese	Teck Ghee	Catholic High School; National Junior College; President's Scholarship and SAF Overseas Scholarship – University of Cambridge (Bachelor of Arts (Mathematics) (Honours); Diploma in Computer Science (Distinction)); John F. Kennedy School of Government, Harvard University (Master of Public Administration (Mason Fellow)); United States Army Command and General Staff College (Graduate (Honours))		Brigadier-General, Singapore Armed Forces; Director of Joint Operations and Plans and Chief of Staff, General Staff, Singapore Armed Forces; *Extensive military career in the Singapore Armed Forces*
Leong Horn Kee	Age: 32 Chinese	Thomson	Tanglin Technical School Colombo Plan Scholarship – Loughborough University of Technology (Bachelor of Technology (Production Engineering and Management) (Honours)); University of London (Bachelor of Science (Economics)); European Institute of Business Administration (INSEAD) (Master of Business Administration)		Project Development Manager, National Iron and Steel Mills Ltd; General Manager, National Iron and Steel Mills Ltd's investment subsidiary; *Deputy Director, Ministry of Trade and Industry*

(cont'd overleaf)

Table I.2 1984 General Election – PAP Candidates Information (cont'd)

Name	Age and Ethnicity	Constituency	Educational and Professional Qualifications	Party / Community / Volunteer / Board Experience	Career
Mah Bow Tan (not voted in)	Age: 36 Chinese	Potong Pasir	St Joseph's Institution; President's Scholarship and Colombo Plan Scholarship – University of New South Wales (Bachelor of Engineering (Honours); Master of Engineering (Operations Research))	Chairman, NTUC Comfort	Deputy Chairman, Singapore Monitor *Public sector experience (including secondments) in the Administrative Service included stints in Mindef, Singapore Bus Service (as GM) and Singapore Monitor (as Chief Executive)*
Ng Pock Too (not voted in)	Age: 39 Chinese	Anson	St Joseph's Institution; Colombo Plan Scholarship – University of New Brunswick (Bachelor of Science (Mechanical Engineering)); Harvard University (Graduate of the Programme for Management Development)	Vice-Chairman, Anson CCC; Chairman, Coordinating Committee for all community activities organised by grassroots organisations in Anson	Political Secretary (Prime Minister's Office); Deputy General Manager, Intraco Ltd; *Chief Executive Officer, Trade Development Board;* *Deputy Director, Economic Development Board*

Table 1.2 1984 General Election – PAP Candidates Information (cont'd)

Name	Age and Ethnicity	Constituency	Educational and Professional Qualifications	Party / Community / Volunteer / Board Experience	Career
Philip Tan Tee Yong	Age: 38 Chinese	Paya Lebar	Outram Secondary School; Degree from Institute of Cost of Management Accountants (self-study)	Member, PAP West Coast Branch; Church Elder active in community and pastoral work; Extensive community work in Bukit Ho Swee area	Cost and Management Accountant of his own personal management consultancy firm; Branch Manager (Business Computer Division) of a multi-national company
Richard Hu	Age: 58 Chinese	Kreta Ayer	Anglo-Chinese School (interrupted due to World War II); University of California (Bachelor of Science (Chemistry)); University of Birmingham (PhD in Chemical Engineering)		Managing Director, MAS; Managing Director, Government of Singapore Investment Corporation; Chairman and Chief Executive of all Shell companies in Singapore and Malaysia; Director, Fraser & Neave; Board Member, Port of Singapore Authority; Lecturer in chemical engineering, University of Manchester

(cont'd overleaf)

Table 1.2 1984 General Election – PAP Candidates Information (cont'd)

Name	Age and Ethnicity	Constituency	Educational and Professional Qualifications	Party / Community / Volunteer / Board Experience	Career
S. Vasoo	Age: 42 Indian	Bo Wen	Gan Eng Seng Secondary School; University of Singapore (Diploma in Social Studies (Distinction)); University of Hong Kong (Master of Social Work)	Member, Community Service, Deeds and Bravery Committee, PA; Vice-Chairman, Toa Payoh Residents' Committee Zone C; Assistant Secretary, Toa Payoh CCC; Panel Member, Video/Film Censorship Committee; Volunteer Policeman, Special Constabulary (Volunteer), Toa Payoh Division Executive Member, Singapore Children's Society; Board Member, Singapore Council of Social Service; Deputy Director, Singapore Council of Social Service	Lecturer, Department of Social Work, National University of Singapore; Psychiatric Nurse, Woodbridge Hospital; Trainee Factory Supervisor, Rubber plantation (Malaysia)
Tang Guan Seng	Age: 36 Chinese	Khe Bong	Thomson Government Chinese Middle School; Nanyang University (Bachelor of Arts (History))		Deputy Chief Editor, Lianhe Zaobao; Chief Reporter, Sin Chew Jit Poh; Assistant Superintendent of Customs, Customs and Excise Department

Table 1.2 1984 General Election – PAP Candidates Information (cont'd)

Name	Age and Ethnicity	Constituency	Educational and Professional Qualifications	Party / Community / Volunteer / Board Experience	Career
Wang Kai Yuen	Age: 36 Chinese	Bukit Timah	St John's Institution (Malaysia); University of Singapore (Bachelor of Engineering (Electrical Engineering) (Honours)); Ford Foundation Scholarship – Stanford University (PhD in Engineering (Control and Systems))	Member, PAP Bukit Merah Branch; Assistant Treasurer, Boon Teck CCMC; Member, ACCORD (Advisory Council on Community Relations in Defence)	Senior Teaching Associate, Institute of Systems Science, National University of Singapore; *Senior Systems Analyst, Stanford Research Institute;* *Engineer, Radio and Television Singapore*
Wong Kan Seng	Age: 38 Chinese	Kuo Chuan	Outram Secondary School; Higher School Certificate, Adult Education Board; Teachers' Training College (Certificate in Education); University of Singapore (Bachelor of Arts (Honours)); National University of Singapore (Diploma (Business Administration); London Business School, University of London (Master of Science (Business Studies))	Member, ACCORD; Chairman, School Executive Committee, Outram Secondary School; Member, Advisory Committee, Outram Secondary School	Personnel Manager, Hewlett Packard Singapore; *Deputy Secretary, Ministry of Defence;* *Prior public sector experience in the Ministries of Defence, Labour and Education (Administrative Service);* *Teacher*

(cont'd overleaf)

Table 1.2 1984 General Election – PAP Candidates Information (cont'd)

Name	Age and Ethnicity	Constituency	Educational and Professional Qualifications	Party / Community / Volunteer / Board Experience	Career
Yatiman Yusof	Age: 38 Malay	Kampong Kembangan	Serangoon English School; Bartley Secondary School; Sang Nila Utama Secondary School; University of Singapore (Bachelor of Arts)	Permanent Chairman, Central Council of Malay Cultural Organisations; Member, Joint Committee for Malay Education; Member, Media Consultative Committee, National Productivity Board; Member, Advisory Committee, Bedok Boys' School;	Editor, *Berita Harian/Berita Minggu*; *Secretary-General, Singapore Malay Teachers' Union*
Yeo Cheow Tong	Age: 36 Chinese	Hong Kah	Anglo-Chinese School; Colombo Plan Scholarship – University of Western Australia (Bachelor of Engineering (Mechanical Engineering)); University of Chicago (Diploma in Management Studies)		Managing Director, LeBlond Makino Asia; Managing Director, Precision Casting Pte Ltd; *Projects Officer, EDB*

Table 1.2 1984 General Election – PAP Candidates Information (cont'd)

Name	Age and Ethnicity	Constituency	Educational and Professional Qualifications	Party / Community / Volunteer / Board Experience	Career
Yu-Foo Yee Shoon	Age: 34 Chinese	Yuhua	Nanyang Girls High School; Nanyang University (Bachelor of Commerce (Economics))	Adviser, Women's Programme Secretariat, NTUC; Longstanding grassroots experience (PAP cadre member since 1973)	Chairman, National Trades Union Congress (NTUC); Executive Secretary, Textile Industries Workers Union; Executive Secretary, Building, Construction and Timber Employees Union; *Earlier career with NTUC*
Zulkifli Mohammed	Age: 36 Malay	Eunos	Monk's Hill Secondary School; Swiss Cottage Secondary School; University of Singapore (Bachelor of Social Sciences (Political Science) (Honours))	President, Central Council of Malay Cultural Organisations (Majlis Pusat); Vice President, Singapore Anti-Narcotics Association's Muslim Counselling Service; Board Member, Singapore Council of Social Service; Member, Board of Trustees, Singapore Cultural Foundation; *Lieutenant, People's Defence Force (Volunteers);* *Founder Member and President, Rotaract Club of Singapore City*	Senior Shipping Executive, Shell Eastern Petroleum (Pte) Ltd; *Earlier career also with Shell Eastern Petroleum*

Table 1.3 1988 General Election – New PAP Candidates

Name	Age and Ethnicity	Constituency	Educational and Professional Qualifications	Party / Community / Volunteer / Board Experience	Career
Abdul Nasser bin Kamaruddin	Age: 31 Malay	Hong Kah GRC	Whitley Secondary School; Swiss Cottage Secondary School; University of Exeter (Bachelor of Arts (Social Studies))	Member, Singapore Malay Youth Library Association (Taman Bacaan); Member, Advisory Council on Youth; Member, Kampong Kembangan Anti-Drug Task Force	Administrative Officer, Singapore Airlines Ltd; *Senior Newscaster, Singapore Broadcasting Corporation*
Charles Chong	Age: 35 Chinese	Sembawang GRC	St Joseph's Institution; Sydney Technical College (Diploma in Aircraft Maintenance Engineering)	Member, NTUC Club Management Committee; Chairman, Singapore Air Transport Workers Multi-Purpose Collective; Alternate Member, National Productivity Board; Panel Member, Industrial Arbitration Court	Administrative Officer and Senior Aircraft Engineer, Singapore Airlines Ltd; *President and General Secretary, Singapore Airlines Staff Union (SIASU)*

Table I.3 1988 General Election – New PAP Candidates (cont'd)

Name	Age and Ethnicity	Constituency	Educational and Professional Qualifications	Party / Community / Volunteer / Board Experience	Career
Chay Wai Chuen	Age: 38 Chinese	Brickworks GRC	St Joseph's Institution; Research Scholarship in Economics – University of Singapore (Bachelor of Arts (Economics) (Political Science) (Statistics); Bachelor of Social Sciences (Economics and Statistics) (Honours); Master of Social Sciences (International Economics)); Commonwealth Scholarship – University of Sussex (Master of Arts (Development Economics))	Branch Secretary, PAP Whampoa Branch; Chairman, Whampoa CCMC; Active in Whampoa grassroots organisations for several years prior	General Manager, Unique Corporation Pte Ltd; *Economist, Monetary Authority of Singapore*
Choo Wee Khiang	Age: 34 Chinese	Marine Parade GRC	River Valley Chinese Middle School; National Junior College; University of Kent (Bachelor of Arts (Accountancy) (Honours))	Secretary, PAP Youth Wing; Vice-Chairman, Kim Seng CCC; Vice-Chairman, Kim Seng CCMC; Adviser, Singapore Children's Art Society	Management Consultant; *Regional Internal Auditor of an multinational engineering firm*
Davinder Singh	Age: 31 Other (Sikh)	Toa Payoh GRC	St Joseph's Institution; National Junior College; DBS Bank Scholarship – National University of Singapore (Bachelor of Laws (Honours)); Supreme Court of Singapore (Advocate and Solicitor)	Member, PAP Youth Wing Headquarters Committee; Member, Advisory Council on the Aged	Lawyer, Drew & Napier

(cont'd overleaf)

Table 1.3 1988 General Election – New PAP Candidates (cont'd)

Name	Age and Ethnicity	Constituency	Educational and Professional Qualifications	Party / Community / Volunteer / Board Experience	Career
George Yeo	Age: 33 Chinese	Aljunied GRC	St Patrick's School; St Joseph's Institution; President's Scholarship and SAF Scholarship – University of Cambridge (Bachelor of Arts (Engineering)); Harvard Business School, Harvard University (Master of Business Administration (Baker Scholar))	Positions on various boards including Singapore Broadcasting Corporation	*Brigadier-General, Singapore Armed Forces;* *Director of Joint Operations and Planning, Ministry of Defence;* *Board Member, Singapore Broadcasting Corporation;* *Chief of Staff, Air Staff, Republic of Singapore Air Force;* *Extensive military career in the Singapore Armed Forces*
Hong Hai	Age: 44 Chinese	Bedok GRC	Muar High School (Malaysia); Colombo Plan Scholarship – University of Canterbury (Bachelor of Engineering (Honours) (Senior Scholar)); John F. Kennedy School of Government, Harvard University (Master of Public Administration); Carnegie-Mellon University (PhD in Economics and Industrial Administration)	Member, Advisory Council on Social and Psychological Defence; Member, Council of the National Arthritis Foundation; Member, Resource Panel, Government Parliamentary Committee for Finance and Trade and Industry	*Managing Director, Wearnes Polytek Holdings Pte Ltd;* *Associate Professor in Business Administration, Department of Business Administration, National University of Singapore;* *Managing Director, Applied Research Corporation;* *Senior Officer, Economic Development Board*

Table 1.3 1988 General Election – New PAP Candidates (cont'd)

Name	Age and Ethnicity	Constituency	Educational and Professional Qualifications	Party / Community / Volunteer / Board Experience	Career
John Chen Seow Phun	Age: 34 Chinese	Hong Kah GRC	Holy Innocents' High School; Anglican High School; Guthrie Scholarship – University of Singapore (Bachelor of Engineering (Electrical Engineering) (Honours)); Commonwealth Scholarship – University of Waterloo (Master of Applied Science; PhD in Electrical Engineering)	Member, PAP Youth Wing; Assistant Secretary, Ayer Rajah CCC; Active community work in the Hong Kah North constituency; Member, National University of Singapore Senate	Senior Lecturer, Department of Electrical Engineering, National University of Singapore; *Senior Officer (Investment Services), Economic Development Board;* *Research Assistant, Guthrie Bhd*
Kenneth Chen Koon Lap (not voted in)	Age: 48 Chinese	Potong Pasir SMC	Bartley Secondary School; Singapore Polytechnic (Diploma in Architecture); Perth Technical College (Graduate of architecture course)	Patron, Potong Pasir CC; Longstanding involvedment in Potong Pasir grassroots organisations; Member, National Crime Prevention Council; Member, Supervisory Panel, Feedback Unit; *Chairman, Sennett CCMC;* *Chairman, Potong Pasir CCC;* *President, Singapore Institute of Architects*	Co-Founder and Senior Partner, Regional Development Consortium Architects Pte Ltd; *Senior Architect, Goh Hock Guan Design (1967–69);* *Stint with an architectural firm in Australia (1965–67)*
K. Shanmugam	Age: 29 Indian	Sembawang GRC	Raffles Institution; National University of Singapore (Bachelor of Laws (Honours)); Supreme Court of Singapore (Advocate and Solicitor)	Member, PAP Central Youth Committee; Active in community work in Chong Boon constituency since 1987	Lawyer, Drew & Napier

(cont'd overleaf)

Table 1.3 1988 General Election – New PAP Candidates (cont'd)

Name	Age and Ethnicity	Constituency	Educational and Professional Qualifications	Party / Community / Volunteer / Board Experience	Career
Lew Syn Pau	Age: 34 Chinese	Tanglin SMC	Anglo-Chinese School; Colombo Plan Scholarship – University of Cambridge (Bachelor of Arts (Engineering)); NTUC/PSC Scholarship – Stanford University (Master of Business Administration)	Second Adviser, Tampines North Residents' Committee; Member, Resource Panel, Government Parliamentary Committee on Labour; Member, National Wages Council; Member, Vocational and Industrial Training Board Adviser, National Iron and Steel Mills Employees' Union; *Extensive experience in the labour movement and trade unions*	General Manager, NTUC Comfort; Secretary for Co-operatives and Business Ventures, National Trades Union Congress (NTUC); Executive Secretary, Metal Industries Workers' Union
Loh Meng See	Age: 39 Chinese	Kampong Glam SMC	Raffles Institution; University of Singapore (Bachelor of Arts (Economics) (Geography)); Australian Institute of Business Administration (Diploma in Business Administration); Chartered Institute of Secretaries and Administrators, UK (Associate); European Institute of Business Administration (INSEAD) (Graduate of the INSEAD Executive Programme)	Vice-Chairman, Kampong Glam CCC; Chairman, Radin Mas CCMC; Active in Radin Mas since 1981; Chairman, Civil Defence Co-ordinating Committee; Vice-President, Singapore Institute of Personnel Management; *Vice-Chairman and Honorary Secretary, Radin Mas CCMC*	Group Personnel Manager, Keppel Corporation Ltd; *Earlier career also with Keppel Corporation*

Table 1.3 1988 General Election – New PAP Candidates (cont'd)

Name	Age and Ethnicity	Constituency	Educational and Professional Qualifications	Party / Community / Volunteer / Board Experience	Career
Low Seow Chay	Age: 38 Chinese	Chua Chu Kang SMC	River Valley Government Chinese Middle School; University of Singapore (Bachelor of Engineering (Mechanical Engineering)); University of Manchester Institute of Science and Technology (Master of Science (Mechanical Engineering); PhD in Mechanical Engineering (Internal Combustion Engines))	Chairman, PAP Chua Chu Kang Branch; Branch Secretary, PAP Fengshan Branch; Honorary Secretary, PAP Suburban East District Working Committee; Secretary, Fengshan CCC; Member, Joint Committee for Continuing Education of the Board of Architects and Professional Engineers Board; *President, Engineering Alumni of Singapore*	Senior Lecturer, Faculty of Mechanical and Production Engineering, Nanyang Technological Institute; *Research Officer, Lucas CAV;* *Engineer, Singapore Automotive Engineering*
Ong Chit Chung	Age: 39 Chinese	Bukit Batok SMC	Victoria School; University of Singapore (Bachelor of Arts (History) (Honours)); Duke University (Master of Arts (Military History)); London School of Economics (PhD in International History)	Second Adviser, Bukit Batok Residents' Committee; Member, Khe Bong CCMC; Active in grassroots activities in Khe Bong constituency for previous 12 years; Member, Oral History Advisory Committee; Member, Resource Panel, Government Parliamentary Committee on Defence and Foreign Affairs; Member, ACCORD; Chairman, Executive Committee, Victoria School	Senior Lecturer in History, Department of History, National University of Singapore; *Head of Military History Branch, Singapore Command and Staff College*

(cont'd overleaf)

Table 1.3 1988 General Election – New PAP Candidates (cont'd)

Name	Age and Ethnicity	Constituency	Educational and Professional Qualifications	Party / Community / Volunteer / Board Experience	Career
Peh Chin Hua	Age: 40 Chinese	Jalan Besar GRC	River Valley High School; Asian Cultural Centre for UNESCO (Japan) (Certificate of Book Experts)	Active in Kim Seng grassroots organisations; Member, Family and Community Life Advisory Council; Founder, Ai Tong Old Boys Association; Member, River Valley High School Advisory Committee; Member, Peh Clan Association; Member, Singapore Ann Kway Association	Group Managing Director, Shing Lee Book Publishers Pte Ltd; *Extensive experience in media/book publishing sectors*
Peter Sung	Age: 48 Chinese	Buona Vista SMC	Victoria School; University of Singapore (Bachelor of Arts (Economics) (Honours)); Teacher's Training College (Certificate in Education)	Honorary Patron, Kim Keat CCMC; *Vice-Chairman, Kim Keat CCMC;* *Chairman, Education Centre;* *Advisory, Malay Cultural Group;* *Treasurer, Advisory Committee, Serangoon Garden South School*	Ambassador to the Philippines, Ministry of Foreign Affairs; *Director, Pilecon Group of Companies;* *Sales Director, Tractors Singapore Ltd, Sime Darby Group;* *Executive, Shell Group;* *Teacher*

Table 1.3 1988 General Election – New PAP Candidates (cont'd)

Name	Age and Ethnicity	Constituency	Educational and Professional Qualifications	Party / Community / Volunteer / Board Experience	Career
Seet Ai Mee	Age: 45 Chinese	Bukit Gombak SMC	Malacca High School (Malaysia); Colombo Plan Scholarship – University of Adelaide (Bachelor of Science (Biochemistry) (Honours)); University of Singapore (PhD in Clinical Biochemistry); Singapore National Institute of Chemistry (Fellow); Royal Society of Chemistry (Chartered Chemist); American Institute of Chemists (Fellow)	Member, Singapore Council of Social Service; Member, Resource Panel, Government Parliamentary Committee on Health and the Environment; President, Singapore Association for the Deaf; Chairman, School Executive Committee, Blangah Rise Primary School; *Chairman, School Management Committee member, Singapore School for the Deaf*	Managing Director and Clinical Biochemist, AML Sci-Ed Consultants Pte Ltd; *Senior Research Fellow, Singapore Institute of Standards and Industrial Research (SISIR);* *Biochemist, Department of Pathology, Ministry of Health;* *Research Fellow and Tutor, Department of Biochemistry, University of Malaya*
Mah Bow Tan (stood unsuccessfully in 1984)	Age: 39 Chinese	Tampines GRC	St Joseph's Institution; President's Scholarship and Colombo Plan Scholarship – University of New South Wales (Bachelor of Engineering (Honours); Master of Engineering (Operations Research))	Member, PAP Potong Pasir Branch; Adviser, Potong Pasir Residents' Committee *Chairman, NTUC Comfort*	Group General Manager (Co-ordination), Singapore Press Holdings Ltd; *Deputy Chairman, Singapore Monitor;* *Public sector experience (including secondments) in the Administrative Service included stints in Mindef, Singapore Bus Service (as GM) and Singapore Monitor (as Chief Executive)*

(cont'd overleaf)

Table 1.3 1988 General Election – New PAP Candidates (cont'd)

Name	Age and Ethnicity	Constituency	Educational and Professional Qualifications	Party / Community / Volunteer / Board Experience	Career
Ng Pock Too (stood unsuccessfully in 1984)	Age: 43 Chinese	Nee Soon Central SMC	St Joseph's Institution; Colombo Plan Scholarship – University of New Brunswick (Bachelor of Science (Mechanical Engineering))	*Vice-Chairman, Anson CCC;* *Chairman, Coordinating Committee for all community activities organised by grassroots organisations in Anson*	*Political Secretary (Prime Minister's Office);* *Deputy Secretary-General, National Trades Union Congress;* *Executive Secretary, Singapore Portworkers' Union;* *Deputy General Manager, Intraco Ltd;* *Chief Executive Officer, Trade Development Board;* *Deputy Director, Economic Development Board*

Table 1.4 1991 General Election and 1992 by-election – New PAP Candidates

Name	Age and Ethnicity	Constituency	Educational and Professional Qualifications	Party / Community / Volunteer / Board Experience	Career
Andy Gan Lai Chiang (not voted in)	Age: 43 Chinese	Potong Pasir SMC	Victoria School; University of Western Australia (Bachelor of Commerce); Western Australia Institute of Technology (Graduate Diploma in Accounting); Australian Society of Accountants (Certified Public Accountant); Institute of Certified Public Accountants of Singapore (Certified Public Accountant)	Secretary and Member, PAP Potong Pasir Branch; Vice-Chairman, Potong Pasir CCC; Chairman, Potong Pasir CCMC; President, Sennett Estate Residents' Association; Member, Potong Pasir PAP Community Foundation Education Centre	Group Financial Controller, North Borneo Timbers Bhd; Director, Carr Futures Pte Ltd, Banque Indosuez; Accountant and Director, HCB Futures Pte Ltd; Auditor, Price Waterhouse, Singapore; Employed in an Australian public accounting firm; Accountant, Tsang and Ong Pte Ltd

Table 1.4 1991 General Election and 1992 by-election – New PAP Candidates (cont'd)

Name	Age and Ethnicity	Constituency	Educational and Professional Qualifications	Party / Community / Volunteer / Board Experience	Career
Harun Abdul Ghani	Age: 52 Malay	Hong Kah GRC	Sultan Idris Training College (Malaysia)	Vice-Chairman, PAP Kolam Ayer Branch; Member, PAP Malay Affairs Bureau; Committee Member, Malay Language Committee, Ministry of Information and the Arts; Member, Local Council for Mosques; Vice-Chairman, Malay Anti-Drug Task Force Committee; Member, Board of Trustees, Industrial and Services Co-operative Society; Deputy President, Perwanit (Young Women and Men Association Singapore); Vice-Chairman, Kolam Ayer CCC; Founder and Secretary-General, Singapore Malay Teachers Union (KGMS)	Political Secretary, Ministry of Home Affairs; *Special Writer, Curriculum Development Institute of Singapore (CDIS)*; *Vice-Principal, Guillemard Primary School*

Table 1.4 1991 General Election and 1992 by-election – New PAP Candidates (cont'd)

Name	Age and Ethnicity	Constituency	Educational and Professional Qualifications	Party / Community / Volunteer / Board Experience	Career
Ho Peng Kee	Age: 37 Chinese	Sembawang GRC	Anglo-Chinese Secondary School; National Junior College; University of Singapore (Bachelor of Laws (Honours)); Harvard Law School, Harvard University (Master of Laws); Supreme Court of Singapore (Advocate and Solicitor)	Vice-President, Consumers' Association of Singapore; Chairman, National Police Cadet Corps Council; Board Member, Ju Eng Home for Senior Citizens; Member of various sub-committees under the Law Society and the Singapore Academy of Law; Member, Management Committee, House of Hope	Associate Professor and Vice-Dean, Faculty of Law, National University of Singapore; Master of Kent Ridge Hall, National University of Singapore; *Lecturer and Sub-Dean, Faculty of Law, National University of Singapore*
Ker Sin Tze	Age: 46 Chinese	Aljunied GRC	Chinese High School; Nanyang University (Bachelor of Commerce); University of Manitoba (Master of Arts (Economics) (Graduate Fellowship); PhD in Economics)	Vice-Chairman, PAP Kim Seng Branch; Vice-Chairman, Kim Seng CCC; Council Member, Singapore Federation of Chamber of Commerce and Industry; Chairman, Singapore Sector, ASEAN-US Business Council; Council Member, Singapore Chinese Chamber of Commerce and Industry; Member, University Council, National University of Singapore; Vice-President, Economic Society of Singapore; *Contributing columnist on socio-economic issues, Sin Chew Jit Poh*	Managing Director, Liang Court Pte Ltd; *Senior Lecturer, Department of Economics and Statistics, University of Singapore;* *Staff Economist, Economic Council of Canada*

(cont'd overleaf)

Table 1.4 1991 General Election and 1992 by-election – New PAP Candidates (cont'd)

Name	Age and Ethnicity	Constituency	Educational and Professional Qualifications	Party / Community / Volunteer / Board Experience	Career
Koo Tsai Kee	Age: 36 Chinese	Tanjong Pagar GRC	Raffles Institution; Colombo Plan Scholarship – University of Newcastle (Australia) and University of New South Wales (Bachelor of Surveying (Honours)); University College London (Master of Science (Engineering) (Distinction) (Hart Prize))	Committee Member, Hong Kah South PAP Community Foundation Project; Member, Advisory Panel for Films, Board of Film Censors	Senior Lecturer, School of Civil and Structural Engineering, Nanyang Technological University
Lim Hng Kiang	Age: 37 Chinese	Tanjong Pagar GRC	Raffles Institution; President's Scholarship and SAF Scholarship – University of Cambridge (Bachelor of Arts (Engineering) (Honours) (Distinction)); John F. Kennedy School of Government, Harvard University (Master of Public Administration (Mason Fellow))		Chief Executive Officer, Housing and Development Board; *Began career with and held various positions in the SAF. Subsequently emplaced on Dual Career Scheme/Administrative Service. Other postings in the Administrative Service included:* *Deputy Secretary, Ministry of National Development;* *Director of Policy, Ministry of Defence*

Table 1.4 1991 General Election and 1992 by-election – New PAP Candidates (cont'd)

Name	Age and Ethnicity	Constituency	Educational and Professional Qualifications	Party / Community / Volunteer / Board Experience	Career
Matthias Yao Chih	Age: 35 Chinese	Marine Parade GRC	St Joseph's Institution; National Junior College; PSC Overseas Merit Scholarship – University of Birmingham (Bachelor of Commerce (Honours)	Chairman, PAP MacPherson Branch; Director, PAP Headquarters; Director, PAP Community Foundation; Secretary, PAP Executive Committee; Member, PAP Publications Committee and PAP Awards Committee; Member, National Youth Council	Political Secretary to Prime Minister Goh Chok Tong; *Political Secretary to First Deputy Prime Minister Goh Chok Tong;* Previous positions in the Administrative Service, including: *Deputy Director (Public Communications), Ministry of Communications and Information;* *Deputy Director (Community Relations), Ministry of Community Development;* *Head of Feedback Unit;* *Deputy Director (Planning), Public Service Division*

(cont'd overleaf)

Table 1.4 1991 General Election and 1992 by-election – New PAP Candidates (cont'd)

Name	Age and Ethnicity	Constituency	Educational and Professional Qualifications	Party / Community / Volunteer / Board Experience	Career
Michael Lim Chun Leng	Age: 30 Chinese	Cheng San GRC	Anglo-Chinese School; Public Service Commission Local Merit Bursary – National University of Singapore (Bachelor of Medicine, Bachelor of Surgery; Master of Medicine (Internal Medicine)); Royal College of Physicians (Member)	Assistant Secretary, PAP Youth Wing Executive Committee; Vice-Chairman, PAP Kebun Baru Branch; Chairman, PAP Kebun Baru Youth Wing; Member, PAP Community Relations Committee; Clinical Supervisor, SAF Medical Services; Member, Resource Panel, Ang Mo Kio Town Council; Visiting Cardiologist, Singapore Coronary Club; *Chairman, NUS Cardiac Rehabilitation Committee*	Cardiologist, National University Hospital

Table 1.4 1991 General Election and 1992 by-election – New PAP Candidates (cont'd)

Name	Age and Ethnicity	Constituency	Educational and Professional Qualifications	Party / Community / Volunteer / Board Experience	Career
Mohamad Maidin Packer Mohd	Age: 33 Malay	Aljunied GRC	Sang Nila Utama Secondary School; Commonwealth Press Union, London (Harry Brittain Fellowship)	Chairman, Malay Affairs Advisory Committee for Aljunied GRC; Assistant Secretary, PAP Headquarters Executive Committee; Member, PAP Youth Wing Executive Committee; Member, PAP Publications Committee; Deputy President, Singapore Malay Youth Library Association (Taman Bacaan); Member, Supervisory Panel, Feedback Unit; Secretary, Malay Journalists Association; Founder Member and Council Member, Mendaki	Political Secretary, Ministry of Information and the Arts; Deputy Director (Research Unit), National Trades Union Congress (NTUC); *Political Secretary, Ministry of Communications and Information;* *Assistant to the Editor, Berita Harian and Berita Minggu;* *Longstanding prior career in journalism*

(cont'd overleaf)

Table 1.4 1991 General Election and 1992 by-election – New PAP Candidates (cont'd)

Name	Age and Ethnicity	Constituency	Educational and Professional Qualifications	Party / Community / Volunteer / Board Experience	Career
R. Sinnakaruppan	Age: 32 Indian	Kampong Glam GRC	Raffles Institution; Nanyang Technological Institute (Bachelor of Engineering (Mechanical Engineering)); Foreign and Commonwealth Office Scholarship – Loughborough University of Technology (Master of Science (Robotics and Flexible Manufacturing Systems))	Assistant Secretary, PAP Kuo Chuan Branch; Member, Kuo Chuan CCC; President, Nanyang Technological University Alumni Club; Member Nanyang Technological University Council; *Member, Action Committee on Indian Education;* *Member, Hindu Endowments Board*	Project Manager, National Semiconductor (S) Pte Ltd; *Manager, Local Industry Upgrading Programme, Economic Development Board*
Umar Abdul Hamid	Age: 31 Malay	Ang Mo Kio GRC	Bartley Secondary School; Singapore Polytechnic (Diploma in Mechanical Engineering); University of Arizona (Bachelor of Science (Electrical Engineering))	Secretary, PAP Malay Affairs Bureau; Chairman, PAP Tanah Merah Branch Youth Wing; Secretary, Mendaki Education Committee; Member, Advisory Panel, Juvenile Court; Vice-Chairman, Majlis Pusat Youth Department; Member, Malay Activities Group Coordinating Council, People's Association	Lecturer, Department of Electrical Engineering, Singapore Polytechnic

Table 1.4 1991 General Election and 1992 by-election – New PAP Candidates (cont'd)

Name	Age and Ethnicity	Constituency	Educational and Professional Qualifications	Party / Community / Volunteer / Board Experience	Career
Kenneth Chen Koon Lap (stood unsuccessfully in 1988)	Age: 51 Chinese	Hong Kah GRC	Bartley Secondary School; Singapore Polytechnic (Diploma in Architecture); Perth Technical College (Graduate of an architecture course)	Chairman, PAP Potong Pasir Branch; Patron, Potong Pasir CC; Adviser to Potong Pasir GROs Member, Supervisory Panel, Feedback Unit; Chairman, Sennett CCMC; Chairman, Potong Pasir CCC; President, Singapore Institute of Architects	Co-Founder and Senior Partner, Regional Development Consortium Architects Pte Ltd; *Brief employment stint in Australia for two years*
Teo Chee Hean (1992 Marine Parade by-election)	Age: 37 Chinese	Marine Parade GRC	St Michael's School; St Joseph's Institution; Awarded the President's Scholarship and the Singapore Armed Forces (SAF) Scholarship; University of Manchester (B.Sc [First Class Honours] in Electrical Engineering and Management Science); Imperial College London (M.Sc [Distinction] in Computing Science); Harvard University (Kennedy School of Government) (Masters in Public Administration – Named a Littauer Fellow)	Member, Ngee Ann Polytechnic Council; Member, Nanyang Technological University Council	Chief of Navy; *Began career with Republic of Singapore Navy (RSN); subsequently emplaced on Dual Career Scheme/Administrative Service;* *Held various Command and Staff Appointments in RSN and the Joint Staff (1973–91)*

(cont'd overleaf)

Table 3.1 1997 General Election – New PAP Candidates

Note: In the lead-up to the 1997 election, candidates the PAP intended to field were given the appointment "Second Adviser" by PA. This was not repeated in subsequent elections.

Name	Age and Ethnicity	Constituency	Educational and Professional Qualifications	Party / Community / Volunteer / Board Experience	Career
Ahmad Mohamed Magad	Age: 43 Malay	Pasir Ris GRC	Presbyterian High School; PSC Scholarship – Fachhochschule Aalen (Aalen University of Applied Sciences) (Ingenieur Grad (Precision Engineering)); Brunel University (Master of Business Administration); Henley Management College (Advanced Post-Graduate Diploma in Management Consultancy)	Second Adviser to Pasir Ris grassroots organisations; Deputy Chairman, Board of Governors, Institute of Technical Education; Member, Public Utilities Board; Co-Founder and Chairman, Association of Muslim Professionals	Managing Director, II-VI Singapore Pte Ltd; Engineering Manager and General Manager, FJW Industries; Training Officer, Economic Development Board Training Institute
Ang Mong Seng	Age: 47 Chinese	Bukit Gombak SMC	Jurong Integrated Secondary School; River Valley Government Chinese Middle School; Nanyang University (Bachelor of Arts (Geography))	Branch Secretary, PAP Boon Lay Branch; Second Adviser to Bukit Gombak GRC; Active involvement in grassroots work in Sembawang GRC in his capacity as General Manager of Sembawang Town Council; Second Adviser to Hougang SMC; Secretary, Boon Lay CCC	General Manager, Sembawang Town Council; General Manager, Bukit Panjang Town Council; Senior Estate Officer, Housing and Development Board

Table 3.1 1997 General Election – New PAP Candidates (cont'd)

Name	Age and Ethnicity	Constituency	Educational and Professional Qualifications	Party / Community / Volunteer / Board Experience	Career
Chan Soo Sen	Age: 40 Chinese	East Coast GRC	Catholic High School; President's Scholarship and Colombo Plan Scholarship – University of Oxford (Bachelor of Arts (Mathematics) (Honours)); Ministry of Finance Postgraduate Scholarship – Stanford University (Master of Science)	Second Adviser to Joo Chiat grassroots organisations; Active collaboration with town councils in his capacity as Business Adviser to EM Services Pte Ltd	Business Adviser to EM Services Pte Ltd; Chief Executive Officer, China-Singapore Suzhou Industrial Park Development Co Ltd; Founder and Executive Director, Chinese Development Assistance Council (CDAC); Career in the Administrative Service, with postings in the Ministry of Defence, Ministry of Finance and Ministry of Home Affairs
Chin Tet Yung	Age: 45 Chinese	Sembawang GRC	All Saints Secondary School (Malaysia); London School of Economics (Bachelor of Laws; Diploma in Economics); University of Oxford (Bachelor of Civil Law); Inner Temple (Barrister-at-Law)	Second Adviser to Nee Soon East grassroots organisations; Chairman, GST Board of Review; Member, Income Tax Board of Review; Member, Police and Civil Defence Services Commission; Member, Board of Trustees, Institute of Southeast Asian Studies; Vice-President, Singapore Academy of Law; Arbitrator and Member, Permanent Court of Arbitration – The International Court of Justice; Member, Drug Rehabilitation Review Committee IV	Associate Professor and Dean, Faculty of Law, National University of Singapore (NUS); Sub-Dean, Faculty of Law, NUS; Senior Lecturer, Faculty of Law, NUS; Lecturer, Faculty of Law, NUS

(cont'd overleaf)

Table 3.1 1997 General Election – New PAP Candidates (cont'd)

Name	Age and Ethnicity	Constituency	Educational and Professional Qualifications	Party / Community / Volunteer / Board Experience	Career
David Lim	Age: 41 Chinese	Aljunied GRC	Anglo-Chinese School; President's Scholarship and Colombo Plan Scholarship – University of Melbourne (Bachelor of Civil Engineering (Honours)); National University of Singapore (Master of Business Administration (Reginald Quahe Memorial Award)); Harvard University (Graduate of the Programme for Management Development)	Second Adviser to Bukit Panjang grassroots organisations in Sembawang GRC	Chief Executive Officer, China-Singapore Suzhou Industrial Park Development Co Ltd; Special Adviser to Chairman of Economic Development Board for Regional Projects and Software Transfer; Executive Vice-President, Sembawang Corporation Ltd; Chief Executive Officer, Port of Singapore Authority; Chief Executive Officer, Jurong Town Corporation; Head, EDB Office, North America; Deputy Director, National Computer Board; *Prior experience in the Administrative Service (Ministry of Defence)*

Table 3.1 1997 General Election – New PAP Candidates (cont'd)

Name	Age and Ethnicity	Constituency	Educational and Professional Qualifications	Party / Community / Volunteer / Board Experience	Career
Hawazi Daipi	Age: 42 Malay	Sembawang GRC	Telok Kurau Secondary School; National Junior College University of Singapore (Bachelor of Arts (Economics) (Geography) (Honours)); Institute of Education (Diploma in Education)	Honorary Secretary-General, Malay Youth Literary Association (Persatuan Persuratan Pemudi Melayu; 4PM); Member, National Arts Council; Member, Arts Fund Committee; *Extensive work in Malay community since school days (including in 4PM)*	Assistant Editor, *Berita Harian*; *Teacher, Ministry of Education*
Heng Chee How (not voted in)	Age: 35 Chinese	Hougang SMC	Raffles Institution; Singapore Police Force Undergraduate Scholarship – Cambridge University (Bachelor of Arts (Honours); Master of Arts); Singapore Police Force Postgraduate Overseas Scholarship – John F. Kennedy School of Government, Harvard University (Master of Public Administration (Mason Fellow) (Lucius Littauer Fellowship Award))	Second Adviser to Hougang grassroots organisations in Hougang SMC	Chief Executive Officer, NTUC Club; Director, Administration and Research Unit, National Trades Union Congress (NTUC); *Superintendent, Singapore Police Force, while holding various appointments including Director of Manpower and Commander of the Geylang Police Division*

(cont'd overleaf)

Table 3.1 1997 General Election – New PAP Candidates (cont'd)

Name	Age and Ethnicity	Constituency	Educational and Professional Qualifications	Party / Community / Volunteer / Board Experience	Career
Inderjit Singh	Age: 36 Other (Sikh)	Ang Mo Kio GRC	Broadrick Secondary School; Temasek Junior College; National University of Singapore (Bachelor of Engineering (Electrical and Electronics Engineering)); University of Strathclyde (Master of Business Administration)	Second Adviser to Kebun Baru grassroots organisations; Chairman, Kebun Baru PAP Community Foundation Committee; Chairman, Ang Mo Kio-Yishun Town Council's Project Development Committee; Member, Nanyang Technological University (NTU) Fund Endowment Committee, NTU Council; Chairman, PAP Siglap Branch Publicity and MP Walkabout Sub-Committees; Chairman, Youth Wing, PAP Siglap Branch; Chairman, Siglap Residents' Committee; Member, Universities Endowment Fund (NUS and NTU); First protem-chairman, Honorary Secretary, NTI Alumni Association	Director of Operations, Texas Instruments Singapore Pte Ltd; Board Chairman, Tri Star Electronics Pte Ltd; General Manager, Customer Service and Original Equipment Manufacturer (OEM) Business, Texas Instruments Singapore Pte Ltd; Earlier career with Texas Instruments Singapore

Table 3.1 1997 General Election – New PAP Candidates (cont'd)

Name	Age and Ethnicity	Constituency	Educational and Professional Qualifications	Party / Community / Volunteer / Board Experience	Career
Lily Neo	Age: 43 Chinese	Kreta Ayer-Tanglin GRC	Methodist High School (Malaysia); University College Dublin, National University of Ireland (Bachelor of Medicine, Bachelor of Surgery, Bachelor of Obstetrics); Royal College of Surgeons, Ireland (Licentiate); Royal College of Physicians, Ireland (Licentiate)	Second Adviser to Kim Seng grassroots organisations; Chairwoman, Queenstown CCMC; Medical Adviser, Queenstown Traders' Association; Active involvement in Queenstown grassroots activities since 1985	Medical Practitioner in private practice
Lim Hwee Hua	Age: 37 Chinese	Marine Parade GRC	Crescent Girls' School; Raffles Institution; Government Overseas Merit Scholarship – Cambridge University (Bachelor of Arts (Mathematics) (Engineering) (Honours)); University of California, Los Angeles (Master of Business Administration (Finance))	Secretary, PAP Women's Wing's Executive Committee; Second Adviser to Aljunied grassroots organisations; Board Member, Maritime Port Authority of Singapore	Head of Singapore Research, Jardine Fleming International Securities Ltd; Investment Analyst, Swiss Bank Corporation; Experience in public service as Administrative Officer with the Ministries of Education, Finance and Law

(cont'd overleaf)

Table 3.1 1997 General Election – New PAP Candidates (cont'd)

Name	Age and Ethnicity	Constituency	Educational and Professional Qualifications	Party / Community / Volunteer / Board Experience	Career
Lim Swee Say	Age: 42 Chinese	Tanjong Pagar GRC	Catholic High School; National Junior College; SAF Scholarship – Loughborough University of Technology (Bachelor of Science (Electronic, Computer and Systems Engineering) (Honours)); Stanford University (Master of Science (Management))	Second Adviser to Buona Vista grassroots organisations; Deputy Chairman, Productivity and Standards Board; Member, Catholic High School Management Committee Chairman, National Computer Board; Director of several government-linked companies including Singapore Technologies Pte Ltd and Chartered Semiconductor Manufacturing Ltd	Director, Administration and Research Unit, National Trades Union Congress; *Managing Director, Economic Development Board (rejoined Administrative Service);* *General Manager, National Computer Board;* *Project Engineer, Ministry of Defence (Administrative Service)*

Table 3.1 1997 General Election – New PAP Candidates (cont'd)

Name	Age and Ethnicity	Constituency	Educational and Professional Qualifications	Party / Community / Volunteer / Board Experience	Career
Ong Ah Heng	Age: 52 Chinese	Nee Soon Central SMC	Chung Cheng High School; Nanyang University (Bachelor of Arts (Government and Public Administration)); University of Arkansas (Master of Arts (Political Science))	Second Adviser to Nee Soon Central grassroots organisations; Member, Bishan-Serangoon Town Council; Director, Chinese Development Assistance Council; *Veteran PAP member since 1964, having served in the PAP Jalan Kayu, Anson and Tanjong Pagar branches and holding multiple Party positions including Secretary, PAP Tanjong Pagar Branch;* *Vice-Chairman, Anson CCC;* *Chairman, Tanjong Pagar CCMC;* *Organising Secretary, People's Association;* *Election Agent to Senior Minister Lee Kuan Yew in the 1976, 1980, 1988 and 1991 General Elections*	Assistant Secretary-General, National Trades Union Congress (NTUC); Director, Administration and Research Unit, NTUC; Executive Secretary, National Transport Workers' Union; *Assistant Director, Administration and Research Unit, NTUC;* *Senior Sports Officer, Singapore Sports Council;* *Organising Secretary, People's Association*

(cont'd overleaf)

Table 3.1 1997 General Election – New PAP Candidates (cont'd)

Name	Age and Ethnicity	Constituency	Educational and Professional Qualifications	Party / Community / Volunteer / Board Experience	Career
Ong Kian Min	Age: 36 Chinese	Pasir Ris GRC	Anglo-Chinese School; Anglo-Chinese Junior College President's Scholarship and Singapore Police Force Scholarship – Imperial College, London (Bachelor of Science (Honours)); University of London (Bachelor of Laws (Honours)); Gray's Inn (Barrister-at-Law); Royal College of Science (Associate)	Chairman, PAP Tampines North Branch; Chairman, Tampines North PAP Community Foundation Committee; Second Adviser to Tampines North grassroots organisations; Member, Supervisory Panel, Feedback Unit	Lawyer and Partner, Shook Lin & Bok; *Legal Assistant, Rodyk & Davidson;* *Senior Police Officer, Singapore Police Force*
Peter Chen Min Liang	Age: 58 Chinese	Hong Kah GRC	Anderson School, Ipoh (Malaysia); Colombo Plan Scholarship – South Australia Institute of Technology (Diploma in Accountancy); Institute of Chartered Accountants in Australia (Fellow)	Second Adviser to Jurong grassroots organisations; Director in various boards (including DBS, Temasek Holdings, EDB, PSA and LTA)	*Retired in June 1996 as Chairman and Chief Executive Officer, Shell Companies in Singapore*

Table 3.1 1997 General Election – New PAP Candidates (cont'd)

Name	Age and Ethnicity	Constituency	Educational and Professional Qualifications	Party / Community / Volunteer / Board Experience	Career
R. Ravindran	Age: 36 Indian	Bukit Timah GRC	Commonwealth Secondary School; National Junior College; National University of Singapore (Bachelor of Laws (Honours); Master of Laws); Supreme Court of Singapore (Advocate and Solicitor)	Second Adviser to Jurong grassroots organisations; Assistant Secretary, Boon Lay CCMC; Member, Political Supervisory Committee, Service Improvement Unit, Prime Minister's Office; Member, Political Supervisory Committee, Public Service for the 21st Century (PS21) Office; Member, Supervisory Panel, Feedback Unit; Member, Executive Council, Tamil Language and Cultural Society; Member, Hindu Endowment Board; Member, Youth Development Wing, Singapore Indian Development Association (SINDA); Member, Indian Anti-Drug Task Force Committee, SINDA; *Chairman, Boon Lay CC Youth Group Executive Committee;* *Assisted at Boon Lay Meet-the-People Sessions since 1993;* *First Vice-Chairman, Central Youth Council, People's Association Youth Movement*	Lawyer (Derrick, Ravi & Partners)

(cont'd overleaf)

Table 3.1 1997 General Election – New PAP Candidates (cont'd)

Name	Age and Ethnicity	Constituency	Educational and Professional Qualifications	Party / Community / Volunteer / Board Experience	Career
S. Iswaran	Age: 34 Indian	West Coast GRC	St Andrew's Secondary School; National Junior College; Colombo Plan Scholarship – University of Adelaide (Bachelor of Arts (Economics) (Honours)); John F. Kennedy School of Government, Harvard University (Master of Public Administration (Mason Fellow))	Second Adviser to Brickworks grassroots organisations; Director, NTUC Childcare Co-operative; Member, Executive Council, Singapore Indian Development Association (SINDA); Chairman, Family Development Wing, SINDA	Managing Director, Temasek Holdings *Director, Strategic Development, Singapore Technologies Pte Ltd;* *Previous positions / secondments in Administrative Service included:* *Director for International Trade, Ministry of Trade and Industry;* *Chief Executive Officer, SINDA;* *Deputy Director, Special Projects, National Trades Union Congress (NTUC);* *Roles in the Ministries of Home Affairs and Education*
Seng Han Thong	Age: 46 Chinese	Ang Mo Kio GRC	Tuan Mong High School; Singapore Institute of Management (Diploma in Management Studies); Brunel University (Master of Business Administration)	Second Adviser to Ang Mo Kio grassroots organisations; Member, 1991 Censorship Review Committee; Vice-President, Seng Clan Association; Trustee, NTUC Childcare Co-operative	General Manager for Special Assignments, Chinese Newspaper Division, Singapore Press Holdings Ltd; *Senior Associate Editor, Lianhe Zaobao;* *Extensive career in journalism for 21 years*

Table 3.1 1997 General Election – New PAP Candidates (cont'd)

Name	Age and Ethnicity	Constituency	Educational and Professional Qualifications	Party / Community / Volunteer / Board Experience	Career
Sin Boon Ann	Age: 38 Chinese	Tampines GRC	Anglo-Chinese School; National University of Singapore (Bachelor of Arts (Political Science) (Sociology)); Bachelor of Laws (Honours)); University of London (Master of Laws); Supreme Court of Singapore (Advocate and Solicitor)	Member, Young PAP Executive Committee; Member, Young PAP Policy Studies Group; Second Adviser to Tampines East grassroots organisations; Assisted Charles Chong (Tampines North), Mah Bow Tan (Tampines East) and George Yeo (Aljunied) in grassroots work; Member of former MP Ong Teng Cheong's campaign team in Kim Keat for the 1980 General Election	Lawyer and Partner, Drew & Napier; *Lecturer, Faculty of Law, National University of Singapore*
Tan Boon Wan	Age: 48 Chinese	Ang Mo Kio GRC	Swiss Cottage Secondary School; Naval Base Secondary School; University of Singapore (Bachelor of Arts (Physics) (Honours)); Imperial College, London (Master of Science (Management); PhD in Management Science))	Second Adviser to Nee Soon South grassroots organisations; *Member, Cairnhill CCC;* *Member, Cairnhill CCMC;* *Extensive involvement in community work since 1980*	Senior Lecturer, Department of Decision Sciences, National University of Singapore; *Marketing Manager, GPG Plastics (S) Pte Ltd;* *General Manager, McGraw-Hill FEP (Nigeria) Pte Ltd;* *Administration Manager, Far Eastern Publishers Pte Ltd*

(cont'd overleaf)

Table 3.1 1997 General Election – New PAP Candidates (cont'd)

Name	Age and Ethnicity	Constituency	Educational and Professional Qualifications	Party / Community / Volunteer / Board Experience	Career
Teo Ho Pin	Age: 36 Chinese	Sembawang GRC	New Town Secondary School; National Junior College; Tan Lark Sye Scholarship – National University of Singapore (Bachelor of Science (Building) (Honours)); NUS Overseas Graduate Scholarship – Herriot-Watt University (Master of Science (Project Management); PhD in Building); Chartered Institute of Building, United Kingdom (Member); Singapore Institute of Building (Fellow)	Vice-Chairman, Young PAP Jurong Branch; Vice-Principal/Assistant Secretary, Jurong PAP Community Foundation Branch; Second Adviser to Bukit Panjang grassroots organisations; Chairman, Advisory Committee, Pioneer Secondary School; General Secretary, Nanyang Community Club; President, Singapore Institute of Building; Active in grassroots work in Jurong since 1982; Committee Member, Nanyang Community Centre; Chairman, Jurong Town CC Youth Executive Committee;	Senior Lecturer, School of Building and Real Estate, National University of Singapore (NUS); *Chief Executive Officer, Jurong Town Council;* *Senior Tutor, School of Building and Real Estate, NUS*

Table 3.1 1997 General Election – New PAP Candidates (cont'd)

Name	Age and Ethnicity	Constituency	Educational and Professional Qualifications	Party / Community / Volunteer / Board Experience	Career
Toh See Kiat	Age: 42 Chinese	Aljunied GRC	Raffles Institution; St Helens Senior High School (Oregon, United States); National University of Singapore (Bachelor of Laws (Honours)); Harvard University (Master of Laws); University of London (PhD in Law); Supreme Court of Singapore (Advocate and Solicitor)	Second Adviser to Serangoon Gardens grassroots organisations; President, Consumers Association of Singapore; Member, Young PAP Executive Committee; Chairman, Young PAP Policy Studies Group; PAP Member since 1983; Member, River Valley CCMC; Member, Tampines North CCC; Member, Helping Hand Drug Halfway House Committee; Town Councillor at Bishan-Serangoon and Eunos-Pasir Ris	Lawyer and Partner, Arthur Loke & Partners; Senior Lecturer (on leave), Division of Business Law, Nanyang Business School, Nanyang Technological University; *Lawyer at several firms;* *Senior Tutor, School of Accountancy, National University of Singapore*

(cont'd overleaf)

Table 3.1 1997 General Election – New PAP Candidates (cont'd)

Name	Age and Ethnicity	Constituency	Educational and Professional Qualifications	Party / Community / Volunteer / Board Experience	Career
Yaacob Ibrahim	Age: 41 Malay	Jalan Besar GRC	Broadrick Secondary School; Tanjong Katong Secondary Technical School; University of Singapore (Bachelor of Engineering) (Civil Engineering) (Honours); National University of Singapore (Master of Science (Civil Engineering); Stanford University (PhD in Civil Engineering)	Member, Islamic Religious Council of Singapore (MUIS); Deputy Chairman, Board of Directors and Executive Committee, Mendaki; Chairman, Programme Advisory Committee on Malay TV, Ministry of Information and the Arts; Member, Inter-Ministry Committee on Dysfunctional Families, Juvenile Delinquency and Drug Abuse; Active involvement with MUIS, Mendaki and the Association of Muslim Professionals since 1990; Youth Member, Muslim Missionary Society (Jamiyah)	Senior Lecturer, Department of Industrial and Systems Engineering, National University of Singapore; Post-Doctoral Research Fellow, Cornell University
Yeo Guat Kwang	Age: 35 Chinese	Cheng San GRC	The Chinese High School; Nanyang Junior College; National University of Singapore (Bachelor of Arts (Social Sciences) (Honours)); Institute of Education (Diploma in Education)	Branch Secretary, PAP Chong Pang Branch; Second Adviser to Punggol grassroots organisations; Active involvement in grassroots work, including the People's Association Youth Movement since 1985	Assistant Director, Administration and Research Unit, National Trades Union Congress; Specialist Inspector for Chinese, Ministry of Education; Head of Department, Anderson Secondary School; Teacher, Nanyang Junior College

Table 3.1 1997 General Election – New PAP Candidates (cont'd)

Name	Age and Ethnicity	Constituency	Educational and Professional Qualifications	Party / Community / Volunteer / Board Experience	Career
Zainul Abidin Rasheed	Age: 48 Malay	Cheng San GRC	Raffles Institution; University of Singapore (Bachelor of Arts (Economics and Malay Studies) (Honours))	President, Islamic Religious Council of Singapore; Director, Mendaki; Member, National Medical Ethics Committee; Member, Advisory Committee, Institute of Policy Studies; Chairman, Kampong Kembangan CC Youth Sub-Committee; Member, Resource Committee, Government Parliamentary Committee for Education; Member, Advisory Council on Community Relations in Defence; Member, Asia Islamic Banking & Finance Advisory Committee, National University of Singapore Council	*Editor, Berita Harian and Berita Minggu;* *Chief Executive Officer, Mendaki;* *Associate Editor, Straits Times;* *Editor, Sunday Times;* *Editor, Singapore Business;* *Research Editor/Manager, Asia Research Bulletin*

(cont'd overleaf)

Table 3.1 1997 General Election – New PAP Candidates (cont'd)

Name	Age and Ethnicity	Constituency	Educational and Professional Qualifications	Party / Community / Volunteer / Board Experience	Career
Andy Gan Lai Chiang (not voted in) (stood unsuccessfully in 1991)	Age: 48 Chinese	Potong Pasir SMC	Victoria School; University of Western Australia (Bachelor of Commerce); Western Australia Institute of Technology (Graduate Diploma in Accounting); Australian Society of Accountants (Certified Public Accountant); Institute of Certified Public Accountants of Singapore (Certified Public Accountant)	Chairman, PAP Potong Pasir Branch; Adviser to Potong Pasir grassroots organisations; Vice-Chairman, Potong Pasir CCC; Chairman, Potong Pasir CCMC; President, Sennett Estate Residents' Association; Member, Potong Pasir PAP Community Foundation Education Centre	Managing Director, Island Horti-Tech Holdings Pte Ltd; Group Financial Controller, North Borneo Timbers Bhd; Director, Carr Futures Pte Ltd, Banque Indosuez; Accountant and Director, HCB Futures Pte Ltd; Auditor, Price Waterhouse, Singapore; Employed in an Australian public accounting firm; Accountant, Tsang and Ong Pte Ltd

Table 4.1 2001 General Election – New PAP Candidates

Name	Age and Ethnicity	Constituency	Educational and Professional Qualifications	Party / Community / Volunteer / Board Experience	Career
Ahmad Khalis	Age: 41 Malay	Hong Kah GRC	Telok Kurau East School; Raffles Institution; National University of Singapore (Bachelor of Laws); Supreme Court of Singapore (Advocate and Solicitor)	General Secretary, Central Committee, Muhammadiyah Association; Member, Medifund Advisory Council; Member, S21 Facilitation Committee; Board Member, Singapore Corporation of Rehabilitative Enterprises; Member, COMPASS (Community and Parents in Support of Schools, MOE); Chairman, Muslim Law Practice Committee, Law Society; Member, Singapore 21 Subcommittee on Senior Citizens and the Young; Founder and Member, Fellowship of Muslim Students' Association; President, National University of Singapore Muslim Society	Partner, Wong Khalis & Partners; Legal Assistant, Kong Chai & Partners

(cont'd overleaf)

Table 4.1 2001 General Election – New PAP Candidates (cont'd)

Name	Age and Ethnicity	Constituency	Educational and Professional Qualifications	Party / Community / Volunteer / Board Experience	Career
Amy Khor	Age: 43 Chinese	Hong Kah GRC	Raffles' Girls Secondary School; Raffles Institution; Tan Lian Boh Scholarship – National University of Singapore (Bachelor of Science (Estate Management)); San Jose State University (Master of Business Administration); University of Reading (PhD in Land Management)	Council Chairperson and President, Singapore Institute of Surveyors and Valuers; Member, Focus Group on Land Allocation, Concept Plan 2001; Board Member, Singapore Land Authority; Member, Advisory Committee, Urban and Redevelopment Authority	Investment Sales Director, Knight Frank Pte Ltd; Director of Consultancy and Research; Knight Frank Pte Ltd; Senior Lecturer, School of Building and Real Estate, National University of Singapore; Property Valuer, Property Tax Division, Inland Revenue Authority of Singapore

Table 4.1 2001 General Election – New PAP Candidates (cont'd)

Name	Age and Ethnicity	Constituency	Educational and Professional Qualifications	Party / Community / Volunteer / Board Experience	Career
Arthur Fong	Age: 37 Chinese	West Coast GRC	Anglo-Chinese School; Anglo-Chinese Junior College; University of Oregon (Bachelor of Science (Management and Finance))	Member, PAP Kampong Chai Chee Branch; Young PAP Branch Chairman, Kampong Chai Chee Branch International Relations Co-ordinator, Executive Committee, Young PAP; District Chairman, Young PAP Marine Parade District; Secretary, Kampong Chai Chee PAP Community Foundation Branch; Vice-Chairman, Finance, East Coast Town Council; Member, Kampong Chai Chee CCC; Member, Kampong Chai Chee CCMC; Chairman, Kampong Chai Chee Sports Club	Assistant Vice-President, The Citigroup Private Bank; Assistant Vice-President, OCBC Private Bank; Relationship Manager, Credit Lyonnais Bank; Business Development Manager, Citibank N.A.; Consultant, Arthur Andersen & Co

(cont'd overleaf)

Table 4.1 2001 General Election – New PAP Candidates (cont'd)

Name	Age and Ethnicity	Constituency	Educational and Professional Qualifications	Party / Community / Volunteer / Board Experience	Career
Balaji Sadasivan	Age: 46 Indian	Ang Mo Kio GRC	Siglap Secondary School; National Junior College; University of Singapore (Bachelor of Medicine, Bachelor of Surgery); Royal College of Surgeons, Glasgow (Fellow); Henry Ford Hospital and American Board of Neurology Surgery (Diploma in Neurosurgery); Harvard University (Fellow); University of London (Bachelor of Laws (Honours))	President, Asian Australasian Society of Neurological Surgery; President, Clinical Neuroscience Society Singapore	Consultant Neurosurgeon, Gleneagles Hospital; Consultant Neurosurgeon, KK Women's and Children's Hospital; Visiting Consultant, National Neuroscience Institute; Consultant Neurosurgeon, Tan Tock Seng Hospital; Clinical appointments at Brigham and Women's Hospital and the Children's Hospital Boston

Table 4.1 2001 General Election – New PAP Candidates (cont'd)

Name	Age and Ethnicity	Constituency	Educational and Professional Qualifications	Party / Community / Volunteer / Board Experience	Career
Cedric Foo	Age: 41 Chinese	West Coast GRC	Tanglin Technical School; Singapore Polytechnic (Diploma in Marine Engineering); University of Michigan, Ann Arbor (Bachelor of Science (Naval Architecture and Marine Engineering)); Neptune Orient Lines Scholarship – Massachusetts Institute of Technology (Master of Science (Ocean Systems Management)); Harvard Business School, Harvard University (Graduate of the Executive Programme in Finance); Kellogg School of Management, Northwestern University (Graduate of the Executive Programme in Finance)	Auditor, Yew Tee CCC; Member, Executive Committee, Yew Tee PAP Community Foundation; Assisted at PAP Yew Tee Branch since 1999	Senior Vice-President (Finance and Administration), Singapore Airlines Ltd; *Executive Vice-President (Finance and IT), Neptune Orient Lines (NOL) Ltd;* *President, NOL USA, NOL Ltd;* *General Manager (Corporate Planning), NOL Ltd;* *Earlier career with NOL*

(cont'd overleaf)

Table 4.1 2001 General Election – New PAP Candidates (cont'd)

Name	Age and Ethnicity	Constituency	Educational and Professional Qualifications	Party / Community / Volunteer / Board Experience	Career
Chong Weng Chiew	Age: 32 Chinese	Tanjong Pagar GRC	Catholic High School; Hwa Chong Junior College; National University of Singapore (Bachelor of Medicine, Bachelor of Surgery)	Member, Executive Committee, Young PAP; District Chairman, Young PAP Ang Mo Kio-Cheng San District; Member, Jalan Kayu CCC; Member, Singapore Buddhist Welfare Services; Medical Director, Grace Health Corner (free clinic); Medical Adviser, Grace Lodge Nursing Home; Medical Adviser, Happy Villa Sheltered Home; Assisted in setting up Bright Vision Community Hospital and Grace Home Care Services	Medical Director, Grace Home Care Services; *Medical Director, Bright Vision Community Hospital*
Cynthia Lee (nee Phua)	Age: 43 Chinese	Aljunied GRC	CHIJ St Joseph's Convent; Catholic Junior College; National University of Singapore (Bachelor of Science (Estate Management) (Honours))	Member, Executive Committee, PAP Women's Wing; Member, Bishan East CCC; Volunteer, Welfare and Education Committee, Toa Payoh GRC	Chief Executive Officer, Bishan-Toa Payoh Town Council; *Chief Executive Officer, Toa Payoh Town Council;* *Senior Manager, ESMACO Pte Ltd;* *Exec/Estates Officer, Housing and Development Board;* *Audit Clerk, Goh, Tan & Co;* *Audit Clerk, Patrick Tay & Co*

Table 4.1 2001 General Election – New PAP Candidates (cont'd)

Name	Age and Ethnicity	Constituency	Educational and Professional Qualifications	Party / Community / Volunteer / Board Experience	Career
Eric Low (not voted in)	Age: 53 Chinese	Hougang SMC	Anglo-Chinese School; Australian Insurance Institute (Diploma in General Insurance)	Chairman, PAP Hougang Branch; Second Adviser to Hougang grassroots organisations; Chairman, Hougang Community Development Council; Honorary General Secretary, National Council of Social Service; Chief Adviser, Students Care Service; Council Member, Singapore Red Cross Society; Chairman, Parents, Children and Youth Committee, National Crime Prevention Council; *Party member since 1985 – served in Telok Blangah and Clementi branches;* *Member, Board of Visitors to SAF Detention Barracks*	Business Development Director, Overseas Assurance Corporation Ltd; *Longstandng career in the insurance industry*

(cont'd overleaf)

Table 4.1 2001 General Election – New PAP Candidates (cont'd)

Name	Age and Ethnicity	Constituency	Educational and Professional Qualifications	Party / Community / Volunteer / Board Experience	Career
Gan Kim Yong	Age: 42 Chinese	Holland-Bukit Panjang GRC	Catholic High School; National Junior College; Overseas Merit Scholarship – University of Cambridge (Bachelor of Arts (Electrical Engineering); Master of Arts)	Member, Siglap South CCMC; Director, Care Corner; Chairman, Community Services Committee, Chen Li Presbyterian Church	Executive Vice-President, NatSteel Ltd; Chief Executive Officer, NatSteel Properties Pte Ltd; Chief Executive Officer, NatSteel Resorts International Pte Ltd; Assistant General Manager, NatSteel Ltd; (other positions in NatSteel Ltd); *Earlier career in the Administrative Service – including positions in Ministries of Home Affairs and Trade and Industry*

Table 4.1 2001 General Election – New PAP Candidates (cont'd)

Name	Age and Ethnicity	Constituency	Educational and Professional Qualifications	Party / Community / Volunteer / Board Experience	Career
Halimah Yacob	Age: 47 Malay	Jurong GRC	Singapore Chinese Girls' School; Tanjong Katong Girls' School; University of Singapore (Bachelor of Laws (Honours)); National University of Singapore (Master of Laws);	Deputy Chairman, Board of Directors, National Trades Union Congress (NTUC) Childcare Co-operative; Member, Board of Directors, NTUC Thrift & Loan Co-operative; Member, Board of Directors, NTUC Healthcare Cooperative; Trustee for nine NTUC-affiliated unions; Adviser for nine NTUC-affiliated unions; Member, Tribunal for the Maintenance of Parents; Member, Board of Governors, International Labour Organisation; Member, Malay Knowledge-Based Economy Advisory Committee; Member, Medifund Committee, Ang Mo Kio Community Hospital; Member, Management Committee, Northland Primary School; *Extensive prior grassroots experience*	Assistant Secretary-General, NTUC; Executive Secretary, United Workers of Electronics and Electrical Industries; Director, Women's Development Secretariat, NTUC; Director, Legal Services Department, NTUC; *Longstanding career with the labour movement since 1978, providing legal services for NTUC and its affiliated unions*

(cont'd overleaf)

Table 4.1 2001 General Election – New PAP Candidates (cont'd)

Name	Age and Ethnicity	Constituency	Educational and Professional Qualifications	Party / Community / Volunteer / Board Experience	Career
Ho Geok Choo	Age: 45 Chinese	West Coast GRC	Tanjong Katong Girls' School; Raffles Institution; University of Singapore (Bachelor of Arts (Political Science) (Economics)); Singapore Institute of Personnel Management (Graduate Diploma in Personnel Management); National University of Singapore (Master of Science (Human Resources Management))	Member, Executive Committee, PAP Women's Wing; Member, Kampong Glam CCMC; President, Singapore Human Resources Institute; Founder Member and Deputy Chairwoman, Singapore Professionals Executives Cooperative; Referee, Industrial Arbitration Court; Member, Resource Panel, Government Parliamentary Committees for Education and Manpower; Member, Promotions Committee, Central Community Development Council	Vice-President, Human Resources, SIA Engineering Company Ltd; Director, Invo-Tech Engineering Pte Ltd; Director, Human Resources, Changi International Airport Services Pte Ltd; Personnel Manager, Minolta Singapore Pte Ltd and City Marketing Sdn Bhd; Senior Personnel Officer, United Overseas Banking Group; Executive Officer, Human Resources Department, Singapore Institute of Standards and Industrial Research

Table 4.1 2001 General Election – New PAP Candidates (cont'd)

Name	Age and Ethnicity	Constituency	Educational and Professional Qualifications	Party / Community / Volunteer / Board Experience	Career
Indranee Rajah	Age: 38 Indian	Tanjong Pagar GRC	Marymount Convent School; Raffles Institution; National University of Singapore (Bachelor of Laws (Honours)); Supreme Court of Singapore (Advocate and Solicitor)	Member, Law Society Inquiry Panel; Member, Law Society Disciplinary Committee; Committee Member, Rules of Court Working Party	Lawyer and Director, Drew & Napier LLC; *Partner, Drew & Napier;* *Junior Partner, Drew & Napier;* *Senior Legal Assistant, Drew & Napier;* *Legal Assistant, Drew & Napier;* *Legal Assistant, Freshfields Singapore*
Irene Ng	Age: 37 Chinese	Tampines GRC	Convent Secondary School (Malaysia); Nanyang Junior College; National University of Singapore (Bachelor of Arts and Social Science); London School of Economics (Master of Science (International Relations))	President, Singles Connect (support group for singles); Member, Governor's Board, Champions of the National Kidney Foundation Award; Involved in grassroots activities in Pasir Ris and Changkat; Member, Workgroup on Employment and Employability, Inter-Ministerial Committee on Ageing Population; Mentor, Creative Arts Programme; Member, Steering Committee, Tampines Regional Library	Senior Manager, Editorial Services Unit, Singapore Press Holdings Ltd; *Senior Political Correspondent, The Straits Times;* *Senior Correspondent, The New Paper;* *Correspondent, The New Paper;* *Journalist, The New Paper;* *Longstanding career in journalism since joining The Straits Times as a journalist in 1986;* *Editor, Kyoto Publication*

(cont'd overleaf)

Table 4.1 2001 General Election – New PAP Candidates (cont'd)

Name	Age and Ethnicity	Constituency	Educational and Professional Qualifications	Party / Community / Volunteer / Board Experience	Career
Khaw Boon Wan	Age: 48 Chinese	Tanjong Pagar GRC	Chung Ling High School (Malaysia); Colombo Plan Scholarship – University of Newcastle, Australia (Bachelor of Commerce; Bachelor of Engineering (Honours) (University Medal)); National University of Singapore (Master of Science (Industrial Engineering))	Board appointments included: Director, Board of Directors, Monetary Authority of Singapore; Director, Board of Directors, Temasek Holdings Pte Ltd; Chairman, Singapore Cable Vision Ltd	Permanent Secretary, Ministry of Trade and Industry; Other Administrative Service postings/secondments included: Principal Private Secretary to Prime Minister Goh Chok Tong; Chief Executive Officer, Singapore General Hospital; Chief Executive Officer, KK Women's and Children's Hospital; Chief Executive Officer, National University Hospital; General Manager, Hospital Corporation of Singapore

Table 4.1 2001 General Election – New PAP Candidates (cont'd)

Name	Age and Ethnicity	Constituency	Educational and Professional Qualifications	Party / Community / Volunteer / Board Experience	Career
Mohammed Maliki bin Osman	Age: 36 Malay	Sembawang GRC	Dunearn Secondary Technical School; National University of Singapore (Bachelor of Arts; Bachelor of Social Science (Honours); Master of Social Science); University of Illinois (PhD in Social Work)	Chairman, Public Affairs Committee, Ang Mo Kio-Cheng San Community Development Council; Adviser, Ulu Pandan Family Service Centre Management Committee; Member, Edusave Advisory Council, Ministry of Education; Member, Madrasah Steering Committee, Islamic Religious Council of Singapore (MUIS)	Assistant Professor in Social Work, Department of Social Work and Psychology, National University of Singapore; *Teaching Assistant, University of Illinois;* *Senior Tutor, Department of Social Work and Psychology, National University of Singapore*

(cont'd overleaf)

Table 4.1 2001 General Election – New PAP Candidates (cont'd)

Name	Age and Ethnicity	Constituency	Educational and Professional Qualifications	Party / Community / Volunteer / Board Experience	Career
Ng Eng Hen	Age: 42 Chinese	Bishan-Toa Payoh GRC	Anglo-Chinese School; National Junior College; National University of Singapore (Bachelor of Medicine, Bachelor of Surgery (Distinction in Social Medicine) (Distinction in Public Health); Master of Medicine (Surgery)); Royal College of Surgeons, Edinburgh (Fellow); Laboratory of Surgical Metabolism, Cornell University Medical Centre, New York Hospital (Research Fellow); MD Anderson Cancer Centre, University of Texas (Clinical Fellow in Surgical Oncology) Academy of Medicine, Singapore (Fellow)	Founder Member, Breast Cancer Foundation;	Private Practitioner (Surgical Oncologist), Mount Elizabeth Hospital; *Consultant Surgeon, Singapore General Hospital*

Table 4.1 2001 General Election – New PAP Candidates (cont'd)

Name	Age and Ethnicity	Constituency	Educational and Professional Qualifications	Party / Community / Volunteer / Board Experience	Career
Ong Seh Hong	Age: 37 Chinese	Aljunied GRC	Dunman Government Chinese Middle School; National University of Singapore (Bachelor of Medicine, Bachelor of Surgery; Master of Science (Applied Finance)); Royal College of Psychiatrists (Member); Academy of Medicine, Singapore (Fellow; Honorary Secretary to the Chapter of Psychiatrists)	Coordinator (Public Affairs and Idea Incubator), Executive Committee, Young PAP; Assistant Secretary, PAP Nee Soon Branch; Vice-Chairman, Nee Soon East CCC; Member, National Youth Council; Honorary Secretary, Foo Hai Buddhist and Welfare Association; Member, Advisory Committee, Institute of Technical Education (Yishun); Member, Advisory Committee, Northland Secondary School; Member, National Committee on Smoking Control	Medical Director, Ren Ci Hospital and Medicare Centre; *Vice-President (Corporate Services), Government of Singapore Investment Corporation Special Investment Pte Ltd;* *Human Resource Manager, Government of Singapore Investment Corporation Pte Ltd;* *Psychiatrist and Registrar, Institute of Mental Health and Woodbridge Hospital;* *House Officer, Ministry of Health*

(cont'd overleaf)

Table 4.1 2001 General Election – New PAP Candidates (cont'd)

Name	Age and Ethnicity	Constituency	Educational and Professional Qualifications	Party / Community / Volunteer / Board Experience	Career
Penny Low	Age: 34 Chinese	Pasir Ris-Punggol GRC	Tanjong Katong Girls' Secondary School; National University of Singapore (Bachelor of Arts (Economics and Sociology) (Statistics)); Singapore College of Life Insurance (Diploma in Life Insurance)	Chairperson, Young PAP Changkat Branch; Secretary, Young PAP North-East District; Actively involved in Meet-the-People sessions in Changkat constituency since 1994; Member, Global Voice Editorial Advisory Board, Financial Planning Association (USA); Committee Member, Society of Financial Service Professionals	Founder and Managing Director, Planners-Hub Consultancy; Financial Consultant and Trainer, IPP Capital Planning Pte Ltd; *Programme Researcher / Producer, Current Affairs Division, Singapore Broadcasting Corporation*

Table 4.1 2001 General Election – New PAP Candidates (cont'd)

Name	Age and Ethnicity	Constituency	Educational and Professional Qualifications	Party / Community / Volunteer / Board Experience	Career
Raymond Lim	Age: 42 Chinese	East Coast GRC	Raffles Institution; Colombo Plan Scholarship – University of Adelaide (Bachelor of Economics (Honours)); Rhodes Scholarship – University of Oxford (Bachelor of Arts (Jurisprudence)); University of Cambridge (Master of Laws)	Founding Member and President, The Roundtable; Board Member, Singapore Broadcasting Authority; Council Member, Economic Society of Singapore; Advisory Board Member, Centre for Commercial Law Studies, National University of Singapore (NUS); Member, Panel of Advisers, Juvenile Court	Managing Director, Temasek Holdings Pte Ltd; *Managing Director, DBS Securities Singapore Pte Ltd;* *Group Chief Economist, ABN AMRO Asia Securities (S) Pte Ltd;* *Group Executive Director, Kim Eng Securities Pte Ltd;* *Journalist, Straits Times;* *Lecturer, Faculty of Law, NUS*
Sitoh Yih Pin (not voted in)	Age: 38 Chinese	Potong Pasir SMC	Serangoon Garden Secondary School; Hwa Chong Junior College; National University of Singapore (Bachelor of Accountancy (Honours)); Institute of Chartered Accountants, Australia (Associate Member); Institute of Certified Public Accountants of Singapore (Fellow)	Member, PAP Punggol East Branch; Chairman, Potong Pasir Community Development Council; Adviser to Potong Pasir grassroots organisations; Branch Secretary, PAP Chong Pang branch; Member, Chong Boon CCC; Member, Supervisory Panel, Feedback Unit; Director, Chinese Development Assistance Council; Member, Governing Council, Singapore Institute of Directors	Co-Founder and Chairman, Nexia TS Public Accounting Corporation; Independent director in several public listed companies; *Early career with KPMG as audit manager*

(cont'd overleaf)

Table 4.1 2001 General Election – New PAP Candidates (cont'd)

Name	Age and Ethnicity	Constituency	Educational and Professional Qualifications	Party / Community / Volunteer / Board Experience	Career
Tharman Shanmugaratnam	Age: 44 Indian	Jurong GRC	Anglo-Chinese School; London School of Economics (Bachelor of Science (Economics)); University of Cambridge (Master of Philosophy (Economics)); John F. Kennedy School of Government, Harvard University (Master of Public Administration; received Lucius N. Littauer Fellow award)	Member, Board of Trustees, Singapore Indian Development Association (SINDA); Member, Community Development Fund Committee, Mendaki	Managing Director, Monetary Authority of Singapore; Deputy Managing Director (Financial Supervision), Monetary Authority of Singapore; Senior Deputy Secretary for Policy, Ministry of Education; Deputy Secretary, Ministry of Education; Director, Economics Department, Monetary Authority of Singapore

Table 4.1 2001 General Election – New PAP Candidates (cont'd)

Name	Age and Ethnicity	Constituency	Educational and Professional Qualifications	Party / Community / Volunteer / Board Experience	Career
Vivian Balakrishnan	Age: 40 Indian	Holland-Bukit Panjang GRC	Anglo-Chinese School; National Junior College; President's Scholarship – National University of Singapore (Bachelor of Medicine, Bachelor of Surgery); National University of Singapore (Master of Medicine (Ophthalmology)); Royal College of Surgeons, Edinburgh (Fellow); College of Ophthalmologists (Fellow)	Council Member, Singapore Medical Association; Chairman, Specialist Training Committee (for all ophthalmologist trainees in Singapore); Member, National Volunteer Centre Committee; Member, Programmes Advisory Committee, Singapore Broadcasting Authority; Member, National Library Board; Co-Chairman, Concept Plan Focus Group on Land Use, Urban and Redevelopment Authority; Member of multiple Editorial Boards for journals such as the Singapore Medical Journal, Asian Pacific Journal of Ophthalmology, and the NUH-Continuing Medical Education Journal	Chief Executive Officer, Singapore General Hospital; Associate Professor, Department of Ophthalmology, NUS; Medical Director, Singapore National Eye Centre; Director and Consultant, Department of Ophthalmology, National University Hospital; Consultant and Head of Paediatric Ophthalmology, KK Women's and Children's Hospital; Specialist Senior Registrar, Paediatric Ophthalmology and Strabismus Service, Moorfields Eye Hospital, Great Ormond Street Hospital for Sick Children and Northwick Park Hospital, London

(cont'd overleaf)

Table 4.1 2001 General Election – New PAP Candidates (cont'd)

Name	Age and Ethnicity	Constituency	Educational and Professional Qualifications	Party / Community / Volunteer / Board Experience	Career
Warren Lee	Age: 41 Chinese	Sembawang GRC	Anglo-Chinese Secondary School; National University of Singapore (Bachelor of Medicine, Bachelor of Surgery; Master of Medicine (Paediatrics)); Royal Children's Hospital, Melbourne (Fellow); Royal College of Physicians (Fellow); Singapore Academy of Medicine (Fellow)	Member, PAP Youth Wing in Hong Kah GRC; Member, Sembawang-Hong Kah Community Development Council; Chairman, Sembawang-Hong Kah Diabetes Education and Care Centre; President, Diabetic Society of Singapore; Board Member and Regional Chairman, International Diabetes Federation; Member of several health/medical-related advisory committees; Chairman, Healthcare Feedback Group, Feedback Unit	Consultant Paediatric Endocrinologist, KK Women's and Children's Hospital; Senior Registrar (Paediatric Endocrinology) KK Hospital / KK Women's and Children's Hospital; Senior Registrar, Paediatric Endocrinology, Singapore General Hospital; Registrar, Paediatrics, Singapore General Hospital; Medical Officer (Paediatrics, Neonatology), Singapore General Hospital

Table 4.1 2001 General Election – New PAP Candidates (cont'd)

Name	Age and Ethnicity	Constituency	Educational and Professional Qualifications	Party / Community / Volunteer / Board Experience	Career
Wee Siew Kim	Age: 41 Chinese	Ang Mo Kio GRC	Raffles Institution; Imperial College of Science and Technology, University of London (Bachelor of Science (Aeronautical Engineering (Honours)); Stanford University (Master of Business Administration); City and Guilds Institute (Fellow)		President (Europe), Singapore Technologies Engineering Ltd; *President, Singapore Technologies Aerospace Ltd;* *Earlier career in Singapore Technologies Aerospace Ltd*
Zainudin bin Nordin	Age: 38 Malay	Bishan-Toa Payoh GRC	Tanglin Technical Secondary School; Jurong Junior College; French-Singapore Institute (Diploma in Electrical Engineering and Industrial Electronics Technology); École Supérieure d'Ingénieurs en Électrotechnique et Électronique (ESIEE), Paris (Diplome d'Ingenieur (Electrical and Electronics Engineering); Master of Engineering (Electrical and Electronics)	Vice-Chairman, Young PAP Marsiling Branch; Assistant Branch Secretary, PAP Marsiling Branch; Associate Member, Marsiling Zone 6 Residents' Committee; *Member, Working Group for Education, Malay/Muslim Knowledge-Based Economy Convention 1999*	Deputy Manager of Electronics Design Centre, School of Engineering (Electronics), Nanyang Polytechnic

(cont'd overleaf)

Table 4.1 2001 General Election – New PAP Candidates (cont'd)

Name	Age and Ethnicity	Constituency	Educational and Professional Qualifications	Party / Community / Volunteer / Board Experience	Career
Andy Gan Lai Chiang (stood unsuccessfully in 1991 and 1997)	Age: 53 Chinese	Marine Parade GRC	Victoria School; University of Western Australia (Bachelor of Commerce); Western Australia Institute of Technology (Graduate Diploma in Accounting); Australian Society of Accountants (Certified Public Accountant); Institute of Certified Public Accountants of Singapore (Certified Public Accountant)	Second Adviser to Geylang Serai grassroots organisations; Chairman, PAP Potong Pasir Branch; Chairman, Potong Pasir Community Development Council; Adviser to Potong Pasir grassroots organisations; Vice-Chairman, Potong Pasir CCC; Chairman, Potong Pasir CCMC; President, Sennett Estate Residents' Association; Member, Potong Pasir PAP Community Foundation Education Centre	Managing Director, Hydroculture-Scape Pte Ltd; Director, Energy Market Company Pte Ltd; Managing Director, Island Horti-Tech Holdings Pte Ltd; Group Financial Controller, North Borneo Timbers Bhd; Director, Carr Futures Pte Ltd, Banque Indosuez; Accountant and Director, HCB Futures Pte Ltd; Auditor, Price Waterhouse, Singapore; Employed in an Australian public accounting firm; Accountant, Tsang and Ong Pte Ltd

Table 4.1 2001 General Election – New PAP Candidates (cont'd)

Name	Age and Ethnicity	Constituency	Educational and Professional Qualifications	Party / Community / Volunteer / Board Experience	Career
Heng Chee How (stood unsuccessfully in 1997)	Age: 40 Chinese	Jalan Besar GRC	Raffles Institution; Singapore Police Force Undergraduate Scholarship – Cambridge University (Bachelor of Arts (Honours); Master of Arts); Singapore Police Force Postgraduate Overseas Scholarship – John F. Kennedy School of Government, Harvard University (Master of Public Administration (Mason Fellow) (Lucius Littauer Fellowship Award)); Awarded Eisenhower Fellowship	Second Adviser to Whampoa grassroots organisations; Chairman, Skills Redevelopment Programme Steering Committee; Chairman, Skills Training Committee, Chinese Development Assistance Council; Member, Infocomm Development Authority; Second Adviser to Hougang grassroots organisations in Hougang SMC	Deputy Secretary-General, National Trades Union Congress (NTUC); Executive Secretary, United Workers of Electronic and Electrical Industries; Assistant Secretary-General, NTUC; Chief Executive Officer, NTUC Club; Director, Administration and Research Unit, NTUC; Superintendent, Singapore Police Force – roles included Director of Manpower and Commander of the Geylang Police Division

Table 5.2 2006 General Election – New PAP Candidates

Name	Age and Ethnicity	Constituency	Educational and Professional Qualifications	Party / Community / Volunteer / Board Experience	Career
Alvin Yeo	Age: 44 Chinese	Hong Kah GRC	Anglo-Chinese Secondary School; Anglo-Chinese Junior College; King's College London, University of London (Bachelor of Laws (Honours)); Gray's Inn (Barrister-at-Law); Supreme Court of Singapore (Advocate and Solicitor; Senior Counsel)	Member, Council of the Law Society of Singapore; Member, Appeal Advisory Panel, monetary Authority of Singapore; Member, Regional Panel of Arbitrators, Singapore International Arbitration Centre; Board Member, Civil Service College; Member, Law Reform Committee, Singapore Academy of Law; Member, Legal Working Group, Economic Review Committee; Member, Citizenship Committee of Inquiry	Lawyer and Managing Partner, Wong Partnership; *Partner, Wong Partnership;* *Associate, Shook Lin & Bok*
Baey Yam Keng	Age: 35 Chinese	Tanjong Pagar GRC	Catholic High School; Hwa Chong Junior College; Economic Development Board Scholarship – Imperial College of Science, Technology & Medicine, London (Bachelor of Science (Biotechnology) (Honours)); Economic Development Board Scholarship – University College London (Master of Science (Biochemical Engineering) (Distinction))	Founding President, The ETCeteras Theatre Group	Second Director, Planning, National Arts Council; *Director, Creative Industries Singapore, Ministry of Information, Communications and the Arts;* *Centre Director (London), Economic Development Board* *Earlier career at EDB*

Table 5.2 2006 General Election – New PAP Candidates (cont'd)

Name	Age and Ethnicity	Constituency	Educational and Professional Qualifications	Party / Community / Volunteer / Board Experience	Career
Christopher James de Souza	Age: 30 Other (Eurasian)	Holland-Bukit Timah GRC	St Joseph's Institution; Raffles Junior College; King's College London (Bachelor of Laws (Honours) (Sweet & Maxwell Prize) (Jelf Medal)); Shell and University of Oxford Scholarship – University of Oxford (Bachelor of Civil Law (Distinction)); Supreme Court of Singapore (Advocate and Solicitor)	Councillor, Central Community Development Council; Youth Volunteer, Eurasian Association; Youth Volunteer, Befriender's Programme, Mendaki; Represented Singapore at hockey	Lawyer and Senior Associate, Commercial and Criminal Litigation Department, Lee & Lee; Assistant Registrar, High Court; Magistrate, Subordinate Courts; State Counsel, Attorney-General's Chambers; Deputy Public Prosecutor, Attorney-General's Chambers; Justices' Law Clerk to Chief Justice Yong Pung How and the Court of Appeal
Denise Phua	Age: 46 Chinese	Jalan Besar GRC	Raffles' Girls Secondary School; Hwa Chong Junior College; National University of Singapore (Bachelor of Arts (English/Political Science)); Association of Certified Accountants (Level I Qualification); Singapore Institute of Management (Graduate Diploma in Personnel Management); Golden Gate University (Master of Business Administration)	Member, PAP Jalan Besar Branch; Founding Chairman, Worldwide Collaborations on Austism Needs (WeCAN)	Full-time volunteer: President, Autism Resource Centre; School Supervisor, and Acting Principal, Pathlight School; Regional Managing Director / Consultant, Centre for Effective Leadership (Asia) Pte Ltd; Director (Human Resources), The Wuthelam Group; Product Manager, Asia Pacific Peripherals Marketing Centre, Hewlett-Packard; (earlier roles at Hewlett-Packard) Assistant Personnel Manager, Maritime Holdings

(cont'd overleaf)

Table 5.2 2006 General Election – New PAP Candidates (cont'd)

Name	Age and Ethnicity	Constituency	Educational and Professional Qualifications	Party / Community / Volunteer / Board Experience	Career
Ellen Lee	Age: 48 Chinese	Sembawang GRC	CHIJ Secondary School; National University of Singapore (Bachelor of Laws (Honours)); Supreme Court of Singapore (Advocate and Solicitor)	Chairman, First PAP Policy Forum; Member, Fengshan CCC; Chairman, Fengshan CC Women's Executive Committee; Member, Fengshan CCMC; Vice-President, Centre for Promoting Alternatives to Violence; Member, Management Committee, Ang Mo Kio Family Services Centre; Adviser, Juvenile Court; Legal Adviser to various clans, temples, trade and martial-arts associations and non-government organisations; *Founder, Chinese Reading Club, Kaki Bukit Prison School;* *Founder, Chinese and English Reading Clubs, Changi Women's Prison;* *Active in community work from several years prior*	Lawyer and Consultant, Ramdas & Wong; *Lawyer, Ellen Lee & Co;* *Lawyer, Lim Kiap Khee & Co*

Table 5.2 2006 General Election – New PAP Candidates (cont'd)

Name	Age and Ethnicity	Constituency	Educational and Professional Qualifications	Party / Community / Volunteer / Board Experience	Career
Fatimah binte Abdul Lateef	Age: 40 Malay	Marine Parade GRC	CHIJ Katong Convent School; Temasek Junior College; National University of Singapore (Bachelor of Medicine, Bachelor of Surgery); Royal Infirmary of Edinburgh, Royal College of Surgeons, Edinburgh (Fellow (Accident & Emergency Medicine and Surgery)); Medical College of Virginia, Richmond and College of Medicine, University of Cincinnati (Fellow; Sub-Specialisation in Emergency Cardiovascular and Neurovascular Care and Prehospital Care Medicine)	Member, PAP Youth Wing; Volunteer at PAP Marine Parade Branch Meet-the-People sessions since 1986; Board Member, Mercy Relief; Volunteer, Red Cross Singapore; Medical Adviser, National Pugilistic and Wushu Federation; Medical Adviser, National Trades Union Congress Sports and Adventure Club; Member, Muslim Healthcare Professionals Task Force, Health Promotion Board; Specialist Volunteer, Singapore International Foundation	Physician and Consultant, Department of Emergency Medicine, Singapore General Hospital; *Consultant, Medical College of Virginia and University of Cincinnati College of Medicine (Ministry of Health-Health Manpower Development Plan);* *Consultant, Royal Infirmary of Edinburgh, Royal college of Surgeons, Edinburgh, and Royal Liverpool (Ministry of Health-Health Manpower Development Plan);* *Various postings at hospitals and polyclinics*

(cont'd overleaf)

Table 5.2 2006 General Election – New PAP Candidates (cont'd)

Name	Age and Ethnicity	Constituency	Educational and Professional Qualifications	Party / Community / Volunteer / Board Experience	Career
Grace Fu	Age: 42 Chinese	Jurong GRC	Nanyang Girls' High School; Hwa Chong Junior College; National University of Singapore (Bachelor of Accounting (Honours); Master of Business Administration (Gold Medal)); Institute of Certified Public Accountants of Singapore (Non-Practising Member)	Board Member, Nanyang Girls' High School	Chief Executive Officer, Southeast Asia and Japan, Port of Singapore Authority (PSA) International Ltd; Chief Executive Officer, Singapore Terminals, PSA Corporation Ltd; Executive Vice-President (Finance), PSA Corporation Ltd; Assistant Director (Finance), PSA Corporation Ltd; Held various positions in Business Development, Corporate Planning and Financial Control, Haw Par Group; Auditor, Overseas Union Bank

Table 5.2 2006 General Election – New PAP Candidates (cont'd)

Name	Age and Ethnicity	Constituency	Educational and Professional Qualifications	Party / Community / Volunteer / Board Experience	Career
Hri Kumar Nair	Age: 39 Indian	Bishan-Toa Payoh GRC	First Toa Payoh Secondary School; National Junior College; National University of Singapore (Bachelor of Laws (Honours)); Supreme Court of Singapore (Advocate and Solicitor)	Volunteer, PAP Taman Jurong Branch Meet-the-People Sessions; Member, Residents' Committee; Volunteer, Club Rainbow; Vice-President, Singapore International Federation; Vice-President (Asian Chapter), Australasian Law Teachers Association; Member, Rules of Court Working Party	Lawyer and Director, Drew & Napier LLC; *Equity Partner, Drew & Napier;* *Junior Partner, Drew & Napier;* *Senior Legal Assistant, Drew & Napier;* *Legal Assistant, Drew & Napier*

(cont'd overleaf)

Table 5.2 2006 General Election – New PAP Candidates (cont'd)

Name	Age and Ethnicity	Constituency	Educational and Professional Qualifications	Party / Community / Volunteer / Board Experience	Career
Jessica Tan	Age: 39 Chinese	East Coast GRC	CHIJ St Joseph's Convent; Catholic Junior College; National University of Singapore (Bachelor of Social Science (Honours))	Volunteer, PAP Serangoon Branch Meet-the-People Sessions	General Manager, Enterprise and Partner Group (Asia Pacific Region), Microsoft Operations Pte Ltd; *Director, Networking Services (Asia Pacific Region), IBM Global Services Pte Ltd;* *Director, Integrated Technology (ASEAN / South Asia), IBM Global Services Pte Ltd;* *Sector Sales Executive, Distribution, IBM ASEAN / South Asia;* *Earlier career with IBM in various positions*

Table 5.2 2006 General Election – New PAP Candidates (cont'd)

Name	Age and Ethnicity	Constituency	Educational and Professional Qualifications	Party / Community / Volunteer / Board Experience	Career
Josephine Teo	Age: 38 Chinese	Bishan-Toa Payoh GRC	Dunman High School; Raffles Junior College; National University of Singapore (Bachelor of Arts; Bachelor of Social Science (Honours) (Rachel Meyer Book Prize)); Economic Development Board-Glaxo Scholarship – London School of Economics (Master of Science (Economics))	Trustee, Administration and Research Unit, National Trades Union Congress (NTUC); *Involved in fundraising/relief efforts for SARS Relief Fund and for the 2004 Indian Ocean Tsunami*	Director of Human Resources, Administration and Research Unit, NTUC; *Director of Human Resources, Agency for Science, Technology and Research (A*STAR);* *Head of Human Resources, Economic Development Board (EDB);* *Manager, Marketing Resources (on secondment from EDB), China-Singapore Suzhou Industrial Park (CS-SIP) Pte Ltd;* *Earlier career with EDB*

(cont'd overleaf)

Table 5.2 2006 General Election – New PAP Candidates (cont'd)

Name	Age and Ethnicity	Constituency	Educational and Professional Qualifications	Party / Community / Volunteer / Board Experience	Career
Lam Pin Min	Age: 36 Chinese	Ang Mo Kio GRC	Anglo-Chinese School; National Junior College; National University of Singapore (Bachelor of Medicine, Bachelor of Surgery; Master of Medicine (Ophthalmology)); Royal College of Physicians, London (Diploma in Aviation Medicine); Royal College of Surgeons, Edinburgh (Fellow)	Councillor, Central Singapore Community Development Council (CDC); Member, Radin Mas CCC; Chairman, Disability Sub-Committee, Social Service Development Committee; Founding Member and Director, Compass Welfare Foundation; Part of evacuation and rescue in Singapore Airlines crash in Taipei in 2000 and SilkAir crash in Palembang in 1997; Medical Commander, Singapore Medical Contingent, United Nations Military Hospital, United Nations Transitional Administration in East Timor	Associate Consultant, Department of Ophthalmology, KK Women's and Children's Hospital; Registrar, Singapore National Eye Centre, SingHealth Pte Ltd; Registrar, Tan Tock Seng Hospital, National Healthcare Group; Aviation Medicine Specialist and Flight Surgeon (Regular Medical Officer), Republic of Singapore Air Force; Medical Officer / House Officer, Ministry of Health

Table 5.2 2006 General Election – New PAP Candidates (cont'd)

Name	Age and Ethnicity	Constituency	Educational and Professional Qualifications	Party / Community / Volunteer / Board Experience	Career
Lee Bee Wah	Age: 45 Chinese	Ang Mo Kio GRC	Sekolah Dato' Dol Said (Malaysia); Notre Dame Convent (Malaysia); Gajah Berang (Malaysia); National University of Singapore; Nanyang Technological University (Bachelor of Engineering (Civil Engineering)); University of Liverpool (Master of Science (Engineering))	Volunteer, PAP Kebun Baru Branch Meet-the-People Sessions; Assistant Honorary Secretary, Kebun Baru CCC; Chairman, Kebun Baru Inter-Racial Confidence Circle; Board Member, Professional Engineers Board; President, Nanyang Technological University School of Civil and Environmental Engineering Alumni Association	Principal Partner, LBW Consultants / LBW Consultants LLP; Assistant Project Manager, Wing Tai Property Management Pte Ltd; Senior Engineer, ST Construction Pte Ltd

(cont'd overleaf)

Table 5.2 2006 General Election – New PAP Candidates (cont'd)

Name	Age and Ethnicity	Constituency	Educational and Professional Qualifications	Party / Community / Volunteer / Board Experience	Career
Lee Yi Shyan	Age: 44 Chinese	East Coast GRC	Maris Stella High School; Hwa Chong Junior College; National University of Singapore (Bachelor of Engineering (Chemical Engineering)); Harvard Business School, Harvard University (Graduate of the Executive Management Programme in Business Administration and Management); Tsinghua University (Graduate of the Management Programme)		Chief Executive Officer, International Enterprise Singapore (formerly known as Trade Development Board); Deputy Chief Executive Officer, SPRING Singapore (formerly known as Productivity and Standards Board); Held senior positions in the fields of Human Resources, Services Development, China Operations and Industry Development (Chemical) in the Economic Development Board; Systems Engineer, Systems and Organisation, Ministry of Defence

Table 5.2 2006 General Election – New PAP Candidates (cont'd)

Name	Age and Ethnicity	Constituency	Educational and Professional Qualifications	Party / Community / Volunteer / Board Experience	Career
Liang Eng Hwa	Age: 42 Chinese	Holland-Bukit Timah GRC	Anderson Secondary School; Singapore Polytechnic (Diploma in Civil Engineering); National Australia Bank Scholarship – University of Melbourne (Bachelor of Commerce (Honours) (Price Waterhouse Book Prize))	Member, Executive Committee, Young PAP; Secretary, Buona Vista CCC; Member, Feedback Supervisory Panel, Feedback Unit; Secretary, Buona Vista CCMC; Vice-Chairman, Residents' Committee; Member, Beyond Condo Sub-Committee, Remaking Singapore Committee	Managing Director, Global Financial Markets, DBS Bank Ltd; *Earlier career with DBS Bank*

(cont'd overleaf)

Table 5.2 2006 General Election – New PAP Candidates (cont'd)

Name	Age and Ethnicity	Constituency	Educational and Professional Qualifications	Party / Community / Volunteer / Board Experience	Career
Lim Biow Chuan	Age: 43 Chinese	Marine Parade GRC	Victoria School; Temasek Junior College; National University of Singapore (Bachelor of Laws (Honours)); Supreme Court of Singapore (Advocate and Solicitor)	Branch Secretary and Member, PAP Jalan Besar Branch; Chairman, Young PAP City North District; Chairman, Young PAP Jalan Besar Branch; Member, Jalan Besar Welfare Fund Committee; Member, Finance and Legal Committee, Jalan Besar Town Council; Secretary, Jalan Besar CCC; Chairman, Jalan Besar SARS Task Force Workgroup; Chairman, Jalan Besar ComCare Workgroup; Member, Central Singapore Community Development Council; Secretary, Central Singapore Joint Social Service Centre	Lawyer and Sole Proprietor, Lim BC & Co; *Founding Partner, Tan Lim & Wong;* *Legal Assistant, Khattar Wong & Partners;* *Legal Assistant, Ong Tan & Nair*

Table 5.2 2006 General Election – New PAP Candidates (cont'd)

Name	Age and Ethnicity	Constituency	Educational and Professional Qualifications	Party / Community / Volunteer / Board Experience	Career
Lim Wee Kiak	Age: 37 Chinese	Sembawang GRC	Chinese High School; Hwa Chong Junior College; National University of Singapore (Bachelor of Medicine, Bachelor of Surgery; Master of Medicine (Ophthalmology)); Royal College of Surgeons, Edinburgh (Fellow (Ophthalmology)); Royal College of Ophthalmologists (Fellow); National Eye Institute, National Institute of Health, United States (Clinical and Research Fellow); Singapore Academy of Medicine (Fellow)	Vice-Chairman, Marsiling CCC; Chairman, Fuchun CCMC; Chairman, Marsiling Residents' Committee Zone 8; Chairman, Young Executive Committee, North West Community Development Council; Chairman, Advisory Committee, Marsiling Secondary School; Member, National Advisory Council Community and Parents in Support of Schools (COMPASS), Ministry of Education *Team Leader, Singapore Medical Contingent, United Nations Military Hospital, United Nations Transitional Administration in East Timor*	Consultant Eye Surgeon, Singapore National Eye Centre (SNEC); Visiting Consultant, Tan Tock Seng Hospital; *Consultant, SNEC;* *Registrar, Singapore Health Services;* *Medical Officer, Ministry of Health*

(cont'd overleaf)

Table 5.2 2006 General Election – New PAP Candidates (cont'd)

Name	Age and Ethnicity	Constituency	Educational and Professional Qualifications	Party / Community / Volunteer / Board Experience	Career
Lui Tuck Yew	Age: 44 Chinese	Tanjong Pagar GRC	Anglo-Chinese Secondary School; Anglo-Chinese Junior College; Singapore Armed Forces Overseas Scholarship – University of Cambridge (Bachelor of Arts (Natural Sciences Tripos (Chemistry)); Fletcher School of Law and Diplomacy, Tufts University (Master of Arts (International Relations); Harvard Business School, Harvard University (Graduate of the Advanced Management Programme)	Volunteer, Institute of Mental Health Bishan Home	Chief Executive Officer, Housing and Development Board; *Other positions in the Administrative Sevice:* *Chief Executive Officer, Maritime and Port Authority of Singapore;* *Deputy Secretary (Land), Ministry of Transport;* *Earlier career in Republic of Singapore Navy; rose to position of Chief of Navy (rank of Rear-Admiral)*
Masagos Zulkifli bin Masagos Mohamad	Age: 42 Malay	Tampines GRC	Bukit Panjang Government High School; National Junior College; Nanyang Technological University (Bachelor of Engineering (Electrical Engineering) (Electronic Engineering) (Honours)); National University of Singapore (Master of Science (Electrical Engineering)); SingTel Postgraduate Scholarship – University of Southern California (Master of Business Administration)	Founder, Mercy Relief; President, Singapore Adult Religious Students' Association (Perdaus); Link Board Member, Ministry of Community Development, Youth and Sports; Board Member, Temasek Polytechnic	Vice-President, SingTel Global Offices, Singapore Telecommunications Ltd; *Earlier career with SingTel*

Table 5.2 2006 General Election – New PAP Candidates (cont'd)

Name	Age and Ethnicity	Constituency	Educational and Professional Qualifications	Party / Community / Volunteer / Board Experience	Career
Michael Anthony Palmer	Age: 37 Other (Eurasian)	Pasir Ris-Punggol GRC	St Andrew's Secondary School; St Andrew's Junior College; University College London (Bachelor of Laws (Honours)); Supreme Court of England and Wales (Solicitor); Supreme Court of Singapore (Advocate and Solicitor)	Volunteer, PAP Bukit Panjang Meet-the-People Sessions since 2005; Honorary Legal Adviser, Eurasian Association; Honorary Legal Adviser, Academy of Principals Honorary Legal Adviser, St Andrew's Schools; Council Member, Singapore Anti-Tuberculosis Association; Chairman, Fund-Raising Committee, Society for the Physically Disabled	Lawyer and Equity Partner, Harry Elias Partnership; Legal Associate, Harry Elias Partnership

(cont'd overleaf)

Table 5.2 2006 General Election – New PAP Candidates (cont'd)

Name	Age and Ethnicity	Constituency	Educational and Professional Qualifications	Party / Community / Volunteer / Board Experience	Career
Muhammad Faishal bin Ibrahim	Age: 38 Malay	Marine Parade GRC	Bedok View Secondary School; Nanyang Junior College; National University of Singapore Scholarship – National University of Singapore (Bachelor of Science (Real Estate Management) (Honours); Master of Science (Real Estate) (Redas Gold Medal)); NUS-Overseas Graduate Scholarship – University of Manchester Institute of Science and Technology (PhD in Management Science)	Chairman, Young PAP North East District; Chairman, PAP Punggol North Branch; Auditor, Punggol North CCC; Council Member, Islamic Religious Council of Singapore (MUIS); Adviser, Young Muslims Secretariat, MUIS; Vice-Chairman, Management Board, Darussalam Mosque; Member, Resource Panels, Government Parliamentary Committees for National Development and the Environment and for Community Development and Sports; Member, Board of Governors, Singapore Polytechnic; Member, Advisory Board and Discharge Committee, Ministry of Community Development, Youth and Sports	Assistant Professor and Programme Director, National University of Singapore (NUS); Senior Tutor, NUS; Valuer, Inland Revenue Authority of Singapore

Table 5.2 2006 General Election – New PAP Candidates (cont'd)

Name	Age and Ethnicity	Constituency	Educational and Professional Qualifications	Party / Community / Volunteer / Board Experience	Career
Seah Kian Peng	Age: 44 Chinese	Marine Parade GRC	Raffles Institution; Colombo Plan Scholarship – University of New South Wales (Bachelor of Building (Honours)); Harvard Business School, Harvard University (Graduate of the Advanced Management Programme); Chartered Institute of Marketing (Fellow)	Member, Jurong Central CCC; Member, Advisory Council on Community Relations in Defence (ACCORD); Member, Family Matters! Singapore; Board Member, Centre for Fathering Ltd; Member, Project Advisory Committee, ComCare Enterprises Fund; Patron, Loving Heart Multi-Service Centre, Jurong Central; Vice-President, Singapore Compact for Corporate Social Responsibility	Deputy Chief Executive Officer and Chief Operating Officer, National Trades Union Congress (NTUC) Fairprice Co-operative Ltd; *Chief Executive Officer, NTUC Media Co-operative Ltd;* *Chief Executive Officer, NTUC Healthcare Co-operative Ltd;* *Senior Manager, Sum Cheong Corporation Pte Ltd;* *Head, Planning and Research, NTUC;* *Special Assistant to NTUC Secretary-General Ong Teng Cheong;* *Head, Budget Department, Ministry of Defence;* *Senior Contracts Executive, Indeco Engineers Pte Ltd*

(cont'd overleaf)

Table 5.2 2006 General Election – New PAP Candidates (cont'd)

Name	Age and Ethnicity	Constituency	Educational and Professional Qualifications	Party / Community / Volunteer / Board Experience	Career
Sam Tan Chin Siong	Age: 47 Chinese	Tanjong Pagar GRC	Tuan Mong High School; Hwa Chong Junior College; National University of Singapore (Bachelor of Arts (Honours))	Secretary, Executive Committee, PAP Bishan East Branch; Chairman, Bishan North PAP Community Foundation Branch; Secretary, Bishan East CCC; Member, Preventive Drug Education Co-ordinating Committee, Ministry of Home Affairs; Member, Joint Consultative Committee on Education, Ministry of Education; Member, Central Singapore Community Development Council (CDC) Harmony Circle, Ministry of Community Development, Youth and Sports; Member, Advisory Committee, Lifelong Learning Endowment Fund; Member, Social Services Committee, Singapore Hokkien Huay Kuan	Executive Director, Chinese Development Assistance Council (CDAC); *Deputy Executive Director, CDAC;* *Assistant Director (Youth), People's Association;* *Head, Social Development Section, People's Association;* *Regional Officer, People's Association;* *Organising Secretary, People's Association*

Table 5.2 2006 General Election – New PAP Candidates (cont'd)

Name	Age and Ethnicity	Constituency	Educational and Professional Qualifications	Party / Community / Volunteer / Board Experience	Career
Teo Ser Luck	Age: 37 Chinese	Pasir Ris-Punggol GRC	Victoria School; Nanyang Junior College; Nanyang Technological University (Bachelor of Accountancy); Temasek Polytechnic (Post-Graduate Diploma)	Member, PAP Policy Forum; Volunteer, PAP Chong Pang Branch and PAP Punggol South Branch Meet-the-People Sessions; Member, Executive Committee, Chong Pang PAP Community Foundation Branch; Member, Resource Panel, Government Parliamentary Committee for Transport; Member, Logistics Working Group, Economic Review Committee; Board Member, National Trades Union Congress Healthcare Co-operative Ltd; Founder, Triathlon Family Club	General Manager / Country Manager, DHL Express (Singapore) Pte Ltd; *Regional Vice-President / Managing Director, Menlo Worldwide Logistics Pte Ltd;* *Earlier employment at Nike Singapore and Coopers & Lybrand*

(cont'd overleaf)

Table 5.2 2006 General Election – New PAP Candidates (cont'd)

Name	Age and Ethnicity	Constituency	Educational and Professional Qualifications	Party / Community / Volunteer / Board Experience	Career
Zaqy bin Mohamad	Age: 31 Malay	Hong Kah GRC	Raffles Institution; Raffles Junior College; B.Eng (Electrical & Electronic) (Nanyang Technological University / ESIEE - Paris); M.Sc (Financial Engineering) / Certificate in Computational Finance (Nanyang Technological University / Carnegie Mellon University)	Volunteer, PAP Kampong Ubi Branch Meet-the-People Sessions; Member, Kampong Ubi CCC; Member, Social Development Feedback Group, Feedback Unit	Director, Solutions (South-East Asia) Avanade Pte Ltd *Business Consultant, IBM Business Consulting Services / PriceWaterhouseCoopers Consulting;* *Senior Consultant, Arthur Andersen*

Table 5.2 2006 General Election – New PAP Candidates (cont'd)

Name	Age and Ethnicity	Constituency	Educational and Professional Qualifications	Party / Community / Volunteer / Board Experience	Career
Eric Low (not voted in) (stood unsuccessfully in 2001)	Age: 57 Chinese	Hougang SMC	Anglo-Chinese School; Australian Insurance Institute (Diploma in General Insurance)	Chairman, PAP Hougang Branch; Adviser to Hougang grassroots organisations; Chairman, Hougang Community Development Council; Chief Adviser, Students Care Service; Council Member, Singapore Red Cross Society; Vice-Chairman, National Crime Prevention Council; Party member since 1985 – served in the PAP Telok Blangah and Clementi Branches; Member, Board of Visitors to SAF Detention Barracks; Honorary General Secretary, National Council of Social Service	General Manager, CISCO Insurance Division, CISCO Security Pte Ltd; Executive Director, Sim Lian Group Ltd; Chief Executive Officer, Marina Country Club Pte Ltd; Business Development Director, Overseas Assurance Corporation Ltd; Longstandng career in the insurance industry

(cont'd overleaf)

Table 5.2 2006 General Election – New PAP Candidates (cont'd)

Name	Age and Ethnicity	Constituency	Educational and Professional Qualifications	Party / Community / Volunteer / Board Experience	Career
Sitoh Yih Pin (not voted in) (stood unsuccessfully in 2001)	Age: 42 Chinese	Potong Pasir SMC	Serangoon Garden Secondary School; Hwa Chong Junior College; National University of Singapore (Bachelor of Accountancy (Honours)); Institute of Chartered Accountants, Australia (Associate Member); Institute of Certified Public Accountants of Singapore (Fellow)	Member, PAP Punggol East Branch; Member, South-East Community Development Council; Chairman, Potong Pasir Community Development Council; Adviser to Potong Pasir grassroots organisations; Branch Secretary, PAP Chong Boon Branch; Member, Chong Boon CCC; Member, Supervisory Panel, Feedback Unit; Member, Resource Panel, Government Parliamentary Committee for Manpower; Director, Chinese Development Assistance Council; Member, Governing Council, Singapore Institute of Directors; Independent director of several publicly-listed companies	Co-Founder and Chairman, Nexia TS Public Accounting Corporation; Earlier career with KPMG as audit manager

Table 6.2 2011 General Election – New PAP Candidates

Name	Age and Ethnicity	Constituency	Educational and Professional Qualifications	Party / Community / Volunteer / Board Experience	Career
Alex Yam	Age: 30 Chinese	Chua Chu Kang GRC	Dunman High School; Victoria Junior College; University of Kent (Bachelor of Arts (Politics and International Relations) (Honours))	Secretary, Young PAP General Branch; Member, Executive Committee, Young PAP; Member, Council Committee, PAP Community Foundation; Vice Chairman, Standing Committee, Northwest Community Development Council (CDC); Member, Yew Tee CCC; Member, Yew Tee CCMC; Board Member, Chinese Development Assistance Council Secretary, Buona Vista CCC; Chairman, Buona Vista CC Youth Wing; Honorary Secretary, HEARTS International	Head, Strategies and Planning / Head, Youth Lab; Consultant, Singapore Industrial and Services Employees' Union; Administrative Officer, National University of Singapore

(cont'd overleaf)

Table 6.2 2011 General Election – New PAP Candidates (cont'd)

Name	Age and Ethnicity	Constituency	Educational and Professional Qualifications	Party / Community / Volunteer / Board Experience	Career
Ang Hin Kee	Age: 46 Chinese	Ang Mo Kio GRC	Bartley Secondary School; Jurong Junior College; National University of Singapore (Bachelor of Arts (Honours))	Chairman, PAP Cheng San-Seletar Branch; Chairman, PAP Community Foundation; Vice-Chairman, Cheng San-Seletar CCC; Volunteer, Ang Mo Kio GRC Meet-the-People Sessions; Member, Chinese Development Assistance Council; Board Member, National Environment Agency; Board Member, Employment and Employability Institute, National Trades Union Congress (NTUC)	Chief Executive Officer, Employment and Employability Institute, NTUC; Chief Executive Officer, Singapore Badminton Association; Director, Singapore Sports Council; Business Development Manager, Worldmine Pte Ltd; Manager, Access Management Group, c/o NCS Pte Ltd; Manager, Singapore Tourism Board; Project and Licensing Officer, Police Headquarters, Singapore Police Force
Ang Wei Neng	Age: 44 Chinese	Jurong GRC	The Chinese High School; Hwa Chong Junior College; Public Service Commission Scholarship – National University of Singapore (Bachelor of Arts; Bachelor of Social Sciences (Honours)); Nanyang Technological University (Master of Business Administration)	Assistant Secretary, Teck Ghee CCC; Active in Teck Ghee grassroots organisations and the organisation of constituency functions; Active in volunteer work in his church	Vice-President and Head of West District, Singapore Bus Services Transit Ltd; Manager, Mcare Lab Pte Ltd; Manager, Hiap Moh Corp Ltd; Manager, BexCom Pte Ltd; Profit Centre Manager, American International Group; Head of Operations and Training, Ang Mo Kio Police Division Headquarters, Singapore Police Force

Table 6.2 2011 General Election – New PAP Candidates (cont'd)

Name	Age and Ethnicity	Constituency	Educational and Professional Qualifications	Party / Community / Volunteer / Board Experience	Career
Chan Chun Sing	Age: 42 Chinese	Tanjong Pagar GRC	Raffles Institution; Raffles Junior College; Singapore Armed Forces Overseas Scholarship and President's Scholarship – University of Cambridge (Bachelor of Arts (Economics) (Honours)); Lee Kuan Yew Scholarship – MIT Sloan School of Management, Massachusetts Institute of Technology (Master of Business Administration (Sloan Fellow))	*Board Member, Civil Service College;* *Board Member, International Enterprise Singapore;* *Board Member, Totalisator Board;* *Board Member, Defence Science Organisation National Laboratories;* *Board Member, Defence Science and Technology Agency;* *Served on boards of several government-linked companies, such as Singapore Technology (ST) Kinetics Ltd, ST Electronics Ltd and Singapore Ordnance Development Engineering Pte Ltd*	Chief of Army, Singapore Armed Forces (rank of Major-General); *Previous roles in SAF included:* *Chief of Staff – Joint Staff, SAF;* *Chief Infantry Officer / Commander, 9th Division;* *Head, Joint Plans and Transformation Department*

(cont'd overleaf)

Table 6.2 2011 General Election – New PAP Candidates (cont'd)

Name	Age and Ethnicity	Constituency	Educational and Professional Qualifications	Party / Community / Volunteer / Board Experience	Career
Chia Shi-Lu	Age: 39 Chinese	Tanjong Pagar GRC	Anglo-Chinese Secondary School; National Junior College; Local Merit Scholarship and President's Scholarship – National University of Singapore (Bachelor of Medicine, Bachelor of Surgery (Brunel Hawes Medal) (Lim Boon Keng Medal); Royal College of Surgeons, Edinburgh (Fellow (Surgery); Fellow (Orthopaedics)); Lee Kuan Yew Scholarship – Imperial College London (PhD in Cartilage Biology; Diploma, Arthritis and Cartilage Biology)	Active volunteer in grassroots work in Aljunied GRC and Hougang SMC under MP Yeo Guat Kwang	Medical Consultant, Department of Orthopaedic Surgery, Singapore General Hospital; Visiting Lecturer, School of Nursing, Nanyang Polytechnic; Adjunct Assistant Professor, Duke-NUS Graduate Medical School, National University of Singapore (NUS); Lecturer, Yong Loo-Lin School of Medicine, NUS; *Registrar, Singapore General Hospital;* *House Officer / Medical Officer, Ministry of Health*

Table 6.2 2011 General Election – New PAP Candidates (cont'd)

Name	Age and Ethnicity	Constituency	Educational and Professional Qualifications	Party / Community / Volunteer / Board Experience	Career
David Ong	Age: 50 Chinese	Jurong GRC	Gan Eng Seng School; Tanjong Katong Secondary Technical School; University of Oregon (Bachelor of Science (Business Administration))	Chairman, Kreta Ayer-Kim Seng CCC; Active in grassroots works in Kreta Ayer-Kim Seng constituency since 1999; Chairman, Active Ageing Council, People's Association; Member, Advisory Committee, Institute of Technical Education College Central; District Councillor, Central Singapore Community Development Council (CDC); Member, Supervisory Panel, Reaching Everyone for Active Citizenry @ Home (REACH); Volunteer, Metropolitan Young Men's Christian Association (YMCA)	Managing Director, RedDot Publishing Inc. Pte Ltd; *Previously employed at:* *Publicis Dialog / Publicis Groupe;* *Planet Marketing Inc. Pte Ltd;* *Reed Elsevier;* *Visa International (Regional Marketing Director);* *American Express Inc;* *CL Computers Pte Ltd*

(cont'd overleaf)

Table 6.2 2011 General Election – New PAP Candidates (cont'd)

Name	Age and Ethnicity	Constituency	Educational and Professional Qualifications	Party / Community / Volunteer / Board Experience	Career
Desmond Choo (not voted in)	Age: 33 Chinese	Hougang SMC	Catholic High School; National Junior College; Singapore Police Force Overseas Merit Scholarship – University of Chicago (Bachelor of Arts (Economics); Master of Arts (Social Sciences))	Second Adviser to Hougang grassroots organisations; *Prior involvement in grassroots activities in Marsiling and Tampines East constituencies*	Deputy Director, Youth Development Unit, National Trades Union Congress; Executive Secretary, Union of Security Employees; Senior Industrial Relations Officer, Singapore Port Workers Union; *Deputy Commander, Clementi Police Division, Singapore Police Force;* *Deputy Director, Foreign Workforce Policy Department, Ministry of Manpower;* *Head, Special Investigation Section, Criminal Investigation Department, Singapore Police Force;* *(Previous roles in SPF)*

Table 6.2 2011 General Election – New PAP Candidates (cont'd)

Name	Age and Ethnicity	Constituency	Educational and Professional Qualifications	Party / Community / Volunteer / Board Experience	Career
Desmond Lee	Age: 35 Chinese	Jurong GRC	Raffles Institution; Raffles Junior College; National University of Singapore (Bachelor of Laws (Honours); University of Oxford (Bachelor of Civil Law); Supreme Court of Singapore (Advocate and Solicitor)	Member, Jurong Spring CCC; Member, Jurong Spring CCMC; Member, Jurong Spring Active Ageing Committee; Lay Member, National Transplant Ethics Panel	Associate Director, Legal and Regulations Department, Temasek Holdings (Pte) Ltd; Deputy Director, Legal Policy Division, Ministry of Law; Deputy Director, Legal Branch, Ministry of Health; Deputy Public Prosecutor and State Counsel, Criminal Justice Division of the Attorney General's Chambers; Justices' Law Clerk to Chief Justice Yong Pung How and the Court of Appeal
Edwin Tong	Age: 42 Chinese	Moulmein-Kallang GRC	St Joseph's Institution; Raffles Junior College; National University of Singapore (Bachelor of Laws (Honours)); Supreme Court of Singapore (Advocate and Solicitor)	Member, Panel of Lawyers, Legal Aid Bureau; Honorary Legal Adviser, Singapore Medical Association; Honorary Legal Adviser, College of Family Physicians; Honorary Legal Adviser, Singapore Table Tennis Association; Member of various committees under the Ministries of Home Affairs and Law; Active in grassroots work in Jalan Besar, Jurong and Marsiling	Lawyer and Partner, Allen & Gledhill LLP; Associate, Allen & Gledhill LLP

(cont'd overleaf)

Table 6.2 2011 General Election – New PAP Candidates (cont'd)

Name	Age and Ethnicity	Constituency	Educational and Professional Qualifications	Party / Community / Volunteer / Board Experience	Career
Foo Mee Har	Age: 45 Chinese	West Coast GRC	Ave Maria Convent School (Malaysia); Loreto Normanhurst (Sydney); University of New South Wales (Bachelor of Science (Psychology) (Honours))	Assistant Secretary, Executive Committee, PAP Women's Wing; Active in various community events and Meet-the-People Sessions in the Cashew Division, Holland-Bukit Timah GRC and PAP Zhenghua Branch; *Actively involved in a wide range of corporate community programs, including advocacy, outreach and fund-raising for various causes*	Global Head, Premium Banking, Standard Chartered Bank; *President and Chief Executive Officer, Thailand Standard Chartered Bank, (Thai) pcl, Thailand;* *Country Head, Consumer Banking, Standard Chartered Bank, China;* *General Manager, Branches, Priority and Offshore Banking, Standard Chartered Bank, Singapore;* *Head, Human Resources and Service Quality, Jardine Transport Group, Singapore;* *Management Consultant, Coopers & Lybrand Management Consultants, Singapore;* *Management Consultant, PA Consulting, Singapore*

Table 6.2 2011 General Election – New PAP Candidates (cont'd)

Name	Age and Ethnicity	Constituency	Educational and Professional Qualifications	Party / Community / Volunteer / Board Experience	Career
Gan Thiam Poh	Age: 48 Chinese	Pasir Ris-Punggol GRC	Hwi Yoh Secondary School; Outram Secondary School; The London Chamber of Commerce and Industry (Higher Stage Group Diploma in Accounting, Costing and Business Statistics); National University of Singapore (Bachelor of Science (Economics, Mathematics and Computer Programming and Applications)); Temasek Polytechnic (Certificate in English / Chinese Translation and Interpretation)	Vice-Chairman, Potong Pasir CCC; Vice-Chairman, Potong Pasir CCMC; *Branch Secretary, PAP Potong Pasir Branch*	Senior Vice-President, Institutional Banking Group, DBS Bank Ltd; *Vice-President, United Overseas Bank Ltd;* *Senior Manager, Maybank Singapore*

(cont'd overleaf)

Table 6.2 2011 General Election – New PAP Candidates (cont'd)

Name	Age and Ethnicity	Constituency	Educational and Professional Qualifications	Party / Community / Volunteer / Board Experience	Career
Heng Swee Keat	Age: 50 Chinese	Tampines GRC	Raffles Institution; Singapore Police Force Overseas Scholarship – University of Cambridge (Bachelor of Arts (Economics) (Honours); Master of Arts (Economics)); John F. Kennedy School of Government, Harvard University (Master of Public Administration (Mason Fellow))		Managing Director, Monetary Authority of Singapore; Permanent Secretary, Ministry of Trade and Industry; Previous roles in Administrative Service included: Chief Executive Officer, Trade Development Board; Principal Private Secretary to Senior Minister Lee Kuan Yew Director, Higher Education, Ministry of Education; Assistant Commissioner, Commander, "J" Division, Singapore Police Force; (Earlier roles in SPF)

Table 6.2 2011 General Election – New PAP Candidates (cont'd)

Name	Age and Ethnicity	Constituency	Educational and Professional Qualifications	Party / Community / Volunteer / Board Experience	Career
Intan Azura binte Mokhtar	Age: 35 Malay	Ang Mo Kio GRC	Raffles' Girls Secondary School; Raffles Junior College; National University of Singapore (Bachelor of Science (Physics)); National Institute of Education, Nanyang Technological University (Post-Graduate Diploma in Education); Nanyang Technological University (Master of Science; PhD in Information Studies); Lee Kuan Yew School of Public Policy, National University of Singapore (Master of Public Administration)	Chairman, Jalan Kayu PAP Community Foundation Branch; Vice-Chairman, Jalan Kayu CCC; Volunteer, Jalan Kayu Meet-the-People Sessions; *Council Member, Islamic Religious Council of Singapore (MUIS);* *Adviser, Research Committee, The Singapore Children's Society;* *Board Member, Singapore Muslim Women's Association (PPIS);* *Member, Scholarships Interview Panel, Mendaki;* *Member, Empowerment Programme for Girls, Mendaki*	Assistant Professor, National Institute of Education, Nanyang Technological University (NTU); Assistant Professor, Abu Dhabi University, United Arab Emirates; Lecturer, Singapore Polytechnic; Part-time Lecturer, NTU; Teaching Assistant, NTU; General Education Officer, Ministry of Education

(cont'd overleaf)

Table 6.2 2011 General Election – New PAP Candidates (cont'd)

Name	Age and Ethnicity	Constituency	Educational and Professional Qualifications	Party / Community / Volunteer / Board Experience	Career
Janil Puthucheary	Age: 39 Indian	Pasir Ris-Punggol GRC	Oundle School (United Kingdom); Queen's University Belfast (Bachelor of Medicine, Bachelor of Surgery, Bachelor of Obstetrics); Royal College of Physicians, London (Member); Specialist Accreditation Board, Singapore (Paediatrician)	Active in Meet-the-People Sessions and other grassroots activities in Radin Mas, Bedok and Pasir Ris-Punggol GRC; Treasurer, Society of Intensive Care Medicine, Singapore	Senior Consultant, Children's Intensive Care Unit, KK Women's and Children's Hospital; Medical Director for Faculty Development and Assistant Professor, Duke-National University of Singapore Graduate Medical School, National University of Singapore; Director, Simulation Centre, KK Women's and Children's Hospital; Director, Children's Hospital Transport Service, KK Women's and Children's Hospital; Associate Consultant, Children's Intensive Care Unit, KK Women's and Children's Hospital; Registrar, KK Women's and Children's Hospital; (Previous roles in hospitals in Australia and the UK)

Table 6.2 2011 General Election – New PAP Candidates (cont'd)

Name	Age and Ethnicity	Constituency	Educational and Professional Qualifications	Party / Community / Volunteer / Board Experience	Career
Lawrence Wong	Age: 39 Chinese	West Coast GRC	Tanjong Katong Secondary School; Victoria Junior College; University of Wisconsin-Madison (Bachelor of Science (Economics)); University of Michigan-Ann Arbor (Master of Arts (Economics)); John F. Kennedy School of Government, Harvard University (Master of Public Administration (Mason Fellow))	Active in youth work in his church; Co-Founder, PromiseWorks (youth mentoring / youth-related work)	Chief Executive, Energy Market Authority; *Previous roles in Administrative service included:* *Principal Private Secretary to Prime Minister Lee Hsien Loong;* *Director (Healthcare Finance), Ministry of Health;* *Deputy Director (Budget) and Head of Economic Programmes, Ministry of Finance;* *(Also positions in Ministries of Finance and Trade and Industry)*
Low Yen Ling	Age: 37 Chinese	Chua Chu Kang GRC	Dunman High School; Temasek Junior College; Nanyang Technological University (Bachelor of Business Studies (Financial Analysis) (Honours))	Volunteer, Hong Kah GRC Meet-the-People Sessions	Director (Professional Services), Economic Development Board; *Business Development Manager, AutoHub Pte Ltd;* *Handled commercial lending accounts in Keppel TatLee Bank and United Overseas Bank*
Ong Teng Koon	Age: 34 Chinese	Sembawang GRC	Raffles Institution; Raffles Junior College; London School of Economics (Bachelor of Science (Economics) (Honours)); Princeton University (Master in Finance)	Grassroots work in Marsiling and Chong Pang; Grassroots work in Chong Pang Constituency; Volunteer, Tampines Home for the Intellectually Disabled	Commodities Trader, Morgan Stanley; *Commodities Trader, Goldman Sachs*

(cont'd overleaf)

Table 6.2 2011 General Election – New PAP Candidates (cont'd)

Name	Age and Ethnicity	Constituency	Educational and Professional Qualifications	Party / Community / Volunteer / Board Experience	Career
Ong Ye Kung (not voted in)	Age: 42 Chinese	Aljunied GRC	Maris Stella High School; Raffles Junior College; Public Service Commission Scholarship – London School of Economics (Bachelor of Science (Economics)); International Institute for Management Development, Switzerland (Master of Business Administration)	Chairman, Employment and Employability Institute, NTUC	Assistant Secretary-General, National Trades Union Congress (NTUC); Executive Secretary, National Transport Workers' Union; Executive Secretary, Singapore Manual Mercantile Workers' Union; *Previous roles in the Administrative Service included:* *Chief Executive Officer, Workforce Development Agency;* *Principal Private Secretary to Deputy Prime Minister, and then later, Prime Minister Lee Hsien Loong;* *Director of Trade and Deputy Chief Negotiator of the US-Singapore Free Trade Agreement, Ministry of Trade and Industry*

Table 6.2 2011 General Election – New PAP Candidates (cont'd)

Name	Age and Ethnicity	Constituency	Educational and Professional Qualifications	Party / Community / Volunteer / Board Experience	Career
Patrick Tay	Age: 40 Chinese	Nee Soon GRC	St Patrick's School; Temasek Junior College; Public Service Commission Local Merit Scholarship – National University of Singapore (Bachelor of Laws (Honours)); National University of Singapore (Master of Laws); Booth School of Business, University of Chicago and Singapore Management University (Graduate of the Executive Development Programme) Supreme Court of Singapore (Advocate and Solicitor); Singapore Mediation Centre (Associate Mediator)	Secretary, Bedok CCC; Secretary, Bedok PAP branch; Chairman, Bedok Community Development and Welfare Fund; Vice-Chairman, Bedok Inter-Racial and Religious Confidence Circle; Councillor, East Coast Town Council; YP Chairman, Bedok branch; Executive Secretary, YP Exco; Longstanding involvement in grassroots work	Executive Secretary, Healthcare Services Employees' Union; Adviser / Senior Consultant, Union of Security Employees; Director, Legal Services Department, National Trades Union Congress (NTUC); Alignment Director, Professionals, Managers and Executives, NTUC; Head, Industrial Relations, Shipbuilding and Marine Engineering Employees Union; Industrial Relations Officer, NTUC; Commanding Officer, Special Tactics and Rescue (STAR) Unit, Singapore Police Force

(cont'd overleaf)

Table 6.2 2011 General Election – New PAP Candidates (cont'd)

Name	Age and Ethnicity	Constituency	Educational and Professional Qualifications	Party / Community / Volunteer / Board Experience	Career
Sim Ann	Age: 36 Chinese	Holland-Bukit Timah GRC	Raffles' Girls Secondary School; Hwa Chong Junior College; President's Scholarship – University of Oxford (Bachelor of Arts (Philosophy, Politics and Economics) (Honours)); Stanford University (Master of Arts (Political Science)); Nanyang Technological University (Post-Graduate Diploma in Translation and Interpretation)	Vice-Chairman, Bukit Timah CCMC; Vice-Chairman, Reading@BT (free children's library), Bukit Timah Community Club; Member, Bukit Timah CCC; Member, National Youth Council; Member, National Arts Council	Director, National Population Secretariat; *Previous roles in the Administrative Service included:* *Regional Director (East China Region), International Enterprise Singapore;* *Deputy Director (Trade), Ministry of Trade and Industry;* *(Also positions in Ministries of Home Affairs and Health)*

Table 6.2 2011 General Election – New PAP Candidates (cont'd)

Name	Age and Ethnicity	Constituency	Educational and Professional Qualifications	Party / Community / Volunteer / Board Experience	Career
Tan Chuan-Jin	Age: 42 Chinese	Marine Parade GRC	Anglo-Chinese Secondary School; Raffles Junior College; Singapore Armed Forces Overseas Scholarship – London School of Economics (Bachelor of Science (Economics)); King's College London (Master of Arts (Defence Studies)); Lee Kuan Yew School of Public Policy, National University of Singapore (Master in Public Policy)	*Commander, SAF Humanitarian Assistance Task Force for the 2004 Indian Ocean tsunami, Meulaboh, Indonesia*	Commander, Army Training and Doctrine Command, Singapore Armed Forces (rank of Brigadier-General); *Previous positions in the SAF included:* Commander, 3rd Division; Assistant Chief of General Staff (Plans); Commanding Officer, 3rd Guards Battalion; Army Attaché in Jakarta; Commander, 7th Singapore Infantry Brigade

(cont'd overleaf)

Table 6.2 2011 General Election – New PAP Candidates (cont'd)

Name	Age and Ethnicity	Constituency	Educational and Professional Qualifications	Party / Community / Volunteer / Board Experience	Career
Tin Pei Ling	Age: 27 Chinese	Marine Parade GRC	Crescent Girls' School; Hwa Chong Junior College; University Scholars Programme – National University of Singapore (Bachelor of Social Science (Honours))	Member, PAP Ulu Pandan Branch; Assistant Treasurer, Executive Committee, Young PAP; Head, Young PAP Media; Chairperson, Youth Executive Committee, Ulu Pandan CCMC; Member, Ulu Pandan Community Development and Welfare Fund Committee; Member, Residential College Steering Committee, University Scholars Programme, National University of Singapore; Chairperson, Organising Committee, National Youth Forum 2006; Member, Youth Organising Committee, 5th ASEAN Ministerial Meeting on Youth 2007; Member, Youth Engagement Committee, 2010 Youth Olympic Games	Senior Associate, Ernst & Young Advisory Pte Ltd

Table 6.2 2011 General Election – New PAP Candidates (cont'd)

Name	Age and Ethnicity	Constituency	Educational and Professional Qualifications	Party / Community / Volunteer / Board Experience	Career
Vikram Nair	Age: 33 Indian	Sembawang GRC	Anglo-Chinese School (Independent); Raffles Junior College; Jardine Foundation Scholarship – University of Cambridge (Bachelor of Arts (Law) (Honours) (Lizette Bentwich Prize)); National University of Singapore (Graduate Diploma in Singapore Law); Supreme Court of England and Wales (Solicitor) Supreme Court of Singapore (Advocate and Solicitor)	Member, Chong Pang CCC; Volunteer, Chong Pang Meet-the-People Sessions; Active in grassroots work in Admiralty Ward; Vice-Chairman and Board Member, Malayalam Language Education Society; Panel Member and Board Member, Partner Connection Fund, Social Development Unit	Lawyer and Associate, Norton Rose (Asia) LLP; Associate, Allen & Gledhill LLP; Business Analyst, McKinsey & Company

(cont'd overleaf)

Table 6.2 2011 General Election – New PAP Candidates (cont'd)

Name	Age and Ethnicity	Constituency	Educational and Professional Qualifications	Party / Community / Volunteer / Board Experience	Career
Zainal bin Sapari	Age: 46 Malay	Pasir Ris-Punggol GRC	St Andrew's Secondary School; Temasek Junior College; Special Malay Bursary – National University of Singapore (Bachelor of Arts (Honours)); National Institute of Education (Post-Graduate Diploma in Education); Nanyang Technological University (Master of Arts (Educational Management))	Member, Joint-Madrasah Education Resource Panel; Member, Censorship Review Committee, Ministry of Information, Communications and the Arts; Member, Education Sub-Committee, Darul Ihsan Orphanage	Director (Special Duty), Industrial Relations, National Trades Union Congress; Superintendent, Ministry of Education; Principal, Mayflower Primary School; Vice-Principal, Mayflower Primary School; Vice-Principal, East Spring Primary School; Head of Department, Tampines Secondary School; Teacher, Tampines Secondary School

Table 6.2 2011 General Election – New PAP Candidates (cont'd)

Name	Age and Ethnicity	Constituency	Educational and Professional Qualifications	Party / Community / Volunteer / Board Experience	Career
Sitoh Yih Pin (stood unsuccessfully in 2001 and 2006)	Age: 47 Chinese	Potong Pasir SMC	Serangoon Garden Secondary School; Hwa Chong Junior College National University of Singapore (Bachelor of Accountancy (Honours)); Institute of Chartered Accountants, Australia (Associate Member); Institute of Certified Public Accountants of Singapore (Fellow)	Member, PAP Punggol East Branch; Adviser, South-East Community Development Council; Chairman, Potong Pasir Community Development Council; Adviser to Potong Pasir grassroots organisations; Member, Resource Panel, Government Parliamentary Committee for Manpower; Member, Governing Council, Singapore Institute of Directors; Board Member, Accounting and Corporation Regulatory Authority; Member, Chong Boon CCC; Branch Secretary, PAP Chong Boon Branch; Member, Supervisory Panel, Feedback Unit; Director, Chinese Development Assistance Council *Independent director of several publicly-listed companies*	Co-Founder and Chairman, Nexia TS Public Accounting Corporation; *Earlier career with KPMG as audit manager*

(cont'd overleaf)

Table 7.1 2015 General Election – PAP Candidates Information

Name	Age and Ethnicity	Constituency	Educational and Professional Qualifications	Party / Community / Volunteer / Board Experience	Career
Cheryl Chan Wei Ling	Age: 38 Chinese	Fengshan SMC	Singapore Chinese Girls' School; Catholic Junior College; Nanyang Technological University (Bachelor Degree (Materials Engineering) Honours); Macquarie Graduate School of Management (MBA); Linde Global Talent Circle (Executive Program at London Business School); Linde Global Leadership Development (eMBA at Oxford Säid Business School)	Chair, East Coast-Fengshan Community Club Management Committee; Member, East Coast- Fengshan Citizen's Consultative Committee; Member, East Coast Town Council; Member, East Coast- Fengshan Youth Executive Committee; Member, East Coast-Fengshan Neighbourhood Committee	VP, Head of Secondary Industries (Corporate Strategy & Market Intelligence), The Linde Group; VP, Head of Global Electronic Specialty Gases, The Linde Group; (Previous roles in The Linde Group); Product Marketing Manager, Kulicke & Soffa; (Previous roles in Kulicke & Soffa)
Ng Chee Meng	Age: 47 Chinese	Pasir Ris- Punggol GRC	The Chinese High School; Hwa Chong Junior College; United States Air Force Academy (Bachelor Degree (Electrical Engineering)); Fletcher School of Law and Diplomacy, Tufts University (Master Degree (International Relations))	Head, National Day Celebrations Committee; Management Committee Member, AMKFSC Community Services; Held directorships in various government and government-linked bodies	Chief of Defence Force, Singapore Armed Forces (rank of Lieutenant-General); Previous roles in the SAF included: Chief of Air Force; Military Private Secretary to the Minister for Defence; Commander, Changi Air Base; Head Air Plans Department; Director of Joint Operations

Table 7.1 2015 General Election – PAP Candidates Information (cont'd)

Name	Age and Ethnicity	Constituency	Educational and Professional Qualifications	Party / Community / Volunteer / Board Experience	Career
Chee Hong Tat	Age: 41 Chinese	Bishan-Toa Payoh GRC	The Chinese High School; Raffles Junior College; University of California, Berkeley (Bachelor Degree (Electrical Engineering and Computer Science); Bachelor Degree (Economics)); Adelaide University (MBA)	Deputy President, Singapore Dragon Boat Association; Volunteer, SCORE Training Committee; Volunteer, WeCare@Marine Parade Initiative	Second Permanent Secretary, Ministry of Trade and Industry; *Previous roles in Administrative Service included:* *Chief Executive, Energy Market Authority;* *Principal Private Secretary to Minister Mentor Lee Kuan Yew;* *(Also positions in Ministries of Education, Transport, Finance and Home Affairs)*
K. Muralidharan Pillai (not voted in; subsequently voted into Parliament – 2016 Bukit Batok by-election)	Age: 47 Indian	Aljunied GRC	Monk's Hill Secondary School; Hwa Chong Junior College; National University of Singapore (L.L.B); National University of Singapore (L.L.M); Double MBA degree, University of California, Los Angeles (UCLA) and NUS	Chairman, PAP Paya Lebar Branch; Adviser, Tamil Language Council; Chairman, Indian Programmes Advisory Committee; Adviser, Board of Trustees of Singapore Indian Development Association (SINDA); Branch Secretary, PAP Bukit Batok Branch	Head of Commercial Litigation, Rajah & Tann Singapore LLP; *Deputy Superintendent, SPF;* *Assistant Superintendent, SPF*

(cont'd overleaf)

Table 7.1 2015 General Election – PAP Candidates Information (cont'd)

Name	Age and Ethnicity	Constituency	Educational and Professional Qualifications	Party / Community / Volunteer / Board Experience	Career
Amrin Amin	Age: 36 Malay	Sembawang GRC	Dunman Secondary School; Tampines Junior College; National University of Singapore (L.L.B); MUIS Scholarship – Columbia University (L.L.M) (Harlan Fiske Stone Scholar)	Grassroots Adviser, (Sembawang GRC (Woodlands)); Member, Association of Muslim Professionals' "Ready for School" Programme; Member, Bursary and Scholarship Body (Prophet Muhammad's Birthday Memorial Scholarship Fund Board (LBKM)); Member, REACH; Member, National Council of Problem Gambling; Member, Board of Governors of Nanyang Polytechnic; Member, Ministry of Social and Family Development's Board of Visitors (Welfare Homes); Member, Marsiling CCC; Member, Chong Pang CCC; Volunteer Tutor, Mendaki Tuition Scheme; Member, Suara Musyawarah Committee	Corporate Lawyer, Joseph Tan Jude Benny LLP; *Corporate Lawyer, Watson, Farley & Williams Asia Practice LLP*

Table 7.1 2015 General Election – PAP Candidates Information (cont'd)

Name	Age and Ethnicity	Constituency	Educational and Professional Qualifications	Party / Community / Volunteer / Board Experience	Career
Cheng Li Hui	Age: 39 Chinese	Tampines GRC	Bukit Panjang Government High School; Anglo-Chinese Junior College; National University of Singapore (Bachelor's Degree, Faculty of Arts); Macquarie University (Masters Degree (Applied Finance)	Vice-Chairperson, Tampines East CCMC; Vice-Chairperson, Tampines East CCC; *Volunteer, Admiralty Constituency;* *Volunteer, Woodlands Constituency;* Councillor, Holland-Bukit Panjang Town Council; *Member, Bukit Panjang Community Kitchen Co-Operative;* *Member, Bukit Panjang CCC;* *Member, NUH Medifund Committee;* *Volunteer, Bukit Panjang PAP Branch*	Deputy CEO, Hai Leck Holdings Limited

(cont'd overleaf)

Table 7.1 2015 General Election – PAP Candidates Information (cont'd)

Name	Age and Ethnicity	Constituency	Educational and Professional Qualifications	Party / Community / Volunteer / Board Experience	Career
Chong Kee Hiong	Age: 49 Chinese	Bishan-Toa Payoh GRC	Raffles Institution; Raffles Junior College; National University of Singapore (Bachelor of Accountancy); Harvard Business School (Completion of Advanced Management Program)	Vice Chairman, Bishan East CCC; Co-Chairman, Healthy Lifestyle Committee; Member, Bishan-Toa Payoh Town Council; Chairman, Home Improvement Programme; Chairman, Neighbourhood Renewal Programme; Chairman, NTUC Foodfare	CEO, OUE Hospitality REIT Management Pte Ltd; *CEO, The Ascott Limited (Ascott);* *CEO, Ascott Residence Trust Management Limited;* *CFO, Raffles Holdings Limited* *Began career with KPMG Peat Marwick*
Chua Eng Leong (not voted in)	Age: 44 Chinese	Aljunied GRC	Anglo-Chinese School; Anglo-Chinese Junior College; University of San Francisco (B.S. (Business Administration (Management))	Chairman, Eunos PAP Branch; Chairman, Eunos PAP Community Foundation; *Assistant Treasurer, Tampines PAP Community Foundation;* *Vice-Chairman, Changkat CC Sports Club*	Executive Director, Standard Charted Private Bank; *Bank Officer, Tat Lee Bank;* *Earlier career at various banks (Tat Lee Bank, OCBC, DBS, Julius Baer)*

Table 7.1 2015 General Election – PAP Candidates Information (cont'd)

Name	Age and Ethnicity	Constituency	Educational and Professional Qualifications	Party / Community / Volunteer / Board Experience	Career
Darryl David Wilson	Age: 44 Indian	Ang Mo Kio GRC	Raffles Institution; Raffles Junior College; National University of Singapore (B.A. (Hons) (English Literature)); Lee Kuan Yew School of Public Policy (Masters in Public Administration); Nanyang Business School, Nanyang Technological University (MBA)	Vice-Chairman, Publicity & Communications Committee (Ang Mo Kio Town Council); Vice-Chairman, Ang Mo Kio-Hougang CCC; Council Member, Central Singapore CDC; Member, Pioneer Generation Taskforce; Member, SG50 Education & Youth Committee; Member, 14th National Youth Council; District Councillor, North-East Community Development Council (CDC); Volunteer, Red Cross; Volunteer, National Volunteer and Philanthropy Centre	Deputy Director, School of Design, Temasek Polytechnic; *Presenter, MediaCorp TV;* *Sportscaster, ESPN Start Sports*

(cont'd overleaf)

Table 7.1 2015 General Election – PAP Candidates Information (cont'd)

Name	Age and Ethnicity	Constituency	Educational and Professional Qualifications	Party / Community / Volunteer / Board Experience	Career
Henry Kwek Hian Chuan	Age: 39 Chinese	Nee Soon GRC	Chinese High School; Victoria Junior College; Stanford University (Bachelor Degree (Economics); Masters Degree in Management Science and Engineering	Grassroots Volunteer, Kebun Baru Constituency; Branch Secretary, Chong Pang PAP Branch; Special Adviser to Chong Pang Grassroots Organisations; Grassroots Volunteer, Chong Pang Constituency; Grassroots Volunteer, Kebun Baru Constituency; Volunteer Tutor, Kaki Bukit Prison School	Co-Founder and Executive Director, Cerulean Capital; Executive Director of Foodtraco Supplies Pte Ltd; Management Consultant, McKinsey & Co; Senior Officer, Infocomms and Media Cluster, Economic Development Board
Lee Hong Chuang (not voted in)	Age: 45 Chinese	Hougang SMC	Chinese High School; Anderson Junior College; Japan-Singapore Institute of Software Technology; National University of Singapore (B. Sc (Computer and Information Sciences))	Chairman, Hougang CCMC; Chairman, Hougang PAP Branch; Chairman, Hougang CC Building Fund; Chairman, Hougang PCF; Vice-Chairman, Hougang CCC; Chairman, People's Association Youth Movement Central Youth Council; Team Manager, National Gymnastics Team; Competition Manager, 28th SEA Games and 1st Youth Olympics Games; Former national gymnast	Senior IT Manager, IBM

Table 7.1 2015 General Election – PAP Candidates Information (cont'd)

Name	Age and Ethnicity	Constituency	Educational and Professional Qualifications	Party / Community / Volunteer / Board Experience	Career
Victor Joseph Lye Thiam Fatt (not voted in)	Age: 53 Chinese	Aljunied GRC	St Joseph's Institution; Catholic Junior College; Colombo Plan Scholarship – University of Adelaide (Bachelor Degree (Honors) (Economics)); Chartered Financial Analyst	Branch Chairman, PAP Bedok Reservoir-Punggol Division (Aljunied GRC); Chairman, Bedok Reservoir-Punggol CCC; Chairman, National Council Against Drug Abuse (NCADA); Board Member (Chairman of Investment Committee), Singapore Chinese Orchestra; Founding Member, Action Community for Entrepreneurship; Chairman, Punggol CCMC; Member, Northeast Community Development Council; Vice President, Singapore Anti-Narcotics Association	CEO, Shenton Insurance Pte Ltd; CEO & Managing Director, WMG Management Pte Ltd; Chief Executive, International Medical Insurers Pte Ltd; Executive Director, CIMB-GK Securities Pte. Ltd; Managing Partner & Founder, Pinnacle Capital; Assistant Director, Ministry of Trade & Industry (Administrative Service)

(cont'd overleaf)

Table 7.1 2015 General Election – PAP Candidates Information (cont'd)

Name	Age and Ethnicity	Constituency	Educational and Professional Qualifications	Party / Community / Volunteer / Board Experience	Career
Louis Ng Kok Kwang	Age: 36 Chinese	Nee Soon GRC	St Gabriel's Secondary School; Catholic Junior College; National University of Singapore (B. Sc. (Biology)); Oxford Brookes University, UK (Masters in Primate Conservation)	Volunteer, PAP Joo Chiat Branch; Committee Member, Kembangan-Chai Chee CCC; Volunteer, PAP Kembangan-Chai Chee Branch; Committee Member, Singapore Animal Welfare Legislation Review Committee; Committee Member, Chong Pang CCMC; Chong Pang Youth Executive Committee, Animal Welfare and Environment Secretary; Volunteer, PAP Chong Pang Branch; Singapore Representative, International Primate Protection League (IPPL); Executive Committee Member of Youth Wing, Jalan Hijau (Nature Society Singapore); Volunteer, Society for the Prevention of Cruelty to Animals (SPCA)	Executive Director, ACRES (Animal Concerns Research and Education Society); Founder & President, ACRES; Consultant, World Society for the Protection of Animals; Consultant, Environment and Animal Society of Taiwan

Table 7.1 2015 General Election – PAP Candidates Information (cont'd)

Name	Age and Ethnicity	Constituency	Educational and Professional Qualifications	Party / Community / Volunteer / Board Experience	Career
Joan Cheng Sim Pereira	Age: 48 Other (Eurasian)	Tanjong Pagar GRC	Convent of the Holy Infant Jesus; Catholic Junior College; National University of Singapore (B.A, Arts and Social Sciences)	*Program Manager, Queenstown CC*	Assistant General Manager, Temasek Cares; *Director of Family Life and Active Aging, People's Association;* Previous roles in People's Association, including senior manager in Queenstown Constituency Office

(cont'd overleaf)

Table 7.1 2015 General Election – PAP Candidates Information (cont'd)

Name	Age and Ethnicity	Constituency	Educational and Professional Qualifications	Party / Community / Volunteer / Board Experience	Career
Rahayu Mahzam	Age: 35 Malay	Jurong GRC	Raffles Girls' Secondary School; Raffles Junior College; National University of Singapore (L.L.B)	Volunteer, Malay Youth Literary Association (4PM); Member, National Youth Fund Advisory Committee; Member, Malay Language Council; Member, National Library Board; Volunteer Probation Officer, Ministry of Social & Family Development; Supervisory Panel Member, National Integration Working Group for Community; Supervisory Panel Member, Malay-Muslim Community Leaders' Forum Planning Exercise (2010/11); Supervisory Panel Member, Censorship Review Committee; Supervisory Panel Member, Feedback Unit; Volunteer, Various Legal Clinics of Muslim Converts' Association (Darul Arqam)	Partner, Heng, Leong & Srinivasan; Accredited Associate Mediator with Singapore Mediation Centre; Deputy Registrar, Syariah Court

Table 7.1 2015 General Election – PAP Candidates Information (cont'd)

Name	Age and Ethnicity	Constituency	Educational and Professional Qualifications	Party / Community / Volunteer / Board Experience	Career
Saktiandi bin Supaat	Age: 42 Malay	Bishan-Toa Payoh GRC	Raffles Institution; Catholic Junior College; University of Melbourne (Bachelor of Commerce (Honours) (Finance)); National University of Singapore (Masters in Applied Economics); Judge Business School, Cambridge University (MBA)	Board Member, SPRING, Singapore; Board Member, Civil Service College; Member, Charity Council; Member, REACH Supervisory Panel; Vice-Chair, Toa Payoh East CCC; Member, Central CDC; Chairman, Community Leadership Forum (CLF) Labs Steering Committee President, Young AMP (Association of Muslim Professionals); Vice Chairman, AMP	Executive Vice President, Global Markets, Global Banking, Maybank Group; Senior Vice President, Head of FX Research, Global Markets, Global Banking, Maybank Group; Vice President (Head), Senior Treasury Economist, United Overseas Bank Group; Lead Economist (Deputy Director), Economic Policy Group, Monetary Authority of Singapore; (Previous roles at Monetary Authority of Singapore)
Shamsul Kamar Mohamad Razali (not voted in)	Age: 43 Malay	Aljunied GRC	Anglo-Chinese School; Anglo-Chinese Junior College; Nanyang Technological University (B.A. with Diploma in Education); National University of Singapore (M.A (Southeast Asian Studies)	Chairman, Ministry of Social and Family Development (MSF) Review Board; Member, Board of Visitors (Children and Young Persons Homes); Member, Nee Soon Central CCC; Secretary, Kaki Bukit CCC Development Welfare Fund	Head of Student Management, Spectra Secondary School; Teacher, Bedok South Secondary School

(cont'd overleaf)

Table 7.1 2015 General Election – PAP Candidates Information (cont'd)

Name	Age and Ethnicity	Constituency	Educational and Professional Qualifications	Party / Community / Volunteer / Board Experience	Career
Sun Xueling	Age: 36 Chinese	Pasir Ris-Punggol GRC	CHIJ St Nicholas Girls' School; Raffles Junior College; National University of Singapore (Bachelor of Social Sciences (Honours) (Economics)); M.Sc, London School of Economics and Political Science	Assistant Secretary, Buona Vista CCC; Assistant Secretary, Youth Sub-Committee of Buona Vista CCC; Member, Young PAP Exco; Volunteer, Buona Vista YP	Director (Investments Group), Temasek International; Director, Deutsche Bank AG (HK); Senior Vice-President, Macquarie Capital Securities HK; Assistant Vice-President, DBS Bank Singapore; Associate, Economics Development Board
Tan Wu Meng	Age: 40 Chinese	Jurong GRC	Raffles Institution; Hwa Chong Junior College; Trinity College, Cambridge University (Medicine and Pathology); National University of Singapore (Master of Medicine (Internal Medicine)); MBBChir-PHD Programme Scholarship (Cambridge University) – UK Medical Research Council's Laboratory of Molecular Biology (PhD (Molecular Biology)); Fellow (Medical Oncology), Academy of Medicine, Singapore	Member, Senja-Cashew CCC; Member, Senja-Cashew Youth Executive Committee; Vice-Chair, Youth Works Sub-Committee, North-West CDC; Councillor, North-West CDC; Young PAP Exco Organising Secretary; Young PAP Regional Chair (Holland-Bukit Timah); Member, Singapore Cancer Society's (SCS) Cancer Care Task Force	Consultant, Parkway Cancer Center; Director (Outpatient Care), NCCS Division of Medical Oncology, SGH; Member, SingHealth Physician Faculty; Member, SingHealth Specialist Outpatient Clinic Task Force

Table 7.1 2015 General Election – PAP Candidates Information (cont'd)

Name	Age and Ethnicity	Constituency	Educational and Professional Qualifications	Party / Community / Volunteer / Board Experience	Career
Yee Chia Hsing	Age: 44 Chinese	Chua Chu Kang GRC	Raffles Institution; Raffles Junior College; Nanyang Technological University (Bachelor of Accountancy)	Member, Ren Ci Hospital Audit Committee; Chairman, Punggol East PAP Branch; Vice-Chairman, Punggol East CCC; Councillor, Nee Soon Town Council; Treasurer, Chong Pang Division CCC; Volunteer, St Andrew's Community Hospital	Head Catalist, Managing Director, CIMB Bank Singapore; Lead Independent Director, First Sponsor Group Limited; Executive Director, Asiaons WFG Securities Singapore; Director (Investment Banking), CIMB-GK Securities Pte Ltd
Melvin Yong Yik Chye	Age: 43 Chinese	Tanjong Pagar GRC	Chinese High School; National Junior College; SPF Scholarship – Nanyang Technological University (Bachelor of Accountancy); University of Leicester (M. Sc. (Criminal Justice))	Founder, Action-Leaders for Community Enhancement (ACE) Club; Secretary, Punggol North CCC; Treasurer, Punggol North CCC; Chairman, Punggol Cove Residents' Committee; Vice-Chairman, Punggol Cove Residents' Committee; Member, National Crime Prevention Council; Member, National Police Cadet Corps Council; Founder, Delta League (nationwide youth engagement programme)	Assistant Commissioner, Singapore Police Force; Previous positions in SPF included: Deputy Director (Planning & Organisation); Director (Administration & Finance); Commander of Clementi Police Division; Director (Public Affairs); Deputy Director (Operations)

(cont'd overleaf)

Table 7.1 2015 General Election – PAP Candidates Information (cont'd)

Name	Age and Ethnicity	Constituency	Educational and Professional Qualifications	Party / Community / Volunteer / Board Experience	Career
Ong Ye Kung (stood unsuccessfully in 2011)	Age: 45 Chinese	Sembawang GRC	Maris Stella High School; Raffles Junior College; PSC Scholarship – London School of Economics (B.Sc. (Economics)); International Institute for Management Development (MBA)	*Chairman, Employment and Employability Institute*	Director (Group Strategy), Keppel Corporation; Deputy Secretary-General, NTUC *Executive Secretary, National Transport Workers Union* *Executive Secretary, Singapore Manual Mercantile Workers' Union* *Previous roles in the Administrative Service included:* *CEO, Singapore Workforce Development Agency;* *Principal Private Secretary to PM Lee Hsien Loong;* *Director of Trade, Ministry of Trade and Industry (roles included Deputy Chief Negotiator, US-Singapore Free Trade Agreement)*
Koh Poh Koon (stood unsuccessfully in 2013 Punggol East SMC by-election)	Age: 43 Chinese	Ang Mo Kio GRC	Maris Stella High School; Hwa Chong Junior College; National University of Singapore (MBBS); Member, Royal College of Surgeons (Edinburgh); National University of Singapore (MMed (Surgery)); Fellow, Academy of Medicine, Singapore; Fellow, Royal College of Surgeons (Edinburgh)	Vice-Chairman, Yio Chu Kang CCC; Adviser, Internal Affairs Committee of Teochew Poit Ip Huay Kuan; *Patron, Punggol East CCC;* *Chairman, Punggol East PCF Kindergarten* Member of numerous local, regional and international medical bodies	Adjunct Clinician Scientist, Institute of Bioengineering & Nanotechnology (IBN), A*Star; Adjunct Assistant Professor, DUKE-NUS Graduate Medical School, Singapore; Clinical Teacher, Yong Loo Lin School of Medicine, National University of Singapore

Table 7.1 2015 General Election – PAP Candidates Information (cont'd)

Name	Age and Ethnicity	Constituency	Educational and Professional Qualifications	Party / Community / Volunteer / Board Experience	Career
Desmond Choo Pey Ching (stood unsuccessfully in 2011 for Hougang SMC and in 2012 Hougang SMC by-election)	Age: 37 Chinese	Tampines GRC	Catholic High School; National Junior College; University of Chicago (A.B. Economics); University of Chicago (A.M. Social Sciences)	Member, National Wages Council; Committee Member, Global Compact Network Singapore's Management Committee; Member, Training Council and Industrial Relations Council; Secretary, Industrial Relations Committee (Service Sector); Trustee, Singapore Shell Employees' Union; Adviser, Union of Security Employees; Executive Secretary, Singapore Union of Broadcasting Employees; Executive Secretary, Attractions, Resorts & Entertainment Union; Second Grassroots Adviser, Tampines East Grassroots Organisations; Second Grassroots Adviser, Hougang Grassroots Organisations	Director, Youth Development Unit, National Trades Union Congress; *Senior Vice-President, Kestrel Capital Pte Ltd;* *Deputy Director, National Trades Union Congress (NTUC);* *Deputy Commander, Singapore Police Force "Delta" Division;* *Deputy Director, Foreign Workforce Policy Department, Ministry of Manpower;* *(Previous roles in SPF)*

APPENDIX TWO: PAP CENTRAL EXECUTIVE COMMITTEE, 1980–2020

PAP Central Executive Committee (CEC) 1980–84

Note: 12 places are filled formally via the election process. By long-standing party tradition, the 13th and 14th highest scoring candidates are usually co-opted into the CEC at the Party Conference itself. Further co-options, and decisions on the filling of CEC office-bearing positions, are usually decided subsequently at the first CEC meeting following the Party Conference.

	16th CEC Party Conference on 7 December 1980	17th CEC Party Conference on 15 November 1982	1983 changes announced 3–4 March 1983
Secretary-General	Lee Kuan Yew	Lee Kuan Yew	Lee Kuan Yew
Chairman	Ong Teng Cheong	Ong Teng Cheong	Ong Teng Cheong
Vice-Chairman	Ong Pang Boon	Ong Pang Boon	Lim Chee Onn (resigned from Cabinet and CEC posts in August 1983 but remained a CEC member until September 1984)
Second Vice-Chairman	Lim Chee Onn	Lim Chee Onn	
First Assistant Secretary-General	Tony Tan (co-opted)	Tony Tan	Tony Tan
Second Assistant Secretary-General	Goh Chok Tong	Goh Chok Tong	Goh Chok Tong
Treasurer	Chua Sian Chin	Chua Sian Chin	Chua Sian Chin
Assistant Treasurer	S. Dhanabalan (co-opted into the CEC)	S. Dhanabalan	Ahmad Mattar
Second Assistant Treasurer	Ahmad Mattar	Ahmad Mattar	
CEC Members (non-office-holders)	E.W. Barker	E.W. Barker	E.W. Barker
	Goh Keng Swee	Ho Kah Leong	Ho Kah Leong
	S. Rajaratnam	Ch'ng Jit Koon	Ch'ng Jit Koon
	Toh Chin Chye		Ong Pang Boon (stepped down from his post of Vice-Chairman)
	Lee Khoon Choy		S. Dhanabalan (relinquished his post of Assistant Treasurer)
Co-opted into the CEC as 13th and 14th highest vote getters at Party Conference	Tony Tan	S. Jayakumar	
	S. Dhanabalan	Lee Yiok Seng	
Members subsequently co-opted			Yeo Ning Hong
			Wan Soon Bee

PAP Central Executive Committee (CEC) 1984–90

	18th CEC Party Conference on 30 September 1984	19th CEC Party Conference on 23 November 1986	20th CEC Party Conference on 8 January 1989
Secretary-General	Lee Kuan Yew	Lee Kuan Yew	Lee Kuan Yew
Chairman	Ong Teng Cheong	Ong Teng Cheong	Ong Teng Cheong
Vice-Chairman	Tony Tan	Tony Tan	Tony Tan
First Assistant Secretary-General	Goh Chok Tong	Goh Chok Tong	Goh Chok Tong
Second Assistant Secretary-General			Lee Hsien Loong
Treasurer	S. Dhanabalan	S. Dhanabalan	S. Dhanabalan
Assistant Treasurer	Ahmad Mattar	Ahmad Mattar	Ahmad Mattar
CEC Members (non-office-holders)	Yeo Ning Hong	Lee Yiok Seng	Ch'ng Jit Koon
	Wan Soon Bee	Ch'ng Jit Koon	S. Jayakumar
	Ho Kah Leong	S. Jayakumar	Lee Yock Suan
	Lee Yiok Seng	Lee Yock Suan	Tan Cheng Bock
	Ch'ng Jit Koon	Tan Cheng Bock	Wong Kan Seng
	S. Jayakumar	Lee Hsien Loong	
Co-opted into the CEC as 13th and 14th highest vote getters at Party Conference	Tay Eng Soon	Wong Kan Seng	Tay Eng Soon
	Lau Ping Sum	Yeo Ning Hong	Yeo Ning Hong
Members subsequently co-opted	Chua Sian Chin (stepped down at the 1984 Party Conference but was subsequently co-opted back into the CEC on 8 February 1985)	Chua Sian Chin (8 January 1987)	

PAP Central Executive Committee (CEC) 1990–95

	21st CEC Party Conference on 18 November 1990	22nd CEC Party Conference on 15 November 1992	Changes announced 14 August 1993
Secretary-General	Lee Kuan Yew	Goh Chok Tong	Goh Chok Tong
Chairman	Ong Teng Cheong	Ong Teng Cheong	Tony Tan
Vice-Chairman	Tony Tan	Tony Tan	S. Jayakumar
First Assistant Secretary-General	Goh Chok Tong	Lee Hsien Loong	Lee Hsien Loong
Second Assistant Secretary-General	Lee Hsien Loong	Wong Kan Seng	Wong Kan Seng
Treasurer	S. Dhanabalan	S. Dhanabalan (co-opted into the CEC and re-appointed Treasurer)	S. Dhanabalan
Assistant Treasurer	Ahmad Mattar	Ahmad Mattar	Abdullah Tarmugi
Second Assistant Treasurer			Lim Boon Heng
CEC Members (non-office-holders)	Ch'ng Jit Koon	Lee Kuan Yew	Lee Kuan Yew
	S. Jayakumar	Ch'ng Jit Koon	Ch'ng Jit Koon
	Lee Yock Suan	S. Jayakumar	Ahmad Mattar
	Tan Cheng Bock	Lee Yock Suan	Lee Yock Suan
	George Yeo	Tan Cheng Bock	Tan Cheng Bock
		George Yeo	George Yeo
Co-opted into the CEC as 13th and 14th highest vote getters at Party Conference	Wong Kan Seng	S. Dhanabalan	
	Aline Wong	Lee Boon Yang	Lee Boon Yang
Members subsequently co-opted into the CEC	Lim Boon Heng	Lim Boon Heng	
	Abdullah Tarmugi	Abdullah Tarmugi	
	Yeo Ning Hong	Yeo Ning Hong	Yeo Ning Hong
	Lee Boon Yang	Aline Wong	Aline Wong

PAP Central Executive Committee (CEC) 1995–2000

	23rd CEC Party Conference on 15 January 1995	**24th CEC** Party Conference on 17 November 1996	**25th CEC** Party Conference on 24 January 1999
Secretary-General	Goh Chok Tong	Goh Chok Tong	Goh Chok Tong
Chairman	Tony Tan	Tony Tan	Tony Tan
Vice-Chairman	S. Jayakumar	S. Jayakumar	S. Jayakumar
First Assistant Secretary-General	Lee Hsien Loong	Lee Hsien Loong	Lee Hsien Loong
Second Assistant Secretary-General	Wong Kan Seng	Wong Kan Seng	Wong Kan Seng
Treasurer	Lim Boon Heng	Lim Boon Heng	Lim Boon Heng
Assistant Treasurer	Abdullah Tarmugi	Abdullah Tarmugi	Abdullah Tarmugi
CEC Members (non-office-holders)	Lee Kuan Yew	Lee Kuan Yew	Lee Kuan Yew
	Lee Yock Suan	Teo Chee Hean	Teo Chee Hean
	George Yeo	George Yeo	George Yeo
	Ch'ng Jit Koon	Ch'ng Jit Koon	Lim Swee Say
	Tan Cheng Bock	Lim Hng Kiang	Lim Hng Kiang
Co-opted into the CEC as 13th and 14th highest vote getters at Party Conference	Teo Chee Hean	Lee Yock Suan	Lee Yock Suan
	Aline Wong	Aline Wong	Aline Wong
Members subsequently co-opted into the CEC	Lim Hng Kiang	Tan Cheng Bock	Loh Meng See
	Lee Boon Yang	Lee Boon Yang	Lee Boon Yang

PAP Central Executive Committee (CEC) 2000–06

	26th CEC Party Conference on 3 December 2000	**27th CEC** Party Conference on 1 December 2002	**28th CEC** Party Conference on 7 November 2004
Secretary-General	Goh Chok Tong	Goh Chok Tong	Lee Hsien Loong
Chairman	Tony Tan	Tony Tan	Lim Boon Heng
Vice-Chairman	S. Jayakumar	S. Jayakumar	Yaacob Ibrahim
First Assistant Secretary-General	Lee Hsien Loong	Lee Hsien Loong	Wong Kan Seng
Second Assistant Secretary-General	Wong Kan Seng	Wong Kan Seng	Teo Chee Hean
Treasurer	Lim Boon Heng	Lim Boon Heng	Mah Bow Tan (co-opted)
Assistant Treasurer	Abdullah Tarmugi	Yaacob Ibrahim	Tharman Shanmugaratnam
CEC Members (non-office-holders)	Lee Kuan Yew	Lee Kuan Yew	Lee Kuan Yew
	Lim Hng Kiang	Lim Hng Kiang	Goh Chok Tong
	Lim Swee Say	Lim Swee Say	George Yeo
	Teo Chee Hean	Teo Chee Hean	Lim Swee Say
	George Yeo	George Yeo	Khaw Boon Wan
			Lim Hwee Hua
Co-opted into the CEC as 13th and 14th highest vote getters at Party Conference	Yeo Cheow Tong	Khaw Boon Wan	Vivian Balakrishnan
	Aline Wong	Tharman Shanmugaratnam	Mah Bow Tan
Members subsequently co-opted into the CEC	Lee Boon Yang	Lim Hwee Hua	Ng Eng Hen
	Mah Bow Tan	Mah Bow Tan	Ho Peng Kee
	Wang Kai Yuen	Wang Kai Yuen	Halimah Yaacob
	Hawazi Daipi	Hawazi Daipi	Teo Ho Pin

PAP Central Executive Committee (CEC) 2006–12

	29th CEC Party Conference on 3 December 2006	30th CEC Party Conference on 16 November 2008	31st CEC Party Conference on 28 November 2010*
Secretary-General	Lee Hsien Loong	Lee Hsien Loong	Lee Hsien Loong
Chairman	Lim Boon Heng	Lim Boon Heng	Khaw Boon Wan
Vice-Chairman	Yaacob Ibrahim	Yaacob Ibrahim	Yaacob Ibrahim
First Assistant Secretary-General	Wong Kan Seng	Wong Kan Seng	Teo Chee Hean
Second Assistant Secretary-General	Teo Chee Hean	Teo Chee Hean	Tharman Shanmugaratnam
Treasurer	Mah Bow Tan (co-opted and re-appointed Treasurer)	Mah Bow Tan (co-opted and re-appointed Treasurer)	Lim Swee Say
Assistant Treasurer	Tharman Shanmugaratnam	Tharman Shanmugaratnam	K. Shanmugam
CEC Members (non-office-holders)	Goh Chok Tong	Goh Chok Tong	Chan Chun Sing
	Lee Kuan Yew	Lee Kuan Yew	Grace Fu
	Khaw Boon Wan	Khaw Boon Wan	Heng Swee Keat
	Lim Swee Say	Lim Swee Say	Denise Phua
	George Yeo	George Yeo	Seah Kian Peng
	Vivian Balakrishnan	Vivian Balakrishnan	Tan Chuan-Jin
			Lee Kuan Yew (Chan Chun Sing)
			Goh Chok Tong (Grace Fu)
			Lim Boon Heng (Heng Swee Keat)
			Wong Kan Seng (Denise Phua)
			George Yeo (Seah Kian Peng)
			Lim Hwee Hua (Tan Chuan-Jin)

PAP Central Executive Committee (CEC) 2006–12

	29th CEC Party Conference on 3 December 2006	30th CEC Party Conference on 16 November 2008	31st CEC Party Conference on 28 November 2010*
Co-opted into the CEC as 13th and 14th highest vote getters at Party Conference	Mah Bow Tan	Mah Bow Tan	Lim Hwee Hua
	Lim Hwee Hua	Lim Hwee Hua	Vivian Balakrishnan
Members subsequently co-opted into the CEC	Ng Eng Hen	Ng Eng Hen	Gan Kim Yong
	Ho Peng Kee	Gan Kim Yong	Indranee Rajah
	Halimah Yacob	Indranee Rajah	Teo Ser Luck
	Teo Ho Pin	Teo Ser Luck	Ng Eng Hen

* Chan Chun Sing, Grace Fu, Heng Swee Keat, Denise Phua, Seah Kian Peng and Tan Chuan-Jin were co-opted on 9 November 2011 following a poll of Branch Chairmen and cadres representing the PAP branches, district committees, the Women's Wing and Young PAP. They replaced CEC members who resigned on 5 October 2011: Lee Kuan Yew, Goh Chok Tong, Lim Boon Heng, Wong Kan Seng, George Yeo and Lim Hwee Hua.

PAP Central Executive Committee (CEC) 2012–18

	32nd CEC Party Conference on 2 December 2012	33th CEC Party Conference on 7 December 2014	34th CEC Party Conference on 4 December 2016
Secretary-General	Lee Hsien Loong	Lee Hsien Loong	Lee Hsien Loong
Chairman	Khaw Boon Wan	Khaw Boon Wan	Khaw Boon Wan
Vice-Chairman	Yaacob Ibrahim	Yaacob Ibrahim	Yaacob Ibrahim
First Assistant Secretary-General	Teo Chee Hean	Teo Chee Hean	Teo Chee Hean
Second Assistant Secretary-General	Tharman Shanmugaratnam	Tharman Shanmugaratnam	Tharman Shanmugaratnam
Treasurer	Lim Swee Say	Lim Swee Say	Lim Swee Say
Assistant Treasurer	K. Shanmugam	K. Shanmugam	K. Shanmugam
CEC Members (non-office-holders)	Heng Swee Keat	Grace Fu	Grace Fu
	Grace Fu	Heng Swee Keat	Heng Swee Keat
		Tan Chuan-Jin	Halimah Yacob
Co-opted into the CEC as 13th and 14th highest vote getters at Party Conference	Tan Chuan-Jin	Halimah Yacob	Tan Chuan-Jin
	Vivian Balakrishnan	Ng Eng Hen	Vivian Balakrishnan
Members subsequently co-opted into the CEC	Halimah Yacob	Liang Eng Hwa	Masagos Zulkifli
	Lawrence Wong	Masagos Zulkifli	Sitoh Yih Pin
	Denise Phua	Lawrence Wong	Murali Pillai
	Seah Kian Peng	Baey Yam Keng	Ong Ye Kung

PAP Central Executive Committee (CEC) 2018–22

	35th CEC Party Conference on 11 November 2018	36th CEC Party Conference on 8 November 2020
Secretary-General	Lee Hsien Loong	Lee Hsien Loong
Chairman	Gan Kim Yong	Gan Kim Yong
Vice-Chairman	Masagos Zulkifli	Masagos Zulkifli
First Assistant Secretary-General	Heng Swee Keat	Heng Swee Keat
Second Assistant Secretary-General	Chan Chun Sing	Chan Chun Sing
Treasurer	K. Shanmugam	K. Shanmugam
Assistant Treasurer	Ong Ye Kung	Ong Ye Kung
CEC Members (non-office-holders)	Tan Chuan-Jin	Tan Chuan-Jin
	Indranee Rajah	Vivian Balakrishnan
	Ng Chee Meng	Lawrence Wong
	Vivian Balakrishnan	
Co-opted into the CEC as 13th and 14th highest vote getters at Party Conference	Ng Eng Hen	Indranee Rajah
	Josephine Teo	Josephine Teo
Members subsequently co-opted into the CEC	Christopher de Souza	Alex Yam
	Desmond Lee	Edwin Tong
	Sitoh Yih Pin	Ng Chee Meng
	Lawrence Wong	Victor Lye

Bibliography

Some sources originated in print form but have also become available online—and in some cases are more conveniently consulted online. My general policy is to provide URLs where available. Originally digital sources (websites, blog posts, etc.) have also been given with the original URL where available. But hyperlinks are mutable and prone to disappearing, frustratingly so for authors, researchers and readers. Where the original is unrecoverable, alternative URLs (for example, to the Internet Archive/Wayback Machine) are given.

Interviews

Ang Mong Seng, 20 May 2013

Baey Yam Keng, 30 Oct. 2015

Dr Vivian Balakrishnan, 14 May 2014

Chan Chun Sing, 12 July 2016

Prof. Chan Heng Chee, 20 Nov. 2012

Dr Chiang Hai Ding, 22 Oct. 2020

Ch'ng Jit Koon, 5 July 2012

Chua Eng Leong, 1 Apr. 2014

S. Chandra Das, 16 Nov. 2012

S. Dhanabalan, 14 May 2013

Harold Fock, 21 Jan. 2014

Arthur Fong, 9 Nov. 2012

Goh Chok Tong, 22 June 2012, 30 Jan. 2013, 30 Nov. 2013, 17 May 2014

Heng Chiang Meng, 3 Nov. 2020

Heng Swee Keat, 6 Apr. 2017

Hwang Soo Jin, 24 Feb. 2014

Prof. S. Jayakumar, 17 Aug. 2012, 29 Apr. 2013

Dr Amy Khor, 2 Dec. 2014

Koh Lian Huat, 12 Aug. 2013

Dr Lau Teik Soon, 27 Oct. 2020

Dr Lee Boon Yang, 12 Mar. 2013, 28 Mar. 2013

Lee Chong Giam, 6 Aug. 2013

Desmond Lee, 3 Feb. 2021

Lee Hsien Loong, 19 Dec. 2014, 1 Dec. 2015

Lee Kuan Yew, 28 Dec. 2011

Lim Hng Kiang, 30 Mar. 2021

Lim Joo Kwang, 5 Aug. 2013

Lim Sah Soon, 21 Aug. 2013

Lim Swee Say, 18 Aug. 2017

Eric Low, 11 Feb. 2014

S.R. Nathan, 12 Sept. 2012

Ong Ah Heng, 16 May 2013

Ong Pang Boon, 9 Jan. 2020
Ong Ye Kung, 2 Jan. 2013, 10 June 2016
Dr Mohamad Maliki bin Osman, 25 Oct. 2017
Dr Ow Chin Hock, 2 Nov. 2012
Zainul Abidin Rasheed, 22 June 2016
K. Shanmugam, 26 Sept. 2017
Tharman Shanmugaratnam, 7 May 2014, 18 Dec. 2015
Inderjit Singh, 9 Feb. 2017
Tan Chuan-Jin, 24 June 2016
Tan Soo Khoon, 11 Apr. 2013
Dr Tony Tan, 11 July 2013
Abdullah Tarmugi, 9 Mar. 2013
Teo Chee Hean, 12 July 2013
Dr S. Vasoo, 3 Apr. 2021
Dr Aline Wong, 27 Dec. 2012
Wong Kan Seng, 16 Apr. 2013
Lawrence Wong, 13 May 2016
Matthias Yao, 22 Aug. 2013
George Yeo, 19 Sept. 2012, 11 Oct. 2012, 22 July 2016
Yatiman Yusof, 21 Oct. 2020

Senior government officials involved in the Economic Strategies Committee, 2017
Officials responsible for the Workfare scheme, 14 July 2014

Personal Communications

S. Dhanabalan, 14 May 2013
Goh Chok Tong, 29 Apr. 2013, 30 Apr. 2013, 17 May 2014, 12 June 2017, 27 Sept. 2020,
    7 Apr. 2021, 21 Apr. 2021
Lau Ping Sum, 1 Mar. 2013, 7 Aug. 2013
Leong Horn Kee, 12 May 2020
Zulkifli bin Mohammed, 23 Oct. 2020
Irene Ng, 22 July 2015
Ng Kah Ting, 8 Nov. 2012, 12 Mar. 2013
Dr Ow Chin Hock, 2 Nov. 2012, 14 Nov. 2012
Zainul Abidin Rasheed, 22 June 2016, 27 Oct. 2020, 20 Nov. 2020
Viswa Sadasivan, 20 Nov. 2013, 13 Aug. 2016
Tang See Chim, 29 Jan. 2013
Teo Chee Hean, 15 Dec. 2017
Dr Aline Wong, 3 Dec. 2020

Oral History Interviews

Interview with Abdullah Tarmugi for "Political History of Singapore 1985–2005" project. Oral History Centre, National Archives of Singapore, Accession No. 003179 (6 reels).

Interview with Chay Wai Chuen for "Political History of Singapore 1985–2005" project. Oral History Centre, National Archives of Singapore, Accession No. 003234 (4 reels).

Interview with Harun Abdul Ghani for "Political History of Singapore 1985–2005" project. Oral History Centre, National Archives of Singapore, Accession No. 002853 (9 reels).

Interview with Jeyaretnam, Joshua Benjamin for "Political History of Singapore 1965–1985" project. Oral History Centre, National Archives of Singapore, Accession No. 002932 (23 reels).

Interview with Dr Lau Teik Soon for "Political History of Singapore 1965–1985" project. Oral History Centre, National Archives of Singapore, Accession No. 001871 (30 reels).

Interview with Lee Khoon Choy for "Political History of Singapore 1945–1965" project. Oral History Centre, National Archives of Singapore, Accession No. 000022 (72 reels).

Interview with Lew Syn Pau for "Political History of Singapore 1985–2005" project. Oral History Centre, National Archives of Singapore, Accession No. 002385 (11 reels).

Interview with Lim Boon Heng for "Political History of Singapore 1965–1985" project. Oral History Centre, National Archives of Singapore, Accession No. 002288 (6 reels).

Interview with Zulkifli Mohammed for "Political History of Singapore 1985–2005" project. Oral History Centre, National Archives of Singapore, Accession No. 002820 (23 reels).

Interview with Mohamad Maidin Bin Packer Mohd for "Political History of Singapore 1985–2005" project. Oral History Centre, National Archives of Singapore, Accession No. 003180 (12 reels).

Interview with Nair, Chengara Veetil Devan for "Political History of Singapore 1945–1965" project. Oral History Centre, National Archives of Singapore, Accession No. 000049 (26 reels).

Interview with Zainul Abidin Rasheed for "Political History of Singapore 1985–2005" project. Oral History Centre, National Archives of Singapore, Accession No. 002281 (8 reels).

Interview with Wan Hussin Bin Haji Zoohri for "Political History of Singapore 1965–1985" project. Oral History Centre, National Archives of Singapore, Accession No. 002862 (12 reels).

Speeches

National Day Speeches

The main source used for National Day Rally speeches is *National Day Rally Speeches: 50 Years of Nationhood in Singapore 1966–2015* (National Archives of Singapore and Cengage Learning Asia, 2017). National Day Rally speeches can also be consulted online at the National Archives of Singapore (NAS) website (www.nas.gov.sg/archivesonline/speeches).

"City of Possibilities, Home for All", PM Lee Hsien Loong, National Day Rally Speech at the University Cultural Centre, 19 Aug. 2007. *National Day Rally Speeches: 50 Years of Nationhood in Singapore*, pp. 583–606.

"First-World Economy, World-Class Home: Setting Fresh Goals", PM Goh Chok Tong, National Day Rally Speech at the Kallang Theatre, 22 Aug. 1999. *National Day Rally Speeches: 50 Years of Nationhood in Singapore*, pp. 389–410.

"From the Valley to the Highlands", PM Goh Chok Tong, National Day Rally Speech at the University Cultural Centre, 17 Aug. 2003. *National Day Rally Speeches: 50 Years of Nationhood in Singapore*, pp. 475–94.

"Global City, Best Home", PM Goh Chok Tong, National Day Rally Speech at the Kallang Theatre, 24 Aug. 1997. *National Day Rally Speeches: 50 Years of Nationhood in Singapore*, pp. 351–67.

"Introducing Safeguards to Protect Singaporeans", PM Lee Kuan Yew, National Day Rally Speech at the Singapore Conference Hall and Trade Union House, 19 Aug. 1984. *National Day Rally Speeches: 50 Years of Nationhood in Singapore*, pp. 111–9.

National Day Rally Speech by Prime Minister Lee Kuan Yew (in Malay), 16 Aug. 1981. https://www.nas.gov.sg/archivesonline/audiovisual_records/record-details/483c0dcb-1164-11e3-83d5-0050568939ad, accessed 17 Feb. 2021.

"New Singapore", PM Goh Chok Tong, National Day Rally Speech at the University Cultural Centre, 19 Aug. 2001. *National Day Rally Speeches: 50 Years of Nationhood in Singapore*, pp. 433–54.

PM Goh Chok Tong, National Day Rally Speech at the Kallang Theatre, 16 Aug. 1992. *National Day Rally Speeches: 50 Years of Nationhood in Singapore*, pp. 253–70.

PM Lee Hsien Loong, National Day Rally Speech at the University Cultural Centre, 22 Aug. 2004. *National Day Rally Speeches: 50 Years of Nationhood in Singapore*, pp. 499–533.

———, National Day Rally Speech at the University Cultural Centre, 20 Aug. 2006. *National Day Rally Speeches: 50 Years of Nationhood in Singapore*, pp. 561–81.

———, National Day Rally Speech at the Institute of Technical Education, 18 Aug. 2013. *National Day Rally Speeches: 50 Years of Nationhood in Singapore*, pp. 723–47.

PM Lee Kuan Yew, National Day Rally Speech at the Kallang Theatre, 16 Aug. 1987. *National Day Rally Speeches: 50 Years of Nationhood in Singapore*, pp. 149–67.

———, National Day Rally Speech at the Kallang Theatre, 14 Aug. 1988. *National Day Rally Speeches: 50 Years of Nationhood in Singapore*, pp. 169–91.

———, National Day Rally Speech, 26 Aug. 1990. *National Day Rally Speeches: 50 Years of Nationhood in Singapore*, pp. 215–37.

"Remaking Singapore: Changing Mindsets", PM Goh Chok Tong, National Day Rally Speech at the University Cultural Centre, 18 Aug. 2002. *National Day Rally Speeches: 50 Years of Nationhood in Singapore*, pp. 455–74.

"Social Stratification and Commitment", PM Goh Chok Tong, National Day Rally Speech, 18 Aug. 1996. *National Day Rally Speeches: 50 Years of Nationhood in Singapore*, pp. 329–50.

"Transforming Singapore", PM Goh Chok Tong, National Day Rally Speech at the Kallang Theatre, 20 Aug. 2000. *National Day Rally Speeches: 50 Years of Nationhood in Singapore*, pp. 411–31.

Speeches by Government Leaders

For speeches by government leaders, I have given the source and, where available, the URL. For speeches by Lee Kuan Yew, I have used the comprehensive 20-volume collection *The Papers of Lee Kuan Yew: Speeches, Interviews and Dialogues* (Singapore: Gale Asia/Cengage Learning Asia, 2013). Several of his speeches can also be consulted online at the NAS website (www.nas. gov.sg/archivesonline/speeches).

Address by PM Lee Kuan Yew on the Eve of National Day on 8 Aug. 1988. "Elected Governments Only as Good as Those Who Choose Them", *The Papers of Lee Kuan Yew, Vol. 10: 1988–1990*, pp. 122–5.

Address by SM Lee Kuan Yew at a Dialogue Session with National Trades Union Congress Leaders on 23 July 2003. "How and Why This Economic Downturn Is Different", *The Papers of Lee Kuan Yew, Vol. 15: 2001–2003*, pp. 443–65.

"Bonding People and Government: The Role of Grassroots Organisations", speech by PM Goh Chok Tong at the Triennial Conference, 29 Apr. 1994. https://www.nas.gov.sg/ archivesonline/speeches/record-details/73ca30d1-115d-11e3-83d5-0050568939ad, accessed 2 May 2021.

"Building a Civic Society", speech by DPM Lee Hsien Loong at the Harvard Club of Singapore's 35th Anniversary, 6 Jan. 2004. https://web.archive.org/ web/20101229193738/http://unpan1.un.org/intradoc/groups/public/documents/ APCITY/UNPAN015426.pdf, accessed 3 May 2021.

"Civic Society: Between the Family and the State", speech by BG (Res) George Yeo, Acting Minister for Information and the Arts and Senior Minister of State for Foreign Affairs, at the NUSS Society Inaugural Lecture, 20 June 1991. *Speeches '91: A Bimonthly Selection of Ministerial Speeches* 15, 3 (1991) (Singapore: Ministry of Information and the Arts): 78–86. https://www.nas.gov.sg/archivesonline/speeches/record-details/70929e71-115d-11e3-83d5-0050568939ad, accessed 3 May 2021.

"Civil Society: Harnessing State-Society Synergies", speech by BG George Yeo, Minister for Information and the Arts and Second Minister for Trade and Industry, at the IPS Conference, 6 May 1998. https://www.nas.gov.sg/archivesonline/speeches/record-details/752a36c9-115d-11e3-83d5-0050568939ad, accessed 3 May 2021.

DPM and Coordinating Minister for National Security Wong Kan Seng, Keynote address at the Singapore Perspectives 2011 Conference, 17 Jan. 2011. https://lkyspp.nus.edu.sg/ docs/default-source/ips/singapore-perspectives-2011-keynote-address-by-mr-wong-kan-seng.pdf, accessed 26 Jan. 2021.

DPM Ong Teng Cheong, Chinese Press Club talk, New Park Hotel, 16 Sept. 1991. https:// www.nas.gov.sg/archivesonline/speeches/record-details/726054b8-115d-11e3-83d5-0050568939ad, accessed 21 Apr. 2020.

First Deputy Prime Minister Goh Chok Tong, speech given at the convention of Malay-Muslim professionals, 7 Oct. 1990. https://www.nas.gov.sg/archivesonline/speeches/ record-details/f550b392-e1b2-11e4-a0fd-0050568939ad, accessed 19 Feb. 2021.

George Yeo, Minister for Information and the Arts and Minister for Health, speech given at the launching of Singapore Technologies (ST) Teleport, 27 Apr. 1995. https://www.nas.

gov.sg/archivesonline/speeches/record-details/717848e5-115d-11e3-83d5-0050568939ad, accessed 21 Jan. 2021.

"Let's Shape Our Future Together", swearing-in speech by PM Lee Hsien Loong, 12 Aug. 2004. https://www.nas.gov.sg/archivesonline/speeches/record-details/7851c88b-115d-11e3-83d5-0050568939ad, accessed 22 Jan. 2021.

Opening address by S. Rajaratnam at the Second Annual Singapore Tamil Youth Conference, 30 Dec. 1989, "Ethnic Counter Revolution", in *The Last Twenty-Five Years 1965–1990*, ed. A. Mani and Malathi Bala. Singapore: Singapore Tamil Youths' Club, 1991, pp. 1–11.

PM and Minister for Finance Lee Hsien Loong, speech at the launch of ComCare at the NTUC Auditorium, 28 June 2005. https://www.nas.gov.sg/archivesonline/speeches/record-details/7c86d3d7-115d-11e3-83d5-0050568939ad, accessed 21 Jan. 2021.

PM Goh Chok Tong, speech given at the Marine Parade National Day Dinner, 27 Aug. 1994. https://www.nas.gov.sg/archivesonline/speeches/record-details/73cb8d43-115d-11e3-83d5-0050568939ad, accessed 3 May 2021.

PM Lee Hsien Loong, remarks at the PA Kopi Talk at Ci Yuan CC, 23 Sept. 2017. https://www.pmo.gov.sg/newsroom/pm-lee-hsien-loong-pa-kopitalk-ci-yuan-cc, accessed 27 Mar. 2021.

———, speech at the NTU Students' Union Ministerial Forum, 15 Sept. 2009. https://www.pmo.gov.sg/Newsroom/transcript-prime-minister-lee-hsien-loongs-speech-ntu-students-union-ministerial-forum, accessed 8 Feb. 2021.

President Ong Teng Cheong, speech given at the swearing-in of the Fifth President at the Istana, 1 Sept. 1993. https://www.nas.gov.sg/archivesonline/speeches/record-details/71dbf6ad-115d-11e3-83d5-0050568939ad, accessed 23 Jan. 2021.

Remarks by PM Lee Kuan Yew at a press conference at the Polytechnic after the results of the General Election were announced on 3 Sept. 1972. "No Intelligent, Constructive Opposition in Singapore", *The Papers of Lee Kuan Yew, Vol. 6: 1973–1974*, pp. 136–40.

Speech by Dr Lee Boon Yang at the opening of the Kallang McNair Residents' Committee Centre on 19 Apr. 1992. Full speech archived at PAP HQ; excerpted in "Boon Yang Defends PAP's 'Votes-for-Upgrading' Strategy", *Straits Times*, 20 Apr. 1992.

Speech by PAP Chairman Mr Ong Teng Cheong at the National Day Celebrations in Punggol Constituency, 6 Aug. 1989. "The Price of Subsidies", *Petir*, July 1989, pp. 12–3.

Speech by PM Goh Chok Tong to Party activists, 24 May 1992. Reproduced in "Pressing Ahead with Our Political Programme", *Petir*, June 1992, pp. 7–8.

Speech by PM Lee Kuan Yew at the Chinese New Year Reception at the Istana on 7 Feb. 1982. "Forging Confucian Values in the Young amidst Rapid Urban Changes", *The Papers of Lee Kuan Yew, Vol. 9: 1981–1987*, pp. 152–5.

Speech by PM Lee Kuan Yew at the Dinner for the Establishment on 25 Sept. 1984. "Principles of Leadership for a Stable Government and Dynamic Society", *The Papers of Lee Kuan Yew, Vol. 9: 1981–1987*, pp. 332–6.

Speech by PM Lee Kuan Yew at the First Ritual for the Observance of the Five Precepts cum Bodhisattva Precept by the Singapore Buddhist Federation at Manjusri Secondary School on 13 Dec. 1988. "Tolerance of Each Other's Religion Is Vital in Singapore", *The Papers of Lee Kuan Yew, Vol. 10: 1988–1990*, pp. 172–5.

Speech by PM Lee Kuan Yew at the National Day Celebrations of the Tanjong Pagar
    Community Centre on 16 Aug. 1984. "Can the One-Man-One-Vote System Continue to
    Work for Singapore?", *The Papers of Lee Kuan Yew, Vol. 9: 1981–1987*, pp. 313–8.
Speech by PM Lee Kuan Yew at the swearing-in of Cabinet at the Istana on 2 Jan. 1985.
    "Political Transition: From Striker to Goalkeeper", *The Papers of Lee Kuan Yew, Vol. 9:
    1981–1987*, pp. 380–1.
Speech by SM Lee Kuan Yew at the CCC National Tribute Dinner on 4 Oct. 1991.
    Reproduced in "How Grassroots Leaders Can Help Mobilise S'poreans for Next Lap",
    Straits Times, 5 Oct. 1991.
Speech by SM Lee Kuan Yew to Nanyang Technological University and National University of
    Singapore students at Nanyang Technological University Auditorium on 15 Feb. 2000.
    "How Will Singapore Compete in a Global Economy?", *The Papers of Lee Kuan Yew, Vol.
    14: 1999–2000*, pp. 163–84.
Speech by SM Lee Kuan Yew to the National Trades Union Congress at the Singapore
    Conference Hall and Trade Union House on 19 July 1996. "Pegging Ministers' Pay
    to That of the Top Earners in the Private Sector", *The Papers of Lee Kuan Yew, Vol. 12:
    1994–1997*, pp. 375–408.
Speech by SM Lee Kuan Yew to the National University of Singapore, Nanyang Technological
    University and Singapore Management University students for the NUS Students'
    Union Senior Minister Forum 2001 at the University Cultural Centre on 15 Oct. 2001.
    "Remaking Singapore for the New Age", *The Papers of Lee Kuan Yew, Vol. 15: 2001–2003*,
    pp. 201–4.
Speech by SM Lee Kuan Yew to the National University of Singapore, Nanyang Technological
    University and Singapore Management University students at the Nanyang Auditorium,
    Nanyang Technological University on 18 Feb. 2003. "What Has the Future in Store for
    Your Generation?", *The Papers of Lee Kuan Yew: Speeches, Interviews and Dialogues, Vol. 15:
    2001–2003*, pp. 379–84.
Talk given by Lim Hng Kiang at Bukit Batok Community Centre Current Affairs Club, 21
    Apr. 1992. Excerpted in "Sharing the Country's Wealth", *Petir*, May 1992, pp. 44–7.
"The National Ideology: A Direction and Identity for Singapore", speech by BG Lee Hsien
    Loong, Minister of Trade and Industry and Second Minister for Defence at the Third
    Alumni International Singapore, Margaux Ballroom, Meridien Hotel, 11 Jan. 1989.
    https://www.nas.gov.sg/archivesonline/speeches/record-details/724e0042-115d-11e3-
    83d5-0050568939ad, accessed 18 Feb. 2021.

Parliamentary Speeches

The relevant notes cite the Official Reports from the Singapore Parliament, accessible at https://
sprs.parl.gov.sg/search/home. Major parliamentary speeches are listed below.

1DPM Goh Chok Tong, speech at the Second Reading of the Maintenance of Religious
    Harmony Bill. Singapore Parliamentary Debates, 23 Feb. 1990, cols 1148–59.
"A Competitive Economy, an Inclusive Society", President S.R. Nathan, address at the opening
    of Parliament, 2 Nov. 2006. Singapore Parliamentary Debates, 2 Nov. 2006.

"Better Health for All", Committee of Supply speech by Gan Kim Yong, Minister for Health, at the 2013 budget debate. Singapore Parliamentary Debates, 12 Mar. 2013. https://www.moh.gov.sg/news-highlights/details/cos-speech-by-minister-for-health-gan-kim-yong---better-health-for-all-(part-1-of-2)-12-march-2013, accessed 20 Oct. 2020.

DPM and Minister for Home Affairs Wong Kan Seng, speech on population at Committee of Supply debate, 4 Mar. 2010. Singapore Parliamentary Debates, 4 Mar. 2010, cols 2928–42.

"Keeping Jobs, Building for the Future", Minister for Finance Tharman Shanmugaratnam, Budget Speech, Singapore Parliamentary Debates, 22 Jan. 2009, cols 1261–1312. https://www.nas.gov.sg/archivesonline/speeches/record-details/8008b212-115d-11e3-83d5-0050568939ad, accessed 26 Jan. 2021.

PM Goh Chok Tong, speech during the debate on the President's Address. Singapore Parliamentary Debates, 5 June 1997, cols 394–411.

"Second Reading Speech by Minister for Law, K Shanmugam on the Protection from Online Falsehoods and Manipulation Bill", 7 May 2019. https://www.mlaw.gov.sg/news/parliamentary-speeches/second-reading-speech-by-minister-for-law-k-shanmugam-on-the-protection-from-online-falsehoods-and-manipulation-bill, accessed 31 Mar. 2021.

Singapore Parliamentary Debates, 14 Dec. 1965, cols 91–117. https://www.nas.gov.sg/archivesonline/speeches/record-details/7835e4e2-115d-11e3-83d5-0050568939ad, accessed 19 Feb. 2021.

Speech by the Prime Minister, Mr Lee Kuan Yew, in Parliament on 23 Feb. 1977, during the debate on the President's Address. Singapore Parliamentary Debates, 23 Feb. 1977, cols 404–54. https://www.nas.gov.sg/archivesonline/speeches/record-details/7394034f-115d-11e3-83d5-0050568939ad, accessed 19 Feb. 2021.

Speech by the Prime Minister, Mr Lee Kuan Yew, on the Motion of Thanks to the Yang Di-Pertuan Negara, 9 Dec. 1963, at the Legislative Assembly. Singapore Legislative Assembly Debates, 9 Dec. 1963, cols 139–51. https://www.nas.gov.sg/archivesonline/speeches/record-details/7411bc17-115d-11e3-83d5-0050568939ad, accessed 19 Feb. 2021.

Speech by the Prime Minister, Mr Lee Kuan Yew, when he moved the Motion of Thanks to the Yang Di-Pertuan Negara, for his Policy Speech on the Opening of Parliament on 14 Dec. 1965.

Party Speeches

The full texts for several speeches given at the Party level are not available in full, and some are archived only at PAP HQ. Where excerpts or a summary of what was said is available either in full or excerpted in a publicly available source (for example, in the *Straits Times* or *Petir*), these sources have been given for readers wishing to consult them.

1st Assistant Secretary-General Heng Swee Keat's speech at 36th Ordinary Party Conference, 8 Nov. 2020. https://www.pap.org.sg/news/1st-assistant-secretary-general-heng-swee-keats-speech-at-36th-ordinary-party-conference/, accessed 2 May 2021.

"4th May Speech at People's Action Party Rally for Holland–Bukit Timah GRC", 5 May 2011. http://vivian.balakrishnan.sg/2011/05/05/4th-may-speech-at-peoples-action-party-rally-for-holland-bukit-timah-grc/, accessed 26 Jan. 2021.

BG George Yeo, speech to Party activists, 25 Apr. 1993. "Young PAP—Recasting the Net", *Petir*, May–June 1993, pp. 10–29.

George Yeo/People's Action Party, "A Personal Message to My Young Singaporean Friends", YouTube, 3 May 2011. https://www.youtube.com/watch?feature=player_embedded&v=zQ87v52GeIg#t=0s., accessed 8 Jan. 2020.

_____, speech at Aljunied GRC rally, May 5 (Part 2), *Todayonline* YouTube Channel, https://www.youtube.com/watch?v=34yLiRUC5rg (accessed 14 Aug 2021).

"New Millennium, New Vision", speech by Secretary-General Goh Chok Tong, at PAP Party Conference, 3 Dec. 2000. *Petir*, Dec. 2000 (Party Conference Special), pp. 2–3.

"Our National Ethic", speech by 1DPM and Minister for Defence Goh Chok Tong at the PAP Youth Wing Charity Night, 28 Oct. 1988. https://www.nas.gov.sg/archivesonline/speeches/record-details/7157e523-115d-11e3-83d5-0050568939ad, accessed 24 Jan. 2021.

"PAP Will Always Be on the Side of Singapore and of Singaporeans", Secretary-General Lee Hsien Loong, speech at PAP 60th anniversary commemorative event at Victoria Concert Hall, 7 Nov. 2014. https://www.pap.org.sg/news/pap-will-always-be-on-the-side-of-singapore-and-of-singaporeans/, accessed 29 Jan. 2021.

"PAP's History through SM Goh's Eyes", SM Goh Chok Tong, speech at Party Conference, 7 Nov. 2004, *Petir*, Nov.–Dec. 2004, pp. 28–47.

PM Goh Chok Tong, address to cadres at the Party Conference on 15 Nov. 1991. "PAP Scours Its Party Branches for Activists Who Are MP Material", *Straits Times*, 30 May 1992.

———, speech at Party Conference on 15 Nov. 1992. "Finding Ministers Is Top Priority", *Business Times*, 16 Nov. 1992; "Why the Urgent Need to Find New Pillars for the Cabinet—PM", *Straits Times,* 13 Dec. 1992; "My Urgent Mission", *Petir*, Nov.–Dec. 1992, pp. 10–9.

———, speech at Party Convention, 11 Jan. 1998. "How to Win an Election: Four Major Lessons from GE 97", *Petir*, Jan.–Feb. 1998, pp. 8–9.

PM Lee Kuan Yew, speech at Party Convention, 23 Jan. 1988 (PAP archive).

———, speech at Party Conference, 18 Nov. 1990, "Preserving Singapore's Unique Political Culture", *Straits Times*, 26 Nov. 1990.

Secretary-General Goh Chok Tong, speech at Ordinary Party Conference, 1 Dec. 2002, at the Kallang Theatre. https://www.nas.gov.sg/archivesonline/speeches/record-details/703d492c-d5d7-11e8-ab1b-001a4a5ba61b, accessed 22 Feb. 2021.

———, speech at the PAP 50th Anniversary Dinner, 23 Oct. 2004, at Suntec International Convention & Exhibition Centre. https://www.nas.gov.sg/archivesonline/speeches/record-details/72933f41-d5d7-11e8-ab1b-001a4a5ba61b, accessed 21 Jan. 2021.

Secretary-General Lee Hsien Loong, speech at PAP Awards and Convention, 19 Nov. 2017. https://www.pap.org.sg/conference-convention/pap-awards-and-convention-2017-transcript-of-speech-by-secretary-general-lee-hsien-loong/, accessed 29 Jan. 2021.

———, speech at 36th Ordinary Party Conference, 8 Nov. 2020. https://www.pap.org.sg/news/secretary-general-lee-hsien-loong-36th-ordinary-party-conference-speech/, accessed 23 Apr. 2021.

Senior Minister of State for Trade and Industry Lim Boon Heng, speech to cadres at Party Conference, 15 Nov. 1992, "Putting Cost of Living in the Proper Perspective", *Petir*, Nov.–Dec. 1992, pp. 64–9.

Speech by Comrade Ong Pang Boon at his 90th birthday dinner, 23 Mar. 2019. https://www.facebook.com/watch/?v=426187534823690, accessed 23 Jan. 2021.

Speech by PAP Secretary-General Lee Hsien Loong at the People's Action Party Convention, 6 Dec. 2015. https://www.pap.org.sg/conference-convention/lets-shape-our-future-together-pap-secretary-general-lee-hsien-loong/, accessed 29 Jan. 2021.

Speech by PM Lee Hsien Loong at Party Convention, 8 Dec. 2013. https://www.pap.org.sg/conference-convention/party-convention-2013-speech-by-pm-lee-hsien-loong/, accessed 28 Jan. 2021.

Speech by Secretary-General Goh Chok Tong at the Ordinary Party Conference, 1 Dec. 2002. https://www.nas.gov.sg/archivesonline/speeches/record-details/703d492c-d5d7-11e8-ab1b-001a4a5ba61b, accessed 16 Apr. 2020.

Newspapers and Magazines

Sources consulted and listed in the notes include the *Straits Times, Sunday Times, Business Times, Berita Minggu, Berita Harian, Lianhe Zaobao, Shin Min Daily News, Channel NewsAsia, Today, New Paper, AsiaOne* and *Singapore Monitor*. Reports from the international press and wire services were also used where necessary. These have not been included in the bibliography.

Various publications of political parties were used and are listed in the notes: besides the PAP's *Petir*, these include the *Hammer* from the Workers' Party, and the *Demokrat* (later, *New Democrat*) from the Singapore Democratic Party.

Books

Asad-ul Iqbal, Latif and Lee Huay Leng, eds. *George Yeo on Bonsai, Banyan and the Tao*. Singapore: World Scientific, 2015.

Bellows, Thomas. *The People's Action Party of Singapore*. New Haven: Yale University Southeast Asia Studies, 1970.

Chan Heng Chee. *The Dynamics of One Party Dominance: The PAP at the Grassroots*. Singapore: Singapore University Press, 1976.

Chee, Julia, Fan Wenjun, Ng Yoke Lin, Tan Bee Leng, June Lin and Joanne Yip (editorial board). *The Papers of Lee Kuan Yew: Speeches, Interviews and Dialogues*, 20 vols. Singapore: Gale Asia/Cengage Learning Asia, 2012–13.

Chee Soon Juan. *Dare to Change: An Alternative Vision for Singapore*. Singapore: Singapore Democratic Party, 1994.

———. *Singapore, My Home Too*. Singapore: Melodies Press, 1995.

Chiang Hai Ding and Rohan Kamis. *We Also Served: Reflections of Singapore's Former PAP MPs*. Singapore: Straits Times Press, 2014.

Chng Tuan Tze, Low Yit Leng and Teo Soh Lung, eds. *1987: Singapore's Marxist Conspiracy 30 Years On*. Singapore: Function 8, 2017.

Corrupt Practices Investigation Bureau. *The Journey: 60 Years of Fighting Corruption in Singapore*. Singapore: Corrupt Practices Investigation Bureau, 2012.

Da Cunha, Derek. *The Price of Victory: The 1997 Singapore General Election and Beyond*. Singapore: Institute of Southeast Asian Studies, 1997.

———. *Singapore Places Its Bets: Casinos, Foreign Talent, and Remaking a City-State*. Singapore: Straits Times Press, 2010.

———. *Breakthrough: Roadmap for Singapore's Political Future*. Singapore: Straits Times Press, 2012.

Desker, Barry and Kwa Chong Guan, eds. *Goh Keng Swee: A Public Career Remembered*. Singapore: World Scientific, 2012.

Editorial Committee under the auspices of the PAP 45th Anniversary Celebrations Organising Committee. *For People through Action by Party*. Singapore: People's Action Party, 1999.

Feedback Unit, Ministry of Community Development and Sports. *Building Bridges: The Story of the Feedback Unit*. Singapore: Feedback Unit, Ministry of Community Development and Sports, 2004.

Fong Sip Chee. *The PAP Story: The Pioneering Years*. Singapore: Times Periodicals, 1979.

George, Cherian. *The Air-Conditioned Nation: Essays on the Politics of Comfort and Control, 1990–2000*. Singapore: Landmark Books, 2000.

George, Cherian and Donald Low. *PAP v. PAP: The Party's Struggle to Adapt to a Changing Singapore*. Singapore: Self-published, 2020.

Goh, Daniel, ed. *Walking with Singapore: The Workers' Party's 60th Anniversary*. Singapore: Workers' Party, 2017.

Han Fook Kwang et al., eds. *Lee Kuan Yew: Hard Truths to Keep Singapore Going*. Singapore: Straits Times Press, 2011.

Henson, Bertha. *GE2020: Fair or Foul?* Singapore: Epigram Books, 2020.

Hill, Michael and Lian Kwen Fee. *The Politics of National Building and Citizenship in Singapore*. London: Routledge, 1995.

Hong, Lysa and Huang Jianli. *Scripting a National History: Singapore and Its Pasts*. Hong Kong: Hong Kong University Press, 2008.

Jayakumar, S. *Governing: A Singapore Perspective*. Singapore: Straits Times Press, 2020.

Jayakumar, Shashi and Albert Lau. *Singapore Chronicles: PAP*. Singapore: Straits Times Press and Institute of Policy Studies, 2019.

Jeyaretnam, J.B. *The Hatchet Man of Singapore*. Singapore: Jeya Publishers, 2003.

Koh, Gillian and Ooi Giok Ling, eds. *State-Society Relations in Singapore*. Singapore: Institute of Policy Studies and Oxford University Press, 2000.

Kuo, Eddie C.Y., Jon S.T. Quah and Tong Chee Kiong. *Religion and Religious Revivalism in Singapore*. Singapore: Ministry of Community Development, 1988.

Lam Peng Er and Kevin Tan, eds. *Lee's Lieutenants: Singapore's Old Guard*. Rev. ed. Singapore: Straits Times Press, 2018.

Lee, Edwin. *Singapore: The Unexpected Nation*. Singapore: Institute of Southeast Asian Studies, 2008.

Lee Kuan Yew. *The Singapore Story: Memoirs of Lee Kuan Yew.* Singapore: Times Editions, 1998.

———. *From Third World to First: The Singapore Story 1965–2000.* Singapore: Times Editions, 2000.

———. *One Man's View of the World.* Singapore: Straits Times Press, 2013.

Lee, Terence and Kevin Y.L. Tan, eds. *Change in Voting: Singapore's 2015 General Election.* Singapore: Ethos Books, 2015.

Legge, James, trans. *The Zuo Commentary on the Spring and Autumn Annals.* Hong Kong: Hong Kong University Press, 1960.

Leong Ching. *Citizens, Conversations & Collaborations: Chronicles of the Citizens' Consultative Committee.* Singapore: People's Association, 2005.

Leong Ching and Irene Ng. *PAP 50: Five Decades of the People's Action Party.* Singapore: People's Action Party, 2004.

Liang Thow Yick, May Lim and M. Rebaczonok-Padulo. *PAP Youth in Action 1986–1991.* Singapore: People's Action Party, 1991.

Lim, Catherine. *A Watershed Election: Singapore's GE 2011.* Singapore: Marshall Cavendish, 2011.

Lim Chong Yah. *Singapore's National Wages Council: An Insider's View.* Singapore: World Scientific, 2014.

Loke Hoe Yeong. *The First Wave: JBJ, Chiam & the Opposition in Singapore.* Singapore: Epigram Books, 2019.

Low, Donald and Sudhir Thomas Vadaketh, eds. *Hard Choices: Challenging the Singapore Consensus.* Singapore: NUS Press, 2014.

Marshall Cavendish. *Up Close with Lee Kuan Yew: Insights from Colleagues and Friends.* Singapore: Marshall Cavendish, 2016.

Mauzy, D.K. and R.S. Milne. *Singapore Politics under the People's Action Party.* London: Routledge, 2002.

Mutalib, Hussin. *Parties and Politics: A Study of Opposition Parties and the PAP in Singapore.* 2nd ed. Singapore: Marshall Cavendish, 2006.

Nathan, S.R. *An Unexpected Journey: The Path to the Presidency.* Singapore: Editions Didier Millet, 2011.

Neo Boon Siong and Geraldine Chen. *Dynamic Governance: Embedding Culture, Capabilities and Change in Singapore.* Singapore: World Scientific, 2007.

王鼎昌：走向总统府之路 (*Ong Teng Cheong: Road to the Istana*). Singapore: Lianhe Zaobao, 1994.

Pang Cheng Lian. *Singapore's People's Action Party: Its History, Organization and Leadership.* New York: Oxford University Press, 1971.

PAP Seniors Group (PAP.SG) Executive Committee. *PAP Pioneers: 50 Ordinary Stories.* Singapore: People's Action Party, 2015.

Peh Shing Huei. *Tall Order: The Goh Chok Tong Story, Vol. 1.* Singapore: World Scientific, 2018.

———. *Standing Tall: The Goh Chok Tong Years, Vol. 2.* Singapore: World Scientific, 2021.

People's Action Party, 1954–1979: Petir 25th Anniversary Issue. Singapore: Central Executive Committee, People's Action Party, 1979.

Quah, Jon S.T., ed. *In Search of Singapore's National Values.* Singapore: Times Academic Press for the Institute of Policy Studies, 1990.

————. *Public Administration Singapore-Style.* Bingley: Emerald Group Publishing, 2010.

Quah, Jon S.T., Chan Heng Chee and Seah Chee Meow, eds. *Government and Politics of Singapore.* Singapore: Oxford University Press, 1987.

Saniff, Sidek. *Life Reflections at Eighty.* Singapore: Opus Editorial, 2018.

Saw Swee Hock. *The Population of Singapore.* 3rd ed. Singapore: Institute of Southeast Asian Studies, 2012.

Seow, Francis. *To Catch a Tartar: A Dissident in Lee Kuan Yew's Prison.* New Haven: Yale University Southeast Asian Studies, 1995.

Singam, Constance, Tan Chong Kee, Tisa Ng and Leon Perera, eds. *Building Social Space in Singapore: The Working Committee's Initiative in Civil Society Activism.* Singapore: Select Publishing, 2002.

Singh, Bilveer. *Whither PAP's Dominance? An Analysis of Singapore's 1991 General Elections.* Petaling Jaya: Pelanduk, 1992.

————. *Is the People's Action Party Here to Stay? Analysing the Resilience of the One-Party Dominant State in Singapore.* Singapore: World Scientific, 2019.

Singh, Bilveer, Walid Jumblatt Abdullah and Felix Tan. *Unmasking Singapore's 2020 General Elections: Covid-19 and the Evolving Political Landscape.* Singapore: World Scientific, 2021.

Tan, Kenneth Paul. *Cinema and Television in Singapore: Resistance in One Dimension.* Leiden: Brill Academic Publishing, 2008.

Tan, Kevin Y.L. *An Introduction to Singapore's Constitution.* Singapore: Talisman Publishing, 2005.

Tan, Kevin Y.L. and Lam Peng Er, eds. *Managing Political Change in Singapore: The Elected Presidency.* London: Routledge, 1997.

Tan, Kevin Y.L. and Terence Lee, eds. *Voting in Change: Politics of Singapore's 2011 General Election.* Singapore: Ethos Books, 2011.

————, eds. *Voting in a Time of Change.* Singapore: Ethos Books, 2021.

Tan Wah Piow. *Smokescreens & Mirrors: Tracing the "Marxist Conspiracy".* Singapore: Function 8, 2012.

Tan-Oehler, Shirley, ed. *The Story of Kampong Ubi.* Singapore: People's Action Party Kampong Ubi Branch and PAP Community Foundation, Kampong Ubi Branch, 1993.

Teo Soh Lung. *Beyond the Blue Gate: Recollections of a Political Prisoner.* Petaling Jaya: Strategic Information and Research Development Centre, 2010.

Turnbull, Mary. *A History of Modern Singapore, 1819–2005.* 3rd ed. Singapore: NUS Press, 2009.

Vasil, Raj. *Governing Singapore.* Singapore: Mandarin, 1992.

Weiss, Meredith L. *The Roots of Resilience: Party Machines and Grassroots Politics in Singapore and Malaysia.* Singapore: NUS Press, 2020.

Welsh, Bridget, James U.H. Chin, Arun Mahizhnan and Tan Tarn How, eds. *Impressions of the Goh Chok Tong Years in Singapore.* Singapore: NUS Press, 2009.

Yap, Jimmy. *We Are One: The People's Association Journey 1960–2010*. Singapore: People's Association, 2010.

Yap, Sonny, Richard Lim and Leong Weng Kam. *Men in White: The Untold Story of Singapore's Ruling Party*. Singapore: Singapore Press Holdings, 2009.

Yee Jenn Jong. *Journey in Blue: A Peek into the Workers' Party of Singapore*. Singapore: World Scientific, 2021.

Book Chapters

Bhaskaran, Manu, Ho Seng Chee, Donald Low, Tan Kim Song, Sudhir Vadaketh and Yeoh Lam Keong. "Inequality and the Need for a New Social Compact", in *Singapore Perspectives 2012: Singapore Inclusive: Bridging Divides*, ed. Kang Soon Hock and Leong Chan-Hoong. Singapore: World Scientific, 2013, pp. 125–76.

Chan Heng Chee. "Postscript: Politics in Singapore, 1984–1986", in *Government and Politics of Singapore*, ed. Jon S.T. Quah, Chan Heng Chee and Seah Chee Meow. Singapore: Oxford University Press, 1987, pp. 309–21.

———. "The Structuring of the Political System", in *Management of Success: The Moulding of Modern Singapore*, ed. Kernial Singh Sandhu and Paul Wheatley. Singapore: Institute of Southeast Asian Studies, 1989, pp. 70–89.

Chia Shi Teck. "Notes from the Margin: Reflections on the First Presidential Election, by a Former Nominated Member of Parliament", in *Managing Political Change in Singapore: The Elected Presidency*, ed. Kevin Tan and Lam Peng Er. London: Routledge, 1997, pp. 188–99.

Ch'ng Jit Koon. "The Role of Grassroots Organisations", in *People's Action Party 1954–1984*. Singapore: Central Executive Committee, People's Action Party, 1984, pp. 180–9.

Chua Beng Huat. "Liberalising Culture", in *Impressions of the Goh Chok Tong Years in Singapore*, ed. Bridget Welsh, James U.H. Chin, Arun Mahizhnan and Tan Tarn How. Singapore: NUS Press, 2009, pp. 436–43.

Clammer, John. "Deconstructing Values: The Establishment of a National Ideology and Its Implications for Singapore's Political Future", in *Singapore Changes Guard: Social, Political and Economic Directions in the 1990s*, ed. Garry Rodan. New York: St. Martin's Press, 1993, pp. 34–51.

Cotton, James. "Political Innovation in Singapore: The Presidency, the Leadership and the Party", in *Singapore Changes Guard: Social, Political and Economic Directions in the 1990s*, ed. Garry Rodan. New York: St. Martin's Press, 1993, pp. 3–33.

George, Cherian. "Internet Politics: Shouting Down the PAP", in *Voting in Change: Politics of Singapore's 2011 General Election*, ed. Kevin Y.L. Tan and Terence Lee. Singapore: Ethos Books, 2011, pp. 146–59.

Gopinathan, S. "Language Policy Changes 1979–1992: Politics and Pedagogy", in *Language, Society and Education in Singapore: Issues and Trends*, ed. S. Gopinathan, Anne Pakir, Ho Wah Kam and Vanithamani Saravanan. 2nd ed. Singapore: Times Academic Press, 1998, pp. 19–44.

Hack, Karl. "Remaking Singapore 1990–2004: From Disciplinarian Development to Bureaucratic Proxy Democracy", in *Singapore from Temasek to the 21st Century*, ed. Karl

Hack and Jean-Louis Margolin (with Karine Delaye). Singapore: NUS Press, 2010, pp. 345–83.

Huang Jianli. "The Head of State in Singapore: An Historical Perspective", in *Managing Political Change in Singapore: The Elected Presidency*, ed. Kevin Y.L. Tan and Lam Peng Er. London: Routledge, 1997, pp. 9–51.

Jayakumar, Shashi, Benjamin Ang and Nur Diyanah Anwar. "Fake News and Disinformation: Singapore Perspectives", in *Disinformation and Fake News*, ed. Shashi Jayakumar, Benjamin Ang and Nur Diyanah Anwar. Singapore: Palgrave Macmillan, 2020, pp. 137–58.

Kassim, Yang Razali. "Winning Over the Malay Community", in *Impressions of the Goh Chok Tong Years in Singapore*, ed. Bridget Welsh, James U.H. Chin, Arun Mahizhnan and Tan Tarn How. Singapore: NUS Press, 2009, pp. 363–74.

Koh, Gillian. "Pruning the Banyan Tree? Civil Society in Goh's Singapore", in *Impressions of the Goh Chok Tong Years in Singapore*, ed. Bridget Welsh, James U.H. Chin, Arun Mahizhnan and Tan Tarn How. Singapore: NUS Press, 2009, pp. 93–106.

Kuo, Eddie C.Y. "Confucianism as Political Discourse in Singapore: The Case of an Incomplete Revitalisation Movement", in *Confucian Traditions in East Asian Modernity: Moral Education and Economic Culture in Japan and the Four Mini-Dragons*, ed. Tu Wei-Ming. Cambridge: Harvard University Press, 1996, pp. 294–309.

Kwok Kian Woon and Low Kee Hong. "Cultural Policy and the City-State: Singapore and the 'New Asian Renaissance'", in *Global Culture: Media, Arts, Policy, and Globalization*, ed. Diana Crane, Nobuko Kawashima and Ken'ichi Kawasaki. New York: Routledge, 2002, pp. 151–68.

Lam Peng Er. "The Organisational Utility Men: Toh Chin Chye and Lim Kim San", in *Lee's Lieutenants: Singapore's Old Guard*, ed. Lam Peng Er and Kevin Tan. Rev. ed. Singapore: Straits Times Press, 2018, pp. 42–79.

Lee Kuan Yew. "What of the Past Is Relevant to the Future?", in *People's Action Party 1954–1979: Petir 25th Anniversary Issue*. Singapore: Central Executive Committee, People's Action Party, 1979, pp. 30–43.

Lim Chong Yah. "From High Growth Rates to Recession", in *Management of Success: The Moulding of Modern Singapore*, ed. Kernial Singh Sandhu and Paul Wheatley. Singapore: Institute of Southeast Asian Studies, 1989, pp. 201–17.

Lim, Linda. "Free Market Fancies: Hong Kong, Singapore, and the Asian Financial Crisis", in *The Politics of the Asian Economic Crisis*, ed. T.J. Pempel. Ithaca: Cornell University Press, 1999, pp. 101–15.

Low, Donald. "What Went Wrong for the PAP in 2011?", in *Hard Choices: Challenging the Singapore Consensus*, ed. Donald Low and Sudhir Thomas Vadaketh. Singapore: NUS Press, 2014, pp. 168–77.

Low, Donald, Yeoh Lam Keong, Tan Kim Song and Manu Bhaskaran. "Economic Myths in the Great Population Debate", in *Hard Choices: Challenging the Singapore Consensus*, ed. Donald Low and Sudhir Thomas Vadaketh. Singapore: NUS Press, 2014, pp. 40–7.

Mutalib, Hussin. "Singapore's First Elected Presidency: The Political Motivations", in *Managing Political Change in Singapore: The Elected Presidency*, ed. Kevin Y.L. Tan and Lam Peng Er. London: Routledge, 1997, pp. 167–87.

Pang, Edwin. "Refreshing the Young PAP", in *Renaissance Singapore? Economy, Culture and Politics*, ed. Kenneth Paul Tan. Singapore: NUS Press, 2007, pp. 231–8.

Quah, Jon S.T. "Singapore in 1988: Safeguarding the Future", in *Singapore 1989*. Singapore: Ministry of Communications and Information, 1989, pp. 1–24.

Rahim, Lily Zubaidah. "A New Dawn in PAP-Malay Relations?", in *Impressions of the Goh Chok Tong Years in Singapore*, ed. Bridget Welsh, James U.H. Chin, Arun Mahizhnan and Tan Tarn How. Singapore: NUS Press, 2009, pp. 350–62.

Rodan, Gary. "State-Society Relations and Political Opposition in Singapore", in *Political Oppositions in Industrialising Asia*, ed. Gary Rodan. London: Routledge, 1996, pp. 95–127.

Seah Chee Meow. "Grassroots Political Participation in Singapore", in *People's Action Party 1954–1979*. Singapore: Central Executive Committee, People's Action Party, 1979, pp. 276–81.

———. "Parapolitical Institutions", in *Government and Politics of Singapore*, ed. Jon S.T. Quah, Chan Heng Chee and Seah Chee Meow. Singapore: Oxford University Press, 1985, pp. 173–94.

Tan, Alvin. "Forum Theatre: A Limited Mirror", in *Building Social Space in Singapore: The Working Committee's Initiative in Civil Society Activism*, ed. Constance Singam, Tan Chong Kee, Tisa Ng and Leon Perera. Singapore: Select Publishing, 2002, pp. 73–80.

Tan Tarn How. "To the Market", in *Impressions of the Goh Chok Tong Years in Singapore*, ed. Bridget Welsh, James U.H. Chin, Arun Mahizhnan and Tan Tarn How. Singapore: NUS Press, 2009, pp. 425–35.

Tan, Tony. "Three Fundamental Principles", in *PAP 50: Fives Decades of the People's Action Party*, ed. Ching Leong and Irene Ng. Singapore: People's Action Party, 2004, p. 8.

Vasu, Norman and Nur Diyanah Binte Anwar. "The Maligned Malays and National Service", in *National Service in Singapore*, ed. Ho Shu Huang and Graham Ong-Webb. Singapore: World Scientific, 2019, pp. 203–25.

Wang, Karyn. "Moving from Survival to Sustainability in the Environment", in *Impressions of the Goh Chok Tong Years in Singapore*, ed. Bridget Welsh, James U.H. Chin, Arun Mahizhnan and Tan Tarn How. Singapore: NUS Press, 2009, pp. 288–98.

Welsh, Bridget. "Does Difference Matter? Particular and National Political Identities in Singapore's 2011 General Election", in *Voting in Change: Politics of Singapore's 2011 General Election*, ed. Kevin Y.L. Tan and Terence Lee. Singapore: Ethos Books, 2011, pp. 91–114.

Welsh, Bridget, James U.H. Chin, Arun Mahizhnan and Tan Tarn How. "Introduction: A Redefined Singapore", in *Impressions of the Goh Chok Tong Years*, ed. Bridget Welsh, James U.H. Chin, Arun Mahizhnan and Tan Tarn How. Singapore: NUS Press, 2009, pp. 1–23.

Yeo, George. "Worldwide Web: Strengthening the Singapore Network", in *State-Society Relations in Singapore*, ed. Gillian Koh and Ooi Giok Ling. Singapore: Institute of Policy Studies and Oxford University Press, 2000, pp. 18–26.

———. "Articles in CUMSA Newsletter", in *George Yeo on Bonsai, Banyan and the Tao*, ed. Latif Asad-ul Iqbal and Lee Huay Leng. Singapore: World Scientific, 2015, pp. 623–7.

Zoohri, Wan Hussin. "Education from 1959 to 2014: The Seeds of the Formation of Mendaki", in *Majulah!, 50 Years of Malay/Muslim Community in Singapore*, ed. Zainul Abidin Rasheed and Norshahril Saat. Singapore: World Scientific, 2016, pp. 159–77.

Journal Articles

Asher, M.G. and Amarendu Nandy. "Health Financing in Singapore: A Case for Systematic Reforms", *International Social Security Review* 59, 1 (2006): 75–92.

Bellows, Thomas. "The Singapore Party System", *Journal of Southeast Asian History* 8, 1 (Mar. 1967): 122–38.

———. "Singapore in 1989: Progress in a Search for Roots", *Asian Survey* 30, 2 (Feb. 1990): 201–9.

Chan Heng Chee. "Singapore in 1985: Managing Political Transition and Economic Recession", *Asian Survey* 26, 2 (Feb. 1986): 158–67.

Chong, Terence. "Globalising on Its Own Terms", *Southeast Asian Affairs* (2006): 265–82.

Da Cunha, Derek. "Singapore in 1998: Managing Expectations, Shoring-Up National Morale", *Southeast Asian Affairs* (1999): 271–90.

Gill, Alisha. "Healthcare Financing: How Should Singapore's Ministry of Health Shift Costs from Private Pockets to the Public Purse?", Lee Kuan Yew School of Public Policy, case study, 2013.

Haque, M. Shamsul. "A Grassroots Approach to Decentralization in Singapore", *Asian Journal of Political Science* 4, 1 (1996): 64–84.

Ho Khai Leong. "Singapore: Campaigning for the Future", *Southeast Asian Affairs* (2007): 297–308.

Khairulanwar, Zaini. "Singapore in 2019: In Holding Pattern", *Southeast Asian Affairs* (2020): 294–322.

Kluver, Randolph. "Political Culture and Information Technology in the 2001 Singapore General Election", *Political Communication* 21, 4 (2010): 435–58.

Koh, Gillian and Ooi Giok Ling. "Singapore: A Home, a Nation?", *Southeast Asian Affairs* (2002): 255–81.

Kuah, Adrian. "Foresight and Policy: Thinking about Singapore's Futures", *Social Space* 6 (2013): 104–9.

Lai Szu Hao. "Communicating to Our Pioneer Generation", *Ethos* 15 (14 June 2016). https://www.csc.gov.sg/articles/communicating-to-our-pioneer-generation, accessed 20 June 2021.

Latif, Asad. "The Internationalisation of Singapore Politics", *Southeast Asian Affairs* (1996): 321–36.

Lee, Terence and Cornelius Kan. "Blogospheric Pressures in Singapore: Internet Discourses and the 2006 General Election", *Continuum: Journal of Media & Cultural Studies* 23, 6 (Dec. 2009): 871–86.

Lim, M.K. "Shifting the Burden of Health Care Finance: A Case Study of Public–Private Partnership in Singapore", *Health Policy* 69, 1 (2004): 83–92.

Lim Xiuhui. "Security with Self-Reliance: The Argument for the Singapore Model", *Ethos* 3 (Oct. 2007). https://www.csc.gov.sg/articles/security-with-self-reliance-the-argument-for-the-singapore-model, accessed 20 June 2021.

Mauzy, D.K. "Leadership Succession in Singapore: The Best Laid Plans . . .", *Asian Survey* 33, 12 (Dec. 1993): 1163–74.

Ng Chee Yuen. "Privatization in Singapore: Divestment with Control", *ASEAN Economic Bulletin* (Mar. 1989): 290–318.

Ng, Irene. "Revisiting S. Rajaratnam's Democracy of Deeds", *Commentary* 25 (2016): 11–20.

Pang Eng Fong. "The Economic Status of Malay Muslims in Singapore", *Journal of the Institute of Muslim Minority Affairs* 3, 2 (1981): 148–61.

Pflug, Jonathan. "Extraordinary Times, Fundamental Principles: The 2009 Budget and the Ministry of Finance's Approach to Countercyclical Economic Strategy", *Ethos* 6 (1 July 2009). https://www.csc.gov.sg/articles/extraordinary-times-fundamental-principles-the-2009-budget-and-the-ministry-of-finance's-approach-to-countercyclical-economic-strategy, accessed 20 June 2021.

Poh, Jacqueline. "Workfare: The Fourth Pillar of Social Security in Singapore", *Ethos* 3 (Oct. 2007). https://www.csc.gov.sg/articles/workfare-the-fourth-pillar-of-social-security-in-singapore, accessed 20 June 2021.

Quah, Jon S.T. "Singapore in 1987: Political Reforms, Control, and Economic Recovery", *Southeast Asian Affairs* (1988): 233–52.

Singh, Bilveer. "Singapore: Change amidst Continuity", *Southeast Asian Affairs* (1994): 267–84.

Sreekumar, T.T. and Shoba Vadrevu. "Subpolitics and Democracy: The Role of New Media in the 2011 General Elections in Singapore", *Science, Technology & Society* 18, 2 (July 2013): 231–49.

Tan, Jason. "The Rise and Fall of Religious Knowledge in Singapore Secondary Schools", *Journal of Curriculum Studies* 29, 5 (1997): 603–24.

Tan, Jason and S. Gopinathan. "An Innovation in Educational Financing", *Change: Transformations in Education* 2 (Nov. 1999): 66–79.

Tan, Kenneth Paul. "Crisis, Self-Reflection, and Rebirth in Singapore's National Life Cycle", *Southeast Asian Affairs* (2003): 241–58.

———. "Democracy and the Grassroots Sector in Singapore", *Space and Polity* 7, 1 (2003): 3–20.

———. "Meritocracy and Elitism in a Global City: Ideological Shifts in Singapore", *International Political Science Review* 29, 1 (2008): 7–27.

———. "Singapore in 2011: A 'New Normal' in Politics?", *Asian Survey* 52, 1 (2012): 220–6.

Tan, Kevin Y.L. "The Elected Presidency in Singapore: Constitution of the Republic of Singapore (Amendment) Act 1991", *Singapore Journal of Legal Studies* (July 1991): 179–94.

Tay, Simon S.C. "Island in the World: Globalization and Singapore's Transformation", *Southeast Asian Affairs* (2001): 279–309.

Yahya, Faizal bin. "Singapore in 2010: Rebounding from Economic Slump, Managing Tensions between a Global City and a Fledgling Nation State", *Southeast Asian Affairs* (2011): 255–70.

Yeoh Lam Keong. "Rethinking a New Social Compact for Singapore", *Ethos* 3 (2007): 7–12. https://www.csc.gov.sg/articles/rethinking-a-new-social-compact-for-singapore, accessed 26 Jan. 2021.

Official Sources

Press Releases

"Additional Buyer's Stamp Duty for a Stable and Sustainable Property Market", Monetary Authority of Singapore media release, 7 Dec. 2011. https://www.mas.gov.sg/news/media-releases/2011/absd-for-a-stable-and-sustainable-property-market, accessed 4 Apr. 2020.

"Additional Measures to Ensure a Stable and Sustainable Property Market", Monetary Authority of Singapore media release, 11 Jan. 2013. https://www.mas.gov.sg/news/media-releases/2013/additional-measures-to-ensure-a-stable-and-sustainable-property-market, accessed 26 Jan. 2021.

"Alternate Authority for the Minister for National Development Instructs POFMA Office to Issue Correction Directions and Targeted Correction Direction", POFMA Office media release, 4 July 2020. https://www.pofmaoffice.gov.sg/documents/media-releases/2020/July/pofma-pr-mnd-04jul2020-01.pdf, accessed 1 Apr. 2021.

"Amendments to En Bloc Sale Legislation Take Effect on 4 Oct 2007", Ministry of Law press release, 3 Oct. 2007. https://www.mlaw.gov.sg/news/press-releases/amendments-to-en-bloc-sale-legislation-take-effect-on-4-oct-2007, accessed 4 Apr. 2020.

"Appointment of Adviser to CCC, CCMCs and RCs in Anson", Statement from the Prime Minister's Office, 23 Dec. 1981. https://www.nas.gov.sg/archivesonline/speeches/record-details/738202a3-115d-11e3-83d5-0050568939ad, accessed 26 Feb. 2021.

"Bumper Launch to Meet Diverse Housing Needs", Housing & Development Board press release, 30 May 2013. http://www20.hdb.gov.sg/fi10/fi10296p.nsf/PressReleases/2B6DE2EB72C9056548257B7B000333F7?OpenDocument, accessed 28 Jan. 2021.

"Employment Situation in Fourth Quarter 2007", Minister of Manpower press release, 31 Jan. 2008. https://www.nas.gov.sg/archivesonline/speeches/record-details/7f58d60a-115d-11e3-83d5-0050568939ad, accessed 26 Jan. 2021.

"Firms to Consider Singaporeans Fairly for Jobs", Ministry of Manpower press release, 23 Sept. 2013. http://www.mom.gov.sg/newsroom/press-releases/2013/firms-to-consider-singaporeans-fairly-for-jobs, accessed 21 Jan. 2021.

"First Reading of the Land Titles (Strata) (Amendment) Bill by DPM S Jayakumar, 27 Aug. 2007", Ministry of Law press release, 27 Aug. 2007. https://www.mlaw.gov.sg/news/speeches/first-reading-of-the-land-titles-strata-amendment-bill-by-dpm-s-jayakumar-27-aug-2007, accessed 26 Jan. 2021.

"Government Statement Relating to Devan Nair's Pension", statement from the Ministry of Communications and Information (1985–1990), 4 Apr. 1985. https://www.nas.gov.sg/archivesonline/speeches/record-details/7390021e-115d-11e3-83d5-0050568939ad, accessed 26 Feb. 2021.

"Household Income Grew amidst Strong Economic Performance", Department of Statistics press release, 13 Feb. 2008. https://www.nas.gov.sg/archivesonline/speeches/record-details/7f0a3c1b-115d-11e3-83d5-0050568939ad, accessed 6 Mar. 2021.

Joint press statement by the Ministry of Home Affairs and Ministry of Information and the Arts, 21 Jan. 1994. Quoted in "Govt Acts against 5th Passage over Performance Art", *Straits Times*, 22 Jan. 1994.

"Keeping Jobs, Building for the Future", Ministry of Finance press release, 22 Jan. 2009. https://www.mof.gov.sg/news-publications/press-releases/Keeping-Jobs-Building-for-the-Future, accessed 26 Jan. 2021.

"MAS Introduces Debt Servicing Framework for Property Loans", Monetary Authority of Singapore media release, 28 June 2013. https://www.mas.gov.sg/news/media-releases/2013/mas-introduces-debt-servicing-framework-for-property-loans, accessed 26 Jan. 2021.

"MAS Restricts Loan Tenure for Residential Properties", Monetary Authority of Singapore media release, 5 Oct. 2012. https://www.mas.gov.sg/news/media-releases/2012/mas-restricts-loan-tenure-for-residential-properties, accessed 26 Jan. 2021.

"Measures to Contain the COVID-19 Outbreak in Migrant Worker Dormitories", Minister of Manpower press release, 14 Dec. 2020. https://www.mom.gov.sg/newsroom/press-releases/2020/1214-measures-to-contain-the-covid-19-outbreak-in-migrant-worker-dormitories, accessed 2 Apr. 2021.

"Measures to Ensure a Stable and Sustainable Property Market", Monetary Authority of Singapore media release, 19 Feb. 2010. https://www.mas.gov.sg/news/media-releases/2010/measures-to-ensure-a-stable-and-sustainable-property-market, accessed 26 Jan. 2021.

"Measures to Further Differentiate Citizens, Permanent Residents and International Students in Education", Ministry of Education press release, 20 Dec. 2009. https://www.nas.gov.sg/archivesonline/speeches/record-details/8087286e-115d-11e3-83d5-0050568939ad, accessed 26 Feb. 2021.

"Ministry of Manpower Introduces the Foreign Employee Dormitories Bill 2014, Annex A: Background on the IMC on FW Management and FW Housing Landscape", Ministry of Manpower press release, 4 Nov. 2014. http://www.mom.gov.sg/newsroom/press-releases/2014/ministry-of-manpower-introduces-the-foreign-employee-dormitories-bill-2014, accessed 26 Jan. 2021.

"More Help for First-Time Home Buyers", HDB press release, 30 Aug. 2010. https://www20.hdb.gov.sg/fi10/fi10296p.nsf/PressReleases/895204e2295bdc394825778e007fa919?OpenDocument&Click=, accessed 4 Apr. 2020.

"More Help for the Needy", MCYS Media Release, 5 Mar. 2008. https://www.nas.gov.sg/archivesonline/speeches/record-details/7f2dc00d-115d-11e3-83d5-0050568939ad, accessed 15 Aug. 2021.

"More Help, Stronger Support, Better Homes", HDB press release, 27 Aug. 2013. https://www20.hdb.gov.sg/fi10/fi10296p.nsf PressReleases/2311677DFDF53AC248257BD40032F6A4?OpenDocument, accessed 26 Jan. 2021.

"National Pledge", National Heritage Board, n.d. https://www.nhb.gov.sg/what-we-do/our-work/community-engagement/education/resources/national-symbols/national-pledge, accessed 13 Aug. 2021.

"Our Singapore Conversation on Healthcare", Ministry of Health press release, 1 July 2013. https://www.moh.gov.sg/news-highlights/details/our-singapore-conversation-on-healthcare, accessed 6 Jan. 2020.

Singapore Police Force, "Police Statement on Reports Lodged against a Candidate Contesting in the General Election 2020", 5 July 2020. https://www.police.gov.sg/media-room/news/20200705_police_statement_cid, accessed 14 Apr. 2021.

Singapore Police Force Statement, 7 July 2020. https://www.police.gov.sg/media-room/ news/20200707_police_statement_others, accessed 14 Apr. 2021.

"Singaporean Citizens Benefit from Record Employment Creation, Securing Good Quality Jobs", Ministry of Manpower press release, 29 Feb. 2008. http://www.mom.gov.sg/ newsroom/press-releases/2008/Singapore-citizens-benefit-from-record-employment-creation-securing-good-quality-jobs, accessed 26 Jan. 2021.

"Statement from the 4G Team on DPM Heng Swee Keat's Decision to Stand Aside as Leader of the 4G Team on 8 April 2021", 8 Apr. 2021. https://www.pmo.gov.sg/Newsroom/ Statement-4G-Team-8-Apr, accessed 30 Apr. 2021.

"Working Together Towards a Responsible and Vibrant Society", MITA's response to recommendations of the Censorship Review Committee, 8 Sept. 2003. https://www.nas. gov.sg/archivesonline/speeches/record-details/77756b8a-115d-11e3-83d5-0050568939ad, accessed 22 Jan. 2021.

Reports, Working Papers, Official Statements and Data

For election results, I have used information and data from the website of the Elections Department Singapore. Also useful is the unofficial resource http://www.singapore-elections.com.

2014 Population in Brief, National Population and Talent Division, Prime Minister's Office, Sept. 2014. https://github.com/isomerpages/isomerpages-stratgroup/raw/master/images/ PublicationImages/population-in-brief-2014.pdf, accessed 6 Jan. 2020.

"Average Monthly Household Income from Work (Including Employer CPF Contributions) among Resident Employed Households by Deciles, 2000–2019 (Table 13A)", Department of Statistics, n.d. https://www.tablebuilder.singstat.gov.sg/publicfacing/createSpecialTable. action?refId=17262, accessed 2 May 2020.

Censorship Review Committee Report 1992, Ministry of Communications and the Arts, 1992. https://eresources.nlb.gov.sg/printheritage/detail/e634b8b0-b986-4c14-9016-b8dcfe12dd6b.aspx, accessed 9 Aug. 2021.

Census of Population 2000—Advance Data Release No. 9: A Decade of Progress, Department of Statistics, 2001.

Collyns, Charles and Abdelhak Senhadji, "Lending Booms, Real Estate Bubbles and the Asian Crisis", IMF Working Paper WP/02/20, Jan. 2002. https://www.imf.org/external/pubs/ft/ wp/2002/wp0220.pdf, accessed 4 Mar. 2021.

ComCare Annual Report for Financial Year 2012, Ministry of Social and Family Development, 2013. https://www.msf.gov.sg/publications/Documents/ComCare%20Annual%20 Report%202012%20(1).pdf, accessed 26 Jan. 2021.

CPF Board Annual Report 2011, CPF Board, 2011. https://www.nas.gov.sg/archivesonline/ government_records/record-details/49f796a0-d636-11e5-b8bb-0050568939ad, accessed 26 Jan. 2021.

CPF Board Annual Report 2013, CPF Board, 2013. https://www.nas.gov.sg/archivesonline/ government_records/record-details/7b64d258-d635-11e5-b8bb-0050568939ad, accessed 13 Jan. 2020.

Department of Statistics Singapore, *Census of Population 1990: Advance Data Release*. Singapore: SNP Publishers, 1991. https://eservice.nlb.gov.sg/data2/BookSG/publish/2/29421d69-75f8-40bb-9775-7d5221375325/web/html5/index.html?opf=tablet/BOOKSG.xml&launchlogo=tablet/BOOKSG_BrandingLogo_.png, accessed 24 May 2020.

Engaging New Media: Challenging Old Assumptions, Advisory Council on the Impact of New Media on Society, Dec. 2008. https://www.mci.gov.sg/~/media/mcicorp/doc/aimsreportdec08engagingnewmediachallengingoldassumptions.pdf?la=en, accessed 26 Jan. 2021.

General Household Survey 1995—Release 1: Socio-Demographic and Economic Characteristics. Singapore: Department of Statistics, Ministry of Trade and Industry, 1996. https://eservice.nlb.gov.sg/data2/BookSG/publish/6/6f08cb77-15fd-417a-96f6-0011ccb3c8c0/web/html5/index.html?opf=tablet/BOOKSG.xml&launchlogo=tablet/BOOKSG_BrandingLogo_.png&pn=49, accessed 29 May 2020.

"HDB Resale Price Index", dataset managed by the Housing & Development Board, 7 July 2015. https://data.gov.sg/dataset/hdb-resale-price-index, accessed 26 Jan. 2021.

"Healthcare Consumer Price Index", dataset managed by the Ministry of Health, 3 Apr. 2017. https://data.gov.sg/dataset/consumer-price-indices-general-and-healthcare, accessed 6 Jan. 2020.

"Healthcare Financing Sources", written reply from the health minister to Parliamentary Question 515 from Gerald Giam, Ministry of Health, 13 May 2013. https://www.moh.gov.sg/news-highlights/details/healthcare-financing-sources, accessed 6 Jan. 2020.

"How Do Singaporeans Benefit from Our Reserves?" Ministry of Finance, n.d. https://www.mof.gov.sg/policies/reserves/how-do-singaporeans-benefit-from-our-reserves, accessed 26 Jan. 2021.

"Improving the Lives of Low-Income and Vulnerable Families in Singapore", Ministry of Social and Family Development, Nov. 2018, pp. 6–7. https://www.msf.gov.sg/publications/Documents/Improving%20the%20lives%20of%20low-income%20and%20vulnerable%20families%20in%20Singapore.pdf, accessed 26 Jan. 2021.

"Income Growth, Mobility and Inequality Trends in Singapore", Ministry of Finance, Aug. 2015. https://www.mof.gov.sg/Portals/0/Feature%20Articles/Income%20Growth,%20Distribution%20and%20Mobility%20Trends%20in%20Singapore.pdf, accessed 1 May 2020.

"Investigation Findings on Flooding of MRT Tunnels between Bishan and Braddell Stations from 7–8 October 2017", Land Transport Authority, 5 Dec. 2017. https://www.lta.gov.sg/content/ltagov/en/newsroom/2017/12/2/investigation-findings-on-flooding-of-mrt-tunnels-between-bishan-and-braddell-stations-from-7--8-october-2017.html, accessed 27 Mar. 2021.

IPS 20th Anniversary Report, Institute of Policy Studies, *Issuu*, 4 July 2011, pp. 4–5. https://issuu.com/ips-singapore/docs/ips_20thann, accessed 9 Oct. 2019.

Khoo Chian Kim, *Census of Population 1980, Singapore—Release No. 3: Literacy and Education*, Department of Statistics, 1981.

Labour Market Report 2013, Manpower Research and Statistics Department, Ministry of Manpower, 2013 (archived by the Ministry of Manpower).

"Lending Booms, Real Estate Bubbles and the Asian Crisis", Charles Collyns and Abdelhak Senhadji, Jan. 2002. https://www.imf.org/external/pubs/ft/wp/2002/wp0220.pdf, accessed 3 May 2018.

Letter Exchange between PM Lee Hsien Loong and DPM Heng Swee Keat, 8 Apr. 2021. https://www.pmo.gov.sg/Newsroom/Letter-exchange-between-PM-Lee-Hsien-Loong-and-DPM-Heng-Swee-Keat, accessed 27 Apr. 2021.

"Merdeka Generation Package". https://www.singaporebudget.gov.sg/budget_2019/budget-measures/merdeka-generation-package, accessed 27 Mar. 2021.

"Payment of Medical Bills Using MediSave Account Monies", CPF Board, *CPF Trends*, July 2011 (archived by the CPF Board).

Population Trends 2013, Department of Statistics, Ministry of Trade and Industry, Republic of Singapore, 2013 https://web.archive.org/web/20140623221822/https:/www.singstat.gov.sg/Publications/publications_and_papers/population_and_population_structure/population2013.pdf, accessed 7 May 2020.

Population in Brief 2009, National Population Secretariat and agencies, 2009. https://github.com/isomerpages/isomerpages-stratgroup/raw/master/images/PublicationImages/population-in-brief-2009.pdf, accessed 14 Aug. 2021.

Population in Brief 2010, National Population Secretariat and agencies, 2010. https://github.com/isomerpages/isomerpages-stratgroup/raw/master/images/PublicationImages/population-in-brief-2010.pdf, accessed 14 Aug. 2021.

Population in Brief 2011, National Population and Talent Division and agencies, 2011. https://github.com/isomerpages/isomerpages-stratgroup/raw/master/images/PublicationImages/population-in-brief-2011.pdf, accessed 14 Aug. 2021.

Reflections of Our Singapore Conversation, Our Singapore Conversation Secretariat, Aug. 2013 https://www.reach.gov.sg/-/media/reach/old-reach/oursingaporeconversation/oursingaporeconversationreflection.ashx, accessed 27 Jan. 2021.

Report of the Advisory Council on Culture and the Arts, Advisory Council on Culture and the Arts, 1989. https://eresources.nlb.gov.sg/printheritage/detail/4574f095-8cae-4e85-81ca-5e57f98af85f.aspx, accessed 2 Mar. 2021.

Report of the Committee on the Problems of the Aged, Ministry of Health, Feb. 1984. https://www.nas.gov.sg/archivesonline/government_records/record-details/c09bde19-86b3-11e7-83df-0050568939ad, accessed 23 Jan. 2021.

Report of the Cost Review Committee, Ministry of Trade and Industry, Sept. 1993. https://www.nas.gov.sg/archivesonline/government_records/record-details/3b0739f8-7958-11e7-83df-0050568939ad, accessed 2 Mar. 2021.

Report of the Cost Review Committee, Ministry of Trade and Industry, Nov. 1996. https://www.nas.gov.sg/archivesonline/government_records/record-details/c5ad6737-73d7-11e7-83df-0050568939ad, accessed 2 Mar. 2021.

Report of the Economic Committee—The Singapore Economy: New Directions, Ministry of Trade and Industry, Feb. 1986. https://eservice.nlb.gov.sg/data2/BookSG/publish/d/d08447b5-ce22-4de2-9d6c-89cd9cb95074/web/html5/index.html?opf=tablet/BOOKSG.xml&launchlogo=tablet/BOOKSG_BrandingLogo.png, accessed 5 June 2020.

Report of the Economic Review Committee—New Challenges, Fresh Goals: Towards a Dynamic Global City, Ministry of Trade and Industry, Feb. 2003. https://www.nas.gov.sg/

archivesonline/government_records/record-details/9a3e288d-da9c-11e6-bb26-0050568939ad, accessed 22 Jan. 2021.

Report of the Economic Strategies Committee: High-Skilled People, Innovative Economy, Distinctive Global City, Economic Strategies Committee, Feb. 2010. https://web.archive.org/web/20170319192204/http://www.mof.gov.sg/Portals/0/MOF%20For/Businesses/ESC%20Recommendations/ESC%20Main%20Report.pdf, accessed 26 Jan. 2021.

Report of the Inter-Ministerial Committee on the Ageing Population, Ministry of Community Development, 1999. https://www.msf.gov.sg/publications/Documents/Materials_IMCReport.pdf, accessed 5 June 2020.

Report of the Select Committee on Deliberate Online Falsehoods: Causes, Consequences and Countermeasures. Parl. 15 of 2018. Presented to Parliament on 19 Sept. 2018. https://sprs.parl.gov.sg/selectcommittee/selectcommittee/download?id=1&type=subReport, accessed 31 Mar. 2021.

Report on the First Triennial Conference for Grassroots Organisations. Bonding People and Government: The Role of Grassroots Organisations, 29 Apr. 1994–15 May 1994, People's Association, 1994.

Report on the Second Triennial Conference for Grassroots Organisations. Grassroots 21: Stronger Community Bonds, People's Association, 1997.

"Resale Statistics", dataset managed by the Housing & Development Board, 7 July 2015. https://data.gov.sg/dataset/hdb-resale-price-index, accessed 26 Jan. 2021.

"Singapore 21: Together, We Make the Difference", Singapore 21 Committee, 1999.

Singapore Census of Population 2000—Advance Data Release No. 7: Household Income Growth and Distribution. https://www.nas.gov.sg/archivesonline/speeches/record-details/7797c138-115d-11e3-83d5-0050568939ad, accessed 15 Apr. 2021.

Singapore Public Sector Outcomes Review, Ministry of Finance, Aug. 2014. https://www.mof.gov.sg/docs/librariesprovider2/past-editions/spor_2014.pdf, accessed 26 Jan. 2021.

"Summary of the Deliberations of the Subject Committee on 'Attracting Talent vs Looking after Singaporeans'", Singapore 21 Committee, 1999.

"T6. Percent Change in Consumer Price Index (CPI) over Corresponding Period of Previous Year, 2019 as Base Year, Annual", Department of Statistics, n.d. https://www.singstat.gov.sg/-/media/files/publications/economy/excel/cpimar20.xlsx, accessed 30 Apr. 2020.

The Report of the Remaking Singapore Committee: Changing Mindsets, Deepening Relationships, Remaking Singapore Committee, 2003. https://eresources.nlb.gov.sg/webarchives/wayback/20070115030050/http://www.remakingsingapore.gov.sg/Full Version of Remake Sg.pdf, accessed 8 June 2020.

The SDP-PKMS Cost of Living Report 1996, Singapore Democratic Party and Pertubuhan Kebangsaan Melayu, 1996.

"Transcript of Remarks by PM Lee Hsien Loong at the Press Conference on Leadership Transition at the Istana on 8 April 2021". https://www.pmo.gov.sg/Newsroom/Transcript-remarks-Lee-Hsien-Loong-Press-Conference-8-April, accessed 1 May 2021.

"Transcript of Senior Minister Goh Chok Tong's Media Interview on 2 May 2011 at 6pm". https://www.nas.gov.sg/archivesonline/speeches/record-details/7ab659e6-d5d7-11e8-ab1b-001a4a5ba61b, accessed 26 Jan. 2021.

"Workfare Income Supplement", *Ministry of Manpower Factsheet*, 11 Mar. 2010. https://
www.mom.gov.sg/~/media/mom/documents/speeches/2010/factsheet%20-%20wis%20
(110310).pdf, accessed 26 Jan. 2021.

World Bank, "GDP Growth (Annual %)—Singapore", n.d. https://data.worldbank.org/
indicator/NY.GDP.MKTP.KD.ZG?end=2018&locations=SG, accessed 23 Jan. 2021.

World Bank, "GDP Per Capita (Current US$)—Singapore", n.d. https://data.worldbank.org/
indicator/NY.GDP.PCAP.CD?end=1984&locations=SG&start=1965, accessed 6 July
2020.

White Papers, Green Papers, Select Committee, Commission of Inquiry Reports

A Sustainable Population for a Dynamic Singapore: Population White Paper (National Population
and Talent Division, Jan. 2013). https://www.strategygroup.gov.sg/media-centre/
population-white-paper-a-sustainable-population-for-a-dynamic-singapore, accessed 27
Jan. 2021.

*Agenda for Action: Goals and Challenges. Misc.2 of 1988. Presented to Parliament by the First
Deputy Prime Minister and Minister for Defence and Ordered by Parliament to Lie upon the
Table.* 15 Feb. 1988. https://www.nas.gov.sg/archivesonline/government_records/record-
details/3e92c6fb-7958-11e7-83df-0050568939ad, accessed 23 June 2021.

*C.V. Devan Nair. Circumstances Relating to Resignation as President of the Republic of Singapore,
Command 8 of 1988.* 29 June 1988. https://www.nas.gov.sg/archivesonline/government_
records/record-details/eb5e9aca-8133-11e7-83df-0050568939ad, accessed 21 Jan. 2021.

*First Report of the Committee of Privileges: Complaints of Allegations of Executive Interference in
the Judiciary, Parl. 3 of 1987.* Presented to Parliament on 21 Jan. 1987 https://www.nas.
gov.sg/archivesonline/government_records/record-details/f4cd4aa0-0537-11e8-a2a9-
001a4a5ba61b, accessed 21 Jan. 2021.

Report of the Commission of Inquiry on Investigations Concerning the Late Mr Teh Cheang Wan.
Singapore: Singapore National Printers (1987). https://www.nas.gov.sg/archivesonline/
government_records/record-details/f1304836-8133-11e7-83df-0050568939ad, accessed
21 Jan. 2021.

*Report of the Committee of Inquiry into the Disruption of MRT Train Services on 15 and 17
December 2011*, Ministry of Transport, 3 July 2012. Executive summary. https://www.
mot.gov.sg/news/COI%20report%20-%20Executive%20Summary.pdf, accessed 27 Jan.
2021.

Report of the Committee of Inquiry into the Little India Riot on 8 December 2013, Ministry of
Home Affairs, 27 June 2014. https://www.mha.gov.sg/docs/default-source/press-releases/
little-india-riot-coi-report---2014-06-27.pdf, accessed 27 Jan. 2021.

Report of the Constitutional Commission 2016, 17 Aug. 2016. https://www.gov.sg/~/media/gov/
elected-presidency/report-of-the-constitutional-commission-2016.pdf, accessed 27 Mar.
2021.

*Report of the Select Committee on the Constitution of the Republic of Singapore (Amendment No. 2)
Bill [Bill No. 41/89].* Presented to Parliament on 15 Mar. 1990. https://sprs.parl.gov.sg/
selectcommittee/selectcommittee/download?id=296&type=report, accessed 23 Jan. 2021.

Report of the Select Committee on the Constitution of the Republic of Singapore (Amendment No. 3) Bill [Bill No. 23/90], Parl. 9 of 1990. Presented to Parliament on 18 Dec. 1990. https://www.nas.gov.sg/archivesonline/government_records/record-details/eba96b29-0537-11e8-a2a9-001a4a5ba61b, accessed 23 Jan. 2021.

Report of the Select Committee on the Legal Profession (Amendment) Bill [Bill No. 20/86], Parl. 7 of 1986. Presented to Parliament on 16 Oct. 1986. https://www.nas.gov.sg/archivesonline/government_records/record-details/fa9b0116-0537-11e8-a2a9-001a4a5ba61b, accessed 21 Jan. 2021.

Report of the Select Committee on the Parliamentary Elections (Amendment) Bill [Bill No. 23/87] and the Constitution of the Republic of Singapore (Amendment No. 2) Bill [Bill No. 24/87], Parl. 3 of 1988. Presented to Parliament on 5 May 1988. https://www.nas.gov.sg/archivesonline/government_records/record-details/982b35cd-0537-11e8-a2a9-001a4a5ba61b, accessed 23 Jan. 2021.

Report of the Select Committee on Verification of Health Care Subsidy of Government Polyclinics and Public Hospitals, Parl. 5 of 1996. Presented to Parliament on 30 Sept. 1996. https://www.nas.gov.sg/archivesonline/government_records/record-details/d82b057d-578d-11e7-9199-0050568939ad, accessed 3 Mar. 2021.

Safeguarding Financial Assets and the Integrity of the Public Services: The Constitution of the Republic of Singapore (Amendment No. 3) Bill, Cmd. 11 of 1990. Presented to Parliament on 27 Aug. 1990. https://www.nas.gov.sg/archivesonline/government_records/record-details/ac86db7a-7aea-11e7-83df-0050568939ad, accessed 23 Jan. 2021.

Salaries for a Capable and Committed Government, Cmd. 1 of 2012. 10 Jan. 2012. Prime Minister's Office. https://www.nas.gov.sg/archivesonline/government_records/record-details/e5fd8a9c-d634-11e5-b8bb-0050568939ad, accessed 27 Jan. 2021.

Shared Values, Cmd. 1 of 1991. Presented to Parliament by Command of the President of the Republic of Singapore. Ordered by Parliament to Lie upon the Table: 2 January 1991. https://www.nas.gov.sg/archivesonline/government_records/record-details/a472b486-7aea-11e7-83df-0050568939ad, accessed 24 Jan. 2021.

The Report of the Electoral Boundaries Review Committee, 1991. Cmd. 12 of 1991. Presented to Parliament by Command of the President of the Republic of Singapore. Ordered by Parliament to Lie upon the Table: 8 August 1991. https://www.nas.gov.sg/archivesonline/government_records/record-details/a8a70f21-7aea-11e7-83df-0050568939ad, accessed 5 Apr. 2021.

White Paper: Competitive Salaries for Competent and Honest Government, Cmd. 13 of 1994. Presented to Parliament by Command of the President of the Republic of Singapore. Ordered by Parliament to Lie upon the Table: 21 October 1994. Prime Minister's Office, 1994. https://www.nas.gov.sg/archivesonline/government_records/record-details/a0bef428-730e-11e7-83df-0050568939ad, accessed 3 Mar. 2021.

White Paper on Constitutional Amendments to Safeguard Financial Assets and the Integrity of the Public Services, Cmd. 10 of 1988. Presented to Parliament on 29 July 1988. https://www.nas.gov.sg/archivesonline/government_records/record-details/ebace2d2-8133-11e7-83df-0050568939ad, accessed 23 Jan. 2021.

White Paper on Maintenance of Religious Harmony, Cmd. 21 of 1989. Presented to Parliament on 26 Dec. 1989 https://www.nas.gov.sg/archivesonline/government_records/record-details/fc4424cf-7957-11e7-83df-0050568939ad, accessed 24 Aug. 2020.

White Paper on the Principles for Determining and Safeguarding the Accumulated Reserves of the Government and the Fifth Schedule Statutory Boards and Government Companies. https://www.nas.gov.sg/archivesonline/government_records/record-details/12ec06c2-4a32-11e7-9199-0050568939ad, accessed 1 May 2020.

White Paper on the Review of Specific Aspects of the Elected Presidency, Cmd. 7 of 2016. 15 Sept. 2016. Prime Minister's Office. https://www.nas.gov.sg/archivesonline/government_records/record-details/1fd8053f-8632-11e6-9af5-0050568939ad, accessed 27 Mar. 2021.

Dissertations

Bellows, Thomas J. "The Singapore Party System: The First Two Decades", PhD dissertation, Yale University, 1968.

Heng, Francis Hua Mong. "Ethnicity and Drug Abuse: The Case of the Singapore Malays", PhD dissertation, University of Hull, 1994.

Sukmawati bte Haji Sirat. "Trends in Malay Political Leadership: The People's Action Party's Malay Political Leaders and the Integration of the Singapore Malays", PhD dissertation, University of South Carolina, 1995.

Manifestos

"A People United: Secure Future, Better Life", PAP 2001 general election manifesto.

"Kuay Teow Hot and Nice", PAP's Aljunied 2011 local manifesto.

"Make Your Vote Count", Workers' Party manifesto 2020, p. 23. https://d3bnzwrhehvhbjiwmja.s3-ap-southeast-1.amazonaws.com/The+Workers+Party+Manifesto+2020.pdf, accessed 22 Apr. 2021.

"Our Lives, Our Jobs, Our Future", PAP 2020 general election manifesto.

"Securing Our Future Together", PAP 2011 general election manifesto. https://papwebcdn.azureedge.net/upload/Issues/1100/20110506pt2.pdf, accessed 7 July 2020.

"Singapore 21: Make It Our Best Home", PAP 1997 general election manifesto.

"Staying Together, Moving Ahead", PAP 2006 general election manifesto. https://web.archive.org/web/20060508021145/http://www.pap.org.sg/uploads/ap/587/documents/papmanifesto06_english.pdf, accessed 7 July 2020.

"The Next Lap", PAP 1991 general election manifesto.

"Together We Progress", PAP 1984 general election manifesto.

"Towards a First World Parliament", Workers' Party 2011 general election manifesto. https://www.scribd.com/doc/52644250/Workers-Party-Manifesto-2011, accessed 8 Jan. 2020.

"You Have a Choice", Workers' Party 2006 general election manifesto. https://issuu.com/wpsg/docs/wp_manifesto_2006, accessed 7 July 2020.

Online Sources

"10 Million Population", Singapore Democratic Party press release, 3 July 2020. https://www.facebook.com/yoursdp/posts/10159188889418455, accessed 1 Apr. 2021.

"Addendum to PAP Resolution 2013", PAP, 8 Aug. 2013. https://www.pap.org.sg/news/
    addendum-to-pap-resolution-2013/?doing_wp_cron=1611800205.78270697593688964
    84375, accessed 25 Feb. 2017.

"Aftermath", 11 May 2011. http://xiaxue.blogspot.sg/2011/05/aftermath.html, accessed 1 Apr.
    2020.

"An Economic History of Singapore, 1965–2065", keynote address by Mr Ravi Menon,
    Managing Director of the Monetary Authority of Singapore, at the Singapore Economic
    Review Conference 2015, Singapore, 5 Aug. 2015. https://www.bis.org/review/
    r150807b.htm, accessed 5 Dec. 2020.

Au, Alex. "On Hougang Field", May 2006. https://web.archive.org/web/20060927151105/
    http:/www.yawningbread.org/arch_2006/yax-581.htm, accessed 7 May 2020.

———. "The Political Parallels to the NKF Scandal", Dec. 2005. https://web.archive.org/
    web/20060117144046/http:/www.yawningbread.org/arch_2005/yax-527.htm, accessed
    5 Dec. 2020.

Chong-Aruldoss, Jeanette. "Inside, Outside . . . Upside Down!", *Online Citizen*, 3 Feb. 2014.
    https://www.onlinecitizenasia.com/2014/02/03/inside-outside-upside-down/, accessed 5
    Mar. 2021.

"CNBC Transcript: Lee Hsien Loong, Prime Minister of Singapore", *CNBC*, 19 Oct. 2017.
    https://www.cnbc.com/2017/10/19/cnbc-transcript-lee-hsien-loong-prime-minister-of-
    singapore.html, accessed 16 Apr. 2021.

"Comment: Openly Discussing Public Service Lapses Will Force Both PAP & Opposition to
    Do Better", *Mothership*, 19 Sept. 2020. https://mothership.sg/2020/09/singapore-public-
    pap-trust-issues/, accessed 30 Apr. 2021.

Constitution of the Republic of Singapore. https://sso.agc.gov.sg/Act/CONS1963, accessed 15
    Sept. 2021.

"Definition of a 'Malay Person' Opens Up a Can of Worms about Mendaki and Apparent
    Double Standards", *Online Citizen*, 24 July 2017. https://www.theonlinecitizen.
    com/2017/07/24/definition-of-a-malay-person-opens-up-a-can-of-worms-about-
    mendaki-and-apparent-double-standards/, accessed 30 Mar. 2021.

"Even if Josephine Teo Doesn't Want to Apologise to Migrant Workers, She Should
    Apologise to Singaporeans", *Online Citizen*, 6 May 2020. https://www.theonlinecitizen.
    com/2020/05/06/even-if-josephine-teo-doesnt-want-to-apologise-to-migrant-workers-
    she-should-apologise-to-singaporeans/, accessed 14 Apr. 2021.

"Ex-Minister Yaacob Ibrahim: Next 4G Leader Should be Chosen 'Yesterday', but They'll
    Likely Need More Time", *Mothership*, 1 May 2021. https://mothership.sg/2021/05/
    yaacob-ibrahim-on-4g-new-leader/, accessed 2 May 2021.

"Finally, Being His Own Man: Goh Chok Tong on Singapore, Asia—and Himself", PM
    Goh Chok Tong, interview with *Asiaweek*, 25 Nov. 1999. https://web.archive.org/
    web/20110130202527/http://edition.cnn.com/ASIANOW/asiaweek/interview/goh.
    chok.tong/goh2.html, accessed 23 Apr. 2020.

"Findings of Survey Conducted by the Institute of Policy Studies", Institute of Policy Studies
    presentation, Feb. 2009. https://lkyspp.nus.edu.sg/docs/default-source/ips/pops-1_
    slides_0209.pdf, accessed 26 Jan. 2021.

"From Quiet, Shy Boy to Leader of the Opposition: Pritam Singh's School Teacher Reflects on his Growth", *Mothership*, 13 July 2020. https://mothership.sg/2020/07/pritam-singh-teacher/, accessed 14 Apr. 2021.

"Fury over 6.9 Million Population Target for Singapore", *Yahoo! News*, 30 Jan. 2013. https://sg.news.yahoo.com/fury-over-6-9-million-population-target-for-singapore-103503070.html, accessed 11 Apr. 2020.

"GE 2020: How The Ivan Lim Scandal Sparked a 'Trial by Internet'", *Vulcan Post*, June 2020. https://vulcanpost.com/703144/ge-2020-ivan-lim-scandal-trial-by-internet/, accessed 14 Apr. 2021.

"GE2020: PAP, WP Candidates for East Coast GRC Address Supporters on Nomination Day", *Channel NewsAsia* YouTube Channel, 30 June 2020. https://www.youtube.com/watch?v=pg_v1KzTXQ&t=179, accessed 27 Apr. 2021.

"GE2020: Why Singapore May Lose, Whatever the Final Score", *Academia SG*, 7 July 2020. https://www.academia.sg/academic-views/ge2020-why-singapore-may-lose/, accessed 2 Apr. 2021.

"GE2020: WP Will Also Be 'Soul Searching' as PAP 'Tries Its Hardest' to Take Back Lost Wards—Pritam Singh", *Yahoo! News*, 12 July 2020. https://sg.yahoo.com/news/ge-2020-wp-will-also-be-soul-searching-as-pap-tries-its-hardest-to-take-back-lost-wards-pritam-singh-144029323.html, accessed 14 Apr. 2021.

George, Cherian. "Time for a Code of Conduct", *Air-Conditioned Nation*, 10 May 2020. https://www.airconditionednation.com/2020/05/10/online-politics/?fbclid=IwAR0hE3u2ShzDUClcGeoje73duAx7vIUoB8iYe9a5QhXqXgsTiLmRkfy98Lc, accessed 2 Apr. 2021.

"George Yeo: Election Not a Power Contest", YouTube, 30 Apr. 2011. https://www.youtube.com/watch?v=BWOiUVB7UM0, accessed 13 Apr. 2021.

Goh Chok Tong, post on MParader Facebook page, 31 Dec. 2017. https://www.facebook.com/MParader/posts/1954247007951289, accessed 31 Mar. 2021.

Heng Swee Keat, Facebook, 2 July 2020. https://www.facebook.com/hengsweekeat/posts/3133213056717198, accessed 1 Apr. 2021.

"Heng Swee Keat's Speech Fumble Makes Him the Subject of Internet Memes", *Independent*, 2 July 2020. https://theindependent.sg/heng-swee-keats-speech-fumble-makes-him-the-subject-of-internet-memes/, accessed 14 Apr. 2021.

"How K. Shanmugam, the Man Who Upholds Some of S'pore's Hardest Laws, Deals with a Crisis", *Mothership*, 17 June 2020. https://mothership.sg/2020/06/k-shanmugam-interview-covid, accessed 6 Mar. 2021.

"Interview with DPM Wong Kan Seng, Minister-in-Charge of Population Issues", 16 Aug. 2006. https://www.strategygroup.gov.sg/media-centre/press-releases/media-interview-with-dpm-wong-kan-seng-on-population-challenge-for-singapore, accessed 26 Jan. 2021.

"Jamus Lim Warms the Cockles of Viewers' Hearts for His GE2020 Debate Performance", *Mothership*, 1 July 2020. https://mothership.sg/2020/07/jamus-lim-warms-the-cockles-of-viewers-hearts-for-his-ge2020-debate-performance/, accessed 2 Apr. 2021.

Ko Siew Huey. "TOC Exclusive: 35 Seconds Too Late—What Happened?", *Online Citizen*, 28 Apr. 2011. http://www.theonlinecitizen.com/2011/04/toc-exclusive-35-seconds-too-late-what-happened/, accessed 20 Oct. 2020.

Koh, Gilbert ("Mr Wang"). "PAP's Cynthia Phua and Her Most Famous Moment as an Aljunied MP", 3 May 2011. http://mrwangsaysso.blogspot.sg/2011/05/paps-cynthia-phua-and-her-most-famous.html, accessed 22 Oct. 2020.

Lee Kin Mun ("Mr Brown"). "Browncast: The Persistently Non-political Podcast No. 6", 1 May 2006. http://www.mrbrown.com/blog/2006/05/browncast_the_p.html, accessed 22 Jan. 2021.

———. "Singapore Gahmen Becomes Famous Overseas for Its French Cooking Skills", 14 Jan. 2009. http://www.mrbrown.com/blog/2009/01/singapore-gahmen-becomes-famous-overseas-for-its-french-cooking-skills.html, accessed 26 Jan. 2021.

Li Shengwu, Facebook, 11 Aug. 2020. https://www.facebook.com/li.shengwu01/posts/10158737911423523, accessed 28 Apr. 2021.

Lim, Catherine. "An Open Letter to the Prime Minister", 7 June 2014. http://catherinelim.sg/2014/06/07/an-open-letter-to-the-prime-minster/, accessed 14 Oct. 2016.

Low, Donald. "Rethinking Singapore's Housing Policies", *IPS Commons,* 3 June 2013. http://www.ipscommons.sg/rethinking-singapores-housing-policies/, accessed 26 Jan. 2021.

Low, Donald, Yeoh Lam Keong, Tan Kim Song and Manu Bhaskaran. "Economics Myths in the Great Population Debate", *IPS Commons*, 8 Feb. 2013. http://www.ipscommons.sg/economics-myths-in-the-great-population-debate/, accessed 27 Jan. 2021.

"Low Thia Khiang's English Speech at the Workers' Party Rally at Bedok Stadium", YouTube, 2 May 2011. https://www.youtube.com/watch?v=wRHRXpRt2lo, accessed 1 Apr. 2020.

"Members' Forum 2019: Secretary-General's Speech—One WP", speech by WP Secretary-General Pritam Singh, 19 Jan. 2020. https://www.wp.sg/members-forum-2019-secretary-generals-speech-one-wp/, accessed 22 Apr. 2021.

"Merdeka Center's Poll of Singaporeans during the GE Campaign Point to Increasingly Engaged and Diverse Electorate", Merdeka Center news release, 27 May 2011. https://merdeka.org/v2/download/news-release-28-may-2011-merdeka-centers-poll-of-singaporeans-during-the-ge-campaign-point-to-increasingly-engaged-and-diverse-electorate/, accessed 26 Jan. 2021.

"Most Singaporeans Would Choose Tharman as the Next Prime Minister: Survey", *Yahoo! News*, 26 Sept. 2016. https://sg.news.yahoo.com/most-singaporeans-would-choose-tharman-1523976433713206.html, accessed 4 Apr. 2021.

"Mr Pritam Singh Supports Alfian Sa'at", Dr Tan Wu Meng, PAP, 19 June 2020. https://www.pap.org.sg/news/opinion-news/mr-pritam-singh-supports-alfian-saat/, accessed 14 Apr. 2021.

"Netizen Defends DPM Heng over 'East Coast Plan', Asks S'poreans for Compassion", *MustShareNews*, 4 July 2020. https://mustsharenews.com/dpm-heng-east-coast-plan/, accessed 14 Apr. 2021.

Ng E-Jay. "NMP Viswa Sadasivan: Did He Just Shake the Foundations of the PAP Facade to the Very Core? (Part One)", 20 Aug. 2009. https://web.archive.org/web/20160331144905/http:/www.sgpolitics.net/?p=3553, accessed 20 Oct. 2020.

"PAP Lost the Youth Vote in Sengkang GRC", *Mothership*, 12 July 2020. https://mothership.sg/2020/07/pap-lost-sengkang-grc-why/, accessed 14 Apr. 2021.

"PAP MP Tan Wu Meng Receives Backlash for Criticism of WP Chief Pritam Singh's Comments on 'Citizens Who Are Loving Critics'", *Online Citizen*, 21 June 2020. https://

www.theonlinecitizen.com/2020/06/21/pap-mp-tan-wu-meng-receives-backlash-for-criticism-of-wp-chief-pritam-singhs-comments-on-citizens-who-are-loving-critics/, accessed 14 Apr. 2021.

"PAP Party Values and Attributes", PAP. https://www.pap.org.sg/ABOUT/Content, accessed 27 Apr. 2020.

PAP Press Statement on Comments Made Regarding the 10 Million Population Falsehood, PAP, 3 July 2020. https://www.pap.org.sg/news/ge2020-news/pap-press-statement-on-comments-made-regarding-the-10-million-population-falsehood/, accessed 14 Apr. 2021.

PAP Press Statement on SDP's False Population Claims, PAP, 2 July 2020. https://www.pap.org.sg/news/ge2020-news/pap-press-statement-on-sdps-false-population-claims/, accessed 14 Apr. 2021.

"PAP v PAP: The PAP Can Do Better on the Policy Side if It Gets Its Politics Right", *Online Citizen*, 12 Nov. 2020. https://www.theonlinecitizen.com/2020/11/12/pap-v-pap-the-pap-can-do-better-on-the-policy-side-if-it-gets-its-politics-right/, accessed 30 Apr. 2021.

"PAP's 35th Central Executive Committee", 23 Nov. 2018. https://www.pap.org.sg/news/paps-35th-cec/, accessed 12 Apr. 2021.

"PAP's Janil Puthucheary, 'I Did Not Do NS . . . Those Are the Facts'", *Online Citizen*, 15 Apr. 2011. http://www.theonlinecitizen.com/2011/04/paps-janil-puthucheary-i-did-not-do-ns-those-are-the-facts/, accessed 26 Jan. 2021.

"People's Action Party Resolution 2013", PAP, 8 Dec. 2013. https://www.pap.org.sg/news/peoples-action-party-resolution-2013/, accessed 28 Jan. 2021.

"PM Lee Hsien Loong on GE2020 Results: 'We Have a Clear Mandate'", *Channel NewsAsia* YouTube Channel, 11 July 2020, https://www.youtube.com/watch?v=BlhusR7McMg, accessed 11 Apr. 2021.

PM Lee Hsien Loong, statement on new Party CEC, 23 Nov. 2018. https://www.facebook.com/pap.sg/posts/2302324019778985, accessed 12 Apr. 2021.

"Police Report Made after Online Commenter Allegedly Threatens Person Who Called Out PAP Candidate Ivan Lim", *Mothership*, 28 June 2020. https://mothership.sg/2020/06/bryant-wong-police-report/, accessed 14 Apr. 2021.

"Pondering the Elections, Why Did the Singapore Democratic Party Lose?", *Asiaweek*, 7 Feb. 1997. http://www-cgi.cnn.com/ASIANOW/asiaweek/97/0207/nat6.html, accessed 8 Sept. 2013.

"POPS (10)—IPS Post-Election Survey 2020", survey by the Institute of Policy Studies, 6 Oct. 2020. https://lkyspp.nus.edu.sg/docs/default-source/ips/pops10_ge2020-survey_061020.pdf, accessed 27 Apr. 2021.

Presidential Elections Act (Chapter 240A). https://sso.agc.gov.sg/Act/PrEA1991, accessed 15 Sept. 2021.

Progress Singapore Party, "A Message from Mr Lee Hsien Yang to All Singaporeans", Facebook, 24 June 2020. https://www.facebook.com/progresssingaporepartyofficial/videos/1731900436976261, accessed 30 Mar. 2021.

"PSP's Tan Cheng Bock: I'm Contesting This GE because PAP Has Lost Its Way", *Mothership*, 2 July 2020. https://mothership.sg/2020/07/psp-tan-cheng-bock-pap-lost-its-way/, accessed 26 Apr. 2020.

"Readers Shout Down ST's Article Criticising Questions over 'Malayness' of Would-Be Presidential Candidates", *Online Citizen*, 21 July 2017. https://www.theonlinecitizen. com/2017/07/21/readers-shout-down-sts-article-to-criticise-malayness-of-would-be-presidential-candidates/, accessed 30 Mar. 2021.

Reflections on Housing a Nation: A Collection of Commentaries by Mah Bow Tan, Ministry of National Development, 2011. https://www.mnd.gov.sg/Reflections%20on%20 Housing%20a%20Nation/Reflections%20on%20Housing%20a%20Nation.pdf, accessed 26 Jan. 2020.

"Remain PM after 70? 'I Hope Not': Prime Minister Lee Hsien Loong, 60, Who Has Held His Post for Eight Years, Would Prefer Not to Retain It Beyond 10 More Years", *AsiaOne*, 30 Sept. 2012. https://www.asiaone.com/print/News/Latest%2BNews/ Singapore/Story/A1Story20120928-374401.html, accessed 16 Apr. 2021.

"Response to TWM Article", Pritam Singh, Facebook, 21 June 2020. https://www.facebook. com/pritam.eunos/posts/3226700714018886, accessed 27 Mar. 2021.

"SDP Tan Jee Say Rebutted against SM Goh 'Personal Attack'—1 May 2011", MediaCorp Channel 5 news report, YouTube. https://www.youtube.com/watch?v=h-jelKjkxLY, accessed 22 Oct. 2020.

Siew Kum Hong. "How Many Portions of Help, Sir?", 31 Mar. 2007. http://siewkumhong. blogspot.sg/2007/03/how-many-portions-of-help-sir.html, accessed 26 Jan. 2021.

"Singapore General Election 2011, Independent Data Release Special: A Survey of Campaign Impressions amongst Singaporean Voters", *Blackbox Research*, May 2011. http://www. blackbox.com.sg/wp-content/uploads/2011/05/Blackbox_GEGraphs_May-2011.pdf, accessed 26 Jan. 2021.

"Singapore Politics Have Been Changed Forever—by Social Media", *Business Insider (Singapore)*, 24 May 2011. https://www.businessinsider.com/singapore-politics-have-been-changed-forever-by-social-media-2011-5, accessed 23 Feb. 2021.

"Singapore's GE2020: The Real Watershed Election?", YouTube, 11 Sept. 2020. https://www. youtube.com/watch?v=M43KVVjzPlU, accessed 30 Apr. 2021.

"SM Goh: Other Ministers May Be Criticised for Particular Policies, but Not George Yeo", *Singapore Election 2011*, 3 May 2011. https://singaporege2011.wordpress. com/2011/05/03/sm-goh-other-ministers-may-be-criticised-for-particular-policies-but-not-george-yeo/, accessed 1 Apr. 2020.

"Some Observations from Ong Ye Kung ST Interview and 4G Leaders' Statement on Succession", *Mothership*, 4 Jan. 2018. https://mothership.sg/2018/01/some-observations-from-ong-ye-kung-st-interview-about-4g-leaders-statement-on-succession/, accessed 14 Apr. 2021.

"South China Morning Post Has a Clear China Agenda", Global Times Singapore, Facebook, 6 May 2020. https://www.facebook.com/GlobalTimesSingapore/photos/a.1064603140 58414/255257585845352/?type=3&theater, accessed 31 Mar. 2021.

"Straits Times Forum: Employers' Practices Leave Foreign Workers Vulnerable to Infection", *Transient Workers Count Too (TWC2)*, 23 Mar. 2020. https://twc2.org.sg/2020/03/23/ straits-times-forum-employers-practices-leave-foreign-workers-vulnerable-to-infection/, accessed 27 Mar. 2021.

"The South Morning China Post's Agenda, and Singapore's Motley Crew of Stooges Are Happy to Help", Global Times Singapore, Facebook, 10 May 2020. https://www.facebook.com/GlobalTimesSingapore/posts/258331475537963, accessed 31 Mar. 2021.

"The Workers' Party in Parliament, 2011–2015", *Workers' Party*, n.d. http://www.wp.sg/wp-in-parliament-3/, accessed 28 Jan. 2021.

"The Workers' Party's Position on Sengkang Candidate Ms Raeesah Khan", PAP, 6 July 2020. https://www.pap.org.sg/news/the-workers-partys-position-on-sengkang-candidate-ms-raeesah-khan/, accessed 14 Apr. 2021.

Tommy Koh, Facebook, 8 Oct. 2019. https://www.facebook.com/tommy.koh.752/posts/2323712111179729, accessed 14 Apr. 2021.

"Transcript of PM Lee's Apology", *Singapolitics*, 5 May 2011. https://web.archive.org/web/20110713072637/http:/www.sgpolitics.net/?p=6756, accessed 26 Jan. 2021.

"Types of Electoral Divisions", Elections Department of Singapore, 15 Apr. 2020. https://www.eld.gov.sg/elections_type_electoral.html, accessed 2 Dec. 2020.

"Vote Wisely", 4 May 2011. http://xiaxue.blogspot.sg/2011/05/vote-wisely.html, accessed 1 Apr. 2020.

"We Can Be Proud of 3Ms", Ministry of Health *Today* forum reply, 7 Apr. 2008. https://www.moh.gov.sg/news-highlights/details/medisave-medishield-medi-crisis, accessed 1 Apr. 2020.

"What Has Happened to Lee Kuan Yew's Values?", *Online Citizen*, 14 June 2017. https://www.theonlinecitizen.com/wp-content/uploads/2017/06/What-Has-Happened-To-Lee-Kuan-Yews-Values.pdf, accessed 23 Apr. 2021.

"What the Fuck, Singaporeans?", 3 May 2011. http://xiaxue.blogspot.sg/2011/05/what-fuck-singaporeans.html, accessed 1 Apr. 2020.

"Workers' Party Won 50.49% Votes in 6 Constituencies It Contested in against PAP", *Mothership*, 12 July 2020. https://mothership.sg/2020/07/workers-party-vote-share-ge2020/, accessed 23 Apr. 2021.

"WP Serangoon Rally (29 Apr. 2011)", *Democracy Singapore*, YouTube, 4 May 2011. https://www.youtube.com/watch?v=NI9C9cZNrDM, accessed 13 Apr. 2021.

"WP's Low: 'There Is a Tiger in the Mountain'", *Today*, YouTube, 27 Apr. 2011. https://www.youtube.com/watch?v=TEm7K5nkC2A, accessed 13 Apr. 2021.

"WP's Sengkang GRC Team Are Young Parents, Pushing for Easier Childcare Access, More Coffee Shops", *Mothership*, 4 July 2020. https://mothership.sg/2020/07/wp-sengkang-team/, accessed 14 Apr. 2021.

"WP's Statement on MediShield Life Review Committee's Recommendations", Workers' Party, n.d. http://www.wp.sg/wps-statement-on-medishield-life-review-committees-recommendations-2/, accessed 28 Jan. 2021.

Yeo Yi Lin. "Update on MediShield Reform: Early Results", MOH Information Paper 2006/013, 1 Nov. 2006. https://www.moh.gov.sg/docs/librariesprovider5/resources-statistics/information-papers/op_on_msh_reform_update_on_early_results_1nov.pdf, accessed 20 Oct. 2020.

"Your Views: What Can We Do to Try to Prevent Another Singaporean from Being Driven to Desperation because He or She Cannot Pay Bills?", *Singapore Media Watch*, 29 Oct.

2006. http://mediawatchsg.blogspot.sg/2006/10/your-views-what-can-we-do-to-try-to. html, accessed 26 Jan. 2021.

Documents from Archives

The National Archives of Singapore is responsible for the collection, preservation and facilitation of the access to Singapore's public records of archival value. It continually reviews with the transferring agencies what records to make publicly accessible as part of its ongoing declassification efforts. I requested and was granted access by the public agencies to a number of records which have not yet been made publicly accessible. NAS facilitated such requests by working with the relevant agencies to obtain the permissions. For such sources, I have added "made available to the author" in the corresponding endnote in order to distinguish them from publicly accessible material. I am grateful to the staff of NAS for their assistance over the years.

The archives of the People's Action Party are not publicly accessible, but they were a rich and important source for this study. I have given as full a reference to the documents consulted from these archives as possible, and hope that it is useful that these references be placed on the public record. I would like to thank the Party for giving me access to these valuable documents.

National Archives of Singapore

Government Files

Correspondence on the origins of Speakers' Corner. Ref. "Speakers' Corner 10.2.99".

Documents from files concerning the thinking of the leadership on Internet regulation. Ref. MITA B01.018.13, 1996.

Documents on the Singapore 21 exercise. Ref. PM Comm/S/13 "Singapore 21 Committee".

"Establishment, Objectives and Functions of Community Development Councils", People's Association information paper, 22 Aug. 1996. Ref. MCD 22-03-42 Community Development Councils Vol. 2.

Files on Chinese language policy. Ref. MOE Education Plan 17.10.88-28.9.94.

Files on housing policy. Ref. ND 311/4-165 Vol. 2.

Files on the Ministerial Committee on Public Housing. Ref. MND 311/13/29 Vol. 3.

Files on the phasing out of religious knowledge. Ref. MOE C07-01-067 Vol. 6.

Government files on the study of religion conducted by the Ministry of Community Development. Ref. MCD 132-06-33 Vol. 3.

Inter Ministry Task Force (IMTF) on Enhancing the Role of CDCs and the Mayors; Minutes of IMTF 16 Aug. 1999. Ref. MCD 22-03-42C.

Lee Kuan Yew, "The Crucial Factor", unpublished draft chapter from planned continuation of memoirs (2008).

Ministry of Manpower files on the challenge of attracting international talent. 2000, Ref. "The International Talent Challenge".

Ministry of Manpower files on the evolution of the workpass framework.

Notes of 85(4) meeting of the Ministerial Economic Committee, 10 Oct. 1985.

Notes of Meeting between PM and Religious Leaders at the Ministry of Community
     Development, 22 Nov. 1989.
Papers on the origins of the Institute of Policy Studies, 30 Sept. 1987, Ref. 005/87.
Transcript of Press Conference on the Feedback Unit, Ministry of Community
     Development, 15 Apr. 1985, chaired by Mr S. Dhanabalan.
Transcript of the 4 Sept. 1988 PAP post-election press conference.
Workfare Income Supplement Scheme (2009). Internal government study. Ref WIS review
     C002.240.0013.V1.

Government Correspondence

Exchange of correspondence between PM Goh Chok Tong and DPM Lee Hsien Loong,
     Aug.–Sept. 2001
Exchange of correspondence between PM Lee Kuan Yew and Goh Chok Tong (cc Ong Teng
     Cheong, S. Dhanabalan, Dr Tony Tan), 20–21 Aug. 1984
Exchange of letters between PM Lee Kuan Yew and Goh Chok Tong (cc Ong Teng Cheong,
     S. Dhanabalan, Dr Tony Tan), 28–30 Aug. 1984
Exchange of memoranda between PM Lee and 1DPM Goh Chok Tong, "Non-constituency
     MPs", 27–28 Mar. 1989
Exchange of memoranda between PM Lee Kuan Yew and S. Dhanabalan, 19 Aug. 1988
Exchange of memoranda between SM Lee Kuan Yew and DPM Lee Hsien Loong (cc
     Cabinet), 18 Dec. 1990
Letter from PM Lee Kuan Yew to all MPs, 26 Sept. 1972
Letters from Zulkifli Mohammed (11 July 1990), Ibrahim Othman (10 July 1990), Ahmad
     Mattar (11 July 1990) and Abdullah Tarmugi (11 July 1990) to PM Lee Kuan Yew
Memo, 1DPM Goh Chok Tong to Minister (Community Development) S. Dhanabalan
     and Minister for Communications and Information Dr Yeo Ning Hong, 22 Jan. 1985
Memo, 1DPM Goh Chok Tong to Minister (National Development) S. Dhanabalan, 6 Feb.
     1988
Memo, 1DPM Goh Chok Tong to Minister (National Development) S. Dhanabalan, 26
     Feb. 1988
Memo, 1DPM Goh Chok Tong to Minister (National Development) S. Dhanabalan, 3
     Aug. 1989
Memo, 1DPM Goh Chok Tong to PM Lee Kuan Yew, 11 July 1990
Memo, BG (Res) George Yeo to DPM Lee Hsien Loong, 17 Dec. 1990
Memo, DPM and Minister (Trade and Industry) Lee Hsien Loong to PM Goh Chok Tong,
     30 Sept. 1991
Memo, DPM Lee Hsien Loong to the "Kitchen Cabinet", 14 Jan. 1991
Memo, Dr Lee Boon Yang to 1DPM Goh, 12 Oct. 1989
Memo, Goh Chok Tong to Lee Kuan Yew, 29 Dec. 1984
Memo, Goh Chok Tong to PM Lee Kuan Yew, 31 Dec. 1984
Memo, Maidin Packer to 1DPM Goh Chok Tong, 6 Dec. 1988
Memo, PM Goh Chok Tong to Chandra Das, 27 Dec. 1991
Memo, PM Lee to 1DPM Goh, 26 Jan. 1988
Memo, PM Lee to SM S. Rajaratnam, "TV in Parliament", 22 Jan. 1985

Memo, PM Lee Kuan Yew to 1DPM Goh Chok Tong, 10 Mar. 1990

Memo, PM Lee Kuan Yew to Goh Chok Tong, "New Town Councils or Mayorates", 24 Oct. 1984

Memo, PM Lee Kuan Yew to Press Secretary James Fu, 23 Aug. 1988. Ref NAS BF 22/88 vol. 2

Memo, PM Lee Kuan Yew to Minister (National Development) Teh Cheang Wan, 12 Feb. 1985

Memo, PM Lee Kuan Yew to Prof. S. Jayakumar, 21 Nov. 1989

Memo, PM Lee Kuan Yew to S. Dhanabalan, 16 May 1985

Memo, Prof. S. Jayakumar to PM Lee Kuan Yew, 18 Aug. 1988

Memo, Senior Minister S. Rajaratnam to PM Lee, 18 Jan. 1985

Memo, SM Lee Kuan Yew to DPM Lee Hsien Loong (cc Cabinet), 18 Dec. 1990

Memo, SM Lee Kuan Yew to PM Goh Chok Tong, 16 Sept. 1991

Memo, SM Lee Kuan Yew to PM Goh Chok Tong, 15 Nov. 1991

Memo, SM Lee Kuan Yew to PM Goh Chok Tong, 24 Nov. 1994

Memo, SM Lee Kuan Yew to PM Goh Chok Tong, 12 Dec. 1994

Note from 1DPM Goh to Minister (National Development) S. Dhanabalan, 20 Mar. 1989, Ref. ND 3/3-7 PT A

Notes from PM Lee to Cabinet colleagues, 17 Aug. 1988 and 19 Aug. 1988

Note from PM Lee to ministers, "Upgrading of HDB Flats", 14 Aug. 1989, Ref. PM 0043/70 vol2, *Refurbishing of HDB Flats* 12.8.89–14.8.89

Note from SM Lee Kuan Yew to PM Goh Chok Tong, "PM's and Ministerial Salaries", 2 Feb. 1994

PAP Archive

"Appointment of Exco of the Young PAP", tabled at 29 May 2004 CEC meeting

Cadre Review Committee Report, 9 Jan. 1993

"Concept Paper on PAP Women's Wing", tabled at CEC meeting, 4 Dec. 1988

Documents on Task Force 97

Documents on Young PAP (2000–04)

Documents pertaining to the 2011 election post-mortem

"Draft Proposal to Streamline the Communication Network between the Government and the People", Ch'ng Jit Koon to Lee Kuan Yew, 30 Dec. 1982

Exchange of letters between 1OS Goh Chok Tong and ASG Lee Kuan Yew, 12 and 13 June 1984

Exchange of letters between SG Lee Kuan Yew and Goh Chok Tong, 6 Dec. 1984 and 9 Jan. 1985

"Exit Management of Retired PAP MPs", prepared by Wong Kan Seng and approved by Goh Chok Tong, tabled at CEC meeting, 19 Oct. 1988

File "31 Oct. 1981 Anson By-Election Defeat—PM's Meeting with MPs and MPs' Reports/ Assessments"

File "Task Force 97 (Dec. 1991–Dec. 1996)"

"Fundraising for PAP HQ", tabled at CEC meeting, 8 Feb. 1995

Internal paper, "Critical Debating by PAP MPs", 29 Apr. 1989

Internal paper, "GRC Organisation for the General Election", 15 Oct. 1997

Internal report, *Enhancing the Roles and Effectiveness of PAP MPs*, 28 Feb. 1991

Interview notes, Lee Hsien Loong, candidate interview panels, 18 May 1984 and 18 July 1984

Letter from PM Lee Kuan Yew to all PAP MPs, 24 Sept. 1988

Letter, "Grassroots Experience", Secretary-General Lee Kuan Yew to all new PAP MPs, 29 Sept. 1988

Letter, Lee Kuan Yew to Goh Chok Tong, 11 Oct. 1984

Letter, Fong Sip Chee to PM Goh Chok Tong, 2 Sept. 1991

Lim Swee Say task group's paper, "Capturing Interest and Winning Loyalties of the Younger Generation", 23 Oct. 2000

Memo, 1OS Dr Ow Chin Hock to ASG Goh Chok Tong, 28 Dec. 1985

Memo, 1OS Goh Chok Tong to Secretary-General Lee Kuan Yew, 24 Jan. 1985

Memo, 1OS Ow Chin Hock to Chairman, HQ Executive Committee Goh Chok Tong, 19 Apr. 1985

Memo, 2DPM Ong Teng Cheong to 1OS Dr Ow Chin Hock, 15 Nov. 1985

Memo, "Appointment of Organising Secretaries", 22 Nov. 1991

Memo, ASG Goh Chok Tong to SG Lee Kuan Yew, 13 May 1986

Memo, ASG Lee Kuan Yew to 1OS Goh Chok Tong, 25 Jan. 1985

Memo, "Candidates", ASG Goh Chok Tong to all PAP MPs, 15 Dec. 1986

Memo, Goh Chok Tong to CEC members, 8 Feb. 1985

Memo, Goh Chok Tong to Secretary-General Lee, 9 Dec. 1987

Memo, S. Dhanabalan (Treasurer) to CEC Members, 11 June 1987

Memo, S. Dhanabalan to CEC members, "Opening of Custodian Account for the Party's Investments in Securities", 17 Oct. 1985

Memo, SG Lee Kuan Yew to ASG Goh Chok Tong, 14 May 1986

Memo, SG Lee Kuan Yew to ASG Goh Chok Tong, 11 Aug. 1988

Memo, "Target Groups of Opinion Makers", 1OS Dr Ow Chin Hock to various MPs and ministers, 28 Sept. 1985

Memo, Yeo Cheow Tong (chairman, Information Committee) to all PAP MPs, 15 Mar. 1985

Memo, "Youth Committee", Goh Chok Tong to BG Lee Hsien Loong, 11 Apr. 1986

Memo and paper, "PAP Youth Wing", BG Lee Hsien Loong to 1DPM Goh Chok Tong, 6 May 1986

Memos between PM Lee and Prof. Jayakumar, 9–10 Feb. 1987

Minutes of 3rd meeting, Refreshing PAP Committee, 29 Apr. 2003

Minutes of 7th meeting, PAP 1991 General Election Task Force, 24 Aug. 1991

Minutes of PAP CEC meeting, 13 Aug. 1984

Minutes of PAP CEC meeting, 13 Aug. 1985

Minutes of PAP CEC meeting, 24 July 1986

Minutes of PAP CEC meeting, 29 Oct. 1986

Minutes of PAP CEC Meeting, 8 Jan. 1987

Minutes of PAP CEC meeting, 10 Sept. 1992

Minutes of PAP CEC meeting, 2 Dec. 1992

Minutes of PAP CEC meeting, 21 Jan. 1993

Minutes of PAP CEC meeting, 31 Mar. 1993

Minutes of PAP CEC meeting, 6 Oct. 1999

Minutes of PAP CEC Meeting, 25 Oct. 2000

Minutes of Party Conference, 3 Dec. 2000

Minutes of PAP CEC meeting, 28 Mar. 2002

Minutes of PAP CEC meeting, 9 Oct. 2002

Notes of Meeting, Wong Kan Seng at Potong Pasir Branch, 28 July 1993, file "Visit by 2ASG
    to Opposition Wards (1993)"

Notes of meeting with MPs, 3 Sept. 1996, from file "Task Force 97 (Dec. 1991–Dec. 1996)"

PAP CEC report, Oct. 1984–Oct. 1986

PAP CEC report, Jan. 1989–Oct. 1990

PAP CEC report, Jan. 1995–Nov. 1996

PAP Post-mortem Report, 1984 General Election

PAP Post-mortem Report, 1988 General Election

PAP Post-mortem Report, 1991 General Election

PAP Post-mortem Report, 1992 Marine Parade By-election

PAP Post-mortem Report, 1997 General Election

PAP Post-mortem Report, 2001 General Election

PAP Post-mortem Report, 2006 General Election

Paper by Dr Hong Hai, "Parliamentary Committees"

Paper, "Establishment of Task Force", approved at CEC meeting, 11 Feb. 1983

Paper, "Some Changes to Party Organisation", 24 July 1986

Paper, "The PAP Foundation", CEC meeting, 3 Mar. 1986

Paper, "The PAP's Public Image and How It Can Be Improved", 24 Apr. 1986

Party documents on the subject of branch performance

Party files on the aftermath of the 1991 election

Party Manifesto (note from BG Lee Hsien Loong to all PAP MPs), 31 Jan. 1987

Personal Statement (from Lee Hsien Loong to PAP Central Executive Committee), 2 June
    1984

Recruitment of MPs, the Party's & MPs' Image, internal report, 1991

Refreshing PAP Report, 8 Sept. 2003

"Remaking and Reshaping PAP and YPAP", tabled at 26/4 CEC meeting, 28 Mar. 2002

Report of the "G" Committee, 14 Aug. 1995

Report of the "O" Committee, 28 July 1995

Report on Cadre Promotion Exercise 1985, tabled at CEC meeting, 13 Mar. 1986

Secretary General Lee Kuan Yew's Speech at the Biennial Party Conference, 23 Nov. 1986

Speech by Party Chairman Khaw Boon Wan at PAP Party Conference, 7 Dec. 2014

Speech by PM Lee Kuan Yew at PAP Malay Affairs Bureau Dinner, 15 July 1990

Speech by PM Lee Kuan Yew at the Party Convention, 23 Jan. 1988

Speech by PM Goh Chok Tong at the PAP Convention, 17 Nov. 1991: "Some Reasons Why
    Good Deeds Cause Resentment, Not Love", *Straits Times*, 23 Nov. 1991.

"Wider Participation by Key Cadres in the Nomination of Candidates for CEC Election",
    tabled at 16 Sept. 2004 CEC meeting

Index